INDUS AGE
The Beginnings

INDUS AGE
The Beginnings

GREGORY L. POSSEHL

PENN

University of Pennsylvania Press
Philadelphia

Published by
University of Pennsylvania Press
Philadelphia, Pennsylvania 19104-4011

Library of Congress Cataloging-in-Publication Data

Possehl, Gregory, L.
     Indus age: the beginnings / Gregory L. Possehl
     p.   cm.
     ISBN 0-8122-3417-0 (alk. paper)
     1. Indus civilization. 2. Pakistan—Harappa Site. 3. Pakistan—Mohenjo-Daro Site. 4. India—History. I.
Title.
PK 119.P62   1999   98-31743
490—dc21   CIP

This book is dedicated to
my colleague, mentor and friend

Walter A. Fairservis, Jr.

His excavations at Kili Ghul Mohammad brought us the
first glimpse of the beginnings of agricultural and pastoral
life in the Subcontinent.

One cannot expect to build great edifices of theory on archaeological evidence without also anticipating their collapse.

Walter A. Fairservis, Jr, *The Roots of Ancient India,* 1971a: xxiv

PREFACE

The earliest cities of the Indian Subcontinent arose on the vast plains of the Greater Indus Valley of Pakistan and India in the middle of the third millennium BC (2500-1900 BC). The two greatest cities of this ancient culture are Mohenjo-daro and Harappa, excavated by the Archaeological Survey of India in the 1920s and 1930s. The Indus or Harappan Civilization stands apart from Mesopotamia and Egypt, other urban systems of the Bronze Age, in a number of ways. First, there is no historical record of the ancient cities of the Indus, even in South Asia's earliest texts, the Vedas. This meant that finding the Harappan Civilization was an adventure in pure archaeological discovery. The nature of archaeology and the politics of the Subcontinent have also inhibited research on this, the largest of the Old World archaic "states," and beginnings of urbanization in South Asia and its somewhat enigmatic "collapse" remain issues of considerable debate. In the end, there is a great deal of misinformation, misinterpretation and misunderstanding about the civilization as a whole. In spite of these lacunae, a good deal more is known of the Harappans than even knowledgeable archaeologists may perceive, much of it based on reasonably solid recent archaeological research. *Indus Age* is a series of books written to advance the knowledge of the Harappan Civilization and present a new view of these ancient peoples to a broad, well educated audience.

I have been studying the Harappan Civilization for over thirty years and have been fortunate enough to have conducted original archaeological field research in Pakistan, Afghanistan and India. For the past decade I have been been excavating Harappan remains in the state of Gujarat in India. *Indus Age* is an opportunity for me to offer my own perspective on the diverse peoples and cultures of ancient India and Pakistan and that is the principal reason I have written it.

Indus Age will appear in four volumes, each carrying a common title, and a unique subtitle. The titles for the unnumbered volumes are

> *Indus Age: The Beginnings*
> *Indus Age: The Mature Harappan*
> *Indus Age: The Writing System*
> *Indus Age: The Transformation*

Audience

For whom has *Indus Age* been written? The answer, though not totally satisfactory, is "anyone interested in the ancient civilization of India and Pakistan." Initially, I was beleaguered by the notion that it was for archaeological colleagues, specialists in the field. But, as the writing progressed, it became apparent that this was not the case and another audience emerged, not necessarily knowledgeable about archaeology, but curious about the Indus Age. It is composed of students, professors and a lay audience with a curiosity about the deeper history of the

Subcontinent. This is really their book and if archaeologists of South Asia find it useful and interesting that is a plus.

Including the concerns of non-archaeologists has had a somewhat serious consequence, precipitated by my educational philosophy. Giving the reader a series of conclusions, opinions and rhetoric to be accepted or rejected, based largely on the forcefulness and conviction of my presentation, is not my aim. What I want to construct is a presentation based on epistemological principles, so that the reader will come to know not only what I believe about the Indus Age but why I believe it. I do this because of a conviction that "why I believe" something is more important than "what I believe." For the non-archaeologist to understand the work at this level I feel that it is necessary to discuss archaeological method, because it has a profound impact on our knowledge of the past. Some of this discussion is so basic to the "expert" that one hopes it does not give rise to questions concerning the appropriateness of these digressions.

Efforts have been made to give this book two qualities. In some ways they run counter to each other. The first is a strong, linear narrative: the story line of the Indus Age. The second is that of a handbook, or an encyclopaedia: a reference work that can be used to find facts quickly and efficiently.

These dual qualities have made it necessary to pay attention to organization. Topics closely related intellectually are often distantly removed in the printed text. I have tried to alleviate this problem by giving particular attention to the index, which is especially important. Abundant cross-referencing of notes and titling, sometimes at the paragraph level, provides signposts to guide the reader through the next, and to facilitate the use of the books.

INDUS AGE: The Beginnings

The present volume is first of the series and will set the stage for the Mature, or Urban Stage of the Harappan Civilization. An Introduction (Part One) presents the theory and philosophy of the series, as well as some definitional and technical information, such as radiocarbon dates, and comments on physical anthropology. This is followed by the story of discovery of the Harappan Civilization.

Part Two of *The Beginnings* starts in the early nineteenth century when the city of Harappa was visited by antiquarians with no knowledge of the older history of Pakistan or India. The realization that the sites in the Indus Valley were Bronze Age, contemporary with the Sumerians, came in 1924 when the Archaeological Survey of India was under the Director Generalship of Sir John Marshall. The story is told of his leadership in organizing the field programs to uncover these cities. New biographical and historical material, some of it from the Archives of the University of Pennsylvania Museum, is presented. The reinvigoration of the Archaeological Survey of India under the guidance of Sir Mortimer Wheeler brings the story of discovery to a close with the Partition of the Subcontinent in 1947.

Part Three of *Indus Age: The Beginnings* is a detailed discussion of Cultural Geography, which offers a regional perspective on the Greater Indus area. Using the concept of a "Region," it develops a cultural geography of the lower Indus Valley and a history of the Indus River; sets up the highlands of Baluchistan and the Northwest Frontier as the environmental homeland of food producing peoples in the Subcontinent; outlines the geography and history of the Sarasvati River; details the lapidary and mineral resources of the Greater Indus Region; and gives a history of the plants and animals utilized by the peoples of the Indus Age.

The final segment (Part Four) is a culture history of the peoples of the Indus Age from the beginnings of food production and domestication of plants and animals to the threshold of civilization in the region. It builds on an innovative, comprehensive chronology for the region with a new terminology for the Stages and Phases of culture history. This culture history draws heavily on the gazetteer of archaeologial sites of the Indus Age that the author has put together over the past decade. Discussion of the early "neolithic" communities and the Early Harappan Stage, which precedes full urbanization at about 2500 BC, is cogent and represents a significant contribution to the study of the Harappan Civilization.

The Size and Length of Indus Age: The Beginnings

Indus Age: The Beginnings was conceived and written as a large book. There are a number of reasons for this. First, archaeologists have learned a great deal about the Indus Age over the thirty years I have been involved in its study. No one has attempted to bring the full mass of data on the Indus Civilization together in one place, and this project offered me an opportunity to change that. *Indus Age: The Beginnings* may change their mind. We do not have all the answers we need, by far, but there is much that we do know, or think we know.

My interest in the history of research on the Harappan Civilization began in the late 1970s (Possehl 1982c). *Indus Age: The Beginnings* is an opportunity for me to tell the story that had built up in my notes on the discovery of the Indus Age.

Something similar is true for the cultural geography of *Indus Age: The Beginnings*. I have access to masses of information gleaned from old District Gazetteers, agricultural reports, census data and personal observations that had never been brought together in one place. This book was the place for me to correct this deficiency and share my information with an audience broader than the students in my classes at the University of Pennsylvania.

The culture history of *Indus Age: The Beginnings* is long, but presents a new, regionally based developmental model for the growth of urbanization in the Greater Indus Region. This is a long complicated story that to be told in detail required extensive exposition.

In the end *Indus Age: The Beginnings* is a long book because it has to be a long book. The same will be true for *Indus Age: The Mature Harappan*.

THE REMAINING VOLUMES IN THE SERIES

The next book in the series is *Indus Age: The Mature Harappan*. This will be a wide ranging discussion of the peoples of this age, their history and way of life. It will begin with a culture history of the Mature Harappan, using the Regions of the Greater Indus Region that were developed in *Indus Age: The Beginnings*. The text will then shift to a consideration of some of the institutions and features of the Mature Harappan: religion, art, technology, subsistence practices, human biology and foreign relations.

This presentation of the Mature Harappan will be unique. There will be a new, detailed overview of the diversity of Harappan religious beliefs. The burial record and insights on disease, nutrition and occupation that have emerged from the modern study of ancient human biology will be fully reviewed. The first integrated study of Harappan art will also be presented with an examination of every major piece, its history, find spot and significance to the understanding of the Harappan peoples. Finally, the Mature Harappan contacts with surrounding peoples in Iran, Central Asia, Mesopotamia and Africa will be explored. A comprehensive review will be made of the Harappan presence in the Arabian Gulf, and new insights concerning their maritime activity along the Saudi Arabian Coast, extending to the Red Sea, will further develop the picture of these peoples.

Indus Age: The Writing System is already available. It is an examination of the undeciphered writing system of the Mature Harappan, the first book length treatment of the subject that does not include a decipherment. This material might have been part of *Indus Age: The Mature Harappan,* but because there is a broad audience interested in historical linguistics it seemed reasonable to create a separate volume on the topic.

The book begins wth a review of the Mature Harappan and the place of writing in it. A typology of Harappan glyptics is presented in well illustrated detail, followed by discussions of the possible survival of the Harappan script in later South Asian writing systems: Megalithic graffiti, the Brahmi script and symbols on punch marked coins. The centerpiece of the book is a review of over forty research efforts on the Indus script, most of which are attempted decipherments. Among these are Colonel L. A. Waddell, 1925: The Harappans, Sumerians and Aryans; G. R. Hunter, 1929: The First Rigorous Treatment of the Script; Sir Flinders Petrie, 1932: Reading the Script as Egyptian Hieroglyphics; G. de Hevesy, 1932: The Indus Script and Writing on Easter Island; Bedrich Hrozný, 1939: A Great Decipherer Takes on the Indus Script; Father Henry Heras, S. J., 1953: The Dravidian Hypothesis; The Russian Team, 1965: Computers and the Indus Script; The Finnish Team, 1969: More Dravidian, More Computers; Iravatham Mahadevan, 1972: Parallelisms, Soma and Indus Writing; S. R. Rao, 1982: The Harappans Invent the Alphabet; Walter A. Fairservis, Jr., 1992: Harappan Chiefdoms.

The assessment of the current state of knowledge on the Indus script highlights the lack of agreement among would be decipherers and the fact that no one has developed an independent test to check the veracity of many of the claims that have been made about the writing system. The assessment leads to the presentation of three principles on which future research on the writing system should proceed: (1) more thorough research on the form of the writing system and its orthography, development of an authoritative sign-list; (2) study of the script within the context of many small-scale research efforts aimed at its implications within Harappan life; comprehensive studies initiated by individuals who attempt decipherment through inspirational genius have little chance of solving this problem; and (3) multiple lines of inference concerning proposed decipherments developed so that identical conclusions developed from two or more independent lines of reasoning can serve as tests for claims of decipherment.

The final book is titled *Indus Age: The Transformation.* One of the most intriguing aspects of the Indus Age is that the Mature Harappan drew to a close with the abandonment of the great cities of Mohenjo-daro and Harappa at approximately 1900 BC. At the same time the distinctly urban features of Harappan life also changed, with the disappearance of writing, the abandonment of the system of weights and measures and that sense of unity of life that came with the Mature Harappan. Older, traditional studies have spoken of the "end of the ancient cities of the Indus" or the "eclipse of Harappan life" as though all of human existence in Pakistan and northwestern India came to an abrupt halt. The world of the Indus Age vastly changed, but life hardly went into a period of eclipse.

Indus Age: The Transformation will review the later phases of the Mature Harappan and discuss the changes that took place region by region, with many new perspectives on the transformation of Harappan life during the early second millennium BC. The older theories of the Harappan eclipse will be examined; the "late" or post-urban world of the Harappans in all of their regions, which draws heavily on the gazetteer of archaeological sites, will be scrutinized. The culture continuity between the Late Bronze Age of the Mature Harappan and the Early Iron Age in the opening of the historical period in the Subcontinent will be outlined. There will be a discussion of early Indian texts as historical documents. The four Early Iron Ages of Pakistan and northern India and the contributions of the Harappan Civilization to historical India and Pakistan will be reviewed.

THANKS ARE DUE TO MANY

This project began with two consecutive years of paid leave from the School of Arts and Sciences at the University of Pennsylvania. This was a key contribution to bringing *Indus Age* into reality.

While I am the author of this book and the *Indus Age* series, there are many people and institutions who deserve special thanks for assisting me in this project. Some of them are: Richard Davis for photographs of Aq Kupruk; the Bernice Pauahi Bishop Museum for a photograph of a *rongogongo*; The Art Institute, Chicago for the photograph of a painting by Gaugin with Easter Island Writing in the background; the American Museum of Natural History for the use of the photograph of the Bull Vase from Damb Sadaat; the Metropolitan Museum of Art for photographs; the National Geographic for photographic services and permission to use photographs, especially the one for the dust jacket of this book; James Blair of the National Geographic Society for permission to use his photographs of seals and other Indus objects; Louis Flam for his photographs of Sindh; Harold Dibble for photographs of the Mount Carmel Caves; Dr. Purushottam Singh for photographs of Jericho; Dr. Walter A. Fairservis, Jr. for photographs and art work, as well as access to his archaeological archives and map collection; Jan Fairservis for art work; The Archaeological Survey of India for many photographs from their extensive archives; Krishna Singh for his graphic skills and tenacity in completing a very large number of artifact drawings and maps; John Syder for his art work and many of the computer graphics; Renwei Huang for her portraits; Fred Schoch and Francine Sarin in the Photographic Studio of the University of Pennsylvania Museum for their assistance and efficiency; the University of Pennsylvania Museum for the use of images from its Photographic Archives and the Archives for making the W. Norman Brown papers available to me; Dr. Sherman Minton for photographs of the *muggar* and *gavial*; the Museum of Fine Arts, Boston for making documents relating to the Chanhu-daro excavation available to me; The British Museum for photographs of objects in its collections; the British Library for permission to reproduce the Rembrandt elephant and materials from the India Office Library. Drawings of the mammals of the Indus Age have been inspired from illustrations of Thomas J. Roberts (1977) and those in S. H. Prater's book (1971).

My companion of many years, Margaret Pugh spent long hours of hard labor editing this work, and if it reads well it is due to her contributions.

Special thanks go to Jon Hastings who has contributed a great deal to my education in computing. He has been a splendid advisor and tutor and always there when I needed him, in Philadelphia or in the field, at Rojdi. His most prominent contribution to *Indus Age* is the special program he wrote which allows the automatic plotting of sites from the Gazetteer of Sites of the Indus Age on to a computerized map in Genric Cadd. This has proved to be an extremely useful tool and I am very grateful to Jon for having done it.

I also want to thank the University of Pennsylvania Press, especially Patricia Smith, the acquisitions editor who backed the project from the moment she saw it. Penn approached this large undertaking with a sense of its importance, and made sure that we had the resources to make it a first class job. My friends and colleagues at Oxford & IBH Publishing in New Delhi were an important part of the formula that made publishing this book a possibility. I have done a lot with Oxford & IBH over the years in my efforts to make my work widely available in the Subcontinent. *Indus Age* is another of these projects, all of which have turned out to be a pleasant success. My brother and sister-in-law Jim and Karen Possehl did the rest.

The following colleagues read and commented on various parts of *Indus Age:* Edward C. Dimock; Robert H. Dyson, Jr.; Walter A. Fairservis, Jr.; Louis Flam; Kenneth A. R. Kennedy;

Patrick V. Kirch; Krishna Deva; B. B. Lal; Erle Leichty; Richard Meadow; Janet Monge; B. M. Pande; Maureen Patterson; Brian Peasnall; Jim G. Shaffer; Burton Stein; Thomas Trautman, Bernard Wailes; Kamil Zvelebil.

Special thanks must go to two of my junior colleagues in the Department of Anthropology at the University of Pennsylvania: Ms. Praveena Gullapalli and Ms. Uzma Rizvi. They stepped in at a critical time and undertook a number of tasks that allowed me to bring this book through the press.

My education has benefited greatly over the years by stimulating and informative conversations about the Indus Age with many colleagues. They are, in alphabetical order: D. P. Agarwal, P. Ajithprasad, B. Allchin, F. R. Allchin, Z. D. Ansari, A. Ardeleanu-Jansen, S. Asthana, G. L. Badam, R. Besenval, K. K. Bhan, R. S. Bisht, B. de Cardi, D. K. Chakrabarti, Y. M. Chitalwala, S. Cleuziou, G. F. Dales, A. H. Dani, M. N. Deshpande, M. A. Dhaky, M. K. Dhavalikar, C. Edens, K. N. Dikshit, L. Dupree, E. C. L. During Caspers, F. A. Durrani, R. H. Dyson, W. A. Fairservis, M. Fentress, L. Flam, H.-P. Francfort, U. Franke-Vogt, K. Frifelt, A. Ghosh, S. P. Gupta, M. A. Halim, K. T. M. Hegde, M. Hoffman, M. Jansen, C. Jarrige, J.-F. Jarrige, J. P. Joshi, M. D. Kajale, M. Kazi, K. A. R. Kennedy, J. M. Kenoyer, R. Knox, P. Kohl, M. Koiso, Krishna Deva, S. Kusumgar, B. B. Lal, M. Lal, C. C. Lamberg-Karlovsky, J. Lukacs, R. H. Meadow, R. N. Mehta, S. Mery, V. N. Misra, M. R. Mughal, B. M. Pande, A. Parpola, A. Patel, D. Potts, G. Quivron, S. R. Rao, S. Ratnagar, P. C. Rissman, V. Roux, H. D. Sankalia, J. G. Shaffer, N. Shaikh, V. Shinde, U. V. Sonawane, G. Stacul, Suraj Bhan, B. K. Thapar, K. P. Thomas, P. K. Thomas, M. Tosi, M. Vidale, Vishnu-Mittre, S. Weber, R. Wright and P. Yule.

The participation of all of these individuals and institutions in this project is very much appreciated. Given the size and scope of the volume this often involved many hours of work. The end product has benefited immensely from their efforts. I should add that not everyone was in full ageement with the points I have attempted to make here, nor were all of their observations integrated into the final product. My readers found much on which to comment and a few things that can be counted as errors. The latter have been corrected, and very gratefully so. In the end, the perspective presented here is my own and I can but thank my friends and colleagues for having done their best to keep me out of trouble. If they have not succeeded, the fault is entirely my own.

GREGORY L. POSSEHL

CONTENTS

LIST OF FIGURES

LIST OF TABLES

LIST OF PLATES

PART ONE

INDUS AGE: THE BEGINNINGS

INTRODUCTION

Origins of settled life in the northwestern sector of southern Asia can be documented near the beginnings of the Holocene, following the retreat of the last great continental glaciers. Over several millennia of growth and change, early villages and pastoral camps grew into the ancient cities of the Indus and the Harappan Civilization (Figure 1.1). These urban centers were a transitory phenomenon, and a great transformation took place when urbanization, and the human complexity that accompanies it, was replaced with a simpler sociocultural form as the citizens of this once proud civilization sought a new way of life (Figure 1.2, Figure 1.3, Plate 1.1). The long period of growth, change, maturation and accommodation, which begins with early villages and camps and ends with the transformation of the Harappan Civilization is called the "Indus Age."

The Indus Age was a part of southern Asia, now dominated by the modern nation states of India and Pakistan. The Indus River and its tributaries are a focal point of life there and this large, diverse geographical setting is known as the "Greater Indus Region." It includes the Indus Valley, the mountainous eastern edge of the Iranian Plateau (Baluchistan and the Northwest Frontier), Gujarat, the Punjab, the Indus-Ganges divide and significant parts of the Thar Desert, particularly in its northern extent. The best general coverage of the Indus Age can be found in sources such as Sir John Marshall's magnificent review of the Indus Civilization, and the early excavations at Mohenjo-daro (Marshall 1931a), as well as more general surveys: Mackay (1948); Piggott (1950); Wheeler (1968); Fairservis (1971a); Allchin, B. and F. R. (1982); Agrawal (1982a); Possehl (1979a, 1982a, 1993c).

There is no entirely satisfactory chronology for the Indus Age, especially for the internal stages and phases of prehistoric life. Present estimates based on radiocarbon dates suggest that it arises at 7000 or 8000 BC with the earliest villages, the domestication of plants and animals and the beginnings of farming and herding societies. The cities, the best known of which are Mohenjo-daro and Harappa, were functioning urban centers for about 500 years and it is convenient, and reasonably accurate, to propose that they can be dated to the second half of the third millennium, or 2500 to 2000 BC. This period is often called the Mature Harappan, or the era of the Indus or Harappan Civilization. The transformation of the Mature Harappan took place within the early centuries of the second millennium and lasted for a very long time. As an archaeologist, I bring the Indus Age to a close in the Early Iron Age of Pakistan and northern India, sometime in the early first millennium BC.

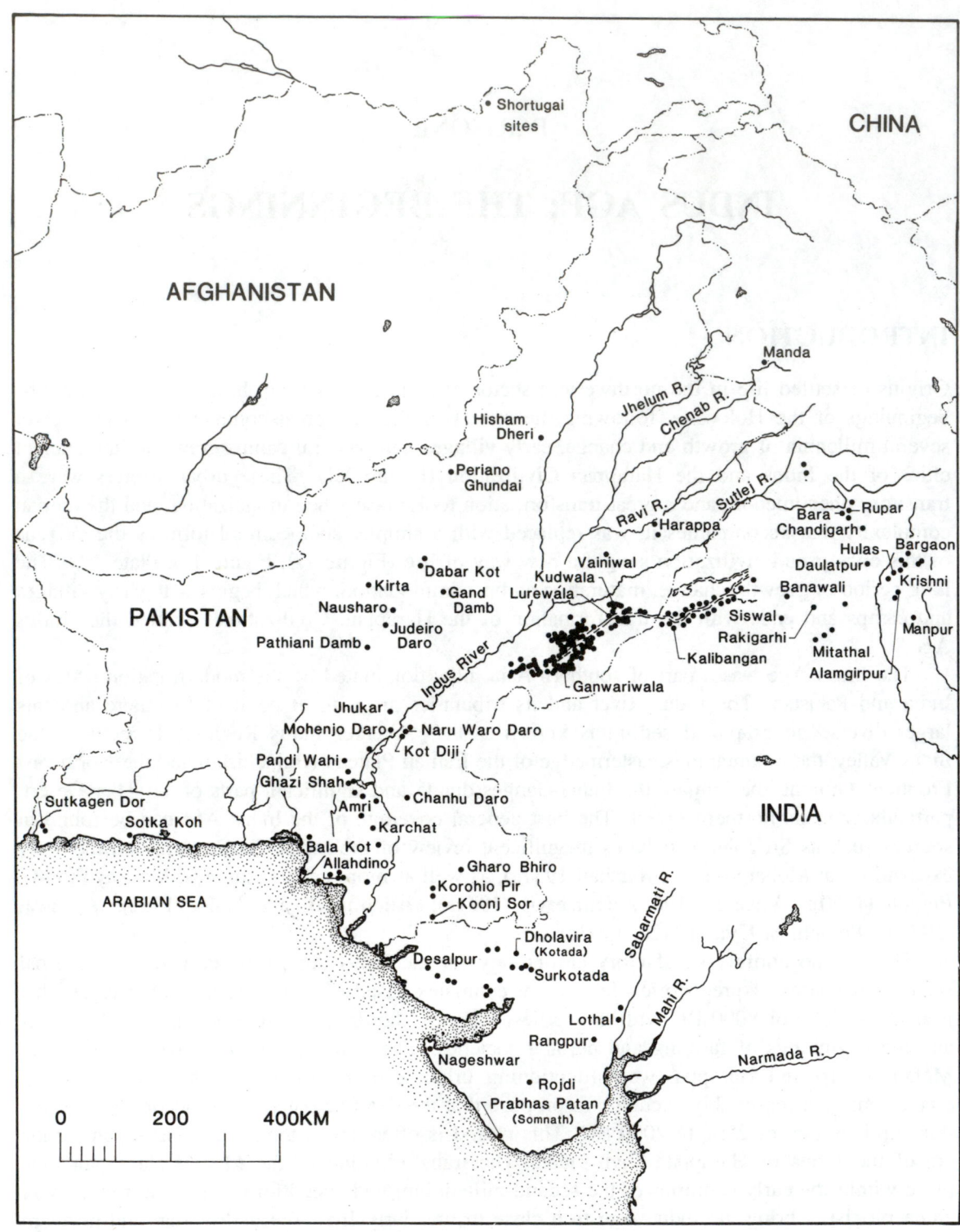

Figure 1.1. Some sites of the Indus Age

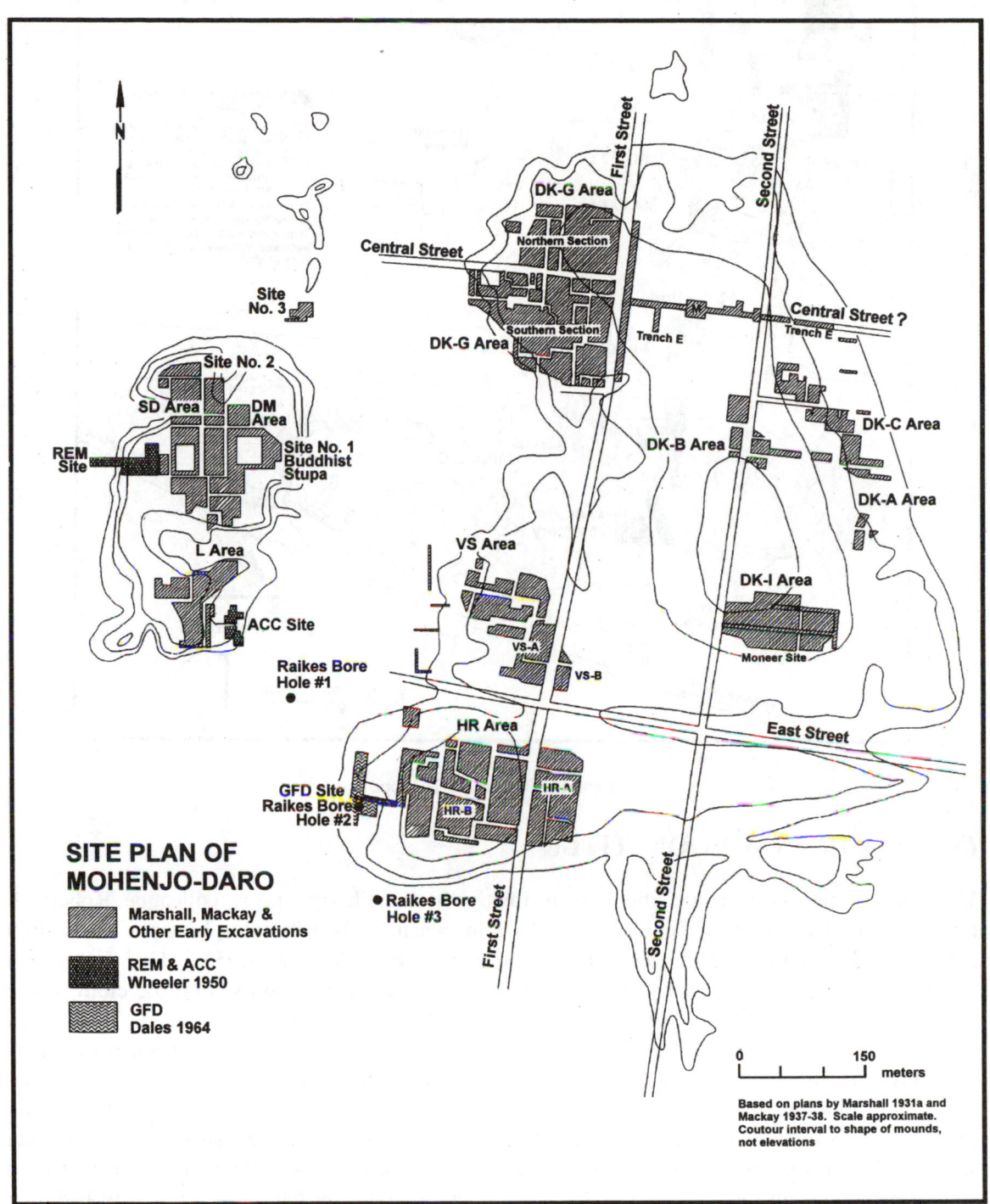

Figure 1.2. Plan of Mohenjo-daro

4

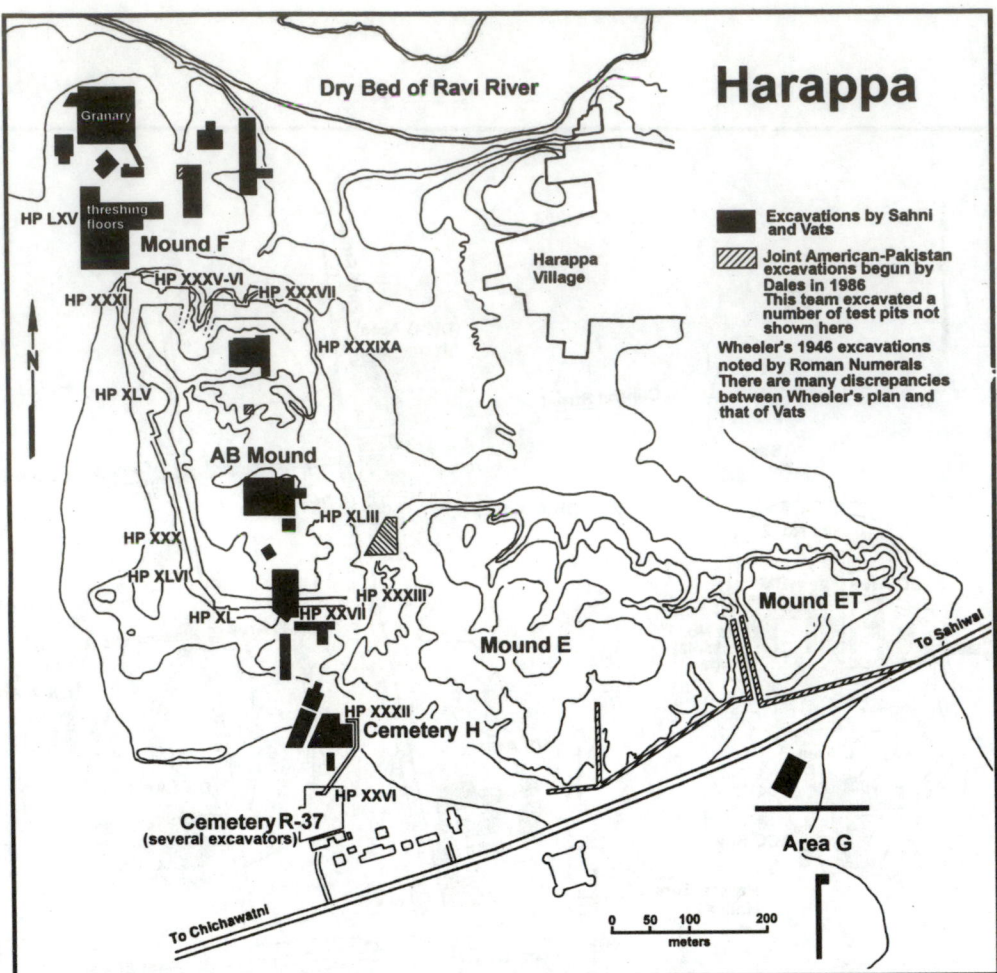

Figure 1.3. Plan of Harappa

INDUS AGE AS A BOOK TITLE

The title for this book came about inadvertently, in the library of my colleague Robert H. Dyson at The University of Pennsylvania Museum, when I was examining his copy of the first edition of Sir Mortimer Wheeler's, *The Indus Civilization* (Wheeler 1953). The dust jacket accidentally came off and to my astonishment I saw that the title embossed on the cloth bound spine was *"The Indus Age,"* yet the dust jacket and the title page clearly read, *"The Indus Civilization."* It appears that the original title was *"The Indus Age"* but had been rejected by Cambridge University Press and Wheeler. This was late enough in the production process that some cloth bindings had been printed with *"The Indus Age"* and some of them at least found their way into circulation. The dust jacket paper they used has a high survival rate and the spine of their books never seems to be revealed except perhaps in a library or on a well used copy. I decided right then, when I first saw the title that Wheeler had once thought to use, that the *Indus Age* would not be lost and I would make it my own when a series of books I had in mind came into being.

The *Indus Civilization* is an excellent title for Wheeler's Supplement to the Cambridge Ancient History which went through three editions (Wheeler 1953, 1960, 1968). His work is focused on the Mature Harappan, the period during which the cities of the Harappan Civilization were living, functioning urban centers.

Wheeler pays scant attention to either the precursor villages and camps in the Greater Indus Region or the transformation of Harappan culture over the course of the second millennium BC.

The *Indus Age* is the right choice for the present series because it will be less time bound than Wheeler's book. A great deal of attention will be devoted to the history of research, the cultural geography, the beginnings of village farming communities and the domestication of plants and animals, as well as the rise of the Mature Harappan Civilization. The Mature or Urban Stage of the Civilization will be explored in a single volume, another will cover the yet to be deciphered writing system. The final volume will explore the demise of the cities, the transformation of Harappan life and the advent of the Early Iron Age in northern India and Pakistan. The notion of an "age" captures this extended period of time, roughly seven millennia, better than Wheeler's "civilization" and the abandonment of his original title turned out to be, for me at least, a good decision, giving me a perfect title for my volumes.

The *Indus Age* is not a title that is entirely free of shortcomings. For example, it brings together chronology and geography, which are independent historical variables. It also tends to isolate a particular period of history in the Subcontinent, suggesting that the *Indus Age* is separate from other developments. A virtue is that it is fresh, not encumbered by years of hackneyed use. Nor does it make use of the outmoded type fossil approach, as in "Harappan Civilization." The sense that the Indus Age is somehow separate from the rest of South Asian history is false, and the presentation has to be made in a way that assuages such a bias.

EARLY INDIAN LITERATURE

The earliest texts in ancient India are the Vedas; four collections of hymns, made up of books, or *mandalas*. Vedic literature includes other works like the Brahmanas, Upanishads and Aryanakas. The earliest Veda is the Ṛgveda, composed and codified to enable the Vedic priests to perform the sacrificial rites necessary for the proper conduct of the life of the Aryan people. The Samaveda is a reordering of certain verses of the Ṛgveda for liturgical purposes. The Yajurveda seems to have come together a century or two later than the Ṛgveda and is an annotated text of "instructions" and sacrificial formulae to be recited by the priest who performs the manual part of the sacrifice. Finally, there is the Atharvaveda, the last and least understood of the Vedas, and probably the most interesting. It is a book of magic; spells and incantations in verse with "...an atmosphere of simple animism and sympathetic magic on a lower cultural level than that of the Ṛgveda, deriving from the plebeian religion of the Aryans and containing many non-Aryan elements" (Basham 1967: 232).

The word *Veda* means "knowledge." In Ṛgveda it is compounded with *ṛc* or "hymn of praise." Taken together the title of this text in English would be something like "Knowledge (consisting) of Hymns of Praise" (Maurer 1986: 5). The Ṛgveda is made up of ten books (*mandalas*) with 1028 hymns. The hymns average about eleven stanzas each. This comes to about 450,000 words.

The date of the Ṛgveda is not clear, although the chronological sequence for the composition of the texts seems certain: Ṛgveda/Samaveda, then the Yajurveda and finally the Atharvaveda. There is also a relative chronology of *mandalas* within the Ṛgveda with Books II through VII being the earliest. These are also called the "Family Books" since they are believed to have been composed by a "family" or patrilineage, of priests. Books I, VIII and X are later additions by various authors. Book IX is generally thought of in separate terms, being devoted exclusively to the deified, potent Soma plant (Maurer 1986: 6). The relative chronology is based on an analysis of the Sanskrit used in the texts and can be taken as a reliable judgment. But, an absolute chronology is not certain.

There is some content of the Ṛgveda that hints at its age. There are references made to metals; certainly gold, silver and lead, probably copper and bronze, but not iron. However, by the time of the Atharvaveda, iron is known (Macdonell and Keith 1912: Vol. 1, 31-2). This can be used to suggest that the Ṛgveda was codified prior to the widespread use of iron in northern India and Pakistan and that the Atharvaveda is on the other side of this time line; nominally 1000 BC or slightly earlier.

Based on the language of the Ṛgveda, its vocabulary and grammar, Vedic Sanskrit can be thought of as the archaic form of this language. The Sanskritists on whose judgment I rely, feel that the date for the codification of the Ṛgveda is not likely to be earlier than 1200 BC nor later than 800 BC. There is some bias toward the later date. These dates are not based on a process of reasoning rich in data and cross-checks. They emerge instead from a sense of how rapidly Sanskrit might have changed, using the grammar of Panini[1] (ca. 5th century BC) as a baseline, and working backward from this point. There are few chronological checkpoints in this process and the period between 1200 and 800 BC emerges as a scholarly judgment; a kind of "ball park guess." But, this range of dates is congruent with the notion that iron may not be mentioned in the Ṛgveda but is in the Atharvaveda, itself only a reasonable or interesting observation, not a hard and fast historical point.

This date for the Ṛgveda is based primarily on language. It gives the approximate date for the codification of the text, but not for the history that may be represented there, which is certainly earlier; how much earlier is simply not known.

The Vedic texts were originally part of an oral literature. They are *sṛuti*, or "heard," and Brahmins were expected to memorize all four books, some parts of which were clearly composed and arranged to assist in this learning process. It can be surmised then that there was a period of composition, when new material was added and older verses edited and changed. But, at some point this flexibility in composition stopped and the priests defined their text as immutable, not to be changed by one word or even one syllable, and the slightest mispronunciation or deviation from the canon was believed to be a sacrilege. It is the language of this codified version of the Ṛgveda that serves as the beginning for a relative chronology of early Indian literature.

Indian tradition is quite strict in its attitude toward learning the Vedas. It was the duty of every Brahmin to memorize perfectly all four texts. There is no mention of writing in the Ṛgveda and this appears to indicate that the society which created these texts was not literate.[2] Memorization was, therefore, the only means for the Ṛgveda and the Samaveda, to be kept alive. In later times, when writing was a part of ancient Indian society, there are proscriptions against writing down the Vedas, something that was respected until Medieval times (ca. 1000 AD), when the tradition began to weaken or sectarian change admitted new views on this literature. Even today there are Brahmins who have memorized their four Vedas, although it is a great rarity. But, as recently as the eighteenth and nineteenth centuries it was more common.

One would think that an oral literature that can be documented for at least two millennia (ca. 1000 BC to ca. 1000 AD) would be subject to change and adulteration. The process of recitation has a kind of flexibility that written forms of transmission do not. Most oral literatures do have rules that govern innovation, and limit it, if only to ensure the integrity of the central theme. But all modern studies of oral or bardic performances (e.g., Parry and Lord 1954; Vansina 1961; Beck 1976; Miller 1976) have documented observable variation between performers and among performances. This same kind of flexibility in oral literature seems to have been shared with ancient bardic traditions such as that of Greece, a superb review of which can be found in Kirk (1975). In general, research on oral traditions informs us that although there may have been an original "genius composer" of an individual treatise to assume that anything more than a version of this is preserved over a long period of time "...seriously misrepresents the complex and continuous process of informal adaptation and elaboration by generations of singers in an oral tradition" (Kirk 1975: 827).

Variation and change in an oral literature is generally thought to result from the reciter's individual style, or taste, and the demands of relevance placed on them by their audiences.

The technical difficulties of sustaining each performance as an exact replica of an earlier one is an additional difficulty. Moreover, oral literature does not exist in a sociocultural or historical vacuum. To survive at all for a significant period of time, it is generally thought that oral literatures must be constantly reshaped within the dynamics of each historical setting.

Some scholars of ancient India believe that the Vedic texts we have today are exact replicas of the same texts that were codified in the first millennium BC. If this is true then much of what we have learned, and was just summarized, about the nature of oral literature in both contemporary societies and those of antiquity, would not apply to the ancient Indian case. How can this be true?

In the end, we do not know how close the contemporary versions of the Vedic texts are to those of the first millennium BC. Since we have no exemplars from the first millennium, there is nothing to be compared to. But, there are some reasons to believe that there are special conditions that apply to the transmission of the Vedic texts that do not apply generally to other oral literatures. Part of this was the education process of the Brahmins.

The main subject of study was the Veda, and long hours were devoted to its mastery. The teacher would instruct by rote, the few students seated on the ground about him and for many hours daily they would repeat verse after verse of the Vedas, until one or more was mastered. Sometimes, to ensure correctness, the hymns were taught in more than one way, first with the words connected, then in their isolated form (*padapatha*), and then with the words interwoven in *ab*, *bc*, *cd*, pattern (*kramapatha*) or in even more complicated ways. This remarkable system of mnemonic checks and the patience and brilliant memories of many generations of teachers and students preserved the Vedas for posterity in much the same form as that in which they existed nearly a thousand years before Christ (Basham 1967: 163).

The Indian Brahmins took the memorization of the Vedas very seriously, and developed means to ensure accuracy and the careful reproduction of the same words and sounds from generation to generation. Careful, even exact oral replication of the Vedas was part of the Hindu faith, institutionalized during the learning process and maintained through peer observation and pressure through the life of a Brahmin. This community of faithful Brahmins was large and they all went through the same learning process, which was standardized to some degree. Deviation from the proscribed path of exact replication would have brought powerful forces of censure to bear on the offender.

There is also good agreement between the written Vedas that exist from Medieval times on, and the oral versions. It is thought that the oral tradition may not have been contaminated by the literate, but we really cannot know for sure. Still, the writing down of the Vedas was not favored, nor widespread, and the observation does have some merit, as a part of the mix of considerations being made here.

The noted Sanskritist J. A. B. van Buitenen told me that in the eighteenth and nineteenth centuries the Europeans who were learning Sanskrit were impressed by the fact that no matter where they went in the Subcontinent, when they heard Brahmins recite the Vedas they heard the exact same thing. From Peshawar to Pondicherry, or Calcutta to Cape Comorin hundreds of thousands, even millions, of Brahmins who had had no direct contact, knew these texts in precisely the same way; certainly the words, centuries down to the last inflection. If this observation is true, and I have not been able to document it in print, the eighteenth and nineteenth tradition of learning the Vedas was very strong; just as strong as it might have been for almost three millennia.

In the end, we cannot know that the Vedic texts we have today are exact replicas of those of the first millennium BC. Given the flexible nature of oral traditions elsewhere this seems to be a highly unlikely happering (see above). But, there are some reasons to believe that this oral tradition is different from most, and that what we have today as texts may be remarkably close to those of deep antiquity.

The Vedas, especially the Rgveda, will be cited in this exploration of the Indus Age, but it should be remembered that these are esoteric ancient texts and not straightforward historical documents. The Rgveda, Samaveda and Yajurveda were composed by priests for the performance of a sacrificial rite; certainly with no thought that in future they would provide archaeologists and historians of ancient India with an insight into the life and society of Vedic times.

The translations from the Vedas used in the *Indus Age* have been taken from Ralph T. H. Griffith (1893, 1895-96, 1896, 1899), Wendy D. O'Flaherty (1981) and Walter H. Maurer (1986). The latter two works are translations of selections from the Rgveda, and not everything I have needed is in either or both of them. The first translation of the Rgveda into English was that of Horace Hayman Wilson, the first Professor of Sanskrit at Oxford University (Wilson 1850-88). The best translation is said to be that by Karl Friedrich Geldner (1951), but it is rendered from the Sanskrit into German and would be inappropriate for this book in that form. I also have reservations about a translation that proceeds from Sanskrit to German and then from German to English. Griffith's translation is the most widely available but it is thought to be flawed in a number of ways from the standpoint of the modern Sanskritist. Where it is possible I have checked the portions of the Rgveda that I want rendered into English in Griffith, O'Flaherty and Maurer, at times checking with Geldner, and settling on the translation that is the most appropriate. To give one a sense of how close different translations can be I give three exemplars of one of the most famous parts of the Rgveda, where social structure and the beginnings of the *varna* system seem to be noted. This is in Book X, Hymn 90, Verses 11-2. I begin with Griffith.

When they divided Purusa how many portions did they make? What do they call his mouth, his arms? What do they call his thighs and feet?

The Brahman was his mouth, of both his arms was the Rajanya made. His thighs became Vaisya, from his feet the Sudra was produced.

Rgveda Book X, Hymn 90, Verses 11-2; Griffith 1896

Professor Walter Maurer translates these two verses in this way:

When they portioned out Purusa, in how many ways did they distribute him? What is his mouth called, what his arms, what his thighs, what are his feet called? His mouth was the Brahmana, his arms were made the Rajanya, what was his thighs was made the Vaisya, from his feet the Sudra was born

Rgveda Book X, Hymn 90, Verses 11-2; Maurer 1986: 272

Professor Wendy O'Flaherty's translation is as follows:

When they divided the Man, into how many parts did they apportion him? What do they call his mouth, his two arms and thighs and feet? His mouth became the Brahmin; his arms were made into the Warrior, his thighs the People, and from his feet the Servants were born.

Ṛgveda Book X, Hymn 90, Verses 11-2; O'Flaherty 1981: 31

I find these to be quite close and that Griffith's work is just fine. But, occasionally Griffith is just wrong. This is the case in an important hymn on Vedic geography, one of the River or Sarasvati hymns (Book X, Hymn 75) where the correct geographical ordering of the rivers of northern India and Pakistan are given.

Professor Maurer got it right with:

Attend to this, my hymn of praise. O Ganga, Yamuna, Sarasvati, O Sutlej, Ravi! With Chenab, O Marudvrdha (confluence of Ravi and Chenab?), with Jhelum, harken! You, O Arjikiya, harken with Susoma.

Ṛgveda Book X, Hymn 75, Verse 5; Modified after Maurer 1986: 203.

Griffith's translation gives the rivers in the incorrect order: Ganga, Yamuna, Sutlej, Ravi, Sarasvati. This is a significant error, since this passage is one that may carry with it some important historical information and is a good example of how these texts can be used productively, if the translators do their jobs correctly.

Those who have studied the Ṛgveda invariably come away with a sense that there is historical information there, but this has to be treated conditionally and with caution. Clearly, there is exaggeration, bravado and self-aggrandizement, all of which are appropriate to the context and familiar in other religious books. But these qualities, and the overall liturgical nature of the work itself, make it difficult to evaluate the Ṛgveda as an historical document. It leaves one with a sense of ambiguity and filled with doubt.

On the positive side there is some geographical information in the Ṛgveda that has been relatively well studied. The rivers that are mentioned in the text can be equated with modern streams, some of which are now largely dry, as in the case of the ancient Sarasvati. The people who composed these hymns were clearly familiar with the Punjab, which they called the "land of the seven rivers." It is the territory from the Indus in the west to the Yamuna in the east, and from the mountains of the north to the panjnad in the south. Sindh was almost unknown to them, and the same is true of the Ganges Valley and Peninsular India.

THE INDUS AGE AND THE MODERN WORLD

Ancient Indian civilization represents one of the three or four enduring great experiments in human organization. It is represented in many ways: social organization, a complex interweaving of philosophy and practical knowledge, concepts of history, kingship, politics and power. One of the most important features is the concept of caste, or in north Indian vernacular "*jati*." Castes are historically deep, lineage-like, endogamous ranked social groups that are closely tied to specific occupations. With that close tie they can be thought of as functional units; specialized parts of a very large, complex organization, each element of which has to perform its job for the whole to operate in a complete, effective, harmonious way. There are elements in many socio-cultural systems that resonate with this form of organization. After all, the lords and ladies of England are organized into lineage-like social groups that are historically deep, ranked in the

European social pyramid and associated with traditional occupations. But, this is simply a form of complex social class. The feature that makes the Indian social order different is the refined philosophical and ideological foundation on which the system rests. The concept most central to the ancient Indian social order is *dharma*, a complex concept with wide meaning. In its broadest sense *dharma* refers to the natural laws of the universe that govern the cosmos, nature and human relations. This is the moral order, the right running world and in this sense there is a relationship to the ancient Egyptian concept of *maat*. These imply positive values like justice, truth, honesty, morality, social ideals and similar concepts. "Basic to dharma in practical life is the notion of karma or willed activity, which determines a man's future incarnation. Closely connected with this concept of dharma is the observance of caste rules for it is only within the caste framework that the observations of dharma may be best observed" (Walker 1968, Vol. 1: 275).

In spite of the occupational interrelationships, the ancient Indian social form was not merely functionalism, nor was it expediency, exploitation or an accident. If we read their texts it was, in fact, the only proper way for human beings to behave, and the complex, mystical concept of *dharma* makes it so. Without the specific philosophical and ideological foundation of *dharma* no system can claim to be based on the principles of caste or *jati*. Other sociocultural systems might look like it, or mimic it, but they are false: it is the philosophy and ideology that define ancient Indian social organization, not the functionalism of *jati*, or *jati*-like social groups.

There is no clear picture of when the caste system began, but it does not seem to be prehistoric. In part this emanates from the definition of caste taken here: historically deep, lineage-like, ranked social groups that are closely tied to traditional occupations, all of which is justified by, and rests upon, a refined philosophical and ideological foundation based on *dharma*. Without *dharma* there can be no caste, and since we can trace the beginnings and history of this concept through the first millennium BC the fully developed system must have its origins there, not in earlier prehistoric times. There was a complex social system of historically deep, lineage-like, endogamous ranked social groups, at least some of which may have been closely tied to specific occupations in prehistoric times, especially during the Mature Harappan. But, the philosophy of *dharma*, essential to the definition of caste used here, was apparently not a part of this social order. We cannot yet read the Indus script and this could change the picture on caste. But, there is nothing in the archaeological record that suggests the philosophical and ideological principles that define caste. The archaeological record has abundant testimony for social class and the functional interrelations of craft and career specialization that can be associated with the Mature Harappan, or possibly even earlier times. But these relationships are universal in complex societies based in ranked social classes and do not define caste.

There is a literary history to *dharma* and the growth of the philosophical and ideological apparatus that defines and justifies the functionalism of caste. Hints at the emergence of this social order are first seen in Book X, hymn 90 of the Ṛgveda, quoted above. The lines describe the society of the times as divided into four functional classes or *varnas*. They are different from *jati*, since many *jatis* taken together are linked to each of these classes, even today. In that sense the text in question is relevant to this discussion.

A. L. Basham has noted that in early Indian literature *varna* is seen far more frequently than *jati*, but by the late Vedic age, in the middle of the first millennium BC, it is possible that "...the first faint trace of caste is to be found in the careful cataloging of trades and professions..." (1967: 149). This is carried forward in the *Laws of Manu*, a work probably compiled just prior to the Christian era. Manu was a great lawgiver who codified the rules governing the behavior, responsibilities, and relationships between the early castes. This was so well done that Manu is

Plate 1.1. Aerial view of the Mound of the Great Bath at Mohenjo-daro. Courtesy of Michael Jansen.

Plate 1.2. Sir John Marshall. Photograph supplied by Bridget and Raymond Allchin.

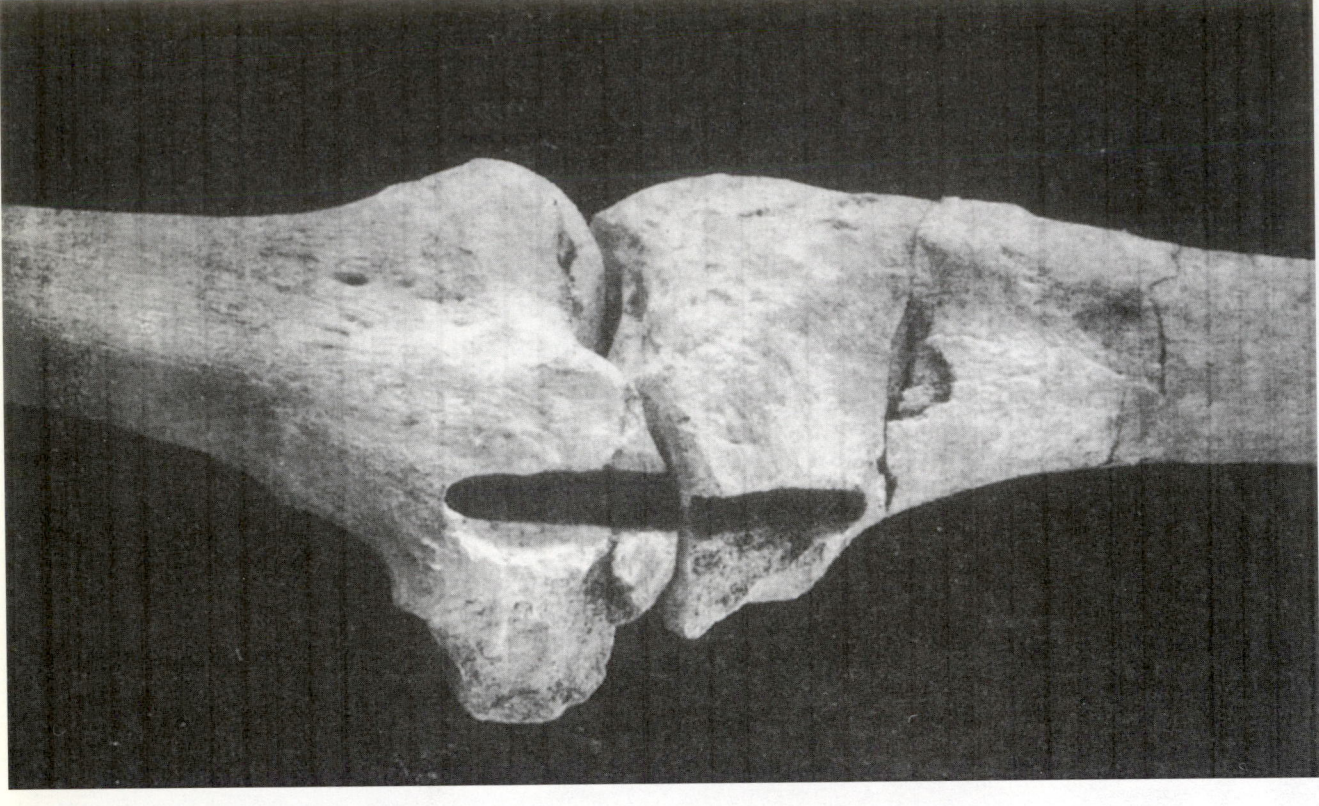

Plate 1.4. Knee joint of a person interred at Kalibangan. Courtesy of Archaeological Survey of India, after A.K. Sharma 1982a: Pl. 27-7.

Plate 1.3. Sir Mortimer Wheeler. Courtesy of Beatrice de Cardi.

regarded as the originator of the *chatur-varna*, or "four classes." "That this rigid four-fold division ever existed outside the lawbooks is disputed by many authorities" (Walker 1968, Vol. 1: 202).

Thus, the notion that the philosophy and ideology that define caste are a product of relatively late historical reflection has a basis in fact. This does not mean that historically deep, lineage-like, ranked, functional social units are a product of the same historical eras. These social classes seem to have deeper roots in the history of the Subcontinent, and although they are not all that is needed to define the Indian caste system, they are an integral part of it. As the story of the Indus Age unfolds it becomes apparent that there is continuity from prehistoric times through early historical South Asia to the present. It is also apparent that the functionalism implied in part by the *jati* system can be seen in the archaeological remains of the Indus Age.

HISTORY OF RESEARCH

The *Indus Age* has been written on historical principles, beginning with a section on the discovery of the ancient cities of the Indus and the work of the early giants in the field; men like Sir John Marshall and, Sir Mortimer Wheeler (Plate 1.2, Plate 1.3). The principal topics in all four books are generally dealt with from the perspective of the history of literature. There are several reasons for approaching the Indus Age in this way, the most important of which is that I enjoy this mode of exposition. This kind of narrative allows me to present and discuss a range of opinions on the Indus Age, both historically and from the perspective of a more contemporary literature. It is especially true for the ideas of my colleagues in India and Pakistan, since so much of their writing is published in books and journals that are not widely available in Europe and America. Over the past 20 years a vast literature on the Harappan Civilization and the Indus Age has appeared, and not all of the good ideas have come from the west.

From an epistemological point of view the reader will begin to see how the various perspectives on this subject have been shaped by what has been said before; why some issues are far better researched than others, why so many cliches about the Indus Age exist and why it has been so difficult to change many of the perceptions about ancient Indian civilization. Most important is the conviction I have about the study of the Indus Age; the study of culture history as a whole. What is known today is so tentative and fragmentary that it should not be assumed that it can be critiqued or managed in a way that comes close to approaching completeness. I have not shied away from offering my own opinion on the subject. There is an important range of well reasoned opinion in most areas of thought and fairness and caution have led me to present those opinions along with my own synthesis.

The downside to a book written from an historical perspective is that the exposition tends to grow. I have decided to ignore this and to proceed with a book that reflects the history of archaeological research on ancient India and Pakistan, and my own philosophy of knowledge.

DATA, SITE REPORTS AND THE LIKE

Archaeological data are very messy because a mass of detail emerges from even very modest excavations. The material from large, long-term programs of excavation as at Mohenjo-daro or Mehrgarh can be staggering. But, it is this detail that forms one of the empirical foundations on which our understanding of the Indus Age stands. No matter what the detail presented here might be, the serious student will *always* return to the original source to conduct publishable research.

The same is true for many of the illustrations in the volumes of the *Indus Age*, most specifically the site plans and maps. Many of the plans have been simplified from those in the original sources, to make them clearer to the general reader. The avoidance of distortion and error has been a goal for those who copied plans and drawings, but copies are copies after all and carry with them all that it implies. The maps showing regional settlement locations are sometimes at a very small scale, with the dot for a settlement location covering several square kilometers, larger than the largest ancient city. Plotting of sites on these maps has not been consciously misrepresented, but they are book illustrations not research documents and this difference needs to be respected. Geographical coordinates have been provided for as many sites of the Indus Age as possible. The serious researcher can use this information to create authoritative documents from the "Gazetteer of Sites of the Indus Age."

DIFFUSION, MIGRATION, FARMERS, HERDERS AND OTHER ITINERANTS

Archaeologists are generally drawn to making formal comparisons between the artifacts in their archaeological assemblages. These are based on similarities among the objects that have been gathered through surface exploration and excavation. Some of the comparisons between these assemblages are close, as between Mohenjo-daro and Harappa during Mature Harappan times. Some are less so, and there is a craft to creating anything like a coherent method, due in part to the fact that there are many dimensions on which artifacts can be compared—shape, decoration, material, the three primary variables. But, shape or form and decoration are not discontinuous variables. They are arranged on multidimensional continua, so the room for variability is very high. The same is true for material, but that can be controlled in better ways; through the use of physical analysis. There is a long-standing sense among archaeologists that the affinity between any set of archaeological assemblages varies directly with the similarities they exhibit in generically related characteristics; e.g., "The more the pots look alike the more closely related the assemblages are" (Binford 1968a: 8). There is a kind of corollary to this that suggests that the degree of relationship can be determined by the ratio of shared versus non-shared traits.

In spite of the fact that there is a good deal of truth in this observation on similarities among assemblages it presents archaeologists with serious problems (Binford 1968a: 8-12). Some of these are methodological or theoretical. How does one establish similarity and does it always mean the same thing (Lowie 1912: 28)? What are the dependent and independent variables in the analysis of artifacts (Binford 1968a: 9)? The method reduces the culture concept to a series of traits that are difficult to assemble into the integrated, or systemic, structure that best characterizes culture. Other inadequacies are simply bad practice, as with the way in which the Midwestern Taxonomic System has been abused (see Binford 1968a: 10-1).

Diffusion has also come into play, with the notion that the "...probability of diffusion having taken place increases directly with the degree of formal resemblance between items and traits" (Binford 1968a: 10). This is filled with conceptual problems. What are the historical and cultural forces that lead to the creation of cultural similarities? How are these creative forces established and maintained? Is diffusion the only mechanism that can be used to explain similarities among archaeological assemblages? What is the role of culture change and independent invention in convergence among archaeological assemblages? Julian Steward presents an interesting view of "diffusion" and "independent invention" that brings them together (1929b).

A deep understanding of the cultural dynamics that are being discussed here has eluded anthropologists. L. Binford proposed that we approach a resolution through a deductive process of hypothesis formulation and testing—"real science" (1962, 1965, 1967, 1968a, 1968c, 1968d). His was a search for the laws of human interaction and culture change, akin to the Laws of Thermodynamics set forth by Sir Isaac Newton. Binford's "new archaeologists" were in hot pursuit of these laws, along with culture process and the systemic view of culture that they proposed. That Binford's search has failed to produce such laws should surprise no one. The New Archaeology never matured into the science envisioned by its adherents. There was a nihilistic quality to some of the discourse, as well as much that was simply wrong. The New Archaeology also polarized archaeology, with positions on both sides far too entrenched and implacable for the good of anyone. On the other hand, the New Archaeology did have some favorable affects. First it brought attention to the need for disciplinary rigor along a number of fronts. Binford's provocation served to challenge virtually every archaeologist's thought. In the end it seems to have played an important role in taking away the worst of the shallow, suspicious, and intuitive "readings of the past." It brought out the need for archaeologists to think of their reconstructions (and culture process in general), in a more rigorous way, paying closer attention to the epistemological foundations of an argument. Formulating hypotheses and subjecting them to tests in the archaeological record proved difficult; but the notion of a test, and of setting up hypotheses, even if they are relatively weak, has proved to be better than what was generally being done in archaeology prior to Binford's proposed revolution. Finally, Binford challenged archaeologists to stop falling back on the negative side of the discipline, complaining for example, that the archaeological record was too incomplete to reconstruct this or that feature of society. He proposed that there was power in positive thought; that all aspects of the prehistoric world were potentially knowable. It was silly of archaeologists to defeat themselves before they started, by holding that anything other than this proposition was true.

The New Archaeology did not resolve the questions that surround the nature of culture process, culture change and the more mundane matters of the reconstruction of the Indus Age that engage me here. But, I have developed some personal rules or thoughts that are less theoretical than they are practical.

First, within the boundaries of a geographical unit like the Greater Indus Region, similarities among archaeological assemblages generally inform us about communication or interaction among the people who were responsible for creating those assemblages. This communication and interaction was undoubtedly made manifest in many ways, both directly and indirectly, through third, fourth, fifth, n... parties. Individual innovations in culture that had value to these peoples were spread in these ways throughout this region; for the most part this communication probably happened very quickly, over a matter of a few years (even weeks and months in some cases), but the acceptance and implementation of change may have taken longer. Such change could be accepted within the variable sociocultural systems of the Greater Indus Region because there were probably some close, underlying sociocultural similarities among these diverse peoples.

There is evidence for variation in the frequency and intensity of the various forms of communication and interaction throughout the Indus Age. But, it never dropped to nil, or even close to it. The region was always alive with activity linking the diverse peoples of the Indus Age— it is just that sometimes it was more alive than others.

The form that this communication and interaction took is not known in detail, or even with much certainty, but we have some hints of a range of activities that can be noted here. These come from the study of archaeology, the historical and ethnographic records and a reading of

14

the cultural geography. Based on the observation that the early history of the Indus Age is one of success and growth, it is reasonable to believe that balanced, symbiotic, relationships favorable to this end were in place. Anthropologists have used the term "exchange systems" to describe relationships that serve to share risk so that if disaster befalls one people in one place, their neighbors can be called upon to assist them. Such relationships enhance survivability (Mauss 1966; Cohen 1974). They also imply interaction, not only in the time of need, but also over protracted periods of time. The mechanism here is exchange, where the regular and predictable interchange of "gifts" is used to sustain a relationship that in part mollifies the hardship of periodic but unpredictable events—flood, crop failure, pestilence, warfare and other disasters.

Seasonality in the lives of farmers and herders is based in part on geography and the fact that adjacent regions can be complementary. The symbiosis of the highlands of Baluchistan and the Northwest Frontier with the Indus lowlands is one of the timeless facts of life within the Greater Indus Region (Figure 1.4). Migration of pastoralists from the mountains in the winter,

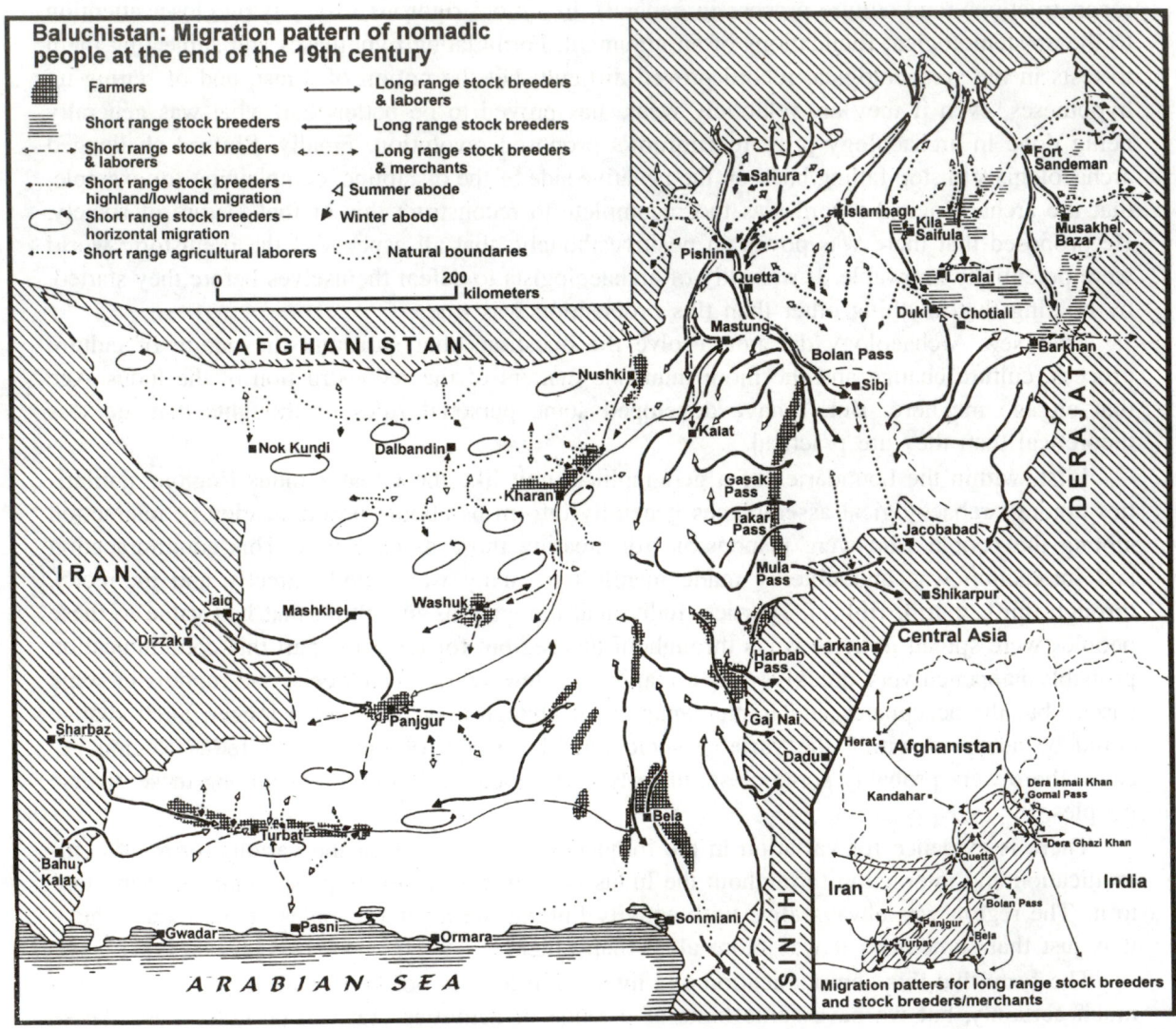

Figure 1.4. Migration between the highlands and lowlands in the Indus region, after Scholz 1983: Figure 5

and back again for the summer, is one of those constant, enduring patterns of movement and interaction that was present during the Indus Age and beyond, into modern times. These nomads are frequently also craftsmen, traders, tinkers, transporters, bards and messengers. They bring news from afar, and bring their children—potential marriage partners for friends whom they pass and live with in the course of their yearly round.

It is clear that the peoples of the Indus Age had a heavy dependence on animals, especially cattle, and to a lesser extent, sheep and goats. In this sense they were pastoralists, whether settled or nomadic. Seasonal nomadism must have been common. Some individuals may have been settled for a part of their life and nomadic at other times. The needs for pasture must have been intense, in some ways documented by Walter Fairservis (1967: 38-9). This leads unmistakably to the proposition that the constant search for pasture might have been one of the most important of the great engines that drove the interaction and communication within the Greater Indus Region. But, it should also be clear that not all of the mobile craftsmen, traders, tinkers, transporters, bards and messengers were embedded within the pastoral component of the subsistence economy. Some of them must have been sustained in other ways, outside of this subsistence regime. The nature of their integration into their own society and the sociocultural system of those around them, however, led to movement, travel, and the spread of products and ideas.

It is in the nature of people to contemplate what I think of as the "thrill of travel;" crossing a river just because the other side is there; visiting a "foreign" place just because it sounds interesting and would be a challenge to go there; going to an island that can be seen only from a mountain top just because no one has ever done it. This is very human stuff, and another of the range of human attitudes and activities that shapes the distribution of artifacts across a landscape like the Greater Indus Region. It implies the movement of people and their possessions as well as their skills.

Another related activity has to do with bards, and people who carry news. These are "professional" wanderers who tell tales, keep an oral folk literature alive and carry to new localities information of happenings in the places they have visited. They tell of famines and plagues, war and peace, marriages and deaths, the comings and goings of the great and near great, even of those who only pretend to such status.

We have little grasp of the details of the social structure of the peoples of the Indus Age; another of the real challenges to those who deal with these ancient peoples. By Mature Harappan times we do have a sense of a social hierarchy and craft and career specialists. There is also a sense of considerable ethnic or social diversity throughout the Indus Age. It comes from the disparate archaeological remains that can be dated to a single Stage or Phase of the history of the Indus Age, as well as from some considerations of physical anthropology.

This serious gap in our knowledge is simply another major challenge for future archaeologists who have chosen to work on the remains of the Indus Age. The life of families everywhere implies the movement of people and bringing new men or women into families after marriage is one source of mobility, even if the pattern is not neolocal. The elder generation may take up residence with the young at or near the end of their productive lives. There is often the sharing of children among dispersed segments of a family or "lineage." There are also the shorter term gatherings for marriages, births, rights of passage and "holidays." There is obviously much more to this dimension of social activity, but this is not the place to create a laundry list of possibilities. We clearly do not know the social forms of the peoples of the Indus Age, and therefore cannot talk about patrilocal post marriage residence, or the form of their lineages and/ or clans, even if they had them. But, what we can say is that the social life of people everywhere implies some degree of movement of themselves and their possessions; the artifacts that archaeologists find spread across the landscape of a place like the Greater Indus Region. They also imply the movement of people with skills to fashion artifacts, who for short periods and long, take up residence in varying locations. Thus, when we look at the geographical spread of artifacts it is not all trade and commerce, transportation specialists and pastoral nomads moving in their search for pasture. Some of it is the ordinary stuff of family business: of acquiring a mate, caring for the elderly, sharing happy or socially important occasions with relatives and friends.

It is these, and related activities, that are the forces of diffusion and migration, whether direct or indirect. The word "diffusion" is not used much in this book, but the study of the Indus Age is certainly concerned with the distribution of artifacts. Since we know that the artifacts themselves did not move in some self-propelled way across the Greater Indus Region, it is mechanisms of the kind noted here that must be invoked to explain these artifactual distributions. While we have little grasp of the specifics of the ancient world in terms of which of these activities or customs was responsible for this or that distributional pattern, we do have a grasp on a range of mechanisms that were used, and that is some progress. And it has been observed that the distributional patterns of artifacts change over historical time.

CHRONOLOGY: Terminology and Dates

Few things are more important in archaeology than chronology and it is with some disappointment that I have to admit that this is one of the most unstable and poorly known aspects of the story of the Indus Age. This disappointment is compounded by the fact that there is no agreed upon terminology for the periods, or Stages and Phases of development of the Indus Age. With the exception of one reasonably good cross reference to the Mesopotamian chronology, the entire scheme of absolute chronology for the Indus Age is based on radiocarbon dates, which presents its own special set of problems and considerations.

There are general discussions of chronology in South Asian archaeology in the following sources: B. B. Lal (1963); Dales (1966c); Meadow (1973); Agrawal and Kusumgar (1974a); Agrawal et al. (1978); Shaffer (1986a, 1992); Possehl and Rissman (1992); Possehl (1993b). Ramachandran (1975) and Possehl (1988, 1989) present lists of radiocarbon dates.

The lack of agreement on the chronology and culture historical terminology of the Indus Age has meant that my colleagues and I have been forced to develop our own schema, with inevitable differences among them. This has resulted in a virtual warren of chronological schemes, so many that even an expert in the field has difficulty keeping up. Good examples can be found in Fairservis (1956a: 349-53), Dales (1966c), Possehl (1977); Shaffer and Lichtenstein (1989), Shaffer (1992), and the recent syntheses by Allchin, B. and F. R. (1982) and Agrawal (1982a).

The use of numbers and/or letters for phases and periods vies with more synthetic attempts that contrast; for example, periods of "integration" with those of "disintegration," or an "Urban" with a "Post-urban Phase." None of these schemes is entirely satisfactory, in part because of the gradual increase in our knowledge and the differing assumptions, disciplinary predispositions and perspectives of those who have created the schema. Chronology and terminology are topics about which there is internal dissension among the experts themselves, each vying for his or her own view of the Indus Age. This seems to arise because each chronological scheme and attendant terms are based on theoretical assumptions about the nature of the archaeological record, the history of the Indus Age and an interpretation of what has been found. Since experts are divided on these fundamental issues the non-expert can be somewhat confused; perhaps discouraged at following the story of ancient India's earliest cities. Still, keeping everyone happy with a chronology and terminology is not a likely possibility.

The Beginnings of a Chronology

The date of the Mature Harappan, the times during which Mohenjo-daro and Harappa were functioning urban centers is based on both comparative analysis with the well documented Mesopotamian chronology, and a growing number of radiocarbon determinations (Possehl 1988, 1989, 1993b). The first absolute chronology for Mohenjo-daro and Harappa was derived from the similarity among seals found at these two sites and in excavations at Ur and Susa (Sayce 1924) as well as through a consideration of certain architectural features (Gadd and Smith 1924: 616). The evidence suggested that the Mature Harappan could be dated as early as 3000 BC and that the civilization had a duration of about 1000 years.

By 1953, with the appearance of the first edition of Sir Mortimer Wheeler's *The Indus Civilization*, revisions to the Mesopotamian chronology had shifted the absolute dates to 2500-1500 BC (Wheeler 1953: 84-93). This early, essentially pre-radiocarbon, chronology was based on the well attested appearance of a wide range of Harappan objects in the west (see Dales 1971, Lamberg-Karlovsky 1972, Asthana 1976, Ratnagar 1981 for general reviews).

The most convincing of these materials are the stamp seals with Indus script (Wheeler 1968: 114-18; Chakrabarti 1978a, 1978b, 1978c), etched carnelian beads (M.G. Dikshit 1949, During Caspers 1972, Reade 1979) and cubical Harappan weights (Ratnagar 1981: 184-86). Other classes of artifacts are also present (inlays, several types of beads, cosmetic implements and some pottery) but the strongest case is made with the more restricted body of data. It is widely agreed that these data are focused on the Akkadian Dynasty (2334-2154 BC), with some indications of slightly earlier contact during the Early Dynastic, as early as the so-called "Royal Graves of Ur," ca. 2550 BC (Chakrabarti 1982). The comparative data then "tail off" into signs of more restricted contact between the Indus Valley and Mesopotamia, heirlooms, or objects that raise methodological problems, possibly even comparisons with dubious chronological value.

Shortly after the appearance of *The Indus Civilization* the 1000 year chronology for the Mature Harappan began to be challenged. Walter A. Fairservis, Jr. (1956b) noted the absence of internal development and change within the Mature Harappan and suggested that the period of time encompassed by these remains could hardly be a millennium. He proposed that the duration of the Mature Harappan was on the order of 500 years, retaining the chronological center on the Akkadian period. By implication, the Fairservis dates for the Harappan Civilization were ca. 2500 to 2000 BC.

By 1964 there were sufficient radiocarbon dates, twenty-four in all, for D. P. Agrawal to suggest that the Fairservis hypothesis for the short chronology could be supported by this data set. Agrawal's analysis of the dates from Kalibangan and Lothal, as well as a few samples from Niai Buthi, Kot Diji and Mohenjo-daro suggested 2500 to 2000 BC (2300-1750 BC)[3] (Agrawal 1964: 950). The calibration revolution in radiocarbon dating had not yet arrived and the Agrawal dates were actually 2300-1750 BC. This chronology still received general acceptance from archaeologists interested in the Indus Civilization (e.g., Wheeler 1968, Allchin, B. and F. R. 1968, Fairservis 1971a), in spite of the fact that it left the Mature Harappan embarrassingly late with respect to the Akkadian Dynasty and the signs of contact with the Early Dynastic.

With the development of calibration curves for correcting the radiocarbon calendar, pioneered by the so-called "MASCA" correction curve from the University of Pennsylvania Museum of Archaeology and Anthropology (Ralph, Michael and Han 1973), the Agrawal chronology has been pushed back into conformity with the Fairservis hypothesis (see also Dales 1966c, 1973; Brunswig 1973, 1975). It is odd that the long, "1000 year," chronology still appears in some contemporary publications, in spite of the fact that for more than thirty years, archaeologists who have the Harappan Civilization as a central part of their scholarly lives have been using a 500 year chronology, generally thought to be almost entirely within the third millennium BC.

Terminology and Chronology

I have a predisposition to think of time in anthropological terms. Thus, the notion of "periods" with hard boundaries has been eschewed in favor of looser notions of "Phases" with "fuzzy" transitions. The use of the term "phase" is found as early as the attempts to define an internal chronology for Mohenjo-daro (Mackay 1937-38: xiv-xv). It reemerges quite clearly in my own work as well as that of Jim Shaffer (Shaffer and Lichtenstein 1989, Shaffer 1992). The scheme of Stages and Phases in relative chronological order that is used for the *Indus Age* is shown in Table 1.1.

TABLE 1.1
The Stages and Phases of the Indus Age

Stage One: Beginnings of Village Farming Communities and Pastoral Camps
      Kili Ghul Mohammad Phase
      Burj Basket Marked Phase

Stage Two: Developed Village Farming Communities and Pastoral Societies
      The Kechi Beg and Hakra Wares Phases are thought to have been generally contemporaneous.
      Togau Phase
      Kechi Beg Phase
      Hakra Wares Phase

Stage Three: Early Harappan
      Four Phases believed to have been generally contemporaneous
      Amri-Nal Phase
      Kot Dijian Phase
      Damb Sadaat Phase
      Sothi-Siswal Phase

Stage Four: The Early-Mature Harappan Transition
      Early-Mature Harappan Transition

Stage Five: Mature Harappan
      Five Phases thought to have been generally contemporaneous
      Sindhi Harappan Phase
      Kulli Harappan Phase
      Sorath Harappan Phase
      Punjabi Harappan Phase
      Eastern Harappan Phase
      Two Related Phases in adjacent regions thought to be generally contemporaneous with the Mature Harappan
      Quetta Phase
      Late Kot Diji Phase

Stage Six: Post-urban Harappan
      Jhukar Phase
      Early Pirak Phase
      Late Sorath Harappan Phase
      Lustrous Red Ware Phase
      Cemetery H Phase
      Swat Valley Period IV
      Late Harappan Phase in Haryana and Western Uttar Pradesh
      Late Harappan-Painted Gray Ware Overlap Phase
      Early Gandhara Grave Culture Phase

Stage Seven: Early Iron Age of Northern India and Pakistan
      Late Pirak Phase
      Painted Gray Ware Phase
      Late Gandharan Grave Culture Phase

Defining Phases and Stages

The Phase of the Indus Age is an archaeological construct based on an assemblage of material culture, which can be associated with a subsistence regime(s), patterns of trade and communication, sociocultural institutions and a geographic area. In some ways the Phase is like the old notion of an archaeological "culture," a term used rarely in today's anthropological archaeology. This is because we know there is a significant difference between the reality of "culture," as it is dealt with in contemporary life, and archaeological reconstructions. In most cases the archaeological reconstruction seems to fall far short of how "cultures" are perceived today and are, therefore, a serious distortion. Thus, using the term does not seem to be justified. I think of culture as the nonbiological means for human adaptation—a definition that may suffer from an overdose of functionalism, along with a dash of Marxism, but it is satisfactory as a kind of working construct.

Phases are then distinct sets of artifacts and the ways in which the people who made them were occupied. The shorthand for the Phase is the regional archaeological assemblage: the pots and pans, tools, weapons, architecture and other artifacts of the ancient past. In many, perhaps most, instances using the assemblage as a proxy for a Phase will work, and it has the advantage of creating an easily defined image for reference. But, the full reality of the Phase is a somewhat larger, more complex notion, especially when integrating the ancient subsistence regimes of the Indus Age.

Phases are not defined by a chronology, either relative or absolute; but a chronology can be ascribed to them. The independent variables in this equation are the artifacts and activities of ancient peoples. The dependent variables are the relative and absolute chronological facts that archaeologists gather as part of their research. The Phase is first defined and the chronology allowed to emerge from observation, analysis and additional data, such as radiocarbon dates. Phases have a distinct, but not always precisely defined, place in the stratigraphic sequences found in the Greater Indus Region. In this sense, they can be thought of as both periods of stability and change or development.

Contending with change within a Phase, even one that is 700 or 800 years long is difficult. Anthropological theory says that no culture would be entirely stable for such a protracted period of time. Still, the present level of sophistication available to handle the Phases of the Indus Age does not really allow us to define just what might be changing in most Phases. The Togau and Kechi Beg Phases, for example, may admit a degree of regional differentiation, but there is nothing that defines an early Togau Phase from a later one. The same is true for the Kechi Beg.

The Phases are, in fact, a kind of ideal construct or model. The variation of the Phase has been collapsed into a form of archaeological "type fossil;" a kind of norm or average that can be thought of as "typical." It is not an entirely desirable way to proceed with archaeological research, but is a candid reflection of the state of development in South Asian protohistory. It is clear that much needs to be done to correct this serious deficiency, and by outlining it in this way I hope that a spirit of research will be generated in students of this discipline to amend it.

The Phase and Stage terminology would seem to focus attention on the relative and absolute chronological beginnings and endings of these constructs. This is true in one particular way: the dates for the beginning and end are given on the principal chronological table. But in creating an archaeological norm or "type fossil" for the Phase, the construct is actually best defined toward its "center" or "mean" than at the edges, the beginning or end. The pictorial representations of the Phases actually depict not the early, emerging assemblage, or the transitional ending one, but something that is "typical" even perhaps "normative." Since the beginnings and endings are difficult to define and date, they are inherently "fuzzy." Improving on this situation is, again, a task for the future.

The Stage in the Indus Age

By gaining some sense of the form that Phases take, one can turn to the relative, stratigraphic sequence of the Greater Indus Region and begin to study which Phases precede or follow others. In reality, this is not quite so linear, because relative and absolute chronology are a part of the mix of features that one examines as a Phase is being constructed. But, it is important to focus on the archaeological assemblage and associated cultural features first and to let chronology emerge as it will. It is often necessary to reconsider and abandon ideas and constructs that at first made sense, but on more informed analysis appear flawed. One must be prepared to modify and rework the definition of Phases in light of new research and to review the stratigraphic record very carefully. No two archaeological assemblages are exactly the same and getting them to fit within a synthetic scheme represents an exercise that is more art than science.

With the Phases defined and their relative stratigraphic positions determined, it is possible to consider them at a somewhat higher level of abstraction; as cultural Stages. The scheme of Stages that unfolded for the Indus Age is almost purely intuitive but it has its roots in Walter Fairservis' 1967 paper in *Novitates*. My experience made it clear from the beginning that the Harappan Civilization, or Mature Harappan was sufficiently well known that it could be thought of as a single cultural Stage within which there were various regional Phases. It was equally obvious that the work of Jean-Francois Jarrige and his team at Mehrgarh had brought us to the point where an initial period of village farming communities and pastoral camps could be defined. The cities seem to anchor one point of development and a beginning point, or threshold, could be established by turning to Mehrgarh I, Kili Ghul Mohammad I and similar sites. This left the question of how to handle the time between the Mature Harappan and the earliest villages of the Kili Ghul Mohammad Phase.

M. Rafique Mughal (1970) defined what he called the "Early Harappan Period" that preceded the Harappan Civilization. He dealt extensively and well with the Kot Diji assemblage, and early materials from northern Baluchistan. But, he did not give the Amri assemblage the importance it should have been accorded. There was also related material that was beginning to come into focus from places like Kalibangan and Mitathal that Mughal did not have access to. But, by using his "Early Harappan Period" as a starting place it was possible to identify four Phases of the Early Harappan Stage that fit the scheme being developed. With a good handle on the Mature Harappan and the four Phases of an Early Harappan it was then possible to turn to the earlier history of the Greater Indus Region.

There seems to have been a protracted period of time between the beginning of the village farming community in Pakistan and the Early Harappan Stage; perhaps about 4000 years. This would have been a long period for a single cultural Stage since, as we read it now, the Early Harappan is close to 600 or 700 years in duration and the Mature Harappan Stage about 500 years. These observations suggested that at least one more cultural Stage was called for; one that preceded the Early Harappan and followed the earliest villages and pastoral camps, which led to the definition of "Stage Two: Developed Village Farming Communities and Pastoral Societies." Deciding on the Phases that would form the beginning of Stage Two was again made easier by the work at Mehrgarh. Period III there is dominated by hard fired red wares, probably made on a fairly fast potter's wheel. One type is called "Togau" and it has a very wide distribution. This period at Mehrgarh also marked a significant increase in craft activity, including evidence for metallurgy, and the maturation of the subsistence system. The following Kechi Beg Phase fit quite snugly into Stage Two since it seems to follow on the Togau and to be chronologically older than the Early Harappan.

With Stage Two in place, the beginnings of the Indus Age could be addressed. A decision had been made that this be coterminous with the beginnings of settled life and the domestication of plants and animals. There was then Stage One made up of the earliest of farmers and herders, followed by Stage Two which was more developed. The next Stage Three preceded the widely known Mature Harappan of the Indus Civilization. The general order and flow of these Stages was satisfactory but there was a sense of unease with the poor fit between the end of the Early Harappan and the beginning of the Mature Harappan. They appear to be different in both style and content. In so many ways, the Early Harappan does not seem to be a "jumping off point" for the urbanization that follows it.

The transition between the Early and Mature Harappan is still not understood very well, but in recent years several archaeological assemblages that appear to bridge these two Stages have been found (Possehl 1993b). The one best documented is at Nausharo (Jarrige 1988a: 200-03). There is another at Harappa (Kenoyer 1991a: 44-50), and a third assemblage at Ghazi Shah (Flam 1993a). In hindsight we can now see that Jean-Marie Casal defined the transition at Amri in his Period II (Casal 1964a: 39-42), a stroke of no small genius. Something like a Transitional Stage may have been found in Haryana at Banawali (Bisht 1982: 116) and Kunal (Khatri and Acharya 1995; GLP's personal observation on the collections). This emerging construct seemed to demand a separate Stage and led to the final modification of the scheme.

The Radiocarbon Chronology

Up to this point relative chronology was used with minimum attention to absolute dates. The method I employed attempted to define Phases in terms of archaeological variables and the things we learn about past peoples that have boundaries in space and relative chronology. It was necessary to bring these defined units into relative stratigraphic association: which Phases were stratigraphically earlier than others, which Phases were stratigraphically later, which seemed to be contemporary with one another. It is an imperfect method because the stratigraphic information needed to be sure of necessary deductions is not always available, but it is a good place to start. It should be reasonably obvious that the process of developing and teasing the present scheme into shape was not a linear, step by step exercise. There was always give and take, looping back to old ideas that needed revision in the light of new information or insights. But, the model of starting with the archaeological assemblages and working out boundaries for them before attacking the absolute chronology was one that could be adhered to with a certain amount of faithfulness.

Turning to absolute chronology is the final step in the process. Archaeologists have learned that constructing a radiocarbon chronology is neither simple nor straightforward. Anomalous dates occur at most sites, sometimes in abundance, as at Mehrgarh and Kalibangan. Some important sites, like Anjira, Kulli and Chanhu-daro, do not have radiocarbon dates, which means that comparative methods have to be used to estimate their ages. Single radiocarbon determinations for a Phase or strata cannot be relied on. A dependable laboratory can make an accurate determination of the point in time when the organism from which the sample has been taken stopped exchanging ^{14}C with the outside environment. This moment is usually thought of as "death." But, a host of uncontrolled variables comes into play that compromises this simple equation. For example, wood is often reused, sometimes for several generations, especially in an arid environment (Schiffer 1986). It is also known that wood from the center rings of a large, very old tree will be dated to an earlier era than the wood from the younger, outer rings of the same tree. Ancient peoples frequently dug in their habitation areas, creating wells, foundation trenches, storage facilities and trash pits which disturbed and redistributed older archaeological strata, and the charcoal in them. This sometimes brought older carbon into association with younger artifacts. The problem is compounded by burrowing animals, especially rodents and worms, both in antiquity and modern times.

Archaeological sites in the making are not static geophysical environments; but neither are the mounds when they have been abandoned. One need only reflect for a moment to realize that these are just the most obvious of the taphonomic (site formation) processes that can disrupt the radiocarbon chronology for an individual site. Even if the archaeologist who collects a radiocarbon sample knows the historical context from which it is being taken, there is no guarantee that the resulting date will provide a correct estimate for this context.

There are ways to ameliorate these problems. Large chunks of wood from very old trees, which may have been parts of living communities for many years, should be avoided as samples to be dated; better to take twigs. Charred grain, fruit pits and pips also make good radiocarbon samples. Carbon samples from trash pits, perhaps containing earth and material from different periods in a site, should not be used. There is also a need to evaluate the radiocarbon dates from individual sites. Single dates are not considered conclusive: they should come in a series. The earliest dates should be at the bottom of a stratified site and progress as one moves up the stratigraphic column. Dates from an individual stratum should be internally consistent and be consistent with dates for similar stratigraphic contexts at other sites. Dates that are completely out of line with their "neighbors" can sometimes be ignored. The process of evaluation has to be controlled and reasoned without being overly manipulative, forcing a conclusion on a data set. There are many sites in the world where a radiocarbon chronology does not seem to have worked. Two sites in the Subcontinent, Kalibangan and Mehrgarh, appear to be in this category.

The calibration of radiocarbon dates is essential, since it has been known from the early 1970s (Ralph, Michael and Han 1973) that the "calendar" of radiocarbon dates is not the same as the "calendar" for the progression of the earth around the sun. The reason for this is not completely understood, but it seems to be related to different amounts of carbon fourteen in the atmosphere. Why the aggregate of carbon fourteen changes is open to debate; but there are now very good curves and tables, some computerized, available for the calibration of dates that turn radiocarbon years into a very good estimate of calendrical years. They are the result of controlled dating of thousands of wood samples of known ages that come from long lived trees like the sequoia, or the bristlecone pine. These samples are first dated by counting the annular tree rings to establish the precise age of the wood. The wood is then run through the radiocarbon dating process. By statistically treating the large number of dates derived from this method, a reliable curve documenting the deviation between true "tree ring" dates and the ^{14}C date is arrived at. For radiocarbon dates older than about 10,000 BP, where the ability to calibrate ends, the usual practice is to simply report the date as "^{14}C years BP;" that it is 'n' number of radiocarbon years old.

Radiocarbon dates in Tables in the *Indus Age* will appear as calibrated dates only. A full date list appears as Appendix B to this volume. Here the information takes three forms: (1) the date computed on the older, inaccurate "Libby half-life" of radiocarbon at 5568 years. The use of this older half-life is the one retained in the official reports given in the journal *Radiocarbon*. As is their convention, this date is given in years "before present" or "bp," which is, by convention, before 1950 AD; (2) the date given by the most accurate half-life of radiocarbon at 5730 years, but as a "bc" (before Christ) or "bce" (before common era) date, with 1950 years subtracted and rounded to the nearest five years; (3) all radiocarbon determinations have been calibrated using the "Calib" computer program (version 3.1) from Prof. M. Stuiver of the Quaternary Isotope Laboratory at the University of Washington, Seattle. The calibrated dates used here are based on the calibration curves he and his colleagues have developed. In conformity with international conventions, calibrated and other "true" calendrical dates will be presented with upper case "BC" or "AD," at times preceded by "cal." Uncalibrated radiocarbon dates will be presented with lower case "bc" or "ad." In the end those of us who deal with the radiocarbon chronology have to be ready to sift and weigh the evidence and follow what one hopes is the preponderance of the data. There is ample room for honest error in this exercise, as well as occasions where one can inadvertently become trapped in various forms of self-fulfilling hypotheses, circular reasoning and bad guesses. This is a somewhat humbling aspect of my profession, but I face up to the challenge resolutely, with no small amount of trepidation.

The absolute chronology for the Stages and Phases of the Indus Age that has been developed for this book is as follows:

TABLE 1.2
The Absolute Chronology of the Indus Age

Stage One: Beginnings of Village Farming Communities and Pastoral Camps	
Kili Ghul Mohammad Phase	7000-5000 BC
Burj Basket-marked Phase	5000-4300 BC
Stage Two: Developed Village Farming Communities and Pastoral Societies	
Togau Phase	4300-3800 BC
**Kechi Beg Phase	3800-3200 BC
**Hakra Wares Phase	3800-3200 BC
**The Kechi Beg and Hakra Wares Phases are thought to have been generally contemporaneous	
Stage Three: Early Harappan Four Phases thought to have been generally contemporaneous	
Amri-Nal Phase	3200-2600 BC
Kot Dijian Phase	3200-2600 BC
Sothi-Siswal Phase	3200-2600 BC
Damb Sadaat Phase	3200-2600 BC
Stage Four: The Early-Mature Harappan Transition	
Early-Mature Harappan Transition	2600-2500 BC
Stage Five: Mature Harappan Five Phases thought to have been generally contemporaneous	
Sindhi Harappan Phase	2500-1900 BC
Kulli Harappan Phase	2500-1900 BC
Sorath Harappan Phase	2500-1900 BC
Punjabi Harappan Phase	2500-1900 BC
Eastern Harappan Phase	2500-1900 BC
Two Related Phases in adjacent regions thought to be generally contemporaneous with the Mature Harappan	
Quetta Phase	2500-1900 BC
Late Kot Diji Phase	2500-1900 BC
Stage Six: Post-urban Harappan	
Jhukar Phase	1900-1800 BC
Early Pirak Phase	1800-1000 BC
Late Sorath Harappan Phase	1900-1600 BC
Lustrous Red Ware Phase	1600-1300 BC
Cemetery H Phase	1900-1500 BC
Swat Valley Period IV	1650-1300 BC
Late Harappan Phase in Haryana and Western Uttar Pradesh	1900-1300 BC
Late Harappan-Painted Gray Ware Overlap Phase	1300-1000 BC
Early Gandhara Grave Culture Phase	1700-1000 BC
Stage Seven: Early Iron Age of Northern India and Pakistan	
Late Pirak	1000-700 BC
Painted Gray Ware	1100-500 BC
Late Gandharan Grave Culture	1000-600 BC

The fact that the study of absolute chronology is one of the most volatile topics in archaeology has already been noted; schemes are constantly changing. Archaeologists are always learning new things that cause them to reevaluate their dating, and different archaeologists examining the same set of "facts" often develop very different chronologies. For example, Jean-Francois Jarrige takes serious difference with the notion of a Late Kot Dijian Phase in the Derajat and Northwest Frontier. This Phase was first defined by K. D. Thomas and F. R. Allchin (1986) based on a stylistic analysis of the artifacts and a long series of radiocarbon dates from sites in that region. These three archaeologists are looking at the same "facts" and reading them in a very different way.

Evaluating the Chronology

The absolute chronology for the Indus Age remains nothing more than a broad outline. There is room for improvement of our dating all through the sequence and this inevitably means that there is room for disagreement among authorities in the field. There is more agreement on the relative stratigraphy, but even here there is margin for debate on particular issues. For example, the relationship between the Hakra Wares Phase and the Early Harappan (Kot Diji and Sothi-Siswal Phases) is not well documented, with only Jalilpur providing a hint of the relative stratigraphy. The scheme presented here could be wrong on this point, but only future field work will resolve it.

Three additional critical points concerning this chronology are:

1. A well run radiocarbon sample from third millennium contexts can be expected to have a one sigma deviation between 100 and 125 years, which is a swing of 200 to 250 years on the central point of the date. The resulting lack of precision in a radiocarbon chronology is a weakness inherent in the method and contributes to the appearance of a linear sequence of change.

2. Some Phases have almost no dates at all, and yet the material has to be accommodated within the relative stratigraphy of a regional sequence, which means that some of the reasoning behind this chronology is necessarily an educated guess.

3. The relative stratigraphy of the Greater Indus Region is still incomplete. For example, in Gujarat there is a "missing millennium" separating the end of the Lustrous Red Ware Phase and the beginning of the Iron Age.

In spite of all these uncertainties, presenting the scheme in its present form has its advantages. The user will not be deceived into believing that the archaeologists who work on Indus material are any wiser than they actually are. No one is fooled into believing that there is a precision to the dating techniques. This scheme also highlights the real need for further work on the chronology of the Indus Age. In some ways, this is routine archaeological research, but it is also fundamental to furthering an understanding of South Asia's earliest farmers and herders. The absolute chronology presented here is as detached from presumptions about the culture history of the Indus Age as I can make it. The dates have been evaluated in a way that it is hoped are free of theoretical presumptions and second guessing. The radiocarbon determinations do not speak for themselves, but every attempt has been made to resist injecting the chronology with impressions of Harappan culture history, rather than the facts as they now stand. No chronology in South Asian archaeology—possibly no archaeological chronology, period!—can be totally free of the bias of the scholar who creates it, so the claims just made are an ideal that has not really been achieved. Objectivity was a goal, and that is the best effort that one can make.

Linear Culture Historical Sequences

The chronological scheme presented in Table 1.2 is basically linear, with patterns of change presented as though they took place simultaneously over vast areas of the northwestern region of the Subcontinent. This is almost certainly not the historical reality of the times. For example, it seems unlikely that the Transition from the Early Harappan to the Mature Harappan began at the same time in all regions of the Early Harappan area, or that the transition from the Togau to the Kechi Beg Phase took place at the same instant wherever they were found. Archaeologists do not really know when, for example, the Kechi Beg Phase, or the one called "Togau" began. Even the notion that Stages and Phases have something called a "beginning" and an "end" is a debatable historical concept. In the first place the archaeological assemblages themselves are not defined with sufficient breadth, or precision, to be endowed with meaning that goes beyond a kind of crude approximation. They are archaeological devices that have to be invoked in the absence of chronological precision. One would err with mistaken concreteness to believe otherwise. Thus, the thought that the Togau Phase, or any of the other Phases and Stages, began in a particular year, let alone a particular month, week, day, hour or minute, is absurd. While history is occasionally played out in a way that leads to the isolation of moments of historical importance that can be fixed with considerable chronological precision, in general this is not the case. Certainly the culture historical sequence outlined here is not likely to have such an event like quality. Given all of this 4300 BC was selected as an approximation of the date for the "end" of the Burj Basket-marked Phase and the shift to Togau times; and 3800 BC was selected as the best approximation for the "end" of the Togau Phase and the shift to the Kechi Beg.

When the Harappan Civilization began, or if it really "began" at all, is not known. At present, 2500 BC is, from the perspective of a twentieth century archaeologist, the best approximation for something that looks like an event. Moreover, using 2500, and the other round numbers, is a constant reminder of our ignorance and serves as an ever present caution not to believe that we know more than we really do.

As chronological control and precision are developed to the point where we are really in control of the dates of the Phases and Stages of the Indus Age, the discussion of chronology will have to move to a new conceptual level. Then we will begin to see what is already sensed; that the Phases and Stages do not have crisp beginnings and endings and some areas will be seen to be more conservative and retain older styles in their artifactual assemblages. The subtleties, vagaries and complexities of the historical record will begin to emerge and defeat the simplistic conceptual schemes of past scholarship. This will demand intellectual innovation, probably the abandonment of Phases and Stages altogether, as we move to handle data sets that are far more particularistic in their detail but still need to be integrated and synthesized.

Dates for some Phases are more securely determined than others. In general, the younger the phase the better our control over its date, but this is not always true. For example, it is apparent that the beginnings of the Harappan Civilization toward the middle of the third millennium BC are better known than the process of eclipse, which seems to take place at different rates and at different times in the various Regions of the former civilization.

Jim G. Shaffer's 1992 chronology for the Indus Valley, Baluchistan and Helmand Traditions is presented in a way that seems to be somewhat "nonlinear," with much overlap between Phases as seen on his Fig. 2 (Shaffer 1992: Vol. II, 426). It is not clear whether this overlap is because of the inherent weakness of the radiocarbon method or an artifact of history. Shaffer is well aware of this.

26

THE GAZETTEER OF SITES OF THE INDUS AGE

My archaeological research has an obvious geographical bias. An effort has been made to avoid determinism in this area, and others as well, but geography is an important element in the mix of factors that play a role in unfolding human history. I also like maps and plans as aids that save words and present history in a visual way (Fig. 1.5). This predilection is complemented by another bias, one that seeks to bring comprehensive order to large data sets, as evidenced in my scholarly life as a part-time bibliographer (Possehl 1979b) and organizer of radiocarbon dates (Possehl 1988, 1989). This affliction also propelled me toward bringing order to information on the sites of the Indus Age.

Most archaeologists would agree, I think, that the concept of a "site" is one of the fundamental building blocks of our discipline. Archaeologists have spent millions of dollars finding and excavating these places. Thus, the non-archaeologist might be surprised to learn that for most of the regions of the world the records for site location, date, size and general character are totally inadequate, in some cases even chaotic. It has been clear from the very beginning of my involvement with the Indus Age that those who study these ancient peoples have lost control over the location, periods of occupation and other information gathered for their settlements. After trying to compile data on cards, sometimes using knitting needles as spindles, I found that computer technology is extraordinarily well suited to handing this kind of intellectual problem. The personal computer revolution in the 1980s placed this technology on my desk and gave me a tool with which to manage the process of building a Gazetteer of Sites of the Indus Age (see Appendix A).

There are about 2600 sites that relate to the history of the Indus Age. The number changes almost daily in the data base used to record them. New places are being discovered each year, and duplicates still have to be removed. The double counting of sites is a serious problem in South Asian archaeology because there is no uniform standard of reporting and many ancient settlements have more than one designation. For example, a mound in Gujarat might be known to some of the farmers in its vicinity as "Hanuman-no-Timbo" (the mound of Hanuman) and be located in Pipal village. It is legitimate archaeological practice to report sites under one or both of these names, the timbo or the village. So one report might be given as "Hanuman-no-Timbo" in Pipal village and a second one simply as "Pipal." Without further information it would appear that there are two sites. Some sites have been reported under their "timbo" name and their village name in different publications, by the same author. It is also true that some inhabitants of any given village, Pipal for example, know a mound under one name (e.g., Hanuman-no-Timbo) and others call it something else (e.g., Nesdi), compounded by the lingering problem of "Pipal."

Assigning the correct relative chronology to a surface collection from one of the sites of the Indus Age is an art. It is widely agreed among professionals that this topic is also filled with confusion, and the information at hand has to be considered an approximation of historical reality, not historical reality itself. There are some surveys that have been conducted with impeccable accuracy and sound record keeping; M. Rafique Mughal's work in Cholistan (Mughal 1997) for example, or the explorations of Jagat Pati Joshi and his team (J. P. Joshi 1986, 1990b). But, they are exceptions to the general pattern.

These problems, and many others, might lead one to despair that this data set will ever be controlled in a precise and accurate way. Experience tells me that the Gazetteer I have assembled is not a finished or polished effort, and much work still needs to done. The version that is published as part of the *Indus Age* will simply be as good as I can make it.

Although the Gazetteer is less than perfect, it is also the best, most comprehensive and accurate document of its type for the Indus Age. Hundreds of hours were spent compiling and checking this data set and the simple mistakes were winnowed out long ago. After much work the Gazetteer has reached a point where it has utility; not final, absolute authority, but utility nonetheless. It is not so encumbered with errors that a reasonable scholar would hesitate (even critically) to use it.

The Gazetteer with its comprehensive coverage of the settlements and the revised chronology for the Phases and Stages allows us to begin to perceive the demographic changes during the Indus Age. It is certainly possible to see graphically the huge increases in the number of settlements over time, from 20 in the Kili Ghul Mohammad Phase to over 500 during the Early Harappan Stage. The size indicated for some of the sites gives us the ability to estimate the net settled area, gaining a foothold on changes in the populations of the Stages and Phases.

A CONSIDERATION FROM HUMAN BIOLOGY

Introduction

The record for human interments of the Indus Age is uneven and that in itself is marked by considerable diversity. Over the years much has been learned about the funerary customs and biology of the peoples of the prehistoric times in India and Pakistan, as H. V. Vallois predicted:

> If there is one region of the world where the existence of a human or pre-human form may one day be demonstrated, it is Southern Asia, which was once vaster than it is today and where life has always been so prolific...Prehistoric anthropological investigations in India have a splendid future before them.[4]

Mehrgarh is the only site of Pre-urban times to have produced a significant number of burials. While these data are useful, it is advisable to use caution when materials from just one site must be used. Sampling, preservation and regionalism are all important factors in shaping the record, and it cannot be assumed that data from a single site are representative of anything other than that place, and even that carries some qualification. For the Mature Harappan the record is a good deal more robust, although there are still serious gaps.

Human Biological Affinities: Historical Perspectives

The Indus Age was discovered at a time when the concept of "race" was still very much current in history and science. In their report on the initial excavations at Mohenjo-daro, Colonel R. B. Seymour Sewell and B. S. Guha used anthropometric measurements and descriptive features of twenty-six skeletons and found four racial groups: Proto-Australoid, Mediterranean, Alpine and the Mongolian branch of the Alpine stock (Sewell and Guha 1931b; Keith 1931). This racial typology of Indus peoples has been widely referenced although the use of racial typology has been discredited for many years.

Except for a few historical references, older racial concepts will not be used here, but physical types will be investigated. The differences are important, and because the notion of "race" remains prominent among some scholars in South Asia (Guha 1935; Chatterjee and Kumar 1962, 1964; Cappieri 1959, 1960, 1965, 1970, 1971; Dutta 1975, 1983) the reasons for its dismissal as a biological concept are meaningful. There are good references to document this position which can be found in contemporary text books on human biology. The ones I like

28

Figure 1.5. Excavated sites of the Indus Age

Key to Figure 1.5

1 Adatjo-daro
2 Ahar
3 Ahichchhatra
4 Ahmadwala Ther
5 Alamgirpur
6 Ali Murad
7 Aligrama
8 Allahdino
9 Ambkheri
10 Amra
11 Amri
12 Anjira
13 Arabjo Thana
14 Atkot
15 Atranjikhera
16 Babar Kot
17 Bagor
18 Bahadrabad
19 Baharia
20 Balakot
21 Balathal
22 Balu
23 Banawali
24 Bandhni
25 Bara
26 Bargaon
27 Bhagratrav
28 Bhagwanpura
29 Bhorgarh
30 Bhudan
31 Bhurtana
32 Binjor One
33 Birkot Ghwandai
34 Bisauli
35 Burj, Patiala
36 Burzahom
37 Butkara One
38 Chandigarh
39 Chanhu-daro
40 Chauro
41 Dabar Kot
42 Dadheri
43 Daimabad
44 Damb Buthi
45 Damb Sadaat
46 Damkot
47 Daulatpur
48 Daulatpur
49 Deh Morasi Ghundai
50 Derawar Ther
51 Desalpur
52 Dhansa
53 Dhatva
54 Dher Majra
55 Dholavira
56 Dwarka
57 Ganeshwar
58 Ghalegay Cave
59 Ghazi Shah
60 Ghuram
61 Gilund
62 Gufkral
63 Gumla
64 Harappa
65 Hastinapura

66 Hathala
67 Hathial West
68 Hulas
69 Islam Chowki
70 Jakhera
71 Jalilpur
72 Jekhada
73 Jhang
74 Jhangar
75 Jhukar
76 Jodhpura
77 Jokha
78 Kalait One
79 Kalako Deray
80 Kalepar
81 Kalibangan
82 Kanewal, Keseri Sing No Timbo
83 Kanewal, Sai No Tekro
84 Kaothe
85 Kapoto Rock Shelter
86 Karez Site
87 Kargushki Damb
88 Kathpalon
89 Kaudani
90 Kechi Beg
91 Khatoli
92 Kherai Graveyard
93 Kili Ghul Mohammad
94 Kohtras Buthi
95 Kot Diji
96 Kotla Nihang Khan
97 Kranai Hill
98 Kudwala Ther
99 Kulli
100 Kunal
101 Kuntasi
102 Lak Largai
103 Lakhabawal
104 Lakhiyo
105 Lakhueenjo-daro
106 Lal Qila
107 Lal Shah
108 Langhnaj
109 Lewan
110 Loebanr 3
111 Lohri
112 Lohumjo-daro
113 Loteshwar
114 Lothal
115 Malvan
116 Manda
117 Manorana
118 Mashak
119 Mehgam
120 Mehi
121 Mehrgarh
122 Miri Qalat
123 Mirzapur
124 Mitathal
125 Moghul Ghundai
126 Mohenjo-daro
127 Moti Pipli
128 Motidharai
129 Mundigak
130 Nagal
131 Nagar
132 Nageswar

133 Nagwada One
134 Nal
135 Naru Waro Dharo
136 Nausharo
137 Niai Buthi
138 Nindowari
139 Noh
140 Nohar
141 Nundara
142 Oriyo Timbo
143 Othmanjo Buthi
144 Pabumath
145 Padri
146 Paijo Kotiro
147 Pandi Wahi
148 Periano Ghundai
149 Pirak
150 Pithadia, Rajkot
151 Pokhran Landi
152 Quetta Miri
153 Raja Karna Ka Qila One
154 Raja Karna Ka Qila Two
155 Rajpur Parsu
156 Rana Ghundai
157 Rangpur
158 Rawalwas Kalan
159 Rehman Dheri
160 Roheljo Kund
161 Rohira
162 Rojdi
163 Ropar
164 Said Qala Tepe
165 Saipai
166 Sandhanawala Ther
167 Sanghol
168 Santhli One
169 Santhli Two
170 Sarai Khola
171 Sarangpur
172 Shahi Tump
173 Shahjo Kotiro
174 Sheri Khan Tarakai
175 Shikarpur
176 Shortughai
177 Siah Damb, Surab
178 Sibri Cemetery
179 Siswal
180 Somnath
181 Sothi
182 Spina Ghundai
183 Sunet
184 Sur Jangal
185 Surain Damb
186 Surkotada
187 Sutkagen-dor
188 Taraghada
189 Tarakai Qila
190 Tarkhanwala Dera
191 Tharro Hill
192 Tigrana
193 Toji Damb
194 Tokaria Timbo
195 Trihni
196 Vagad
197 Valabhi
198 Warthan
199 Zekhada

best were written by Kenneth A. R. Kennedy, a scholar who works in South Asia (Kennedy 1970-71, 1976).

The traditional concept of "race" refers to a large body of people who share many biological (physical) features that can be used to distinguish them from other people who live within their region or in surrounding regions. Physical anthropologists and others who deal with human biology have found that by and large human physical features rarely, if ever, form the kind of large population clusters that the concept of race implies.

The pattern of biological features within most regions is better characterized by variation in physical form than by homogeneity. When larger world patterns are studied, such as those of physical features between geographical regions, the pattern that emerges is not clusters of co-varying traits, but rather gradual clines of change for each trait analyzed. For example, the tendency for humans of light skin color to be found in the northern latitudes which gradually gives way to darker pigmentation moving south toward the equator. These clines are never wholly regular and there are always a healthy number of exceptions, demonstrating that the clustering of human biological traits among significant numbers of people is itself the exception rather than the rule.

Humans do form biological populations and these share many physical features, but they are seldom of a size that approaches that proposed for races. The notion of relatively small populations with distinct features is important in the early culture history of the Indus Age, even if the changes suggested by them are not fully understood. Some changes may be due to the isolation of small populations and operation of the evolutionary process of genetic drift.

More theoretically, the physical features that have been selected to construct racial typologies are phenotypic expressions that combine genetic makeup with acquired environmental factors. This manifestation is not necessarily the sole expression of the genetic composition of the individual being examined. The actual genetic composition, or genotype, of an individual is complex, but one thing is certain, the phenotypic expression that can be seen and measured in an individual does not directly reflect the genetic composition of that human. For example, blue eyes are an expression of two genes for blue, but brown eyes result from either a brown-brown pairing or a brown-blue combination. Thus, the genetic makeup of an individual with brown eyes cannot be determined from that observation alone.

Many, perhaps most, biological features result from a complex set of genetic interactions and are not the product of a simple one on one genetic constitution. In addition, the environment can shape features that are genetically constituted. The overall shape of the cranium, a classic topic for racial study, results from the genetic control of five very large and many smaller bones. The final shape of a human head is the result of an immensely complex biological interaction where similar outcomes can result from significantly different genotypes. People with round heads (brachycephalics) must be seen as a genetically diverse group and not homogenous in that they all share a single gene for "round headedness." It is also clear that there are environmental influences on cranial shape, the most important of which are nutritional and developmental factors.

A good example of a misinterpretation of cranial measurements is given by Kennedy (1982a: 293). He cites B. S. Guha's (1935) thought that a "foreign intrusion" could be used to account for the low incidence of mesocrany and brachycrany among the Harappan skulls available to him. This kind of historical interpretation is not in harmony with the biological reality that indicates that cranial form is a result of both genetic and environmental factors. In the end, changes in nutrition may have a greater effect on cranial shape than elements that migrate into a population's gene pool. On the other hand, there still seems to be some mystery in craniology. The following from Kenneth A. R. Kennedy gives some insight into this topic:

> One is also aware that brachycranialization has continued as an evolutionary trend in world populations during the last 10,000 years. While specific causes for this phenomenon continue to be elusive, the fact of brachycranialization is established by the prehistoric skeletal record. It is a response to some stresser yet to be identified. Brachycrany which is evidenced in low frequency in cranial specimens from Harappa and Lothal cannot be cited as a hallmark of racial identity for segments of these populations...Recognition of the evolutionary fact of brachycranialization bears on the question of the biological identity of the ancient Harappans whom, it now appears from multivariate analysis, were a relatively homogenous population (K.A.R.K. citing P. C. Dutta 1972; Kennedy 1982a: 293-94).

Many important things can be learned from the human remains of the Indus Age, even if it is no longer acceptable to indulge in speculations about racial history. Perhaps the most useful set of the inferences that comes from the study of human remains concerns the diet and health of the population.

Contemporary Approaches

Contemporary physical anthropology/skeletal biology is concerned with much more than the notion of "race" or biological affinity; although the topic of biological affinity remains of general interest to the field. It is equally concerned with the reconstruction of biological profiles and the demography of extinct populations. They attempt to reconstruct rates of mortality, fertility, fecundity, morbidity, degrees of biological affinity between ancient and modern populations, profiles of health and disease, patterns of nutrition. They can say a great deal about physical traumas, wounds, broken bones and the like, as well as the incidence of disease and markers of biological stress that appear in bones and teeth. Where "race" was once the focus of this aspect of physical anthropology, today it is a broad field with a diversified research agenda aimed at presenting us with a solid morphometric and statistical analysis of human skeletal remains.

Contemporary Approaches: Diet and Nutrition

Stable isotopes are providing an important approach to the history of human biology and nutrition. It is a subject still under development and genuine historical conclusions are not yet available from such studies, but by using stable isotopes such as Strontium ^{90}/calcium ratios it is theoretically possible to sketch out the balance between meat and vegetable matter in the diet. This can be thought of as the individual's, or a population of individuals, position in the food web. While problems remain in perfecting the laboratory tests for this technique, especially when concerned with the influence of chemical alteration during the period the specimen was buried, (so-called "diagenesis") there is great promise here, evidenced by the work undertaken by the team of palaeoanthropologists working at Harappa (Hemphill 1993; Kennedy 1993; Lovell 1993a, 1993b; Lukacs 1993).

Signs of biological stress can also be detected in bones by examining them for Harris lines, signs of rickets and by looking at permanent teeth for the pattern or alteration of growth. Teeth are useful dietary and health indicators and thanks to the work of Prof. John Lukacs we have a good picture of dental patterns and pathologies from several South Asian sites. Some occupations also have a remodeling effect on the human skeleton and dentition and progress has been made

32

in adducing interesting conclusions on this topic. For example, the pattern of wear on the teeth of a woman from the cemetery at Harappa allows us to believe that she was a basketmaker (Kennedy 1993).

Contemporary Approaches: Funerary Practices

The study of the interments themselves can yield insights into the apparent social status of individuals based on wealth reflected in the value of associated grave goods. In many mortuary sites upper class individuals reveal from skeletal analysis their degree of attainment of full ontogenetic potential as well as reduction in the magnitude and frequency of markers of occupational stress caused by a lifetime of heavy labor. This kind of research has not been particularly useful in the study of the Indus Age because graves are not usually very well equipped with the worldly riches of these ancient peoples; however, with a sufficiently large sample collected from a number of sites this too, might change. The best study is by Kennedy and Caldwell (1984). One thing does seems to be apparent from this record: within the Mature Harappan Phase we appear to have a diversity of practices relating to the disposition of the dead. There are a number of social and historical dimensions that could be related to this, but the most plausible working hypothesis suggests that it relates to the ethnic diversity of the population of this vast area, with peoples of differing ethnic history practicing their own mortuary customs.

Sites With Human Skeletal Remains

The list of the principal sites of the Indus Age through the Mature Harappan where burials have been found is given in Table 1.3. It is not intended to be a list of sites where the odd bone or two have been found, but does include places where burials have been reported.

A Caution on the Survivability of Bones

Bone, even though it is 60% mineral, is not a stable material. Depending on local soil and environmental features it often is not well preserved in archaeological settings. A brief review of some of the principal caveats in this area follows.

When bone is excavated a dramatic change in its environment occurs and skeletal material that may have had a secure "home" in the soil is likely to become unstable. This change often brings about rather rapid deterioration (e.g., a slightly acidic soil will demineralize bone). The unearthing of bone, at least unfossilized specimens, almost always brings with it the notion that the bone will be compromised as a scientific specimen unless thorough and painstaking preservation methods are undertaken. In the 1920s and 1930s these methods were not known, and the bones, both human and animal, were often not cared for except for a cursory surface cleaning. They were more likely to be tossed in a basket, allowed to dry in the sun (a virtual death knell!) and packed away with the thought that someone, someday might take a look at them. There are some exceptions, as in E. J. H. Mackay's excavations in DK-G Area of Mohenjo-daro (Mackay 1937-38: 116).

Bones that might have been reasonably sturdy specimens in the field when observed by the excavators, are often delicate, sometimes only a powdery stain in the bottom of a box, by the time they reach the laboratory. Thus, discrepancies between field reports and the scientific laboratory study of bones, human skeletal series included, should be expected. This includes the deterioration, even the complete loss, of significant parts of the skeleton.

TABLE 1.3
Sites of the Indus Age through the Mature Harappan with Burials

Site	District
Allahdino	Karachi
Bagor	Bhilwara
Binjor Three	Ganganagar
Burzahom	Srinagar
Chandigarh	Chandigarh
Chanhu-daro	Nawabshah
Dabar Kot	Loralai
Daimabad	Ahmednagar
Damb Buthi	Dadu
Damb Sadaat	Quetta-Pishin
Dauda Damb	Kachi
Derawar Ther	Bahawalpur
Dher Majra	Ropar
Gemuwala Dehar	Bahawalpur
Gumla	Dera Ismail Khan
Harappa	Sahiwal
Isplinji Two	Sarawan
Kalibangan	Ganganagar
Kashi Qalat Cemetery	Makran
Kulli	Jhalawan
Langhnaj	Mehsana
Lothal	Ahmedabad
Mahra Sharif	Dera Ismail Khan
Mehi	Jhalawan
Mehrgarh	Kachi
Moghul Ghundai	Zhob
Mohenjo-daro	Larkana
Nagwada One	Surendranagar
Nal	Jhalawan
Periano Ghundai	Zhob
Rampara Two	Bhavnagar
Randal Dadwa	Rajkot
Rojdi	Rajkot
Ropar	Ropar
Sarai Khola	Rawalpindi
Shahi Tump	Makran
Sibri	Kachi
Sur Jangal	Loralai
Surkotada	Kutch
Sutkagen-dor	Makran
Tarkhanewala Dera	Ganganagar
Uchali	Rawalpindi
Waddanwala	Bahawalpur

Additional damage occurs when the bone is curated, moved from museum to museum, or intramurally from storage to laboratory and back. The effects of these actions should not be minimized, since they can dramatically alter delicate components on the bones and in the cranium as well as "high spots" where the bone comes into contact with packing materials and boxes. These "high spots" are the points from which physical anthropologists take many of their measurements and when they are gradually "sanded" away it compromises the usefulness of an individual specimen. Curation inevitably leads to the loss and misplacement of specimens or body parts, further complicating the systematic study of specimens.

In many instances, an almost complete skeleton may be unearthed, lacking only a few bones. An evaluation of such specimens requires critical study, because it cannot be assumed that this reflects the burial condition of the specimen. Body parts can be missed in excavation, which was especially true in the early years of the discipline, when screens were not used and digging was a more hasty process than it is today. They can be lost (misplaced or deteriorated) in transport to the site lab and from there to storage and the study laboratory. Selected body parts might also be preserved differently in the ground in which they are buried.

There can be important micro differences in burial environments that might lead to the disappearance of all, or some, of the extremities. For example the feet might be in a position slightly closer to the surface and subjected to more rain, or located in a part of the ground more wet than the cranium because of local underground drainage patterns. Water is an enemy of preservation because porous materials like bone expand when they are wet and contract when they dry. The more frequently this "accordion" action takes place the more general the deterioration will be. The action of animals, particularly carnivores and rodents, has to be considered. The carnivores might get only a portion of a partly buried body and gnaw on it, removing some bones. The hyaena is a nefarious scavenger of this sort, a trait caught by Rudyard Kipling in his grisly little poem "The Hyaenas:"

> After the burial parties leave
> And the baffled kites have fled; The wise hyaenas come out at eve
> To take account of our dead.
> How he died and why he died
> Troubles them not a whit. They snout the bushes and stones aside
> And dig till they come to it.

Burrowing animals, such as rodents, might happen across a buried meal while busily digging a new home. Careful examination shows the tooth marks left by such predators to have distinctive shapes and patterns, allowing the knowledgeable physical anthropologist an opportunity to identify them.

Finally, archaeologists have come to find that sometimes objects, skeletons included, move around within the archaeological midden in which they are buried. Frost action in cold climates, can produce significant motion in the lateral dimension as well as depth. But, even in warm climates, especially when the midden is wet, things do seem to move about, sometimes just a little, or a few inches or feet. When skeletal parts move about in a container containing the remains of the deceased it is generally called "coffin burn" by forensic specialists. This kind of underground action has not been extensively studied and is therefore not well understood, but it can cause the separation of some bones from their parent skeletal structure and lead to the "jumbling-up" of the skeleton, especially where a number of specimens are found together, as at Mohenjo-daro with the HR-Area Tragedy, or the Long Lane Group.

Humans also damage skeletal specimens, later graves cutting into earlier interments, pit digging, or foundation laying among other things. Every archaeologist who works in South Asia is aware that somehow the advent of the Iron Age changed humans from relatively stable people into voracious pit diggers!

There is a host of taphonomic, post-depositional and archaeological processes that confuse the record of human burial and the resulting skeletal series. What is presented here is cautionary: one should not expect that the preservation of skeletons will be good, that field remarks will be in complete agreement with laboratory observations or that missing and scattered body parts can uncritically be assumed to indicate violence, amputations or dismembering.

Another Caution on Determining Physical Injury

As this survey unfolds, settings where violence occasionally is suggested by the human remains will be noted. The famous "massacre scenes" at Mohenjo-daro are an example. Finding convincing marks of violence on the skeleton is sometimes possible, but only an expert can determine this (Kennedy 1996). It cannot be assumed, for example, that a skull found slightly removed from its apparent torso is conclusive evidence for decapitation, or that missing long bones signify amputation. Similarly, breaks and abrasions might indicate violence, but they too can be caused in many ways, some while the skeleton was in the ground, others in transport after the specimen has been removed from the ground. It is also true that not all fatal, or nonfatal, wounds leave marks on the skeleton.

Wounds that damage bone and have healed during an individual's life can be identified. As the bone knits and closes, a process called "resorption" takes place. The edges of the wounded, damaged bone become rounded and extra tissue is sometimes generated around it. Wounds suffered close to death, where the bone has not had a chance to heal, have sharp edges. A good example of this comes from a knee wound on one of the skeletons from Kalibangan seen in (Plate 1.4). Assessing this is the business of the professional physical anthropologist and is a subject that requires training and great skill, along with a critical evaluation of the archaeological context and the osteological materials themselves. Kenneth A. R. Kennedy, has used the phrase "an exacting science" (1984a: 427). He has an excellent discussion of this general topic in his consideration of signs of trauma and disease among the Harappans (1984a, 1996).

THE REGIONS OF THE INDUS AGE

The *Indus Age* offers a number of points of departure from the familiar view of ancient Indian civilization. The chronology of stages and phases is one of these. Another is the use of "Regions," first introduced in Possehl (1992a). The geographical regions are cultural and natural areas that appear to have historical legitimacy and utility. They serve as structural references to help divide the ancient landscape in the northwest of the subcontinent for discussion of cultural geography as well as the Mature Harappan Stage.

From the perspective of cultural geography, Regions are useful tools and nothing more. But, in looking at the variations in the archaeological assemblages over roughly one million square kilometers covered by the Mature Harappan, there is significant variation from place to place. There is the classic, Sindhi Harappan in the Indus Valley and Kutch, which shares much with the sites in the West Punjab and Bahawalpur or Cholistan. This assemblage is different from the Mature Harappan found elsewhere.

It is clear from a number of sources that the environment of the Greater Indus region during the Indus Age was quite different from today. There may have been little climatic change between then and now, but the environment, and hence the ecology, of this vast region is none the less different. The impact of humans has been immense with land clearing and cultivation on a gigantic scale, often done in tandem with irrigation systems on a significant scale. The latter systems have significantly increased the land of the region that can sustain reasonably productive agriculture. Poorly designed and operated irrigation systems have also led to immense problems of salinity and other maladies of the natural world that poison farm land and lead to much diminished productivity, even outright abandonment. Thus, irrigation is also responsible for the loss of agricultural land. What this means to the archaeologist is that areas that may have been highly productive in deep antiquity are now salt encrusted deserts. These observations lead to the conclusion that while there has probably been a net increase in highly productive farm land within the Greater Region since the Indus Age, there has also been a very substantial reshuffling of the location of productivity. Some land that was not farmed during the Indus Age is farmed today, and some that was highly productive then is no longer suitable for cultivation. Added to this is the predation of domesticated animals on grazing and browsing lands and the impact of a human population that is now numbered in hundreds of millions, when in the archaeological past it was enumerated in millions, or even only in hundreds of thousands.

Archaeologists have also learned that the river system in the northwestern corner of the Subcontinent is not today what it was during the Indus Age. The lower course of the Indus river has migrated, as any mature stream will do. But, the rivers of the Punjab were in different places, and there apparently was a river system of some size that is now dry. This is called the Ghaggar-Hakra today, but in ancient times it was the Sarasvati. The full history of this drainage system is not yet known in any detail, or with much security. It is believed that the change in these river courses was caused by local crust movements spawned by the plate tectonics of the encounter that the Subcontinent's landmass has with Asia. Stream capture on a substantial scale was involved here. Since it seems that the region was so different in these terms it has been decided to let many of the illustrations in this book reflect this fact, even though one can predict with some confidence that there will be revisions to this portrayal in the future. So the reader should take these illustrations as a reflection of the spirit of difference, rather than its complete documentation. They are admittedly speculative and that is one of the dimensions of archaeology that one must grapple with in an appropriate way.

SPECULATION

There is a great deal of hard archaeological data concerning the Indus Age: the architecture, pottery, metal artifacts, seals and figurines along with important evidence in the form of settlement patterns, size and location. A book of such facts might be interesting to a small audience, but because most people want to know the meaning of these "facts" or hard evidence, a significant portion of what is presented in the *Indus Age* is, of necessity, speculative.

Speculation is a relative concept, something on which reasonable scholars can disagree, and it is not entirely clear in all instances where the boundary between fact and speculation lies. One can come to a point where virtually all archaeological thought can be relegated to speculation. This begins with a consideration of the immense gaps in the archaeological record that come through a lack of preservation of many materials; the very small samples taken from an excavation site, the incomplete analysis of these small samples, the removal of entire sites and site clusters from the landscape. We can say that we have hard data, facts, but the backdrop against which we evaluate so much of their significance is an unknown, possibly unknowable, black box. Moreover, much of archaeological, or historical reasoning, is inductive functionalism and, therefore, tautological.

It often happens that progress in scholarship ends with the first utterance from "impeccable authority," and this makes for poor archaeology. The evaluation of fact and/or speculation should look to the content of a statement and the reasoning that supports it. We should be less interested in what is "believed" and pay increasing attention to why proposals are advanced and how they are epistemologically supported. What my colleagues believe about the Indus Age is of little concern to me, but I am immensely interested in why they believe it.

NOTES

1. Panini's grammar, his *Astadhyayi*, is a work of great genius but does presuppose a long history of grammarians preceding it (translated by Vasu 1990, Cardona 1988). He worked at Taxila, a city famous for its learned men, in about the 4th or 5th century BC, possibly as early as 500 BC. The grammar itself is written in a meta-language, which systematically lays out over 4000 grammatical rules for Sanskrit. As A. L. Basham has observed: "The great terseness of Panini's system makes his work very difficult to follow without preliminary study and suitable commentary" (1967: 388). But, this is the first work of scientific linguistics and is a magnificent achievement of ancient Indian civilization. While some *pundits* of antiquity took difference with Panini, all on minor points, his work was so comprehensive and authoritative that it was universally accepted. No one who moved in the higher, literary and religious circles of ancient Indian society would have dared to deviate from Paninian standard Sanskrit. This also meant that the language could only shift and change within the confines of Panini's rules and it was more or less fixed. The language that Panini described, or defined "...began to be called *Samskrta*, 'perfected' or 'refined', as opposed to the *Prakrtas* ('unrefined'), the popular dialects which had developed naturally" (Basham 1967: 388-89).

2. Literacy might have been present but that Vedic society prohibited the writing of sacred texts. This could be the case, but is a distant possibility since the texts do not mention things like reading and writing. Nor are there words for scribe or scribal tools and products or any other reference that would lead one to believe that literacy was a part of the Vedic world.

3. All radiocarbon determinations have been calibrated using the "Calib-3" computer program from Prof. M. Struiver of the Quaternary Isotope Laboratory at the University of Washington, Seattle. The calibrated dates used in this paper are based on the calibration curves he has developed in conjunction with his colleagues. In citing radiocarbon dates, the international convention has been adopted of using lower-case letters for uncalibrated measurements, as "bc" or "bp", and capitals preceded by "cal." for measurements calibrated into "real" dates in calendar years, as BC or AD.

The CALIB computer program has also made it possible to easily compute a mean or average date for individual sites with more than one date and also for all of the dates from all of the sites within the four periods under discussion here.

4. I wish to thank Kenneth A. R. Kennedy for drawing my attention to this quote, and for his review of significant portions of this manuscript. Dr. Janet Monge also gave time to making the physical anthropology presented here both accurate and understandable.

PART TWO

THE DISCOVERY OF THE INDUS AGE

INTRODUCTION

The discovery of the ancient cities of the Indus is a story of archaeological exploration on a grand scale. Prior to the excavations at Harappa and Mohenjo-daro in the 1920s, the earliest secure date in the history of India and Pakistan was the spring of 326 BC, when Alexander the Great made his raid into the northwestern provinces of the Subcontinent. There was no hint, even in the earliest ancient Indian texts, that there had been a period of urbanization during the Bronze Age of the Greater Indus Valley and Baluchistan, including the fertile plains of Sindh, Gujarat, Punjab, Haryana, northern Rajasthan and western Uttar Pradesh, extending as far west as the Dasht River on the modern border between Pakistan and Iran (Figure 1.1). No one suspected that the remains of this civilization would be found buried within the mounds of what was then western India. This historical context is significantly different from the discovery of other ancient states, where historical documents, including the Bible and standing monuments, clearly pointed to the Sumerians, Dynastic Egyptians and those who once inhabited the Shang settlements of northern China.

Part Two of the *Indus Age* presents a history of Harappan archaeology to about the time of the independence of India and Pakistan in 1947. The nineteenth century explorations that led to the discovery of the ancient cities of the Indus are reviewed but more important are the early excavations of Mohenjo-daro and Harappa, as well as the explorations undertaken by Sir Aurel Stein. The story ends with the termination of Sir Mortimer Wheeler's term as Director General of the Archaeological Survey of India (30 April 1948), which followed the partition of British India.

An Approach to the "Discovery of the Indus Age"

This history of research focuses on the discovery of the Bronze Age of Pakistan and India, and the personalities who played key roles. Following the story of discovery it moves to a consideration of how Sir John Marshall and his colleagues in the Archaeological Survey of India went about expanding their knowledge of the Indus Civilization through the excavations at Mohenjo-daro and Harappa. Some consideration of archaeological methodology comes into play in this discussion, since later field workers, most notably Sir Mortimer Wheeler, severely criticized the manner in which these two key sites had been dug. By the time the early work at the two cities had matured, the formulation of the first paradigm on the Harappan peoples was presented by Marshall in his monumental work *Mohenjo-daro and the Indus Civilization* (1931a). The great world depression of the 1930s had its effect on the Archaeological Survey of India, as did Marshall's retirement. In the middle of World War II the Viceroy of India made an important change in leadership at the Survey by bringing in R.E.M. Wheeler, an entirely new personality and player in the archaeology of the Subcontinent. The story ends with the Wheeler years, his reform of the Archaeological Survey of India including the training program he instituted for excavation, a set of methods still with the field archaeologists of India, Pakistan, Sri Lanka and Bangladesh. Wheeler, and his colleague Stuart Piggott, who was never with the Archaeological Survey of India, replaced Marshall's paradigm or interpretation of the Harappan peoples with a new set of thoughts that have been with us since the 1950s. In some ways the *Indus Age* is an attempt to pursue the process of paradigm construction with some new perspectives on the Indus Civilization that take into account the vastly increased amount of data that is available today, compared to Wheeler's era, as well as a more anthropological approach. This history is essential to set the scene for the remaining volumes of this work.

More Race, Language and Culture

The usual date given for the discovery of the Indus Civilization is 1924, the year Sir John Marshall's article in the *Illustrated London News* announced the new discoveries at Mohenjo-daro and Harappa.[1] Archaeology had begun to mature by this time and the excesses of interpretation of prehistoric materials had gone by the wayside. The true antiquity of humans was understood to go back to a time when animals now extinct were alive and Darwinian biological evolution was firmly in place. Things like "fairy arrows" and the search for the lost tribes of Israel and Noah's ark no longer dominated the field. But the relationships between prehistoric peoples and their cultures were far from understood, and race was an important concept for archaeologists, historians and colonial administrators. Moreover, because systematic archaeology was the invention of Europeans and Americans, the relationships between prehistoric peoples and the Old Testament lingered on even in an age that might be thought of as "scientific."

Sir William Jones was a noted eighteenth century scholar and jurist of the Calcutta High Court. In 1786 he proposed an historical relationship between Sanskrit, Greek and Latin. This appeared as a part of his "Third Anniversary Discourse" to the Asiatic Society of Bengal, the institution which he founded in 1784. In one of the most widely quoted paragraphs in the annals of linguistic history he noted:

> The *Sanscrit* language, whatever may be its antiquity, is of a wonderful structure; more perfect than *Greek*, more copious than *Latin*, and more exquisitely refined than either, yet bearing to both of them a stronger affinity, both in the roots of verbs and in the forms of grammar, than could possibly have been produced by accident; so strong indeed that no philologer could examine them all three, without believing them to have sprung from some common source, which, perhaps no longer exists; there is a similar reason, though not quite so forcible, for supporting that both the *Gothic* and the *Celtic*, though blended with a very different idiom, had the same origin with the *Sanscrit*; and the old *Persian* might be added to the same family, if this were the place for discussing any question concerning the antiquities of Persia (Jones 1788: 348-49)

This insight brought together not just Latin, Greek and Sanskrit, but virtually the entire range of Indo-European languages. This was a new kind of intellectual thought, and it is a mark of Jones' genius that he was able to see it.[2]

We now know that Jones was not the first to notice coincidences between Greek, Latin and Indian languages. In 1583 an English Jesuit by the name of Thomas Stevens working in India noted the structural similarities between Greek, Latin and the languages of North India.

Two years later (1585) an Italian merchant Fillipo Sasseni observed that there was much in common between Sanskrit and the European languages because in Sanskrit "we can find many of our nouns, especially numbers: 6, 7, 8 and 9, God, serpent and others." By the seventeenth century scholars were also accepting the similarities between Greek and German, and Franciscus Rapelengius argued for the association of German and Persian (Mallory 1989: 273, fn. 1).

These are small, isolated observations, not on the scale of the Jones synthesis. Moreover, we have little reason to believe that Jones even knew of them, so the insight of the man is not compromised here (see Mukherji 1968, for more on Jones).

The languages of South India were also the subject of research. The first substantial argument that they were distantly different from Sanskrit and most of the languages of north India was put forth by Francis Whyte Ellis in 1816, thirty years after the Jones proposal for Indo-European (Ellis 1816). These have come to be called "Dravidian."

> Philologists had already concluded that many of the inhabitants of India, especially in the south and remoter parts of central India, were speakers of languages that were non-Aryan in origin and inferior in linguistic terms. The Rev. Robert Caldwell (1814-91) used the term Dravidian (from the Sanskrit, Dravida, used to name a country or people of south India and to distinguish peninsular India, north India or Uttarapatha or south India from the Deccan or Daksinapatha and the north) to designate, one might say invent, a new family of languages. He argued that the Dravidian languages are 'essentially different from and independent of, Sanskrit' (Inden 1990: 59).

The Dravidian languages were defined substantially after their Indo-European counterparts, but well prior to the discovery of the Indus Age, and both language groups were deeply involved in the interpretation of the archaeological remains: were they Harappans Indo-Europeans; were they Dravidians; were they other peoples?

There is no doubt that Sir William Jones was a genius, but he had his bias. As D. K. Chakrabarti has noted concerning the archaeology in the early nineteenth century of South Asia.

> There were two basic theoretical traditions in the beginning. On the one hand there were explorers and surveyors like Rennell, Buchanan and Mackenzie interested in objective reporting and plotting of sites, and on the other were scholars like William Jones whose basic problem was to link the history of India to the other early centers of civilization in the light of the Biblical theory of creation. The theoretical ideas of this period exerted far more profound influence on the subsequent course of ancient Indian historical researches than is usually realized (Chakrabarti 1988: 44).

Chakrabarti has made another important observation concerning nineteenth century ideas about the history of India. In the first half of this period India was thought to be a center, which then changed.

> If to William Jones the centre of population, knowledge, language and all the arts was Iran, some of his contemporaries made India the centre of all things. One has to refer to T. Maurice and people like Pierre Sonnerat to realize this. Right up to the middle of the nineteenth century different culture influences along with actual migrations of people were supposed to have gone out of India. From the middle of the nineteenth century onwards an entirely opposite hypothesis was generally given: India was at the receiving end of various cultural influences and migrations of people emanating from the regions further west (Chakrabarti 1988: 21).

Chakrabarti suggests that this reversal of opinion has something to do with the establishment of the British Raj following the 1857 mutiny, a point too coincidental not to be overlooked, but something he does not pursue (1988: 21).

The common ground of both positions noted by Chakrabarti is that migration was a potent agency of history; at first emanating from India, then bringing things to it; something that was part of the implications that flowed from research on the Indo-European family of languages. The discovery of this language family had a far reaching set of consequences, that have played an important role in the history of research on India, perhaps South Asia generally. One should see W. Halbfass (1988) and R. Inden (1990) for the South Asia story and E. Said (1979 and 1993) for more general considerations. The discovery that Sanskrit and its modern relatives such as Hindi, Urdu, Punjabi, Bengali, Gujarati and Sindhi, along with Avestan and its modern counterpart Farsi, on Persian were closely related to Greek, Latin and most of the modern European languages was a surprise to the broad linguistic community and historians, but it set in motion an unanticipated line of theory. This had to do with the Aryan race, proposed to be the people who spoke the languages of the Indo-European family. European intellectual and moral superiority was a foregone conclusion to most savants of the nineteenth and early twentieth century. The success of European colonialism, Christianity and the Industrial Revolution proved that. This condition of innate superiority was seen in the Classical Greeks and to have been carried forward by Rome. With the discovery of the Indo-European family of languages there was evidence for an even earlier history, one set within a prehistoric past that only archaeology could uncover. The Aryans, or Indo-Europeans, must have also been blessed with this "superiority" since they too were successful conquerors of vast lands, from the Bay of Bengal to the outer islands of Scandinavia and the United Kingdom.

Thus, race and language became intimately associated. In India, because of the endogamous nature of caste, it too was part of the mix and added to it were more subtle notions of nationhood and culture, militancy, intelligence and legitimacy. In the late nineteenth and early twentieth centuries many reputable scholars thought of history in terms of races (biological populations) that spoke particular languages, each with its own culture and national character. The mature version of this position is nicely reviewed by Ronald Inden (1990: 56-66). As a part of his discourse he focuses on Herbert H. Risley Commissioner of the 1901 Census of India, Honorary Director of the Ethnological Survey of the Indian Empire and author of *The People of India* (1915).

> Risley asserts that his racial types are not to be equated with the languages after which he names them, and cautions his readers not to see correlations between head shapes and intelligence. None the less, the retarded racial history that he has provided for India enables him to reach conclusions such as this, with respect to racial characteristics and their social manifestations.
>
> Thus, for those parts of India where there is an appreciable strain of Dravidian blood it is scarcely a paradox to lay down, as a law of the caste organization, that the social status of the members of a particular group varies in inverse ratio to the mean relative width of their noses (1915: 29) (quoted from Inden 1990: 61).

Although not everyone was in agreement with Risley and his followers, the literature on human variability, in India and elsewhere, is filled with this kind of thought. In spite of the disclaimers that even a Risley could make, as noted above, when they stated their case they saw a relationship between physical type and many social manifestations. Even great archaeologists were not immune.

V. Gordon Childe spent a good portion of his intellectual life studying Indo-Europeans. In the last two paragraphs of his widely read *The Aryans* he observed:

> ...The lasting gift bequeathed by the Aryans to the conquered peoples was neither material culture not a superior physique, but that which we mentioned in the first chapter—a more excellent language and the mentality it generated...

At the same time the fact that the first Aryans were Nordics was not without importance. The physical qualities of that stock did enable them by the bare fact of superior strength to conquer even more advanced peoples and so to impose their language on areas from which their bodily type was almost completely vanished. This is the truth underlying the panegyrics of the Germanists; the Nordics' superiority in physique fitted them to be the vehicles of a superior language (Childe 1926: 211-12).

The date of publication of this book is important, since 1926 places it at the height of Sir John Marshall's campaigns at Mohenjo-daro; on the doorstep of the discovery of the Indus Civilization.

The somewhat reductionist version of this thought *vis a vis* South Asia is that there was an Aryan race, with its own distinct set of culture traits that spoke Indo-European languages. They had expanded from an original homeland by migration and conquest to occupy the vast area that has already been outlined. This success in prehistoric times served to reinforce, if not prove, the hypothesis of European superiority. Peoples like those of India having become so debased by institutions such as caste that they no longer figured in the mix.

This position on history, human biology, language and culture is flawed in many fundamental ways. Something I have come to think of as the "Golden Rule of Historical Linguistics" comes to us from Franz Boas, who demonstrated in his monumental work *Race, Language and Culture* (1940) that these three elements are independent historical variables that characteristically shift, diverge, mix and change over even short periods of time. The study of history tells us that it is rarely if ever the case that they remain together, as an association of biological and cultural traits; the Eskimo being a rare exception. But vestiges of theory implying that this Golden Rule is not so live on, even in work by men of distinction (e.g., Renfrew 1987). Moreover, race as it was used in the nineteenth and early twentieth centuries has been totally discredited as a useful concept in human biology. No authoritative scientist today who studies human variation would use the concept or term in new productive research, except possibly disciplinary history.

In the end, there is no reason to believe today that there ever was an Aryan race that spoke Indo-European languages and was possessed of a coherent or well defined set of Aryan or Indo-European cultural features. But, this was not the case when the Indus Civilization was discovered. In the nineteenth century, extending to the 1920s and 1930s, the races of humanity were still legitimate concepts, the innate superiority of some people over others was still a legitimate notion (although declining in its currency). Boas had not yet placed the "Golden Rule of Historical Linguistics" before the scholarly community. Thus, there is much writing about Aryans and Indo-European and the Harappan Civilization and of its relationship to Egypt and especially Sumer. Many scholars have proposed that the civilizations of Harappa and Sumer were related, possibly one and the same. Even Sir John Marshall used the term "Indo-Sumerian Civilization" until 1925-26 (Marshall 1925-26: 75; see also Marshall 1926-27a: 53).

I have never found a discussion of the assumptions or "theory" on which the notion of an "Indo-Sumerian" civilization could be founded. But the thought is certainly part of the history of research on the Harappans, as illustrated by:

...the "Sumerians"—those foremost civilized and civilizing ancient people whose monuments and high art of five thousand years ago are the wonder of the modern world—were the long lost Early Aryans; that the Phoenicians were not Semites as has been hitherto supposed, but Aryans and the chief colonizing branch of the Sumerians; and that the people who colonized and civilized India, as well as those who colonized and civilized the Mediterranean, North-western Europe and Britain and who were ancestors of the Britons, were likewise Aryan and belonged predominantly to the Phoenician branch of that race (Waddell 1925a: v).

This quote from Colonel Waddell may hold a clue to the answer to this question. It was either known or assumed that the civilization of Sumer was earlier than that of Mohenjo-daro and Harappa. Therefore, one of two cases might pertain: if the Aryans were the first great colonizers and conquerors of Europe and Asia up to the Subcontinent, then it made sense that the Sumerians were simply another Aryan people; or in order to preserve the notion of Aryan supremacy the Sumerians, the first builders of cities and the first to know the art of writing had to be Aryan. One cannot decide exactly how this logic actually worked from Waddell or others like George Barton (1928a, 1928b, 1930), G. R. Hunter (1934) and C. L. Fabri (1937) who proposed or implied this relationship. Whatever the case, there is a lot lacking in the clarity of thought here, possibly a certain amount of politics and the reinforcing of the myth of "Aryanism" and a supposed "superiority" there.

The notion of Aryan superiority was carried to extreme by the National Socialists in Germany during the 1930s and 40s, but its historical roots go back to the second half of the nineteenth century (Poliakov 1977: 71-105; Mallory 1989: 266-72). Even physical anthropologists of high standing such as Rudolf Virchov and Thomas Huxley pursued the isolation of a blond, round-headed Aryan race.

The Aryans and racial concepts in history are very much a part of Indian thought, with distinguished men like Bal Gangadhar Tilak who found the Aryan home in the arctic (Tilak 1904). Some of the recent books that touch on this subject are often concerned either with Aryans in isolation or linking the Indus Civilization to modern Hinduism through them (see Chandra 1980; Deshmukh 1982; Kashyap 1984; Sethna 1992; S. S. Misra 1992).

Thus, race was very much a part of the intellectual environment within which the Indus Civilization was discovered. In the early years of research on race, up to World War II at least, there is evidence for much discussion of the topic. But, none of the important, productive archaeologists who have worked on this civilization have demonstrated much interest in the subject: Sir John Marshall,[3] M. S. Vats, Rao Bahadur K. N. Dikshit, E. J. H. Mackay, N. G. Majumdar, Sir Mortimer Wheeler, Stuart Piggott, A. Ghosh, Y. D. Sharma, Walter Fairservis, George Dales, S. R. Rao, B. and F. R. Allchin, B. B. Lal, B. K. Thapar, Jagat Pati Joshi, A. H. Dani, S. P. Gupta, D. P. Agrawal, K. N. Dikshit. This has meant that the best literature on the Harappan Civilization is not tainted by racism or Aryanism. Racism is there in the secondary literature, but the best is relatively free of it.

Paradigms of the Discovery of the Indus Age

The "Discovery of the Indus Age" is built around a pair of organizing principles, set within the chronology of discovery. The first concerns tracing the development of the major paradigms that have been employed for understanding the Indus Civilization. This is the intellectual history of Harappan archaeology. It was consciously decided not to venture seriously into the comparative side of this topic, but to stick fairly close to a story of our progressive understanding of the Indus Civilization. Second, the "Discovery of the Indus Age" is solidly biographical. There is a concern for the people who were involved in this work; their background, training and personalities. This form of presentation emerged in part from the strengths of the author. It is also a story that has not been told before, so that there is inherent legitimacy and freshness as well.

The greatest deficiency in this form of presentation is that the "Discovery of the Indus Age" is not based only on the overall intellectual history of colonial India and Pakistan. Although this larger theme is not totally ignored, it is not a robust part of the narrative. As desirable as it might have been to approach the history of archaeology in the Subcontinent from this perspective, it is not one of my strengths nor was it found possible to create a history that would be completely satisfying to all intellectual pursuits. Rather than compromise, the "Discovery of the Indus Age" focuses on the archaeological paradigms and personalities, which presents history with real people as the actors.

Michael Jansen is another archaeologist of the Indus peoples who has written on the history of research in a similar way. His 1986 book has much to recommend it. Many of the topics touched on in this Part of the *Indus Age* are also discussed there, with Jansen's own twist to the story.

The First Visit to an Harappan Site

There are several good sources for the history of Indian archaeology, some of which also focus on the discovery of the Harappan Civilization and related prehistoric remains in the Subcontinent: (Cumming 1939; Marshall 1939; Ghosh 1953a, 1961; S. Roy 1953; T. N. Roy 1961; Chakrabarti 1981, 1988; Krishna Deva 1982; Pande 1982; Possehl 1982c; Jansen 1986, 1987). They tell us that the story of discovery actually begins in March or April 1829 (Masson 1843: Vol. I, 402-54)[4] when a man known as Charles Masson visited the huge mound adjacent to the modern village of Harappa, near an abandoned course of the Ravi River in Sahiwal District (formerly Montgomery District) of the Punjab. Masson traveled in the western borderlands of British India in the 1820s and 1830s as an antiquarian from the state of Kentucky in America. He had just entered the Punjab from Bahawalpur and parts west and left this impression of the place.

Charles Masson's Description of Harappa in 1829

A long march preceded our arrival at Haripah (Harappa) through jangal of the closest description. East of the village was an abundance of luxuriant grass, where, along with many others, I went to allow my nag to graze. When I joined the camp I found it in front of the village and a ruinous brick castle. Behind us was a large circular mound, or eminence, and to the west was an irregular rocky height, crowned with remains of buildings, in fragments of walls, with niches, after the eastern manner. The latter elevation was undoubtedly a natural object; the former being of earth only, was obviously an artificial one. I examined the remains on the height, and found two circular perforated stones, affirmed to have been used as bangles, or armrings, by a faquir of renown. He has also credit for having subsisted on earth, and other unusual substances, and his depraved appetite is instanced in testimony of his sanctity. The entire neighborhood is embellished with numerous pipal trees, some of them in the last stage of lingering existence, bespeaking a great antiquity, when we remember their longevity. The walls and towers of the castle are remarkably high, though, from having been long deserted, they exhibit in some parts the ravages of time and decay...There was ample room on the summit to receive the party and the horses belonging to it. It was impossible to survey the scene before us, and to look upon the ground on which we stood, without perceiving that every condition of Arrian's Sangala was here fulfilled, the brick fortress, with a lake, or rather swamp, at the north-eastern angle; the mound, protected by a triple row of chariots, and defended by the Kathi before they suffered themselves to be shut up within their walls; and the trench between the mound and fortress, by which the circumvallation of the place was completed, and whence engines were directed against it. The data of Arrian are very minute, and can scarcely be misapplied to Haripah, the position of which also perfectly coincides with what, from inference, we must assign to Sangala. (Masson 1843, Vol. I: 453-54).

Hariyupiya

Archaeologists have no idea what the original name of the city adjacent to the modern village of Harappa was, but it is certainly not Sangala. Sir Mortimer Wheeler (1947b: 78-82) has suggested that the name can be found in the Ṛgveda as "Hariyupiya":

> This one great power of thine our eyes have witnessed, wherewith thou slewest Varashikha's children.
> When by the force of thy descending thunder, at the mere sound, their boldest demolished.
> In the aid of Abhyavartin Chayamana, Indra destroyed the seed of Varashikha.
> At Hariyupiya he smote the vanguard of the Vrichivans, and the rear fled frightened.
> Ṛgveda Book IV, Hymn 27, Verses 4-5; Griffith 1896

The suggestion that "Hariyupiya" and "Harappa" are one and the same is little more than a bold assertion, not to be taken too seriously (B. Roy 1928; Dani 1950). A great deal of time separates the principal Mature Harappan occupation of Harappa from the apparent time of the composition of the Ṛgveda. Moreover, we do not have a clear understanding of the historical nature of the vedic texts as a whole, and etymological "games" have their own dangers. Any thought that the Aryans, as invaders suggested by the Ṛgveda, brought Harappa, or the Harappan Civilization to its knees is not an hypothesis which is supported by archaeologists working in the field today.

T. G. Aravamuthan has proposed that the name was derived from Mesopotamia:

> Far away in Iraq, a little to the east of the Tigris and on the site of the modern town of Karkuk, there stood a city the name of which has been variously spelt as Arrapha (Smith 1927: 88) and Arrapkha (Langdon 1929: 432). The pronunciation of the name of this city is almost identical with that of Harappa. Though the Iraqian city does not seem to have been known during the period of Ur (3000 BC; Langdon 1929: 423) it appears to have been taken by the kings of Gutium about 2400 BC (Langdon 1929: 439) so its antiquity must be earlier than the latter of these two dates (Aravamuthan 1942: 67).

Arrapha is the ancient name for the modern Iraqi city of Kirkuk, but this use of the science of etymology does not seem to be sound. Is it really conceivable that a city of the Indus Civilization would have derived its name from a Mesopotamian place, let alone, that the name would have survived over 4000 years of history?

More on Charles Masson

The Vedas were not known to Masson but classical literature was, especially the history of Alexander the Great's visit to the Punjab, as noted in his writing. His association of the ruins at Harappa with Sangala is incorrect, but it was something that Masson never gave up, and the search for Sangala continues to this day (Ashfaque and Sultana 1989). On the other hand, Masson was an insightful man of considerable energy, with a deep interest in antiquarian science. He made a sound contribution to the history of South Asian archaeology and it is appropriate to cite briefly his contributions.

Masson's visit to Harappa was not his only discovery of archaeological significance (Whitteridge 1986; Possehl 1990a). During his time in British India he recorded many sites, made a magnificent collection of ancient coins and conducted excavations in the Buddhist stupas of the region. The site of Begram, near Kabul, once known as Kapisa, attracted his attention. This ruined city was once the summer capital of the Kushan Dynasty, contemporaries of the Romans, Parthians and Han Chinese, who played an important role in the regulation of the Silk Road trade in the early centuries of the Christian Era. Masson thought that Begram might be the city of Alexandria ad Caucasum, founded by Alexander the Great. Reports indicated that many coins were to be found in the cultivated fields that covered the low, rolling mounds of the long deserted city and Masson began to collect them. His start in 1833 was slow, but by 1837 he had ca. 80,000 coins and other precious objects from Begram (Masson 1842: Vol. III, 149) that were forwarded to the Honorable East India Company, which had provided some support for Masson's work (Masson 1834, 1836a, 1836b, 1842, Vol. III: 149).[5] Most of these coins related to the Greek rulers and those who succeeded them who used the western script on some of their coins. Little was known then of the early history of Afghanistan, Bactria and northwestern Pakistan. The great Kushan Dynasty, for example, had not yet been discovered. This collection, and other inscriptional materials from the northwest of Pakistan and Afghanistan, allowed James Prinsep to make impressive progress on the dynastic history of the region and to define the Kushan Dynasty.[6]

In addition to his numismatic interests Masson sketched a number of Buddhist stupas which he called "topes" (Figure 2.1). At the site of Koh Takht Shah, near Kabul he found a number of interesting relics and birch bark documents in the Kharosthi script of the early centuries of

Figure 2.1. Masson's Sketch of Tope, or Stupa, Number Three at Bimaran. Courtesy of the India Office Library

the Christian Era. Masson also worked in and around the city of Jalalabad, to the east of Kabul, where he excavated Buddhist monasteries and stupas at this center of Buddhist culture and ancient trade. The site of Hadda in this area is an especially revealing monastery because of its splendid sculpture in Indo-Mediterranean style. At Bimaran, also near Jalalabad, he renewed excavation at a stupa that had been abandoned by an unlucky earlier investigator and uncovered a gold reliquary which is one of the most beautiful finds ever to come from Afghanistan[7] (Plate 2.1).

Masson was also an early visitor to Bamiyan in central Afghanistan where he left the following penciled inscription in a small cave to the west of the larger of the two colossal Buddhas:

> If any fool this high samootch explore
> Know Charles Masson has been here before (Hackin 1933: 2).

This bit of doggerel was even signed and dated 1833, as seen in Plate 2.2.

Bamiyan is a Mahayana Buddhist monastic site and trading center of about the 2nd to 7th centuries A. D. It is located in a broad, well watered valley of great beauty, that is also a crossroads of central Afghanistan. The routes to the north connect to the Silk Road, then east to China through Chinese Turkestan or west to the Mediterranean. From Bamiyan itself one can move into modern Pakistan and on to India via places like the ancient sites of Hadda and Taxila, or west into Persia. Bamiyan was a large and busy place. When the Chinese pilgrim Hsuan Tsang visited there in 632 A.D., exactly 1200 years before Masson's excursion, it was organized around ten separate monasteries with a total of over 1,000 monks. The central features of Bamiyan are two colossal standing Buddhas. The earlier is 38 meters high and dates to the 3rd-4th century. The other is 55 meters high and was carved about a century later (Figure 2.2; Plate 2.3).

The Unmasking of Charles Masson

Masson's papers are now in the India Office Library, London. They disclose an interesting

Figure 2.2. Masson's Drawing of Bamiyan. Courtesy of the India Office Library

48

reality: this man was not born with the name Charles Masson, nor was he from Kentucky. He was actually James Lewis, born on February 16, 1800 in Aldermanbury, near London (Kaye and Johnson 1937: 191; Whitteridge 1986: 1; see also Ross 1933).[8] Following a brief stint with the King's 24th Regiment of Foot, he reenlisted as a private soldier in the Army of the East India Company. Masson gave his age at the time as nineteen when, in fact, he was almost twenty-two. There are no surviving likenesses of the man, but the recruiting register describes him as five feet five inches tall, fresh-complexioned, with hazel eyes and brown hair (Alder 1975: V). He sailed for Bengal in January of 1822 on board the *Dutchess of Athol*. He served in the Bengal Regiment of Horse Artillery and fought at the siege of Bharatpur near Agra. Major-General Hardwicke, commandant of Bengal Artillery, employed Masson to catalog his collection of zoological specimens. Some time after the siege of Bharatpur, on July 4, 1827, Masson deserted the army. He headed west to Bahawalpur, the Punjab and Lahore under the guise of an American. One of his earliest stops was at Harappa.

Masson's later years in Afghanistan, following his 1835 pardon for desertion, were not happy ones. The Great Game was in full swing, and the First Afghan War (1838-42) was approaching. The pardon had come with the stipulation that he provide his masters with political information on Afghanistan. This not only interfered with his archaeological research but was repugnant to him personally. The political climate brought him into contact with a number of important figures, not the least of whom was Sir Alexander Burnes, the second European to visit Harappa and to publish it as an archaeological site (1835a: Vol. I, 117-18).

Figure 2.3. Sketch of Sir Alexander Burnes, from Burnes 1835a

Sir Alexander Burnes

In 1831, Lieutenant Alexander Burnes made an historic journey up the Indus River (Figure 2.3). The ostensible reason for this voyage (Burnes 1833-34, 1834, 1835a, Vol. I) was to deliver a gift of five horses and a carriage from the King of England to Ranjit Singh, the powerful Sikh ruler of the Punjab. Coincidentally, Burnes also took the first scientific observations on the Indus River and its tributaries and prepared a chart of its course.

In the course of the journey Burnes visited the site of Amri, and was the first man to publish it as an archaeological site. He left the following curious description: "Near the modern village...there is a mound of earth about forty feet high, which the traditions of the country point out as a halting-place of a king, who ordered the dung of his cavalry to be gathered together, and hence the mound of Amree (sic)" (Burnes 1835a: Vol. I, 51).

While in the Punjab Burnes went to Harappa, just four years after Masson's visit.

His observations on the site are not at significant variance from Masson:

> About fifty miles eastward of Toolumba, I passed inland for four miles to examine the ruins of an ancient city, called Harappa. The remains are extensive, and the place, which has been built of brick, is about three miles in circumference. There is a ruined citadel on the river side of the town; but otherwise Harappa is a perfect chaos, and has not an entire building: the bricks have been removed to build a small place of the old name hard by. Tradition fixes the fall of Harappa at the same period as Shorkote (1300 years ago), and the people ascribe its ruin to the vengeance of God on Harappa; its governor, who claimed certain privileges on the marriage of every couple in his city, and in the course of his sensualities, was guilty of incest. At a later period, Harappa became a Mahommedan town; and there is a tomb of a Saint of the 'faithful,' eighteen feet in length, the assigned, but fabulous, stature of the deceased. A large stone of annular form, and a huge black slab of an oval shape, which lie near the grave, are said to represent the ring and its gem of this departed giant, and to have been converted from more valuable to their present base materials. Where such fables are believed, we must cease to hope for even reasonable fiction. I found some coins in these ruins, both Persian and Hindoo, but I cannot fix its era from any of them (Burnes 1835b: Vol. I, 117-18).

THE BEGINNINGS OF DISCOVERY: Sir Alexander Cunningham and Harappa

The two early notices of Harappa, by Masson and Burnes, have historical importance primarily because they came to the attention of Sir Alexander Cunningham, the first Director General of the Archaeological Survey (Figure 2.4).

In 1875, Cunningham reported that he visited Harappa on three occasions: "In 1853, and again in 1856, I traced the remains of flights of stairs on both the eastern and western faces of the high mound to the northwest, as well as the basement of a large square building" (1875: 106). In this report he noted the size of the site [four kilometers (2.5 miles) in circuit] and the height of the mounds (12 to 18 meters). He also noted, with considerable regret, that many of the features he had seen earlier had disappeared: "...the whole have now been removed to form ballast for the railway. Perhaps the best idea of the extent of the ruined brick mounds of Harapa [sic] may be formed from the fact that they have more than sufficed to furnish brick ballast for about 100 miles of Lahor [sic] and Multan Railway" (1875: 106-107).

The wanton plunder of Harappa stirred Cunningham to carry out a modest excavation there, which apparently

Figure 2.4. Sketch of Sir Alexander Cunningham

50

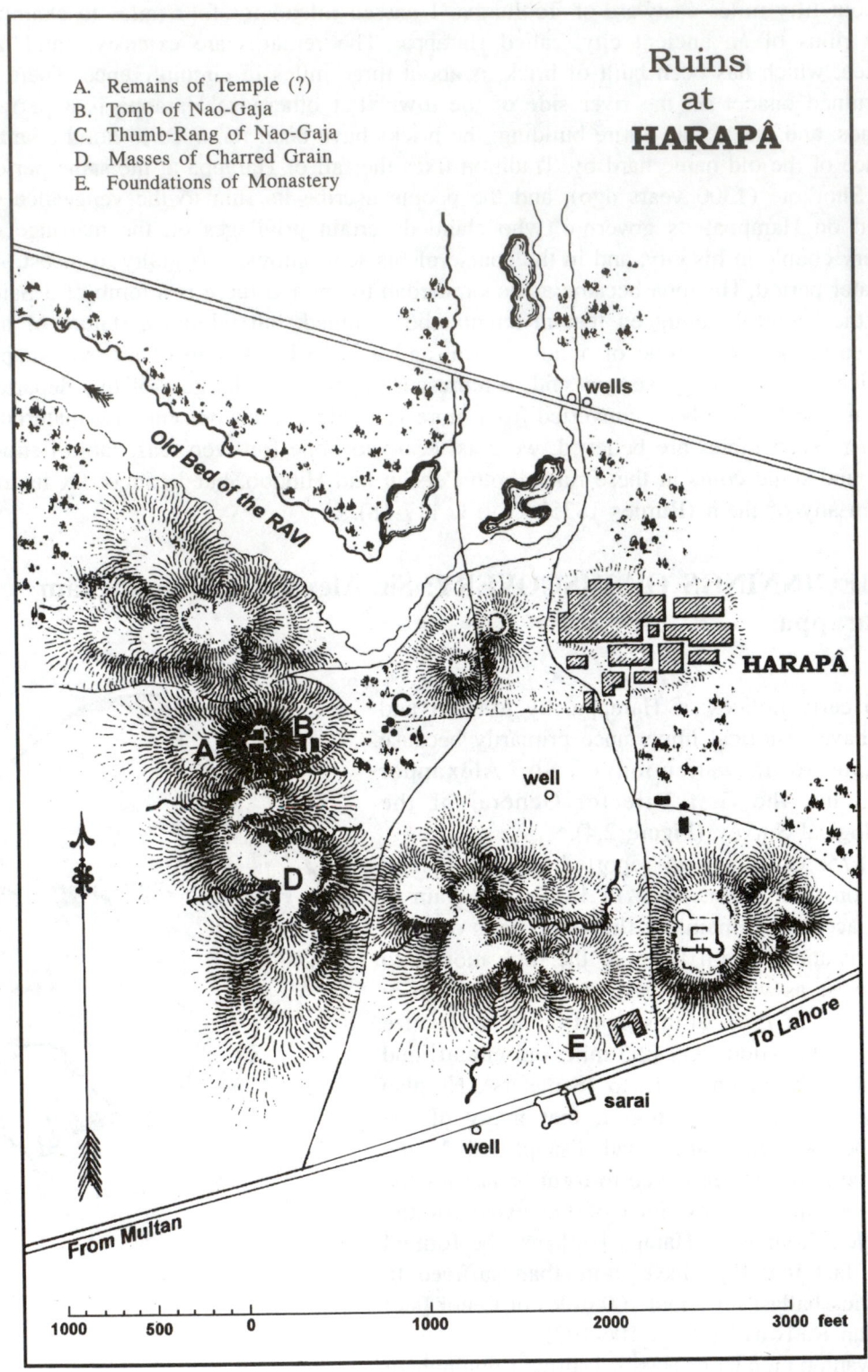

A. Remains of Temple (?)
B. Tomb of Nao-Gaja
C. Thumb-Rang of Nao-Gaja
D. Masses of Charred Grain
E. Foundations of Monastery

Ruins
at
HARAPÂ

wells

Old Bed of the RAVI

HARAPÂ

C

A B

well

D

E

sarai

well

To Lahore

From Multan

| 1000 | 500 | 0 | 1000 | 2000 | 3000 feet |

Figure 2.5. Alexander Cunningham's plan of Harappa, from Cunningham 1875

was only a minor success. But, his report on this work includes the first site plan and his designations of the principal areas at Harappa (A-B, C, D, and E) are still used today (Figure 2.5).

The Brick Robbers

The complete details of this abominable act of vandalism at Harappa are not known, although in the course of his excavations, M. S. Vats found evidence for the earth moving, including the fish plates for the tracks of a light railway that was apparently used in the brick robbing operation (1940: 3). In his autobiography, a Scottish engineer by the name of John Brunton (Figure 2.6) describes his direction of the construction of the Sind Railway in the later half of the 1850s (Brunton 1939). This construction work was faced with the same peril as in the Punjab. Where to find ballast?

My own servants and tent-pitchers amounted in number to 35-from whom tents and provisions had to be collected with a supply of camels to carry them. Then there were my horses for riding the marches, so altogether when we collected at Hyderabad it formed a rather imposing procession. Before leaving I had learnt the position of an old ruined city, called Brahminabad in the "Great Desert" of Scinde—it lay about 15 or 16 miles from the selected course of the left bank line, away in the Desert of rolling banks of sand. I had been much exercised in my mind how we were to get ballast for the line of Railway. If all I heard were true, this ruined city, built of brick, would form a grand quarry for ballast, so I determined to visit it and judge for myself, for we cannot in India any more than in England, trust to hearsay (Brunton 1939: 121).

Figure 2.6. Sketch of John Brunton, from Brunton 1939

At another point in the book Brunton mentions that his brother Robert was supervising the construction of the Lahore to Multan section of the Western Railway (1939: 83). It is reasonable to presume then, that it was Robert Brunton who ordered the dismantling of Harappa, the same fate that John Brunton planned for Brahminabad.[9] There is testimony from Sir Aurel Stein that Kalibangan was also once used as a quarry for bricks: "...it appears that according to information...received from Mr. Warren, an employee of the Bikaner State Railway, much had been removed from the mounds for ballast in constructing the railway" (Stein 1943a: 51).

In all fairness, it should be added that the Harappans themselves, plundered their sites for used bricks and there is evidence for it in DK Area at Mohenjo-daro: "...a stack of bricks against the eastern wall of the western wing of the Palace (Block 1) provided eloquent proof of the collection of bricks from the lower levels to build the houses of later date. This stack included bricks of various sizes, to many of which the mud mortar still adhered" (Mackay 1937-38: xiii). Does life really ever change?

The First Three Harappan Stamp Seals

Cunningham acquired a stamp seal, which today can be identified as a typical Harappan type (Figure 2.7; see also Plate 2.4). This object, now in the British Museum, was the property of a man known only as "Major Clark" and Cunningham had the following to say of it:

> The seal is a smooth black stone without polish. On it is engraved very deeply a bull, without hump, looking to the right, with two stars under the neck. Above the bull there is an inscription in six characters, which are quite unknown to me. They are certainly not Indian letters; and as the bull which accompanies them is without a hump, I conclude that the seal is foreign to India (Cunningham 1875: 108).

Cunningham missed the significance of the object, but then nothing was known of the early periods of India history at the time. However, this seal, and others like it were to be the key finds in uncovering the Indus Civilization, hidden in the city mounds of the Punjab and Sindh.

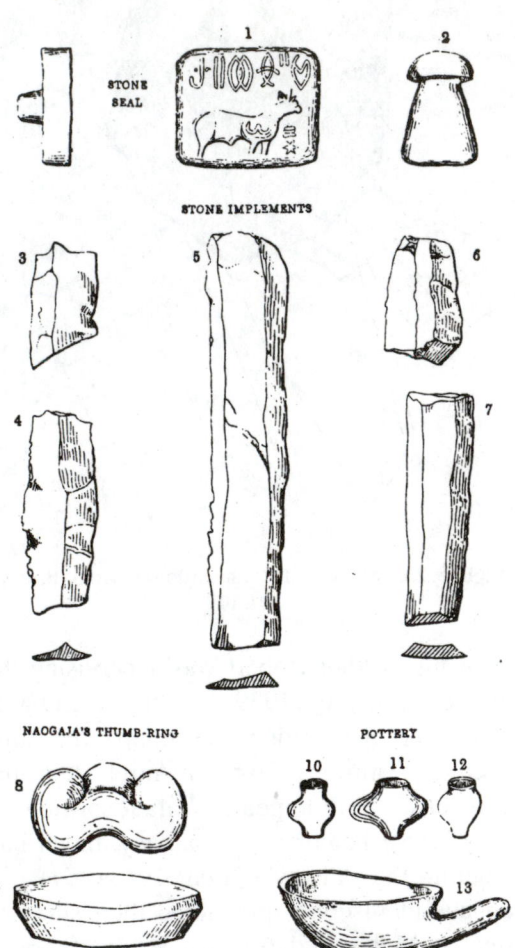

Figure 2.7. Cunningham's finds from Harappa, from Cunningham 1875

In 1886, M. Longworth Dames published a second seal from Harappa which had been acquired by an Education Inspector by the name of J. Harvey (Plate 2.4). In his one page note Dames discusses and illustrates Cunningham's (or rather Major Clark's) seal and the new find, as well as some interesting, but obscure bibliography.

J. F. Fleet published a third seal from Harappa (1912) which had been acquired by Mr. T. A. O'Connor, then the District Superintendent of Police. O'Connor excavated at the site in 1886 and this seal came from his work there. The Fleet paper is important for two reasons: (1) he reveals that all three seals were in the British Museum, where they are today, and (2) the Cunningham-Clark seal is published accurately as a photograph of the impression, and not as Cunningham's rather crude drawing.

Two more Indus seals came to the notice of the Archaeological Survey of India prior to 1924, when the significance of Mohenjo-daro and Harappa was first realized. These were published by Sir John Marshall (1922: Pl. XI, Nos. 22 and 23) in the *Cambridge History of India*. Marshall's professional intuition was working at full speed when he said in connection with these objects: "The potter's art, on the other hand, had been practiced throughout India from time immemorial, and in the Punjab and North-West, which were in closer touch with Persia and Mesopotamia, it is likely enough that burnt bricks were used at a more remote age. In this connection a special interest attaches to certain seals of unknown date and origin which are said to have been found from time to time among the remains of brick structures at Harappa in the Montgomery District of the Punjab. The majority of the seals are engraved with the device of a bull with the head outstretched over some uncertain object, possibly in the act of being sacrificed, and all of them bear legends in a pictographic script, which remains to be deciphered" (Marshall 1922: 617-18) (Figure 2.8).

There are two more Harappan seals that came into private hands prior to the discovery of the Indus Age (Bissing 1927; Coomaraswamy 1929). The first was purchased in Cairo in 1912, but probably comes from Damascus, or that region of the Near East (Bissing 1927: 21). It is a "unicorn" and seems to be slightly damaged (Figure 2.9). The second seal is also a "unicorn." It is said to have been purchased by Professor H. D. Griswold from a coin dealer in the Punjab in 1910 or 1912 (Figure 2.10). It was given to the Museum of Fine Arts, Boston in 1929, not having been published prior to that date. Since neither of these came to scholarly notice, unlike the other seals from Harappa, they played no role in unraveling the mystery of the civilization from which they came.

Other Early Exploration at Harappan Sites

In Baluchistan, there were other men interested in the history of ancient India and Pakistan who investigated Harappan sites in this region and published the results of their findings. The two places in question are Sutkagen-dor and Dab Kot, both seen by colonial officers before the turn of the century.

Sutkagen-dor[10]

In 1875, Major E. Mockler first noticed the great Harappan site of Sutkagen-dor in the Dasht Valley of the Makran (Mockler 1877). This is the westernmost of the Mature Harappan sites, within 35 kilometers of the modern border between Pakistan and Iran.

Mockler returned to the site in February 1876 and conducted a modest excavation. He uncovered the remains

Figure 2.8. Drawing of Marshall's seals from Harappa published in 1922

Figure 2.9. Bissing's "unicorn" seal purchased in Cairo, after Bissing 1927

Figure 2.10. Drawing of the Boston unicorn seal, after Coomaraswamy 1929

54

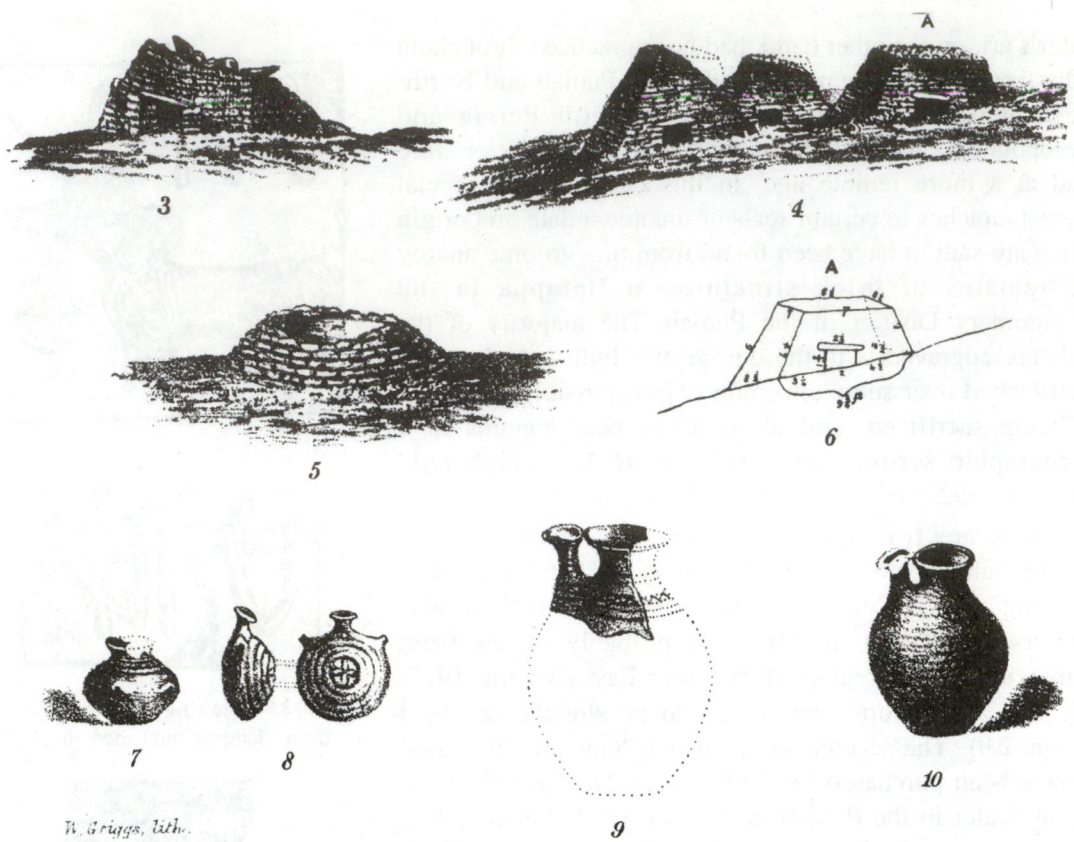

Figure 2.11. Artifacts from Sutkagen-dor excavated by Major Mockler, after Mockler 1877

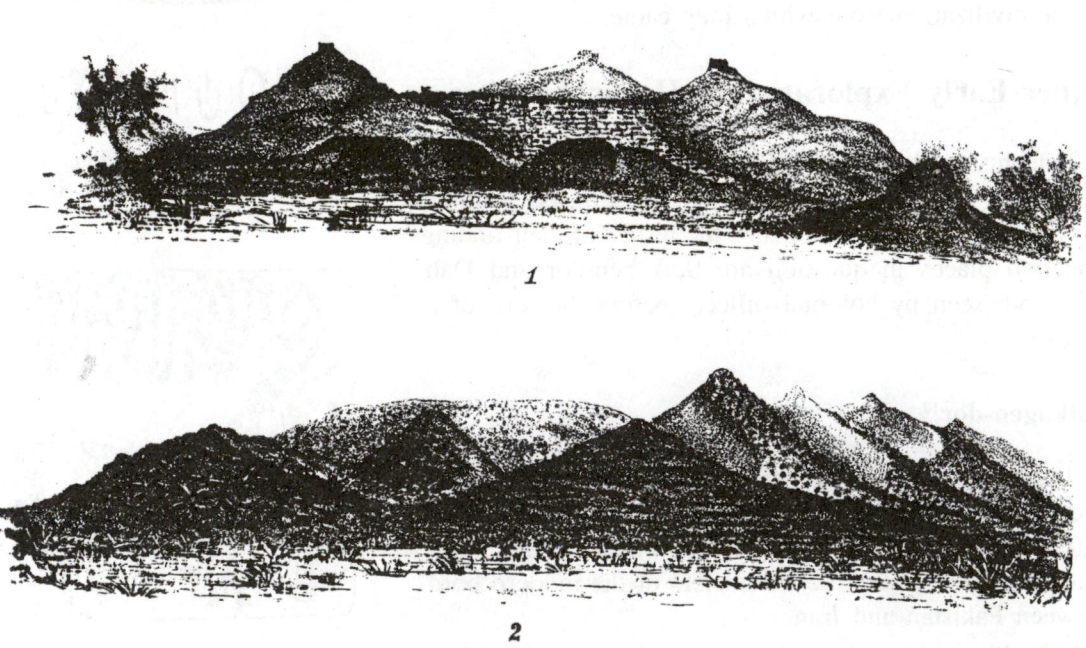

Figure 2.12. Major Mockler's sketch plan of Sutkagen-dor, after Mockler 1877

of a "house" made of burnt bricks, which are close to the dimensions of bricks at Mohenjo-daro. "Everywhere charcoal, bones (principally of fish), pottery and stone knives .were found, but nothing else...Fragments of pottery were imbedded (sic) even in the very lowest walls; and below their foundation, stone knives, bone, and pieces of copper were met with in great quantities" (Mockler 1877: 125). He also published one plate of his finds and a sketch of the place, but he had no appreciation of its true antiquity. Mockler was not lucky enough to find one of the stamp seals with the Indus script (Figure 2.11, Figure 2.12).

Because of its position on the far western flank of the Indus Civilization, Sutkagen-dor has received some attention from archaeologists. Sir Aurel Stein was there twice, first in 1928 (Stein 1931: 60-71) and again in and 1932 (Stein 1937: 70-1).

George Dales conducted a small excavation at the site in 1960 (Dales 1962a, 1962b, 1964, Dales and Lipo 1992) and in recent years Roland Besenval of the Centre National de la Recherche Scientifique, working with an Italian research team, has been to the site in connection with his explorations in the Makran, which began in 1987 (Besenval 1992; Besenval and Sanlaville 1990; Besenval and Marquis 1993). It was clearly an important settlement, and we now know from Besenval's work that there are other Harappan sites in the vicinity. It is not today, and never was, directly on the beach of the Arabian Sea. Still, Sutkagen-dor was a frontier settlement, in the sense that it was established on an ancient border between southeastern Iran and the Harappan domain, and the sea. It must have played a dual role in overland commerce and sea trade.

Dabar Kot

The great mound of Dabar Kot on the Thal plain of Loralai District in Baluchistan has been a prominent part of local history for many years. The impressive size of the mound (46 hectares and 35 meters high), and the fact that it sits on a plain making it so clearly visible, account for this. It was first recognized as an archaeological site in 1898 by Dr. Fritz Noetling, a palaeontologist with the Geological Survey of India. He visited the site in 1898 and made a collection, which includes one very fine chipped stone arrow head (Noetling 1899) (Figure 2.13).

Noetling had no idea of the age of his finds, but he seems to have been a man with a great curiosity about the past, no matter how recent in geological terms. As part of his study of the geology of Baluchistan he visited Periano Ghundai in 1897 and Rana Ghundai in 1898, where he made collections and published small reports (Noetling 1898a, 1898b, 1899).[11]

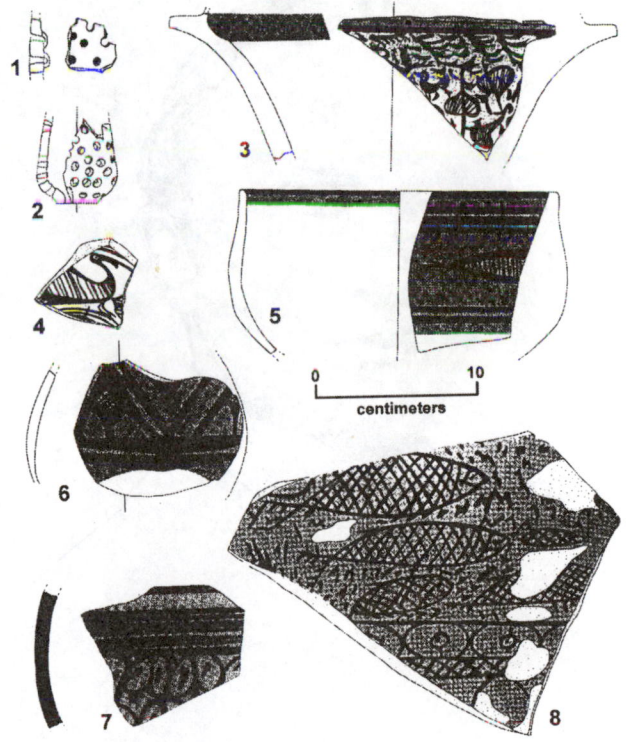

Figure 2.13. Pottery from Dabar Kot collected by Dr. Noetling, after Pedde 1993a

Sir Aurel Stein also visited Dabar Kot, the first time in 1904, on his early reconnaissance in Baluchistan (Stein 1905: 52). He returned for a small excavation in 1927 (Stein 1929a: 55-64) when he was able to suggest that the early levels of the site might well correlate with the recent finds from Mohenjo-daro (1929a: 64).

In more recent years Walter Fairservis went to Dabar Kot and attempted to present a coherent stratigraphy from sherds pulled from Stein's sections (Fairservis 1959: 308-28) (Plate 2.5). A young German scholar, Friedhelm Pedde has also been there and published his observations (Pedde 1993a, 1993b: 29).

Prehistoric archaeology in the western region of British India was clearly not being ignored, but it was being done on a more or less ad hoc basis. What was needed was direction and coordination and that meant the sponsorship of the colonial government. This was to come in 1902 with the appointment of John Marshall as Director General of the Archaeological Survey of India.

THE APPOINTMENT OF JOHN MARSHALL

Lord Curzon of Kedleston (Figure 2.14) became Viceroy in 1899. One of the things he turned to immediately was the British administration of India's cultural heritage. Part of the plan he developed called for the rejuvenation of the Archaeological Survey of India. This meant a new person would be needed for the post of Director General and Curzon wanted someone young and vigorous. On 21 February 1902 the Government announced the appointment of John Marshall[12], a 26 year old student of Greek archaeology, as the new Director General (Ghosh 1953a: 31). He came to the position with splendid recommendations and a fine background in Mediterranean archaeology. Marshall had been trained in field archaeology at Knossos, under the tutelage of Sir Arthur Evans and had been recruited in part, because this background would allow him to bring the best and most recent methods of excavation to India.

The Survey was organized then, as today, into geographical areas of responsibility, called "Circles," each headed by a Superintendent Archaeologist (after ca. 1962 called Superintending Archaeologists). The boundaries of the Circles have shifted over the years, and the number has grown in a reasonably steady way, but their nomenclature has remained descriptive, although today they use

Figure 2.14. Sketch of Lord Curzon

the principal city within each Circle as its name, rather than the region, as in the "Agra Circle."

It is often overlooked by those interested in archaeological field research that the Government of India had as its highest priority for the new Archaeological Survey of India the administration and conservation of monuments. Marshall was to conduct a national survey to assess the condition of monuments, to get on with the job of preserving them, and ensure that they were not used for inappropriate purposes. Excavation, exploration and epigraphy were placed in the second rank of priorities, although they were not to be neglected, as Curzon indicated in an address to the Asiatic Society of Bengal in 1900 (Curzon 1900).[13]

Interest in Harappa During the Marshall Era

The three seals from Harappa with the enigmatic script, published by Cunningham, Dames and Fleet, were known to all of the professional archaeologists in the Subcontinent, even if they did not understand their historical significance. Marshall is said to have taken an interest in them even before his appointment as Director General. He was on home leave in 1906, and pursued his interest at that time because the seals were in the British Museum (Vats 1940: 11). Harappa was a place with potential importance and there were two early assessments of the place. The first was undertaken by Pundit Hira Nanda Sastri in 1909, on the instructions of J. Ph. Vogel, Superintendent Archaeologist of the Northern Circle of the Archaeological Survey of India. The Pundit's report on the site was not enthusiastic, at least as far as excavation potential was concerned (Sahni 1920-21a: 9). Sir John Marshall sent his closest colleague in the Survey, Harold Hargreaves, for another assessment of the mounds in 1914 (Majumdar 1939: 99). This eventually led to Sahni's first digging there (Sahni 1920-21a, 1920-21b). The history of research at Harappa is reviewed in Possehl (1991).

Clues from Other Sites

The fact that prior to 1920 there had been excavation at sites of the Mature Harappan has already been noted. They did not produce the distinctive stamp seals like those found at Harappa, and this critical clue did not lead Marshall and his colleagues to make the needed connection. There was actually a third site that was known and excavated by one of Marshall's own people.

This is Kalibangan, visited by the Italian scholar Luigi Pio Tessitori in April 1917. He undertook a small excavation there in 1918 (Tessitori (1918-19: 23, 1920, 1921). Kalibangan had been earlier noted as an important ancient place by Lt. Col. James Tod, who called it "Kali-bang" (Tod 1829-32: Vol. II, 167). Tessitori called the site "Kali Vangu" in his survey report (Tessitori n. d.) and "Kali Banga" in the *Annual Report of the Archaeological Survey of India* (Tessitori 1918-19: 23). There is no indication that he understood the antiquity of this site, hardly a fault, given the paucity of information on India's prehistoric past at that time. The discovery of the Indus civilization would have to await a return to Harappa with confirmation from Mohenjo-daro. Stein used Tessitori's manuscript, which was never published (Tessitori n.d.), as part of the data he had for his "Ghaggar-Hakra" tour (Stein 1943a; S. P. Gupta 1989).

Luigi Pio Tessitori

Tessitori was born in Udine, Italy on December 22, 1887 and died at Bikaner on November 22, 1919 at age 31, before he could publish a report on his work at Kalibangan (Della Casa and

Figure 2.15. Luigi Pio Tessitori, after Della Casa and Sagramoso 1990, cover illustration

Sagramoso 1990; Marshall 1918-19) (Figure 2.15). He came to India in 1914 and approached the Asiatic Society of Bengal to work on their project of collecting manuscripts in Rajasthan, which had been started by H. P. Sastri. Tessitori was trained as a Sanskritist and was apparently very adept at the mastery of languages. His article entitled "Notes on the Grammar of the Old Western Rajasthani with special reference to Apabhramca and to Gujarati and Marwari" is an example of this ability. It was published in nine installments of the *Indian Antiquary* (Tessitori 1915, 1916).

Tessitori had a great love for Rajputana and his "Bardic and Historical Survey" (Tessitori 1914, 1917-18, 1918-19, 1920, 1921) contributed much to our knowledge of this region through the collection, classification, editing and publication of manuscripts he recovered from villages, towns and cities, mostly in the Princely States of Jodhpur and Bikaner. These were published in four principal monographs (Tessitori 1917a, 1917b, 1918, 1919). He is also said to have written a "History of Bikaner" which I have not been able to trace.

Tessitori's principal involvement in archaeology was along the Sarasvati. He explored some eighty-five sites and excavated at Rang Mahal, in addition to Kalibangan (1920: 254-55). The collections resulting from this work were never properly handled, due to the principal's premature death. Although he was not primarily an archaeologist, his interests in this part of Rajasthani history demonstrates the breadth of his talent, and his ability to deal with multiple sources of data.

Sir John Marshall had much respect for Tessitori. Writing from the editor's chair of the *Annual Report of the Archaeological Survey of India* he noted: "The death of this brilliant young scholar, which took place at Bikaner in November last, almost immediately after his return from Italy, is one which will be deeply regretted by all who remember the charm of his personality, the single-heartedness of his life, and his intense devotion to his work in Rajputana. His loss indeed is irreparable; for there is no one living who possesses the special knowledge which Dr. Tessitori brought to bear on his Survey of the bardic chronicles; and even as regards the archaeological work which he was doing, it will be no easy matter to replace him" (Marshall 1918-19: 22).

There is a short note on Tessitori's scholarly work in India by R. S. Sharma (1990) which is included as a paper from the proceedings of a conference held on the topic in Udine on November 12-14, 1987 (Della Casa and Sagramoso 1990).

Rai Bahadur Daya Ram Sahni Excavates at Harappa

Another Superintendent Archaeologist of the Northern Circle of the Archaeological Survey of India, was Rai Bahadur Daya Ram Sahni[14] (Figure 2.16). He knew of the seals from Harappa and noted; "Systematic explorations may yield more records in these characters and may thus provide a clue to their true nature and the interpretation of these curious epigraphs" (Sahni 1916-17: 7).

Sir John Marshall enabled Sahni to excavate at Harappa in the 1920-21 winter field season. The actual work began in the beginning of January 1921 and continued until the middle of February (Sahni 1920-21a: 9). Sahni opened trenches on the mound labeled "A-B" on General Cunningham's plan (see Figure 2.5), as well as on the northernmost mound, now labeled "F." On mound "F" he dug a trench 150 meters (500 feet) long down to a depth of 3.5 meters

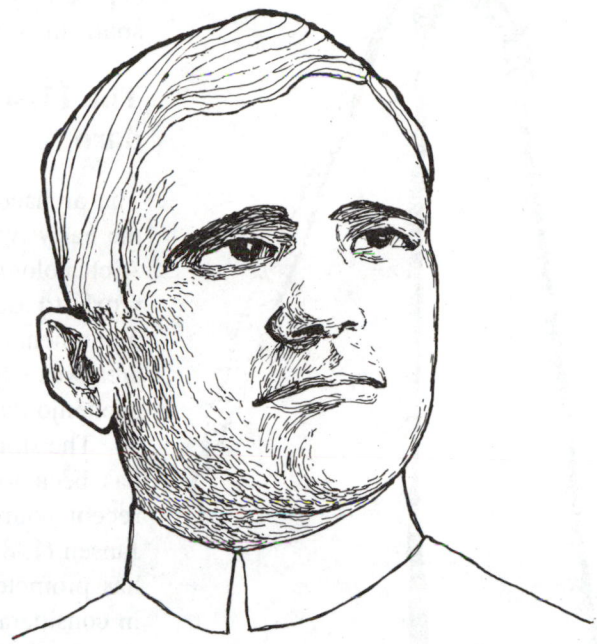

Figure 2.16. Sketch of Rai Bahadur Daya Ram Sahni

(12 feet) and found a great deal of disturbed material, with little architecture surviving the railroad's plunder (Plate 2.6). He did, however, find three more Harappan seals (Sahni 1920-21b: Plate XIII, b, c, d), none of which was a zebu, so the presence of the unhumped bull remained a misleading mystery.

By the end of the season Sir John Marshall felt sufficiently confident of the Harappa work that he could state: "Thus, although the results attained so far are undoubtedly meager, they are important in that, according to Sahni, they prove that the Harappa seals and their curious pictographic legends belong to the pre-Mauryan epoch; and it is to be remembered that the digging to date has pierced only the topmost levels" (1920-21b: 17). This was, of course, a somewhat conjectural conclusion at that time, but it was to be proved correct. It was also of extraordinary importance since it was the first documentation of South Asian history prior to the arrival of the Greeks at Taxila in the spring of 326 BC.

Lack of funds prevented the Survey from vigorously moving ahead with this work until 1923-24 and 1924-25 (Marshall 1923-24: 47), when the Rai Bahadur continued his probings of Mounds F and A-B. He expanded trenches opened in 1920-21 and used rain gullies at the site to reach early levels. In 1923-24, Sahni continued his excavations on Mound F where he came across the remains of a large building, the scope of which he did not understand. During the next season he returned to the same area of Mound F and exposed a great deal more of the structure which he called the "area of the parallel walls." In his preliminary report (Sahni 1924-25: 76-77) he confessed that he had no concept of its function, but the building on Mound F has since come to be called the "granary." In 1923-24, Sahni found a copper ear cleaning implement with parallels at Ur and Kish (Sahni 1923-24: Pl. XIX, 22; Figure 2.17).

Sahni's first three seasons of excavation at Harappa bring to a close what can be thought of as the first phase of research at the site. Archaeologists were hunting for a solution to the mystery of the seals from Harappa, but they had not yet uncovered their true significance, or

Figure 2.17. Copper toilet implement from Harappa with Mesopotamian parallels, after Vats 1940: Plate CXXV, 1

the fact that there was an entire civilization waiting to be exposed by the spade. This was really to come from the south in Sindh, at Mohenjo-daro.

The First Phase of Exploration at Mohenjo-daro

The archaeology of Sindh was comparatively unknown in the early twentieth century, and Marshall's Superintending Archaeologists for the Western Circle had a great deal of work to do. As part of the general assessment of monuments called for by the Viceroy, Lord Curzon, the area was explored and inevitably, the huge city mounds of Mohenjo-daro outside Dokri were discovered.

The story of the discovery of the Harappan Civilization has been told in many ways by many people. The most recent sources are: Pande (1982), Possehl (1982c) and Jansen (1983, 1986, 1987). Jansen's work at Mohenjo-daro has prompted him to review the history of research there in considerable detail and there is no one who knows more than he does about this interesting topic.

The Meaning of the Name "Mohenjo-daro"

There has been some research on the meaning of the name "Mohenjo-daro." Some of it is worth reviewing, since several renderings of the site name are in the literature. M. H. Sorely has noted that:

> It is commonly written "Mohenjo-daro" as if there was some connection with Mohan, the Hindu divinity, which was one of the avatars of Krishna. Actually Mohenjo-daro is a pure Sindhi expression. It should be written correctly as Muyan-jo-Daro or Moenjo-Daro, Moen or "muyan" being the inflected, objective plurals of the past participles of the verb "maran" to die. "Muo," the singular form means "the dead man." "Daro" is the ordinary Sindhi word for a mound, or a heap, and is philologically connected with the Pak-European root which appears in cognate form in numerous European languages. The root meaning is "to place" or "to pile up" or "to heap" so that "Moenjo-daro" is the highly accurate and at the same time, most picturesque description of what the place in reality is, namely "the Mound of the Dead Men (Sorely 1959: 111; see also Jansen and Urban 1984b: 5).

The words "damb" in Baluchi and "dheri" in Pashto are cognate with "daro." The word for "mound" in Brahui, a Dravidian tongue of Baluchistan, is "ghundai," as in the site of Periano Ghundai (Witch's Mound). For a time it was the policy of the Department of Archaeology in Pakistan to render the name of Mohenjo-daro as Sorley suggests: "Moenjo-daro." They have now returned to the form "Mohenjo-daro," which is used here, except in direct quotes where each author's original rendering is retained. Mohenjo-daro is also the spelling that is familiar to most people and the one found in Sir John Marshall's monumental work on the site: *Mohenjo-daro and the Indus Civilization*. It has tradition behind it, even if in a technical sense it might not be precisely correct. It is also reasonable to doubt that D. R. Bhandarkar thought that the place was connected with the avatar "Mohan."

Devadatta Ramakrishna Bhandarkar Discovers Mohenjo-daro

D. R. Bhandarkar (Figure 2.18), one of Marshall's young Superintendent Archaeologists, visited Mohenjo-daro in the winter of 1911-12 (Bhandarkar 1911-12), and can be credited with the "discovery" of the site.[15] Bhandarkar was the son of the famous Poona Indologist, Sir Ramakrishna Gopal Bhandarkar (Puri 1981). The younger man had moved first towards a career in law, but switched to ancient history and archaeology. In 1911-12, he was Superintendent of the Western "Harappan" Circle of the Archaeological Survey of India. Bhandarkar's visit to Mohenjo-daro was part of a comprehensive survey of ancient sites and monuments within his Circle which had been ordered by Sir John Marshall. He described the site as follows:

Figure 2.18. Sketch of D. R. Bhandarkar

> I also visited what is called Mohen-jo-daro, seven miles east of Dokri in Larkhana district. We had received glowing accounts of this spot, and I had great hopes of finding it to be as interesting as the ruins of the Mirpur Khas stupa before they were dug out. But on visiting the place I was greatly disappointed. Here are spread the remains of an old place for about three-fourths of a mile. Near the western edge is a tower on a mound nearly seventy feet high from the ground-level, from which the mound gradually rises. Of the top portion only the inner core has remained, consisting of sun-dried brick work. The bottom of it appears to have been reached most probably by treasure hunters, who, I was told, frequently excavated the most promising sites here. Close by towards the west and south are six mounds, but of far less height, and there seems to have been a river once running between the tower mound and other heaps. On the north side of the tower again are vestiges of an old brick road running up. The bricks as a rule are of modern type and not of large dimension like the old. There are no doubt some here which look old, but they are few and far between. Not a single carved moulded brick was I able to discover here. What a contrast to the Mirpur Khas stupa, where cart loads of such bricks were found before it was excavated! The probabilities, therefore, are that the Mohen-jo-daro does not represent the remains of a Buddhist stupa or of any ancient monument. According to the local tradition,

62

these are the ruins of a town only two hundred years old, and the daro or tower itself a part of the bastion guarding its west side. This seems to be not incorrect, because the bricks here found, as just said, are of the modern type, and there is a total lack of carved terra-cottas amidst the whole ruins (Bhandarkar 1911-12: 4-5).

Rakal Das Banerji at Mohenjo-daro

Figure 2.19. Sketch of R. D. Banerji

Bhandarkar was followed by Rakal Das Banerji, a gifted and energetic man, as Superintendent Archaeologist of the Western Circle (Figure 2.19). During the field season of 1919-20, one year prior to Sahni's initial probing of Harappa, Banerji visited Mohenjo-daro. He was in the midst of a comprehensive reassessment of the antiquarian remains in his Circle, which might have been a way of 'checking-up' on Bhandarkar.[16] Banerji left the following description of the site:

The ruins at Mohen-jo-daro lie at a distance of 6 miles from the Railway Station at Dokri on the Rohri-Kotri Section of the N. W. Railway. The locality does not seem to have attracted notice before though the height of the mound and the extensity of the ruins is well known in the neighborhood. The ruins cover an area of about 2 square miles and are visible from a distance. They are not mentioned in the revised list of ancient monuments in the Bombay Presidency, but were visited by my predecessor in 1913 (sic).

The ruins consist of vast mounds of burnt bricks surrounded by smaller ones. In the centre of this area is a very high mound about 80 or 90 feet above the level of the surrounding country. This is called Muhen-jo-daro. The top of the entire mound consists of debris and brick bats but here and there loose debris has slipped away exposing straight walls of burnt bricks. This mound is about 600 feet in length and 200 in breadth. In one place on this mound there is the drum of a stupa made of sun-dried bricks. Only the shell of the drum remains as the core has been excavated to a depth of some 30 to 40 feet by treasure seekers. The inhabitants of the surrounding village have dug out and removed bricks from this mound from time immemorial and do so even now. Some of these people who do not acknowledge to have excavated this mound for bricks within the last ten or twelve years, state that when they dug for bricks previously, they found the entire mound to consist of a huge platform, of burnt bricks on which were built numerous round hemispherical objects of burnt as well as sun-dried bricks (?votive stupas).

Close to this platform of stupas there is another high mound which is the second largest in this place. This appears to have been a temple or monastery as the old villagers state that they found rows of small square chambers arranged around a square courtyard in this mound. Search among the ruins led to the discovery of numbers of carved bricks but no human figures or images were found. The villagers are unanimous in stating that no coins have ever been found in any of these mounds. These two mounds are surrounded by numerous small mounds which represent the ruins of the village or township which had grown around this stupa and temple in the height of their glory. The stupa at this place is much higher than the stupas at Depar Ghangro or Mirpur-Khas and appears to have been the largest and highest Buddhist stupa in the country of Sindh. The stupas and the surrounding ground is full of saltpetre or some other salt which is carried away and sold as a manure. The digging for bricks and the removal of this sort of manure constitute a serious danger to the structures that may lie under the covering of loose brick bats and debris and therefore steps ought to be taken to stop excavation in this area immediately (Banerji 1920-21) (Plate 2.7, Plate 2.8, Plate 2.9, Plate 2.10, Plate 2.11, Plate 2.12, Plate 2.13, Plate 2.14, Plate 2.15, Plate 2.16).

Banerji picked up a flint scraper from the surface of Mohenjo-daro which was of some significance to him. Over the next three years he visited many sites in Sindh and by December, 1922 he came to the conclusion that Mohenjo-daro was a very ancient site (1926: 2).

My estimate of the antiquity of Mohen-jo-daro was confirmed by an accidental discovery at Ghaibi-daro. During a shower of winter rain a portion of one of the mounds slipped down accidentally exposing a square tower or bastion of some brick building in the interior, inside which were arranged a number of large sized round-bottomed jars in a super-imposed row...I went to the top of the mound and carelessly introduced my right hand into the topmost one which was still unbroken. I felt a sharp pain and on withdrawing my hand found my little finger to be bleeding. The Brahuis who had accompanied me thought that I had been bitten by a snake. They broke the jar and found that it was covered with alluvium at the top in which a small sharp scraper of flint was firmly embedded, on which my middle (*sic*) finger had struck. Below the layers of alluvium there was a row of nine smaller jars arranged in four rows, with pointed bottom, each of which contained a small crucible-shaped reliquary, containing a single unburnt bone of the human body surrounded by miniature necropolitan pottery of the same type as that discovered later on in Rooms No. 27 and 39 of site no 1 at Mohen-jo-daro. This was the first discovery of neolithic or sub-neolithic stone implements underground and not on the surface. The discovery at Ghaibi-daro proved definitely that knives or scrapers of neolithic flint was associated with pre-historic pre-cremation burials and the specimens found by me at Reti, Alor, Mithodoro, Dhamraho, Badin and Mohen-jo-daro were not exactly chance finds. This discovery prompted me to start the excavation of Mohenjo-daro immediately... (Banerji 1926: 16-7).

Banerji's Excavation at Mohenjo-daro

There is some confusion regarding the date of Banerji's first excavation at Mohenjo-daro. Marshall clearly indicates in the *Annual Report of the Archaeological Survey of India, 1923-24*, page 48, that Banerji first dug there in the field season 1921-22 (see also Marshall 1931a: 10, 123, 125); but Banerji's preliminary report for the Archaeological Survey on this work is found in the Annual Report for 1922-23, and there is no indication that it is out of chronological order (Banerji 1922-23: 102-04). Moreover, Banerji tells us that he made the decision to excavate the site in 1921-22, and revisited it in December 1922 (Banjeri 1926: 26): "The ruins of three of the islands were excavated during the working season of 1922-23" (Banerji 1926: 27).[17] This is confirmed by K. N. Dikshit who called his excavation in 1924-25 "the third season" (Dikshit 1924-25: 63). That is Banerji was season one, Vats two and Dikshit three. In this same report Dikshit states that Site 2 was excavated in 1922-23 (1924-25: 71). These points would seem to argue against the possibility that Banerji excavated in 1921-22 and 1922-23. On the other hand, Marshall was quite clear about the first season of excavation and it is curious that he was so adamant about "1921-22." Marshall was not given to make mistakes of this sort, and one senses that this was an issue between him and his Superintendent in the Western Circle.

A report on this work at Mohenjo-daro was prepared by Banerji and submitted to the Director General for publication in about 1926. It includes the story of discovery, his excavations at the site and many observations about other ancient sites in Sindh (Banerji 1926). The original manuscript consisted of 166 typescript pages, plus many illustrations. This document was retained by the Office of the Director General until 16 January 1930, when it was returned to Banerji, the illustrations said to be missing.[18] Banerji was then the Manindra Chandra Nandi Professor at Banaras Hindu University. The manuscript clarifies a number of things that were not apparent earlier (Possehl 1982c) and contains much useful historical information; although Marshall's observation that it is "diffuse" is also true.[19]

The Director General was on home leave from mid-March to mid-December 1923, so he missed some of the activity relating to the early finds from Mohenjo-daro (Spooner 1922-23: 3, fn). Marshall gave the prestigious George Birdwood Lecture to the Royal Society of Arts while in England and worked at the British Museum. This Birdwood Lecture was chaired by Marshall's patron, Lord Curzon, who was then Secretary of State for Foreign Affairs, and quite proud of his appointment of Marshall and the work of the Survey (Curzon 1923: 659). But, 1922-23 was a year of financial retrenchment, with a budget cut for the Archaeological Survey of India of three lakhs (Spooner 1922-23: 1).

More Stamp Seals from Mohenjo-daro

Banerji's excavation began at Site 1, along the eastern retaining wall of the stupa; a very productive area (Figure 2.20, Figure 2.21, Figure 2.22). During this work, Mr. N. S. Chikte, who was in charge of the trench, discovered "...two seals with pictograms or ideograms of the same class which had been discovered up to date, only at Harappa..." (Banerji 1926: 29). In another publication he notes:

> The most important discovery of the season was a seal of soapstone, found on the staircase on the riverside, at the bottom of the eastern retaining wall of the tower. This seal bears in the centre the figure of a one-horned quadruped, which has been identified by Dr. D. B. Spooner as the unicorn. The fragment of a similar seal was discovered in a drain at the same place and a third specimen was discovered on a small shrine to the north-east of Site No. 1. These seals bear ideograms or pictograms like the seals discovered at Harappa (Banerji 1922-23: 103).

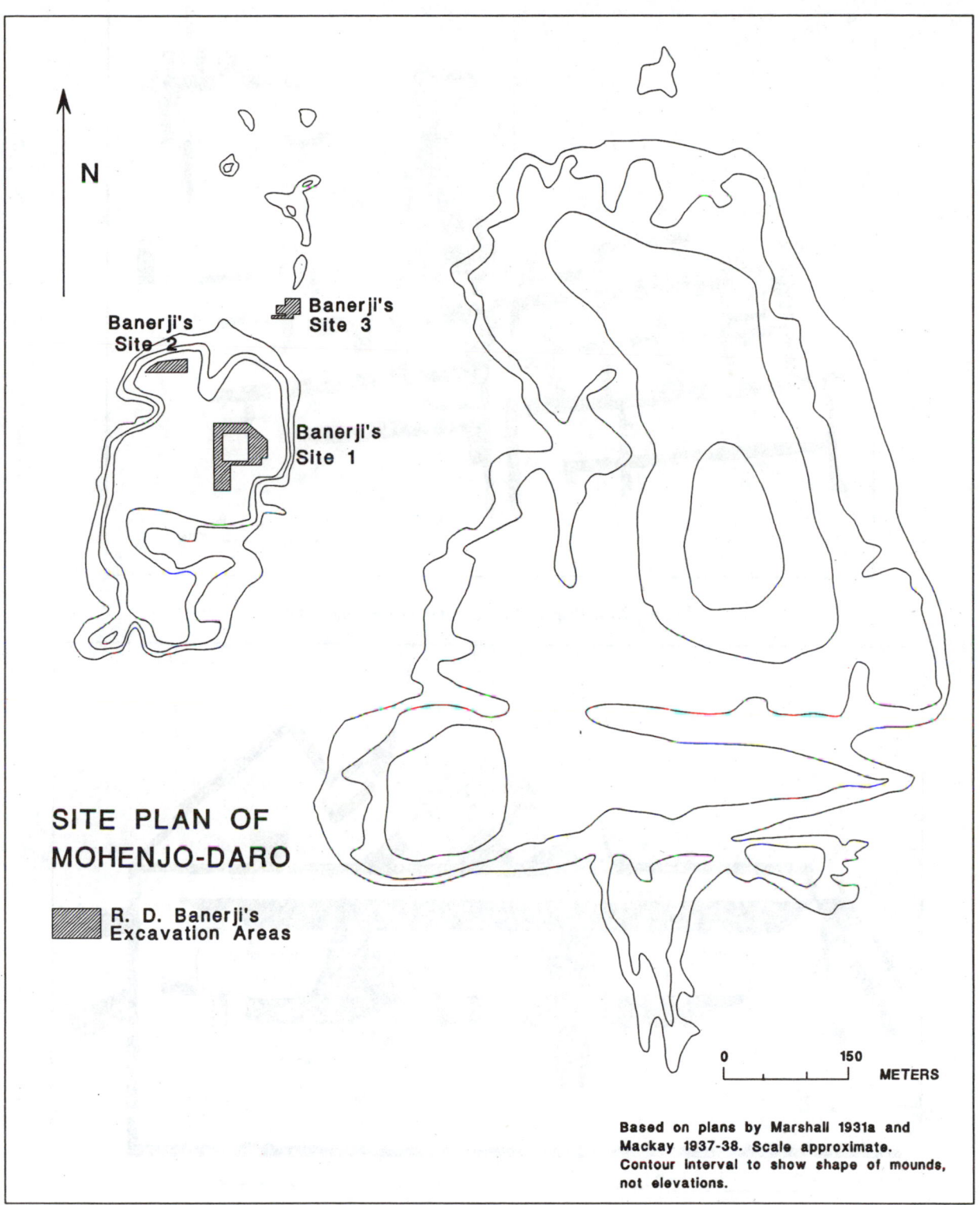

Figure 2.20. Plan of Mohenjo-daro showing Banerji's excavation sites

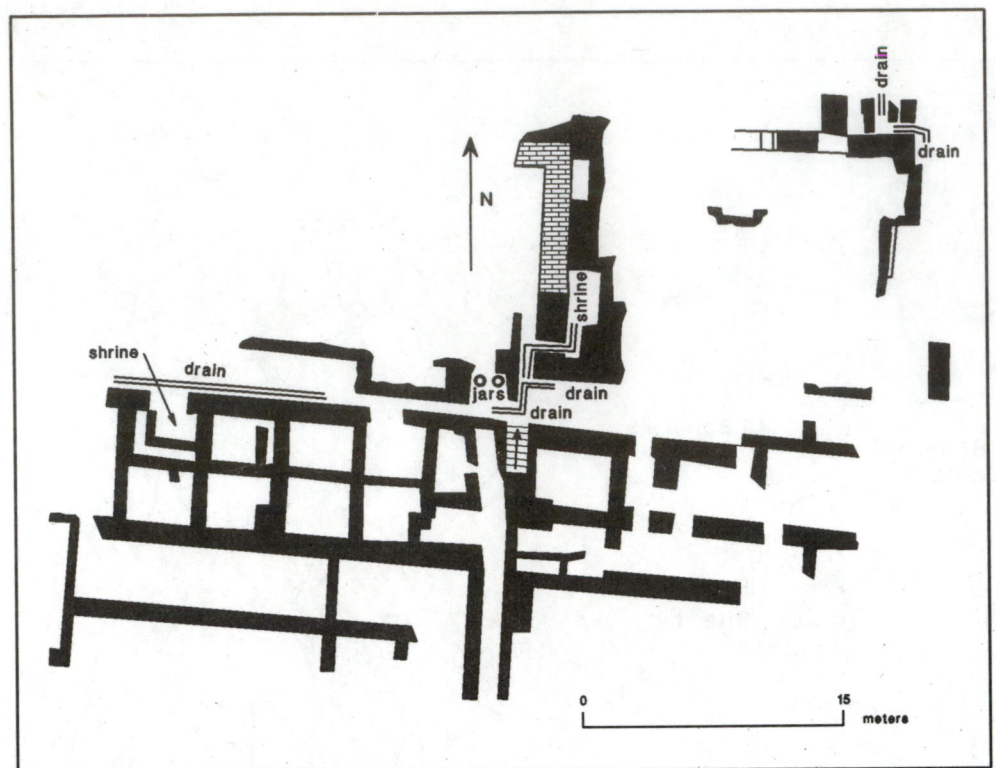

Figure 2.21. Plan of Site 2, after Jansen 1983: 31

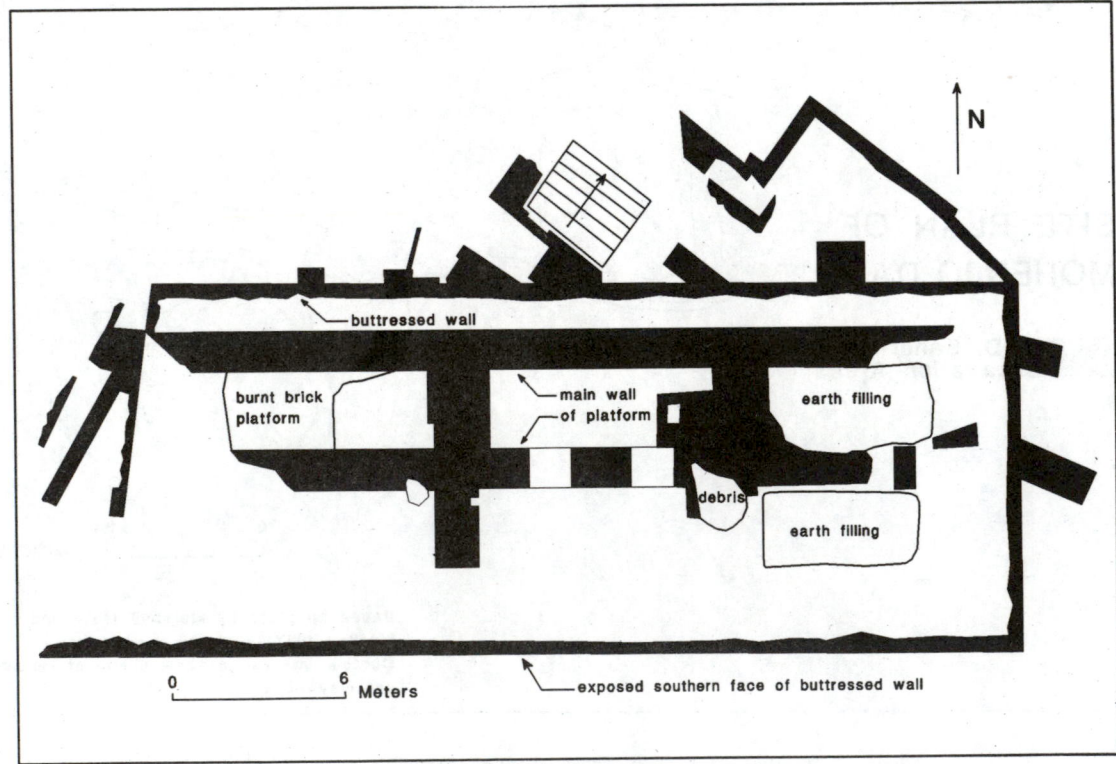

Figure 2.22. Plan Site 3, after Jansen 1983: 32

The investigation of the eastern retaining wall was an important step, since it relates to the question of defenses and fortifications around the Mound of the Great Bath, as well as the Mature Harappan preoccupation with the raising of platforms. As seen in the *Indus Age: The Mature Harappan*, these are knotty problems and it is to Banerji's credit that he carried out work that helps resolve it.

Banerji's Insights

Banerji's health was not good at the time of his work at Mohenjo-daro and as a consequence there was some delay in the publication and dissemination of this important material (Marshall 1923-24: 48). In the end, Banerji suggested that there were affinities between the finds from Mohenjo-daro and Minoan antiquities. This has been proved wrong, but his discrimination of several strata below the stupa and the tie between Mohenjo-daro and Harappa was a very significant contribution to the archaeology of the day. Equally to the point is the incredible coincidence between the timing of Banerji's excavation and the work at Harappa. Between 1919-20 and 1923-24 there was a great flurry of serious archaeological activity around the two sites which had heretofore been largely ignored. It is almost as if R. D. Banerji knew that there was a relationship between Mohenjo-daro and Harappa after his initial visits to the site.

THE DISCOVERY OF THE HARAPPAN CIVILIZATION

In the summer of 1924 Marshall arranged for the finds from Mohenjo-daro to be brought to his headquarters where they could be compared directly with those from Harappa (Marshall 1923-24: 48).

That the finds from the two sites belonged to the same stage of culture and approximately to the same age, and that they were totally distinct from anything previously known to us in India was at once evident. So impressed indeed was I by their novel character that I lost no time in publishing an account of them in the *Illustrated London News*, my hope being that through the medium of that widely read journal I might succeed in getting some light thrown on their age and character by archaeologists in other countries. This hope, I am glad to say, was at once fulfilled. In the following issue of the *Illustrated London News* appeared a letter from Professor Sayce[20] pointing out the close resemblance between these objects from the Indus Valley and certain Sumerian antiquities from Southern Mesopotamia, and a week later there appeared in the same journal a longer article from the pens of Messrs. Gadd and Sidney Smith giving a more detailed comparison of the pictographic script and other antiquities found in the two countries. Some of the analogies suggested by these two writers are fanciful, but most of them are undoubtedly correct and there can now no longer be any doubt that the Punjab and Sind antiquities are closely connected and roughly contemporary with the Sumerian antiquities of Mesopotamia dating from the 3rd or 4th millennium before Christ. Simultaneously also the same conclusion was reached by Dr. E. Mackay, Director of the American Expedition at Kish, who in an unpublished letter to me pointed out the similarity between the ceramic wares found at Mohenjo-daro and at Kish, and also brought to my notice that a seal identical with those found at Harappa and Mohenjo-daro had been discovered in the debris beneath a temple at Hammurabi's time (Marshall 1923-24: 48).

EARLY EXCAVATIONS AT MOHENJO-DARO AND HARAPPA

The results of Marshall's review of material from Mohenjo-daro and Harappa clarified the situation in a way which spurred the Archaeological Survey of India to action. The 1923-24 field season saw significant new digging at both sites, which firmed Marshall's conviction that there was a great civilization there but, Mohenjo-daro was the site with the greatest promise. The brick robbing had destroyed much of the architecture at Harappa and so the Survey's main efforts were in Sindh.

Field Methods of the Archaeological Survey

True stratigraphic excavation was not practiced in Indian archaeology until Sir Mortimer Wheeler introduced the technique in 1944. Mohenjo-daro and Harappa were excavated using arbitrary levels above or below an established point. For Marshall's work this established point was simply a measurement below local ground surface. This was changed to a fixed datum point for all measurements by E. J. H. Mackay, who followed Marshall at Mohenjo-daro. Both methods inevitably lead to the mixing of artifacts from different depositional units and thus destroy the cultural contexts and associations among objects. At the time of these excavations this system was still used in many parts of the world, but the excavation methodologists of the day, Wheeler among them, had determined that arbitrary levels were unnecessary if careful digging was done, and that they should be abandoned.

When Marshall arrived in 1925-26 he had Mohenjo-daro gridded into one hundred foot squares, which were in turn subdivided into twenty-five, twenty foot squares. This system served well for horizontal control, although it was altered by Mackay, who preferred to use building and room numbers (Mackay 1937-38: xiii).

Sections were rarely drawn, and the reading of stratigraphy from them was an unknown art. Mackay introduced the screening of earth at his Chanhu-daro excavation, which must have increased the recovery of small objects (Mackay 1948: Plate XXX). Still, the notion of counting things in South Asian archaeology in a statistical fashion would have to wait many years before it was introduced by Walter Fairservis in his 1950-51 excavations in the Quetta Valley.

Small finds (seals, copper objects, figurines, beads, etc.) were recorded in three dimensions when they were found at Mohenjo-daro. Placing them in exact architectural context is difficult however, since for Marshall's years one has to have a very accurate rendering of the surface of the site at each point for the find to be properly registered within the earthen matrix of the city.

Marshall, and many other archaeologists, had a model for stratigraphy in their minds when they were working. At Mohenjo-daro it involved the notion of major stratigraphic units: a Late Period, preceded by an Intermediate Period, which was preceded by the Early Period. Each of these was arbitrarily divided into three subunits. As a whole the Mohenjo-daro scheme was:

LATE PERIOD
Phase I
Phase II
Phase III
INTERMEDIATE PERIOD
Phase I
Phase II
Phase III
EARLY PERIOD
Phase I
Phase II
Phase III

All of this was determined prior to full excavation of the site, so that Marshall and his successors would have to force the data from their excavation into the scheme that they had created. If they already knew the history of the site, one wonders why they bothered to dig it.

There was some alteration of this scheme necessitated by the extensive digging there. Mackay introduced a 'Ia' and 'Ib' to the Late Period, and noted that "...'Late III Phase' should be regarded as the uppermost stratum of the Intermediate Period. The evidence that the Late III Phase was in absolute continuity with the Intermediate I Phase, but that it was itself terminated by a complete evacuation of the city on the occasion of a great flood, is indisputable..." (Mackay 1937-38: xiv).

These methods and concepts were very much a part of Old World archaeology of the 1920s and 30s. Marshall and his colleagues were working within the norms and methods of their time, although the men on the cutting edge of field methodology had begun to insist on change. Wheeler, and his colleague Stuart Piggott, were to be very critical of these methods, sometimes in an extreme way (but see O'Flaherty 1970).

Marshall's Senior Field Staff

By 1925 Marshall had brought together a team of archaeologists on whom he could rely to conduct the semi-autonomous work required by excavation at either Mohenjo-daro or Harappa. They were Superintendent Archaeologists (or soon to be), in charge of a Circle of the Survey; trained in conservation, excavation, exploration and administration. Some scholars have suggested that they were supposed to be "supermen," or "jacks of all trades," so thinly stretched that they could not perform any of these jobs adequately (Woolley 1939a: 2). Without making a judgment on this point it can be said that Superintending Archaeologists hold the key jobs in the Survey and the variety of their daily responsibilities is certainly an attraction to the position.

The senior man in this "senior staff" was Harold Hargreaves. He was the person on whom Sir John relied to carry out difficult tasks and to advise him about the inner workings of the Survey. Hargreaves was generally posted in the Northern or the Frontier Circle, and carried out exploration in Baluchistan and excavated the famous prehistoric site of Nal (Hargreaves 1925-26a, 1925-26b, 1929). As it turned out, he managed to excavate Sampur near Mastung and Nal in the Spring of 1925 and then joined the Mohenjo-daro team to work there during the 1925-26 Winter field season. Hargreaves succeeded Marshall as Director General, but with Marshall still very much on the scene (see Note 45 on succession in the Survey).

The other recurring personalities in the field team were all Indian, until Ernest J. H. Mackay was brought to the Survey. They were Daya Ram Sahni, made a Rai Bahadur early in his career for his distinguished service to the Government of India, and whose initial excavations at Harappa have already been noted; Kashinath Narayan Dikshit[21], who was to become a Rao Bahadur, another trusted senior man; and Madho Sarup Vats, who worked at Mohenjo-daro, and later undertook eight seasons of excavation at Harappa. All three of these men became a Director General of the Survey and were clearly gifted individuals. The final person who should be mentioned is Nani Gopal Majumdar, whose life was tragically cut short in 1938 while on service in the Archaeological Survey. His obituary in the *Madras Mail* of 12 November 1938 notes that he was touted to be a future Director General of the Archaeological Survey of India (Anonymous 1938a).[22]

This is the cast of senior men who played the most prominent roles in the early years of excavation at Mohenjo-daro and Harappa, and each in his own way, left a mark on our understanding of these cities and the civilization of which they were a part. The problem orientation of the various field seasons at Mohenjo-daro are reviewed in the annual preliminary

70

reports that each excavator was expected to prepare. They are summarized below (see also Jansen 1986, 1987).

By the mid-1920s the Archaeological Survey of India was not staffed by large numbers of Europeans. Marshall and Hargreaves were the only westerners to play a role in the work at Mohenjo-daro until E. J. H. Mackay arrived. No Europeans were involved in the large scale excavation of Harappa, following Cunningham's probes, until Wheeler went there in 1946. Archaeology in Colonial India was a thoroughly Indianized operation by the time the Indus Civilization was being investigated. It was the Sahnis, Dikshits, Vats', Majumdars, Siddiqis', Dhamas and Moneers who did the work. True, for a time the Director General was British—Marshall then Hargreaves—but this soon changed and on 29 July 1931 Rai Bahadur Daya Ram Sahni was appointed Director General (Ghosh 1953a: 39)[23]. In terms of leadership being given to Indians the Archaeological Survey was well ahead of other Governmental institutions in British India.

Mohenjo-daro 1923-24

Superintendent Archaeologist Madho Sarup Vats (Figure 2.23) (Plate 2.17)[24] was sent to Mohenjo-daro in 1923-24 because Banerji was in poor health. Vats excavated two long trenches, one north-south, the other east-west in what came to be known as "VS Area" (Vats 1923-24: 51-2; Marshall 1931a: 11), the "VS" coming from his name. The site on the first plan of Mohenjo-daro (Figure 2.24) was called "Site 4," following on Banerji's Sites 1-3. This work demonstrated that Mature Harappan material was all over the surface of this part of the Lower Town, not covered by later occupations (Plate 2.18). Vats also discovered good stratification of the remains down to the water table.

Figure 2.23. Sketch of M. S. Vats

Mohenjo-daro 1924-25

Superintendent Archaeologist K. N. Dikshit (Figure 2.25) excavated at Mohenjo-daro in 1924-25 with more funds, and consequently more labor, than his predecessors (Dikshit 1924-25). He worked in the areas that would be designated "DK" (the DK coming from Dikshit) in the Lower City. Another of Dikshit's trenches (Area F) was on the the high mound to the west, where Banerji had worked. This trench was over-shadowed by other digging on the Mound of the Great Bath and has somewhat disappeared as an operation, the "DK" designation not being applied to it.

Dikshit also published the first site plan of Mohenjo-daro with his substantial preliminary report (Dikshit 1924-25: Pl. XVI; Figure 2.25). His excavation areas were lettered Site A through Site F. Sites (or Areas, or Trenches) A, B, C, and D were in the central portion of the Lower City. Site E is a very long trench that spans the width of the Lower City. It was ca. 450 meters long and yielded a series of striking and

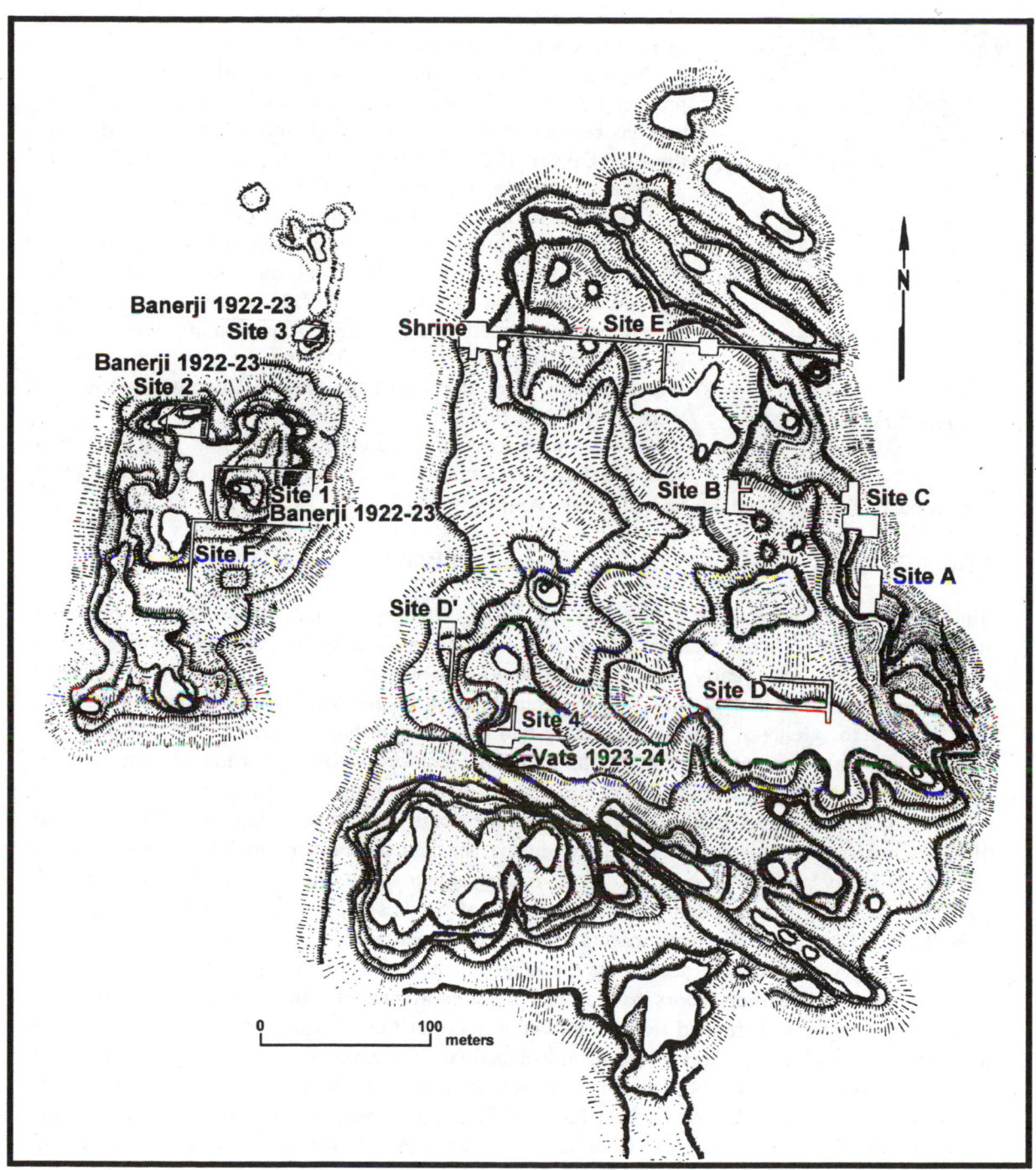

Figure 2.24. The first map of Mohenjo-daro. Prepared by K.N. Dikshit during the third field season, 1924-25

Figure 2.25. Sketch of K.N. Dikshit

important antiquities as well as what Dikshit called a "temple" or "shrine" on the western end (Dikshit 1924-25: 68-9) (Plate 2.19). Site F, as noted, was on what has come to be called, the Mound of the Great Bath. Dikshit also did some minor clearing in Banerji's Site 2 (Dikshit 1924-25: 71).

Trench E revealed the so-called "jewelry block" which produced masses of small finds, including a necklace or girdle that has become one of the most frequently illustrated finds from the site (Dikshit 1924-25: 69-70, Pl. XXb; Mackay 1931a: 520-22; Marshall 1931a: Pl. CLI, b10; Plate 2.20).

The small finds poured in during this season: "The quantitative results of the operations were no less striking than the character of the remains disclosed. The total number of small finds registered during the season was 7,152, far exceeding the number of antiquities recorded during a single season at any other ancient site in India" (Dikshit 1924-25: 71). At the same point in his report Dikshit notes that 146 examples of Harappan glyptic art were included in this total.

It was the presence of this archaeological "loot" that led Ernest J. H. Mackay to concentrate on the northeastern part of the Lower City around Trench E, which he called DK Area.

Mohenjo-daro 1925-26: The Big Season of Work

Sir John Marshall spent only one season excavating at Mohenjo-daro (1925-26) and he never worked at Harappa. Taxila was the center of Marshall's intellectual life, and he was engaged in excavations there on a yearly basis. But, Mohenjo-daro was the "hot" site. It was the focus of international attention and commanded the consideration of the Archaeological Survey of India and its Director General. Marshall probably had little choice but to give up Taxila for a year and concentrate on the new city in Sindh. The concentration of forces at Mohenjo-daro was so complete that digging at Harappa was suspended for this season.

Marshall had proper staff quarters and facilities built at Mohenjo-daro between 1925 and 1927. A *pukka* road was constructed between the site and the railway station at Dokri, eleven kilometers away. Adequate quarters, work rooms and a small museum were also prepared. Much of this was made possible by the support of Sir Leslie Wilson, Governor of Bombay (Marshall 1931a: 11-3). Earlier excavation teams had been forced to live under canvas, which was a very trying existence, destroying the health of both R. D. Banerji and K. N. Dikshit.

The results of earlier labors had proved the importance of Mohenjo-daro, and Marshall assembled a large, well-funded team to initiate digging at the site on a scale that had not been attempted before. The members of this team included H. Hargreaves, who was then Superintendent of the Frontier Circle; K. N. Dikshit, Superintendent of the Western Circle; Superintending Archaeologist Rai Bahadur Daya Ram Sahni; Officiating Superintendent M. S. Vats; Assistant Superintendent B. L. Dhama and Mohammad Sana Ullah, the Survey's Archaeological Chemist. These were all gazetted officers of the archaeological establishment. In addition, Marshall recruited N. G. Majumdar, a brilliant young curator from the Rajshahi Museum in Bengal. A. D. Siddiqi, Marshall's aide at Taxila also came to Mohenjo-daro. They were joined by other experienced men from the Taxila excavations: K. N. Puri, Q. M. Moneer and J. K. Ray (Marshall 1925-26: 73-4). Puri and Moneer were destined to play a continuing role at Mohenjo-daro and in the archaeology of Sindh and Baluchistan. Large scale excavation at a major site inevitably generates some tension. Decisions have to be made that are not always appreciated by everyone. Some of this seems to come through in Marshall's recounting of the role that K. N. Dikshit played in the 1925-26 field season:

> To Mr. K. N. Dikshit, my Superintendent in the Western Circle, my thanks are due for the assistance that he rendered over the preliminary preparations throughout the summer and autumn of 1925...Mr. Dikshit had already been excavating for a season (1924-25) at Mohenjo-daro on a quasi-independent footing and not unnaturally felt some disappointment when it was decided to extend the scope of the operations and place them under other control. In spite of his disappointment, however, he threw himself into the new scheme with praiseworthy energy and afforded much help over getting together the requisite labor, materials, supplies, etc. Unfortunately, after the excavations had started, his health broke down, he lost heart in the work, and eventually withdrew on medical leave before he could complete the plans or write up the report. Recently, however, Mr. Dikshit has supplied me with a rough note on his section of the digging and this note has been utilised by Mr. Ernest Mackay in writing up the account given below of the Dk Area (Marshall 1925-26: 73).

Conspicuous by his absence from Mohenjo-daro during the 1925-26 excavations was R. D. Banerji, who had been moved, perhaps "banished," to the Eastern Circle in Bengal (Banerji 1925-26). His health was also bad and he seems to have been "in dutch" with Marshall. This posting away from Mohenjo-daro was a harbinger of things to come.

Sindh was an important place in the 1920s. There was another large project there, that corresponds almost exactly in time with the early digging at Mohenjo-daro. This was the construction of the Lloyd Barrage at Sukkur, which began in 1923 and opened in 1932. It is one of the world's largest dams, being 1532 meters (5000 ft.) long.

The excavation camp had at least one distinguished visitor during this season. Sir Aurel Stein, who was about to undertake his explorations in Swat (Stein 1930), spent thirty-six hours on a train to reach Mohenjo-daro. He found the visit very instructive, and would draw on his firsthand knowledge at many points in his career, especially his excavations at Dabar Kot, an Harappan site near Duki in Baluchistan (Stein 1929a: 55-64). The visit also gave him an opportunity to discuss his proposed explorations in Waziristan (Stein 1929a) and Gedrosia (Stein 1931) with the Director General (Mirsky 1977: 423).

Labor for the 1925-26 Season

Marshall's financial resources for this season allowed him to hire between 1000 and 1200 laborers. Only about 300 of these were available locally. The rest were procured from labor contractors in Karachi. Most of the latter were Makranis, said to have migrated to Karachi with their families because of famine. They were small and weak; according to Marshall not a match for the Sindhis, whom he much admired (1925-26: 74). So did Sir Charles Napir, the conqueror of Sindh. He called the Sindhi warrior of the mid-nineteenth century "'...wild, picturesque fellows with their brilliantly coloured trappings, very like stage banditti', slung with shields and sabres and draped in brightly coloured shawls and silks, with turbaned heads or gold Sindian caps, and the exceeding grace of all...scarcely could an ugly Scindian (sic) be seen, fine manly countenances, with eyes of fire and teeth of snow" (P. Napier 1990: 51).

In an interesting aside Marshall (1925-26: 74) acquaints us with some of the human details of this season of work. First, the wages for local labor, that is Sindhis residing in the vicinity of Mohenjo-daro, were 11 annas per day for adult males and eight annas for women and children.

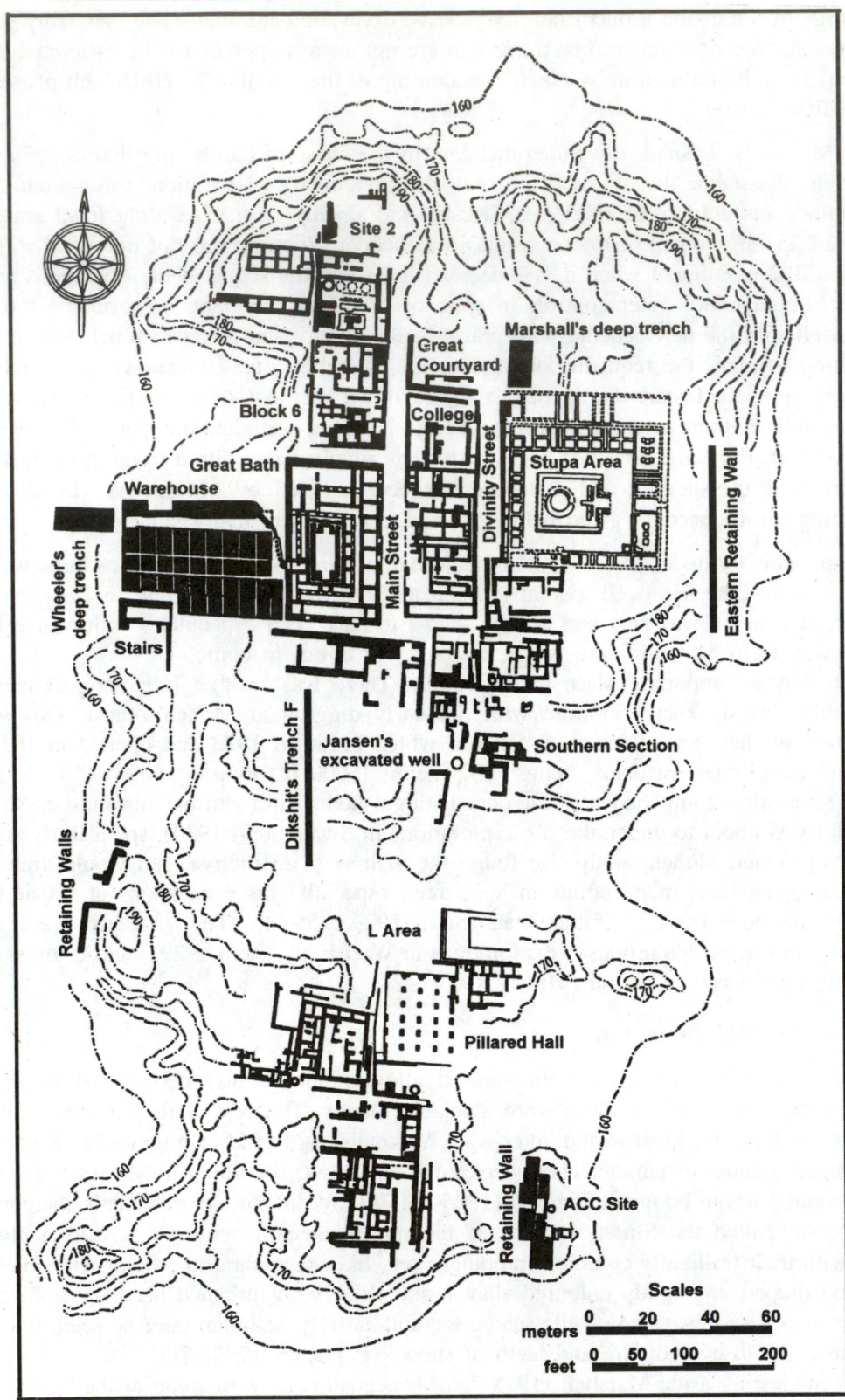

Figure 2.26. Plan of the Mound of the Great Bath at Mohenjo-daro

Among the contract laborers, adult males were paid 14 annas, women 11 annas and children eight. There were 16 annas to the rupee and this system harkens back to the tradition of binary counting present in the weights of the Harappan Civilization.[25]

Marshall notes that the labor contractors were responsible for the welfare of their employees, but they made no provision for housing or medical support as they should have. As winter deepened and the cold persisted, pneumonia and other troubles began to take a toll, as did an outbreak of small pox. Isolating the small pox was relatively easy, housing was another matter. This was solved by the construction of "dugouts," which were subterranean living quarters excavated into the alluvium. These were placed on the western side of the site, where the Marshall camp and facilities were located. Some of the dugouts were sited to the west of the Mound of the Great Bath, and as E. J. H. Mackay has noted, proved that there were no extensive archaeological deposits there (Mackay 1937-38: 5), except for those very close to the modern edge of the mound (Wheeler 1968: section facing p. 44). Marshall met the cost of these facilities partly from his excavation grant and partly by dunning the contractors. He also procured the temporary services of a Sub-Assistant Surgeon from the Medical Department to care for his battalions of men, women and children.

The labor was parceled out to the excavators who worked on their own turf: Hargreaves in HR Area, Vats in VS Area and Dikshit in DK Area. Sir John also took a team of laborers for his own excavation efforts. He was assisted by B. L. Dhama, the Assistant Superintendent Archaeologist in Rajasthan and Central India and his old "Number One" from Taxila, A. D. Siddiqi. They worked in the SD Area (Siddiqi) on the northern half of what Marshall called the "Stupa Mound" and what is now known as the Mound of the Great Bath (Plate 2.21, Figure 2.26).

Figure 2.27. Sketch of the Priest-King

By the end of the season significant portions of the Lower Town had been opened up; plans of many buildings drawn and artifacts discovered. It was Marshall's only season of excavation at the site, but he discovered the Great Bath, surely one of the most significant finds in all of the digging at Harappan sites (Marshall 1931c: 12-3) (Plate 2.22). HR Area was exposed and VS Area (the old Site 4) very substantially expanded (Plate 2.23). Many classic Harappan style artifacts came to light at this time, including the so-called "Priest King" which emerged from Dikshit's excavations in DK-B Area, in a building that the excavators thought may have been an *hammam* or hot bath (Mackay 1925-26: 90-1, Pl. XLIIIa; Plate 2.24, Plate 2.25, Figure 2.27).

The Term "Indo-Sumerian" Dropped

In the earliest discussions of the Harappan Civilization (those prior to 1926) the term "Indo-Sumerian Civilization" was frequently used. This came about for a number of reasons, not the least of which was that it was fairly clear that the finds were not related to Egypt, and Sumer gave researchers their only comparative material. The undeciphered Harappan script was a key element in this judgment. On the other hand, the Indus Valley and Mesopotamia are within striking distance of one another and it seemed likely that they were somehow in contact.

The Sumerians and Akkadians of the third millennium BC have played an important role in the interpretation of Harappan remains, and right from the beginning. In fact, T. G. Aravamuthan (1942) derived the name "Harappa" from an Assyrian town. There were also scholars who worked on the yet to be deciphered Indus script who believed that it could be understood in terms of Sumerian or Akkadian (Gadd and Smith 1924; Waddell 1925a, 1925b, 1926; Barton 1928a, 1928b, 1929, 1930; Pran Nath 1932, 1986; Hunter 1934; Mitchiner 1978; Punekar 1984). One relatively recent researcher speaks of the "Hindu States of Sumeria" (Sankarananda 1962), and another the close biological and cultural connections between the two populations (Subharayappa 1995). There is also much of Mesopotamian civilization in the Wheeler-Piggott paradigm, so the use of this Near Eastern Civilization as a model for understanding the Indus is far from dead as an issue. In 1925-26 the term "Indo-Sumerian" was dropped by Sir John Marshall; a wise decision on his part that is not always acknowledged:

> And here I may say parenthetically that I shall use the term 'Indus' henceforth to designate the particular culture of the chalcolithic period which I have hitherto designated Indo-Sumerian, since the latter term is likely to imply a closer connection with Sumer than now seems justified (Marshall 1925-26: 75; see also Marshall 1926-27a: 53).

While Marshall attempted to make "Indus Civilization," not "Indus Valley Civilization," the standard, he was never quite successful. Some (e.g., Mackay and Vats) saw his term as parochial, and objected by noting that the civilization extended well beyond the confines of the Indus Valley, even if Marshall never intended a close geographical connotation for his name. Mackay preferred the notion of "Harappa Culture" taking the archaeological tradition of using the "type fossil" concept to name archaeological assemblages. G. R. Hunter, one of the early scholars working with the Indus script (Hunter 1929, 1932, 1934) seems to have coined the term "Proto-Indian." The term was picked up by M. S. Vats, following his excavation at Rangpur (Vats 1934-35: 38). "Proto-Indian" is still current with some scholars, more so in Russia, and particularly with those involved with the Indus script and other iconographic topics.

It is within this historical context, with the appearance of Indus artifacts, especially seals, some with script, at Ur, Kish and other sites (Mackay 1925b, 1931b, 1933a, 1933b; Scheil 1925; Langdon 1932; Gadd 1932, 1933; Frankfort 1933, 1939), that the material links between Mohenjo-daro, Harappa and Mesopotamia were being documented. Large scale excavations at Ur and Kish were very important in this story and the leaders of these expeditions were destined to play a role in the history of archaeology in the Subcontinent; Sir Leonard Woolley, of Ur, as a reviewer of the effectiveness of the Archaeological Survey of India (see below and Possehl 1993a) and Stephen Langdon, an American Professor at Oxford, as a student of the Indus script (see below and Possehl 1996a: 79-80, 84, 90-100).

These well documented material contacts improved the general chronology of the Harappan Civilization, but Marshall and his colleagues also recognized the uniqueness of the ancient civilization in India and Pakistan. These were times when many connections between the diverse cultures and peoples of prehistoric Asia were being sorted out. Some of the ideas presented in this process of finding one's way were grandiose. T. J. Arne, for example, observed in an organ of the Geological Survey of China, that the pottery collected in Zhob by Dr. Fritz Noetling of

Plate 2.1. The Bimaran reliquary. Courtesy of the British Museum.

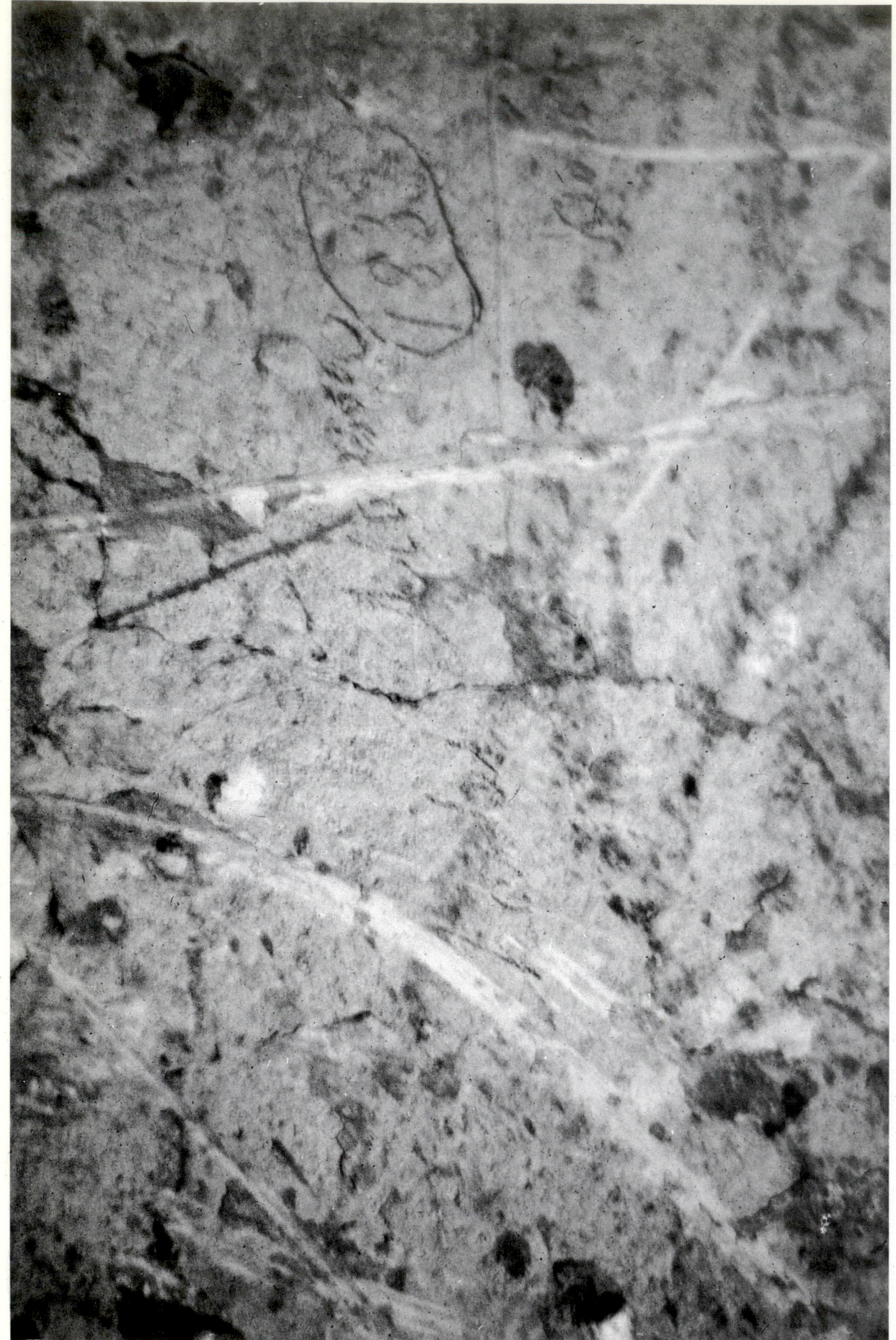

Plate 2.2. Masson's signature, author's photograph.

Plate 2.3. Bamiyan. Courtesy of Pierre Fraley.

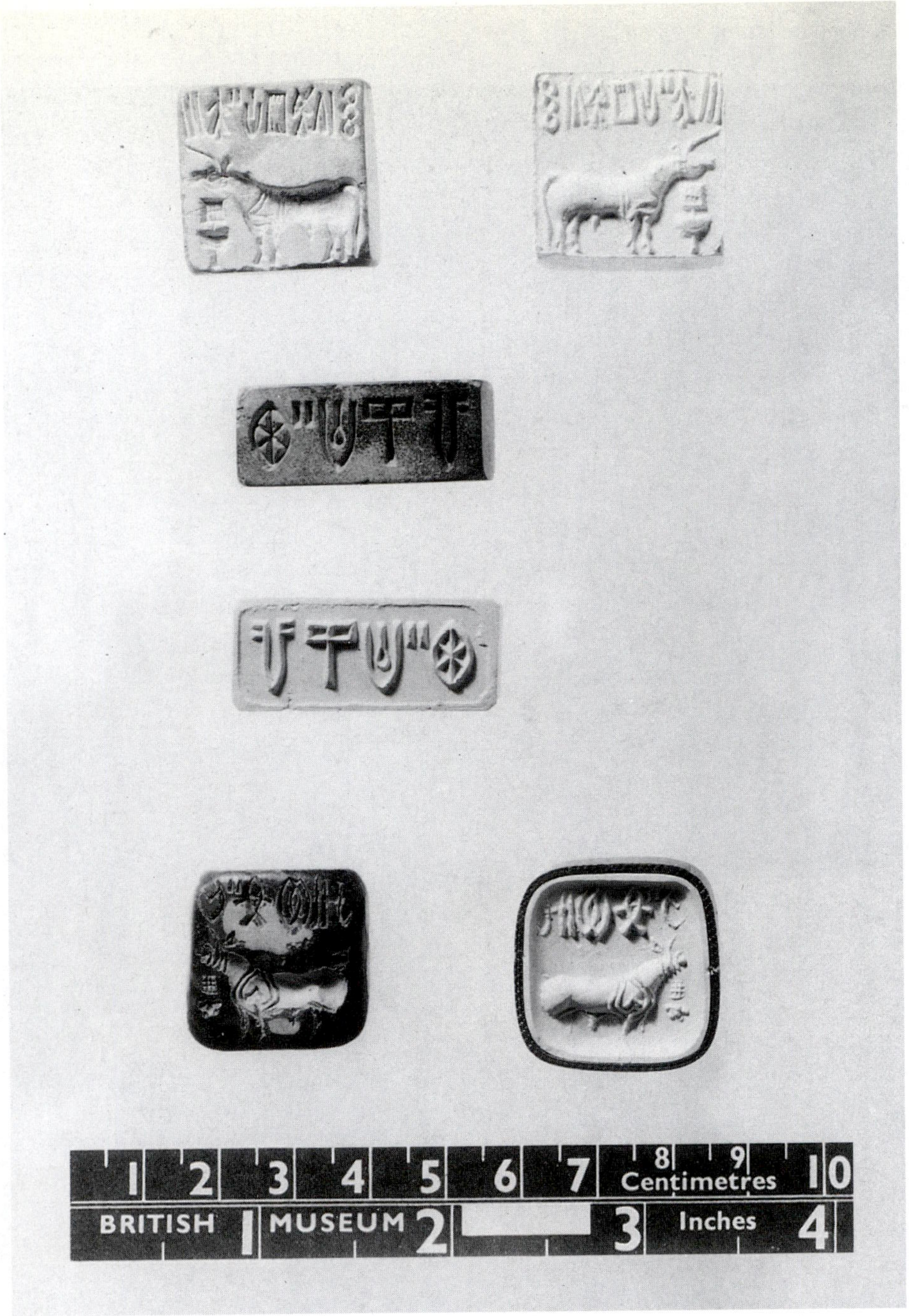

Plate 2.5. Walter A. Fairservis, Jr., photo by Nicholas Jacobs.

Plate 2.4. The first three seals from Harappa. Courtesy of the British Museum.

Plate 2.6. Sahni's 1921 trench on Mound F at Harappa. Courtesy of the Archaeological Survey of India, Punjab Volume 27, Old Negative Number 2738.

Plate 2.7. Mound of the Great Bath at Mohenjo-daro, called "Site 1" by R. D. Banerji. Courtesy of the Archaeological Survey of India, Sind Photographic Volume 2, 1916-19, Old Negative Number 6025.

Plate 2.8. The Stupa and Mound of the Great Bath at Mohenjo-daro under early excavation, called "Site 1" by R. D. Banerji. Courtesy of the Archaeological Survey of India, Sind Photographic Volume 2, 1916-19, Old Negative Number 6023.

Plate 2.9. The Stupa on the Mound of the Great Bath at Mohenjo-daro, called "Site 1" by R. D. Banerji. Courtesy of the Archaeological Survey of India, Sind Photographic Volume 2, 1916-19, Old Negative Number 6029.

Plate 2.10. The Stupa on the Mound of the Great Bath at Mohenjo-daro, called "Site 1" by R. D. Banerji. Courtesy of the Archaeological Survey of India, Sind Photographic Volume 2, 1916-19, Old Negative Number 6028.

Plate 2.11. The retaining wall on the eastern side of the Mound of the Great Bath Mohenjo-daro, just as it was traced out. Courtesy of the Archaeological Survey of India, Sind Photographic Volume 3, 1922-25, Old Negative Number 6041.

Plate 2.12. Banerji's "Site 2" in the foreground, with a view of Site 1 and the Stupa on the Mound of the Great Bath at at Mohenjo-daro. Courtesy of the Archaeological Survey of India, Sind Photographic Volume 2, 1916-19, Old Negative Number 5027.

Plate 2.13. Banerji's "Site 2" on the northwest corner of the Mound of the Great Bath at Mohenjo-daro. Courtesy of the Archaeological Survey of India, Sind Photographic Volume 2, 1916-19, Old Negative Number 5027.

Plate 2.14. Banerji's "Site 3" to the north of the Mound of the Great Bath at Mohenjo-daro, before excavation. Courtesy of the Archaeological Survey of India, Sind Photographic Volume 3, 1922-25, Old Negative Number 6082.

Plate 2.15. Banerji's "Site 3" to the north of the Mound of the Great Bath at Mohenjo-daro, after excavation. Courtesy of the Archaeological Survey of India, Sind Photographic Volume 3, 1922-25, Old Negative Number 6085.

Plate 2.16. The mounds of Mohenjo-daro before excavation. Courtesy of the Archaeological Survey of India, Sind Photographic Volume 3, 1922-25, Old Negative Number 6096.

Plate 2.17. M. S. Vats excavating a hoard of copper-bronze artifacts in VS Area. Courtesy of the Archaeological Survey of India, Sind Photographic Volume 7, 1925-26, Old Negative Number 234.

Plate 2.18. M. S. Vats' Site 4 after excavation in 1924. Courtesy of the Archaeological Survey of India, Sind Volume 3, Old Negative Number 6270.

Plate 2.19. Dikshit's "Temple" at the western end of his Trench E. Courtesy of the Archaeological Survey of India, Sind Volumes, Old Negative Number 763/92.

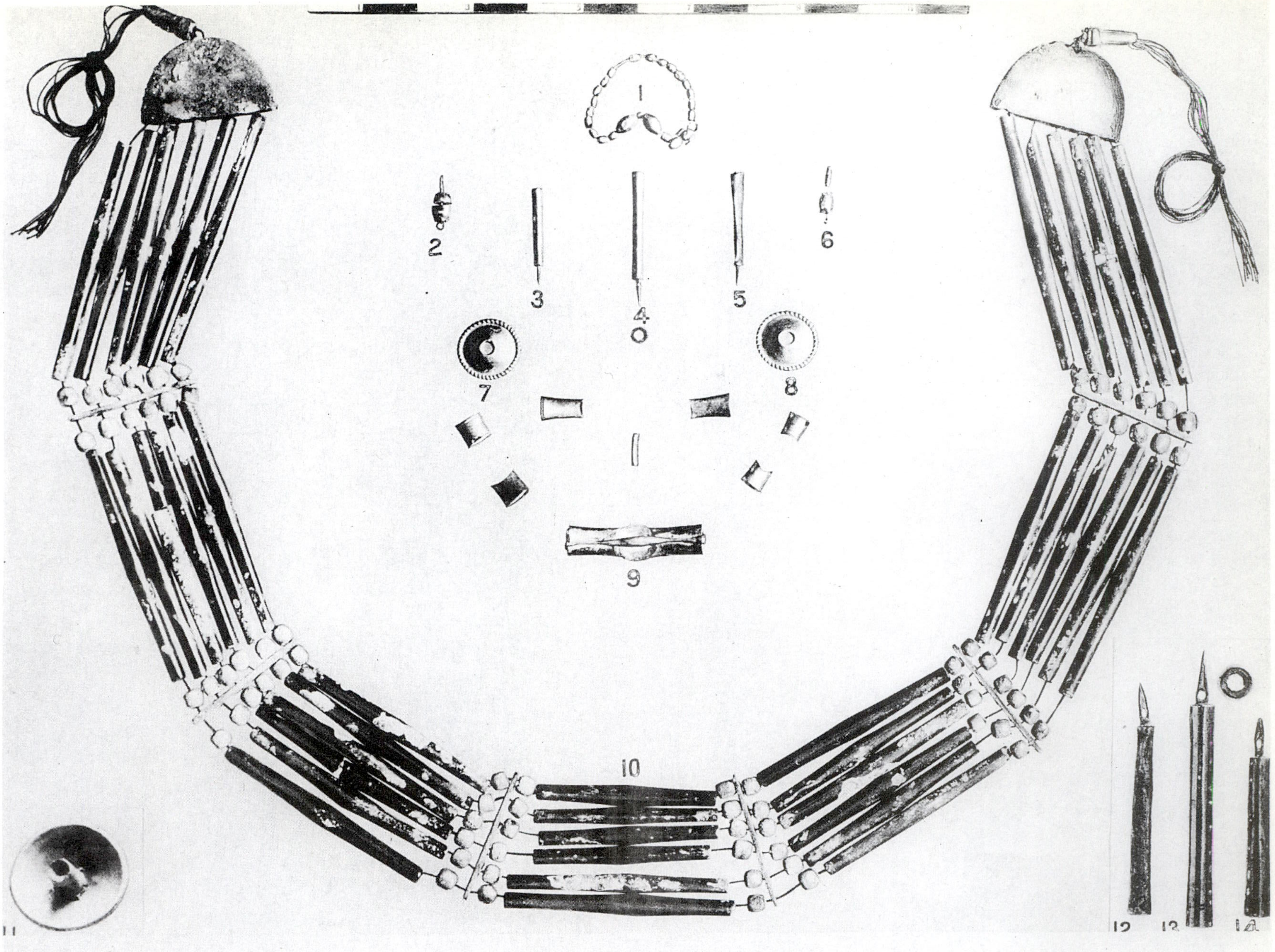

Plate 2.20. Necklace from the hoard in Area E, DK Area, after Marshall 1931a: Plate CLIb.

Plate 2.21. Mound of the Great Bath at Mohenjo-daro, with the Great Bath in the foreground, the Granary behind it and the plains of the Indus Valley in the background, author's photograph.

Plate 2.22. The Great Bath at Mohenjo-daro, author's photograph.

Plate 2.23. The northwest portion of VS Area from the west, after Marshall 1931a: Plate LVII, a.

Plate 2.24. Chamber 1, Block 2 of DK-B Area, where the Priest King was found. Courtesy of the Archaeological Survey of India, Old Negative Number 766-92.

Plate 2.25. A workman handing over the Priest King at the time of excavation in 1, Block 2 of DK-B Area. Courtesy of the Archaeological Survey of India, Old Negative Number 766-92.

Plate 2.26. (Left) Ernest J. H. Mackay at Kish in 1923-24. Mackay is at the left. Stephen Langdon in the center and the project's "topographer" Colonel W. H. Land is on the right. Courtesy of the Field Museum of Natural History, Chicago, Negative Number OX 213.

Plate 2.27. (Bottom left) The Bronze Dancing Girl from HR Area, before cleaning. Courtesy of the Archaeological Survey of India, Old Negative Number 370/88.

Plate 2.28. (Bottom right) The Bronze Dancing Girl from HR Area, after cleaning. Courtesy of the National Museum, New Delhi.

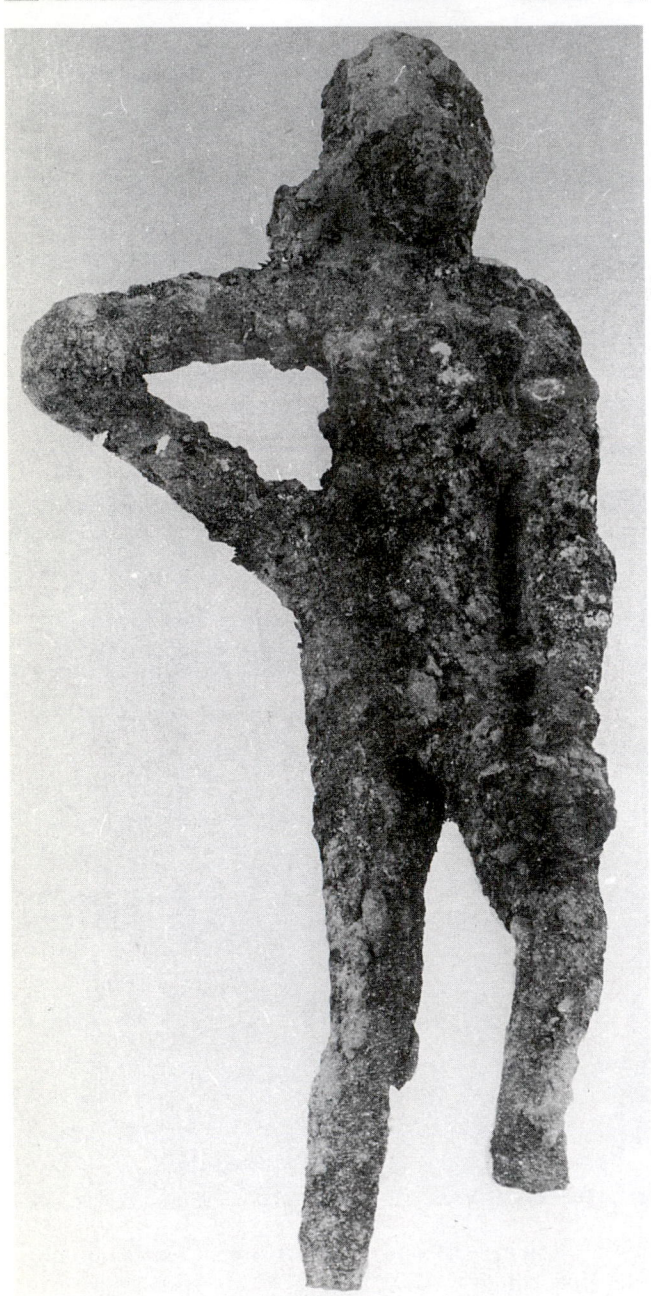

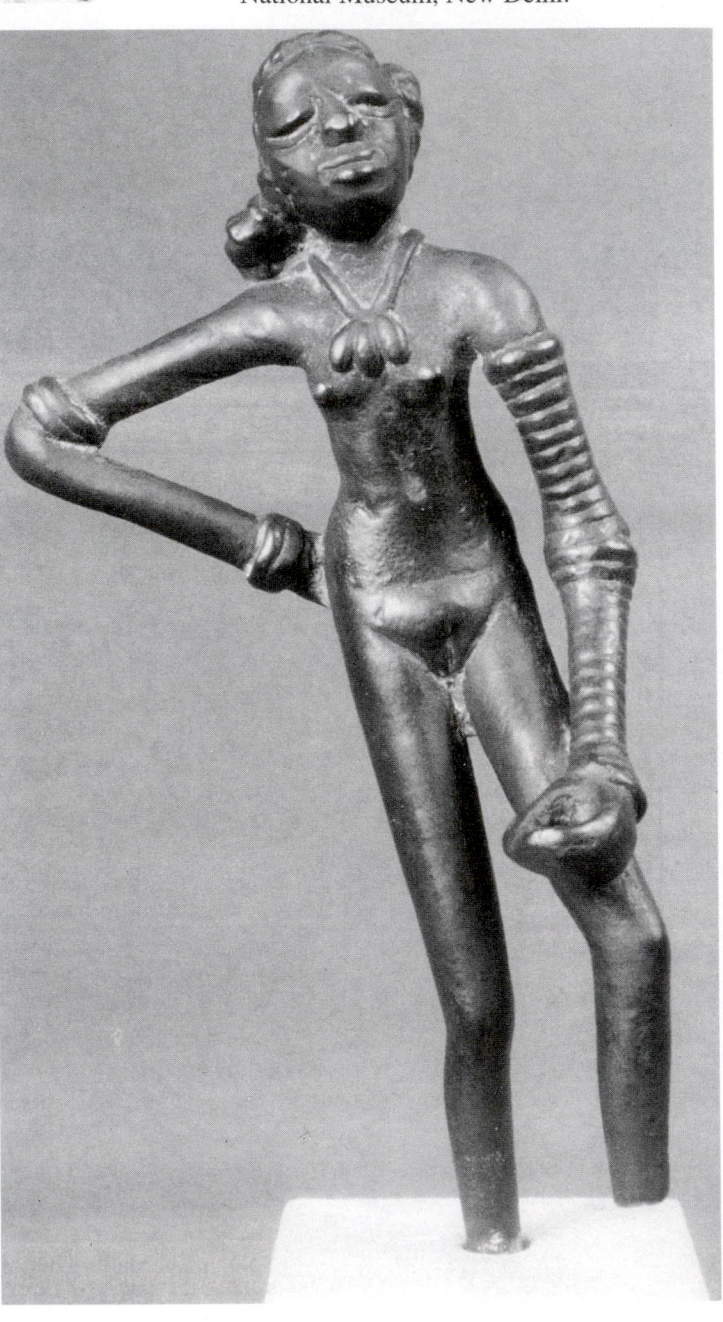

the Geological Survey of India "...all remind one to a surprising extent of the Honan pottery, perhaps, more so than any pottery...with the exception of sherds from Abu Shahrain (Mesopotamia)" (Arne 1925: 20).

The Need for New Leadership at Mohenjo-daro

No matter what the importance, or success of the Mohenjo-daro program, the Director General needed to get back to his work at Taxila, which was not published until 1951 (Marshall 1951). This pressing necessity called for a serious bit of planning to insure the investment that was being made at Mohenjo-daro. Mohenjo-daro had been the subject of five excavation seasons directed by four different officers of the Survey, each of whom had many other responsibilities. With Marshall's research at Taxila, he could not afford to take on a second major excavation, and still manage the Survey. It was also clear that the archaeologists working at the site needed someone there who was familiar with, preferably trained in, Mesopotamian archaeology. There were finds at Mohenjo-daro that suggested Mesopotamian connections and the spectacular excavations at places like Ur and Kish, contemporary with the Indus Civilization, were producing data that had to be controlled. This lack of manpower, and the need for a Mesopotamian specialist, suggested to Marshall that he should recruit a new man for the staff of the Survey, which brought Ernest J. H. Mackay to India (Marshall 1931a: 13).

Ernest John Henry Mackay[26]

Ernest J. H. Mackay was a seasoned, veteran archaeologist when he was asked to join the Archaeological Survey of India. He had been trained in field archaeology in Egypt by Sir Flinders Petrie, beginning in 1907, and completed a photographic survey of the Theban tombs there between 1913 and 1916. Mackay then moved on to excavate tumuli in the Arabian Gulf (Mackay 1929b). Mackay's career in Egyptology even touches the United States. Records in the Archives of the University of Pennsylvania Museum indicate that he was an Assistant Curator of Egyptology there in 1921-22. He served in the army in Palestine during the First World War and from 1919 to 1922 was Custodian of Antiquities for the government there. In 1922, Mackay became field director of the Field Museum-Oxford University Archaeological Expedition to Mesopotamia, where he excavated Jamdat Nasr (Mackay 1931c) and the important Sumerian city of Kish (Mackay 1925a, 1929a) (Plate 2.26). Mackay demonstrated an interest in the Harappan Civilization in early correspondence with Sir John Marshall and a paper on Indo-Sumerian connections (Mackay 1925b). He arrived at Mohenjo-daro in time for the beginning of the 1926-27 field season.[27]

Mackay returned home to England when the work at Mohenjo-daro was completed to write his report on the excavations. While there he was recruited to excavate Chanhu-daro for the Museum of Fine Arts, Boston and the American School for Indic and Iranian Studies in 1935-36 (Mackay 1943). Dorothy Mackay, his wife, assisted him in his later field work, especially at Chanhu-daro. Mackay died at his home in Whitleaf Monks Risborough, Bucks on Saturday, 2 October 1943 at the age of 63 (Anonymous 1943), but before he died he saw his last site report, *Chanhu-daro Excavations, 1935-36* (Mackay 1943).

Mohenjo-daro 1926-27

Marshall (Marshall 1931a: 13) informs us that since Mackay was unfamiliar with the local conditions in India (let alone those of rural Sindh) and the ways of Indian administration, he could not be expected to take on the direction of a major excavation successfully, without a partner. For this reason he was joined by Rai Bahadur Daya Ram Sahni as Co-Director for the 1926-27 field season. The notion of partnership comes mainly from Marshall's account of the arrangement. Sahni states it this way: "Mr. Ernest Mackay, who had recently been recruited from Mesopotamia, arrived at Mohenjo-daro on the 26th November and for about a week assisted me on the Hr. site, after which I placed him in charge of the separate area south of the Stupa mound" (Sahni 1926-27: 60). Whatever the arrangement, the two men wrote separate preliminary reports, which were substantial documents (Sahni 1926-27: 60-88; Mackay 1926-27: 89-97).

Sahni went to work on the Lower City and succeeded in opening up a total area of ca. 140 meters by 120 meters, most in HR Area, but it included part of the adjacent VS Area. He made good progress in linking up roads and lanes between these parts of the city. It was during this season that the beautiful bronze dancing girl (Plate 2.27, Plate 2.28) was found (Sahni 1926-27: 81, Pl. XII, c,d; Marshall 1931a: Pl. XCIV, 6, 7, 8), along with one of the exquisite jewelry hoards in HR Area (Sahni 1926-27: 70-1, Pl. XII, a, b; Marshall 1931a: Pl. CXLIX).

In January 1927, Mackay began working in L Area, ca. 28 meters south of the Stupa on the Mound of the Great Bath. He uncovered the so-called "Assembly Hall" and other architectural remains that are not well understood, even today. He also found three pieces of limestone sculpture: a seated torso (L-950), a reasonably well preserved bust (L 898) and a very poor, abraded head, possibly of a woman (L-127) (Figure 2.28, Figure 2.29, Figure 2.30, Plate 2.29, Plate 2.30).

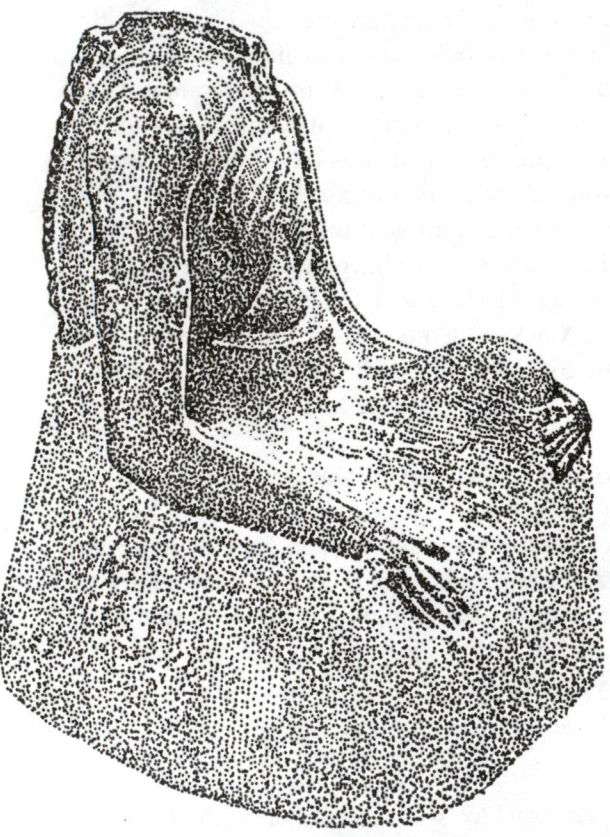

Figure 2.28. Seated Man from Mohenjo-daro, L 950

Mohenjo-daro 1927-31: The Final Four Large Seasons of Work

The remaining four major seasons of work during the early period of excavation at Mohenjo-daro were completely in Mackay's charge. The results are described in his *Further Excavations at Mohenjo-daro* (Mackay 1937-38); the finds from 1926-27 had been incorporated into Marshall (1931a). In addition, there are some stray finds that were first published by Marshall in *Mohenjo-daro and the Indus Civilization* that came from Mackay's work, even after the 1926-27 season. The "Proto-Siva" or Mahayogi seal (Number 420) and the Seal of Divine Adoration (Number 430) are good examples. Things of this kind are generally noted in the text and footnotes, but paging through the reports and assuming that everything illustrated there can be attributed to Marshall's work, or even Mohenjo-daro, can lead to mistakes and is a dangerous pastime. Even a few objects from Harappa and Baluchi sites are figured in Marshall's Plates and are not always adequately flagged for the reader.

Mackay's labor force was 600 men, about

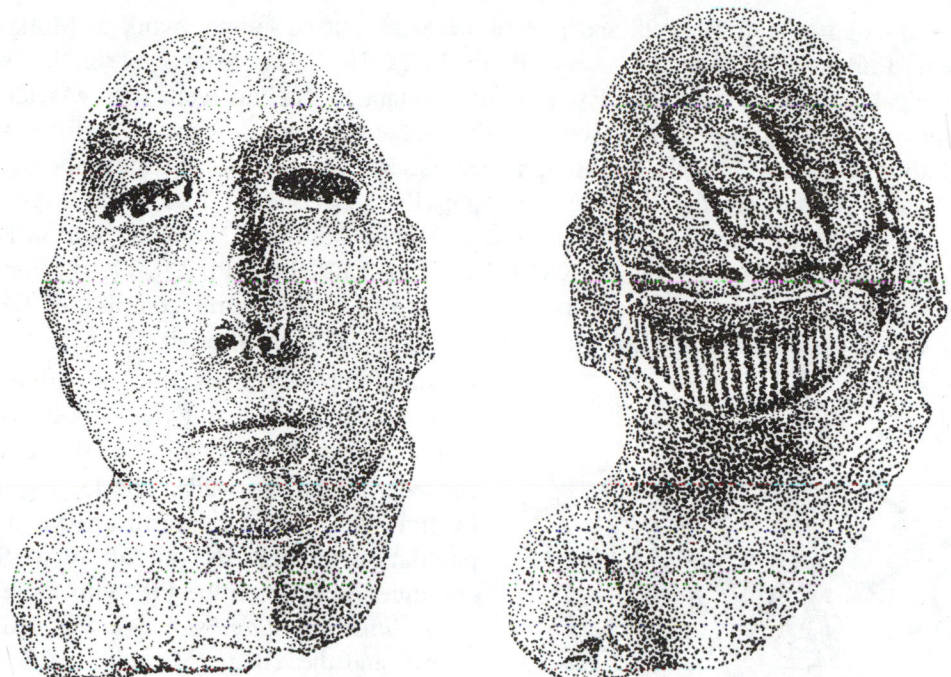

Figure 2.29. The Stern Man of L Area, Mohenjo-daro, L 898

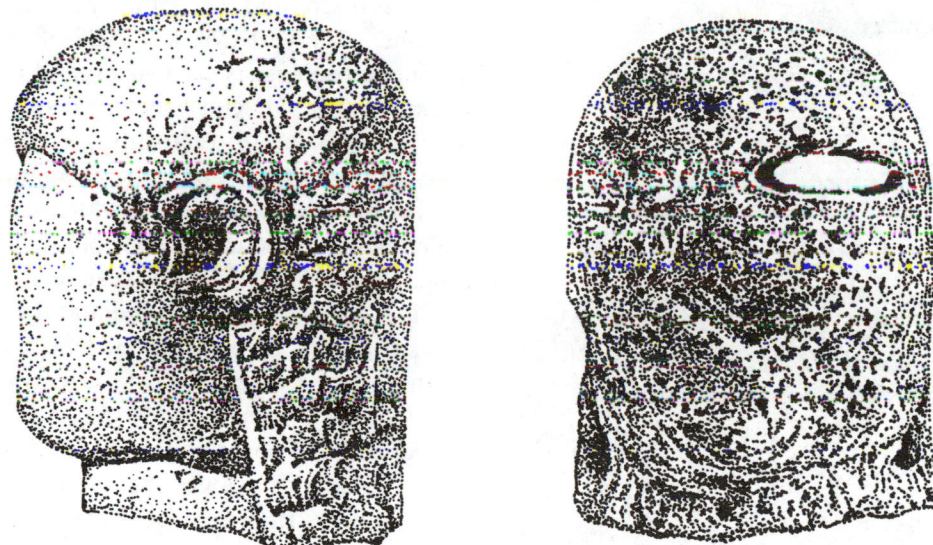

Figure 2.30. The Lady of L Area, Mohenjo-daro, L 127

one-half that of the 1925-26 season. They were mostly Sindhis from surrounding villages, who returned home following their work at the site. But some Brahuis from as far away as Kalat joined up, and were well regarded by Mackay for their strength and intelligence. There is no mention of labor contractors and the complications engendered by the huge labor force that Marshall employed (Mackay 1937-38: xii).

Mackay, who seems to have been on a long leash, went to the rich DK Area and expanded Dikshit's operation (Plate 2.31). He also did the first deep digging of any scale at the site, and thereby gained some sense of the stratigraphy of the northern part of the Lower City. N. G.

80

Majumdar assisted him in 1927-28 and part of 1928-29, but he left the work at Mohenjo-daro to excavate Jhukar, 25 kilometers away (Plate 2.32). H. L. Srivastava, a scholar with the Archaeological Survey of India, and Excavation Assistant K. N. Puri were with Mackay for all four seasons of work. He had one season of additional supervision of excavation from Mr. Devi Dayal Mathur, who was mainly a photographer. C. R. Roy, a physical anthropologist from Calcutta, was with him for the 1928-29 campaign (Plate 2.33, Plate 2.34, Plate 2.35).

The famous "Proto-Siva" seal and the "Seal of Divine Adoration" came to light in DK Area in 1928-29, (Mackay 1928-29: 74-5, Pl. XXVII, f, g; Marshall 1931a: Pl. XII, 17, 18; Figure 2.31, Figure 2.32). Mackay also succeeded in clearing a vast architectural complex in DK Area, which gives the visitor to Mohenjo-daro a real sense of walking through an ancient city. The splendidly preserved baked brick buildings stand today much as they did over 4000 years ago. One can enter houses, walk up flights of stairs and peer down into wells. The feeling and aura is that of a living community, with the population temporarily out of town. Sir John continued to pour on the PR, with more articles in the *Illustrated London News* (Marshall 1928a, 1928b) and the *Times* (Marshall 1928c).

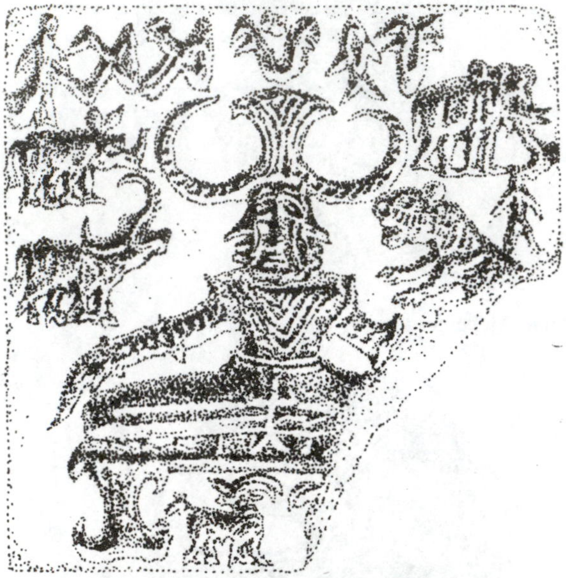

Mackay's seasons were long: 1927-28, December 22 to March 9; 1928-29, October 24 to March 26 and he employed up to 600 workmen each year (Mackay 1937-38: xi). Three or four archaeologists each supervised nearly 200 workmen. The Director was also responsible for the supervision of recording, conservation, registration of finds and general administration of the project and its camp. It was a huge undertaking. Modern standards of archaeological research could not possibly sustain it.

T. E. Lawrence was in India at the time and Mackay struck up a correspondence with him. Both were veterans of Mesopotamian archaeology (Garnett 1939: 551-53, 565-66). Mackay issued an invitation to visit Mohenjo-daro, recalling Lawrence's experience at Carchemish. Regrettably, Lawrence had to decline, but told two of his colleagues in the British Air Force of the opportunity, since Mackay was generous enough to extend it to "friends." Lawrence was in Karachi, and the Air Force had holiday leave, so his buddies, Heir and Jones, headed north for Christmas 1927, returning by 18 January 1928 when Lawrence wrote to Mackay:

> They came back in great form, delighted with themselves, and the object of general envy and admiration.

Figure 2.31. Drawing of the "Proto-Siva" seal

Figure 2.32. Drawing of the seal of Divine Adoration

I am sorry they stayed so long. It was a tax upon the kindness of Mrs. Mackay and yourself. However you have acquired merit. If the Recording Angel has not made due entries on your conduct sheets, please call me as witness (Garnett 1939: 565).

W. Norman Brown also visited Mackay at Mohenjo-daro in 1928. This was their first meeting but there would be more since they were to work together on the Chanhu-daro project in 1935-36.

In 1931, financial problems put an end to the large scale excavations at Mohenjo-daro. The final field season started on 3 November 1931 with Mackay planning to investigate Site 3 to the north of Mound of the Great Bath, which he thought might be a part of the city wall (Mackay 1930-34: 70). He put four gangs of men to work there but in the middle of the afternoon on November 6th he was told to suspend work and close down his operations before anything more than preliminary clearance had been done. This was clearly an abrupt decision not anticipated when the planning for the season had been under way.

Mohenjo-daro: 1931-38

Small scale work continued at both Mohenjo-daro and Harappa during the 1930s, although Vats managed more at Harappa than occurred in Sindh (Mackay 1948: 2-3). The happenings at Mohenjo-daro during this period are historically more "interesting" than those at Harappa, because the work at the southern city was never published, nor did it have a real leader. Vats took care of both of these essentials at Harappa.

At the end of April 1932 Mackay asked K. N. Puri, who was Custodian of the Mohenjo-daro Museum, to dig a trial trench as deep as he could go in the interior of DK-G Area. The ground water was at its lowest then and it was a good opportunity to explore the lowest levels. He selected Block 7, Room 3 for his work which is noted by Mackay (1937-38: 44; see also Mackay 1930-34: 71). Puri reached ground water on May 10 and excavations were suspended. He found continuous Mature Harappan occupation, and some of the important Reserve Slipped Ware towards the bottom of the excavation.

We learn from a short report by Q. M. Moneer that excavations also proceeded in the DK-I Site, which has come to be known as the "Moneer Area."

> While supervising the preparation of a conservation estimate at Mohenjo-daro—writes Mr. Moneer—I utilized a period of leisure between January 15th and February 6th, 1934, to resume the trial excavation of the DK-I Site, where work had been started by Mr. K. N. Puri, the Custodian of the Mohenjo-daro Museum, about the beginning of December 1933. This is a small mound measuring about 250 feet from north to south and 120 feet from east to west and is bisected by a nine foot wide street that runs across it from north to south (Moneer 1930-34: 72).

The "Moneer Area" is now a prominent part of the Mohenjo-daro story and there is a short bibliography on it (Dales 1982, Urban 1987). The area was drawn up by Wheeler as part of his general stocktaking of the site in 1950 (Figure 2.33). The Aachen/IsMEO team cleaned and cleared the area of vegetation and accumulated debris and did some fairly intensive surface explorations. Jansen has plans for a report on the area which will salvage much information. The work by Puri and Moneer followed the first digging by K. N. Dikshit in 1924-45 when he placed his Trench D there (Dikshit 1924-25). More was to come after Moneer departed.

K. N. Puri returned to DK-I in 1936-37. He put in a trench that was 45 by 37 meters, all in the late levels. Three hundred antiquities, including 26 seals, were found. The discovery of a large

Figure 2.33. Moneer Area as drawn by Wheeler (above) and the Jansen Team (below), after Urban 1987: Figures 6 and 7

83

number of beads, 16 small weights, and a pair of small copper scale pans together with a fulcrum in a room directly accessible from a lane suggests that it was a lapidary shop (Puri 1936-37: 41).

The most poorly documented of the excavations in DK area is the one in DK-B that was undertaken between April 9th and 14th 1938. This unpublished week of work is documented by a field notebook that has been located by Michael Jansen. It was signed by A. Rahman. A brown limestone head was found and only recently published (Ardeleanu-Jansen 1984: 140). All of this documents the tremendous interest in Mohenjo-daro in the 1930s and how eager archaeologists were to excavate there. Mackay had certainly done his job of instilling the work ethic in men like Puri and Moneer.

There was work other than excavation to do at Mohenjo-daro. The museum had to be tended, and the conservation of the excavated remains needed immediate attention. In 1935-36, we learn from M. S. Vats that the deep trenches around the stupa were filled to prevent accidents. He also engaged in rebuilding and filling gaps in the walls of the Great Bath and adjoining rooms. As an experiment to control the destructive effects of saltpeter he placed two courses of mud brick on the tops of conserved walls in the SD Area. Enameled "protection" notice boards were also posted in two parts of the site for the guidance of visitors (Vats 1935-36: 21). The next year, Mr. Moneer was allowed to activate the conservation plan he developed in 1934.

Moneer rightly notes that: "The most urgent problem for the conservator here is the destructive action of saltpeter (Sindhi *kallar*) which permeates the soil and is the deadliest enemy of brickwork" (1936-37: 21). He had noticed that the bricks that were slightly overburnt in antiquity seemed to survive best so he began to make new over fired bricks for the conservation program. The DK Area was, in general, the site of the deepest excavations and he went to work there, repairing and underpinning walls and trying to save the drains (Moneer 1936-37: 21-2). No one has solved the salt problem at Mohenjo-daro. This destructive force continues to ravage these remains and the Government of Pakistan has put a halt to renewed excavation on any substantial scale until it is satisfied that the problem is under control. It just makes no sense to uncover vast new areas of the city, if they are only going to crumble in a few years following the research.

After November 6, 1931 Mackay devoted himself to the preparation of what was to be *Further Excavations at Mohenjo-daro*. All of the objects had to be checked, tallied, field measurements confirmed and tables prepared (Mackay 1930-34: 71). Mackay moved on to Chanhu-daro for one final excavation in the Indus Valley during the cold season of 1935-36, and then had that report to write as well (Mackay 1943). Excavation at Mohenjo-daro was not to be resumed until Wheeler returned there in 1950.

EXPLORATIONS IN SINDH: A Bright Beginning, A Tragic Ending

There is an interesting relationship between archaeological explorations in Sindh and the excavation at Mohenjo-daro. A brilliant young Bengali scholar, N. G. Majumdar (Figure 2.34) from the Varendra Research Society's Museum

Figure 2.34. Sketch of N. G. Majumdar

in Rajshahi participated in the Mohenjo-daro excavations. His talent and intellect brought him to the attention of Sir John Marshall, Daya Ram Sahni and E. J. H. Mackay, all of whom supported his appointment to the Archaeological Survey of India as an Assistant Superintendent.

On 2 January 1928 Mackay gave him the opportunity to conduct an independent excavation. This would be a "trial" dig at the site of Jhukar, 25 kilometers north of Mohenjo-daro (Majumdar 1927-28: 76-83, 1934: 5-18). Jhukar was first visited by R. D. Banerji in 1918-19 (Banerji 1918-19: 58), who thought it was a Buddhist stupa. Majumdar's initial excavation of Mound B at the site brought to light a settlement of Kushan age, just like the material from the Stupa Area on the Mound of the Great Bath at Mohenjo-daro. The pottery is very much like that of modern Sindh, and not so different from some prehistoric wares. His excavations at Jhukar were the first to make this point.

Unfortunately, Majumdar expended a great deal of time on Mound B, five or six weeks, and just as he was about to wind things down he decided to have a look at Mound A. Here he found the same Kushan material, but below this were two strata with buildings made of baked bricks just as at Mohenjo-daro. He christened these "Early and Late Jhukar." We now know that the "early Jhukar" is a settlement of the Mature Harappan. His "Late Jhukar" is called simply "Jhukar" and is the Sindhi Post-urban Harappan. The two are distinguished almost exclusively on the style of the painted pottery. The situation needs to be fully reviewed, but in his first try Majumdar established an important chronological distinction and has given us the first indication of the cultural materials that followed the Mature Harappan in Sindh.

In 1929-30 and 1930-31 Majumdar returned to Sindh to continue his explorations and small-scale excavations. He discovered many sites and those he first investigated make a list of distinguished Indus settlements: Chanhu-daro, Amri, Ghazi Shah, Lohumjo-daro, Ali Murad and Pandi Wahi (Figure 2.35). At Amri, during Christmas 1929, he also established the chronological relationship between the Early Harappan, Amri-Nal Phase material and the Mature Harappan, setting the stage for the debate on the origins of Indus urbanization.

Other interest was expressed in the archaeology of Sindh, with exploration being undertaken; some by scholars not affiliated with the Archaeological Survey of India. Henry Cousens wrote a substantial monograph on the antiquities of Sindh (1929). While his work does not contain many references to the prehistoric remains it is an important general source, and an early effort at organizing the regional archaeology of the Subcontinent. G. E. L. Carter, an officer in the Indian Administrative Service visited Tharro Hill, an important site in southern Sindh (1932) and G. S. Ghurye visited Kot Diji and made a substantial collection that is now in the Prince of Wales Museum, Bombay (1936).

Majumdar's research in the Sindh Kohistan was resumed on 17 October 1938, six and a half years after completing his initial survey, when he left Delhi for Johi, a tahsil headquarters in Dadu District ninety kilometers southwest of Mohenjo-daro. He first moved to the Gaj Nai Canal Bungalow and then, on November 7th, to a tent camp just off the Gaj Nai itself (a nai is a hill torrent in Sindhi). During his time in the field Majumdar discovered six new prehistoric sites, including Roheljo-kund, a settlement of the Amri-Nal Phase, which just precedes the Mature Harappan in Sindh and Baluchistan (Krishna Deva and McCown 1949).

November 1938 was an important month in the history of the Archaeological Survey of India. Majumdar resumed his field work in Sindh and Sir Leonard Woolley arrived in India to conduct a review of the Survey. Woolley came with his wife Katharine on 6 November 1938 and stayed for three months. The resulting report (Woolley 1939a) caused something of a sensation and is reviewed in detail later in Part 2.

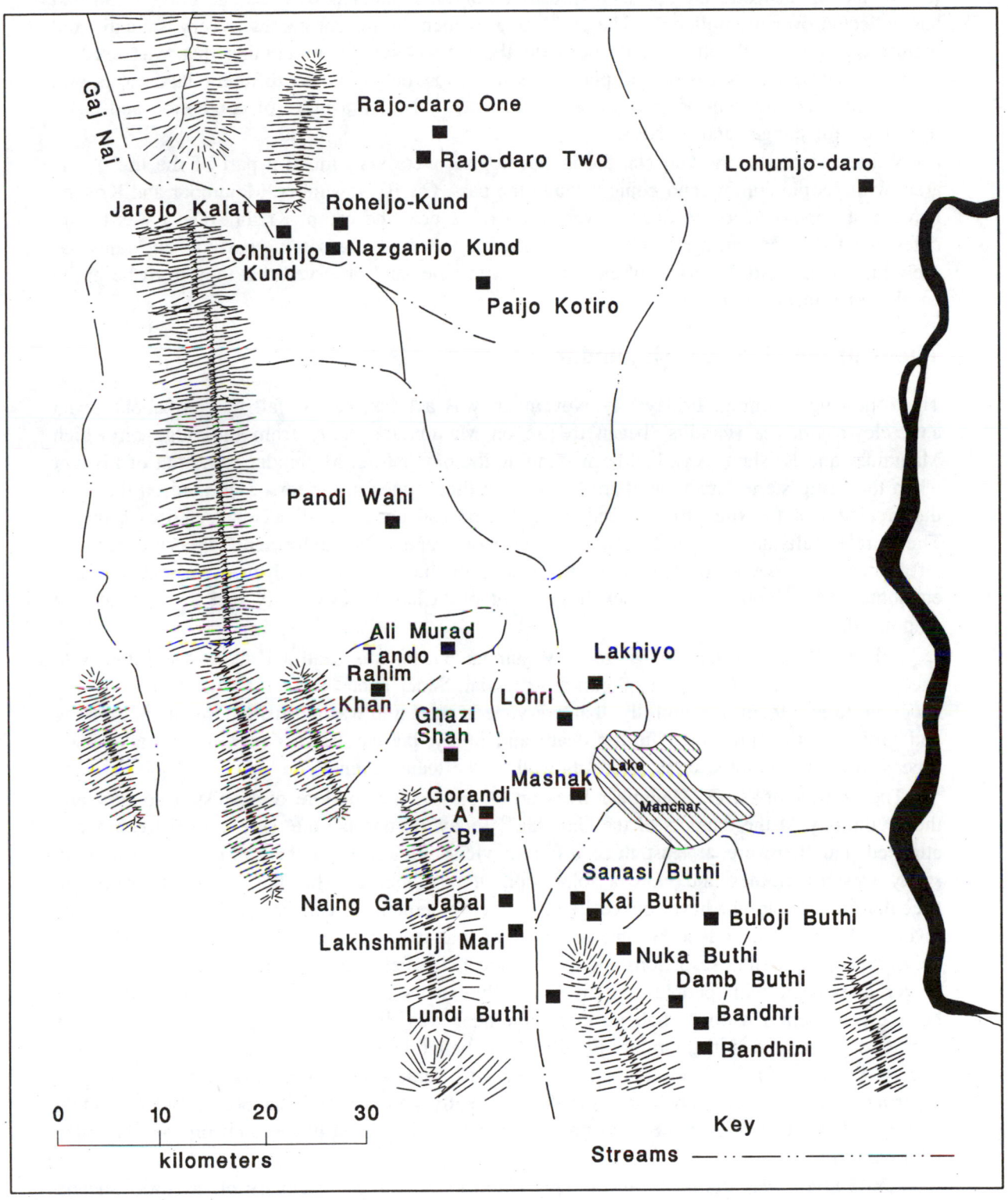

Figure 2.35. Sketch map N. G. Majumdar's sites at the Gaj Nai and in the vicinity of Lake Manchar

Majumdar's camp was established near the point where the Gaj Nai cuts through the outer face of the Sindh Kohistan, and then spreads its braided channels over a huge gravely fan that has collected over the millennia. The cut through which the torrent passes is very dramatic and picturesque and is a natural route between the plains and the mountains that was used in prehistoric times. It is a strategic place; the transition between two different landscapes and historically, two different peoples. As a consequence it is also a place of contention and has a reputation for danger and mystery.

While camped at the Gaj Nai the archaeologists were very much a part of the life of the area, with people coming and going through the pass. On 10 November, Majumdar and Krishna Deva, just appointed to the Survey, were on a ridge near the camp. Krishna Deva was taking notes dictated by Majumdar. His back was turned to the track of a passing party when Majumdar drew his attention to the group of eleven men with rifles and observed that they must be in the employ of a local *zamindar*.

The Murder of N. G. Majumdar

The following morning, Friday[28] 11 November, was a brisk, sunny, fall day. At about seven a.m. eleven *dacoits* (bandits) began to fire on Majumdar's camp from the ridge on which Majumdar and Krishna Deva had been standing the day before. Majumdar came out of his tent when the firing started and was immediately shot three times in the torso. He died on the spot: the precision of the fire probably indicated that he had been specifically selected as a target. The team's draftsman, Aravinda Chatterji, and photographer, Manindra Sen Gupta, immediately left their tent to determine the nature and source of the shooting. Both were wounded in this encounter. Sen Gupta had an index finger shot off: Chatterji eventually had to have an arm amputated.

Krishna Deva was the first to go to Majumdar but he was dead and there was little to do except to cover the body. The exploration jamandar, Sadar Din,[29] shouted to the *dacoits* to stop shooting; telling them (untruthfully) that everyone in the camp was a Muslim. His quick thinking and prompt action prevented further death and injury, but the *dacoits* managed to take 2000 rupees in cash and some other goods as well as the team's camels.

The murder of N. G. Majumdar lives on as part of the folklore of Kohistan country and the mythology of the dangers of the Gaj Nai.[30] Today, no one is quite sure why the camp was attacked and there are at least three different views. It is known that Majumdar dressed in spiffy western clothes and wore a solar topi, or pith helmet. This has led some people to speculate that he might have looked like a law enforcement officer, or a representative of the revenue department, and he became a target for that reason. Others have noted that Sindhis, being rural people, had suspicions and unsophisticated beliefs about outsiders and the "western" power associated with people who lived in white tents and wore pith helmets. This could have given them reason to believe that Majumdar was divining or digging for gold in his sites and robbery was the motive. Finally, local belief holds that excavating old sites might release the evil *jins* or ghosts trapped there. This same fear might have been a cause, or contributed to, the attack on Majumdar. No one really knows why it happened, but it brought an untimely end to one of the most promising careers in the early research on the Harappan Civilization.[31]

While Sindh was the center of the real action involving the discovery of the most ancient civilization in South Asia, interesting things were also happening at Harappa. M. S. Vats, another of the young luminaries of the Archaeological Survey of India, was hard at work there.

CONTINUED EXCAVATION

The Work of M. S. Vats

Rai Bahadur Daya Ram Sahni undertook three seasons of independent excavation at Harappa between 1920-21 and 1924-25. He had made a good start at the site, but there was a lot left to do, in spite of the ravages of the railroad brick robbers. There was no excavation there in 1925-26, presumably because of the very large scale of the program at Mohenjo-daro, when Marshall joined the field team, and brought so many of his colleagues with him. Sometime in 1925-26 M. S. Vats became the Superintendent Archaeologist for the Northern Circle, and settled in to address the task of excavating Harappa (1930-34a-f) and conducting a bit of exploration (Vats 1930-34g). He undertook eight seasons of work at this site, which extended to the end of the 1933-34 field season. They are summarized season by season, in Appendix C. There are several points concerning the historical significance of this period and Mr. Vats's special contribution to Harappan archaeology. Photographs from the early excavations at Harappa give a sense of the shape of the mounds and the manner of excavation (Plate 2.36, Plate 2.37, Plate 2.38, Plate 2.39, Plate 2.40, Plate 2.41, Plate 2.42, Plate 2.43, Plate 2.44).

The stratification of Harappa has always been confusing, in part due to the predations of the brick robbers. Vats settled on a scheme not unlike the one used at Mohenjo-daro, but with a special, perhaps even diabolical, twist. The Vats scheme is given in Table 2.1.

TABLE 2.1
M. S. Vats' Stratigraphy at Harappa
after Vats 1940: 9-10

	Mound F Strata	Mound AB Strata	Area J Strata	Area G Strata	Cemetery H Strata
Late I	I	I	I	I	I
Late II	II	II	II	II	II
Late III			III	III	
Late IV					IV
Intermediate I		IV	III	III	
Intermediate II	V			IV	
Intermediate III	VI				
Intermediate IV	VII				
Early I			VIII		

The perplexing part of this scheme comes from the fact that while there is a correlation in the terminology (e.g., Late I and Late II) for the relative stratigraphy, different parts of the site have an independent absolute chronology. Thus, Late I and II in Area J are dated by Vats to "circa 2850 to 3500 BC" while Late I and II in Cemetery H come to "circa 2000-2500 BC" (1940: 10). This is an impossibly intricate setup but it has to be understood in order to read effectively Mr. Vats' key report (1940).

The labels used to designate the various excavation areas at Harappa, such as Mound F or Cemetery H, have also been a source of some confusion, or at least puzzlement. The system began with Sir Alexander Cunningham's first excavation there in 1872-73, when he published a sketch plan of the site. He designated various mounds with letters: A through E (Cunningham 1875: Pl. XXXII). Later experience at the site led workers to conclude that Cunningham's mounds A and B were in reality a single feature, thus the designation AB Mound. During the

88

later excavations there, undertaken by Rai Bahadur Daya Ram Sahni and Madho Sarup Vats, the scheme was extended by giving unlettered mounds designations F through J. The upper case letter 'I' was omitted for some reason, possibly because so many Roman Numerals were in use. It was during this period that the site was also gridded into 100-foot squares for purposes of coordinating the excavation. The squares "...running west to east being numbered A, B, C, etc., and similarly those going north to south, 1, 2, 3, and so on" (Vats 1940: 8). Using this system we can account for the designation of the Mature Harappan Cemetery R-37 at the site (Figure 2.36).

Mound F was the best preserved of the excavation areas probed in the early years; the seasons prior to Sir Mortimer Wheeler's work there in 1946. Rai Bahadur Daya Ram Sahni had excavated in this area, just south of an abandoned bed of the Ravi River, before Vats came to the site. This area has a complex set of remains that Sahni and his successor chose to call "the area of the parallel walls;" because they did not know their function (Plate 2.45). In 1926-27, Sir John Marshall resolved this issue. He notes in the annual report on the activities of the Survey, that this architectural complex seems to have been a storage facility since it could be favorably compared to storage rooms associated with Cretan Palaces (1926-27a: 53) (Figure 2.37). Marshall's training at Knossos with Sir Arthur Evans, gave him the necessary experience to make this connection and it is one of the clearest examples of how training in archaeology shapes our interpretation of remains. From the day of Marshall's judgment until the present, this building has been called "the granary," in spite of the fact that there is almost nothing to support his conclusion (Figure 2.38).

Parts of Harappa were very rich in their small finds. In one year Vats exposed 4,690 square meters and found 350 seals and other inscribed objects (Vats 1926-27). In 1928-29, the famous red jasper torso of a nude male was found on Mound F (Plate 2.46). This statuette is an extraordinary piece of workmanship with beautiful lines and carries with it a sense of the Hellenistic. It was attributed to the Harappan Civilization by Vats, but this was disputed by Marshall (Vats 1928-29).[32] There was a search for additional parts of the piece, but it proved fruitless (Vats 1929-30a).

Vats was responsible for excavating the first large cemetery associated with the Harappan Civilization. It was found south of the AB mound and the ground was designated Cemetery H. K. N. Sastri discovered Cemetery H. He reported that following a heavy downpour during the monsoon of 1927: "...the tops of a few burial jars cropped up above the ground surface. The writer, who was at that time in charge of the archaeological sites and the Museum at Harappa, reported the discovery to M. S. Vats, the then Superintendent, Archaeological Survey, Northern Circle, Lahore. In February 1928, he excavated the area all around the find spot of the aforesaid jars and recovered another group of seven burial jars" (Sastri 1965: 1).

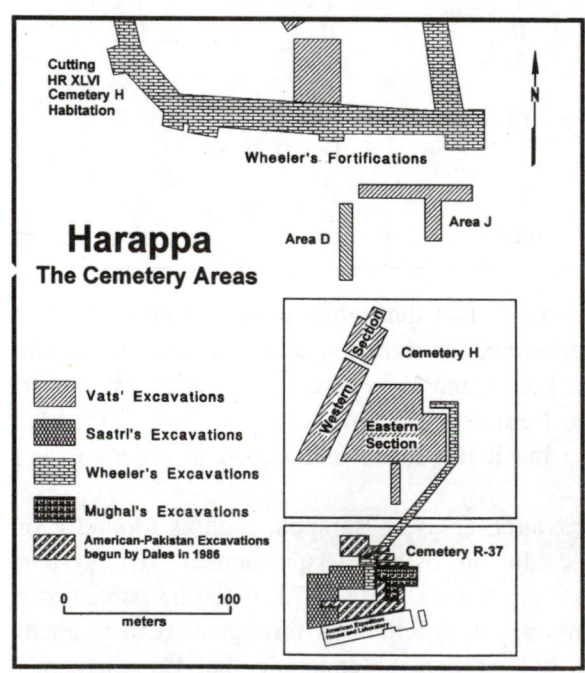

Figure 2.36. Plan of the Cemetery Areas at Harappa

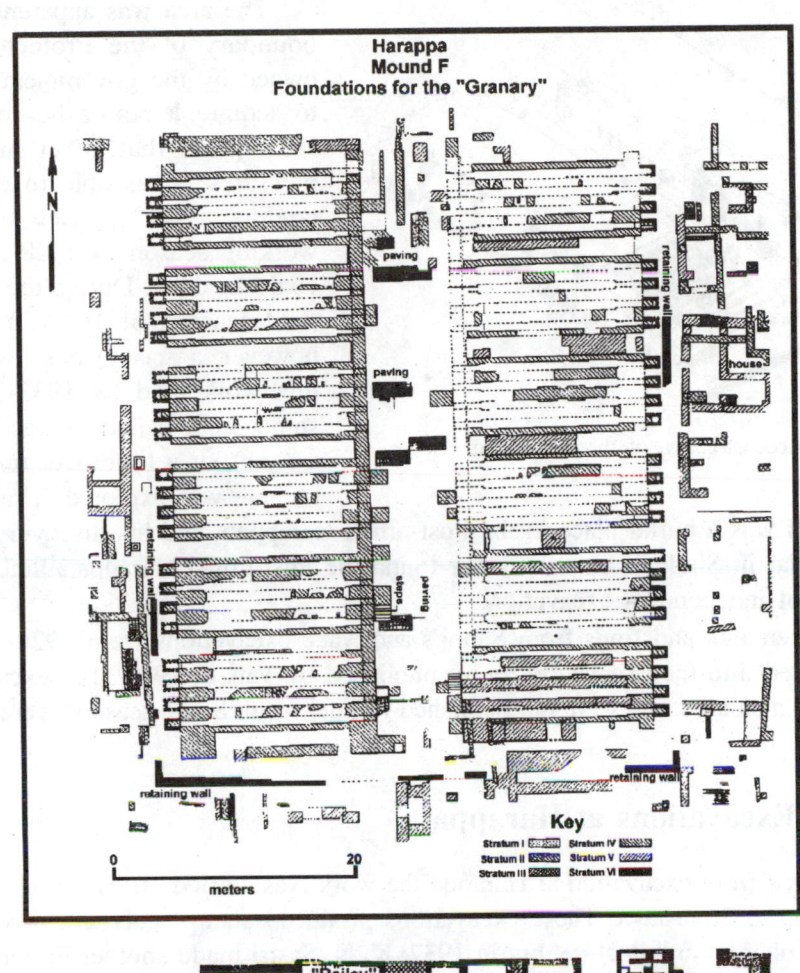

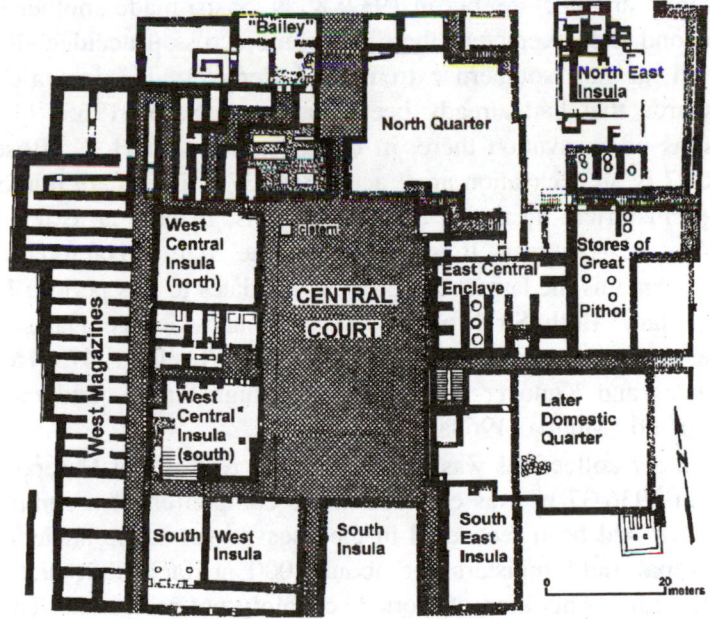

Figure 2.37. Above, plan of the Granary at Harappa. After Vats 1940: Plate 3. Below, plan of the West Magazines in the Palace of Knosses. After Evans 1921 : Figure 152

90

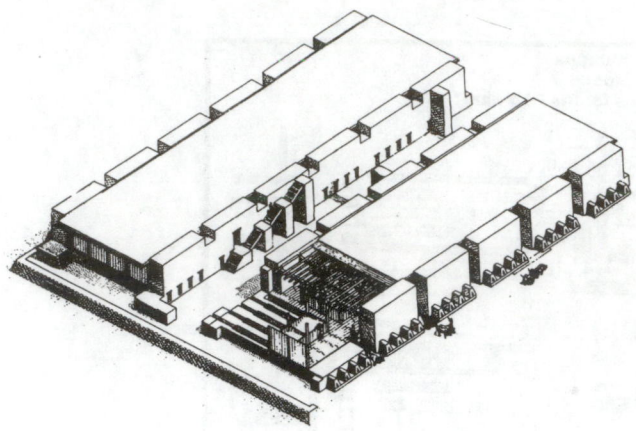

Figure 2.38. Reconstruction of the Granary at Harappa

The area was apparently outside the boundary of the Protected Monument owned by the government and Vats had to acquire it before he could dig there. He reports that: "Yet in spite of the pressures I was able to exert, the land could not be acquired till late in the working season of 1928-29, when little could be done. During the following two field seasons of 1929-30 and 1930-31, however, a special push was made with this work, and by 1933-34 an area of some 3,800 square yards (3,475 square meters), or a little over three-quarters of an acre was explored" (Vats 1940: 203).

Cemetery H was a burial place in the Post-urban Harappan, and his discovery is parallel to that of Majumdar in Sindh, where the latter found the Post-urban Harappan Jhukar material in his first piece of independent excavation.

All of the remains and finds from Sahni's and Vats' excavations from 1920-21 to 1933-34 were incorporated into the excavation report published by Vats in 1940. The excavations in the 1930s, while on a small scale, were not published in final form. Some seasons were not published at all.

Subsequent Excavations at Harappa

When Vats retired from excavation at Harappa the work was carried on by Dr. H. Nazim, M. H. Kuraishi and H. L. Srivastava. These excavations produced stamp seals and other small finds, without much coherent architecture, but in 1937, K. N. Sastri made another important discovery at Harappa; the second Indus cemetery there. He came across it accidentally while supervising the digging of a pit, at the "southern extremity of Cemetery H," in which to rebury a large quantity of pot sherds that had already been examined (Sastri 1965: 1). Sastri went on to conduct four seasons of excavation there, in collaboration with H. K. Bose (Sastri 1957: 39-40).[33] Cemetery R-37 is an excavation area; actually R-37 is its square number, not a "cultural" designation with prehistorical meaning. This cemetery is, in fact, an extension of Cemetery H and dates to the Mature Harappan. It is the first of the Mature Harappan cemeteries to have been discovered and remains the largest cemetery which dates to this period. There is no cemetery known at Mohenjo-daro. Both Sir Mortimer Wheeler and George Dales invested substantial resources to further an understanding of Cemetery R-37 (Wheeler 1947a; Hemphill, Lukacs and Kennedy 1991; Dales and Kenoyer 1993b). M. R. Mughal also conducted an excavation in Cemetery R-37 in 1966 (Mughal 1968a).

Work with the older collections was also part of the research at Harappa. We learn from H. L. Srivastava that in 1936-37 he was engaged in the completion of a comprehensive list of ca. 25,000 antiquities that had been recovered in the excavations at the ancient city. This included consulting the original field registers for about 1000 artifacts that had lost their numbers (Srivastava 1936-37: 138). This kind of work is certainly not recreation. The demands for care, cross-checking and an imaginative use of written sources, drawings and photography are nothing short of exhausting.

Sir Mortimer Wheeler at Harappa

The day in May 1944 was hot at Harappa, so hot that R. E. M. Wheeler, the newly appointed Director General of the Archaeological Survey of India, was advised to be on the site only between the hours of 5:30 and 7:30 AM (Wheeler 1955: 190). As he approached the looming AB Mound, promptly at dawn, he was astounded by its size and was immediately struck by the fact that it must have been a Citadel, put in place to protect the inhabitants of the city from attack. The presence of a Citadel at Harappa would be revolutionary if true, since the prevailing opinion was that the Harappans were a remarkably peaceful people, energetically engaged in commerce. The lack of palaces, or anything even approaching this kind of social isolation for any class, suggested quite a different social structure from the contemporary peoples of Egypt, Mesopotamia, or even Crete.

A few minutes of scraping at the surface of the AB Mound revealed the presence of brick lines and Wheeler felt that his initial impression was probably right. As he said in his autobiography: "A few minutes' observation had radically changed the social character of the Indus civilization and put it at last into an acceptable focus" (1955: 192).

A radical change in the way in which the Harappan Civilization would be viewed came to Wheeler as an inspiration, before he had been at the site more than an hour or two. His first principle of interpretation, the often unstated assumption that guided him in his synthesis of the Harappan Civilization, was not something thoughtfully pieced together over a period of months or years, drawing on detailed reading and research; it was a simple revelation.

This insight was immediate and compelling to Wheeler, sufficiently so that he dug the site. In 1946 he took one of his field schools there to test his new ideas. The title of his report (Wheeler 1947a) "Harappa 1946: The Defenses and Cemetery R-37" is fully descriptive of what was addressed during this single season of work. He found a revetment and bastions on the Citadel, and was able to trace the fortifications to some degree. At a more human level, the excavation team discovered cart tracks below Cemetery H, with an axle length matching modern Sindhi vehicles of this type (Wheeler 1947a: 85, Pl. XXXV,B). His stratigraphic work in a trench between Cemetery H and Cemetery R-37 demonstrated that this R-37 was earlier than Cemetery H, and that there was a substantial alteration of the site in the period separating these two archaeological assemblages.

By the time the excavation was complete Wheeler felt that he had the beginnings of an understanding of the Harappans as a whole and his report contains his earliest synthetic statement on them (1947c: 74-8). It was also the venue for him to suggest that Aryan invaders had put a violent end to the cities of Mohenjo-daro and Harappa and that: "On circumstantial evidence, Indra stands accused" (Wheeler 1947b: 82).

The excavation of Harappa was interrupted after Wheeler's single season. M. Rafique Mughal did one season of digging in Cemetery R-37 in 1966 (Mughal 1968a), but in 1986 Professor George F. Dales initiated a long term project there, with the cooperation of the Pakistan Government (Plate 2.47). They have been able to define the Early Harappan and Transitional occupations at the site and to vastly expand our knowledge of the human remains through a reinvestigation of Cemetery R-37 (Meadow 1991a; Hemphill, Lukacs and Kennedy 1991).

M. S. Vats Excavates Rangpur

In 1934, M. S. Vats conducted the first protohistoric excavations in Gujarat. His work took place at the important site of Rangpur on the Peninsula of Saurashtra and was done at the invitation of the Thakore Sahib of Limbdi State. Vats put in three trenches and found a great deal of pottery but little architecture. He thought that the pottery could be classed as Indus black and red ware with similar shapes and decorations. The presence of triangular terracotta cakes and perforated vessels added to this conviction (Vats 1934-35). But, he also noted that some of the pottery was more "evolved" than that found in the Early and Intermediate periods of Mohenjo-daro or Harappa. "Provisionally it may be taken to correspond with the Late Period of the Indus Valley sites or perhaps intercalcated between that and the date of the Cemetery H at Harappa" (Vats 1934-35: 38). So began the myth that the Harappan sites of Gujarat should be properly classed as "Late Harappan."

Rangpur was not forgotten and was returned to by G. S. Ghurye in 1936 (Ghurye 1939) and M. G. Dikshit in 1947. Dikshit felt that the site should be classified as "Post-Harappan" (M. G. Dikshit 1950, see also 1957). S. R. Rao excavated there for three seasons beginning in 1953-54 and brought the site back within the Harappan fold (Rao 1963a). Rao also excavated Lothal, the famous port (Rao 1979, 1985). Mention should be made of the work at Somnath promoted so well by Bendapudi Subbarao. He was a student of H. D. Sankalia who died early in his career, shortly after founding the Department of Archaeology and Ancient Indian History at the Maharaja Sayajiro University of Baroda and publishing a landmark study of prehistoric India and Pakistan (Subbarao 1958) (Plate 2.48). It was within this context that the Gujaratis, then part of the State of Bombay, founded a Department of Archaeology under the leadership of P. P. Pandya (Figure 2.39).

Vats went on from Rangpur to conduct research in Khairpur State of Sindh at Diji-ji-Tikri (Vats 1935-36a) and Kotasur (a.k.a. Naru Waro Dharo; Vats 1935-36b) (Plate 2.49).

Figure 2.39. Sketch of P. P. Pandya, first Director of Archaeology in Gujarat

Hellmut deTerra and T. T. Paterson at Burzahom

In 1935, the geologist-archaeologists Hellmut deTerra, T. T. Paterson, and P. Teilhard de Chardin, working through the Carnegie Institution of Washington D.C., Yale and Cambridge Universities, as well as the American Philosophical Society, undertook a trial excavation at Burzahom in Kashmir, 16 kilometers northeast of Srinagar (deTerra and Paterson 1939: 233-35, Plate XXIV). They recognized it as an Iron Age Megalith and discussed the possible "Neolithic" affinities of their finds. Their excavation was set in the context of their investigation of the Himalayan glacial sequence and the palaeolithic archaeology of the Indian Subcontinent, and in that sense was something of an aside in the overall research plan. With the geologists working in the mountains and E. J. H. Mackay busily excavating at Chanhu-daro, 1935-1936 was a busy time for American sponsored archaeological research in colonial India.

Plate 2.29. The Seated Nobleman of L Area as it was excavated. Courtesy of the Archaeological Survey of India, Old Negative Number 795-92.

Plate 2.30. General view of L Area, author's photograph.

Plate 2.31. DK-G North partially excavated, from the southwest. Note the rail cars near the horizon. They were used to move excavated earth. Courtesy of the Archaeological Survey of India, Old Negative Number 1088/92.

Plate 2.32. Antique photograph of Jhukar. Courtesy of the Archaeological Survey of India, Old Negative Number 1137/92.

Plate 2.33. Central street in DK Area, looking north, author's photograph.

Plate 2.34. West Street in DK Area, looking west, author's photograph.

Plate 2.35. A courtyard and wells in DK Area, author's photograph.

Plate 2.36. Harappa, general view of Mound A-B, from the north. Courtesy of the Archaeological Survey of India, Punjab Photographic Volumes 508/86.

Plate 2.37. Harappa, view of Mound A-B. Courtesy of the Archaeological Survey of India, Punjab Photographic Volumes 509/86.

Plate 2.38. Harappa, Mound B under excavation. Courtesy of the Archaeological Survey of India, Punjab Photographic Volumes 440/86.

Plate 2.39. Harappa, area to the west of Naugaza's Tomb under excavation, Mound A-B. Courtesy of the Archaeological Survey of India, Punjab Photographic Volumes 510/86.

Plate 2.40. Harappa, concentration of bones and pottery, Trench A(f) Harappa. Courtesy of the Archaeological Survey of India, Punjab Photographic Volumes 432/86.

Plate 2.41. Pit 1 at Harappa with a drain of bricks on edge. Courtesy of the Archaeological Survey of India, Punjab Photographic Volumes 499/86.

Plate 2.42. Harappa, excavations to the west of Naugaza's Tomb, Mound A-B. Courtesy of the Archaeological Survey of India, Punjab Photographic Volumes 450/86.

Plate 2.43. Harappa, Mound F, photograph published by Vats as "Lingham in situ in Trench A(i)"; Vats 1940: Plate Xc. Courtesy of the Archaeological Survey of India, Punjab Photographic Volumes 435/86.

Plate 2.44. Harappa, general view of Mound F before excavation, from the southwest. Courtesy of the Archaeological Survey of India, Punjab Photographic Volumes 503/86.

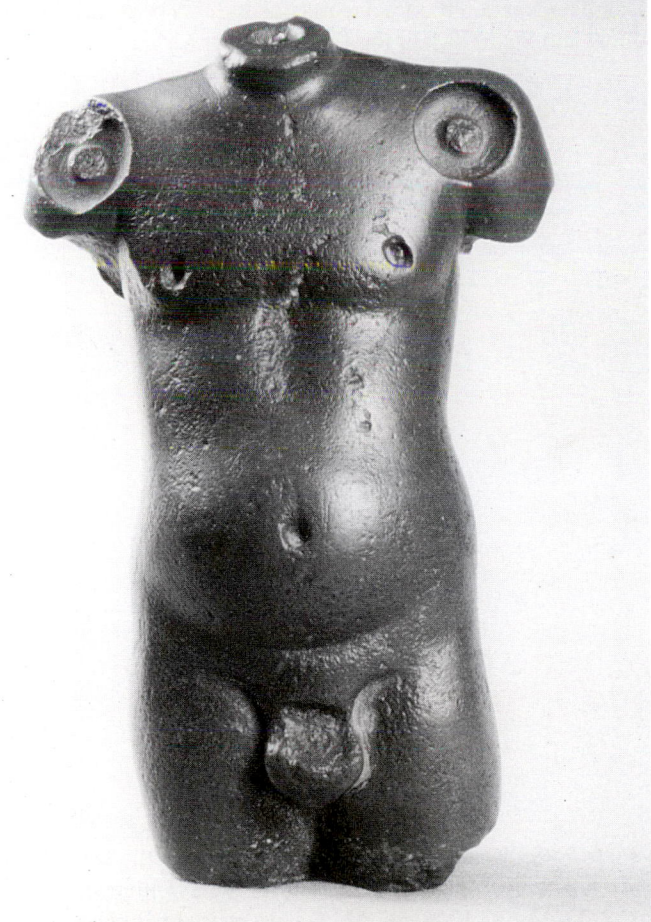

Plate 2.45. Harappa, area of the "parallel walls," trench A(6) from the southeast, at Harappa. Courtesy of the Archaeological Survey of India, Punjab Photographic Volume 463/86.

Plate 2.46. The red jasper torso from Harappa. Courtesy of the National Museum, New Delhi.

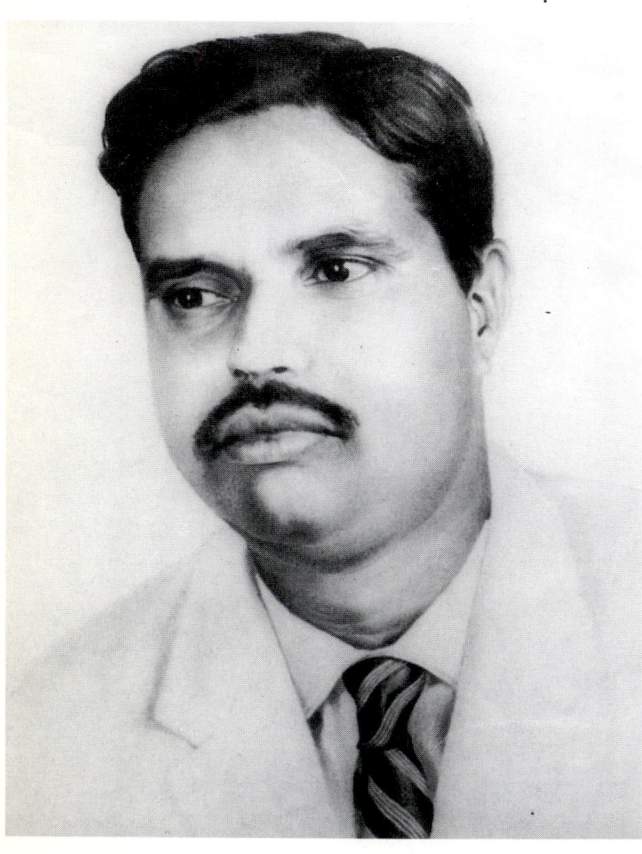

Plate 2.47. George F. Dales at Harappa instructing three Pakistani students on the finer points of Indus terracottas. From left to right the students are: Ghulam Jamil Ahmed, Shokat Ali Shad and Shahid Mehmood. Courtesy of Mrs. Barbara Dales.

Plate 2.48. Bendapudi Subbarao, founder of the Department of Archaeology and Ancient History at M. S. University of Baroda. Courtesy of K. K. Bhan, M. S. University of Baroda.

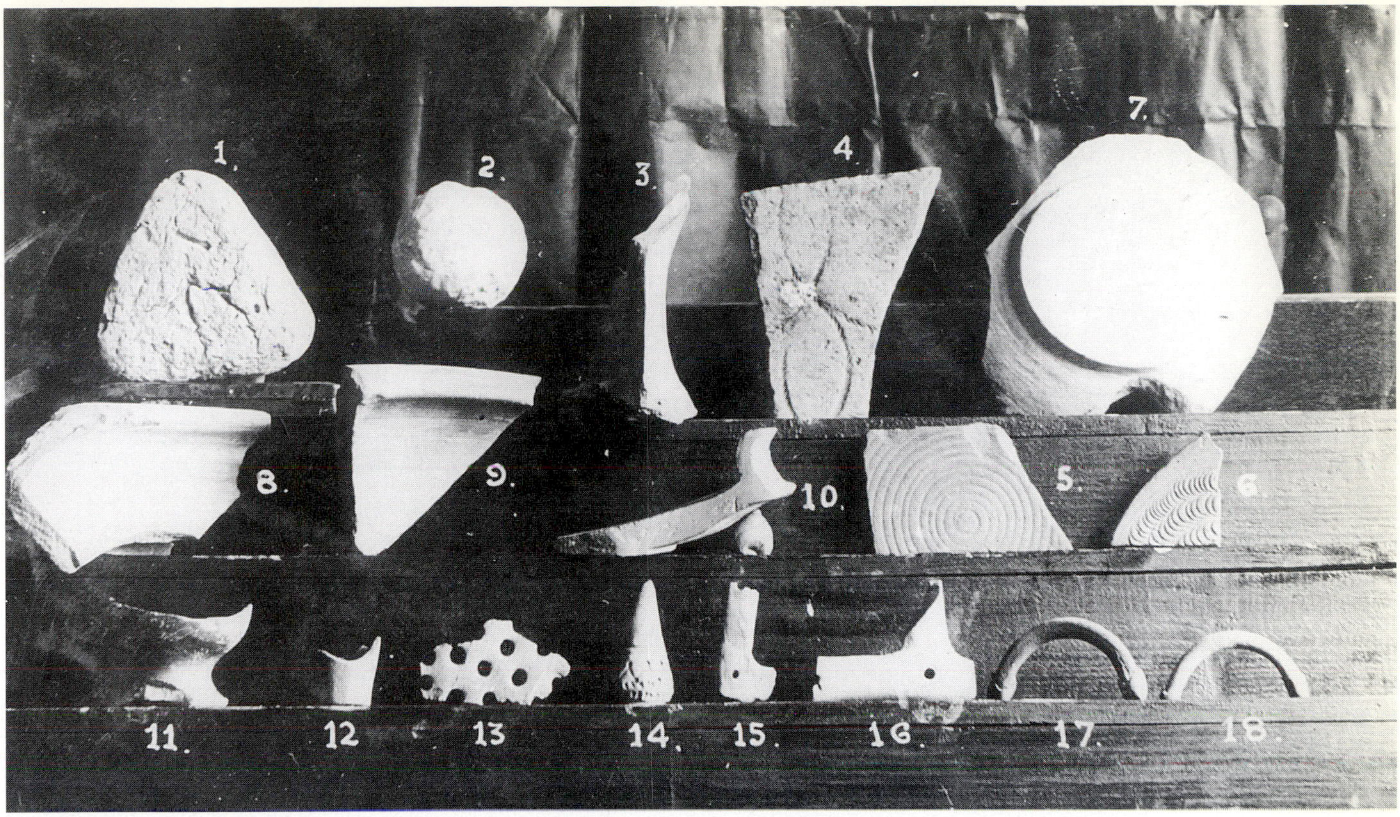

Plate 2.49. Finds from Diji-ji-Tikri. Courtesy of the Archaeological Survey of India, Old Negative Number 1121/92.

Plate 2.50. Chanhu-daro Mound I from the South. Courtesy of the Archives of the University of Pennsylvania Museum.

Plate 2.51. Work in progress at Chanhu-daro. Courtesy of the Archives of the University of Pennsylvania Museum.

Plate 2.52. The furnace in the craft area at Chanhu-daro. Courtesy of the Archives of the University Pennsylvania Museum.

Plate 2.53. Pot with the human cranium and other finds from Chanhu-daro. Courtesy of the Archives of the University of Pennsylvania Museum.

Plate 2.55. B. K. Thapar. Courtesy of Mrs. B. K. Thapar.

Plate 2.54. Aerial view of Las Bela, with the mounds of the Kulli site of Edith Shahr. Courtesy of Walter A. Fairservis.

Plate 2.56. The Taxila School of Archaeology, 1944.
Key to names, giving current or recent academic posts: 1. Dr. P. Banerjee, Asst. Director, National Museum, New Delhi; 2. Dr. Ajit Mookerjee, formerly Director, Crafts Museum, New Delhi; 3. Prof. S.R. Das, Dept. of Archaeology, Viskwabharti University; 4. S.C. Chandra, d. 1961 while a superintendent of the Survey; 5. Prof. B.N. Puri, Dept. of Ancient History, Lucknow University; 6. Prakas Majumdar, formerly of the University of Calcutta; 7. B.K. Thapar, Director General, Arch. Survey of India; 8. Prof. A.H. Dani, Retired Head, Dept. of Social Sciences, Islamabad; 9. Dr. D.R. Patil, formerly a superintendent of the Survey; 10. Dr. Bhanst, formerly of the Dept. of Sanskrit, University of Punjab.

Plate 2.57. Wheeler's deep trench on April 7, 1950. Courtesy of the Pakistan Department of Archaeology.

Plate 2.58. The area of Wheeler's deep trench today, with podium of the granary in the background, author's photograph.

Plate 2.59. Gordon Childe on the right, with Frederick E. Zeuner. Courtesy of the Director, Institute of Archaeology, University College London, University of London.

Plate 2.60. Walter A. Fairservis, Jr. at work at Allahdino in 1977. Courtesy of Jan Bell Fairservis.

Later excavation was undertaken at Burzahom for nine seasons (between 1960-61 and 1973-74) by T. N. Kazanchi of the Archaeological Survey of India. He demonstrated that the early village at the site had affinities with the North Asian "Neolithic" and could be dated to the third millennium, extending into the opening centuries of the second millennium. He found important human burials, along with those of domesticated dogs. Two Kot Dijian pots were also found, one with the important "horned deity" motif related to the famous pot from Kot Diji (Khan 1965: Figure 16) and the so-called "Proto-Siva" seal (No. 420) from Mohenjo-daro (Mackay 1937-38: Pl. XCIV, 420).

THE INDUS SCRIPT AND EASTER ISLAND

By this time much interest in the Indus script had been generated. Colonel L. A. Waddell published a wrong-headed book on the topic as early as 1925. Professor George A. Barton of the University of Pennsylvania followed this with something much more useful, but basically descriptive (Barton 1928a, 1928b, 1929, 1930). Stephen Langdon, who was the power behind the Oxford-Field Museum Expedition at Kish where Indus seals were found, had more than a casual interest in the Harappan Civilization and worked in earnest on the Indus script (Langdon 1931, 1934a). He also supervised the Oxford PhD dissertation of G. R. Hunter, who wrote the first serious study of the script (Hunter 1929) published in book form in 1934. Alan S. C. Ross, who wrote on the numeral system of the Indus script (Ross 1938, see also A. S. C. Ross 1936, 1939), also studied at Oxford and worked with Langdon.

Langdon involved himself in the controversy over the Indus and Easter Island scripts, precipitated in 1932 when Professor Paul Pelliot informed the Academie des Inscriptions et Belles-Lettres that Monsieur Guillaume de Hevesy, an Hungarian living in France, had found correspondences between the script of Mohenjo-daro and the writing inscribed on the wooden tablets of Easter Island (Figure 2.40; Sir E. Denison Ross 1932; de Hevesy 1932, 1934a, 1934b, 1934c, 1938a, 1938b; Imbelloni 1939: 61).

In all other matters Langdon seems to have been a sober, conservative scholar, but for whatever reason, he liked the idea that there was an historical connection between Easter Island and the Indus Civilization: "Since Sir John Marshall's book was published, M. G. de Hevesy has called attention to script of Easter Island...There can be no doubt concerning the identity of the Indus and Easter Island scripts" (Langdon 1934a: ix). Since this was clearly going to be a controversial matter, Langdon assisted others with an investigation of Easter Island, with special emphasis on its script. He allowed, possibly even recruited, the leader of his excavations at Kish, Louis Charles Watelin to be the leader of the 1934-35 Franco-Belgian Expedition to Easter Island (Lavachery 1935). The staff of this research project included Alan S. C. Ross and Alfred Metraux, a Swiss anthropologist who specialized in the study of Polynesia. He was also the husband of another important anthropologist, Rhoda Metraux.

Watelin died of pneumonia, in Chile, on his way to the Pacific and the expedition failed on this tragedy (Langdon 1934b: 9); however, Alfred Metraux decided to critique M. de Hevesy's hypothesis (Metraux 1938a, 1938b). This was effective, but drew out the politics of the time, with G. R. Hunter coming to de Hevesy's support: "It is with considerable surprise, not to say disgust, that I have read Mons. Metraux's criticism of you...I have found in every case without exception when you have taken signs from my work you have faithfully reproduced them with scrupulous, and indeed remarkable exactitude...With regard to Mr. Metraux's strictures on your reproduction of Easter Island signs I can only say that there also I am impressed with your skillful and accurate draftsmanship of the few Easter Island signs that I have had time to check up with photographs of originals" (Hunter in de Hevesy 1938b: 809-10).

94

Figure 2.40. M. de Hevesy's chart comparing the Indus with the Easter Island script [de Hevesy 1935, Pl. III]

The story of the 1934-35 Franco-Belgian Expedition to Easter Island has yet to be told, and it is certainly worthy of a serious scholarly investigation. The relationship between S. Langdon, A. Ross and G. R. Hunter on one hand, and Metraux on the other, also might well be better documented, since Ross was in the field with Metraux.

W. NORMAN BROWN ENTERS THE FIELD AT CHANHU-DARO

A number of scholars and institutions interested in Indian archaeology wanted to conduct field work there. From the very beginning of the Archaeological Survey of India foreign excavation teams had been a matter of concern to its officials. By 1934, the Government of India had decided to test these waters and to allow "outsiders" to excavate. The door was not thrown open, but was slightly ajar and an American team managed to slip through.

W. Norman Brown and Archaeology

One of the great institution builders in the study of Indology in America was Professor W. Norman Brown of the University of Pennsylvania (Figure 2.41). Brown was determined to further American involvement in the archaeology of the Subcontinent. His involvement goes back to September 1922 when the Archaeological Institute of America appointed him its representative in India with the following note: "It is the intention of the Institute to raise an endowment fund with which it is hoped that an American School of Classical Studies may be established in India (R. V. D. Magoffin to Brown September 6, 1922).[34] With the opening of work at Mohenjo-daro, Brown wanted American scholars to be a part of the rapidly unfolding story of prehistoric life in Sindh. He eventually received a concession for the excavation of Chanhu-daro, which was directed by Ernest J. H. Mackay. Following the excavation, Mackay recalled the following course of events:

Figure 2.41. Sketch of W. Norman Brown

> The amendment of the Ancient Monuments Act of India, some three years since, to permit outside universities and archaeological bodies to excavate in that country gave to the American School of Indic and Iranian Studies and the Boston Museum of Fine Arts the opportunity to carry into effect a long cherished dream. In 1934, Professor W. Norman Brown, President of the former body, visited India and negotiated with the Government of India a concession to excavate the mounds

of Chanhu-daro in Nawabshah District of Sind, to the east of the Indus. Already a preliminary investigation has been made this past winter season, in which I was assisted by several members of the Indian staff formerly at work at Mohenjo-daro, and in the latter half of the season by my wife. The first season's excavations have proved of surprising value (Mackay 1935-36: 38).

Behind this simple, straightforward paragraph hangs a tale, more complex, even tortured, than suggested by Mackay. It begins in 1928 when Brown first met Mackay at Mohenjo-daro where he went to see an excavation in progress. He was on one of the first fellowships granted by the John Simon Guggenheim Memorial Foundation (Rocher 1978: xix), conducting his research and planning further American involvement in the scholarship of the Subcontinent through the American School of Indic and Iranian Studies. This institution was the "parent" of the American Institute of Indian Studies, which survives today as principal vehicle for American scholarship in India. Building this Institute was no simple task, and Brown's key role in it is outlined by R. Rocher (1978: xix-xxi).

Brown wanted to undertake an archaeological project in India (Brown to Archaeological Survey of India, 18 June 1934). The School of Indic and Iranian Studies was to be Brown's vehicle for the promotion of American involvement in the Subcontinent. It was presented to the Government of India in 1927-28 and received favorable notice (Coatman 1927-28: 40). The principal officials were Brown as President, Franklin Edgerton of Yale as Vice-President and Mortimer Graves of the American Council of Learned Societies as Secretary-Treasurer.

As early as 1930, letters in the Archives of The University of Pennsylvania Museum indicate that Museum Director Horace H. F. Jayne, invoking Brown's name, had been in correspondence with Mackay while he was still at Mohenjo-daro. Jayne expressed a desire, on the part of the Museum, to conduct archaeological excavations in British India and sought Mackay's opinion. In this exchange Mackay is a warm, informative partner. He noted that the antiquities laws of India would not permit a foreign excavation, but suggested that this might change in the near future.

The law was amended in 1932 (The Ancient Monuments Preservation Act, 1904 by Act No. 18, 1932): the gate opened, and so did contact between Prof. Brown and Mackay. Beginning in January 1934, there is a marked increase in the correspondence between these two men, including one (Brown to Mackay, 7 April 1934) with the following observation: "We have long felt that we should like to see an American archaeological expedition in India, and that the most profitable field would be that of the Indus Valley or possibly Baluchistan." This is followed by questions such as: "Would you be willing to head such an excavation?" "Have you a site in mind?" "Why do you think it would be a good site?" "Do you advise a reconnaissance excavation?" "How much money would be needed for it?"

The response to Brown's offer was both cordial and complete (Mackay to Brown 18 April 1934). First, Mackay states that he would be happy to lead an American expedition to India. Second, Amri was his choice of sites, in fact, Mackay informs Brown, "...I have already applied for a concession to excavate this site, though as yet I have no money." He also discusses other Sindhi sites with potential for excavation such as Ali Murad, Ghazi Shah and Chanhu-daro and Nal in Baluchistan. Mackay recommended that Brown apply for permission to work at all of these sites "...making it clear, however, that the intention is not to seize upon them all but to look for one that is really worth excavating."

These sites had been excavated on a trial basis by N. G. Majumdar, but published only in a preliminary way in the annual reports of the Archaeological Survey of India and as snippets elsewhere. In a letter of April 18 Mackay offers some other tips to Brown on how he might go about making headway with the fabled Indian bureaucracy and he includes a budget of 3280 Pounds Sterling (about $17,000 at the time) for a five month field season. The sum included Mackay's salary.[35]

Money was a serious problem because of the Great Depression and Brown attempted to put together a consortium of museums that could undertake the project and share in the finds. In Brown to Mackay on May 25, 1934 we see that he had in mind the Museum of Fine Arts in Boston (possibly half the budget), the Metropolitan Museum of Art (also possibly half the budget), the Toledo Museum of Art (possibly $2500), the Worcester Museum of Art (possibly $2000) and The University Museum of the University of Pennsylvania (possibly $2000). He added: "If all these museums come in, we shall be embarrassed with too much money."

Brown's "agent" at the Museum of Fine Arts was Ananda Coomaraswamy, to whom he wrote on May 3, 1934, including a detailed six page proposal with Mackay's budget. This went to the "Museum Committee" of their trustees and on June 7, 1935 Brown appeared at their committee meeting and made his pitch. He must have been effective since they: "Voted that the museum appropriate $17,000 for one year's excavation at a site in the Indus Valley and at the end of the year it will consider whether it will be possible to continue" (Minutes of the Museum Committee, Museum of Fine Arts, June 7, 1934). The complete success of this trip must have been both a relief and a joy to Brown, buoying his confidence that this venture would be a success. The Museum Committee's action was reaffirmed by the full trustees of the museum on April 8, 1935, the same meeting at which the Museum of Fine Arts-University Museum joint excavations at Rayy, near Tehran, Iran were approved.

Thus, Boston became the only financial supporter of the proposed expedition to Sindh. All the other institutions were off the hook, but the Museum of Fine Arts became the sole beneficiary of this aid and the substantial collection of material from Chanhu-daro that they now possess is testimony to their foresight.

The Director of the Museum of Fine Arts at the time was Edward Jackson Holmes, grandson of poet Dr. Oliver Wendell Holmes and nephew of the justice of the same name. Securing the permit was not going to be easy and Director Holmes and his successor G. H. Edgell, gave strong support throughout the entire affair.

There was some behind the scenes side play in Boston when Harvard University got into the act. Langdon Warner, the explorer of Inner Asia, suggested to Holmes that Richard S. F. Starr, who had just excavated at the Mesopotamian site of Nuzi for Harvard, be incorporated into the Chanhu-daro excavation team (Warner to Holmes ca. 27 June 1934). He wanted to ensure that American archaeological knowhow would be represented along with its money. The all British excavation team at Ur, financed in a significant way by The University Museum, had been a source of some abrasion and Warner wanted to prevent a recurrence of this in India. For reasons that are not apparent, Starr was not included on the excavation, nor was any American in the field. Mr. Starr went on to Princeton where he wrote a dissertation on the painted pottery of the Indus Civilization (Starr 1941).

Brown opened negotiations with the Archaeological Survey of India as soon as he had his money: "Our plan, if we are granted permission to excavate Amri, is to operate during the full season of 1934-35" (Brown to Archaeological Survey of India, 18 June 1934). As it turned out this was pushing things a bit too fast and he had to go to India to get his excavation permit. He arrived on August 23, 1934 (he did not leave until 17 May 1935!) to begin the negotiations. Brown was a man of boundless enthusiasm and energy and one can imagine that he had plans for some research as well, but the year was mostly devoted to securing the permit to dig. The

American Council of Learned Societies paid for this part of the Chanhu-daro program, as part of its participation in the American School of Indic and Iranian Studies.

The Antiquities Law had been changed, but the rules for implementing it were not complete. This was finally accomplished by Notification F. 41-1/33 (Government of India 1934). Moreover, the American School was the first application and it would be the case to set precedents and get the bureaucracy thinking in terms of foreigners and archaeological excavation. The rules were published in *The Gazette of India* on 15 September (Government of India 1934: 1103-105), just as N. G. Majumdar's monograph *Explorations in Sind*[36] (Majumdar 1934) was becoming available. This book had a disagreeable revelation about Amri and on 11 September 1934 Brown sent the following telegraphic message to Mackay in England:

> Proofsheets Majumdar's report available today state Mohammadan graves top Amri mound, villagers objected excavation, he could only explore edges STOP Therefore chances our excavation imperiled STOP Would Chanhu-daro be acceptable, three seals found there STOP You cable facts your opinion Holmes Boston asking him cable me instructions Cecil Hotel Simla STOP We could ask option both sites. Brown (Brown to Mackay, 11 September 1934).

This revelation of the graves at Amri caused a flurry of correspondence between Simla, England and Boston that was finally settled when the Trustees of the Museum of Fine Arts left the choice of site to the men in the field, asking only that it be a place with a good chance of producing exhibitable works of art (Brown to Mackay 20 October 1934).[37] Chanhu-daro was Mackay's recommendation, made to Brown on 1 November 1934, two days after Majumdar's monograph on Sindh had reached him at home in England.[38] The formal application for excavation was duly amended to reflect the preference for Chanhu-daro and the process lumbered forward. At one time Brown called on the assistance of the Mr. E. C. Mieville, Private Secretary to Viceroy the Marquess of Willingdon to inch the elephant along.

By mid-December hopes for a 1934-35 field season were slipping away, although the permit seems to have been almost in hand. Brown to Mackay of 18 December states: "Is sufficient season left to justify starting excavation, cable care Maidens Hotel Delhi." Mackay to Brown of 19 December 1934 states: "If travel by P & O Rajputana nine weeks work possible STOP Perhaps fairer to Boston if start October, wier (sic) decision."

It was not until 3 April 1935 that the license is noted as granted. The Director General of the Survey at that time was Blakiston and he notes in a letter to Brown: "I do not see any special urgency in the matter of sending the license which I have already promised you. The license will probably have to be printed and it will in any case be given to you on your return to India or to Dr. Mackay as you may like when ready and before commencement of the work." Given the time and energy that Brown had put into securing this license, one might well wonder if he shared the same lackadaisical attitude that the Director General had in this matter.[39]

Prof. Brown left India from Bombay on 17 May 1935 and was in London on 10 June, when he wrote the following letter to Mackay:

> Please copy out and send to me the text of the Chanhu-daro license. But do not copy out the rules attached to the license. You might, however, compare the rules as there presented with the printed (gazetted) rules to see that they correspond. Here are copies of letters I am sending to India. Everything looks clear now. If any mail comes to me in your care, open it and act as circumstances indicate. With my best to both you and Mrs. Mackay.

THE CHANHU-DARO EXCAVATION

Mackay arrived at Chanhu-daro on 23 October 1935 to begin his excavations. Over the course of the field season he found evidence for a considerable amount of craft activity at the site, including the making of beads and square stamp seals. The Post-urban Harappan was also investigated, with the exposure of the Jhukar habitations. Later, materials of the so-called Jhangar and Trinhi Cultures were also discovered. These are still not well understood but Chanhu-daro remains the best documented excavation for their study, inadequate as that may be. Chanhu-daro is still an important site for understanding Harappan technology and the emergence of the Post-urban Harappan in Sindh.

Mackay and his wife Dorothy, also an author who dealt with the Indus Civilization (D. Mackay 1945), left British India for good, following the conclusion of the Chanhu-daro excavation. On 23 April 1936, they sailed from Karachi for England (Mackay 1943: i-ix). Mackay published a final report on Chanhu-daro (Mackay 1943) and several papers (Mackay 1935-36, 1936a, 1936b, 1937b, 1937c; see also Ghosh 1937; Brown 1938, 1939).

A young student of Indian archaeology, H. D. Sankalia, was at Chanhu-daro for almost a month during the excavation (Figure 2.42). Sankalia was to emerge as one of the giants of this field, but he departed from this project well before its conclusion (Mackay 1943: vii). In his autobiography Sankalia discusses his time there, which was not much to his liking (1978: 21-4). He had attended classes given by Sir Mortimer Wheeler at the University of London and had toured sites in England with him. This thoroughly imbued him with the necessity of three-dimensional recording and stratigraphic excavation. Since Mackay understood none of this, Sankalia was put off by the field methods he saw being employed at Chanhu-daro. Moreover, he was still quite young and he admits that he did not take full advantage of this special opportunity (see also Lal, Prof. B. B. 1989).[40]

Between January 19 and 28, 1936 Mackay had an American visitor as well. He was the young linguist, Murray B. Emeneau, whose work with Dravidian, especially the etymological dictionary he compiled with Thomas Borrow, would contribute to efforts to decipher the Indus script. Emeneau wanted to hear Brahui, and because many of Mackay's laborers spoke the language, Emeneau took this as a convenient opportunity to see an excavation in progress and to conduct his linguistic field work (Mackay 1943: vii; M. B. Emeneau, personal communication 1988).

Chanhu-daro produced evidence for the stratigraphic relationship between the Mature Harappan and the Post-urban Harappan, as well as more information on the still enigmatic Jhangar and Trinhi "cultures." But most important has been the insight into Harappan crafts that emerged from the discovery of bead- and seal-making facilities at the site (Plate 2.50, Plate 2.51, Plate 2.52, Plate 2.53).

Figure 2.42. Sketch of H. D. Sankalia

The Museum of Fine Arts Withdraws Financial Support

Boston's share of the finds from Chanhu-daro had reached the Museum of Fine Arts about June 1, 1936 and was immediately examined by their staff. While it is a fine collection of Indus material, including seals, some wonderful painted pottery, copper and bronze implements and important evidence for Harappan craftsmanship and technology, it is not exactly material that an internationally important art museum would be enthusiastic about. There was praise for Mackay's conduct of the excavation and his administration of the project, but there was no excitement about the finds. They were nice and the project was sound, but in the times of the Great Depression it was clear that priorities would have to be examined: Was Chanhu-daro worth supporting, given other potential projects?

The question was discussed by the Museum Committee in its meeting of 5 March 1936 and a decision put off to its April agenda. At this time it recommended: "...not to continue beyond the present season that work of the Indus Valley Expedition" (Minutes of the Museum Committee 5 March and 2 April 1936). Some of the competition for funds involved archaeological work in Iran. When Chanhu-daro was dropped as a project, the Museum of Fine Arts went to Persepolis on a joint project with the Oriental Institute at the University of Chicago.

How to Publish a Report on Chanhu-daro

The obligation to publish a report on the excavations became evident as Mackay began to send chapters of this document to Norman Brown in Philadelphia. It was a problem, because no provision had been made for it in Mackay's original budget of $17,000; typical for the field. In one letter, Director G. H. Edgell confesses that: "...I had forgotten about the publication of the Chanhu-daro material" (Edgell to Brown April 13, 1940), but he was a man of honor and would face up to this challenge, with Brown as a partner: "I have no sympathy with the museum that works for plunder alone..." (Edgell to Brown October 17, 1940). Another insight comes from a handwritten note at the top of the letter Brown sent to him with the budget of $4484.12 for the costs of the report. It reads: "This is one of the times that I wish that we had an adequate endowment for publications, as the museum undoubtedly shares with the American School of Indic and Iranian Studies the responsibility for publishing the results of the Chanhu-daro excavations" (on Brown to Edgell October 14, 1940).

In the end a deal was struck between Brown's "School," the Museum of Fine Arts, the American Council of Learned Societies (Anonymous 1941: 529) and the American Oriental Society to bring out the book. It appeared in 1943, when America and England were deep into World War II. Mackay acknowledges receipt of his ten author's copies in a letter to Brown dated June 19, 1943. Among those to whom he sent copies were Gordon Childe, Max Mallowan, Sidney Smith and his alma mater, Bristol University. Mackay died on October 2, 1943, an archaeologist who published everything he dug, a rare thing and something for which he can be admired.

Ernest J.H. Mackay, Chanhu-daro and Sir John Marshall

Toward the end of Mackay's tenure in British India there are signs of strain in his relationship with Sir John Marshall. There is nothing that documents this in a direct, or outlandish, way; life in the Survey was too gentlemanly for that, but indications abound. For example, in Marshall's great book on the excavations at Mohenjo-daro (Marshall 1931a), Mackay is virtually the only person to whom he directs a negative footnote. This can also be seen in the preliminary report on the Chanhu-daro excavations where Mackay suggests that the term "Harappa Culture" be substituted for "Indus Valley Civilization" (Mackay 1935-36: 39). The following appears as a footnote on the same page: "This suggestion of Dr. Mackay has not found favor among other scholars, notably Sir John Marshall—Editor." It can be chilly in the shadow of a giant!

In 1939 Sir John Cumming edited *Revealing India's Past*, a publication that can be seen as a tribute to Marshall and his years as Director General of the Survey. The strains between Marshall and Mackay are evident here as well. Mackay is, first of all, not a contributor. Moreover, his work is hardly mentioned; Chanhu-daro gets seven lines (Majumdar 1939: 108-09). His contribution to the excavations at Mohenjo-daro are dismissed with: "In 1926 the work at Mohenjo-daro was continued by Daya Ram Sahni and E. J. H. Mackay, and from 1927 to 1931 it was conducted by the latter" (Majumdar 1939: 102), and a bit later: "E. J. H. Mackay prepared a report of the later excavations..." (Majumdar 1939: 108).

There is no evidence that the basis for this strain was anything other than the personalities of two strong willed men. Mackay was an aggressive digger and scholar. He chose to publish his own syntheses of the Harappan Civilization in 1935 and this could be seen as rivaling Marshall's thoughts in *Mohenjo-daro and the Indus Civilization*. Marshall himself was generous in many ways, but he seems to have been a man who had a low tolerance for competitors and managed the Survey in a way that did not produce a true successor. Sir Mortimer Wheeler, in a biographical review of Marshall, repeats a phrase that has somehow become attached to the man: ...he was a tree under which nothing grew (Wheeler 1971: 699, see also Wheeler 1958).[41]

Sir John's relationship with Sir Aurel Stein was also strained from its beginning in 1904. But, Stein was a giant, with an international reputation. Mackay was just a good field man. While both Stein and Marshall went to great lengths to present a public face of politeness, it is clear that this was a facade. Once more, two ambitious, energetic men, sharing interests, having to work together within the confines of a small institution, is not necessarily a good mix. This aspect of Stein's life is nicely captured in Mirsky's biography (1977: 214-17).

SIR AUREL STEIN'S GREAT SURVEYS

Sir Mark Aurel Stein was one of the world's greatest archaeologists (Figure 2.43). His explorations in British India, Iran and Chinese Turkestan are a record of discovery unparalleled by any other archaeologist. The fabulous discoveries he made in China lie outside the scope of this book, but are his crowning achievements. More modest perhaps, but to the professional just as important, are his explorations in British India, and their later extension into Iran. These too, are filled with remarkable discoveries, especially for the understanding of the Protohistory of this region. They did not, however, produce the vast

Figure 2.43. Sketch of Sir Aurel Stein

treasure of art and documents that came from Turkestan and have consequently taken a back seat to those flashier finds. Stein's achievements were justly rewarded, but not without some trial.[42] The exploration of British India undertaken by him has an episodic quality. It can be seen from afar as having a structure, but it did not come together as a single piece of work. The work began in 1904-05 (Stein 1905) with a hasty reconnaissance on the borderlands when he visited Bannu and Mahhaban in the Northwest Frontier (1905: 4-10, 19-34), Dabar Kot near Duki (1905: 53), sites in Pishin and the mound of Nal in Kalat. The complex story of the famous Nal site in Kalat is available in the summary of the excavations there. J. Mirsky reveals that Sir John Marshall *sent* Stein to Nal in 1904 (Mirsky 1977: 215-16), but the visit is not mentioned in either Marshall's report on Nal pottery (Marshall 1904-05) or in H. Hargreaves' report on his excavations there in 1925 (Hargreaves 1929). Stein returned to Nal in April 1928, and camped there for two nights (Stein 1931: 166-67), yet he makes no reference to having been at the site before. In any event, the hasty tour of 1904-05 was overshadowed by his more detailed research in the region and in retrospect can be seen as a prelude to the important explorations.

There were three tours in the western borderlands of Pakistan that formed a chain of passage for the explorer, stretching from northern Swat, deep within the Hindu Kush, down the spine of the Northwest Frontier and Baluchistan to the border of Pakistan and Iran near the coast of the Arabian Sea. These can be catalogued as follows:

Swat Tour   :   9 March to 16 May 1926
Waziristan Tour :   16 January to 12 April 1927
Gedrosia Tour   :   28 November 1927 to 15 April 1928

A brief synopsis of these tours provides a picture of Stein's accomplishments.

The Tour of Swat

Stein calls Swat one of his happiest field experiences (1930: 104), but he was a mountain man and Swat is one of the most dramatic, picturesque places in the world. The people were friendly and helpful and the work went well. Alexander the Great's eastern campaign was one of his favorite topics and Swat gave him an opportunity to contribute to this aspect of South Asian scholarship (Stein 1927, 1928b, 1928c, 1929b, 1932, 1937: 1-44, 1943b). Stein moved north from Peshawar all the way to Kalam at the far end of the Swat Valley, and then on a wide loop to the east to investigate stupas and a place called Pir-sar. During this tour he explored Udegram, one of the cities that the great Macedonian visited and most important, he found the citadel of Aornos, at the modern Pir-sar, that had been besieged by the Greeks. Swat was a major Buddhist center and important new information on stupas and monasteries resulted from this work. Actually, there are two reports on the tour: the first, a report on Alexander's campaign (Stein 1929b); the second, an archaeological memoir, more descriptive of his finds (Stein 1930). There is little Protohistory in the formal report, but the Italian Archaeological Mission to Swat has followed his pioneering explorations with much more intensive work and has found that there were Neolithic and Bronze Age settlements in the valley which have a bearing on the Harappan Civilization.

The Tour of Waziristan

Stein made a proposal to explore the mountainous valleys of Waziristan while on home leave in May 1925. The name comes from the Waziri tribe of the region. He began in Dera Ismail

Khan, on the Indus and covered Bannu, as well as Zhob and Loralai Districts, ending at Quetta (Stein 1929a, Figure 2.44). This region of Pakistan is filled with sites of the Chalcolithic Age, and Stein was the first to record many of them. His most impressive triumphs were the first serious investigations at Periano Ghundai, Rana Ghundai, Sur Jangal, Kaudani, Moghul Ghundai and Dabar Kot. The German scholar Dr. Fritz Noetling, with the Geological Survey of India, had visited Periano Ghundai in 1897 as well as Rana Ghundai and Dabar Kot in 1898 (1898a, 1898b, 1899), but had not excavated any of them.

Dabar Kot is a huge site in the hills of Loralai District. It appears that there is a full-fledged Mature Harappan occupation, that lies near the base of the mound. Stein did not have a natural liking for prehistoric materials, nor was he a patient excavator (Krishna Deva 1982: 393; see also Stein 1931: 4), but he wrote an enthusiastic letter to Marshall about Dabar Kot: we found "...layers upon layers of debris marking occupation from prehistoric times onward. The materials for the study of successive types of painted pottery were abundant. Structural remains, all in stamped clay or mud bricks were difficult to interpret; but beside them we found a well-made drain of big bricks, recalling in a small way what I saw at Mohenjo-daro" (Archaeological Survey of India, 16 March 1927; Mirsky 1977: 452). There was also a small stupa at Dabar Kot. When Stein excavated it he found a relic casket sitting on the living rock, with small gems set in gold along with pearls. Inscribed pottery, with both the Brahmi and Kharosthi scripts, were Kushan in type and demonstrate the spread of their influence into Baluchistan. The stupa at Dabar Kot and the one on the Mound of the Great Bath at Mohenjo-daro are probably contemporary.

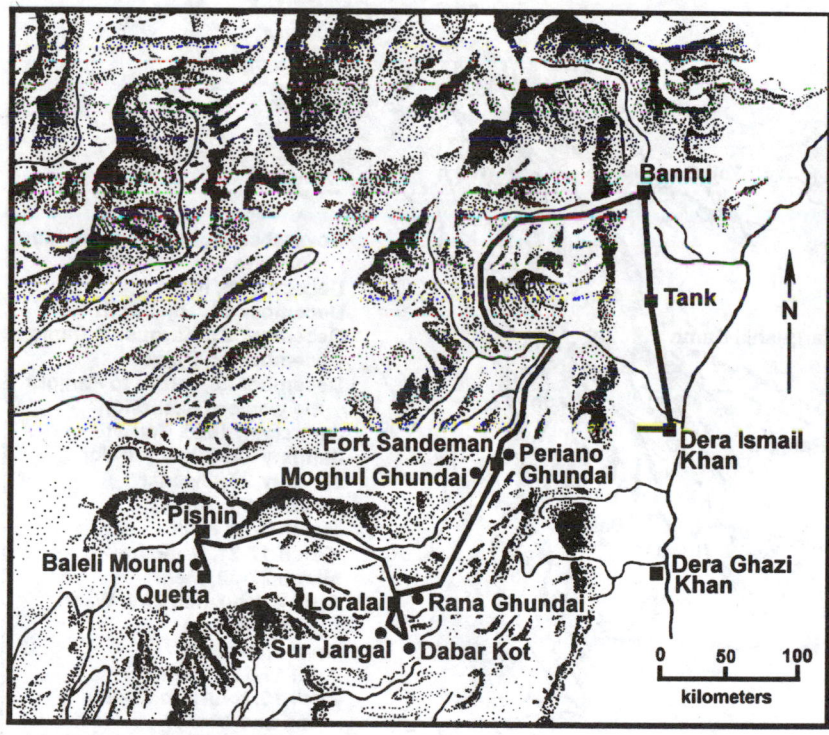

January 11, 1927, arrival in
    Dera Ismail Khan
January 14, move to Tank
January 16, Bannu area
January 26, Fort Sandeman
February 26, Rana Ghundai
February 27–March 8, excavation at
    Dabar Kot
March 17-20 excavation at
    Sur Jangal
March 30, arrival in Pishin
April 12, collecting at Baleli Mound
    and end of tour in Quetta

Sur Aurel Stein's Waziristan Tour, 1927
After Stein 1929

Figure 2.44. Sketch map of Stein's Waziristan tour

The Tour of Gedrosia

The tour of Gedrosia, the Greek name for southern Baluchistan and Makran, was Stein's most productive on the Indo-Iranian borderlands. He began on 28 November 1927, in Quetta where the Waziristan tour had ended and worked his way south to Kalat and Surab, then west to the Rakhshan Valley (Figure 2.45). A direct march over the Central Makran Range took him south to the market center of Turbat, Miri Qalat and the site of Shahi Tump, near the great river intersection of the Makran, where the Nihang and Kej join to form the Dasht River. A "detour" to Sutkagen-dor and burial cairns on the coast preceded his procession up the Kej Valley to Kolwa and the mound of Kulli. From there it was north, up the "stair-step" mountains of Kalat, to Mehi, Nal, a detour into Wadh and Drakalo, then home to Quetta.

Stein excavated six sites on this tour that lie within the scope of this book:[43] Kargushki Damb, Kulli, Mehi, Nundara (Siah Damb), Shahi Tump and Sutkagen-dor. In the course of his reconnaissance he defined the Kulli Complex, now seen as the highland manifestation of the Mature Harappan (Possehl 1986a) and revealed a new, and still not well understood, Nal phase at Nundara. At Shahi Tump he found Bronze Age burials, apparently cut into a Kulli habitation site. The curious Shahi Tump Gray Ware, associated with tall cups shaped like modern beer glasses, and rotund jars of the same coarse buff fabric. For years the chronology of Shahi Tump eluded our chronological grasp, but the French research team working with the Italians in Makran is now

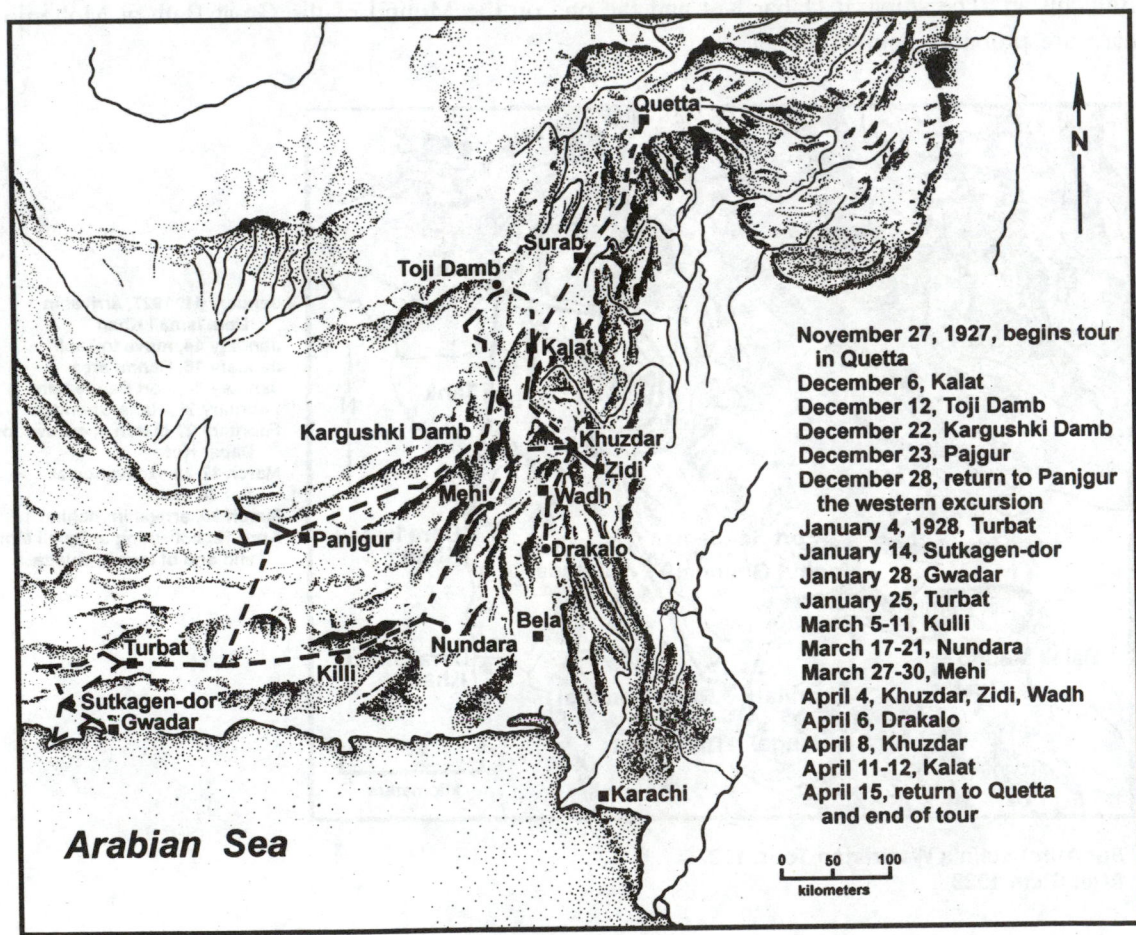

Figure 2.45. Sketch map of Sir Aurel Stein's Gedrosia tour

sorting this out (Besenval 1992; Besenval and Sanlaville 1990; Besenval and Marquis 1993). Stein's record of success is an admirable one, especially in only four and a half month's work.

Stein's excavation methods are antiquated by modern standards, and he seldom used a spade with a sense of scientific problem orientation or for specific goals. Nor did he seek virgin soil, except when he suddenly came upon it. At times he employed large numbers of workers; 90 in his three day excavation of Mehi (Stein 1931: 153). These deficiencies, along with a lack of section drawings, drawings of his ceramics and the preliminary nature of his work in the Indo-Iranian Borderlands have meant that it is often difficult to evaluate his research. But, it is equally clear that he recorded some spectacular archaeological sites, many, perhaps most, of which have not been revisited by any other archaeologist since the Stein era.

Stein's Other Tours in the Subcontinent

Two other reconnaissance projects that Stein undertook in the Subcontinent have a bearing on our understanding of the Harappan Civilization. The first took place in 1940-41 along the now dry Ghaggar-Hakra River, known in ancient times as the Sarasvati. The second tour was in 1943 and covered Las Bela and southern Gedrosia. Las Bela is a rich valley fronting the Arabian Sea just west of Karachi. On both of these exploratory tours Stein was accompanied by Krishna Deva of the Archaeological Survey of India, who had been with Majumdar in October and November 1938, during his final reconnaissance.

The Sarasvati Tour

The Sarasvati tour began on 17 December 1940 when Stein arrived in Bikaner City (Figure 2.46). The exploratory phase ended on 11 March 1941 with his departure from Bahawalpur. He was back for a short tour in December 1941 and January 1942, when he excavated three sites: Kalepar, Ahmedwala Ther and Kudwala Ther. Neither of these two phases of work was ever fully published by Stein. He died in Kabul on 26 October 1943. There is a preliminary report (Stein 1943a) which is a typescript, without a map, or illustrations (also published as Gupta 1989, with additional notes). The return visit to the Sarasvati in 1941-42 is not mentioned in the 1943a manuscript, where Stein says of Kalepar: "I fully realized the opportunity which this site offered for fruitful trial excavation; but the difficulty of collecting adequate labor from the scattered camps of graziers without great loss of time was obvious...So I felt reluctantly obliged to leave this tempting task for some future investigator..." (1943a: 120)

Stein recorded fifty-eight prehistoric sites and notably, the early historic, (Kushan Period) mound at

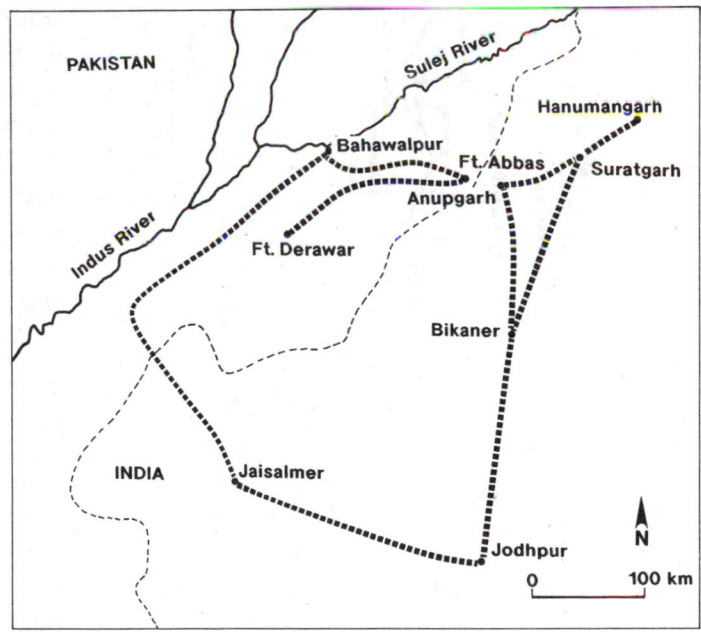

Figure 2.46. Sketch map of Stein's 1940-41 survey of the Lost Sarasvati

106

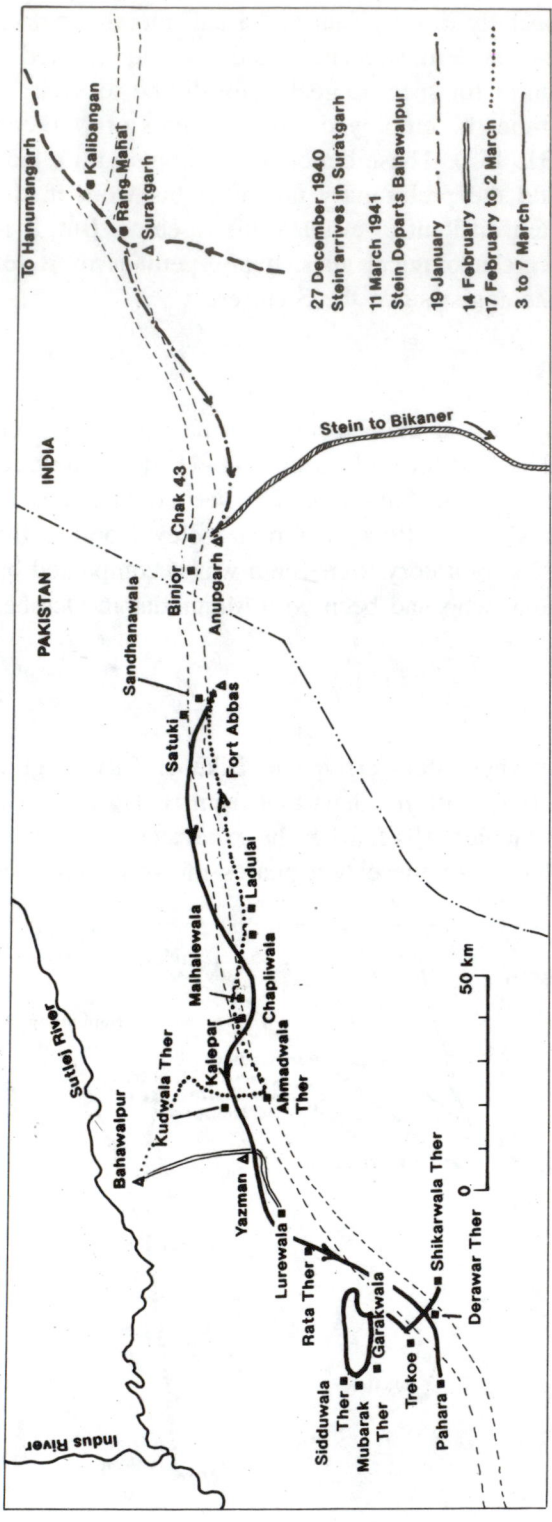

27 December 1940
Stein arrives in Suratgarh

11 March 1941
Stein Departs Bahawalpur

19 January — · — · —
14 February — ·· — ·· —
17 February to 2 March ········
3 to 7 March ————

Stein to Bikaner

To Hanumangarh

Kalibangan
Rang Mahal
Suratgarh

INDIA

PAKISTAN

Binjor — Chak 43
Anupgarh
Sandhanawala
Satuki
Fort Abbes

Ladulai

Malhalewala
Chapliwala
Kalepar
Ahmadwala Ther
Kudwala Ther

Sutlej River

Bahawalpur

Yazman

Lurewala
Rata Ther
Sidduwala Ther
Mubarak Ther
Garakwala
Trekoe
Pahara
Shikarwala Ther
Derawar Ther

50 km

0

Indus River

Figure 2.47. Detail of Stein's route along the Lost Sarasvati

Rang Mahal. His finds on the Sarasvati were sufficiently important that, in spite of the lack of publication, other researchers were drawn back into the area. His notes on places like Trekoe, Kalepar, Sandhanwala Ther and Kalibangan were again, pioneering observations (Figure 2.47).

In her biography, Mirsky (1977: 539-40) notes that Stein did return to this region: in (Stein to Mrs. Allen, 10 November 1942) he states, "I propose to go down to Bahawalpur about the beginning of December & hope to be free for the move to Las Bela in early January." This was clearly the plan for phase two on the Ghaggar-Hakra. Mirsky also located a report by Krishna Deva in which he says that Stein and he had excavated Trekoe, Kalepar and Sandhanwala Ther (Archaeological Survey of India, Krishna Deva to Dikshit, 24 January 1943).

Tracking Stein on the Ghaggar-Hakra Survey, and gaining some sense of the chronology for his sites, has been made easier by later work, that also sampled the settlements he visited, but sometimes with different names! (Figure 2.48). These later explorations were undertaken on the Indian side of the border by A. Ghosh of the Archaeological Survey of India in 1950-53 (Ghosh 1952, 1953b, 1956, 1959, 1989b) (Figure 2.49).

Dr. Katie Feroz Dalal (Frenchman), a PhD student at Deccan College, followed in Ghosh's steps in 1970, with some additional research in the region, including an excavation at Binjor One (Dalal 1980).

Ghosh's Pakistani colleague, M. Rafique Mughal surveyed sites in Bahawalpur Division between 1974 and 1978. Their work provides important information needed to understand Stein's manuscript. For example, we know that Stein's wares from the key site of Kalepar are what Mughal calls Early Harappan (equivalent to Ghosh's "Sothi" found in the earliest settlement at Kalibangan). Kalepar is also known as "Bhoot," meaning "ghost;" appropriate for an archaeological site!

107

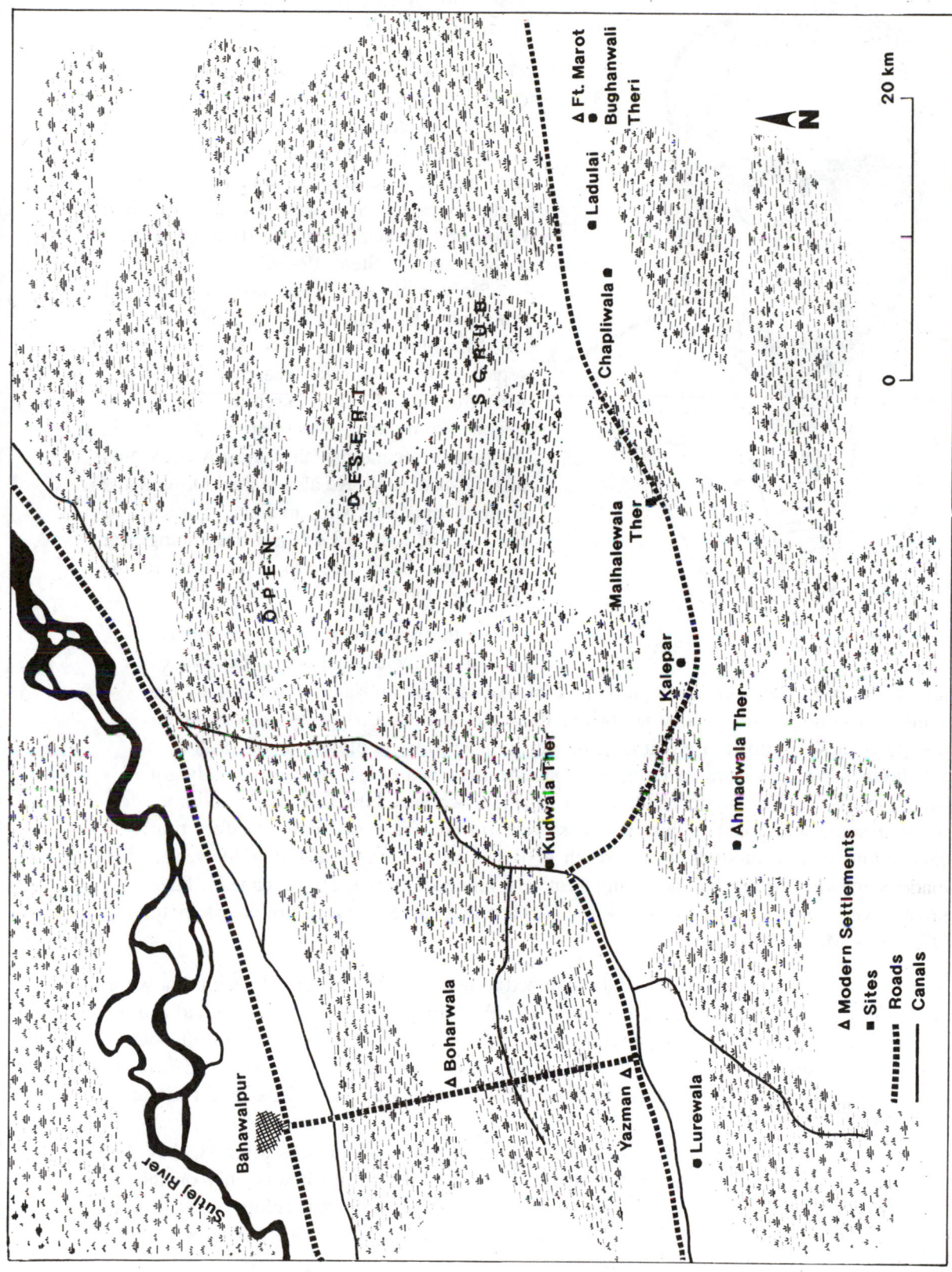

Figure 2.48. Some of Stein's sites in Cholistan

108

Figure 2.49. Sketch of A. Ghosh

The Tour of Las Bela and Southern Gedrosia

The exploration of Las Bela and Southern Gedrosia was a minor affair compared to Stein's other forays into the field. But he was eighty-one years old and, while he loved his time in the country, he was no longer as vigorous as he once was. There is no final report on this small tour, but Stein did prepare a short article (Stein 1943b).

Sir Aurel was back on the track of Alexander. He wanted to trace the route that the Macedonian army had taken when it separated from Admiral Nearchus and headed west from Las Bela, through the Makran for Persia. From January to March 1943 he did his best to reconstruct this ancient track, and largely succeeded. He also visited Ormara and some of his "old" sites in Jhau, first seen on the 1927-28 tour of Gedrosia. Beginning near Bela City, Stein describes the tour to the Director General:

...the first few days' survey suffice to allow us to trace a number of ancient sites in the vicinity. Reserving trial excavations for later, I set out to the southwest mainly with a view to tracing the exact route followed by Alexander on his march into Gedrosia, thus linking up our tour with my explorations of 1928-29[44] in Makran. We first went to Ormara on the Arabian Sea coast, then up the Hingol Valley to Jhau in Jhalan (sic. Jhalawan GLP) and hence back here to Bela. In addition, in Jhau some additional prehistoric sites were traced. We now hope to effect trial excavations at two mounds within reach of Bela. Altogether these four odd weeks, made somewhat trying by increasing heat and mode of travel, all on camels, have proved very instructive in many ways (Archaeological Survey of India, Stein to Dikshit, 4 March 1943).

The two sites he excavated in Las Bela included a mound of the historical period known as Karia Pir, and a prehistoric settlement called Niai Buthi. Donald E. McCown, who had a brush with archaeology in this region, prepared a manuscript on the pottery from Niai Buthi, which seems to have vanished (McCown 1946b). Walter Fairservis was back in Bela in 1959-60 and did some further work at Niai Buthi. He determined that it was part of the Kulli Complex (Fairservis 1961b) (Plate 2.54).

Stein died in Kabul, Afghanistan on October 26, 1943, twenty-four days after Mackay died in England. It had been Stein's dream to explore this remote land, and it was only on the eve of his death that the needed time and permissions were available. The best eulogy to Stein is by his old friend, and tax collector, C. E. A. W. Oldham (1944), with whom Stein had spent a pleasant time on a 1899 visit to Gaya (Mirsky 1977: 100).

SIR AUREL STEIN: Summary

Stein's contribution to the archaeology of India and Pakistan was immense, rivaling that of Sir Alexander Cunningham and Sir John Marshall. Krishna Deva tells us that he was "proud of his association with the Archaeological Survey of India" and "wedded to field exploration" (1982: 392). Being a man without a family he had the freedom, both personal and financial, to pursue these desires and he made the most of this opportunity. While his excavation methods may have lacked finesse, he was a gifted writer, able to bring his finds alive for a broad audience and to explain complex historical and geographical matters in a graphically simple prose.

While there is little doubt that Stein and Marshall had a strained relationship, they also found it possible to contain this emotion. Marshall knew that the overall mission of his Survey was enhanced by Sir Aurel's presence and the magnificent reports he produced on his exploration. On his side Stein was also aware that Marshall's goodwill was necessary if he was to keep working in peace, and for financial support to keep him in the field and to publish his monographs. Thus, Marshall's retirement, in the middle of Stein's great Baluchistan tour, cannot pass without notice.

SIR JOHN MARSHALL AND THE INDUS CIVILIZATION

To understand the continuing developments in the archaeology of the Indus Age, and archaeology in British India generally, requires some sense of Sir John Marshall, his tremendous presence in the field and his apparent success as the head of the Archaeological Survey of India. By 1931, there was a kind of paradigm that had developed for this extraordinary body of material and the two cities from which it had been derived. This early synthesis was largely the creation of Marshall himself, but was expanded upon by both Ernest Mackay and V. Gordon Childe. Sir Mortimer Wheeler and Stuart Piggott challenged this interpretation in more than a minor way, and theirs in turn has come under some critical comment in more recent years. Therefore, some attention to the progress of our "imaging" of the Indus peoples in their historical context is necessary.

Marshall's Paradigm for the Indus Civilization

Marshall put forth his synthesis of the Harappan Civilization in the opening chapters of his monumental work *Mohenjo-daro and the Indus Civilization* (1931a). His first concern was for the physical environment and he proposed, along with others of his time (Huntington 1924; de Terra and Hutchinson 1936: 9), that the climate was different during the Bronze Age in Pakistan and northwestern India. Marshall supported this with the following evidence: 1) baked bricks were used as protection against heavier rainfall, 2) street drains were used to carry off the rainwater, and would not be needed under today's dry conditions, 3) the lion, a dry country animal, may be completely absent in the representations of animals. Finally, Sir Aurel Stein had found the remains of flourishing Bronze Age communities in Baluchistan that led him to conclude that there was a substantially larger population in this region during those times. Stein attributed this in large part to a wetter climate (Stein 1931: 131-32). His position was supported by V. Gordon Childe with this observation: "The lavish use of baked brick in prehistoric cities would seem a needless extravagance under modern rainless conditions" (1934: 205). The climate of these ancient times is still a matter of some debate, but does not seem to have been either markedly wetter, or drier during Harappan times. The best critical assessment of this portion of the Marshall paradigm was done by Robert Raikes and Robert Dyson (1961).

On the cultural side he saw a striking uniformity at Mohenjo-daro and Harappa. "Though these two spots are some four hundred miles apart, their monuments and antiquities are to all intents and purposes identical" (Marshall 1931a: 91, cf. 102-03). Once again, Childe concurs: "...astonishingly homogenous...The agreement is so complete that every remark in the subsequent description would apply equally to either site...(Childe 1934: 205-06).

Marshall went on to say that the Harappans were just as individual (interestingly, he used the term "national" in this context) as the other civilizations, shown by the character of the domestic architecture and monuments like the Great Bath. The "remarkably naturalistic quality" of Indus art is another feature, but so is the painted pottery. The use of cotton, instead of flax and the quality of the writing system were also seen as unique, national markers for the Indus (Marshall 1931h: 95). "But behind these and manifold other traits that are peculiar to the Indus civilization and give it its national character, is a tissue of ideas, inventions and discoveries which were common property of the then civilized world and cannot be traced to their respective sources" (1931h: 95). These shared features included: domestication of animals; cultivation of wheat, barley and other grains; growing of fruits; irrigation by canals; building of houses; organization of society in cities; spinning and weaving of textiles and dying them in various colors; the use of the potter's wheel and the decoration of wares; river navigation; the use of wheeled vehicles; the working of metals; writing; fashioning of ornaments from faience, ivory, bone, shell and semiprecious stones (Marshall 1931h: 95).

The Harappan Civilization was centered in Sindh and the Punjab, but he did not think of the two metropolitan centers as "twin capitals." There was some evidence for an extension of the civilization into Saurashtra (Kathiawar for him), although there was sparse evidence available from the east, since little work was done there. It is interesting to see that he thought in terms of a diffusion of the Harappan Civilization from Sindh to the west, into Baluchistan (Marshall 1931b: 2, 1931h: 96).

The script was much like other quasi-pictographic scripts of the era, but its similarity had misled those who wished to decipher it. Four attempts, each using another of the scripts, (Sumerian, Proto-Elamite, Minoan and Hittite) as a model had failed by 1931 and Marshall cautioned against the use of this methodology (1931e: 41).

He found no reason to connect the language of the Indus people with Sanskrit, or its culture with the Aryans. In fact, he argued forcefully, and correctly, that the Indus Civilization was earlier than the Vedic Period and that these cultures were the products of different peoples. Marshall, speaking on the Harappan language, said that so vast an area probably contained the native speakers of more than one language (1931e: 42) but that it was likely that these were within the Dravidian group.

Marshall's discussion of Indus religion was the longest and most complex of all his statements on these ancient peoples. (Marshall 1931f; also Marshall 1931g). He saw a cult of the Great Mother Goddess evidenced by figurines, some of which were toys, and others votive offerings, or less likely, cult images for household shrines (1931f: 50), with parallels in Western Asia and the Aegean. Tribal society in twentieth century India suggested to him that this practice was pre-Aryan. There was a great Male God, Pasupati or the Proto-Siva (1931f: 52-3); a position that is not universally accepted today (Srinivasan 1975-76, 1984; but see Sullivan 1964 and McEvilley 1981). He saw evidence for the worship of icons or gods on seals also, and concluded that the Indus people not only anthropomorphized their gods but worshipped cult images of them as well.

The most interesting and provocative insight offered with regard to these two sets of Harappan deities is Marshall's guarded and qualified suggestion that they represent the beginnings of Saktism:

> The underlying principle of saktism is a sexual dualism, which has been aptly described as 'duality in unity.' In this development of the primitive mother worship, the goddess was transformed into a personification of female energy (*śakti*) and, as the eternal productive principle, (*prakṛiti*), united with the eternal male principle (*purusha*) and became the creator and Mother of the Universe (*Jaganmata* or *Jagad-amba*), including the gods themselves (Marshall 1931f: 57).

This position has been forgotten in many attempts to understand the Indus belief system, but has considerable merit as a beginning point. Once again, Marshall finds some evidence for this in the Western Asian Bronze Age (1931f: 57-8).

There were also three kinds of cult stones at Mohenjo-daro and Harappa: the phallic, baetylic and the *yoni* ring stones. Larger phallic and baetylic stones were intended for worship; the smaller ones were amulets for carrying on the person. Rebirth and, by implication, an absolution of sin was achieved by physically going through a *yoni* ring stone (1931f: 58-63). Evidence for the worship of natural phenomena, trees, animals and water, was also introduced by Marshall.

Mackay in his book on the Harappans, *The Indus Civilization* (1935), which was revised by his wife Dorothy Mackay in 1948 and reissued with the title *Early Indus Civilizations*, presents a far more descriptive image of these peoples. His insights, some of which have great charm (e.g. the wear on the corners of buildings at Mohenjo-daro caused by the passing of people and animals, the polish on the floors of the baths in individual houses) do not even seek to deal with issues that Marshall discussed. Two Mackay notes are, however, contributions to what I have termed the "Marshall Paradgim":

> "Although in the material used and in the stability and carefulness of their construction these burnt-brick cities were certainly the equal to any later work found in India or elsewhere, they are far from remarkable for beauty, refinement, or decorative value. One house is so like another, with its plain, unrelieved walls, that to the modern eye something seems sadly lacking in the mental and spiritual equipment of the builders. Except for floods and occasional raids, there must have been little to upset the humdrum routine of these busy communities of traders, a state of affairs which doubtless brought about the atrophy of the artistic sensibilities of their members" (Mackay 1948: 49-50).

The thought that peaceful Harappan burghers were so consumed with commerce and profit that other parts of their culture atrophied is first presented by Mackay. His second note is of the bronze dancing girl from Mohenjo-daro:

> "...remarkable bronze figure...found by Rai Bahadur Daya Ram Sahni. The dancer, who from her features is obviously an aboriginal type, may represent the predecessor of the dancing-girls (*devadasis*) who are attached to so many temples in modern India. The status of these girls is considered quite an honorable one..." and the ancient bronze "...may represent a temple-dancer of Mohenjo-daro" (Mackay 1948: 73).

V. Gordon Childe, the preeminent interpreter of ancient civilizations joined the Marshall Paradigm in his *New Light on the Most Ancient East* with the following:

"No multiplication of weapons of war and battle-scenes attest the futile conflicts between city-states as in Babylonia nor yet the force whereby a single king, as in Egypt, achieved by conquest internal peace and warded off jealous nomads by constant preparedness.

We cannot even define the nucleus round which accumulated the surplus wealth of capital involved in the conversion of the village into the city. Neither sumptuous temples, as in Sumer, nor monumental tombs, as on the Nile, serve to mark out the divine or deified disposer of this surplus without any need of appeal to written documents...one can indeed distinguish between industrial and commercial quarters, between the lowly abodes of artisans and shopkeepers and the larger mansions of prosperous burghers. But no temple nor palace dominates the rest though the total areas excavated would compare favorably with those explored in Mesopotamia. The visitor inevitably gets an impression of a democratic bourgeois economy, as in Crete, in contrast to the obviously centralized theocracies and monarchies hitherto described. Yet that there was an efficient and enduring authority is clear enough. The cities were carefully laid out on a deliberate plan, and the plan was adhered to strictly during several phases of reconstruction so that the streets were always maintained at a constant width. The cities were provided with elaborate corbelled drains, running to sumps...(1934: 207-08).

There is little or no mention of warfare, or internecine conflict in Marshall's account of the Harappans. Nor, with the exception of religion, does he dwell on the great institutions of Harappan life: the details of politics, economics and the social fabric of the peoples themselves. In this sense, the presentation is weak, but then so was the data set and the conceptual framework within which Marshall would have found himself as a man of his times.

There are three things that come through in Marshall's essays as theoretical positions, that were largely implicitly held. First, the Harappan Civilization was a member of a class of civilizations, most closely related to Sumer and the Proto-Elamites. It was "natural" that parallels would be found because of geography and this close relationship. Although it was not sufficiently close for the Harappans to be termed "Indo-Sumerian" the connection was real and important. He even included a simple list of finds that indicated close contact between the Indus and the Tigris-Euphrates (Marshall 1931h: 103-05). There was a continuity between the twentieth century and these distant peoples and he was justified in using historical and ethnographic observations to further his understanding of the Indus peoples. It also helped him to interpret the language and ethnic or biological diversity of the Indus population. Finally, Marshall was a scholar with a commitment to the epistemology of his field. We are not presented with a *fait accomplis* in terms of his propositions concerning the Harappans, but rather a reasoned argument, backed by a sophisticated use of other peoples work and insights. Even when he is wrong, as in the case for a wetter climate, Marshall offers his reasons for believing as he does, and this is a trait of considerable scholarly merit—certainly not found in all discourse on this civilization, even today.

In spite of some limitations *Mohenjo-daro and the Indus Civilization* is an extraordinary report on an archaeological site, especially if judged against the standards of its day. First, it is thorough. There are full reports on the technical and scientific side of archaeology with separate articles written by experts on the fauna, flora, human remains, metals and the like. Second, it is both a descriptive and empirical report on the excavations as well as a synthetic work, one that seeks to relate the facts of the excavation to a larger set of ideas that give real meaning to the stones and bones. Combining descriptions and ideas in this way is an art and Marshall should be given a great deal of credit for orchestrating his three volumes in such a way as to hold these two levels of thought separate from each other in order to keep "fact" from "fiction." While it is true that Mohenjo-daro was not excavated on a stratigraphic basis, and this was a method current by 1920, the report on the excavation is ahead of its time in many ways which speaks well of the Archaeological Survey of India and its leadership.

Marshall's Retirement and the Crisis of Management

Sir John Marshall was an extraordinarily successful Director General of the Archaeological Survey. The discovery of the Harappan Civilization is one part of this success, important in its own right, but he had accomplished much more. The Survey traditionally devotes at least half of its resources to conservation, a fact which has, so far, received scant attention in this story of the discovery of the Harappan Civilization. On this front, Marshall cleared a shanty town surrounding the Taj Mahal. Similar efforts had been made at Fatehpur Sikri, Sanchi, tombs of the Mughal Emperors and South Indian tombs, temples and palaces. Hundreds of monuments of all types and different ages had been cleared of debris, structurally stabilized, gardens laid out and planted. Some derelict structures had even been brought back to function within the Indian economy. The Survey found that "living" buildings rather than uninhabited "museums" were better maintained, and thus survived longer. Marshall had developed a works code and published a pamphlet (Marshall 1907), then a book, on the principles of conservation (Marshall 1923a). Millions of rupees had been spent to preserve thousands of years of Indian history. This is the task that occupied most of the Director General's time and took most of his energy and resources. Marshall also had some great success, comparable to Mohenjo-daro and Harappa, in other excavations. At Taxila, he exposed (and conserved) nine hectares (22 acres) of the ancient Sirkap Mound as well as working at the earlier Bhir Mound, and later Sirsukh settlement. The Jaulian Monastery was also excavated, conserved and published along with the Dharmarajika Stupa. The Taxila project was a huge undertaking; Mohenjo-daro pales in comparison. There were also significant excavations at many other places. A short list includes:

Besnagar: one of the longest lived centers of Indian culture in Madhya Bharat with evidence for occupation from Chalcolithic times through the present. The city is also the location of the famous Heliodorus Pillar.

Brahmanabad (Mansura): the great Medieval city in Sindh.

Hampi: the ceremonial center of the Vijayanagara Empire in Karnataka.

Mathura: one of the cultural centers of the Kushan Empire. There is evidence for occupation at Mathura from the Iron Age (Painted Grey Ware) to the present.

Nagarjunakonda: a great Buddhist center on the Krishna river in Andhra Pradesh. There is evidence for occupation from Early Historical through Medieval times.

Pagan: once a capital of Burma with hundreds of Buddhist monuments.

Rajgir: capital of the Mauryan Empire.

Sanchi: one of the earliest and most important Buddhist centers. There is a large stupa, and associated monastic complex. This is one of the most beautifully conceived and decorated set of monuments in the Subcontinent.

Sarnath: site of the Buddha's first sermon, it is also the site of an Ashokan pillar and stupa, and many later structures. There is evidence for occupation from Mauryan times through the Medieval period.

Takht-i Bahi: a magnificent hilltop Buddhist monastery overlooking the confluence of the Indus and Kabul Rivers. This excavation revealed some of the most beautiful Gandharan sculpture ever to come to light.

Site museums were also a Marshall innovation. He had been exposed to them as a young scholar in Greece, where these institutions were first built. In British India they were established at Mohenjo-daro, Harappa, Taxila, Sarnath and Nalanda. These were to come under fire, when Sir Leonard Woolley undertook his evaluation of the Survey in 1938-39. But, in spite of Woolley's recommendation they were not closed or so reduced in scope that they were no longer museums. These galleries and repositories are a tribute to Marshall's intelligence and farsighted perspective on the need to serve the interests of the regions where he excavated.

The Epigraphic section of the Archaeological Survey of India is a story in and of itself. In the Marshall years they prospered and many hundreds of inscriptions were found, recorded and published.

In the end, we have to see Marshall as a giant. Whatever his weak points, his accomplishments were immense. He excavated and published his work. He instituted a national conservation program and built site museums. He made a concerted effort to recruit and train Indians, who were then integrated into Marshall's programs. He took the Archaeological Survey of India from a small bureaucracy, in 1902, and built it into a large, capable organization, the first example of massive state sponsored archaeology in the world. He did this through his own genius, and his ability to raise money.

It is widely recognized that Marshall was supported by Viceroys and their advisers, but he created the atmosphere that made them see that this support was in their best interests. The world economy, and thus tax revenues, were also healthy during the Marshall years. There was money to be spent on culture and history. The coincidence of his success with this prosperity cannot be dismissed, but it is not the only reason for it.

In some ways, Marshall might even be seen as having been too successful, too much the great man, perhaps indispensable in the minds of some. But, he had to retire and decisions had to be made concerning leadership in the Survey. There is evidence that the process was difficult and led to ambiguity in the highest office of the Survey. There was no clear leader and the people who occupied the office of Director General were compromised in terms of their ability to be decisive.

The *Annual Report of the Archaeological Survey of India, 1927-28* contains a brief review of Sir John Marshall's tenure of 26 years as Director General, written by his friend and colleague Harold Hargreaves (Hargreaves 1927-28: 1-3). Marshall retired from the position of Director General in September 1928 when "...he was placed on Special Duty in order to provide him with an opportunity of writing and publishing the materials collected by the Archaeology Department and himself during this long period of office" (Hargreaves 1927-28: 1). Hargreaves tells us that Marshall planned to write the reports on Mohenjo-daro, Harappa and Taxila, and on the monuments of Sanchi, Mandu, Delhi, Agra and Multan (Hargreaves 1927-28: 1). Marshall continued his monumental excavations at Taxila and must have begun editing *Mohenjo-daro and the Indus Civilization* almost immediately, since this three volume work appeared in 1931.

His retirement left a vacuum in the leadership of the Survey. Directors General were named, to be sure. Hargreaves followed Marshall, but Hargreaves was given the offending title "Officiating Director General" and Marshall was retained in India, very much on the scene.[45] *The India Office and Burma Office List* (see note 34) is a reasonable, although not infallible, source to document the leadership in the Survey. Personnel are also noted in the various *Annual Report of the Archaeological Survey of India*. It is a telling note to observe that Marshall was listed first in the *India Office List...*, initially under the title "Director General" with his "Officiating Director General" listed below him. Even when his title was publicly changed to "Officer on Special Duty" he took precedence over the Director General!

With Marshall still in India as the honored "old man," the Director General's position and power were clearly compromised, and this must have been felt by everyone, from *chowkidars* to Superintendent Archaeologists. We learn that in 1934 (some years after his "retirement" in 1928) Marshall was issuing invitations to come to India to work. In a letter to Mr. Guillaume de Hevesy, he who proposed a link between the Indus script and that of Easter Island we learn that Marshall wrote the following in reference to the Harappan Civilization: "I hope that France and other countries will not wait further to send their own expeditions to take an active part in the exploration of these prehistoric antiquities" (de Hevesy 1934a: 3). It seems that Marshall found it hard to let go of the reins of power. Without strong, confident leadership, the Survey could not prosper and as long as Marshall did not withdraw, both physically from India and symbolically from his position as "Officer on Special Duty," nothing would change.

Wheeler suggested something like this in his autobiography, *Still Digging*:

> Marshall was of a temperament which hinders the confident delegation of responsibility, and hinders therefore the adequate training of subordinates to assume responsibility. It may be that something in the air of Edwardian India, some germ surviving from the India of the Moghuls, had entered into Marshall's system. Certain it is that, when I reached India in 1944, Marshall was still a remote king-god of whom the worshipers had no intelligent comprehension, and sought none (1955: 182).

I am in agreement with Wheeler on this matter, except for one important point: training. There seems to be some evidence that Marshall was concerned with training and was even good at it. When Marshall "retired" he had capable and adequately trained men to take on the responsibility of leading the Survey, he just did not allow them to exercise this gift. In light of this, Wheeler's statement might be amended to read: Marshall was of a temperament which hinders the confident delegation of responsibility, and hinders therefore his ability to relinquish office in a way which respects the needs of others and the fact that inevitably there must be new leaders.

It is not clear however, that this failing in Marshall was entirely his fault. There is some evidence that the men closest to him promoted the Marshall legend and played a role in creating the ambiguity which surrounded the Director General's office. In retrospect it appears that some of this may not even have been done in their own self-interest.

ARCHAEOLOGICAL DOLDRUMS IN THE 1930s

Marshall's successors faced serious problems that were nonexistent during his tenure. With the collapse of the world economy in 1930, the new men at the top of the Survey found the prosperity of the Marshall years gone. Now they had to battle not only the Marshall legacy, but serious budget cuts as well. The Great Depression of the 1930s stripped the Survey of the resources necessary for serious field research. Even clever, parsimonious Superintendents, were finally left with so little money that they could not even "fudge" a bit of excavation from their independent budgets, and grants for such work became increasingly small. This brought to an end the kind of small scale work that had been managed at Mohenjo-daro and Harappa. A. Ghosh (1953a: 39-48) tells us that Harold Hargreaves became Director General on 8 October 1928 and that Rai Bahadur Daya Ram Sahni took the office on 29 July 1931. He was followed by J. F. Blakiston on 1 June 1935. Rao Bahadur K. N. Dikshit was the next Director General, and had the misfortune to hold this office at the time of the Woolley inspection.[46]

The situation dragged on until 1937, by which time things had deteriorated to a point that the Viceroy, Lord Linlithgow began to think that he needed an outside review of the Archaeological Survey of India. He decided to invite Sir Leonard to advise him on the state of

116

the Survey, with the aim of improving its operations. Woolley was world famous. He had enjoyed great success in Egypt and Mesopotamia, especially with his spectacular finds from the "Royal" Cemetery of Ur,[47] the excavation of which had been sponsored by the British Museum and The University of Pennsylvania Museum. Many of the finds from the "Royal" Cemetery have Harappan parallels, or were made in Harappan workshops, so this site plays an important role in understanding ancient trade, commerce and contact associated with the lands of Dilmun (modern Bahrain), Magan (modern Oman) and Meluhha (the greater Indus Valley, or the Indus Civilization). Woolley's inspection was a major event in the administrative history of British archaeology and was announced in the prestigious journal *Nature* (Anonymous 1938b, see also Woolley 1939b). A review of Woolley's visit and the report that he submitted has been published (Possehl 1993a), so the focus here can be more pointed, although there is a clear overlap between this section and the article.

The Woolley Report

Sir Leonard Woolley (Figure 2.50) was one of the most famous archaeologists of his day, an international figure in archaeology when he arrived in India, on 6 November 1938, with his wife Katharine (Ghosh 1953a: 43) to complete a review of the Archaeological Survey of India. N. G. Majumdar had just returned to Sindh Kohistan and was murdered within a week of the Woolley's arrival. These were not good times for the Survey.

The Woolleys' travel began immediately and the pace was hectic until the tour ended on 11 February 1939. Unfortunately Mrs. Woolley was unable to complete the review. She became ill and had to return to England. By the tour's end, Sir Leonard had visited forty-five places, including all of the Survey's museums and important sites such as Mohenjo-daro, Harappa, Taxila, Sarnath, Nalanda, Nagarjunakonda and Paharpur. He journeyed up the Indus Valley to the Northwest Frontier, the Tibetan border, East Bengal (now Bangladesh) and South India. On the journey from Karachi to Lahore some of his observations were made from a spotter aircraft. All of this was done in just under 100 days. Woolley's sound health combined with energy and stamina were legend in the field (Mallowan 1977b). His biographer notes that at the end of the tour:

> They travelled to Ceylon by way of Bombay and Madras to catch the boat home at the end of the month. By the time they arrived in England, Woolley had completed a devastating report for Lord Zetland, the Secretary of State for India (Winstone 1990: 216).

Figure 2.50. Sketch of Sir Leonard Woolley

The Woolley Report caused a sensation.

Virtually every Indian newspaper carried a major story when it was released. In England, *The Times* gave it prominent coverage in its edition of Thursday 13 July 1939 (Anonymous 1939a). War was brewing. Nevil Chamberlain was appeasing and Sir Leonard was appraising. The report on the state of the Archaeological Survey of India took more space that morning than politics. Such was Woolley's power and appeal. It is interesting that *The Times* story focuses on the culture, historical implications of Woolley's report. It mentions the "administrative" problems, but the story leads off with a consideration of the historical gap between the end of the ancient cities of the Indus and the beginnings of historical India as this was understood in 1939, diffusing the real criticism directed at the institution.

Woolley's report was noted twice in the 28 October 1939 issue of *Nature*; first in an article on anthropology and archaeology in India (Anonymous 1939b) and then as an abstract in a separate article (Anonymous 1939c; see also Anonymous 1939d and Woolley 1939a for more in *Nature*). The prestigious George Birdwood Memorial Lecture of the Royal Society of Arts was delivered by Sir Leonard on 1 December 1939. The topic was Indian archaeology but the tone of this presentation (Woolley 1940) was entirely different from his report to the government. It focused not on the Archaeological Survey of India and its problems, but on Indian art and architecture, especially in the south. This was, perhaps, more appropriate to his audience at the Royal Society.

Woolley's Points Concerning the Archaeological Survey

Introduction

The final printed pamphlet of forty-seven pages was titled *A Report on the Work of the Archaeological Survey of India* (Woolley 1939a). It is a complex document, and not always internally consistent. There is also a great sense that both the observations and reporting were done in haste and that this was not entirely due to a shortage of time. In the end it was suppressed; Jacquetta Hawkes says "...withdrawn for a time..." (1982: 231). Wheeler observes: "With the fatal timidity and vacillation which characterized the last years of the British Raj in India, the Woolley Report was issued and immediately withdrawn" (1955: 184). This pamphlet is now difficult to find, even in research libraries.[48]

The impact of the document is difficult to judge. Even if it had not been suppressed, the attention and resources of the Government of India were turned to World War II almost immediately after its release. This meant that implementation of Woolley's recommendations, if any were planned, were set aside, without respect to its withdrawal. It would be unfair to say that it did not serve some useful purposes, but to hold that: "Woolley's report revolutionized the archaeology of India in the long run..." (Winstone 1990: 219), is a gross exaggeration. After all, none of the advice for opening India to foreign missions received serious consideration nor did his stinging recommendations for destroying archaeological site museums. The report has generally been played down in historical writing on Indian archaeology (Ghosh 1953a; S. Roy 1953; Chakrabarti 1988); not necessarily because it is a rare document.

The following review of Woolley's observations and recommendations are not always favorable to this distinguished field archaeologist. This is not to indicate that the Archaeological Survey of India was a healthy organization when Woolley visited that country. It was not, and some of the problems were severe. It is therefore doubly regretful that Woolley's report was crafted in a way that failed to pinpoint the real problem, which was leadership and an inability to come out from behind the shadow of Sir John Marshall. But equally important, having missed the point, Woolley chose to phrase his evaluation in such an offensive way that his recommendations had to be suppressed. Wheeler theorizes that this withdrawal was due to "timidity and vacillation" (1955: 184); another view might legitimately see this as a "prudent act," done in recognition of the report's wrong-headedness and often disagreeable tone.

A kind of summary statement of Woolley's findings can be seen in the following statement:

> I was persuaded that while the present achievements of the Department did indeed compare unfavorably with what had been done in the years prior to 1930 when Sir John Marshall was Director General, the cause of this was simply the financial stringency; no staff could be really successful under existing conditions and probably the present staff was doing as well as in such conditions any staff could do. Before I reached India a careful study of the reports of the Department covering the years 1923 to 1935 had tended to weaken that assumption. I have now visited, alone or with my wife, all the archaeological museums of the Central Government as well as provincial and other museums, have inspected a very large number of the historical monuments for whose upkeep the Department is responsible, and have examined and made detailed notes of some three dozen archaeological sites including most of those on which the Department is doing or has recently done work of any importance; and I have been forced to the conclusion that the lack of money is not the principal reason for the set-back in the progress of archaeology in India. The Department has been starved financially and more money must be spent if its work of exploration is to be put upon a proper basis; that is a fact which cannot be gainsaid. But a mere increase of the grant unaccompanied by other changes would actually do more harm than good, for the truth is that the Department is altogether lacking in men trained for the work which they have to do (Woolley 1939a: 1-2).

Woolley's mandate from the Government of India was very broad, a virtual *carte blanche* to examine the entire Survey.

> At an early date I pointed out that the "general points" mentioned in item (1) might well be of crucial importance; e.g., it would be impossible to recommend excavation and the consequent amassing of antiquities in the hands of the Government or other bodies if no sufficient means existed for their conservation and exhibition, so that the question of museums was intimately connected with the inquiry; and it would be futile to recommend excavations if there were not sufficient funds for the work, so that the finances of the Department would also have to come under review; and again, excavations if not properly conducted are worse than useless in that they involve the destruction of historic evidence, so that the capacities of the staff would have to be adjudged (Woolley 1939a: 1).

While he found the personnel in the Archaeological Survey to be lacking in training, and had to battle personnel policies that played against them as well, they were well intended public servants.

> I have encountered everywhere plenty of enthusiasm, intelligence and learning; it is the experience and the training that have been lacking and for this the members of the staff are not to blame (Woolley 1939a: 2).

Training the Survey's staff was clearly a problem that Marshall had experienced, and dealt with, probably on a daily basis. Moreover, most of his people were recruited because they were thought to be intelligent and enthusiastic. This desire to work, could lead untrained people to make mistakes, and that was to be avoided. Dilip Chakrabarti located a letter from Sir John to Superintendent Archaeologist K. N. Dikshit dealing with an incident that bears upon this issue. He has reprinted the note in its entirety (1988: 237-38) therefore only a portion is included here. It is dated Camp Bombay, the 19th July 1925 and begins:

> I am just visiting the Elephanta Caves and write this on the spot. The Public Works Department are excavating the tank at the western end of the Caves and a variety of interesting objects have been found in the mud during the last few days, one of them being a large copper vessel with an inscription. The Custodian, who seems to me a very worthy little man, has apparently received no instructions as to how he is to handle these antiquities. Obviously the proper course for him is to keep a register of them and hand them over to you without any attempt at cleaning them. As a fact he has already cleaned the copper vessel, and in my opinion considerably depreciated its value, but that is not his fault, as he clearly believed that he was doing the best. I shall be glad if you will give him explicit and immediate instructions about these matters... (Chakrabarti 1988: 237).

This small incident is just one example of the concern that Marshall had for training. Recruiting really smart, educated people for jobs as relatively poorly paid public servants was not easy, given competition from commerce and industry. Just finding people who could read and write and were willing to serve in the Survey was something of a triumph when it was done. The issue was large and had to be faced up to every day by Marshall and his senior colleagues. To some degree it still exists; but this fact should not be taken to suggest that it is something that has been ignored, today, or any time in the past. Training and qualifying people for jobs in the Archaeological Survey of India or the Pakistan Department of Archaeology is simply a huge job and not the kind of issue that will just go away because administrators decide to pay attention to it.

Outside reviewers can be invaluable sources of new insights and opinions on institutions. This is clearly the well intended spirit in which Woolley was invited to undertake his review of the Archaeological Survey. But sometimes outside reviewers, by the nature of their disposition and/or experience, come to these tasks with their own agendas; rigid opinions about what is right and wrong, and how institutions should be structured and operate. If this is the case, then the results can be less than optimal. To use Sir Leonard's words, they can "actually do more harm than good" (1939a: 2; see above).

Woolley thought that part of the problem in the Survey arose from the fact that, "Every member of the staff is expected to be proficient in the work of conservation and excavation, may at any time be put in charge of a museum, and is in addition saddled with a mass of clerical and office work for which he has no special qualifications. In short each member is expected to be a super-man..." (Woolley 1939a: 2).

Some Analysis of the Woolley Report

It is not possible to do a thorough review of the Woolley report, because it is a very broad document. However, there are three areas where Woolley spent a great deal of time reporting on the facts as he saw them and making recommendations to the Viceroy and the Secretary of State for India. These are listed in approximately the same order he presented them in his report:

1. Excavation
a. Evaluation of the work
b. Selection of sites
c. Training and qualifications of personnel
d. Excavation by non-Government bodies

2. Conservation

3. Museums

This review of Woolley's report will follow his order.

Excavation: Evaluation of the work

Sir Leonard's report on the excavations undertaken by the Survey are a central concern of this book and it is important to explore his views as thoroughly as possible.

The following condemnation of Indian excavation work is found at the beginning of the report and sets the tone for Woolley's remaining observations: "In the matter of excavation I have on most sites which I have visited found that the methods employed were bad, trained observation conspicuous by its absence, and the results in consequence incomplete and untrustworthy" (1939a: 3). Paragraphs 53 through 55 of the report are a detailed substantiation of this point, including one section titled "Proof of inexperienced officers in the methods of excavation." It would be unfair to say that all that Woolley suggests here is incorrect. The Survey in 1938-39 had a variety of people in the field, some of whom were more qualified than others. But some of his evaluations are clearly out of line. For example, those made at Harappa, given as one of his "proofs," can be challenged, even from this distance.

He states: "Thus at Harappa the whole character of the buildings has been misunderstood and the scantiness of burnt brick construction found has been attributed entirely to the plundering of the site whereas there is plenty of evidence to shew (sic) that burnt brick was employed for foundations only and that superstructures were in crude brick..." (1939a: 27). This is a novel suggestion, not shared by any other archaeologist who has visited or excavated at Harappa, including Wheeler. Certainly buildings with "crude brick" superstructures, even wooden ones, probably existed at Harappa, but the notion that baked bricks were only used for foundations does not seem plausible. His further observation that the small baked brick structures in the foundations of what has come to be called "The Great Granary" were "battered buttresses" and not "air vents" does not make sense either. The archaeological aspects (not the functional) of this building seem to have been well understood from the preliminary reports and in Pundit Vats' publication (1940: Pl. VI; see Figures 2.37 and 2.38). One might wonder if there is a linguistic gap here between a native speaker of English and a native speaker of Hindustani, since in some ways, the foundations in question are small "battered buttresses," at the same time functioning as ventilation access for the foundations of this building. Moreover, K. N. Sastri was in charge of Harappa at the time and he was a well seasoned officer, who, if interviewed in this case, would have almost certainly given a satisfactory explanation of this building.[49]

Excavation: Selection of sites

The Survey, especially under Sir John Marshall, had excavated sites in all of the major regions of British India. The pattern of excavation meant that some periods of time were highlighted in one region at the expense of others, simply because of the nature of the finds. The Harappan Civilization, for example, was much better known than the Neolithic period in the western borderlands. The "Greek" through Gandharan Period was well known in the northwest, but the same time period yielded scanty remains of indigenous cultures in Central and Southern India. One has to see India as a large, complex historical mosaic, not a simple, linear historical sequence. The task of reconstructing this mosaic for the past 10,000 years, when humankind began to take up farming and live in villages is immense for such a vast region. In fact, it remains incomplete fifty years after Woolley's report.

The Survey's strategy, which is clearly Marshall's strategy, for piecing together this history is given by him in his somewhat autobiographical essay in *Revealing India's Past*.

> I should like to explain, however, why at that period, whenever we had any time at all for excavation, we busied ourselves chiefly with well-known Buddhist *sangharamas* (monasteries) and did not turn our attention to the larger city sites where we could hope for discoveries of an entirely different and perhaps more illuminating order. The reason was twofold. In the first place we were at that time better informed—thanks to the Chinese pilgrims and the researches of earlier archaeologists—about these Buddhist monuments generally than about any other class of remains, and it seemed to me safer therefore, to start with these and make sure of our ground before groping our way further into the unknown. The other reason, which I do not hesitate to confess, was that we were more likely to get spectacular finds on these Buddhist sites than anywhere else, and such finds were absolutely indispensable to us, if we were to interest the public in our work and secure more adequate funds for it" (Marshall 1939: 25).

Marshall also realized the wisdom of excavating in several regions of the country, and not allowing any one place to dominate his excavation strategy. This can be seen in abstracts from his annual reports, taken from years of prosperity, when the Survey was very much involved in excavation. Excavation and research were conducted at:

1926-27: Taxila, Punjab
Harappa, Punjab
Mohenjo-daro, Sindh
Nalanda, Bihar
Bulandi Bagh, Bihar
Paharpur, East Bengal (Bangladesh)
Andhra Pradesh, three trial excavations
Pagan, Burma
Hmawaza, Burma
Kalagangon, Burma
Research in the Northwest Frontier

1927-28: Taxila, Punjab
Harappa, Punjab
Mohenjo-daro, Sindh
Jhukar, Sindh
Sarnath, Uttar Pradesh
Nalanda, Bihar
Paharpur, East Bengal (Bangladesh)

Nagarjunakonda, Andhra Pradesh
Pagan, Burma
Hmawaza, Burma
Research in the Salt Range, Northwest Frontier and
West Bengal

1928-29:   Taxila, Punjab
Harappa, Punjab
Dallin rescue excavation, Punjab
Mohenjo-daro, Sindh
Nalanda, Bihar
Mahasthan, East Bengal (Bangladesh)
Paharpur, East Bengal (Bangladesh)
Murshidabad District, West Bengal
Nagarjunakonda, Andhra Pradesh
Hmawaza Burma

As can be seen from this list Marshall was also in favor of sustained excavations at his sites, rather than flitting from place to place.

The policy had changed by the time Woolley came to evaluate the Survey. Constant budget cuts meant that grants became scarce and the grand excavations that the Survey once could afford had to be abandoned. But the policy (plan) remained one that emphasized work in as many regions of British India as funds could reasonably sustain. This plan of work came under heavy fire from Woolley. He prefaces the section of his report with these words: "In reviewing the work done by the Department in recent years I have been disagreeably impressed by the lack of any coherent plan for its archaeological activities" (1939a: 4). He then goes into a somewhat detailed review that reveals that there was consistent effort made to undertake small scale excavations at a number of sites, generally delegated to the Superintendent and Assistant Superintendent Archaeologists. These excavations were directed toward documenting the diversity of ancient Indian history, filling in the culture historical mosaic, and learning something about as many parts of the country as could be achieved within the budgets allocated. The Survey probably could have saved all of its funds to keep one major excavation under way, but there was a kind of "diplomacy" in going about things in a regional way that is very South Asian in nature. These "Indian" ways of doing things completely escaped Woolley, who never seems to have taken heed of, or understood, what is usually stated as "Indian conditions."

Woolley spends some time reviewing the need to establish a relative chronology for India, which he refers to as "historical correlation." Speaking for the small scale work at many sites he opines: "I consider the work done there to be sufficient or the results of future work unimportant...because it is a mistake to concentrate on a particular period when the great need is for correlation" (1939a: 6). In spite of the documentation that Woolley attempts to bring to bear on this charge (1939a: 4-6), he was almost certainly mistaken in this judgment. While it was true that there were immense gaps in the archaeological history of the Subcontinent in 1938-39, the strategy that was employed on the meager financial resources available during the Great Depression would have eventually yielded the kinds of historical insights that Woolley's plan envisioned. The Survey just went about the task in a different, more diffused way. Places like Besnagar, Sarnath, Taxila and others, were being excavated and had great depth of occupation that produced results that filled the undeniable need of correlation. But, this task takes time. It was not complete in 1938-39; it is not complete today. For example, there is still a gap of about a millennium between the end of the Harappan Tradition (Lustrous Red Ware) and the earliest documentation of the Iron Age in Gujarat.

It should be clear at this point that the real error of the Woolley recommendation was not so much that he proposed "correlation" and deep digging as the research strategy to set things straight in India, but that he saw this as the only strategy. In reality, archaeology at the national level is best pursued when "correlation" and deep digging go hand in hand with horizontal excavation; when both strategies are pursued in an integrated, thoughtful way. It is the lack of a sense of balance, that multiple strategies are called for, that is the true failure of Sir Leonard's recommendation on excavation.

Excavation: Training and qualifications of personnel

The 1939 report contains several recommendations that would improve the Archaeological Survey's position in terms of recruiting new talent. Some of this has to do with severe age requirements in Indian law for employment, which are real impediments to employment and advancement, and it is good that Sir Leonard made his point. Woolley also advocated hiring student apprentices and using volunteers, to find new talent for archaeology in the Subcontinent. He wanted real men, with a commitment to the field, not armchair office bodies, waiting for morning tea. The first season of training "...ought to involve such physical drudgery that only a real enthusiast will survive it and persist" (Woolley 1939a: 17).

Excavation by Non-Government Bodies

The Archaeological Survey of India was founded and matured with a strong sense of its mission to discover, disseminate and preserve the cultural history of the country. There is some implication in the history of this institution that its mission was also perceived as an exclusive right, not to be shared with other organizations, especially non-Indian bodies. The Viceroy, Lord Curzon once said: "The last thing we want is the continental expert with a spade in his hand. We will excavate our own sites" (T. N. Roy 1961: 88).

This attitude has led to a long history of tension between the various national "departments" of archaeology and outside agencies, whether they are South Asian universities, museums or foreign teams. Most of this tension has been resolved today, and there are vigorous programs of archaeology at many South Asian universities and museums, all well coordinated with the archaeology department of the central government. There are also foreign teams working in most of the countries of South Asia, including India. In fact, Pakistan has a long and distinguished history of welcoming European and American excavators.[50] But, in 1939, in spite of the seeming success of the Chanhu-daro excavation in 1935-36, it was clearly an issue and Woolley devoted a large portion of his pamphlet to it (1939a: 9-16).

His recommendations were strongly in favor of allowing non-governmental bodies, including foreign teams, the right to explore and excavate, as long as "Indian interests" were preserved. The report proposes specific amendments to the Antiquities Act (1939a: 13-5) and discusses a division of finds. He was in favor of being generous to foreign institutions since it would lead to a dissemination of Indian culture and promote an understanding in foreign countries of the Subcontinent's rich, diverse cultural heritage.

Woolley on Conservation

"In the matter of the conservation of standing monuments the Department, following carefully the precedents laid down in the past, has done and is doing admirable work to which I can give unstinted praise; only where the preservation of excavated buildings is concerned for which the precedents are more doubtful, have they indulged in an exaggerated policy which is wasteful financially and its result scientifically deplorable" (Woolley 1939a: 2-3). Paragraph 50 (1939a: 24) of his report deals with the documentation of these practices and it is titled: "The practice of the Department radically wrong."

Once more Woolley uses strong language in concert with strong opinions on what is right and wrong when one addresses a nation's cultural heritage. He attempts to justify his use of words like "wasteful, deplorable" and "radically wrong" with observations he made during his tour. At Mohenjo-daro (he spells the site name his way: "Mohendjo-daro") the following is noted:

"At Mohendjo-daro I examined carefully what purported to be a well-preserved private house of about the 26th century B.C. and it was only after some time that I was able to realize that no single brick visible in it was more than five years old. Fraudulent reconstruction similar to this though not so thoroughgoing has been carried out over the whole vast site of Mohendjo-daro: it has cost and costs a large sum of money; it is not in the interest of the layman, for of the few who annually visit the place none examine the whole of it: for the archaeologist destroys the value of the ruins; it is not in the interest of future generations who would want to see the buildings of 2600 B.C., not of 1935 A.D.; and it is useless, because it cannot be permanent (1939a: 25).

No one can defend conservation work that produces fakes and forgeries in ancient monuments, and from the very beginning it was, and remains, the policy of the Archaeological Survey of India and other national departments of archaeology to avoid this pitfall. In the Survey's *Conservation Manual for the Care of Ancient Monuments* (Marshall 1923a) the following is found as a statement about authenticity.

Archaeological, Public Works, or other officers charged with the execution of conservation work should never forget that the reparation of any remnant of ancient architecture, however humble, is a work to be entered into upon with totally different feelings from a new work or from repairs of a modern building. Although there are many ancient buildings whose state of disrepair suggests at first sight a renewal, it should never be forgotten that their *historical value is gone when their authenticity is destroyed*, and that our first duty is not to renew them but to preserve them (Marshall 1923a: 9-10, original emphasis).

In fact, Woolley held that the restoration of excavated remains is futile and a waste of money since this work can never be permanent. He states that these:

"...are necessarily in a ruined state and they possess an archaeological interest and very rarely any aesthetic value. The invariable policy of the Department has been to conserve such remains, and it has applied to the work the same or nearly the same principles as it applies to monuments of artistic importance referred to in paragraph 43. That is a disastrous error. The two problems are radically different and the same rules cannot hold good for both; the undiscriminating and unintelligent adherence to precedent has here resulted in a gross waste of public money and the defeat of scientific aims (Woolley 1939a: 22).

I have had the pleasure of seeing Mohenjo-daro and the wonderful sense of walking through an ancient city is an experience that cannot be duplicated at any other site of the third millennium BC. Here one can walk down lanes, look into people's homes, peer down wells, even sit on the 'stoop.' To simply rebury such a treasure makes no sense at all. The references in the report to budgetary savings that might be had from altering this portion of the conservation policy is not well stated and somehow smacks of pandering to the civil servant segment of Woolley's audience.

Perhaps the problem we confront in this portion of the Woolley Report comes down to the fact that Woolley came to India in 1939 with European values. He confronted Director General Rao Bahadur K. N. Dikshit, who saw things somewhat differently. Woolley, as an Englishman found the preservation of excavated remains in India to be wasteful and futile, these remains being best suited for reburial. Dikshit was an Indian who found the preservation of his cultural heritage to be a worthwhile undertaking, even if these efforts would not be permanent.

Woolley on Museums

The Woolley Report also has strong words for the Museums maintained by the Archaeological Survey at some of its major excavated sites.

> In 1904 the Archaeological Department built a museum at Sarnath to house the movable antiquities discovered in the course of the excavations there which could not be preserved *in situ*, thus initiating a policy of local museums on excavated sites which has been followed ever since; the Department now owns museums at Sarnath, Nalanda, Taxila, Mohendjo-daro, Harappa, Nagarjunakonda and Pagan (the last not included in my survey), these all being local archaeological museums; in addition it controls the Archaeological Section of the Indian Museum, Calcutta, the Central Asian Antiquities Museum, Delhi, and historical museums in the forts of Delhi, Lahore, etc.

> The policy of founding local museums on archaeological sites was borrowed from Greece, the only country which has adopted it with any consistency, and was deliberately approved for India, and I am aware that so recently as 1937 it received[51] the blessing of the Indian Museums conference held at New Delhi; but what may be suitable for a small country like Greece where distances are short and communications reasonably easy is not necessarily suitable for India. Here the policy is condemned by the fact that these local institutions only too often fail to perform any of the functions of a museum (Woolley 1939a: 28).

According to the report, there are three functions of archaeological museums: housing and preservation of antiquities, advancing science through the study of the antiquities by scholars, and use as educational centers where the general public can learn. Woolley then measures the success of the site museums he visited against this yardstick. They come off badly, of course. The need for conservation staff at each of the museums does not come close to meeting the needs of the individual collections; the labels are ill-contrived (if present at all); the exhibits poorly conceived; some of the museums are remote and have few visitors. In the end Woolley condemns the entire scheme, dismissing the very notion of an archaeological museum as a *reductio ad absurdum* (Woolley 1939a: 29).

Woolley then makes recommendations for individual museums, which can be summarized as follows (Woolley 1939a: 30-1):

Sarnath: To be maintained for the use of students and not the public. Collections to be disbursed. Objects not from Sarnath to be removed.

Taxila: If reorganized the museum should remain. The coins of precious metals might be better moved to Delhi.

Mohenjo-daro: Close. Disburse the collection.

Harappa: Close. Disburse the collection.

Nalanda: Exhibit a small amount of material that is of local interest and disburse the treasures, especially the priceless bronzes. The museum clerk, not a trained Curator, to be placed in charge of the scaled-down installation.

Nagarjunakonda: Halt the process of bringing a site museum into existence.

The concept of a site museum has been debated and to some degree the discussion continues. The arguments against them are cost and the remoteness of many, which discourages visitors. Being out of the way also means that they can be difficult to protect and properly administer. The concerns of local parties, however, lead to complaints that their cultural heritage is being pillaged by some poorly defined "center" that excavates (stronger language, like "violates," might even be used) the remains of their forefathers and then takes them off to a metropolitan museum that is already so stuffed with material that it cannot be properly exhibited. These parties press for some kind of sharing of their heritage which might lead to the construction of local museums, frequently at the excavated site itself.

Efforts were made to mollify the problems inherent in the site museums of colonial India. In the *Annual Report of the Archaeological Survey of India, 1936-37* we learn the following:

In view of the impending publication of Mr. Mackay's report on the Further Excavations at Mohenjo-daro the proposal to distribute the duplicate antiquities from Mohenjo-daro to various museums in India was mooted. Mr. C. L. Fabri and Mr. U. C. Chattacharya were temporarily engaged in the work of sorting out, selecting and listing antiquities. In the first instance seven representative sets were prepared and listed, two sets were fuller than the rest; one interned for the Central Government Museum and the other for the Bombay Government. These sets have been distributed as follows:

Collection No. 1	Government of Bombay, Prince of Wales Museum, Bombay
Half of Collection No. 2	Indian Museum, Calcutta
Half of Collection No. 2	Central Asian Antiquities Museum, New Delhi, Govt. of India
Collection No. 3	Government Museum, Madras
Collection No. 4	Reserved for proposed Provincial Museum of Sind
Collection No. 5	Provincial Museum, Lucknow
Collection No. 6	Patna Museum, Patna
Collection No. 7	Central Museum, Nagpur (Puri 1936-37).

In South Asia local parties and interests are generally very strong, and there is a tendency to cater to them: "Indian conditions" again. Whether Marshall realized this or not when he founded the first South Asian site museum at Sarnath in 1904, he made a wise move because his decision was so much within the sociocultural norms of the culture in which he was operating. The wisest advice on site museums should have been directed toward improving, not destroying them. If the conservation and restoration of collections was poor, then each museum should have a conservator or a central conservation-restoration laboratory created where finds could be brought, treated and then returned to the site museum.

Recent history has shown that Woolley's recommendations were not acted upon and the museums at Mohenjo-daro and Harappa were not closed. A Museum at Nagarjunakonda was built and others followed it. Today there are thirty site museums in India alone and several others in Pakistan. Local interests, not central interests, were served. As noted above, representative pieces from all of these sites are located in large museums in the great metropolitan centers of South Asia, and one need not go to Mohenjo-daro or Harappa to see very good, perhaps even the best, material from these two major Indus cities.

Even the remote museums have visitors. From the following quote from the *Annual Report of the Archaeological Survey of India* for 1930-34 it can be seen that visitors are important.

> During the season 1931-32, the Museum at Mohenjo-daro was very popular; and though a charge was made for the admission of visitors it apparently did not prevent even the poorer townspeople and village folk from coming to see it. A striking feature was the number of visitors from outside Sind, both Indian and from abroad, who came to the Museum on their way from Lahore to Karachi, or *vice versa*. The retention of a local museum at Mohenjo-daro as an adjunct to the site itself is,—in Mr. Mackay's opinion—really necessary; for despite its apparent isolation it is being used with profit by visitors far and wide (Mackay 1930-34: 74).

One positive recommendation that came out of this portion of the report was an appeal for a "National Museum" in Delhi. There was a growing sense of this need in other circles as well, but Woolley's was an important voice in keeping the issue alive. Today there are fine institutions in Delhi and Karachi, that serve this important function.

The Need for an Adviser on Archaeology

If Woolley found serious fault with the Archaeological Survey of India, he was willing to offer suggestions to solve them. One of his pleas was for an "Adviser in Archaeology." His point was reasonable and logical, if his assessment of the state of this organization was correct: "If the present efforts of the Department can be so characterized it is manifest that the staff, before it can train others, must itself be trained; I therefore recommend the employment of a temporary Adviser on Archaeology who could deal with all the points at issue" (Woolley 1939a: 3). Woolley himself was offered this post but he turned it down.[52] He was an independent man, who usually worked on a contract basis, and the thought of joining a bureaucracy had absolutely no appeal.

Some see the appointment of Mortimer Wheeler to the post of Director General of the Survey, a result of this recommendation. That may be true, but there are points that suggest that if there was a connection it was distant. First of all, Wheeler was not brought to the Survey as an "Advisor on Archaeology" but as the Director General. Moreover, none of the documentation I have seen regarding Wheeler's appointment makes reference to Woolley, or the 1939 report he prepared, except remarks that in 1939 Woolley privately spoke of Wheeler as the man for the job, but without Wheeler's knowledge (Wheeler 1955: 184).[53]

The Indian Response to the Woolley Report

The Indians, of course, were furious at this report and the Director General, Rao Bahadur K. N. Dikshit looked for a powerful voice to defend the Archaeological Survey. Sir Aurel Stein was the logical spokesman, but the Woolleys had recently been his host and the situation demanded a certain level of diplomacy in his response. He wrote:

> W's report is a remarkable piece of work in many ways, considering the short time during which he had to make observations all over this vast continent and his naturally inadequate knowledge of Indian conditions. Many of his remarks are just, some of his criticisms less so. The main fact he could scarcely be expected to dwell on in print, viz. that while Marshall worked under all the difficulties inherent in bureaucratic

mentality, administrative machine and want of an example of state-aided research in archaeology at home etc., he did achieve great things; but he could not create foundations sound enough to assure safe and satisfactory progress under much weakened and less well-prepared successors. Complete "Indianization" is now practically achieved. History will judge whether it will be of benefit to India (Stein to Andrews, 13 February 1940, in Mirsky 1977: 523).

I have found no public statement on this from Stein, but his private sentiments seem clear from his letter. Krishna Deva (personal communication, February 1992) has indicated that the senior members of the Archaeological Survey of India read Woolley's report and discussed it among themselves. They were, however, inhibited from making public comment, since this might have been interpreted as criticism of the government, which was left to politicians in those days, not to public servants. One has to assume that Stein's points and others were brought out in conversation with key officials, rather than written, which led to the suppression of the report and it was withdrawn. In the end, the Woolley Report seems to have had a minimal impact on the Archaeological Survey, except for one element; Dikshit undertook an excavation at Ahichchhatra aimed at the correlation problem.

Woolley's Recommendation to Excavate Ahichchhatra

A large scale excavation at the famous site of Ahichchhatra took place during World War II (1940-44), under the direction of Rao Bahadur K. N. Dikshit. Woolley referred to the site as Rangpur, the name of the adjacent village in his report. The ancient name is Ahichchhatra (also Adichchhatra, Ahichhatra) meaning "The Canopy of Serpents." It is a huge mound on the east bank of the Ganga in Uttar Pradesh. Ahichchhatra is mentioned in the *Mahabharata* and was capital of North Panchala. Sir Alexander Cunningham conducted a brief excavation there (Cunningham 1871), that was followed by other digging (Fuhrer 1891-92).

Woolley recommended that a deeply stratified site should be found, where a pottery sequence could be recovered to help in the correlation of historical periods in north India. Ahichchhatra fit that description and Dikshit excavated there for four seasons. He was assisted by A. Ghosh and several scholar-traineees including Krishna Deva, K. C. Panigrahi and F. A. Khan, later to become Director of the Pakistan Department of Archaeology and the excavator of Kot Diji. They exposed the fortification wall and excavated two temple mounds inside the city. Deep digging at the fortification produced evidence for nine major strata and more or less continuous occupation from Painted Gray Ware times (ca. 800 BC at this site), to the Medieval Period (ca. 1000 AD). A final report on this work has never appeared as a single document, but many of the finds have been published (Ghosh 1946; Panigrahi 1946; Krishna Deva and Wheeler 1946a, 1946b; V. S. Agrawala 1947-48; M. G. Dikshit 1952). It was also in the course of this work that Painted Gray Ware and Northern Black Polished Ware were first formally defined (Krishna Deva and Wheeler 1946a, 1946b). Later excavation there, in 1963-64 and 1964-65 revealed a "Late Harappan" Ochre Colored Pottery habitation that would have preceded Painted Grey Ware (IAR 1963-64: 43-4, 1964-65: 39-42).

Closing Remarks

This review of the Woolley Report is not intended to imply that Woolley was wrong to point out problems faced by the Archaeological Survey of India in 1938-39, but rather to question the inflexibility and tone of his recommendations. When an experienced man offers "proofs" that are not "proofs" but only opinions based on shaky observations and interviews, causing a sensation may reflect badly on him. It was, after all, a hasty trip to a huge country, reviewing a very substantial institution with hundreds of employees and a tradition that goes back to the mid-nineteenth century. It leaves the impression that Sir Leonard Woolley was a man of strong opinions, not all of which have survived the test of time.

In some ways an era in Indian archaeology drew to a close with the death of Sir Aurel Stein in 1943 and the end of the Ahichchhatra project 1944. World War II was still a very intense conflict, but it was increasingly clear that the Allies would emerge victorious. It meant that the Indian government could again turn its attention to archaeology.

A NEW ERA IN SOUTH ASIAN ARCHAEOLOGY

The Appointment of Sir Mortimer Wheeler as Director General

Whatever took place between 1939 and 1943 in the Archaeological Survey of India did not seem to improve things, at least in the eyes of the Viceroy's office. In June of 1943, Lord Wavell, the Viceroy sent the following to Leo Amery, Secretary of State for India.

> Post of Director General of Archaeology falls vacant next year and the Member for Education, after discussion with me, is extremely anxious to get a man...from home for succession. I fear condition of the department is quite lamentable. It contains no one of any quality and level of its work is low...I do not know if Mortimer Wheeler who I understand is at present serving in the Army would be possible...(Hawkes 1982: 230).

Wheeler was a Brigadier in the Army, serving with the artillery in North Africa. The government tracked him down and by 7 August 1943 he wrote from Tripoli to his friend Sir Cyril Fox:

> ...The other day I was returning to my tent in the evening sun when my Corps Commander (General Sir Brian Horrocks) dashed along with a signal in his hand and the remark — I say, have you seen this — they want you as (reading) 'Director General of Archaeology in India.' Why, you must be rather a king-pin at that sort of thing. You know, I thought you were a regular soldier' (Wheeler 1955: 141).

Wheeler wanted the post, but he also wanted to stay on with the artillery until the long awaited invasion of Italy had been accomplished. His almost immediate reply to the India Office (and others) read:

> I have the honor to accept the post of Director General of Archaeology, India which the India Office has offered me, if my release from the Army be sanctioned in due course. I do not desire that my release shall take effect before 30th Nov. 43 provided that until that date I am retained in a theatre of active operations (Hawkes 1982: 221).

With India still not far off Wheeler, back in Algiers, ran into two colleagues, one of whom would be very much a part of the new era in Indian Archaeology, Stuart Piggott (Figure 2.51), the other his television collaborator, Glyn Daniel. Daniel has left his recollection of this meeting:

> ...looking across the crowded room we saw Wheeler talking to Harold Macmillan, then Minister resident at Allied HQ in Africa. Wheeler saw us and came over to talk. He asked us what we were doing in Algiers and we explained. "Air Photo Interpretation." He said, his eyes flashing and moustache bristling, "women's work." I hope you find something better to do (Hawkes 1982: 222).

Wheeler left for England, where he attended to personal matters and began planning what he would actually do as Director General.

Wheeler's Arrival in India

In February 1944 Wheeler set off for India, sailing back through the Mediterranean he had just left. His ship docked in Bombay and he immediately caught a train north to Delhi, pausing there only to solicit the assistance of Daniel and Piggott. Both decided, for their own reasons, not to join him in the Archaeological Survey of India.[54] Then, without skipping a beat, Wheeler was off to his new office in Simla. His first day on the job revealed his sometimes theatrical behavior. Wheeler recounts:

> On the top floor of the gaunt Railway Board building where the Archaeological Survey was then housed at Simla, I stepped over the recumbent forms of peons, past office windows revealing little clusters of idle clerks and hangers-on, to the office which I had taken over that morning from my Indian predecessor. As I opened my door I turned and looked back. The sleepers had not stirred, and only a wavering murmur like the distant drone of bees indicated the presence of drowsy human organisms within. I emitted a bull-like roar, and the place leapt to anxious life...One after another my headquarters staff was ushered in, and within an hour the purge was complete. Bowed shoulders and apprehensive glances showed an office working as it had not worked for many a long day. That evening one of the peons (who later became my most admirable Headquarters Jemadar) said tremulously to my deputy's Irish wife, "Oh, memsahib, a terrible thing has happened to us this day..." (Wheeler 1955: 186).

A tall, theatrical, sometimes intimidating man, Wheeler was not someone to stand in his predecessor's shadow. This comes through in the biography by Jacquetta Hawkes (1982) and in a very fine, short treatment on his personality by Sir Max Mallowan (1977a: 237-39). Wheeler lost little time in beginning to set the Archaeological Survey straight. While he speaks favorably of Woolley's report (1955: 182-85), Wheeler had his own plan to implement, and it differed in many respects from the older man's vision of Indian archaeology. Wheeler did not close the site museums, for example, but strengthened them and established a Museums Branch of the Survey (Ghosh 1953a:43). He also closed the work at Ahichchhatra and never sent the Survey back to this huge, complex, deeply stratified site that, after discussions with A. Ghosh, I have come to think of as a "monster." There were many Wheeler innovations, most of them important: the Museums Branch was one, but he also reinvigorated the publication program with a new journal called *Ancient India*. He brought the conservation program more closely under the Survey itself, rather than being shared with the Public Works Department, and created the post of Executive Engineer in his headquarters in addition to a Superintendent of Gardens and a Joint Director General. He also reconstituted the Excavations Branch, closed since 1932. But most important, there was the Wheeler persona, self-confident, even bold, energetic and powerful as a bull, ready to seize the Survey and create a new future for archaeology in the Subcontinent. Pantywaist reports and recommendations be damned, he was prepared to lead, and lead he did.

Wheeler's Training Excavations

Wheeler worked in many directions to bring the Survey along the path he had laid out, but the keystone of the plan was a series of training excavations. These were the forums within which he would tutor new leaders, and his personal supervision of the schools would allow him to spot talent and bring it along. Wheeler's unconventional ways and great enthusiasm for his new job generated two sets of responses, as he noted: "My older staff groaned at the willful and pernicious unconventionality of the newcomer. The younger staff which I proceeded to recruit responded with a high spirit that was my greatest reward" (Wheeler 1955: 187). And the schools worked, the students from Taxila, the first excavation, undertaken in 1944-45, provided the leadership for the Archaeological Survey of India and the Pakistan Department of Archaeology for many years following independence.

There were four training excavations between 1944 and Partition in 1947. The students were taught the Wheeler method of controlled, stratigraphic excavation and recording. This was laid out in early issues of *Ancient India* and then brought together in *Archaeology from the Earth* (1954). In addition, the students received tutoring in on-site photography, surveying, drawing, reading and recording of stratigraphy as well as the history of the region in which they worked, but the most important thing was the model of leadership that Wheeler gave them. This is not to suggest that he was a placid, pleasant man; nothing is farther from the truth. Wheeler was easily annoyed, even by trivial mistakes, and this could turn into a kind of rage. It is said that he would shout, rant and rave, use abusive language and stamp about calling everyone a fool. Some of these outbursts are said to have been real shows, quite theatrical in nature, sometimes even out of line.[55] No one was immune from his outbursts and Professor B. B. Lal recalls a number of incidents to which he was a party that involved many people, including Lady Wheeler (Lal 1984).

Those who were with him feel that Wheeler was convinced that "Indians" were indolent and it was his job to get them to work. Furthermore, the older staff of the Survey, men like A. Ghosh, Krishna Deva and V. S. Agrawala, were told that they would have to unlearn much of their training to fit within the Wheeler team. The new trainees, including B. B. Lal, A. H. Dani, F. A. Khan, and B. K. Thapar (Plate 2.55) can be seen as Wheeler's favorites. He had them early in their careers and could instill his values and knowledge. They were the future of the Survey and the men on whom he counted to make the long term changes that were necessary.

Although Wheeler's theatrical nature stayed with him to the end of his term as Director General, there is testimony to the fact that he did mellow over time. He came to realize that the Survey was not entirely moribund and that "Indians" were willing to work. He could also display a deep sense of caring and commitment to those who served with him in Indian archaeology. The best students caught this aspect of his personality, not the more superficial act. Wheeler was also fair, and while it might have been difficult to argue with him, if the point was well taken, even by one of the students, he would be the first to acknowledge it (Lal 1984: ix). It is interesting, but no one has ever told me that Wheeler was liked by these colleagues, whether senior or junior, but he was deeply respected.

The training schools that Wheeler organized were a tremendous success and the excavation results can be quickly summarized:

Taxila

The first of the excavations took place at Marshall's site of Taxila in 1944-45 (Plate 2.56). Most of the excavation effort was directed at finding the early levels of Bhir Mound, the portion of the settlement visited by Alexander the Great in 326 BC (Wheeler 1976: 32-5).[56] One trench was also laid on Sirkap Mound to investigate the place of the so-called "Kachcha Kot" (Dilapidated Fort) in relation to the main Sirkap occupation. This excavation was never published as a single report, although A. Ghosh published the Sirkap trench and determined that there were essentially two Sirkaps, an Indo-Greek city of the second century BC and a Saka or early Parthian city of the first century BC (Ghosh 1947-48). A hoard of coins and jewelry of ca. 300 BC was also found in the Bhir Mound excavation and was published by G. M. Young (1946) in the brand new *Ancient India*.

Arikamedu

On a hot day in May 1944 Wheeler arrived in Madras, prophetically, at the same time as a stray Japanese bomber. His "discovery" of Roman amphorae and Arretine Ware in the museum there has been told in amusing detail elsewhere (Wheeler 1976: 35-41). A year (April-June 1945) after the discovery he held his second training school at the site, which like Taxila, was familiar historical ground to him. Arikamedu is just off the shore of the Bay of Bengal in Pondicherry, the former French possession in South India. This site has been identified as a seaport of the early centuries AD. French antiquarians had been excavating there for a number of years, with indifferent results. Wheeler's work was published (Wheeler, Ghosh and Krishna Deva 1946) and reveals that he found the remains of a warehouse of ca. 50 AD and a facility for dying inexpensive cloth, of about the same period.

Harappa

By 1946 Wheeler was prepared to tackle a new historical context and went to Harappa, which he had visited in May of 1944. The story of this visit to the site is important and is fully told in *Still Digging* (Wheeler 1955: 190-92). It is important because when he saw the height and contours of the AB Mound he immediately saw what he thought of as a citadel, and within hours had completely changed the principal organizing notions for the Harappan Civilization from one of peaceful peoples to those of war. In 1946, Wheeler set to work excavating the defenses, Cemetery R-37 and found the first evidence for an Early Harappan occupation there. A report was published on this work (Wheeler 1947a) which contained the first expression of the "Aryan Hypothesis" for the demise of the Indus Civilization (1947b).

Both Krishna Deva and B. B. Lal have told me that this hypothesis seems to have been developed from information Wheeler took from V. S. Agrawala. Agrawala was selected to be the tour guide and lecturer for visiting dignitaries who came to Harappa during the excavations. He spoke of the R̥gveda and references in it to warfare and the conquest of towns and cities and speculated that it might have been the reason for the demise of the Harappan Civilization. Thus, credit for this hypothesis, now quite dead as an historical notion, seems to belong to V. S. Agrawala, not Wheeler.[57]

Brahmagiri and Chandravalli

On the eve of Partition, Wheeler took his students to the south again (March-June 1947) to excavate megaliths at Brahmagiri and the site of Chandravalli which was found to be largely contemporaneous with Arikamedu and is a site of the Satavahana period. Roman coins were found there along with the now important Russet-colored Ware (Wheeler 1947-48).

It is interesting that Wheeler went back to Taxila as his first venture into the field. Woolley (1939a: 6) felt that, while continued work there was desirable, Taxila would have to wait its turn, while new sites were uncovered. D. K. Chakrabarti notes that: "Taxila was chosen as the venue of this training because of its infrastructural advantages..." (1988: 176). Wheeler was, however, the preeminent excavator of Roman (Classical) sites in England, and Taxila would at least produce materials with which he was familiar. The basic history of the site and Gandhara were also known to him, sufficiently so that a bit of boning up would get him by. It certainly was not Ahichchhatra: set deep within India, a material culture totally unfamiliar to him, steeped in the complexities of Indian culture, Sanskrit literature, Hindu and Buddhist religion, the Epics. How could he lead, direct and train, if he was in fact the student? One can think of no better site in the whole of the Subcontinent, that would have given Wheeler a chance to both learn about India and conduct his field schools, than Taxila.

This hypothesis might even be tested by the fact that his second training excavation was at the Indo-Roman port of Arikamedu in Tamil Nadu. It was not until the eve of Partition, three years after having arrived in India, that he dug Brahmagiri and faced up to Indian history in a deeper sense.

These intensive training excavations produced a cadre of competent field archaeologists who fanned out into government service and universities. The only significant person who was not a part of the training schools was H. D. Sankalia who, in a different context, was trained as a field man by Wheeler, not E. J. H. Mackay, as has been suggested (Chakrabarti 1988: 177).

South Asian archaeology owes a great debt to Wheeler. These training excavations instilled in a generation of field workers the need for clear problem orientation, discipline and sound recording.

Wheeler turned over his office to Dr. N. P. Chakrabarti on 30 April 1948. The new Director General is most noted for organizing the Delhi venue of a large exhibition of Indian materials that had been taken to London in 1947, under the sponsorship of the Royal Academy. The exhibition was important because of its great size and scope and was the collection around which the National Museum of India was formed. The best material from Mohenjo-daro and Harappa had been incorporated into the exhibition, including the "Priest King," the best of the two bronze dancing girls from Mohenjo-daro, the red jasper torso from Harappa and many stamp seals. It all returned to Delhi and when the exhibition closed the Pakistanis, justifiably, asked that at least some of these treasures be repatriated to their country. F. A. Khan, one of the original students at Wheeler's training excavations, went to Delhi and a *partage* was arranged. The "Priest King" and "Seal of Divine Adoration" were given to the new Pakistan nation, but the Indians kept the "Proto Siva" (Mahayogi) seal, the best bronze dancing girl from Mohenjo-daro, and the red jasper and black stone torsos from Harappa. The minor finds and ceramics were evenly distributed. Pakistan, after all, had the sites and could dig for many years generating huge new collections. India at the time had little, if nothing, to compare. Today, both the National Museums of India and Pakistan have very fine collections from the two key sites of the Harappan Civilization, Mohenjo-daro and Harappa, as well as materials from their own excavations.

Following Partition, Wheeler continued to work in South Asia. The Government of Pakistan made him an Archaeological Adviser, and he undertook two more excavations: one season of work at Mohenjo-daro in 1950 (Wheeler 1950a, 1950b, 1950c; 1950d; Alcock 1952, 1986; Dales 1986) and Charsada in 1958 (Wheeler 1962) in the Northwest Frontier. Wheeler also published a popular book on the archaeological heritage of Pakistan at this time (Wheeler 1950e).

The 1950 excavation of Mohenjo-daro was conducted by Wheeler with Leslie Alcock as his assistant. A. H. Dani was also part of the team and he supervised much of the work at the ACC Site in the southeastern corner of the Mound of the Great Bath (Alcock 1986: 496). Alcock was to go from Mohenjo-daro to work with Walter Fairservis' team in the Quetta Valley where he played a central role in the excavation of Damb Sadaat. Although the excavation of Mohenjo-daro in 1950 is technically outside the time frame for detailed exposition in this Part of the *Indus Age* it is too important to be ignored, since the development of the Wheeler-Piggott Paradigm hinged on it in part.

The excavation set for itself three objectives (Wheeler 1955: 223-25): training Pakistani archaeologists; investigating the Mound of the Great Bath to see if defenses comparable to Harappa could be found and finally, investigate the lowest levels of Mohenjo-daro. The work took place between February and April 1950 and the training aspects were apparently less than a success (Wheeler 1955: 228). Alcock found towers in his area, that could be interpreted as fortifications (1986: 500, see also Alcock 1952), but the work in the REM area on the western side of the Mound of the Great Bath did not reveal anything of the kind. Wheeler did, however, find what he thought was the Great Granary of the city, and this fit with his notions of what the Indus Civilization was all about (Wheeler 1968: 43-6). The deep digging began with the laying out of a trench on February 20, 1950, at plain level, west of the "Granary." By April 7, the ground water had sufficiently undermined the sides of this trench that it was no longer safe to work in, and it was abandoned, with a pond now in the bottom (Plate 2.57, Plate 2.58). This exercise did not reach virgin soil, but did get to −40.00 meters above mean sea level. Excavations in a well on the Mound of the Great Bath reached −38.17 meters above mean sea level, still within an archaeological midden, which is the lowest excavation at Mohenjo-daro (Ardeleanu-Jansen 1993a: 13). Drilling has gone a bit deeper (Jansen 1987: 19). The deep trench did give evidence for continuity of occupation from levels well below modern plain level, as well as for a large mud brick bund, just removed to the west from the podium of the "Granary." It did not sustain the notion that the Mound of the Great Bath was surrounded by fortifications, let alone protection for Priest Kings.

The Wheeler-Piggott Paradigm for The Harappan Civilization

It has been noted that Stuart Piggott did not join Wheeler in the Archaeological Survey of India but he did study archaeology while in British India and was a frequent contributor to the new *Ancient India*. He and Wheeler set about creating a new paradigm for the Harappan Civilization, that differed substantially (though not entirely) from the one that had been put forward by Marshall, Mackay and V. Gordon Childe in *Light on the Most Ancient East* and the various editions of *New Light on the Most Ancient East* (Childe 1928, 1934; Plate 2.59).[58]

The new paradigm had begun at Harappa on Wheeler's first visit to the site, before he had even begun to excavate there. He saw in the AB Mound a Citadel, to defend the inhabitants of the city from attack. During times of peace the city's priests and godhead were proposed to have been there. Based on what Wheeler knew of Mesopotamian civilization, the times "...produced in India a social organization not altogether unlike those of the contemporary West" (Wheeler 1947c: 74); and "In Sumer, the wealth and discipline of the city-state were vested in the chief deity, i.e. in the priesthood or a priest-king. The civic focus was the exalted temple, centre of an elaborate and carefully ordered secular administration under divine sanction" (Wheeler 1947c: 74). This led Wheeler to think of the Harappan Civilization in a similar way: "It can no longer be doubted that, whatever the source of their authority—and a dominant religious element may fairly be assumed—the lords of Harappa administered their city in a fashion not remote from that of the priest-kings or governors of Sumer and Akkad. In other words, the social structure of Harappa conformed in principle with that of the other great riverine civilizations of the day" (Wheeler 1947c: 76). Here we have returned very close to something that Sir John Marshall wisely abandoned in 1926: "Indo-Sumerian Civilization."

Piggott follows this line of thought, but is more subtle in his treatment of Sumerian matters (Figure 2.51). His version of the paradigm is found in his book *Prehistoric India* (1950: 153): "A state ruled by priest-kings, wielding autocratic and absolute power from two main seats of government, and with the main artery of communication between the capital cities provided by a great navigable river, seems, then, to be the reasonable deduction from the archaeological evidence of the civilization of Harappa."

Wheeler pursues other dimensions of the Indus Civilization in *Five Thousand Years of Pakistan* (Wheeler 1950e). This is a book meant for a wide audience but in it he uses phrases like the following to characterize his understanding of the Harappan Civilization: "All is orderly and regulated...dull, a trifle lacking in the stimulus of individuality" or the "...absence or suppression of personality in its details from street to street" and "This sense of regimentation..." (Wheeler 1950e: 28). In another place he refers to the "...astonishing *sameness* of the civilization...Another quality of it is its *isolation*" (Wheeler 1950e: 29, original emphasis).

The new excavations at Harappa, and the potency of the two younger scholars, led Childe to revise the 1953 edition of *New Light*...:

Figure 2.51. Sketch of Stuart Piggott

No multiplication of weapons of war and battle scenes attests internecine conflicts between city states as in Mesopotamia, nor yet the force whereby a single king, as in Egypt, achieved by conquest internal peace...At the moment the two cities of Harappa and Mohenjo-daro stand out like twin capitals in a single "empire" among a number of smaller sites—provincial townships, fortified villages, and possibly frontier posts and factories...That a "ruler" dwelt in the citadels is clear, and the attachment thereto of great granaries concretely expresses his economic power; like the Sumerian city-god or the divine pharaoh he concentrated the real wealth produced by the city's dependent territories (Childe 1953: 174).

The presence of Citadels, and the lack of evidence for warfare, posed a problem for Wheeler and Piggott. Without evidence for arms and warfare, where was the enemy, from whom were the Priest Kings protecting themselves? This problem was addressed by Wheeler in the first edition of *The Indus Civilization* (1953).

The Indus Civilization inevitably derived its wealth from a combination of agriculture and trade. How far these sources were supplemented and enlarged by military conquest is at present beyond conjecture, but it is to be supposed that the wide extent of the civilization was initially the product of something more forcible than peaceful penetration. True, the military element does not loom large amongst the extant remains, but it must be remembered that at present we know almost nothing of the earliest phase of the civilization.

As at present known, fortifications at the two major cities are confined to the citadels; it is not apparent that the Lower City was in either case fenced. This in itself suggests that the function of the armed citadel may have been as much the affirmation of domestic authority as a safeguard against external aggression. Until, however, the negative evidence in respect of the Lower City is stronger than it is at present, too much stress may not be laid upon this interpretation (Wheeler 1953: 52-3).

The problem with envisioning the high mounds at Mohenjo-daro and Harappa as citadels has not improved since 1953, and the concept has been dropped by most modern interpreters of the Harappan Civilization. Since it is not known what kind of architecture was on the summit of the AB Mound at Harappa it is difficult to be definitive there. But the Mound of the Great Bath at Mohenjo-daro seems to have been a place of ritual, the elevation being a symbol of the auspicious, rather than a safeguard against attack. It was also a place of storage, and this does bring an important economic function into the domain of the religious establishment. The striking juxtaposition of the tank and a storage facility adjacent to one another at Lothal might be seen as conforming to the Mohenjo-daro arrangement.

The third edition of *The Indus Civilization* contains reference to "foreigners" and an "immigrant regime" (1968: 39 and 40) with regard to the building of the Citadel at Mohenjo-daro. This is not a well developed theme in Wheeler's writing, but it is there and was a part of the historical mix of factors that he felt were a part of the Indus Civilization.

Some prominent features of the Marshall Paradigm were carried forward in the Wheeler-Piggott interpretation. Obviously, a strong analogy with Sumer and Egypt is a feature of both paradigms and the same justification for its use is given: the three civilizations were all members of a larger class of historical phenomena. A wetter climate was also postulated and the sameness of the remains was highlighted in both views. There is little difference between these interpretations in their treatment of Harappan craft production and "science."

The overall view of these two syntheses emerge as radically different. With Marshall we learn of Harappan trade, commerce and shared ideology; with Wheeler and Piggott we are informed about priest-kings, temple complexes, state granaries and the nature of theocratic power. Marshall's effective use of his knowledge of the Indian tradition and ethnographic analogy disappears from later reasoning, being replaced by a comparative method and notions like "Indo-Sumerian Civilization." The Wheeler-Piggott Paradigm changed Marshall's Harappans from austere, peaceful, even boring, urban merchant burghers, whose beliefs were harbingers of Indian ideologies, into a people victimized by despotic priest-kings who wielded absolute power from remote citadels where they safeguarded themselves and the gods who justified their authority.

To a degree the *Indus Age* is directed toward creating a new interpretative scheme to replace the Wheeler-Piggott Paradigm. This short review is intended only to place the work of these scholars in a direct historical context, especially with respect to Marshall.

There is another British scholar-administrator who made a contribution to the understanding of the Indus Civilization. His work is well known to most archaeologists, because it is important, but it seems to have been missed by many. This seems to be a good place to begin to redress this situation.

A British Civil Servant Explores Sindh

The archaeological history of Sindh has been enhanced through the work of Hugh Trevor Lambrick[59], a civil servant and devoted student of the region and its people. His "amateur excursions in archaeology" provide a great deal of information on the archaeological remains in the Sindh Kohistan, the outer Kirthar Range and Thar Parkar (Lambrick 1941, 1942a, 1944, 1946). His travels and observations concerning human settlement in the desert fringe separating the Indus flood plains from the Thar Desert are still our only source of information on protohistoric habitation in this region (Lambrick 1964: 70-99). Much of this work is drawn together in his book on Sindh, which should be considered "must reading" for any serious student of the Indus Civilization.

Lambrick had a very sound grasp of the relationship between geography and human settlement; seen best in his two volumes on the history of Sindh (1964, 1972). His narrative on the Indus Civilization, its relationship to the Indus River and its flood plains remains the most valuable single source on the topic (1964: 70-99). In addition, Lambrick wrote a critical paper debunking the theory that floods destroyed Mohenjo-daro and led to the eclipse of the ancient cities of the Indus (Lambrick 1967) as well as a contribution to an understanding of the internal stratigraphy of Mohenjo-daro (1971). There is no overall, grand theory in Lambrick's work, as with the Wheeler-Piggott Paradigm. Instead, one finds a well stated, reasoned, even commonsensical approach to understanding the past, backstopped by important observations, spanning his career in the field when he was administering the census, dealing with irrigation and civil unrest (Plate 2.60).

There is an undoubted originality to Lambrick's research in archaeology and ancient history. His gift for stating much of his discussion in terms of cultural geography has enhanced his field observations. These, it has to be admitted, are at times maddeningly imprecise and unfortunately, he never published anything like a gazetteer of his finds, with illustrations of the artifacts. Still, there is a utility to the overall contribution and he represents a fine example of how an "amateur" can contribute to the discipline of archaeology.

Another Near Eastern Archaeologist Appears on the Scene

Donald Eugene McCown was a brilliant student of archaeology at the Oriental Institute of the University of Chicago (Figure 2.52). Trained by A. T. Olmstead, Henri Frankfort and Erich Schmidt he wrote a dissertation that has become an archaeological classic: *The Comparative Stratigraphy of Early Iran* (McCown 1942).

In February 1945, Donald McCown was a Captain in Signals stationed in Paris. It was from here that he applied for a John Simon Guggenheim Memorial Foundation Fellowship to "...define and put into relative sequence the cultures of Baluchistan...thereby continuing a study of earlier Iranian cultures...throwing light on the origins of the Harappa culture and explaining contact between that civilization and Mesopotamia." The Guggenheim Foundation awarded him a "post-service" fellowship on April 5, 1945. This meant that he could take up the work when he was discharged from military

Figure 2.52. Sketch of Donald E. McCown

service, which took place on July 7, 1945. In 1946, he was back at the Oriental Institute and wrote a memorandum to Director John A. Wilson on August 12 of that year. In it he laid out a scheme for work in Baluchistan and a program for understanding the origins of the Harappan Civilization and its contacts with Sumer. The Guggenheim Fellowship is not mentioned here but the Guggenheim proposal is clearly a part of it.

The program under consideration is concerned with the Harappa civilization in three ways: a) the determination of its origin and possible kinship with Near Eastern civilizations, b) establishing its chronological position in relation to Mesopotamia, on which the chronology of all the Indus-Baluchistan cultures largely depends, and c) ascertaining how much influence was exerted between Sumer and the Harappa civilization.

McCown wanted to excavate Ghazi Shah, one of Majumdar's sites near Lake Manchar. He wanted to be in the field for the first season, excavating between November 1946 and February 1947.

Realizing that the Subcontinent was rapidly moving toward independence and the creation of the Pakistan nation, McCown proposed an alternative program for this period, in Iran, at the site of Tall-i Jangal, just south of Persepolis.

Professor Wilson responded to McCown's proposal on August 21, 1946 in a prudent tone, acknowledging that it made good archaeological sense, but he did not want the young scholar to become embroiled in the vagaries of Indian Partition and the Institute had commitments to work at Luxor and Megiddo. Moreover, Wilson was soon to step down as Director and he did not want to tie the hands of his successor with a brand new project, in a part of the world in which the Oriental Institute had never worked.

In the end, McCown sailed alone for India on November 26, 1946, using the resources from his Guggenheim to support him for a year. He spent most of his time in Delhi, but visited sites in the Punjab (probably Harappa) and Sind (Mohenjo-daro, Ghazi Shah, Pandi Wahi?) and Quetta, where he undertook a small survey that revealed previously unreported sites. In a report to the Guggenheim Foundation of May 18, 1947 he says:

> Some of the materials which bear on my problem, particularly finds made by Sir Aurel Stein on the last explorations before his death, are unpublished. These Dr. Wheeler persuaded me to work up for a Memoir of the Archaeological Survey of India. I was loathe to take up any more work, but he had no one else to deal with them and their publication is essential and preliminary to my Baluchistan study. So I spent a month longer in India that I had originally planned.

McCown spent some time while in India with Stuart Piggott, who holds McCown's work in high esteem (personal communication July 1995). His time there led to several publications dealing with Rana Ghundai, Harappan sites and most important, he joined with Krishna Deva to publish the findings from N. G. Majumdar's last, tragic tour in 1938 along the eastern face of the Kirthar Range to the Gaj Nai (Krishna Deva and McCown 1949). A manuscript was prepared for the Survey that described the pottery found by Sir Aurel Stein at the Amri-Nal and Kulli site of Niai Buthi in Las Bela, excavated during Stein's last explorations (McCown 1946b). This document was read by Beatrice de Cardi (1965: 128), but it has since disappeared. He also prepared an introduction to Brigadier E. J. Ross' report on Rana Ghundai (McCown 1946a).

In May 1947 McCown was in Baghdad, on his way home from India. It was from here that he wrote to the Guggenheim. He also wrote to Thorkild Jacobsen on May 12, discussing mostly work in the Near East, but observing: "As you know the Guggenheim Fellowship is for a year, so I am morally, if not legally, committed to work on that project until next November. Had it been possible to dig in the Indus Valley next winter, this would have been in line with the Guggenheim and would have provided new information for which it would have been worth delaying the Baluchistan book. If I am to work in Iraq before the Guggenheim is finished I really should have Mr. Moe's permission to interrupt the Guggenheim."

In the end Donald McCown never returned to India. He went off to work at Nippur (McCown and Haines 1967; McCown, Haines and Biggs 1978), eventually dropping out of archaeology altogether. McCown's later years were spent with the National Security Agency, drawing on his background in signals. But, he had a near encounter with the archaeology of the Subcontinent in the Wheeler era, and this at least deserves some notice.

As an aside, Donald's brother, Theodore D. McCown also has an Indian connection. Theodore made a career as a Physical Anthropologist at the University of California, Berkeley, and co-authored the report on the famous Neanderthal remains from the Mount Carmel Caves in Israel (McCown and Keith 1939). He searched for fossil man with Deccan College in the Narmada Valley, conducting two expeditions there, the first in 1957-58 then again in 1965-66.

PARTITION, INDEPENDENCE AND MORE RECENT DIGGING

The discovery of the Indus Age would be incomplete without some recognition of more recent projects that have played a role in shaping our perceptions of the Harappan Civilization. This research is not so distant from us that it can be considered historical, yet it is very much a part of the substance of this book. There are several undertakings that deserve special notice because of their overall impact on our understanding of the Indus Age. They will be enumerated more or less in the order in which they were initiated.

At Partition the archaeologists in the new Indian nation were isolated from the Indus Civilization. Most of the sites, and the two great metropolitan centers, were in equally new Pakistan. This led Indian archaeologists to begin an intensive period of exploration followed by excavation of key sites. The first of these was undertaken by S. R. Rao, of the Archaeological Survey of India, who began intensive exploration in Gujarat. This led to the excavation of Rangpur and Lothal (Rao 1963a, 1979, 1985). These two bodies of work, which were multi-year programs, brought to light important new material that redefined the borderlands of the Harappan Civilization. Rao's explorations and excavations set protohistoric archaeology in this region on a new course and his site of Lothal has proven to be an extremely important place in terms of understanding the Mature Harappan. Rao's work in Gujarat has been carried forward by Jagat Pati Joshi and his explorations and excavations in Kutch, especially at Surkotada and more recently by R. S. Bisht at Dholavira.

In 1955, a year after Rao began his excavations at Lothal, his colleague and Director of Archaeology in Pakistan, F. A. Khan, initiated a project at Kot Diji (F. A. Khan 1959a, 1964, 1965). The Kot Diji Project defined this aspect of the Early Harappan and documented the relationship between the Kot Dijian assemblage and the Mature Harappan. An expansion of the work at Kot Diji was also undertaken by the Pakistan Department of Archaeology at Sarai Khola (M. A. Halim 1972a, 1972b; Mughal 1972i, 1972j).

Kalibangan was taken under excavation for nine seasons (1960-61 to 1968-69) by B. B. Lal and B. K. Thapar, both of whom had participated in the Wheeler field schools (Lal and Thapar 1967; Lal 1979, 1981; Thapar 1973a, 1973b, 1975). This was the first horizontal excavation of an Early Harappan settlement and informed us about the nature of both the Early and Mature Harappan in the Sarasvati Valley.

140

The most important excavation of an early food-producing village in the Subcontinent began in 1974-75 when Jean-Francois Jarrige undertook the excavation of Mehrgarh. At least thirteen seasons of work have been completed in collaboration with the Government of Pakistan. There is a huge bibliography for this project, the most important of which is the compilation of all of the preliminary reports into a book (C. Jarrige, J.-F. Jarrige, Meadow and Quivron 1995) with a splendid introductory essay by the project Director J.-F. Jarrige (1995a). Other bibliographic information is as follows: J.-F. Jarrige (1981, 1982, 1983, 1984a, 1984b, 1986, 1987a, 1987b, 1988a, 1988b, 1989, 1990a, 1990b, 1990c, 1991a, 1991b, 1992, 1993a, 1993b, 1994a, 1994b, 1995a); C. Jarrige (1984, 1991, 1992, 1994); Jarrige and Lechevallier (1979, 1980); Jarrige and Meadow (1980, 1992); Lechevallier (1984); Lechevallier, Meadow and Quivron (1982); Lechevallier and Quivron (1981, 1985); Meadow (1981, 1984a, 1984b, 1986, 1989a, 1991b, 1993a); Quivron (1980); Santoni (1980, 1984, 1988, 1989); Sellier (1989, 1992).

M. R. Mughal's tremendously important exploration of Cholistan between 1974 and 1978 has proven to be the single most important survey in the history of the Indus Age. He discovered an astounding number of sites along the Ghaggar-Hakra river that have revolutionalized our understanding of the settlement patterns of the Indus Age (Mughal 1980a, 1981, 1982, 1984, 1990a, 1992b, 1992c, 1994, 1997).

A team from Aachen Germany led by Michael Jansen, at times paired with a team from IsMEO, always working closely with Pakistani counterparts, has been conducting a program of research at Mohenjo-daro since 1979. This has produced significant insights into this ancient urban setting and the role of Mohenjo-daro within the overall context of the Harappan Civilization (Jansen 1979, 1983, 1984a, 1984b, 1985, 1989a, 1989b, 1993a, 1993b; Jansen and Urban editors 1984, 1985, 1987, Jansen and Tosi editors 1988; Jansen, Mulloy and Urban editors 1991; Urban and Jansen editors 1983; Halim and Vidale 1984; Ardeleanu-Jansen 1984, 1987, 1989, 1992, 1993a, 1993b).

Finally, there is the reinvigoration of the excavations at Harappa that began in 1986 by the joint American-Pakistani team which has done much to tighten our control of the internal periodization and chronology of this site as well as offering important insights into its economy and craft production (Meadow 1991a; Dales and Kenoyer 1987, 1988, 1989, 1990, 1992a, 1992b, 1993a, 1993b).

One note on the excavations at Amri by Jean-Marie Casal (Figure 2.53) is in order. This was a very well known site and Casal dug there from 1959-62 (Casal 1964a). He confirmed Majumdar's sequence and defined a Transitional Period (his Amri II) between the Early Harappan, Amri-Nal materials and the Mature Harappan. His Transitional Period did not receive the attention it should have during his lifetime, but it was a bold insight on his part, that is reshaping notions of Indus urban beginnings today.

Figure 2.53. Sketch of Jean-Marie Casal

One of the most interesting, important parts of the story of the Harappan Civilization is actually taking place outside of the Subcontinent. It is the discovery of Harappan materials in the Arabian Gulf, especially in Bahrain, the United Arab Emirates and Oman. There is a substantial body of literature on this topic, which is nicely presented in (Cleuziou 1980, 1981, 1984, 1986, 1989a, 1989b, 1992; Cleuziou and Tosi 1986, 1988; Cleuziou, Reade and Tosi 1989; Edens 1993; Frifelt 1976, 1979, 1985, 1986, 1989; Al Khalifa and Rice editous 1986; Potts 1983, 1990, 1993; Ratnagar 1981; Tosi 1986a, 1986b, 1986c). It is also discussed in the volume on the Mature Harappan in this series. This research tells us about Harappan seafaring ventures and the foreign commerce of all of the ancient peoples of this world region.

There has been a great deal more work than that just outlined here. The excavations at many places were not highlighted—Shortughai, Said Qala, Kili Ghul Mohammad, Anjira, Miri Qalat, Gumla, Rehman Dheri, Lewan, Islam Chowki, Jalilpur, Banawali, Bhagwanpura, Mitathal, Ropar, Hulas, Allahdino (Plate 2.64), Ghazi Shah, Somnath, Kuntasi, Zekhada, Nagwada, Nageswar, even Rojdi, Babar Kot and Oriyo Timbo—could easily have been noted.

This later history played the predominant role in reshaping our perceptions of the Indus Civilization. Materials excavated prior to Partition play a substantial part in contemporary understanding of the Harappan Civilization but the new materials have greatly expanded the geographical horizons of this civilization, even beyond the limits of the Subcontinent. The earlier syntheses, which drew almost exclusively on materials from Mohenjo-daro and Harappa, have been transcended in a most fundamental way.

WHAT IT MIGHT ALL MEAN

This is a long story of discovery with many details, each of which is significant, but could overshadow the bigger story. Therefore, it seems important to extend this historical journey to convey some enduring ideas which the story as a whole contributes to understanding the Harappan Civilization.

Perhaps the first and most important point is the discovery itself. The ancient cities of the Indus had been forgotten for millennia, but then one day in 1924, there they were, sprung as a new entity upon an unsuspecting world. This act of discovery is not something which can be associated with ancient Egypt or Mesopotamian Civilizations, each of which had been a known part of the unbroken historical record. It seems to have had several consequences, one of the most significant is the way in which the civilization was analyzed. Lacking the deep historical traditions that formed boundaries and gave shape to regions, the Harappan Civilization grew from the knowledge of two sites, and archaeological methods were used to guide this process. In fact, something closely akin to the "type fossil" method, derived from paleontology, was used. As sites were discovered their material inventories were compared to Mohenjo-daro and Harappa and if they were close, they were added to the inventory of sites, if they did not fit the Harappan pattern they were excluded. This method led archaeologists to see an immense Harappan world, all of which was treated as an undifferentiated whole, since the type fossil method tends to minimize differences and emphasize similarity. To some degree this striking aspect of the Harappan Civilization is an artifact of discovery and not necessarily inherent in the fabric of the civilization itself.

The type fossil method is akin to, but different from, the kind of comparative archaeological study that has been applied to many sets of archaeological remains, the so-called "Uruk expansion" for example (Algaze 1993). Comparative methods have great utility, but when they are used to minimize differences, sometimes erasing them altogether, as in the type fossil notion, problems can arise. It has happened in the history of the Harappan Civilization, where sites were examined and were declared to be either identical with the type fossil as defined through the excavations at Mohenjo-daro, or outside these bounds. It was a black and white situation, with no room for gray. A good example of this occurred with the various early excavations at Rangpur in Gujarat. The principal question that archaeologists were seeking to answer through excavation was: is this a settlement of the Harappan Civilization?

This is an important point, and approaching it from a slightly different direction may serve to clarify and expand it. No one has ever gone about organizing the material culture of ancient Near Eastern civilization using the same "type fossil" method that was applied to the Indus. It would be an immense task and probably would not repay the effort in intellectual terms. My guess, and the guess of those who have more experience there than I, is that the boundaries of this set of ancient states would be vastly expanded. Thus, while the Harappan Civilization is much larger than the heartland of civilization in southern Mesopotamia, it is not likely that it is that much larger than the area inhabited by all third millennium civilizations in greater Mesopotamia or the Near East.

The greater Mesopotamian material is not handled within the "type fossil" paradigm because so much is known about it that this would be an unproductive way to pursue the historical problems on which archaeologists work. A great deal is known about ancient geography and the shape of states from written records and the continuity in history suggests powerfully convincing ways of organizing our thoughts concerning them. Lacking these insights for the Harappan Civilization, archaeologists have proceeded as best they could at organizing their material. The "type fossil" method was a good standard in its day, but as a result a very large archaeological entity has emerged. The Harappan Civilization, in that it was ever a single unified polity for any length of time, is probably larger than is justified. There is a contrast with Near Eastern Bronze Age civilization which emerges. In spite of the degree of similarity and coherence in material culture that unites these archaeological assemblages and could be favorably compared to the Indus Civilization, archaeologists there have managed to deal with cultural diversity. They understand that in antiquity, greater Mesopotamia was rarely politically united, and then only for very short periods of time. Seen from this perspective one might question the wisdom of including the so-called Harappan sites in Saurashtra, as well as those to the east of Kalibangan, within the same organizing scheme that might be used for Sindh and the Punjab.

Having discussed the size of the Harappan Civilization in these terms it should be evident that the so-called sameness of Harappan remains has emerged as a result of the same methodology. If the Harappan Civilization is large, then the "type fossil" method demands that it be homogeneous, because that is the way the method works. If the "type fossil" method is abandoned, if differences are emphasized rather than similarities in material culture, or if we seek to define our ancient cultural units using criteria other than pottery, figurines, beads, etc., then the civilization will tend to break up into smaller units, and the homogeneity of the former entity will disappear, by definition.

It can be simply, clearly and convincingly asserted that the remains of the Harappan Civilization are no more astonishingly homogeneous than those of Dynastic Egypt. Since the Egyptians were well known archaeologically it may seem somewhat odd that the issue of homogeneity came to be associated with the ancient Indian civilization and not the inhabitants of the Nile. But it did, and that seems to be a serious distortion of an archaeological reality.

Another important historical point relates to the way in which the excavations of Mohenjo-daro and Harappa dominated the thought on this ancient sociocultural system. In fact, until the excavations at Kalibangan and Lothal began to mature in the 1960s, it could be said, with only small footnotes to the contrary, that the two cities stood for the entire civilization. It is hardly necessary then to explain why the thinking on these ancient peoples was so urban oriented, so dominated by the perspective of the city.

It is also clear that there is considerable scope for the role of the individual scholar to be considered in the discovery of these remains. Rakal Das Banerji's energy, and arrogance, his determination to see his rival, D. R. Bhandarkar, shown the fool, was a fundamentally important driving force behind his first visit to Mohenjo-daro and his decision to excavate there. Marshall, in his own methodical way, sent Hargreaves to Harappa on a reconnaissance that had no particular focus, other than because stamp seals had been found there. He then put Sahni into the field at Harappa, just as Banerji was beginning to learn something about Mohenjo-daro. That both sites came to the fore together in 1922-24, is a coincidence of astounding magnitude; sufficiently so that one has to suspect that there is an historical relationship behind this event.

In spite of his close association with this civilization, especially Mohenjo-daro, Sir John Marshall actually worked at the site for only one season, and never lent his spade to Harappa itself. While one would suspect that he visited Harappa, I know of no document that could be used to prove it.

I am also struck by the relatively even pacing of the excavation and exploratory work, even admitting that the excavation at Ahichchhatra was not thought of as an Harappan site until Y. D. Sharma excavated there in 1964.[60] But, the progress of discovery is a relatively even process, with a significant increase in the overall level of activity after Partition in 1947.

The early work at Harappan sites such as Major E. Mockler's excavation at Sutkagen-dor in 1876, Fritz Noetling's survey of Dabar Kot in 1898, followed by Sir Aurel Stein's visit in 1904, and L. P. Tessitori at Kalibangan in 1917 and 1918, produced collections of distinctive Harappan pottery and related artifacts. Admittedly the work was poorly published, if published at all, but the material was there. Its significance was totally unknown then and piecing together a relatively complete history of these early ventures in Harappan archaeology is essentially a product of contemporary scholarship.

NOTES

1. Some of this material also appears in *The Indus Age: The writing system.* The treatment in the present book is more detailed.

2. Discussions with Professor Thomas Trautman were useful in clarifying a number of issues in this portion of the text. He also led me to the Ellis reference.

3. Marshall has one article that deals with this subject: "Influence of Race on Early Indian Art" (Marshall 1923b). Some of his thoughts are quite extreme (1923b: 663). But this paper, which resulted from the George Birdwood Memorial Lecture at the Royal Society of Arts, Chaired by Lord Curzon, was delivered before the significance of Mohenjo-daro and Harappa was known, and Marshall's thought on these peoples was quite reasonable, although not entirely free from now defunct racial concepts.

Another of the Birdwood Lectures was delivered by Sir Leonard Woolley on 1 December 1939 (Woolley 1940). This followed his review of the Archaeological Survey of India, that, as will be seen, was a condemnation of Marshall's leadership.

4. There are problems with the chronology of Masson's travels in his writings. He was a deserter and seems to have concealed the date of his departure from the services of the East India Company.

5. The story of Masson's relationship with the East India Company, and how it came to support his research is long and interesting, nicely outlined in (Whitteridge 1986).

6. Horace H. Wilson has a very good essay tracing in complete detail the story of discovery that led Prinsep to his insights (Wilson 1841: 1-50).

7. The Bimaran reliquary is in the British Museum and usually on display in their South Asian galleries.

8. The *Bengal Muster Rolls* documents the desertion of Lewis on 4 July 1827 (Whitteridge 1986: 2; see also Kaye and Johnson 1937: 1273-274). His position as a deserter may be the reason for his generally cavalier treatment of dates. Masson's unmasking by Captain (Sir) Claude Wade as a deserter is also well documented in papers in the India Office Library (Kaye and Johnson 1937: 1276-277). Masson returned to England in 1842 and died on 5 November 1853 in Lower Edmonton at the age of 53 (Whitteridge 1986: 165)

Confirmation of the fact that Charles Masson was James Lewis may be best seen from the fact that he (Masson) accepted a pardon for desertion offered in the name of James Lewis. The pardon is dated 9 February 1835 [India Office Library, correspondence from the Secret Committee to the Governor General (L/P & S/5/547)].

9. The city is better known today as Mansura and has recently been the site of renewed excavation by the Pakistan Department of Archaeology.

10. The name of this site is correctly rendered "Sutkagen-dor," not "Suktagen-dor" given in Stein (1931: 60). Stein corrects his own mistake (Stein 1937: 71) with the following: "I may take this opportunity to record that the proper pronunciation of the local name as now heard from nomadic Baluch of the neighborhood was Sutkagen-dor (as also given by Major Mockler 1877: 122), from *sutka* 'burnt' prevailing in the local Baluch dialect over *sukta* as the equivalent of Persian *sukhta*. The name owes its origin to the red coloring which the great amount of well-burnt potsherds strewing the ground gives to the whole site as seen from a distance."

11. The collections from these three sites are now in the Museum fur Indische Kunst, Berlin and are the subject of a Masters Thesis by Friedhelm Pedde, a student at the Free University of Berlin (Pedde 1993a and b).

12. Marshall's full name was John Hubert Marshall (1876-1958), but he rarely used even his middle initial. He married Florence, daughter of Sir Harold Bell Longhurst (surgeon-dentist) shortly before leaving for India and they had two children, a son and a daughter (Wheeler 1971: 699). Marshall was trained in the Classics at Cambridge and was a Gold Medalist in Greek there. He moved on to the British School in Athens and gained a reasonably broad exposure to the eastern Mediterranean, traveling in Greece, Southwestern Turkey and Crete. This background is important because it is clear that Marshall's greatest triumphs in field archaeology were in part those that traced the history of the Greeks in the Subcontinent, at Taxila and Charsada (his first excavation in British India), for example. His experiences with the Bronze Age of Crete also influenced his early synthesis of Harappan remains.

Marshall and Aurel Stein were admitted as Companions of the Indian Empire on 24 June 1910 (His Majesty, The King Emperor 1911: 33). Marshall was Knighted in 1914 and is noted in a comprehensive list of members of the Order of the Indian Empire in the following way: Doctor Sir John Hubert Marshall, Kt., M.A., Litt. D., F.S.A. (Government of India 1937: 72).

13. It is curious that this speech was not published by the Society, but rather in Curzon (1900), one of the *Annual Reports for the Northern Circle of the Archaeological Survey of India*. Since it is a rare document it was thoughtfully reprinted in Chakrabarti (1988: 227-36).

14. Rai Bahadur was Mr. Daya Ram Sahni's title. It is an honorific conferred by the Government of India on Indians for service to the state. The award was intended for recognition of accomplishments beyond the exemplary, even for years or decades of service. Muslims took the title "Khan Bahadur." Non-Muslims from the north generally became "Rai Bahadur" and those from the south took "Rao Bahadur".

15. The notion of discovery in site survey is often curious. The people who lived around Mohenjo-daro knew it was there all along. They even did a bit of their own brick quarrying for house construction. The credit due to Bhandarkar is really for publishing the place as an archaeological site and thereby bringing it to the attention of a larger, professional audience.

16. It is clear from an overview of Banerji's writing that he had little respect for Bhandarkar; a fact that was confirmed by Mr. A. Ghosh on June 24, 1979 at an archaeological conference in Srinagar, Kashmir. I have been told that Banerji referred to Bhandarkar as as "*burgi*," a derogatory Bengali term for Maharatta soldiers and brigands. Banerji seems to have delighted in finding fault with his predecessor, and his probing of Mohenjo-daro may have been motivated in part, to show that Bhandarkar had been totally wrong concerning the significance of the site.

Banerji was a brilliant, energetic man, gifted with a fine memory. But he was also vain, and cursed with the worst traits of his *zamandari* background, some of which, like the abuse of alcohol, may have adversely affected his health and longevity. Banerji came a cropper with virtually all of his colleagues, including Sir John Marshall. In the end, Banerji was "...suspended with effect from the 16th August 1926, and has since been removed from Govt. service with effect from that date" (Marshall 1926-27b: 246).

Bhandarkar, on the other hand, was a gentlemanly Maharashtran; a meticulous, patient, perhaps even slow, scholar. He was much respected by his colleagues and a portrait of him hangs in the Department of Archaeology at Deccan College in Pune.

17. Banerji requested Mr. J. L. Rieu, I. C. S., Commissioner of Sindh, to turn over Mohenjo-daro to the Archaeological Survey of India in 1922. This was accomplished under order No. 321-AHR.D dated 10-1-23 and Banerji took possession of the place from the Assistant of the Deputy Conservator of Forest in Sindh. Banerji also had a contour plan of the site prepared, the whereabouts of which is unknown to me (Banerji 1926: 26).

18. I have been informed by Dr. Jansen that he has located these illustrations and will seek to publish them.

19. This observation was made in the cover letter from Harold Hargreaves dated 16 January 1930, when the manuscript was returned to Banerji. The letter is reproduced in Banerji (1926) as an unnumbered page at the beginning of the book.

20. It is somewhat ironic that an Assyriologist, Archibald H. Sayce should have made such an important contribution to Harappan archaeology. His letter to the editor of the *Illustrated London News* of 27 November 1924 does in fact make the point that the Harappan Civilization was contemporary with the "...age of the Babylonian King Mansitusu to that of the Third Dynasty of Ur" (Sayce 1924: 526; reprinted in Possehl 1979a: 108). This pushed the known dates for ancient Indian history back from the age of Alexander the Great to the third millennium BC. Sayce's letter was published in the issue of the *Illustrated London News* directly following Marshall's article announcing the discoveries at Mohenjo-daro and Harappa (Marshall 1924; article published on 20 September 1924; reprinted in Possehl 1979a: 105-07). In the next issue there was an article by C. J. Gadd and Sidney Smith discussing the system of writing and the chronological matters highlighted by Sayce (Gadd and Smith 1924; article published on 4 October 1924; reprinted in Possehl 1979a: 109-10). Since it is likely, or at least logical, that the Gadd and Smith article was intended to follow directly the publication of the Marshall announcement,

146

it seems that there are some grounds to suggest that Sayce, a powerful man in the intellectual circles of his day, somehow managed to have his insight into the chronology of the Indus Civilization published both alone and prior to the same announcement by the two younger scholars.

Sayce was one of those Assyriologists who "got in on the ground floor" of the discipline and made a contribution to the decipherment of the so-called "Vannic" texts of eastern Anatolia. Trained in the church, the Reverend Sayce also wrote much on Palestinian and Biblical archaeology. A small obituary by Sidney Smith (1933) contains some additional information and a bibliography of his major works, which number not fewer than 25 books.

21. There are two men who work with the Archaeological Survey of India, who have published on the archaeology of the Indus Civilization under the name "K. N. Dikshit." The older of these two men was Kashinath Narayan Dikshit who became Director General in 1938. He was a Maharashtran and received the title "Rao Bahadur." The younger man, Kailash Nath Dikshit, rose to be a Joint Director with the Archaeological Survey of India. He comes from Uttar Pradesh.

22. Two other Europeans figured prominently in the Marshall era at the Survey. D. Brainard Spooner was a distinguished scholar, specializing in historical periods. He played an important role in administration, was admitted to the Order of the British Empire, but never became Director General. J. F. Blakiston was also a scholar of historical archaeology and a trusted Marshall lieutenant. He was Director General from 1 June 1935 to 21 March 1937, when Rao Bahadur K. N. Dikshit took office. Blakiston played an important role in the American excavations of Chanhu-daro in 1935-36 and visited the site between 21 and 23 January 1936 when it was being excavated by Mackay (Mackay 1943: vii-viii).

23. The actual succession dates are as follows (Ghosh 1953a):
John Marshall
    11 February 1902, Appointment announced (Ghosh 1953a: 31)
    22 February 1902 reached India (Ghosh 1953a: 31)
    1915 Knighted (Ghosh 1953a: 31)
    6 September 1928 relinquishes his post as Director General
    and is placed on Special Duty (Ghosh 1953a: 38)
    Retires 19 March 1931 (Ghosh 1953a: 38)
    Leaves India on 15 March 1931 (Ghosh 1953a: 38).
Harold Hargreaves
    8 October 1928, appointed (Ghosh 1953a: 39)
Rai Bahadur Daya Ram Sahni
    29 July 1931, appointed (Ghosh 1953a: 39)
J. F Blakiston
    1 June 1935, appointed (Ghosh 1953a: 40)
Rao Bahadur K. N. Dikshit
    21 March 1937, appointed (Ghosh 1953a: 41)
    Sends out Majumdar (Ghosh 1953a: 41)
    Woolley appointed for a review (Ghosh 1953a: 41)
    6 November 1938 to 11 February 1939, Woolley in India (Ghosh 1953a: 41)
R. E. M. Wheeler
    1944, appointed (Ghosh 1953a: 43)
    1952, Knighted (Ghosh 1953a: 43)
D. N. P. Chakravarti
    30 April 1948, appointed (p. 45)

M. S. Vats

      30 June 1950, appointed

A. Ghosh

      2 March 1953, appointed

24. This photograph is from the archives of the Archaeological Survey of India. It shows Vats excavating the large hoard (VS 1450) of copper-bronze implements in VS Area during the 1925-26 field season (Sahni 1925-26: 94, Plate XXXVIII, f; Sahni 1931b: 228-30). Excavating in a coat and tie is no longer in fashion.

25. To put this in more understandable terms for the modern reader, the rupee at the time was worth about one fifteenth of a pound sterling, which in turn was worth ca. \$5.15. This yields a rupee worth a little more than 34 American cents.

26. Mackay is a Scotts name which should be pronounced not "Mac"-"Kay," but "Maceye." Ernest John Henry was born 5 July 1880 and died 2 October 1943, soon after having received a copy of his final site report on Chanhu-daro. He appears to have been a native of Bristol and attended grammar school and university there (BA 1918, MA 1922 and D.Litt 1933). Since he was abroad during much of this time his education would have been somewhat irregular and might form the basis for a small study. Between 1907 and 1912 Mackay trained in archaeology in Egypt with Sir Flinders Petrie. Over the next three years he was engaged in the photo-documentation of the Theban tombs. Mackay remained in the Middle East during World War I as an army captain from 1916-1919. In this capacity he served as a member of the Army Commission for the survey of ancient monuments in Palestine and Syria. He served as Custodian of Antiquities, Palestine Government, 1919-22. His next assignment took him to Mesopotamia as part of the Oxford University-Field Museum excavations. He directed excavations for them at Jemdet Nasr and Kish from 1922-25. The British School of Archaeology in Egypt appointed him to excavate tumuli on the Island of Bahrain in 1925. The Archaeological Survey of India appointed Mackay a Special Officer between 1926 and 1931 when he was engaged in the excavations at Mohenjo-daro. He returned to England following this appointment but went back to the Subcontinent in 1933-36 to undertake the excavations at Chanhu-daro for Professor W. Norman Brown of the University of Pennsylvania and his American School of Indic and Iranian Studies. Following this he returned once again to England to write his report. Mackay's wife Dorothy Mary Simmons accompanied him to Chanhu-daro, and assisted with various recording duties. He published one popular book on the Indus Civilization (1935) which was enlarged and updated by Mrs. Mackay in 1948. The Mackays had one son.

27. Although he was not on the site, Mackay made a contribution to the preliminary report for the 1925-26 field season by taking K. N. Dikshit's rough notes on the DK Area excavation and turning them into a narrative (Mackay 1925-26).

28. Most of the information concerning the events on this tragic morning were related to me by Mr. Krishna Deva, who was with Majumdar at the time.

Majumdar's death is officially recorded in the *India Office and Burma Office List* (1940: 661) as having taken place on Friday 11 November 1938. It is strange that Majumdar is listed in the 1939 edition of this book as Superintendent, Archaeology Section, Indian Museum Calcutta.

29. Sadar Din was one of the most respected men in the Archaeological Survey of India and later the Pakistan Department of Archaeology. He served Majumdar and a host of other archaeologists, including Sir Mortimer Wheeler during his time as Director General, and Walter Fairservis when the Second Afghan Expedition worked in the Quetta Valley, Zhob-Loralai, Afghanistan and Seistan. I had the good fortune to meet Sadar Din in Karachi late in the

summer of 1964, when he came to give his *salaams* to Fairservis in the Metropole Hotel. For a photograph of this remarkable man see Wheeler (1976: 18).

30. This was a nasty band of *dacoits*. They passed by Majumdar's camp again that day, having just killed a local *zamindar* and another man. A local Superintendent of Police followed them, but this pursuit was not vigorous. Krishna Deva recalls thinking that the police seemed to be more interested in pushing the *dacoits* ahead of them, out of their jurisdiction in Dadu District, than in capturing the culprits. Some of the *dacoits* were apprehended later and put on trial in Dadu two years after the murder. Krishna Deva gave testimony at this trial and recalls that the guilty parties were given eleven years in prison.

Dr. Louis Flam has traveled widely in this area and much of my information on the modern folklore of the case is from his information and detailed discussions with me.

31. Not a part of local lore is the thought that communal feelings played the predominant role in this murder.

32. The "Buddhist" levels at Harappa, which are more clearly adumbraded in the preliminary reports on Harappa, than they are elsewhere, would be the "home" for this piece if it is "Hellenistic" in style. My own opinion on the torso is that it is probably Mature Harappan in age.

The small debate between Vats and Marshall, concerning this piece, recalls the present, much larger debate concerning the date of the so-called "Daimabad Bronzes."

33. Some of Sastri's documents were found by George Dales in the Harappa Museum during one of his recent excavation seasons at the site. This invaluable source of new information on Cemetery R-37 should be available in studied form sometime in the future. M. S. Vats takes some notice of Cemetery R-37 in his report on earlier work at the site (Vats 1940: 200, fn. 1). He equates the pottery of his fractional burial in Area G 289 (Vats 1940: 197-202) with that of Cemetery R-37 and correctly implies that the new burials belong to the Mature Harappan era.

34. The correspondence referred to in this section is all on file with these Archives as well as the Archives and Library of the Museum of Fine Arts, Boston. I thank both of these institutions for making the materials available to me.

35. This came to $17,000 as the Pound Sterling in 1934 was trading at about $5.15. Mackay's "personal emoluments per annum" were stated as 1000 Pounds Sterling.

36. Majumdar's monograph (1934) is actually published with the name N. C. Majumdar on both the cover and title pages. It is thus frequently miscatalogued.

37. There is also a telegram from Mackay to Brown, dated 6 November 1934: "Advise big (sic) Chanhudaro while waiting Amri permit."

38. A small historical connection can be made here. Mackay's copy of this monograph is currently in my personal library. It is very clearly inscribed: "To Dr. E. Mackay, MA, PhD. With best compliments, N. G. Majumdar, 11.10.34."

39. Prof. Brown was clearly exasperated by the process of securing the permission to excavate Chanhu-daro. At one point, when the serious problem with graves at Amri had come out, he noted that "This has been a hectic week" (Brown to Mackay 17 September 1934). He was in Delhi for Christmas that year, staying in Maiden's Hotel near the Red Fort. In Brown to Mackay, 24 December 1934 he makes a startling observation about the Director General, Rai Bahadur Daya Ram Sahni: "It is all a bit maddening, because about 2 1/2 months of delay is due directly to Sahni's incompetence. I am glad he is out—he has been a bad mistake, and I think everyone realizes it, although of course no one is going to say so, and my remarks are entirely confidential."

40. I once spoke to Dr. Sankalia about Chanhu-daro. He was somewhat close-mouthed on the topic, simply noting that my observations were correct.

41. Given the fact that it was widely known that Wheeler had little respect for Marshall's management of the Archaeological Survey of India and felt that he was an incompetent, old fashioned excavator, it is somewhat odd that *The Times* and the editors of the *Dictionary of National Biography* selected him to review his career. These institutions have a reputation for being more even handed in their selection of reviewers.

42. Stein was admitted as Companion of the Indian Empire on 24 June 1910 (His Majesty, The King Emperor 1911: 33), the same day as John Marshall. Two years later, on 14 June 1912, Stein was elevated within the Order to Knight Commander (His Majesty, The King Emperor 1913: 14). The elevation of Stein to Knight Commander may have been part of the original plan for honoring these two men. Some of my older colleagues, who knew both Marshall and Stein, have pointed out that Marshall, for all his hard work and accomplishments, was still a figure of national stature within British India, while Stein achieved no small amount of international luster. Their sense of the politics of these knighthoods indicates that it was probably not possible to separate their stature from the start, especially given the fact that Marshall was the Director General and Stein, a Superintendent Archaeologist under his supervision (The India Office and Burma Office List 1910: 34). Thus, the initial even-handed treatment, followed by the elevation of Stein, may have been seen as something to which Marshall, and his supporters, could not object.

43. The burial cairns at Jiwanri and Spet-bulandi (White Mound) are places associated with historical times.

44. See Stein 1931.

45. The colonial Government of India issued something titled *The India Office and Burma Office List* on an annual basis. This is not always completely accurate: N. G. Majumdar was listed as Superintendent Archaeologist at the Indian Museum in 1939, the year following his death. But, the "Office Lists" do give a sense of the changes at the top of the Archaeological Survey, including the rank of Superintendent Archaeologist. Because the Survey was moving toward a crisis, which was said to be a crisis of leadership, it is worthwhile to see how much ambiguity surrounded the office of Director General for many years.

Archaeological Survey of India, 1927
Director General of Archaeology:
Sir John H. Marshall, M.A., Kt., C.I.E.
    J. F. Blakiston (officiating)
Deputy Director General of Archaeology:
    Rai Bahadur Daya Ram Sahni
(The India Office and Burma Office List 1927: 25)

Archaeological Survey of India, 1928
Director General of Archaeology:
    Sir John H. Marshall, M.A., Kt., C.I.E.
Deputy Directors General of Archaeology:
    J. F. Blakiston, Rai Bahadur Daya Ram Sahni
(The India Office and Burma Office List 1928: 25)

150

Archaeological Survey of India, 1929
Director General of Archaeology:
        Sir John H. Marshall, M.A., C.I.E.
        H. Hargreaves (officiating)
Deputy Directors General of Archaeology:
        J. F. Blakiston, Rai Bahadur Daya Ram Sahni
(The India Office and Burma Office List 1929: 25)

Archaeological Survey of India, 1930
Director General of Archaeology:
        Sir John H. Marshall, M.A., C.I.E.
        H. Hargreaves (officiating)
Deputy Directors General of Archaeology:
        Rai Bahadur Daya Ram Sahni, J. A. Page
(The India Office and Burma Office List 1930: 26)

Archaeological Survey of India, 1931
Director General of Archaeology:
        Sir John H. Marshall, M.A., C.I.E.
        H. Hargreaves (officiating)
Deputy Directors General of Archaeology:
        K. N. Dikshit, J. A. Page
(The India Office and Burma Office List 1931: 26)

Archaeological Survey of India, 1932
Director General of Archaeology:
        Rai Bahadur Daya Ram Sahni
Deputy Directors General of Archaeology:
        K. N. Dikshit, J. A. Page
(The India Office and Burma Office List 1932: 26)

Archaeological Survey of India, 1933
Officer on Special Duty:
        Sir John H. Marshall, C. I. E.
Director General of Archaeology:
        Rai Bahadur Daya Ram Sahni
Deputy Directors General of Archaeology:
        Khan Bahadur Zafar Hasan, J. A. Page
(The India Office and Burma Office List 1933: 26)

Archaeological Survey of India, 1934
Officer on Special Duty:
        Sir John H. Marshall, C. I. E.
Director General of Archaeology:
        Rai Bahadur Daya Ram Sahni
Deputy Directors General of Archaeology:

Khan Bahadur Zafar Hasan, J. A. Page
(The India Office and Burma Office List 1934: 48)

Archaeological Survey of India, 1935
Officer on Special Duty:
     Sir John H. Marshall, C. I. E.
Director General of Archaeology:
     Rai Bahadur Daya Ram Sahni
Deputy Director General of Archaeology:
     Khan Bahadur Zafar Hasan
(The India Office and Burma Office List 1935: 48)

Archaeological Survey of India, 1936
Officer on Special Duty:
     Sir John H. Marshall, C. I. E.
Director General of Archaeology:
     J. F. Blakiston
Deputy Director General of Archaeology:
     Khan Bahadur Zafar Hasan
(The India Office and Burma Office List 1936: 48)

Archaeological Survey of India, 1937
Officer on Special Duty:
     Sir John H. Marshall, C. I. E.
Director General of Archaeology:
     J. F. Blakiston
Deputy Director General of Archaeology:
     Khan Bahadur Zafar Hasan
(The India Office and Burma Office List 1937: 48)

Archaeological Survey of India, 1938
Director General of Archaeology:
     Rao Bahadur K. N. Dikshit
Deputy Director General of Archaeology:
     M. S. Vats
(The India Office and Burma Office List 1938: 18)

Archaeological Survey of India, 1939
Director General of Archaeology:
     Rao Bahadur K. N. Dikshit
Deputy Director General of Archaeology:
     M. S. Vats
(The India Office and Burma Office List 1939: 18)

Archaeological Survey of India, 1940
Director General of Archaeology:
     Rao Bahadur K. N. Dikshit
Deputy Director General of Archaeology:

M. S. Vats
(The India Office and Burma Office List 1940: 18)

The India Office and Burma Office Lists for 1941, 1942, 1943 and 1944 were not published (The India Office and Burma Office List 1945: iv).

Rao Bahadur K. N. Dikshit was Director General through all of this period.

Archaeological Survey of India, 1945
Director General of Archaeology:
    R. E. Mortimer Wheeler, M. C., D. Litt.
(The India Office and Burma Office List 1945: 8)

Archaeological Survey of India, 1946
Director General of Archaeology:
    R. E. Mortimer Wheeler, M. C., D. Litt.
(The India Office and Burma Office List 1946: 8)

Archaeological Survey of India, 1947
Director General of Archaeology:
    R. E. Mortimer Wheeler, M. C., D. Litt.
(The India Office and Burma Office List 1947: 8)

46. Dikshit served from 21 March, 1937 until the arrival of R. E. M. Wheeler in 1944. Wheeler handed the Director General's office to Dr. N. P. Chakravarti on 30 April 1948, who in turn relinquished it to M. S. Vats on 30 June 1950. A. Ghosh received charge from Vats on 2 March, 1953 (Ghosh 1953a: 45-8).

47. This cemetery area at Ur was once thought to contain the graves of Mesopotamian kings and queens, in part because they contained so much gold, lapis lazuli and other luxury goods. We know the names of many of the high status individuals interred there, sometimes accompanied by human sacrifice. As more came to be known of the succession of kings in Mesopotamia it became clear that the "royal" personages in the "Royal" Tombs of Ur did not appear on king lists, prepared for secular purposes. The chances that this was due to insufficient data have diminished, essentially to zero, and it is now felt that the individuals interred in the "Royal Graves of Ur" were probably the high priests and priestesses of the Moon Temple on top of the great ziggurat of Ur, not far from the 'Royal' Graves. The best date for this cemetery is 2650-2550 BC.

48. Until 1993, when it was republished (Possehl 1993a), many officers in the Archaeological Survey of India had never seen it. I am told that there was not a single copy in all of Pakistan until a photocopy was sent there in the late 1980s.

49. Since Sastri was on the site, one wonders if Woolley was, in reality, finding fault with a comparatively junior person who may have been unqualified to explain these things to the visitor. In the end, we can wonder who actually was answering Woolley's questions when he gathered his "proofs," perhaps they were site *chowkidars*.

50. The French have been working in Pakistan on a continuing basis since Jean-Marie Casal began the excavation of Amri in 1959. The Italian Mission in Pakistan has worked in Swat since 1966. American research there has been more discontinuous, but both George Dales and Walter Fairservis have spent substantial amounts of time in the field in Pakistan at places such as Damb Sadaat, Balakot, Allahdino and Harappa.

51. Here Woolley documents this fact: "This Conference recommends that small museums should, as in the past, be maintained at the different archaeological sites where important excavations have been carried out or where important monuments exist, so that the materials kept in such museums may be studied in proper surrounding and perspective, duplicate antiquities being housed in the principal museum of the province or distributed to such other museums as require them, provided these are considered by the Archaeological Survey to be sufficiently well established to use and look after them properly...". (Resolution X).

52. This is widely stated in India, and it is a reasonable thing to have happened. Krishna Deva, who had just joined the Survey when Woolley appeared, is the most definitive source.

53. Jacquetta Hawkes, Wheeler's biographer, makes the following, undocumented claim: "There is no doubt that Leonard Woolley had privately recommended that Dr. Mortimer Wheeler should be offered the role of European Adviser..." (1982: 231). There is some evidence that this may have happened before the War, but if that is true then Wheeler had completely forgotten about it by 1943 (see Hawkes 1982: 220-21, 231-32).

54. The author met Piggott in July 1996 at his home "The Cottage" outside of Oxford. I confirmed that Wheeler had invited Piggott and Daniel to join him in the Archaeological Survey of India. Piggott declined, apparently opting for the Army rather than Wheeler's overbearing manner.

55. Krishna Deva has related to me that on one occasion Mr. A. Ghosh was about to resign in despair over Wheeler's browbeating, but never took a formal step. On another occasion, toward the end of Wheeler's term, Krishna Deva and V. S. Agrawala were working on a large exhibition of Indian Art to be displayed in the Viceroy's Residence. Wheeler somehow managed to become exasperated by Agrawala's performance and he began to abuse him, referring to Agrawala, ca. 50 years old at the time, as "boy." When the reprimand came to an end, Agrawala offered Wheeler his verbal resignation, indicating that a written note to that effect would be immediately forthcoming. Krishna Deva, the third person present, recalled that Wheeler then left the room, but returned shortly thereafter and apologized to Agrawala by saying: "Please excuse this English barbarian, I didn't mean to hurt you."

56. It should be added that renewed excavation at the site did not require the enlargement of the Museum and other facilities (Woolley 1939a: 30).

57. Wheeler makes reference to Childe's thought on the matter (Childe 1934: 223). If one reads Childe's full statement it is clear that he was not proposing that the Vedic Aryans destroyed Harappa or any of the other Indus settlements, simply that they may have buried their dead in a cemetery near the city of Harappa.

58. Frederick E. Zeuner had rather extensive experience in South Asian Archaeology. He explored the Teri dunes of Tamil Nadu in 1949 and was deeply involved in other research in the region in the early 1950s. He was a visiting scholar at Deccan College, and worked in Gujarat, especially Langhnaj (Zeuner 1950, 1951, 1952, 1953, 1959). Zeuner also played an extensive role in the education of Dr. Bridget Allchin (Zeuner and Allchin 1956).

59. H. T. Lambrick, "Brick" to his friends, was born 20 April 1904 and died 31 August 1981. He was educated at Rossall and Oriel Colleges, Oxford and received a first in modern history. This placed him at the head of the Indian Civil Service list and in 1927 he left for Sindh where he served until Partition in 1947. Lambrick was responsible for publishing the 1941 census of Sind (1942b). He also played a key role in putting down the guerrilla warfare of the fanatical sect of Hurs who terrorized the province in the early 1940s. His novel, *The Terrorist* (1972) emerged from this experience. Lambrick was appointed C.I.E. in 1944. Upon

154

his return to England he rejoined Oxford as a Spaulding Senior Research Fellowship in Indian History at Oriel College, where he was also Treasurer (1951-55). He retired from Oriel in 1971 and was awarded the Richard Burton Medal in 1978.

Biography interested Lambrick and he published two books, both on important personages in Sindh: Sir Charles Napier (1952) and John Jacob of Jacobabad (1960).

60. Ochre Colored Pottery was only found at Ahichchhatra in 1964-65 and the discovery was a surprise to everyone.

PART THREE

THE CULTURAL GEOGRAPHY OF THE INDUS AGE

INTRODUCTION

The peoples of the Indus Age occupied an immense area. During the Mature Harappan it was the largest Bronze Age civilization of Asia or Africa. The first civilization in India and Pakistan covered an area of about one million square kilometers, a bit smaller than the Regions of Cultural Geography used in this book, which are estimated at 1,310,000 square kilometers. The estimate of one million square kilometers of the Mature Harappan compares to about 200,000 square kilometers for southern Mesopotamia, the combined regions of Sumer and Akkad. The Akkadian Dynasty seems to have about doubled their area by conquest, bringing their Empire up to a tract that may have been as large as 400,000 square kilometers. The kingdom of Mari and other early "Mesopotamian" states might have occupied an additional 100,000 square kilometers outside Akkadian control. The size of Elam is difficult to determine, but an estimate of 200,000 square kilometers seems to be a reasonable approximation.[1] Thus, the combined size of all Near Eastern archaic states that would have been contemporary with the Harappan Civilization falls considerably short of that of the Mature Harappan. By comparison Egypt in the Old Kingdom was tiny at ca. 17,100 square kilometers (Butzer 1976: 83), but geographical size is certainly not the only important measure of historical significance.

The Greater Indus Region covers all of Pakistan, except for the northern-most mountainous areas, as well as southern Afghanistan. On the Indian side it encompasses virtually all of Gujarat and the western fringe of southern and central Rajasthan. In northern Rajasthan it includes the old drainage of the Sarasvati and Drishadvati rivers; the Punjab, Haryana and the northern Ganga-Yamuna Doab in Uttar Pradesh (Figure 3.1).

An understanding of the Indus Age depends, to some degree, on an appreciation of the historical and cultural geography of this region. Geography is the stage on which peoples of the Indus Age played out their lives. It set limits on activities and within those limits moulded, formed and influenced, but did not determine, many of the options and opportunities with which they lived. It is also important to have an acquaintance with the vocabulary of the Greater Indus Region, the names of mountains and valleys, rivers and *nadis*, plants and animals found there and how and when the seasonal precipitation comes and goes.

The Role of Modern Boundaries

The study of the Indus Age makes it necessary to some degree to set aside the modern boundaries

156

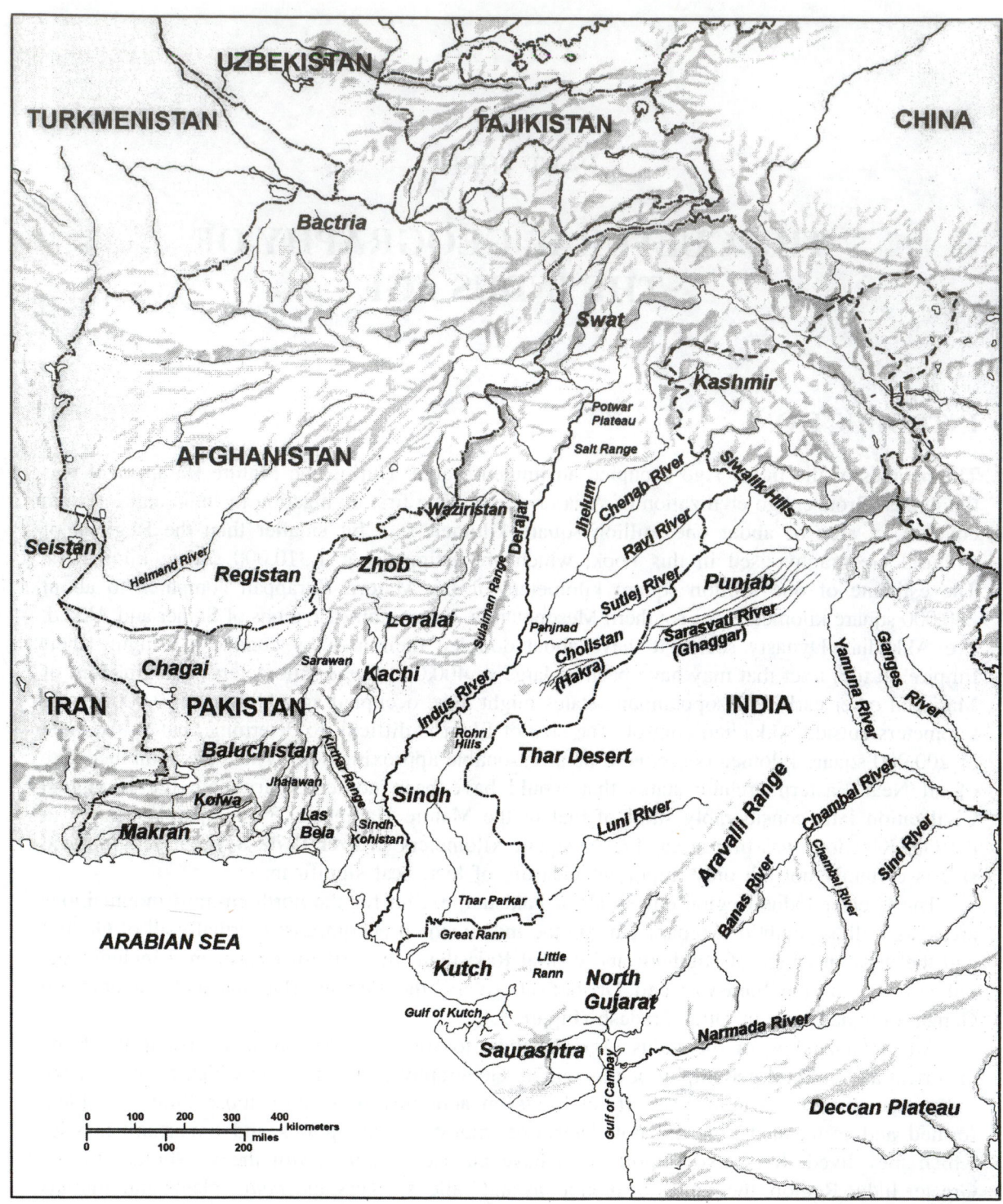

Figure 3.1. Map of the Greater Indus Region

between the nation states of South Asia, as well as the internal borders of their constituent states, provinces and districts. The cultural geography of the Indus Age is not completely divorced from these borders but they are not always useful when studying the history of this region. There are some interesting correspondences between modern political geography and ancient times. For example, it should not be considered a coincidence that the Mature Harappan site of Sutkagendor is the western-most settlement of the Indus Age and also on the modern border between Pakistan and Iran. Settlement patterns suggest that there is a boundary between the domains of the Early and Mature Harappan that approximates the modern boundary between India and Pakistan where it crosses the Sarasvati River course. But, these are exceptions and on the whole the modern system of national, state, provincial and district boundaries have little to do with the organization of life during the Indus Age. Relaxation of the boundaries of the modern world allows an examination of the Indus Age on its own terms. It lets the Indus Civilization "shape itself," based on excavated material and a series of theoretical propositions and assumptions controlled by scholarship, rather than modern politics.

The Historical Importance of Size

The gross dimensions of the Greater Indus Region (ca. 1,000,000 km^2) are important in several respects. For instance, the simple consideration of how the sense of being "Harappan" was maintained over such vast distances, given the transportation limitations of the times. It is interesting that the Mature Harappan painted pottery style was sustained over all parts of this vast area for about six hundred years. The same is true for the seals, bead forms and brick proportions and sizes. On a more human level, it must be assumed that the people who inhabited the ancient settlements of the Indus Age thought of themselves as belonging to, and participating in, some form of cultural unity. During the Mature Harappan there were surely Harappan "southerners" and "northerners," "city folk" and "country folk," "farmers" and "herders." There is every probability that what is seen as the Harappan Civilization in an archaeological sense was, in historical reality, an ethnically and linguistically diverse collection of peoples. From the archaeological record one senses that in spite of this differentiation, we are still seeing a single ancient culture at some level of abstraction. How were the norms of this culture maintained over such immense distances? What kept it all together?

The answer to these questions is obviously "communication," either direct, face to face contact, or a more indirect form. Without some convention of communication, areas that are geographically removed from one another tend to take their own course of culture change and gradual differences will emerge. The two most obvious mechanisms that can be documented that would have sustained the mid-range and longer communication networks are the movements of pastoral nomads, and other itinerants, some of which are tied to seasonal changes, and the internal commerce of the Indus Age.

The Diversity of Lifeways and Peoples

The Greater Indus Region is an area of the world within which there is great diversity of lifeways. Most of these people are sedentary farmers, almost all of whom also depend to some degree on domesticated animals (i.e., pastoralism). Some village based farmers also rely on pastoralism to a marked degree. The archaeological record of the Indus Age is replete with the remains of farming villages and the towns and cities of the times. Less clearly perceived are the camps of peoples with other adaptations, hunters and herders, some of whom were mobile and nomadic.

Pastoralists, Nomadic and Otherwise

The ethnographic and ethnohistoric records of the Greater Indus Region inform us that there is today, and was in the historical past, a great deal of mobility among the peoples represented there. Some of this mobility is based on pastoralism, but this is far from the only livelihood. These are exceedingly complex lifeways, not easily characterized by a set of cultural typologies. The nomadic peoples of this region are not well studied. Among the best sources are the District and Provincial Gazetteers of the late nineteenth and early twentieth centuries. There are three good collections of essays that address issues of pastoralism in the Subcontinent: L. Leshnik and G. Sontheimer (1975), P. K. Misra and K. C. Malhotra (1982); an issue of *Studies in History* edited by Shereen Ratnagar in 1991 (see also Ratnagar 1987 and 1991); several monographs: S. Westphal-Hellbusch and H. Westphal (1968), B. Suryavanishi (1962), Pehrson (1966) and R. P. Khatana (1992). The proceedings of a conference on nomads in Central Asia (Francfort 1990) is also relevant as are O. Aurenche (1984), H. Koster and C. Chang (1994a and 1994b) and O. Bar-Yosef and A. Khazanov (1992). The ecology of pastoralism is learned best from Brian Spooner (1971, 1973), R. Dyson-Hudson and N. Dyson-Hudson (1980), T. J. Barfield (1993) and A. Khazanov (1994), with additional notes on the Subcontinent in W. A. Rodgers (1991).

The term "pastoral nomad(s)" can be thought of as a person(s) engaged in the management of grazing or browsing animals in a way that leads to migration or movement from place to place. One reason for movement among these peoples is the search for fresh pasture, but this is not always the only motivating factor. There are also settled pastoralists in this region. These are people who are settled in one place and manage their animals from this base. In some instances, as in parts of Baluchistan and the Northwest Frontier, farmers and pastoral nomads are one and the same, because some people there live in villages and undertake cultivation for part of the year and are pastoral nomads for the remainder. Other pastoral nomads are less dependent on cultivation and might live a mobile life for the whole year. In the end the amount of "mobility" involved in pastoral nomadism is highly variable at any given point in time. The degree and type of mobility also seems to be something that shifts and changes over time for any given group. No one is quite sure just how much "mobility" in this form of human adaptation it takes for a group to be appropriately called "pastoral nomadic."

There are other nomads in the Greater Indus Region, who may keep some animals. These are itinerant traders, tinkers, and many kinds of craft specialists: potters, timber cutters, charcoal makers, miners, metal smiths, money lenders, bards and story tellers and others. There are also many "mixings and matchings." Pastoral nomads may always have been an element in regional trade and transport, others might have indulged in charcoal making or some other occupation for some of the year. The ethnohistoric record informs us the money lenders may also have been petty traders and fortune tellers/magicians who often kept cattle. The set patterns are there, and they are important, but the diversity of viable lifeways at this level is immense, especially in the pre-modern world.

The pastoral nomads of Pakistan and northwestern India are generally called *maldhari*, usually translated "cattle-keeper" or "cattle-breeder." They keep other animals, too: sheep, goats, camels, water buffalo and horses.

The people of the region believe that all of them originally were *maldhari*, even the Rajput and Kathi. The meaning of *maldhari* perhaps denotes those who emphasize cattle-breeding rather than cattle-tending. Conditions permitting, they may also practice agriculture. Certain groups breed cattle exclusively and traditionally. No definite line can be drawn between them and other groups who have access to animals for subsistence needs and still practice agriculture (Westphal-Hellbusch 1975: 123).

Observations determine that there were, and still are, many *maldhari* in Gujarat and they control vast herds of cattle and other animals. Informants in Bhavnagar District have indicated that until quite recently, possibly as late as the 1950s, they controlled the breeding stock for cattle in the region. The *maldhari* sold only castrated males to farmers or "outsiders," and very closely controlled the reproduction of their own animals. The sterile bullocks they sold were valuable and this generally implied that there was financial debt between the *maldhari* and the farmers. Servicing this debt was built into the seasonal round of the pastoralists, as was the selling of animals. These were important considerations that promoted mobility (nomadism) and broadened the social and economic roles played by pastoral nomads.

Maldhari control over cattle fertility has changed in recent times. The *panchayat* of Srinathgadh village, adjacent to the archaeological site of Rojdi, is the proud owner of a magnificent, fertile, bull of the *kankreji* breed. His sperm is available to the cows of the village on payment of a servicing fee by their owners to the *panchayat*. The *maldharis* are now left out of it.

Citing a few examples might help to understand the complexity of pastoralism, pastoral nomads and other itinerants in the Greater Indus Region. Many of these examples come from the Gazetteers, given the thin ethnographic documentation of pastoral nomads.

The Baluchistan Provincial Gazetteer says that "Nearly all the highland population of the country takes part in periodic migration—towards the plains in the autumn and toward the highlands in the spring" (Government of India 1908c: 24). Many of these migrants engage in the transportation of goods while on the move. On the plains they find pasture for their animals and engage in agricultural work, mostly harvesting crops. Some of them, Afghans are specifically mentioned, move all over the subcontinent, even to Chinese Turkistan. The involvement of Afghan pastoral nomads in the subcontinent is summarized in D. Balland (1991, with a map of movement in Figure 1). F. Scholz has a map that summarizes the patterns of movement (1983: Figure 5) (Figure 1.4).

This generalization can be made a bit more specific, admitting some variation in the pattern. In northern Loralai District the inhabitants of Duki, Bori and Barkhan are generally settled. The large prehistoric/historic site of Dabar Kot is in Duki. But in other parts of Loralai there is "...a constant flow of migration due to the nomadic habits of the tribes, the variations in climate, and the periodic visitations of scarcity and drought, which compel the inhabitants to seek more favored localities" (Minchin 1907e: 56). Some pastoral nomadic people of Loralai go to the plains to find pasture in the winter, especially to Kachi and the Derajat. But the eastern parts of the region are relatively low, especially Duki and Chamalang, and many peoples go there during the winter for pasture and "...to engage in trade and transport or work as laborers" (Minchin 1907e: 57).

In the adjacent Marri-Bugti country there is also movement to the plains in the winter; to the Derajat (Dera Ghazi Khan), and also to Kachi (Sibi and Jacobabad). The compiler of this gazetteer notes that many Marris have permanently settled in Sindh, especially Larkana, Rohri and Jacobabad (Minchin 1907i: 35). There is also a good monograph on the Marri Baluch (Pehrson 1966) that has details on the specifics of their system of agriculture as well as of pastoral nomadism.

H. T. Lambrick, a long time resident of Sindh as a colonial administrator, who also did some archaeology, observes the following about Marri-Bugti country:

Overlooking the abodes of Bijar Khan and his freebooters, in Eastern Kachhi, stands a rugged mountain mass, a huge bastion to the gateway of the Bolan. This forbidding region is divided between the most war-like of all the Baluch tribes, the Marris to the north and the Bugtis to the south; their respective headquarters, Kahan and Dera, being situated in two upland valleys separated by a broad range. The only access to the interior of this country from the west is through the intricate defiles by which these valleys drain down to the plain; from the south the Bugti country can be penetrated by the pass of Duz Khushtak, but on this side it is protected by miles of sandy wilderness and several formidable ranges must be passed.

The characteristics of India's great western barrier are here found in all their grimness; sharp foothills rising from a wilderness of drift sand: long stony plateaux intersected by water courses full of boulders and shingle: ranges thrusting up almost perpendicularly and deeply cleft by avulsion or the passage of torrents: naked saddlebacks scored by innumerable ravines. In this harsh land there is little vegetation, yet the sparse grazing supports large numbers of sheep, goats and cattle; cultivation is confined to patches of alluvium in the valleys, some of them watered by small perennial streams. The Bugtis were accustomed to sell the produce of their flocks and herds in Sind, purchasing cloth, grain and other necessaries in return; but their livelihood depended largely, and the Marris' almost wholly, on loot (Lambrick 1960: 40).

These observations on Loralai and Marri-Bugti country document two interesting points. First, not all of the movement is temporary and pastoral nomads make permanent moves, sometimes settling down. The Sindh Gazetteer of 1907 gives some statistics on non-Sindhis resident there (Aitken 1907: 156). Baluchis lead the list with 64,913 people. Next are Rajasthanis (64,306); then Kutchees (51,779), Punjabis (31,631) down to 1,565 Europeans. Second, raiding and banditry are part of life and should not be forgotten as historical factors that shape the lives of most people in this are old. This kind of behavior need not be seen as "invasions" or "war," nor is it true that all of the hill tribes of Baluchistan and the Northwest Frontier were as dependent on loot as the Marris and Bugtis were. But, raiding and banditry were present, not as historical determinatives of 19th century history, but as factors with which the people of the plains had to contend. This same condition may well have pertained to earlier, even prehistoric times, allowing, of course, for the fact that at times it may have been more intense and frequent than the 19th century, and at other times less so.

The movement is not all highland to lowland for the winter, lowland to highland for the summer, but most of it is, as in Sarawan. Sarawan District of Kalat is home to a people known as Brahui. Today they number over 300,000. Kalat is their traditional capital. The Brahui are a farming-herding people whose language is usually classified as Dravidian, the language family of modern South India. The status of Brahui as a purely Dravidian tongue has recently been questioned (McAlpin 1980, see also McAlpin 1981). Asko Parpola has an interesting discussion of the Brahui (1994: 160-75). Some believe that they represent a remnant group, left behind as Dravidians retreated south (Stein 1931; Bray 1909-34: Vol. 2, 42; Marshall 1931i: 109). Others see them as relatively recent migrants from Central India (Bloch 1924; Elfenbein 1983, 1987). J. Elfenbein (1987) proposes a migration from the vicinity of the Narmada River, through Gujarat and Sindh to Kalat about 1000 years ago. This issue in the culture history of the Greater Indus Region is unresolved, and no one knows whether the Brahuis are a vestigial group who have been in their present location since the Bronze Age, or whether they came from Central India, or elsewhere.

Virtually all of the Brahuis move to the plains for the winter, with the exception of those who live in valleys where agriculture is secure. The outline of the system is described in F. Scholz (1972, 1974). The dry farming tracts of eastern Sarawan are entirely abandoned during the winter. Moving by way of the Bolan Pass, and other routes through the Kirthar Mountains, these Brahui go to Kachi with their families and animals to pasture their flocks. A few practice agriculture on land they own there, but most engage in pastoral pursuits in Kachi and the rest of Sindh. They take jobs as farm day laborers and hire out their camels for transport. "The migration commences at the end of October and almost all the people have moved down by the end of November after sowing the spring crop, returning again to the highlands in March, when pasture is abundant and the crops are coming up" (Minchin 1907g: 45-6). This last point is important because it documents that many pastoral nomads in Baluchistan engage in agriculture on land that they own; they are not only day laborers. There is also some migration within Sarawan: "A few people from the western part of the district, especially the Langavs visit Nushki during the spring for pasture, and large caravans go from Mastung and Mungachar to Panjgur for dates in the winter" (Minchin 1907g: 46).

The ethnoarchaeology of Kachi has been presented by F. Andouze and C. Jarrige (1991), with useful drawings of seasonally used structures of several types. They also compare their data and findings with pastoral nomads from Iran, Qatar and Syria.

A similar pattern of movement takes place in Quetta-Pishin (Hughes-Buller 1907a: 55): down for the winter, up for the summer. But, Quetta is a comparatively large valley, and more people stay there for the winter. Many peoples in Pishin, presumably those in the upland areas of this track "...spend the summer in their hamlets, but in winter move to the Pishin plain with their flocks in search of pasture" (Hughes-Buller 1907a: 55).

The population in Chagai District, on the border with Iran, is said to have been four-fifths pastoral nomads at the turn of the century (Hughes-Buller 1907b: 47). They moved about their domain for the year, venturing out only when there was a scarcity of pasture. Some of them then went to Kachi, or south to Kharan District.

There is also transhumant migration from the valleys of the Northwest Frontier to the Punjab. A large, contemporary ethnic group, known as Gujjars, are a farming-pastoralist people. They are one element in a complex mix of peoples from the mountains of northern Pakistan, especially Swat, across to Jammu and Kashmir in India, and beyond. There is a monograph on one small Gujjar group, who call themselves "Gujjar Bakarwals" from the large herds of goats (*bakri*) (Khatana 1992).

Las Bela is a small, triangle of low land jutting into southern Baluchistan. It fronts the sea, and Sonmiani Bay. The gazetteer has the following to say about migration there:

> The inhabitants of Las Bela are not subject to periodic migrations like the Brahuis. In years of drought and famine, however, they migrate temporarily to Karachi, Nagar Thatha, Mirpur in Sind, and to Kathiawar (Saurashtra in Gujarat, GLP) and Jamnagar (a district of Saurashtra, GLP) in Bombay, where they work as day labourers and return to their homes as soon as the conditions in their country are favorable. Periodical immigrants are the Brahuis from Wad, Nal, Kolwa, Jau (Jhau), and Ornach, who come in the autumn and work as field labourers and return to the highlands early in April. The Makranis, principally the Nakibs, visit the Bela State in small numbers in the cold weather and bring with them dates and pomegranates from Panjgur territory and exchange them for cotton cloth or European manufacture. A small number of Makranis also visit Omara whence they return towards Panjgur in the spring with dried fish and cotton cloth (Minchin 1907d: 46).

162

Sindh, with its multitude of settled people from Baluchistan, is filled with people who use pastoral resources. Most farmers have a bullock for the plow; the more successful keep many bullocks. Some farmers have significant herds of cattle, often tended by pastoralists who are paid for their services, taking care of cattle of several "farmers", as well as their own. The Sindhi management strategy is for the principal pastoral resources belonging to a family to be cared for by some members of that family: brother(s), son(s) or nephew(s). They keep the animals on a full time basis, possibly taking other animals from relatives and associates, while other family members keep the farm. These nomadic people are constantly on the search for pasture, and move into eastern Sindh/western Rajasthan and Cholistan in years with a good monsoon (Din 1904: 231) and venture as far as Kutch and Saurashtra. They are usually close to home in Sindh during the winter.

Rajasthan is, on the whole, a much drier environment than Sindh, except for Sindh's eastern margin. In the western parts of the Thar Desert migration was an annual event for most of the rural population prior to Partition in 1947. The *kharif* harvest was predominant and once it was gathered, in September or October, the population was on the move, to Sindh, Gujarat, the Punjab and elsewhere, to pasture their flocks of cattle, camels, sheep and goats and seek employment in fields, or use their camels for transport (Government of India 1908e: 29). The pattern here, as in Baluchistan, was for a large segment of the population to be settled for part of the year, and mobile for the other. P. S. Kavoori (1991) presents interesting tabular information documenting this movement, which was extensive. To the north, in Bikaner, the Sindhi pattern of animal keeping was found; some animals being rented out to specialist castes, others to familial segments. There were a few pastoral nomads who followed this lifestyle almost entirely full-time. Of one group, the Raths, it is said, "...they cultivate but little land, and their chief occupations are pasturing their own cattle, and stealing the cattle of other people" (Government of India 1908e: 406).

The western Punjab had its own system of interwoven pastoralism and agriculture in the eras prior to the irrigation schemes built by the British in the nineteenth century. There is no good single source describing this system, but interesting coverage of the ethnology of the area is found in the District Gazetteers of the Punjab, especially under headings such as "People" and "Tribes, Castes and Leading Families" (Government of India 1884a-f, 1895, 1898, 1899, 1915, 1921, 1926, 1932).

The situation in Gujranwala District at the end of the 19th century was described as:

Thus the district may be divided into two distinct portions—one the cultivated portion or *des*, and the other the grazing tract of *bar*. The former comprises...the land...on the banks of the rivers to the south. The latter contains that large, uncultivated tract which runs right athwart the Doab and down its centre. In their general aspect, productions, and capabilities these tracts differ greatly, as well as in the character and habits of the inhabitants. In the *des* we find agriculturists of settled habits, with rights and property in the soil, and deriving their chief support from their cultivation; whilst the people of the *bar* are graziers, leading a nomad life; possessing little or no landed property, and subsisting more on the profits derived from their cattle than their land. In the former we find the soil good, water near the surface, wells numerous, cultivation superior, agriculture thriving, proprietors fairly industrious, village large...The *bar* may be described as a flat, level tract covered with rich grass and thickly dotted over with bush jungle...The general resources of this district may be thus classified— agricultural produce from the *des*; and the spontaneous products, as wood, grass, etc., together with the profits derivable from grazing, and milch kine, from the *bar* (Government of India 1884c: 3–4).

The Montgomery District Gazetteer of 1884 has the following to say of a tribe of :

all Mohammadans and their favorite occupation is the breeding and grazing of cattle. They are locally known by the name of Jats, in contradistinction to the more settled inhabitants, who call themselves ryots[2] or subjects...two (tribes) are chiefly confined to the Sutlej, but the others only possess land on the Ravi, and graze their herds in the two doabs adjoining the river" (Government of India 1884g: 51).

Spate and Learmonth quote sections from an unpublished paper attributed to E. S. Lindley, a canal official in Pre-Partition India:

A typical *Bar* of the western Punjab was a desolate place; the surface mostly bare, in places hard and smooth and almost impervious to water when rain fell, in places powdery with saltpetre, and in places growing some grass after rain. Belts of such open ground alternated with belts dotted with small hardy trees or shrubs, which tended to collect the moving sand and dust to form sandhills that in places formed a miniature Sahara...Animal life is represented by snakes, lizards and a few gazelles...a few pastoral nomad tribes lived a free but hard life, living precariously by their camels which could eat anything, and their cattle that seem able to exist on the smell of grass roots, finding sport and occupation in stealing cattle from each other and from riverine neighbors. The water-table was 80 to 120 ft. (24-37 m) below the surface; in the shallow valleys of a plain that is perfectly level to any but a trained eye, the collection of annual rainfall of less than 6 inches gave better grazing, and these Janglis ("Jungle Folk") had their regular camping places, at wells they had made...holes, dug, up to four feet in diameter and going into the bowels of the earth...the huts were of reed screens..." (Spate and Learmonth 1967: 520).

Based on these, and reports in the Punjab Gazetteers and other places, it is possible to reconstruct a pattern of farming and pastoralism in the West Punjab where farmers, with some animal resources, inhabited the land near the rivers, even in the entrenchments, where natural irrigation and cultivable soils were found. The doabs, or *bar*, were vast pastures occupied by pastoral nomads. There is just enough documentation to show that there was a well developed symbiosis between the people who utilized these two environments; farmers using the pastoralists to care for some of their animals and taking pastoral products from them such as clarified butter, wool, hides, meat; pastoralists relying on the farmers for grain and other products. Cattle stealing is just another form of symbiosis which appears to be reasonably well documented as a part of life there. In today's economy the very high rupee value of water buffaloes has placed them in the esteem of thieves as well. These ethnohistoric observations are the basis for understanding ancient settlement patterns in the Punjab (Possehl 1984).

There are many pastoral nomads in Gujarat, especially Kutch. The principal castes today are *jats*, *charans*, *bharvards* and *rabaris* (Westphal-Hellbusch 1975). The acknowledged, traditional occupation of these peoples is the herding and management of grazing and browsing animals, but as with most castes, it is often not the occupation that they pursue. For example, many *rabaris* in North Gujarat are farmers who work for daily wages. There is also variation among them as to the animals they herd. The *rabaris* in the Barda Hills and Gir Forest of Saurashtra tend to breed cattle and water buffalo. The low, hilly tracts are home for them during the cold, dry season and they live in small villages called *nes* made up of a few huts. At other times of the year they are in lower areas, with their animals (Government of Bombay 1884: 137). *Rabaris* in northern and western Saurashtra keep huge herds of goats, with a few sheep mixed in. The goats are profitable today, because there is a strong market for them in the Arabian Gulf, where

164

they are shipped to be eaten. *Rabaris* are also found in considerable numbers in Rajasthan; some are known for their camel breeding.

> Camel-breeders have a tendency to withdraw from social entanglements. They like to absent themselves and their herds to half-deserts where their animals are best suited to live. A camel-breeder can live for weeks or months on camel milk alone. The herd offers him all he needs to live. His frame of mind is in harmony with this type of physical withdrawal. Camel-breeders avoid contact with villagers. Once or twice a year they may visit fairs to sell young animals and buy what is necessary for the household (Westphal-Hellbusch 1975: 129; see also Government of Bombay 1880: 29-30).

There are three principal patterns of settlement and movement for the pastoral nomadic castes of Gujarat. The most prominent is for the core of several families to live in a permanent village, or villages, in association with farmers. The core family is made up of the old and very young, along with some women. There are often no working males in this core; they are moving with the herds. The nomadic element of the family is comprised of males and the young and mature women. Contact is maintained between the sedentary core and the camp, but it is possible for some males to remain away from "home" for two, even three years at a stretch (Westphal-Hellbusch 1975: 129).

A second, less common pattern is for these people to have no settled life at all, living the entire year in a camp. It is a hard life, especially for the very old. Both of these organizational forms mean that some of the people are more or less constantly on the move, searching for pasture, using their animals to fertilize fields, selling animals, servicing their debt with settled people. With the exception of some camel breeders, they have close relationships with villages that count on them for ghee (clarified butter), wool, hair, manure and young animals.

The third form of adaptation is poorly documented in the literature. It involves settled pastoralism, usually mixed with some farming. The principal source of these people's livelihood are pastoral resources, but everyone lives at home, in a permanent village, most of the time anyway. The men and boys pasture the animals by day and return home with them at night. They might extend their stay away from the village with the herds for a day or two, even a week or a month, living simply, with minimal shelter, maintaining contact with their village. If this happens within the context of a village with many castes, the nomads may settle into the role of being caretakers for the animals of the village, earning income for their efforts. There are single caste villages of "settled nomads." One of these is named Chiroda (Plate 3.1). It is adjacent to the archaeological site of Oriyo Timbo where I learned something about this lifestyle while excavating. This settled state contributes to the broadening of the economic base for these people. They engage in day labor, buy land and begin to farm it, and take up trades.

The three forms of adaptation described here for Gujarat are in fact norms. There is wide variation within and among them. For example, a village of otherwise "settled nomads" may be partially the place of residence for some family cores for the first of the adaptations described here.

A Caution on Analogy

When the archaeological evidence is presented it will be seen that there is testimony for pastoralism, even pastoral nomadism during the Indus Age. Archaeologists do not know much about the details of this adaptation during those times, but there is a strong sense that there was a range of variation in the adaptation, then as now. This survey is not intended to provide rigid models for the reconstruction of the past, but to outline a range of variation that presents ideas about how subsistence adaptations might have worked in the past. The system of food production during the long history of the Indus Age was dynamic, constantly shifting and changing over time. It has to be assumed that there are many sociocultural forms that were developed there, over the thousands of years involved, that are not documented by the ethnographic, or near-historical record. Limiting ourselves to the narrow confines of ethnographic analogy is a serious error. The principles of adaptation, the rules that apply to symbiosis, should be looked at to reconstruct the true range of variability in sociocultural forms, not only those few that emerge from anthropological investigations, notes of government servants, historians and travelers. These observations apply to other itinerants in the Greater Indus region as well.

Other Itinerant Peoples: tinkers, traders, bards and the like

There are many kinds of nomadic peoples in the Greater Indus Region, even some who live without pastoral resources. Others use pastoral resources as a secondary component to their livelihood. Some people there use animals in highly specialized ways. Nomadic peoples are found all over the region, but the following from the Kutch (Cutch) District Gazetteer of 1880 documents the range of such itinerants:

> Of the classes who in ordinary seasons move about the province, the chief are, of artisans, carpenters, blacksmiths, coppersmiths, masons and weavers who with little capital go from town to town offering their services or selling their wares; of carriers, Hairs with their bullock carts, Charans, Lohanas, and Memans with their pack bullocks, potters with their asses, Sindhis with their camels; and of the lower classes, shepherds. Ods, or wandering diggers, cotton cleaners, and laborers, especially field laborers in harvest time. Of immigrants, polishers, blacksmiths, known as Gadalias, and Ods, come from Marwar and return within the year; and in the cold and hot seasons traders from Cabul and coppersmiths from Kathiawar come and sell their fruit and brass vessels, and return before the rains set in (Government of Bombay 1880: 103).

There is a fine treatment of the *gadulia lohars* (from *gadulia* or bullock cart and *lohar* or blacksmith) (P. K. Misra 1975). This caste is found all over northwestern India, especially Rajasthan. They are smiths who also trade in cattle.

Bards and storytellers are often itinerant. They have been poorly studied, but are important in many ways, especially as in regional communication networks. Joseph Miller (1976) has a long paper on bards in Rajasthan. The bards of this region, extending into Gujarat and Sindh are called "*bhopa*" and "*charan*" castes also involved in pastoralism, especially camel keeping today (Balfour 1885: Vol. 1, 280; Westphal-Hellbusch 1975: 127). One of the main bardic stories is of Pabuji and his helpers, the Thoris. They engage in a series of adventures that are regularly expanded and embellished within the context of the immutable part of the story which is about procuring camels for the dowry of Kelan, the daughter of Buro, Pabu's stepbrother (Hartkamp-Jonxis 1979). The Bhopa are regarded in Rajasthan as the hereditary guardians of history and pedigree. Edward Balfour sees three different functions of bards in India: historians, genealogists and court minstrels (1885: Vol. 1, 280). Sir Richard Burton mentions bards in his observations on Sindh. He notes that "In former times they used to accompany the head of the house into battle armed with sword and shield, with the Surindo or Rebec in hand, praising the brave and overwhelming cowards with satire and abuse...One of the Talpur family, who had not distinguished himself for bravery at the battle of Meeanee, was so much tormented by their ironical praises that he pays them liberally to keep out of his presence" (Burton 1851: 303).

Music is often involved in the intricacies of interrelated activities. Castes with music as part, or all, of their traditional occupation, are generally well respected, especially the bards, when they have a tradition of recording, preserving and protecting heritage. Balfour notes that they would associate themselves with caravans, ensuring the safe conduct of goods, at times free of local duties and taxes. By extension, members of these castes could function as individuals, carrying large sums of money and important messages, with freedom of movement and great honesty (1885: Vol. 1, 208).

Sedentary village farming communities and pastoral nomadic camps were important, complementary forms of adaptation during the Indus Age. They emerge out of the process that led to the establishment of the food producing/domestication revolution. The ethnographic and ethnohistorical record show that farmers without pastoral resources and activities, and pastoralists who undertake no agriculture at all are rare in the Greater Indus Region as well as Central Asia, Iran and the Near East. These food producing peoples should be imagined to be on a continuum of subsistence activities; at one end farmers, without pastoral resources and at the other pastoralists, without any engagement in agriculture. These are extreme forms of adaptation. Most food producers are not in this highly specialized category. The vast majority are somewhere in the middle, a blend of farmer and herder, directly engaged in making use of both cultivated plants and domesticated animals. Almost all contemporary, or near contemporary pastoral nomads in the Greater Indus Region can be included as part-time farmers, if their activities are reviewed over a sufficient period of time, a century or more, no matter what is going on at any given moment.

It is apparent that farmers and nomads, and all of the peoples who complement these ways of life, in the region from the Mediterranean to the Ganges, are characteristically interdependent. Sometimes the farmers and the pastoral nomads may be one and the same people; the farming and the pastoral nomadism being seasonal aspects of a single way of life. I have observed many Baluchis, Brahuis and Pathans who visit the Indus Valley in the winter as pastoral nomads, and return to their mountain villages in the spring to farm and herd. Characteristically, farmers use pastoralists to maintain their village farming form of adaptation and the pastoralists use farmers to maintain their pastoral way of life (Plate 3.2) which leads to symbiosis and sharing of resources.

Additional Thoughts on Nomads and Itinerants

Anthropologists generally study their "people" over short periods of time: a season, a year, perhaps returning for a short time at a later date. Their observations are often so time-bound that long term adaptive strategies may not be revealed. It is clear, however, that the farmers from the Mediterranean to the Ganges all have the requisite skills and knowledge to be pastoral nomads, and the pastoral nomads, in their own right, have the requisite skills and knowledge to be farmers. We are aware from many studies, the classic being F. Barth (1961), that this knowledge is frequently used, and farmers do become pastoral nomads, and pastoral nomads become farmers. This transformation of lifeway takes place at the level of individuals, families, even whole lineages or "tribes."

There is diversity within the multidimensional continua of activities that these subsistence strategies imply. Variability comes in many forms: mobility, the role of the seasons and structuring lifeways, in the plants and animals that are used, in changing ways, with differences in intensity. These dimensions of variability, and others, make for dissimilarities of peoples and ways of life that an anthropologist observes as a visitor to the region.

From this exposition the typology of "farmer" and "pastoralist" or "pastoral nomad" is of limited use because these adaptations are not static. They are simply points on a vast multi-dimensional configuration of adaptations and sociocultural forms. There is shifting of lifeways over time, along many dimensions of variability. This yields many forms of adaptation that would be called "intermediate" if the typology were used, but these adaptations are not "intermediate" at all. They are perfectly viable ways of life, conforming in harmony with the sociocultural, historical and environmental conditions that gave rise to them. Some of this shifting is short term, perhaps seasonal. But much of it is long-term, involving scores of years if not centuries; more in keeping with the time dimensions of the Indus Age than with contemporary anthropological study.

Cultural ecology can be informative about the nature of many subsistence relationships, but it has limits. The movement of pastoral nomads is not propagated solely by a search for fresh pasture. The exchange of farm products for those of the pastoral herd is not an example of ecological complementarity alone. Much more is represented in these relationships. Various maldhari peoples of Gujarat traditionally moved to find pasture, as well as to service debt with settled peoples, and provide them with the fertility of their bulls. If the movement of some of these pastoral nomads is traced, one finds that they leave pastures to move on to new ones. The vacated pastures are then immediately occupied by another group of pastoralists, which implies that the movement to "new" pasture takes place for some reason other than the exhaustion of one that others had just exploited.

One must turn to the theory of exchange systems to begin to get a more complete understanding of the interrelationships between the subsistence adaptations (Bates and Lees 1977). Exchange systems are complex phenomena and function in many ways as outlined in Marcel Mauss (1966), Marshall Sahlins (1965, 1972), Manning Nash (1966), Philip Curtin (1975) and Annette Weiner (1992). Exchange relationships are generally long-term, measured in generations not days, and involve reciprocity:

> In reciprocal exchange...trading partners engage in little or no bargaining and supply-and-demand adjustments take long time periods to work out. This sort of exchange often rests on fixed sets of trading partners, who after many sequential exchanges have established the connection of trust that in the long run, not in a single exchange, equivalences will be worked out. The trading partners may be individuals or nearly equivalent units of social structure....The advantage of reciprocal trade must be manifest in a deferential supply of goods and services, not in profit or disproportional gain (Nash 1966: 31).

Annette Weiner's (1992) thesis is that the secret of success in these complex relationships is not to have everything come out exactly even but to manipulate the system, using power, cunning and charisma to form "profit." This allows the successful participants in exchange systems to build wealth so that they can redistribute it.

These relationships are also personal, face to face, and can be socially charged. One dimension of exchange systems seems to be resolving problems of a differential supply of goods and services; to get metals from the mountains to the coast and fish from the sea to the mines. Although this immediate economic benefit of exchange systems is important, there are usually other payoffs.

Exchange networks give individuals and communities access to a wide range of goods: food, clothing, fuel; but some goods have a high ascribed value: precious metals, jewelry, symbols. Those who control the distribution of these "special" products can use them to create and maintain a following, thereby ensuring their position in society. The exchange of this kind of important wealth often takes place as part of a predictable cycle of movement, as with pastoral nomads, or as part of ritual or ceremonial life. In this way exchange systems play a role in the validation of status and rank, and if the ethnographic record is an adequate reference this takes place in societies which are even minimally differentiated. In these systems notions of profit and loss are measured not only in terms of material products but against a more generalized social backdrop. Such systems are also characterized by subjective attitudes toward exchange since every transaction carries with it not only the economic component but is itself a statement about the social position of the participants.

Expanding this perspective to what Sahlins (1972:199) has called the "intertribal sector" reveals another dimension, or function, for exchange systems. This has been noted by Levi-Strauss in the following way: "There is a link, a continuity, between hostile relations and the provisions of reciprocal presentation. Exchanges are peacefully resolved wars and wars are the result of unsuccessful transactions" (1969:67). Important wealth is therefore not only the currency of social ritual, it is also the currency of "intertribal" alliances. This, of course, closely parallels the process of alliance formation noted in regard to the "validation principle." Such intertribal alliances are useful, at times essential, arrangements which allow relatively small groups to draw on extended resources in times of crisis, such as war. They are also devices which serve to spread the risk of environmental disaster as noted by Piddocke (1965) for potlatching and Ford (1972) for exchange systems in the American southwest. In both instances material goods, exotic products, frequently utilized in a ritual context, were moved within an alliance network on a relatively predictable schedule as a hedge against periodic but unpredictable misfortune. The actual materials, while often important adjuncts to ceremonial life, are essentially the surface indicators of deeper ecological, political and economic alignments (Possehl 1986a: 80).

The set of relationships that pastoralists have with surrounding peoples, with different adaptations, is far deeper and more complicated than a simple need for food grains and other farm products. The range of goods and services exchanged is much wider. Products of long-distance trade are involved. Political alliances are formed and maintained, marriages arranged, news spread. Exchanges of goods and gifts take place between friends and allies and each individual exchange reinforces, revalidates these bonds. Exchange relationships are a form of insurance, enhancing survivability by spreading the risk of environmental disaster (drought, flood, pestilence), warfare and other undesirable events.

There is another category of nomadic, or semi-nomadic, people in South Asia that is deeply involved in exchange. It is the hunting and gathering groups that also figure in the story of the Indus Age.

Hunter-gatherers

In India, hunters and gatherers survive into modern times. Following the food producing revolution some people with this way of life occupied marginal environments, but not all of them. Some hunter-gatherers of the Indus Age seem to have lived side by side with farmers, pastoralists (nomadic and otherwise), and other peoples. What we find in the archaeological and ethnohistorical record is that hunter-gatherers quickly adapted to the use of domesticated animals, especially cattle and goats. Thus, determining just who is a hunter-gatherer and who is not can be difficult, and illustrates the limited use of this kind of typological approach to anthropological data. There is also evidence that prehistoric hunter-gatherers obtained food grains, either by "trade" or cultivation, or both. While they continued to hunt and gather for much of their livelihood they were also herders, and formed important relationships with settled farmers, pastoral nomads and the others in the region. The key to hunter-gatherer survival in South Asia lies not in isolated self-reliance, but on the establishment of a symbiotic relationship with the peoples around them. They hunted wild animals and gathered forest products that were traded to their neighbors for agricultural, animal and craft products, like grain, milk, metal implements and cloth. Richard Fox has expressed this relationship in the following way:

Rather than being independent, primitive fossils, Indian hunters-and-gatherers represent occupationally specialized productive units similar to caste groups such as carpenters, shepherds or leather-workers. Their economic regimen is geared to trade and exchange with the more complex agricultural and caste communities within whose orbit they live. Hunting and gathering in the Indian context is not an economic response to a total undifferentiated environment. Rather it is a highly specialized and selective orientation to the natural situation: where forest goods are collected and valued primarily for external barter or trade, and where necessary subsistence or ceremonial items—such as iron tools, rice, arrow heads, etc.—are only obtainable this way. Far from depending wholly on the forest for their own direct subsistence, the Indian hunters-and-gatherers are highly specialized exploiters of a marginal terrain from which they supply the larger society with desirable, but otherwise unobtainable forest items such as honey, wax, rope and twine, baskets, and monkey and deer meat. Unlike the Australian aborigines or the Paiutes, their economic processes and well-being are dependent on the barter of these items for the crops and crafts of their more complexly organized plainsmen neighbors. The economic activity of Indian hunting-and-gathering groups is more akin to the specialization of caste hereditary occupation, than it is to the generalized environmental response of the Australians or Paiute (Fox 1969: 141-42).

If data from the archaeological record is combined with what can be gleaned from ancient and medieval history and the ethnographic past, it appears that the enthnographic setting of the Greater Indus Region during the Indus Age must have been rich, with a diversity of peoples, lifeways, cultural traditions, occupations and probably languages.

The Integration of Complementary Ways of Life

The integration of the diverse lifeways in the Greater Indus region in ethnographic or ethnohistorical times is one of the clearest indications of the resilience of life there. It is especially remarkable when the system taken as a whole is so dynamic, so filled with change and alteration over time. Families, even whole groups ("lineages") might settle as farmers for some years and then find a shift to pastoral nomadism advantageous or necessary. Nomadic potters might find a permanent village in which to settle, perhaps for a few years or a generation or two, and then resume an itinerant life, with the possibility that pottery making would have slipped in importance for the family's livelihood and identity. A traveling bard might settle in one place in retirement. Following F. Barth's observations (1961) success could transform a nomadic pastoralist into a settled landowner and farmer, or failure in pastoral nomadism might find another pastoral nomad forced into impoverished day labor in a farmer's field. Shifts within this multidimensional system of lifeways can be short-term (seasonal, yearly), long-term (generations) and many time spans in between.

Measuring the rate at which shifts between a nomadic and settled way of life takes place is a difficult, perhaps even problematic, endeavor. Just how much movement constitutes "nomadism", for example? In a study of modern Indian pastoral nomads, especially in Rajasthan and Gujarat, S. S. Prasad has documentation for the fact that between two-thirds and three-quarters "...of the pastoral families that now migrate told that their grandfather did not practice a migratory way of life" (1994: 134). This indicates that these parts of the subsistence regime are quite pliable, and change relatively fast.

There is another dynamic dimension to the peoples of this world region; it is physical movement, especially on the short-term. Some of this mobility is based in geography, environment and ecology. The lowlands of the Indus Valley and Punjab are juxtaposed to mountains of Baluchistan and the Northwest Frontier Province. The symbiosis between these regions is itself a powerful engine of movement. It has been an intimate link since the beginnings of plant and animal domestication, and even before. The mineral resources of the relatively barren mountains can be contrasted to the productivity of the plains in terms of plant and animal resources. The search for new pastures and farm land led peoples east of the Indus plains and south into Gujarat. Trade and commerce, possibly modest in scale in the early stages of the Indus Age connected the sea coasts to the interior, eastern Iran and Central Asia to the Indus Valley.

It is increasingly clear that the peoples of the Indus Age, especially the Mature Harappan, wherever they have been found, were cattle breeders and keepers *par excellence*. The hard evidence for this comes in a number of forms. There are the pastoral camps in Cholistan, Saurashtra, Kutch, Gedrosia, and to some extent Sindh and the Punjab. There is also the testimony of the faunal remains, figurines and other imagery which consistently document cattle as a prominent part of the lives of the peoples of the Mature Harappan. It may be wrong, therefore, to think of the Mature Harappans as primarily peasant farmers, living in neat Sindhi and Punjabi villages, even though we have evidence for such settlements. The emerging picture of Mature Harappan life indicates that many of these peoples were mobile cattle keepers, craft and career specialists working the highlands and the lowlands on a seasonal round, or moving from Saurashtra to Sindh, or Sindh to Cholistan and other places, in search of pasture and their livelihood. The case is especially strong for a large number of pastoralists camp sites in Cholistan (Mughal 1994, 1997).

The documentation in the district gazetteer series, and an examination of topography, leads to the conclusion that the Punjab, especially the western Punjab, was basically pasture land for cattle keepers until the last half of the nineteenth century A.D. This observation is also sustained by the fact that medieval copper land grant tablets, so important for the documentation of the transfer of agricultural land, have never been found there (R. Thapar, personal communication). The *bar* and *des* were substantially different in the nature of their resources. Pastoralism in the *bar* and agriculture in the *des* was the pattern until massive late nineteenth century irrigation schemes brought water to the *bar*. Because irrigation on this scale was not a part of the Indus Age, it stands to reason that Mature Harappan peasant farming comments, as well as those of earlier stages, would have been restricted to the well-watered *des*, leaving the *bar* open for use as pasture in the complex mixes of pastoralism that were probably present then, as now. These observations in cultural geography would seem to be an explanation for the interesting pattern of prehistoric settlement found in much of the western Punjab (Possehl 1984), and seem, to some degree, to be sustained by recent exploration in the region.

Some years ago it was observed that Harappan settlement patterns tend to be either clusters of sites, clearly interrelated like those in Cholistan (Mughal 1997), or Kutch District of Gujarat, or isolated settlements (Possehl 1979c). The extremes of this isolation are illustrated at places like Sutkagen-dor, Manda or even Shortughai, Balakot or a pair of sites like Ahmad Khan Dheri and Ahmad Khan's Dheri in Rajasthan (Figure 3.2). West Punjab has already been discussed, with village farming communities associated with the river entrenchments, not the *bars* separating them, just as is the case for Harappa itself.

Given the presence of a Mature Harappan cultural style over about one million square kilometers, as well as the coherence of earlier regional Phases, we can infer a very substantial base of interaction and communication for the peoples of the Indus Age. Intense, regular communication between diverse regions is the basis on which these cultural patterns were developed and sustained. They are also a key to understanding culture change. Taking these

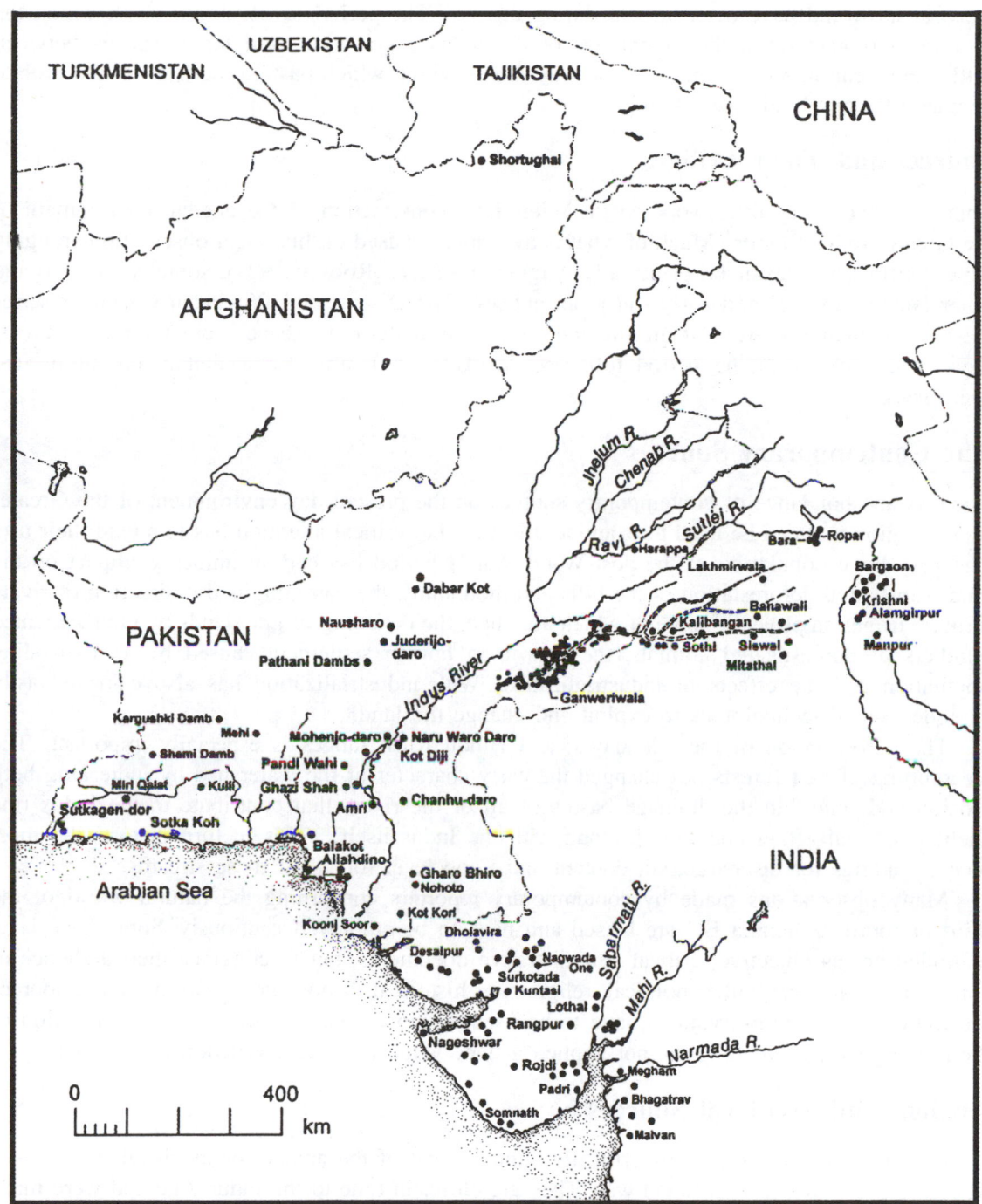

Figure 3.2. Map of Mature Harappan sites

observations on interaction it would seem to be farfetched to imagine that the immense areas and the spaces between the Mature Harappan site clusters and isolates were uninhabited during this time. It is more reasonable to see them as the niches within which a very large number of pastoralists would have been present during this era. The period of development on which the Mature Harappan rests, the beginnings of the Indus Age, with even larger spaces between settlements, can be viewed in the same way: times within which pastoral nomadism and mobile peoples of many kinds were living.

Sources and Their Utility

There has been very little work on the scientific reconstruction of the ancient environment of the Greater Indus Region. Much of what is available is based on historical observations ranging from the time of Alexander, principally Arrian's *Anabasis* (Robson 1929), some early Arab and other Islamic sources and early European notices. The District and Provincial Gazetteer series are also invaluable sources of information on the pre-modern landscape. Contemporary sources, those that come from the period following World War II, are also available, but of limited usefulness.

The Contemporary Sources

There is an abundance of contemporary sources on the present day environment of the Greater Indus Region that can be used to examine this area, but critical attention has to attend their use. The very large population of the post-World War II period has had an immense impact on the land: substantial deforestation of the hills and mountains, the damming and redirection of rivers through irrigation projects, some of which are huge, the denuding of grasslands by unprecedented numbers of domesticated animals, the growth in human settlement caused by an expanding population and the effects of industrialization. With industrialization has also came a vastly extended set of technologies to exploit and change the land.

The deforestation of the Himalayan and Hindu Kush ranges is especially important. The clearcutting of vast forests has changed the early character of the watershed by increasing both erosion and runoff in the drainage basins of all of the rivers that contribute to the Indus (the Jhelum, Chenab, Ravi and Sutlej, along with the Indus itself). This in turn distorts the most recent readings for discharge, silt content and flood level for all of these streams.

Many observations made by contemporary reporters concerning the natural world of the third or fourth millennia BC are biased and have to be employed cautiously. Some have been compiled not as objective, critical administrative documents, but to convince their audience of some particular issue, either political, religious or historical. It does not mean that these sources are useless, but the observations have to be used within the context of a critical evaluation of their strengths and weaknesses, not applied at face value to a reconstruction of the past.

Ancient and Medieval Sources

If modern sources are somehow critically tainted, what of the ancient or medieval documents? They are useful but in a different way. They are closer in time to the Indus Age and were made prior to the population explosion, massive irrigation works and industrialization. They were also made at a time when the inhabitants of the Subcontinent used relatively simple technologies, much more akin to those of the Bronze Age than to those of the very recent past. Just as in modern times they also might reflect a particular bias, therefore a critical approach to these sources is needed.

The "Best" Sources

There is another body of material that comes from a time and institutional context that seems to minimize (never eliminate!) the need for critical assessment. It consists of documents of the late nineteenth and early twentieth centuries, compiled and composed by intelligent men, most of whom were trained in scientific objectivity, who were part of the scientific age. The documents are largely administrative reports and gazetteers written for governmental use, generally in the context of economic development and colonial rule. These sources have the advantages of science and its values of accuracy, precision, tight definition and systematic presentation. They come from an age that predates the population explosion of recent decades and although they were written in the mature years of the industrial revolution, much of this change had not yet come to the rural areas of South Asia. They avoid the problems inherent in using data from the past forty or fifty years and preserve a sense of reliability, but are deficient in many cases because they were prepared to enhance the effectiveness of colonial rule. The data, such as those on rainfall or river discharge rates and other time dependent observations, can be thin and may use archaic terminology, especially in the systematic nomenclature of plants and animals. Many of the reports and gazetteers were compiled by men of sound, general, probably public school education, who more than likely knew the classics better than geology. But they were good, some even skilled, at using specialized sources and the soundness of their education and training led them to avoid making errors of excess. It is also true that these reports and gazetteers were generally vetted among a population of administrators, introducing a set of checks and balances that kept outright errors and gross misunderstandings of the cultural geography of the day to a minimum.

The Routes in and around the Greater Indus Region

As in most parts of the world in premodern times, before the construction of roads, communication routes in the Greater Indus Region follow the form of the land. They follow rivers, streams and valley bottoms, are channeled through low points in mountain crests; at times they are one and the same, as the *Gaj Nai* in western Sindh where a river has flowed through a fault in a mountain face for millennia creating a valley through which pastoral nomads, travelers, traders, tinkers, all manner of humanity, travel between the Indus Valley and the mountains of Baluchistan. A historical study of these routes led to the creation of the accompanying illustration, a visual accompaniment to explain the orientation of travel (Figure 3.3). J. F. Jarrige and M. U. Hassan are owed a debt for their illustration of the western portion of the study (Jarrige and Hassan 1989: 151); M. Rafique Mughal and Farzand A. Durrani for conversations.

ANIMALS AND PLANTS OF THE INDUS AGE

Introduction

Life during the Indus Age was dependent upon a diverse suite of domesticated animals and plants. The people were farmers of wheat (*Triticum* sp.) and barley (*Hordeum distichum*) who kept domesticated animals, principally the zebu (*Bos indicus*), sheep (*Ovis aries*), goats (*Capra hockeys*) and water buffalo (*Bubalus bubalis*). Whether the peoples of the Indus Age domesticated the pig (*Sus domesticus*) is in some doubt, but there are plenty of wild pigs (*Sus scrofa*) from these times. The productivity of domesticated plants and animals was complemented by hunting and gathering as evidenced by the remains of wild ungulates such as the chital or spotted deer

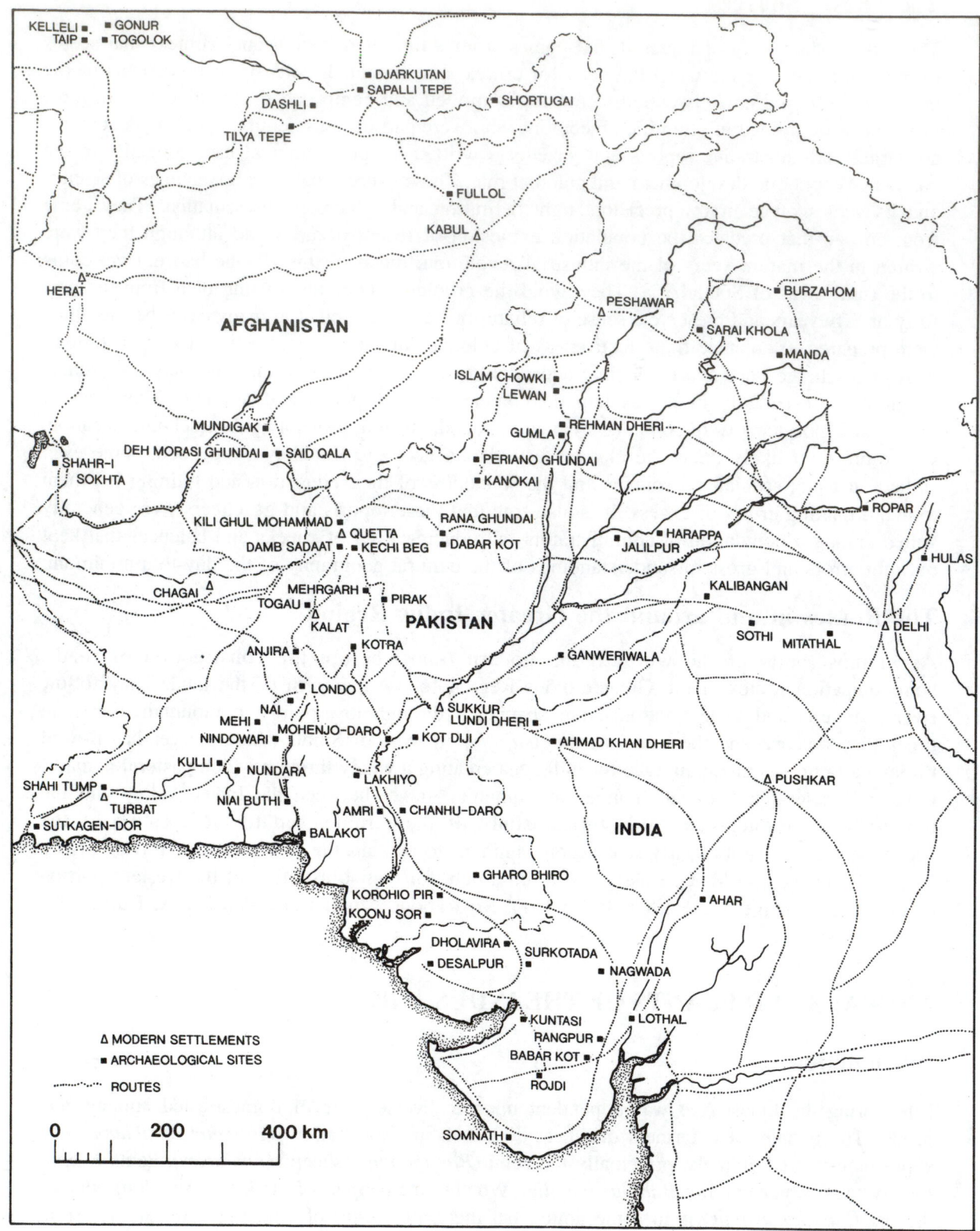

Figure 3.3. Routes in and around the Greater Indus Region

(*Axis axis*), Indian gazelle or chinkara (*Gazella bennetti*), nilgai (*Boselaphus tragocamelus*), blackbuck (*Antelope cervicapra*) and onager (*Equus hemionus*) in the zoological record of virtually every excavated site. There is also evidence that the elephant (*Elephas maximus*), rhinoceros (*Rhinoceros unicornis*), tiger (*Panthera tigris*) and Asiatic lion (*Panthera leo*) were well represented in the Greater Indus Region during the Indus Age. The Indian jujube, generally known as *ber* (*Zizyphus jujubata*) is a wild plant with a red fruit and a hard, cherry-like seed that seems to have been consumed in quantity from the eighth millennium B.C. to the present. It makes tasty eating on archaeological excavations. But, it was the domesticated species that provided the bulk of the food for the inhabitants of early villages and camps and the later cities and towns.

The best general sources on the mammals of the Greater Indus Region are: Ellerman and Morrison-Scott (1966); Prater (1971); Roberts (1977); Corbet and Hill (1992). There are two excellent books on the birds: Ali and Ripley (1983) and Roberts (1991-92). Information on plants is more scattered. A good general source is Anonymous (1953, 1957, 1961), especially since Sindh was a part of the Bombay Presidency, and is well represented in these books.

Domesticated Mammals

Cattle[3]

The zebu (*Bos indicus*) (Plate 3.3, Plate 3.4) the humped South Asian cattle, was the most important animal of the Indus Age. The remains of cattle are generally predominant in all of the sites of the time and by the Mature Harappan they can be expected to constitute about half of the faunal remains from any given site. There is some ambiguity about the presence of a second kind of cattle in the Greater Indus Region during the era. It is the unhumped *Bos taurus*, which was the predominant breed in the west . There are many unhumped "taurine" cattle figurines from Harappan sites (Figure 3.4), as well as in somewhat later contexts (Figure 3.5). There are other examples of unhumped bulls in steatite (Figure 3.6, Figure 3.7). The famous Indus stamp seals have the so-called "unicorn," an animal that appears to be the representation of an unhumped bull (Plate 3.5, Plate 3.6). There is a total of 1218 bull seals for Mature Harappan not counting the so-called "short-horned bull" (Mahadevan 1977: 793). Of these, 54 are clear zebu seals, the remaining 1164 are the so-called "unicorn."

These animals, *Bos indicus* and *Bos taurus*, are closely related and their osteological remains are difficult to differentiate. They may actually be the same species (Corbet and Hill 1992: 264; Grigson 1985). Some parts of the cranium are different in these two animals, but this is not part of *Bos* anatomy that is found frequently in the archaeological record. The situation at present is that there seem to be artifactual representations (figurines, imagery on seals, drawings on pottery) of *Bos taurus* but no bones (Grigson 1984).

The presence of so much imagery of unhumped cattle in the Mature Harappan, in the absence of confirming osteological evidence, is one of the unresolved issues in the study of the Indus Age.

The biological significance of the hump at the shoulders of the zebu is not understood. There is one suggestion that it may have some physiological value in a hot climate (Sundersen 1976), but this is far from certain. Based on paintings and engravings of these

Figure 3.4. Figurine of an unhumped bull from Mohenjo-daro, after Ardeleanu-Jansen, Franke and Jansen 1983: 69

Figure 3.5. Two *Bos tarus* gold figurines from the Quetta Treasury, after Jarrige and Hassan 1989: Figure 8

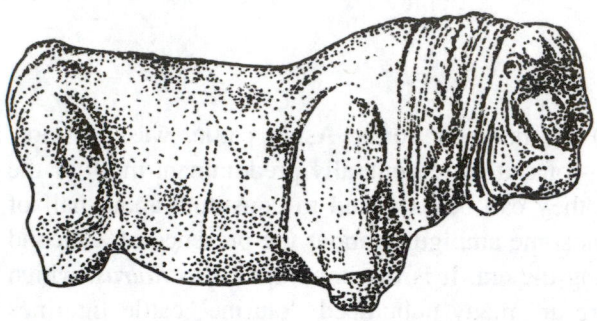

Figure 3.6. Steatite figurine of an unhumped bull from Mohenjo-daro, after Marshall 1931a: Plate XCVII, No. 23

animals at places like Lascaux and Egyptian tombs, it is known that the Pleistocene and early Holocene cattle in Europe, the Near East and North Africa were unhumped. The earliest evidence for a humped breed comes from the faunal remains at Mehrgarh I (Meadow 1984b: 37), along with a figurine from Mehrgarh II (Meadow 1984b: 36). There is no direct evidence to suggest that the Pleistocene *Bos* of the Subcontinent, commonly called *Bos namadicus*, was humped, but most believe this to have been the ancestor of the zebu (Corbet and Hill 1992: 263).

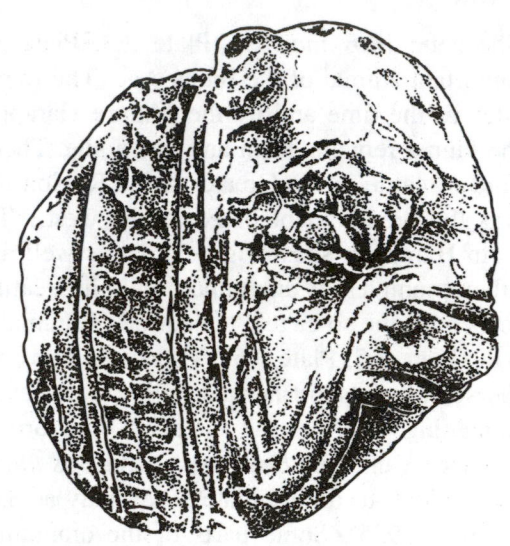

Figure 3.7. The face of one of the steatite bull figurines after, Anonymous 1989: Figure 325

There are hundreds of terracotta cattle figurines and some very good examples in steatite. An exceptional example in copper bronze comes from Kalibangan (Plate 3.7). There are many bull figurines made as puppets, with a separate, movable head hinged at the shoulders (Plate 3.8). Puppets of other animals also exist as do examples on wheels (i. e., Chanhu-daro; Mackay 1943: Plate LVIII, Nos. 11, 12, 15, 17, and 19 for a vehicle; Banawali, Bisht 1982 Plate 10.23). This kind of toy is a distinct innovation of the Mature Harappan and seems to have been a Harappan delight, designed to entertain children and their adult playmates. The Kulli Phase bull figurines are almost always painted, those from the other domains are almost always plain. There are no Kulli puppets.

It can be inferred that bullocks were used for traction, to pull carts and the plow, both of which are documented by terracotta models, including the bulls themselves (Plate 3.9). Carts are further documented by ruts in ancient streets at Harappa (Wheeler 1947a: Pl. XXXV, B; Kenoyer 1991a: 49), and there is direct evidence for traffic wearing away the walls of buildings at Mohenjo-daro. "Corners of some of the smaller by-ways show evidence of having been rubbed by pack-animals or by the clothing of passers-by, and in some cases the angles of a building were purposefully rounded-off so that pack-loads should not become dislodged, a device which has also been observed in ancient Ur" (Mackay 1948: 20, see also Mackay 1937-38: 88, 101). Most westerners are not accustomed to thinking of cattle as pack animals, but they are still used in the Subcontinent for this purpose. Cattle undoubtedly were used for their dairy products but the water buffalo may have provided such products too. Cattle were also a source of meat since many bones are charred and have butcher marks on them.

Cattle were of extraordinary importance to the people of ancient India and Pakistan. In part, this inference comes from the bones themselves. One of the consistent patterns from sites of the Indus Age is the percentage of cattle bones that can be assigned to the genus *Bos*. We learn from Richard Meadow (1993a: 312-13) that by the end of Mehrgarh Period IB cattle bones make up more than one-half of the total faunal assemblage. This drops a bit in the later periods at the site, but is still higher than one would expect from a fourth or third millennium Near Eastern faunal assemblage. Cattle comprise up to 75 percent of the mammalian fauna from the third and fourth millennium sites of Jalilpur and Balakot.

The same high percentage of cattle bones has been found from sites of the Indus Age in Gujarat.

These high figures for cattle are all the more remarkable because Meadow also demonstrates that cattle remains, as compared to those of sheep and goats, are probably consistently underrepresented in the archaeological record. This is due to the reproductive pattern of *Bos* and the resulting culling of young animals from the herd (Meadow 1993a: 313). Thus, the high percentage of cattle that is calculated from our faunal studies probably underestimates the true herd size.

Cattle imagery is also the most prevalent aspect of Harappan art: the seals, figurines, painted Kulli pottery, Damb Sadaat and Late Kot Dijian pottery. Given these observations it is fair to say that cattle were more than likely a prominent form of wealth for these people and must, therefore, have been a source of great prestige (Fairservis 1986, 1992: 133-39).

Water Buffalo

Wild water buffalo (*Bubalus arnee*) and the domestic form (*Bubalus bubalis*), native to India and Southeast Asia, are present in the Indus Age, although not in numbers approaching those of cattle (Figure 3.8) (Plate 3.10). According to S. H. Prater (1971: 247-48) the water buffalo survives in the wild in the Nepal Terai, the plains of the Brahmaputra and Assam, and in Bustar District of Madhya Pradesh and adjoining parts of Orissa. The male of the species can be very aggressive, charging without cause, and with little warning. Females with young are aggressive in their protection behavior; a trait which also characterizes the domesticated breed.

The horns of the wild water buffalo are massive, larger in males than females. They develop a wide sweep, bending around to form a semicircle, with a small space between the pointed tips. There is a gradation of angle, from a relatively vertical set to one which sweeps back to the shoulders, almost parallel to the ground. Horn size is very much reduced in the domesticated breeds and shaped by shaving and controlling the direction of growth, partly as a "brand" for identification of the animals. The distinctive sweep of the horns has been captured effectively by ancient artists in both the Greater Indus Region and Mesopotamia (Plate 3.11, Plate 3.12). There is a striking similarity in the pose of the water buffalo in these two regions and it can be

TABLE 3.1
Selected Mammalian Remains from Harappan Sites in Gujarat

Site	Cattle	Sheep/ Goat	Pig	Buffalo	Deer	Other	No.	Source
Oriyo	84.7%	13.9%	1.4%	— —	— —	— —	1190	Rissman 1985: 128 & 197
Dhatva	76.4%	0.2%	2.7%	3.0%	12.8%	4.9%	657	Shah 1975
Kanewal	ca. 50%	— —	— —	— —	— —	— —	— —	Shah 1980
Khanpur	62%	— —	— —	— —	— —	— —	— —	Thomas 1984
Nageshwar Urban Phase)	49.9%	20%	0.5%	11.4%	— —	— —	971*	Hegde, et al. 1990: 47
Prabhas Patan	55%	— —	— —	— —	— —	— —	— —	Thomas 1984
Rangpur (all periods)	78%	11%	8%	2%	— —	— —	1847	Bhola Nath 1963
Rangpur (Urban Phase)	68.3%	19%	5.1%	7.6%	— —	— —	79	Bhola Nath 1963
Rojdi (all phases)	74.5%	15.9%	9.6%	— —	— —	— —	804	Possehl et al. 1985
Lothal all phases	56.3%	20.4%	18.2%	4.5%	0.3%	0.3%	4,602	Bhola Nath and Rao 1985: 636-50

* Total bone count for both periods.]
(Table modified from Rissman 1985: 128 and 197)

expected that the motif was shared, coming through the activities of the Middle Asian Interaction Sphere.

There are 14 stamp seals with water buffalo on them (Mahadevan 1977: 793). Some depict combat with humans (Figure 3.9), reaffirming the aggressive nature of the wild animal. Water buffalo figurines are relatively rare, but there is one magnificent example from the so-called "Daimabad Bronzes," which are, unfortunately, of uncertain date (Dhavalikar 1982) (Figure 3.10). A very fine water buffalo in copper-bronze comes from Mohenjo-daro (Mackay 1937-38: Plate LXXI, No. 23).

There is every reason to believe that during the Indus Age wild water buffalo inhabited the flood plains of Sindh and extended at least as far north as the wetlands of the Panjnad. Wild water buffalo are reported from the aceramic period at Mehrgarh (Period I) (Meadow 1984b: 35). The domesticated water buffalo is probably present by Mature Harappan times, but the history of human control over this animal is not yet known (Meadow 1991b: 55). It is highly likely, however, that members of the wild breed were still in the Indus Valley throughout the prehistoric period, possibly along with feral animals that had escaped from their domiciles. This is evidenced by the combat scenes on Indus seals, although there is room for other interpretations.

The water buffalo is a prolific producer of milk, with very high butter fat content. It can also be used for traction; pulling plows and carts. Its need for water renders it somewhat less

Figure 3.8. A water buffalo

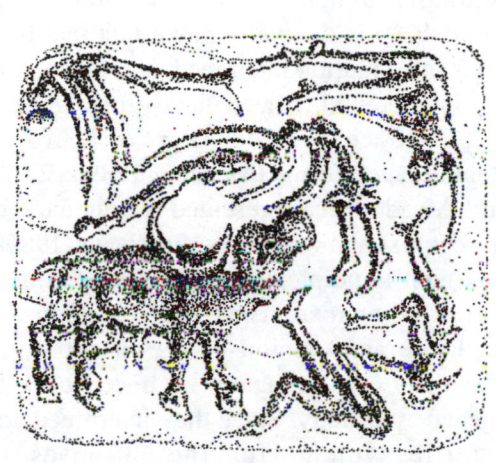

Figure 3.9. Seal portraying combat with a water buffalo, after Mackay 1937-38: Plate XCVI, 510

Figure 3.10. Water buffalo from the Daimabad bronzes, after Yule 1985: Plate 3

adaptable than the bullock, and for this reason it is not widely used as a pack animal. Water buffalo evolved in environments with standing and slowly running water: ponds, swamps, large rivers with ample backwater and remnant lakes. They are accustomed to wallowing in these places, cooling themselves during the heat of the day and refreshing their skin, which will crack and deteriorate unless it gets its daily renewal by soaking, making them not good animals for pastoralists to keep outside relatively wet environments. In this way the water buffalo is a good index of stable sedentism in well watered places. This was the environment where the buffalo occurs in quantity; which is one of the reasons that it figures prominently in the review of the cultural geography of the Greater Indus Region.

180

Sheep

There are two wild sheep in the Greater Indus Region, the Urial, or Shapu (*Ovis vigni*) (Figure 3.11) and Argali or Mouflon (*Ovis ammon*) (Figure 3.12). These are very closely related animals and natural hybridization between the two has been known to occur. But there is some normative difference in habitat and it is convenient to refer to two different animals, in some contexts.

The Urial (*Ovis vigni*), has a broad distribution from the Eastern Mediterranean and Anatolia, across the Iranian Plateau to South Asia, extending north into Central Asia. It is considered to be the wild ancestor of the domesticated form *Ovis aries*. Within the Greater Indus Region wild sheep are known from the Salt Range and Punjab hills, all through the mountains of Baluchistan, Waziristan, the Northwest Frontier and Sindh Kohistan.

Ovis ammon is found to the north of the Urial. It is an animal of high remote mountains, where there are cold winds and arid conditions. They are known to range to altitudes of 6100 meters in the Pamirs and are common above 4500 meters. Today *Ovis ammon* are found in the mountains of northern Pakistan and India, as well as northern Afghanistan. In antiquity these sheep may have inhabited the higher mountains of eastern and central Afghanistan and Northern Waziristan (see Schaller 1977 for a study of modern wild sheep and goats in the Subcontinent).

Figure 3.11. Wild sheep

Figure 3.12. Marco Polo's sheep

Adding a dimension of confusion to the nature of sheep is the well-known fact that both the Urial and Mouflon interbreed, and bear fertile young, in the wild. Sheep have great genetic plasticity, attested by the diversity of both wild and domesticated forms (Meadow 1989b: 28-9). Richard Meadow has presented a summary of the present taxonomic position for sheep (1989b: 28-9), which is perplexing, at least to the non-specialist, because the proliferation of nomenclature and opinion on the taxonomy of these animals can ultimately be traced back to their genetic plasticity. Since they interbreed and bear fertile young, for the purposes of archaeology and human use, it might be acceptable to consider them one species, and leave the sophistry of binomial nomenclature to the zoologists.

Sheep bones, along with those of goats, are common elements in faunal collections from virtually every site of the Indus Age. Their close biological affiliation makes a separation of the bones of these two animals somewhat vexing for zooarchaeologists, and often leads to the frequent category (not a special animal!) "sheep-goat."

Sheep have been purposely bred to produce wool and early forms of the animal would have been hairy, like their wild counterparts. They are a source of meat and produce passable milk, to which the palate can be tamed. Hearty animals, they adapt well to migration and travel, are tolerant of drought and poor pasture and fit well into the kind of pastoral nomadism that the peoples of the Indus Age practiced. They mature quickly and therefore do not engender significant amounts of investment, like cattle and buffalo.

There are fine representations of sheep in Indus sculpture and it is curious that there are no sheep on Indus stamp seals. H. F. Friederichs proposed that the animal with the curly horns on the Seal of Divine Adoration was a sheep (Friederichs 1933), but I agree with Mackay, it

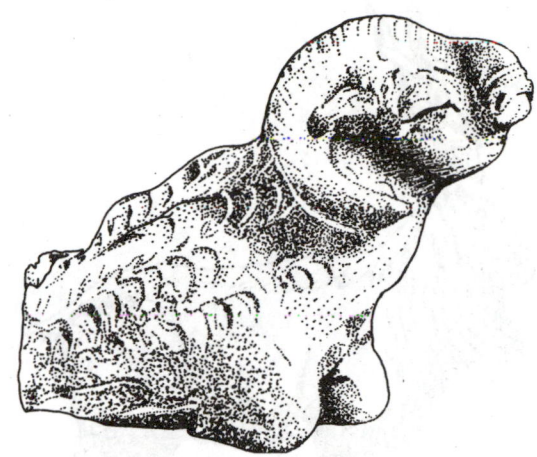

Figure 3.13. Ram figurine from Mohenjo-daro, after Mackay 1937-38: Plate LXVI, No. 23

Figure 3.14. Caprines from Nal and Siah Damb II, after Hargreaves 1929: Plate XVII, Nos. 61 & 63; de Cardi 1965: Figure 16, No. 5

is more likely to represent a goat, although the foreshortened face is more primate-like than any of the artiodactyls (Mackay 1937-38: 671). Mackay notes that unmistakable sheep figurines are comparatively rare in Indus sites (Mackay 1937-38: 291), but it is often difficult to separate them from goats (Figure 3.13). The problems of identification of these animals in terracotta parallel those in bone. Various examples of the animal will be found in Mackay (1937-38: Plates LXXX and LXXXVIII).

Nal type pottery from the Gedrosia Region has some animals that cannot be identified as either sheep or goats. Three of these are illustrated as a transition for this discussion (Figure 3.14).

Goats

Figure 3.15. Wild goat

Domesticated goats (*Capra hircus*) were among the most important and productive animals for the ancient farming and herding communities of the Greater Indus Region. There are three wild goats in the region today: the Persian Wild Goat (*Capra aegagrus*), the Markhor and the Ibex (Figure 3.15, Figure 3.16, Figure 3.17). These are a closely related species with somewhat overlapping ranges (Plate 3.13).

Figure 3.16. The Markhor   **Figure 3.17.** The Ibex

The domesticated goat (*Capra hircus*) is now thought to be the descendent of the Persian Wild Goat, *Capra aegagrus*. The wild form is found from the eastern edge of the Iranian Plateau, into Turkmenia and west to Anatolia and the Greek Islands. Herds of wild goats are found today in southern Baluchistan, but in prehistoric times they would have ranged far north into Afghanistan and Central Asia. The animal can be found in arid highlands with poor pasture and in areas close to sea level. It is known in the eastern foot hills of the Kirthar Range and adjacent plains and would have been found in Sindh Kohistan in antiquity.

The cousin of *Capra hircus*, the Markhor (*Capra falconeri*), is a somewhat more regional animal, found in Central Asia, Afghanistan, Kashmir, the Punjab and Baluchistan. It is the goat with the large "cork screw" horns. They are adaptable to high altitude conditions and those at sea level, and are found on the arid, treeless plains at the base of the Sulaiman Range. They also inhabit the oak scrub forests of Chitral and the pine and juniper forests of northern Baluchistan and south Waziristan.

The Ibex exists from the Alps of Northern Italy, all the way across the Near East, Caucasus, Iran, Central Asia into Chinese Turkistan and also occurs in North Africa. In the Greater Indus Region it has been recorded in the northern Punjab, northern Baluchistan and Waziristan and Afghanistan. Today, the distribution of the animal is in the high altitudes of the Himalaya, Hindu Kush, the Pamirs and Altai and in the Safed Koh of the Northwest Frontier Province.

Some evidence for the domestication of the goat comes from Snake and Horse Caves in Northern Afghanistan (Dupree 1964, 1972a, 1972b; Shaffer 1978a: 73-81; Meadow 1989b), where a date of ca. 9000 to 10,000 BC is suggested for early food producing peoples. Domesticated goats are also found at Mehrgarh Period I and Kili Ghul Mohammad I in Quetta.

Goats reproduce well and are not fussy, difficult to maintain animals and like sheep. It is a small animal that matures quickly and does not require the kind of investment that a buffalo or bullock would. They are highly mobile and agile and are tolerant of drought and poor pasture, making them excellent animals for pastoral nomads. Goat milk is agreeable and nutritious and goat hair is a valuable product. They are also good to eat and there is abundant evidence for their consumption in antiquity.

A goat, or goat-like creature, occurs on several Indus seals or sealings; as already noted, the Seal of Divine Adoration. The corkscrew quality of the horns suggests the Markhor, but they are laid flat, parallel to the ground, not a natural attitude for a rack of horns on this animal. Moreover, the face of the animal on the seal is foreshortened, taking on a strangely human quality and it might be that it was intended to be more (or less) than a goat. Other goats on Indus seals include M-271 (Joshi and Parpola 1987; Mackay 1937-38: Plate XCIX, No. 670) with a goat-like face but with the horns of the goat on the Seal of Divine Adoration; L-48 (Joshi and Parpola 1987; Rao 1985: Plate CLIX, A, 3) with the goatee of the male animal and two others from Kalibangan (K-34 and K-37 in Joshi and Parpola 1987), both of which stand in front of the fish sign of the script. Mahadevan lists 37 seals with a goat or goat-antelope motif (1977: 793), since there is some ambiguity between the Harappan portrayal of these two animals in this medium.

Mackay mentions a splendid bronze goat (Mackay 1937-38: 292) (Figure 3.18). He could not have known this, but goats in this wonderfully lively attitude have good parallels in Bactria and Central Asia, and this is probably an import (see Middle Asian Interaction Sphere). Goats (or sheep) can be found on the plates in Mackay (1937-38: Plates LXXX and LXXXVIII).

Figure 3.18. Bronze goat from Mohenjo-daro, after Mackay 1937-38: Plate LXXIV, Nos. 18-9

The Gaur

The Gaur (*Bibos gaurus*) or Indian Bison (Figure 3.19) is a massive animal with a distinctive ridge down the center of its shoulder area. It is a hill animal found in peninsular India, including the Western Ghats. The modern distribution begins in southern Maharashtra, but in antiquity it probably extended north into Gujarat and southern Rajasthan, and might have included the Indus Valley. It is also an animal of the Himalaya and a northern distribution across to Afghanistan is a possibility.

Osteological remains of the Gaur have never been confidently identified at a site of the Indus Age. This is in part because the comparative osteology of the animal is poorly defined and many bones could be confused with those of *Bos* and *Bubalus*.

It has been hypothesized that the "short horned" animal on the Indus seals is a Gaur (Mackay 1937-38: 327, 669-71) (Plate 3.14). It is the second most popular motif with 95 cases (Mahadevan 1977: 793). With two exceptions (Mackay 1937-38: Plate LXXXVII, No. 229, Joshi and Parpola 1987: 303, No. K-28) the animal is shown with the head

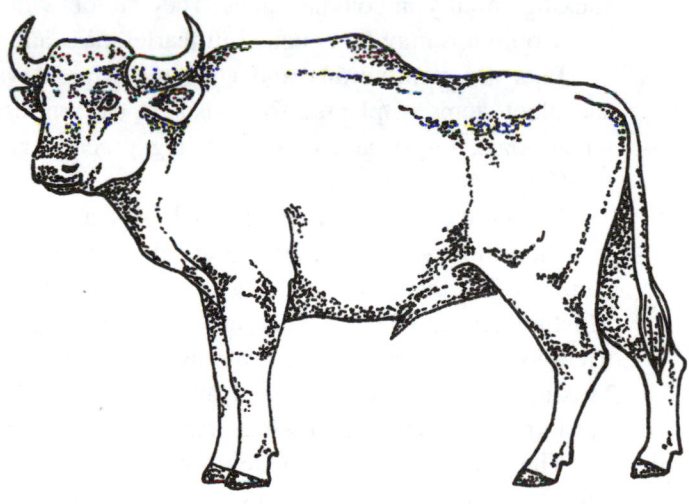

Figure 3.19. The Gaur

lowered over a basket or bowl, in what can legitimately be called a feeding position.

> The suggestion was made in the first book that the so-called 'manger' was probably of basket-work finds some support in No. 370 where the woven pattern is clearly seen. Moreover, roughly made basket-work mangers are seen in any Sindhi village of to-day, though not of the same pattern as those on the seals. It is possible that some of these 'mangers' were made of clay, though no such vessels have actually been unearthed (Mackay 1937-38: 327).

The equation of the short-horned bull with the Gaur is reasonable, although there is no example where the distinctive ridge at the shoulders is shown in a convincing way. However, there are obviously four closely related animals in the iconography of the seals: the zebu, the unhumped bull or "unicorn," the water buffalo and the short-horned beast. Because the "unicorn" is clearly not the Gaur, and the others correlate with known animals, a process of elimination leads to this conclusion. If the provisional identification of the short-horned bull with the Gaur is accepted it would be the second "real" animal on the seals for which there are no osteological remains in the archaeological record (see Grigson 1984 on the "unicorn" and Possehl 1990c for a reply).

There is one terracotta figurine from Mohenjo-daro that Mackay also identifies as the Gaur, but this seems unlikely. It is more likely a water buffalo (Mackay 1937-38: Plate LXXVII, No. 5). The photograph was taken at an odd angle, however. It is the ridge on the back that needs to be seen, not necessarily the markings on the horns, which in this case are definitely like those on the water buffalo (for a credible photograph of the Gaur see Prater 1971: Plate 58).

Pigs

Wild pigs (*Sus scrofa*) (Figure 3.20) are found in virtually all the major regions of Asia. They are best adapted to disturbed, soft, wet soils where they can root for food and wallow during the day to cool off. In prehistoric times they would have been seen in all of the Indus Valley, as well as Gujarat, the Punjab, Haryana, northern Rajasthan and Uttar Pradesh. Recent irrigation schemes have increased the wetlands of Pakistan and northwestern India and the pig population has flourished in these areas. Lake Manchar and its vicinity was known as particularly good pig sticking country in colonial times. They are oblivious to human threat and will attack if provoked. Their oblivion may be couched in fearlessness and they are dangerous and aggressive if hunted.

Pigs are omnivorous and consume a great variety of seeds, roots, tubers, fruit and the succulent stems of plants. They also eat carrion, eggs, small reptiles, rodents, insects, fungi and mushrooms. Grass and other standing green vegetation on the surface is considered "famine food" for these rooters.

Larger carnivorous animals find pigs a favorite prey and the absence of these predators from the Subcontinent in later years can account, in part, for the increase in the pig population. Humans find them edible although their meat has to be thoroughly cooked to avoid trichinosis. Muslims and Jews have proscriptions against eating pork, apparently because of the presence of trichinosis and the animal's omnivorous eating habits, even consuming scatological matter. Muslims find pigs unclean and the thought of eating pork is repugnant to them. Pakistan has been known to engage in widespread eradication campaigns to control the pig population there.

The male of the species develops enlarged canine teeth. The uppers are comparatively short and thick, but the lowers grow large and curve into formidable, dangerous tusks. Pig ivory is useful and it should not be neglected as a probable source of raw material for the craftsmen of the Harappan Civilization. Pig bristles are also made into brushes to paint pottery and for use in decorative purposes.

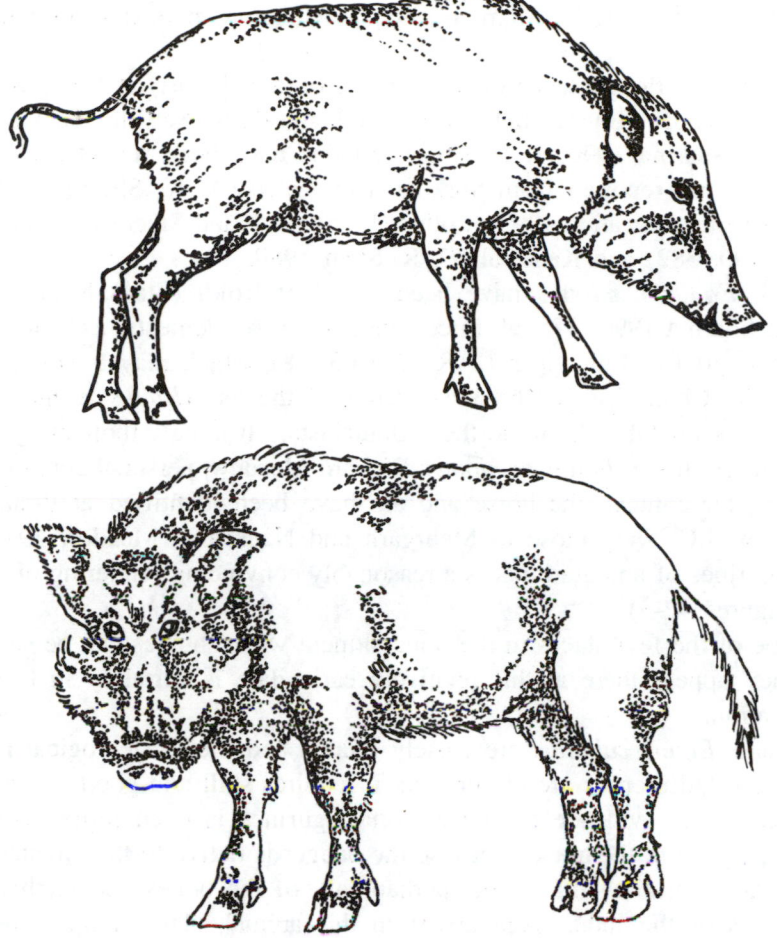

Figure 3.20. The wild pig, two views

Pigs are intelligent, tough, resourceful and fecund. The subspecies in the Subcontinent bears litters of four to six, with good survival rates. This is due in part to their social habits and mutual protection, with two or three sows, their young and a male comprising a herd, or sounder. This productivity, and reproductivity, is one of the reasons that man has been attracted to the pig and the use of its flesh, ivory, bristles and leather. There may be domesticated pigs (*Sus domesticus*) at sites of the Indus Age, but they are far from common. This changes in the Iron Age, but for earlier times the pig remains and representations seem for the most part to be the wild form (Meadow 1989b: 172; 1996).

During the Mature Harappan there are figurines of pigs, although they are far from common. One from Mohenjo-daro is illustrated by Marshall (1931a: Plate XCVI, No. 22). A somewhat unsatisfactory pig figurine is presented as Plate 3.15 from the archives of the Archaeological Survey of India

The Horse and Ass

It is not yet certain that the peoples of the Indus Age, even the Mature Harappans, had access to the domesticated horse (*Equus cabalus*). This has engendered some debate among faunal analysts (see especially Rissman 1986: 19 and Bokonyi 1996) who are challenged by Meadow and Patel 1997 and Anthony 1996) (Plate 3.16). The presence of the ass or Onager (*Equus hemionus*) is more certain (A. K. Sharma 1993; S. Bokonyi, personal communication 1992) (Figure 3.21).

There are claims for the presence of the horse (*Equus caballus*) at Harappa, (Prasad 1936, Bhola Nath 1959), Ropar (Bhola Nath 1968), Mohenjo-daro (Sewell and Guha 1931a) and Kalibangan (A. K. Sharma 1990: 382). Horse remains have been reported from Bronze Age sites in Gujarat and are reported from Surkotada in Kutch (A. K. Sharma 1990; S. Bokonyi 1996 and personal communication 1992), Lothal (Bhola Nath and Sreenivasa Rao 1985), Malvan (A. K. Sharma 1990: 382) and Kanewal (D. R. Shah 1980: 74).

The bones of *Equus hemionus* have been found at Rojdi (Stack-Kane 1989: 183) and Surkotada (A. K. Sharma 1990: 375, all three subperiods). A "domestic ass" has been identified in a preliminary report for Kalibangan (IAR 1964-65: 38), which may be *Equus hemionus*. B. S. Guha and B. K. Chatterjee (1946: 316) identified the ass (*Equus asinus*) and the horse (*Equus caballus*) at Rana Ghundai in northern Baluchistan. It is now thought by some that only the onager was present there (*Equus hemionus*; Richard Meadow, personal communication 1989).

In a slightly later context, the horse and ass have been identified at Pirak, a site of the second millennium B.C., very close to Mehrgarh and Nausharo (Meadow 1979b). There are also terracotta figurines of an equid that is a reasonably convincing rendering of *Equus caballus* (Enault 1979: Figures 92-3).

Gujarat is one of the few places in the Subcontinent where horses can be successfully bred. The fact that they appear there at this relatively early date is certainly in keeping with this historical observation.

The onager and *Equus caballus* are closely related and their osteological remains are not easily distinguished. Differences are present, but it requires skill and good comparative material to determine them. The evidence from terracotta figurines is even more difficult to use in distinguishing the ass from the horse. Because the onager is native to the Greater Indus Region, there is a reasonable certainty that some, perhaps all, of the bones and teeth found so far at archaeological sites of the Indus Age are from this animal. The onager was part of their environment and it is not surprising that the Harappans made terracotta figurines of them.

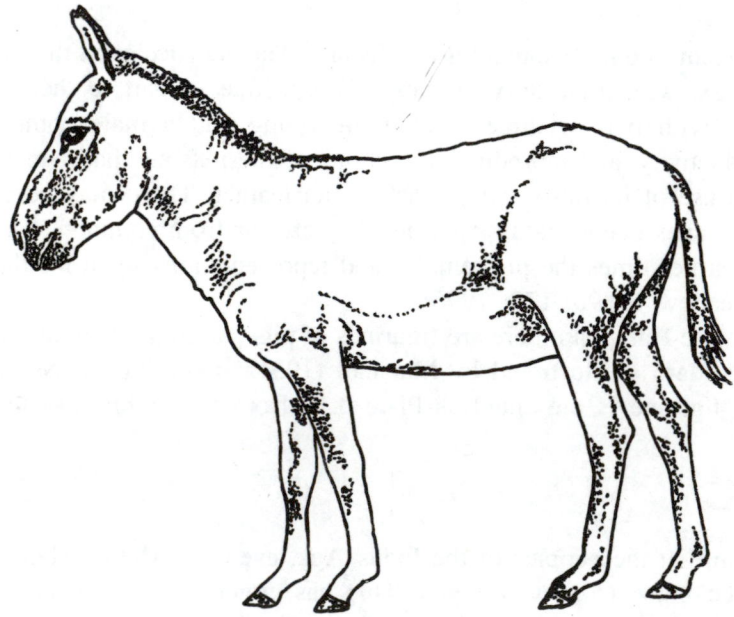

Figure 3.21. The Onager

The case is not the same for the horse (*Equus caballus*). This animal is reliably believed to be the domesticated form of a smaller animal known as the tarpan or Przewalski's horse, *Equus przewalskii* (Figure 3.22) which is at home to the north of the Indus region in Chinese Turkistan, Mongolia, Central Asia, the Trans-Caspian and Ukraine in the west. It is not native to the Greater Indus Region. The time and place for the domestication of the true horse (*Equus caballus*) is not known. The subject has been clouded and confused by the politicized history of the Aryans and their migrations.

The earliest direct testimony for human control of horses comes from the Chalcolithic site of Dereivka on the Dnieper River of the Ukraine. The evidence from Dereivka comes in the form of bit wear on the premolars of a stallion. The associated occupational level has been dated by a series of seven radiocarbon determinations to 4200-3800 cal. BC (Anthony and Brown 1989, 1991; Anthony 1991; Telegrin 1995). The mandible from the stallion was later tested which resulted in an anomalous radiocarbon determination of ca. 3000 cal. B.C. (Telegrin 1995). The mandible and skull of the stallion had been stabilized and preserved with a thick coat of lacquer and glue when it was first put in a museum some 25 years ago. It may be that the presence of these organic materials contaminated part of the specimen that was used for this anomalous date.

David Anthony and Dorcus Brown have carried out experiments comparing the type and degree of wear on the archaeological specimen with their modern control samples. These tests suggest that the stallion had been fitted with a hard bit for a minimum of 300 hours (Brown and Anthony 1995). The use of the bit suggests either riding or driving. If the Dereivka bitted horse is as early as ca. 4000 B.C. it would come centuries before the earliest evidence for wheeled vehicles. Thus, Anthony and Brown think that this horse was ridden.

Bit wear has also been found on five horse premolars from the site of Botai in Kazakhstan (Brown and Anthony 1995). This settlement of pit houses yielded a faunal collection of some 300,000 specimens that was 99% horse bones. Botai has been dated to 3300-2900 cal B.C. by five radiocarbon determinations. "Botai Culture" sites have no evidence for domesticated animals other than horses and dogs; although there is some evidence for camels, their domesticated status has not been determined.

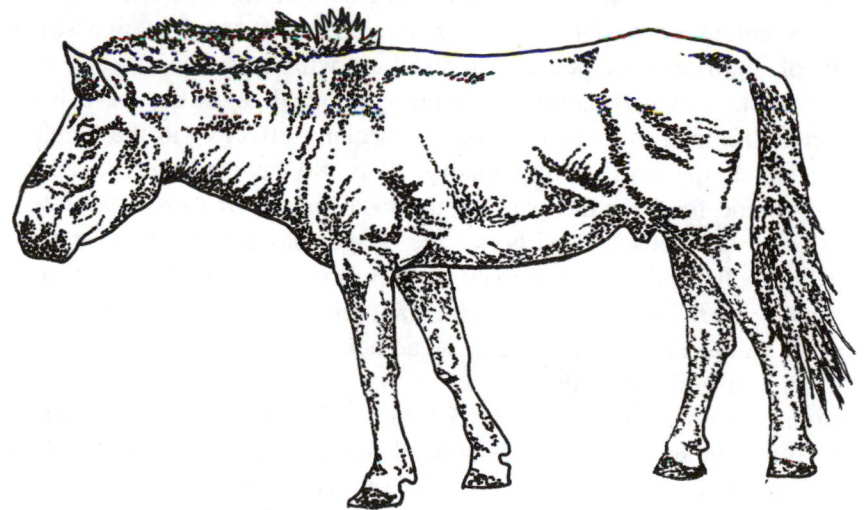

Figure 3.22. Przewalski's horse

The earliest stage of wheeled vehicles in this region comes from the Sintadshta and Petrokova Cultures on the upper Tobol-Ishim drainages of the northern steppe zone of Russia and Kazakhstan. Sites of this type have evidence for chariots with spoked wheels pulled by horses. They date to ca. 2100-1800 cal B.C. and represent the early development of the so-called "Andronovo Horizon" that was in contact with Bactria and Margiana (Anthony and Vinogradov 1995; Parpola 1995; Kuzmina 1994).

If *Equus caballus* was brought to the settlements of the Mature Harappan, it can be demonstrated by tracing a history of their movement out of the Ukraine and Kazakhstan south into the Subcontinent. Finding the remains of *Equus caballus* in northern and southern Afghanistan, or Seistan, for example, would strengthen the case for horses at Mohenjo-daro and Surkotada. One thing that seems clear is that the Harappans could not have domesticated this animal because its wild progenitor was not part of their environment. Failing the demonstration of the southern migration of *Equus caballus*, by whatever means, for whatever purpose, the local equid of the Indus Age was *Equus hemionus*, and that is probably the beast represented by the bones found in the archaeological sites of this age.

One might wonder why horses, *Equus caballus*, have been a topic of discussion in Harappan studies and why it seems to be important for this animal, not just the onager, to be present at Mature Harappan sites. Some hint of this may be found in the following passage from S. R. Rao:

> It is argued sometimes that the Harappans were non-Aryans as they had no knowledge of the horse and did not use rice, both of which played a dominant part in the daily life of the Aryans. This argument is not tenable anymore because horse bones have been found in the late levels of Harappa (Bhola Nath 1959: 358) and Mohenjo-daro (Wheeler 1960: 65), and now in the Mature Harappan levels at Lothal (S. R. Rao 1973) and Surkotada. Terracotta figurines of horse occur at Rangpur (S. R. Rao 1963a: 137-38) as well as Lothal. The earliest occurrence of rice in India is at Rangpur and Lothal in the mature Harappan levels. Obviously, horse and rice must have been known to the Harappans as early as 2200 BC (S. R. Rao 1979: 219).

Onagers are fast and skittery, wary of humans. Mountstuart Elphinstone commented on those in Bikaner, which he saw on his way to Kabul in 1809: "It resembles a mule rather than an ass, but it is the colour of the latter. It is remarkable for its shyness, and still more for its speed: at a kind of shuffling trot peculiar to itself, it will leave the fleetest horses behind" (Elphinstone 1819: Vol. I, 10). Because they represent a challenge they have been vigorously pursued by hunters. Riflemen in jeeps have been especially effective in the hunt. T. J. Roberts recounts a story that at the turn of the century 70 or 80 onagers were machine-gunned in Bahawalnagar to provide food for the army of the local prince (Roberts 1977: 161).

Smaller than the usual domesticated horse, the onager has a handsome reddish-brown coat with a creamy white belly and legs. The mane is dark brown. S. H. Prater claims that onagers can be readily tamed when young, but are recalcitrant and vicious when mature (1971: 228). If that is the case they might have found a place as a pack animal in Harappan times. Their flesh is edible and the hide useful for leather.

The onager is native to the Greater Indus Region and its name in Hindi and Urdu is *ghor khar*. It survives in the region today only as a small remnant population in the Ranns of Kutch (Ali 1946), but there may be a few remaining in southern Baluchistan (Roberts 1977: 161). Onagers are still found in the central deserts of the Iranian Plateau. In prehistoric times they

Figure 3.23. Equid figurines from Lothal and Rangpur

Figure 3.24. Possible horse figurine from Mohenjo-daro, after Mackay 1937-38: 289, Pl. LXXXVII, No. 11

would have been well represented in western India and much of Pakistan, in areas below the Hindu Kush. Their range extended north through Afghanistan, into Central Asia and Chinese Turkistan. In the nineteenth century onagers were observed in the Kirthar Piedmont, Sindh Kohistan, Kohat, Bannu and other low valleys of Baluchistan as well as the Punjab, Bahawalpur, Rajasthan and Gujarat.

Horse figurines are said to be present at Lothal (S. R. Rao 1985: 483-84, Pl. CCVI, B & D) and Rangpur (S. R. Rao 1963a: 137, Fig. 50) (Figure 3.23). There is also one possible horse figurine from Mohenjo-daro (Mackay 1937-38: 289, Pl. LXXXVII, No. 11) (Figure 3.24), but even Mackay calls this identification "purely tentative." These identifications are dubious and while they seem to represent some form of equid they are not sufficiently realistic in their rendering of an animal that one could distinguish *Equus hemionus* from *E. caballus*. Horses and asses are useful as draft animals. There is no indication that they were ridden during the Indus Age, nor has attention been paid to bit wear, that would indicate the harness.

Domesticated Dogs

Domesticated dogs have been found at many Mature Harappan sites, including Mohenjo-daro (Sewell and Guha 1931a: 650-52), Alamgirpur (Bhola Nath and Biswas 1969: 43), Lothal (Bhola Nath and Sreenivasa Rao 1985: 640) and Rojdi (Stack-Kane 1989: 183). The specimens from Mohenjo-daro compared favorably with the prehistoric dog found at Anau in Central Asia (Duerst 1908) and the modern Indian *dingo* (*Canis familiaris dingo*).

E. J. H. Mackay (1937–38: 286; 1948: 143) draws attention to several breeds of dogs that are apparent in the figurines, especially from Mohenjo-daro. One has pointed ears and either a curled tail or one hanging down (Figure 3.25). The second has an upright tail and prick

190

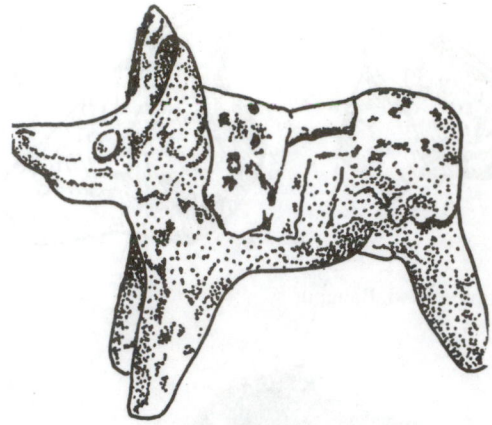

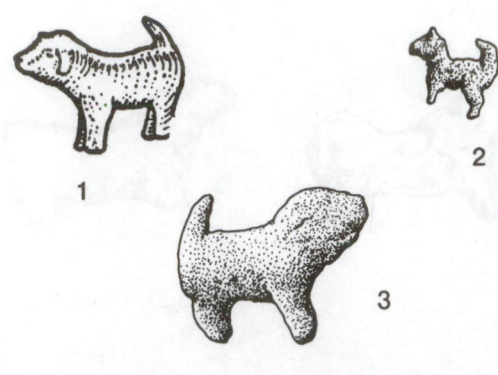

Figure 3.25. Terracotta figurine of a dog from Mohenjo-daro, after Mackay 1937-38: Plate LXXVII, No. 22

Figure 3.26. Copper-bronze figurines of a second breed of dog with an upright tail and prick ears from Mohenjo-daro, Nos. 1 and 2 after Mackay 1937-38: Plate LXXIX, Nos. 5 & 6, drawings from Yule 1985: Tafel 2; No. 3 from Lothal, after S. R. Rao 1985: Figure 117, No. 4

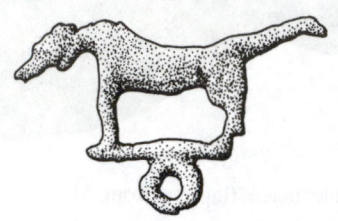

Figure 3.27. Terracotta figurine of a dog from Mohenjo-daro, after Marshall 1931a: Plate XCVI, No. 16

Figure 3.28. A figurine of a dog that resembles the modern Afghan Hound, after Mackay 1937-38: Plate LXXIX, No. 19, drawing from Yule 1985: Tafel 2

ears (Figure 3.26). A third looks much like a bulldog and has been very difficult to illustrate, but the original photograph can be seen in (Marshall 1931a: Plate XCVI, No. 17) (Figure 3.27). Finally, there is an animal that looks something like the modern Afghan Hound (Figure 3.28).

The presence of collars on some of the animals (Plate 3.17) as well as a terracotta figurine of a dog tied to a post (Marshall 1931a: Pl. XCVI, No. 18) all reinforce the zoological findings. Mackay (1937-38: 286) suggests that some of the collars are large enough to be used as protection against attacks by panthers, practiced in the India of his day.

There is nothing particularly remarkable about the Harappan dogs and they compare well with those from Elamite contexts, in Mesopotamia and as far afield as that shown on the famous Gebel el-Arak handle.

There are also domesticated dogs in the Northern Neolithic of Kashmir and northern Pakistan. Some appear to have been purposely buried. K. Gollan (1985) has suggested that Kashmir might provide a kind of laboratory for tracing the domestication of these creatures.

There is another canid that appears in the record of the Indus Age which is generally called the *dhole* or *cuon* (*Cuon alpinus*), also known as the Red Dog of India (Hawkins 1986: 177-78) (Figure 3.29). It has been found throughout peninsular South Asia from the Nilgiri Hills to Kashmir and extends to eastern Central Asia, Siberia, parts of China and all of Korea. Bones of a *cuon* have been found at Rojdi (Stack-Kane 1989: 183). An interesting note on this animal

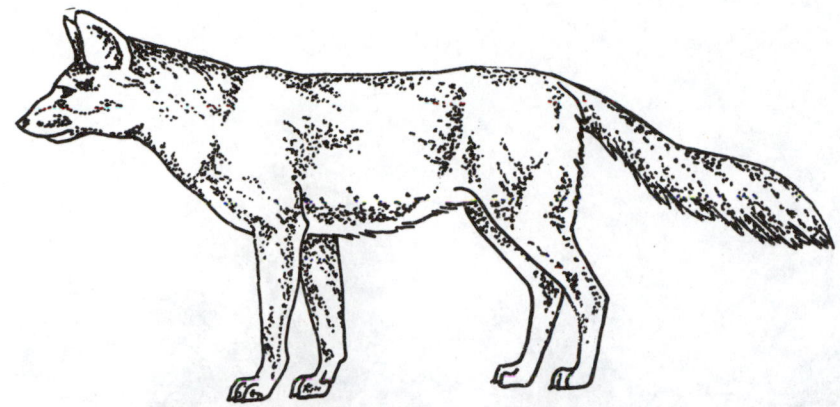

Figure 3.29. The *cuon*

may be in a Mesopotamian text, which relates the receipt of a multicolored, or reddish, dog of Meluhha as tribute to Ibbi-Sin. A statue was made of it and taken to the temple as a votive gift to Nanna. The name of the dog translates "He bites!" (Ur Excavation Texts VIII; Sollberger 1965, Vol. 2: 37, lines 9-13; Possehl 1996c: 143)

House Cats

There are not many signs to show that the Harappans had domestic house cats. The only evidence comes from Rojdi (Stack-Kane 1989: 183), where the identification of the bones of *Felis catus* is qualified. The following quote on a tablet from Nippur indicates that the Mesopotamians felt that the cats of Meluhha were special in some ways:

> The donkey of Anshan, The...of Parahse, the cat of Meluhha, the elephant of the steppe, (are the creatures) which bite off a willow(?) as though it were a leek (Lambert 1960: 272-73).

This could refer to a wild species, tamed to live close to humans; we just do not know. It would be curious if the cat was missing from the inventory of domesticated animals because the wild progenitor of the domesticated animal *Felix lybica* (see Figure 3.41) is in the region. It is a good rodent hunter which would have been helpful in the community, and the cuddly quality of the kittens makes pet keeping a mechanism through which domestication could have taken place.

This short discussion of dogs and cats of the Indus Age would be incomplete without mention of the foot imprints that Mackay found on a brick from Chanhu-daro. In his discussion of these remains Mackay quotes from a letter by Dr. Glover M. Allen, who examined the object:

> The two tracks on the brick must have been impressed when it was freshly laid out to dry in the sun. The one...is that of a cat, while the other...is that of a dog. Claw marks seem to be indicated on that of the dog but not in the case of the cat's. The deep impress of the pads and their spread indicate the speed of both animals. Here then is a record of a prehistoric dog chasing a large prehistoric cat, the dog's imprint slightly overlapping the cat's shows that he came second (Mackay 1943: 222).

Dr. Allen thought the cat might have been *Felis viverrina* the Fishing Cat, based on the size of the foot imprint (see Figure 3.43 for an illustration of the Fishing Cat).

192

Figure 3.30. A young Indian elephant in a Rembrandt sketch probably made in 1637. Courtesy of the British Museum, REM 06

Elephants

The Indian elephant *Elephas maximus* (Figure 3.30, Figure 3.31) is very much a part of the Greater Indus region, with good evidence for ivory working on an extensive scale during the Indus Age (Plate 3.18). There are also figurines of elephants in terracotta (e.g. Mackay 1937-38: Pl. LXXIX, No. 13) and metal (the Daimabad Bronzes, Figure 3.32) and the actual bones in various sites. In addition there are 55 stamp seals with an elephant motif (Mahadevan 1977: 793). A truly magnificent hollow terracotta elephant was found at Nausharo III, Mature Harappan (Figure 3.33). This is a part of a three-headed composite beast (C. Jarrige 1992: 134-35).

Elephant remains have been found at Mohenjo-daro (Sewell and Guha 1931a: 653), Harappa (Bhola Nath 1959), Lothal (Bhola Nath and Sreenivasa Rao 1985: 641), Surkotada (Period IC; A. K. Sharma 1990: 380), Chanhu-daro (Mackay 1943: 14) and Kalibangan (IAR 1964-65: 38). One massive rib from Rojdi has been identified as possibly that of an elephant (Stack-Kane 1989: 183). The earliest reported elephant remains in the Greater Indus Region come from aceramic of Period I at Mehrgarh (Meadow 1984b: 35). Therefore, there is little doubt that the elephant was one of the wild animals of the Indus Valley in prehistoric times. It has been included here, along with other domesticates, because it is easily tamed. Some of the seals suggest that a number of the elephants depicted had been decorated with paint and some draped in cloth or other material by their owners, indicating a very close relationship with the Indus peoples.

Figure 3.31. A mature Indian elephant

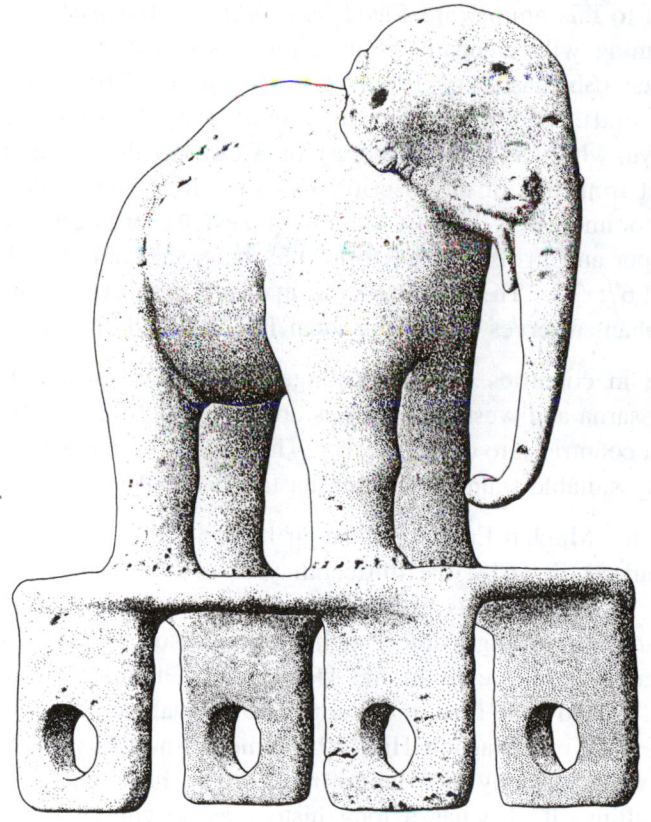

Figure 3.32. The elephant from the Daimabad Bronzes, after Yule 1985: Plate 2

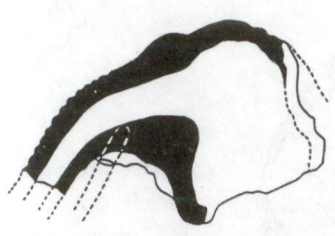

Figure 3.33. Terracotta figurine of an elephant from Nausharo Period III, after C. Jarrige 1992: 132-33

There is no conclusive evidence for domestication; even the modern Indian elephant is wild in a technical sense. Domesticated animals are those that have a genetic constitution different from their wild counterparts. This is not the case for the Indian elephant, who is loosed to mate in the wild and then recaptured. Their genetic makeup is therefore no different from their wild kindred and they are simply a good example of an animal tamed for human use.

Historical reference to elephants occurs in the Ṛgveda Book 10, Hymn 40, Verse 4 (Griffith 1896) which concerns hunting two wild elephants. The Atarvaveda (Book 3, Hymn 22; Griffith 1895-96) praises the pachyderm's strength (S. D. Singh 1963). Alexander the Great met war elephants in his Indian battles in 326 BC. In fact Porus, the King he defeated in his last great battle, attempted to escape on one (Arrian, Book V; Robson 1966: 43-54). Interesting and important references to this animal are found in *Kautilya's Arthashastra*. For example, the art of capturing and taming wild elephants is mentioned; also using them in war, which implies that they were ridden (Shamashastry 1960: 48-9, 399-400). The *Arthashastra* is an ancient Indian text on statecraft, said to have been compiled by Kautliya, the prime minister of Chandragupta Maurya, who was a contemporary of Alexander the Great. The vocabulary of this text varies somewhat from that of the inscriptions of the Mauryan Asoka, and it contains other terms that became common only in post-Mauryan times. According to A. L. Basham this text is definitely pre-Gupta and in its present form may be a substantial elaboration on Kautilya's original (Basham 1967: 79). The *Arthashastra* includes a short section on the creation and maintenance of elephant reserves within the ideal Indian kingdom, which ends with:

> Elephants bred in countries such as Kalinga, Anga, Karusa and the East are best; those of the Dasarna and western countries are of middle quality; those of Saurashtra and Panchajana countries are of low quality. The might and energy of all can, however, be improved by suitable training (Shamashastry 1960: 49).

Somewhat later, the Mughal Emperor Jahangir hunted wild elephants in the Dohad areas of Panch Mahals in Gujarat in 1618, the thirteenth year of his reign (A. Rogers tr. and ed. H. Beveridge 1909-14: Vol. II, 47). His grandson, Aurengzeb was born in the royal camp during this sojourn to Gujarat. According to the Panch Mahals District Gazetteer of 1879, "...in 1645, seventy-three elephants were caught in the Dohad and Champanir forests" (Government of Bombay 1879: 210). Dohad is an area in eastern Panch Mahals, on the border with Maharashtra. Champanir is at the base of Pavagadh Hill, 40 kilometers northeast of Vadodara.

If the elephant was tamed by the Harappans it would have made an excellent animal for heavy lifting and pulling. It also has a long history as an animal of war, but it needs good training and very strong, forceful handling in combat, because it has been known to panic in battle. Ivory, most of it thought to be elephant ivory, was extensively used by the Harappans and their predecessors for a host of objects, some of which are shown in Plate 3.19.

Camels

The one humped Dromedary Camel (*Camelus dromedarius*) (Plate 3.20) is used in the Subcontinent today. The camel is an extraordinarily durable and useful riding and pack animal as well as a source for traction. Its milk and flesh are both consumed. Camels are highly tolerant of arid environments, can go for long periods without drinking and will eat rough plant life eschewed by many other animals. Their large feet are adapted for movement through soft sandy terrain. They are important in Pakistan, especially Sindh, Baluchistan, the Northwest and Punjab. In India the camel is found throughout Kutch, North Gujarat (but only occasionally in Saurashtra), Rajasthan, the Punjab and Haryana: there could hardly be a better fit with the geography of the Mature Harappan. There are no wild Dromedary Camels anywhere.

In Hindi/Urdu the Dromedary Camel is *unt* or *oont* in older transliterations. In British colonial times it was widely used by the army and something of the animal is captured in these few lines from Rudyard Kipling's "Oonts."

> Wot makes the soldier's 'eart to penk, what makes 'im to perspire?
> It isn't stand'n up to charge nor lyin' down to fire;
> But its everlastin' waitin' on a everlastin' road
> For the commissariat camel an' 'is commissariat load
> O the oont, O the oont, O the commissariat oont
> With 'is silly neck a-bobbin' like a basket full o' snakes
> We packs 'im like an idol, an' you ought to 'ear 'imgrunt
> An' when we get 'im loaded up 'is blessed girth-rope breaks

The camels of Sindh have a good reputation. James Burnes, the physician brother of Sir Alexander Burnes, visited the court of Sindh at Hyderabad in 1827. As he passed through Thar Parkar in southeastern Sindh he noted: "In these inhospitable tracks, and all along the Delta of the Indus, the camels of Sinde, so famed throughout the whole of Asia, are reared..." (1829: 35).

The two-humped Bactrian Camel (*Camelus bactranus*) is not used in the Subcontinent today, although it is found in Central Asia and extends all through Turkistan and east to Mongolia. It is not known with certainty whether there are wild Bactrian camels today, or only feral specimens, or breeds in between.

Reviews of the camel in an archaeological context are available from Ripinsky (1975, 1982, 1983), Meadow (1984c), Sathe and Atre (1989) and Bulliet (1975). Camel bones have been recovered from Mohenjo-daro (Sewell and Guha 1931a: 660; Meadow 1984c); Harappa (Prashad 1936: 58-9; Bhola Nath 1962); Surkotada (A. K. Sharma 1990: 380); Kanewal (Shah 1980: 75), Kalibangan (IAR 1964-65: 38); and possibly Rojdi (Stack-Kane 1989: 183), but they do not occur at Mehrgarh (Meadow 1984c: 136). The remains that have been examined within the context of the Indus Civilization and its predecessors have generally been identified, or thought to be *Camelus dromedarius*, which Richard Meadow has called into doubt (1984c: 136). Meadow does not question the presence of the camel, but believes that there is a chance that those in the Indus Valley during the Indus Age were Bactrian beasts. He has a review (1984c: 136) of the occurrence of the two species of camels within the Greater Indus Region and adjacent areas. Camel bones and figurines with two humps document the presence of *Camelus bactranus* in Turkmenia during Namazga IV times (early third millennium) (Masson and Sarianidi 1972: 109). Bactrian camels also occurred at Anau (Duerst 1908) and there is good evidence for this animal at Shahr-i Sokhta (Compagnoni and Tosi 1975).

Sathe and Atre (1989: 305) feel that "...Harappans did not use the camel, although they

196

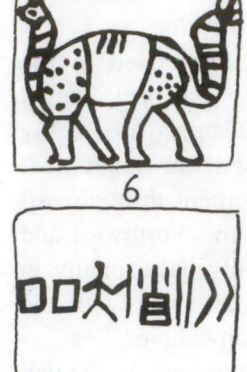

Figure 3.34. Possible camel on a copper tablet from Mohenjo-daro, after Mackay 1937-38: Plate XCIII, No. 8

might have known it by their contacts with the west..." This is possibly too severe a judgment given the range of sites with camel bones, but it is still not entirely clear how important the camel was in the Indus Age.

I know of no figurines or other positive representations of camels in Indus art. One of the copper tablets from Mohenjo-daro has a composite animal, with the long, drooping neck of a camel, but a hump is not clearly shown and there are heads and necks on both ends (Mackay 1937-38: Pl. CII, No. 6) (Figure 3.34).

It is of considerable interest for Indus archaeology that the camel figurines from Pirak, near Nausharo and Mehrgarh on the Kachi Plain, are all *Camelus bactranus*. Period I at Pirak dates to ca. 1700 B.C., just within the Post-urban Harappan of the Harappan Cultural Tradition, but there is little if any continuity between the Mature Harappan and this site. These would have come from Central Asia, or might have been endemic to the Greater Indus Region. Jim Shaffer has suggested that the site of Shortughai was established, in part, to allow the Harappans access to a reliable supply of the Bactrian camel (Shaffer 1987).

Richard Bulliet, in an interesting and important book on the camel, has made the point that there is no evidence that the Dromedary camel was present in South Asia prior to the first millennium B.C., the evidence pointing to the exclusive use of *Camelus bactranus* (Bulliet 1975: 188).

The uncertainty of the early identification of faunal remains, the Pirak figurines and Bulliet's synthesis all seem to point in one direction. The camels of the Mature Harappan were probably Bactrian. Somewhat farther afield, but still of interest, is the fact that the camel on the pick-axe from Stein's excavations at Khurab, grave E (Stein 1937: Pl. XVIII, E, i, 258; K. R. Maxwell-Hyslop 1955; Zeuner 1955) has now been identified as a Bactrian variety (Lamberg-Karlovsky 1969: 167-8). The object should date to ca. 2000 B.C. An even earlier Bactrian camel may be evident from Tepe Sialk III$_4$ (Ghirshman 1938: Pl. LXXXIX, A2).

It is possible to make qualitative distinctions between *Camelus dromedarius* and *Camelus bactranus*, so the case should be placed back in the faunal laboratory for final resolution.

Wild Mammals

Many wild animals have been found in Harappan contexts. They come in the form of bones from animals that were hunted, as well as representations on seals and other objects. No wild animal represents the Subcontinent better than the tiger.

Tiger

The tiger *Panthera tigris* (Figure 3.35) is now extinct in the Greater Indus region. In earlier times it was distributed over vast areas of the Subcontinent, occupying all areas except the deserts. Its range to the west is interesting, and it is not widely known that it is found across southern Turkistan, the upper Murgab, the lower Amu-Darya and lower Syr-Darya and ranges west to southeastern Tanscaucasia (see Ellerman and Morrison-Scott 1966: 318 for documentation).

The tiger is an animal of the forest and jungle; the lion inhabits the desert and savannah grasslands. In prehistoric times the tiger would have pushed down into the riverine jungles of Sindh and the Punjab (Plate 3.21). It was not common in Sindh in the 19th century, but: "It is found in Khayrpoor (Khairpur) State, but there are not many records of it causing destruction.

Figure 3.35. The Indian tiger

In Lower Sind nothing is heard of it. From Sukkur upwards it is occasionally said to issue from its cover, which is the dense fringe of Tamarisk bushes and long grasses along the banks of the river, visit the cultivated parts and carry away stray cattle" (Murray 1884: 26).

Tigers are still abundant in eastern India and on some game preserves. George Schaller's classic *The Deer and the Tiger* (Schaller 1967) is an insightful study of behavior and ecology.

Figure 3.36. Seal with the horned tiger, after Mackay 1937-38: Plate LXXXIX, No. 360

This animal is a skilled hunter, and occasionally preys on humans, much more so than the lion. According to W. T. Blanford, quoting in part "Forsyth," man-eating tigers are animals that have become fat and heavy, or very old, or disabled by a wound. A tigress, left with cubs in an area of poor game will also turn to prey on humans, said to be "the easiest animal of all to kill" (Blanford 1888-91: 65). There are many myths about man-eaters, including the inevitable notion that one taste of human flesh renders the beast permanently habituated to this meat, and that a tigress who has turned to human prey will bring up her cubs to do the same (Blanford 1888-91: 65). The tiger is thought to usually attack humans from behind, and Indians in the eastern states are known to wear masks on the back of their head, facing backwards watching for an onrush, as a way to ward off attack. This was no joking matter in the nineteenth century, and many people were killed by tigers each year: "Thus, in Lower Bengal alone in six years 1860-66, 4218 persons were killed by these animals" (Blanford 1888-91: 65).

I. Mahadevan records 21 tiger seals within the Indus corpus. Five of these are horned beasts (Mahadevan 1977: 793) (Figure 3.36). There is an important motif that runs through the representation of the tiger in Harappan art. It is the beast, head turned back over a shoulder, looking at a human with an outstretched arm, in a tree (see Plate 3.21a). Seals showing combat between humans and tigers are also present (Figure 3.37). Pinwheels of animals are also found in Harappan seals and one is of three intertwined tigers (Plate 3.22).

Lion

There is, at present, one surviving population of the Asiatic lion *Panthera leo* in the Gir Forest of Saurashtra (Figure 3.38). The former Nawabs of Junagadh, who formed a preserve for hunting, are responsible for later turning it into a national facility dedicated to the preservation of this remnant population of about 200 specimens (Plate 3.23).

Figure 3.37. Human-tiger combat seal, after Mackay 1937-38: Plate CXI, No. 357

The Asiatic lion was once found in Mesopotamia, all of Iran, most of Pakistan and northern India, stretching as far east as Bengal and as far south as the Narmada River. According to W. T. Blanford (1888-91: 57), in the mid-nineteenth century they were common around Ahmedabad in Gujarat and Mount Abu on the Gujarat, Rajasthan border. Kills were recorded in the Allahabad area of the central Ganges in 1864 and 1866. They occurred in Haryana, Kandesh and some parts of Rajasthan (e. g., Kota) in the early nineteenth century. A lion, thought to be the last in Sindh, was shot near Kot Diji in 1810 (Kinnier 1920). The late Amir of Bahawalpur revealed that lions were hunted in the thorn jungle of the Hakra River around Fort Derawar at the turn of the century (Roberts 1977: 156).

There are no clear representations of lions in Harappan art, and I know of no bones or teeth of this animal that have been found in archaeological contexts. There are representations of felids that could be lions, or a wide range of other cats. Tigers are there because the Harappans

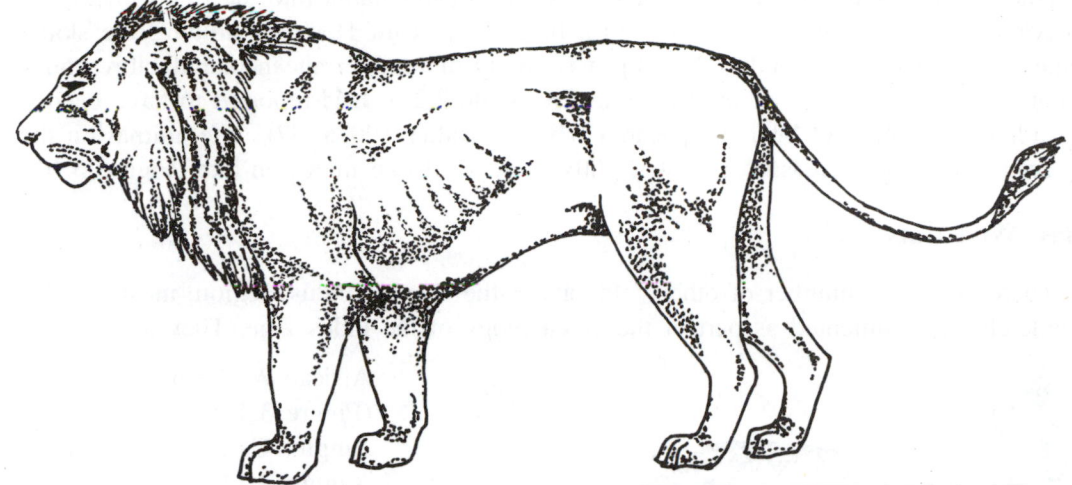

Figure 3.38. The Asiatic lion

Figure 3.39. Felids on a sealing from Harappa, Vats. 1940: Pl. XCIII, No. 304

often took pains to show the stripes. But, there is nothing with the distinctive features of a lion; the ruff, for example, or the slightly bushy end to the tail. Marshall (1931g: 70) draws attention to a a possible pair of lions on a sealing from Harappa (Figure 3.39) with two animals on their hind legs "greeting" one another. These are cats of some kind, but there is nothing "Leo" about them and it is doubtful that they are lions. Mackay (1931d: 391) gives the definitive statement: "...the lion is not represented on any of the seals." A composite figurine from Nausharo III (C. Jarrige 1992: 134-35) may have one element representing a lion, but it could also be a tiger. There is no way of knowing for sure.

In Mesopotamia the lion was represented in many contexts, including seals where it is often shown attacking herds of antelopes, on the front piece of a lyre from the Royal Graves of Ur and as sculpture in the round. Lion hunts are one of the more dramatic representations on

Figure 3.40. Gold cup from the Quetta Treasury, after Jarrige and Hassan 1989: Figures 6 and 7

Assyrian Reliefs, and document their abundance in Mesopotamia into the first millennium B.C. Excavations in the Quetta Miri produced a bronze statue of Hercules holding the skin of the Nemean lion in his left hand. This object is surely of Mediterranean manufacture and should be dated to about the turn of the Christian Era (Plate 3.24). It is reported to have been sent to the Indian Museum, but later disappeared (Hughes-Buller 1907a: 47). The animal on the gold cup from the Quetta Treasury is just slightly more wolf-like than lion-like (Figure 3.40).

Other Wild Cats

There is a large number of other wild cats in the Greater Indus Region, most of which are completely undocumented as part of the archaeology of the Indus Age. They are:

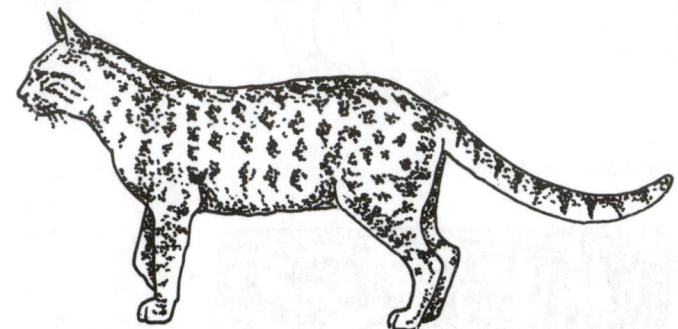

Figure 3.41. *Felis lybica*

African Wild Cat, *Felis libyca* (Figure 3.41)
Jungle Cat, *Felis chaus* (Figure 3.42)
Sand Cat, *Felis margarita*
Pallas' Cat, *Felis manul*
Lynx, *Felis lynx*
Caracal, *Felis caracal*
Leopard Cat, *Felis bengalensis*
Fishing Cat, *Felis viverrina* (Figure 3.43)
Leopard or Panther, *Panthera pardus* (Figure 3.44)
Cheetah, *Acinonyx jubatus*

A spotted animal that could be a leopard is found on the painted pottery of Siah Damb II (Figure 3.45). Spotted cats are also motifs on the pottery of Tepe Hissar (Schmidt 1937: Plate XXI, No. H 4797), and various sites of the Central Indian Chalcolithic and Central Asia, as at Kara Tepe, Namazga II (S. P. Gupta 1979: Vol. II, 93). This has been reviewed in part by by H. D. Sankalia (1969, 1974: 491).

Most are small cats, not to be thought of as human predators. They are also nocturnal, for the most part, but would have been very much a part of the environment. The lack of their presence in the archaeological record should be noted as a significant omission. The most glaring omission is that although there are representations of tigers, especially on Indus seals, there

Figure 3.42. *Felis chaus*

Figure 3.43. *Felis viverrina*

Figure 3.44. *Panthera pardus*

Figure 3.45. Spotted cat? on painted pottery from Siah Damb II, after de Cardi 1965: Figure 16, No. 15

is no record of the lion. The only record, the Fishing Cat, is from an imprint on a brick at Chanhu-daro (Mackay 1943: 222).

Rhinoceros

The most prominent occurrence of the rhinoceros *Rhinoceros unicornis* (Figure 3.46) within the context of the Harappan Civilization is as a device on the standard stamp seals. According to I. Mahadevan (1977: 793) there are 40 inscribed objects with a rhinoceros, including the square stamp seals, copper tablets (Mackay 1937-38: Pl. XCIII, No. 7) and sealings (Mackay 1937-38: Pl. XC, No. 13b, Pl. CI, No. 1b, Pl. CIII, No. 13) (Plate 3.25). There are also some good examples of terracotta rhinos (Figure 3.47) as well as one from the Daimabad Bronzes (Figure 3.48).

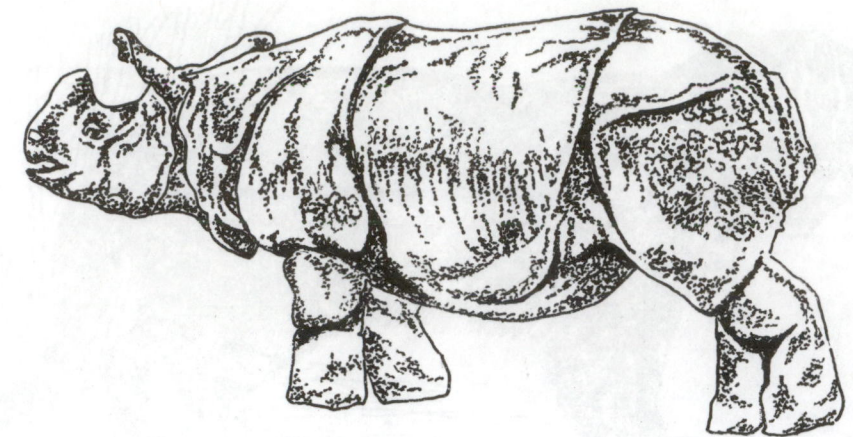

Figure 3.46. The Indian rhinoceros

Figure 3.47. Terracotta model of a rhinoceros from Mohenjo-daro, after Marshall 1931a: Pl. XCVII, No. 8, see Bautze 1985: 407 for documentation

Today the rhinoceros is found along the eastern borderlands of the Himalaya (Bihar, Bengal Duars, Cooch Bihar) and in Nepal. It is fond of wetlands, tall grass and reeds (see Dutta 1991: 70-100 for habitat information). The fourteenth century traveler Ibn Battuta, who reached the Indus River on 12 September 1333 (Haig 1887: 393) reported seeing a rhino on the northern border of Sindh and the Punjab: "After crossing the river of Sind called Banj Ab, we

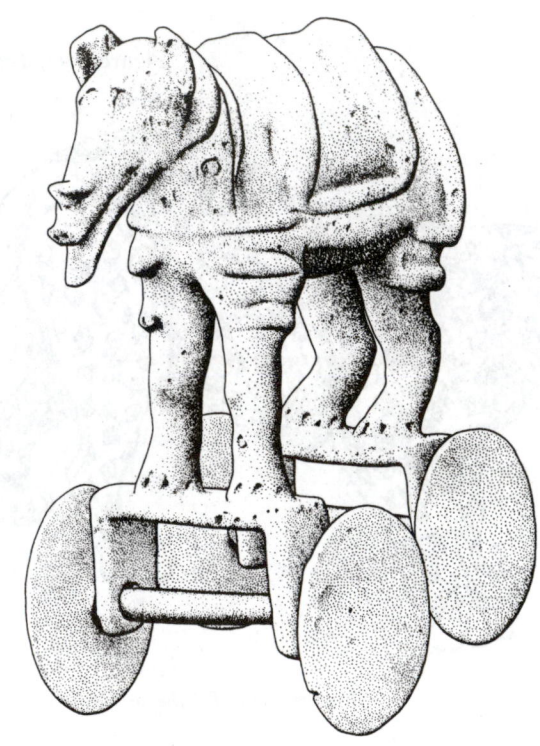

Figure 3.48. Rhinoceros from the Daimabad Bronzes, after Yule 1985: Plate 3

entered a forest of reeds, following the track which led through the midst of it, when we were confronted by a rhinoceros" (Gibb 1957: 596).

The first Great Mughal, Babar, hunted the rhino. In his memoirs, the *Babar Nama* he notes: "In the course of my expeditions into Hindustan, in the jungles of Peshawar and Hashnagar, I frequently killed the rhinoceros" (Leyden and Erskine 1921: 211). On one of these hunts we are told that a rhino tossed the horse of a young man named Maksud a full spear's length. The young man took the new name "Rhinoceros Maksud" away from this encounter (Leyden and Erskine 1921: 211). In 1514 the Raja of Cambay, Mahmud Bagada, sent the King of Portugal

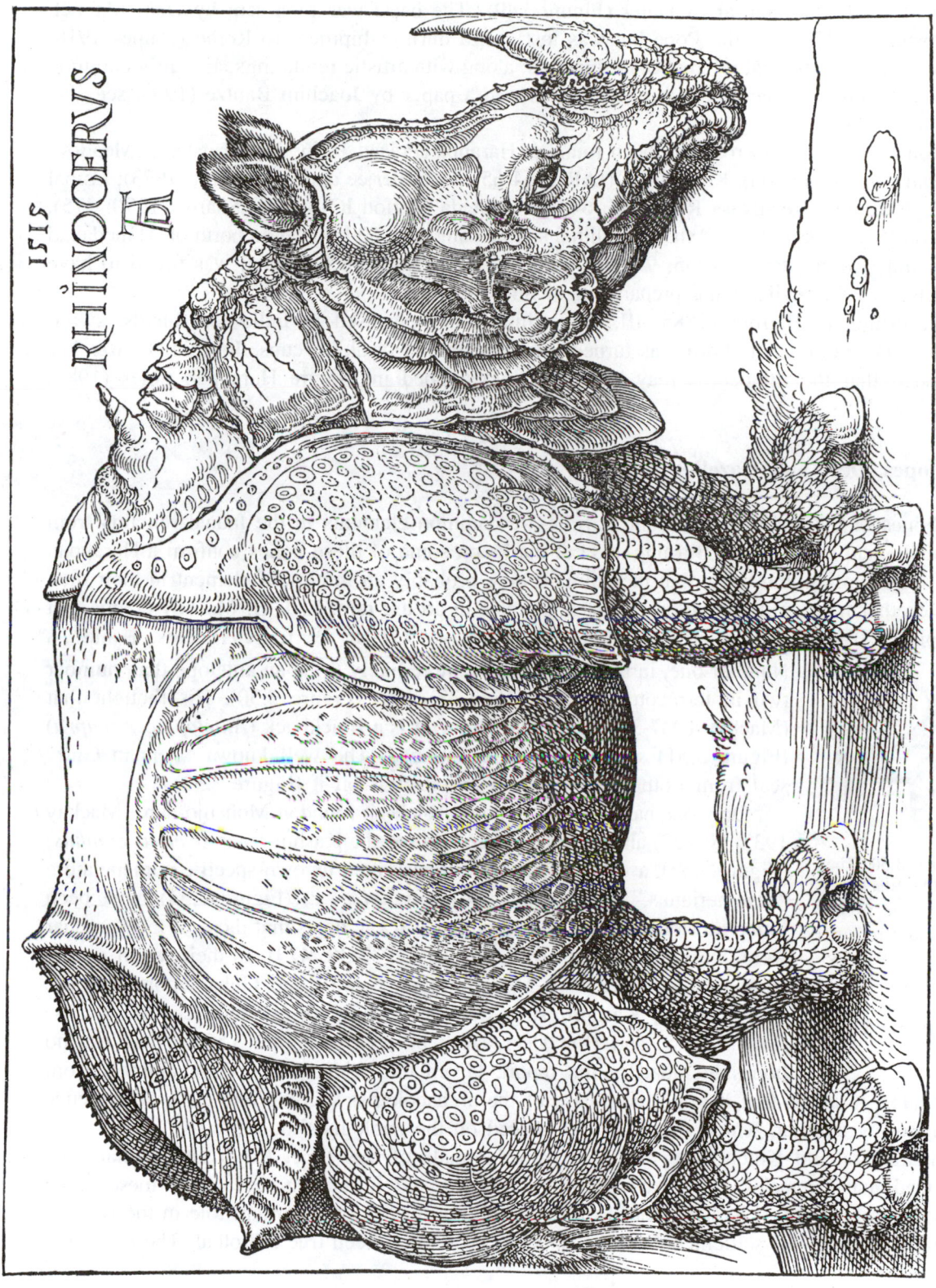

Figure 3.49. Albrecht Durer sketch of *Rhinoceros unicornis*, AD 1515, after Knappe 1964

an Indian rhinoceros, through the good offices of Alfonso d'Albuquerque. This animal was sketched by the German artist Durer (Figure 3.49). The beast was then sent by Dom Manuel, the Portuguese King, to the Pope but was lost at sea during shipment to Rome (Dames 1918: Vol. 1, 124-25).[4] Textual references to rhinoceri, along with artistic renderings, are fairly common in ancient India and have been brought together in a paper by Joachim Bautze (1985, see also Cockburn 1883).

Bones of the rhinoceros have been found at Harappa (Prasad 1936: 31), Nausharo (Meadow, personal communication), Kalibangan (IAR 1964-65: 38; Banerjee and Chakrabarti 1973); Lothal (Bhola Nath and Sreenivasa Rao 1985: 642), Surkotada (Period IC) (A. K. Sharma 1990: 375), Kanewal (Shah 1980: 74) and the microlithic site of Langhnaj, 60 kilometers north of Ahmedabad in Gujarat (Clutton-Brock 1965: 9-10). One of the scapulae from Langhnaj was found to have been used as an anvil for the preparation of microlithic tools.

According to Balfour (1885: III, 406), rhino hide was used in India for shields, sword handles and ramrods. Its horn was turned into goblets and drinking cups. Joachim Bautze has suggested that the rhinoceros may have been worshipped in Mature Harappan times (1985: 407).

Antelopes, Deer and Gazelles

The bones of the antelope, deer and gazelle are common elements in the faunal remains from archaeological excavations. Burning and cut marks on some of these bones confirm a Harappan interest in hunting and show that the animals were probably an important element in their diet. On the other hand, representations of these animals in art are rare. E. J. H. Mackay claims that two pieces from Mohenjo-daro are antelopes (Mackay 1937-38: Pl. LXXVII, Nos. 1 and 2).

Figure 3.50. The possible Blackbuck in bronze from Mohenjo-daro, after Mackay 1937-38: Plate LXXVII, No. 1, drawing from Yule 1985b: Tafel 2

Number one, in bronze, is clearly more likely to be an antelope than number two in terracotta (Mackay 1937-38: 285) (Figure 3.50). His thought that (Mackay 1937-38: Pl. LXXX, No. 4) it is a Blackbuck (*Antelope cervicapra*) (Figure 3.51) should also be questioned. The well known "Persian Gulf" seal from Lothal has a pair of artiodactyls on it (Figure 3.52).

Only one handle made of antler has been found at Mohenjo-daro (Mackay 1937-38: 423) although the antlers of both the Kashmir stag (*Cervus elaphus*) (Figure 3.53), a variety of red deer once given its own specific nomenclature "cashmerianus," and Sambhar (*Cervus unicolor*) (Figure 3.54) have been found at Mohenjo-daro and Harappa. Mackay notes that those of the Sambhar were "very common indeed" (Mackay 1937-38: 423). In their report on the zoological remains from Mohenjo-daro, Sewell and Guha report only the antlers of the Kashmir stag, Sambhar, Chital or spotted deer (*Axis axis*) (Figure 3.55) and Hog Deer, (*Axis porcinus*) (Figure 3.56). There are no bones included in the report. Given the evidence for these animals from other sites, it seems that it might be a case of the archaeologist keeping one class of evidence and ignoring another, which should not be placed on the zoologists' door step.

Saurashtra and Kutch have abundant game animals of this type. Rojdi and Lothal both produced many remains. The excavations at Rangpur and Surkotada reveal that these game animals rarely occur. It is clear from Rojdi that hunting played an important role in the lives of the inhabitants of this settlement, and the same seems to have been true at Lothal. The following

Plate 3.1. Settled *rabaris* working at Oriyo Timbo, winter 1982, author's photograph.

Plate 3.2. Part of a large camp of Pathans from Baluchistan at Lakhueenjo-daro, Sukkur, winter 1995-96, author's photograph.

Plate 3.3. *Bos indicus* hooked to a Sindhi cart, photograph from E.J.H. Mackay.

Plate 3.4. *Bos indicus* at Lothal, author's photograph.

Plate 3.5. A typical "unicorn" seal from Mohenjo-daro, after Marshall 1931a: Plate CIII, No. 11. Courtesy of the Archaeological Survey of India and Asko Parpola.

Plate 3.6. A zebu seal from Mohenjo-daro, after Marshall 1931a: Plate CXI, No. 340. Courtesy of the Archaeological Survey of India and Asko Parpola.

Plate 3.7. *Bos taurus* from Kalibangan in copper-bronze, after Thapar 1975: 29. Courtesy of the Archaeological Survey of India.

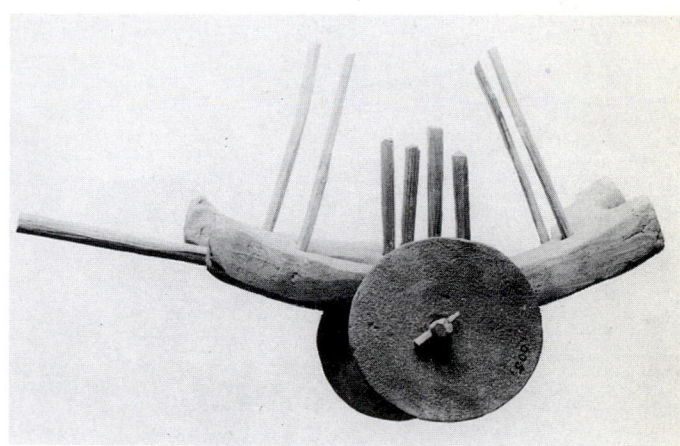

Plate 3.8. Bull puppet figurine from DK Area, Mohenjo-daro. Courtesy of the Archaeological Survey of India, Old Negative Number 797/92.

Plate 3.9. Terracotta cart from Chanhu-daro. Courtesy of the Archives, the University of Pennsylvania Museum.

Plate 3.10. The head of a water buffalo, showing the distinct curvature and ribbing of the horns.

Plate 3.11. Water buffalo on an Indus seal, after Mackay 1937-38: Plate XCIX, No. 663. Courtesy of the Archaeological Survey of India and Asko Parpola. Photo by Erja Lahdenperä for the Corpus of Indus Seals and Inscriptions Project of the University of Helsinki.

Plate 3.12. Water buffalo on a Mesopotamian seal. From Asko Parpola 1994. The Hero with locks of hair slakes the thirst of the water buffalo with water flowing from the pot of Enki. Inscribed "Sargalisarrim King of Akkad, the scribe is your servant". A late Akkadian cylinder seal c. 2200 BC. Musee de Louvre AO22303 (Collection de Clercq. Collon 1987: No. 529).

Plate 3.13. A goat on an Indus seal from Lothal, after S. R. Rao 1985: Plate CLIX, A, 3. Courtesy of the Archaeological Survey of India and Asko Parpola. Photo by Erja Lahdenperä for the Corpus of Indus Seals and Inscriptions Project of the University of Helsinki.

Plate 3.14. Indus stamp seal with the short-horned bull, after Marshall 1931a: Plate CX, No. 310. Courtesy of the Archaeological Survey of India and Asko Parpola.

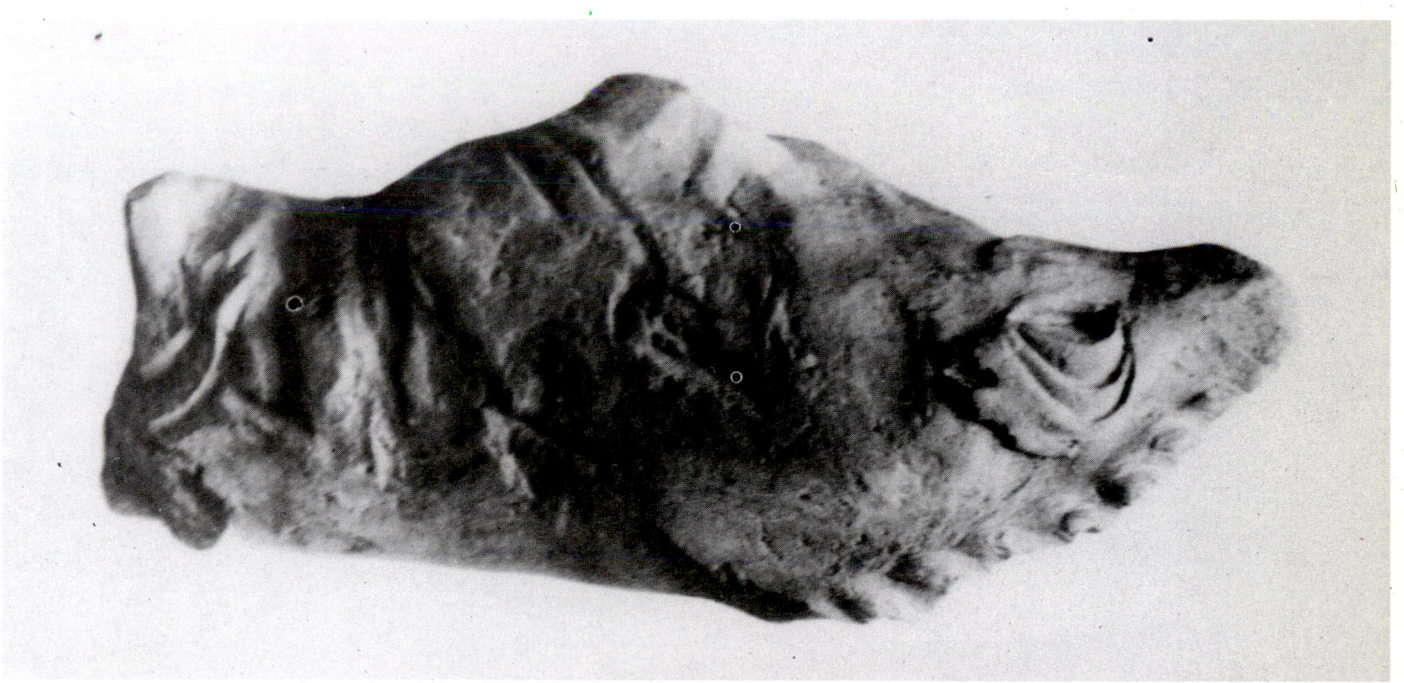

Plate 3.15. A figurine of a pig from Mohenjo-daro. Courtesy of the Archaeological Survey of India, Old Negative Number 1111/92.

Plate 3.16. The domesticated horse, this one being the Kathi breed, author's photograph.

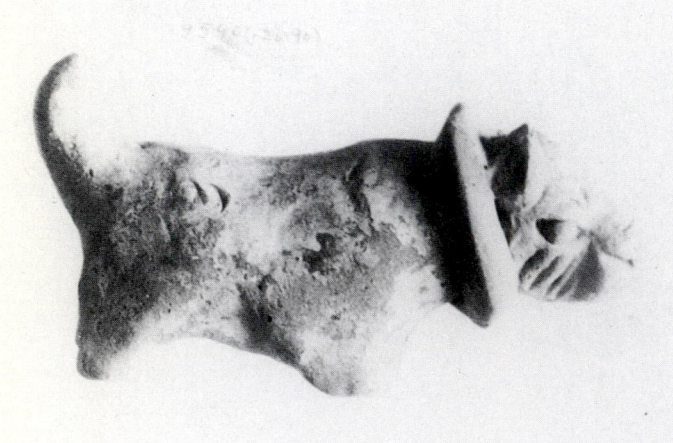

Plate 3.17. Terracotta figurine of a dog with a collar, after Mackay 1937-38: Plate LXXIX, No. 15.

Plate 3.18. An elephant seal from Mohenjo-daro, after Mackay 1937-38: Plate XCIV, No. 648. Courtesy of the Archaeological Survey of India and Asko Parpola.

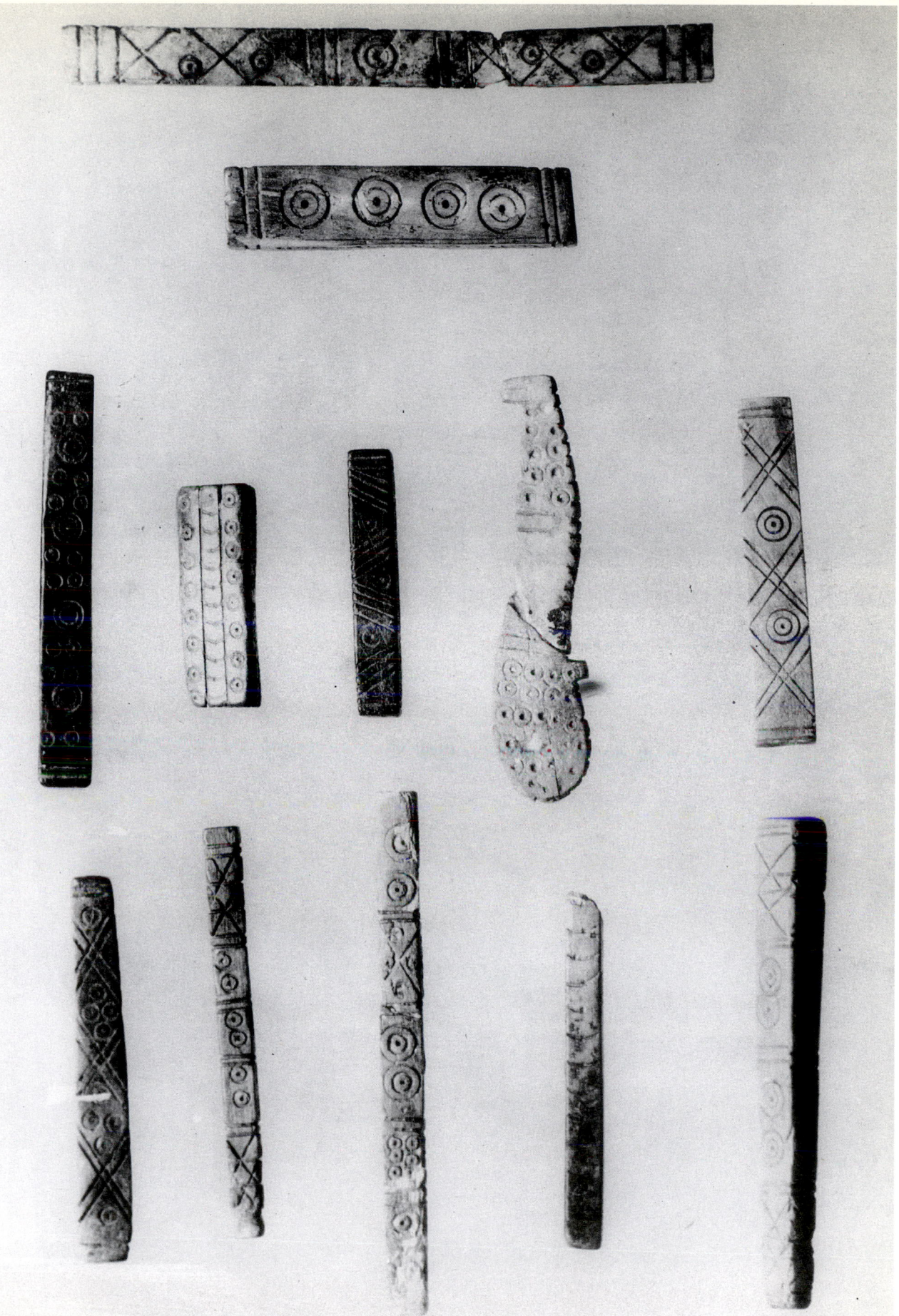

Plate 3.19. Ivory objects from Mohenjo-daro. Courtesy of the Archaeological Survey of India, Sind Volumes, Old Negative No. 800/92.

Plate 3.20. A Dromedary camel in upper Sindh today, author's photograph.

a

b

Plate 3.21. Two tiger seals, (a) from Kalibangan, (b) from Mohenjo-daro. Courtesy of the Archaeological Survey of India and Asko Parpola; Mohenjo-daro seal after Mackay 1937-38: Plate LXXXVII, No. 259.

Plate 3.22. A pinwheel of tigers, after Marshall 1931a: Plate CXII, No. 386. Courtesy of the Archaeological Survey of India and Asko Parpola.

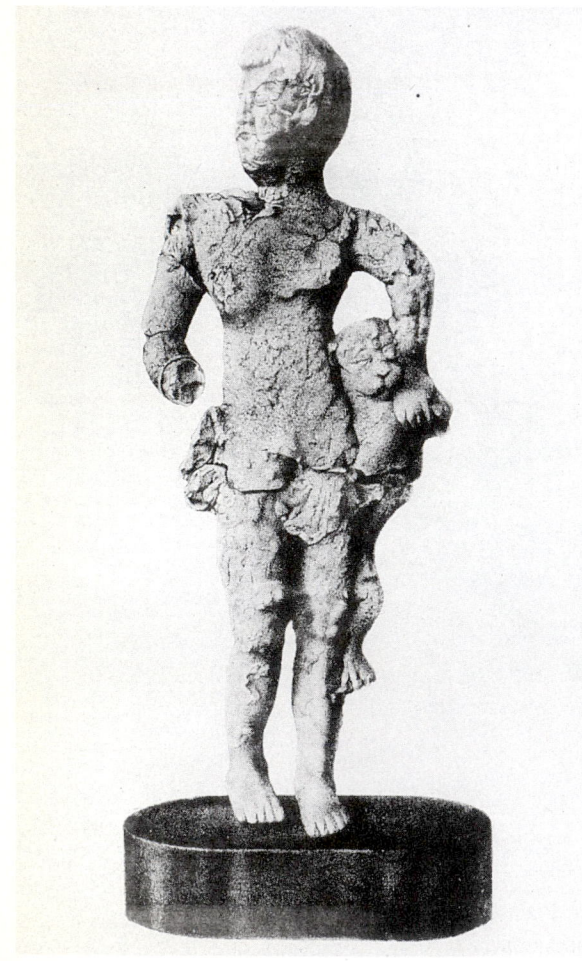

Plate 3.23. Three Asiatic lions camouflaged in the Gir Forest of Saurashtra, author's photograph.

Plate 3.24. Drawing of Hercules holding the skin of the Nemean lion, from Hughes-Buller 1907a, frontispiece.

Plate 3.25. Rhinoceros on a seal from Harappa, after Vats 1940: Plate XCI, No. 253. Courtesy of the Archaeological Survey of India and Asko Parpola.

Plate 3.26. A Mughal miniature of a Nilgai, ca. 1630-40. Courtesy of Mr. and Mrs. John Gilmore Ford.

Plate 3.27. The Indian Red Jungle Fowl. Courtesy of VIREO, Philadelphia Academy of the Natural Sciences.

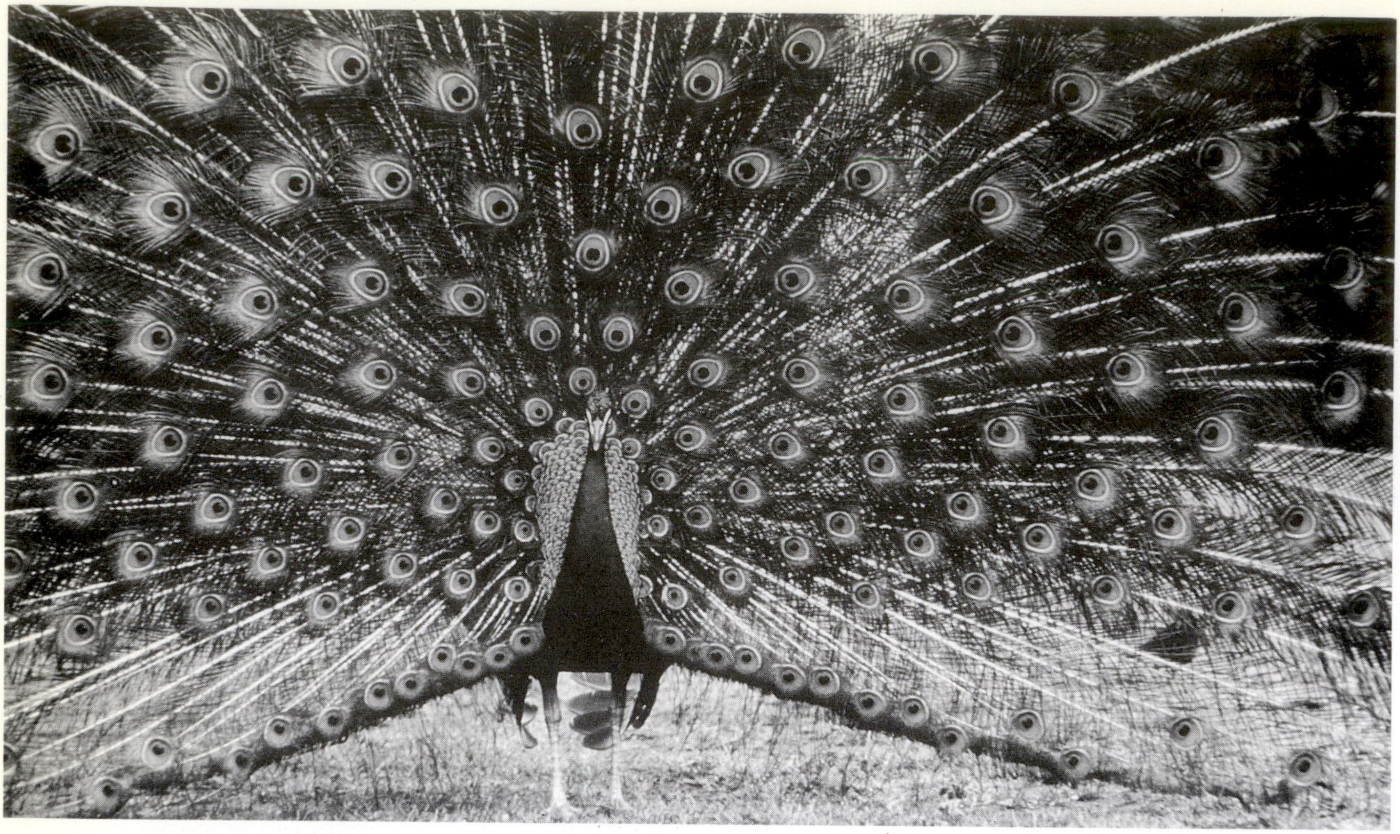

Plate 3.28. The Indian Peafowl. Courtesy of VIREO, Philadelphia Academy of the Natural Sciences.

Plate 3.29. Peacock on a sherd from the Sorath Harappan site of Atkot. Courtesy of the Gujarat State Department of Archaeology.

Plate 3.30. Seal number 93 with a duck in a circle, after Marshall 1931a, Plate CIV, No. 93. Courtesy of the Archaeological Survey of India, Old Negative Number 652/89.

Plate 3.31. The *gavial*. Courtesy of Dr. Sherman Minton.

Plate 3.32. The *muggar*. Courtesy of Dr. Sherman Minton.

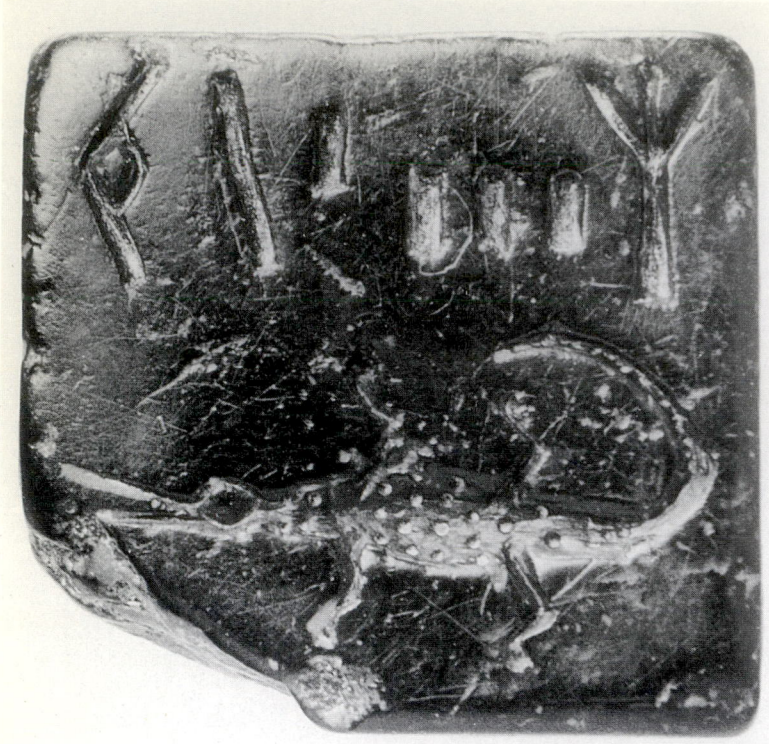

Plate 3.33. A seal from Mohenjo-daro with a gavial, after Marshall 1931a: Plate CXI, No. 361. Courtesy of the Archaeological Survey of India and Asko Parpola.

Plate 3.34. A fish motif on a jar from Nal, after Hargreaves 1929: Plate XXb. Courtesy of the National Museum, New Delhi and George F. Dales.

Plate 3.35. The Salt Range, author's photograph.

Plate 3.36. Lake Manchar. Courtesy of Louis Flam.

Plate 3.37. Bolan Pass in a mid-nineteenth century lithograph.

Plate 3.38. The Kachi Plain, author's photograph.

Figure 3.51. The Blackbuck

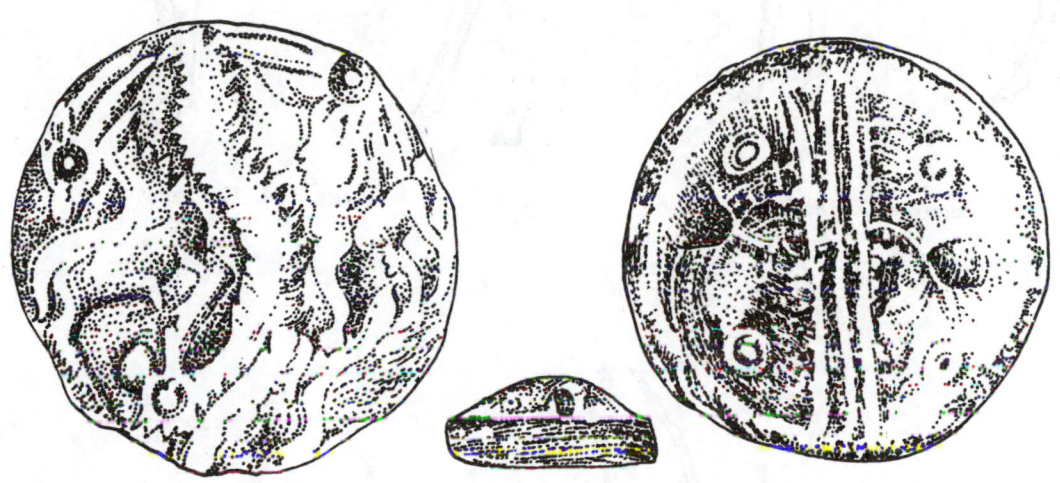

Figure 3.52. Persian Gulf Seal from Lothal, after S. R. Rao 1963b

list draws on Stack-Kane (1989) for Rojdi, Bhola Nath and Sreenivasa Rao (1985) for Lothal, Bhola Nath (1963) for Rangpur and A. K. Sharma (1990) for Surkotada.

Four-horned Antelope (*Tetracerus quadricornus*) (Figure 3.57) Rojdi
Hog Deer (*Axis porcinus*) Rojdi
Chital or Spotted Deer (*Axis axis*) Rojdi, Lothal, Surkotada
Basasingha or Swamp Deer (*Cervus duvauceli*) Rojdi, Lothal
Sambhar (*Cervus unicolor*) Rojdi, Lothal, Rangpur III
Nilgai or Blue Bull (*Boselaphus tragocamelus*) (Figure 3.58) Rojdi, Lothal (Plate 3.26).
Blackbuck (*Antelope cervicapra*) Rojdi, Lothal,
Indian Gazelle or Chinkara (*Gazella bennetti*) (Figure 3.59) Rojdi

Figure 3.53. The Kashmir Stag

Figure 3.54. The Sambhar

Figure 3.55. The Chital

Figure 3.56. The Hog Deer

Figure 3.57. The four-horned
Antelope

Figure 3.58. The Nilgai

208

Figure 3.59. The Chinkara

The Nilgai is a strange looking animal, once abundant in Saurashtra. In fact, the name "Rojdi" is Gujarati for the female of this species. The proportions of the animal are such that the front legs are longer than the back, giving it a sloping profile, not quite as exaggerated as the giraffe. The front is deer-like, the rear more like a bull or cow—the proverbial animal put together by a committee.

This class of game animal is well represented in Harappan art, especially on painted pottery. There is an excellent example of an animal, probably a Blackbuck, on a cup from Rangpur IIC (Figure 3.60). Rows of other animals, possibly Blackbuck but could also be wild goats or some other artiodactyl, are very common on pottery from Kulli sites (Figure 3.61). Painted pottery from Northern Baluchistan, especially in the so-called "Jangal

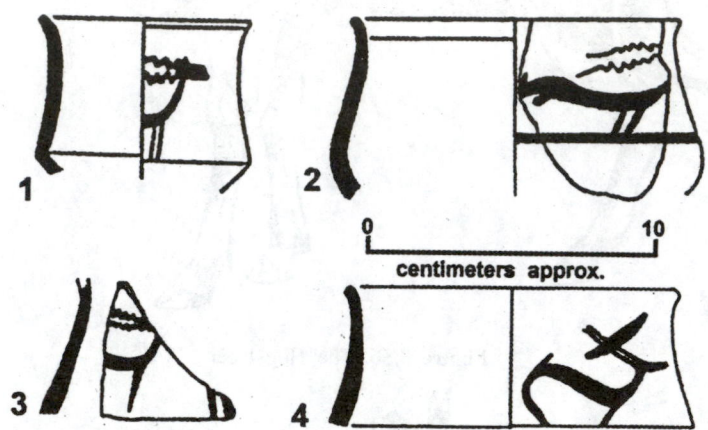

Figure 3.60. Blackbucks on Lustrous Red Ware from Rangpur and Oriyo Timbos ca. 1600 BC, Post-urban Harappan; Nos. 1-3, S. R. Rao 1963a: Figure 34, Nos. 50, 51, 53; No. 4, Rissman and Chitalwala 1990: Figure 18, No. 80

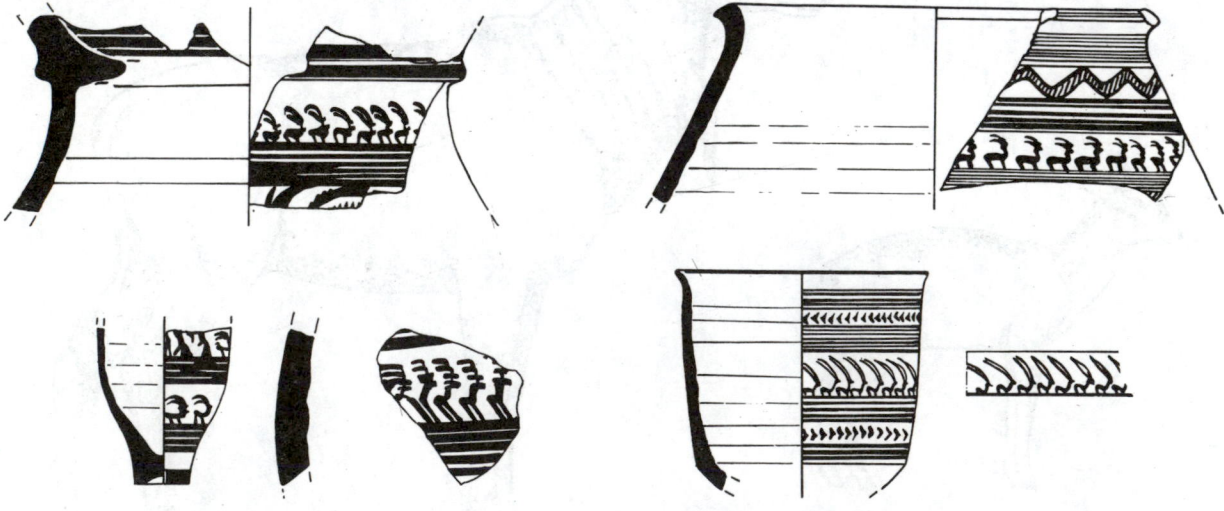

Figure 3.61. Various animals in rows on pottery from Kulli and Mehi, Kulli Phase, after Stein 1931

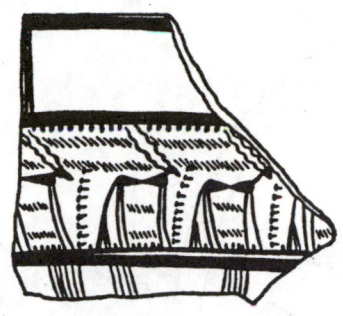
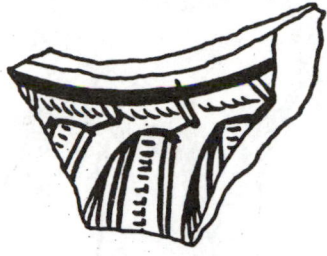

Figure 3.62. Jangal painted pottery from Rana Ghundai with game animals, Kechi Beg Phase, after Fairservis 1959: 392

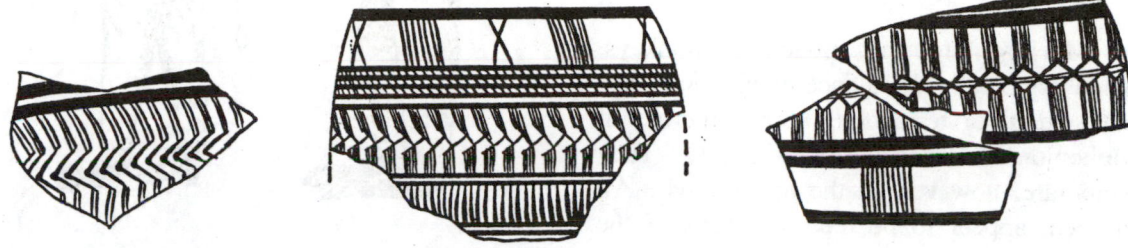

Figure 3.63. Jangal painted pottery with stylized animals from Rana Ghundai, Kechi Beg Phase, after Fairservis 1959: 393

Painted Style" are decorated in a similar way, again with animals that may be Blackbucks (Figure 3.62). These designs begin in a stylized way and seem to appear in even more exaggerated forms, as in (Figure 3.63). There is an attractive bronze Blackbuck from Mohenjo-daro (Mackay 1937-38: Pl. LXXVII, No. 1). The animal next to this (No. 2) is said by Mackay to be an example of the same animal in terracotta (Mackay 1937-38: 285), but this is not convincing. The animals on a bronze pin from Mohenjo-daro (Mackay 1937-38: Pl. C, Nos. 3 and 10) are not clearly identifiable, although Mackay (1937-38: 539) believes they are Blackbucks.

Monkeys

There were probably two monkeys in the Greater Indus Region during the Indus Age: the Rhesus Macaque (*Macaca mulatta*) (Figure 3.64) and the common Langur or Hanuman monkey (*Presbytis entellus*) (Figure 3.65). The Rhesus monkey has a shorter tail, is stouter and has a more clean shaven look. The langur has a long tail, which is a distinctive feature, and a "bushy" face.

Shereen Ratnagar (1981: 149-53) discusses monkey figurines extensively since they occur in both Mesopotamia and the Indus. She lists 23 monkey figurines from Harappan (seven examples), Mesopotamian (eleven examples) and Iranian sites (five examples) from Early Dynastic to Larsa times. She argues that it appears likely that the bulk of the Early Dynastic to Larsa Period monkey figurines in Mesopotamia depict Indian primates based on the appearance of the figurines which have the look of the rhesus macaque or the baboon. She eliminates the baboon because it is African and ties between Mesopotamia and Africa are extremely weak (1981: 152-53).

210

Figure 3.64. The Rhesus Macaque

Figure 3.65. The Langur

Mackay notes that models of monkeys, made principally of faience or vitreous paste but seldom of terracotta, were numerous at Mohenjo-daro (Mackay 1937-38: 293). They were rare, however, in the upper levels. All of them appear to be representations of the rhesus species (Figure 3.66). Mackay illustrates (1937-38: Plate C, No. 13, p. 540) two monkeys of steatite in an embrace on a pinhead. This is said by Mackay (1937-38: 540) to be like another from Mohenjo-daro (Marshall 1931a: CLVIII, No. 5) but the photograph is indistinct. Illustrations of another monkey from Mohenjo-daro can be found in Marshall (1931a: Pl. XCVI, No. 11). Vats published one monkey from Harappa (Vats 1940: Pl. LXXVIII, No. 35, Monkey on a stick).

No monkey bones have been found at sites of the Indus Age.

Pangolins

Two species of pangolins, or scaly anteaters, are found in the Subcontinent. The Chinese species is confined to the mountains of the eastern states, but the Indian Pangolin (*Manis crassicaudata*) (Figure 3.67) is found all over the remainder of the region to the south of the Himalaya. It is a smallish animal: the

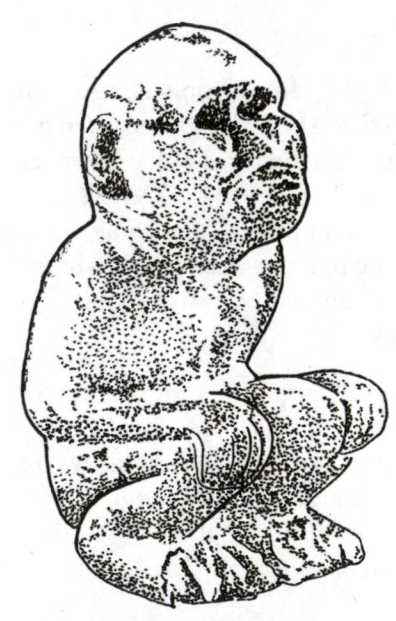

Figure 3.66. Monkey figurine from Mohenjo-daro, after Marshall 1931a: Pl. XCVI, No. 13

adults are 60 to 75 cm in length with a 45 cm tail. It is covered with heavy scales which are its principal form of physical protection. Pangolins are nocturnal and spend their days in burrows they have dug for themselves, or curled up among rocks. Their diet consists almost exclusively

Figure 3.67. The Indian Pangolin

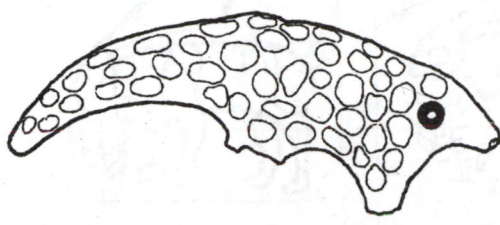

Figure 3.68. Terracotta model of a Pangolin from Harappa, after Vats 1940: Pl. LXXVIII, No. 26

of ants and termites and they seem to be especially fond of the eggs of these insects. They have short, powerful limbs, with formidable claws which they use to dig for food. "Tearing down a breach in a termite mound with powerful claws of its forelimbs and thrusting its long narrow head inside, the animal reaches for the buried comb-like fungus 'gardens' which usually lodge swarms of these insects, eggs, young and adults" (Prater 1971: 303).

There is only one occurrence of the pangolin in the art or remains of the Harappan Civilization. This is a terracotta from Harappa (Vats 1940: Pl. LXXVIII, No. 26) (Figure 3.68).

The Porcupine

The Indian Crested Porcupine (*Hystrix indica*) is part of the Greater Indus Region and its remains

Figure 3.69. The Indian Crested Porcupine

are occasionally found in archaeological vestiges of the Indus Age. The quills would have been useful in daily life as tools (needles and punches), and decoration on clothing (Figure 3.69).

Hares

While not common in the art of the Indus Age hares (never rabbits) are represented, and are fairly common throughout the Greater Indus Region. The principal examples are terracotta figurines (Figure 3.70) and engravings on the copper tablets of Mohenjo-daro (Figure 3.71). They are also found on the so-called miniatures from Harappa (Figure 3.72).

Figure 3.70. Figurine of a hare, after Marshall 1931a: Pl. XCVI, No. 9

Figure 3.71. Hare on two copper tablets, after Mackay 1937-38: Plate CXVIII, Nos. 5 & 6

Figure 3.72. Hares on miniatures from Harappa, after Vats 1940: Plate XCV, Nos. 421 & 425, drawings from Parpola 1985a, Figure 17e & f

Squirrels

The woodlands of South Asia are inhabited by a variety of squirrels that scurry and hop about during the course of a day. Two small representations of these animals were found at Mohenjo-daro (Marshall 1931a: Pl. XCVI, No. 7; Mackay 1937-38: Pl. LXXVII, No. 20), with others from Harappa (Vats 1940: Pl. LXXVIII, Nos 28-30) (Figure 3.73). The representation in Marshall (1931a) is an especially lifelike miniature masterpiece in faience. They seem to depict either *Funambulus pennanti*, the Northern Palm Squirrel or *Funambulus tristriatus* the Jungle Striped Squirrel. Both would have been in the Greater Indus Region in antiquity.

Figure 3.73. A squirrel figurine from Harappa, after Vats 1940: Plate LXXVIII, No. 29

Wolves, Jackals and Hyaenas

Remains of the Indian wolf (*Canis lupus*) (Figure 3.74) have been found at a number of sites, including Surkotada IB, and Lothal. These may have been hunted and killed, or could be the remains of tamed animals admitted to the human community on their good behavior. The gold cup from the Quetta Treasury (Figure 3.40) has a row of four animals, all very much alike, that

Figure 3.74. The Indian wolf

Figure 3.75. The Asiatic jackal

214

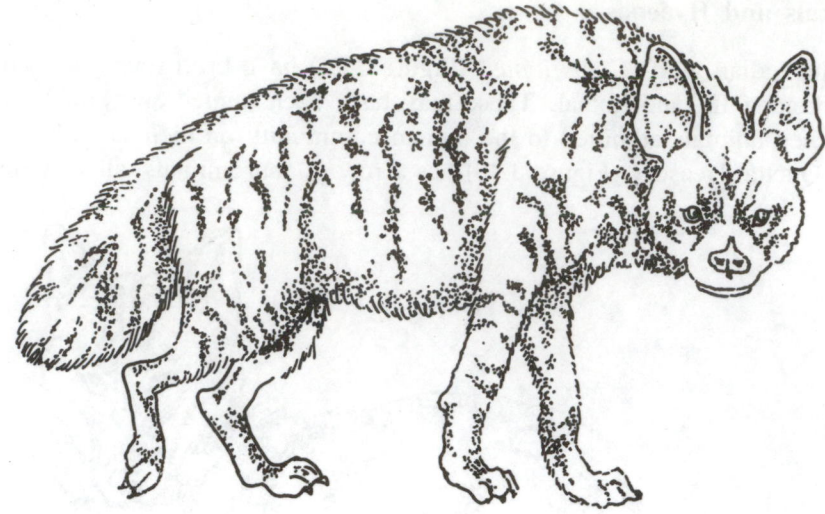

Figure 3.76. The striped hyaena

one might expect to be lions. On close examination, however, they seem to be more wolf-like than lion-like. The first point is the bushy tail, not at all like the long, slender tail of a lion, with a slightly bushy end. There is a ruff at the neck and head and it suggests a lion; but a wolf in an agitated state, with hair on end, develops a ruff as well, and the animals on the gold cup are in pursuit. The snout of this animal is long and narrow, more like the wolf than the fuller faced lion.

I know of no artifactual representations of the Asiatic jackal (*Canis aureus*) (Figure 3.75) or the striped hyaena (*Hyaena hyaena*) (Figure 3.76). The remains of these animals do occur in sites of the Indus Age as in Surkotada IA and IC (A. K. Sharma 1990: 373) and Rojdi (Stack-Kane 1989: 183) for the jackal. Ganeshwar (IAR 1983-84a: 72) and Jokha have hyaena bones (D. R. Shah 1971).

The Fox

The common red fox (*Vulpes vulpes*) (Figure 3.77) is very much a part of the natural world of the Greater Indus region. I know of no remains of this animal from one of the ancient sites of this area, nor is there an artifact that represents it. It, like the lion, is interesting because of its absence from the record, one of the animals that was culturally filtered out of the lives of the peoples of the Indus Age.

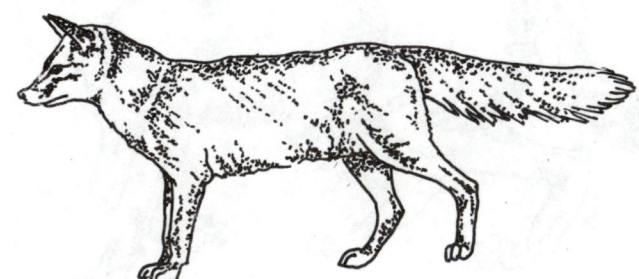

Figure 3.77. The common red fox

Bears

There are two bears in the Greater Indus Region. The Asiatic Black Bear (*Selenarctos thibetanus*) (Figure 3.78) is still found in Pakistan, Baluchistan and through the mountainous north of the country (Roberts 1977: 108). The Brown Bear (*Ursus arctos*) is found in the Himalaya today, even to the north of the Asiatic Black Bear. There is a report of *Ursus arctos* from Period III at Amri (Poulain-Josien 1964: 168). Given the distribution of the bears in Pakistan and India this might well be *Selenarcos thibetanus*. Bears do not figure in the art of the Indus Age.

Figure 3.78. The Asiatic Black Bear

Dolphins

The *Bulhan* (Figure 3.79) is a blind dolphin that inhabits the Indus River, and would have extended into its tributaries in the Punjab in prehistoric times. It is classified with its relative in the Ganges drainage as *Platanista gangetica* (*Su-su*) by Indian biologists. But those in Pakistan consider it to be a separate species *Platanista indi*. There is a small, vestigial eye, but it finds its way by a sonar system. It is a smallish dolphin: the adults are about 2.5 meters long, with a long snout and two rows of sharp, conical teeth. It appears to swim on its side and use echo location to navigate and find its food (Pilleri 1980; Roberts 1977: 310). The evolutionary heritage of the *Bulhan* goes back to the sea, but today it is found only within the Indus River. Modern damming and bunding have divided and segmented the small, endangered population of several hundred. Earlier in the century the gazetteer of Sindh informs us that:

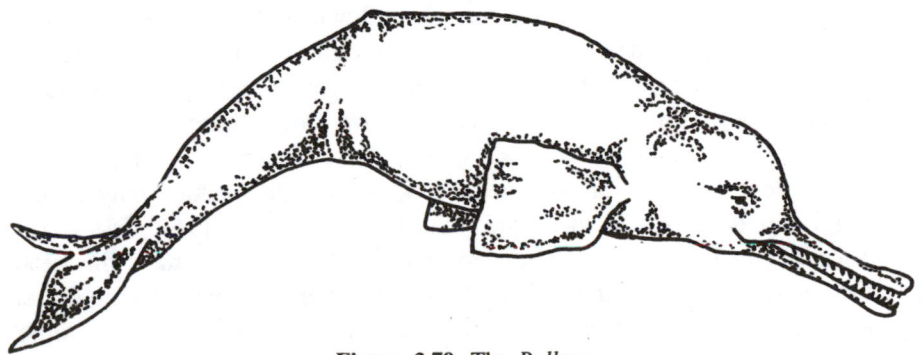

Figure 3.79. The *Bulhan*

Its oil is a specific for rheumatism and the *Muhanas* (boatmen) burn it in lamps. Some castes eat the flesh. The porpoise is caught with the aid of trained otters, which are turned loose in some pool near the bank of the river where there are fish. The blind porpoise hears the noises that they make and hurries up (not to eat the otters, but to share their feast) when a stout, bell-shaped net is clapped on it and it is speared through the meshes (Aitken 1907: 52-3).

There is, to my knowledge, no record of this animal in the Indus Age. But it would have been known to the inhabitants of the riverine settlements of the time and it would not be surprising to have some evidence emerge in the archaeological record someday.

The Birds

Introduction

There are two important birds in the Indus age, the peafowl (*Pavo cristatus*) and the chicken (*Gallus gallus murghi*), the domesticated form of the Red Indian Junglefowl. Each is important in its own way, but both were clearly part of the Mature Harappan world. There is a short article covering the ornithology of the Harappan Civilization and related materials that is not too dated, but is very empirical (V. V. Rao 1972-73).

The Mesopotamians speak of a bird of the land of Meluhha, which can be presumed to have been the Greater Indus Region. It was called either *dar-me-luh-ha* or *dar-me-luh-ha-musen*. They speak of the birds themselves as well as ivory models of them: "Three mana of ivory, cut, out of which 1 small male figure, 3 small female figures, 1 dar-musen-me-luh-ha, a bird" (UET III; Legrain 1947: 228, no. 757). The Sumerian bird *dar-musen*, with its Akkadian equivalent *tarru* (Meissner 1981: 1331) and *ittidu* is known with several variations. One of them, the *dar-me-luh-ha-musen*, whose Akkadian equivalent *su-la-mu* seems to signify that it is black. This rules out the peafowl as a candidate for this bird. Under domestication the Indian Red Junglefowl could have undergone rapid color change from its wild state: its tail is black and the under parts brownish black. But, no one knows if this happened. Benno Landsberger (1962: 148) believes that the *dar-me-luh-ha-musen* was a "frankolin" or the Persian Black Partridge (*Francolinus francolinus henrici*). This is also the identification in the *Chicago Assyrian Dictionary* under the entry *ittidu*. This largely jet black bird is found from Sindh, across the Iranian Plateau, into the Near East and Turkey (Ali and Ripley 1983: 99-100); but it is also native to Mesopotamia and one might legitimately wonder why it would therefore be called a *dar-me-luh-ha-musen*. (see Ratnagar 1981: 69 for discussion).

One interesting, and plausible point, can be gleaned from Landsberger, whether he intended this interpretation or something else. In *The Curse of Agade* there is a reference to: "Meluhhans, people of the black mountains, brought exotic wares down to her..." (Cooper 1983: 53; lines 48, 49). The association between "Meluhha" and the color "black" is found elsewhere in Mesopotamian texts and the reference to a black bird might draw on this allusion.

In a Mesopotamian epic known as *Enki and the World Order* there is reference to *dar* birds of the foreign lands or mountains which are said to have a carnelian, or possibly just a red beard (Falkenstein 1964: 105). In this same text Enki says of Meluhha: "may your bird be the *haja*-bird, may its call be heard in the royal palace" (Falkenstein 1964: 75, 105), which led Falkenstein, in a gigantic leap of association, to claim that the *haja*-bird is the peacock. Since there is no epistemological basis for this identification, other than Falkenstein's assumption, it cannot be sustained, in spite of having been repeated in recent works on the topic (Ratnagar 1981: 69-70).

Chickens *Gallus gallus*

The modern domesticated chicken is descended from the Indian Red Jungle Fowl, a beautifully colored bird (Plate 3.27). The male is a glossy deep orange-red, with long, yellowish neck feathers. The tail is shiny metallic black with long, arching sickle-shaped feathers. The under parts of the wild bird are blackish brown. This magnificent creature shares little with the white broiler stock now raised around the world.

The contemporary, and near contemporary, distribution of *Gallus gallus* is disputed. Salim Ali and Dillon Ripley (1983: 120) extend its range all across the northern Punjab, from the Ganga-Yamuna area to the banks of the Indus. T. J. Roberts finds no evidence that this bird has ever existed in Pakistan (1991-92: Vol. 1, 342). It is also found in the Western Ghats of Gujarat (Ali and Ripley 1983: 120). It has been said that its wild distribution is coincident with that of the *sal* tree (*Shorea robusta*) and the swamp deer (*Cervus duvauceli*) which was certainly an inhabitant of Sindh, especially around Sukkur, and the Panjnad as well, putting it farther south than the modern distribution. *Sal* forest is found in the Eastern Region and would have brought man and the Jungle Fowl together in this region (Spate and Learmonth 1967: 550). The Rawalpindi District Gazetteer reports Red Jungle Fowl in the area as late as 1907 (Government of the Punjab 1907: 28).

The bones of chickens have been found at Mohenjo-daro (Sewell and Guha 1931a: 662), Harappa (Prashad 1939: 15), Rupar (Bhola Nath 1968), Lothal (Bhola Nath and Sreenivasa Rao 1985: 639-40), Kalibangan (IAR 1964-65: 38), all three periods at Surkotada (A. K. Sharma 1990: 380), and Rojdi (Stack-Kane 1989: 183). The Rojdi evidence comes in the form of one very well preserved leg bone with a magnificent spur, marking the male from the female.

Some terracotta figurines are said to be representations of chickens. It would probably be agreed that they are birds, but the notion that they are *Gallus gallus murghi* may not be true in all cases (Figure 3.80). Mackay thought that the figurine in Figure 3.80, with the feeding container in front of it, could be evidence for domestication, or at least the keeping of tame fowl (Mackay 1937-38: 296).

The Indus script includes bird logographs. The only way to make a definitive judgment on the kind of bird intended to be represented is for all of them to be reproduced. In some instances an examination of the original is necessary, since there is some defacement and the creatures were not rendered in a lifelike way. The concordance of the script, with standardized signs and variation among them reduced, should not be consulted.

Figure 3.80. Terracotta bird figurine of a chicken, after Mackay 1937-38: Plate LXXX, No. 20

Figure 3.81. Stamp seal with two bird signs, after Marshall 1931a: Plate CXI, No. 338

Figure 3.82. Painting of a cock on a potsherd from Tutankhamun's tomb, after Carter 1923

218

Figure 3.83. A peacock in a tree, after Hutchins 1985: 198

Compare Stephen Lang-don's hand-drawn signs for birds with those from the Mahadevan Concordance (1977: 32). Ernest J. H. Mackay (1948: 143) has claimed that one of the seals has two cocks in a fighting attitude which might indicate that this was a sport to the Indus people. It may be that he is referring to a place where bird signs are doubled, (Marshall 1931a: Pl. CXI, No. 338) (Figure 3.81) but seeing a "fighting attitude" on this seal would be difficult.

By the middle of the second millennium the chicken had traveled far. There is one, for example, painted on a pot sherd from Tutankhamun's tomb (Figure 3.82).

Peafowl

Peafowl (*Pavo cristatus*) (Plate 3.28) are found all over the Subcontinent, except in Baluchistan and the higher ranges of the Himalaya (Figure 3.83). Salim Ali and Dillon Ripley (1983: 125) believe that they have been introduced into Sind, Uramkot, Mirpurkas, Hyderabad and Sehwan and are now semi-feral. If this is true then it would have followed their temporary extinction there since they are well represented in the Sindhi Harappan painted pottery style (Figure 3.84, Figure 3.85). There is also a little terracotta figurine from Harappa that may be a peacock in full plumage display (Vats 1940: Plate LXXVIII, No. 14; Plate 3.29).

In the wild state, the peafowl prefers moist and dry deciduous forest in the vicinity of streams. The semi-feral, semi-domesticated bird is attracted to the outskirts of human settlements and cultivated land. Females of the species are plain in comparison to the much flashier males which have a brilliant blue neck and a long train of large multicolored feathers which can be ostentatiously displayed as an open fan. His beauty is compromised somewhat by an ugly *may-awe* call which, when first heard might cause one to wonder at such a contradiction in nature. Peafowl are fast runners and may prefer to escape their enemies on foot. They are interesting fliers, not given to long flight and migration by air. "They rise with a loud flapping of wings, even an old cock with his long, heavy train rocketing almost vertically to clear the tree tops.

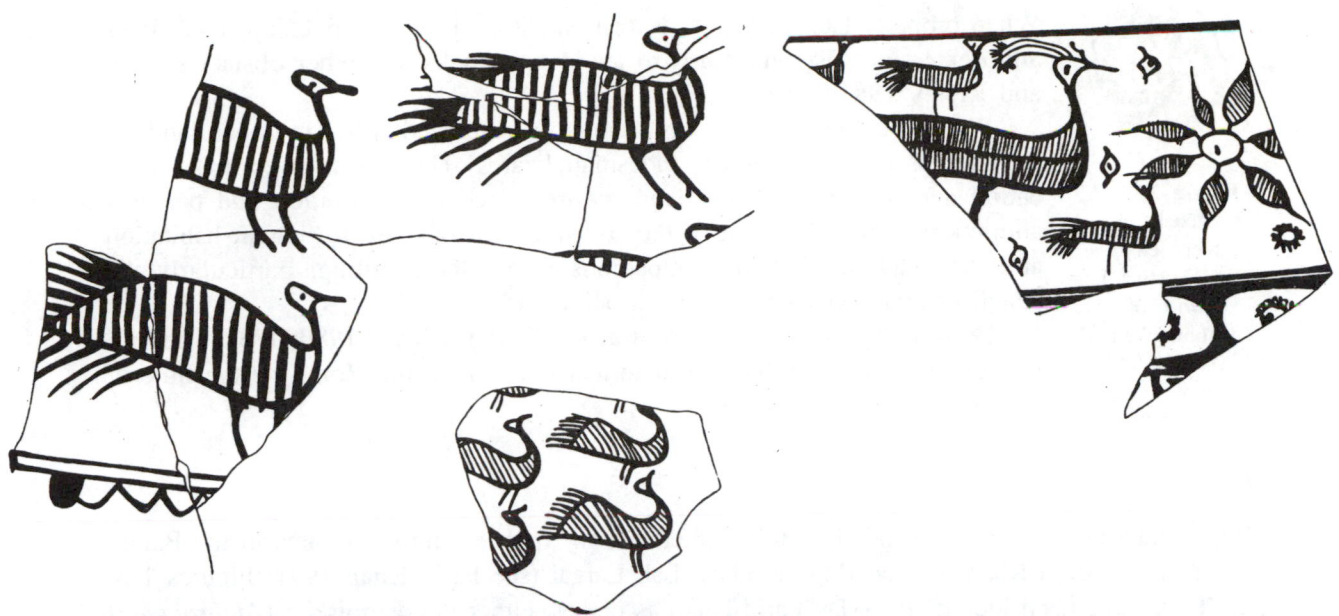

Figure 3.84. Peacocks on painted pottery of the Mature Harappan of Chanhu-daro, after Mackay 1943: Plate XXXII, Nos. 4, 8 & 9

Figure 3.85. A large storage jar with peacocks from Chanhu-daro, after Mackay 1943: Frontpiece, drawn from Fairservis 1971a: Figure 62

220

Figure 3.86. A peacock on a silver denarius of Faustina I, wife of Antoninus Pios, AD 141, after Zeuner 1963: 457

When properly launched they fly fast and strongly with rapid flaps and glides and dexterous twists and turns to avoid tree-trunks and other obstacles" (Ali and Ripley 1983: 125).

Peafowl are omnivorous, and scratch in cultivated fields and open land for their meals of seeds, insects and small lizards. They themselves make good eating and their magnificent feathers are prized for decoration and personal adornment. The cultivation of the soil draws them close to human habitation and they can be pleasant companions in a village setting; particularly the beautiful males when they want to show off.

Peafowl bones may be present at Rojdi (Stack-Kane 1989: 183). The bird was exported far and wide in historical times, reaching Rome by the time of Christ (Figure 3.86).

Cranes

Representations of birds are found on the painted pottery from a number of sites in the Bannu Basin: i. e., Sheri Khan Tarakai (Figure 3.87), Lak Largai (see Farid Khan 1991: Figures 1 & 2). They have been identified by Dr. Farid Khan as cranes, either the demoiselle (*Anthropoides virgo*), or the common crane (*Grus grus lilfordii*, Farid Khan 1991: 97). There is a long history of capturing cranes for pets in this part of Pakistan and in an interesting article, Khan hypothesizes that the representations on pots of these distinctive long-legged birds might take this tradition back into prehistoric times. He has also suggested (F. Khan personal communication) that perforated stones found at these same sites in Bannu may have been weights used in the bola-like instrument that is thrown to capture them.

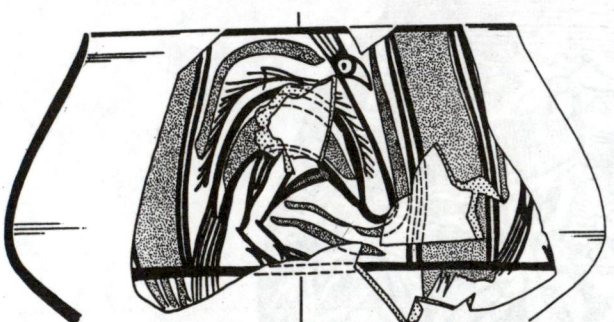

Figure 3.87. Crane from Sheri Khan Tarakai, after Farid Khan 1991: Figure 2

Millions of cranes, along with many other birds, migrate through the Greater Indus Region on their way to and from East Africa where they spend their winters to avoid the snows of Siberia, their summer habitat. Whether or not they were captured by the ancient inhabitants of the Bannu Basin is another matter, but Farid Khan makes an interesting case for this possibility.

Birds of Prey

There is a wide variety of birds of prey: kites, hawks and falcons in the Greater Indus Region. There are no remains of any of these birds in the faunal record, but there is one representation on one side of a seal from Harappa (Figure 3.88). It is an important seal. It has the shape of a stepped cross and

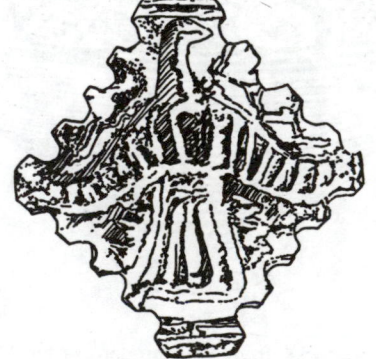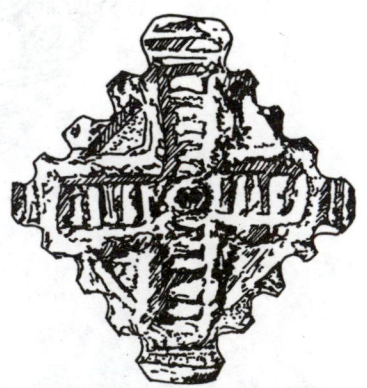

Figure 3.88. Seal from Harappa with a bird of prey, after Vats 1940: Plate XCI, No. 251

seems to belong to the class of artifacts that are part of the Middle Asian Interaction Sphere. Vats (1940: 302) speaks of two other representations, each a kite, (Plate LXXVIII, No. 10 & 11), but they are not convincing representations of this bird.

Other Birds

The excavation reports on Mohenjo-daro and Harappa and many other sites are filled with figurines of birds, most of which defy further identification. There is, however, one very fine representation of the Indian Parakeet (Figure 3.89). Two species of this bird, one large, the other small, are found all over South Asia (Figure 3.90). Mackay claims that a figurine from Mohenjo-daro is a representation of a pheasant (1937-38: 299, Plate LXXI, No. 3), which he was able to have confirmed by the Zoological Survey of India. There is a delightful little terracotta figurine from Harappa of a man carrying a bird in his arms that appears to be a duck (Vats 1940: Plate LXXVI, No. 14). Somewhat more certain is one of the signs of the Indus script that looks like a duck inside a circle. This occurs only once in the corpus of Indus writing and was found on a seal excavated by M. S. Vats in 1923-24 at Mohenjo-daro (Plate 3.30).

Bird figurines were popular at the larger Indus sites. Figure 3.91 illustrates several examples of terracotta figurines of birds that seem not to be identifiable by species.

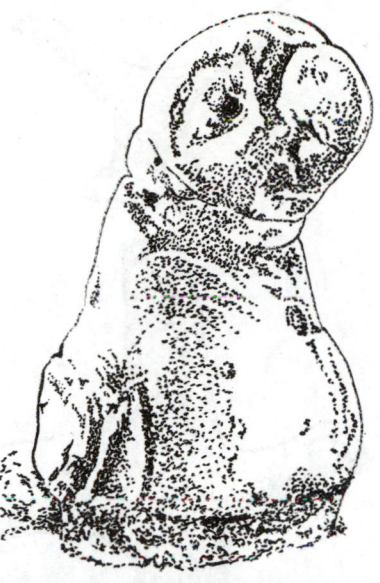

Figure 3.89. Figurine of the Indian parakeet, after Marshall 1931a: Pl. XCVI, No. 2, drawn from Anonymous 1989: Figure 316

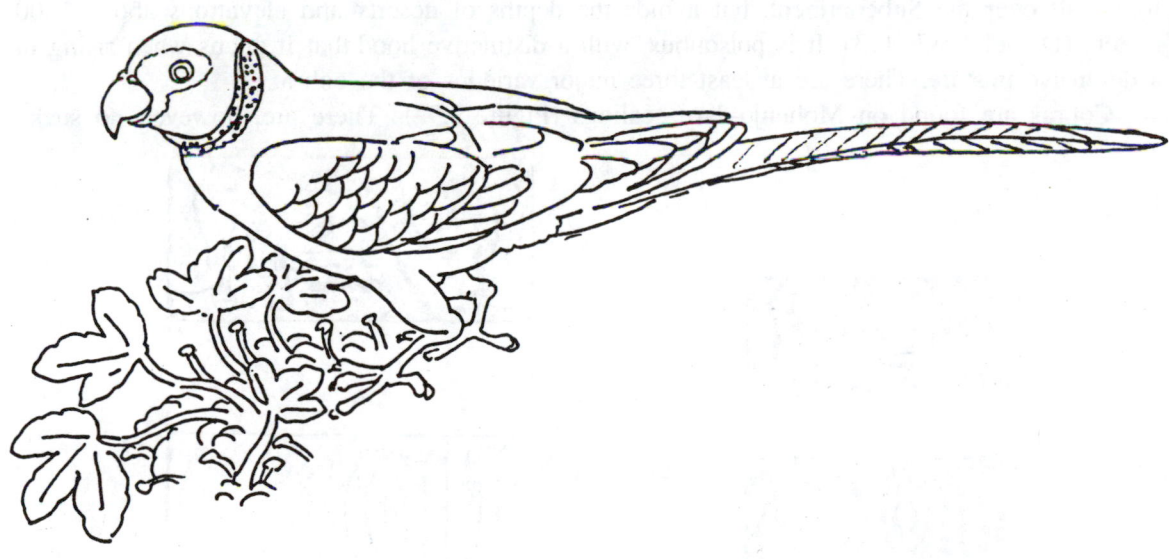

Figure 3.90. An Indian parakeet, after Hutchins 1985: 163

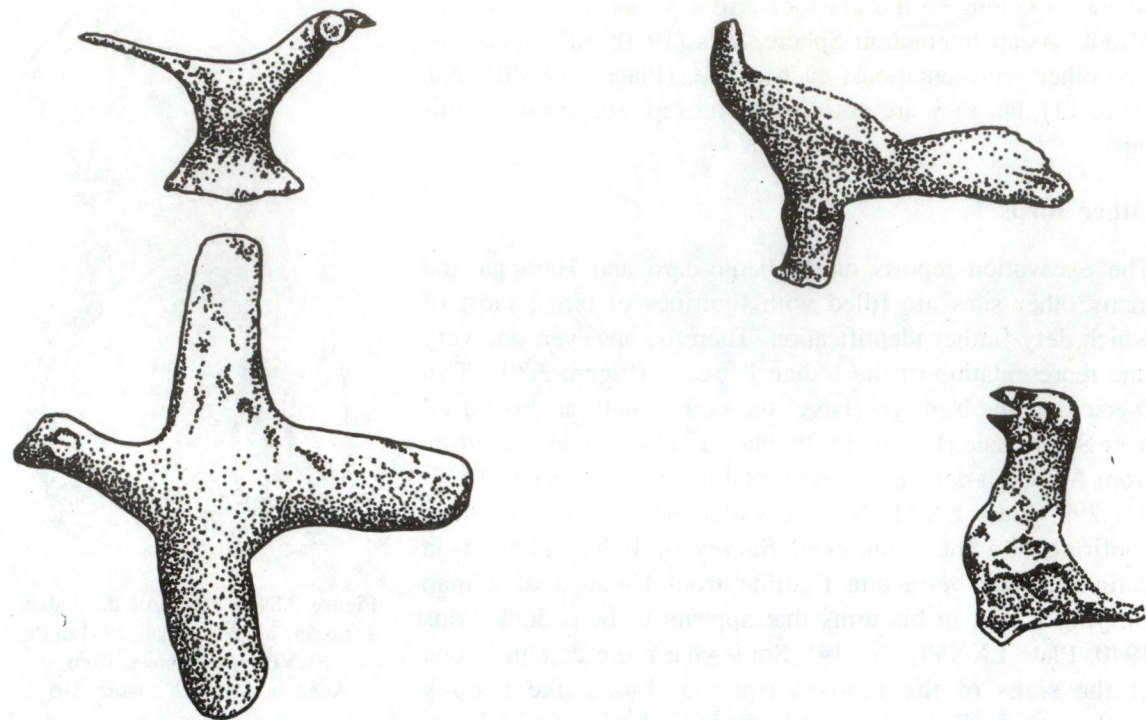

Figure 3.91. Miscellaneous bird figurines from Mohenjo-daro, after Mackay 1937-38: Plate LXXX, Nos. 21, 22, 23 & 26

The Reptiles and Amphibians

Snakes

The only snake relevant to this discussion is the well-known Indian cobra (*Naja naja*). It is found all over the Subcontinent, but avoids the depths of deserts and elevations above 1800 meters (Daniel 1983: 113). It is poisonous, with a distinctive hood that it opens when rising in a defensive posture. There are at least three major varieties of the cobra.

Cobras are found on Mohenjo-daro sealings (Figure 3.92). There are, however, no snake

Figure 3.92. Snakes on seals, after Mackay 1937-38: Plate CII, No. 9; Marshall 1931a: Plate CXVIII, No. 11

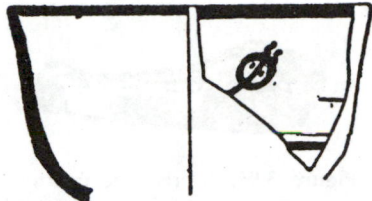

Figure 3.93. Sherd from Anjira IV with a possible snake, after de Cardi 1965: Figure 17, No. A10

figurines; the one at Harappa (Vats 1940: 73, Plate LXXVIII, No. 23) is a doubtful example. Snakes are not prominent in the pottery repertoire, but they are found in Period IV at Anjira and Siah Damb on a type of pottery called Anjira Ware. These are not painted, but raised, wavy ridges on the body of the pot that terminate in snake heads, with two eyes indicated by small holes. B. de Cardi's photographs are very convincing (1965: Plate VIII). One sherd, also of Anjira IV, may have a snake painted on it (Figure 3.93).

Snakes are a prominent part of the iconography of Central Asia during the second and third millennia. There was considerable intercourse between this area and the Greater Indus Region during much of the Indus Age. Snakes are also present on the carved soft stone vessels of the Intercultural Style (Kohl 1974, 1975, 1976) of the third millennium. In fact, the snakes on Anjira Ware may be indicative of yet more evidence for interaction between Gedrosia and Central Asia, as known from the Dashli material at Mehi and the Central Asian cemetery at Khurab (Hiebert and Lamberg-Karlovsky 1992). Considering the Mature Harappan participation in this interaction, it is somewhat surprising that the motif is not more prominent in the Greater Indus Region.

Lizards

Given the healthy populations of lizards in the Greater Indus Region it is unusual that they are not represented in the iconography of the Indus Age. The house gecko is particularly conspicuous by its absence.

Turtles

There are two soft-shelled river turtles that appear in the faunal records of the Indus Age. These are the Gangetic Soft-shell *Trionyx gangeticus* and the Indus Soft-shell *Chitra indica*. The Gangetic Soft-shell can grow to be very large, 1.5 meters in length, and is a wary sunner along the banks of rivers and *dhands*. It has a slightly smaller cousin that also inhabits the southern areas of the Greater Indus Region. *Chitra indica* is smaller, but not unlike the Gangetic turtles. Turtle flesh is eaten by tribal peoples.

Turtles do not appear on Indus seals, but there are figurines and some bones (Sewell and Guha 1931a: 662). Mackay (1937-38: 287) tells us that three representations have been found at Mohenjo-daro (Marshall 1931a: Plate XCVI, No. 15; Mackay 1937-38: Plate LXXX, No. 6 and Plate LXXVII, No. 21), with one more from Harappa (Vats 1940: Plate LXXVIII, No. 21) (Figure 3.94). There might also be a turtle on a terracotta sealing from Mohenjo-daro (Mackay 1937-38: 360: Plate CI No. 2) Mehrgarh Period VIIC has significant numbers of bones from river turtles (*Trionyx gangeticus*; Meadow 1984b: 35).

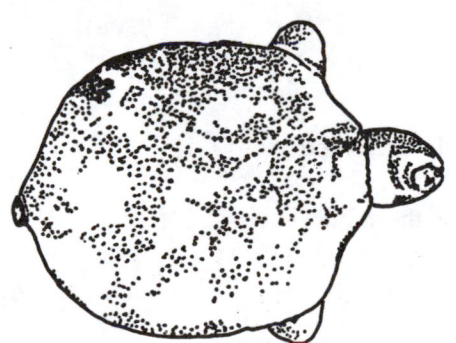

Figure 3.94. Turtle figurine from Mohenjo-daro, after Mackay 1937-38: Plate LXXVII, No. 21

Crocodiles

There are two crocodiles in the Greater Indus Region, especially the Central Region. The most striking is the *gharial* (*Gavialis gangeticus*), *sesar* in Sindhi

(Plate 3.31). It is a large fish eating beast that can grow to six meters in length. H. T. Sorley says: "...this crocodile does without any doubt feed on corpses..." (1959: 63). It has a long narrow snout, its most distinguishing characteristic. There are many representations of the *gharial*, or *ghavial*, in the art of the Mature Harappan and it would have been a very prominent and dangerous animal for the peoples of the Indus Age.

Figure 3.95. A crocodile figurine, after Marshall 1931a: Plate XCVI, No. 14

The other crocodile is the *muggar*, *Crocodilus palustris*, called *wagu* in Sindhi (Plate 3.32). It has a broad snout, and is smaller than the *ghavial*, rarely reaching four meters in length. It is a dangerous character, but shy and not easily approached. *Muggars* inhabit still and slowly moving backwaters, canals and *dhands*. They were once found all through Sindh, extending west to the Hab River, where Walter Fairservis observed them in 1959 and where H. T. Sorley shot one some years earlier (1959: 64).

Mangho Pir, or Pir Muggar, is a place where *muggars* have been kept in captivity for many decades. They live in some ignominy in a walled pool of dirty water. Sorley reports that in the mid-nineteenth century: "Kincade records that 'General Nicholson won bets by crossing Mangho Pir (tank) hopping from the back of one crocodile to another" (1959: 64).

There are a number of Indus seals with the *gavial* on them (Plate 3.33) as well as one terracotta figurine that seems to represent this beast (Figure 3.95). The *muggar* does not seem to be present.

Fishes

It is known from the faunal remains that the peoples of the Indus Age were fishermen. Aitken tells us:

> There are probably few shores to which fish resort in greater number and variety than the coast of Sind. The Indus, one of the few rivers in India which flow all the year around and one which as yet obstructed by no weirs, attracts those species, like *Palla*, which breed in fresh water...the fisher's craft has been carried on at and about Karachi from time immemorial on a scale so much in excess of local requirements that the salting of fish for export has also become a great trade (Aitken 1907: 61).

The sea fish of commercial value in the nineteenth century are discussed by Aitken (1907: 65-6). Some of the most important are:

pomfret	*Stromateus cinereus* and *S. niger*
punner	*Drepane punctata*
Several species of *Cybium* which are said to be "highly esteemed"	
palla	*Clupea ilisha*
Several species of *Polynemus*, also said to be good for the table	
mullet	*Mugil waigiensis*
sole	*Synaptura orientalis*
Bombay duck	*Harpodon nehereus*

He observes that : "*Pristipoma hasta* (Sindhi, *Dothar*) and others of the genus, *Scioena sina*, and perhaps *S. miles* (Sindhi *Sua*) salted in greater number than any other fish" (Aitken 1907: 66). The first is a grunt that has the modern scientific name of *Pomadasys hasta* and was found in great quantity in the Mature Harappan levels of Balakot (Meadow 1979a: 297).

Less esteemed but freely eaten are 'Cat fish' *Arius thalassinus* and others (Sindhi *Khago*), and Sharks (Sindhi, *Mangro*) of several species and the Sawfish (Sindhi *Mor-Mangar*). The flesh of sharks is considered to be very strengthening and they are salted for export in great numbers (Aitken 1907: 66).

"The Freshwater Fisheries of Sind are extensive and rich and have three claims on the care of the Government, first as an almost indispensable source of food for poor and rich, secondly, as a means of livelihood to a large section of the people, and thirdly, as a source of revenue" (Aitken 1907: 71). Over sixty species of fish are known in the Indus and fresh waters of Sindh. By far the one of most commercial value is the palla (*Clupea ilisha*) which is a sea fish of the same genus as the herring that ascends the Indus in great numbers in February and March so that it can spawn. It is said to be the very best fish for the table in Sindh if not all of the Subcontinent (Aitken 1907: 73). After the palla comes a carp (*Labeo rohita*) and various catfish of the *Wallago* and *Mystus* genera, the latter documented from excavations at Harappa (Belcher 1991: 114, 1993).

There is little fishing in the main branch of the Indus River. The strength of the current and the friability of the banks are unfavorable to this occupation. The backwaters, old channels, canals and *dhands* are much better (Aitken 1907: 75). Lake Manchar is a good fishing spot and the pools of the Hab River are said to have contained fish of sufficient size and quantity that they were worth the trip. The means of taking fish is highly variable, but includes hook and line, used everywhere, and nets, that are cast and staked in the water. Harpoons, spears and the hands are also used. In the Gulf of Kutch it is reported that fish are caught by trapping them in stone boxes. These are structures built in the shallows that are covered by high tides. When the tides recede some fish are left behind in the water-filled boxes where they can be easily taken by hand or net (Government of Bombay 1884: 106).

River orientation to life in Sindh is one of those more or less natural things for people living beside a stream like the Indus. Some of this comes through in Herodotus when he speaks of the peoples of India, or Sindh in his terms:

> There are many Indian nations, none speaking the same language; some of them are nomads, some are not; some dwell in river marshes and live on raw fish, which they catch from reed boats. Each boat is made of one single length between the joints of a reed. These Indians wear clothes of rushes; they mow and cut them from the river, then plait them crosswise like a mat, and put it on like a breastplate (Herodotus Book III, 98; Godley 1926).[5]

Sunder Lal Hora has a series of papers on the exploitation of fish in ancient India and Pakistan (Hora 1951a, 1951b, 1952, 1954-55 and 1956). The papers cover a wide range of times and topics, even touching on the Indus Age. Fish imagery is very much a part of the Indus Age. Period VII Mehrgarh also has fish motifs on the pottery, with fish swimming among water plants (Jarrige, Jarrige, Meadow and Quivron 1995: 185). The Kulli repertoire is especially rich, as is the earlier Nal corpus of pottery from the same region (Hora 1956) (Figure 3.96, Figure 3.97) (Plate 3.34). Chanhu-daro also has one sherd with fish painted on it. (Figure 3.98). There are small tokens from Harappa in the shape of a fish, inscribed with a few Indus characters (Figure 3.99). Some examples in ivory were found at Mohenjo-daro (Marshall 1931a: Plate CXXXII, 19, 20, 32, 40; Mackay 1937-38: Plate CXLI, No 48).

The modern notion of a barbed fish hook, with a loop to take the line seems to have been invented by the Mature Harappans (H. Sarkar 1953; Hora 1954-55, 1956). Sixteen fish hooks

226

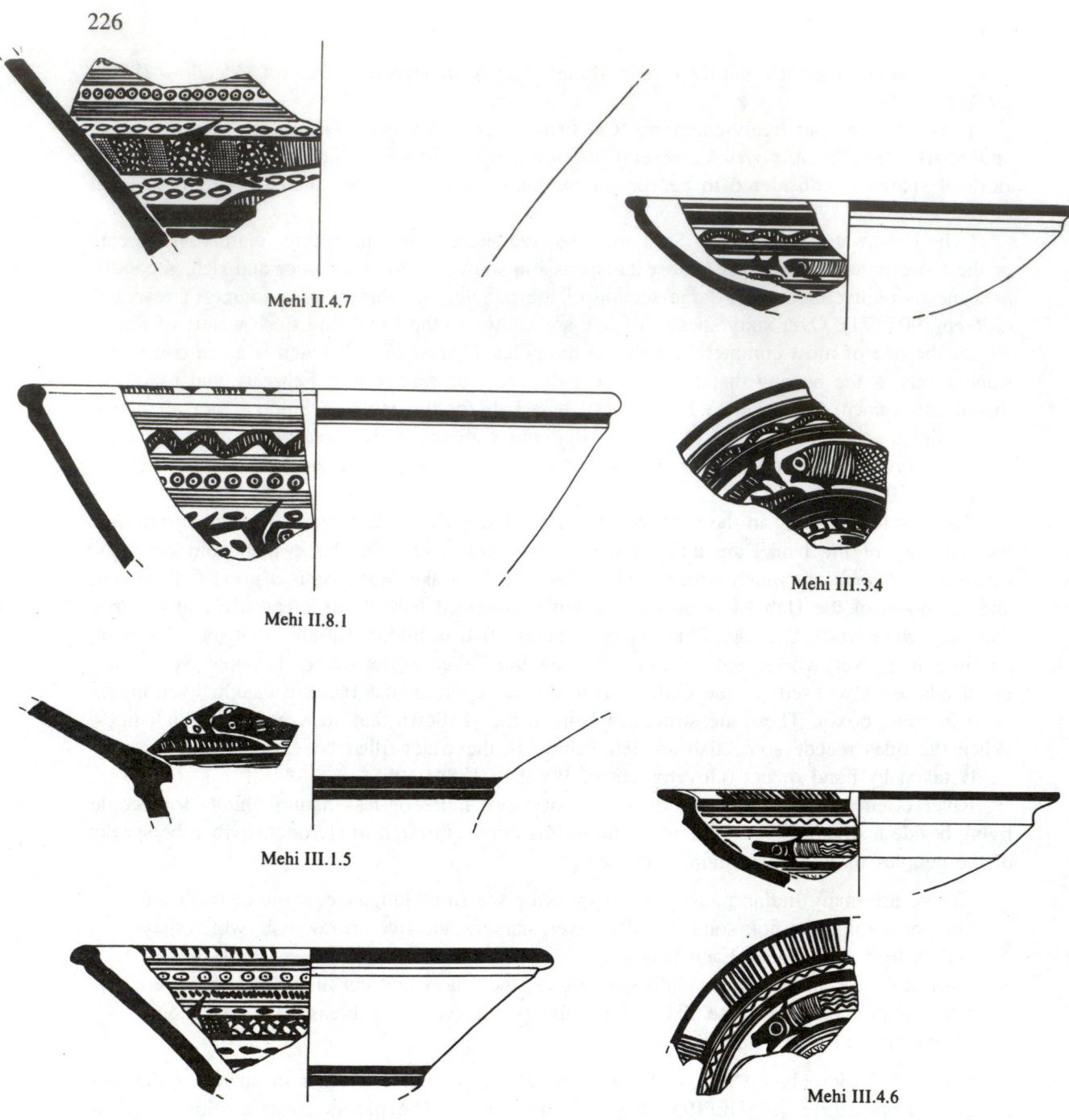

Mehi II.4.7

Mehi II.8.1

Mehi III.3.4

Mehi III.1.5

Mehi III.4.6

Mehi I.1.8

Figure 3.96. Fish designs from Mehi after Stein 1931

from Mohenjo-daro, with or without loops and or barks, were published by Marshall (1931a: Plate CXLIII, Nos. 24-5) and Mackay (1937-38: 472, Plate CV, Nos. 16, 24; Plate CXXI, No. 43). Harappa produced only one (Vats 1940: Plate CXXV, No. 8) and Chanhu-daro seven (Mackay 1943: Plate LXXIII, Nos. 5-8, 17-8). There is a very large example from the Sorath Harappan site of Padri in Saurashtra (Shinde and Thomas 1993).

S. N. Raghunath (1984) has proposed that the large brick-lined enclosure at Lothal, sometimes

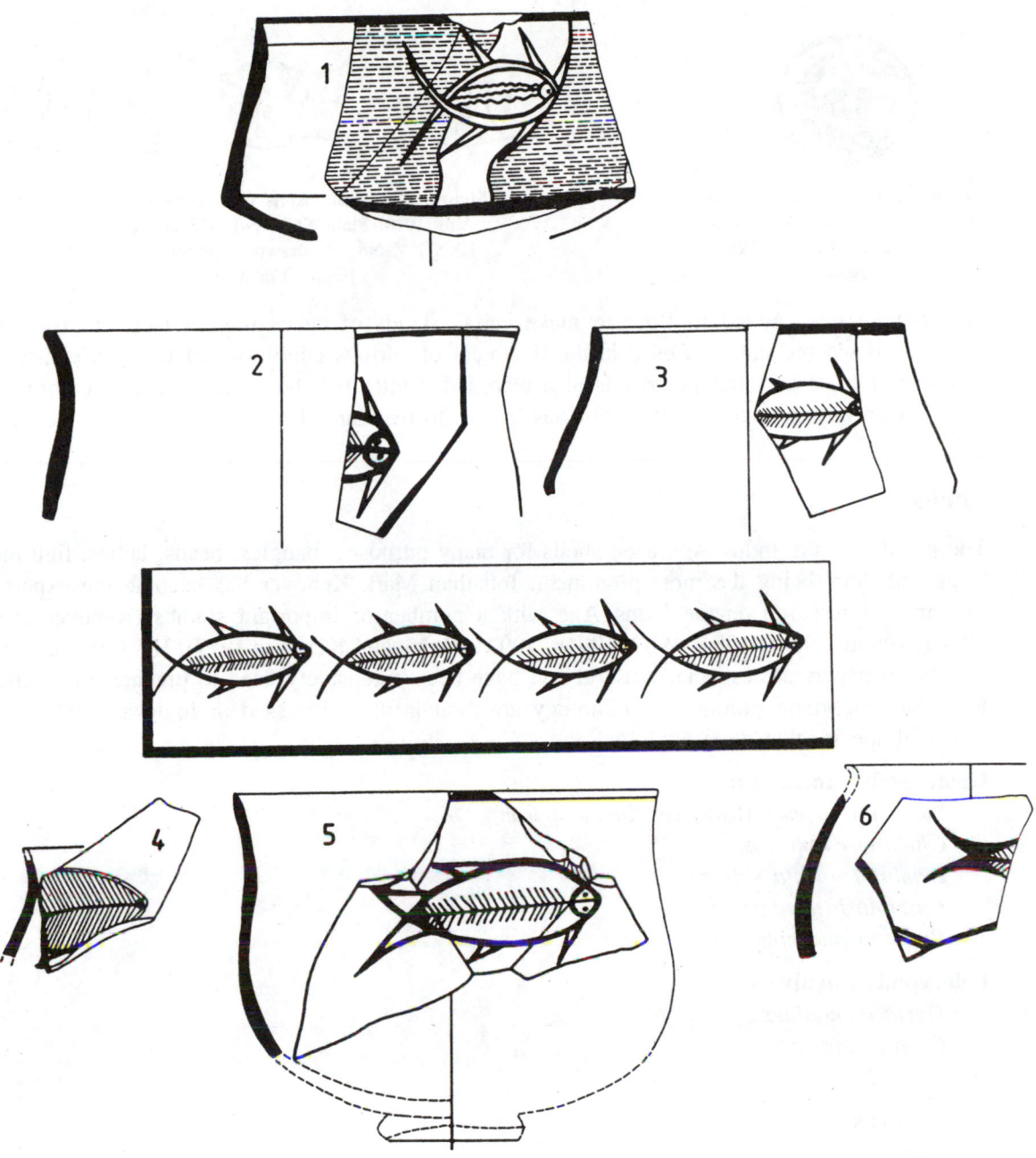

Figure 3.97. Fish on pottery from Rehman Dheri, after Durrani 1988: Figure LIV

called a dockyard, was a "fishing engine" or tank. It is another interesting suggestion for the use of this facility.

Cuttle bones, internal shells of fish of the family Cephalopoda, were found at the site of Othmanjo Buthi in Sindh by N. G. Majumdar (Prashad 1934: 155-57). These bones have many uses, as documented by ethnographic observations in South Asian villages. They are used as natural sand paper for finishing wood and polishing surfaces. They are also ground to a powder and made into a paste applied to the skin as protection against the ills of prickly heat, other skin afflictions and mumps. Cuttle bones are given to birds as food and in some parts of the

228

Figure 3.98. Fish motif on a sherd from Chanhu-daro, after Mackay 1943: Plate XXXIII, No. 4

Figure 3.99. Fish tokens from Harappa, after Vats 1940: Plate XCV, No. 428 and Plate LXXXIV, No. ab, drawn by Parpola 1985: Figure 17a & b

Punjab they were added to flour to make certain kinds of cakes more crispy. In *Ayurvedic* medicine powdered cuttle is used in the treatment of various conditions of the eye, ear, throat and skin. Its use as tooth powder is also recorded. Cuttle fish bones are a useful commodity and it is intriguing to realize that this was known to the Early Harappan peoples of the Sindh Kohistan.

Shells

The peoples of the Indus Age used shells for many purposes: bangles, beads, ladles, figurines, rings and inlay being the most prominent. Jonathan Mark Kenoyer has become the expert in this area of research on the Indus Age with a number of important studies (Kenoyer 1983, 1984a, 1984b, 1984c, 1985, 1989, 1991b, 1992a; Dales and Kenoyer 1977). His (1984a, 1984b and 1985) papers are especially useful and have been extensively used to prepare this section. Fine, but important, points in terminology are thoughtfully discussed in Joglekar (1990). The principal species that were exploited are:

Gastropods (univalves)

Turbinella pyrum (formerly *Xancus pyrum*)
Chicoreus ramosus
Lambis truncata sebae
Fasciolaria trapezium
Pugilina buchephala

Pelecypods (bivalves)

Tivela damaoides
Castilla impar
Meretrix casta

Other shells

Dentalium
Cyprae (Cowries)
These may now be discussed in this order.

Gastropods

Turbinella pyrum is a sacred shell with a special position in Hindu ritual. It is properly the "shankha" or "chank" (Figure 3.100; see Joglekar 1990 for a discussion of religious and zoological terminology). It is the most common shell at Mohenjo-daro and was widely used during the Indus Age, reaching the far north of the Greater Indus Region (Khan, Knox and Thomas 1991a: 38, 59) and Shahr-i Sokhta in Iran (Durante 1977). This shell is restricted to the waters surrounding the Subcontinent. It is not found in the Arabian Gulf. The preferred habitat is a sheltered bay, with shallow water (up to 20 meters). Today the species is concentrated around

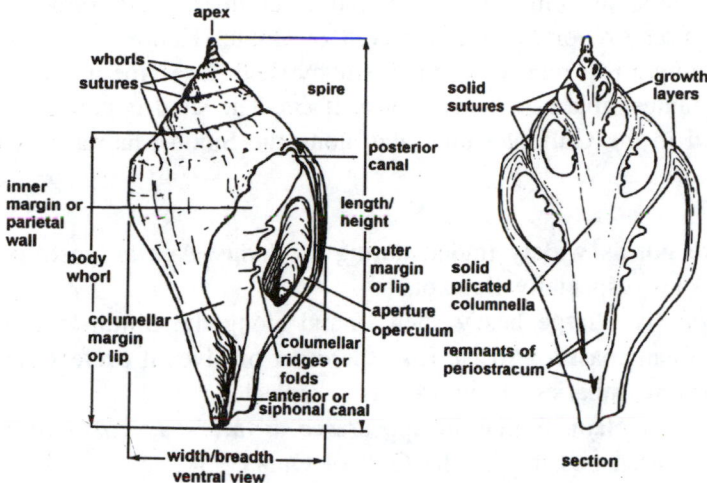

Figure 3.100. *Turbinella pyrum*, after Kenoyer 1984b: Figure 2

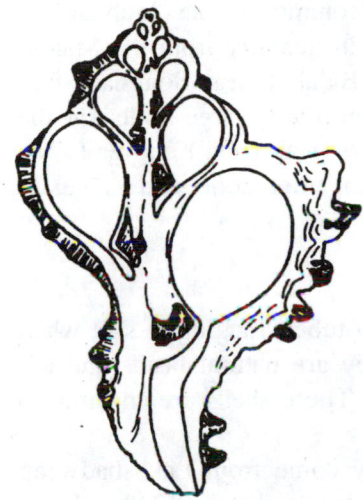

Figure 3.102. Internal structure of *Lambis truncata sebae* after Kenoyer 1984b: Figure 3

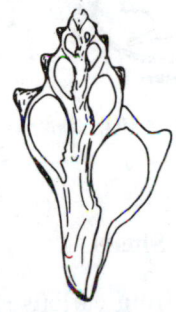

Figure 3.103. Internal structure of *Fasciolaria trapezium* after Kenoyer 1984b: Figure 3

Figure 3.101. Internal structure of *Chicoreus ramosus*, after Kenoyer 1984b: Figure 3

Sri Lanka and the Gulf of Mannar. It extends up the east coast from there, to the mouth of the Godavari River. It is not common along the western coast of peninsular India, but there are concentrations in the Gulf of Kutch and along the Makran Coast to Pasni (Kenoyer 1984b: 100).

Chicoreus ramosus (Figure 3.101) is a shell which is larger than the shank, but has a thinner body. The species has a wide distribution in the Indo-Pacific region, but colonies are found along the southern side of the Gulf of Kutch. It also occurs along the Sindh and Makran coast. One source is reported in the Gulf of Oman (Kenoyer 1984b: 100).

Lambis truncata sebae (Figure 3.102) is the largest, most massive sea shell found at Mohenjo-daro. It is found throughout the Pacific area, also occurring in bays from the Gulf of Kutch across the Sindh and Makran coasts to the Gulf of Oman and south to the Red Sea. The other sub-species of this shell, *Lambis truncata truncata* is found in South India and on the east coast of Africa, including Zanzibar (Kenoyer 1984b: 100-01).

Fasciolaria trapezium (Figure 3.103) looks like and lives like *Turbinella pyrum*. Mixed

230

colonies of the two species are known. This shell is more susceptible to burrowing animals and many of the specimens from archaeological sites are damaged in this way. The species is found in South Indian waters, the Gulf of Kutch, but is comparatively rare along the Sindh and Makran coasts. It is also reported from the Gulf of Oman (Kenoyer 1984b: 101).

Pugilina buchephala is a relatively small, stubby shell. Its shape and unconsolidated sutures make it somewhat undesirable as a source for artifacts. The shell is common to the Indo-Pacific region and is found in the Gulf of Kutch and along the Sindh-Makran coast.

Bivalves

Bivalve shells were not as widely traded during the Indus Age as gastropods, but they were worked at coastal sites, especially Balakot.

Tivela damaoides is a large heavy shell, found along the Sindh-Makran coast, extending along the Saudi Arabian coast to Africa. Like the other bivalves it prefers clean saltwater and is found along beaches at estuaries. They are easily collected.

Castilla impar is a clam similar in appearance to *Meretrix casta*. It is found along the Sindh and Makran coasts, possibly in the Gulf of Oman.

Figure 3.104. *Meretrix casta* after Dales 1979a: 268

Meretrix casta (Figure 3.104) is different from the aforementioned shells. It is a simple clam-like bivalve, a shell common to the Arabian Sea coast and recovered in quantity from the Mature Harappan levels of Balakot near Sonmiani Bay where it was used, on a very large scale, for the manufacture of bangles (Dales and Kenoyer 1977). It inhabits the lower tidal zone and is easily collected.

Other Shells

Shells from various species of the genus *Dentalium* are long hollow tubes, ranging in size when mature from about eight to sixteen centimeters. Being hollow, they are natural beads and are commonly found at sites of the Indus Age, beginning at Mehrgarh. These shells are endemic to the Gulf of Cambay.

Money cowries are not found at sites of the Indus Age. They come from Lakhshadweep and Maldive Islands, East Africa and seas farther east. Balfour tells us that in 1740 a rupee bought 2400 cowries, in 1756 the price was 2560 and that by 1870 it was 5760 cowries per rupee in Madras (1885, Vol. 1: 835). Ibn Battuta observed that the natives of the Maldive Islands used cowries for money and exported them to Bengal in exchange for rice. The price was as high as 400,000 shells per gold dinar (Gibb 1929: 243).

Pearls

Although not a shell, the pearl does come from a shellfish. This is not to suggest that we have a pearl from a site of the Indus Age, but there is an inscription for King Irdanene of Uruk with mention of "fish-eyes" from Meluhha (Falkenstein 1963: 10-11). It is widely believed that Meluhha was the Harappan Civilization and that "fish-eyes" was the Akkadian designation for pearls. Pearl oysters are known from the Gulf of Kutch extending around Saurashtra to Jamnagar and Bhavnagar. By the 19th century there was little trade due, it seems, to over exploitation, but in prehistoric times the situation would have been different (Government of Bombay 1884: 93).

MINERAL RESOURCES IN AND AROUND THE GREATER INDUS REGION

The peoples of the Indus Age had access to a wide range of exotic stones and minerals. References have been made to many of these in the discussion of the individual Regions, and Appendix D presents information in an abbreviated form. Full documentation will be found in the Appendix. There are good, general references to this section (Watt 1908; Coggin Brown and Dey 1923; N. L. Sharma and Ram 1964; Government of India 1964; Asthana 1982; Government of India 1985). Not every stone or mineral will be discussed; just a key few that are important because of their place in the archaeological record.

The most recent mineral exploration in Pakistan is covered in a publication on computer disk. It is titled "Mineral Commodity Sources for Ancient Peoples of the Lower Indus River Valley" which was compiled by G. Schmidt and R. Williams Mathews as Open File Report of 92-519, by the U. S. Geological Survey.

Metals

At least eight metals were known to people of the Indus Age: copper, tin, arsenic, gold, silver, electrum, antimony and lead. Of these only the first five will be discussed.

Copper

There was certainly no shortage of copper during the Indus Age. There is evidence for its use from the very beginning of the village farming community at Mehrgarh I (Jarrige, Jarrige, Meadow and Quivron 1995: 246). The melting, possibly smelting, of copper may begin in Mehrgarh II, with the appearance of what seems to be copper slag (Jarrige, Jarrige, Meadow and Quivron 1995: 319) but it is certainly present in Period III there (Jarrige, Jarrige, Meadow and Quivron 1995: 249) where thirteen broken crucibles were found to contain copper residues. Copper was abundant enough in Mature Harappan times for these peoples to have used it for large storage containers, frying pans and other household, utilitarian needs.

There are many sources of copper in and around the Greater Indus Region, but two of them are prominent. To the east is the so-called "Khetri Belt" which stretches from the Udaipur region of southern Rajasthan to the vicinity of Jaipur, west of Delhi (Figure 3.105). There are many mines in this area and it seems to be the best candidate for the principle source of copper during the Indus Age (Chakrabarti 1987: 66). The second source is in Baluchistan, especially Kalat and Chagai, where old slag heaps from copper smelting are present (Government of India 1908c: 48-9; Hassan 1989; Marshall 1931a: 677-78. Robat, Malik-i Shah Koh, Saindak, Ras Koh are places noted on Figure 3.105. Hughes-Buller collected "massive malachite" from the Wad Valley and Pab Hills of Jhalawan (Minchin 1907a: 162). The other occurrences of copper in the Greater Indus Region would have complemented these two primary sources.

There is a third potential source of copper in the Indus Age, but it lies outside the Greater Indus Region. It is the copper of Oman, or Magan as it was probably called in antiquity (Peake 1928; Weisgerber 1980, 1983, 1984). This topic has not been completely researched, but it is possible that Magan copper was used during the late Early Harappan and the Mature Harappan Stages.

Tin

Tin is not terribly important to the peoples of the Indus Age in and of itself. Its utility lies in its alloying properties with copper to make bronze. Adding three or four percent of tin to

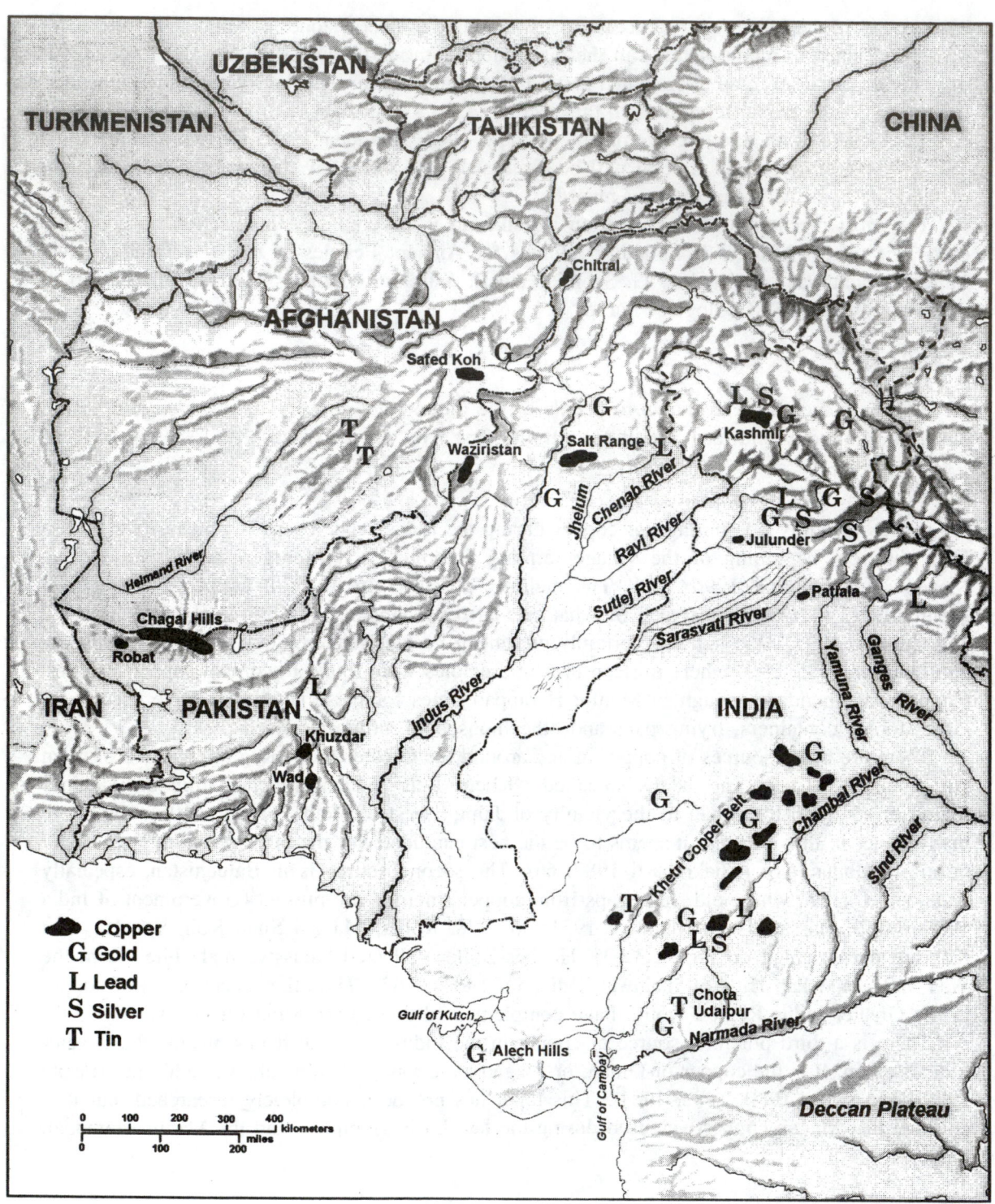

Figure 3.105. Metal resources of the Indus Age

copper produces a harder metal and one that casts better because the tin inhibits the metal's ability to take on oxygen. The base bibliography on tin and the Indus Age is: (D. P. Agrawal 1969, 1969-70, 1971, 1976, 1982c, 1982d, 1984; Dayton 1971; Muhly 1973; R. K. Sinha 1975; Berthoud et al. 1977; Salah, et al. 1977; Franklin, Olin and Wertime 1978; Hegde 1978; Chakrabarti 1979, 1987; Schuiling 1983; Stech and Pigott 1986).

There is little tin in Pakistan and northwestern India. Most of it is found in the southern Khetri Belt, with an extension south into Gujarat (Sabarkantha and Panch Mahals). Discussions on this with K. T. M. Hegde (personal communication 1989; see also Hegde 1978) led to the conclusion that there may well have been placer tin in the rivers of the western Ghats during antiquity and that this has been so completely worked out that the evidence is gone. It would have taken millions of years for those deposits to accumulate and they could have been totally exploited in a few decades.

There is no tin in Baluchistan; however, there are major reserves in central Afghanistan (Salah, et al. 1977: 165-90). Afghan tin is now seen as the most likely source for the peoples of the Indus Age. D. N. Wadia mentions the import of tin from Burma in historical times (1966: 117-18).

D. K. Chakrabarti focuses on the occurrence of tin in the Chotanagpur and Bastar and areas of eastern India (1979, 1987: 67-8). Although it is true that the metal is present there, it seems from the geographical orientation of the peoples of the Greater Indus Region that these sources are too far away, and in the wrong direction. They cannot be ruled out, by any means, but the sources in Gujarat, Rajasthan and the major one in Afghanistan have to be given priority as the most likely places for tin to have come into the Indus Age.

Arsenic

Arsenic is important to the Indus Age in the sense that it too, can be combined with copper to produce bronze. The ores of arsenic are principally realger and orpiment. *The Wealth of India* (Government of India 1985: Vol. 1 435) reports the following sources of arsenic: Kashmir (Lashteal, Barali and Zaskar); Haryana (Gurgaon District); Uttar Pradesh (mountainous districts); Rajasthan (associated with the copper mines near Khetri, at Batai and Bagor); Gujarat (Panch Mahals District). This report also mentions arsenical ores in eastern India (Bihar and West Bengal; Agrawal 1971: 150).

Arsenical bronzes occur with high frequency during the Mature Harappan and arsenic was an important mineral to the Harappan smiths (Agrawal 1971: 150-52). There is some doubt that it was ever mined separately, the alloy emerging from the arsenic which sometimes occurs naturally in copper ore. The close association of arsenic with copper in the Khetri Belt suggests that this may have been at least one of the sources of arsenic during the Indus Age.

Gold

The substantial, medieval and modern gold reserves of the Subcontinent are found in southern India, the Kolar and Hutti Gold Fields. These deposits and the allure of the metal have generated a good general bibliography on the subject: (Pascoe 1931; Munn 1934, 1936; B. K. Rao 1961; F. R. Allchin 1962, 1981; Anonymous 1963; Lahiri 1968; Chakrabarti 1987: 69; Gonda 1991; Craddock 1991; Nanda 1992; Ansari 1993).

The South Indian gold is found by deep, hard rock mining. Kolar mines average 2745 meters in depth (Nanda 1992: 3). Because of this and the distance from the Greater Indus Region, the South Indian source of gold has never had an appeal, at least as the primary one for the peoples of the Indus Age. Another reason for eschewing the far south as a source comes from Herodotus.

The India of Herodotus had a reputation for having a wealth of gold: "All this abundance of gold, whence the Indians send the aforesaid gold-dust to the king..." (Herodotus Book III, 98, Godley 1926), which followed this observation about India as part of the Achaemenid empire:

> The Indians made up the twentieth province. These are more in number than any nation known to me, and they paid a greater tribute than any other province, namely three hundred and sixty talents of gold dust (Herodotus Book III, 94, Godley 1926).

Two things are apparent from this information. First, India paid the Persian King a great deal in gold, and second, the gold was in the form of dust, not the solid product of hard rock mining. Herodotus includes his well-known thoughts on how the Indians procured this gold dust:

> Other Indians dwell near the town of Caspatyrus and the Pactyic country,[5a] northward of the rest of India; these live like the Bactrians; they are of all Indians the most warlike, and it is they who are charged with the getting of the gold; for in these parts all is desert by reason of the sand. There are found in this sandy desert ants not so big as dogs, but bigger than foxes; the Persian king has some of these, which have been caught there. These ants make their dwellings underground, digging out the sand in the same manner as do the ants in Greece, to which they are very like in shape, and the sand which they carry forth from the holes is full of gold. It is for this sand that the Indian set forth into the desert (Herodotus Book III, 102, Godley 1926).

N. E. Afghanistan. Caspatyrus (for Caspapyrus) is probably Kabul. "Pactyic country" may well be "Paktun country" the land of the Pushtus.

Herodotus describes the organization of the men and women riding into the desert, retrieving the sand. The account ends with:

> Most of the gold (say the Persians) is got this way by the Indians; there is some besides that they dig from mines in their country, but it is less abundant (Herodotus Book III, 105, Godley 1926).

This all seems to be more than a bit far fetched, but the predominance of gold dust may remain a reasonable conclusion. An examination of the sources of gold found in Appendix B will reveal that there are many sources of placer gold in Pakistan, Afghanistan and some in northwestern India. It is still panned from the Indus (Ansari 1993). That it is in somewhat short supply today might simply reflect the fact that the lode deposits were worked out by the peoples of the Indus Age and their descendants who sent so much of their wealth to the Persian Kings.

Silver

Silver in the Greater Indus Region has a spotty distribution. There is an arc of sources that begins near Udaipur and traverses through the Khetri Belt into the outer Himalaya into Kulu, Kashmir and across to Afghanistan, extending as far as Herat. The best bibliography on sources of this metal are (D. K. Chakrabarti 1987; Craddock, et al. 1989; Hassan 1989; see Falk 1991 for literary references to silver).

Silver is sometimes associated with lead and copper ores, and these co-occurences might be the source of Indus silver. It was not in wide use, if judged from the amount of silver recovered in excavation, and this low frequency of occurrence seems to match rather closely the relatively small number of ore bodies.

Afghan Metals

Afghanistan's richness in metals can be underlined by a quote on the resources around the site of Mundigak in the south-central part of this country:

> Recent geological reconnaissance in south-western Afghanistan has located substantial deposits of lead, copper, silver and gold together with iron mineralization and alluvial cassiterite (tin). This last occurrence has been confirmed by a French archaeo-metallurgical survey that has also evidenced the antiquity of mining in the whole area (Berthoud, et al. 1977) (C. Jarrige and Tosi 1981: 123).

Other Resources

The people of the Indus Age manufactured objects from a wide range of stone. The most important are carnelian, lapis lazuli, turquoise, steatite, limestone and chert.

Carnelian (chalcedony)

Properly speaking, carnelian is a manufactured, not natural, product. It is the red stone that emerges when chalcedony is heated and it almost never occurs in the natural world. The raw material, chalcedony, is a highly silicious stone, that could go by the generic title "agate." It is associated with the basalts of Gujarat and the Deccan and is still found in abundance in many of the river beds of Saurashtra. The stone tends to be large and there is little doubt that one of the sources of the stone for the long Indus beads was the rivers of Gujarat. There are also modern sources of large agates at Rajpipla on the Narmada River (Possehl 1982d).

The agate beds in the rivers of Gujarat have been worked for at least four millennia, and they still produce a commercial product. The supply of this raw material must have been much greater during the Indus Age.

Agates of much smaller sizes are found in the streams and talus slopes of the Hindu Kush (Tosi 1980; Jarrige and Tosi 1981: 137), as well as in Baluchistan, specifically the Wad Valley and Pab Hills (Minchin 1907a: 162). This is likely to be the material used at places like Mundigak, but seems to be an unlikely source for a place like Chanhu-daro, given the size of the beads from that site.

Lapis Lazuli

Lapis lazuli is a deep blue stone, easily worked and beautiful to see. It comes in many grades, from the deep blue pure stone to coarser varieties with many inclusions which generally blemish the mineral. There is a large bibliography on the trade in lapis lazuli, which describes the sources: Hermann (1968); Tosi (1970, 1974a); Sarianidi (1971); Piperno and Tosi (1973); D. K. Chakrabarti (1978); Hermann and Moorey (1980-83); Wyart, Bariand and Filippi (1981); Majidzadeh (1982); Delmas and Casanova (1990); Casanova (1992, 1994).

Lapis lazuli, or properly lazurite (occasionally "lasurite"), is a member of the sodalite group of minerals (Dana 1949: 587-90). Sodalite and lapis lazuli are chemically very similar, differing only in that sodalite has a chlorine atom which in lapis lazuli is substituted with sulfur and a variation on the amount of sodium (Pough 1976: 230-31). Both minerals have a range of color, which is available in Dana (1949: 588-89). The range for sodalite is: "gray, greenish, yellowish, white; sometimes blue, lavender-blue, light red." For lapis lazuli it is: "...rich Berlin-blue or azure-blue, violet-blue, greenish blue."

Another blue stone is lazulite discussed by Dana in the phosphate group of minerals (1949:

717-18). Its color is given as "...azure-blue, commonly as fine deep blue viewed along one axis, and a pale greenish blue along another." We learn from the same source that "The name lazulite is derived from an Arabic word, *azul*, meaning heaven, and alludes to the color of the mineral."

There were four potential sources of lapis lazuli in the Indus Age. The one most frequently cited is in Badakhshan Province of northeastern Afghanistan at the Sar-i Sangh mines (Salah, et al. 1977: 281). The area has nine lapis lazuli zones, 20 to 300 meters long and one to eight meters thick. There is also lapis lazuli in the Pamir/Lake Baikal region to the east of Badakhshan. This source is defined in Ivanov (1976). Recently, a source has been discovered in the Chagai Hills of eastern Baluchistan (Delmas and Casanova 1990). The credit for bringing it to public attention goes to Jean-Francois Jarrige, who learned of it from his Baluchi and Brahui friends (Jarrige, personal communication). The Ural Mountains of Russia are the fourth source for lapis lazuli.

It was believed for many years that all lapis lazuli in ancient India came from the Badakhshan source, but recent analysis of the lapis from Shahr-i Sokhta has shown strong evidence that three sources were utilized: Badakhshan, Pamir and Chagai Hills (Delmas and Casanova 1990: 502). The Ural Mountain source does not seem to have come into play. Analysis of lapis from Tepe Siyalk, by the same team, indicates that an additional source exists since there was little correlation between the lapis examined from there and any known mine (Delmas and Casanova 1990: 502; Casanova 1992: 53).

Further sourcing of lapis lazuli from other sites would be helpful; however, it may be that the Indus Age peoples were also drawing on these sources of this beautiful stone. The Chagai Hills source, so near the rich copper mines there, would appear to be a leading candidate in our revised thinking.

Turquoise

The distribution of turquoise in prehistoric times is reasonably well understood. Two basic references on this subject are: Tosi (1974b); Bulgarelli (1981). There is one source of turquoise in India; the Ajmer Hills of central Rajasthan (Fentress 1976: 309). Turquoise is also reported in the Chagai Hills, along with the lapis (Meadow, 1996 personal communication). There are several sources scattered through the mountains of Central Asia in the desert area known as the Casal Kum. This has been researched by archaeologists who have found evidence for exploitation of some of the mines since the third millennium BC (Bulgarelli 1981: 65; Vinogradov, Lopatin and Mamedov 1965). Northern Iran has known sources: Nishapur, Damghan and Sar-i Cheshme (Bulgarelli 1981: 67). There is also turquoise in southeastern Iran around Kirman and Yazd (Asthana 1982: 274; Pogue 1915: 40).

It is not clear which of these sources, or others, were drawn upon for the turquoise found at sites of the Indus Age. There is not a lot of it, but turquoise has been found at Mehrgarh (Jarrige and Lechevallier 1979), Rehman Dheri (Durrani, Ali and Erdosy 1991: 105) and Mohenjo-daro (Mackay 1931a: 523, 525).

Steatite and Other Soft Stones

Steatite and other soft stones in its 'family' are widely distributed in the Greater Indus Region (see Government of India 1985: Vol. 10, 32-6 for Indian sources). The principal localities that may have been used are: Gujarat (Sabarkantha District with extensive, high quality beds); Jammu & Kashmir (Riasi and Udhampur Districts); Rajasthan (many sources; commercial mines work today in Udaipur, Bhilwara and Jaipur Districts, in the Khetri Copper Belt); Uttar Pradesh (mountain districts); all from Government of India (1985: Vol. 10: 33-5). There is good steatite in

Pakistan, in the Northwest Frontier Province near Peshawar and at Abbotabad in the northwestern Punjab (Coggin-Brown and Dey 1923: 25). There is also steatite, or a related stone in northern Baluchistan, Zhob District, fifty kilometers north of Fort Sandeman (Pithawala 1952: 202).

This group of stones was widely available to the peoples of the Indus Age, who would have had a large series of choices as a source for their lapidary crafts.

Limestone and Marble

Limestone is an abundant mineral throughout South Asia. The Rohri Hills of upper Sindh, which stretch from Sukkur to Kot Diji, are composed of limestone and the great amount of this stone at Mohenjo-daro is thought to have been mined from this source. Limestone and marble occur in some abundance in Kutch, Saurashtra, throughout Rajasthan and in the Vindhyas. These minerals are also found in Baluchistan and the Salt Range.

Although pure limestone and marble are white in color, local conditions may add impurities and these minerals have a wide range of color in nature.

Alabaster and Gypsum

Alabaster and limestone are related in the sense that they are derived from lime. True alabaster is the hydrated sulfate of lime. It will not effervesce in the presence of hydrochloric acid. Hydrous sulfate of lime is a form of gypsum and this is what goes by "alabaster" today. According to Pascoe (1931: 679) it is widespread in South Asia. There are significant occurrences in the Kamard area of central Afghanistan just north of Bamiyan. Here, a fine, translucent stone occurs in beds over six meters thick. It also occurs in the Kirthar range, west of Mohenjo-daro and in Kachi. In Baluchistan it is found in the Bugti and Marri Hills, where Dabar Kot is located. Gujarat also has significant quantities of quality alabaster in Kutch, Saurashtra and Rewa Kantha. Alabaster is found in the Salt Range as well as in Rajasthan, in many localities. The mineral also occurs in the Vindhyas.

Gypsum plaster, or "plaster of Paris" is first documented at Mohenjo-daro. Alabaster was used for sculpture and manufacturing bowls and jars. Some of the objects called "alabaster" may be "marble." Like marble, alabaster in a pure state is white, but local impurities give it many different colors.

Chert

There is a large quantity of chert in the Rohri Hills of upper Sindh, near Sukkur, which is the principal source of this material in the Subcontinent. Rohri chert has a distinctive type of banding, resembling tree rings, or the layering of the flesh of some fish. It is believed that this is a good visual marker for this source. Chert is also reported in the Kirama Hills of the Punjab and from the limestones of Saurashtra and Kutch in Gujarat. An Italian archaeological team, headed by Paolo Biagi, is conducting an extensive survey of the Rohri Hills (Biagi and Cremaschi 1988, 1990, 1991) following an informative reconnaissance in the 1970s (Allchin, Goudie and Hegde 1978).

Salt

Salt, sodium chloride, is an essential part of the human diet. A substantial inland reserve of this mineral within the Greater Indus Region is in the Salt Range of the northwestern Punjab (Plate 3.35). There are millions of tons of pure rock salt in these hills which cover in excess of 7500 square kilometers. Abundant surface exposures of the rock salt makes locating the mineral and extracting it very simple. Other reserves of rock salt are found in Kohat and in southeastern

238

Sindh (Wadia 1966: 155). Vasant Shinde (1991) has suggested that his Sorath Harappan site of Padri was occupied by people who extracted salt from sea water as part of their livelihood. Marine derived salt would have been the single largest reserve of this mineral for the Indus peoples. There is also an interesting account from the nineteenth century of an indigenous Indian method of extracting salt from river sands which might be very ancient, although not documented in the archaeological record of the Indus Age (Burt 1834).

Summary

There are many other materials that were used by the peoples of the Indus Age. Only the most prominent have been focused on to provide a sense of their source localities. There is much more that could be done in this area of archaeological research in South Asia, and it would yield many interesting and important insights concerning trade and transport. It would also assist archaeologists in assessing the cost of products.

DOMESTICATED PLANTS

Wheat and Barley

Wheat and barley are still two of the principal food grains of the Greater Indus Region. The primary food grains of the Indus Age were also wheat (*Triticum* sp.) and barley (*Hordeum distichum*), both known to have been domesticated at Mehrgarh in the aceramic era in the seventh millennium BC. They are winter grasses with a wide distribution across the Iranian Plateau to the west. In the wild, they survive best in upland environments with disturbed soils; talus slopes and the like. Because they mature in the winter, under cold conditions, they are not well adapted to the summer monsoon growing season of much of the Subcontinent. In the initial period of domestication wheat seems to have been the predominant food grain. It may have been displaced by barley at some sites during the Mature Harappan. (Figure 3.106, Figure 3.107, Figure 3.108).

These two plants were primary food grains of early villages and camps, but they were accompanied by other early domesticates, such as lentils (*Lens* sp.), the pea (*Pisum* sp.), the chickpea (*Cicer* sp.), (Figure 3.109), flax (*Linum* sp.) and others. A book by Daniel D. Zohary and Maria Hopf (1988) reviews this in considerable detail, although the discussion of South Asian materials is not particularly strong. The pulses, annual legumes cultivated for their seed, are an especially interesting group of plants because they are able to fix atmospheric nitrogen in symbiosis with the

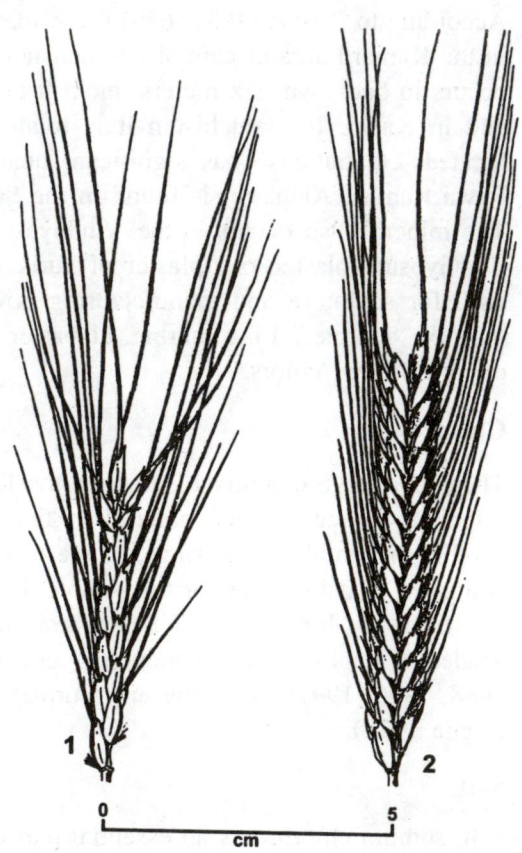

Figure 3.106. 1. Wild einkorn, *Triticum monococcum boeotieum*; 2. Cultivated einkorn, *Triticum monococcum monococcum*, after Zohary and Hopf 1988: Figure 2

Figure 3.107. Ear of club wheat, *Triticum aestivum compactum*, after Zohary and Hopf 1988: Figure 5

bacterium *Rhizobium* found on their roots (D. Zohary and Hopf 1988: 83). They add nitrogen to the soil, rather than consume it, and if these plants are rotated and mixed with the food grains, higher yields are achieved through increased soil fertility. The pulses are also good sources of plant protein, whereas the primary food grains are rich in starch. It is not surprising then that pulses, notably the lentil (*Lens culinaris*), chickpea (*Cicer arietinum*) and pea (*Pisum* sp.), are all associated with the earliest evidence for cultivation (Zohary and Hopf 1973).

Distribution of Wild Ancestors

The search for the earliest records of food production and domestication has been guided by several principles. One of the most important has been to look in those regions within which the wild ancestors of modern domesticates are found. This was most clearly articulated by Robert J. Braidwood (1975: 103-04) when he structured his excavations in the "hilly flanks" of the Fertile Crescent, the foothills of the Zagros and Anatolia, where he proposed that wild wheat and barley coexisted with wild sheep, goats, pigs and cattle. This complex, which Braidwood called "a constellation of potentially domesticable plants and animals" is found from the Taurus Mountains and the eastern shores of the Mediterranean Sea, all across the Iranian Plateau to Pakistani Baluchistan, the Northwest Frontier and Afghanistan.

Figure 3.108. 1. Ear of wild barley, *Hordeum vulgare spontaneum*; 2. Ear of cultivated two-rowed barley, *Hordeum vulgare distichum*; 3. Ear of six-rowed barley, *Hordeum vulgare polystichum*, after Zohary and Hopf 1988: Figure 14

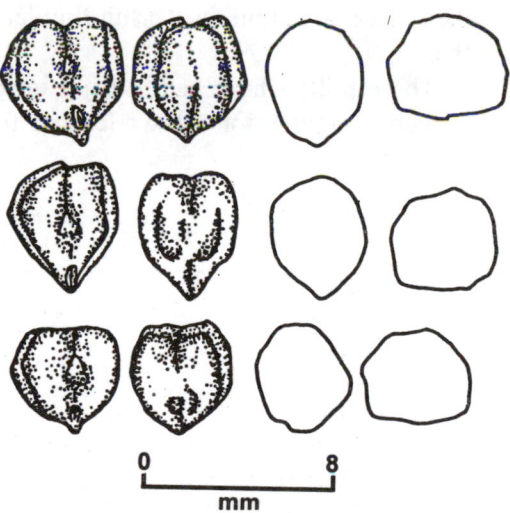

Figure 3.109. Cultivated chick pea *Cicer arietinum*, after Zohary and Hopf 1988: Figure 29

Based on modern (20th century) survey, wild wheat might not have quite as wide a distribution as barley (Vavilov 1949-50; D. Zohary and Hopf 1988: 16-52) and the palaeobotanists have yet to find evidence for it in Baluchistan or Afghanistan. Wild barley, however, is present (Harlan and Zohary 1966). But, the theory and methods to be employed in establishing the early Holocene distribution of these (and other) plants is in flux today. This is nicely reviewed in D. Zohary and Hopf (1988: 1-11, especially 6-9). One thing seems to have been settled; centers of plant diversity can no longer be equated uncritically with places of domestication, as proposed by Vavilov 1949-50 (see D. Zohary and Hopf 1988: 1; D. Zohary 1970; Harlan and deWet 1971). The most recent, comprehensive statement on the distribution of vegetation in the Near East is van Zeist and Bottema (1991), but see also M. Zohary (1973).

Wheat and barley are both represented all through the Regions of the Indus Age, from the very beginning of the village farming community. As a generalization, it is fair to say that these people were wheat and barley farmers who concentrated on the keeping of cattle. But, there are other important plants and animals that complemented these subsistence resources. The most important is a class of grasses we have come to call "millets."

Millets[5b]

African millets in Asia have been discussed in a number of sources (Krishnaswamy 1951; Mehra 1963, 1991; Allchin, B. and F. R. 1968: 266; Hutchinson 1976; Mehra and Arora 1985; Vishnu-Mittre 1974; Possehl 1986b). The term "millet" is used for grasses with large heads of spherical seeds. It is not a term related to the taxonomy of the plants involved, and "millet" has a generic quality about it. African millets are plants that mature and bear seeds in the summer, compared to the domesticated cereals of the Asian neolithic (wheat and barley) that are winter grasses. Cultivators in the Subcontinent were given an option for summer, monsoon cultivation through the introduction of African millets. This option was not available with native plants, seed plants that matured in hot weather without large seeds. The African plants, with their Hindi-Urdu names, are: sorghum or *jowar* (*Sorghum bicolor*), pearl millet or *bajra* (*Pennisetum typhoides*), and finger millet or *ragi* (*Eleusine coracana*). They brought an opportunity for real change in the subsistence regime in South Asia. At present their introduction is thought to have taken place sometime in the third millennium BC, associated with the Mature Harappan (2500-2000 BC).

These millets have had a major impact on the subsistence system of the Subcontinent. The production figures for the six leading food grains are given in Table 3.2.

TABLE 3.2
Production of Cereals in India, 1988-89
Figures in thousands of tons

Rice	70.667
Wheat	53.995
Jowar	10.518
Maize	8.332
Bajra	7.787
Ragi	2.379
All cereals	156.550
Government of India 1990: 46	

The African millets, third, fifth and sixth on the list, account for 20,684 thousand tons of grain, or just over 13 percent of the total.

Botanists interested in the history of domestication have discussed the home area for the three grasses (Harlan and Stemler 1976; Harlan, deWet and Stemler 1976; Harlan 1992) and it appears to be established that it is Africa (Jauhar 1981: 10-1; N. Krishnaswamy (1951). A recent article by Jack Harlan (1992) has two maps that are important for understanding the domestication and spread of sorghum and pearl millet (Figure 3.110, Figure 3.111).

The taxonomy of wild Pennisetum is complex with some division of opinion on classification, even at the level of the genus:

> The species of Pennisetum and Cenchrus show a more or less continuous variation with respect to several morphological features, implying some leakage of genes and introgression of characters between the two genera. In view of close similarities between the species of Pennisetum and Cenchrus, some taxonomists, e.g., Correll and Johnston (1970), do not recognize Pennisetum as a distinct genus. Most modern taxonomists, including...Bor (1960), DeLisle (1963), Clayton (1972) and Gould (1975), do treat Pennisetum as separate genera (Jauhar 1981: 5).

The origins of domesticated Pennisetum may be polyphyletic, with several related grasses playing a role. The matter is somewhat complex, without a full consensus on the part of botanists, outlined in (Jauhar 1981: 9-10).

Little is known of the domestication of these millets in Africa. There is a short review of recent literature and findings by Jouke Wigboldus (1996: 2) which indicates that sorghum was being exploited by humans in the Sudan in the fifth millennium BC but may not have been domesticated (Haaland 1987, 1995, in press; Klichowska 1984; Krzyzaniak 1978, 1991). Sorghum is also reported in the Natal in the third millennium (Davies and Gordon-Grey 1977). The finger millet reported from near Aksum, Ethiopia in the mid-fifth to third millennium may not be reliable. Overall, knowledge of the domestication of these plants, or even their use in antiquity by humans, is not very penetrating. This is a challenge to archaeologists working there, and those who attempt to develop a story of their dispersal from the homeland should be cautioned.

African Millets in the Subcontinent and Beyond

The current archaeological documentation of African millets in South Asian contexts is shown on Tables 3.3, 3.4, and 3.5.

TABLE 3.3
Early Occurrences of Sorghum or *jowar* (*Sorghum bicolor*)
in South Asia

Rohira	Early Harappan 3200-2500 BC	IAR 1983-84: 177
	Sothi-Siswal	Kajale 1991: 173
Ahar Ic	Banas Period 2000-1500 BC	Vishnu-Mittre 1969
Daimabad	Savalda Period 2000-1900 BC	Kajale 1991: 173
Hulas I	Late Harappan, 2000-1700 BC	IAR 1986-87: 132
		Saraswat 1993: 5-6
Rojdi C	Late Sorath Harappan 2000-1700 BC	Weber 1991: 128-29
Senuwar	Neolithic & Neolithic/ IA & IB Chalcolithic, ca. 2000-1200 BC	IAR 1990-91: 103
Pirak I	Bronze Age 1900-1600 BC	Costantini 1979

242

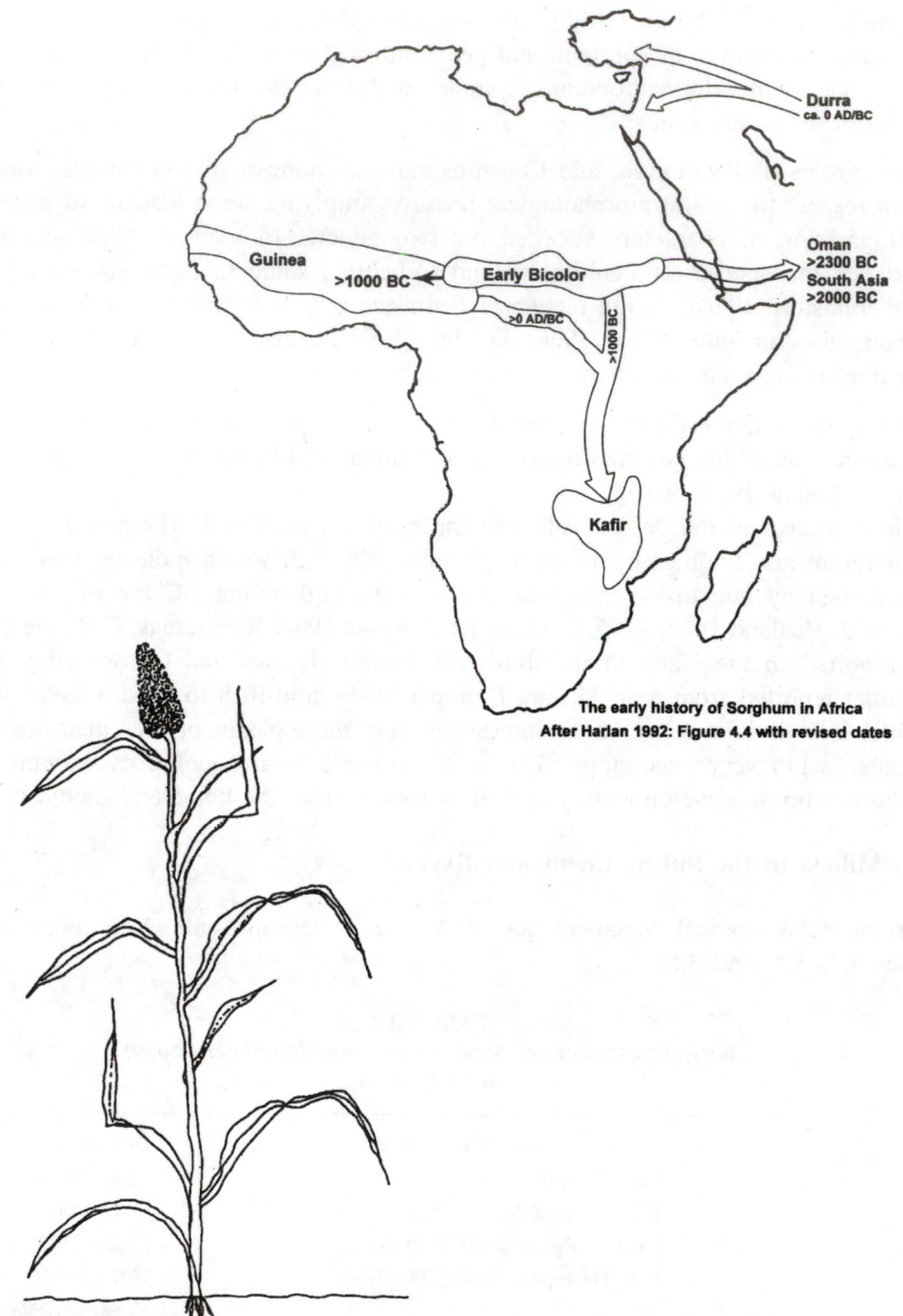

Durra
ca. 0 AD/BC

Guinea

>1000 BC

Early Bicolor

>0 AD/BC

>1000 BC

Oman
>2300 BC
South Asia
>2000 BC

Kafir

The early history of Sorghum in Africa
After Harlan 1992: Figure 4.4 with revised dates

Sorghum bicolor or **jowar**
After Reddy 1994: Figure 4-6.
Mature plants are just over two meters in height

Figure 3.110. The evolution and diffusion of sorghum, after Harlan 1992, Figure 4.4

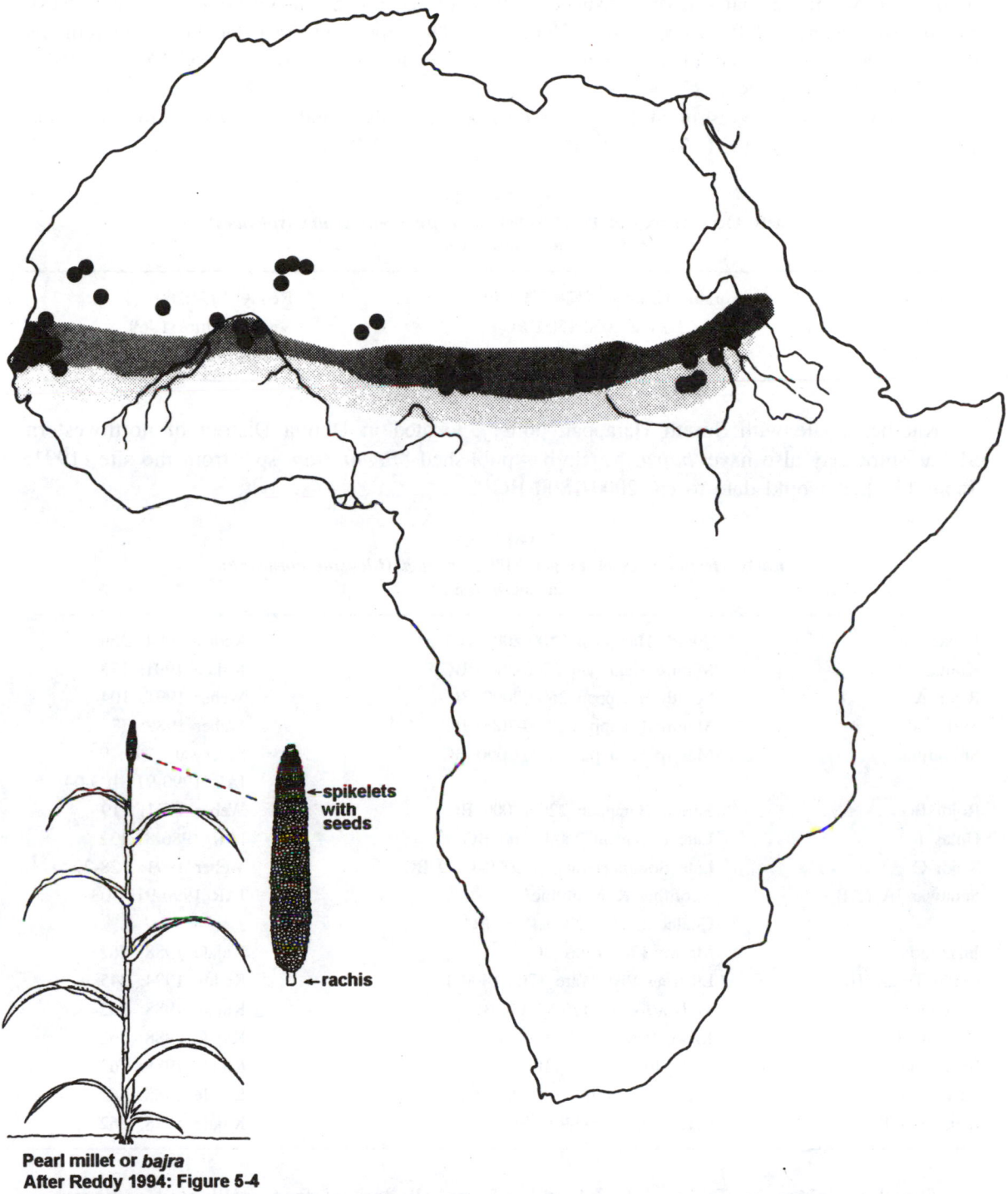

Pearl millet or *bajra*
After Reddy 1994: Figure 5-4
Mature plants are just over two meters in height

Figure 3.111. The distribution of pearl millets. Circles indicate the location of wild pearl millet, *Pennisetum violaceum*; dark shading is the northern pearl millet belt; light shading, areas in which pearl millet is grown, but in which sorghum is the dominant crop, after Harlan 1994: Figure 4.6

The sorghum from Rohira is somewhat out of place chronologically. There are three periods of occupations there that are of relevance to this discussion: Sothi-Sisawl (Early Harappan), Mature Harappan, and Bara (Post-urban Harappan). The report on the palaeobotanical remains makes it clear that the samples submitted by the excavators come from Period IA, the Sothi-Siswal occupation (IAR 1983-84: 177).

Sorghum may be present at Inamgaon during the Malwa and/or Jorwe occupations, ca. 1700-700 BC (Kajale 1991: Table 13-1).

TABLE 3.4
Early Occurrences of Pearl Millet or *bajra* **(***Pennisetum typhoides***)**
in South Asia

Babar Kot	Sorath Harappan 2500-2000 BC	Reddy 1994:269
Ahar Ic	Banas Period 2000-1500 BC	Vishnu-Mittre 1969
Rangpur III	Lustrous Red Ware 1700-1400 BC	Ghosh and Lal 1963:169

Kaothe, a site with Sorath Harappan pottery, located in Dhulia District of northwestern Maharashtra may also have *bajra*. Kajale has published "*Pennisetum* sp." from the site (1991: Table 13.1). It would date to ca. 2000-1800 BC

TABLE 3.5
Early Occurrences of Finger Millet or *ragi* **(***Eleusine coracana***)**
in South Asia

Babar Kot	Sorath Harappan 2500-2000 BC	Reddy 1994: 269
Kuntasi	Mature Harappan 2500-2000 BC	Kajale 1991: 173
Rojdi A	Sorath Harappan 2500-2000 BC	Weber 1991: 104
Surkotada	Mature Harappan 2500-2000 BC	Weber 1989: 77
Shikarpur	Mature Harappan 2500-2000 BC	Saraswat 1993: 9
		IAR 1990-91: 103-04
Rojdi B	Sorath Harappan 2200-2000 BC	Weber 1991: 119
Hulas I	Late Harappan 2000-1700 BC	IAR 1986-87:132
Rojdi C	Late Sorath Harappan 2000-1700 BC	Weber 1991: 128-29
Senuwar IA & B	Neolithic & Neolithic/	IAR 1990-91: 103
	Chalcolithic c. 2000-1200 BC	
Inamgaon I	Malwa 1700-1400 BC	Kajale 1988: 762
Oriyo Timbo II	Lustrous Red Ware 1700-1400 BC	Reddy 1994: 245
Sonegaon	Malwa/Jorwe (1700-1300 BC	Kajale 1988: 762
Daimabad	Jorwe Period 1400-1100 BC	Kajale 1988: 762
Inamgaon II	Early Jorwe 1400-1100 BC	Kajale 1988: 762
Paiyampalli	Southern Neolithic c. 1400 BC	Kajale 1988: 762
Inamgaon III	Late Jorwe 1100-900 BC	Kajale 1988: 762

The dates given in Tables 3.3, 3.4 and 3.5 are all derived from calibrated radiocarbon determinations and represent a kind of "standard" or widely recognized chronology for the Subcontinent (Possehl and Rissman 1992; Shaffer 1992).

An evaluation of the data presented in these Tables is important. There are a number of independent palaeobotanists now working in the Subcontinent. The pioneering work of Vishnu-Mittre laid the foundation, and there are now Indians, Europeans and Americans all working together, not only on the African millets, but on a broad range of palaeoethnobotanical problems. The occurrence of these millets is neither sporadic, nor thin. They occur at no less than 16 archaeological sites, in Pakistan, and Northern, Middle and Southern India. At some places they are abundant, represented by thousands of individual seeds, as with *ragi* in Rojdi A (Weber 1991: 151). The archaeological documentation of these plants in South Asia, during prehistoric times, at least as early as the mid-third millennium B.C., is strong and flourishing.

Further critical analysis of the data set also reveals that the identification of millets from Ahar is somewhat in doubt, and it should be noted that the authoritative paper by Kajale (1991) does not recognize them. This seems to be based on an observation by H. D. Sankalia made in the report on his Ahar excavations: "Looking to its stratigraphic position, viz the top layers of Phase Ic, Period I, in squares which were admittedly disturbed, it would be advisable to be cautious, and not to infer the use of *Jawar* in the prehistoric Ahar, but in the Early Historic Period c. 100 BC-AD" (Sankalia, Deo and Ansari 1969: 236). Rice and millet are found together in Phase Ic at Ahar. There is also one instance where *jowar* (and rice) occur in Phase Ib, below Ic, so the situation may not be as ambiguous as Sankalia thought (Vishnu-Mittre 1969: 234). The *bajra* from Babar Kot consists of one broken seed and needs further substantiation. The *bajra* from Rangpur was a mass of carbonized seeds, and appears secure, but "lonely" as an attestation.

African millets also occur in prehistoric contexts in the Arabian peninsula; although the occurrence of sorghum from RH5, dated to ca. 4800 B.C. (Nisbet 1985: 417) has been withdrawn. Hili 8 in Oman has sorghum. It comes from Phase IIe, which can be dated to 2330-2250 B.C. (Cleuziou and Costantini 1980). Cleuziou says that sorghum was probably cultivated around Hili. Costantini has also documented the presence of these millets in Yemen at sites dated to the second half of the third millennium B.C. (Costantini 1990).

Millets signal a new form of adaptation in the subsistence regime of the Indus Age. They significantly escalated the flexibility and adaptability of the Indus peoples, by increasing the productivity of the monsoon (*kharif*) growing season, and introduced the double cropping revolution to the ancient world. They may also inform us about long distance, inter-regional contacts.

It has been observed that agriculture began in South Africa when the winter grasses reached the region. In a discussion of hunter-gatherer/pastoral adaptations in South Africa Andrew B. Smith makes the following point:

> The Khoikhoi were unable to expand their subsistence base towards a...strategy which would have given them greater parity with the immigrating colonists. One reason for this is that they were occupying a winter rainfall zone and all African domesticated plants are summer rainfall crops, e.g. sorghum and millet. Only with the introduction of winter crops from Europe, i. e. wheat, barley and rye, did agriculture begin in the Western Cape (Smith 1984-87: 420).

This is just opposite to the situation pertaining to the Subcontinent.

Because modern farming practices can play a role in revealing things about the ancient world, those places within the Greater Indus Region where millets are grown today, especially *jowar* and *bajra*, provide important information. A series of Tables has been prepared for selected Districts within the Greater Indus Region that are presented as part of the discussion of the Regions of the Indus Age (see below). The area of wheat and barley cultivation (*rabi* crops) and that for *jowar* and *bajra* (*kharif* crops) in these Districts is given as an index for the relative potential for these cereal grains. There are great differences by region in modern cultivated areas. But, it is also clear that all four of these food grains are of significant importance for the region as a whole.

Rice

Rice (*Oryza sativa*) is the most popular food grain in the Subcontinent today. Its history is therefore of special interest to many archaeologists. Wild rice, the nomenclature used here is *Oryza rufipogon*, is pan-tropical in distribution and found generally in the Ganges Valley, the Indus River system and in Gujarat. The archaeological record in India suggests that the wild form was used by hunting and gathering peoples there. When rice came under cultivation is not yet certain, but a date preceding the Mature Harappan cannot be supported given the present evidence. The genus *Oryza* is a "plastic" one with much continuous variation, which has led to a proliferation of taxonomic terminology. Domesticated rice often grows close to stands of the wild plant, offering abundant opportunities for hybridization.

A list of the early occurrences of rice in the Subcontinent is given in Table 3.6.

The tentative identification of rice at Kalibangan has been withdrawn (Vishnu-Mittre and Savithri 1973).

The earliest abundant use of domesticated rice in the Subcontinent comes from Pirak, which begins at ca. 1800 BC. There is much rice at the site at this time, and it was apparently the staple crop. There are problems with the identification of rice and the chronology of its occurrence at the sites that are earlier than Pirak I. The qualifications for rice being present during Period I at Ahar are the same as those stated for the *jowar*, above. Some extraordinary claims for the antiquity of cultivated rice in the mid-Ganges Valley have been made (G. R. Sharma et al. 1980: 22-4). Rice at Mahagara and Koldihwa has been said to date to the 7-6th millennium BC (G. R. Sharma et al. 1980: 23). Unfortunately these claims, as they stand today, do not withstand careful scrutiny.

Mahagara is situated in the Belan Valley (G. R. Sharma et al. 1980: 133-200). The site has 2.6 meters of habitation debris, with architecture represented by floors, 4.3 to 4.6 meters in diameter, surrounded by post holes. Pottery includes the distinctive Cord Impressed Ware, Burnished Red Ware, Burnished Black Ware and a Rusticated Ware. Groundstone querns, milling stones, adzes, celts and chisels were found. A microlithic chipped stone industry utilized chert and chalcedony. Rice is reported from the Neolithic levels of the site (Sharma et al. 1980: 182) but it may not be domesticated. K. R. Alur reports sheep/goat, cattle, horse, deer and wild boar. The sheep/goat may be domesticated, but Alur feels that the cattle were domesticated with some wild individuals (Alur 1980: 220). There are four radiocarbon determinations for the Mahagara Neolithic in Table 3.7 with calibrated ranges ca. 1700-1200 BC, in line with the chronology of Pirak I; however, the domesticated status of the Mahagara rice is in doubt.

TABLE 3.6
Early Occurrences of Rice in South Asia

Neolithic

Baraunha	Eastern Neolithic	IAR 1982-83: 149
		IAR 1983-84: 177
Manigara	Eastern Neolithic	IAR 1983-84: 178
Chopani Mando	Vindhian Neolithic	G. R. Sharma et al.
		1980: 23, 69
Mahagara	Vindhian Neolithic	IAR 1981-82: 106
		IAR 1982-83: 149
Koldihwa	Vindhian Neolithic	IAR 1975-76: 80, 88
		IAR 1983-84: 178
Gufkral	Northern Neolithic	Kumar 1988: 79
Semthen	Northern Neolithic	Buth, Bisht and Gaur 1982

Mature Harappan

Lothal	Lothal A	Ramesh Rao and Lal 1985
Rangpur	Period IIA	Ghosh and Lal 1963

Post-urban Harappan

Pirak	Period I	Costantini 1979
Hulas	Late Harappan	IAR 1979-80: 114
		IAR 1982-83: 149-50
Un	Late Harappan	IAR 1979-80: 114
		IAR 1982-83: 150
Atranjikhera	OCP, Black and Red Ware	Chowdhury 1983
		Phase(?), PGW(?), NBP

Chalcolithic

Ahar	Chalcolithic	Vishnu-Mittre 1969:230
Koldihwa	Chalcolithic	IAR 1974-75: 80
Mahisdal	Late Chalcolithic	IAR 1982-83: 150
Chirand	Chalcolithic	Vishnu-Mittre 1971: 20
Navdatoli	Malwa Assemblage	Clutton-Brock, Vishnu-Mittre
		and Gulati 1961:18-9,
		43-4, 51-2
Inamgaon	Malwa-Jorwe	Kajale 1988: 735, 783
Oriup	Black and Red Ware(?)	Kumar 1988: 61
Pandu Rajar	Neolithic/Chalcolithic	Kumar 1988: 68
Dhibi		
Barudh	Black and Red Ware	Kumar 1988: 61
Baidipur	Black and Red Ware	Kumar 1988: 61
Mahisdal	Black and Red Ware	Vishnu-Mittre 1974:17
Sonpur	Chalcolithic	Vishnu-Mittre 1974:17
		IAR 1970-71: 5-6

Late Bronze Age–Early Iron Age

Pirak	Period II	Costantini 1979
Pirak	Period III	Costantini 1979
Hastinapura	PGW	Chowdhury and Ghosh
		1954-55: 120-24
Noh	Black and Red Ware Assemblage	Vishnu-Mittre 1974:17
	PGW	Vishnu-Mittre and
		Savithri 1974
Hallur	Southern Neolithic	Vishnu-Mittre 1971
		Megalithic Overlap 125-32

Later Occurrences

Narhan	Pre-NBP (700-600 B.C.)	IAR 1984-85: 162
Narhan	NBP (500-400 B.C.)	IAR 1984-85: 162
Narhan	Early Historic (1-2nd C. AD)	IAR 1984-85: 163
Sringaverapura Period I,	1050-1000 BC	IAR 1982-83: 149
		IAR 1983-84: 178
Sringaverapura Period II,	950-700 BC	IAR 1982-83: 149
		IAR 1984-85: 161

TABLE 3.7
Radiocarbon Dates for Rice in the Vindhian Region

Mahagara

BS-128	1Σ cal BC 1737 (1613) 1511
	2Σ cal BC 1879 (1613) 1404
PRL-407	1Σ cal BC 1683 (1527) 1442
	2Σ cal BC 1869 (1527) 1328
PRL-409	1Σ cal BC 1731 (1518) 1396
	2Σ cal BC 1888 (1518) 1134
PRL-408	1Σ cal BC 1527 (1436) 1320
	2Σ cal BC 1731 (1436) 1138

Koldihwa

PRL-224	1Σ cal BC 7505 (7303) 7033
	2Σ cal BC 7698 (7303) 6614
PRL-100	1Σ cal BC 6190 (5991) 5764
	2Σ cal BC 6454 (5991) 5591
PRL-101	1Σ cal BC 5432 (5256) 5051
	2Σ cal BC 5573 (5256) 4807
PRL-223	1Σ cal BC 1734 (1527) 1429
	2Σ cal BC 1882 (1527) 1312

Another site is Koldihwa ca. 85 kilometers southeast of Allahabad on the Belan River, opposite Mahagara. The site has three periods: Iron Age, Chalcolithic and Neolithic (Sharma et al. 1980). There is little evidence for architecture at Koldihwa; some burnt clay lumps with impressions of "screens" or mats being the most suggestive. There is Cord Impressed and associated wares of the Vindhian Neolithic, as well as ground stone celts, a Neolithic blade industry and microliths (Sharma et al. 1980: 135). Remains of rice in pottery have been identified by Vishnu-Mittre and Te-Tzu Chang as domesticated (Sharma et al. 1980: 135-36).

The general similarity of the artifacts suggests that the rice from Koldihwa should be dated to the Vindhian Neolithic of the second millennium BC. The earlier dates from Koldihwa (PRL-100, PRL-101 and PRL-224) could aberrations; but it is more likely that they are indications of an earlier, unreported occupation at the site.[5c]

Similarities in material culture, especially the ceramics, further suggest a close temporal and cultural relationship between Koldihwa and Mahagara. There are other sites in this region with similar artifacts (e.g., Kunjhun II, Kunjhun River Face, Lekhahia I) which seem to fit together as a recurring set of features which date to the second millennium BC. This material has been summarized in Possehl and Rissman (1992: 473-75).

Rice in the Mature Harappan

There are two sites of the second half of the third millennium where rice has been reported: Lothal and Rangpur. The single occurrence at Lothal is reported by Ramesh Rao and Krishna Lal (1985: 679, 682-83). This unnumbered sample of impressions on clay with fragments of husk and leaf comes from Phase II of Lothal A (c. 2350-2200 BC). Some of the husks were identified as *Oryza* sp. There is wild rice in the Lothal area so there is no guarantee that this was the domesticated form.

The rice from Rangpur (Ghosh and Krishna Lal 1963: 171-72) comes from Period IIA Sorath Harappan (c. 2500-2200 BC). This single sample consisting of husks was also identified as simply *Oryza* sp. The authors of the report believe that "From the nature of their use, it appears the husks were mixed with the mud as a binding-material for the purpose of plastering" (Ghosh and Krishna Lal 1963: 172). Given the geographic proximity of Lothal and Rangpur these impressions could be derived from the wild variety.

Naomi Miller has suggested that many of the palaeobotanical samples that we find in the archaeological record are derived from the use of dung cakes as fuel. The burning of the dung cake resulting in the carbonization of the seeds that the animal(s) ate. This is a very attractive idea, and worth reading (Miller 1984; Miller and Smart 1984). If we were to apply Miller's hypothesis to the rice remains from Lothal and Rangpur we could conclude that the seeds were found as a result of Mature Harappan animals (probably cattle and water buffalo) grazing in fields of wild rice and other grasses. The dung from these animals was used as fuel and the carbonized husks made their way into the archaeological samples via some set of taphonomic moves through the trash cycle of the inhabitants of the two sites.

The present state of our knowledge does not present a strong case that rice was used as a domesticated food grain during the Mature Harappan. On the other hand, by the early second millennium the data set in hand can be used to document its use as a food grain. At Pirak, L. Costantini has observed that:

> Rice is the only alimentary plant that is present in all four sectors where soil samples were taken containing burnt grains, impressions and fragments of unburnt husks. In Sector 3G(14) a considerable layer of archaeological deposit was revealed that was absolutely full of rice impressions. It is very compact soil consisting of small clayey layers alternating with thin, tightly packed layers of rice straw (Costantini 1979: 329).

Later occurrences of rice are numerous, as is the record for cotton.

Cotton

Gossypium herbaceum is thought by some to be the wild ancestor to Old World cottons. It is endemic to South Africa (Phillips 1976: 196), although this as a place of origin for all Old World cottons is contested (Santhanam and Hutchinson 1974: 90). The domesticated form is called *Gossypium arboreum*. There are weedy, "feral" varieties of *G. arboreum* in the fields of India and Pakistan. These have a range of variation but it cannot be shown that they are truly the wild progenitors of the *deshi* cotton of the region today. There is a wild species of cotton in Pakistan called *G. stocksii* which yields short, useful fibers. G. Willcox has suggested that this could have been the cotton used during the Indus Age (1992: 293). Sindh and Gujarat, especially Saurashtra, have deep traditions as cotton growing areas (Hutchinson 1976: 136). Santhanam and Hutchinson (1974) suggest that cotton was first brought under cultivation in this area.

Cotton is not a product mentioned in the Ṛgveda, leading one scholar to believe that this proves that this text predates the Indus Civilization (Sethna 1981). There are many references to cotton from the middle of the first millennium onwards in Indian literature (Gopal 1961; Ayyar and Aithal 1964).

There is a long history to the belief that ancient India was the home of cotton, as indicated by the fact that the usual word for this material in west Asian languages is "Sindhu" or some variation of it. The earliest textual reference in the Near east is Sennacherib's (705-681 BC) mention of "trees bearing wool" that were "sheared" and the "wool" woven into garments. This reference comes in regard to the King's description of gardening around his palace at Nineveh (King 1909; Meissner 1910: 491; Luckenbill 1924: 111, 116; Oppenheim 1964: 94). P. Talon

250

has suggested that this cotton was not widely cultivated, given the cold winters of Assyria and was essentially a "hot house plant" kept for the amusement of royalty (1986: 77). There are two references to cotton in Herodotus. The first is "There too there grows on wild trees wool more beautiful and excellent than the wool of sheep; these trees supply the Indians with clothing" (Book III, 106, Godley 1926). The second reference is to Indian troops in Xerxes' army wearing "garments of tree-wool" (Book VII, 65, Godley 1926). Later references are included in the "Periplus of the Erythraean Sea." In the chapter dealing with the Gulf of Cambay and Broach the author-navigator tells us:

> Beyond the gulf of Baraca is that of Barygaza and the coast of the country of Ariaca, which is the beginning of the Kingdom of Nambanus and of all India. That part of it lying inland and adjoining Scythia is called Abiria, but the coast is called Syrastrene. It is a fertile country, yielding wheat and rice and sesame oil and clarified butter, cotton and the Indian cloths made therefrom, of the coarser sorts. Very many cattle are pastured there, and the men are of great stature and black in color. The metropolis of this country is Minnagara, from which much cotton cloth is brought down to Barygaza (Schoff 1912: 39).[5d]

Thus the history of cotton in the Subcontinent is very deep, with strong lines of continuity. A recent excavation in the Near East may have, however, thrown some new light on this place of primacy.

Excavations at Dhuweila in eastern Jordan have produced evidence for cotton that has radiocarbon dates indicating an calibrated age of 4450-3000 BC (Betts 1988; Betts, et al. 1994). Since the dates were taken on the fabric of the cotton itself the problem of association does not apply to this case.

In the end, there is not nearly enough known about the wild ancestors of cotton to be confident that we know where wild cotton was growing at the opening of the Holocene and the early millennia of this era. It should also be assumed that further excavation with a problem orientation aimed at documenting the palaeobotanical resources of ancient peoples of Asia and Africa will throw more light on the human use of this important genus of plants.

Cotton was identified at Mohenjo-daro during the early campaigns there. The first was part of a bag(s) or wrapper(s) in which two silver vessels were found as part of a large hoard in HR-Area, House VII, Room 8 (Sahni 1931a: 194, Plate CXL, Nos. 2 & 3; Mackay 1931e: 585-86). Ernest J. H. Mackay found more of the material, also preserved in the corrosion salts of metals: (Table 3.8)

TABLE 3.8
Some Occurrences of Cotton at Mohenjo-daro

remains of a bag (noted above)	Sahni 1931a:194
cord wound around a copper blade	Mackay 1937-38:441, DK 8376
fabric adhering to a razor	Mackay 1937-38:441, Plates CXVIII No. 7 and CXXV, No. 41
a fine cord wrapped around a copper rod	Mackay 1937-38:441 DK 5844

The technicalities of their identification are given in (Gulati and Turner 1928, 1929; Turner and Gulati 1929a, 1929b).

Cotton has also been suggested to be present at Balakot on the basis of Gossypium-type pollen (McKean 1983: 230-32, 245-47). The sample with the Gossypium-type grains comes from Layer 4, which would make it rather late in the Mature Harappan. McKean argues as effectively as she can that this pollen resulted from cultivated cotton.

Lorenzo Costantini has observed that cotton was used at Mehrgarh during Period II. Several hundred charred seeds were associated with a fireplace in one of the compartmented buildings there (Jarrige, Jarrige, Meadow and Quivron 1995: 248). This was a provisional identification, included in the preliminary report for the 1978-79 field season, and the work on these seeds needs further study.

A single carbonized cotton seed was also found at Hulas, in the "Late Harappan" or Post-urban Stage there (IAR 1986-87: 132).

The *deshi* or traditional method of cotton cultivation in Sindh is known as *belai* (Sorley 1968: 413; McKean 1983: 246-47). Under this simple system the plant is grown as a *kharif* crop, planted in summer following the inundations of the Indus and picked in November. Sorley also describes a second, more intensive system of *kharif* cultivation for cotton on the Indus plains (1968: 412), as well as a *rabi* (winter) method. None of these three methods has technological bars that would have prevented its use during the second half of the third millennium.

Sesame

Sesame (*Sesamum indicum*) is a plant indigenous to the Greater Indus Region. An early identification of sesame seeds comes from Harappa, where a lump of sesame seeds was found at the eastern end of Trench V on Mound F, at the northern end of the site, where the "Granary" is located. Vats places it 1.8 meters (six feet) below the surface in Stratum 2, or the Mature Harappan (1940: 467). The identification of the lump of seeds was made by staff of the Punjab Agricultural College, Lyallpur. This sample is apparently no longer available for study (Vishnu-Mittre and Savithri 1982: 206). Contrary to G. Willcox (1992: 293), other finds of sesame have been made in the Subcontinent, prior to the time of writing his paper. There are five sites, counting Harappa: (Table 3.9)

TABLE 3.9
Early Occurrences of Sesame in South Asia

Harappa	Mature Harappan	Vats 1940: 467
Lothal	Mature Harappan	Ramesh Rao and Lal 1985: 678-79, 683
Senuwar	Chalcolithic	IAR 1990-91: 103 c. 1200-600 BC
Narhan	Northern Black Polished Ware, mid-second millennium	IAR 1984-85: 162
Sringaverapura	Painted Grey Ware, early second millennium	IAR 1982-83: 149 IAR 1983-84: 178

The sample from Lothal is published with a (?), but Ramesh Rao and Lal do note in the summary: "The clay impressions have yielded *Oryza* sp. and an undetermined monocot, while the seeds are probably of a millet and *Sesamum indicum*" (1985: 683).

Sesame is *til* in most of the modern languages of the Greater Indus Region. This word is

252

also the generic term for "edible oil" demonstrating sesame's place of primacy in this sector of South Asian culture. It is an essential ingredient in Hindu ceremonial life as well as cooking. The plant is intolerant of frost, drought and prolonged heavy rain. It does well in the sandy alluvium of Rajasthan, clayey soils and the black cotton soils of Gujarat and Central India. Today it is often generally a *kharif* crop and inter-cultivated with *jowar*, *bajra* and cotton as a hedge against total loss (Vishnu-Mittre and Savithri 1982: 216).

India is the world's leading producer of sesame today, with heavy production in Rajasthan (Kalibangan, etc.), Uttar Pradesh (Hulas and other sites in Saharanpur District) and Gujarat (Lothal, etc.) (Anonymous 1992: 940-41). It was a staple in Sindh and exported in some quantity in the nineteenth century (Aitken 1907: 380). The crop was a part of the agricultural economy of Sahiwal District at the end of the nineteenth century (formerly Montgomery) where Harappa is located (Government of India 1884g: 103).

Dates

Dates (*Phoenix dactylifera*) were known to the early cultivators of the Greater Indus Region. The fruit is a dietary staple in the Makran, that part of the Greater Indus Region where it is most extensively grown today and in recent times.

Two date seeds come from Mehrgarh, Periods I and II, one of them in association with the cotton that may be there (Costantini 1984: 32). Date seeds occur in Early Harappan context at Rohira (IAR 1983-84: 177). Seeds were also found in VS Area of Mohenjo-daro (Mackay 1931e: 587). No seeds were found at Harappa but there are two faience sealings from Mound F that are said to be in the shape of date seeds (Vats 1940: 467 and Plate LXXXIV, ap). The later attestation from Sringaverapura is in the form of date palm leaf impressions. These occurrences are summarized in Table 3.10.

TABLE 3.10
Early Occurrences of Dates in South Asia

Mehrgarh	Periods I & II	Costantini 1984: 32
Rohira	Period IA	IAR 1983-84: 177
	Sothi-Siswal	
Harappa	Mature Harappan	Vats 1940: 467
Mohenjo-daro	Mature Harappan	Mackay 1931e: 587
Sringaverapura	Period II	IAR 1982-83: 149
	950-700 BC	IAR 1984-85: 161

The date palm is an important plant today, and in historic times in the Greater Indus region. The leaves are a useful fiber, and are woven into mats. The wood, not structurally very solid, is used for light duty objects. The date fruit is an important source of food, for urban and rural peoples alike. While it seems that the people of the Indus Age knew the date, they do not appear to have made extensive use of it, at least as the present data admit.

THE SEASONS AND SEASONALITY

The climate of the entire Greater Indus Region has two pronounced seasons: hot and cool. These correspond in a general way to the summer and winter seasons of North America and Europe. Each season has its own pattern of rainfall and other characteristics that are important to agriculture, animal husbandry and the pace of life (see Spate and Learmouth 1967:46-72 for a general description). There are some things that characterize the Greater Indus Region with the advent of electricity, improvements like motorized *punkas* (fans) and home air conditioners.

The Greater Indus Region Hot Season

There is nothing as legendary as the heat of the Subcontinent. It can be truly oppressive in some places; Mohenjo-daro is one of them. The heat begins in the Greater Indus Region in March and April, with bright sunny skies. It peaks in May and June by the end of which some clouds may begin to form, partially blocking the sun, which brings down the temperature.

The complex problem of climatic change in the Greater Indus Region is found in detail elsewhere (see below). There is no evidence that the rainfall and temperature regimes were significantly different during the Indus Age from today.

In March and April, the early hot weather, there is a *rabi* crop of wheat and barley to be harvested, processed and stored. Then the fields have to be prepared for the rains, which will come in July. Daytime temperatures in March and April are typically in the 100-110°F (38-43°C) range; tolerable but hardly a comfortable working environment. The nights are cool (60-65°F; 16-18.5°C) and the humidity rather low (ca. 40-50% at 8 AM and 20-30% 4 PM) (Spate and Learmouth 1967: 52). But temperatures are on the rise, beginning as early as February, and by the end of April they generally pass a point where even sedentary activities are uncomfortable. Concentration is difficult, nerves are easily frayed and as a consequence intensive work is not a realistic undertaking. The temperatures are on the average elevated, commonly reaching 140°F (60°C), with a corresponding rise in humidity. This is a period of hot day time winds; so hot that the evaporation of perspiration does not feel cool. Indoor rooms are stifling, building walls and roofs are hot to the touch, tools and pots left in the open quickly become too hot to use. It is also a period of dust, and the sky over the Greater Indus Region in May and June takes on a brassy color, with kites and vultures riding the thermals of rising air, seeking to go high enough to find comfort.

Two changes in work habits are quite apparent. First, the mid-day hours are times of peace and quiet, as most people seek refuge from the sun, on cool porches, verandahs and under broad leaf trees like the banyan. There is also an increase in night time and early morning activity, when it is cooler. Virtually everyone sleeps out of doors; on roofs, verandas, at road sides. Since misery loves company, the late evening hours, between 10 PM and midnight, are times of socializing, commiserating, joking, laughing; nothing too strenuous, and the best part of pretty weather days. These and other points are made in an amusing little book on the climate of Karachi "and how to live in it" (Pithawala and Shamshad 1953).

I have been at Mohenjo-daro in July, with little monsoon cloud cover, and the days were truly oppressive. Keeping track of the temperature would probably have been worse than just getting through the day, so I chose not to know how hot it really was. The staff of the guest house there put beds with mosquito nets on the roof for the nights, which served to get me out of a room, but I, my bed, clothes and the mattress were soon soaked in perspiration and I found it better simply to go to the parapet surrounding the roof and try to take advantage of the occasional wisp of air that passed by.

The following couplet captures the Sindhi hot weather scene very nicely:

When both Sehwan and Sibi grill so well
What good was there, O Lord, in making hell
(Kincaid 1925: 1)

The pre-monsoon months can also be periods of cyclonic violence. Temperature and moisture gradients can develop storms, large and small. Dust devils are a common sight, and may reach proportions that can move furniture and create mini dust storms that only serve to aggravate already frayed nerves. Some of these disturbances are very powerful, far exceeding the notion of a little "dust devil." They also appear suddenly, out of nowhere. Spate and Learmouth (1967: 53) have a description of these *andhis*. They are on a kind of weather continuum with the smaller storms, but in Bengal, can reach the upper atmosphere at 15.25 kilometers (50,000 ft.). The *andhis* are generally short in duration but they are violent, with winds that can bring down trees and damage houses and bring heavy rain. There are lightning strikes and loud claps of thunder. Since the storms generally do not cover broad areas, the flash-boom sequence is instantaneous, even overlapping, which can be quite unnerving; like a kind of battlefield scene.

There one sits on a hot, early June day, and all of a sudden becomes engulfed in a cyclone of high winds and violent rain, with furniture and the daily wash swirling round in the air, lightning strikes everywhere (flash-boom, flash-boom) and then a tree on its way down. Even if the falling tree really came down from the wind, the power and force of the lightning-thunder sequences makes it seem as if it was the atmospheric artillery that did the damage. It is disconcerting, and given the general humor of those who have to live through it, not at all amusing. The rain, of course, is too local to be significant in terms of agriculture, and although it may provide an hour, or even a day of relief from the heat, it is basically not helpful.

Greater Indus Region Hot Season Rains: the southwest monsoon

July sees the beginning of the southwest monsoon in the Greater Indus Region.[6] It starts with rains in South India a month earlier, by early or mid-July reaches as far north as Gujarat, and a week or two later works its way farther north to the Punjab. First there are clouds that bring relief from the depths of the heat, then there is rain. Ancient India's most accomplished poet, Kalidasa (ca. 400 AD), expressed it this way:

The day is miserably hot,
the night is worn and thin:
separated, with contradictory motion
like man and wife at odds.

The birds loosen their shoulder feathers with darting beaks,
dispel their body heat by lowering ruffled wings;
with crouching legs seize upon the nest,
barely avoiding a sudden toss
from the buffet of the summer gale.

Above the fledgling of the wild goose,
although he rests in coolness of a flowering water-lotus,
the loving mother bird will hold her wings,
a handsome white umbrella.
The little parrot, parched with thirst,
resting on a fair maiden's bosom,
will sip at the necklace of pearls which grace her breasts
in hope that they are water.
(From Ingalls 1968: 96-7)

The term "monsoon" seems to have been taken from the Arabic *mausim* for season. It refers to winds that blow from the southwest, across the Indian ocean, gathering moisture which falls as rain when it encounters the South Asian subcontinent. These ocean winds have been used by sailors to cross the Indian Ocean from Africa to India in the summer for 5000 years. The monsoon strikes the South Asian landmass at an angle and the Indus River Valley is just on the western edge of its effect. Monsoon rain there and in Baluchistan is weak and very unreliable. In fact Mohenjo-daro receives, on average, only about 10 centimeters of rain per year and the area would be a desert if it were not for the life-giving floods of the river. Gujarat is positioned to take some advantage of monsoon precipitation, and dry cropping is possible there, as it is in the eastern (Indian) side of the Punjab, and the modern states of Haryana and Uttar Pradesh (see Fein and Stephens 1987).

The monsoon winds are gentle and typical monsoon rainfall is not accompanied by wind. The predominant image of the monsoon should be of a light to medium rain, falling straight down, from a still sky. It rains for a while, a few minutes or an hour or two and then it stops, and may be renewed again.

Historically, the onset of the monsoon is seen as an auspicious time, a time of relief and joy, reinvigoration and playfulness. But, the monsoon itself, between June and November, is a period of considerable ambivalence; on the one hand the rains have come and that relieves the heat and discomfort and renews agricultural life, but at the same time it is a period of fear that the rains will fail, the heat will persevere, the crops will not thrive. Roads are muddied, bridges can be out and travel is difficult; snakes and vermin will have been driven from their underground homes to prey on the unwary.

> The monsoon rains constitute the pivot of the agricultural year... the abundance or scarcity of rain during this period determines whether or not this year's crops will be bountiful...In the context of agricultural production, then, temporal and climatic auspiciousness is manifested as 'wetness," which ramifies into 'fertility,' 'succulence,' and 'plenty.' 'Dryness' during this season is 'untimely' and hence connotes 'sterility,' 'harshness,' and 'scarcity' (Pugh 1983: 45).

Due to its "wetness," something that might be thought of as a positive virtue, the monsoon is an inauspicious time for the celebration of marriages, and other life-cycle rituals, since communication is so difficult, if not dangerous. It thus connotes things such as "isolation" and "loneliness."

The farmers, however, know better and there is a great deal of folk literature in both north and south India to attest to this (K. Singh 1987; Murton 1987). There is a positive literature of the monsoon bringing rains and an abundant harvest, sustaining life by replenishing rivers, wells and tanks, always with the caution of the disaster that follows the failure of the rain. Classical Sanskrit poetry deals with the monsoon, mostly, it seems, with regard to the plight of lovers.

> When an adventure comes visiting upon a rainy day,
> her make-up washed by raindrops from her eyes
> and thin blue sari clinging to her breasts,
> showing the natural beauty of her body;
> blessed is the lucky lover
> who helps her change her dress.
> [Yogeshvara (700-800 AD), from Ingalls 1968: 104-05]

The Cold Season in the Greater Indus Region

Like in many other parts of the world the transitions between the hot and cool seasons are generally short, sometimes so short that the people living through the change fail to recognize the transition because it seems to them to be so abrupt. In South Asia there is no spring and fall which separates summer from winter in a European or North American sense.

The thought of cold weather in India or Pakistan is foreign, the searing heat of the Subcontinent being such a part of literature and history there. But, it does get cold, sometimes deadly cold, even in the lowlands. Certainly the mountains of Baluchistan and the Northwest, with valley floors above 1500 meters (5000 feet) have freezing weather and snow. Nights are especially harsh and Charles Masson, the man who published the first description of Harappa, suffered from them in the Quetta area. In one day he was robbed twice:

> My shoes alone escaped, being either too large or too small for their (the thieves) several feet (Masson 1842, Vol. I: 309). [Thus he was left] ...destitute, a stranger in the center of Asia, unacquainted with the language—which would have been useful to me—and from my colour exposed on all occasions to notice, inquiry, ridicule and insult (Masson 1842, Vol. I: 309-10).

It was winter and the cold was intense, leaving a coating of ice three quarters of an inch thick on the top of a bucket.

> I suffered accordingly, and ventured to approach the fires (of my caravan companions), invitation being out of the question...I was rejected from all of them: some alleging I was a Kafir, others no reason at all (1842, Vol. I: 313).

He did manage some wood for a fire and he sat before it with his knees pulled up to his chest.

> Towards morning, my situation being observed by a Mogal soldier in the service of Khadar Khan, he came and threw over my shoulders a postin, or great coat...made of the skins of dumbas, or large-tailed sheep...I endeavored to rise and return thanks, when I found that, what with the heat of the fire in front, and the intensity of the cold behind, my limbs had contracted, fixed in the cramped position in which I had been so long sitting (Masson 1842, Vol. I: 316).

Mr. Masson suffered the effects of this grueling night for the remainder of his life.

It freezes elsewhere, in the Punjab and Haryana, but not in Gujarat. Even in these warmer places the cold can cause discomfort and problems with exposure for poor people who do not have the resources to protect themselves. Moreover, the Indian and Pakistani mentality is one that is congruent with the literary image of their land. It is heat, not cold that they prepare for, and most people only manage through the deeper cold of January and February as best they can.

There are some days in the winter that are delightful, especially in Sindh and Gujarat. When the weather is not too cold the region can be extremely pleasant, even invigorating; but at the back of one's mind always looms the inevitable: better enjoy this as much as possible, the hot weather is on the way.

The cold season brings a second period of rain to much of the Greater Indus Region. This precipitation is more important in the west than in the east. The winter rains come on the westerlies that start in the Mediterranean, bring snow to the ski slopes of Lebanon, water the fields of Syria and cross the whole of the Iranian Plateau. They are weak by the time they reach Pakistan, but there is still enough rain that the wheat and barley fields of Baluchistan and the Northwest can survive in most years. It rains in the winter on the Kachi Plain and the Punjab. Winter rain in Gujarat comes in some years, but there it is not a blessing since the precipitation is accompanied by violent winds and is highly localized. This is a perverse kind of weather, not a farmer's rain.

The hot and cold seasons are both agricultural periods, with different attributes across the geographical diversity of the Greater Indus Region. The winter growing season is generally called *rabi* and that of the monsoon is generally referred to as *kharif*, terms that will be used here. In modern Hindu thinking this is all deeply embedded in cyclical thought about seasonality (Wadley 1983), rolling progressions, that are ultimately paralleled in the theory of the transmigration of souls and larger Hindu cosmological eras.

The Importance of the *Rabi* and *Kharif* Seasons

The principal *rabi* crops are wheat and barley, both winter grasses. These are the cereals on which the earliest food producing communities in both the Subcontinent and western Asia depended. They are endemic to the Near East, and wild barley extends to the western borders of the Greater Indus Region. Wild wheat may not reach that far east. The history of these domesticated plants is covered in Part IV of this book.

The principal *kharif* crops are the millets, especially sorghum or *jowar* and pearl millet or *bajra*. These are summer grasses, adapted to the climate of the southwest monsoon.

The relative importance of each of these crops today may be an index of long term adaptive strategies. They also say something about the amount of monsoon versus winter rain, and the long term trends here. The relative dependence on them in the various Regions of the Harappan Civilization will be given consideration.

The balance among domesticated animals has a similar importance. Cattle require more water than sheep or goats. Water buffalo are even more demanding of water, and need to be fully immersed each day to maintain their good health. Water buffalo are also not good migratory animals, and where they occur in quantity can be used as a rough index of sedentarism. Pigs are also indices of sedentarism, but the relatively recent ascendancy of Islam in significant parts of the Greater Indus Region has distorted this correlation, and it cannot be used reliably, as derived from modern statistics and ethnographic observations. But, the relative balance between cattle, sheep, goats and water buffalo will be noted for the various Regions of the Harappan Civilization as possible insights into the ancient adaptations there.

THE QUESTION OF CLIMATIC CHANGE AND THE HARAPPAN CIVILIZATION

Although the climate of the Subcontinent has not been entirely stable since the close of the last great glacial period, the evidence at hand does not suggest that these two seasons were ever replaced by another climatic regime within the Late Holocene, or the period under discussion. Nor is there evidence for significantly more rainfall during the Mature Harappan, in spite of some claims (Stein 1931: 9; Marshall 1931b; Ramaswamy 1968; G. Singh 1971, 1977; G. Singh, Joshi and Singh 1972; G. Singh, Chopra and Singh 1973; G. Singh, R. J. Wasson and D. P. Agrawal 1990; Wasson, Smith and Agrawal 1984). The principal monograph on G. Singh's first phase of work is G. Singh, Joshi, Chopra and Singh (1974). By using the word "significantly" in this context it is meant to imply a sufficient increase in rainfall that would have a measurable, positive effect on crop yields and the production of grasslands for pasture.

Modern weather records, widely available in the Subcontinent since 1901 (Krishna Rao 1962), with many stations recording for much longer, have been examined in some detail, using reasonably sophisticated statistics (Krishnan and Thanvi 1982). The results of these examinations are unequivocal: "Rainfall variability in the Indian arid zone does not indicate any secular trend" (Ramakrishna 1988: 99).

There has been some discussion of climatic change in the older archaeological literature since the flourishing village farming communities of Baluchistan in the prehistoric eras seemed to indicate a more convivial environment. In his discussion of Kolwa, a broad, fertile valley of Makran where the famous site of Kulli is located, Sir Aurel Stein had the following to say:

> The open and for the most part drainageless tract of Kolwa forms for some 80 miles a natural continuation of the Key Valley proper, from which it is separated by an almost imperceptible watershed. It contains by far the greatest dry-crop area of Makran, and its export of barley to other parts in years of good rainfall is considerable. Yet how rare such rainfall is and how precarious its cultivation in Kolwa, is shown by the very scanty population of the tract being practically all nomadic. All the more interesting is the evidence which the explorations to be described below have revealed as to Kolwa having in pre-historic times been the seat of a large and thoroughly settled population. The contrast between massively built stone structures traceable at more than one ancient site of Kolwa and the wretched huts of palm—matting which house practically the whole of even the settled population of the Kej Valley as elsewhere in Makran, is striking and illustrated how great the change which has come over this whole region (Stein 1931: 9).

Sir John Marshall proposed the position in some detail in the opening chapter of *Mohenjo-daro and the Indus Civilization* (Marshall 1931b: 2-4). The basic elements of the position he took noted that the high density of prehistoric villages in Baluchistan can be accounted for only by a more productive environment, now severely constrained by the lack of water: Stein's point. It has already been noted that elephants, tigers and rhinoceri are all depicted on seals and are animals which prefer a wet habitat. The lion, a dry land animal, is conspicuous by its absence from Indus imagery. Baked bricks were used as protection from rain. the sun-dried variety being susceptible to erosion in climates with heavy rainfall. Moreover, the large drains at Mohenjo-daro must have been there to handle something more than the scanty rainfall of today's environment. The acceptance of this position seems to be one of the few points of agreement shared by Sir Mortimer Wheeler and Marshall as noted in Wheeler (1953: 4-8; see also Piggott 1950: 135).

The "higher rainfall hypothesis" was thoroughly critiqued in the 1960s, first in a classic article by Walter Fairservis (1961b). Robert Raikes and Robert Dyson (1961) also examined the proposal and found it wanting, as did Farzand Durrani (1965).

The Higher Rainfall Hypothesis Revived

Using historical records of the monsoon and a reconstruction offered by Lamb, Lewis and Woodruff (1966), C. Ramaswamy proposed, in 1968, that a shift in the deep, upper atmosphere troughs regulating the monsoon led to "...frequent active monsoon conditions over the entire Indus Valley..." during the Mature Harappan (Ramaswamy 1968: 629). Ramaswamy's proposal did not receive much support, but in 1971 Gurdip Singh published a paper based on palynological research at four lakes in Rajasthan which served to further the revival of the higher rainfall hypothesis for the Mature Harappan (G. Singh 1971). This stimulated a renewed interest in the subject (Bryson 1975; Bryson and Swain 1981; Swain, Kutzbach and Hastenrath 1983). Singh proposed more rainfall for the period 2500-1800 BC. A period of rather marked aridity began at ca. 1800 BC and by implication, the eclipse of the ancient cities of the Indus was caused by a decrease in mean annual precipitation. Actually, these schemes look very much like those proposed in the 1930s (e.g. deTerra and Hutchinson 1936: 9).

A team headed by G. Singh returned to the Didwana salt lake basin in 1980 (G. Singh,

Wasson and Agrawal 1990; Wasson, Smith and Agrawal 1984). This produced some additional data, and is an important contribution to the study of the palaeoclimate of the northwestern regions of South Asia.

G. Singh's work has been widely recognized in the archaeological literature because of its implications for the history of the Harappan Civilization. It deserves a full review because there are reasons for it to be questioned.

The Palynological Research at the Salt Lakes in Rajasthan

Singh's original research took place at Sambhar, Didwana and Lunkaransar and Pushkar Lakes (Figure 3.112). The first three lakes are salty. Pushkar is filled with fresh water. The relevant pollen samples were taken from the salt lakes.

The pollen samples were gathered by digging pits in the dry lake beds. The resulting profiles were sampled at 2.5 to 10 cm intervals. Samples for radiocarbon dating were taken from the same face as the pollen samples, in the form of short monoliths of material, 10 to 15 cm in thickness (G. Singh, Joshi, Chopra and Singh 1974: 471). The same basic method was used at the second visit to Didwana (G. Singh, Wasson and Agrawal 1990: 351-52).

According to records with the India Meteorological Department (1962) Sambhar Lake (26° 55' N - 75° 11" E) received an average of 494 mm of mean annual precipitation between 1901 to 1950. Rainfall at Didwana Lake (27° 24' N - 74° 35' E) averaged 357 mm for the same period. At Lunkaransar Lake (28° 30' N - 73° 45' E) the average was 233 mm. Surface drainage plays an important role in supplying these lakes with water. Sambhar, for example is now fed by four rivers, the Menda, Rupnagar, Kharian and Khandel which, with some smaller streams, have a catchment area of ca. 6500 square kilometers (Holland and Christie 1909: 154).

A summary of the study resulting from the work of the first Singh team is given in Table 3.11.

TABLE 3.11

Results of Palynological Research at Four Thar Desert Lakes

Estimated Date	Lake Environment	
1000 AD-today	Rajasthan lakes saline	Present aridity
1000 B. C.	Lakes begin to turn saline	Beginning of present aridity
1400-1000 B. C.	Lakes contain fresh water.	Aridity ameliorates
1800-1400 B. C.	Sambhar Lake begins to turn saline; increase in halophytes.	Aridity continues and spreads east
ca. 1800 B. C.	Lunkaransar Lake begins to dry-up.	Onset of aridity
3000-1800 B. C.	Grassy steppe savanna with good tree growth. Obstacle dunes, parabolic dunes developed from the sand washed away from sand shields.	Moist Phase with ca. 500 mm more a rain than today.
7500-3000 B. C.	Poor plant cover	Dry Phase; but not as dry as today
ca. 7500 B. C.	Indication of large scale use of fire by man. Probable beginning of cultivation with	Cerealia-type pollen.
8000-7500 BC	Pollen indicates fresh water lakes	Moist phase with more rain than today
ca. 240 mm more		

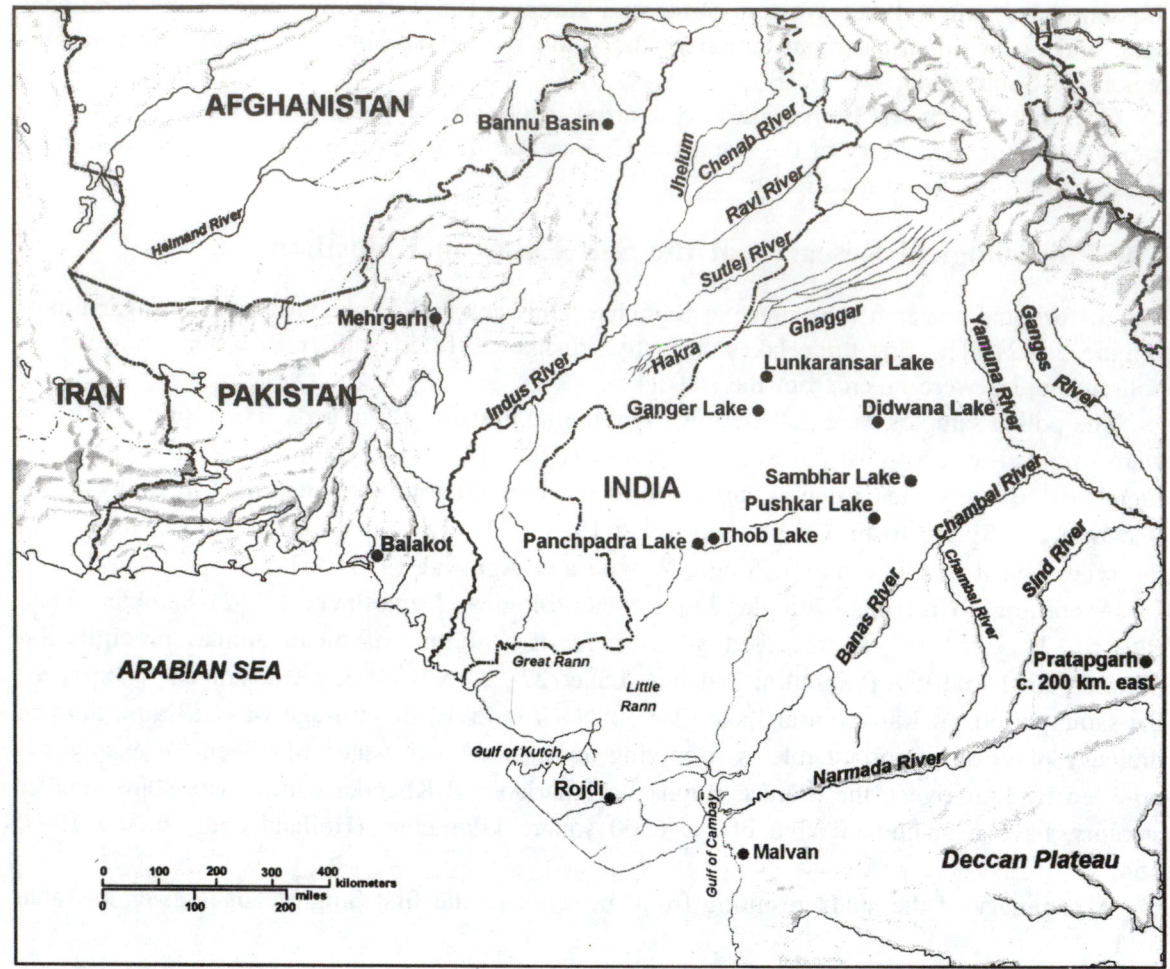

Figure 3.112. Locations where palaeoenvironmental research has been conducted

This sequence of events is in partial agreement with the work of a cooperative venture in palaeoclimatology called COHMAP (Cooperative Holocene Mapping Project), a multi-institutional consortium of scientists studying the Quaternary and Neogene climate of the earth. Their model and data show that the northern tropics, especially Asia and Africa, had an orbitally increased amount of summer solar radiation between 10,000 and 4000 B. C. which enhanced the contrast between the sea and land masses producing strong summer (southwest) monsoons. This accounts for the high lake levels (COHMAP 1988: 1043).

A more general kind of correlation has been advocated by D. P. Agrawal, at least for the glacial and early Holocene times:

> A comparison of $^{18}O/^{16}O$ measurements on *Globorotalia ruber* and *G. menardil* from the Undermine Sea and the Arabian Sea cores shows that during the last glacial maxima (c. 18,000 B.P.) and at c.10,000 B.P. the southwest monsoon was weaker than today but the northeast monsoon was stronger. During this time the Persian Gulf region, Rajasthan, and the Zagros mountains were drier than today (Agrawal 1987: 2).

The second phase of work undertaken by the Singh team at Didwana produced a sequence that can be summarized as follows in Table 3.12.

TABLE 3.12
Results of G. Singh's Palynological Research at Didwana

Estimated Date	Lake	Vegetation
younger than 2230 BC	Ephemeral lake grassland	Semi-arid savannah
2230-4420 BC	Moderately deep	Sub-humid fresh water
4420-5510 BC Savannah grassland		Fresh water followed fluctuating fresh and salt
5510-12000 BC	savannah grassland	Fluctuating fresh and Shrub, salt water
Older than 12000 BC Arid steppe		Hypersaline

(adapted from G. Singh R. J. Wasson and D. P. Agrawal 1990: 353)

The second phase of work at Didwana is important because a much more substantial attempt was made to use terrestrial plants to reconstruct the environment around the lake. These included *Aerva* and *Calligonum* which grow in dry areas. *Artemisia* (sagebrush) which is a bush that thrives under conditions of winter rainfall, *Prosopis* and *Oldenlandia* are also included. This effort is important because it shifts the burden of the evidence from assessing the aquatic flora within the lakes themselves, to the correlation of the environment within the lakes with the surrounding vegetation.

A general observation on the chronology is needed if the research is to be used for the reconstruction of culture history. The two sequences have to rely on relatively few radiocarbon determinations. These are given in Table 3.13 (G. Singh, Wasson and Agrawal 1990: 354; IAR 1978-79: 109). It is a weakness in the entire scheme, and no one should believe that it is possible to use the chronological schemes offered in the Singh et. al publication with complete confidence.

An examination of the chart presented in G. Singh, Wasson and Agrawal (1990: 353) is important for two reasons. First, the column which reflects the water level of Didwana Lake over long periods of time, derived from Wasson, Smith and Agrawal (1984), moves back and forth in the time period ca. 4000 to 5500 BC. Significant changes are also evidenced in the millennia prior to this period. Is it really possible for the water level in these lakes to change so quickly and erratically if long term variations in rainfall (e.g., climatic change) was the only factor influencing this variable? After this period the water level curve is very stable. Second, an examination of the terrestrial pollen does not seem to indicate climatic change. *Aerva* starts out as an abundant pollen and then goes flat. *Oldenlandia* moves around, but does not tell us much, and the same could be true for *Prosopis*.

These lakes are complex bodies of water. Today, some are fresh, some are salty. At times

TABLE 3.13
Radiocarbon Dates from Salt Lakes in Rajasthan

Number	Calibrated Radiocarbon Date (some uncalibrated due to age)	Stratum/ Phase
Didwana Lake		
PRL-650	12,450+360 -340 bp	Wet Phase
PRL-649	1Σ cal BC 8350 (8085) 7958	Wet Phase
	2Σ cal BC 8841 (8085) 7633	
PRL-648	1Σ cal BC 6188 (6102, 6099, 6045) 5956	Wet Phase
	2Σ cal BC 6385 (6102, 6099, 6045) 5763	
PRL-647	1Σ cal BC 5754 (5579) 5340	Dry Phase
	2Σ cal BC 5996 (5579) 5081	
PRL-645	1Σ cal BC 5197 (4902, 4876, 4854) 4686	Wet Phase
	2Σ cal BC 5284 (4902, 4876, 4854) 4457	
PRL-646	1Σ cal BC 4911 (4719) 4469	Fluctuating
	2Σ cal BC 5202 (4719) 4342	Climate
PRL-644	1Σ cal BC 2871 (2577) 2457	Dry Phase
	2Σ cal BC 2913 (2577) 2200	
WIS-415	1Σ cal BC 1291 (1196, 1181, 1165, 1141, 1139) 1049	-120 to 130 cm
	2Σ cal BC 1393 (1196, 1181, 1165, 1141, 1139) 993	
Lunkaransar Lake		
WIS-405	1Σ cal BC 8415 (8335, 8306, 8262) 8091	II-III, arid
	2Σ cal BC 8825 (8335, 8306, 8262) 8035	
WIS-386	1Σ cal BC 4343 (4319, 4288, 4258) 4164	Late III, arid
	2Σ cal BC 4436 (4319, 4288, 4258) 4045	
WIS-387	1Σ cal BC 3958 (3930, 3875, 3808) 3777	Early IVa, arid
	2Σ cal BC 3986 (3930, 3875, 3808) 3698	and windy
Sambhar Lake		
TF-887	1Σ cal BC 8088 (8027) 7941	Early III, arid
	2Σ cal BC 8333 (8027) 7705	
TF-698	1Σ cal BC 7501 (7422) 7097	Early III, arid
	2Σ cal BC 7578 (7422) 7010	
TF-738	1Σ cal BC 7249 (7033) 6711	Mid-III, arid
	2Σ cal BC 7424 (7033) 6561	
TF-886	1Σ cal BC 6354 (5983) 5688	Mid-III, arid
	2Σ cal BC 6591 (5983) 5442	
TF-884	1Σ cal BC 5191 (4942) 4834	Late III, arid
	2Σ cal BC 5230 (4942) 4722	
TF-739	1Σ cal BC 3372 (3334, 3152, 3145) 3038	Mid-IVa, arid
	2Σ cal BC 3618 (3334, 3152, 3145) 2912	and windy
TF-883	1Σ cal BC 3295 (3018, 2990, 2927) 2889	Mid-IVa
	2Σ cal BC 3359 (3018, 2990, 2927) 2698	

two lakes, one salty the other fresh, are in close geographical proximity as witnessed by freshwater Pushkar's proximity to salty Didwana, Sambhar and Lunkaransar. Over the past century a number of hypotheses have been advanced to account for the salt in some of these lakes and there is a small bibliography on this topic that has been summarized in Sinha (1977). Basically, there are four hypotheses on the origin of these lacustrine salts: (1) it is marine and results from the regression of the Tethys Sea, (2) the salt derives from brine springs in the region, (3) it is windborne, from the Arabian Sea and the Ranns of Kutch, and (4) G. Singh's hypothesis that it results from the concentration of salt through the evaporation of lake water with dissolved salts in it.

The first three hypothesis have been discredited in a number of ways in Sinha (1977). The Singh hypothesis is also questioned, most seriously from the following observations. The three salt lakes are all grouped together within a very small region of an Indian State. They are under one climatic regime. On the other hand there are freshwater lakes in this same region, flourishing under the same climatic conditions that produces the hypersalinity in the lakes that have been studied by the geoclimatologists. The freshwater bodies are Pushkar Lake at Ajmer, one of the best known pilgrimage sites in India, and the lesser known Lake Gajner 30 kilometers south of Bikaner City (Erskine 1909: 310). The evidence seems conclusive that climate is not regulating the salt content of the lake waters.

There is contemporary evidence that water enters the lakes in Rajasthan from local rainfall, drainage, and ground water. Further observation shows that water leaves these basins through both evaporation and subsurface drainage. The salinity of the lake water is therefore the result of a balance between rainfall and surface drainage on the one hand and subsurface conditions on the other. A change in total average annual rainfall, surface drainage or subsurface drainage, will change the halite content of these bodies of water. The best hypothesis is that salinity levels in the lakes is regulated by subsurface drainage.

Changes in Salt Content of the Lakes due to Subsurface Drainage

Changing surface and subsurface drainage patterns in this region may well result from large-scale tectonic activity brought about by the collision of the Indian peninsula with the larger Asian land mass. This point is of particular importance to the present assessment of the pollen data because there appears to be a change in lake salinity at ca. 2000 B. C. Singh and his collaborators interpret this increase as a decline in mean annual rainfall, possibly brought about by the shift in the southwest monsoon. It is, without doubt, one phenomenon that might lead to increasing salinity. But, it is also true that at ca. 2000 B. C. there is geological evidence for major changes in surface, and probably subsurface, drainage in northern Rajasthan, eastern Punjab, Haryana and western Uttar Pradesh; an event that led to the desiccation of the Sarasvati Riverine system, the rejuvenation of the Sutlej River and the creation of the Yamuna River.

It would be remiss not to mention a review of the Holocene environment of northwestern India and Pakistan by V. N. Misra (1984). We reach much the same conclusion: there is basic climatic stability between the Mature Harappan and today.

Other Places Where Palaeoenvironmental Work Has Been Done

There are data from four other sources of palaeoenvironmental reconstruction, three of them based on pollen. These are not entirely consistent among themselves but do tend to indicate that the environment of the third millennium was not so different from the present. There is also an implication that the science of reconstructing the ancient environment of the Greater

Indus Region is very young and a great deal of work needs to be done before consistent patterns of climatic variability begin to emerge over this vast area.

Balakot

The first of these reconstructions comes from Balakot near Sonmiani Bay in Pakistan where Margaret McKean (1983) undertook some palynological research aimed at reconstructing the ancient environment. Her conclusion from a comparison of ancient and modern pollen samples covering the Early Harappan and the Mature Harappan is: "...occupation during both cultural periods existed under essentially modern climatic conditions" (McKean 1983: v).

Malvan

The second study was undertaken as part of the archaeological excavations at Malvan, in South Gujarat, by J. P. Joshi and F. R. Allchin (F. R. Allchin and J. P. Joshi 1970, 1995; J. P. Joshi and F. R. Allchin 1972). The palynological research conducted by Vishnu-Mittre and Chayya Sharma at an oxbow lake in the vicinity of the Bronze Age archaeological site has shown considerable environmental stability. The entire pollen sample revealed that an open grassland of Cheno-Amaranths, along with several other herbaceous elements, surrounded the lake. Distant arboreal forests are also suggested. There is good evidence for the occasional drying up of the lake, for reasons that are not fully understood. Over all, the pollen sequence suggests little environmental change. However, this is undated and there is no sense of the time depth covered by this sample (Vishnu-Mittre and Sharma 1973).

Nal Lake, Gujarat

Vishnu-Mittre and Sharma (1978) tested Nal Lake ca. 60 km southwest of Ahmedabad. Their reconstruction there indicates lake level stability between 3000 and 1500 BC, with a disappearance of pollen between 1500 BC and 1819 AD when the lake was revived.

Mehrgarh

Stephanie Thiebault undertook the examination of wood charcoal from Mehrgarh (Periods VI and VII) and Lal Shah, the Period VII kiln site (Thiebault 1989, 1992). The species she identified are still endemic to the region, although *Juniper*, for example, would only be found at higher elevations in the Quetta Valley. There is little, or nothing, to suggest higher rainfall in the past from this data set. The macrobotanical analysis at Mehrgarh leads to the same tentative conclusion (Costantini and Biasini 1985).

Rojdi

The joint team from the Gujarat State Department of Archaeology and the University of Pennsylvania Museum undertook an intensive program of palaeobotanical research (Weber 1991). While palaeoenvironmental reconstruction was not the principal aim of this research it was a topic that received some attention. From an analysis of thousands of seeds from about 100 different plants there is nothing at Rojdi to suggest that the environment during the third and early second millennia was significantly different from today.

Bannu Basin

There is another view on the climate of the Indus Age that deserves notice. Some attention has been paid to the ancient environment of the Bannu Basin in Pakistan as part of the joint archaeological work being undertaken there between the University of Peshawar and a team from the United Kingdom. Although it is clear that the drainage of this valley has undergone significant changes, they seem to be late glacial or early Holocene in age (Thomas 1986a: 22, see also Thomas 1986b). Helen Rendell suggests that: "Several lines of evidence point to the existence of moister conditions within the basin 3000 to 5000 years ago. In addition to an increase in aridity since that time, there is evidence that the major phase of incision within the basin occurred within the last 300 years..." (H. Rendell in Allchin, Allchin, Durrani and Khan 1985: 12). Rendell's colleague on the Bannu Basin Project has put this in a good context by noting:

> Any climatic shifts which might have led to a more even distribution of rainfall through the year, or to an increase in the amount of winter rain, would have had a distinctly beneficial effect on past arable agriculture. All this is speculation: it must be stressed that we have no unambiguous evidence that late Holocene climates were markedly different from the climate of the Bannu Basin today. This is not, of course, to say that climates have remained the same through much of the later Holocene time in this area; we just do not know (Thomas 1986a: 22-3).

Central Gangetic Plain

Somewhat outside the Greater Indus Region, H. P. Gupta (1976) collected a pollen sequence from an oxbow lake in Pratapgarh District of Uttar Pradesh. It is in the vicinity of sites that may have played a role in the development of agriculture on the mid-Gangetic Plains (Sharma, Misra, Mandal, Misra and Pal 1980). His conclusion can be summarized as follows: "The climatic sequence, as determined from the biostratigraphy of the lake-basin, has been grouped into four phases (I-IV). The general vegetational pattern is rather uniform and is tipped more towards open savannah forest with vast stretches of grasslands and a few scattered stands of arboreal vegetation" (Gupta 1976: 115). Gupta's chronology is not tightly controlled, but there is some reason to believe that his conclusions would cover the third millennium BC.

The Environmental Reconstruction

The history of the lakes in Rajasthan is still little understood. Sinha (1977) has noted that the entire subject has been an odd and unfortunate mix of armchair speculation with just enough field research to keep the debate alive. What is needed is a vigorous program of problem oriented field study to resolve the more or less empirical gaps in our knowledge. It is only with the completion of a program of field study that the interpretation of pollen data such as contributed by G. Singh and his team will be secure. A step in that direction has recently been taken by B. C. Deotare and M. D. Kajale (1996). Their cautious approach to the fluctuating hydrological conditions in Panchpadra and Thob Lakes between Jodhpur and Barmer in western Rajasthan include alternatives to variation in rainfall as explanations of lake levels.

The position taken here is that there was no significant difference in the rainfall regime in the period from ca. 7000 BC to 1000 BC as compared to today's long term pattern. Rainfall is dynamic, like other features of the environment, and this position admits differences in yearly patterns, as well as longer term "cycles" of drought and rainfall abundance, in the range of scores or even a hundred years or so. The conclusion reached from the available data, is that changes in rainfall, or climate, should not be seen as an explanation for major historical events, such as the eclipse of the ancient cities of the Indus.

The relationship between rainfall and a larger environmental reconstruction is more complex. We know from a host of reliable sources, including archaeological excavations, historical observations and data collected by scientists, that today's landscape in the Greater Indus Region is different from that of even the nineteenth century. The immense irrigation works of Sindh and the Punjab are good examples of this. The large and interesting literature on colonial period hunting in India is indicative of an abundance of game, both mammals and birds, on the plains of the Greater Indus Region, especially Sindh, the Punjab, Rajasthan and Gujarat. The situation, by some accounts, was not so different from the vast herds of animals on the savannahs of Africa.

An Aside on Hunting

During the colonial period in India a vast number of animals were killed for sport by hunters, mostly British and the native nobility[7]. One hunter, James Inglis, quotes an article from the *Saturday Review* of January 15, 1887, which notes that the wild animals of India were dangerous creatures that had caused many deaths, of both humans and livestock. He records that "1,835 tigers, 1,874 bears, and 6,278 wolves were killed off last year, as compared with 2,196, 2,000, and 6,706 respectively in the preceding twelve months" (Inglis 1888: 37). Hunting was supported by government grants. The death tally noted above equaled a sum of Rs. 224,126 in "Government grants bestowed for these protective measures" (Inglis 1888: 37). Fixed rates were set for the killing of various animals: Rs. 30 for a tiger and Rs. 70 for an elephant (Sanderson 1864: 41). A hunter notes that elephants had caused many problems in South India, and that "the Government had issued an order for all elephants to be killed, and offered a reward for each elephant, male or female" (Hamilton 1892: 152). In 1864 George P. Sanderson provided a list of popular Mysore area game. This includes elephants, bison or gaur, tigers, panthers, leopards, cheetah, bear, wolf, striped hyena, wild dog, sambar, spotted deer, barking deer, Indian antelope, Indian gazelle, wild hog, crocodile, jackal, fox, common jungle cat, leopard-cat, otter, porcupine, mouse deer, and hare (Sanderson 1864: 13). He also notes that the following animals of Indian sport are not found in the Mysore region: rhinoceros, wild buffalo, nilgai, and ibex (Sanderson 1864: 14). In relation to small game, there seem to have been a few favored methods of hunting. One described by Hamilton is the beating method; "[w]e generally took a line through the low jungle with a dozen or so beaters, and shot everything we came across" (Hamilton 1892: 35). Another method involved starting fires in forests to flush out animals (Inglis 1888: 663).

Daily accounts of hunts provide a picture of the extent of the killing of wildlife. One tally for a morning's bird hunt included "a florican, a Brahminy duck, a wild goose, a brace of lalseer, or red tufted mallard, several pintails, grey duck, and teal", as well as "two or three sandpipers, goggle-eyed plover, two beef-steak birds, or black ibis, and a couple of curlew" and "a brace of snipe, a blue fowl, two grey partridges, a brace of hares, and two green pigeons" (Inglis 1888: 41). On another day in 1875 in an area near Nepal hunters shot "three tigers, one boar, four deer, eight sandpipers, nine plovers, two mallards, and two teal" (Inglis 1888:627, 641). The next day, their bounty included "one tiger, one florican, one mallard, and two widgeon" (Inglis 1888:652), as well as six deer which they shot, but did not take with them (Inglis 1888:643). The third day of this particular hunt, counts the day's total at "one tiger, seven hog-deer, one bear, seventeen jungle fowl, five florican, and six hares" (Inglis 1888:663).

Hunters prided themselves on having bagged large numbers of animals. Recall the earlier notice of using machine guns to hunt onagers in Bahawalpur. Nineteenth and early twentieth century documents of "shooting parties" regularly record the slaughter of hundreds of mammals and thousands of birds. About the Indian bustard, Hamilton mentions that "one sportsman has killed over a thousand of these birds with the rifle" (Hamilton 1892: 17). Inglis notes with respect that his hunting club included a planter, Joe, who had "witnessed the death of over three hundred tigers, scores of them falling to his own gun" (Inglis 1888: 35). Inglis' friend, George S., remarks in a letter that he has recorded in his journal killing fifty-two tigers on various hunts (Inglis 1888: 593). The animals were often killed and left in the jungle after their trophy parts were taken. Relating the killing of his first elephant, Hamilton explains that after the shooting, "we cut off her tail, and went away highly delighted" (Hamilton 1892: 144).

It is interesting that these sportsmen largely ignore the effects of their sports on the Indian environment. They were aware of animals which were rare, and delighted in these finds. One particularly memorable quote comes from Hamilton "I was fortunate enough when shooting on the Pulneys, to come across and shoot three does of a rather rare antelope known as the mountain antelope; and again on the 26th of November, 1863, I shot a buck of the same species" (Hamilton 1892: 13). Another time Hamilton speaks of his hunting a black leopard in 1857. After explaining how he killed it, Hamilton notes that "the black variety is scarce in Southern India. I only saw one other during all the years I was on the hills." (Hamilton 1892: 227). Inglis remarks, after relating the story of the slaying of a rhinoceros, that rhinos "were formerly much more common in these jungles, but of late years very few have been killed" (Inglis 1888: 557).

There seems to be a naive assumption that there was an endless supply of wildlife in India. The *Saturday Review*, after relating the tallies of slaughter, assures prospective sportsmen that "this bag need not make the sportsman in quest of game lose heart, provided he has at his disposal those three coveted requisites—time, health, and money" (Inglis 1888: 37). In some ways this was simply the acceleration of a process that began much earlier with the introduction of firearms into the Subcontinent, but taken as a whole it can be said with confidence that the density and distribution of game animals is a mere shadow of what it would have been in the prehistoric period. There are many examples of this involving animals which were important during Mature Harappan times. In Pakistan alone, there was once an abundance of lions, tigers, elephants, rhinocerii, onager, nilgai and blackbuck. Now these animals are either extinct there, or limited to a few individuals who stray across the modern border with India in Thar Parkar or along the bed of the ancient Sarasvati (Roberts 1977).

Pasture Lands and Animals

Reducing the number and distribution of wild mammals has had an effect on the availability of pasture but the growing human population and their husbanding of domesticated mammals has more than compromised this as a conservation measure. The presence of relatively large human populations in the Greater Indus Region since ca. 7000 BC, accompanied by their cattle, sheep, goats, water buffalo and later camels and horses has had the effect of slowly but perceptibly depleting the landscape of its grass resources. This should not be viewed as catastrophic since many plants respond well to grazing, browsing and periodic burning.

The presence of domesticated animals must be seen in concert with man's search for fire wood and timber for wood working and architecture. Clearing land and draining swamps for agriculture, along with the harboring of other land for villages, towns and cities are involved as well. Taken as a whole, it can be seen that we have good reason to imagine that over nine millennia the Greater Indus Region is different today from the prehistoric era under consideration.

Summary

Since the environmental reconstruction of the Greater Indus Region from ca. 7000 BC to 1000 BC has received so little systematic attention, it is not yet possible to offer a reconstruction of this landscape based on anything other than a kind of reasoned speculation. Assuming that the rainfall regime from 7000 BC to 1000 BC was pretty much as it is at present, we have the ability to hold this important variable constant; within the parameters of its own dynamic. The recent massive irrigation facilities and the agricultural areas that they foster should also be removed from the reconstruction. A reconstructed regional drainage pattern has to be managed, but some progress has been made there. Many more game animals are implied, and the distribution pattern for many (most?) of them expanded into areas where they are now extinct. Finally, in the absence of more particular data, the density of tree and grass cover has to be increased, with the environment generally much "fluffed up." Of course, this is unacceptable as a reconstruction of the ancient environment of the Greater Indus Region. But for now, there is little else that can be done. The topic represents a research challenge for those who take a serious interest in the study of prehistoric life in South Asia.

THE REGIONS OF CULTURAL GEOGRAPHY FOR THE INDUS AGE

The cultural geography of the Harappan Civilization (Possehl 1982b, 1992a), especially as expressed in regionalization, is one direction my research has taken. It is an expression of the cultural ecology (Steward 1955, Helm 1962, Netting 1971) of the Indus people (Fairservis 1961b, 1967) which finds its roots to some extent in the culture area concept (Kroeber 1939). Of course, this is not the only way that archaeologists organizing multiregional data sets should organize their materials (Barth 1956).

It has become increasingly apparent that the Harappan subsistence regime was both complex and differentiated (Vishnu-Mittre and Savithri 1982, Meadow, 1993a, 1993b) and that some of these patterns seem to have been coincident with the stylistic geography of the ceramic corpus. What is emerging is an ancient cultural mosaic, documenting important aspects of Harappan cultural diversity.

Much remains to be done on the reconstruction of the Harappan subsistence regime. There are several domains of the Harappan Civilization where there is virtually no excavated data on which a reconstruction can be based. Other Regions, such as the Southern (Gujarat) and Central Regions are places within which some archaeological work has been done and there is more data with which to work.

The scale of the Indus Civilization was one of two striking aspects of Harappan cultural geography that was immediately apparent to the earliest investigators of Mohenjo-daro and Harappa. The other can be thought of as the "sameness" of the Harappan remains, wherever they were found. Ernest J. H. Mackay captured this in his early synthesis of Harappan remains when he noted: "The wares of the Harappa people possess in a marked degree that utilitarian aspect which is such a dominant feature of their architecture, and if the mentality of a people can be correctly gauged by the pottery they make, the people of Mohenjo-daro and Harappa must have been singularly lacking in imagination" (Mackay 1948: 120). This aspect of the civilization, dealing with the monotony of this important ancient people, began to change in the late 1960s.

There is no doubt that the so-called uniformity of the Harappan culture in depth has been exaggerated and is due as much to archaic methods of research as to any inherent conservatism in the ancient craftsmen. The excavations on the Mohenjo-daro citadel in 1950 showed that change and evolution are clearly recognizable in the Indus ceramic and that, in particular, there was a lowering of technical standards in the later phases (Wheeler 1968: 94).

This study of the Indus Age is directed toward the definition and clarification of the realities of Harappan life. An investigation of the "Sameness Paradigm" is part of it.

The Selection of Names for the Regions

Considerable thought has been given to the selection of names for the Harappan Regions. Jagat Pati Joshi (1984: 51) chose a neutral, descriptive set of terms for his investigation of the internal geography of the Harappan Civilization: Northern (West Punjab); Eastern (East Punjab, Haryana, northern Rajasthan and western Uttar Pradesh); Central (Bahawalpur); Southern (Sindh); Southwestern (Baluchistan) and Southeastern (Gujarat); a legitimate choice of words and somewhat coincident with the domain terminology used here. In fact, it is not unusual for peoples to refer to their own geography using these neutral terms. In modern India there is a Northern State (Uttar Pradesh), a Central State (Madhya Pradesh) and a Southern State (Andhra Pradesh). Objection to this approach is probably a matter of taste.

There are seven regions of the Indus Age, as follows:

> The Central Region
> The Gedrosia Region
> The Southern Region
> The Northwestern Region
> The Northern Region
> The Eastern Region
> The Hakra Region

The cultural and historical geography of these regions within the Greater Indus Region will be explored in the following sections. Some emphasis is placed on bringing out the character of the terrain, the modern rainfall regime, the balance between pastoral and settled life and the natural resources that are present. For the Gedrosia and Northwestern Regions additional attention is paid to the plants and animals that seem to have played a role in the domestication process, as well as natural variables that are shared with the greater Near East (Figure 3.113).

THE CENTRAL REGION

The Central Region (Figure 3.114) is an area of central importance to the Indus Age and is the largest of the Regions at 140,000 square kilometers. It derives its name from the centrality of the lower reaches of the Indus River, united below the Panjnad. It is not entirely congruent with the modern province of Sindh in Pakistan and although the style of the Harappan remains found there during the Mature Harappan is termed the "Sindhi Harappan," this should not be taken as a reference to the modern Sindh speakers or their contemporary province.

The southern boundary of the Central Region is the Arabian Sea and the Ranns of Kutch, wherever they may have been located in antiquity. This boundary extends as far west as Balakot,

270

Figure 3.113. The regions of cultural geography for the Indus Age

but not into the Welpat area of Las Bela, which is Gedrosia and Kulli country. The western boundary skirts the uplands of modern southern Sindh and goes up the Baran Nai to Lake Manchar (Plate 3.36). From there it abuts the Kirthar Range, extending to the base of the Bolan Pass (Plate 3.37), low around the Marri-Bugti Hills and north to about the 29th meridian at the Panjnad. The boundary crosses the united "River Sindhu" and moves south skirting the edge of the deep Thar Desert, extending east to encompass the Mature Harappan sites of Ahmad Khan

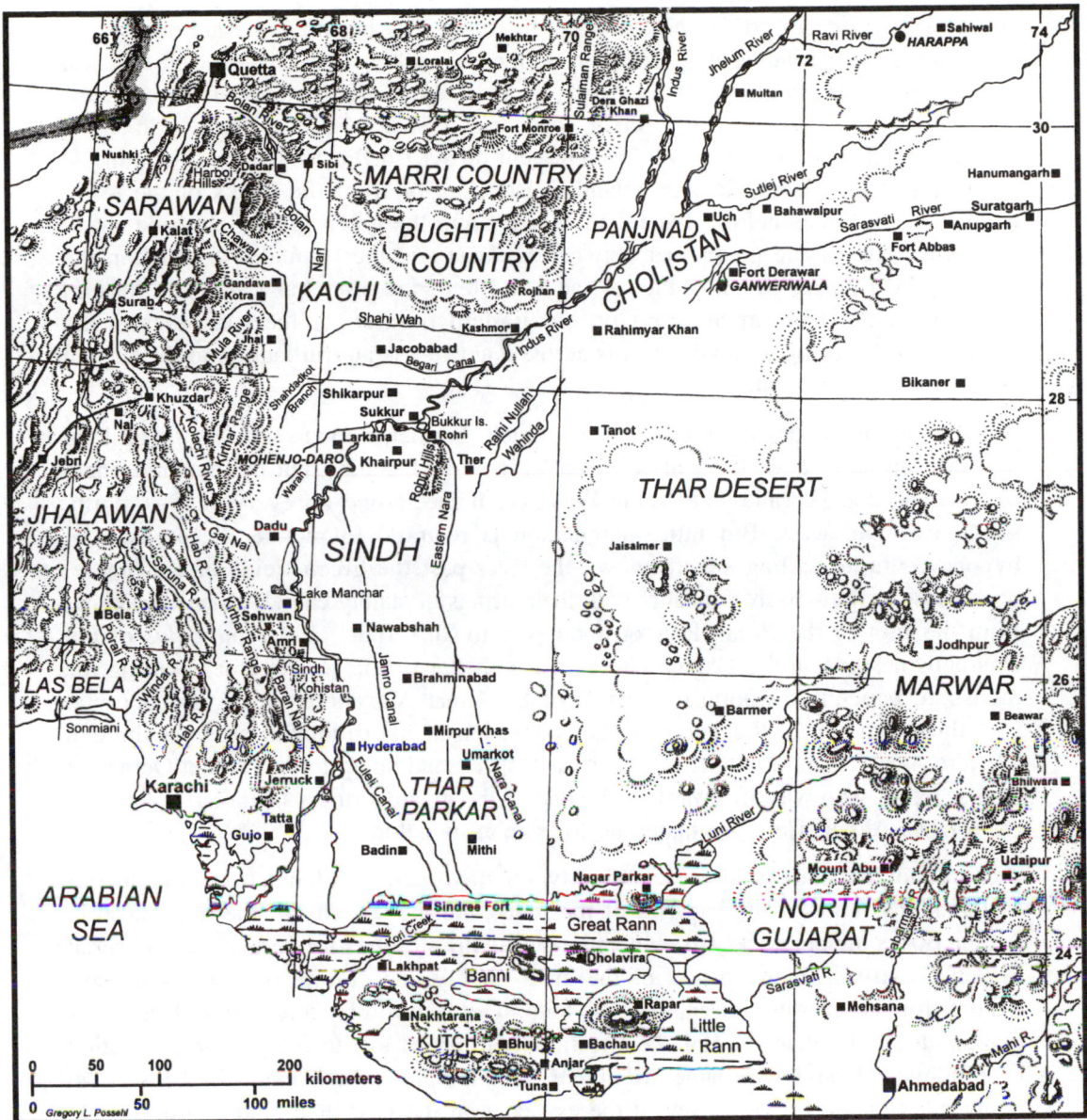

Figure 3.114. The Central Region

Dheri and Ahmad Khan's Dheri, but does not enter the Hakra Region. It extends down to the Ranns of Kutch, encompassing the Mature Harappan sites of Gharo Bhiro, Korohio Pir and Koonj Sor and uses the northern edge of the Great Rann, wherever it too, may have been in antiquity, as the final leg of its eastern border. From the perspective of cultural geography Kachi is an extension of the Indus plains. It is also an extraordinarily important place, within the Central Region.

The area admits some geographic diversity but is dominated by the plains of the Indus River. Kachi, now a District of Baluchistan, is also included since it is geographically part of the plains, not the mountains.

The Indus Valley is a place of great beauty and many people have become deeply attached to it:

Be the fact good or bad for the Province, fact it is. The beauties of Sind are not for the stranger, or casual visitor. He, perhaps merely seeking the shortest and quickest route to some temporary post up North, or possibly to his permanent home in the damp, grey West, notices only torrid heat, arid wastes, blinding glare, suffocating dust, and a coastal Port somewhat reminiscent of Suez or Port Said. Not for him the enchanting views from the little island at Bhukkar, or from the banks of the lower reaches of the Indus below Hyderabad. Not for him the green grain fields and shady forests that fringe the great river between Larkana and the Capital. Not for him the scent of the Kumbar Road, or the myriad bird life of the Munchar Lake. Not for him the moonlight on the great desert on our Eastern frontier; or the sunrise from the Indus delta, throwing its golden shafts across Karachi's beautiful lagoon to the rugged sky-line of the Hub hills.

But for the old Sindhi these things mean much. Further, nobody who has lived long in Sind, can have failed to be affected not only by its beauties, but by the atmosphere of romance that pervades the whole Province. It meets one on every side — north, south, east and west. But little imagination is required to picture the argosies of bygone centuries sailing silently down the river past the green fields of Kushmore: or the old caravans from Kandahar with their strings of stately camels slowly emerging from the foot of the Bolan Pass on their way to Shikarpur: or the *buggalas* of old Nearchus nestling in the Chinna Creek in the shelter of the Oyster Rocks during the monsoon, patiently awaiting the arrival of the Great Alexander shortly to appear at the Ghizree mouth of the Indus on the conclusion of his triumphal progress through Western Asia! Then, too, think of the circumstances leading up to the birth at Oomerkot of that infant who was afterwards to be one of the greatest rulers in Indian history, — the mighty Akbar. Here are materials for romances galore.

We are not dependent, however, simply on historical incidents to stimulate our imaginations. Though the vagaries of the Indus and the severity of the hot season in the interior combine quickly to obliterate man's puny strivings for permanency, material evidence exists in many places of the great vitality and culture of those who have lived before us in this ancient land of Sind. The beautifully coloured and perfectly glazed tiles and pottery of Hala bear testimony to an art lost to the present generation of Sindhis; whilst the ornamented graves and temples which can still be seen in many parts of the Province, reveal the existence in the past of a God-fearing people with well developed notions of sculpture and architecture. Who can regard the wonderful tombs on the Makli Hill at Tatta or the ruins of the great city of Brahminabad without realising that those responsible for these things must have been, in their day, well advanced in social and civilised life, and deserving of the respect of the present generation (Webb *in* Kincaid 1925: vii-viii).

J. Abbott, an officer in the Indian Civil Service who served in Sindh early in this century, wrote a small book about the land he quite obviously had come to love (Abbott 1924). The province was annexed to British India in 1843, as part of the aftershock of the First Afghan War (1838-42). It was ruled as a division of the Bombay Presidency until 1936. The people of Sindh have their own particular character. Sindhis are noted for their independence and a particular astuteness in business. This combined with the distance (both physical and mental) between Karachi and Bombay gave Sindh and the Sindhis a kind of reputation. They were self-reliant, suspicious of outsiders and resistive of outside interference. They were smart and given to a touch of secretiveness among themselves. Moreover, among the Sindhis, all of them, no matter how bad, had virtues that outsiders could never possess; there was a sense of family. At the time of annexation to British India the country was about three-fourths Muslum, the rest being mostly Hindus, with a very small Parsee community. The lines between the communities could be drawn quite hard, but there was mixing and blending as well. In an account of the powerful Muslum Pir Pagaro and his following of Hurs we learn that:

> And we would see the landowners, lords of vast estates who at other times seemed such magnificent people, humble themselves before him; the very shopkeepers of Sanghar would vie with one another for some mark of his condescension as if they too, though Hindus, were his disciples (Lambrick 1972: 22).

Perhaps as a result of this sense of family, and a fierce desire to run their country their way, Sindhi politics have a reputation of being blatantly dishonest and filled with collusion. In fact, the expression "Sindhi politics" has come to stand for political corruption and the worst kind of local brokering; something that modern times have not quite shaken from the place.

The nature of Sindh was graphically portrayed by Richard Burton in four books on the province (1829, 1851a, 1851b, 1877), one of which (Burton 1851a) carries in its subtitle the notion of an "unhappy valley." The province had an interesting reputation, and no small amount of bad press. But, it also had its friends and admirers, among them the aforementioned J. Abbott. He, and others, set about to present another image of the valley and one of his essays begins with the following:

> Sind is a valley of many silences, and these proclaim the limits in which its restricted life-flow wanders. Silence of the desert and the immensity of light without shade; silence as of drowsy forenoon of those peaceful stretches of the river that have no allurement for the fisher; silence more solemn of the dreary wastes where the river joins the sea on a lonely and uninviting coast; but it has no silence so profound as the silence of the hills. For the desert has its nomads and its shrines—be they but seldom tended—the paths of men cross it and the fields of men adjoin it; the delta has its dwellers who love its level solitude with an ancient love, and far-faring boats drop down upon the flood from one busy center to another through the recurrent silences of the river; but the hills have no share in the labors of the valley and the sound of human industry never reaches them to break their impenetrable stillness (Abbott 1924: 9).

Abbot's book appeared just as the large-scale excavations of Mohenjo-daro were getting under way. It seems likely that Sir John Marshall and his senior staff knew of this work. It is clear that Marshall himself had a high regard for his Sindhi workers, but a low regard for the Sindhi labor contractors.

Why Kachi is Politically a Part of Baluchistan

Kachi (Plate 3.38) came to be administered by the Khans of Kalat in the eighteenth century when Mughal power had largely decayed. With this relaxation, the Brahui of Kalat were freed, to some degree, from external interference. In 1730 Mir Abdulla, the Ahmadzai Khan of Kalat turned an acquisitive eye to the Indus Valley and Kachi. He assembled a force and invaded the district, which at that time was part of the dominions of a Sindhi, Nur Muhammad Kalhora. Mir Abdulla descended into Kachi by way of the easy Bolan route. Dadar was taken and plundered and Mir Abdulla advanced to a place called Jandrihar near Sanni. The Kalhora *naib* of Gandava marched against him with a superior force and a fierce battle ensued at Jandrihar. Mir Abdulla's army fought well, but their leader was killed in action.

In 1739, Nadir Shah of Persia invaded India and occupied Delhi. In the treaty he made with one of the last Mughals, Emperor Muhammad Shah, Mughal provinces to the west of the Indus River were ceded to the Persians. Much of this territory was Nur Muhammad's and he decided to revolt. His attempts to this end were ineffective and short-lived and he was almost immediately captured by Nadir Shah (Minchin 1907b: 18).

In 1740 Nadir Shah delivered Nur Muhammad to Mohabat, Khan of Kalat, the son of Mir Abdulla. This was done to establish a friendly tie between the Persians and Brahuis by enabling Mohabat to avenge the death of his father. But rather than committing murder, the Brahui chief took Kachi as an atonement. Thus, Kachi is spoken of as having been acquired by Kalat and the Brahuis for the blood of Mir Abdulla (McConaghey 1907: 26). It is still theirs today, and is called the "Breadbasket of Baluchistan" by virtue of its size and the manner in which the Brahui manage its resources.

The Name of the River: History and Etymology

The most ancient name of the greatest of rivers in Pakistan is the "Sindhu." In the Ṛgveda this may mean simply "stream" but in most cases it clearly refers to a river *par excellence*, the Indus itself (Macdonell and Keith 1912: Vol. 2, 450).

> Flashing and whitely gleaming in her mightiness she
> moves along her ample volumes through the realms.
> Most active of the active Sindhu unrestrained,
> like a dappled mare, beautiful, fair to see.
> Ṛgveda Book X, Hymn 75, Verse 7; Griffith 1896[8]

Sindhi speakers today still refer to the river as Sindhu or Sindh; although *darya*, the Persian equivalent is also used, a reflection that this is now an Islamic country and Persia and Persians remain powerful cultural forces (Abbott 1924: 21-7; Lambrick 1964: 100-02; Plate 3.39). The river has also been called the "Mirhan of Sindh" and the "Ab-i-Sindh" (Raverty 1892b: fn. 307),[9] although the term "Mihran of Sindh" is overused and has been applied in a number of ways that confuse the original meaning of this term. The modern romanized rendering of the provincial name, without the pleasant aspirant "h" ending, which is discernible in the country speech of the region, is "Sind," and "Indus" is a simple derivation of this word. From "Indus" one derives the modern name "India." The etymological relationship between "Sindhu" and "Hindu" should be clear enough to need no further exposition. While "Hindustan" is still used in contemporary vernacular languages in the northern part of the entire Subcontinent, "Bharat" is frequently used to designate the land of "India," especially within Hindi speech communities. "Bharat" is derived from the home of the ancient Bharata Tribe in the east Punjab.

While cognizance of the Indus River in the Ṛgveda is certainly the first written notice of this stream, it is not a source of useful historical information. There are several Greek, or Persian notices of "India," which for them is the modern area of Sindh, let alone the entire subcontinent. To the north of their "India" and our Sindh, was "Gandhara" with its capital of Taxila.

The earliest Greek source on the Subcontinent seems to be attributable to a man named Scylax, who was in the employ of the third Achemenid ruler, Darius I. His document, now lost, came from a voyage down the Indus beginning at a town probably on the Kabul River (in "Pactyis" or "Pakhtun" country) and ending about two and one-half years later in Egypt. Herodotus tells us the following about Darius and Scylax:

But as to Asia most of it was discovered by Darius. There is a river Indus, which of all rivers comes second in producing crocodiles. Darius, desiring to know where this Indus issues into the sea, sent ships manned by Scylax, a man of Caryanda, and others he trusted; these set out from the city Caspatyrus and the Pactyis country, and sailed down the river towards the east and the sunrise till they came to the sea; and voyaging over the sea westwards, they came in the thirtieth month to that place whence the Egyptian king sent the Phoenicians afore-mentioned to sail around Lybia. After this circumnavigation Darius subdued the Indians and made use of this sea. Thus it was discovered that Asia, saving parts toward the rising sun, was in other respects like Lybia (Herodotus IV. 44; Godley 1926: 243, 45).

This reconnaissance by Scylax is one of the great lost works on ancient India. There are a few more bits and pieces that are summarized in English by Karttunen (1989:65-8). His story has a later parallel in the history of the Indus with the voyage of Lt. Alexander Burnes up the river from the Arabian Sea (Burnes 1833-34, 1834).

We know from Herodotus (III, 94; Godley 1926: 123) that India, specifically Sindh, became the twentieth province of the Persian Empire and that it paid a greater tribute than any other province: 360 talents of gold dust. Cambyses, the predecessor of Darius I, also controlled parts of the Subcontinent including Gandhara and the western Punjab (Olmstead 1948: 144-45).

The sixth century geographer Hekataeus makes note of the Indus, and a tribe he called the "Opiai" with their capital on its banks. He notes a vast desert "beyond," or to the east of the Indus Valley, knowledge of which seems to have come from Scylax's voyage (see also Karttunen 1989: 69-73).

The first historical source that survives to any extent is the *Indika* of the infamous Ctesias the Cnidian (McCrindle 1882). This Greek physician was in the employ of the Achaemenid kings Darius II and Artaxerxes Memnon. It is claimed that he came to Persia about 416 BC and remained there for 17 years. Ctesias attended the wounds of Artaxerxes Memnon inflicted by the latter's brother Cyrus during the rebellious battle of Cunaxa on September 3, 401 BC (Olmstead 1948: 374).

The *Indika* of Ctesias does not survive in full. It is most completely preserved as an abstract undertaken by the Byzantine Patriarch Photios during his exile in Armenia, in the last decade of the ninth century AD (*Bibliotheke* Photii, LXXII; McCrindle 1882: 5). Other ancient authors had access to the original text, and these can be found in McCrindle's book on the manuscript (McCrindle 1882).

Ctesias was not a critical author and his *Indika* is therefore one of the most fantastic documents to come from antiquity. It includes some of the most preposterous, uncritical retelling of bazaar gossip and travelers' tales that one can imagine (Karttunen 1981 for a critical review). But, as with many ancient documents, there is something to be gleaned from the work and there are some interesting facts, including the seasonality of the monsoon (McCrindle 1882: 33) and the interesting fat-tailed sheep of the region (McCrindle 1882: 17). Ctesias also notes that cotton comes from Sindh (McCrindle 1882: 24-5) and that there is a large lake in "..the middle of India (Sindh)..." on which the inhabitants sail their boats and rafts, hunt with bows and arrows, which they use with great skill. These folk also hunt with hawks; an early reference to falconry. He further suggests that the lake produces oil (McCrindle 1882: 15-6). H. T. Lambrick believes that this lake may be Manchar and that the oil is in reality fish oil (1964: 102); although there are petroleum seeps along the western mountainous border of the Indus Valley, especially north of Sehwan (see below).

Christian Lassen has also presented a review of the veracity of Ctesias' comments on Sindh

(Lassen 1874, Vol. 2: 641-65). He tends to see a glimmer of truth in some of the Greek's statements, but is highly critical of the work as a whole, and of Photios' abridgment. He also notes, correctly, that for the most part Ctesias is simply reporting what Persians told him about "India" and did not visit the country himself, or interview its inhabitants as a source of information.

These sources, and the Persians in his army, gave Alexander the Great a great deal of information on Sindh and the Punjab when he made his raid into the Subcontinent in the Spring of 326 BC. He and other Greeks did not consider this region beyond the known world. The land beyond the Punjab and across the western desert of the Indus River was the unknown; the sense of being on the edge of the earth and about to move into a genuinely foreign environment, a place with such fantastic people and animals as to defy imagination, may go far in explaining why Alexander's army wanted to call it quits, and go home. They placed their commander in such a position that he had no choice but to accede to their wishes. But, the Great Macedonian was going to do it his way and he took them on a voyage down the Indus River.

Natural History: The Central Region

A discussion of some of the natural history for the Central Region is called for. Interesting and important extensions of this summary are available in Aitken (1907) and Roberts (1977), as well as District Gazetteers.

Vegetation

The Indus flood plains were home to the usual species of trees found in the lowlands of the northwestern Subcontinent. This is a variety of acacia, especially *Acacia arabica* or *babul*, mixed with *kandi* (*Prosopis spicigeria*) and *sissu* or *tali* (*Dalbergia sissoo*) a very fine timber tree, *neem* (*Azadirachta indica*), *ber* (*Zizyphus jujuba*), tamarisk (*Tamarindus indica*), and other trees of lesser importance. The largest tree of the prehistoric forest was probably the *pipal* (*Ficus religiosa*). Well developed gallery forests would have been found in the meander flood plain, far enough removed from the floods to allow trees to survive and well enough watered to have them prosper. Rich stands of reeds and other useful plants would be found around oxbow lakes and other wet features of the plains (Plate 3.40).

Two additional plants, useful in dyeing cloth are endemic to the region. The first is *Rubalia cordifolia*, Indian Madder, or *manjit* in most Indo-European languages of the Subcontinent. It yields a simple dye which can be manipulated to gain colors from red to brown, with a mauve possible as well. The other is indigo, from the plant *Indigofara tinctoria*, which yields a blue coloring, widely used in the ancient world. The true home of this plant seems to be obscure, but it was cultivated in many places in the Subcontinent. In the Greater Indus Region this included the southern Punjab, near Multan and the Panjnad, as well as Sindh and Gujarat.

The botany of the Subcontinent is extremely well studied and there are many good sources. The ones on which I rely most are Anonymous (1953, 1957 and 1961), a three volume compilation of the flora of the old Bombay Presidency, which included Sindh and Gujarat. These are excellent sources of nomenclature, vernacular terminology, description and distribution of plants. Watt's *The Commercial Products of India* (1908) is also a mine of information as is Balfour's "Cyclopaedia" (1885).

E. H. Aitken (1907: 40-8) considered the forests of Sindh to be an important resource in the province. In his time they covered 2,500,000 hectares (6,000,000 acres). These were found along the river course and in Sukkur District, and the Upper Sindh Frontier in the north of the

Province. The principal detached forests were found in patches along the Eastern Nara and around Hyderabad.

Mammals

The Central Region would have been home to the lowland species of mammals of the Greater Indus Region; the elephant and rhino would have been there, along with the lion and tiger, as well as other cats. The Indus River, and its lakes and backwaters would have teemed with fish, which appear to have been important in the subsistence regime all through the Indus Age. The specifics of these resources have already been discussed (Plate 3.41).

Minerals

Dominated by a broad, deep, mature river valley, the Central Region is rich in fertile earth and water, but shy in mineral resources. Aitken notes the presence of alum, building stone, carbonate of soda, sulfate of strontia, coal, gypsum, iron and the like (1907: 77-84). He does not mention the limestone resources of the Rohri Hills which are associated with massive amounts of high quality chert. The limestone of Mohenjo-daro seems to have come from this source as well as the heavy concentration of chert found at this site and many others in the Greater Indus Region. The chert from Rohri is banded in a very distinctive way, resembling the layering in the flesh of fish. This distinctive signature for the chert in this large source seems to be a reliable marker for determining the source of specimens that have been turned into artifacts. There is also petroleum, or bitumen, in the area, especially around Sibi. These scattered sources appear to have been used all through the Indus Age.

The Flood Plains of the Indus River

The Indus is a very large, complex river as we know it today. The same would have been true in antiquity, but important features of location and course would have been different and these would have had, by the nature of systems, an effect on other variables such as volume and direction of flood. Since the later decades of the nineteenth century, the Indus has been a managed stream, with massive bunds across it, huge, intricate canal systems tapping it, man-made levees holding in check the flood waters and directing its central course. The exercise is called "river training" and it has been extremely effective in changing the nature of the river that would have flowed through Sindh when Mohenjo-daro was a flourishing metropolis.

It is not known exactly what the Indus was like during the Indus Age or where it flowed in those days. But, there are several older descriptions of the Indus that were made before the massive engineering works of the late nineteenth century were in place and these are excellent introductions to the river. The first is the original voyage by a European up its source through Sindh by Alexander Burnes (1833-34, 1834 and 1835a, see also 1835b). J. MacMurdo's three papers give a sense of the early river (1834a, 1834b, 1839) as do the accounts of Magrath (1839) and Tremenheere (1867). For the delta see Carless (1837, 1838a), Haig (1894) and Wilhelmy (1968a). M. Yusuf has a perspective on the Indus delta and the Ranns of Kutch (1987). The modern river is reviewed in Fraser (1958), Pithawala (1959), Lambrick (1964), Shroder (1993) and especially Jorgensen, Harvey, Schumm and Flam (1993) and Flam (1993b). The palaeocourses of the river have also been studied and we do have some idea on where it might have flowed in prehistoric times. It is an immensely interesting and important subject. The approximate contours of the modern river are shown in (Figure 3.115).

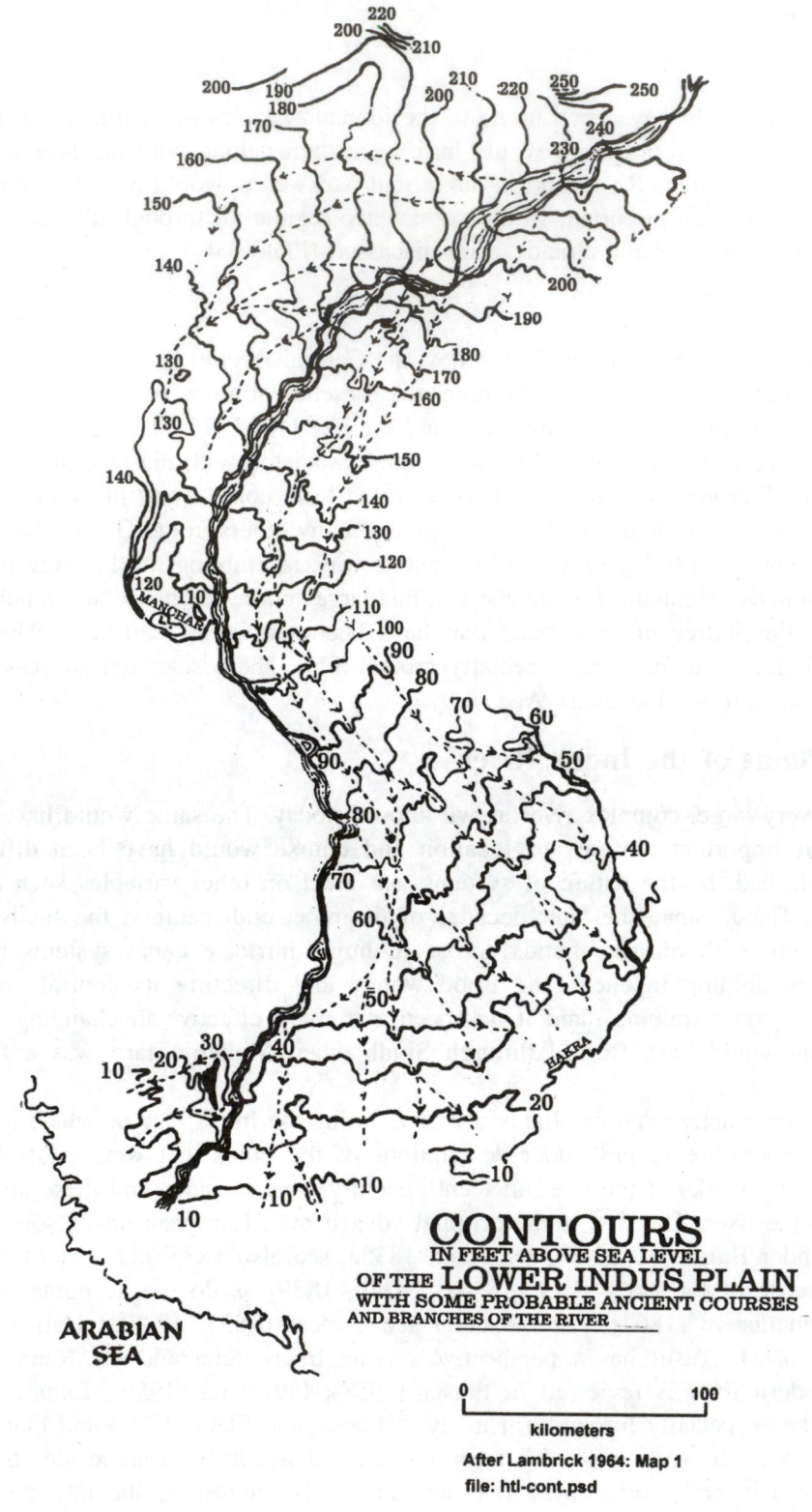

Figure 3.115. Contours of t' Indus Valley, after Lambrick 1964: Figure 1

The source of the Indus River was found by Sven Hedin in 1907 at the sacred spring of Singikabab near the Manasarover Lake in Tibet at an elevation of 5165 meters (16,946 feet) (Pithawala 1959: 67). The lake also gave birth to the Sutlej River, which joins the Indus after its long course through the Himalaya and the Punjab. The Indus initially flows west, then northwest where it is joined by the Ka-erh Chu. The combined river flows 600 kilometers through Ladakh (Plate 3.42, Plate 3.43) past Skardu and into Gilgit before it makes a great arcing turn to the south, at the same time dropping precipitously out of the confinement of the great mountains. Along this path the river has been fed by many smaller mountain torrents found in this vast watershed. Still confined to a well defined bed, the Indus flows south through Pakistan's Northwest Frontier Province and is joined at Attock by the waters of the Kabul River. Passing south through the Salt Range it enters the Punjab plains and is joined by the Tochi-Kuram and Zhob-Gomal streams. At this point the modern Indus, for the most part, flows within a deep entrenchment and is not a widely meandering river. Below the Salt Range the Indus begins to be navigable, at least by small country craft. Passing Dera Ghazi Khan, the Indus enters the Central Region at a point known as the panjnad; the traditional name of the point where the five rivers of the Punjab (Jhelum, Chenab, Ravi, Beas and Sutlej) join the Indus.[10]

Some Geographical Features of the Mature Indus River

Below the panjnad the Indus would have been a mature, meandering river, confined to a single channel during the winter low water months, but inundating a vast flood plain during the summer floods. As such, it has several geographical features shared with other large mature rivers of the world that are important in determining the nature of the Indus and the implications for human settlement and exploitation. These geographical features are also applicable to the Punjab and have a general usefulness in understanding rivers. Moving out from any given course of the main stream these begin with the banks of the river itself, then to the active flood plain, the meander flood plain, the cover flood plain, and finally the piedmont plain to the west and desert fringe to the east. Most of these features have been discussed by Fraser (1958).

The Banks of the Indus River

The immediate banks of the Indus River in the Central Region are transitory features and can be dangerous to human settlement. During the summer inundation, the chances of devastating floods are present. These will not strike everywhere at the same time, or even the same year, but the chances of settlement on the banks being wiped out on the short term are high. Moreover, the banks have a reputation for being soft and frequently collapsing of their own accord during low water, and so even in winter, the danger of cataclysmic demise awaits those who venture too near the Indus.

There are places where the banks are low and boats can ply the stream during low water and fishing and commerce can proceed. Those who utilize these natural facilities are used to moving frequently, following the deeper channels, staying away from high banks of new alluvium. Good locations are those with access to the subsidiary channels of the stream where boats and goods can be moved during the yearly inundation.

The pattern of alluvial buildup along the active course of the Indus, and other rivers like it, is such that the riverbed and its banks may rise above the surrounding plain if they remain in one place for a number of years. A natural levee is thus formed. When the river changes course it actually slips off its bed over the levee and the fact that water does not find it easy to flow up hill means that it is generally impossible for it to regain its former course and will seek a new channel, lower down from the old one. The Indus Valley is covered with these old natural levees which may be micro-features on the landscape but do impound some water and can form seasonal lakes.

Other lakes are formed when one of the loops of the meandering river is pinched off. Meanders tend to grow through the erosion of their longest outer bank, gradually narrowing the neck separating successive meander loops. "In time of flood the neck may be breached and the ends of the loop silted up, the river taking a new 'preferred,' straighter course" (Whitten and Brooks 1972: 331). These are called oxbow lakes, because their loop outline has the general shape of the bow in a harness when an ox is used for traction. These provide good fishing and habitat for plants (reeds, palms and grasses) and animals (birds, shellfish, fur-bearing mammal species) of great use to the inhabitants of the valley. The modern village of Hasanwahan, just east of Mohenjo-daro, is located on the edge of a very fine example of an oxbow lake.

The vegetation along the present banks of the Indus tends to be either larger remnants of older plants that matured prior to the river taking its current course, or annual plants that can survive the flood dynamics of this location.

The Active Flood Plain of the Indus River

The active flood plain is that part of the plain immediately adjacent to the actual river channel that has a very high probability of being flooded on an annual basis. I. S. Fraser describes it:

> The active flood plain might be described as the summer bed of the river as almost all this land is inundated during that season. The position of channels and river bars are continually changing within this land form. Erosion and deposition take place on a vast scale during the flood season and the surface form becomes stable only after the water-flood has receded. During the low water season the active flood plains have a level or very slightly undulating surface, scarred by numerous active or abandoned channels...Although the active flood plains are flooded annually, they do not merit the term 'waterlogged.' The soil is sufficiently permeable to allow excess water to drain off soon after the flood-water recedes... (Fraser 1958: 29).

This is an area that is virtually continuous along both sides of the active river course and is covered by rich, new alluvium. It is flat or lightly undulating, with many new scars resulting from the transitory flood channels of recent inundations (Plate 3.44, Plate 3.45). The area tends to be well drained and the soils soft near the ground surface. Dry cropping during the *rabi* (winter) cultivation season is possible (Fraser 1958: 29).

The Meander Flood Plain of the Indus River

Farther removed from the active river bed, at least in a near historical sense, across the banks and active flood plains on both sides, one meets the meander flood plain.

Meander flood plains are found beside active flood plains of existing major rivers and beside recently abandoned river courses. They are usually long belts lying parallel to river courses, but by no means continuous along all rivers (Fraser 1958: 28).

> The slightness of the gradients of the rivers of the Indus Plains is responsible for the formation of numerous bars, meander scrolls, levees and oxbow lakes. These features continually change until the river which forms them moves to a new bed. Then they become stable, their pattern stenciled on the land surface and remaining so unless they become obscured by a mantle of more-uniform alluvium (Fraser 1958: 28).

The Cover Flood Plain of the Indus River

The cover flood plain of the Indus River is the largest expanse of recent alluvium. Cover flood plains are composed of recent alluvium and some are still in the process of formation. They are the flood plains longest abandoned by flowing rivers, and the former channels, bars and other riverine features have been blanketed by more recent riverine deposits. The landscape and surface materials of the cover flood plains are the result of repeated sheet flooding accompanied by vertical accretion (Fraser 1958: 28).

This is still flood plain and some of this area is flooded. The cover plain receives mostly slow moving sheet floods with only the finest alluvium, but again, this is an area that can be invaded by the active river flood and is not a safe haven for villages. The face of the cover flood plain is older than the active or meander plains and has been subjected to substantial periods of gentle flooding, and has been slightly leveled by wind erosion. It is relatively flat with few features of relief visible to the naked eye. The lowest points collect more water by flood and some winter rain, and therefore more silt, by their very nature filling in the shallow spots, further leveling the terrain.

It can be difficult to separate the cover from the meander flood plain and in practice, the two often form a continuum with bars, old meander scars and levees gradually flattening and becoming less prominent features of the land as one moves from an area of more active meander to a cover plain (Fraser 1958: 28).

The area around the modern town of Larkana and the ancient city of Mohenjo-daro has been for sometime slightly higher ground than the rest of the active and meander flood plain of the Indus river. Sometimes it is not flooded, and is often referred to as "the island" among the Sindhis themselves.

The Western Piedmont Plain of the Indus River

From the perspective of the Indus River, the western piedmont plain is the area where the orogeny, erosion and redeposition from rivers and hill torrents of the Gedrosia Region predominate. South of the Lakhi Hills and Bado Range human habitation is very thin, almost negligible. The hill torrents, or *nais* in Sindhi, are important sources of water, and are the most convenient passes through the front of the Kirthar Range as at the Gaj Nai, just above Lake Manchar. But to the north, running to Kachi, is a zone of significant human habitation and many of sites of the Pre-Mature and Mature Harappan are located there.

The various passes through the Kirthar Range are foci for local drainage and a substantial amount of erosion, as well as natural passes between the hills and plains. Over the millennia these have built up their own alluvium on the western edge of the mountains. The largest passes are associated with the Gaj Nai, Mula and Bolan Rivers and these cuts through the Kirthar Mountains have been powerful forces in molding local communications, trade and transhumance. Some of the smaller springs are hot, and carry calcareous minerals which form tufa deposits that block and then redirect the local courses of the *nais*. The *nais* have been used for local irrigation all along the Kirthar Piedmont, probably from the period of early experimentation with farming. The most substantial of the piedmont soils covers the Kachi Plain, an area over 10,000 square kilometers, which is due primarily to the action of the Bolan River and Western Nara, assisted by the Mula River and the many *nais*.

Sindh Hollow, Lake Manchar and the Nais

There are several features of the Indus Valley which deserve special notice. The first is the so-called "Sindh Hollow." Lambrick (1964: 26), Postans and Knight (1844) discuss these features as they were seen in the mid-nineteenth century. In most flood seasons a branch of the Indus River took a course flowing due west as it passed the southern end of the Marri-Bugti Hills, filling a long trough between the Kirthar Mountains and the central plains of the valley. Because of its enduring nature this wide but shallow trough came to be known as Sindh Hollow. It seems to be a very old feature of the western side of the Indus Valley. The dependability of the annual inundation and the renewal of silt means that it was prime farming land in ancient times. The Western Nara now flows in this trough, which was a prominent feature of the early Indus.

An inundation basin on the western side of the Indus, called Lake Manchar, can be seen as a terminus of sorts for Sindh Hollow. E. H. Aitken described these features in 1907: "It now issues from the river (Indus) near the village of Akil in the Larkana Taluka, 8 miles east of Larkana. The distance from the head of the Nara to the Manchar is 83 miles in a straight line, but 153 1/2 miles measured along its course. It formerly started much farther north, but between 1860 and 1880 some 20 miles of it were eroded by the Indus till it came to be fed from the latter near the village of Akil" (1907: 286). Aitken also notes that the Western Nara was useful for navigation during the less violent periods of summer flood, since the flow of this stream was managed by headworks and was significantly lower than the main course of the Indus (1907: 288). The Western Nara also overspills its bed during some floods and the resulting natural channels make it a useful stream for irrigation (Aitken 1907: 287).

In Sindhi parlance, Lake Manchar is simply a very large *dhand*, or seasonal water body. It varies in size from year to year depending on the flood of the Indus and to a much smaller degree, runoff from snowfall in Baluchistan. The archaeological explorer N. G. Majumdar was there in December 1930 and informs us that the lake is normally 15 to 20 kilometers in diameter (1934: 60) or 25,000 to 30,000 hectares in surface area. It swells enormously as a result of the summer inundation, reaching a maximum size of several thousand hectares. When the flood waters recede there is normally something on the order of 10,000 hectares of irrigated land. In addition to providing a reliable source of water and significant tracts of naturally irrigated land, Lake Manchar is also a source of fish, fowl and reeds. The *dhand* and surrounding area has been a focus of human habitation on the edge of the Indus Valley since the beginnings of food production and probably much earlier (see Figure 3.129).

One of the best known of the Manchar Lake sites is a mound in the village of Trihni known as Lal Chhato (Majumdar 1934: 61-3), in which Majumdar put some small test pits. The exact age and affiliation of this settlement is not known, but it seems to be part of the Indus Age. When Majumdar first visited there on December 8, 1930, it was still submerged in about 2.5 meters of water. "This water, we are told, considerably dries up after the winter months. The mound is then exposed to a much greater height and becomes accessible from Trihni by land" (Majumdar 1934: 61). He also dug at the site of Mashak in the village of Shah Hassan at Lake Manchar in December 1930, following the excavation at Trihni. The site is a Mature Harappan settlement (perhaps with some Trihni Ware) and was found in shallow water, but still within the bounds of the lake at that time of year. Two other potential archaeological localities were investigated in Lake Manchar: Rohindo and Madi But. They were well known to the *mohanas* (boatmen) and were still completely below water in December (Majumdar 1934: 64).

The existence of sites that are ca. 4000 years old within the bounds of Lake Manchar tests one's intuitive notions about alluvial processes in mature river valleys such as the Indus. It is clear that there has been no huge buildup of silt in the lake over this period of time or Trihni and Mashak would have been long hidden, unless they are huge sites, with only the "tip of the iceberg" showing today; and there is no indication that is the case. Many alternatives exist to explain this. Four alternatives that have come to mind are that the lake might be a relatively recent formation; the lake, or something like it, was in existence in antiquity and has been rejuvenated in more recent historical times; there might be a long term balance in depositional and erosional processes in the lake, with a natural "flushing" system relieving it of silt, but still not strong enough to remove archaeological sites, or the Indus Valley is just not as well understood as some would lead us to believe. One thing is clear, however, the presence of these sites demonstrates in a reasonably conclusive way that the present Western Nara, leading into the Manchar basin, could never have been a main course of the Indus.

This area was also visited by Charles Masson, the explorer who first visited Harappa in 1826. The visit took place in 1831 during a trip from Kalat through the Mula Pass and down the "outside" of the Kirthar Range, past the Gaj Nai and on to Sehwan and Trihni (Masson's "Trenni," the inhabitants of which were noted in Masson's day for their proclivity of stealing dogs from passing caravans), and to the mounded village of Bubak where Majumdar halted about 100 years later on December 7, 1930 (Majumdar 1934: 59; Masson 1842: Vol. II: 141). Masson did not recognize any of the prehistoric mounds, but he did spend time examining the fort at Sehwan, noting that it was an ancient site and finding a minor antiquity, a copper earring (1842: Vol. II: 142-46).

Majumdar made the following observations concerning these sites in the lake:

> Our explorations around the Manchar Lake now prove for the first time the existence of a lake-dwelling people in Sind, during the later part of the Indus period. That their settlements were on the verge of the lake shows that they could not have been primarily an agricultural people. In fact, the western bank of the Manchar abuts on rocky beds, leaving very little margin for cultivation. The people living on its neighborhood must have been, therefore, compelled to depend largely on fish and such other game as the lake could afford. Their ways of subsistence could not have been much different from those of the people living in the Manchar area at the present day. Fishing is their principal avocation, and they like to be as near the water as possible. Many of them live in boats with their families, or in huts constructed on platforms on the surface of water. These huts have a curious likeness to the Neolithic and Chalcolithic pile-dwellings of the lakes of Switzerland and other European countries. Whether the ancient lake-dwellers of Manchar use to have similar pile-houses it is difficult to say with the data available. The pits and trenches excavated on Lal Chhatto and Mashak mounds have not revealed any brick or stone, nor was there any indication to show that these lake-dwellings were made of these materials. The cuttings reveal a deposit of pure silt; and the find of household objects like pottery, etc. in this silt deposit is unaccountable, unless we suppose the existence of wooden or mud houses built on an elevation made of earthwork. It may therefore be supposed that the little islands like Lal Chhatto and Mashak were the predecessors of the modern fishing hamlets of Lake Manchar (Majumdar 1934: 65).

H. G. Raverty notes that similar conditions exist in the area around the panjnad town of Alipur where the Jhelum and Chenab join just above the confluence of this united stream with the main Indus body: "...from June to September...all the district to the southwards...is under water and the only means of communication is by boats. During this time the inhabitants, washed out of their dwellings, live on small platforms raised on poles, with one or more of which each homestead is provided, called *machan* in Hindi and also *manchan*...(they) are often not able to leave them for weeks together" (Raverty 1892b: 155).

In colonial times Lake Manchar was perhaps best known as a place for hunting birds, especially in the winter when tens of thousands passed through on their annual migration to more tropical regions.

284

As the floods subside Lake Manchar is drained by the Aral Wah (river), 27 kilometers in length, connecting it to the main channel of the Indus. "But the Aral does not always run in one direction. During the inundation, when the level of the Indus is much above that of the Manchhar (sic), its current is reversed and it becomes a feeder of the Lake and a much more important one than the Nara, the waters of which are dissipated in irrigation. As soon as the inundation subsides, the Aral again serves to discharge the Lake" (Aitken 1907: 288).

There is also a Nara to the east of the main Indus channel flowing along the western fringes of the great Thar Desert. This is an old river bed shown as the "Eastern Nara" on most maps, although it has many other names: Hakra, Sakra, Wandan, Dahan, Dadhawah and Wahind to name a few. It is now a major canal, irrigating many thousands of hectares. The origins of this channel and its relationship with the Indus is not fully understood. It might be that this modern course is the lower portion of an ancient river called the Sarasvati in Vedic literature, a topic dealt with in some detail in the discussion of the Eastern and Hakra Regions.

The Eastern Nara and the Desert Fringe of the Indus River

To the east, the alluvium of the Indus seems very old and is interdigitated with silts from the Eastern Nara. The area is extremely complex, therefore interesting and deserving of greater study. An early memoir on it was written by Alexander Burnes (1835b). The land surface is old and is now largely covered by shifting sand dunes so large that they can choke rivers. The sands hold seasonal lakes or *dhands* that are now used by pastoral nomads for agriculture and domestic water. The presence of a scatter of small prehistoric archaeological sites in this desert fringe is evidence that the same was probably true during the Indus Age (Lambrick 1964: 88–9).

It is an area that can be thought of as outside the main zone of flooding of the Holocene Indus with its own history of subsidiary (Hakra) river activity. Behind, or to the east of the desert fringe of the Central Region, is the Great Indian Desert. It is a separate Region in which the Harappan Civilization was active during the Early and Mature Harappan.

The Indus River

Within the plains of modern Sindh the Indus River is a fully mature stream. It has a reputation as a powerful, violent, unpredictable river. Sindh, as far as the amount of rainfall is concerned, is a desert, so there is little water added from this source. A sampler of statistics gives some impression of the size of the Indus, especially as it compares to other mature rivers. The observations for the Indus have been taken from Pithawala (1959: 74-110), where the full set of numbers are available. Some expeditious facts about the Indus from this source:

1.	Total length	2900 km
2.	Length in Sindh, with meanders	ca. 1000 km
3.	Discharge, maximum	885,165 cu ft/second
4.	Discharge, minimum	17,568 cu ft/second
5.	Discharge, average maximum	ca. 400,000 cu ft/second
6.	Maximum highwater at Sukkur	+5.40 meters
7.	Maximum highwater at Kotri	+7.35 meters
8.	Total silt per year carried past Sukkur (average for 29 years)	9,937,000,000 cu ft.
9.	Total silt per year carried past Kotri (average for 29 years)	8,229,000,000 cu ft.
10.	Average silt carried	1,000,000 tons/day
11.	Maximum velocity in Sindh	3.2 meters/second

A typical year for the floods at Sukkur, in the early 20th century, finds that March is low water time with the Indus flowing slowly at 70,000 cu ft/second (cusecs). As April with hot weather approaches, the water starts to rise due to the beginning of the Himalayan snow melt. The flow increases to 100,000 to 110,000 cusecs. By May it is double the April values at ca. 200,000 cusecs. June values at 280,000 cusecs would be typical and July figures at 350,000 cusecs. Virtually all of this water is snow melt from the winter falls in the mountains, and in July the river tends to level off, possibly even drop a bit in its level and flow. But, as the southwest monsoon reaches the drainage areas of the Punjab and fore slopes of the mountains, rainfall contributes to total volume and the Indus is on the rise again in August, often up to 600,000 cusecs, with the average about 400,000.

The maximum discharge rate for the Indus is ca. 885,000 cusecs. It has been suggested that the physical properties (climate and hydrology) of its drainage basin theoretically could combine for a maximum flow of ca. 950,000 cusecs. Such an event would be terribly destructive, even cataclysmic, especially in Sindh, where it would wreak havoc throughout the entire region. The large-scale clear cutting of timber resources undertaken in the past 20 years in the Himalayan and Hindu Kush Ranges tends to increase both the runoff and erosion of all of the rivers, contributing to the Indus flow in Sindh which has increased the probabilities of a 950,000 cusec flood. This wanton destruction of a natural, viable watershed may well raise the ante and admit the possibility of a yet unthought of 1,000,000 cusec event.

A Comparison of the Indus and the Nile Rivers

Just as Egypt is said to be the "Gift of the Nile" it could be said that Sindh is the "Gift of the Indus." These two great rivers share many characteristics but there are important differences as well, many of which have been brought out in a book comparing works in these two valleys in the scientific age just prior to modern times (Buckley 1893). The annual inundation of the Nile is much more steady and deliberate than the Indus (Lambrick 1964: 22). The Nile is measurably smaller, with an average maximum discharge of about 300,000 cusecs, compared to the Indus with ca. 400,000 cusecs. The Indus also carries significantly more silt. This can be measured in two ways. The proportion by weight of silt to water in the Indus is one part in 237, but for the Nile it is one part in 666. The total volume of silt carried by the Indus during the 100 days of inundation has been estimated to be ca. 119 million cubic yards, the same statistic for the Nile would be only 40 million cubic yards (Buckley 1893: 36-7).

The Indus Plains

The Indus in the Central Region flows through, and has filled, a geological syncline or down warp, formed when the main peninsular land mass of India had its "bump" with the rest of Asia. This syncline is the western edge or scar resulting from this intercontinental "accident." Its partner is the Ganga Valley, also a deep syncline filled with alluvium on the nose of the intercontinental collision which began in the Mesozoic age of dinosaurs and continues unabated today.

The accumulation of alluvium in Sindh has not been steady, but much of the sediment came during the Holocene after the retreat of the last continental glaciers about 10,000 years ago (Brinkman and Rafiq 1971: 18). It is now estimated in parts to be 600 meters deep (Lower Indus Project 1966: 16, for detail see Lower Indus Project 1965a, 1965b, 1965c, 1965d, 1965e). Over the millennia the area below the panjnad has been crossed and crossed again by the meandering Indus and its floods. It can be inferred that it has flowed close to the Kirthar Range to the west and tens of miles to the east of the present bed, reaching into the modern Thar

Desert. The approximate alignment of the easternmost Indus alluvium is a sinuous track, not perfectly defined by field geology.

To the unaided eye the Indus Valley is perfectly flat. It is true that there are two natural limestone outcrops that disturb this vista. The Rohri Hills in the north extending from the Sukkur Gap to just south of Kot Diji and a set of smaller hills at Ganjo near Hyderabad. These are relatively small bumps in the overall scheme of the plains and they appear to be very flat. In fact, the old alluvial areas in the northeastern Central Region stretch away in a grand vista in all directions, as flat as a calm sea, so flat that the curvature of the earth might be detected.

The Indus has been in its mature stage, with broad meanders, for many millennia, probably for all of the Holocene. It is a river particularly known for its changes of course and realignment of channels, because the slope of the valley itself is steep enough to generate a strong, eroding flow, but gentle enough to promote meandering. It is also well documented that the soils of Sindh are friable and loose, easily eroded and moved by floods subsequent to their original deposition. A chart of distances measuring the river course against the direct distance of travel for the premodern period is shown in Table 3.14.

TABLE 3.14
Distances in Sindh

	Direct By River Miles	kilometers	Ratio
Kashmore to Sukkur	117	188	1 to 1.49
Sukkur to Sehwan	169	272	1 to 1.61
Sehwan to Kotri	122	196	1 to 1.50
Kotri to delta head (Aitken 1907: 10)	122	196	1 to 1.55

One of the physical properties of mature rivers like the Indus is that the absolute length of the meandering river course is a constant. The pinching off of an oxbow in one place implies an equal lengthening of the river in another. This seesaw action of shrinkage and growth is further reason for the unpredictability of the Indus.

Indus Floods

The Indus lies quiescent for much of the year, flowing within its principle channel, although at any given time many subsidiary channels are also carrying water and there are even more *dhoroes* or dry beds. As the water rises and flow increases, the pre-flood charging of all channels takes place, first to the north, then progressing south, down the valley. Sooner or later the water tops the bank of the main stream at a low point or some spot of weakness in the natural levee of the stream. Water initially pours fast through such a gap, further opening the breach through erosion. But the water soon slows and as it does it drops its burden of sand and silt, first leaving the heavier material, then the lighter as it progressively fans out across the country side. The Indus Valley alluvium is generally coarser in the north than it is in the south, although both sand and silt occur in all flood deposits. The fact that the greater volume of the silt, and the larger, coarser materials, carried by the flood waters, drop out while still close to the main stream explains how the natural levees are formed. These levees can be thought of as a single ridge with the channel of the quiescent, winter river, incised within it.

The floods of the Indus are varied in another way that helps to explain how humans benefit from natural phenomena. At times, the flood waters are so concentrated and powerful that as they move forward they heavily scour the land, digging a new low channel in the flood plain, even throwing off subsidiary channels. These courses are documented best from nineteenth century maps of the Kalhora and Talpur dynasty irrigation canals of Sindh. The lack of backfill spoil along the courses, as well as their convoluted routes are compelling evidence (Lambrick 1964: 27) that, for the most part, these Sindhi dynasties let nature dig their irrigation works. The same may have been true during the Indus Age, since it is the smart way to produce an irrigation system in this valley.

The concentrations of silt left by the full recession of water in the farthest reaches of these channels is deep, and extraordinarily fertile. The soft rich earth is used for agriculture without preparation by farmers who hunt down these temporary *sailaba* fields under one of the traditional Sindhi systems of production.

The pace of flooding during any particular year is such that as breaks occur in the upstream reaches, with water and silt drawn off, the pressures to breach in the lower reaches of the stream are diminished. Chance plays some role in this process. Floods moving to the east or west of the stream may mean that the opposite side of the river will remain wholly or comparatively unaffected by that annual inundation, so that in any given year only parts of the valley are likely to be flooded and some areas go dry for several years in a row. But, the floods are generally a blessing and from the earliest times of recorded history the Indus Valley has been famine free. Such is the predictable productivity of this great green machine for agriculture.

The years for very high water and serious flooding in the Indus Valley are: 1841, 1858, 1861, 1874, 1882, 1897, 1903, 1914, 1917, 1921, 1924, 1929-30, 1942, 1944, 1945 and 1948 (see Inverarity for 1861). The worst of the historical floods were not caused by high precipitation and snowfall in the Himalaya but by natural catastrophes there. For example, the flood of 1841 began with the collapse of an ice bridge on the Shyok tributary to the Indus in the Fall of 1840, which formed a temporary lake 19 kilometers long 800 meters wide and 120 meters deep. When the dam was breached it sent a wall of water down the river. It took two days to reach Attock which it passed as a wall of thick, muddy water nine meters high (Snelgrove 1967: 37). The flood of 1858 was also caused by a temporary obstruction deep within the mountains. It is said that the river rose 20 to 25 meters at Attock and caused the Kabul River to flow backwards for a time (Snelgrove 1967: 38). In 1926, 1929 and 1932 the Chong Kudun glacier advanced across the Shyok branch and formed a barrier 120 meters high which later burst, releasing an unspecified body of water (Snelgrove 1967: 38). Landslides and ice on the upper reaches of the Indus system represent a considerable long-term danger to the inhabitants of Sindh and these would have probably been "invisible" to the ancient inhabitants there.

The 1874 flood was not linked to a natural catastrophe but it washed away 80 towns and villages and a large portion of the city of Jacobabad (Snelgrove 1967: 38). The 1942 flood left 400,000 people homeless. These flood waters covered 16 talukas in upper Sindh spreading over 8000 square kilometers. It was a sudden, violent surge of water that carried everything it encountered before it, destroying roads, bridges, railways, entire villages, farmsteads and fields. The flood proceeded south and abated only when it reached Lake Manchar, the safety valve for Indus floods (Pithawala 1959: 94).

These exceptional floods cause great damage, and seem to occur with some frequency. The inhabitants of the Indus Valley, especially within the Central Region, must have learned to cope with them, in spite of the great danger. Although they cannot be predicted on a yearly basis, severe floods can be thought of as a constant, endemic phenomenon: they are going to happen, and happen frequently. The people who have lived on or adjacent to the flood plains for millennia have gone through a long period of adaptive adjustment and know their river very well. These exceptional events are, and always have been, part of their lives and the fact that they continue to occupy intensely flooded land suggests that their adaptation is sound. Archaeologists should remember this when they theorize that it was the vagaries of the Indus River, and its unpredictable flood regime, that drove the ancient inhabitants of Mohenjo-daro and other Indus Civilization cities and towns from their homes. After all, if Mohenjo-daro and the Indus Civilization are said to be the "Gift of the Indus," could it also have been the source of its demise?

Navigation of the Indus

The history of navigation of the Indus begins with the withdrawal of Alexander the Great down the river, organized by his admiral, Nearchus. There are no technical data in any of the accounts to aid in understanding the navigation of the river, but Arrian seems to make navigation a simple chore, if only because he draws little attention to it.

The mission of Lt. Alexander Burnes in 1831 (Burnes 1833-34, 1834, 1835a) was ostensibly to deliver a carriage and horses to Ranjit Singh, the great Sikh ruler of the Punjab at that time. To get the cargo to him the British petitioned the Amirs of Sindh for permission to bring them up the river by boat, affording the British government a view of the waterway. After a false start, Burnes reached Tatta on April 12th. From there it was a six day journey to Hyderabad. They sailed on to Sukkur where the party halted for about a month. Moving to the Ravi, they finally reached Lahore on July 18th. Burnes compiled statistics on the river and drew an accurate map of the Indus. His mission was called a harbinger of conquest at the time when a Sindhi native was heard to lament "Alas! Sinde is now gone, since the English have seen the river, which is the road to its conquest" (Burnes 1834: 38). In spite of the presence of southerly winds to push Burnes' craft up river the journey was slow because they had to be pulled upstream by human power linked to the boat by ropes. Navigation in the delta is difficult because of the constantly shifting channels, although there is good depth in the active courses. Burnes noted that sailing between the upper delta and Sehwan is easy, but above Sehwan the river is shallow and more difficult.

The Indus is a river which can be sailed during the low water period. It is treacherous during full flood and is avoided by all sailors during this period. One can sail down the Indus with relative ease, although the collapse of the banks is a constant danger.

Burnes was a spirited character of his day, gifted in languages and courage, he visited Amri and Harappa as part of his journey up the Indus. He was, however, five years behind Charles Masson. Burnes was also among the first Europeans to visit Bokhara, which resulted in a book that was a "sensation" in England and contributed to his receiving a knighthood. Sir Alexander played a major role in the so-called "Great Game." He met an untimely death at the hands of a Kabul mob on the evening of November 2, 1841, during the British occupation of Afghanistan in the First Afghan War.

Lieutenant John Wood was the first to take a steam boat up the Indus. He accomplished this in 1835 and it allowed him to make a detailed survey of the Indus River, published in 1838.[11] It is an important historical document, in some ways more useful to an archaeologist or historian than Burnes' account. For example, Wood has a reliable report that at times the Indus in Sindh can be forded, although it is not an event of any certainty (Wood 1838: 569-71). In the nineteenth century, large grain boats with sufficient draft had to be charted in great detail to avoid grounding. The fords are temperamental, shifting features, even within a single season, and Lieutenant Wood was able to document only one good example in 1836-37, near Hala, just above Hyderabad.

Given the prominence of the Indus River Central Region it is not surprising that the prehistoric inhabitants of the Central Region possessed boats. These are documented by three representations at Mohenjo-daro and a model from Lothal.

1. Mohenjo-daro, (Mackay 1937-38: Pl. LXXXIX, A). This is a seal with a boat engraving (Figure 3.116).
2. Mohenjo-daro, (Mackay 1937-38: Pl. LXIX, No. 4). Graffiti on pottery representing a boat (Figure 3.117).
3. Mohenjo-daro, (Dales 1968: 39). A three-sided sealing with a boat on one side (Figure 3.118).
4. Lothal, (Rao 1985: 505, Pl. CCXX and CCXXIIIA). This is a terracotta boat model from the Mature Harappan (Figure 3.119).

Mackay described the two representations of boats he found at Mohenjo-daro in the following way:

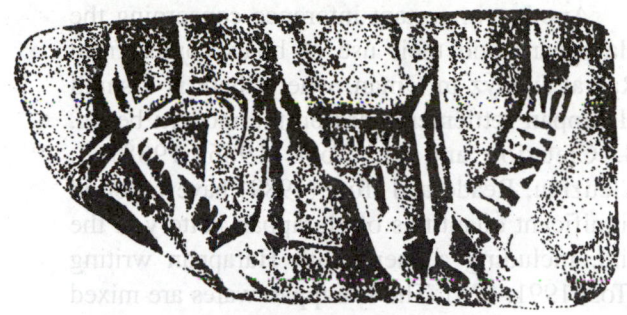

Figure 3.116. Boat from Mohenjo-daro, after Mackay 1937-38: Pl. LXXXIX, A

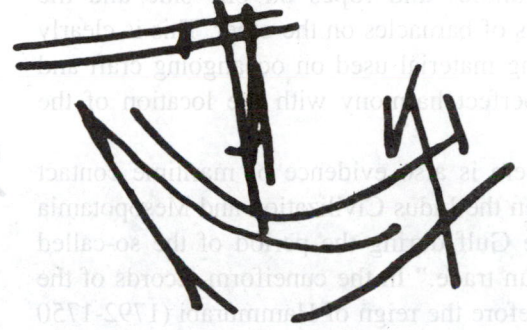

Figure 3.117. Boat from Mohenjo-daro, after Mackay 1937-38: Pl. LXIX, No. 4

Figure 3.118. Boat from Mohenjo-daro, after Dales 1968: 39

We have, however, found two representations of boats. One is roughly scratched on a potsherd and apparently has two yards on its masts. The other is carved on a seal and the bindings of its hull suggest that this boat was made of bundles of reeds, as were so many contemporary craft of ancient Egypt. It is mastless, which perhaps indicates that it is a river boat. The one, if not two, uprights at either end of the cabin carry flags or emblems, and a seated steersman holds a pair of oar-like rudders, as on the modern Indus craft. This vessel, it is interesting to note, is singularly the one portrayed on the well known Gebel-el Arak ivory knife handle, which, though found in Egypt, is thought to have been an importation, possibly from Elam. Of these boats the one with the mast could have been used for sea travel (Mackay 1934: 422).

The third Mohenjo-daro boat (Figure 3.118) is also small and lacks a mast. Judging by its looks, it is a river craft. The Lothal model appears more like a sailing dinghy than a ship and with a flat bottom would hardly have been a safe, useful craft on the open sea.

290

Another important inference concerning the Harappans and their use of boats comes from Ras al Junayz in Oman, where there is a small Harappan settlement hard on the modern beach. S. Cleuziou and M. Tosi (1986, 1988) S. Cleuziou, Reade and Tosi (1989) have reported significant quantities of Harappan pottery at the site, including a sherd with Harappan writing (Tosi 1991: 124). The Harappan wares are mixed with indigenous ceramics. Among the other finds are pieces of bitumen with the impressions of reed bundles and ropes on one side and the remains of barnacles on the other. This is clearly caulking material used on oceangoing craft and is in perfect harmony with the location of the site.

There is also evidence of maritime contact between the Indus Civilization and Mesopotamia via the Gulf during the period of the so-called "Dilmun trade." In the cuneiform records of the time before the reign of Hammurabi (1792-1750 BC) there are five references to Meluhhan boats. The most famous is a boast by Sargon of Akkad (2334-2279 BC) which has been translated by Samuel N. Kramer (1964: 49).

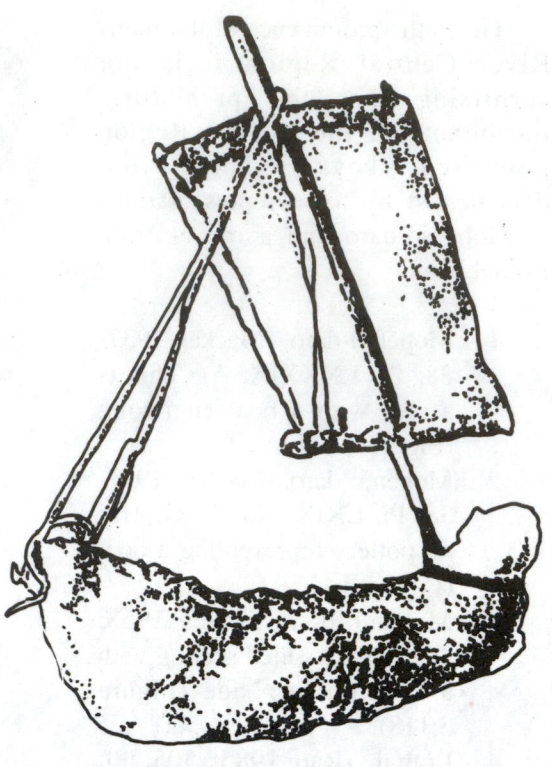

Figure 3.119. Boat from Lothal, after Rao 1985: 505, Pl. CCXX and CCXXIIIA

> The ships from Meluhha,
> the ships from Magan,
> the ships from Dilmun
> he made tie-up alongside
> the quay of Akkad.

The original of this inscription is published in (Hirsch 1963: 37-8).

The History of the Indus River and Its Ancient Courses

Introduction

It has been clear from the beginning of research on the Harappan Civilization that knowing the courses of the Indus River in the Central Region, during the Indus Age, was imperative to understand fully these ancient peoples. But finding these courses has proved to be an elusive goal. The Indus River has been shown to be a volatile body of water, constantly in motion, shifting its bed from here to there, depositing massive amounts of alluvium as it moves from place to place on the plains of its mature valley. To think of "the course of the Indus River during the Mature Harappan" is to chase a chimera. There surely was no one "course" but there must have been many during the Mature Harappan and they were even numerous in the millennia that preceded it.

H. T. Lambrick has some interesting things to say about the nature of the Indus in his important book *Sind: A general introduction*. He notes the following concerning the meandering of the Indus and its effects on the inhabitants of Sindh:

What is remarkable, in view of what we know of the movements of the Indus during the last twenty centuries, is not that part of the site of Mohen-jo-Daro was flooded out on more than one occasion, and rebuilt on almost the same plan as before, as is duly mentioned; but that the city could have flourished almost continuously through so long a period as a thousand years. For it is the local withdrawal of the waters of the Indus, and not their temporary excess, that brings calamity in Sind; and with the exception of Sehwan (Aror survives as a village) it is doubtful if any of its living towns have achieved an unbroken period of existence as long as that of Mohen-jo-daro. All the other places mentioned by the Arab geographers of the tenth century AD are unidentifiable, or lie in ruins; changes in the course of the Indus have been the most important cause of the abandonment, as of the foundation, of these and most other towns in Sind before and since, up till the nineteenth century (Lambrick 1964: 72-3).

He also cites a specific instance when he recalls that the town of Nasarpur, one of the principal markets of middle Sindh in the first half of the eighteenth century, did not recover from its abandonment by the Indus in 1758 (Lambrick 1964: 94, fn 16).

This same sense of the transitory nature of the river is given by D. A. Holmes as part of his study of the history of the Indus:

"The remains of...Mohenjo-daro lie south of Larkana, but its proximity to the right bank of the modern river is purely coincidental. It can only be assumed that the inhabitants built their city at no great distance from the river, or a major branch of the river...Our knowledge of the later vagaries of the Indus shows that the prosperity of any one district is somewhat transient, being primarily dependent on the location of that aberrant river" (Holmes 1968: 375).

Since Medieval times there has been one fixed point in the lower course of the Indus River. Some 200 kilometers below the panjnad the modern Indus flows through the Sukkur Gap, a break in the limestone ridge known as the Rohri Hills. The river proceeds through a gorge, at the mouth of which is the rugged island of Bukkur. The stream is reduced to a mere 550 meters in width by taking this course. Since it must still accommodate the same volume of water as the broader stream the Gap is consequently deep: over 20 meters (Lambrick 1964: 19-20). The Indus has flowed through the Gap for as much as a millennium, as attested by Muslim geographers (Elliot 1871: 554; Lower Indus Project 1965b: Vol. 2, Appendix V: 15; Lambrick 1964: 182-3, 1967: 489-90; Holmes 1968: 379). According to Lambrick the first mention of Bukkur is in the first quarter of the thirteenth century, in the history of Malik Nasr-ud-Din Kabacha when the island was a fortress. H. M. Elliot gives the following:

Kabacha though he was an Amir under the Ghorian kings, and governor of the country of Sind, yet was presumptous enough to aspire to independence. When Kabacha with twenty thousand of his followers were encamped on the bands of the Indus within one parasang of Uch, Uzbec Pai with seven thousand men, suddenly fell upon them at night, defeated, and dispersed them. Kabacha embarked in a boat for Akar and Bakar (two island forts in his possession), while the Uzbec descended upon his camp...(Elliot 1871: 554).

In a note on the passage, Elliot claims that "...the *Tarikh-i Alfi* says plainly, 'He (Kabacha) went towards the island of Bakar.' Altogether, I make little doubt that the famous island-fort of Bhakkar is the one indicated" (Elliot 1871: 554, note 2). Elliot's "Bhakkar" is, of course, our Bukkur (Plate 3.46, Plate 3.47).

There is some suggestion that prior to having been seized at the Sukkur Gap the river flowed to the north, around Sukkur. "The explanation of the river's faithfulness to this narrow bed lies in the attractive power of the gorge itself. Its bottom lies some sixty feet below flood level, and thus much deeper than the bed a little way up stream; we should here regard the natural capillarity of the water as an unbreakable chain pulled relentlessly down into it" (Lambrick 1964: 20). The recent river courses at Sukkur were illustrated by Lambrick and show very well the variability of the courses above the gap, as opposed to relative stability on the near, down side (Figure 3.120).

The significance of the Sukkur Gap lies in its relative permanence as a fixed point for the modern and Medieval river. Once it was captured by the passage through Rohri Hills the Indus was not free from this point in its course. It seems that the Indus did not flow here in the fourth century BC since none of Alexander's historians draw attention to the drama of this passage. Two inferences can be drawn from these observations: the Indus did not flow through the Sukkur Gap during the Indus Age and the capture there took place sometime between the fourth century BC and the thirteenth century AD.

In its unmanaged state there is a sense that the Indus meandered within a *particular zone* over relatively long periods of time, perhaps several centuries. While the Indus is known for the unpredictability of its flood, the course of the river is not completely haphazard, meandering here and there without any sense of order over the long run. If this hypothesis is valid, and it has not been proven, then there would be some justification in seeking the zone, or zones, that were active in Pre-urban and Mature Harappan times.

For the sake of consistency with the vocabulary of authors who have dealt with this topic, the term "course" will be used in place of a "zone" through which the river flowed in antiquity. The courses are to be thought of as broader than the active flood plain of the Indus, reaching out to the meander flood plain, or a relatively wide area within which the river might have flowed for a protracted period of time.

Scholars Who Have Studied This Problem

There are five scholars who have made serious attempts to describe the ancient courses of the Indus: R. D. Banerji, Maneck B. Pithawala, H. T. Lambrick, D. A. Holmes and Louis Flam.

R. D. Banerji

R. D. Banerji's observations on the ancient courses of the Indus are the least systematic of these efforts, but the pioneering effort is certainly worth recognition. His views are presented in a work written in 1926 but not published until 1984, well after his death (Banerji 1984). The maps that accompanied the original manuscript have been lost, so there is no choice but to rely on the narrative, which is not entirely coherent without the illustrations.

Banerji speaks of at least eleven old beds of the Indus between the modern river and the Kirthar Range (1984: 14-5). He also made interesting attempts to link settlement location and river courses as an aid in dating the history of the river (1984: 1-17). His efforts are rather crude by today's standards, really emerging from his own very strong intuition, but they should be recognized as a beginning for interest in this important topic.

Maneck B. Pithawala

Maneck B. Pithawala's thoughts on the ancient beds of the Indus River are far more systematic and important than Banerji's. Pithawala's work on Sindh (1959) and his contributions to the geography of Sindh, and Pakistan generally, have proved to be very useful. His reconstructions

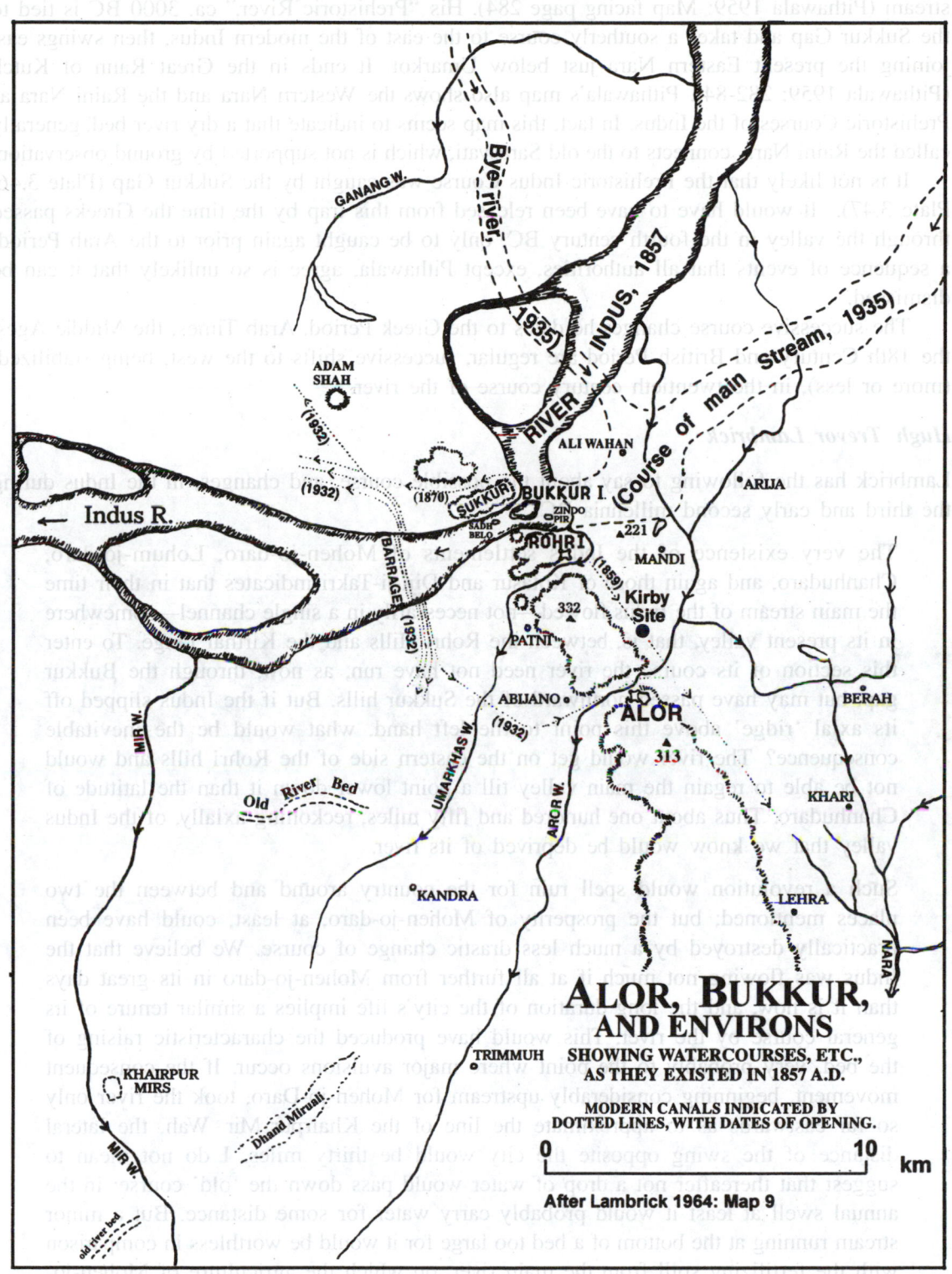

Figure 3.120. Indus River at Sukkur, with old channels, after Lambrick 1964: Figure 9

take a long perspective on the history of the Indus, attempting to reconstruct even the Pleistocene stream (Pithawala 1959: Map facing page 284). His "Prehistoric River," ca. 3000 BC is tied to the Sukkur Gap and takes a southerly course to the east of the modern Indus, then swings east joining the present Eastern Nara just below Umarkot. It ends in the Great Rann of Kutch (Pithawala 1959: 282-84). Pithawala's map also shows the Western Nara and the Raini Nara as Prehistoric Courses of the Indus. In fact, this map seems to indicate that a dry river bed, generally called the Raini Nara, connects to the old Sarasvati, which is not supported by ground observation.

It is not likely that the Prehistoric Indus Course was caught by the Sukkur Gap (Plate 3.46, Plate 3.47). It would have to have been released from this trap by the time the Greeks passed through the valley in the fourth century BC, only to be caught again prior to the Arab Period; a sequence of events that all authorities, except Pithawala, agree is so unlikely that it can be dismissed.

The successive course changes he dates to the Greek Period, Arab Times, the Middle Ages, the 18th Century and British Period are regular, successive shifts to the west, being stabilized, (more or less), in the twentieth century course of the river.

Hugh Trevor Lambrick

Lambrick has the following to say about the possible course, and changes, in the Indus during the third and early second millennia BC:

> The very existence of the Indus settlements of Mohen-jo-daro, Lohum-jo-daro, Chanhudaro, and again those of Kotasur and Diji-ji-Takri indicates that in their time the main stream of the Indus flowed—not necessarily in a single channel—somewhere in its present valley, that is, between the Rohri Hills and the Kirthar range. To enter this section of its course the river need not have run, as now, through the Bukkur gap, but may have passed northward of the Sukkur hills. But if the Indus slipped off its axial 'ridge' above this point to the left hand, what would be the inevitable consequence? The river would get on the eastern side of the Rohri hills and would not be able to regain the main valley till a point lower down it than the latitude of Chanhudaro. Thus about one hundred and fifty miles, reckoning axially, of the Indus valley that we know would be deprived of its river.

> Such a revolution would spell ruin for the country around and between the two places mentioned; but the prosperity of Mohen-jo-daro, at least, could have been practically destroyed by a much less drastic change of course. We believe that the Indus was flowing not much if at all further from Mohen-jo-daro in its great days than it is now, and the long duration of the city's life implies a similar tenure of its general course by the river. This would have produced the characteristic raising of the bed, very probably to the point where major avulsions occur. If the consequent movement, beginning considerably upstream for Mohen-jo-Daro, took the river only so far eastwards as to approximate the line of the Khairpur Mir Wah, the lateral distance of the swing opposite the city would be thirty miles. I do not mean to suggest that thereafter not a drop of water would pass down the 'old' course; in the annual swell at least it would probably carry water for some distance. But a minor stream running at the bottom of a bed too large for it would be worthless in comparison with the fertilizing spill from the main river, on which the agriculture of Mohen-jo-daro must have mainly depended; and if the Indus had moved more than twenty miles to an appreciably lower bed, the overflow thereafter could not have extended to the plains around the city (1964: 80-1).

For Lambrick the third millennium course of the Indus ran around the northern side of the Rohri Hills and then south, passing close to Mohenjo-daro. At some point the river slipped off this course, with a dramatic shift to the east, abandoning Mohenjo-daro and its inhabitants, leading to the demise of the city and presumably, the civilization as well.

There are certainly ample palaeochannels in the Indus Valley to accommodate Lambrick's hypothesis, but dating these channels is difficult and he does not address this key problem. We are left with a piece of speculation that may sound like a good idea, but lacks a carefully crafted chronology. This problem in chronology has received attention from others, D. A. Holmes and Louis Flam, whose reconstructions of the former channels of the Indus are much more systematic.

D. A. Holmes

D. A. Holmes' position on the ancient courses of the Indus was determined when he was a member of a team that studied the Indus Valley, partly by means of aerial photography (Holmes 1968). His survey was conducted in the context of agricultural development, but interesting observations on palaeochannels of the Indus emerged from the work and the maps in the 1968 paper are extremely useful. Holmes' results were integrated into Flam's discussion of the Holocene palaeochannels of the Indus (1981a).

Louis Flam

Louis Flam's observations on the ancient courses of the Indus (Flam 1981a: 38-75, 1993b) begin with the notion that the present river course has been so controlled through massive bunding, along almost its entire length, that it can now be considered a man-made geographical feature (Memnon 1963: 15). This river training may have one positive attribute for historical study in that it has so limited the massive flooding of the river that older scars and depressions have been preserved, rather than having been obliterated by the natural action of the river. Flam's approach shares some features with Lambrick. He makes extensive use of historical sources and field observations, but Flam has an advantage. He has had access to aerial photography (Holmes 1968; Lower Indus Project 1965b) where a number of fragmentary, but interesting Holocene river courses have been delineated with reasonable certainty. These are major landscape features, presumably a reflection of the Indus flowing in this position over a protracted period of time.

Using Flam as a guide, and adding some pieces of information from other sources, the principal Holocene channels are as follows:

I. The Western Side of the Modern River, above Lake Manchar
    1. Jacobabad Course
    2. Shahdadkot Course
    3. Warah Course
    4. The Western Nara
    5. Kandhkot Course
    6. Dadu Course
    7. Modern Course of the Indus

II. Southern Indus Plain and Delta
    1. Khairpur Course
    2. Shahdadpur Course
    3. Sanghar Course
    4. Samaro Course

5. Dhoro Badahri Course

6. Modern Course of the Indus

These courses are shown on (Figure 3.121). Many of them have been turned into modern irrigation canals, for a portion of their length. Very smart to have let Mother Nature do the digging and leveling!

Following arguments put forward by Butler (1950), Pels (1964) and Schumm (1968), Flam considers the Jacobabad, Shahdadkot, Warah, Sanghar and Samaro-Dhoro Badahri Courses to

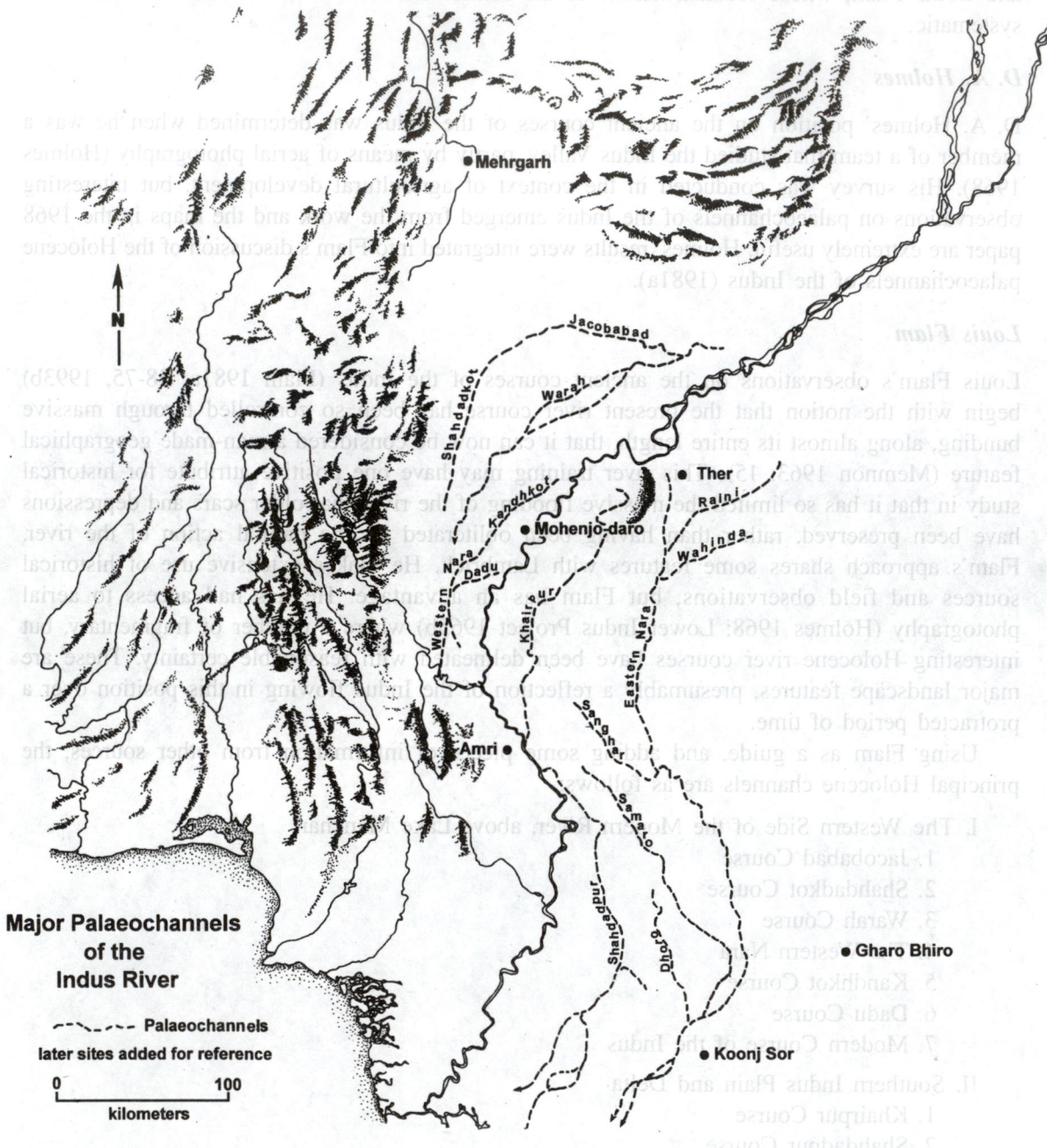

Figure 3.121. Palaeochannels in Sindh

be the oldest Holocene course remnants of the Indus River. The Kandhkot, Khairpur and Shahdad Courses are ancestral to the present course but not as old as the former channels (Flam 1981a: 53).

The Jacobabad-Shahdadkot-Hamal Lake Course (Flam 1981a: 53-4)

The Jacobabad Course emerges from the modern river near Kandhkot, ca. 80 kilometers above Sukkur. It runs west past Jacobabad and is finally covered by the Kachi Plain piedmont alluvium. The Shahdadkot Course begins southwest of Jacobabad and disappears just south of Shahdadkot after a run of ca. 70 kilometers. The Hamal Lake course seems to take off near the point where the Jacobabad-Shahdadkot Courses end and Holmes offers the following tentative conclusion: "There is thus evidence of a distinct river system running around the northwestern flank of the Indus alluvial plain, south to Manchar Lake, now partly obscured by the advance of the piedmont alluvial plain" (1968: 371).

The Wara Course and Western Nara (Flam 1981a: 54-5)

The Wara Course is a "...broad zone of extensive high bar deposits and clearly defined channels" (Holmes 1968: 371) that occur between the modern river and the Jacobabad-Shahdadkot Course. As with the latter, it begins at about Kandhkot but rather than pointing west it moves to the south and west across the plains where it more or less disappears opposite Mehar. Along the southern portion of its course there is an encroachment of the Kirthar Piedmont alluvium which fills and thus obscures this feature. "The Lower Indus Project report (1965b: 406) further characterizes the Wara Course as larger, more prominent, and more recent than the Jacobabad Course" (Flam 1981a: 68-9). The Wara Course is also geographically close to the Western Nara when they are in the vicinity of the town of Mehar. It may be that at some point in the past these channels were joined here, extending the flow of the Wara Course to the vicinity of Lake Manchar.

The Kandhkot, Western Nara and Dadu Courses (Flam 1981a: 55-7).

Another major feature on the aerial photographs of the western side of the Indus in upper Sindh is a channel called the Kandhkot Course which is: "...for most of its length a single channel, narrow, deep and winding, running parallel to the modern Indus river from Kashmore, through Kandhkot which is located on its bank, to the south of Shikarpur, where it is cut by the modern Indus" (Holmes 1968: 371). It is evident that this ancient course of the river took a broad turn to the east and that the continuation of its ancient course is not to the eastern side of the modern course.

The Western Nara and a more southern course near Dadu are spill channels of the Kandhkot course. Holmes is of the opinion that neither of these channels was ever a major course of the Indus, "...as supposed by some earlier workers..." (1968: 372).

The Khairpur and Shahdadpur Courses (Flam 1981a: 56-77)

On the eastern side of the river there are two disconnected, but compellingly united, palaeochannel scars in the cover flood plain: the Khairpur and Shahdadpur Courses. The Khairpur Course is the more northerly of these channels and begins just below Sukkur, opposite the point where the Kandhkot Course is cut by the modern stream. The Shahdadpur Course "...emerges from the modern river about eight kilometers below Sarkand and can be traced just west of Shahdadpur, east of Tando Adam and south to Tando Allahyer. It has the same features of the deep, winding channels and high bar deposits as the Khairpur Course and is probably a continuation of it" (Holmes 1968: 373).

The Sanghar, Samaro and Dhoro Badahri Courses (Flam 1981a: 57)

Three ancient courses of the Indus, Sanghar, Samaro and Dhoro Badahri, are on the eastern side of the river, generally to the south of Nawabshah. They are of interest because none seems connected to the Kandhkot-Khairpur-Shahdadpur Course, nor were they active channels of the Eastern Nara (Flam 1981a: 57). Holmes is of the opinion that the Sanghar Course is "...old, perhaps the oldest course visible in the region..." (1968: 373) and it shares many physical features with the Jacobabad Course. It is narrow and seems to have resulted from the flow of a large, stable river which carried the heavy floodwaters of a major branch of the Indus, if not the main stream itself. The Sanghar Course also exhibits "...all the characteristics of an infilled deltaic distributary, as encountered in Lower Sind" (Holmes 1968: 373).

The Samaro Course is visible just southeast of Nawabshah and moves southeasterly to Samaro town. It passes the now abandoned Medieval city of Brahmanabad. A join with the Eastern Nara is made via the scoured out Dhoro Badahri Course (Holmes 1968: 373).

Other Palaeochannels of the Indus

D. A. Holmes and the Lower Indus Project have detected other courses as part of their research on the Indus River (see Holmes 1968: Figure 2). They pertain to later historical periods of Sindh.

A Proposed Chronology for the Holocene Palaeochannels

Introduction

It is one thing to isolate channel scars, bar formations and other evidence for former courses of the Indus river but to give each of these a date is another matter. The following reconstruction has been taken from Flam's work (1981a: 38-75), with some minor modifications. This chronology for the former courses of the Indus does not fully conform with that proposed by Holmes (1968: 375-80).

Flam bases a significant part of his argument for the chronology of the various courses on the nature of long-term fluvial processes in river valleys like the Indus (Flam 1981a: 58-65). These have to do with variables such as slope, competence, geological bed, climate and the availability of water. They are all interrelated, dynamic forces which play important roles in determining the erosional and depositional processes of the Indus (and other rivers like it) as well as the character of the meander pattern and the river's ability to stay in one channel. S. Schumm (1965, 1968, 1969) has shown that changes in hydrologic regimen are reflected in the width/depth ratio of a bed, the river's sinuosity, its gradient and the sediment load. It should be clear that width/depth ratios and sinuosity are things that can be seen on aerial photographs and are therefore important variables in charting the changing patterns of river hydrology and from this, the chronology of its beds.

Flam's bibliography has many good references to help in investigating the Indus fluvial processes in particular and river hydrology in general. The technical side of Indus River history is important because what follows is a very tentative proposal which could be revised by insights gained from further field exploration and a sound understanding of river hydrology.[12]

The Early Holocene Course: ca. 8000-4000 BC

All of the major sources (Holmes, the Lower Indus Project and Flam) seem to agree that the Jacobabad and Shahdadkot Courses to the west of the modern Indus and the Sanghar Course on the eastern side share many physical characteristics and are the oldest Holocene remnants of the former bed of the Indus (Figure 3.122). Flam takes this observation and suggests the following:

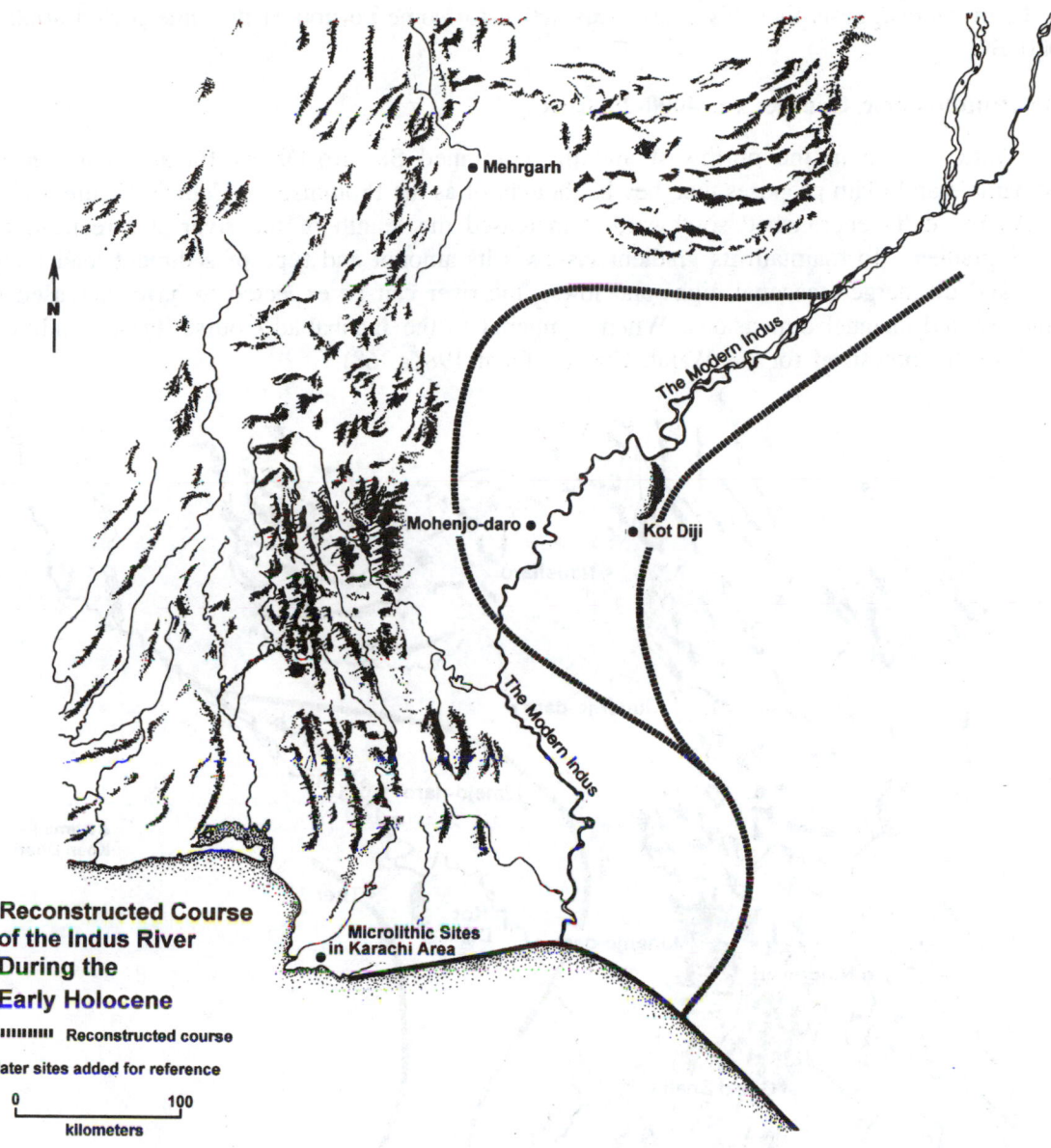

Figure 3.122. Reconstructed course of the Indus River System during the Early Holocene

The environmental characteristics of the early Holocene provides some aid in securing a date for the Jacobabad-Sanghar Course. It has been suggested that the early Holocene coast line of the Lower Indus Basin was located north of Hyderabad. One of the two oldest remnants on the southern subregion of the Lower Indus Basin, the Samaro-Dhoro Badahri Course probably would have been under the sea during most of the early Holocene. The hydrologic regime, gradient and type of sediment load which has been indicated for the early Holocene phase can be favorably compared to the channel characteristics of the Jacobabad-Shahdadkot-Sanghar Courses. That is, the broad zone of bar and channel deposits, the coarse-textured (sand?) sediment load and the adjustments of grade of the Jacobabad Course correlate well with the hydrologic regimen, sediment type and gradient descriptions of the early Holocene phase in the Indus drainage system (Flam 1981a: 66-7).

Flam also suggests that this course was active for some portion of the time period 8000 to 4000 BC.

The Protohistoric Course: ca. 4000-2000 BC

The Wara Course in the northwest and the combined Samaro-Dhoro Badahri courses are comparable and Flam proposes that they be thought of as the Protohistoric Course (Figure 3.123).

As the delta encroached southward it increased the length of the river and reduced the river's gradient. To maintain its gradient vis-a-vis its amount and type of sediment load (silty-clay) and discharge (seasonal highs and lows), the river can be expected to have increased its sinuosity and channel dimensions. When compared to the Jacobabad Course, these conditions are those hypothesized for the Warah Course (Flam 1981a: 68).

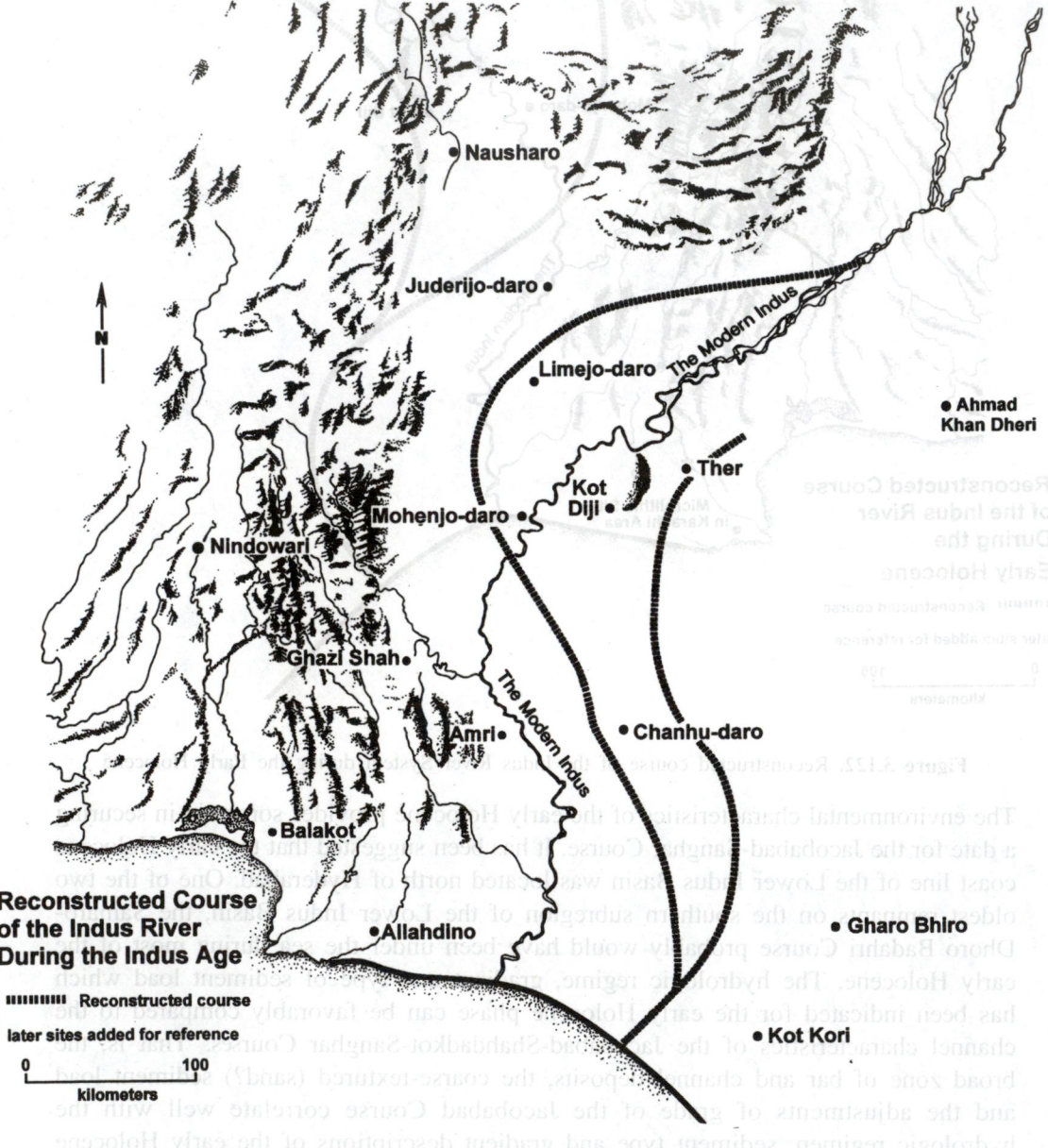

Figure 3.123. Reconstructed course of the Indus River System during the Indus Age

Plate 3.39. The Indus River near Mohenjo-daro at sunset. Courtesy of James Blair.

Plate 3.40. The Indus plains at Mohenjo-daro, author's photograph.

Plate 3.41. Goats under a tree in Kachi, author's photograph.

Plate 3.42. The confluence of the Indus (left) and Zaskar (right) Rivers at Leh, Ladakh. Courtesy of Michael Searle.

Plate 3.43. The Indus River in the Leh Valley, Ladakh. Courtesy of Michael Searle.

Plate 3.44. The Indus River during flood in middle Sindh, author's photograph.

Plate 3.45. The Indus at Sukkur.

Plate 3.46. The Indus at Bukkur Island in a mid-nineteenth century lithograph.

3.47. The Indus between Bukkur Island and Rohri, looking north, up the Indus, author's.photograph.

Plate 3.48. The Diwana Dam. Courtesy of Walter Fairservis.

Plate 3.49. The northern pass into the Isplenji Valley, with unexcavated caves in the background. Walter Fairservis with his back to the camera, author's photograph.

Plate 3.50. Isplenji Valley, from the top of the site of Isplenji One, author's photograph.

Plate 3.51. The Welpat area of Las Bela with the Hab River in the background. Courtesy of Walter A. Fairservis, Jr.

Plate 3.52. The Hab River in the foreground with the Amri-Nal and Kulli site of Karpas Buthi (LB-14) just above it. Courtesy of Walter A. Fairservis, Jr.

Plate 3.53. The Kalubhar River in eastern Saurashtra, author's photograph.

Plate 3.54. The central plain of Saurashtra, author's photograph.

Plate 3.55. Mount Girnar in southern Saurashtra, author's photograph.

Plate 3.56. The thickly forested area of the Gir Forest, author's photograph.

Plate 3.57. A stream in the Western Ghats, on the route from North Gujarat to Udaipur, author's photograph.

Plate 3.58. The Little Rann of Kutch, author's photograph.

Plate 3.59. Sketch of Sindree made by Captain Grindlay, after Sir Alexander Burnes 1835a: Vol. I, between pp. 308 and 309.

Plate 3.60. The Nal Depression, author's photograph.

Plate 3.61. Quetta Miri in a mid-nineteenth century lithograph.

Plate 3.62. Black tent camp in the Quetta Valley.

Plate 3.63. Khojak Pass in a mid-nineteenth century lithograph.

Plate 3.64. The Khyber Pass just to the east of Kabul, author's photograph.

Plate 3.65. The conifer forests of Ziarat in Zhob, author's photograph.

Plate 3.66. The Ravi River in full flood, July 1966, author's photograph.

Plate 3.67. The Indus River at Attock, author's photograph.

Plate 3.68. The Indus at Mianwali during the winter low water period, south of Attock, author's photograph.

Plate 3.69. The plains of the Northern Region, north of Attock. Photograph taken from the Buddhist monastic site of Takht-i Bhai, author's photograph.

Plate 3.70. The Potwar Plateau at Sarai Khola, where it has been deeply eroded, author's photograph.

Flam conjectures that the Western Nara (which he calls "Sind Hollow") is part of this course, but that does not seem to be correct, at least as far as an extension deep enough to reach Lake Manchar is concerned (see Flam 1981a: Figure 16). If the main course of the Indus River ever flowed into the Lake Manchar hollow it would have cut between the Lakhi Hills and the Bado Range and possibly between the Bado and Bhit Ranges. High ground is there, testifying that the river never flowed there. Thus, the map of the "Indus River During the Indus Age" (Figure 3.123) differs somewhat from the Flam reconstruction given in his Figure 16 (1981a).

The "Greek River"

A review of Greek sources on Sindh shows that the Indus had a course different from either the Early Holocene or Protohistoric river (Figure 3.124). It has been noted that authorities agree

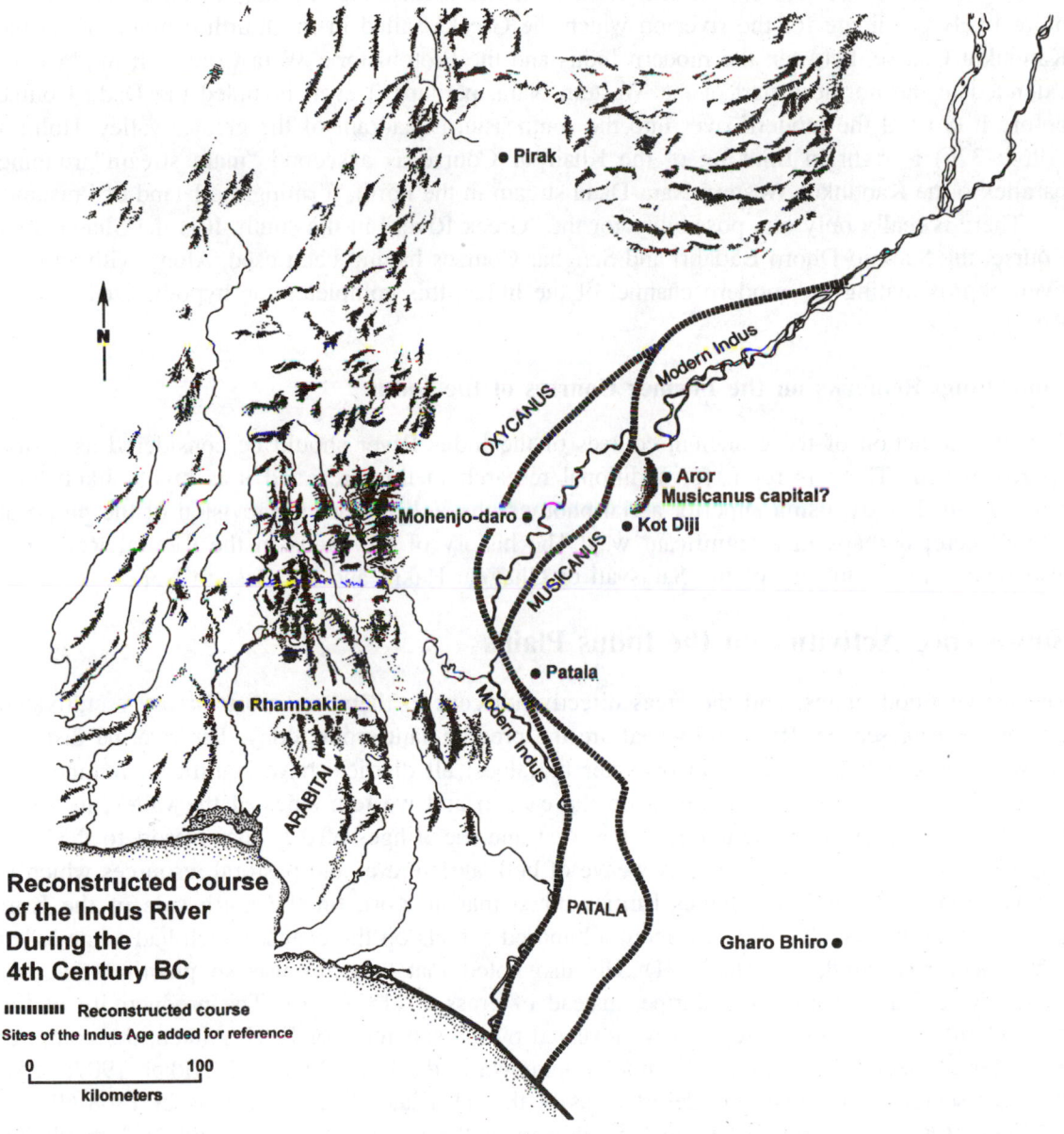

Figure 3.124. Reconstructed course of the Indus River System during the 4th Century BC, the "Greek River"

(Lambrick 1964: 108; Holmes 1968: 375) that in the fourth century BC the Indus did not flow through the Sukkur Gap, as it does today. This dramatic passage is not likely to have escaped all of the written observations on Alexander's sail down the Indus. Arrian, for one, speaks of Sindh as being composed of two large islands, Prasiane in the north and Pattala in the south, noting: "At Pattala the stream of the Indus parts into two large rivers, both of these retaining the same name 'Indus' till they reach the sea" (Arrian VI.17.2; Robson 1929, Vol. 2: 157).

Holmes (1968: 376) has created a map that reflects these observations, but he uses the Jacobabad Course of the northwestern arm of the "Greek River" bringing it through Lake Manchar. This is not acceptable on two counts; the Jacobabad Course is said to be the oldest, or one of the oldest courses, in that quadrant of Sindh, and it is highly unlikely that a major course of the Indus ever flowed through Lake Manchar given the presence of Protohistoric sites there. The floods are just too violent for the fragile archaeological sites to have survived. A more likely candidate for the river on which the Greeks sailed in the fourth century BC is the Kandhkot Course, between the modern Indus and the Protohistoric Wara Course. It might have extended to the northern part of the Western Nara, perhaps it even included the Dadu Course before it crossed the modern river into the southeastern quadrant of the greater valley. Holmes (1968: 376) is right in thinking of the Khairpur Course as a second "main stream" running parallel to the Kandhkot-Western Nara-Dadu stream in the north, forming the Island of Prasiane.

There is really only one possibility for the "Greek River" in the south. It is the Shahdadpur Course, the Samaro-Dhoro Badahri and Sanghar Courses having been used. Along with another river, approximating the modern channel of the Indus, this completes the hypothesized "Greek River."

Concluding Remarks on the Former Courses of the Indus

The reconstruction of these ancient courses of the Indus River should be considered as a first approximation. There is room for additional research in this area and it is highly likely that more detailed study, using superior aerial photography will lead to the revision of the proposal offered here; perhaps in a significant way. The history of the Indus in the Central Region is also related to the history of the Sarasvati or Ghaggar-Hakra and the Eastern Nara.

Subsistence Activities on the Indus Plains

The active flood plains, and the areas directly adjacent to them are most intensely cultivated during the *rabi* season. Rice and wheat are the predominant crops today. The riverine districts of Sindh have a large population of water buffaloes; all districts have significant numbers of cattle. Sheep and goats are important on the eastern and western sides of the valley, in Sindh Kohistan and the Kirthar Piedmont in the west and the fringes of the Thar Desert to the east. The subsistence system is a complex weave of both agricultural and pastoral resources which is highly productive. In 1827, James Burnes noted that at Kori, on the north side of the Kori Creek of western Kutch: "We saw about a hundred camels on the beach, which had come laden with ghee from Sinde..." (1829: 31). He also noted that "...grain was so plentiful that our horses were fed with rice, cut unripe, instead of grass..." (1829: 36). The productivity of the premodern agro-pastoral system is also revealed by the statement of E. H. Aitken, the compiler of an early Gazetteer on Sindh: "Famine is unknown in the Indus Valley..." (Aitken 1907: 255); however scarcity does visit the desert areas of the Thar and Thar Parkar, as in 1868-69 and 1898-99. But, for the most part Sindh is the gift of the Indus, and it is a violent, but reliable provider.

The traditional method of cultivation is described in Aitken (1907: 236). If possible, the land is wetted after the inundation, plowed once or twice and then rolled or patted to prevent evaporation of the trapped moisture. Wheat is sown in November and December and harvested in April.

There is another interesting form of cultivation in the areas in and near the active flood plain of the Indus. New beds are scoured where the water moves the most rapidly. These new beds can form complex dendritic patterns, the ends of which are shallow and broad, on the scale of a good farmer's field. These areas are soaked with moisture and covered by *kacho* the fertile, light alluvium from the receding floods. This soil is amazingly fertile. A month or two after subsidence of the waters, the banks exposed beside the Indus will be green with countless sprays of tamarisk seeded from the adjoining jungles; and if these are not washed away in the following flood season, there will be a dense growth of low bushes in a year's time. Even the best land in the canal-irrigated area, which is perennially refreshed with a modicum of Indus silt, is seldom equal in productivity to the best riverine kacho...(Lambrick 1964: 17).

Prior to the large-scale canalization of the nineteenth century it was a custom in Sindh for *kacho* to be hunted down and planted, often without plowing, the seeds of wheat and barley most often being broadcast and left to mature on their own.

As seen in Table 3.15 the *kharif* season millets, jowar and bajra are not significant contributors to the agricultural regime in Larkana (Mohenjo-daro) and Nawabshah Districts (Chanhu-daro). It is wheat, and in the past barley, that are the principal food grains, and this is in agreement with the palaeobotanical records from Mohenjo-daro. The area is also cattle and water buffalo country, as shown on the table. These two observations made today, may well hold true for the very distant past.

TABLE 3.15
The Agricultural Regime on the Indus Plains

DistrictPlant or	Acres or Animal Animals	Page in Number of	Report
Larkana	wheat ·	173198	331
Larkana	jowar	19906	421
Larkana	bajra	400	421
Larkana	cattle	236107	764
Larkana	water buffalo	203189	764
Larkana	sheep	94417	784
Larkana	goats	79586	784
Nawabshah	wheat	232881	331
Nawabshah	jowar	87075	421
Nawabshah	bajra	31407	421
Nawabshah	cattle	305201	764
Nawabshah	goats	214857	784
Nawabshah	sheep	213266	784
Nawabshah	water buffalo	180891	764

From: *Pakistan Census of Agriculture 1960*, 1963

Canal Irrigation in Sindh During the Mature Harappan

One of the unresolved issues confronting the study of the Indus Age is whether significant canal irrigation works were associated with the agricultural regime. The question is not whether they were able to dig ditches to drain swamps and move small amounts of water to and from their fields, but rather the bigger problem of moving water from the active river course(s) to different, higher, riverine environments, outside of the valley area that would have been naturally flooded. This is an important, two-fold issue. It has to do with the question of an elite population's capacity to gather and manage large labor forces, as well as the salinization of agricultural fields, with its consequent drop in productivity.

There are some things that are known about irrigation in the Indus Age. At Mehrgarh Period II (Burj Basket Marked times): "The charred seeds of wheat and barley belonging to the species *Triticum sphaerococcum* and *Hordeum sphaerococcum* that, according to L. Costantini, grow only on irrigated fields, also were collected from the ashy layers" of Period II (Jarrige, Jarrige, Meadow and Quivron 1995: 318-19). This is followed with evidence for a ditch of significant size that was filled with Mehrgarh Period IV trash (Jarrige, Jarrige, Meadow and Quivron 1995: 451 and 461). This seems to indicate a date of Togau or Kechi Beg Phase use.

Louis Flam proposes that there were three different forms of irrigation in Sindh Kohistan and along the Kirthar front (1981a: 151-52) during the Early and Mature Harappan Stages. The first used the natural flooding of a hill stream to irrigate land, similar to a form of cultivation widely practiced on the Indus flood plain known as *salaiba* and documented at the site of Kohtrash Buthi. The second form, documented at the site of Kai Buthi made use of small, shallow ditches to gently guide spring water out onto a flat area that was used for cultivation. His third irrigation practice involved an investment in bunding, either a low earthen wall, locally known as a *kach* system or a *gabarband*, documented at the site of Nuka.

Gabarbands and Irrigation

Dams and *bunds*, both large and small, are among the most interesting features of the Sindh Kohistan, the adjacent Kirthar Area and Baluchistan (the Gedrosia Region). There are thousands of *gabarbands* throughout these areas, especially in Sarawan, Jhalawan and along the Hab River and its tributaries. They are an important feature of agricultural technology first met with in Sindh Kohistan.

There are two small papers on these features (Hughes-Buller 1903-04; Raikes 1965b). The name *gabarband* can be translated "Zoroastrian dam," *gabars*[13] being Zoroatrians or fire-worshippers, *band* being a general word for a dam, or enclosing earthwork intended to conserve water. These irrigation facilities are built of stone and have proved very difficult to date. Some of them are modern. The Brahuis and Baluchis of the region use dams, which they build. These are not literally *gabarbands*. There is an association between some of the *gabarbands* and prehistoric sites. Walter Fairservis found a stone dam associated with an Amri-Nal site at Diwana on the upper Hab River[14] (Fairservis 1961b: Figure 1; Figure 3.125, Plate 3.48). Given the location of the site with respect to this dam, and the absence of other settlement in the vicinity, except for a modern village where the inhabitants denied any familiarity with the dam, it seems that this feature and the site can be associated. The association between *gabarbands* and prehistoric settlements has been well studied by Louis Flam (1981a) and he suggests that it is reasonable to assume that this technology begins in the Amri-Nal Phase in the first half of the third millennium BC. This is based on his research on *bands* in the Sindh Kohistan and Kirthar Mountains, where there are no Togau Phase sites, but good associations between these irrigation features and Amri-Nal sites.

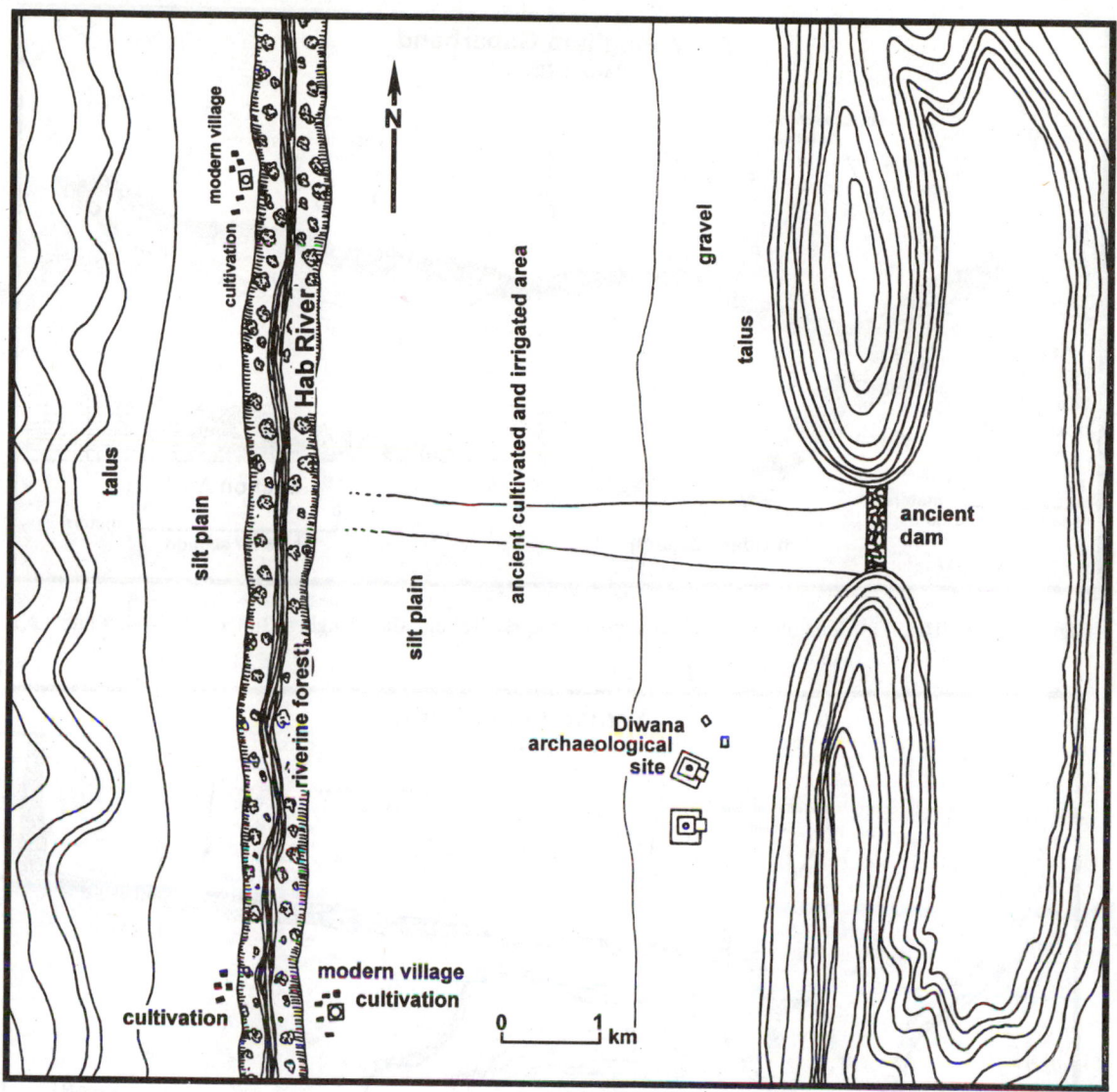

Figure 3.125. The placement of the dam at Diwana on the upper Hab River

The very large *gabarbands*, with ornamental stone work seem to be later, probably much later, and they may represent the results of Partho-Sassanian investment in this region during the early centuries of the Christian Era (Possehl 1975). This time period is marked by the appearance of Londo Ware in the region and it is one of great prosperity and sedentism with a large number of sites in Kalat and Makran. The fact that the Parthians and Sassanians were also *gabars* is relevant. The history of stone dam building may have a duration of over two millennia, implying that each of the *gabarbands* needs to be independently dated and that there is no chronology for them which has sufficient historical precision to be generally useful (Figure 3.126, Figure 3.127).

One of the consistent, but not universal, features of the *gabarbands* is that they were not full-scale dams, intended to hold back the full flood of a river or stream. Many were built to check and direct the flood waters and frequently were constructed to hold water in a way which allowed alluvium to build up behind them, creating a small, but fertile and naturally watered

306

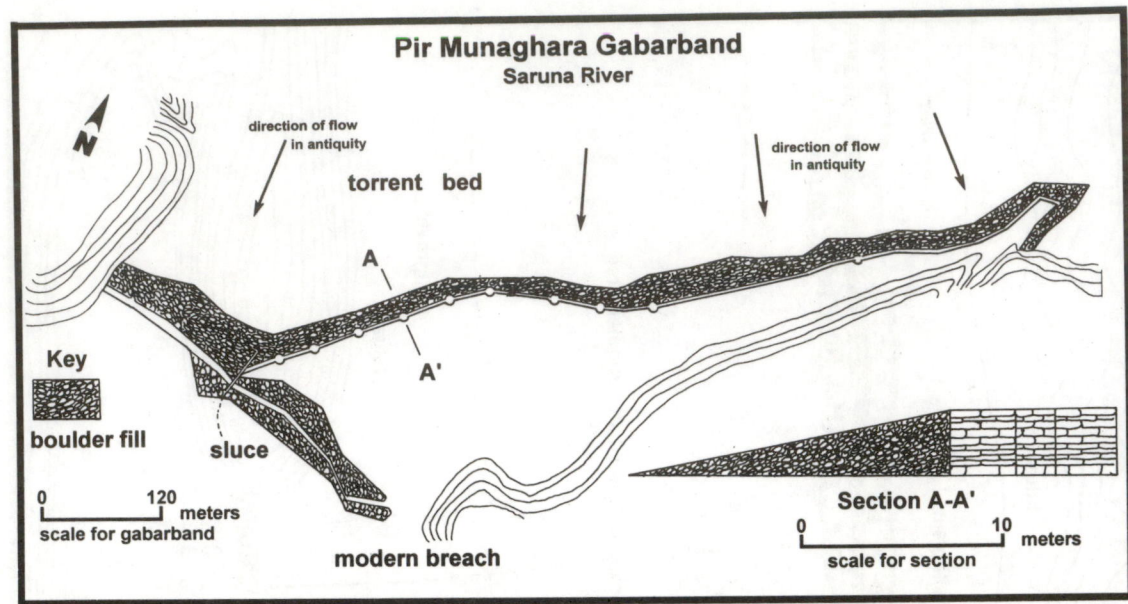

Figure 3.126. The Pir Munaghara *Gabarband* in the Saruna Valley, after Hughes-Buller 1903–04: Plate LXI

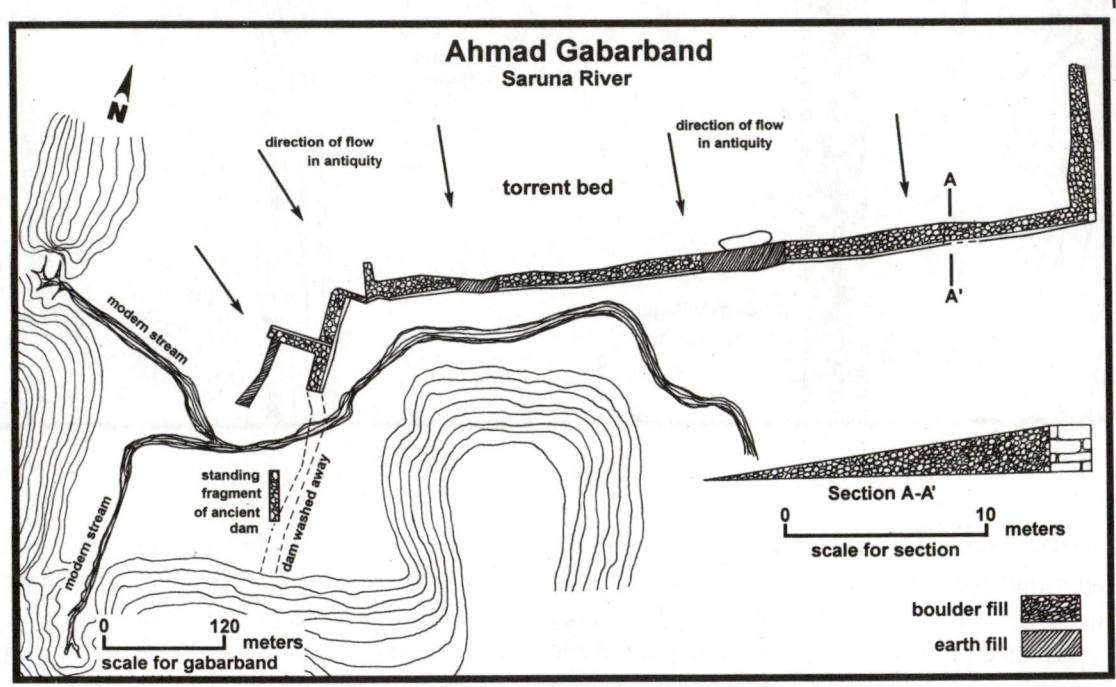

Figure 3.127. Plan of the Ahmad *Gabarband* in the Saruna Valley, after Hughes-Buller 1903–04: Plate LXI

agricultural field (Figure 3.128), which might be as large as a hectare or two. In many instances several small *gabarbands* have been constructed in a row, down one side of a valley, or with advantage being taken of good locations for siting on either or both sides of a valley. The intention of the builders then, was not to impound water so that it could be taken off and moved a great distance, as a modern irrigation facility would do, but to slow and direct water. Equally important, it was intended to build up alluvium, conserving soil and creating an

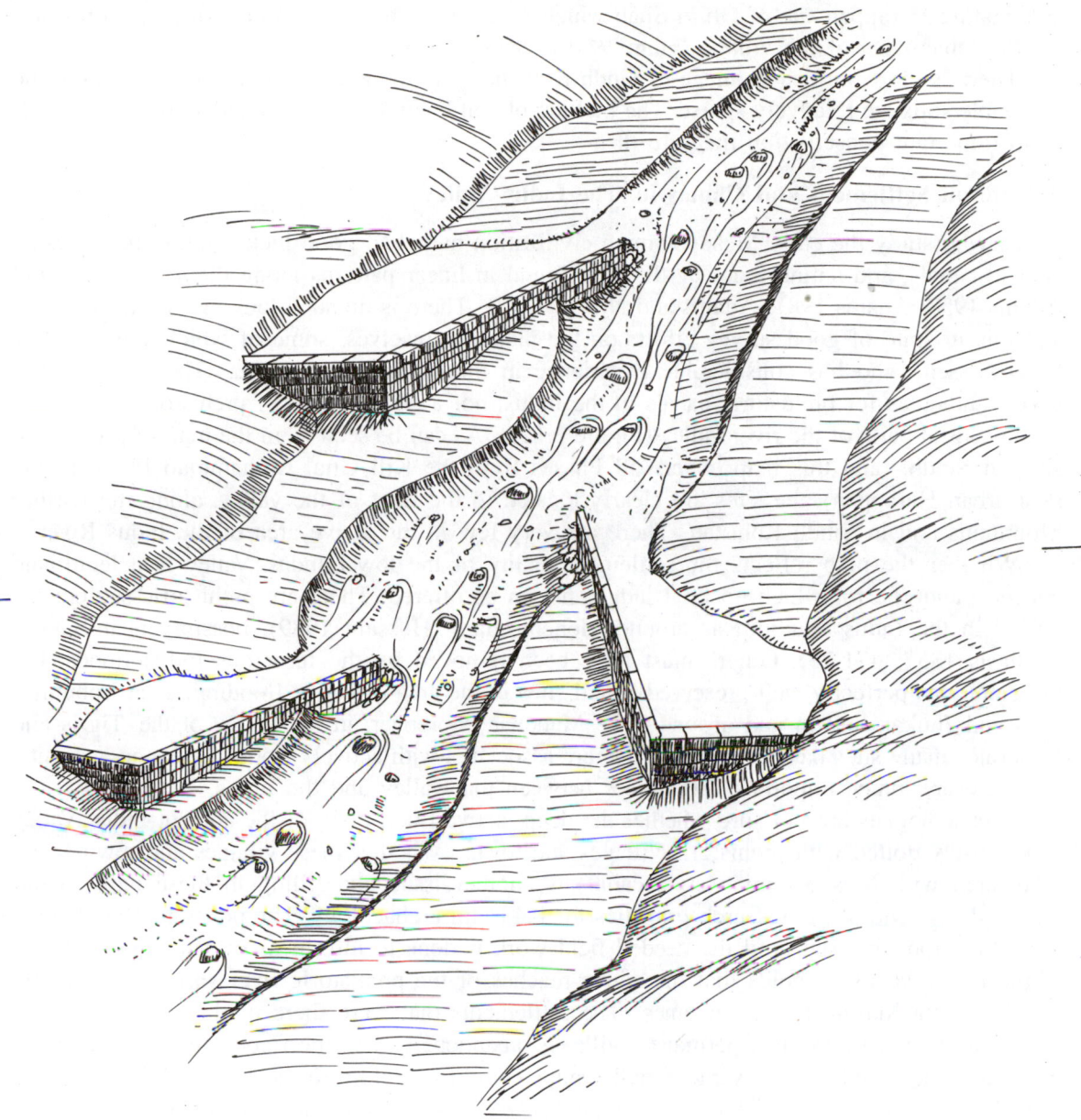

Figure 3.128. Alignment of *gabarbands* used to create fields

agricultural field in a region of thin stony soils, with insufficient rainfall for reliable dry farming. The form of a *gabarband* is generally "L" shaped, with a "wing" of some kind on the upstream, river side intended to catch and direct water into the *gabarband's* catchment area.

Springs and Irrigation

The Sindh Kohistan and Kirthar Piedmont are dotted with springs, some of which are hot. This water is frequently in limestone areas. The limestone is dissolved in the water as it rises to the surface, then left behind as a tufa evaporate. The heads of these springs are masses of stony debris, and cascades of tufa, with piping that often channels the flow of water far from its source (Flam 1981a: 108; Blanford 1880). There is a good perennial spring near the Amri-Nal and Mature Harappan site of Ghazi Shah which would have been one source of irrigation water for the inhabitants of the village (Flam 1981a: 281).

There is more surface drainage in Sindh Kohistan than the Kirthar area to the north, but the cultivable soils are relatively sparse. The buildup of soil behind low bunds and stone *gabarbands* is an important conservation measure then.

A Note on Settlement and Canals in The Indus Valley

Those who study the early Mesopotamian civilization have had good luck finding the traces of ancient canals, and dating them by the sites found in linear patterns along them (Jacobsen and Adams 1958; Adams 1981; Adams and Nissen 1972). There is no such luck in the Indus Valley, and this in spite of good survey efforts on the plains themselves, some of which was done by Hans Nissen, who has considerable experience in the Mesopotamian area. There are neither good candidates for prehistoric canals in the Indus, nor a good record of prehistoric settlement in the central parts of the river valley (Figure 3.129). As can be seen from the map of prehistoric sites in Sindh, (and this map covers all Phases from the Kili Ghul Mohammad Phase to the Post-urban Harappan), the sites are clearly located to the west of the valley, along the Kirthar Mountains and in Sindh Kohistan. There are very few in the active area of the Indus River.

Whether the map reflects the settlement reality of the lower Indus Valley is a legitimate concern, and one for which no final judgment can be offered. There are prehistoric settlements buried in the Indus alluvium as around Mohenjo-daro (Hussain 1989); possibly near Sukkur (Bellasis 1857: 471-73). Others must have been removed by the ferocious Indus floods, but there are also perfectly well preserved, small sites in the area of active flooding, as at Lohumjo-daro and Jhukar, and in and around Lake Manchar. Moreover, in the valley of the Tigris and Euphrates many sites have been found that are associated with actively flooded areas in antiquity, but there are many, important differences between that valley and the Indus.

Archaeologists are not sure whether the deep, active flood plain of the ancient Indus Valley was densely dotted with prehistoric villages and towns. Whether these villages and towns were associated with Mesopotamian style canals is another issue and filling in these gaps in our knowledge is one of the research priorities for Pakistani archaeology. The position taken here is a kind of stopgap, used until the needed field work is done to inform us of settlement patterns of the Indus Valley. It holds that the active reaches of the prehistoric river valley were lightly settled during Mature Harappan times. The settlements that were there might have been more temporary and seasonal than permanent villages, abandoned when the floods approached, and if necessary, sacrificed to this event. Small groups could then return to their general area with the subsidence of the floods, to chase down their *kacho* fields or rejuvenate more developed farming lands. They might even have returned to their former settlements if they still existed. The system, as now seen, was disbursed and segmented, dependent on small-scale groups, loosely coordinated movement and intercommunity activity. Given this position there is little room for the Harappans and their predecessors to have excavated large-scale irrigation canals.

The historical record of Sindh does show that old courses of the Indus, especially subsidiary channels like the Western Nara, have been used as irrigation facilities. It is possible that these were also used during the Indus Age. But, there is so little evidence for human settlement deep in the active areas of the Indus Valley, that this proposition is difficult to test. If one believes these field data then there is hardly a need for canal irrigation to support a dense population; if not then the question remains open. Such is the state of the archaeology of the Indus Age.

Salts accumulate from irrigation because farmers allow water to stand in fields, letting it

Figure 3.129. Prehistoric settlements in Sindh

evaporate, thus concentrating the minerals that were dissolved in the water. Over a period of decades this can render large tracts of land completely infertile. Proper irrigation is a cycle, with water brought to fields, which are saturated and the excess water taken away and allowed to return to the parent stream.

Under the natural flood of the Indus, this cycle would not have been present. First the floods themselves flush surface salts from fields. Possibly more important, the floods unbridled by dams, bunds, headworks and canals do not return to the same localities for decades on end. Thus, the evaporation that takes place is of sufficiently short duration that the fertility of the land is not compromised.

Some Subregions in Sindh

The Kirthar Piedmont, Sindh Kohistan

The Kirthar Piedmont and Sindh Kohistan are interesting and important areas for the study of the Indus Age. The Kirthar Mountains are a barrier to communication and channel movement between Baluchistan and the Indus Valley into the passes occupied by hill torrents (*nais*). The Sindh Kohistan ("Sindh Mountain Country") is also an important area for travel. It is a shortcut to the south which avoids the Indus Valley, striking directly for the Karachi area, the Arabian Sea Coast and the Makran.

Because this region is as much crossed through as it is lived in, it has strategic importance as the link between Baluchistan and the Indus Plains. The survival of Baluchi nomad-farmers is dependent on winter access to the Indus Valley, and conversely, the health of valley herds of cattle, sheep and goats is dependent on summer access to mountain pastures. Reliable access to the passes is therefore necessary. This is compromised, or at least conditioned, by the notion that these points in the landscape have strategic value and their control, by one or another group gives them an advantage over their neighbors; certainly their foes. Historically, this has led to a certain tension in the region, which has never been completely free from feuding, raiding and a low level of general conflict. But, just as important, this has never been so prevalent over a long period of time that the symbiotic rhythm of transhumance has been compromised.

Perhaps the single most striking feature of this region is Lake Manchar, which seems to have been much the same feature of the Indus Age as it is today.

The subsistence regime of the Kirthar Piedmont and Sindh Kohistan is totally different from that of the Indus plains, even admitting significant variation within its own environment. This region has been most extensively studied by Louis Flam (1981a, 1981b, 1982a, 1982b, 1984, 1986a, 1986b, 1993b) and his dissertation is recommended to those who are interested in more than the condensed view given here.

The ground water of this area is generally brackish and is not an irrigation resource. Rainfall is unreliable and relatively low, 100 to 200 millimeters per year, compared to 400 to 600 millimeters for Saurashtra. This is mostly monsoon rainfall and is reflected in the fact that millets are an important crop. There is wheat grown in Dadu District, but mainly in the eastern canal irrigated zone along the Indus. To be successful, rainfall and runoff have to be managed and this is done with low earthen bunds and some dams, *gabarbands*. Runoff is captured and also diverted by these structures, which are known to have been completely swept away by unusually strong rains.

The Kirthar Range and Sindh Kohistan area is pastoral territory, with good pasturage and seasonal access to the adjacent uplands. Cattle are the single most important animal, although sheep and goats are present in considerable numbers. Relatively few water buffalo are present and it is an area with a good balance between *kharif* and *rabi* season cropping; again observations from the modern world that may hold true for distant antiquity.

TABLE 3.16
The Agricultural Regime in Kirthar Area and Sindh Kohistan

DistrictPlant or	Acres or Animal	Page in Number of Animals	Report
Dadu	jowar	136331	422
Dadu	wheat	127132	332
Dadu	bajra	4540	422
Dadu	goats	273424	785
Dadu	cattle	226326	765
Dadu	sheep	210076	785
Dadu	water buffalo	90274	765
Karachi	jowar	15438	426
Karachi	wheat	1898	336
Karachi	bajra	490	426
Karachi	cattle	67460	771
Karachi	goats	43190	791
Karachi	sheep	6330	791
Karachi	water buffalo	4960	771

From: *Pakistan Census of Agriculture 1960*, 1963

The predominant crop in this area is jowar, the cultivation of wheat in Dadu District, taking place on the eastern side where irrigation is available. Therefore, there is a contrast to the adaptation on the deeper alluvium of the Indus Valley, as seen on Table 3.16 above. The bunds and *gabarbands* are used to catch the western fringes of the monsoon rain to bring in one crop. Ibn Battuta, the great 14th century traveler was in Sindh in 1334 and while at Sehwan observed that: "...the food of the inhabitants consists of sorghum and peas, of which they make bread. There is a plentiful supply of fish and buffalo milk, and they eat also a kind of small lizard stuffed with curcuma" (Book II, Chapter VI; Gibb 1929: 185-86; "curcuma" is arrowroot). Wild food still played a role in the diet of the people of Sindh in Medieval times.

The area is poor in mineral resources (Flam 1981a: 100-19).

The Kachi Plain

"The plain of Kachi is generally spoken of as an awful desert of which no good is to be hoped..." (Minchin 1907b: 59). So runs the cliché, which is far from the truth. Kachi is a very flat, alluvial plain, surrounded on all but the southern side by mountains. Many small torrents flow from these hills, but there are three rather large rivers: the Bolan, Nari (Western Nara) and Mula Rivers. The area is extremely hot during the summer, often reaching over 120° F. Winters are pleasant, sometimes cold, with some rainfall. The Bolan Pass is one of the most important routes from the Indus Plains to the highlands and in prehistoric times Kachi was something of a crossroads of cultures because of this strategic location.

Agriculture is more dependent on summer monsoon rainfall than on the winter westerlies;

although winter archaeological excavations do seem to be rained out on a reasonably regular basis. According to the District Gazetteer: "By far the largest and most important crop is *juar* (jowar)...It forms the staple food-grain of the people" (Minchin 1907b: 67). Modern records show a relative balance between *rabi* and *kharif* cultivation, undoubtedly a reflection of better irrigation technology. Other crops include bajra, pulses of the genus *Phaseolus*, sesamum, cotton, wheat and barley; all well documented in the context of the Indus Age. Rice is not mentioned, but was an important crop in the Iron Age, as documented at Pirak (Costantini 1979, 1981).

> Cultivation can be said to depend to an appreciable extent on rainfall, and only a fringe of permanently irrigated lands exists near the hills. The largest proportion of the crops are raised from the floods which disgorge their waters on to the plain, the chief sources of irrigation being the Nari, the Bolan, the Sukleji, the Mula and the Dhoriri. At the same time it must be admitted that cultivation is precarious, for, if the summer rains fall in the hills, the centre of the country remains bare of crops and most of the population must migrate to find its means of livelihood in Sind (Minchin 1907a: 58).

The Kachees have made substantial investments in bunds and dams within the mountain valleys that surround their plain. This conserves water and allows large heads of water to be built up, insuring a flow to the most distant fields.

TABLE 3.17
The Agricultural Regime in the Kachi

District	Plant or Animal	Acres or Number of Animals	Page in Report
Sibi	wheat	149703	334
Sibi	jowar	107052	424
Sibi	bajra	8981	424
Sibi	sheep	268705	788
Sibi	cattle	162635	768
Sibi	goats	195634	788
Sibi	water buffalo	15326	768

From: *Pakistan Census of Agriculture 1960*, 1963

Thar Parkar and the Eastern Desert

In spite of the general aridity of the region, Thar Parkar and the fringe of the Thar Desert bordering the Indus Valley, is a place with some agriculture. In the traditional pattern it is concentrated around the many *dhands* or lakes that dot the area during the *kharif* season. On the accompanying Table 3.18 it can be seen that this area relies heavily on bajra as a food grain, but any good millet would do.

The *dhands*, and a bit of monsoon rainfall, promote the growth of grasslands in Thar Parkar and it is good cattle and goat country, with some sheep tagging along.

> It affords grazing for large numbers of camels and goats, and the desert is unrivaled for the excellence and variety of its grasses. These are scarcely perceptible for many months together, but as soon as the rain falls start up in sudden luxuriance. The sand is then covered with a tenuous veil of green, and the desert beautiful and prosperous. The grass is so superior to that of the irrigated plains that large herds of cattle are driven into the desert to be fattened" (Lambrick 1964: 8).

The *dhands* of the eastern desert, especially those adjacent to central and northern Sindh, are found in natural hollows swept clean of the sand that rest on hard alluvial clays. The water accumulates in these low areas as percolation from rain falling over a huge expanse of loose sand. The *dhands* that have existed for any time at all are soon rendered alkaline because of the evaporation of moisture, but the water trapped by suspension in the surrounding sand is sweet. The *dhands* are essential watering holes.

The population of water buffalo is small and perhaps would have been even smaller in the past. The figures on Table 3.18 are probably an artifact of some canal irrigation brought into the region since the nineteenth century.

Thar Parkar is the natural corridor to Kutch, whether the route is directly over the salt wastes, or around the eastern end, to the north Gujarat Plain. The abundance of luxurious pasture here in the summer *kharif* season suggests that this might have been the preferred season for movement through the area.

TABLE 3.18
The Agricultural Regime in Thar Parkar

Plant or Animal	Acres or Number of Animals	Page in Report
bajra	871569	422
wheat	194940	332
jowar	30326	422
goats	583949	786
cattle	501892	766
sheep	239228	786
water buffalo	78418	766

From: *Pakistan Census of Agriculture 1960*, 1963

The Central Region: Concluding Statement

Sindh and the Indus River are important for an understanding of the nature of the Harappan Civilization, its beginnings and transformation. The history of the river is just now becoming a subject of serious research and the key questions of irrigation, subsistence practices and settlement patterns are only beginning to come into focus. A discussion of cultural geography has provided a forum within which all of this could be brought together as a single contemporary source on the Regions of the Indus Age.

THE GEDROSIA REGION

Introduction

The southwesternmost of the Regions of the Indus Age is located in the mountains of Pakistani Baluchistan, known as Gedrosia to the Greeks (Figure 3.130). It is arid upland country incised by deep river valleys, flanked by rugged hills and mountains. Geographically, the region is part of a vast plateau stretching from the western edge of the Indus Valley to the eastern edge of the Tigris; a line approximating the modern boundary between Iraq and Iran. In the north of the

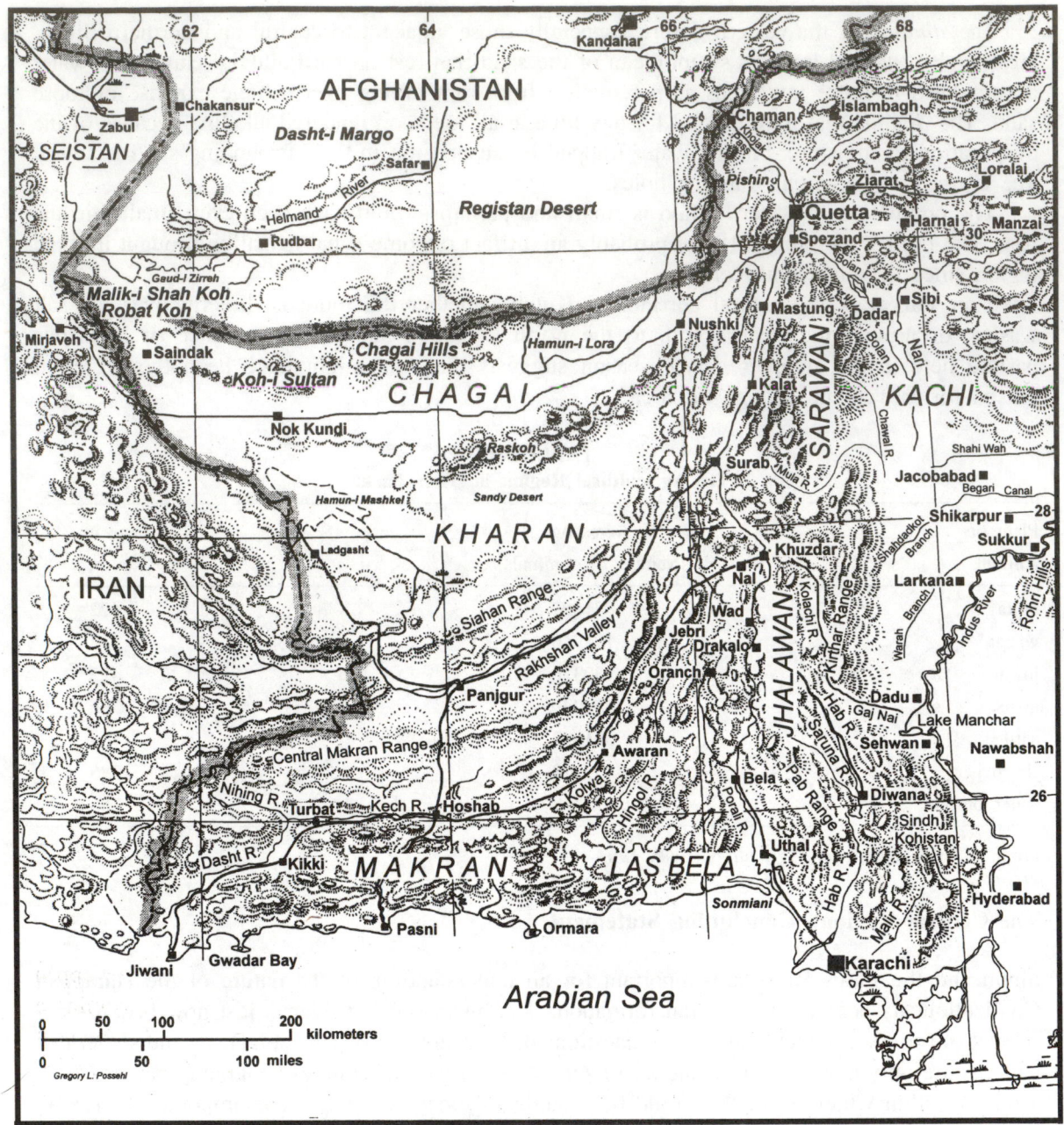

Figure 3.130. The Gedrosia Region

Region most of the precipitation comes in the cold months, as the winter westerlies that bring moisture to the Middle East and Iran arrive with snow. The southern parts fall within the weak, western shadow of the summer, southwest monsoon and have the benefit of two seasons of rainfall. There is an advantage to two seasons of rain because both are unreliable but independent, and if one fails there is no implication that the other will fail as well. The region is semi-arid. For the most part, the plants here are xerophitic species, well adapted to the precarious nature of the rainfall and armed to the leaf tip with spikes and spines.

The way of life in this region is pastoral nomadic, with village settlement in the better watered valleys, especially where simple irrigation or water catchment can be managed. The villages are also the seats of political power, in part because tribal leaders like to be situated in predictable locations, if this is possible. The Brahui and Baluchi pastoral tribes raise large numbers of sheep, goats and some cattle, as well as undertaking some cultivation. They spend their summers in the relatively cool hills of their homeland and the winters in the Indus Valley where they find employment as agricultural laborers (sometimes on archaeological sites) and gain access to pasture for their flocks.

The symbiosis between the Gedrosia and Central Regions is strong. In ecological terms these are complementary regions with different but related plant and animal communities. The changing of seasons led to the migration of wild animals and variation in the maturation cycle of the plants. Winter is the time of bounty in the valley, summer in the adjacent mountains. The suffocating heat of the valley in the summer is as debilitating as the biting cold of the mountains in winter.

The Gedrosia and Northwestern Regions are both within the zone where the wild progenitors of modern domesticated plants and animals can be found: cattle, sheep, goats, pigs, barley and perhaps wheat. It is possible that these Regions and the adjacent Indus lowlands played an independent role in the domestication process and the establishment of early village life and pastoral camps.

The present settlement pattern here is a significant distortion of the "traditional" arrangement because large diesel and electric pumps have been brought into many valleys and are tapping very deep ground water, some of which could be considered fossil. This has led to a settling down of the population, forsaking their tents for permanent villages.

The Depth of Human Settlement in the Gedrosia Region

There is a long history of settlement in the Gedrosia Region, which is probably home to some of the earliest village farming communities of the Indus Age. A complete, unbroken sequence of habitation has been uncovered, up to and including the Kulli Complex of the Mature Harappan. The Region was densely inhabited during this time and the Kulli settlements represent a highland expression of Indus urbanization. They have been described by Stein (1931), Casal (1966, 1968), de Cardi (1983), J.-F. Jarrige (1983), C. Jarrige (1984) and Possehl (1986a). Vessel forms of the ceramics of the Kulli Harappan are to some degree Sindhi Harappan, decorated in obvious Kulli style. The large, round-eyed Kulli bull is the most distinguished motif. The so-called "Kulli canister," is a distinctive, important vessel form that is not shared with the larger Harappan ceramic corpus. The distribution of Kulli sites does not extend into Iranian Baluchistan. Survey work in southeastern Iran still has many gaps, but the work that has been done (Stein 1937; Prickett 1986; Lamberg-Karlovsky, personal communication) has not yet produced a Kulli site and the major excavation at Tepe Yahya yielded only limited evidence for contact with the Indus Civilization. The present southern border between these two modern states was in all probability a border in the third millennium as well.

The area of the Gedrosia Region is about 115,000 square kilometers, remembering that today the edges of this, and all of the other Regions, are "fuzzy" and were probably "fuzzy" and shifting in antiquity. The eastern border of the Region connects Sutkagen-dor near the Arabian Sea coast to the vicinity of the modern town of Kalat, where the northernmost Kulli site, Damb Zerger (de Cardi 1983: 24) is located. It is a distance of ca. 640 kilometers. The eastern edge is taken to be the Sindh Kohistan and Kirthar range; 430 kilometers from the Arabian Sea to the Mula Pass.

From the perspective of cultural geography the Gedrosia Region is the most complex of all the Regions of the Indus Age, with five subregions in the mountainous environment of the Region as a whole.

Natural History: The Gedrosia Region

Human life in the Gedrosia Region has been structured to a major degree by the shape of the land. The hills and mountains separate valleys and rivers of diverse nature. Most of the water courses are small and not perennial. The overall structure of the Region can be seen by looking south from the relatively high knot of mountains and valleys in the north around Kalat and the Harboi Hills. These give way and open up in a finger or fan-like way, as one moves south. To the east there is a series of parallel river valleys (Hab, Porali, Hingol) with streams flowing almost due north-south. But to the west the rivers flow increasingly on a northeast-southwest track. There is also a drop in altitude as one moves south, from Kalat to the sea, stair stepping down the spine of Gedrosia. The structure is remarkably like looking down at one's right arm with the thumb straight and fingers spread open; the Arabian Sea nipping on the tips. The thumb and palm form the high thick mass of the Kirthar and Pab Ranges. The gap between the thumb and index finger becomes the triangular valley of Las Bela; the Hingol Valley the space between the next two fingers, and so on to the Dasht Valley.

Many of the small valleys and some of the larger ones, are basins of interior drainage which can be salt wastes. But, geology is such that under some conditions drainage is good, and the salts do not accumulate through evaporation and a fertile playa or *hamun* forms which is suitable for cultivation. Some of them are small, a few hectares in size. Others are large, like the one in Isplenji, just south of Quetta, on the frontier of the Gedrosia Region, which is 60 or 70 square kilometers (Plate 3.49, Plate 3.50). These *hamuns* are formed of fine alluvium carried into well drained basins. They have fertile soil and by their nature are better watered than other parts of the micro-geomorphology. They are excellent for agriculture and have been one of the small scale geographical variables that have structured agricultural life and the location of ancient settlements since the opening of the food producing era. They are also very flat and hard during the dry season, giving them a race course quality where modern archaeologists can test their driving skills at high speed.

Vegetation

The mountains, for the most part, are barren. "Phytogeographically speaking the Baluch territory as a whole is part of the Irano-Turanic and Sudanese regions... The vegetation of these territories is characterized by plant associations in which *Pistacia* and *Amygdalus* form the so-called 'steppe-forest' with trees and bushes extremely sparse and far apart. Like *Pistacia* and *Amygdalus*, the thicker formations of *Juniperus* also form 'steppe-forests'" (Costantini and Biasini 1985: 16-7). Under the right conditions the juniper groves can be dense and old. However, an overall view of the larger plants leads to the impression that it is *Acacia, Tamarix, Euphorbia*, and *Zizyphus* country. The vegetation of the Gedrosia Region has been described as "...very scanty and consists of desolate scrub...woody, stunted, thorny, not above a foot high, with round cushion-like outlines, bleached stems and few leaves, they look like the skeletons of plants...it is the measure of as desolate and offensive a vegetation as can be imagined" (Minchin 1907d: 16-7). This is perhaps more severe than objective. The vegetation has never seemed "offensive" to me, although the landscape certainly can be desolate in places. In fact, the lack of solid ground cover lends a breathtaking beauty to the country, that is captivating and draws one along on a journey from one spectacular prospect to another. More systematic lists of plants are available in the botany sections of the District Gazetteer series.

From an historical perspective it should be noted that the Gedrosia Region was home to wild barley (*Hordeum spontaneum*) and possibly wheat (*Triticum* sp.). These are both winter grasses found on the greater Iranian Plateau and mountainous Afghanistan. They are well adapted to disturbed soils in mountainous areas and the winter precipitation of the higher, northern areas of Gedrosia.

Wheat and barley are cultivated as winter *rabi* crops, although they do not necessarily dominate as food grains. Sorghum or *jowar* (*Sorghum bicolor*) is grown in quantity as a *kharif* crop especially in the southern districts (Las Bela and Makran) where the summer monsoon has some effect. Dates (*Phoenix dactylifera*) are also cultivated, and eaten, in vast quantities in the sorghum area. Onions (*Allium cepa*) and a wide variety of pulses are cultivated as condiments.

There are also edible wild plants that are important for understanding human settlement in the area. The jujube, *ber* (*Zizyphus jujubata*) is part of the undomesticated local botany. Some hill slopes, in the higher elevations to the northern end of the Region have good stands of pistachio. There is a wild prune (*Prunus eburnea*), a wild almond and an olive in the northern portion of the Region and substantial quantities of wild cumin (*Curcuma longa*) are also found.

Mammals

These mountains and valleys are home to many animals that were exploited in antiquity. The mammals of Pakistan have been documented in an excellent way by T. J. Roberts (1977). Hork, and the District Gazetteer series are sound guides to a comprehensive view of the mammal life of the Gedrosia Region. The animals that played a role in the story of the Indus Age include a wide range of creatures. There are a number of important predators like the Indian wolf (*Canis lupus*), Asiatic jackal (*Canis aureus*), common fox (*Vulpes vulpes*); black bear (*Selenarctos thibetanus*), striped hyaena (*Hyaena hyaena*), jungle cat (*Felis chaus*), leopard (*Panthera pardus*) which would have been found there and would then, as now, represent something of a danger to humans, especially the unwary.

The tiger (*Panthera tigris*) is not likely to have been found in the Region, except perhaps for Las Bela, but the Asiatic lion (*Panthera leo*), long extinct in the area, might have been present in the Gedrosia Region during prehistoric times.

The Indian pangolin or anteater (*Manis crassicaudata*) and porcupine (*Hystrix indica*) are both shown in Harappan art.

Animals that were likely to have been hunted for their meat and other useful products, but were never domesticated, include the Indian gazelle or chinkara (*Gazella bennetti*), the Persian gazelle (*Gazella subgutterosa*) and the markhor (*Capra falconeri falconeri*).

The animals that humans domesticated at the opening of the Indus Age are found in the wild in the Gedrosia Region: the wild goat (*Capra aegagrus*), wild sheep or urial (*Ovis vigni*), wild pig (*Sus scrofa*) and onager (*Equus hemionus*). Not very much is known about the wild cattle of this region, but, it would be included in this list. Roberts (1977: 161) has made an interesting point about the distribution of the onager: "The Baluchistan name for the ass, as in adjoining Iran, is 'ghor kar.' The prevalence of place names in Kalat and southwestern Baluchistan having the prefix or suffix ghor and khar, testifies to the extent to which the animal was familiar and wide spread in former times." He also notes that as late as 1964, tracks of the animal had been found in Baluchistan, although this elusive animal was not seen.

Minerals

There is a great deal of coal in the Gedrosia Region, not that the ancient peoples of South Asia used it (Minchin 1907g: 133-36). More important is the presence of old slag heaps from copper smelting in Sarawan and at many locations in the Chagai Hills. There is also lapis lazuli in the

Chagai Hills, and the use of this source has been documented at Shahr-i Sokhta (Delmas and Casanova 1990; Casanova 1992, 1994). The old notion that the only ancient source for lapis lazuli was in the Badakshan region of northeastern Afghanistan has been shown to be incorrect. There is no tin in Baluchistan; however there are major reserves in central Afghanistan (Salah et al. 1977: 165-90). The copper resources of Baluchistan appear to have been substantial. There is still profitable copper mining at Sandak, but most of this resource has been worked out today. The major sources of copper were in the Chagai Hills and Kalat (See Appendix D for documentation). R. Hughes-Buller found malachite in the Wad Valley and Pab Range (Minchin 1907a: 162). Baluchistan has to be counted as one of the two principal sources of copper during the Indus Age. The second area was the Khetri Belt of mines in Rajasthan.

The Subregions and Subsistence

Kalat

Kalat is the largest subregion within the Gedrosia Region. This is Brahui territory, tribal peoples who speak a Dravidian language, akin to those concentrated in South India today. Their land is rugged and mountainous, with some fertile valley bottoms, but good summer pasture. The capital city, "Kalat", is the center of Brahui tribal power in the region and has been a fortified citadel for many years (Figure 3.131).

Some sense of the modern food production system can be had from the statistics on the following table. It shows the balance between wheat, a winter *rabi* crop and the millets of the *kharif* season. The wheat is often sown and then left to mature on its own through the winter, while the people who planted it migrate to Sindh in search of pasture for their sheep and for work, another timeless fact of life in this Region. Mastung was once a renowned producer of melons and grapes. In the mid-nineteenth century five varieties of grapes were grown; one a fine, fleshy, white variety measuring 3.2 centimeters (one and one-quarter inches) long (Hughes 1877: 67).

TABLE 3.19
Subsistence Regime in Kalat

Plant or Animal	Acres or Number of Animals	Page in Report
jowar	336662	425
wheat	216094	335
bajra	90	425
sheep	344480	789
goats	273480	789
cattle	158360	769
water buffalo	2260	769

From: *Pakistan Census of Agriculture 1960*, 1963

The Kirthar Front

The Gedrosia Region presents a mountainous "front" to the Indus Plains, called the Sindh

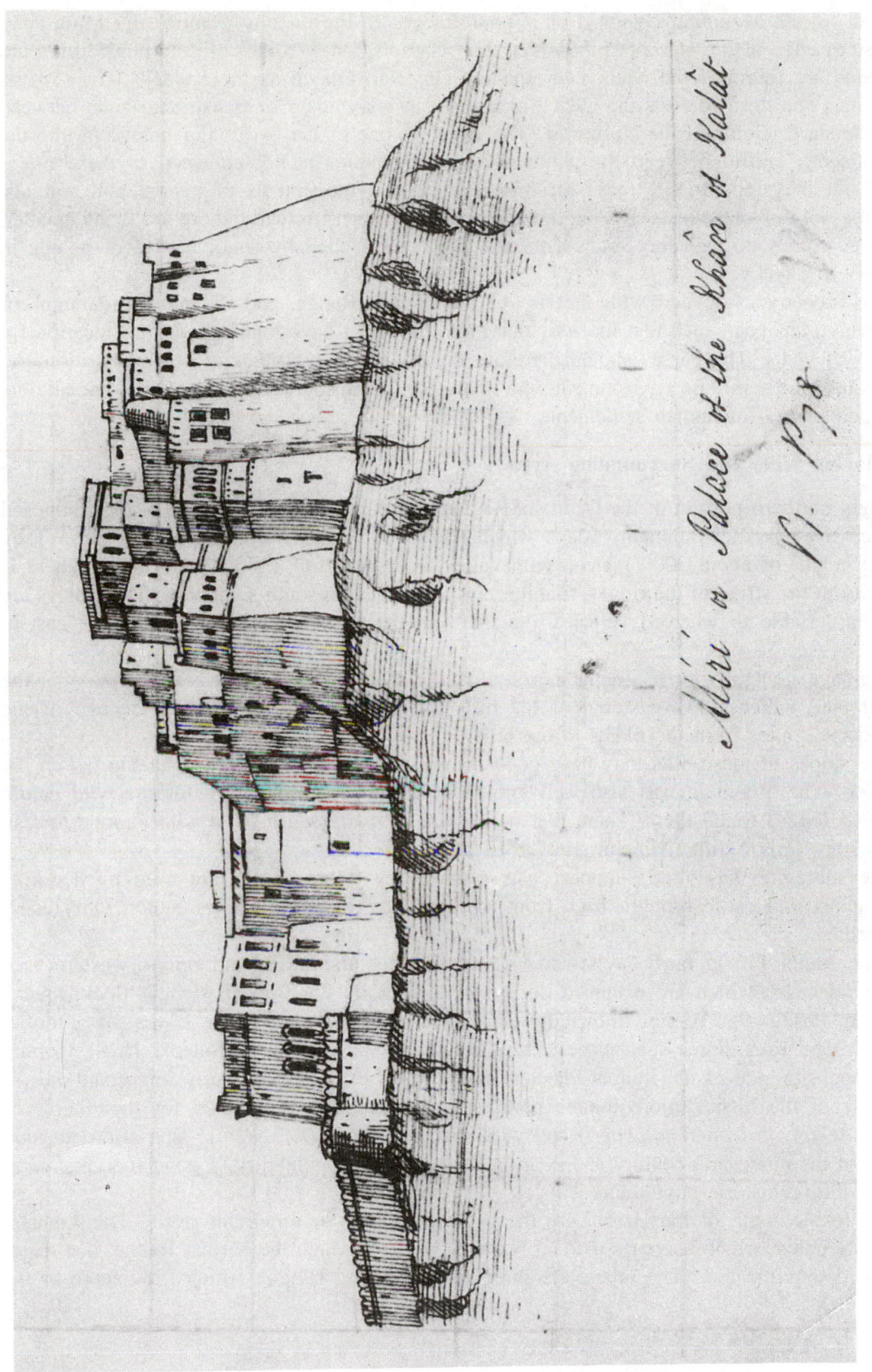

Miri or Palace of the Khan of Kalat

V. P78

Figure 3.131. Kalat as drawn by Charles Masson, courtesy of the India Office Library

Kohistan (Sindh Mountain Country) or Kirthar Range. To the far north, above the Mula Pass, the eastern edge of the Harboi Hills serves this function. Major routes of communication onto the plains are found at the Mula Pass and the Gaj Nai, known as the Kulachi River in the mountains. The third route is the great Bolan Pass, in a boundary or transitional zone between the Gedrosia Region and the Northwest. The Bolan is one of the two major gateways into the Subcontinent. Traffic between the plains and the mountains is not confined to these major routes, but they tend to be tracks for massive seasonal movements of people and animals, providing not only ease of access but a ready supply of water. Actually, there are many smaller, well used routes through the Sindh Kohistan that are travelled by small parties of people in their day to day lives.

The orogeny associated with the rise of the Kirthar Range, and the other mountains of Baluchistan, has been such that the *nais* that pass through it have maintained their location for millions of years. The passes should therefore be thought of as routes of communication and fixed points in a semi-arid environment with relatively secure sources of water and some alluvial soil; good places for human settlement.

The Harboi Hills and Surrounding Area

The high, northern portion of the Gedrosia Region is dominated by the Harboi Hills, composed of successive, parallel mountain ridges which rise step fashion from the Kachi Plains. They reach a height of about 3000 meters, with valley floors 1000 to 1500 meters lower. There is regularity to the strike of the ridges, running north-northeast to south-southwest. The valleys are readily accessible to wheeled vehicles and there are foot paths across the hills from east to west.

Drainage generally flows to the north, into the Bolan River, a notable exception is the Chawal Nai, which flows east out of the hills into Gandava in Kachi. This is one of the "secondary" routes from the plains to the hills.

The slopes of these hills may have good stands of juniper, sometimes pistachio, as on the Siah Koh. The mountain was also well known in the nineteenth century for the wild cumin (*Curcuma longa*) found there. There is a wild prune (*Prunus eburnea*), a wild almond and an olive in the Harboi Hills (Minchin 1907g: 10-2).

The subregion has good summer pasture on valley floors, which are used by herds of sheep, goats and cattle brought back from the lowlands during the hot weather. One hill is described:

"The Melbi hill is fairly well wooded with juniper and olive, and on its western face are several caves which are occupied during the winter by Phalwanzai Mengal flockowners" (Minchin 1907g: 9). To my knowledge no one has investigated these caves as potential archaeological sites. Some such places, like the famous Shanidar Cave (Solecki 1978), in Iraq, on the opposite side of the Iranian Plateau, have proved to be spectacularly important sites.

Many of the higher, more remote parts of this subregion were noted for their herds of markhor (*Capra falconeri falconeri*) and wild sheep or urial (*Ovis vigni*). This afforded good hunting in the nineteenth century and is an indication of the availability of good food resources here for the prehistoric population.

Just to the south of the Harboi are the headwaters of four important rivers. The Kulachi, previously noted, which becomes the Gaj Nai as it passes through the Kirthar Range, is a major route of communication. The others are the Hab, Porali and Hingol, which flow south to the Arabian Sea.

The Hab River, Porali River, Hingol River and Las Bela

The Hab River is the easternmost of the streams that flow north-south in the Gedrosia Region (Plate 3.51, Plate 3.52). It, along with its tributary, the Saruna River, are perennial for the most part and debouche directly into the Arabian Sea, not the Indus. This valley is, for the most part, very rugged country, without significant flood plain or cultivation. There are two interesting archaeological sites in the valley. One is an Amri-Nal settlement at Diwana (Fairservis 1961b: 9-11) associated with an ancient dam for storing water and silt runoff. The second is a small Mature Harappan site at the mouth of the river near Hab Chowkie. The Hab is an important route from north to south, especially in its upper reaches, where access from the east, the lower India plains, can be had from the vicinity of Lake Manchar. The upper Hab and Saruna Valleys have a significant concentration of *gabarbands*, and are a kind of "type area" for these structures.

The Hab is separated from the Porali River to the west by the Pab Range, a series of largely disarticulated hills and low mountains. The Porali is also perennial and drains through the important, fertile valleys of Wad, Ornach and Las Bela. Las Bela with its broad triangular area known as the Welpat, is particularly good land, at least for the Region. The word "las" means "plain" and Las Bela can be taken to mean "good" or "fertile plain," a clear indication of how the inhabitants feel about their home country. For an early account of Las Bela see Carless (1838c, 1839). The Welpat plain around Bela is watered not only by the Porali, which takes to braided channels here, but from smaller *nais* originating in the mountains to both the east and west. There are also a great many wells used for irrigation and domestic purposes.

The traditional crops of Las Bela are the usual millets, sorghum, (*jowar*) and pearl millet (*bajra*). "The most important crop is *jowar*...which forms the staple food grain of the people (Minchin 1907d: 78). The millets are cultivated along with mustard, *rai* (*Brassica juncea*) and sesame, *tal* (*Sesamum indicum*). The rainfall and runoff of Bela are associated with summer rainfall and this valley of 16,680 square kilometers falls within the westernmost shadow of the southwest monsoon, the mountains around it being just high enough to bring the rain. Wheat and barley, *rabi* crops, are grown in very limited quantities (Minchin 1907d: 78).

Agriculture in Las Bela is made possible during the southwest monsoon by the presence of dams, *gabarbands*, or simply *bands*, and their smaller counterparts *kirai*. Today these are built and maintained on a cooperative basis, with some involvement of state officials. The Porali River in Las Bela had three *gabarbands* and about 13 *kirai* at the turn of the century and all rivers in the valley are said to be dammed at some point (Minchin 1907d: 91). When the floods come these dams hold water which is then fed off to the fields of individual cultivators. This is done in succession, with the upstream dams filling first, taking their share and the water then being allowed to move on. Since the *kirai* only block a portion of the flow, no breaching mechanism is necessary, but the larger works are provided with some mechanism to allow water to pass through, or around them.

These dams, which vastly increase the utility and effectiveness of the summer rainfall, are an important technological feature in securing the food supply for the inhabitants of Las Bela. The introduction of *jowar* and *bajra*, from Africa, apparently in the third millennium BC, was also an important ingredient in the evolution of the modern agricultural regime.

TABLE 3.20
Subsistence Regime in Las Bela

Plant or Animal	Acres or Number of Animals	Page in Report
jowar	113735	426
wheat	5662	336
bajra	3354	426
goats	235870	790
cattle	93300	770
sheep	82970	790
water buffalo	4210	770

From: *Pakistan Census of Agriculture 1960*, 1963

Las Bela has a substantial coast line and at least one good port at Sonmiani located on a sheltered bay of the Arabian Sea. Adjacent to the open sea is another feature, known as Miani Hor, which is a shallow bay, with access to the sea, but separated from it by a large sand bar. This *hor* is a source of diverse maritime products and has been exploited since the Bronze Age, as evidenced by the remains at the Early and Mature Harappan site at Balakot (Meadow 1979a). Ormara, 200 kilometers west of Sonmiani, is another port associated with the political, not geographical, aspect of Las Bela.

The coast of Las Bela, as well as the Makran to the west and reaching as far as Gwadar, have a geographical curiosity, mud volcanoes, *buttam* in Baluchi (Minchin 1907d: 11) (Figure 3.132). These features are variable in size ranging from a few meters to 100 meters in diameter

Figure 3.132. Lithograph of mud volcanoes in Las Bela, from the 1853 edition of Sir Charles Lyell's *Principles of Geology*

and up to the same height. They resemble stubby volcanic cinder cones but because of their soft, unconsolidated sides often have deeply incised water gullies there. The caldera are filled with mud and belch methane gas at various times, often as frequently as 25 second intervals. They are not a particular danger to humans but the gases are noxious and a source of malodorous discomfort. The volcanoes are short-term, transitory features appearing here and there, even in the sea, bubbling along for a time and then falling to permanent quiescence. There is no evidence that they were objects of attention to the Harappans or Kullis; however, it must be that they were part of their ancient landscape and it would not be surprising to find some evidence, possibly in art, of their representation.

Between the Hab and Porali Rivers is a small stream known as the Windar, associated with an important prehistoric site at Balakot and shallow lake called Siranda. The Windar was dammed in historical (prehistoric?) times and provides irrigation for the surrounding plain. The excess runoff is directed to Siranda Lake, to keep it full and fresh (Minchin 1907d: 8-9).

Las Bela and the Windar Valley are two of the places through which Alexander the Great passed with his army in 326 BC on his return to Babylon. Arrian refers to the fact that Alexander built a harbor and dockyards on a lake near the mouths of the Indus. Most readings place this lake in the general drainage of the Indus, but there is a slight chance that it was Sonmiani Bay, in part because the lake in question had ocean fish in it (Arrian VI.20, Robson 1929, Vol. 2: 163-64). George Dales noted that the top of Balakot was covered with the remains of ruined kilns or furnaces and hundreds of post holes and stone alignments. These were mixed with some pottery that could be Hellenistic or Buddhist in date and iron trilobite arrowheads (Dales 1979a: 271). There is also Islamic pottery in some quantity, so no certain date can be given to this jumbled mass of material. But, one can at least wonder if the top of Balakot was selected as elevated ground, with good breezes to fan the furnaces of Alexander's smiths at the new dockyard, assisting Admiral Nearchus with the maintenance of his fleet and rearming Alexander's army.

Las Bela is the location of a number of Kulli sites, most of which were recorded by Walter A. Fairservis, Jr. in the course of his 1959-60 work there (Fairservis 1961b). Many of these are located along the Porali just above the point where it debouches on to the Welpat. Fairservis calls these sites, taken together, "Complex A."

To the east, across the low, dissected Mala Range, is the Hingol River. This is an extremely complex system of streams, with several names, depending on the particular portion of the drainage which is being examined: e.g., Nal, Gidar Dhor. The headwaters of the Hingol reach far to the north into the southern portion of the Harboi Hills, to the north of Khuzdar, a distance of ca. 400 kilometers as the crow flies.

The greater Hingol River system is home to many important archaeological sites including Mehi, Nundara (Jhau) and Nal. It is not however, a valley system renowned for its agricultural potential and the principal occupation of the nomads who live and pass by is the raising of sheep, goats and a few cattle.

Karachi appears not to have been an important place in antiquity, although it is entirely possible that a site of the Indus Age lies within the built up area of the municipality. For a history of this important harbor of colonial times see A. F. Baillie (1890).

The Makran

An area known as the Makran lies across the southern, seaward side, of the Gedrosia Region. It includes the entire drainage of the Kech and Dasht Rivers, up to the watershed of the Rakhshan

Valley and the Makran Coastal Range, including the relatively small Bhari River flowing to Pasni on the coast and the Basul just to the west of Ormara. According to the 1921 census the region had ca. 1.7 persons per square kilometer (2.7 per square mile).

Henry Field has a good summary of material on this subregion (Field 1959: 7-76) and the Makran District Gazetteer (Hughes-Buller 1906) is a fine source of information as well.

The landforms here are composed of relatively soft clays interbedded with harder calcareous strata. The heavy erosion of these barren formations has led to many unusual, even fantastic hill formations.

The Makran is the land of the Ichthyophagoi whom Alexander met on his passage out of Las Bela and the region in which so many of his troops were lost (Arrian IV, 24-28; Robson 1929: Vol. 2: 177-91). The description of this portion of Alexander's return to the west is instructive in that it describes a country much like the one we see today; rather bleak, waterless, except for oases, a land of little food and a place of danger for large numbers of uninvited guests. Arrian tells that of the men in the army only "...a few out of many were saved; but most of them fell into the sand, like men who perished in the sea" (Arrian IV, 25.3; Robson 1929, Vol. II: 181). Some of those who did not perish in the sand died by drowning:

> The army received also a further disaster, which perhaps more than anything else distressed both the troops, and their horses and transport animals. During the trade winds there is very heavy rain over the land of the Gedrosians, as also over India, not so much over the Gedrosian plains as over the hills, whither the clouds are borne by the wind and are poured out in rain, not rising above the crests of hills. Now the army bivouacked near a small stream, in fact for the sake of water, and about the second watch of the night the stream which flowed here became swollen with rains, the rains themselves having fallen out of sight of the army, and came down with so great a spate of water that it drowned most of the women and children from among those which followed the army, swept away all the royal pavilion and its contents, and so many of the transport animals as had survived; and indeed the troops themselves were saved only with great difficulty, with their weapons only, and not even all of these (Arrian IV, 25; Robson 1929: 182-83).

Agriculture in the Makran

The District Gazetteer series has some interesting things to say about the food habits of the population during the late nineteenth century. Dates, sorghum and fish were the staples of the diet. Dates were apparently taken in great quantity in a variety of different guises. Fish were sometimes consumed raw, just as reported by Arrian in his description of the Ichthyophagoi. Fish were also dried and then boiled at meal time, the broth consumed before the meat. A fish meal was prepared and made into cakes and eaten as a kind of "bread." *Jowar* cakes were eaten as unleavened bread at meals later in the day, not in the morning. Fish and dates so dominated the diet of the common folk that it was a standing joke that when strangers came they had no taste for these foods, especially the Brahui. But after a few days they adapted to it and went about with a dried fish or two stuck in their turbans and dates stuffed in their pockets (Hughes-Buller 1906: 109-10). Rice and wheat were eaten only by the wealthy, as was flesh of sheep and goats. Barley was cultivated in the eastern portion of the Makran, especially Kolwa. The rich kept zebus (*Bos indicus*) for milk but poorer families relied on the lactations of sheep and goats for this product. There is no mention of hunting.

TABLE 3.21
Subsistence Regime in Makran

Plant or Animal	Acres or Number of Animals	Page in Report
wheat	15240	335
jowar	40446	425
bajra	No report	425
goats	127260	790
sheep	108460	790
cattle	31820	770
water buffalo	140	770

From: *Pakistan Census of Agriculture 1960*, 1963

The flora of Makran is similar to the rest of the Gedrosia Region but the highland trees, like juniper and pistachio, are gone. They have not been replaced by like species and due to the scanty, unpredictable rainfall there is less ground cover. There is a good deal of *Euphorbia*, *Acacia*, *Zizyphus jujubata*, *Tamarix*, *Capparis aphylla*, *Prosopis spicegera* and *Salvadora oleoides*.

The wild goats and sheep of the northern highlands disappear with the juniper, except for the higher, northern portions of this zone in the Central Makran Range, bordering the Rakhshan Valley. Other animals common in the nineteenth century included the Indian wolf (*Canis lupus*), Asiatic jackal (*Canis aureus*), striped hyaena (*Hyaena hyaena*), common fox (*Vulpes vulpes*), leopard (*Panthera pardus*), Indian gazelle or *chinkara* (*Gazella bennetti*) and wild pig (*Sus scrofa*).

The greater Kech (Kej) Valley is one of the two foci for human habitation in this region; the other is the immediate coast of the Arabian Sea. It includes the Kolwa area, as well as the Nihing and Dasht Rivers, which is the new name given to the stream after the joining of the Kech and Nihing.

When Sir Aurel Stein was there in January 1928 he reported that the Kech Valley contained fully one-third of the population of the Makran. This accounts for the reason that the region is often referred to not simply as "Makran" but rather "Kech-Makran," an observation that dates to Medieval times when the great Venetian, Marco Polo, made note of the place. His observations are of interest because they refer to the commercial and sea going nature of the people.

> Kesmacoran is a kingdom having a king of its own and a peculiar language. Some of the people are Idolators, but the most part are Saracens. They live by merchandise and industry, for they are professed traders, and carry on much traffic by sea and land in all directions. Their food is rice and corn, flesh and milk, of which they have great store. There is no more to be said about them...And you must know that this kingdom of Kesmacoran is the last in India as you go towards the west... (H. Yule 1926: 401).

The seafaring orientation of this area can also be documented by the fact that Gwadar came into possession of the Sultanate of Oman and did not revert to Pakistani sovereignty until four years after the British withdrawal from the Subcontinent. This close historical tie between the Makran and Oman seems to go back to Harappan times since there is a coastal village at Ras al Junayz that has Harappan materials, including a copper stamp seal and ceramics (Cleuziou, Reade and Tosi 1989: Figure 18). The Makran Gazetteer (Hughes-Buller 1906: 64, 89) also documents the immigration of a tribe known as the Barr who came from Bahrain to Pangur within historical times.

There are sea terraces along the Makran Coast. They have been studied by Rodman Snead (1963, 1966, 1967, 1969, 1993), but are not yet well dated. If the latest estimates are correct they were formed well before the Indus Age, in two episodes at ca. 30,000 ^{14}C years BP and ca. 23,000 ^{14}C years BP (Snead 1993: 327). This would imply that the famous Mature Harappan site of Sutkagen-dor was not a port.

Not well documented are the presence of substantial numbers of east Africans on the Makran and in Gujarat as well. They are generally called *siddis* and further point up the close ties between the western coasts of the Subcontinent and those of east Africa. It should not be assumed that these are necessarily recent developments since they may begin with the sea trade on the Indian Ocean during the third millennium BC.

Settlement in the Kech and Nihing Valleys is made possible by the presence of the rivers with a chain of oases along them. These are formed around large pools in the riverbed, which are likely to have been man-made and are reportedly well maintained. Dates are grown here along with *jowar*, wheat and vegetables (Hughes-Buller 1906b: 109-10).

Kolwa is a natural extension of the Kech Valley, some 130 kilometers long and 25 kilometers wide. To the naked eye the two valleys are contiguous, but there is a slight difference in the watersheds that makes them stand apart on hydrological grounds. Kolwa is a vast *hamun* or playa and this accounts for its agricultural potential when there is rain. According to Stein, Kolwa is by far the greatest dry crop area in Makran and he notes that its export of barley (a winter crop) is considerable in years with good rainfall. There are few permanent settlements in Kolwa today, which is in contrast to the prehistoric past when great settlements like the mound of Kulli were inhabited: "The contrast between the massively built stone structures traceable at more than one ancient site of Kolwa and the wretched huts of palm-matting which house the whole of even the settled population of the Kech valley as elsewhere in Makran, is striking and illustrates the great change which has come over this whole region" (Stein 1931: 9).

The Mature Harappan site of Sutkagendor is in the Makran on the Dasht River, close to the Pakistan-Iran border. Roland Besenval, an archaeologist with CNRS, has had an opportunity to conduct surveys in this area and has found other Mature Harappan sites in the region stretching up the Dasht River to Turbat. Other coastal settlements are known at Sotka-koh, Balakot and Allahadino, near the Arabian Sea coast at Karachi. Farther on, the coast of Gujarat was also occupied, even across the Gulf of Khambhat.

Concluding Remarks: The Gedrosia Region

The Gedrosia Region is among the most desolate of the areas within the Greater Indus Region. But, there is great diversity here and the area has an attractive quality to it, both from the perspective of the landscape and the independence of the people who inhabit it. It is a key region with the natural resources that enabled man to domesticate plants and animals and develop the arts of farming and pastoralism. The complementary environments of the Central and Gedrosia Regions fostered an interdependence through transhumance which may have been as much a part of prehistoric subsistence, economics and politics as it is today.

THE SOUTHERN REGION

Introduction

The Southern Region (Figure 3.133) is largely coincident with the boundaries of the State of Gujarat. The Region encompasses about 150,000 square kilometers. The area discussed here includes a variety of environments ranging from salt flats of Kutch and the sandy alluvium of north Gujarat to the rich teak forests of the Western Ghats. It is essentially a lowland area

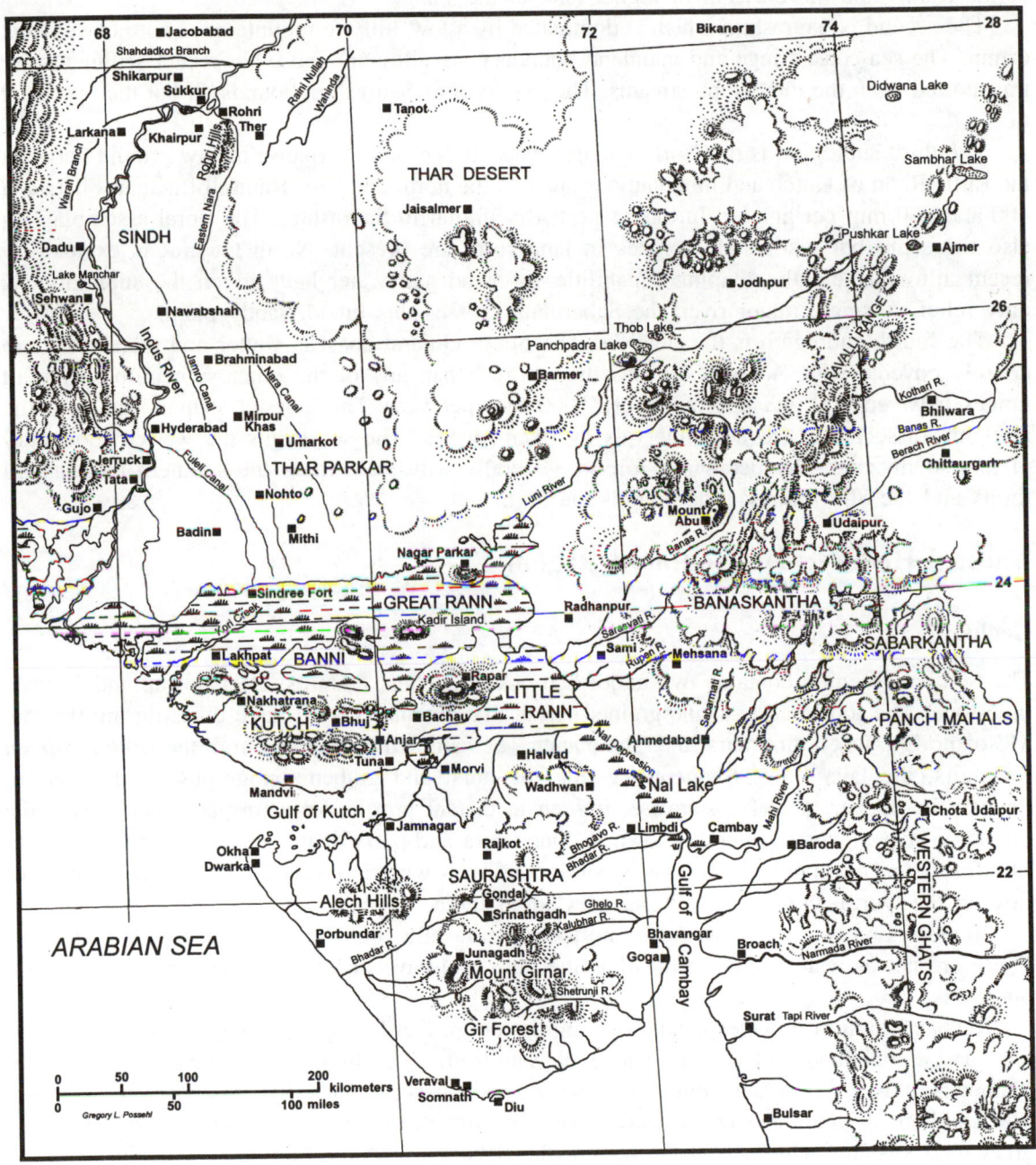

Figure 3.133. The Southern Region

appended to peninsular India that stands apart as a region of the subcontinent. It is bounded on the north by Sindh and mountains, on the east by mountains alone and on the south and west by the sea.

Subregions

There are four subregions within the Southern Region, which form cultural and environmental units.

The first is Kutch. There are two physiographic parts of this fascinating place: the salt flats of the Ranns and the crescent of higher land to the south.

The second is Saurashtra which is dominated by a low, hilly to mountainous core of volcanic origin. The sea coast fringe and mainland boundary are alluvium and other recent sediments are transported from the interior by streams. The sea coast of Saurashtra bounds all but the mainland tie.

The third subregion is the North Gujarat Plain. It is a broad expanse of low ground between the Little Rann of Kutch and mountainous areas to the north and east. Rainfall fluctuates between 400 and 800 mm per annum. In this respect it is similar to Saurashtra. The floral assemblage is also the same but distinct differences in land form are present. North Gujarat is exclusively recent alluvium and the shaping capabilities of wind and water have given the subregion its only relief. A single major river, the Sabarmati, crosses this broad, sandy plain.

The fourth subregion is the smallest. The South Gujarat coast is wetter and therefore more densely covered with *Acacia-Capparis* thorn forest than any of the other subregions. Rainfall ranges between 800 and approximately 1000 mm per year. This coastal strip is flat with the alluvium dissected at frequent intervals by river courses. The sea forms the western boundary of this small zone. Dry deciduous forests, generally with teak, mark the southern and eastern limits and the 800 mm isocline bounds the north.

Natural History: The Southern Region

Geology

The Southern Region contains two major bedrock geological features: Deccan trap and Jurrasic limestone. The trap rock is a fine grained basalt that emanated from huge dikes during the late Mesozoic Era, when dinosaurs ruled the planet. The name "trap" derives from the Dutch *trappen* for stairs, the lava flows frequently giving the horst and graben topography of the Deccan Plateau the appearance of a staircase, if seen in distant profile. Trap formations dominate the lithology of peninsular Gujarat, known as Saurashtra and parts of the southern mainland coast. The formation on mainland Gujarat is contiguous with what is probably the largest single lava flow in the world, the Deccan Plateau of Central India.

Jurassic limestones are found in northern Saurashtra and the adjacent Kutch highlands. These are not as nearly as widespread as the traps and have played little part in soil formation processes.

Recent alluvium is widespread, covering the entire North Gujarat Plain, as well as most of the coastal mainland and the sea fringe of Saurashtra. The highly productive North Gujarat Plain which is covered with dunes is riverine, mostly very sandy Sabarmati River alluvium. The southern or mainland coast is also covered with deep fertile alluvium, a product of the great river systems which cross the region: the Sabarmati, Mahi, Tapi and Narmada.

Soils owe a great debt to the bedrock geology of the region. Associated with the Deccan trap are the so-called "black cotton soils." These black to brown loams have played a significant role in prehistoric subsistence adaptation. They are the product of *in situ* formation on the trap and have a wide distribution in central and western India. Black cotton soil varies in depth and is usually loam to clay in mixture with calcareous concretions invariably present. They are usually deficient in phosphorous, nitrogen and organic matter but sufficient in potash and lime (Radhawa et al. 1968: 17). Black cotton soils are well known for their ability to absorb considerable amounts of moisture, which makes them excellent for dry cropping.

In several parts of Gujarat the black soils have been eroded and their character changed by stream transportation. In other areas, especially North Gujarat, alluvium has been derived from wind and water erosion of the Aravalli Range to the north in Rajasthan. Soils in north Gujarat are often sandy and may have a high salt content, especially in areas which are frequently flooded and have poor drainage.

The Southern Region is surrounded on two sides by high ground. The Aravallis cross the north, at their southern terminus and the Western Ghats along the eastern boundary, extending south to the end of peninsular India. The northern slopes are gentle, with open deciduous woodlands; however, to the east, slopes are steep with abundant vegetation, especially in the south of Gujarat where rainfall is high. As would be expected with a narrow coastal plain abutting such mountains, rivers and streams are generally short and seasonally turbulent. Passes through the Western Ghats afford passage of larger rivers such as the Narmada.

Minerals

The Southern Region is not rich in minerals, but there are several products that we know were used during Early and Mature Harappan times that are available here. There are the reserves of translucent stones with a very high silica content, that can be called agates, for convenience. Chalcedony, that turns red when heated and is then known as carnelian, is found in some abundance here. The source of these stones are the geodes and other precipitates associated with the Deccan trap and today this material is found in river gravels, some of which are old and now covered with alluvium. Agate nodules are widely available in Kutch, and in all of the stream beds of Saurashtra. The best modern mines are at Rajpipla, on the Narmada River, and they supply the stone for the famous lapidary industry at Cambay (Government of Gujarat 1964f; B. Allchin 1979a; Possehl 1982d; Kenoyer 1986; Kenoyer, Vidale and Bhan 1991; Karanth 1988, 1990, 1992; see Janaki 1980 for history). The Southern Region seems to have been the principal source of chalcedony for the bead-making industry of Mature Harappan times.

There is some copper and a bit of tin in north Gujarat, very close to the modern border between Gujarat and Rajasthan. The tin reported in Panch Mahals, in the Western Ghats, was placer tin, which might have been available in some quantity in antiquity. It would have taken millions of years for the metallic lumps of tin to accumulate and they could all have been collected in just a few centuries, or even decades, mostly erasing the evidence for a resource that was once quite rich.

Pearls of good quality but poor luster are found in the Gulf of Kutch, Junagadh and Bhavnagar (Government of Bombay 1884: 94). There might have been an ancient trade in these objects, if the Akkadian word for "fish eyes" is a pearl.

Rivers

The Narmada is one of the largest and most holy of India's rivers. It has been a traditional boundary between north and south throughout much of Indian history and is the only major river on the subcontinent which flows from east to west. The Narmada is deeply entrenched for most of its course. It does not have the broad alluvial plain associated with so many Indian rivers. During much of the year it does not even fill its entrenchment bank to bank, but meanders within a well defined channel. Periodically, however, it does broach its banks and spills water and alluvium over vast areas. Unfortunately, these events are violent and destructive. Because of the vagaries of the monsoon, the great differences in seasonal water levels and the deep entrenchment, the Narmada has never had irrigation potential except with the construction of modern dams.

The most important river in the Region is the Sabarmati, which flows south from its source in the Aravallis to the Gulf of Cambay. It has been a source of some natural *sailaba* irrigation in its southern reaches, especially in Kheda District.

Saurashtra is an area of radial drainage, the small rivers of the subregion moving out to the sea from the central upland area (Plate 3.53, Plate 3.54). Given the small catchment areas of these streams they are generally not classed as perennial, although all except the smallest do have surface water in their beds all year, and in the best of times there is some flow from month to month throughout the year. The monsoon rains are a fickle phenomenon and when they hit hard, with great showers of rain these small rivers are engulfed and devastating floods can result, eliminating whole villages along their banks. This would have been a particular hazard during the prehistoric occupation of Saurashtra because there is a very strong tendency for Sorath Harappan settlements to be located within 100 meters of these streams (Possehl 1980: 50-6).

Rainfall

Rainfall in Gujarat is almost exclusively dependent on the monsoon. Saurashtra and North Gujarat receive between 400 and 700 millimeters. This is sufficient for dry cropping, especially in Saurashtra with its moisture retentive black cotton soils. South Gujarat receives more rain, ca. 800 to 1500 millimeters. Rainfall is especially high in the southern part of the subregion, near the border with the modern state of Maharashtra.

TABLE 3.22
Rainfall at Various Stations in Gujarat 1901-50

	Mean	80%
Ahmedabad	779.8 mm	563 mm
Bhavnagar	620.0	436
Bhuj	340.4	150
Bulsar	1805.7	1242
Dhandhuka	606.0	400
Dhrangadhra	507.3	283
Jamnagar	466.3	255
Rajkot	594.3	450
Veraval	524.5	266

India Meteorological Department 1962

Flora

The flora of Gujarat is, on the whole, small, grassy or shrub-like plants characteristic of the South Asian dry forests. Three major floral complexes have been defined: *Salvadora-Prosopis*, *Acacia-Capparis*, and *Anogeissus-Terminalia-Tectona* (Gaussen et al. 1968; G. L. Shah 1974). The first two complexes are characteristic of the lowlands, with widely spaced shrub and thickets, even savannah-like zones, with the *Salvadora-Prosopis* complex being more tolerant of both salt and aridity. The third complex is a dry deciduous forest. In several parts of the state the teak element is missing but the remainder of the complex occurs intact. Altitude and the resulting greater precipitation, partitions this complex from the other two, but these plant complexes can be partitioned using other criteria as well. Forests of teak and other species that are found on the higher hills such as the Gir area are predominately Indo-Malayan and Indian plants. Thickets and areas with shrubby vegetation with *Prosopis, Salvadora, Acacia, Capparis, Euphorbia*, such as the sandy plains of the North Gujarat western complex, are abundant (Meher-Homji 1970).

The arch of intermittent high ground along the entire southern coast (the hills at Palitana, Gir, Girnar near Junagadh and Barda to the west) still supports true forests (Plate 3.55). This is particularly striking in the protected environment of the Gir Forest and Animal Preserve. Gir and Mount Girnar are dominated by teak and members of the *Anogeissus* and *Terminalia* genera (Gaussen et al. 1968: 34-8). Both of these are very large deciduous trees. At times these forests form a closed canopy, especially in protected Gir (Plate 3.56). Less densely vegetated parts of the Gir Forest are shown in Plate 3.23, where the lions reside. This seems to be an enduring pattern for Saurashtra since there is a very good correlation all over western India between dry deciduous forests and elevation. These hill ranges should, therefore, be thought of as forest areas in the third millennium BC.

There is also high ground to the north, with Mount Abu and the passage into Udaipur. This is generally thought of as part of the Western Ghats. Although the hills can be rugged, the passage is not especially difficult. The area is well endowed with tree cover, even today, as well as perennial streams (Plate 3.57).

Dichanthium annulatum and *Cenchrus ciliaris* are the most important grasses in Saurashtra. *Dichanthium* is also one of the most important grasses in all of western India and plays a salient role in animal husbandry wherever it is found. R. O. Whyte (1964: 118) suggests that an open *Dichanthium annulatum* grassland is the grass subclimax for North Gujarat, probably Saurashtra and parts of South Gujarat as well. His work is corroborated inferentially, by that at Agra by N. N. Sen[15] and at Nurpur by N. P. Mohan[16] where grassland successions have been studied. In the vicinity of the Nal Depression large areas may contain *Ischaemum rugosum* and *Iseilema colonum*. Both of these are wet adapted grasses, the former often found as a weed in wet rice fields (Whyte 1964: 120). When drainage is improved, a succession terminating in *Dichanthium annulatum* is achieved.

Lowland Gujarat has a very close botanical affinity with the Central and Gedrosia Regions to the west, an important continuity which helps to understand some of the underlying affinities between the various domains of the Harappan Civilization.

The mammalian fauna in this part of India has not been well studied. A great variety of ungulates are present, including: nilgai (*Boselaphus tragocamelus*), blackbuck (*Antelope cervicapra*), chital or spotted deer (*Axis axis*), wild water buffalo (*Bubalus bubalis*), elephant (*Elephas maximus*), rhinoceros (*Rhinoceros unicornis*), lions (*Panthera leo*) and tigers (*Panthera tigris*).

There is an abundance of bird life, including migratory cranes, storks, ducks and other water fowl, during the winter. They come to rest in the shallow pools of the many rivers that drain from the central highlands of Saurashtra, and find Nal Lake in the area north of Lothal, an amiable stopping place.

Kutch and the Nal Depression

Kutch has always been a very special place, somewhat remote from both Sindh and peninsular

India, yet a place that is traveled through and is a port of call for maritime commerce as well. Today it is securely and certainly a part of India. There is a separate Kutchee language, somewhat different from both Sindhi and Gujarati.

The Mature Harappan settlements in Kutch were all within the Sindhi Harappan fold (i.e., Desalpur, Pabumath, Shikarpur, Surkotada, and Dholavira). They have classic Sindhi Harappan painted pottery, stamp seals, etched carnelian beads. While there is a strain of "local" material culture at these places, the predominant theme is still Sindhi Harappan. These settlements are distinguishable from the contemporary Sorath Harappan sites of Saurashtra and other sites on the North Gujarat Plain at places like Nagwada. The Sindhi Harappan sites extend as far as Lothal, along the so-called "Nal Depression;" all of which merely documents what is historically self-evident: Gujarat and Sindh, as neighboring regions are culturally related. This is determined in part because they lie to the west of the Great Indian Desert, their closeness promoted by propinquity. In some ways it is useful to think of the Ranns as an extension of the Indus River delta (Wilhelmy 1968).

The main landmass of Kutch is a spine of hills flanked by a narrow area on the south, where it borders the sea. This is igneous Deccan trap and limestone, and not a significant watershed. On the north the land slopes gently into the Ranns. It is pasture land and the area known as "Banni" has been home to pastoral nomads for millennia.

Kutch and the Nal depression are discussed in the present geographical context based on archaeological criteria. The similarity of places like Lothal, Surkotada and Dholavira, to Mohenjo-daro and Chanhu-daro, is striking. Their dissimilarity to places like Rojdi, Babar Kot, Rangpur, Atkot and other Sorath Harappan sites is just as striking and justifies the scheme adopted here.

The Ranns

The Ranns of Kutch are the most dramatic feature of the area (Plate 3.58). These are vast, absolutely flat salt wastes, that are flooded during the summer monsoon because of high tides and increased flow from the rivers that feed them. The tides retreat, the river flow decreases and the water left behind evaporates, leaving salts and fine alluvium. There are small islands of high ground, for example Kadir, where the huge Sindhi Harappan site of Dholavira is found, that support permanent settlement in the midst of these wastelands. They are dangerous to cross, with many soft, unstable "swamps" concealed below innocuous surfaces of salt, but over the centuries stable, consolidated routes have been found. Each year these are renewed and marked by lines of small stones and the bones of dead animals, which guide those on an adventurous journey who, if they stray from this path, may find themselves as part of a guidepost for a future generation of travelers.

Were the Ranns a Sea During Mature Harappan Times?

The Ranns cover about 25,000 square kilometers, ca. 20,000 and ca. 5000 for the Great and Little Ranns, respectively. This is a little over half of the total of 42,900 square kilometers for the present district, which itself is a remarkably good natural geographical feature. The Ranns are never exactly the same size from year to year. Moreover, in many places the boundary between Rann and other land cannot be placed precisely. The area is tectonically active and there is a possibility that the Ranns may have been lower, and therefore permanently linked to the sea in prehistoric times, as advocated by Billimoria (1947). This is a possibility but it has not yet been demonstrated, in spite of some geophysical work on the problem (Wynne 1872; Silveright 1907; Sah and Kar 1969; Murty, Kulkarni and Gupta 1969; Roy and Merh 1977; S. K. Gupta 1977a; Lele 1982; Ratan and Chandra 1982). All of the early historical authors are either ambiguous on this point or direct their comments to other topics, summarized in J. P. Joshi (1990a: 9-12). The anonymous author *Periplus of the Erythraean Sea* of the late first century AD, refers to the Gulf of Kutch under the name *Erinion* and speaks of adjacent areas: "Beyond the river Sinthus (Indus) there is another gulf, not navigable, running in toward the north; it is called Erinion; its parts are called separately the small gulf and the great; in both parts the water is shallow, with shifting sandbanks occurring continually and a great way from shore; so that very often when the shore is not even in sight, ships run aground..." (Schoff 1912: 38). It is easy to see that this was a reference to the Ranns (Sankalia 1981) especially in light of the observation that the *Periplus...* was written by a sailor who was in the region during the monsoon, when the Ranns would have been flooded.

Large fish vertebra have been found at some Kutch Harappan sites (e.g., Pabumath, Y. M. Chitalwala, personal communication 1988). This is an important observation; however we know that the Harappans during the Mature Phase were able to move fish over large distances, undoubtedly in salted and/or dried form, since a marine species of catfish has been found at Harappa (Belcher 1991: 114).

Earthquakes in Ranns: The Allah Bund

Kutch has been subjected to violent earthquakes. One, in 1819, caused the formation of a ridge called the "Allah Bund" (Allah Dam) that has been used as an example of the way in which tectonics can form natural dams, with the potential to change the course of rivers, even those as large as the Indus (Raikes 1964). This was used to reinforce an argument that the Mature Harappan came to an end through the damming of the Indus and the resulting floods and accumulation of silt. The bibliography on the Raikes hypothesis is as follows: Raikes (1964, 1965a, 1967, 1979, 1984); Raikes and Dales (1977, 1986); Dales (1965c, 1966a, 1966b). The critiques of the hypothesis have appeared as: Lambrick (1967); Possehl (1967); Wasson (1984, 1987). The Raikes hypothesis still receives some notice; therefore, the geographical background to the formation of the Allah Bund is appropriate. The story of the disastrous Kutch earthquake of 1819 has not yet been told in an archaeological context.

The earthquake of 1819 was an unusual event in that it did not occur on, or near, the edge of one of the earth's continental plates. Earthquakes of this type are comparatively rare, and have not been well studied (Johnston and Kanter 1990). Tremors of this kind take place in areas of very old faulting that have been covered and stabilized for millions of years, and are somehow rejuvenated. The famous, and violent earthquakes at New Madrid in the Mississippi Valley in 1811 and 1812 were also mid-plate events, felt as far away as the East Coast of the United States. One of them is said to have collapsed a scaffolding around the Capitol Building in Washington DC (Johnston and Kanter 1990: 70).

> The New Madrid and Kutch earthquakes are only the most prominent elements in our data set of 800 stable-continent events of a magnitude = 4.5 or more. The number may seem large, but it is the sum of a global record covering centuries or millennia (Many more earthquakes of magnitude = 4.5 or greater take place along plate boundaries in just a year) (Johnston and Kanter 1990: 71).

The Kutch quake occurred on June 16, 1819, with aftershocks lasting until about November 20th or later the following year. It was well documented because of its severity and the dramatic changes it caused in the landscape (Burnes 1835a: Vol. I, 308-28; Lyell 1853: 459-64; Oldham 1926; Abdul Ali 1935). Abdul Ali (1935) collected reports sent to the Bombay Presidency. One from J. MacMurdo, the Collector at Anjar, dated June 17th states:

It is with sincere regret that I have to inform you that this place was visited by an Earthquake yesterday evening at 10 minutes before 7 o'clock. The effects of the shock, which lasted nearly two minutes have been the leveling of the Fort Wall to the ground. Not a hundred yards of the wall remain in any one spot, and the guns, towers, etc. are all hurled in one mass of ruin (Abdul Ali 1935: 468).

Similar damage was done in Bhuj, the capital of Kutch, where the fort and palace were destroyed along with 7000 houses. Mr. MacMurdo further reported to Bombay:

A number of phenomena are said to have occurred at the moment of the shock, but I shall only remark that, which appears to be the most striking. The Runn and Bhunee on the North of Cutch between that province and the isolated district Kaioria which was quite dry, was suddenly filled with a sheet of water, the extent of which on the East and West was not known, but its breadth was generally about six miles, and its depth gradually increased to upward of 21–5 feet, after which, in a few hours, the waters subsided to about half that quantity. Horsemen who crossed this tract on the day following the shock, describe a number of cones of soft sand elevated above the water, the tops of which were bubbling with air and water when they passed (J. MacMurdo to Government of Bombay, June 23, 1819 *in* Abdul Ali 1935: 472).

There was a small fort maintained by the Rao of Kutch for customs purposes on the border between Kutch and Sindh, at a place called Sindree, just where the Phurraun branch of the Indus drains into the Great Rann. The Phurraum course would seem to be the modern Fuleli Canal. Alexander Burnes describes the fort as a brick structure about 150 feet square (1835a: Vol. I, 311). Following the earthquake it was:

Overwhelmed by an inundating torrent of water from the ocean, which spread on every side, and, in the course of a few hours, converted the tract, which had before been hard and dry, into an inland lake, which extended for sixteen miles on either side of Sindree. The houses within the walls filled with water, and eight years afterwards I found fish in pools among them. The only dry spot was the place on which the bricks had fallen upon one another. One of four towers only remained, and the customs-house officers had saved their lives by ascending to it, and were eventually transported to dry land by boat on the following day (Burnes 1835a: Vol. I, 312).

Burnes procured an unpublished sketch of Sindree that had been made by a Captain Grindlay in 1808, which was redrawn and published in his memoir (1835a: Vol. I, insert between pp. 308-09) (Plate 3.59). Half of the sketch appeared in Sir Charles Lyell's 1853 edition of *Principles of Geology* (1853: 461), where there is a discussion of the Kutch earthquake (Lyell 1853: 459-64). In fact, in *Principles...* it is learned that it was Sir Charles's interest in this violent act that spurred Burnes to add the memoir on Kutch to the second edition of his *Travels Into Bokhara* (1835a: Vol. I 308-28). In 1838 Lyell asked his friend Captain Grant to revisit Sindree and make a plan of the place. Grant also made a sketch from about the same spot that Captain Grindlay stood (Figure 3.134).

Just to the north of Sindree, a roll of earth was raised six to eight meters high, and at least 120 kilometers long (Johnston and Kanter 1990: 72). Burnes examined this and noted that it should not be imagined to be "a narrow stripe like an artificial dam" since at one point it could be seen to be 25 kilometers (16 miles) broad (1835a: Vol. I, 315).

The Allah Bund remains a prominent feature of the Indo-Pakistan border along northern Kutch. It was the subject of field research by a team of Indian scientists between 10 and 13

Figure **3.134.** Captain Grant's sketch of Sindree in 1838, after Lyell 1853: 463

March 1993 (Patel 1993; Kale 1993). They confirmed the unconsolidated nature of this roll in the earth (Kale 1993: Figure 2): "The Allah Bund is a dissected scarp facing south and drained by numerous southerly flowings, often beheaded gullies. The scarp trends nearly east-west for a considerable distance. The northern part has a gentle slope up to 2 meters towards the north. The southern dissected scarp, with an exposed height of 1.5 meters abuts abruptly against the flat, salt encrusted surface of the Rann" (Kale 1993: 5).

"For several years after the convulsion of 1819, the course of the Indus was very unsettled, and at length, in 1826, the river threw a vast body of water into its eastern arm, called the Phurraun, above Sindree; and forcing its way in a more direct course to the sea, burst through all the artificial dams which had been thrown across its channel, and at length cut right through the 'Allah Bund'..." (Lyell 1853: 462). This was the first flood challenge to the structural integrity of the Allah Bund, and the Indus cut through it like a hot knife through butter; such is the strength of unconsolidated alluvium.

The Wasson critique of the Raikes hypothesis (1984, 1987) stresses the fact that the static pressure against the proposed natural dam on the Indus would have produced a result that is the same as that documented for the Allah Bund. It could not have withstood the first significant flood; sufficient evidence to lay to rest once and for all Raikes' proposition.

During the winter months the Ranns are a resting place for millions of birds on their annual migration from Siberia to East Africa. It is still possible to stand at the edge of one of the Ranns and see flamingos transform the once white surface into an undulating sea of pink. There are also millions of ducks, cranes, storks and spoonbills. Prehistoric sites in Kutch, and elsewhere, have a meager record of bird remains. While the faunal analysis of sites of the Indus Age has not been directed toward recovering and analyzing bird remains, the bones of the larger birds are quite robust, especially crania, beaks, leg bones and the major "struts" in the wings. They would be better preserved and more noticeable than rodents, and there is a good record of these small mammals. Thus, the wealth of birds as a resource may well have been left largely untapped for some cultural reason during the Indus Age. Birds on this same migration pattern made use of Lake Manchar in Sindh as well a lake in the Nal Depression.

The Nal Depression

The Nal Depression is a shallow channel that links the Little Rann of Kutch to the head of the Gulf of Cambay (Plate 3.60). It is ca. 110 kilometers long and barely perceptible to the eye; the change in vegetation is the most prominent feature of its landscape. Near the center is Nal Lake, from which the Depression takes its name. It fluctuates in size with the seasons, dry for most of the year, but there is water there during the monsoon that drains into the Little Rann. D. N. Wadia has suggested that until late glacial or Holocene times this depression might have been an arm of the sea (Wadia 1966: 310, 400). Pollen data from Nal Lake indicate that it was large and fresh from about 3000 to 1500 BC, when it seems to have become smaller, possibly even drying up (Vishnu-Mittre and Sharma 1978). This would be due to tectonics, and might lead one to believe that Wadia's hypothesis is sound, but establishing a chronology for low periods presents a challenge not yet taken.

Lothal, a southernmost Sindhi Harappan settlement, sits within the Nal Depression, placing it at the end of a natural communications link between the Cambay area and Sindh, a perfect setting for a trading and manufacturing center. Lothal seems to have have been flooded on occasion (S. R. Rao 1979: 252; S. Pandya 1981, 1982, 1987, 1991), a reflection of its low elevation near the mouth of the Sabarmati River and the southern end of the Nal Depression. The site is now only about 12 meters above mean sea level. The settlement might have been a bit closer to the Gulf of Cambay if S. K. Gupta's hypothesis that the sea level around Saurashtra was two to six meters higher during Mature Harappan is correct (1977b). But the overall environment around the site seems to have been remarkably similar to the one we see today (Raghunath 1977).

The Subsistence Regime

The present day inhabitants of the Southern Region are predominantly farmers and herders. Investments in cash crops of groundnuts and cotton have altered the older subsistence economy based on food grains and vegetables. In fact, these new endeavors have proved to be profitable enough for the small scale farmer to make a considerable investment in creating new agricultural land. This is done by taking refuse soil from the vicinity of the village, combining it with borrowed soil from the better endowed fields and dumping it on the barren slopes of the low-lying rocky hills. In addition, some villages have taken considerable precautions against erosion to assure minimum surface movement of the soil. High profit cash crops however, have not completely changed the pattern of sowing good grains. Small plots of millets (moth, jowar and bajra), vegetables and even sugar cane characterize most areas. These are usually grown in sufficient quantity to assure domestic consumption, with little or none remaining for local sale.

These village based agriculturalists often maintain considerable numbers of domesticated animals, especially cattle and goats, with just a few sheep. Other people own no land and generally derive their income and subsistence from their animals, some of whom may be taken on rent from settled farmers. The three principal castes of this type are *charans*, *bharvards* and *rabaris*. The latter caste is widespread, found all over Gujarat, into Rajasthan and Sindh. Given the pronounced seasonality in this Region, with a very dry period climaxing in April and May, some movement of people and their animals is part of the regimen. Prior to the Partition of the Subcontinent they moved freely from Saurashtra to Sindh and back. Today they venture east on to the Deccan Plateau, as well as making a round of their own state, extending north into Rajasthan.

Some of the motivation for the movement of these pastoral peoples is not founded in cultural ecology and the search for pasture, but involves a purely sociocultural function, with the groups acting as a mobile integrative force, bringing together peoples in diverse localities (Dave 1965: 10-2). These pastoralists are not well studied (Westphal-Hellbusch 1975 has some bibliography). They are numerous and in evidence everywhere in Saurashtra and the other subregions. They are important to the archaeologist when considerations of cultural similarities and differences are addressed. Widespread similarities in material culture, such as those expressed in the Harappan tradition, have a foundation in institution and interaction. Pastoralists with physical mobility and wide ranging spatial contact with a variety of communities and individuals could lead to the integration of this civilization.

Even with the expansion of fields the modern settlement pattern for the Southern Region retains some of the features of the mid-nineteenth century landscape. Map studies indicate that within an area of intensive archaeological exploration, all villages shown on a map compiled in

1869 were still inhabited and there had been only one new settlement built in spite of a considerable increase in population.

Modern Agricultural Statistics

The same tables for the cultivation and husbanding of key plants and animals can be constructed for the Southern Region as were prepared for the Central and Gedrosia Regions. The task here is to illustrate the comparative emphasis that the local (Region level) environment and culture place on *rabi* and *kharif* season crops and the balance between cattle, sheep, goats and water buffalo. Because so much of this partitioning of resources is closely related to (not determined by) rainfall and the two cyclonic events of western South Asia, the figures presented in the tables give some indication of an important environmental and cultural variable.

Kutch

The inhabitants of Kutch are, for the most part, cattle pastoralists as indicated by the roughly half million cattle enumerated on Table 3.23. They are concentrated in Banni, a rich pasture area on the south side of the Great Rann. The diverse peoples of KUTCH now move their cattle into Saurashtra and east onto the Deccan Plateau. In pre-Partition times they migrated to Sindh as well, and a few still do, without a visa. The breeding of camels is also important in today's (and the pre-modern) economy. The camel breeder's life is a tough one, largely away from settlements, living on camel's milk and little else.

Cattle are the wealth of Kutch today, and it seems that the same was true in prehistoric times given the substantial numbers of this animal documented from sites of the Indus Age. Agriculture is poorly developed in the area, with just enough farming being done to quash rumors that it is a dead art in the district. Poor, unreliable rainfall and meager subsurface water support a sparse *kharif* crop with the two most productive millets being planted. There is almost no wheat grown.

TABLE 3.23
The Agricultural Regime in Kutch

Plant or Animal	Acres or Number of Animals
bajra	21357
jowar	17425
wheat	1520
cattle	460289
goats	200147
sheep	180707
water buffalo	80489

Government of Gujarat 1964a: 21-2

Saurashtra

The heavy emphasis on millets, jowar and bajra, are apparent in both the districts of Saurashtra selected for Tables 3.24 and 3.25. Very little *rabi* season wheat is grown, and all of that is irrigated from wells, a practice that may have begun in Mature Harappan.

TABLE 3.24
Subsistence Regime in Bhavnagar District

Plant or Animal	Acres or Number of Animals
bajra	296410
jowar	291523
wheat	85970
cattle	347486
sheep	195146
water buffalo	135839
goats	113779

Government of Gujarat 1964b: 23-4

TABLE 3.25
Subsistence Regime in Rajkot

Plant or Animal	Acres or Number of Animals
jowar	294648
bajra	199294
wheat	54743
cattle	404368
sheep	240811
goats	141735
water buffalo	114641

Government of Gujarat 1964c: 23

North Gujarat

Mehsana District in North Gujarat was selected as the subregion within the Southern Region to illustrate modern cropping and husbandry practices. The clutch of Anrata Chalcolithic and other sites in the estuaries of the Banas, Sarasvati[17] and Rupen Rivers, hard by the eastern edge of the Little Rann of Kutch are located in this district, which is the justification for its selection.

TABLE 3.26
Subsistence Regime in Mehsana District

Plant or Animal	Acres or Number of Animals
bajra	436379
jowar	298076
wheat	106848
water buffalo	385257
cattle	363472
goats	98647
sheep	42697

Government of Gujarat 1964d: 22

South Gujarat

Surat District was selected to illustrate modern subsistence practices in this subregion. The huge number of cattle in the area, probably a reflection of the rich pasture and vegetation as well as the dominance of jowar in the agricultural regime are noteworthy. There is no other district in the entire Greater Indus Region where *kharif* planting is so dominant.

TABLE 3.27
Subsistence Regime in Surat District

Plant or Animal	Acres or Number of Animals
jowar	235215
wheat	26319
bajra	3681
cattle	719362
goats	211162
water buffalo	201786
sheep	26473

Government of Gujarat 1964e: 25

Summary

The Southern Region is an area of balanced subsistence practices, and is a very good example of the cultural and ecological integration of farmers and herders, outside a mountainous area where transhumance predominates. The strength of the southwest monsoon, and the corresponding lack of significant precipitation from the winter westerlies makes this area the one Region within which *kharif* season cultivation predominates, and would have been among the first areas within which the African millets were integrated into the South Asian subsistence regime.

These observations reflect the constants in the life of this Region and will be used as the fundamental basis for a reconstruction of prehistoric life in the region.

THE NORTHWESTERN REGION

Introduction

The Northwestern Region (Figure 3.135) consists of Baluchistan north of Kalat: Quetta-Pishin, Zhob, Loralai and Marri-Bugti country and major portions of the present Northwest Frontier Province and Swat, with an outlier in southern Afghanistan, to accommodate Mundigak, Said Qala and a few other places. The domain extends out to the Chagai Hills, one of the areas rich in minerals. It is the largest of the Regions at approximately 300,000 square kilometers. In many ways it resembles the Gedrosia Region, with mountains and narrow valleys, restricted cultivable soils and the same suite of native fauna and flora. The Vale of Peshawar has no protohistoric archaeology, but it is, or could be, considered part of the Northwestern domain as well.

Within historical times the southern districts of the Region have been a transitional area between Baluchistan to the south and Pathans to the north. But, in Waziristan, Bannu, Kohat and Dera Ismail Khan one is in Pathan country proper, the least tractable region of British India

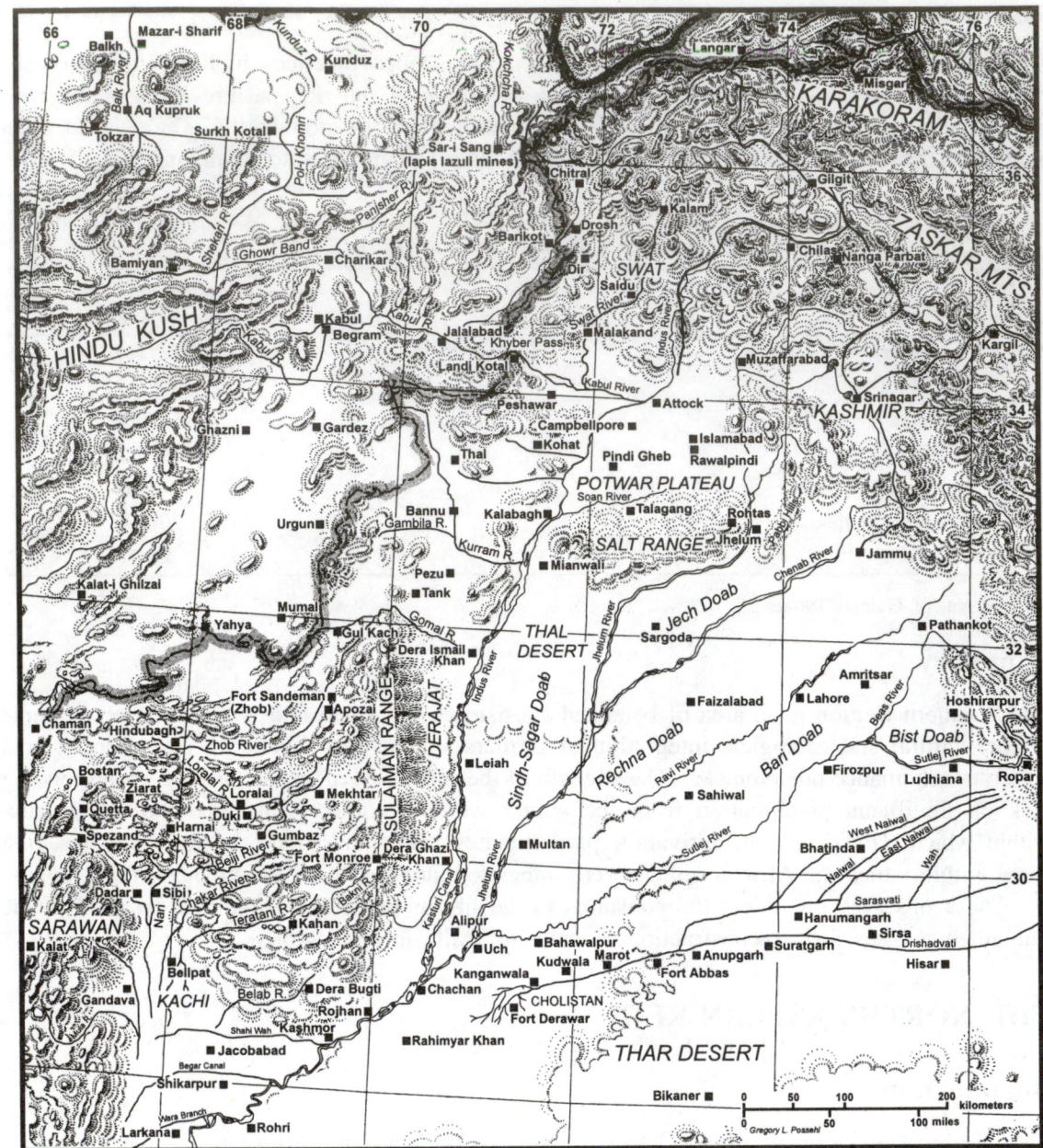

Figure 3.135. The Northwestern Region

and the subject of many fine stories of daring-do on both sides. The Pathans code of ethics, *pakhtunwali* demands that guests, even a deadly foe, be given hospitality, and fugitives afforded protection. Most important, any insult to a Pathan, his family or *khel* must be avenged. Feuding is therefore an endemic pastime in the region, even today. One Commander in Chief of the Punjab during Colonial times thought: "Now these tribes are savages—noble savages, perhaps— and not without some tincture of virtue and generosity, but still absolute barbarians..." (Quoted in Farwell 1989: 194).

There is a deep boundary separating Zhob-Loralai from the Gedrosia Region that begins in protohistoric times and is seen principally in pottery styles. There is a clear relationship between the two regions, but north and south are just as clearly stylistic zones, with the potters in each place adopting a different set of motifs and some vessel forms, as marks of their own identity. These cultural features are the best reasons for separating this domain from the Kulli province.

The Indus River is the eastern border of the Northern Region. This part of its course has been described in the discussion of the Northern Region.

The Subregions

Quetta-Pishin

The joined valleys and Quetta and Pishin (generally just called "Quetta") are taken as the southern boundary of the Northwestern Region, since the Kulli materials do not reach this far north, and it was a center for a distinctive way of life during the Indus Age (Plate 3.61). The valley's role as an old route of communication is made clear by the journey of two early European travelers, Steel and Crowther, who were in what they called "Pesinga" on 1 July 1614, on their way from Ajmer to Isfahan (Hughes-Buller 1907a: 33) (Plate 3.62).

A Major Route of Communication

The Bolan Pass rises gently off the Kachi Plain and enters the mountains at the northern end of the Kirthar Range. Its easy course is sometimes quite flat, spread broad with huge boulder fans inside the pass itself. It breaks through the mountains cleanly and suddenly at about 1550 meters above sea level into a broad, flat valley, surrounded by high peaks, that rise abruptly off the valley floor. A direct route through Quetta, to Pishin farther west, is a little over 100 kilometers, to the Khojak Pass. This is the route through the low mountainous western edge of the valley system, that borders the Registan Desert and leads on to Kandahar in Afghanistan. The Khojak Pass, while steep and rugged in places, involves only a drop of 1000 meters over the space of 15 or 20 kilometers (Plate 3.63). It is an easy passage for men and animals. In short, the Bolan-Quetta-Pishin-Khojak route is, and was, an easy, fast route from the plains of the middle Indus Valley to the southern plain of Afghanistan. From there one could head northwest, then north skirting the mountainous center of Afghanistan, to Central Asia, another easy, unimpeded interregional route; or start at Kandahar, head north to Ghazni and on to Kabul. This easterly route is joined by other trails coming together from Zhob, the Gomal Valley, the Kabul River and Khyber Pass.

The general track of the modern road in the Khyber Pass is one of the traditional routes of travel and invasion into the Subcontinent. The general northwestern corner of the Subcontinent has been an entry point for millennia; although it is not known just when it began (Plate 3.64). When the Middle Asian Interaction Sphere was part of life in the Greater Indus Region, in the second half of the third millennium and slightly later, the route to southern Afghanistan from a place like Mohenjo-daro would have certainly started with the Bolan and proceeded as described.

Endowed with a Superior Environment

The Quetta-Pishin Valley is situated at between about 1500 and 1600 meters above sea level. It is basically flat or undulating, and enjoys a very tolerable summer climate that is warm, occasionally hot, but dry. There is almost never summer rain, or enough that can be counted on for agriculture. The winters can be cold and it frequently freezes, as many an unprepared traveler has paid for.

Cold is the greatest threat for families, and flock owners sometimes suffer large losses of sheep from the severe winter cold; but the district is well protected from famine due to good irrigation as long as there is autumn and winter precipitation. If failure for two or three consecutive years occurs then there can be shortages. Crop failure in Sind or the Punjab also has an effect on Quetta supplies. Visitations of locusts and wheat rust are problems as well. The wheat rust results from heavy rain on a southeast wind coming when the ears of grain are ripe (Hughes-Buller 1907a: 211).

The winter westerlies bring rain and snow to the area, which produces a good crop of wheat and barley. The altitude and climate are agreeable for orchard crops like apples and other fruits. The Quetta-Pishin district Gazetteer lists the following: vine, apricot, mulberry, peach, pomegranate, quince, pear, almond, plum, fig, apple, damson, walnut (Hughes-Buller 1907a: 109). The rainfall also provides for pasture and this in turn, with the annual transhumant migration to the Indus lowlands, provides for relatively large herds of sheep, goats and cattle.

The Pishin Lora and the Hana River are both perennial streams in the valley that are additional water resources for farmers and herders. Quetta also has many artesian wells (Hughes-Buller 1907a: 149) and small streams that emanate from the foothills of the mountain ranges surrounding the valley floor.

Table 3.28 gives the statistics for the seven key plants and animals that are being tracked in terms of cultural geography.

TABLE 3.28
The Agricultural Regime in Quetta

Plant or Animal	Acres or Number of Animals	Page in Report
wheat	113041	349
jowar	242	424
bajra	40	424
sheep	110360	788
goats	201409	788
cattle	24311	768
water buffalo	1669	768

From: *Pakistan Census of Agriculture 1960*, 1963

The trivial nature of the *kharif* season crop is especially apparent in these modern statistics. Given the rainfall and temperature regimes, there is little reason to believe that the situation would have been different during the Indus Age.

In addition to these domesticated resources the Quetta area is endowed with reserves of juniper. The berries are used for perfume and the trees supply superior wood (Hughes-Buller 1907a: 171). Wild pistachio trees are found on the hills of the Chiltan and other ranges. Pistachio bears fruit after ca. 25 years and these trees were owned even though they were wild, and could be given as compensation for blood-money or as part payment of bride-price. The fruit is eaten fresh or dried (Hughes-Buller 1907a: 171-72, 175).

Quetta is subject to earthquakes. Major events occurred in ca. 1888, 1892, 1900, 1902 and 1935. The 20 December 1892 earthquake, was a very powerful event and Capt. (later Colonel Sir) A. H. McMahon followed a resulting fissure for 200 kilometers, from the Khojak Pass rail tunnel to Nushki, passing through the Lora River. Old men told McMahon that similar faults had occurred at least three times during their lives (Hughes-Buller 1907a: 30-1). The 1935 quake was also devastating (West 1936), destroying among other things the McMahon Museum in Quetta City, with the treasures from Nal.

The Depth of Settlement in Quetta-Pishin

The Quetta-Pishin interconnected valleys are immensely important and have sustained village life and pastoral nomadism for many millennia. The aceramic remains at Kili Ghul Mohammad Period I are undoubtedly contemporary with the remains from Mehrgarh, at the base of the Bolan Pass. These document settled life here as early as the seventh, or eighth millennium BC. The natural resources necessary for the food producing revolution are all here, with the exception perhaps of wild wheat, and the Quetta-Pishin Valleys were of the regions that seem to have been on the cutting edge of this revolution in the Subcontinent. While archaeological work has not yet documented this fact, the same is probably true for the Zhob-Loralai and Marri-Bugti Country, just to the north of Quetta.

Zhob-Loralai and Marri-Bugti Country

The principal geographical feature of the Region is the Sulaiman Range, which fronts the Punjab on its eastern side. It begins at the Gomal Valley and terminates in southern Marri-Bugti Country 400 kilometers south of its beginning. The backbone of the range is a single high ridge with its highest peak, Takht-i-Sulaiman ("Throne of Solomon") at ca. 3400 meters. Sir Thomas Holdich has a fine description of this terrain:

> From the Gomal River to Jacobabad there stretches one continuous chain of mountain peaks, which although now distinguished by many local names, may well be known by their ancient designation of Sulimani. They are, and they have ever been, through the ages of an immense past, the original habitat of the Pakhtun or Pashtu speaking mountaineers whom we now call Pathans. The Sulimani system is not a water parting; it is not a central divide that throws off the beginning of a great system of drainage east and west. The slopes of the Sulimani hills, both east and west, drain equally to the Indus, and it is the drainage of the western slopes that, turning suddenly and bursting through the main chain of central limestone ridges, forms those terrific gorges and rock-bound mountain gates which are our only means of access to the traversable valleys of the western plateau. The main Sulaiman ridge, which is the dominating feature of the Indus frontier south of the Gomal, lies back from the foot of the hills some 30 miles—which 30 miles of gradual descent from the plateau to the plains is packed close with narrow, rugged, sun-scorched, treeless ridges, composed chiefly of recent clays and conglomerates, which preserve an approximate parallelism in their strike, likening the whole system to a gigantic gridiron. Narrow little 'subsequent' valleys between these sharp-backed ridges contribute an intermittent flow of brackish water to the main arteries and these again, as before described, break transversely across the general strike of the minor ridges ere they debouche into the Indus plain (Holdich 1904: 36-37).

There are no large rivers in the Northwestern Region, but the Zhob River is perennial and has probably supported agricultural settlement since the beginning of food production and herding in the region, especially the cluster of sites around Fort Sandeman, including Periano Ghundai and Moghul Ghundai (Stein 1929a: 31-41; 43-9; Fairservis 1959). It arises in the eastern watershed of the Pishin Valley and flows for ca. 385 kilometers to a junction with the Gomal.

It is a broad, shallow, sluggish stream for much of its course, with shallow pools 50 or 60 centimeters deep and 30 to 60 meters wide appearing in many places (Minchin 1907h: 17-8).

Behind the Sulaiman Range is a series of lesser ranges with various strikes, more east-west in the west, and more parallel to the Sulaiman in its proximity. Some valleys are broad and fertile, as in the Thal Plain, the location of the Harappan site of Dabar Kot (Stein 1929a: 55-63).

The hills and mountains of Zhob-Loralai (Plate 3.65) and Marri-Bugti Country is more suited to pastoralism than agriculture. But the valley bottoms do afford some cultivation, generally confined to the *rabi* season, as in the Gedrosia Region. Subsistence statistics from 1960 in Loralai will illustrate this in Table 3.29.

TABLE 3.29
The Agricultural Regime in Loralai

Plant or Animal	Acres or Number of Animals	Page in Report
wheat	71243	333
jowar	33244	423
bajra	4424	423
sheep	495580	787
goats	142794	787
cattle	97905	767
water buffalo	1383	767

From: *Pakistan Census of Agriculture 1960*, 1963

The very few numbers of buffalo, so needful of water and shade and intolerant of a nomadic life, is particularly striking here.

Waziristan is a mountainous area of four reasonably fertile valleys along the modern border between Afghanistan and Pakistan. In terms of environment and subsistence this area is much like the other parts of the Region.[18]

The Bannu Basin

The Bannu Basin is a roughly circular valley about 50 kilometers across. A joint archaeological project has been undertaken there since the mid-1980s with participants from the University of Peshawar and the United Kingdom. They have paid close attention to the environment, both ancient and modern.

The basin has diverse environments, ranging from dune fields and huge boulder fans, associated with the Kurram and Gamblia River drainage, to relatively rich agricultural fields. There is some evidence that part of the Basin was filled with lakes in the not too distant past (Thomas 1986a: 23).

Kenneth D. Thomas has conducted a survey of modern cultivation there (Thomas 1986a, 1986b). His survey and the material presented in Table 3.30, indicate that this is a *rabi* crop area, with a heavy emphasis on wheat. Cattle predominate among the animals, with comparatively few water buffalo. There is only a modicum of irrigation and most of Bannu depends on rainfall, and rainfall runoff irrigation (*sailaba*) for agriculture. Thomas mentions that there is a *kharif* crop, but it is of much less importance than the *rabi* crop and it cannot be planted everywhere in the valley (1986a: 26).

TABLE 3.30
The Agricultural Regime in Bannu

Plant or Animal	Acres or Number of Animals	Page in Report
wheat	303284	323
jowar	4183	413
bajra	2734	413
cattle	111286	754
sheep	73130	774
goats	64901	774
water buffalo	22860	754

From: *Pakistan Census of Agriculture 1960*, 1963

Kohat

Kohat is a splendid small place, elevated enough to be almost comfortable in the summer, and low enough to have tolerable winters. This is Pathan country that even the Great Mughals only nominally controlled. The valley is rhomboid in shape and approximately 95 by 80 kilometers. Within the rhomb are a succession of broken hill ranges with an east-west trend forming smaller valleys, five to ten kilometers in width. There are no major rivers in Kohat, but numerous hill torrents, mostly active in the winter, afford limited potential for modern irrigation, but do recharge the water table.

There are few mineral resources in Kohat: rocksalt and placer minerals. These may have come from deposits in Zhob District (Minchin 1907h: 24).

The area is covered with thin grasslands and what little forest there is, is stunted. But when there is rain it immediately springs to life and becomes verdant, and in the summer vast hillsides of wild flowers provide a spectacular view. Large tracts of wild, or at least uncultivated, sesame can also be seen.

The *Imperial Gazetteer* notes that of the 7700 square kilometers in Kohat, only 2316 are available for cultivation (Government of India 1908a: 173). These few hectares are in the valley bottoms, with good loam. As seen in the accompanying table, Kohat is a *rabi* crop area.

TABLE 3.31
The Agricultural Regime in Kohat

Plant or Animal	Acres or Number of Animals	Page in Report
wheat	214491	323
bajra	44528	413
jowar	4171	413
goats	185987	773
cattle	172016	753
sheep	121046	773
water buffalo	7065	753

From: *Pakistan Census of Agriculture 1960*, 1963

The Derajat

The Derajat is the low plain between the mountains of the Northern Region and the Indus River. It is so named because it contains the three Deras: Dera Ismail Khan, Dera Fatah Khan,

Dera Ghazi Khan. These settlements (*deras*) take their names from the Baluchis called in to take the area in *jagir* during the fifteenth century.

As a whole the area is low and hot, with poor monsoon showers and a small amount of winter rain. The treeless plain is not even well provided with grass and the pasture resources are minimal. One might legitimately wonder what a *jagir* in this place would be worth. Some settlement is afforded where hill torrents from the Sulaiman Range cross the plain on their way to the Indus. There are only two cities: Dera Ismail Khan and Dera Ghazi Khan.

The Derajat is, however, a major route of communication from the Panjnad north to the Potwar Plateau. There are tracts that lead west into Zhob-Loralai and on to Afghanistan that pass through Dera Ghazi Khan, Dera Ismail Khan and Bannu. Its role as a relatively high speed corridor of communication, up the western side of the Indus is probably the single most important culture historical feature of the Derajat.

Dera Ismail Khan: The Gomal Valley

Dera Ismail Khan is the principal settlement on the plain of the Gomal River. This plain is a triangular wedge ca. 90 by 90 by 60 kilometers that cuts into the mountains of this Region just above the beginning of the Sulaiman Range. The watershed of the Gomal reaches west into Afghanistan, but its major tributary is the Zhob River, coming in from the south. The Gomal Valley is also flat and treeless with a very hot summer and almost no relief from monsoon cloud cover, let alone rainfall. The valley is drier than either Bannu or Dera Ghazi Khan (Government of India 1908a: 197). Its floor is covered mostly by a dense, hard clay that is not easily penetrated by water. These hard flat lands are called *pat*. Sustained rainfall will soften this soil and it becomes a tenacious mastic. The country is impassable during this time.

Over the long term this valley has been occupied by village farming communities, especially in the east, near the modern city, which has been documented by excavations at Rehman Dheri (Durrani 1988; Durrani, Ali and Erdosy 1991) Gumla and Hathala (Dani 1970-71). The work at Gumla indicated that the first settlement was an aceramic village, comparable to Mehrgarh I and Kili Ghul Mohammad I.

The Gomal River affords good communication to the uplands of Waziristan and into Zhob-Loralai. A low pass gains access to Bannu to the north via the modern settlement of Tank.

There is some irrigation from the Gomal and in most years water from it is completely consumed and never reaches the Indus. This valley is also a *rabi* crop zone, with a heavy dependence on wheat and a good population of cattle.

TABLE 3.32
The Agricultural Regime in Dera Ismail Khan

Plant or Animal	Acres or Number of Animals	Page in Report
wheat	283821	324
jowar	35948	414
bajra	26764	414
cattle	312823	754
goats	164857	774
sheep	133043	774
water buffalo	34048	754

From: *Pakistan Census of Agriculture 1960*, 1963

Dera Ghazi Khan

Dera Ghazi Khan[19] is administered as part of the Punjab today. Like Dera Ismail Khan to the north, it is an alluvial tract, but this time it is because of the Indus and the other rivers of the panjnad. Although it is hot and normally would be quite desolate, with only about 300 millimeters of annual rainfall, D. G. Khan's (as it is called in the vernacular) proximity to the Indus has given it deep alluvial soils, annual flood water and it is extensively cultivated. Most of the land in the Derajat portion of the modern district is irrigated in some way. Extensive plantations of dates are found along the Indus in this area.

Lieutenant John Wood, who was in Dera Ghazi Khan on his 1835 journey up the Indus by steamer, noted that the town of D. G. Khan was six and one half kilometers (four miles) from the Indus, and could be approached for much of the year via a large navigable canal. It was frequently threatened by flood and was surrounded by a bund, for protection. "It is the largest town on the Indus...Its merchants, though they do not speculate largely, have an extensive agency, and a considerable command of money. The country around yields heavy crops of grain, and the staples of cotton and indigo..." (Wood 1838: 575).

Wood's description is perhaps a bit glowing, because the area is not one of the more productive parts of the Greater Indus Region. However, due to the deep alluvium, which is replenished from both the floods of the Indus and its tributarics, as well as the hill torrents that enter the plain from the west, the area is agriculturally viable if water can be brought to the land. Within historical times this was done by canals, some of which, as reported by Wood, are quite large. Whether this was a practice during Protohistoric times is in some doubt.

This is another *rabi* crop area, with agricultural statistics much like that of Loralai, at least in terms of the proportions of resources *Pakistan Census of Agriculture 1960* (1963).

TABLE 3.33
The Agricultural Regime in Dera Ghazi Khan

Plant or Animal	Acres or Number of Animals	Page in Report
wheat	385304	329
jowar	124467	419
bajra	38703	419
cattle	675475	761
sheep	524196	781
goats	219990	781
water buffalo	76471	761

From: *Pakistan Census of Agriculture 1960*, 1963

In spite of the wetlands near the Indus River there are very few water buffalo here and the sheep-goat population is large in relation to cattle. This is probably a reflection of the general aridity of the area, and the rugged terrain that surrounds the small, relatively fertile lowland zone.

Natural History: The Northwestern Region

The plants and animals of the Region are very much like those of the Gedrosia Region.

The only mineral of any importance is rock salt, which is available in Kohat, in an extension of the Salt Range, most of which is in the Northern Region. Since it is basically on the surface, this supply of salt would have been a valued commodity in ancient times, the region being so far from the sea (Government of India 1908a: 49). Salt tracts are also found at the northern end of the Zhob drainage and were worked in the nineteenth century (Minchin 1907h: 185). There is also some red ochre in Hazara District, in the mountains to the north of this Region (Government of India 1908a: 49). Small amounts of chromite exist in the Hindubagh (now called "Islambagh") area of Zhob District and petroleum has been reported just east of Zhob City in the Dahana Sar area (Minchin 1907h: 186-87). Serpentine and associated asbestos are reported from the Zhob Valley (Minchin 1907h: 185-86). There is good, abundant coal in Loralai (Minchin 1907e: 226-30). A small amount of copper is reported from Waziristan (Fentress 1976: 307).

Summary

Several features of this Region stand out. The communication link along the Indus, through the Derajat is important, since it links Sindh with the northwest of the Greater Indus Region. Curiously, Dera Ghazi Khan has not yet been explored by archaeologists, but it should be. Visitors to the area have reported mounds there. The complex of sites found in the Thal area, Fort Sandeman, Bannu and Dera Ismail Khan may well indicate that this is a region within which environmental factors have played a considerable role in the clustering of human settlement, with a more widespread pastoralism filling the spaces between the village farming communities.

THE NORTHERN REGION

Introduction

The Northern Region is approximately 180,000 square kilometers and is partly coincident with the modern Province of West Punjab (Figure 3.136). The western Hakra River tract of the Sarasvati will be a separate entity because of its environmental features as well as its historical and culture importance. The decision not to name this area the "Punjab" is because there is another Punjab in India and there is reason to distinguish between the two from the perspective of culture history, although both "Punjabs" share many physical features. In pre-Partition days they were a single political unit, which reflects many of the similarities in environment, history and language. The name "Punjab" comes from "five rivers" or literally the "five waters," that flow through it. From west to east these are generally stated to be: the Jhelum, Chenab, Ravi, Beas and Sutlej (Plate 3.66). A more ancient name for the region is "*Saptasindhava*" or "the seven" which includes the Indus as well as the now largely dry Sarasvati (Ghaggar-Hakra). "Seven rivers" is applied to other river systems and the seas of India as by Virgil in the *Aeneid*: "...even as [the] Ganges, rising high in silence with its seven peaceful streams..." (Virgil, Book ix, 30; Fairclough, translator 1935: Vol. 2, 115).

The rough boundaries of the Northern Region are the Sutlej River on the east and south, and the Indus on the West. The Potwar Plateau and Salt Range are included. The foothills of the outer Himalaya mark the northern boundary.

There is a geographic continuity from west to east as one crosses the Indus and leaves the mountains of the Northwest Frontier and moves east to the Ganges valley. There are no sharp divides, barriers, or abrupt changes in land form, rainfall, temperature, fauna or flora. In most respects the Northern Region is one unit, without subregions.

The Middle Course of the Indus River

The Indus enters the Region from the north, across the Potwar plateau, moving to Attock, where it is joined by the Kabul River and then passes through the Salt Range onto the lowlands of the western Punjab (Plate 3.67). Its course for the entire distance is basically straight and almost due south. For some of its run along the western boundary of the Northern Region the Indus is deeply entrenched, flowing within the confines of high walls of alluvium. In other places it is almost level with the plain on both sides (Plate 3.68). The river is broad and shallow on the Potwar, somewhat braided and studded with islands and sandbanks. It is fordable in the low water cold season, although this is said to be a dangerous undertaking. The Kabul River joins the Indus at a point where the two streams are about equal in volume and their joined waters enter a much narrower define and gain speed, taking on the additional waters of the Haroh River from the Murrie Hills. During the summer this confluence can be a wild confusion of waters, with high water, strong currents and much splashing about; best observed from a distance. Attock is also the approximate midpoint in the total course of the river, being ca. 1400 kilometers from its source and about 1500 kilometers from the sea (Government of India 1908b: 196-97).

The Indus is navigable throughout its course separating the Northern and Northwestern Regions, although during low water, sailors are at their peril of grounding among the shifting bars. Still, country boats ply the course in all seasons, avoiding only the years or times of exceptionally violent floods or unusually low flow.

A Note on Drinking Water

Drinking water, in many parts of the Greater Indus Region is affected by severe summer flooding, especially from the rivers of the Punjab. Most people prefer well water to river water, for reasons of health. Lieutenant John Wood has given the following as part of his 1835 journey on the Indus River:

> The inhabitants prefer well-water to that of the Indus. When the river has been falling for four or five successive days, to drink the nulla water is almost certain to bring on an attack of illness: this the Natives attribute, and I think very properly, to the vegetable matter which on such occasions must be brought into the watercourse by the drainage of the inundated districts (Wood 1838: 574).

This wisdom, based on simple observation, has probably been known for millennia and Wood's report only confirms it.

Landform and More Rivers

The Northern Region as a whole is an immense rolling plain, about 300 kilometers north-south and east-west as well. All of the area is under 370 meters, with the minor exception of the rugged, broken hills near Sangla and Kirana on either side of the Chenab River, which rise in jagged pinnacles as high as 512 meters. These hills are so small that they are little more than visual curiosities, affecting neither rainfall nor the grass area of the land suitable for human use. The fall of the rivers is also gentle; less then one meter to the kilometer in the north, where it is the steepest. In most of the area the slope is about 30 centimeters per kilometer and in the extreme southwest, where it approaches the lower valley it drops to half of that (Plate 3.69).

The principal physiographic features of the Region are the entrenched rivers and the humpbacked doabs. Doab is a Hindi-Urdu word: "From *Do*, two, and *Ab*, water, a country lying between two rivers, a mesopotamia" (Balfour 1885: Vol. I, 963). The Doab (with a capital 'D') is the space separating the Indus from the Ganga-Yamuna drainage, and there are many minor doabs. In the Punjab, doab land is also called *bar*. The doabs of the Northern Region are named, said to have originated in Mughal times, with the Emperor Akbar.

> Sindh Sagar Doab separates the Jhelum
> Jach or Chaj Doab separates the Jhelum from the Chenab
> Rechna Doab separates the Chenab from the Ravi
> The Bari Doab separates the Ravi from the Sutlej-Beas

There has been a great deal of change in the modern West Punjab from the aboriginal conditions. The vast canal system has brought land clearing and agriculture to huge areas that were once grasslands. Long-term exploitation by men and animals has trimmed trees and nipped grass, increasing erosion and sand cover, as noted by the quote from Mr. Lindley. Some have suggested that much of this degradation was due to climatic change (i. e., Marshall 1931b: 2-5; Mackay 1948: 29 and 37); but:

> The weight of modern opinion appears to be against desiccation in the true sense of an actual climatic change; but prolonged human interference with natural drainage, deforestation of the Siwaliks, and so on have undoubtedly led to marked deterioration in ground-water conditions and so in vegetation. The accounts of Alexander's campaigns and Mogul hunts bear witness to considerable forest growth; and today on the more arid margins strong winds and frequent but torrential rains have led to a serious spread of shifting sands and more serious if less spectacular deterioration of good cultivated land (Spate and Learmonth 1967: 519).

These tributaries to the Indus are large rivers in and of themselves and should not be thought of as benign little streams that combine to form one mighty river with the violent, unpredictable habits ascribed to the Indus in Sindh. Sir Alexander Burnes speaks of this when he reports passing the Sutlej in January 1932, on his way across the Punjab to Bokhara.

> The people informed us that about fifty years ago the Sutlege had been hemmed in among the mountains, by a hill falling upon its bed. After an obstruction for some weeks, it vomited forth its imprisoned stream with great destruction. A similar case occurred about eight years ago, in the Ravee, or river of Lahore. It did little injury, and the terror of the inhabitants was excited only by the black earthy color of the water which forced itself over the obstructing mound. The Sutlege has altered its course at no distant period, and swept some of the villages on its banks. Near the existing point of union between the rivers, we passed the dry bed of the old Sutlege which is said to have joined the Hyphasis at Feerozpoor...In a country subject to such changes, how are we to look for an identity between the topography of modern and ancient days? (Burnes 1835a: Vol. II, 5).

How are we to look for identity indeed! It takes care and perseverance, but with time and effort a sufficiently precise reconstruction can be approximated which would be useful to the archaeologist. That time is not here yet, but some progress is being made.

The Sindh Sagar Doab, also known as the Thal Desert, is a sandy desertic tract, which has responded very well to recent irrigation. In prehistoric times it would have been a desert, the driest most unusable area in an otherwise productive region. There are, however, Kot Dijian sites in this sandy terrain and it was inhabited.

The soils of the Northern Region are sandy loams for the most part. There are sandy tracts, as in the Thal, and patches of clayey soils. The modest rainfall has meant little leaching of the soil and the soil responds well to agriculture if enough water is made available, either through unusually abundant rainfall or irrigation.

In the north, with the steeper gradients and somewhat deeper entrenchments, the river courses have been relatively stable, but as one moves south there has been much long term variation. "The Chenab used to flow east of Multan...Ancient Multan stood on two islands in the Ravi, and in Tamerlane's time the Ravi joined the Chenab Below Multan" (W. A. Wood 1924: 13). Recent geophysical exploration in the vicinity of the site of Harappa on the Ravi has shown a very large oxbow turn in the river. The date for this feature has not yet been determined, but it admits the possibility that the Harappa city was on the northern rather than the southern bank of the river in ancient times (Pendall and Amundson 1990a, 1990b, 1993). Prior to the nineteenth century, when extensive canals were driven down the spines of the doabs to open up new agricultural lands, cultivation took place within the entrenchments of the rivers on the *kadir* or new alluvium. In some places the entrenchments are wide, 10 kilometers or so, but can also be quite narrow, a few hundred meters. Given the scale of the Northern Region they represent only a small percentage of the total land area, but were sufficiently productive to provide farm products for the region as a whole. In times before the canals, most of the Northern Region was a rich savannah-like grassland, with green strips of riverine land traversing it at periodic intervals. The pastures were exploited by the many cattle keeping peoples of the area who used the riverine strips for cultivation and as reliable sources of water for themselves and their large herds.

Quotes from the Punjab Provincial Gazetteer will provide further documentation of the condition of the region. The first comes from a description of Montgomery District, now called Sahiwal, where Harappa is located.

> On either side of the Ravi is a strip of riverain cultivation; here inundation canals carry the water for varying distances up to 23 miles, population is fairly thick, and cultivation good. South of this track stretches the Dhaia or central ridge of the District. Absolutely bare in a dry season, the track produces a good crop of grass if rains are plentiful (Government of India 1908b: Vol. 2, 2).

The next piece comes from a description of Lyallpur District, now called Faisalabad. The District comprises most of the high table-land between the Chenab and Ravi rivers, and is now irrigated by the Lower Chenab Canal. It contains a few proprietary villages near the Ravi in the south and on the Jhang (District) border; the rest of the District consists of villages built on crown waste and colonized by Government (Government of India 1908b: Vol. 2, 219).

In the Gujranwala District Gazetteer there is a wonderful description of the land. The author speaks of *des* and *bar*, the former being agricultural tracts along the rivers, the latter, *bar*, is the grazing land between the rivers, with rich pastures, inhabited by pastoral nomads (Government of India 1884c: 3-4 and below Part 4).

The first of the quotes tells of the settlement along the Ravi bed, making use of inundation canals. It also speaks of the pasture that was available. The second is useful in documenting the new colonization that took place in the nineteenth century by virtue of the new canals, that transformed the older "aboriginal" landscape into what we see today.

The Salt Range

Huge deposits of rock salt are found on the surface as well as in deep deposits in a low range of hills, known as the Salt Range or the Makhialah Hills. It forms the northern boundary of the Thal Desert, extending from the Indus, northeast for about 120 kilometers.

The Salt Range is the southernmost rampart of the Himalayas in Pakistan. It is a single ridge for most of its length, with a steep, forbidding southern face and about 500 meters of relief, on the average. The highest peak, Sakesar Hill, is at 1524 meters above mean sea level. This bleak and barren, rugged crest separates the dissected, varied uplands of the Potwar Plateau, from the monotonous alluvial plains of the Indus and its tributaries (Fraser 1958: 200).

The principal interest to humans in the area, are the enormous deposits of rock salt which may be the largest known (Spate and Learmonth 1967: 502). The Kerwa Mines tap five seams of almost pure rocksalt totaling 275 feet in thickness. Potash salts and gypsum are also present in appreciable quantities. The salt at or near the surface attracts, and keeps water, both rain and humidity, forming large "stains" on the ground, generally purple in color. But, just beneath this surface material is hard rock salt, of good quality, that can be mined using simple tools. This formation may have provided salt for the prehistoric population of what is now northern Pakistan. A Kot Dijian site at Musakhel, on the southern edge of the Salt Range was probably occupied in Late Kot Dijian times, as well as during the Kot Dijian, Early Harappan Stage.

The Potwar Plateau

The Potwar Plateau is a heavily dissected region north of the Salt range at about 350 to 580 meters above mean sea level. The rivers of the region are generally found at the bottom of deep erosion gullies and small valleys, making them unsuitable for irrigation. It has been referred to as a "ridge and trough" upland (Fraser 1958: 174). The area enjoys comparatively good rainfall, 380 to 635 mm, a quarter to a third of which falls in the winter. Snow, while rare, is not unknown (Spate and Learmonth 1967: 500). Owing to the unreliability of the monsoon rains, this is still a *rabi* crop area, with wheat and barley prevailing. I. S. Fraser has called it more favorable to dry cropping than most other parts of the Indus Plains (1958: 179-80), helped along by frequent plowing, terracing and bunds to control runoff.

The subregion has a rich history centered on the Taxila Valley, near Islamabad, the capital of Pakistan. Its three ruined cities of Bhir Mound, Sirkap and Sirsukh cover a thousand years of history from the presence of the Acheamenid Persians through the visit of Alexander the Great and beyond. Kot Dijian and Late Kot Dijian sites, especially the well excavated mound at Sarai Khola at the mouth of the Taxila Valley, attest to the presence of village farming communities in the area from the fourth millennium, if not earlier (Plate 3.70).

The famous Soan River flows through the Potwar Plateau and the initial research of Hellmut De Terra and T. T. Paterson (1939) has yielded abundant evidence for early man there. Palaeolithic research in this area, as well as the nearby Pabbi Hills, has been carried forward by a British team (B. Allchin 1981, 1986; Rendell 1984; Dennell 1984, 1990, 1991; Dennell et al. 1993) which has some very early dates for tool making, suggesting that the region has an important role to play in understanding the evolution of human behavior.

The Mountains of the Northern Region Borderlands

The mountains north of the Subcontinent are not included here as a separate domain of the Harappan Civilization because of scant evidence for human occupation. Settlements of the so-called "Northern Neolithic" are present in Kashmir (Plate 3.71) and a certain amount of interaction between them and the plains is known because of the Kot Dijian Pot found at Burzahom

(Figure 4.82) and the presence of Northern Neolithic sites on the Plains, most notably at Sarai Khola. I have visited other sites, farther south in the Thal Desert area, with this kind of pottery. The hills rise rapidly from the Potwar Plateau, as at Murrie, just north of Taxila (Plate 3.72).

The mountains, not the deep ranges and valleys, but the near front, as far as the Vale of Kashmir was an area known to the Harappans, from the Early Harappan Stage. The area did provide some resources for them. The Himalaya, literally "Land of Snow" in Sanskrit was an object of awe and veneration in early Indian civilization, as seen in the following bit of Sanskrit verse from the Medieval poet Murari (c. 800-900 AD) dealing with Siva's abode of Mount Kailasa:

> This is Mount Kailasa, where the jeweled ground
> so sparkles as to rob the trees of shadow,
> but renders them their shadow once again
> by their reflections in it;
> where the moonbeams issuing from Siva's crown
> are strong enough to place the seal of sleep
> on lotuses, although the sun
> has ventured close enough to touch them with his hands.
> (Ingalls 1968: 294)

On leaving the Potwar Plateau in the direction of Kashmir, one is first confronted by the famous Siwalik Hills. They make a relatively gradual transition to the Pir Panjal Range, the southern front of the Himalaya in the region of the Northern Region. There is a sharp rise in slope at this time and then an equally precipitous fall into the deep, well watered Vale of Kashmir. Altitudes associated with the Pir Panjal Range are passes at about 3500 meters, with the highest monadnocks reaching 4725 meters (Spate and Learmonth 1967: 430). The valley, at only 1585 meters, has been the scene of very powerful erosional forces, bringing alluvium down from the mountain slopes, but also as the recipient of significant amounts of wind blown loess. Much of the alluvial geology of Kashmir is found in the *karewas*, flat-topped terraces, generally Pleistocene, with clay and silt interbanded with loess and marl, showing that the modern lakes in the valley have gone through significant fluctuations in their water level.

The principal resource that the outer Himalaya, including Kashmir and surrounding valleys, provided for the Early and Mature Harappan seems to have been timber, especially the tall cedars and pines useful in the construction of larger buildings. Sockets for wooden beams are commonplace at Mohenjo-daro as is evidence for timber and brick construction in the area excavated by G. Dales in 1964 (Dales 1965a: 148-49) and the podium of the "Granary" (Wheeler 1968: 55). Wheeler's reconstruction of the building above the baked brick foundations that is seen today is an entirely wooden structure. It is widely believed that trees would have been floated down the rivers, into the Northern Region, as far as Mohenjo-daro. The great mound of Rupar, located at the point where the Sutlej River breaks onto the northern plains, might have been founded at this strategic location to protect a route between two subregions and to monitor and regulate Harappan commerce with the mountain peoples.

There is also some gold in Kashmir along with copper, silver, agate, amazonite methyst, quartz and slate.

Rainfall

The westerlies influence the region, with declining winter rain as one moves from west to east.

On the average Peshawar gets 132 mm in this season and Lahore only 69 mm (Spate and Learmonth 1967: 519). But, the influence of the southwest monsoon increases in the east, with Lahore receiving 125-150 mm of summer rain, in addition to the winter precipitation. The rainfall in this region could be thought of as averaging between about 130 and 150 mm, similar to Gujarat in the total amount, but spread between two independent cyclonic events and therefore somewhat more reliable.

Natural History: The Northern Region

The Northern Region is blessed with grasslands and light forest coverage of *Acacia*, *Salvadora*, and *sissoo*. The riverine entrenchments are favored with better tree and grass coverage than the doabs, but the overall character of the early era would have been one of open savannah.

In prehistoric times the region was home to the elephant, rhinoceros, lion and tiger, and two kinds of bears, as well as a wide range of ungulates. The antler of the Kashmir Stag (*Cervus elaphus*) has also been found at Mohenjo-daro (Sewell and Guha 1931a: 659-60). These are not associated with bones of the animal and it is widely, and reasonably, believed that the antlers were imported for their medicinal qualities. There are grouse, partridge, quail and pheasants (Government of India 1908b: Vol. 1, 12-3). *Kunj* or damoiselle cranes are abundant in the winter. The Jungle Fowl was still said to be found in Rawalpindi District (Punjab Government 1907: 28). They also note the presence of the sharp nosed, fish eating crocodile, the *ghavial* (*Gavialis gangeticus*) and its blunt nosed cousin, the *mugger* (*Crocodylus palustris*) in all of the major rivers. The blind Indus porpoise was said to be common (Punjab Government 1915: 13).

Because of their importance in the domestication process it is interesting that in Mianwali District, along the Indus River near the Salt Range, markors are said to have been present in small numbers but the wild sheep or Urial (*Ovis vigni*) was quite common in the Salt Range, the Bhangi Khel and Paniala Hills. The Thal is full of *Chinkara* (*Gazella bennetti*). There are numbers of hog deer (*Axis porcinus*) especially in the south of the district in Bhakkar. Wild boar are found in the riverine tracts (Government of the Punjab 1915: 13). The abundance of game in the Northern Region, and the Punjab generally, made it a splendid hunting ground in Mughal and Colonial times.

The Imperial Gazetteer discusses an abundant bird life.

Natural Resources of the Northern Region

Salt is the major mineral resource of the Northern Region, but oil is found in Mianwali District. Ten springs produce small quantities of thick, dark green sulphurous liquid oil (Government of the Punjab 1915: 138-39). It is used as bitumen. Oil is also reported from Attock District (Government of India 1908b: Vol. I, 78).

Gold is found in minute quantities mixed in the sand of the Indus and is extracted by a laborious process of washing. The yield is very small, 370 ounces in 1904. A hard day's work would yield two to four annas (Government of India 1908b: Vol. 1, 77; Government of Punjab 1915: 139). Workers at Mohenjo-daro in 1925-26 were paid much better; men received 11 annas per day and women and children eight. An anna is one-sixteenth of a rupee and the rupee of that day was worth about thirty-four American cents.

Some copper is reported from the Salt Range (Government of the Punjab 1883a: 14). The outer Himalaya have also produced copper, but this seems to be farther to the east, in the Eastern Region.

Subsistence Information

The subsistence regime of the Northern Region today is based on the cultivation of wheat and the tending of cattle. This is the *rabi* pattern, and is a reflection of the importance of the winter westerlies as a source of moisture. There is, however, some balance to the agricultural system and *kharif* season millets are also grown; in this case mostly as fodder. Some statistics from three districts of the region are given as evidence for this pattern. Harappa is in Sahiwal District.

TABLE 3.34
The Agricultural Regime in Campbellpur

Plant or Animal	Acres or Number of Animals	Page in Report
wheat	664373	324
bajra	122986	414
jowar	69842	414
cattle	535050	755
sheep	232816	775
goats	199068	775
water buffalo	60119	755

From: *Pakistan Census of Agriculture 1960*, 1963

TABLE 3.35
The Agricultural Regime in Sahiwal District*

Plant or Animal	Acres or Number of Animals	Page in Report
wheat	710533	328
bajra	47339	418
jowar	5063	418
water buffalo	727262	760
cattle	623143	760
sheep	399323	780
goats	144312	780

From: *Pakistan Census of Agriculture 1960*, 1963
*Called Montgomery District in the Census

TABLE 3.36
The Agricultural Regime in Multan District

Plant or Animal	Acres or Number of Animals	Page in Report
wheat	983011	328
jowar	232158	418
bajra	158453	418
cattie	1046539	760
sheep	694101	780
water buffalo	520349	760
goats	276939	780

From: *Pakistan Census of Agriculture 1960*, 1963

THE EASTERN REGION

Introduction

The Eastern Region which is approximately 400,000 square kilometers, is now entirely in India (Figure 3.136). It is a tract known for its fertility. The Region includes the Indo-Gangetic Divide east of the Sutlej River, as described by O. H. K. Spate and A. T. A. Learmonth (1967: 534-45), the Ganga-Yamuna Doab, and encompasses the modern Indian states of Punjab, Haryana

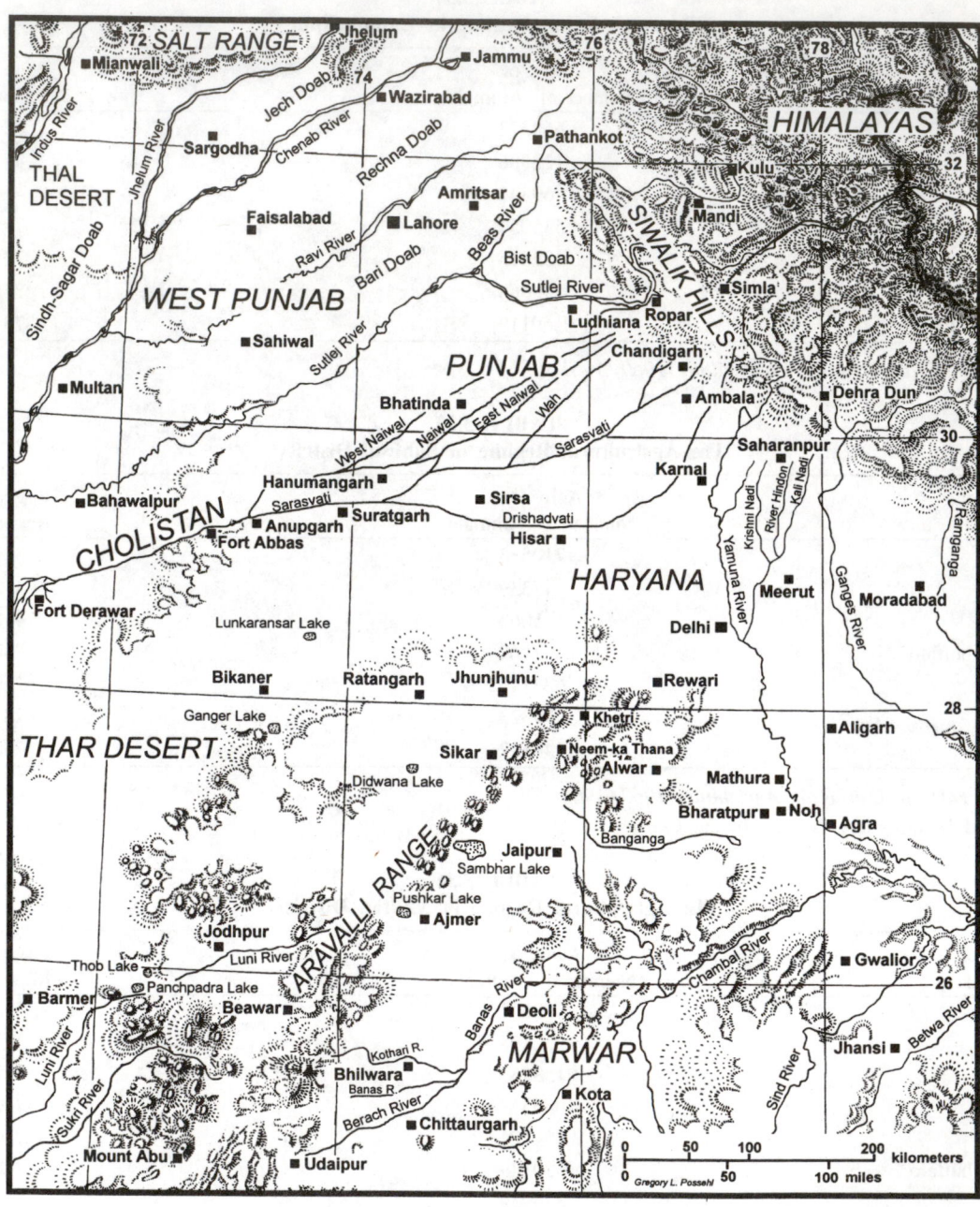

Figure 3.136. The Eastern Region

Plate 3.71. The Vale of Kashmir near Burzahom, author's photograph.

Plate 3.72. The Murrie Hills just north of Taxila, looking south toward the northwestern plains of the Northern Region, author's photograph.

Plate 3.73. The Ghaggar in Hisar District, Haryana during the monsoon of August 1994, author's photograph.

and the Territory of Delhi. The Ganga-Yamuna Doab, almost to the confluence of these two rivers, is included in the Eastern Region because of the Early, Mature and Post-urban Harappan sites there. In an anomalous way the Region extends as far south as the Agra-Bharatpur area, west to Jaipur, north to Sikar on to Haryana as shown on the Map of Regions.

Landform

On the whole the land is flat, although there are hills and some escarpments in the southeast. According to Spate and Learmonth "...the terrain is simply the usual alluvial monotony" (Spate and Learmonth 1967: 534-35). To the north, where the low Siwaliks meet the plains there has been very broad and extensive erosion. In Hoshiarpur District there are a hundred streams that meet the plains, all of which are dry except when it rains. These *chos*, as they are called, carry sand and heavier alluvium down from the mountains and form an immense "pan fan" all along the northern boundary of the Region (Spate and Learmonth 1967: 535). But the plains themselves are fertile alluvium, and much like the land of the Northern Region; one immense doab.

In the southeastern part of the Eastern Region one meets with far more aridity than in the north in the Punjab and Haryana. A purely geographical consideration would place this part of the Eastern Region in the Thar Desert, but in terms of ancient culture and geography it belongs here.

The Upper Sarasvati Drainage

The origin of the Upper Sarasvati is found in the Eastern Region, in the 160 kilometer stretch of Siwalik ridge between the Sutlej and Yamuna. With the exception of a few streams at either end of this feature the drainage here is dissipated into agricultural fields or finds its way to the Sarasvati (Spate and Learmonth 1967: 536). This is a complex dendritic drainage system; its history goes back to the end of the last glacial period. The combined effects of erosion, deposition and tectonic movement have led to changes in the flow in this or that palaeochannel and it should not be assumed that the drainage system of today is a reflection of anything more than a few hundred years (only a few decades in some areas) of riverine history.

The precise history of the various palaeochannels of the Upper Sarasvati has not yet been worked out, just as the history of the main Sarasvati after being joined by the Drishadvati, is not completely understood. It is clear, however, that the headwaters and upper catchment of the Sarasvati is in the Siwaliks and one of the challenges is the reconstruction of this riverine environment during the Indus Age.

The Ganga-Yamuna Doab

The area between the Ganga and Yamuna Rivers is a long, (ca. 650 kilometers) relatively narrow, (ca. 100 kilometers in the north) fertile plain of deep rich alluvium. In Saharanpur District, at the upper end of the doab, there is an abundance of archaeological sites, especially during Mature Harappan and Post-urban times. Rainfall is over 900 mm per year and the area is noted for its considerable agricultural production.

The Ganga-Yamuna doab is itself broken into a series of five minor doabs. These are formed by the courses of the Katha Nala, Krishni Nadi, River Hindon and Kali Nadi as they drain south, following courses that parallel the Ganga and Yamuna in a general way, but they are tributary to the Yamuna.

Prior to the clearing of the land for cultivation this would have been an area of forest and thicket, rich in animal life, with small lakes in fossil river scars and hollows in the landscape.

It would have included trees of substantial size, like *sissoo* (*Dalbergia sissoo*), along with *sal* (*Shorea robusta*) and *khair* (*Acacia catechu*). There is a good correlation between the distribution of the Indian Jungle Fowl and *sal* forest. This region is one where Harappans and the progenitor of the domesticated chicken would have certainly come together. Fire must have been used extensively to clear the land in Mature Harappan times, although there is one Early Harappan site at Nawanbans, just east of the Yamuna in Saharanpur District, so the process was begun in an earlier era. The Ganga-Yamuna doab was widely settled in Mature Harappan times, perhaps living side by side with other peoples, some food producers, other hunter-gatherers. But the Harappan inhabitants did not venture across the Ganges to the east. The Ganges thus forms a good geographical and cultural boundary for the Mature Harappan.

Natural History: The Eastern Region

The natural history of the Eastern Region is very much like that of the Northern Region, but the Ganga-Yamuna doab receives more rainfall than the Northern Region. The southeastern area of the Eastern Region is considerably drier, which would affect the natural history and comparability to the Harappa area.

Minerals

The Eastern Region is not rich in minerals. It has been reported that copper has been mined in Jullundur and Patiala Districts (Fentress 1976: 307), and in the outer Himalaya, in Kangra (Government of the Punjab 1883b: 17), Kulu, and the former Simla Hill States, which are now in Himachal Pradesh. Some copper is also found deeper in the mountains, in the Chandra Valley, for example (Government of India 1908b: 78). These mountainous areas are on the borders of the domain, but the resource was there, and the Early and Mature Harappans certainly had a great deal of copper available to them.

Rainfall

The Indo-Gangetic Divide is an area with both summer and winter rainfall, although the winter rains are of less importance than the monsoon. Modern irrigation is reserved for the *rabi* wheat crop throughout the area. Mean annual rainfall from 1901 to 1950 is given on Table 3.37 for various cities scattered through this Region.

TABLE 3.37
Rainfall in the Eastern Region

Agra	664.8 mm
Delhi	660.1 mm
Jaipur	597.9 mm
Sikar	441.4 mm
Ludhiana	647.9 mm
Ferozepore	426.7 mm
Saharanpur	936.1 mm
India Meteorological Department 1962	

Subsistence Information

Except for the southeastern desert area, the Eastern Region is well irrigated today and is known for its agricultural productivity. Spate and Learmonth have noted for their "Indo-Gangetic Plains" that:

> The region is one of the most cultivated in India, with well over half the total area of some 40,000,000-45,000,000 acres (16,000,000-18,000,000 hectares) cultivated, and double cropping adds 20-25% to this figure. Forests are under a million acres and current fallows (nearly half in the dry southwest) show a marked decline as compared to the Indus Plains; so also, unfortunately do fodder crops (Spate and Learmonth 1967: 550).

Food crops predominate in this Region, with wheat at the top of the list, indicating the strong *rabi* season cast to the agriculture here. Wheat is followed by rice, barley, jowar and bajra (Spate and Learmonth 1967: 551). Rice replaces wheat and barley to the east of the Ganga. It is clear that by the Mature Harappan, these people had extended themselves to the edge of the region within which their principal *rabi* food grains were viable (Fairservis 1961b: 28).

Wheat, barley and rice have been found in Harappan or Post-urban Harappan contexts at Hulas (IAR 1982-83: 149-50 and IAR 1983-84: 177-78). Jowar and bajra have not been identified, but *ragi*, a plant of the millet family, has been found in a preliminary way in these same reports. With the extensive irrigation facilities removed from the landscape, the agricultural regime for the Mature Harappan finds agreement with the grosser outlines of the modern situation.

THE HAKRA REGION

Introduction

The remains of a once great river crosses the modern border between India and Pakistan near the city of Anupgarh (Figure 3.137). In Vedic times it was the Sarasvati, literally "Chain of Pools" the holiest of Indian rivers in this age. Sarasvati is also an Hindu deity, the wife of Brahma and the goddess of learning, music and poetry. Today the river is often called the Ghaggar-Hakra.[20] A lot has been written about the "Lost River of the Great Indian Desert," not all of it entirely accurate or unclouded (e.g., Wadia 1966: 392-93).

Describing the boundaries for the Hakra Region is difficult. It is centered on the Sarasvati bed and includes some land to either side. The eastern beginning has been tied to the junction of this stream and the Drishadvati, at about Kalibangan, largely as a matter of convenience. The southern end is also more or less arbitrary, coinciding with the area where the ancient river system seems to disappear into the sand and alluvium of northern Sindh. This is in the vicinity of the modern town of Rahim Yar Khan. There are no subdivisions within this Region; it is the smallest of the Greater Indus Region at about 25,000 square kilometers.

There is an especially close relationship between the Sarasvati and the Eastern Region. The headwaters of the river, the central feature of the Hakra Region, lie in the East outside its boundaries. However, the only way to make sense of the nature and history of this once great stream is to treat the river as a whole, or a system with many sources that shift over time.

Lt. Col. James Tod observed in his *Annals and Antiquities of Rajasthan*:

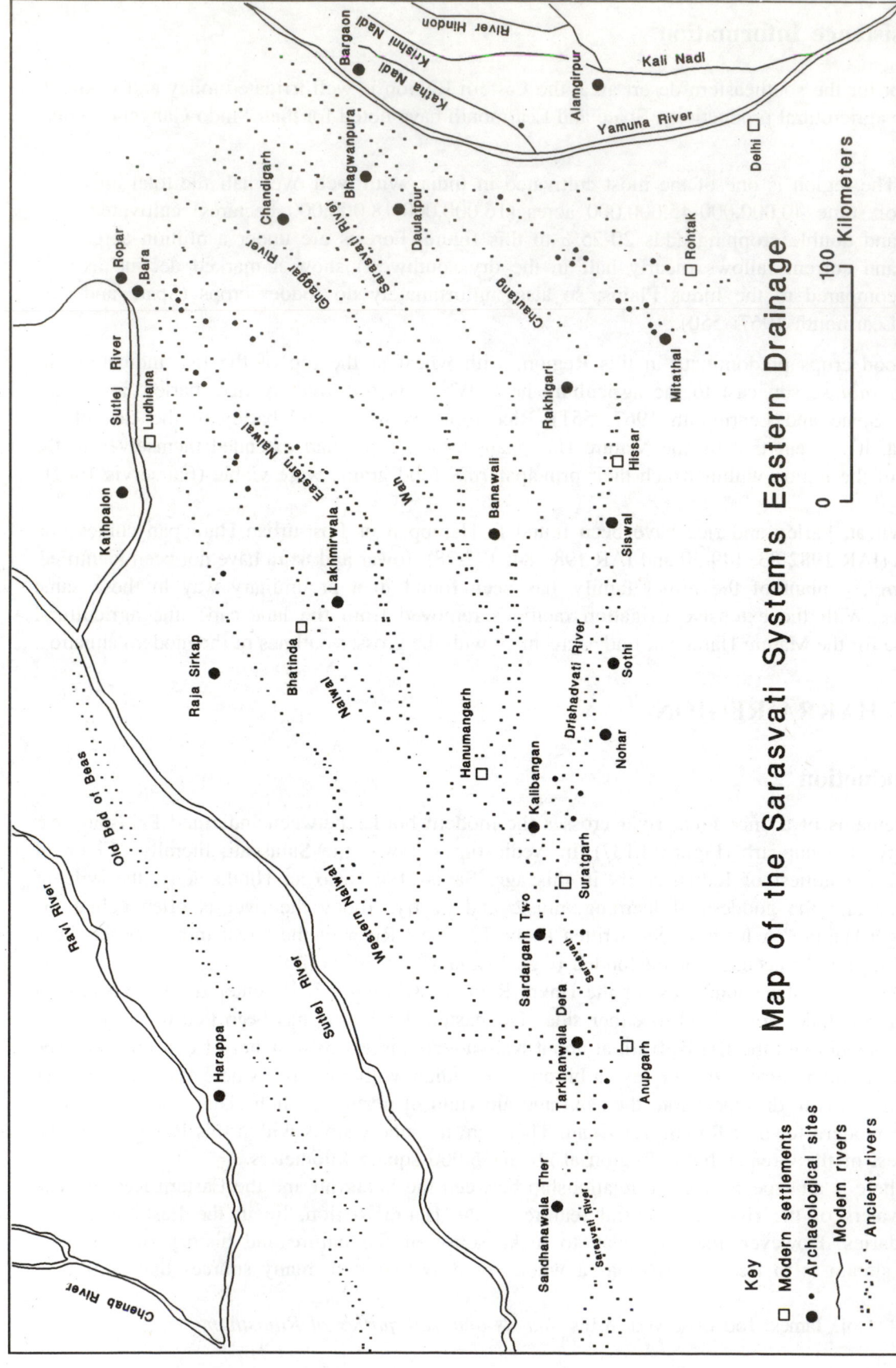

Figure 3.137. Map of the Sarasvati system's eastern drainage, after Pande 1977: Figure 2.21

Amidst these ruins of the Johyas the name *Sekunder Roomi* (Alexander the Great) has fixed itself, and the desert retains the tradition that the ruin called *Rung-mahal*, the 'painted palace' near Dandoosir, was the capital of a prince of this region punished by a visitation of the Macedonian conqueror. History affords no evidence of Alexander's passage of the Garah, though the scene of his severest conflict was in that nook of the Punjab not remote from the lands of the Johyas. But though the chronicler of Alexander does not sanction our indulging in this speculation, the total darkness in which we appear doomed to remain with regard to Bactria and the petty Grecian kingdoms on the Indus, established by him, does not forbid our surmise, that by some of these, perhaps by the descendants of Python, such a visitation might have happened (Tod 1829-32: Vol 2. 144).

"*Rung-mahal*," more frequently rendered "Rang Mahal" today, is a huge archaeological site about eight kilometers east of Suratgarh, on the south bank of the Sarasvati. Its principal occupation was in the early centuries of the common era, and it would be associated with the Kushan domination of northern India. A Swedish archaeological team excavated there in 1952-54 and Rang Mahal Ware has come to be an important ceramic marker for the Kushan Age (Rydh 1959).

Archaeological Exploration in the Region

The earliest archaeological investigation of the region was undertaken by L. P. Tessitori 1917 and 1918. Good reviews of the archaeological data are available from a number of sources (Suraj Bhan 1973; Pande 1977). K. N. Dikshit in a series of papers has reviewed the archaeological and geophysical evidence (Dikshit 1979a, 1980, 1984a, 1984b, 1987).

The Justification for a Separate Region

In modern geography the Hakra Region would not be justified as a separate region either in physical or historical geography. Its independent status during Mature Harappan times has to be considered.

One of the sites discovered by Mughal is ca. 80 hectares in size. It is called Ganweriwala and compares in total area with both Mohenjo-daro and Harappa. The site remains unexcavated, but doubtless it will rank with the others as the third Harappan city. Ganweriwala was built in Cholistan at a place that is equally distant from Mohenjo-daro and Harappa, so in terms of locational geography the even spacing of these urban centers suggests that each had its own hinterland or Region. This aspect of ancient geography and the density of settlement, especially during the Mature Harappan, justify thinking of the region as a separate Region of the Indus Age.

Some Thoughts on Terminology

This is the "Hakra Region" and the river system, the "Sarasvati," in recognition of the antiquity of this term. It has not been possible to trace the antiquity of the names Ghaggar and Hakra, but they seem to be medieval in origin. Tod derived "Hakra" from "Sankara" or serpent (1829-32: Vol. 2, 144, fn 3) which would be congruent with the etymology of "nalla" for a small river or stream being derived from "naga," snake or cobra. He observed that, "The natives of these regions cannot pronounce the sylabant; so that... the 's' is converted into 'h'" (1829-32: Vol. 2, 144, fn. 3), an extremely common sound shift in north India.[21]

Modern Geography and River History in Northern Regions of the Greater Indus Region

Remote sensing has demonstrated that the riverine history of the northern Regions of the Greater Indus Region, including the Thar Desert, is long and complex; concisely summarized by S. M. Ramaswamy, P. C. Bakliwal and R. P. Verma (1991). The discussion of the course of the Sarasvati, and other recent rivers of the Punjab, Haryana, northern Rajasthan and Cholistan (e.g., Naiwal, Ghaggar-Hakra, Sabi) is fraught with terminological confusion. First, there is a modern river bed, kilometers wide in some places and heavily cultivated, that the people of Haryana refer to as "Sarasvati." During the monsoon parts of this channel carry small amounts of water, most of which is quickly captured for irrigation. Thus, the river that today's people call "Sarasvati" is not entirely dead. To the west of the Sarasvati, is another channel that the modern people of the region call "Ghaggar." This carries considerable water during good monsoons, such as that of 1994 (Plate 3.73). The Ghaggar and the Hakra, its continuation in Pakistan, are sometimes thought of as the modern courses of the Sarasvati, but the beds of these rivers are different geographical features, at least in their upper reaches. Farther west there are other rivers, the Wah, the Eastern, Central and Western Naiwal, all of which had some part in the drainage of the Punjab and Haryana during the Indus Age.

There is an earlier, Pleistocene history of drainage in this region. Ramaswamy, Bakliwal and Verma (1991) have found that: "The occurrence of well developed tentacles of paleochannels in the vast Indian Desert and the final arm of the paleochannel as the Ghaggar in the Anupgarh-Ganganagar plains show that the River Sarasvati flowed close to the Aravalli hill ranges, met the Arabian Sea in the Rann of Kutch... (1991: 2605). The chronology for this river is not yet known, but it may well be generally "Pleistocene" and it should not be ruled out as a river which had an impact on human life in the region. There is much to be learned about this topic and it represents another challenge to those interested in serious, problem oriented research in South Asian archaeology.

The History of the Sarasvati: Setting up the Problem

The Sarasvati River occurs in the Ṛgveda in many places and it corresponds phonetically to the Iranian "Haraqaiti," which would be the modern Helmand River of southern Afghanistan (Macdonell and Keith 1912: Vol. II, 434-37). The name Sarasvati continues to be used in Puranic literature; for example in the *Sathapatha Brahmana* and *Taittiriya Samhita*. This river was holy, in fact the "foremost of rivers" (*naditama*):

> Foremost mother, foremost of rivers, foremost of goddesses, Sarasvati, We are, as 'twer, of no repute and dear Mother, give thou us renown. In thee, Sarasvati, divine, all generations have their stars. Be, glad with Sunahotra's sons: O Goddess grant us progeny. Ṛgveda Book II, Hymn 41, Verses 16-17, modified after Griffith 1896. The Sarasvati is venerated, and it is powerful, both as a destroyer of foes and as a mighty river: Yea, this divine Sarasvati, terrible with her golden path, foeslayer, claims our eulogy. Whose limitless, unbroken flood, swift-moving with a rapid rush, comes onward with tempestuous roar. She hath spread us beyond all foes, beyond her Sisters, Holy One. As Surya spendeth out the days. Yea, she most dear amid dear streams, Seven-sistered, graciously inclined. Sarasvati hath earned our praise. Guard us from hate Sarasvati, she who hath filled the realms of earth. And that wide tract, the firmament! Seven-sistered, sprung from threefold source, Five Tribes prosper, she must be invoked in every deed of might. (Ṛgveda Book VI, Hymn 61, Verses 7-12; Griffith 1896).

The image created in the Ṛgveda for the Sarasvati River is one of a powerful, full flowing river, not easily reconciled with the literal meaning of the name "Chain of Pools." The discrepancy cannot simply be dismissed; swept under the carpet. It is a good example of how difficult it can be to use the Ṛgveda, and the vedic texts generally, as historical sources.

It could be that when the composers of the Vedas first came to the Sarasvati it was a river of great magnitude, and these recollections are what we read in their texts. But over time the stream was robbed of its headwaters and dried up, becoming a chain of pools. For whatever reason, the name was changed and Sarasvati is the name that was preserved in the texts; awkward to be sure, but probably not insurmountable. This carries with it an interesting chronological implication: the composers of the Ṛgveda were in the Sarasvati region prior to the drying up of the river and this would be closer to 2000 BC than it is to 1000 BC, somewhat earlier than most of the conventional chronologies for the presence of Vedic Aryans in the Punjab.

The geography of the Ṛgveda is centered on the Punjab, and the reference, "seven sisters," is to the "*Saptasindhava*" the "seven rivers" of the region. Portraying the river as full flowing and mighty, indeed the foremost of rivers, has suggested that the Sarasvati is the Indus, in at least some passages of the Ṛgveda. Ralph T. H. Griffith was of this opinion (1896: Vol. 1, 677), as was Professor R. von Roth, according to Sir Aurel Stein (1942: 176). Today, this is a distinctly minority opinion, thanks to the work of several scholars who have dealt with the identification of the Vedic River Sarasvati. It is summarized well in Macdonell and Keith (1912: Vol. II, 434-37). There are a number of points that suggest that the modern dry river bed with the name Sarasvati was also the ancient river, not the least of which is the historical continuity presumed in the nomenclature itself. In a key passage of the Ṛgveda, the so-called "River Hymn" in Book X, Hymn 75, the author enumerates a series of rivers, evidently in order, beginning from the east: Ganga, Yamuna, Sarasvati, Sutlej and Ravi. This correctly places the Sarasvati between the Yamuna and the Sutlej and reinforces the argument for the continuity of the name.

> Unto you, O Sindhu, they go, as do mothers to a child, as do lowing cows with their milk. As a warrior king both wings of his army, do you alone lead when you seek to attain the van of these headlong streams.
>
> Attend to this, my hymn of praise. O Ganga, Yamuna, Sarasvati, O Sutudri (Sutlej), Parusni (Ravi)! With Asikni (Chenab), O Marudvrdha (confluence of Ravi and Chenab?), with Vitasta (Jhelum), harken! You, O Arjikiya, harken with Susoma.

Ṛgveda Book X, Hymn 75, Verses 4-5; Maurer 1986: 202-03.[22]
Macdonell and Keith add to this:

> But there are strong reasons to accept the identification of the later and earlier Sarasvati throughout. The insistence on the divine character is seen in every hymn. which refers to it as the support of the five tribes, and corresponds well with its further sacredness. Moreover, that hymn alludes to the *Paravatas*, a people shown by later evidence of the Pancavimsa Brahmana to have been in the east, a very long way from their original home, if Sarasvati means Indus. Again, the *Purus*, who were settled on the Sarasvati, could with great difficulty be located in the far west. Moreover, the five tribes might easily be held to be on the Sarasvati, when they were, as they seem to have been, the western neighbors of the *Bharatas* in Kurukshetra, and the Sarasvati could easily be regarded as the boundary of the Punjab in that sense (Macdonell and Keith 1912: Vol. II, 436).

The River System We See Today

The first focused discussion of the history of the Ghaggar-Hakra and its connection with the ancient Sarasvati came in an anonymous article in an 1874 issue of the *Calcutta Review*. It was written by Surgeon-Major C. F. Oldham (see R. D. Oldham 1887: 322, fn. *), who also wrote another distinguished article on the subject (1893).[23] In his first paper the Surgeon-Major correctly sees the identity of the Ghaggar-Hakra and the Sarasvati and suggests that in antiquity there was a connection between the Sutlej-Beas drainage and that of the Sarasvati (see also C. F. Oldham 1893: 55). This was supported by R. D. Oldham (1887: 333). They also speak of the Hakra as receiving water as a kind of extension of the Yamuna at the same time (R. D. Oldham: 1887: 333, with citations). Both the Sutlej capture and the Yamuna connection to the Hakra are issues of some contention in the study of the Sarasvati River.

Today this is a complex river system that begins in the Siwalik Hills of the Eastern Region. Sir Aurel Stein describes it:

> The Sarasvati, called *Sarsuti* in Hindi, is formed by the junction in the Ambala District of the Punjab of a number of smaller streams descending from the outer Himalaya range of the Siwaliks. The river bed is filled mainly by the drainage of the monsoon-rains which that hill-range receives in abundance. Its water is made by dams to irrigate much ground in Ambala District. Thence it passes along the western portion of the Karnal tract, the sacred Brahmatshi of tradition, into the easternmost part of Patiala territory. There it ceases to carry a perennial flow of water.
>
> The wide bed of the river next enters the Hissar District and continuing its southwestern course carries summer floods of a volume varying in accordance with the intensity of the monsoon to the northeastern border of Bikaner. At a distance of some 12 miles before reaching that border, a weir constructed in 1897 now holds up the flood water to form the artificial lake of Otu (Stein 1943a: 7-8).

In its upper course the main branch of the Sarasvati also passes Thaneshwar and is later joined by the Chautang, the ancient Drishadvati. By this time it is headed more or less in a westerly direction for the Pakistan border.

The dry, flat river bed is generally lined with sand dunes on both sides. These can be high, over 30 meters at Suratgarh, and Sir Aurel Stein notes that others approach 100 meters (1943a: 13). The width of the bed is rarely, if ever, less than three kilometers, and may exceed six in places.

According to Spate and Learmonth:

> These are not true river banks, but as it were aeolian levees, accumulations of windblown sand trapped by vegetation on the riverine strips once seasonally flooded. 'The gradually rising accumulation of driftsand, usually protected by some growth of scrub, has prevented the onward march of the dunes and thus preserved the dry bed from being smothered' (Stein 1942: 175). But it is unlikely that this broad bed was ever completely filled with water; the fertility of its loamy levels when water can be brought to them, and its striking definition between the bordering sand-ridges, are responsible for the local belief in the existence of a river of the first magnitude. This is very unlikely, but that water once flowed well down to Bahawalpur is attested beyond doubt by numerous settlement-mounds, and it is often held that the East Nara in Sind is the continuation of the Hakra, beheaded by the Sutlej (Spate and Learmonth 1967: 536; see also Stein 1943a: 12-5).

A. Ghosh never published a full report on his explorations of the Sarasvati, but in his first preliminary report he differs with this observation on the apparent edges of the old river.

> That they represent river-banks is proved by the existence on them of a large number of shells, kindly identified for me by the Zoological Survey of India as *Zootecus insularis* (Ehr.), *Indonaia caerula* (lea) and *Parreysia* sp. Some of these, being fresh-water shells, must have got deposited on the banks of the river when it was alive. Small dunes, accumulating at the tops of the sand-banks, and consisting of finer sand drifted from the banks themselves and outside, are of secondary formation (Ghosh 1952: 38).

With this Ghosh gives an important, but not necessarily conclusive, piece of evidence that needs to be taken further with more systematic work and research by both malacologists and geologists. Field survey and collection should easily settle the matter with which he differs.

Local tradition abounds concerning the mighty river that is said to have filled the *faux-*banks. Sir Aurel Stein tells us that one of the Mature Harappan sites near Anupgarh carries two names: Mathula Theri and Mallavali Theri. "The designation of Mallavali (the 'mound of the boatman'), suggests connection with the story about the ferry boats for which the Mathula ridge is supposed to have once served as a landing place" (Stein 1943a: 71-2). Another mound in the vicinity, this one of Rang Mahal date, is called Jandewala and "...is supposed to have been named after the boatman whom local belief assumes to have taken his boat across the Ghaggar river from Juhanzwala to Mathula" (Stein 1943a: 76). Stein also observed that the inhabitants of the Ghaggar-Hakra riverine tract had no problem at all distinguishing river bed from desert tract (1943a: 14, fn. 1).

James Tod observed something similar, when he commented that the traditions of the region assert that:

> ...these regions were not always either arid or desolate, and the living chronicle...which dated its deterioration from the drying up of the *Hakra* river, which came from the Punjab, and flowing through the heart of this country, emptied itself into the Indus between Rory Bekher and Otch (Tod 1829-32: Vol. 2, 144).

The Very Early Courses of the Sarasvati

The best synthesis of geographical data on the Sarasvati was done by Herbert Wilhelmy (1969). His approach is essentially one that depends on geography and medieval and modern history to determine the sequence of active courses in a relative way from early to late. He uses early literary evidence and some archaeological data to attempt to date these courses, which is much out of date, principally because he could not draw on the explorations in Cholistan by M. R. Mughal.

The geological exploration and the examination of landsat imagery have contributed to unraveling the early, probably Pre-Pleistocene, history of the Sarasvati. Bimal Ghose and his colleagues (Ghose, Kar and Husain 1979, 1980) have noted that the geological map of Rajasthan and Ajmer compiled by B. C. Roy (1959) indicates that the area to the west of the Aravalli Mountains is basically covered with deep alluvium, except for a few rock outcrops dating from Precambrian to Eocene times. With these exceptions, it is all riverine and aeolian material, and in that sense the area is a geological extension of the Indus Valley. The Indus itself could not have been responsible for so much work, and the entire riverine system emanating from the Himalaya from the Northwest Frontier to the Ganges, as well as Aravalli streams must be examined to answer the question of the sources of so much alluvium.

The Luni is the only river of any note in the Thar Desert and the Ghose team demonstrates that while it contributed something to this long-term process, it is not large enough to have been the major influence (Ghose, Kar and Husain 1980: 9). There is, however, evidence for many fossil river beds in the Thar Desert and by using landsat imagery it was possible to piece together some continuities between surface features that are otherwise isolated and cut off from each other.

Photo-reconnaissance enabled the team to propose that what we see today as the combined headwaters of the Ghaggar, Sarasvati and Chautang originally flowed past Nohar and joined the Luni 450 kilometers to the south (Figure 3.138). There are at least two major phases (courses) in this area, and it can be reasonably proposed that they are both quite old, several hundreds of thousands, if not millions, of years earlier than the Mature Harappan. Then the river was forced, again at about Nohar, to turn to the west. It was a major course adjustment, caused by the encroachment of sand according to the authors (Ghose, Kar and Husain 1980: 10). Their chronology for these events is not well developed, and they suggest for the later phases, those associated with channels numbered 3-5, that archaeological data should be of use.

Combined with the work of other scholars, this reconstruction outlined in the Central Region, suggests that there were three major early rivers in the Sindh-Rajasthan area: the Indus flowing close to the Baluchistan Mountains, the Early Sarasvati flowing in the east, along the Aravallis and a "Nara" flowing somewhere between, generally placed fairly close to the Indus.

Other Rivers of Note in the Area

The Drishadvati or Chautang

The Drishadvati River is a major factor in the Ghose, et al. (1980) reconstruction, and that of many others as well. It is a dry river; in some places its bed approaches five kilometers in breadth. It rises in the Siwaliks, close to the Sarasvati and they flow parallel to one another for some distance, but the Chautang takes a more southerly course. It then turns west, past Hisar and the well known archaeological sites of Siswal, Sothi and Nohar. It joins the Sarasvati near Suratgarh, with the sites of Kalibangan and Rang Mahal occupying places of prominence at this strategic junction. This river is reliably identified as the ancient Drishadvati, and was noted in passages in the Ṛgveda. It would have been a major contributor to the full flow of the Sarasvati as it made its way west, across the Indian frontier with Pakistan and into Cholistan.

The Naiwal

The Naiwal drainage system is complex and far from being understood in terms of its history. Three principal courses are generally presented, labeled the West Naiwal, Naiwal and East Naiwal, which begin just to the east of Ropar, near the point where the Sutlej enters the Punjab plains. Three dry beds run more or less parallel to one another, passing through Bhatinda District. The streams never meet, but join a common bed as a broad depression that runs east-west to the northeast of Hanumangarh. Following this short, but broad route, the joined Naiwal then enters the main Sarasvati beg.

Wilhelmy (1969) has proposed that the three Naiwal courses are early evolutionary stages of the Sutlej, with a gradual northwestern migration of this river. This places the Eastern Branch as the earliest and the west as the latest. Capture by the Beas River then moved the stream much farther to the north, prior to the Sutlej taking its present day middling course.

These views of the Naiwal may be too simplistic. Landsat imagery shows a far more complex

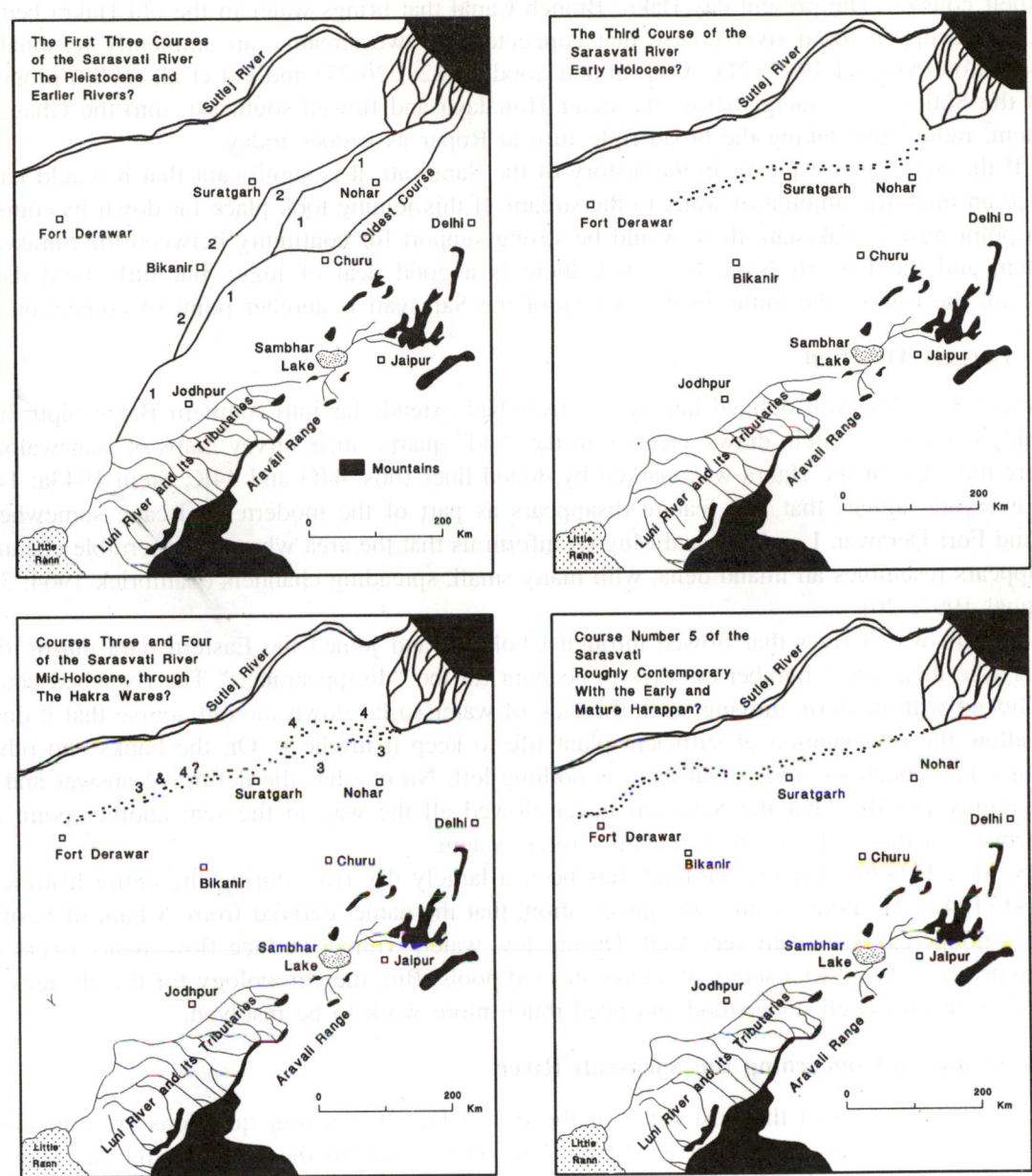

Figure 3.138. The early history of the Sarasvati, after Ghose, Kar and Husain 1980: Figure 2

set of river beds and fluvial features that may not form three well defined courses at all (Pal, et al. 1980: Figures 4 and 5). This is largely an empirical problem and it should be possible to create accurate maps of these features through an examination of satellite and other air imagery, combined with ground checking. In any event the drainage across this portion of the Punjab was important in forming the modern Sutlej River.

The Sutlej

A simple map reconnaissance reveals that the Sutlej River runs parallel to the Sarasvati for some distance and that the two streams are perilously close for much of the southerly portion of their courses. The present day Hakra Branch Canal that brings water to the old Hakra bed is said to occupy a fossil river course that connected the two streams, an eminently reasonable proposition (Mughal 1997: 21). Agrawal and Sood (1982: 226-27) and Pal et al. (1980) propose that the Sutlej once emerged from the outer Himalaya and flowed southeast, into the Ghaggar system, rather than taking the broad right turn at Ropar as it does today.

If the Sutlej was a player in the history of the Sarasvati, it is significant that it would have added an immense amount of water to the stream. If this joining took place far down its course, at a point now in Pakistan, there would be strong support for continuity between the Sarasvati system and the Eastern Nara, for which there is a good deal of logic, but little field data. Overall, the role of the Sutlej in the history of the Sarasvati is another point of contention.

The Largely Dry Bed

That a reasonably well defined largely dry river bed extends far into southern Bahawalpur has already been noted. Stein draws attention to the "old" quarter inch survey maps of Bahawalpur, where the edge of the Hakra was marked by dotted lines (nos. 44G and 44K; Stein 1943a: 14), but everyone agrees that this feature disappears as part of the modern landscape somewhere around Fort Derawar. Lambrick and Mughal inform us that the area where a discernible channel disappears resembles an inland delta, with many small, spreading channels (Lambrick 1964: 31; Mughal 1997: 26).

If there was a river that flowed through Cholistan and joined the Eastern nara during the Indus Age there are a number of ways to account for the "disappearance." The river bed could be choked with modern, moving sand, the lack of water so far down the old course that it does not allow the rejuvenation of sufficient plant life to keep it in check. Or, the banks and other features have been so eroded that there is nothing left. No one has the definitive answer and it is certainly possible that the Sarasvati never flowed all the way to the sea: another point of contention in the study of this fascinating river system.

S. M. Ali holds that the Sarasvati has been a largely dry river during the entire historical period (1942). He notes, with some justification, that the name, derived from "Chain of Pools" suits a nonperennial stream very well. During low water, without surface flow, many rivers of this type are reduced to a series of interconnected pools. But, the chronology for the changes in this river are not well understood and need much more work to be resolved.

Four Problems Concerning the Sarasvati River

Questions abound about the Lost River of the Indian Desert, but four questions are critical in understanding the environment of the Indus Age. These concern the mechanisms that control the water supply for the Sarasvati. There is also the question of whether the Sarasvati ever flowed directly to the Arabian Sea. The courses of the river system are also at issue and finally, since the river is "lost" today, what the chronology was for its drying up.

What Has Controlled the Course Changes and Drying-up?

The source of water for the Sarasvati is, in part, obvious and the drainage from the Siwaliks is and was the source for this riverine system. But, the Sarasvati was apparently an immense river in the past which means that some consideration be given to an additional source or sources. There is no convincing reason to believe that there was greater rainfall during the Indus Age.[24] The environment however, was different; several millennia of agriculture, grazing, tree felling and irrigation have altered the landscape. S. I. Siddiqi (1944, 1945) proposed that many of the changes in the Ghaggar-Hakra system have been caused by these agencies. While Siddiqi and Ali are right to point out these important agencies of environmental change, and they may have had an effect in historical times, it is hard to imagine that they were powerful forces molding the character of such a large riverine system in the remote past, or even during the Early and Mature Harappan.

The possibility of additional watershed contributing significant amounts of water to the Sarasvati is more difficult to determine. The modern drainage sits between two large rivers, the Yamuna and the Sutlej, and water from their sources could have dramatically affected the character of the Sarasvati. Tectonic movement could have shifted the water from either or both of these rivers into the Sarasvati bed, a notion that was met with when the question of subsurface drainage was used as a regulator of the water supply for the lakes of Rajasthan.

Plate tectonics have demonstrated that the landmass of peninsular India and Pakistan has joined with Asia, the suture being along the Burmese border, then across the Ganga Valley and Himalayan front and south along the Northwest Frontier and Baluchistan Mountains. The Ganga flows in a broad, deep syncline that has been filled with alluvium. The Himalaya have been pushed back and thrust up as part of this process. The Indus River flows in another syncline, a down warp and a tear as the Subcontinent pushes north. Over time, this "bump" of two continents has caused a great deal of tectonic activity, with earthquakes rumbling across the hills and plains.

The doab between the Ganga and Indus drainage is a low divide, about 500 kilometers wide, from Delhi to Bahawalpur. The relief is so small that slight shifts in surface contours can cause significant shifts in surface and subsurface drainage. When the area was being surveyed as part of the assessment of its irrigation potential, line levels were taken that accurately demonstrate this point (Baker 1840). A more simple approach is to examine the altitudes of airports and other facilities from ONC one to one million air charts. These suggest that representative elevations along the Yamuna River are in the area of 213 meters (700 feet) above mean sea level. Those along the Sutlej are in the 168 meters (550 feet) to 183 meters (600 feet) range. In the doab, moving generally east to west, readings like the following prevail: Bhiwani, 219 meters (720 feet); Hisar 213 meters (700 feet); Sirsa 198 meters (650 feet); Suratgarh 213 meters (700 feet); Fort Abbas 164 meters (537 feet). The Himalaya, with peaks approaching 9000 meters and many above 6000 meters, are within 160 kilometers (100 miles) of Delhi. But in the doab, raise the west a few meters (30, 40, 60) and the drainage heads east down the Ganga to the Bay of Bengal. Conversely, push up the east by the same modest amount and the drainage heads west down the Indus to the Arabian Sea. These are trivial changes, when the orogenic processes associated with the Himalayas are considered, and over the long run, one suspects that tectonics determined how much water flowed east down the present Ganga-Yamuna system and how much flowed west, then south down the Indus Valley. These changes do not necessarily have to be abrupt, nor need they have been directional, in the sense that there was a progressive shift of water from east to west, or west to east. But, right now, it seems that during the Indus Age the Sarasvati was a large river and that water that now flows in the Yamuna and/or Sutlej Rivers made it so. Over time these waters were withdrawn and the Sarasvati became smaller, eventually dry. The agency for these changes was the tectonic reshaping of the doab separating the Yamuna from the rivers of the Punjab. Developing a chronology for these changes is incomplete.

The Capture by the Yamuna

Many people who have studied this problem are in agreement that at one time the Chautang

River almost certainly carried a substantial amount of water that now would be counted as part of the watershed of the historical Yamuna River (e.g., "Nearchus" 1875: 351). The date for this however, is very much in debate. H. Wilhelmy's maps (1969: A, facing page 86) show an early Chautang drainage emanating from the Siwaliks at about Hardwar, with a smaller Yamuna drawing on streams farther to the east, and not coming together as a major river until it reached the vicinity of Indraprastha, modern New Delhi. Wilhelmy's active Chautang runs parallel to the Eastern Naiwal (his Vedic Sutlej); between them is the Sarasvati. While the chronology is almost certainly not right, this reconstruction of a series of active waterways is an eminently reasonable one. I place this confluence of streams somewhat earlier than Wilhelmy does.

D. N. Wadia has proposed that the Yamuna flowed through the Punjab in the Vedic era, under the name Sarasvati. "In the course of time it took a more easterly course and ultimately merged into the Ganges at Prayag. It then received the name of Jamuna" (Wadia 1966: 392).

H. T. Lambrick left no doubt as to his reconstruction:

> It becomes fairly clear that the Jamuna was at one time a contributor, by way of the ancient bed of the Chitang, itself a mile wide. The low watershed between the Indus-Hakra and the Ganges basins at the present time runs between the Chitang and the Jamuna; but the latter, an 'alluvial' river from the High Himalaya, formerly ran along this ridge, and overspilled indifferently to either hand, later slipping off the ridge to the eastward. The Chitang unites with the Ghaggar or Hakra at Bhatwar (Lambrick 1964: 30).

Pal et al. (1980), Agrawal and Sood (1982) and Agrawal (1982b) and Robert Raikes (1968a) are all in agreement concerning the near term relationship between the Sarasvati and the Yamuna. Raikes has a rather elaborate scheme, with another chronology suggesting a kind of cyclical alteration of water flowing into the Sarasvati, then being cut off, then returning again (Raikes 1968a: 290).

Marie-Agnes Courty tends to see any connection between the Yamuna watershed and the Sarasvati, via the Chautang, as very distant. This could be as old as the late Pleistocene, or the Early Holocene, but was long abandoned by the time the first villages appeared in the area in the third or fourth millennium BC (Courty 1985: 259). This is based on the presence of well developed terraces in the upper Yamuna, indicating a long history for the river in its present course, and the fact that Yamuna type alluvium is deep within the soil profile of the Chautang.

Some of her views are summarized:

> Yamuna-like rivers, rising from the Himalaya, stopped flowing in the study area well before the Protohistoric period. This assessment is based on the lack of Yamuna type alluvium at a depth less than 8 m below the present day floodplain and especially by its absence below the Protohistoric sites. Alluvium deposited during the early Holocene, just below the Protohistoric period, was similar to the Ghaggar one (Courty 1989: 259; see also Courty 1985: 30-1).

Courty's data are important and cast doubt on the chronology proposed here for the connection between the Chautang (Drishadvati), and the rest of the Sarasvati. But, the case has not yet been proved and for purposes of illustration I will continue to show this as the first stage in riverine sequence of the Indus Age, dated the Early Harappan Stage (ca. 3200-2600 BC). The proposal is provisional, however, and comes with reservations.

The Sutlej Drainage

The two principal nineteenth century commentators on the drying up of the Sarasvati have already been noted: C. F. Oldham (1874, 1893) and R. D. Oldham (1887). They both believed that the Sarasvati was fed from the Sutlej River, R. D. Oldham the more vigorous of the two in putting forth this view, since he had opposition (see also Siddiqi 1945). The principal objection of the day came from a Settlement Officer by the name of J. Wilson, who claimed that the bed of the Hakra, as seen today, is too small and lacking in depth to have ever taken the full flow of the Sutlej, which my own observations and Plate 3.76 seem to confirm. Oldham quotes a long passage from Wilson's report on settlement in Sirsa District (Wilson 1884 *in* R. D. Oldham 1887: 334), only some of which is abstracted here. It is learned that in Mr. Wilson's opinion the Hakra, he calls it the Sotar, is too shallow, and lacks the marks of violent flood action that large rivers of the Punjab have. He also notes that the soil types of the Hakra are very different from the sandy silt of the Sutlej, the Hakra being fine, fertile alluvium:

> The soil is all rich alluvial clay, such as is now being annually deposited in the depressions which are specimens of these numerous pools which have given the Sarasvati its name, 'the river of Pools'; and there seems little doubt that the same action as now goes on, has been going on for centuries, and the numerous mountain torrents of the Indo-Ganges watershed, fed, not by the snows but by the rainfall of the Sub-Himalayan ranges, wandering over the prairie in many shallow channels, joined in the Sotra or Hakra valley and formed a considerable stream, at first perhaps perennial but afterwards becoming absorbed after a gradually shortening course, as the rainfall decreased over the lower Himalayan slopes, and as the spread of irrigation in the submountain tract intercepted more and more of the annual floods... (Wilson 1884, quoted in R. D. Oldham 1887: 334).

Oldham recalls that there is no evidence for less rainfall in the past, at least in the time scale he was dealing with and that alluvial processes change over time. Another anonymous charge concerned different levels between the Hakra and the Sutlej. The Sutlej is lower and because water does not easily flow up hill, it would have been impossible for it to "fall" into the Hakra bed. Oldham treats this in terms of long-term alluvial processes and that such variation is "normal" (R. D. Oldham 1887: 335). He then concerns himself with the Greek literature on the Punjab and notes that Arrian does not mention five rivers in the area, but only four, omitting the Sutlej. He infers from this that it flowed in an independent channel, the Hakra, and there was no panjnad in that era (R. D. Oldham 1887: 336). From Ptolemy he finds reference to a "divarication" of the Indus which he takes to be the point where the Hakra was formed (R. D. Oldham 1887: 336-37). In addition to pursuing the Sutlej hypothesis R. D. Oldham also traced out the subsidiary courses of the Sarasvati, especially the Naiwal branches in Bhatinda and adjacent Districts, where three very large Mature Harappan sites have recently been reported at Lakhmirwala, Hasanpur Two and Gurnikalan One (J. P. Joshi 1986). There is more in the article, but it should be clear enough that Oldham was a lively and capable man when it came to making a point.

H. T. Lambrick, who sees both Yamuna and Sutlej water contributing to the flow of the Sarasvati has noted how complex the history of the two rivers might be:

> On the opposite, that is the right bank, there are traces of flood channels from old beds of the Sutlej, or it may sometimes have been the entire Sutlej River, joining the Hakra in three widely separated places. The furthest upstream and least distinct of these seems to have come in at Bhatnir, some twenty-five miles above the junction of the Chitang. Next in order, an ancient winding bed of the Sutlej, unites with the Hakra at Walhar (Fort Abbas GLP), just within the border of Bahawalpur. This appears

to derive from an old course of the Sutlej which flowed past Bhatinda and Malot, and its general alignment has been followed by the Hakra Branch Canal. The third of these connecting channels runs down from about 20 miles ENE of Bahawalpur City, and meets the Hakra near Kudwala. Its general direction has been followed by another irrigation canal, the Desert Branch; but we have been told that it was previously 'a large dry channel called Vahind, a feeder of the Sankara' (Buckley 1893: 156). Thirty miles or so below this junction, in the neighborhood of Derawal, the single wide bed of the Hakra seems to develop into a sort of delta of smaller channels (Lambrick 1964: 30-1).

These are huge swings for the Sutlej but again, in relatively flat terrain that is also tectonically active such things can happen.

Wilhelmy (1969) as well as Bimal Ghose and his team also have found evidence that the Sutlej has, from time to time, contributed water as a western confluence of the Sarasvati (Ghose, Kar and Husain 1979, 1980: 10).

Given the evidence, it is reasonable to propose that the Sutlej watershed was an important source of water for the Sarasvati system during the Indus Age. Three stages in the evolution of the modern Sutlej might be identified and roughly correlated with the Eastern Naiwal, the Naiwal itself and the western Naiwal. This should be qualified by recalling that Pal, et al. (1980) have illustrated satellite imagery indicating more complexity in the fluvial history of Bhatinda and surrounding Districts than such a simple typology might indicate.

My reconstruction of the history of the Sutlej connection to the Sarasvati basically follows that of Wilhelmy (1969), with a revision of chronology. The work of Pande (1977), Lambrick (as noted) and the archaeological research in Cholistan conducted by M. Rafique Mughal (1981, 1982, 1990a, 1994, 1997), have also been used.

Did the Sarasvati Ever Flow to the Sea?

There is no direct, physical evidence to suggest that the Sarasvati ever flowed uninterrupted to the Arabian Sea, as proposed by D. N. Wadia (1966: 393; Mughal 1994: 51)[25]. This is discussed and illustrated by H. Wilhelmy (1969: 90, Figure 4), who suggests a distant connection, well before the Indus Age. But there are some tantalizing observations that keep this issue alive, the first of which is the almost compelling logic for the continuity of the river. After all, great rivers do not normally simply stop in the middle of nowhere, although the Amu Darya, for example, never reaches the sea, so it does happen. The Vedic pundits thought that the Sarasvati went to the sea: "Pure in her course from the mountains to the ocean, alone of streams Sarasvati hath listened" (Ṛgveda Book VII, Hymn 95, Verse 2; Griffith 1896: Vol. II, 99; see also Ṛgveda Book VI, Hymn 61, Verse 2). Given the other thoughts on this river that one finds in the Ṛgveda, this observation has to be treated critically, not literally.

On the other hand, both M. R. Mughal (1997: 26) and H. T. Lambrick (1964: 31) have pointed to an inland delta in the vicinity of Fort Derawar (his Derawal), that can be sustained on the scene by anyone with a knowledgeable eye. Another delta feature can be seen on landsat imagery. One of the palaeochannels in Pakistan:

> "...ends as a shallow depression near Beriwala. On the landsat imagery the lower course looks as if it debouched into the sea, but obviously it was unlikely that the sea was so far inland in Mid-Holocene. It is possible, however, that the chain of tectonic events which diverted the Sutlej and the easterly rivers away from the Ghaggar, caused a depression into which the Ghaggar, deprived of its major source of water, died into a lake-like depression (Agrawal and Sood 1982: 236).

Given the absence of human habitation around this feature near Beriwala, it was probably a delta that formed earlier than the time periods referred to here (Figure 3.139). But, the delta around Fort Derawar is another matter. This was densely settled during Hakra Wares times as well as during the Mature Harappan (Mughal 1990c: Figures 3 and 5; 1997: 9). The settlement patterns for these periods in the Fort Derawar area show the kind of dense, widespread, definitely not linear, pattern that such a delta would support (Mughal 1982: Figures 7.1 and 7.2; (Figures 3.140, Figure 3.141, Figure 3.142, Figure 3.143)."

Some attempt has been made to link up possible courses of the ancient river using the alignment of sites. These settlement data suggest that there were actually two courses for the river in the vicinity of Fort Derawar. Modern maps show a bifurcation of old channels at a place called Kanganwala, ca. 16 kilometers northeast of this fort (see Figure 3.140), which is taken here to have been a possible point where the river split during the Indus Age. It should be noted, however, that all of the reconstructions used here are based only on the logic of the settlement map, they have not been confirmed on the ground, or even through the use of aerial photography. The former is a necessary step for a final reconstruction.

The presence of the inland delta southwest of Fort Derawar suggests that all, or most, of the Sarasvati's water was "sopped up" in this area where it would have been used for intensive agriculture and pastoralism. There seems to have been enough water to support intensive agriculture but not enough to push through to the Eastern Nara, during the second and third millennia BC.

From Fort Derawar, for about 150 kilometers in a southwesterly direction, there is nothing that resembles the remains of an ancient river; just sand dunes and old alluvium. But then, in the middle of the desert, about 50 kilometers southeast of the modern city of Rahim Yar Khan, something new can be seen; the well developed course of not one, but two rivers, the Raini Nullah and the Wahinda (Wilhelmy 1969: Figure 4). Lambrick has described this important junction:

> The Raini on the whole deserves its title of 'Nullah,' for it is a deep water course, not more than forty yards wide in places, with steep banks some fifteen or twenty feet high. The country on either side—hard alluvium with sand hills—slopes down to it perceptibly from either side. The bed of the Wahinda on the other hand is wide and flat, and in many places difficult to recognize among the drift sand. One has the impression that great floods occasionally rolled down the Wahinda, filling up all the open places between the sand hills for miles, and not perhaps progressing to a very great distance southward; but that more often the spill water kept to the Raini—far exceeding its capacity for a while, but flowing down the steeper declivity, and scouring out the central nullah (Lambrick 1964: 31-2).

The Raini Nullah and the Wahinda flow in a long "hollow" lower than the Indus on the west and the Thar Desert on the east. Their waters today are completely assimilated by irrigation and they do not join the major river course of the desert fringe, the Eastern Nara, although there is no insurmountable problem in seeing this as a continuum in the prehistoric past.

Based on the presence of the Fort Derawar inland delta that was densely settled in Hakra Wares and Mature Harappan times, along with the lack of physical evidence for a dry river bed between Fort Derawar and the Raini/Wahinda, it seems unlikely that the ancient Sarasvati flowed to the sea during these times. The absence of a river scar suggests that the same is true for later periods. It is not even likely Sarasvati flowed to the sea in this westerly course, in very ancient times, prior to the Hakra wares Stage (3800-3200 BC). The early history of the drainage system

374

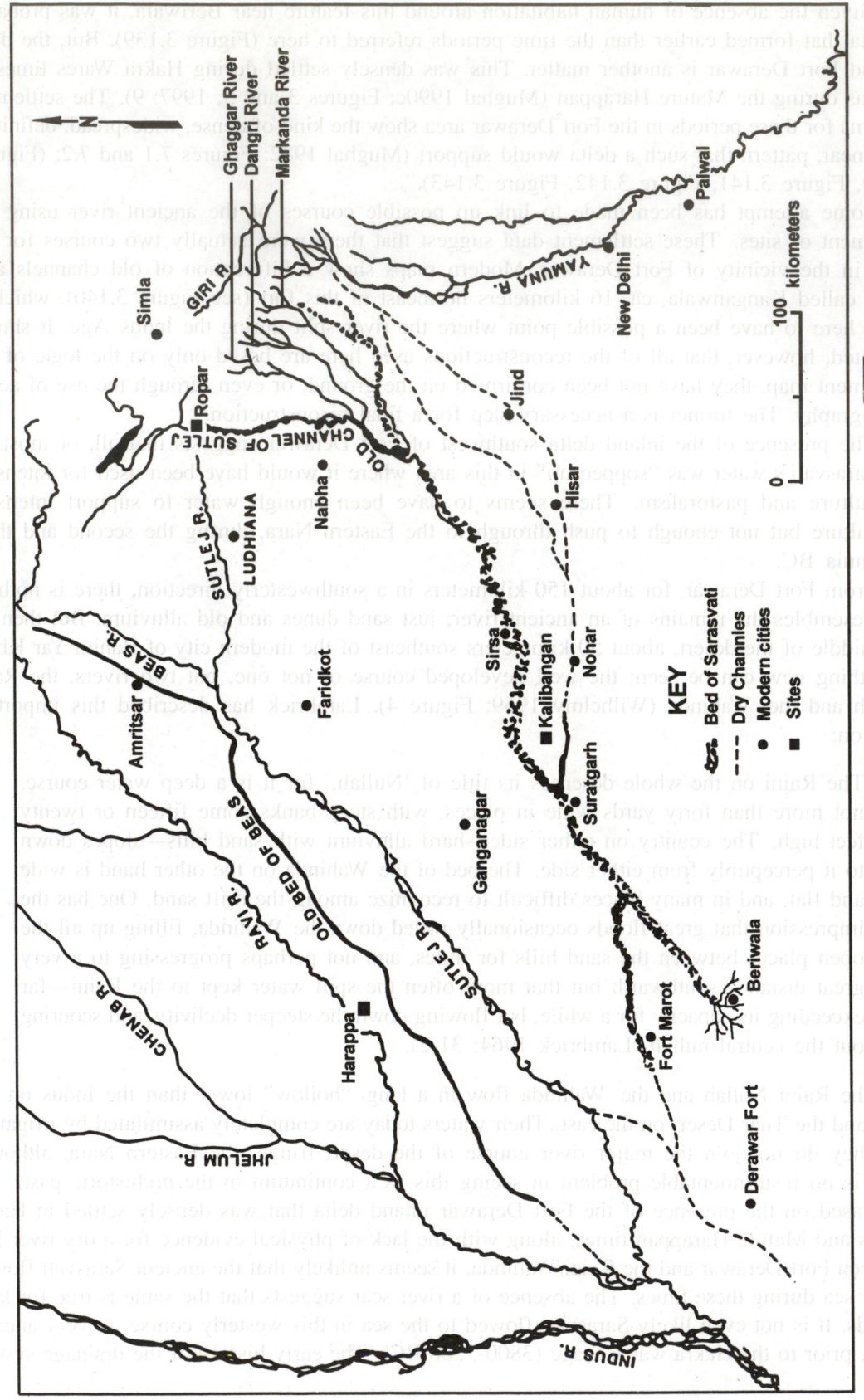

Figure 3.139. The Sarasvati with the inland delta shown near Beriwala

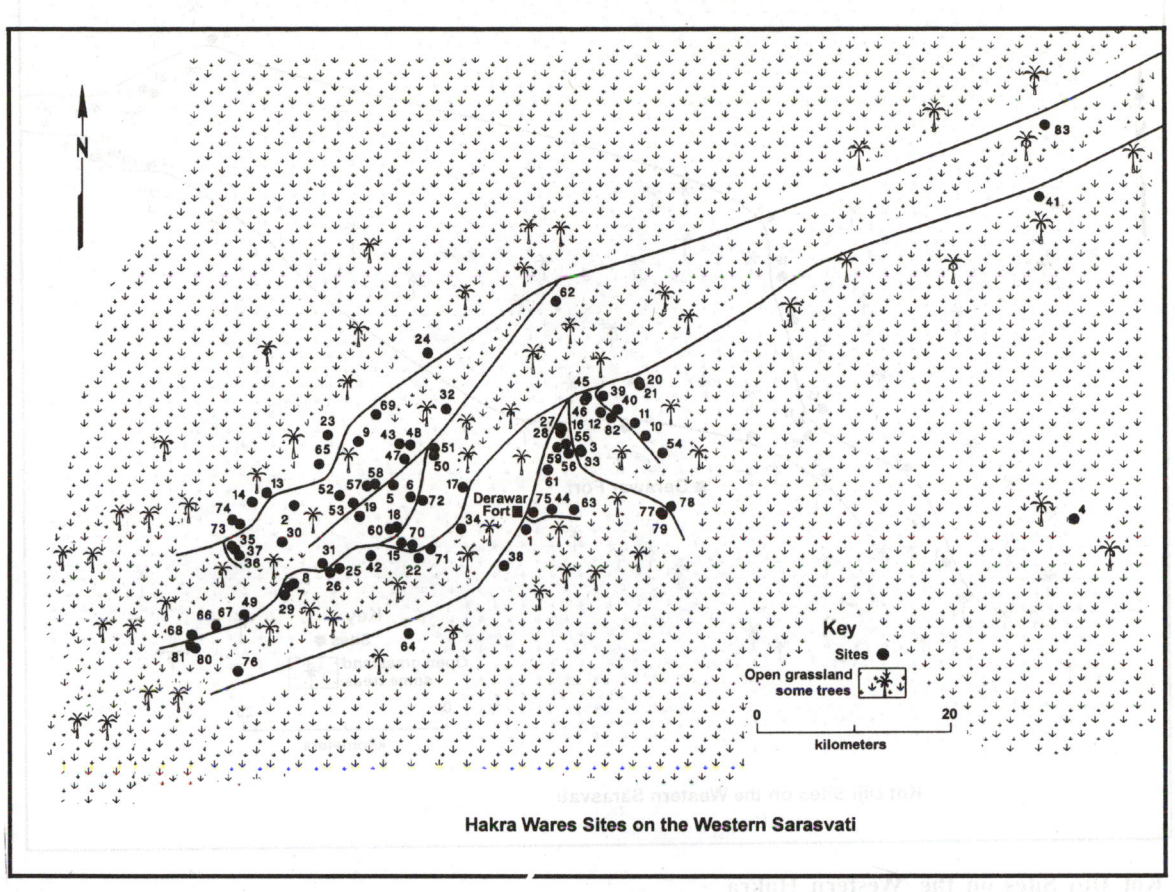

Hakra Wares Sites on the Western Sarasvati

Hakra Wares Sites on the Western Sarasvati

1. Abduwali	2. Ashi One	3. Akkanwali Theri	4. Ambrawali
5. Azimwala Two	6. Azimwali 'C'	7. Badakwala Four	8. Badalwala Four
9. Baggewali	10. Bahilawala 'B'	11. Bhilawala 'C'	12. Bandwali
13. Bhootanwala 'C'	14. Bhootanwali Two	15. Chandnewala 'C'	16. Changalawala 'C'
17. Chaudhryanwala	18. Chikrala	19. Chore	20. Dabli East
21. Dabli West	22. Darkhanwala Ther	23. Gajjuwala Two	24. Hotewala Two
25. Jafawala Three	26. Jafawala Two	27. Jalwali'A'	28. Jalwali 'B'
29. Jangipur	30. Jawaiwala Two	31. Jhalar	32. Kalharwala 'B'
33. Khan Kandewala 'D'	34. Khanpuri Two	35. Khiplewali	36. Khiplewali Three
37. Khiplewali 'D'	38. Kikri Two	39. Killianwali	40. Killianwali 'D'
41. Kuchanwala	42. Lakhman	43. Lathwala Two	44. Litanwal Four
45. Lundewali Four	46. Lundewali Three	47. Luppewala	48. Luppewala Three
49. Mehwali Two	50. Merechi Kanda	51. Merechi Khanda Two	52. Musafarwali
53. Musafarwali Two	54. Naharnwala	55. Naharwali	56. Naharwali 'B'
57. Niwaniwala Three	59. Oinwala Ther	60. Parhara	61. Payunewala Bhit Three
62. Payunewala Bhit Two	63. Qadir Bux Theri	64. Rahmanwali	65. Sadwala Kanda
66. Safuwala Two	67. Safuwal Three	68. Safuwala Two	69. Sanukewala Two
70. Sherwala Three	71. Sheruwal Two	72. Shidiwala 'A'	73. Sohniwali Two
74. Sohniwali Two	75. Thoom Thali	76. Thoriwala	77. Turawewala 'B'
78. Turawewali Theri	80. Valwala Two	81. Valwali	82. Waddenwali
83. Wariyal 'C'			

Figure 3.140. Map of Mughal's Hakra Wares settlements in the vicinity of Fort Derawar, after Mughal 1990c: Figure 3; 1997

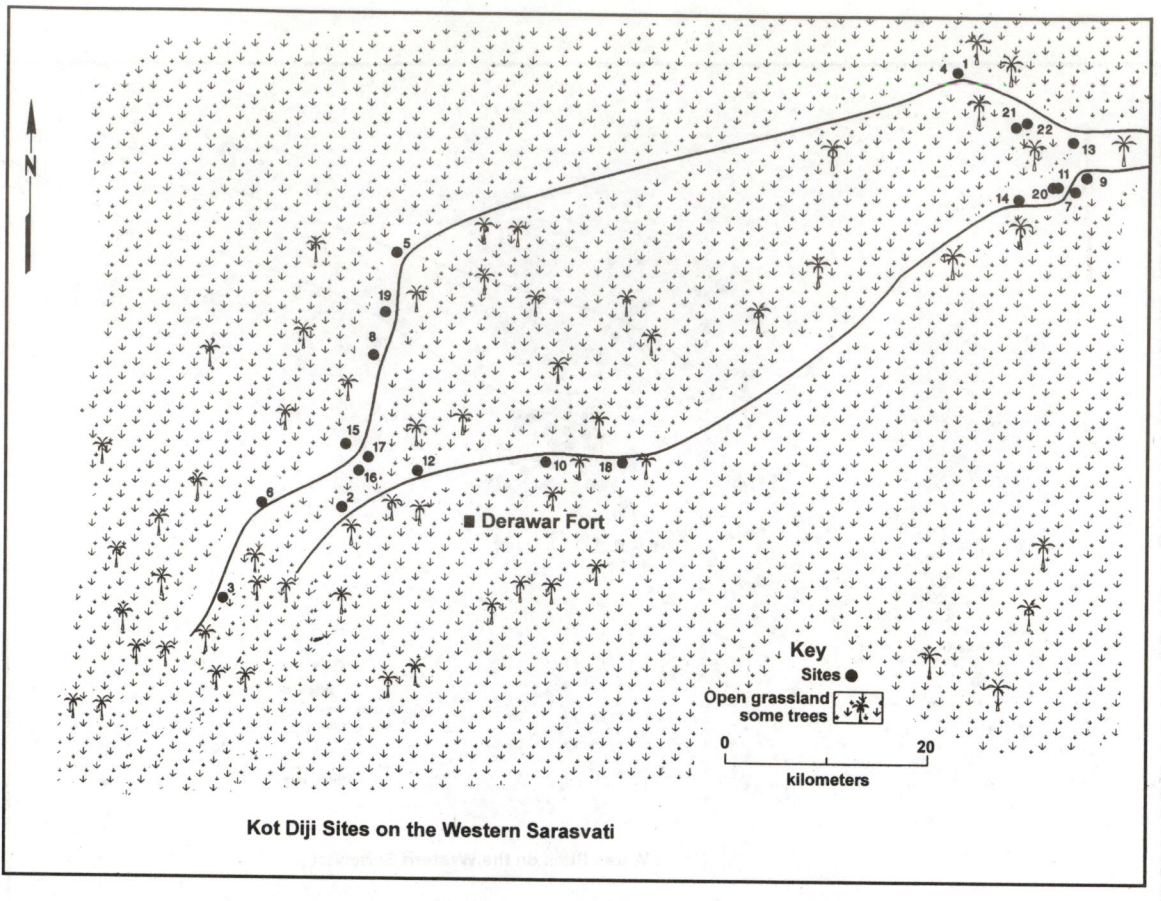

Kot Diji Sites on the Western Sarasvati

Kot Diji Sites on the Western Hakra

1. Ali Mohammad Wala Ther	2. Azimwali 'B'	3. Badalwala Three	4. Chak 045
5. Chak 076	6. Gemuwali	7. Guddal 'B'	8. Hotewala Ther 'A'
9. Januwala	10. Januwali Dhar	11. Jatoiwala 'A'	12. Jhumtiwala
13. Kaliwaryal	14. Kuchanwala	15. Lathwala	16. Luppewala Two
17. Merechi Kanda Three	18. Naharnwala	19. Sidduwali 'C'	20. Wakkarwala
21. Wariyal 'A'	22. Wariyal 'D'		

Figure 3.141. Map of Mughal's Kot Diji settlements in the vicinity of Fort Derawar, after Mughal 1990c: Figure 4

seems to have been documented to the east, in Rajasthan as shown on Figure 3.138 and discussed in Ghose, Amal Kar and Husain (1980). The Pleistocene, possibly the Tertiary, history of the Sarasvati/Drishadvati drainage is well southeast of the now dry beds, and the river system seems to have progressively moved to the north and west. Thus, in spite of the alignment of the Sarasvati with the Eastern Nara it may well be that these two rivers were never one. If there was a river connection tying the Eastern Nara-Raini-Wahinda to the Himalaya it would have probably been via one of the ancient beds of the Sutlej-Beas, but this again in Pleistocene or even earlier times.

The Eastern Nara has been an active river course for millennia, but seems to have had its ebbs and flows, as it were. As with many of the old river courses on the plains of the Indus and its tributaries, this has now became a managed stream, rejuvenated by irrigation engineers, and is more of a canal than a river. It has been straightened, leveled, and the flow of water regulated by headworks behind the Lloyd Barrage at Sukkur (Fraser 1958: 348). In the nineteenth century Eastern Nara was not a vital stream, and the Sukkur headworks was constructed in the mid-1850s. One of the supervisors of this project was Captain J. H. Kirby who came across a buried settlement in August 1855 that may date to the Mature Harappan (Bellasis 1857: 471-73; see also Burnes 1835; Jacob 1857 and Fife et al. 1857). Water was regularly introduced into the Eastern Nara in 1857, and the transformation of another river into an artifact, at the hands of irrigation engineers, continued unabated from that date.

Circumstantial evidence suggests that the main course of the Indus River has flowed down this eastern course from time to time, over the millennia; just as it has flowed to the west, close to the Kirthar piedmont. The best reconstruction for the main course in the third millennium BC (Figure 3.123) places it farther west than its present bed, leaving the Eastern Nara an open channel, almost certainly a smaller stream than the Indus proper, but still an active water course, moving along the edge of a desert. It is not known where the water came from. Was it a connection to the main Indus course, perhaps just above the northern end of the Rohri Hills? Did it follow today's man-made connection or was it a connection to the Sarasvati? These are the best hypotheses. The connection to the Sarasvati seems to be the most reasonable, keeping in mind that no one really knows the answer. It certainly deserves attention as one of the more significant problems in the reconstruction of the environment of the Greater Indus Region during Early and Mature Harappan times.

Where Did the Ancient Sarasvati System Flow?

Kalibangan is one of the premier Early and Mature Harappan sites on the middle Sarasvati. It sits on the alluvial scarp above the bed of the river at the strategic junction of the Sarasvati with the Drishadvati. This location, out of the river bed and at the junction of the two principal streams, is convincing testimony to the proposition that these rivers were active, perennial rivers at the time the site was occupied (ca. 3200-2000 BC). Low water flow, during the winter, may have reduced their flow in a significant way, perhaps even to a chain of pools in some years. But during the monsoon they would have been active, meandering within the present banks lined with sand dunes, perhaps even filling these with water from time to time. There are some qualifications for the Drishadvati because the French exploratory team has demonstrated that there are Bronze Age archaeological sites within the bed of this river (Francfort 1992: 95-6). But the Drishadvati is broad and there is ample room for an active river of at least modest size to be squeezed into this topography, without harming the archaeological remains.

Using archaeological settlement data, the research and insights of H. T. Lambrick, H. Wilhelmy, and a host of Indian and Pakistani scholars, along with some internal logic, three stages in the life of the Sarasvati River system have been illustrated. The first is the river at ca. 3000 BC. The second illustrates the river during the Mature Harappan (2500-2000 BC). The third stage is for the Post-urban Harappan in the region (c. 2000-1500 BC), (Figure 3.144, Figure 3.145, Figure 3.146). The chronology for this scheme is actually founded in archaeological data and the study of settlement patterns of the Indus Age.

What is the Chronology for the Drying Up of the Sarasvati?

Robert Raikes, the hydrologist who conducted archaeological exploration, along with his other professional duties, and who proposed the famous, but now discredited theory, that a natural dam on the Indus River caused the abandonment of Mohenjo-daro and other settlements at Sindh (Raikes 1964), carried out a brief environmental survey at Kalibangan in 1968 (Raikes

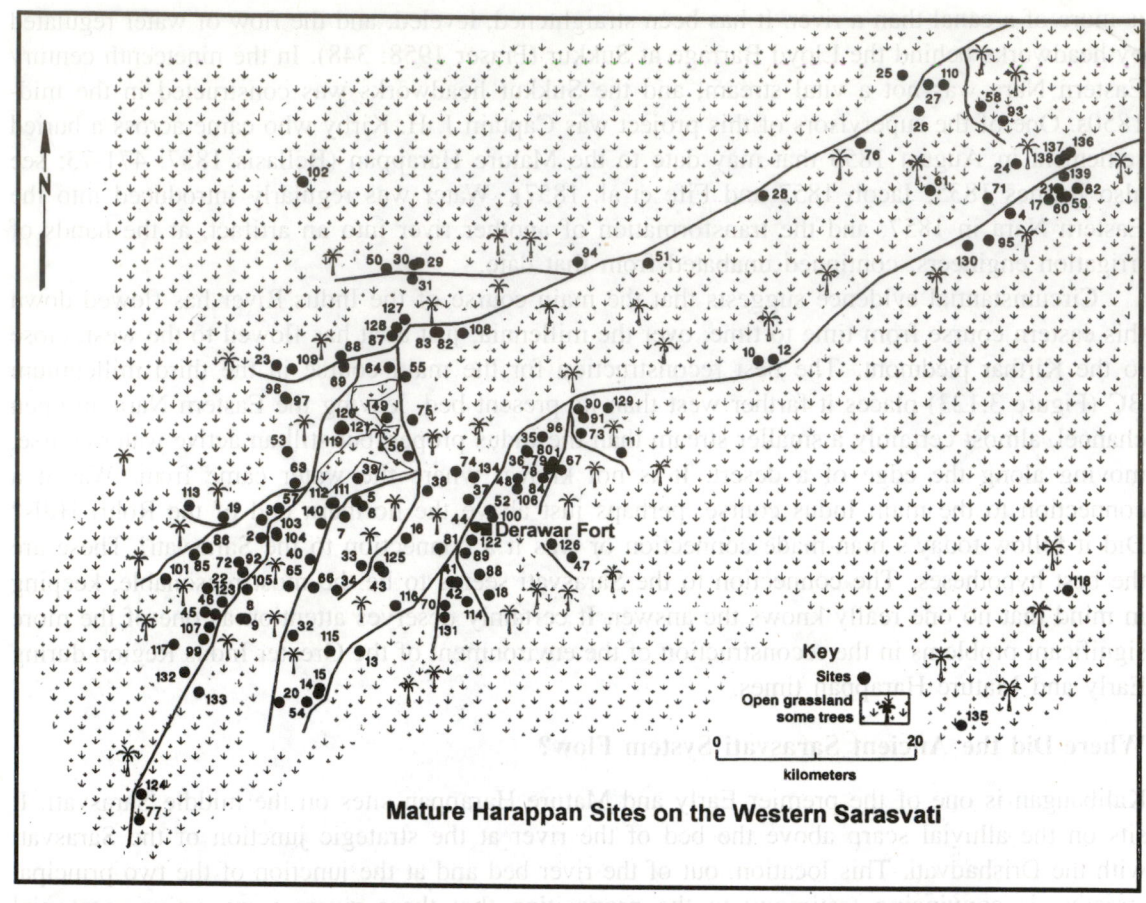

Mature Harappan Sites on the Western Sarasvati

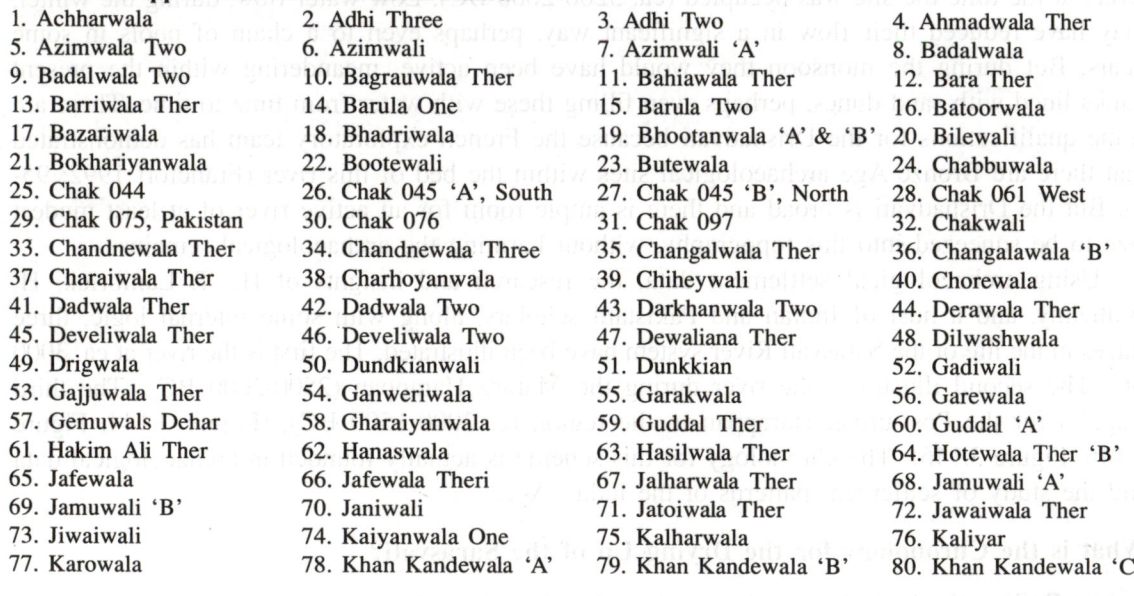

Mature Harappan Sites on the Western Hakra

1. Achharwala	2. Adhi Three	3. Adhi Two	4. Ahmadwala Ther
5. Azimwala Two	6. Azimwali	7. Azimwali 'A'	8. Badalwala
9. Badalwala Two	10. Bagrauwala Ther	11. Bahiawala Ther	12. Bara Ther
13. Barriwala Ther	14. Barula One	15. Barula Two	16. Batoorwala
17. Bazariwala	18. Bhadriwala	19. Bhootanwala 'A' & 'B'	20. Bilewali
21. Bokhariyanwala	22. Bootewali	23. Butewala	24. Chabbuwala
25. Chak 044	26. Chak 045 'A', South	27. Chak 045 'B', North	28. Chak 061 West
29. Chak 075, Pakistan	30. Chak 076	31. Chak 097	32. Chakwali
33. Chandnewala Ther	34. Chandnewala Three	35. Changalwala Ther	36. Changalawala 'B'
37. Charaiwala Ther	38. Charhoyanwala	39. Chiheywali	40. Chorewala
41. Dadwala Ther	42. Dadwala Two	43. Darkhanwala Two	44. Derawala Ther
45. Develiwala Ther	46. Develiwala Two	47. Dewaliana Ther	48. Dilwashwala
49. Drigwala	50. Dundkianwali	51. Dunkkian	52. Gadiwali
53. Gajjuwala Ther	54. Ganweriwala	55. Garakwala	56. Garewala
57. Gemuwals Dehar	58. Gharaiyanwala	59. Guddal Ther	60. Guddal 'A'
61. Hakim Ali Ther	62. Hanaswala	63. Hasilwala Ther	64. Hotewala Ther 'B'
65. Jafewala	66. Jafewala Theri	67. Jalharwala Ther	68. Jamuwali 'A'
69. Jamuwali 'B'	70. Janiwali	71. Jatoiwala Ther	72. Jawaiwala Ther
73. Jiwaiwali	74. Kaiyanwala One	75. Kalharwala	76. Kaliyar
77. Karowala	78. Khan Kandewala 'A'	79. Khan Kandewala 'B'	80. Khan Kandewala 'C'

Contd. on next page

Figure 3.142. Map of Mughal's Mature Harappan settlements in the vicinity of Fort Derawar, after Mughal 1990c: Figure 5

1968a). He worked with R. K. Karanth of the Geological Survey of India and the staff of the Archaeological Survey of India. Four bore holes were excavated in the bed of the Sarasvati due north of Kalibangan. An analysis of recovered materials suggests that "The general hypothesis, which emerges from the calculations..., is of alternating capture of the Yamuna by the Indus and Ganges systems respectively. That the low and almost indiscernible watershed between the two systems and the slow migration of the Yamuna across its floodplain under the influence of *coriolis* force (or deflection force due to the earth's rotation) would result inevitably in a right-bank avulsion somewhere near where Indri now stands" (Raikes 1968a: 289). Table 3.38 gives the stages and dates:

TABLE 3.38
The Changes in the Sarasvati River at Kalibangan

Westward diversion to Indus 2500-1700 BC (coinciding with Harappan occupation)	750 years
Eastward diversion to Ganga 1750-1100 BC (coinciding with abandonment)	650 years
Westward diversion to Indus 1100-500 BC (coinciding with Painted Gray Ware sites)	600 years
Eastward diversion to Ganga 500-100 BC (coinciding with abandonment)	400 years
Westward diversion to Indus 100 BC-500 AD (coinciding with Early Historic)	600 years
Eastward diversion to Ganga in about 500 AD (coinciding with abandonment)	

(Raikes 1968a: 290)

The notion that the abandonment of Kalibangan, and many other Mature Harappan sites in its region, was due to changes in the flow of the Sarasvati is widely accepted. Whether or not the system switched back and forth according to Raikes' model is somewhat in doubt. Given the research of the Indo-French Archaeological Mission in the bed of the Chautang, where

81. Khanpuri	82. Khetranwali One	83. Khetranwali Two	84. Khingarwali
85. Khiplewala	86. Khiplewala Two	87. Khohi Siddhuwali	88. Kikri
89. Kikriwala Ther	90. Killianwali 'B'	91. Killianwali 'C'	92. Kippianwala
93. Kudwala Ther	94. Kuruwala	95. Lal Patel	96. Lundewali Ther
97. Lunida One	98. Lunida Two	99. Mahawala Ther	100. Mahiwali
101. Mashinewala	102. Mehmudabad	103. Mehrianwala Ther	104. Mehrianwali Two
105. Mehrindawala Ther	106. Mehruband Ther	107. Mehwali	108. Mirana
109. Mubarak Ther West	110. Naujhalwala	111. Niwaniwala Ther East	112. Niwaniwala Two
113. Noor Shah Ther	114. Qasaiwala	115. Rappwala Ther	116. Runwali
117. Safuwala Four	118. Sanghewala	119. Sanukewala	120. Sanukewala Three
121. Sanukewala Two	122. Sauransanda	123. Sheikhri Two	124. Sheikhwali
125. Sheruwala Ther	126. Shikarwala Ther	127. Siddhuwali 'B'	128. Siddhuwali 'D'
129. Sullewala	130. Tarsoolwala	131. Tharulawala Ther	132. Tharwala
133. Thoriwala	134. Trekoe	135. Waddanwala	136. Wariyal Ther
137. Wariyal 'E'	138. Wariyal 'F'	139. Wariyal 'H'	140. Wasuwala Ther

380

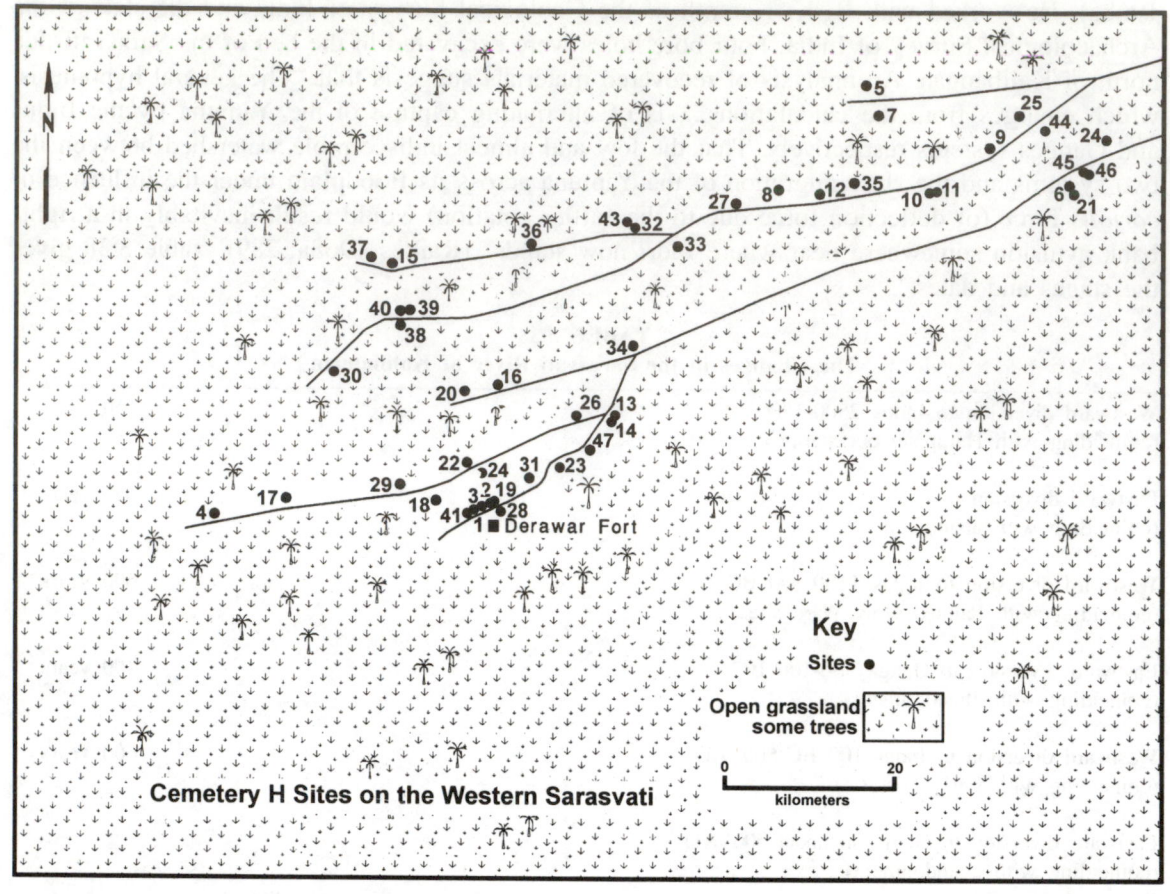

Cemetery H Sites on the Western Sarasvati

1. Bazariwali 'A'	2. Bazariwali 'B'	3. Bazariwali 'C'	4. Bhootanwali
5. Boharwala Ther	6. Bokhariyanwala 'A'	7. Chak 051	8. Chak 061 East
9. Chak 069	10 Chak 088 'A' West	11 Chak 088, Pakistan	12 Chak 107
13 Cheelanwali	14. Cheelanwali 'B'	15. Dabli Theri	16. Daiwala
17. Gemuwala ther	18. Khetwal Ther	19. Kudwala Ther	20. Lomriwala
21. Lundewali Two	22. Lurewala	23. Magrejewali	24.Marechiwala
25. Mubarakwala Ther	26. Payuna Bhit	27. Ratta Ther	28. Rawewala
29. Rohatwala	30. Shahiwala	31. Shaikhanwala Ther	32. Siddhuwala Ther
33. Siddhuwali 'E'	34. Siddhuwali 'F'	35. Singharwali	36. Trekoe
37. Turanwala	38. Wariyal 'B'	39. Wariyal 'G'	40. Wariyal 'H'
41. Wavriwala			

Figure 3.143. Map of Mughal's Cemetery H settlements in the vicinity of Fort Derawar, after Mughal 1990c:
Figure 6

many Protohistoric sites were found, it seems that this route between the Yamuna watershed and the westward drainage was shut off early as a major water course; a course of more than just local importance. Since the Chautang route is the most plausible from the geographical point of view, the data from the bore holes at Kalibangan should be reinterpreted.

M. Rafique Mughal believes that during the Early Harappan period the Hakra River was perennial since there are sites located all along its course, from the northeast to southwest, beyond Fort Derawar (Mughal 1990c: 146). His observation can still be supported.

381

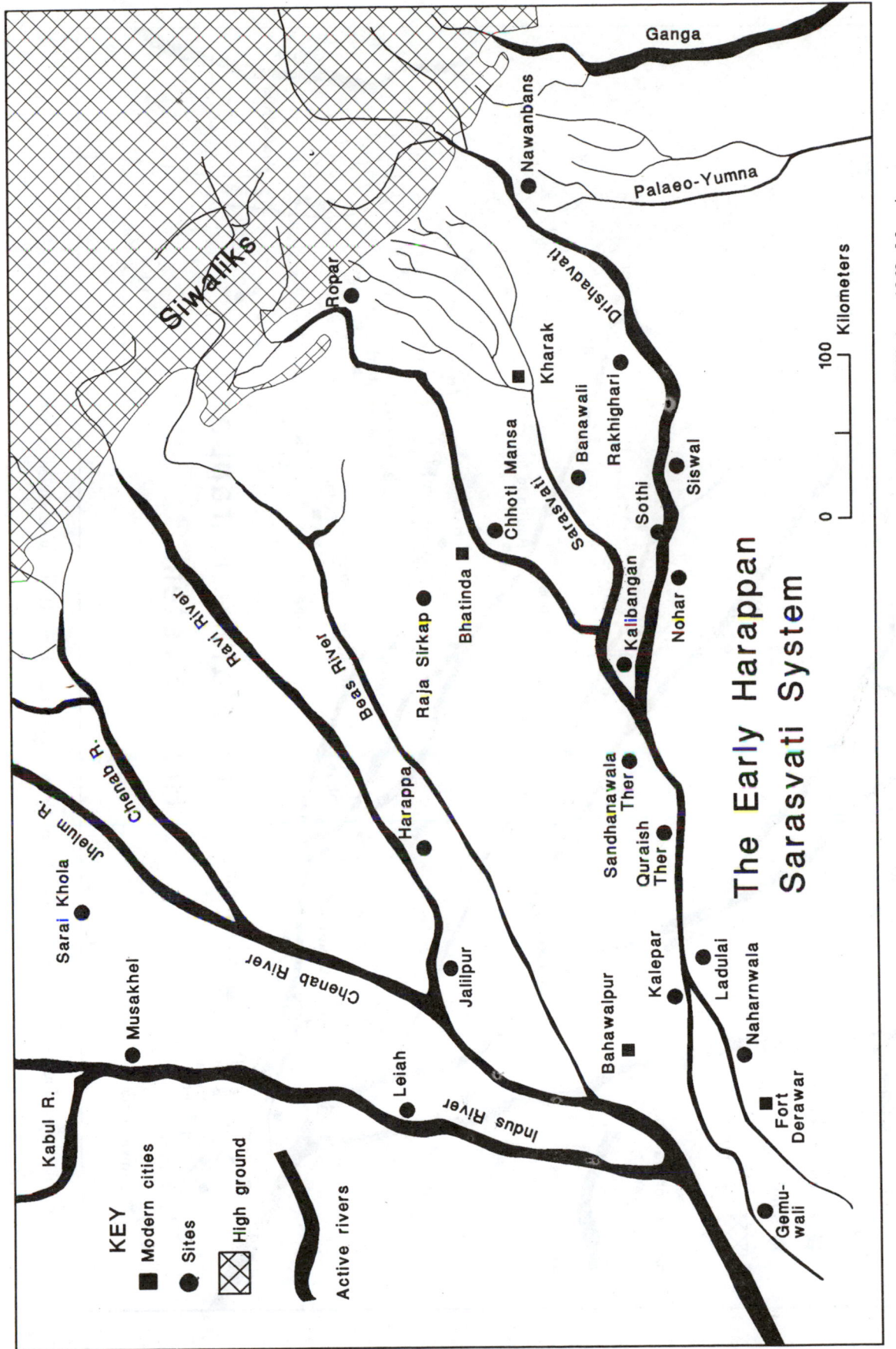

Figure 3.144. The Sarasvati River system during the Early Harappan Stage, modified from Wilhelmy 1969: Map A

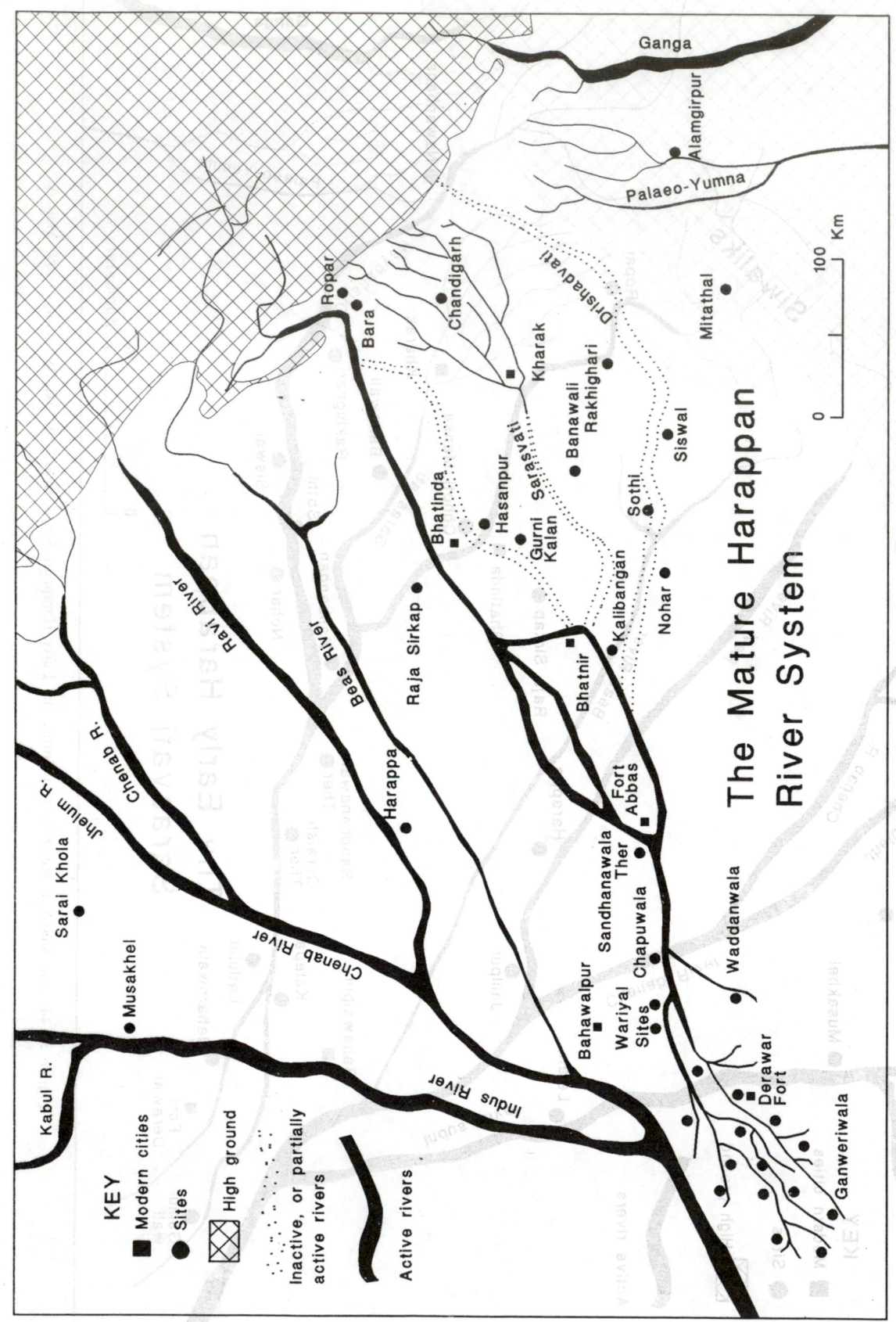

Figure 3.145. The Sarasvati River system during the Mature Harappan, modified from Wilhelmy 1969: Map B

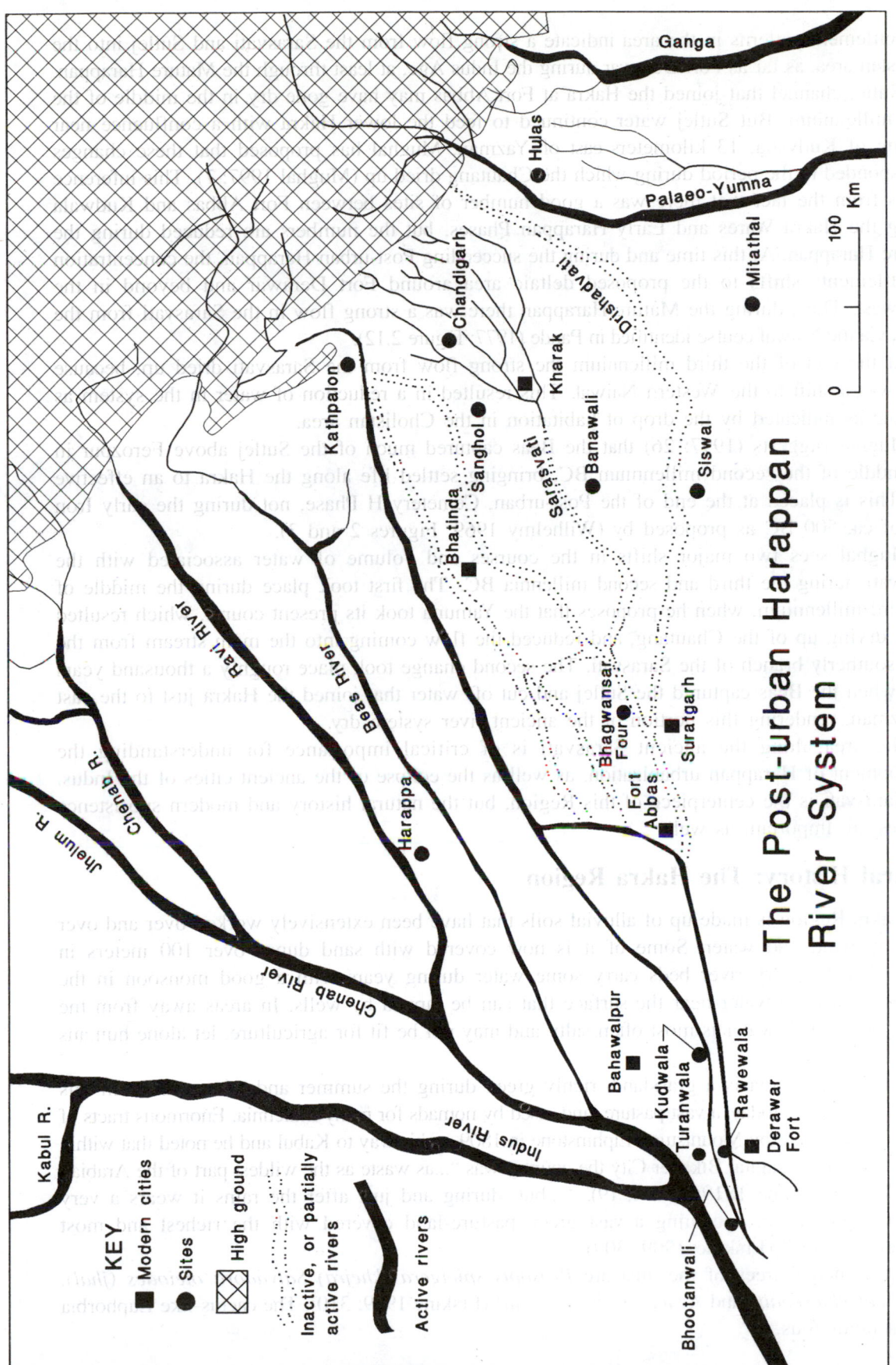

Figure 3.146. The Sarasvati River system during the Post-urban Harappan, modified from Wilhelmy 1969: Map C

Settlement patterns in the area indicate a strong flow from the Sarasvati and Sutlej into the Cholistan area, as far as Fort Derawar during the Indus Age, at least through the Mature Harappan. The Sutlej channel that joined the Hakra at Fort Abbas may have gone dry in the middle of the third millennium. But Sutlej water continued to feed the lower Hakra with a confluence near the site of Kudwala, 13 kilometers east of Yazman. Mughal has proposed that these changes corresponded to the period during which the Chautang dried up (Mughal 1997: 7). This inference comes from the fact that there was a good number of sites between Fort Abbas and Kudwala during the Hakra Wares and Early Harappan Phases, but the numbers are reduced during the Mature Harappan. At this time and during the succeeding Post-urban Harappan, the concentration of settlements shifts to the proposed deltaic area around Fort Derawar and beyond in the southwest. Thus, during the Mature Harappan there was a strong flow in the Sarasvati from the Sutlej, via the Naiwal course identified in Pande (1977: Figure 2.12).

At the end of the third millennium the strong flow from the Sarasvati dried up, because there was a shift to the Western Naiwal. This resulted in a reduction of water in the system as a whole as indicated by the drop of habitation in the Cholistan area.

Mughal suggests (1997: 26) that the Beas captured much of the Sutlej above Ferozpur in the middle of the second millennium BC, bringing settled life along the Hakra to an effective halt. This is placed at the end of the Post-urban, Cemetery H Phase, not during the early Iron Age of ca. 500 BC as proposed by (Wilhelmy 1969: Figures 2 and 3).

Mughal sees two major shifts in the courses and volume of water associated with the Sarasvati during the third and second millennia BC. The first took place during the middle of the third millennium, when he proposes that the Yamuna took its present course, which resulted in the drying up of the Chautang, and reduced the flow coming into the main stream from the long, southerly branch of the Sarasvati. The second change took place roughly a thousand years later, when the Beas captured the Sutlej and cut off water that joined the Hakra just to the east of Yazman, rendering this portion of the ancient river system dry.

The area along the ancient Sarasvati is of critical importance for understanding the development of Harappan urbanization, as well as the eclipse of the ancient cities of the Indus. The Sarasvati is the centerpiece of this Region, but the natural history and modern subsistence regimes are important as well.

Natural History: The Hakra Region

The Hakra Region is made up of alluvial soils that have been extensively worked over and over again by wind and water. Some of it is now covered with sand dunes over 100 meters in height. The low, dry river beds carry some water during years with a good monsoon in the Siwaliks and have water near the surface that can be tapped by wells. In areas away from the river systems well water is most often salty and may not be fit for agriculture, let alone humans and animals.

Much of the area is a grassland, richly green during the summer and winter rains. In this sense it was, and is today, a vast pasture land, used by nomads for many millennia. Enormous tracts of sand were seen here by Mountstuart Elphinstone in 1809 on his way to Kabul and he noted that within a few yards of the capital Bikaner City the country was "...as waste as the wildest part of the Arabian Desert" (Elphinstone 1819: Vol. I, 19). "...but, during and just after the rains it wears a very different appearance, becoming a vast green pasture-land covered with the richest and most succulent grasses" (Erskine 1909: 309).

The principal trees of the area are *Prosopis spicigera* (*khejra*) *Salvadora oleiodes* (*jhal*), *Acacia catechu* (*khair*) and *Acacia arabica* (*babul*) (Erskine 1909: 310). The cactus-like Euphorbia (*tor*) is ubiquitous.

The animal life in the area is not so different from the Northern Region. Of special interest is the frequent note that the onager was present in some numbers in older times (Erskine 1909: 311) and that hunting them was thought to be good sport. Wild pigs (*Sus scrofa*) abounded in the bed of the Ghaggar, where there was good, soft soil in which they could root. Blackbuck (*Antelope cervicapra*) and the Indian Gazelle or Chinkara (*Gazella bennetti*) were plentiful (Erskine 1909: 311-12).

One of the reasons that this area is so dry is that it is caught on the edges of both the southwest monsoon and the winter westerlies. Bikaner receives 306 millimeters of rain in the average year and Ganganagar 238 millimeters. These are averages for 50 years, 1901-51 (Krishna Rao 1962). Bahawalpur receives about 152 millimeters (Din 1904: Table 4). As in many desert areas, the difference between day and night time temperatures can be great and it is said that it freezes in winter in Bikaner (Erskine 1909: 312-13).

The mineral resources of this Region are virtually nonexistent, except for a few quarries of various kinds of specialized stone, apparently not used in antiquity. Tod mentions an unctuous clay that comes from Kolath: "It is used chiefly to free the skin and hair from impurities and the Cutchie ladies are said to eat it to improve their complexions" (1829-32: 158).

The Subsistence Regime

The subsistence regime in this Region is somewhat varied today, generally due to the extensive spread of irrigation, in most cases making use of now extinct river beds. We have no systematic accounts of the early regime, but some useful data for reconstruction are available from the older District Gazetteers and other sources. Two areas for which these sources are available are Bahawalpur and Bikaner.

A general statement about the agriculture in the Indian arid zone is as follows:

> Despite water scarcity being a limiting factor in crop production, about 45 per cent of the total land area (320,000 sq km) of the Indian arid zone is sown to crops annually. More than 85 per cent of the area is rain fed and is subject to the vagaries of the monsoon...Crop production in the rainfed areas is unstable and risky, leading to low and unremunerative yield levels. *Bajra* (*Pennisetum typhoides*), *kharif* pulses, *jowar* (*Sorghum bicolor*) and sesamum are the principal crops grown (Mann and Singh 1977: 215).

Bajra occupies 60 percent of the rain fed cultivated area. Transplanting bajra substantially increases yield and is a hedge against the failings of the early monsoon (Mann and Singh 1977: 217-18).

Bahawalpur

The Gazetteer for Bahawalpur is a font of information on agriculture, animal husbandry and geography (Din 1904). It describes three agricultural zones in the district:

1. pure desert in the south
2. a central tract, chiefly desert, not capable of cultivation, considerably higher than the river valleys
3. the alluvial tract, along the Sutlej, then Chenab then Indus Rivers. (Din 1904: 1)

The wells in all areas, except along the rivers are salty and not suitable for irrigation and 67% of the district was uncultivable.

TABLE 3.39
The Agricultural Regime in Bahawalpur District 1903-04

Plant or Animal	Acres or Number of Animals
wheat	338,585
jowar	54,458
bajra	57,407
cattle	328,660
sheep-goat	581,242
water buffalo	64,260

From: Din 1904: 220 and Table 22

Although the absolute numbers have changed considerably the area is still a wheat growing, *rabi* crop area, with a large number of cattle, sheep and goats. This is shown in 1960 statistics.

TABLE 3.40
The Agricultural Regime in Bahawalpur District

Plant or Animal	Acres or Number of Animals	Page in Report
wheat	245049	329
jowar	44482	419
bajra	31706	419
cattle	330649	762
sheep	183521	782
water buffalo	119591	762
goats	118177	782

From: *Pakistan Census of Agriculture 1960*, 1963

Statistics for subregions within Bahawalpur may be available, but the testimony of the Gazetteer compiler indicates that these figures reflect the high productivity areas near the Indus and irrigated tracts, and that the *kharif* growing season was the important one in Cholistan.

The Gazetteer gives some interesting insights into the diversity of cultivars. For example, there were 15 varieties of wheat in the district, along with 11 varieties of jowar and two of cotton (Din 1904: 221, 223, 225). Wheat, barley and jowar are all used as fodder but bajra was only eaten by humans as a famine crop. Dates were an important crop and were abundant with 773,088 trees (Din 1904: 13).

This has to be considered a marginal agricultural area, except for the irrigated and riverine tract. In the past however, it was a vast pasture land, as indicated by the following observation: "In the rainy season the Cholistan is one stretch of grass...People take their cattle to the banks of the well-known *tobhas* and pay the proprietors a nominal rate of *bhunga*, so that the Cholistan in the rains is a vast common pasture for the Sindhians" (Din 1904: 231). The rains in this context mean the monsoon and it is a good indication of the symbiotic relationship between the desert and Sindh in the past and would have applied equally well to Protohistoric times as it does in the early twentieth century. Cholistan was one more place for Sindhi herders to take their herds when the floods engulfed the Indus Valley.

Bikaner

Today Bikaner is on the Indian side of the border, to the south of the Sarasvati. Southern and eastern portions form a vast sandy tract known as *bagar*. The name Bikaner is derived from *ner* or habitation and the founder Rao Bika in 1488[26] (Erskine 1909: 309).

There do not seem to be agricultural statistics comparable to those for Bahawalpur, although there is one contemporary study of land use there (Sen, Gheeslal, and Abraham 1982). The following table, 3.41, with figures for plantings in one good and one bad year give some indication of the numbers.

TABLE 3.41
The Agricultural Regime in Bikaner 1901-02 and 1905-06

	1901-02	1905-06
	Good year	Bad year
wheat	8040	5943
jowar	6076	1387
bajra	370,587	5920

From: Erskine 1908: 91

"In by far the greatest portion of the state, there is only one harvest (the *kharif*), and the principal crops are *bajra*, *moth*, *jowar*, *til*, and a little cotton. The cultivation of *rabi* or spring crops, such as barley, gram, rape-seed and wheat, may be said to be confined to the Suratgarh *nizamat* in the north and the Reni *nizamat* in the east" (Erskine 1909: 343). Tod's observations also reflect the importance of bajra in the area, stating that "The bajra of the desert is far superior to any grown in the rich loam of Malwa..." After a good monsoon they can save enough of the grain for two years' consumption (Tod 1829-32: 155).

Wheat was especially grown in the Ghaggar bed, around Hanumangarh, and there were plantations of the wild berry *ber* (*Zizyphus jujuba*; Erskine 1909: 311).

Cattle, sheep and camels were the most numerous animals, and in the west and northwest practically the only income for pastoral tribes there. The whole of Bikaner is a pasture land of considerable renown, especially the grazing around Hanumangarh and to some extent around Lake Chhapar (Erskine 1909: 345). Sheep are kept in large numbers for wool, which is plentiful enough to be exported (Erskine 1909: 345-46).

THE CULTURAL GEOGRAPHY OF THE GREATER INDUS REGION

Concluding Remarks

There are seven common threads that run through this discussion of the Regions of the Indus Age.

The character of the terrain in each Region and its subregions, mountains, plains, deserts or rolling savannahs, has been presented descriptively. The images are useful in visualizing the land of the Greater Indus Region; its dissimilarities, the possible impediments to travel and uses.

The discussion of landforms was done within the concept of the region, which I call the "Regions" of the Indus Age. They serve to illustrate the diversity of the Greater Indus Region, and make a point of arguing against the supposed uniformity of the Indus Civilization. These cultural and geographical areas will come up again in the exploration of the Mature Harappan.

Although modern farming and herding practices are not a totally satisfactory reflection of past practices of this kind, they can be instructive in reconstructions if carefully and critically evaluated. Time has been given to this topic, using an inventory of *rabi* and *kharif* plants (wheat, *jowar* and *bajra*) and four important domesticated animals (cattle, sheep, goats and water buffalo) for this purpose. The presentation concerns the relative importance of *rabi* and *kharif* crops, and the important but poorly understood problem of African millets in the Greater Indus Region during the Indus Age. Modern patterns are also a way to demonstrate the relative importance of cattle in the region today, just as they were during the Indus Age, as well as those areas where sheep and/or goat pastoralism was important. The special limitations, but immense productivity of the water buffalo, is also significant, even if relatively small numbers are evidenced in the prehistoric faunal record.

The conclusion that seems to best fit the data on the issue of climatic change, as they are known today, seems to be that in an overall sense the climate of the Indus Age was not too different from today, if there was any difference at all. The monsoon was in place, and it rained in the eastern part of the Greater Indus Region during the summer, in some places with sufficient regularity and intensity for dry cropping to be practiced. As one moves west the strength and reliability of this weather system decreased. But, in the west there was winter precipitation, especially in the mountains of the Gedrosia and Northwestern Regions, and that was the source of prosperity there.

This does not imply that the environment was the same in 3000 BC as it is today. Many millennia of burning, grazing, tree felling, swamp draining and clearing land for the plow have had an immense impact on the land. In general, the Greater Indus Region is a more barren area than it was in the distant past.

The major riverine systems of the region, especially the *Saptasindhava*, the "seven rivers": the Indus, Jhelum, Chenab, Ravi, Beas, Sutlej and Sarasvati, have received considerable attention. The discussion was extended to include comments on the Drishadvati and the Eastern Nara. It should be clear that the drainage map of the Indus Age would be considerably different from the one that we have today and that relying on modern maps is a perilously unreliable activity for the student of the Indus Age. Moreover, there is good reason to believe that this drainage system was not stable through all of the history of the Indus Age and that there were important changes that took place, especially toward the end of the Mature Harappan.

The maps for these changes are not satisfactory enough to be used as representations of the ancient landscape, and the modern drainage pattern has been used as the background for most of the site distributions. But, in time this will change as our knowledge of ancient hydrology in Greater Indus Region is refined.

The plants and animals of Greater Indus Region which include the domesticates, their wild predecessors and others that were simply a part of the environment of the Indus Age, have been investigated. The domestication process was a key turning point in the history of mankind and the role that Greater Indus Region played in it was important. Demonstrating that the plant and animal "raw materials" were in the region for this great transformation is an essential first step in the explication of this story. Some animals were noted because they make good eating and we know they were hunted, like the blackbuck, chital and nilgai. Others have a significantly different distribution today than they would have during the Indus Age: the elephant, tiger, Asiatic lion, rhinoceros. Others like the blind Indus dolphin, the *bulhan* are merely a curiosity. The fish resources of the Greater Indus Region are an important source of food and have not been very well handled by archaeologists. Interest needs to be stimulated in this important foodstuff (Belcher 1991, 1993, 1994a, 1994b, 1994c; Desse 1989; Desse and Desse-Berset 1990). Highlighting it here might further this end.

Shells were treated in some detail because they were an important raw material during the Indus Age, in fact constituting one of the important industries of the Mature Harappan, especially with *Turbinella pyrum* the shankh and *Meretrix casta*.

Mineral resources were noted and an appendix has been compiled to list the source areas for various minerals and other natural products that the peoples of the Indus Age are known to have used.

These topics are all important for understanding the lifeways and cultural processes of the Indus Age. They have been presented here as a prelude to a discussion of the archaeological history of these peoples.

NOTES

1. Thanks are due to Richard Zettler who assisted me with these estimates, which are clearly just ballpark guesses at this time. But, I hope that we have come up with figures that are reasonable approximations.

2. Ryot is generally translated "farmer" or "cultivator." According to *Hobson-Jobson* (Yule and Burnell 1903: 777) the etymology of the word goes back to one meaning "a herd at pasture" but came to mean "subjects" (collectively). In the nineteenth century it was used by native speakers for "subject" but in Anglo-Indian usage it came to mean "a tenant of the soil" or an individual occupying land as a farmer or cultivator.

3. The zebu (*Bos indicus*) has been considered a separate species of domesticated animal for many years. However, a modern authorative source on the mammals of India (and Southeast Asia; Corbet and Hill 1992), which is the best source for the current binomial nomenclature of these animals has merged the zebu with the rest of domestic cattle (*Bos taurus*). They recommend: "When it is considered desirable to use scientific terminology for domestic cattle the recommended form is '*Bos taurus* (Jersey)', '*Bos taurus* (zebu)', etc. (Corbet and Hill 1992: 264). Without getting into an argument about what is right, or even best, the older terminology (zebu, *Bos indicus*) will be retained in this work and the other books of the *Indus Age*. To change this terminology would only lead to confusion in the mind of the readers, almost none of whom are either zoologists or scholars trained in faunal analysis.

4. The primary source for this story seems to be deBarros (1563-1615, Vol. II, Book x, Chapter 1), as indicated in Dames 1918: Vol. 1, 125). I have never located this book, but I have seen deBarros (1945-46: Vol. 4, 114-15) where it is recounted.

5. This quote from Herodotus would appear to present reasonable, believable information. But his information on India has an uneven quality, as noted in the following observation by James Douglas:

> Then there is a story in Herodotus that "Darius sent for a certain race of Indians who eat their fathers." We Indians can swallow a good deal, but are inclined to make faces at this *piece de resistance*: so we repeat the ditty:——

> Herodotus, Herodotus
> You could not spell, you ancient cuss;
> The priests of Egypt gammon'd you,
> Which was not very hard to do.
> But don't you think you'll gammon us,
> Herodotus, Herodotus!

(Douglas 1893b: Vol. 2, 352; the citation to Herodotus and the Indian cannibals will be found in Book III, 38, see also Book III, 99 for more supposed ancient Indian cannibalism, Godley 1926).

James Douglas was a British bank agent who devoted much of his mature life to the history and lore of Bombay and its Presidency. His writings on this topic appeared in venues such as the *Times of India*, the *Pioneer* and the *Bombay Gazette*. They were brought together in two volumes by Douglas (1893).

5a. Pactyic country today is probably the land of the Pathans, eastern Afghanistan and the Northwest Frontier Province of Pakistan.

5b. A portion of this discussion will also appear in Possehl in press a and in press b.

5c. The Sharma team occasionally quotes PRL-224 as a Neolithic date. A check of the original documentation for this date will reveal that when it was submitted to the laboratory it was thought to have come from an Iron Age pit (D. P. Agrawal et al. 1977: 231). There is just too much confusion in the documentation of Koldihwa for it to be used as an authorative source.

5d. I have selected Schroff's translation of Chapter 41 of the "Periplius" because it seems to me to be the best. That by Huntingford (1980: 43-4; 68) calls the fabric mentioned in the text "flax cloth" which seems unlikely for the Gujarat region, where cotton is such a stable. The Casson translation does not make this mistake (1989: 40).

6. There is a fine collection of essays on the monsoon that can be recommended (Fein and Stephens 1987).

7. The following section on Colonial Period hunting was researched by Ms. Jacqueline Fewkes, who also prepared a very useful draft of the text used here.

8. This is a much more poetic translation than the others I have found.

9. Raverty's wonderfully detailed, contentious literary review of the Indus River (1892a) was reprinted in 1979 and pagination in citations has been taken from the reprint (Raverty 1892b).

10. Panjnad derives from "panj" the word for five. This survives in English in the word "punch" a drink traditionally made of five ingredients. This refreshment may have originated among the factors at the East India Company establishment at Surat who made a drink of spirit, lime or lemon juice, spice, sugar and rose-water. The pentaploa of the Greeks was similar in that it is also composed of five ingredients, in this case wine, honey, cheese, meal and oil (Balfour 1885, Vol. 3: 311).

11. Lieutenant Wood also found the source of the Oxus or Amu Darya River in 1838 at a lake called Sir-i-Kol in the Pamirs at 4725 meters (15,500 feet). He lived to tell the tale after a vicious winter journey by a small party of determined, frost-bitten men. Wood published this account (1841) and in the same year he received the Patron's Medal from the Royal Geographical Society for this feat. Wood was apparently both modest and extremely hard working, "laid back" in today's vocabulary. John Keay has described him as someone whose life "...gives the impression of a man running away from his achievements" (1977: 148). For a short biographical note on Mr. Wood see (Balfour 1885: Vol. III, 1086-87).

12. Flam is also currently working with a team of very competent hydrologists headed by Prof. Stanley Schumm, so he has had the advantage of working closely with scholars who have technical expertise in these matters.

13. There is a very good discussion of the finer points of meaning for *gabar* in Balfour's *Cyclopaedia of India*....

14. This dam may have been first published by Ralph Hughes-Buller (1903-04: 196). His article on *gabarbands* is signed "E. Hughes-Buller" but it was clearly written by the great *savant* of Baluchistan, Ralph Hughes-Buller. This would have been a hand written manuscript and the "R" must have been mistaken for an "E."

15. N. N. Sen, "Notes on grassland ecology in Uttar Pradesh." (1952). Cited in R. O. Whyte (1964: 119)

16. N. P. Mohan, "A short note on the principle types of grassland in Uttar Pradesh." (1942). Cited in R. O. Whyte (1964: 119).

17. This is another Sarasvati River, still active. It flows across the North Gujarat Plain.

18. Waziristan was one of the areas of the Northwest Frontier Province that was most resistant to British administration and it was the subject of much irritation to Calcutta and later, Delhi. The Government of the Punjab even formed a special army, called the Punjab Field Force, more popularly "Piffers," to deal with the problems of this territory. Until 1886 this unit reported to the Lieutenant Governor of the Punjab, not to the Commander-in-Chief, India, the head of the Army of Bengal.

Brigadier E. J. Ross was stationed in this area from 1935 to 1940, as commander of British troops in Zhob and Loralai, headquartered at Fort Sandeman. Rana Ghundai is just 13 kilometers east of this position and while attempting to pacify the Pathans, Ross found time to study this mound and make a significant contribution to the archaeology of the Zhob Valley (Ross 1946).

19. Known as "Dera Ghastly Khan" to British troopers in the Indian Army. It was said to be home to vicious scorpions and huge spiders called "jerrymungulums," whose bite caused those unfortunate enough to have the experience to bleed from the ears (Farwell 1989: 197).

20. There are other names for the river in this area, Sotra and Choya being the most common by my observation. Twentieth century publications have more or less standardized this terminology, but those who live near this old river still enjoy the variety of their own dialectical habits.

21. Tod notes that this sound shift turns the name "Jahilmer" into "the hill of fools" rather than the "hill of Jasil" (1829-32: Vol. 2, 144, fn. 3).

22. The translation of this Hymn in Griffith (1896) is quite defective. He manages to put the rivers out of geographical order, listing them as: Ganga, Yamuna, Sutlej, Ravi and Sarasvati. This verse, number five, is very widely known and the fault lies with Griffith, not Vedic geography.

23. While these two men are probably related in a family sense, they do not appear to have been intimates. C. H. Oldham was a physician and R. D. Oldham was with the Geological Survey of India, where he wrote on the Sarasvati as well as compiled a memoir on the Kutch earthquake of 1819, which formed the Allah Bund, thus contributing to theories on the demise of the Harappan settlements in Sindh (R. D. Oldham 1887, 1926; Raikes 1964 for the beginning of the theory on the damming of the Indus).

The articles in the *Calcutta Review* were generally not credited, however C. H. Oldham's paper there is so widely known, and its authorship acknowledged for so many years, that it is a convention to list it under his name, although it appears nowhere in volume LIX of that periodical.

24. R. D. Oldham has noted that M. de Saint Martin proposed that climatic change had caused the drying of the Sarasvati. I have not been able to trace this source, but Oldham rejected it, noting: "...there is no historic evidence of such enormous climatic change as this implies..." (1887: 333).

25. A version of this section also appears in a festschrift planned for Beatrice de Cardi.

26. James Tod (1829-32: Vol. 2, 137) says 1459. Tod has a small account of the founding of the former principality (1829-32: 137-38) and two chapters on the Bikaner area, which includes a portion of the Sarasvati bed.

PART FOUR

THE BEGINNINGS OF THE INDUS AGE

INTRODUCTION

FARMING AND CITIES: Setting the Scene

The mastery of agriculture and management of domesticated animals was one of the great revolutions in human history. It involved the combined arts of food production and domestication which led to significant changes in human society, increases in population and biological changes to human populations, not all of which were positive. The beginnings of village life and the symbiosis between settled peoples and pastoral nomads, so important in understanding ancient India and Pakistan, begins here. The revolution ultimately set the scene for the rise of urbanization in South Asia and the Old World in general.

The potency and vigor inherent in food production and domestication were critical in sustaining the large populations implied by urbanization. There is a link, a deep causality, between the development of food production and domestication and the rise of city life, with a single unbroken historical narrative involving the development of early villages and pastoral camps and the transition to urbanization in the Greater Indus Region.

Scholarly non-archaeologists, unfamiliar with the archaeological record and the way in which archaeologists compile the culture historical sequences they present, prompt the inclusion of some diverse issues that are the antecedents to understanding the South Asian rise of food production and domestication. Some of the issues are conceptual; the nature of food production as opposed to domestication and the consequences of sedentism. Other issues are culture historical. The documentation of food production and domestication in the Near East is coming together as a good example of a (probably not "the") sequence of events that precedes the development of farming and pastoralism. The Near Eastern material is familiar to many archaeologists and in a discussion of the South Asian route to food production and domestication it provides a backdrop for a full understanding of the significance of the archaeological findings there. Non-archaeologists should share this background so that they can fully appreciate the finds in the Subcontinent.

What follows is a reasonably complete presentation in terms of issues and empirical detail, rather than a 'streamlined' version, so that a number of important problems can be brought into sharp focus. Among the most important is the complex set of intersecting questions concerning diffusion, independent invention and the timing of the food producing revolution in India, Pakistan and Afghanistan. The discussion preceding "getting to the heart of the matter," the South Asian material, is of necessity a bit long. Those who are impatient can move ahead and concentrate on other sections in which they have a special interest.

DEVELOPMENT OF FOOD PRODUCTION AND DOMESTICATION

THE "NEOLITHIC": An Outdated Term

In well established, but outmoded terminology, the beginnings of food production and domestication defines the "Neolithic." This term cannot be avoided completely because it refers to a simple, technological concept and a theory of culture history that emanated from 19th century scholarship. The Neolithic was defined as the era within which ground stone tools and pottery made their first appearance in local archaeological sequences. The great synthesizer of Old World archaeology, V. Gordon Childe revised this definition, when he proposed the Neolithic as the period within which humans first used domesticated plants and animals and settled into villages (Childe 1936). This shifted the definition from a technological stage to one relating to the settlement and subsistence system of a people. For some time it was thought that Childe's new Neolithic was probably coincidental with the appearance of ground stone tools and pottery, but as we learned more about human prehistoric life it has become clear that there are many parts of the world where the initial appearance of domesticated plants and animals is uncorrelated with particular types of material culture.

Robert Braidwood, the eminent archaeologist whose work and thought shaped a generation of research on the problem of plant and animal domestication in the Near East, further refined Childe's nascent ideas and placed the most important locus of change not on the subsistence system, per se, but on the evolution of what he called the "primary village farming community" and sedentarism (Braidwood 1952, 1975). In fact, Braidwood's scheme for the concepts and vocabulary used in dealing with the prehistoric world eschewed the traditional sequence of linear technological stages for the early history of humans (i.e., Palaeolithic, Mesolithic, Neolithic), for concepts like an era of hunting and collecting, the primary village farming community and era of towns. The terms used in the *Indus Age* are more compatible with Braidwood's scheme than those of Childe and his predecessors; however, it has not been possible to abandon the older vocabulary altogether.[1]

There are a number of difficult tasks that prehistoric archaeologists face, not the least of which is the selection of terminology for periods, phases, eras and the like. To be successful, to convey the full intended meaning and thus be adopted by a broad range of researchers, culture historical terms need to resonate with older terminology, yet break with the past in a way which creates new meaning. Terms that use the notion of a Neolithic will be preserved in some of the long regarded formal names for archaeological assemblages of the Subcontinent; "Northern Neolithic" (Burzahom, Gufkral, Sarai Khola I); or the "Southern Neolithic" (which is not Neolithic at all). These are both important cultural traditions of food producing peoples in the Subcontinent; although the Southern Neolithic is somewhat (not totally) peripheral to the Indus Age.

There is a third cultural tradition of food producers in eastern India, and probably Bangladesh, that seems to be related to Southeast Asia as found at places like Spirit Cave (Gorman 1970a, 1970b, 1977) in northwestern Thailand and the Padah Lin Caves (Thaw 1971) in Burma; again, largely peripheral to the Indus Age. The food producing tradition of most of the peoples of the Indus Age is associated with the uplands of the Iranian Plateau and Afghanistan and is based on the wheat/barley and sheep/goat/cattle constellation of domesticated plants and animals. This is clearly related, in some yet to be understood ways, to the larger Near Eastern pattern of early food production. It should not be interpreted as a certainty that there was a diffusion of farming and herding from the Near East to South Asia and these connections need not be thought of as historical. But, the plants and animals used by the peoples in Pakistan, Afghanistan and northwestern India were much the same as those used on the Iranian Plateau, extending all the way to the Mediterranean Sea and beyond (Figure 4.1).

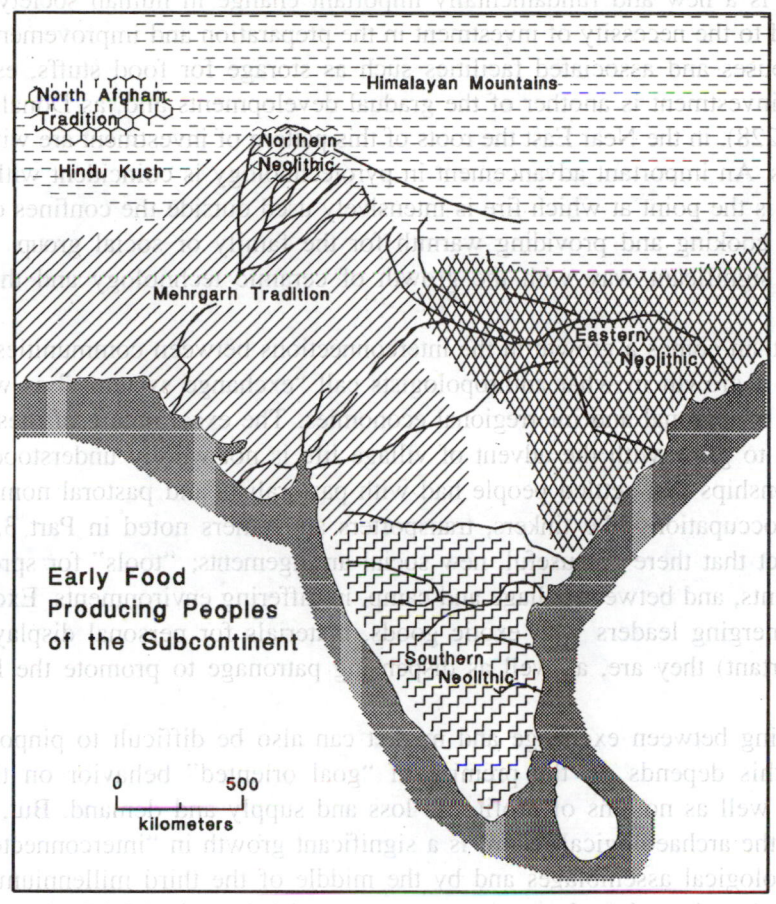

Figure 4.1. Early traditions of food producing peoples in Pakistan, Afghanistan and India

SOME CONSEQUENCES OF FOOD PRODUCTION AND DOMESTICATION

It is widely agreed that the importance of the food production and domestication revolution lies in the profound consequences that it brought to human life. Based on the thoughts of V. Gordon Childe (1936), Robert Redfield (1953), Esther Boserup (1965, 1981), Robert J. Braidwood (1975), Philip E. L. Smith (1972a), and others, a series of changes and implications can be outlined that focus on three interdependent phenomena: sedentism, changes in human social organization and alterations in human demographic patterns. Settling down into villages and the symbiosis that sedentary peoples have with pastoralists and hunter-gatherers is widely regarded as the single most important act, and it clearly had an impact on other factors. But, in the end, this is a set of historical forces that act in a systemic way, with an abundance of feedback and interlocking patterns of change.

Sedentism

The advent of food production and domestication is not the first time that people settled into "villages" but it does seem to mark a period when this "settling in" was accompanied by an elaborate investment in facilities, and an emphasis on the definition of productive land, house plot and village site ownership. The degree of emphasis on land and investment in land and other facilities, is a new and fundamentally important change in human society. Much of this seems to be tied to the necessity of investment in the preparation and improvement of cultivation plots and in houses and associated facilities such as storage for food stuffs, especially grain. The pattern of investment is another of the gradual developments and, as Donald Henry points out (1989: 151-228), in the Near East the roots of this pattern of investment are with sophisticated hunter-gatherers. An important advancement in pyrotechnology is coincident with the discovery of plaster. This is the point at which fire is intensively used outside the confines of the domestic hearth, beyond cooking and providing warmth for the family or social group. This was then expanded in a significant way with the growth of ceramic technology and the discovery of metallurgy.

With sedentism comes a growth in the interconnections between communities (villages) that seem to reflect a growth in what anthropologists call "exchange systems," as well as markets and the growth of regional and interregional economies. The exact nature of these systems, and why they seem to grow with the advent of village life is not wholly understood; however the complex relationships that settled people had with pastoralists and pastoral nomads, as well as emerging new occupations like tinkers, transporters and others noted in Part 3, are important here. We suspect that there are useful, new social arrangements; "tools" for spreading the risk among settlements, and between village and camp, in differing environments. Exchange systems also provide emerging leaders with exotic goods, materials for personal display to show how different (important) they are, as well as dispensing patronage to promote the loyalty of their followers.

Differentiating between exchange and market can also be difficult to pinpoint because, to some degree, this depends on the premise of "goal oriented" behavior on the part of the participants, as well as notions of profit and loss and supply and demand. But, one thing that can be seen in the archaeological record is a significant growth in "interconnectedness" among regional archaeological assemblages and by the middle of the third millennium BC (ca. 2500 BC) interregional trade and exchange became a powerful force in Middle Asia, the area from the Mediterranean to the Indus and from Central Asia to Arabia.

Changes in Human Social Organization

The revolution brought by food production and domestication is best thought of in terms of its impact on the way in which people organized themselves, and how this in turn led to further changes. What is observed in the archaeological record is first, the development of sedentary villages with new and significant investment in architecture and storage facilities, paralleled by an increase in the size of regional populations. The relationship between sedentism and population size, or growth, and the role of changing social structure is not well understood. All three are important, just as environmental factors are, especially at particular times in regional histories. It seems reasonable that these factors, and others, form a complex web of interlinked causal relationships and that none is totally independent of the other.

In this sense the older search for single "prime movers" in culture change has been (or should be) abandoned and our thoughts focused more on the nature of shifting changes in an interconnected set of historical forces, all of which were acting in concert to yield particular day to day and longer term historical trajectories. These sequences are neither simple nor linear. Rather they are multidimensional, with connectedness among large numbers of trends and patterns, each of which has an effect on the others. The trends and patterns, and therefore the effects, are dynamic and never in total equilibrium, such as might yield a linear, additive outcome. While additive change must be considered part of the historical process, it is complemented by punctuated times of change with many kinds of feedback and the kind of interconnectedness that characterizes complex systems.

The settled village and pastoral communities that seem to be part of the early history of food production and domestication called for new means of social control and community leadership. An overall assessment of the ethnographic record suggests that the flexible bilateral kinship systems of hunters and gatherers seem to have given way to more rigidly defined lineage systems, with property rights closely tied to group membership. There was also a change in the value of children, since in farming and herding societies they can perform simple but important tasks, requiring little training or experience; guarding flocks and fields against predators and loss. Frank Hole reached many of these same conclusions in his study of early social structure in western Iran (1968: 260-62).

A new phenomenon, militarism, seems to arise within the context of food production and domestication, although the exact point at which it becomes a significant political force can be debated. However, there is a view that suggests that community investment in fortifications, as might have been found at Jericho in the Jordan Valley (Kenyon 1957), can be seen in this light.[2]

Craft and career specialization also originates within the historical context of early agriculture and herding. We see a progressive growth in numbers of craftsmen and community leaders, which have paralleled growth in the size of communities. The increasing sophistication in the suite of artifacts that emerges is impressive at times and seems to indicate a growing knowledge of natural processes and primitive chemistry or alchemy. The further development of pyrotechnology, first with the production of plaster, then pottery and finally metallurgy and glass must also have involved specialization. The pyrotechnological "ladder" of development has been very well outlined by T. Wertime (1973), Gourdin and Kingery (1975) and Kingery, Vandiver and Prickett (1988).

The reasoned, if hypothetical, view is that the organization of human societies changed from family groups, arranged in small flexible units, to larger communities, with new patterns of leadership, new and stronger mechanisms for social control, increases in career specialization, craft sophistication and the accompanying specialization that is implied by this increased knowledge. These social changes are the most important to be brought about by the development of food production and domestication. To clarify this, and place these massive changes in some perspective, other changes can also be addressed.

Demographic Changes

Perhaps the implication most discussed in the development of food production and domestication is a general rise in population and other demographic changes (Cohen and Armelagos 1984). This can be seen in the archaeological record as an increase in the number of settlements and an overall growth in the size of individual places. J. Lawrence Angel has observed: "With the beginning of farming, some stabilizing of general health occurred, with at least maintenance of female longevity near the hunting period norm. This promoted a slight excess of survivals over deaths in juveniles and consequently a fairly rapid population increase" (1984: 62). But, this change was uneven and it should not be assumed that the shifts, on average, were anything like those that the world is experiencing today.

Robert Carneiro and Daisy Hulse (1966), in an interesting but rarely cited note, comment on the historical implications of long-term population growth. They begin their assessment of the rate of population growth during the early food producing era in the Near East by assuming a population of about 100,000 at 8000 BC. While no one knows for sure, most archaeologists would accept this as a reasonable, but not necessarily precise, figure. If one factors in a one-half percent per year growth rate for 4000 years an astounding 46,200,000,000,000 people would have been present in this region at 4000 BC (Carneiro and Hulse 1966: 178). This is, of course, a totally unrealistic figure. The world today has a population of only about six billion people. But, even a relatively small percentage growth rate such as 0.15% yields 40,200,000 for the same time interval, 8000 to 4000 BC; far too many people in the minds of most archaeologists to be considered accurate. Most scholars concerned with ancient demographics in the Near East would say that a million or a million and one-half people might have been present in the Near East at about 4000 BC. The average growth rate that yields 1.5 million people at 4000 BC, if one starts with 100,000 at 8000 BC, is ca. 0.07% per year (Carneiro and Hulse 1966: 178).

The figures that Carneiro and Hulse present should not be taken as an indication that the population of the Near East grew at a relatively constant rate, like one and one-half percent, over long periods of time (several centuries or a millennium).

Looking at averages such as this is in some ways artificial. It may well have been the case that populations grew rapidly for short periods of time (a century) and then crashed, for reasons of migration, epidemics, warfare or other catastrophes. As proposed by Bennet Bronson (1977: 37-40), the long term demographic curve is probably best characterized by a series of peaks and valleys, frequently crossing the line of an average growth rate, but rarely adhering to it for long. Still, computing the average has some heuristic value since it is a cautionary observation. Even given the productive power of agriculture and domesticated animals and the fecundity of *Homo sapiens*, we should be careful not to overstate the rate of growth that would have been attained over long periods of time.

Many countries in the world today have annual population growth rates of over one percent per year. Carneiro and Hulse (1966: 180) note that the average annual rate of increase for the population of the world for the period from 1950-60 was 1.8 percent. From an archaeological view of time this is a short term phenomenon but it is apparent from the mathematics of this game that it is an unrealistic rate to be sustained for a large number of consecutive generations.

The conclusion drawn from all of this is that the advent of food production and domestication did spur a population increase that on average, is probably higher than the rates that preceded it. If judged by modern standards (those attained since the end of World War II), this rate would have been quite modest.

Not only did the population grow but there must have been a significant redistribution of people. Agricultural and pasture land is not necessarily the best for hunting and gathering and people would have gravitated away from the latter into the former. Swamps were drained, light savannah grasslands plowed and some of this brought people into environments that might have been downright dangerous.

In one study of prehistoric demographics, J. Lawrence Angel looked at the population for Çatal Hüyük, an early village in southern Turkey situated near wetlands, which seems to have been the location of their fields (Angel 1971). This was an environment that had been avoided by earlier hunters and gatherers. Çatal Hüyük village was there because it was well watered and fertile; excellent agricultural land. But it was also home to mosquitoes who brought malaria with them. This disease had a devastating effect on the inhabitants of Çatal Hüyük who must have suffered terribly (Angel 1971: 84-9). The food producing revolution did not always lead people to enviable environments and to some degree the population increase might also have brought a shortening of the average life span for some populations.

The new diet also brought changes in health. The most obvious is a marked increase in dental caries. The softer, carbohydrate rich foods stuck in the mouth and did their progressive damage, much as today. Changes in the kinds of roughage, "nut cracking" and other hard chewing foods had an affect on dental health and digestive processes as well. It also seems, over a period of millennia, to have reduced the musculature of the face, leading to cranial features that are more gracile and less prognathus—very attractive by modern standards.

Living close together in their new villages, the sedentary populations began to have to cope with settlement sanitation and new diseases like cholera, small pox, chicken pox, mumps and measles that require relatively large host populations to thrive. Mass killers like plague have their starts in the growing, settled communities. Even in the eighteenth century AD child mortality could be extremely high. "The poet Thomas Gray (1716-1771), famous as the author of 'Elegy Written in a Country Churchyard' was the sole adult survivor among his parent's twelve children" (J. Cohen 1995: 42). And, we can turn to the opening lines of Thomas Nashe's poem of 1600 "A Litany in Time of Plague."

> Adieu, farewell, earth's bliss;
> This world uncertain is;
> Fond are life's lustful joys;
> Death proves them all but toys;
> None from his darts can fly;
> I am sick, I must die,
> Lord, have mercy on us!

It is highly likely, given the very poor sanitation and lack of scientific knowledge about the causes of disease, that many of these early settlements, especially the largest, were centers of population loss, largely due to disease. They may well have sustained their size by significant migration to them.

Kenneth A. R. Kennedy has devoted his career to the study of the ancient populations of the Subcontinent and has had an opportunity to study first hand almost all of the human skeletal remains from this region. In a 1990 summary of his findings he contrasts the human biology of the hunting and gathering peoples with those of settled, agricultural peoples, the Mature Harappans included. He begins with six points concerning the biology of hunter-gatherers, which can be summarized as follows:

1. The hunting and gathering peoples of South Asia have pronounced muscular-skeletal robusticity.

2. Pronounced sexual dimorphism may be present, with or without striking differences in stature. This is due to muscular-skeletal robusticity.

3. Ontogenetic growth seems to have been maximized and there is a low incidence of signs of arrested growth: Harris lines, dental enamel hypoplasia.

4. While teeth often show marked wear, there is a relatively low incidence of dental caries, tooth suppression, and malocclusion.

5. There is a low incidence of markers of infectious disease on bones. While signs of anemias and other problems brought by deficiency of iron, protein and other minerals and vitamins are present, they are low compared to food producing peoples.

6. The incidence of traumatic lesions are low. (Kennedy 1990: 64, 66).

In everyday language the South Asian hunter-gatherers were large, big-boned people, with marked differences in appearance between males and females. They were also pretty healthy, with good teeth, a reliable food supply and few signs of broken bones and wounds. Kennedy contrasts these features of food producing peoples of the same region. In summary:

1. There is a reduction in sexual dimorphism.

2. The incidence of nutritional stress, as seen on bone and teeth, is greater.

3. While there is less tooth wear, there is an increase in the incidence of dental caries, abscesses, malocclusion and tooth suppression.

4. There is an increase in pathological signs of infection, nutritional deficiency, even genetic abnormalities.

5. Food producing peoples in South Asia have more traumatic lesions than their hunting/gathering counterparts (Kennedy 1990: 66).

The food producers were a smaller, more gracile people, with less apparent difference between males and females. In broad terms they were not as healthy as the hunter-gatherers, having bad teeth, more sickness and higher incidence of broken bones and wounds. It might even be that in some ways their food supply was not as reliable, especially given the larger size of the population. These observations make it clear that in South Asia "...the socioeconomic transition from food-gathering to food-producing lifeways demanded a very high biological price. This price was paid by modifications of skeletal and dental anatomy, patterns of growth and development, the advent of specific pathological conditions and higher incidents of lesions inflicted by accidents and intention to maim and kill" (Kennedy 1990: 66, see also Kennedy 1984b). There is little reason for us to believe that these conclusions are restricted to the Indian Subcontinent, and would appear to be a kind of universal biological truth as applicable to the Near East, for example, as anywhere else (Cohen and Armelagos 1984a, especially Cohen and Armelagos 1984b: 586-94; Rathbun 1984; Angel 1984).

FIRST AFFLUENT SOCIETY: Hunting/Gathering May Not Be All Bad

Having introduced some qualifications to the proposition that the development of food production and domestication was a "step forward" in the human career, it might be enlightening to continue on that track and consider an idea that is somewhat fashionable in anthropology today. It proposes that hunters and gatherers were members of the "first affluent society," a suggestion that came out of innovative ethnographic research that started in Africa in the late 1960s (Lee 1968, 1969, 1972a, 1972b; Lee and DeVore 1968, 1976; Woodburn 1968; Sahlins 1972). Richard Lee and his colleagues documented the subsistence system of the !Kung San Bushmen and found that these hunter-gatherers devoted only about one-third of their "work week" to subsistence activities and the rest to family and friends. Furthermore, due in part to the bountiful supply of a nut from the *mongongo* tree, they were comparatively well provisioned, in spite of the fact that they lived in the Kalahari Desert, with only fifteen to twenty-two cm of annual rainfall.

One interesting thing that came out of these studies of Kalahari people is that the gathering of vegetable foods, almost exclusively the women's responsibility, provided the bulk of the food supply. The buzz words became "man the hunter" who was really "woman the gatherer." Without doubting the data from the !Kung and other peoples, one wonders if this might be the case for hunter-gatherers in general—the thought of a vegetarian Eskimo comes to mind. Of course, the Arctic is a special environment, not one that is characteristic of all hunter-gatherers, but then neither can the Kalahari Desert be thought of as "average" or "typical."

The investigators in Africa also found that during a three year drought in neighboring Botswana, when 100,000 cattle were lost and relief food to farmers reached 200,000 persons, the Bushmen hardly noticed, but they did help the Bantus who came into their area to gather. While we cannot be sure, it seems probable that this kind of symbiosis between peoples with different subsistence systems may well have been part of the prehistoric past, even in the eras when agriculture and animal husbandry were relatively new arts. There is a resiliency to well adapted hunter-gatherers who cautiously maintain a low population density that allows them to face "disasters" like drought with a minimum of adversity. The historical record documents something quite different for many food producers who live in a less resilient, more "brittle" world.

The insights into the amount of time that the Kalahari foragers spent at subsistence related tasks (their work) was coincidental with the appearance of another hypothesis put forward independently by Esther Boserup (1965). She proposed that increasingly intensive agricultural practices, from slash and burn systems, through single cropping to multiple cropping of a farm plot in a single year, were accomplished only by diminishing returns on the labor invested in subsistence activities. There was less food output per labor hour as intensification increased, which implied that the intensification of agricultural practices to produce more food, did so at greater labor cost. This would (could?) be implemented only when the size of a population demanded it.

Some researchers (e.g., Cohen 1977a, 1977b, 1984; see also Spooner 1972) found Boserup's thesis very attractive and thought that it might be extended back into pre-farming times. Agriculture itself might demand more labor than hunting and gathering, as suggested by Lee and his collaborators, and that the "Neolithic Revolution" resulted only from an increasing population. Thus, population pressure, sometimes combined with environmental stress, became an important theoretical issue in understanding the development of sedentism and pastoral nomadism (Binford 1968b; Smith 1972b)

The research on the !Kung spawned a number of other investigations of hunter-gatherers, including some studies that claim to demonstrate, in theory at least, that their diet would be healthy, well balanced, with better protein than early farmers, who soon ended up with a diet based on large amounts of carbohydrate (Barnicot 1969; Yudkin 1969; see also Cohen 1984). The intensified "foraging" strategies of antiquity may have provided a very good, balanced, reliable food supply with relatively low labor inputs (Hayden 1981a, 1981b). All of which seems to suggest that the life of a hunter-gatherer might have been quite good: ample leisure time, a balanced diet, a reliable food supply. Things could have been worse!

Other experiments, spawned by more purely archaeological interests, suggest the same thing for those peoples of the ancient Near East who found wheat an attractive food. Agricultural scientist Jack Harlan located a stand of wild wheat in Turkey (Harlan 1967). It was a good, sturdy field, visited just prior to full maturity. He decided to harvest this stand as an experiment, to see how much food grain could be taken from it. Harlan made five half-hour runs. Stripping heads of grain by hand yielded two kilograms of seed heads per hour. Using a reconstructed "Neolithic" sickle upped the yield to two and one-half kilograms per hour. About half of this yield was edible seed and it can be estimated, for convenience, that the yield from wild stands would have been about one kilogram per hour of work for each adult gathering the wild cereal. If one person consumed the equivalent of about one-half of a kilogram per day (about one pound) this would come to the consumption of ca. 180 kilos per year. According to Harlan's experiment one person could gather this amount, a year's supply of food grain by:

working 12 hrs for 15 days
working 10 hrs for 18 days
working 8 hrs for 22 1/2 days

Of course there would have been loss, due to spoilage and pests, but one can see that the wild cereal was, or could have been, a very productive plant. There is a consequence or two, however. First, even the minimum of 180 kilograms of grain is a heavy, bulky mass. For a family of five it comes to 900 kilos, or 1980 pounds, about a ton; hardly something that could be thought of as portable. Thus, if it was to be consumed all year around, some provision for storage would have to be made, and this implies a degree of sedentism, to maintain access to the food supply, and to protect it from poachers, human or otherwise.

It is also fair to add, that Harlan's experiment with cooking or processing the wild wheat was not as successful as the harvest. Whatever he tried, Harlan came up with a pretty unpalatable mess, at least according to his American tastes.

The Backlash to the Revisionist Position on Hunter-Gatherers

The revisionist position on affluent hunter-gatherers did not go unchallenged, it may have smacked just a bit too much of Rousseau's "noble savage." It was also out of line with the intuitive feelings of some anthropologists. This came in the form of questions concerning the quality of life and health of hunter-gatherers. Mark Cohen has said:

> ...there are...unresolved issues concerning hunter-gatherer health and nutrition: whether, as has been claimed, hunter-gatherers were and are indeed relatively unviolent (see Ember 1978); whether the shift from hunting and gathering to farming affected the work load, relative to health, and the status of women (Draper 1975); whether apparent latitudinal variations in hunter-gatherer diets are indeed representative of prehistoric conditions (Lee 1969; compare Ember 1978); whether a decline over time in the percentage of meat in the human diet and an increase in vegetables (particularly small seeds and vegetable starches) and of seafoods, which are apparent in the archaeological record (Cohen 1977; Hayden 1981a; Yesner 1980), are real or an artifact of preservation (see Kamminga 1981)...(Cohen 1984: 3).

Since the surviving hunting and gathering groups in today's world are so few and therefore so special, it stands to reason that they may not be representative of hunters and gatherers from the eras preceding the Holocene, when all humans seem to have had this type of adaptation. The ethnoarchaeology of modern hunter-gatherers should be used with some caution, mindful that all ethnographic analogy has its pitfalls (Binford 1967, 1968c).

What seems to emerge from this research is that hunting and gathering could be a very productive livelihood, with dependable food supplies, a balanced diet and a very good quality of life. But, it is also apparent that this was not always the case. To conclude that ancient hunting and gathering peoples represent the first "affluent society" may be true, but probably only for some, surely not all of them.

THE NATURE OF FOOD PRODUCTION AND DOMESTICATION

The new "Neolithic" is defined by the appearance of domesticated plants and animals that are manipulated in a subsistence system that can be called "food production" rather than hunting and gathering. Domestication is a biological phenomenon. Plants and animals that are domesticated are genetically different from their wild counterparts because of human intervention in their reproductive patterns. For the most part, this means that domesticated plants and animals look different from wild examples, since the phenotypic expression of the genes is affected. Sometimes the changes in domesticated plants and animals are extreme, so extreme that the domesticated species cannot survive, or even breed, without the assistance of humans. Yellow Delicious apples fall into this extreme category, but some exotic breeds of show dogs would also. Many domesticated plants and animals, however, would manage to survive without human intervention and this is where the notion of "feral" comes into play for domesticated species that have returned to their wild state. Mustang horses in the American west are good examples of feral animals, but so are wild dogs and cats that can do quite well on their own. Many domesticated plants, "wander" back to the wild, and in Baluchistan it is possible to find feral wheat and barley sprouting on the back dirt of an archaeological excavation.

Food production, in contrast to hunting and gathering, is a way of manipulating plants and animals, as well as resources like soil, water, fire and fertilizer to assure a food supply. With food production humans use new forms of planning, foresight, knowledge and investment to assure productivity. Such systems involve a great degree of intervention into the natural world, as opposed to the untended system that "Mother Nature" governs and from which hunters and gatherers benefit. One has to qualify this as somewhat arbitrary because the amount of human intervention that separates food producing subsistence systems from those that are not, has never been defined (Harris 1972: 183, 1989; see also the early chapters in Harris and Hillman 1989). Food production, by conventional definition, involves things like plowing or preparing soil for planting, weeding, cultivation, possibly irrigation, and protecting maturing crops from predators. With animals it means assisting in the birthing process, the castration of some males, protecting herds from predators, scouting for water and the best pasture ahead of herds, breeding and taming animals for the harness. But most of these criteria turn out to be matters of degree and not necessarily matters of kind. There is a continuum of relationships here, about which David Harris has been particularly astute (1989: 16-23; see also A. K. Chase 1989). We know, for example, that many hunter-gatherers dig up tubers, harvest only part of the plant and rebury the rest (an "eye"), so that the plant can be reharvested the next time it comes to maturity (Cohen 1977a: 18-27; Yen 1989: 59). This can be seen as a simple form of horticulture. The extensive use of fire as an agency of a subsistence system can have immense benefits for the productivity of a landscape in terms of rejuvenating grasses, clearing weeds, supplying fertilizer and clearing fields of vision (Lewis 1972; Pyne 1991; Yen 1989: 57-8). In Australia they are observations on the harvesting of *Panicum* that suggest that the aborigines not only reaped good returns from this plant, but extended its range to increase productivity (Yen 1989: 58). Some Australian aborigines use ground stone food processing tools to break down the seeds that they gather (Cane 1989). J. Harlan (1989a) has described the use of wild grasses in Africa that fall into a category that is usually called "famine plants." These are immensely useful and humans have a very close relationship with them, in some ways as close a relationship as we have with plants that are conventionally thought of as domesticated, giving further credence to the notion that we should look to a continuum of relationships between humans and plants. There is also a well documented example of Eastern Mono Shoshonean hunter-gatherers using stream irrigation to increase the yield of wild plants along its banks.

Not only did they (Eastern Monos) gather wild seeds and roots, but in certain localities they took the pains to increase the yield of several of the more prolific seed plots by irrigation. They did not till the soil, plant or cultivate. They merely intensified by irrigation what nature had already provided. Although they thus lacked the other essentials of an agricultural complex, they had made one significant advance. They had in fact undertaken irrigation on a considerable scale (Steward 1929a: 150).

This is a good example of "hunter-gatherer" subsistence management. Within the Mono sociocultural (tribal) contexts it is important but it does not fit into a larger pattern that suggests "agriculture." The irrigation among the Eastern Monos and the more widespread practice of replanting tubers are simply isolated examples of the kinds of behavior that farmers use, and

404

are useful insights in two ways: 1) these activities can be seen as possible developmental steps that would link "pure" hunting and gathering to entrenched cultivation, and 2) they offer a caution that anthropological typologies are of limited utility if peoples, ancient and modern, are thought of in terms of ideal types. There are many more ethnographic examples of this kind of behavior among hunter-gatherers, as noted in L. Keeley (1995).

There is a correlation between food producing subsistence systems and the use of domesticated plants and animals. With the full advent of the primary village farming community, and the evolution of pastoralism, human dependence on domesticated species was very great, almost total in some "mature" cases. As the system of farming and animal keeping developed into today's world, that dependence could be dangerous. Looking at the production of food on a worldwide scale there were six animals, or groups of animals that each produced over a million tons of meat per year (Harlan 1976: 91): pigs, cattle, poultry, sheep, goats and buffalo (in that order), but of the 113.1 total metric tons just about 75% of the productivity came from two animals, pigs and cattle. Plants are a bit different. The thirty or so principal plants yielded about 2360 million metric tons of produce (Harlan 1976: 90). But the top seven producers (wheat, rice, corn, potato, barley, sweet potato and cassava in that order) accounted for about 71% of the total yield. Thus, nine plants and animals constitute three-fourths of the world's food supply—this vulnerability is part of the legacy of the "Neolithic Revolution."

There are, however, two sides to the issue. The legacy is good because these plants and animals have been brought to a point where they can provide food for the billions of people now living. It is bad because out of the millions of plant and animal species, we are dependent on so few. If something catastrophic should happen to just one or two of them, our extreme dependence could be turned into disaster for those same billions of people. There may be little resiliency in this subsistence regime.

It is probably true that even the most highly evolved subsistence systems, like that of the twentieth century United States, still involves some hunting and gathering. Gathering wild black berries and other fruits that are turned into jam is still a subsistence activity enjoyed by many. Hunting and fishing still provide sustenance for the population as a whole. But, viewed against the backdrop of wheat and corn production, along with that of cattle, pigs and poultry, these numbers, even for fishing, are pretty small fry.

The deviations from these norms are also important. For example, the Lapp reindeer is biologically a wild animal but manipulated in a way that most archaeologists would agree is a form of food production. The Indian elephant is a wild animal, left to breed in the wild and then recaptured, tamed and used in parts of a subsistence system that falls into the same category. What about birds like peacocks and parrots, kept in captivity for long periods of time, or even the worldwide distribution of the "wild" urban pigeon? The lumber industry is dependent on trees that seem to be wild, but replanting after cutting is now the norm. As one begins to look more deeply into the notions of food production (or raw material production in the case of sylvaculture) and domestication, the distinctions among various management techniques become slightly fuzzy and the notions of wild, domesticated and feral are not necessarily as clear as they might at first be thought.

EARLY DOMESTICATES: Near East and South Asia

Placing the center of research on the early domestication of plants and animals in the habitats of the wild progenitors may have been Braidwood's greatest contribution to research on the "neolithic." Focusing the search on such habitats, whether it is his Near Eastern "constellation," the millet area of Africa (Harlan 1989b, 1992), or the corn/bean/squash regions of the Americas, makes good sense but presents a problem that has not been addressed adequately. Using the modern distribution of these wild ancestors may not reflect the Late Glacial or Early Holocene distribution of the same species. In large part, due to the density of research in the Near East, archaeologists are beginning to come to grips with the problem there, but it has been a major research effort, involving a massive amount of work.

As noted in the discussion of cultural geography, botanical surveys in the 20th century have indicated that wild wheat might not have quite as wide a distribution as barley (Vavilov 1949-50; Zohary and Hopf 1988: 16-52; Harlan and Zohary 1966). Palaeobotanists have yet to find evidence for wild wheat in Baluchistan or Afghanistan. Wild barley, however, is present. One might legitimately wonder if the modern distribution of wild wheat informs us about the distribution of this plant at the end of the last glacial period. There are some confusing bits of data that suggest that the whole story of this distribution may not be known, even in the Near East, as Naomi Miller notes, at Tell Mureybit, an early village farming community in Syria.

The earlier levels have roasting pits that contained concentrations of wild einkorn. There is little doubt that these grains represent food remains, but Mureybit lies outside the modern range of wild einkorn. As a result the finds have been adduced either as evidence for early cultivation or as evidence that the Syrian desert was moister than it is now. Sherratt (1980) suggests that people could have farmed the relatively moist river flood plain in this otherwise marginal environment. Based on the presence of cerealia pollen from the archaeological deposits Leroi-Gourhan (1974), concludes that there were cultivated fields at the base of the site, presumably einkorn. An alternative explanation for the cereal pollen on the site is that it arrived adhering to the harvested wild grains. (cf. Robinson and Hubbard 1977). Van Zeist and Woldring's (1980) palynological study strongly supports the view that the climate was moister then than today, so the einkorn finds might have been collected from the wild (Miller 1991: 140).

These observations can be seen as an indication that the modern distribution of wild wheat and barley does not inform us of the distribution of these plants at the beginning of the Holocene. Thus, it is premature to insist that the Indo-Iranian borderlands were outside the distribution of wild wheat 10,000 years ago.

Even if wild wheat was not present on the Indo-Iranian Borderlands this region could still have played a key role in the domestication process. The genetic history of free threshing wheats, those most useful to humans, involves genetic crosses with the genus *Triticum* and with a related plant, goat-face grass (*Aegilops squarrosa*), found all across the Iranian plateau. Richard H. Meadow has made the point that: "The necessary conditions for an emmer X ("and") *Aegilops* cross...could have been met anywhere the latter appeared as a weed in fields where emmer was cultivated. Therefore, *T. aestivum* could have originated as easily in the Pakistan area as in northwest Iran and, in fact, it seems quite likely that free threshing wheat of the west was *T. turgidum* cf. conv. *durum* and that of the east *T. aestivum*" (Meadow 1993a: 301).

A South Asian center for the domestication of plants and animals is an old concept, going back to the famous Russian botanist Nicoli Vavilov (1949-50, 1957). Lorenzo Costantini and Loredana Costantini Biasini have made the following observation that is pertinent to the present description of the genetic resources of Baluchistan for the promotion of the domestication of plants and the establishment of early village farming communities:

> Phytogeographically speaking the Baluch territory as a whole is part of the Irano-Turanic and Sudanese regions. The areas included in the Irano-Turanic region, with a continental climate of widely ranging daily and annual temperatures, low rainfall and two distinct seasons, i.e., hot dry summer and bitterly cold winter, are the northern

portions of Baluchistan lying in the Irano-Anatolian or Armeno-Iranian province of the eastern Irano-Turanic sub-region (Zohary 1973: 90). The vegetation of these territories is characterized by plant associations in which *Pistacia* and *Amygdalus* form the so-called 'steppe-forest' with trees and bushes extremely sparse and far apart. Like *Pistacia* and *Amygdalus*, the thicker formations of *Juniperus* also form 'steppe-forest.' ...from the agro-ecological standpoint Baluchistan represents a transitional zone. Although including it among the Indo-Pakistan regions, Vavilov (1957: 87, 180) described a number of features it shares with the Irano-Turkestan area (Costantini and Biasini 1985: 16-7).

This is essentially the description of Baluchistan found in Cultural Geography, Part 3 of this book. As Jean-Francois Jarrige has observed, it may indicate that Baluchistan, possibly including the Northwest Frontier areas of Pakistan, along with Afghanistan, might have been part of a large geographical area within which the wild progenitors of potentially domesticable plants would have been found (Jarrige 1995a: 64). These are characterized by the additional presence of pistachio (*Pistacia*), almond (*Amygdalus*) and juniper (*Juniperus*) as significant elements of a steppe-forest in a climate with hot, dry summers and cold, wet winters.

OTHER IMPORTANT CONSIDERATIONS

A Lack of Knowledge About the Evolution of Plants and Animals

There is an imperfect evolutionary history of the plants and animals that have been domesticated, even in Braidwood's "constellation" or the corn/bean/squash complex of the Americas. The early history of goats and sheep, for example, is not known in sufficient detail for anyone to sit back and confidently believe that we know it all. In fact, Sebastian Payne once proposed that sheep are all simply domesticated goats, some of which have been retained by human communities and others returned to the wild as feral animals. They continued to evolve along their own lines into the "wild" animals we see today (Payne 1968). This proposal has been withdrawn, of course, but such notions of ancient biological change, guided by human intervention, long lost to history except for the archaeological and palaeontological record, is a possibility for many species and should not be ignored when archaeologists formulate the problems that they intend to test in the field and laboratory.

The same might pertain to the evolutionary history of the winter grasses, wheat and barley, that were key species in early agriculture in the Near East and South Asia. These plants just "show-up" in the archaeological record and it is assumed that the varieties that we call "wild" are genetically pristine, having come into existence through natural selection completely independent of human intervention. This may be the case, but it needs to be, and can be, tested. What if wheat and barley are plants that Pleistocene "gatherers" used, even in the absence of ground stone tools. The use that such "gatherers" made of these plants could have played a major role in shaping their genetic constitution and evolution. This would imply that the "wild" plants we see today (and in the archaeological record) are in fact feral, significantly changing the manner in which the archaeological record should be read. Of course, it cannot be said that this was true, but much more needs to be known about the evolutionary history of plants like wheat and barley before archaeologists and palaeobotanists can speak with true confidence about their domestication.

Scholars interested in the history of plant domestication have studied the modern distribution of these organisms in some detail (Vavilov 1949-50; Harlan and Zohary 1966; Zohary 1970;

Zohary and Hopf 1988; Harlan 1971, 1976). The contemporary, or near contemporary, distribution of wild wheat and barley is reasonably well known, especially for the Near East to the west of the Zagros. The interior parts of Iran, Central Asia, Pakistan and Afghanistan have been studied, but not with the intensity of the more westerly area. These are studies of modern patterns of occurrence; the manner in which they relate to deep antiquity, say 10,000 or 12,000 years ago, is a matter of speculation. Is the contemporary, or near contemporary, distribution of wild wheat, for example, a good proxy for the distribution of this plant at the beginnings of the Holocene? In spite of many assurances, we really do not know. Maybe it is a good proxy, but maybe it is not.

The Early Domestication of Plants and Animals Not Now Important

Many plants and animals have been domesticated, or played a significant role in the Indus Age. There is a tendency to believe that today's subsistence economy, or at least that of an "ethnographic present," is an adequate guide for the formulation of archaeological research strategies and that what we need to look for is the history of the plants and animals that are in use today. This assumption, or approach, ignores the possibility that plants and animals that are not significant contributors to food producing economies now are historically relevant, and has been shown to be unsound in a number of places. For example, a group of plants of the genus *Chenopodium* seems to have been as economically important in the archaic farming system of eastern North America (Smith 1989) as it was in Saurashtra during the Mature Harappan (Rojdi B) (Weber 1991: 119; see also Vishnu-Mittre and Savithri 1976 and 1982: 214, for similar evidence from Surkotada in Kutch). In fact, the entire Rojdi subsistence system is characterized by a reliance on a number of plants that are not economically important today. The same is true in the New World for a number of gourds. Thus, to use the present day as a model to understand this aspect of the domestication process could lead one down the 'garden' path.

There are a number of other concerns which include the idea of a "hearth of domestication" as well as complex matters of diffusion and independent invention. Our human relationship with plants and animals is more complex than notions such as "domesticated/undomesticated" or "hunting-gathering/food producing" can accommodate. These relationships are on a set of continua or interaction zones which shift over time in an ecological and environmental context. They are not starkly defined in "black and white," but involve complex shades of grey, which occasionally become dense enough to determine that a relationship has crossed some still poorly defined line suggesting "food production and domestication."

METHOD: How are Domesticated Plants and Animals Identified?

One of the serious methodological issues that archaeologists interested in the beginnings of food production and domestication must face up to is the manner in which this subsistence form can be identified. The shift from a mobile hunting and gathering economy to life in sedentary villages is certainly archaeologically detectable, but this does not help much with the identification of evolution of mobile pastoralism. Finding these camps is much more difficult than finding an early village. Unraveling what was happening inside the villages and camps only doubles the difficulties inherent in addressing the problem. Archaeologists have become very good at collecting artifacts and plotting architecture, but they are also very good about collecting animal bones, antler, horn cores, shell and other animal remains, as well as materials from plants: seeds and pollen. Seeds, once they have been carbonized are like coal, and although they are fragile and easily crushed and abraded, they are very stable and will not rot. Wet sieving, and flotation methods have been perfected and using them makes it possible to recover all manner of things: seeds, twigs, charcoal, very small pieces of detritus from chipping stones, even the exoskeletons of insects.[3] By using these methods we can determine, in part, what plants and animals were used by the people who occupied the sites we excavate. It is even possible, if the data are consistent among a number of different sites of the same period, to get a sense of the proportional importance of various species within the spectrum of plants and animals in use. However, this is specialized business, and one must be cautious not to jump to conclusions by using the results from only one or two excavated sites, or from many sites that lack genuine comparability. While it is comparatively easy to identify the genus of plants and animals, distinguishing the domesticated varieties from their wild counterparts is far more difficult. But, there are highly skilled people engaged in archaeozoology and palaeobotany, and many institutions have fine comparative collections and herbaria of modern and securely identified ancient material that can be used to identify newly excavated specimens.

Closely related species always present problems to biologists working with archaeological materials. For example, in the Greater Indus region the skeletons of domesticated (and wild) sheep (*Ovis aries*) and goats (*Capra hircus*) look very much alike, and only certain bones can be used to distinguish one from the other. Thus, many reports contain three categories: "sheep," "goats" and a peculiar archaeological animal, the "sheep/goat" accommodating those bones that are surely one or the other, but cannot be ascribed to either animal with certainty. It has recently been learned that the blackbuck (*Antelope cervicapra*), an animal with a wide distribution in South Asia, has a skeleton that is also very much like these animals, further complicating the business of identification (R. Meadow, personal communication).

Experts have developed specific criteria that help to determine whether particular plants and animals were domesticated or wild. Many (not all) of these "rules" are based on the consideration that domestication involves human interference in the reproductive cycle. This changes the genetic make up of these species which in turn will change their appearance, or phenotypic expression of the genetic code. Domesticated goats look different from their wild relatives and the same is true for sheep, wheat and barley. Some of these changes are preserved in the skeletons of animals and plant parts that can be recovered in excavation. The criteria that can be used to distinguish domesticated from wild plants and animals have been clearly presented by Sandor Bokonyi, an archaeozoologist of great distinction (Bokonyi 1969).

Animals

1. Animals found far outside their native ranges — This is a good indicator, provided the native range of the animal is securely known, and there are reasonable data suggesting that environmental change has not altered this in the distant past. Wild sheep and goats are upland and mountain creatures and when their remains are found far removed from these environments, as in a lowland desert, it can be reasonably asserted that humans brought them there and if the distance is great enough, it might not be as dead kills.

2. Morphological changes in the bony parts of animals — Included is a general reduction in the size of some animals, such as cattle. Changes in the shape and curvature of horn cores is also present, as are changes in toe bones, and stress markers peculiar to domesticated animals. There might also be increased variation in the animals, as in domesticated dogs.

3. Changes in the proportion of age grades from those found in wild herds — The theory is that adult animals are those that: (1) reproduce, and (2) are workers and have accumulated the investment of their owners. Therefore, young animals are killed more frequently, and this can be seen in faunal assemblages.

4. Changes in the proportion of sex grades not found in the even distribution of wild population — This proposition rests on the theory that female domesticated animals are important for the reproductive process in a way that males are not, and that the females will therefore always be kept alive in preference to males. Older males for work animals, like bullocks and water buffalo are also important, so the burden for food, if this approach has credence, falls on young males, whose bones should turn up with a higher frequency than any sex/age grade. Although this is good theory, distinguishing male from female animals based on their skeletal parts is very difficult and can only be done from a few body parts.

5. Artistic representation of domesticated animals — It occasionally happens, but is not important in the early phases of the development of food production and domestication.

6. Artifacts associated with domestication — They can be useful and might occur directly in the archaeological record, or their use inferred from the skeleton. For example, bits occur as artifacts and their use can be inferred from the jaw bones and teeth of animals that were equipped with them, since they wear away these body parts.

Plants

1. Plants found far outside their native ranges — It is an especially good device provided the native range of the plant is securely known, and there are reasonable data suggesting that environmental change has not altered this in the distant past. Wild wheat and barley are upland and mountain plants and when their remains are found in river valley settlements far removed from these environments it is reasonable to believe that humans brought them there to be planted and used.

2. Change in the morphology of plants; a useful criteria — It frequently happens that humans breed out the natural seeding qualities of the plants. In the grasses, it means that the brittle features of the mature plants that allow them to seed themselves by easily falling to the ground are lost. Humans do not want shattered seed heads on the ground, when they try to harvest mature plants with a sickle. Wild plants frequently have seeds wrapped in a tough glume, used to nourish and protect the seed in the self-planting and germination cycle. We breed plants in a way that selects against the tough threshing problem.

3. Domesticated seeds are frequently larger than their wild counter parts — This happens for two reasons: (1) humans tend and protect their fields and may even bring water to them to increase yield, part of which comes from larger, healthier seeds; (2) humans select larger seeds for replanting, hoping to assure good yields in this way.

4. Occasional representation of domesticated plants in ancient art — It is not important in the early phases of the development of food production and domestication.

6. Just as with animals, artifacts associated with plant domestication can be useful — Artifacts might occur directly in the archaeological record, or their use inferred from the archaeological record. Sickles, grinding stones to make flour and winnowing tools are such artifacts. It may seem curious to some, but stone blades that have been used to cut grass develop a shine, called "sickle sheen" that is not actually burnishing, but a deposit of silica that comes from the stalk of the plant. The friction of cutting generated just enough heat for this transfer to be made, over hundreds of cutting strokes, of course. Imagine biting down on a piece of straw (ripe grain) and drawing it quickly through the teeth. The heat from friction is considerable, enough in fact that this should be done cautiously, since it might hurt. Ground stone food processing tools are also important implements to suggest the harvest and use of food grains, remembering that ground stone tools are useful for processing other materials as well.

Richard H. Meadow (1993a: 296-98) has discussed the methods for distinguishing wild from domesticated species at the early village site of Mehrgarh in Pakistan. He observes that the strongest case comes when multiple lines of evidence add up to the same conclusion. Moreover, we should be looking most closely at morphological changes and proportions of sex and age grades, especially from a place like Mehrgarh, which is close to the native range of the plants and animals involved in the domestication process, but slightly outside of it in most cases.

Defining and then observing the very earliest phase of food production and domestication is not easy. The genetic expression of change in both plants and animals took time to surface. This is especially true for larger mammals with longer terms between generations. Thus, the techniques that rely on morphological changes to bones and plant parts will be effective only after human manipulation has been well established. Progression from hunting and gathering to food production and domestication may involve some subtle variations in the way in which humans manipulated the species and even the study of sex/age grades for animals might not be capable of detecting the earliest experiments. It is generally agreed that there are some reasonably good methods available to archaeologists to identify early food production and domestication but even the best of them may be fallible if invoked alone. Conclusive results can be achieved best when several sets of observations imply the same conclusion.

EARLY FOOD PRODUCTION AND DOMESTICATION: Differing Views

There is anything but unanimity on where and when the food production and domestication "revolution" took place, or, for that matter, whether it was a revolution at all. Explaining it in sociocultural terms is a subject that is even more widely debated.

Where

The question of where food production and domestication took place is more complicated than might be thought at first. Clearly, the domestication process took place in or near those areas where the wild progenitors of the early domesticates lived. In the Near East the great civilizations of antiquity (Sumer, Babylonia, Egypt) took their livelihood from wheat and barley along with cattle, sheep, goats and pigs. The fact that all of these plants and animals, along with others suspected of having been involved in early agriculture and pastoralism were native to the same region, led archaeologists to focus on the region from the beginning.

Such reasoning has given rise to the concept of "hearths" of domestication, so clearly articulated by the geographer Carl O. Sauer (1952). These were defined by Sauer in terms of the biological diversity and richness of these world regions in terms of the presence of a number of plants and animals that are known to have been domesticated (Sauer 1952: map facing 74).

The notion of "hearths" has fallen out of fashion in the discussion of the early domestication of plants and animals. It is true, in part, because when one takes a close look at the natural world, a series of gradually changing clines rather than centers is found, as the notion of a hearth seems to imply. It also seems to divide the world into regions that are "haves" and "have nots" with respect to the plants and animals that have been suited for domestication, which appears to be only partially true. Still, there is a germ of truth in Sauer's ideas, even if they do not represent a final answer, and he should not be forgotten.

The Near East, or the lands of James Henry Breasted's "Fertile Crescent," is one of the areas with the "constellation of potentially domesticable plants and animals" defined by Braidwood. Sauer also defined the Near East as a hearth, based on the presence of these same plants and animals. The region was so distantly removed from the Greater Indus Region that he gave the latter an independent status. Sauer envisioned a third hearth in eastern India, extending to mainland Southeast Asia. Central and northern China was a fourth hearth for Sauer as were the Ethiopian highlands. In the New World Sauer envisioned a great hearth from Mexico, south along the great cordillera to Chile.

Not all researchers who deal with the question of "agricultural origins" would agree with Sauer's proposal of multiple hearths in the Old World, or even the notion of a "hearth" at all. But there is a geographical dimension to the origins of domestication, and that is something on which virtually all researchers agree (e.g., Harlan 1971, 1976, 1977). Some (not all) archaeologists still prefer to see one or two regions, generally the Near East and East Asia as "The Hearths" where food production and domestication first began. Then, in some yet to be explained way, diffused, or "spread" to other parts of the Old World, sometimes using new plants and animals as villages and pastoral camps were established in new environments. It is generally agreed that food production and domestication in the New World is a slightly later, but independent, process of adaptation. In the Old World the question is whether there was one hearth or many, and as a result what role diffusion might have played. These observations are interlinked and remain points of contention and debate.

When

The date for the earliest food production and domestication is also a point of contention. It has been assumed for several generations that, whatever the cause, the earliest evidence would be found in the Holocene; the period that followed the retreat of the last continental glaciers 10,000 to 12,000 years ago. Changes associated with the retreat of the glaciers brought the world's climate into its present dynamic equilibrium. It was once thought that the early Holocene was hot and dry in the Near East and that this stress was a causal factor in the development of food production and domestication (Childe 1936; summarized in Braidwood 1975: 95-7). This is no longer a viable proposition. However, theories based on environmental stress are still in vogue when the origins of the "Neolithic" are discussed.

What little was (and is) known of late glacial "epipalaeolithic" archaeology in the Near East and South Asia does not suggest that these peoples were making extensive use of domesticated species, or even species of plants and animals that were later domesticated. They did not live in villages nor did they have ground stone food processing tools. In the Near East, later peoples who had houses, ground stone tools and pottery, did use Braidwood's constellation of plants and animals and it appeared that the task for archaeological research was to close the gap between the epipalaeolithic assemblages and the early villages.

Childe presented the idea that there was a "Neolithic Revolution," implying that there was a short period of intensive cultural change that transformed hunter-gatherers into village based farmers and mobile herders. The time period within which there was a changeover was thought to be short. Some believe that this position is suspect. The economic prehistorian Eric Higgs and his followers, proposed that there would be no discontinuity between the economies we call hunting and gathering and those called pastoral and agricultural (Higgs 1972, 1975; Higgs and Jarman 1972; Jarman and Wilkinson 1972). From Higgs' point of view, pastoralism involving domesticated animals is simply a new theme within a more general set of predator/prey relationships, with humans caring for and protecting the animals they once killed directly. Tending of animals is seen as an effort to increase the dependability of the food supply by providing a reliable, renewable source of animal resources. At least one new product, milk, not found in a purely hunting environment, would also be available within the context of food production. The same could be true for human relationship to plants; cultivation being an effort to tend the plants thereby assuring a more bountiful yield.

The Higgs position suggests that the beginnings of both food production and domestication may be delicate and involve only slight modifications in human behavior, animals and plants. Thus, a distinct threshold, or a "revolution" separating hunting and gathering from pastoralism and agriculture, might not exist at all, since they may be on a very slow continuum of change. Seen from this perspective, the food production relationship and domestication in some form may go back many millennia to the last glacial period.

The interdependent questions of "when did it happen?" and especially "why did it happen when it happened?" remain unanswered. Why humans came to domesticate plants and animals at some particular point in history remains somewhat of a mystery. It seems to be a phenomenon that developed just after the opening of the Holocene in several regions of both the Old and New Worlds. Why it did not occur earlier is not known. The Higgsians, of course, hold that these special relationships were in place in the Pleistocene, and that the new development was the village farming community, not food production and domestication. Such are the unresolved conceptual debates.

VIEWS ON THE DEVELOPMENT OF FOOD PRODUCTION IN SOUTH ASIA

There is some evidence for two opposed views on the development of food production and domestication in the Subcontinent (see Gupta and Kesarwani 1983 for a review). One begins with the observation that the western borderlands of Pakistan have the same suite of potentially domesticable plants and animals that were available in the Near East; sheep, goats, cattle, barley and possibly wheat. With these resources in place there, it is highly likely that a process took place in the region independent of the Near East. The South Asian "Neolithic" was an autochthonous development. It can be thought of as the "revisionist position" contrasted to the second view, the "standard position," which holds that the development of food production and domestication took place in the Near East about 8000 or 9000 BC and from there diffused into Europe, across the Iranian Plateau into Central Asia and the Indian Subcontinent.

S. P. Gupta and Arun Kesarwani have undertaken a review of these two positions (1983) and concluded: "...the theory of diffusion of Neolithicism from the Fertile Crescent to various parts of the world stands completely discredited and has been replaced by the theory of independent origins at various places..." (Gupta and Kesarwani 1983: 105). This may be a slight overstatement, but it does offer a pointed version of one position.

The View Taken Here: Expanding the Geographical Dimensions of the Nuclear Zone

It has been clear for many years that the wild progenitors of the plants and animals on which Near Eastern, South and Central Asian civilizations are founded are quite widely distributed. The animals (sheep, goats, cattle) and plants (barley and possibly wheat) are all found in the uplands of the area ranging east from the Mediterranean Sea, between the Arabian Gulf and the plains of Central Asia. The region is dominated by (but not limited to) the Iranian Plateau and Hindu Kush of Afghanistan. This region between the Indus River and the Mediterranean Sea, the Arabian Gulf and the deserts of Central Asia (Figure 4.2) where the ranges of Braidwood's constellation of potentially domesticable plants and animals overlap, can be seen as a vast interaction sphere in prehistoric times. This is the expanded nuclear zone for Near Eastern, Iranian, Central and South Asian domestication. The domestication of those plants and animals on which Near Eastern, South and Central Asian civilizations were founded, took place in the zone proposed here. Interaction within this zone may have been so intense and regular that it

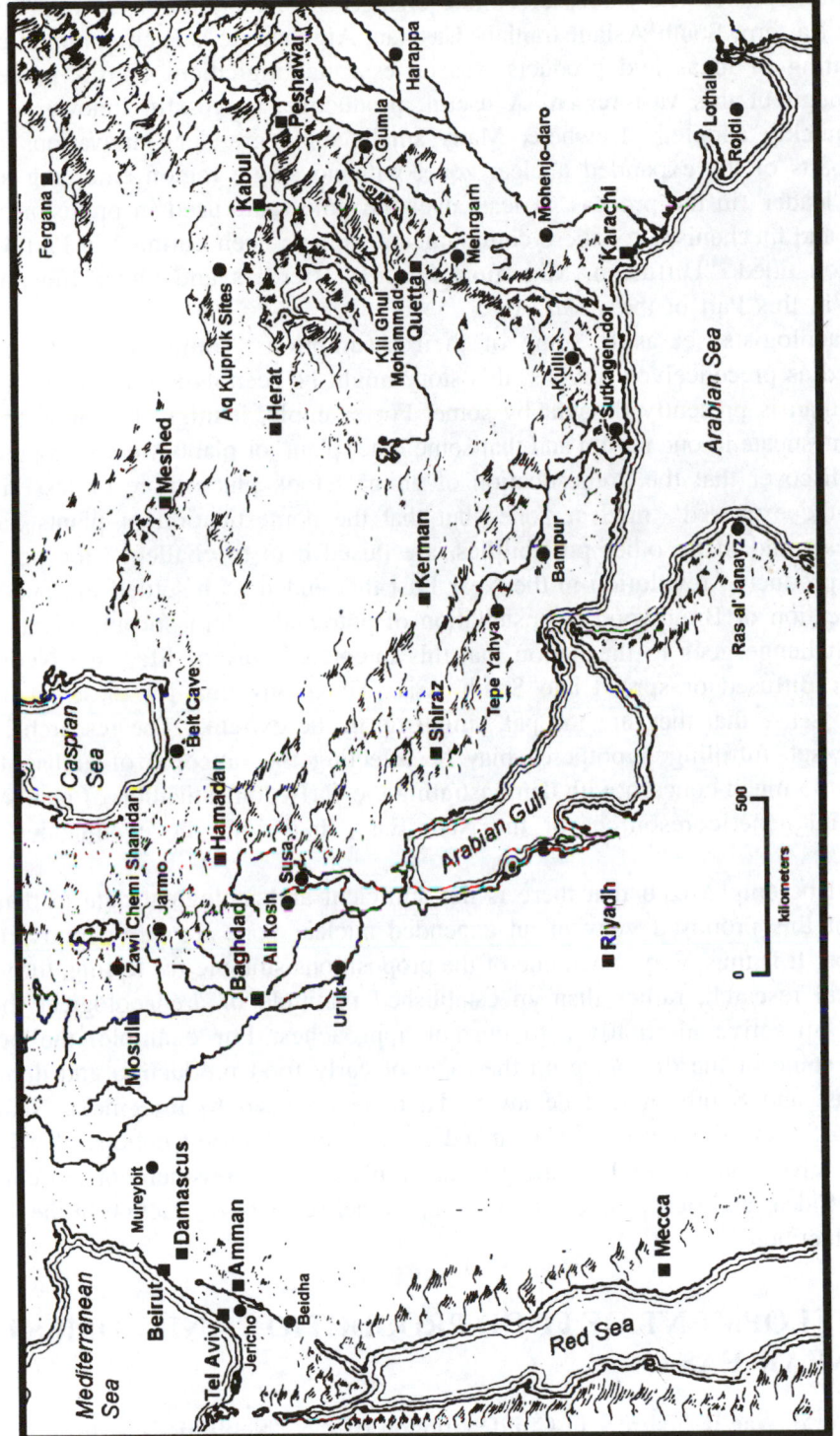

Figure 4.2. The Middle Asia region with potentially domesticable plants and animals on which the Indus Age was founded.

will be found that there is no predominant early center of innovation within it; the ideas and products of early experiments with plants and animals having been rapidly disseminated within the interaction sphere. The forces of culture change and adaptation were regional, rather than local (Near Eastern, South Asian, Iranian, Caspian, Afghan, etc.). Rich communication and the prolific sharing of ideas and products was an essential ingredient in this process of culture change throughout this vast region. A useful, productive, successful innovation in one place could be quickly adopted elsewhere. Many small, some grander, innovations took place in numerous parts of the expanded nuclear zone, with no single region emerging as a clear and consistent "leader" in the process, at least over the time scale used in prehistoric archaeology. The means and mechanisms of these communications have been outlined in Part 1 of this book, in the section titled "Diffusion, Migration, Farmers, Herders and Other Itinerants." More is found later in this Part of the *Indus Age*.

If archaeologists set aside some of their assumptions, some of which might even be characterized as preconceived notions, this story might be seen as a good deal more interesting and varied than is presently thought by some. For example, it might be found that wheat was an early domesticate in one region and that some other plant, or plants were being used elsewhere. We might discover that the domestication of animals took place more or less simultaneously throughout the expanded "nuclear zone" but that the domestication of plants has a different history. These, and many other possibilities, are raised here to challenge the notion that there was a food producing revolution in the Near East that ended with settled life and encompassed the domestication of Braidwood's constellation of potentially domesticable plants and animals. A further challenge goes to the notion that this integrated way of life, "the Neolithic village" subsequently diffused or spread into South Asia. The motivation for these challenges comes from a deep sense that they are too pat, simplistic in the extreme. The research has reached a point where self-fulfilling hypotheses may be affecting the outcome of archaeological work. There is far too much concern with demonstrating the early domestication of plants and animals, or the special genetic resources of the Near East, than with the evenhanded testing of a proposition.

It should be emphasized that there is not sufficient archaeological data to demonstrate the usefulness of this proposed view of an expended nuclear zone for early food production and domestication. It is thus, very much one of the propositions suitable for testing, through extended archaeological research, rather than an established platitude of archaeological theory. But, it holds some attractive alternatives to current approaches. For example, the polarities that characterize some of the discourse on the topic of early food production and domestication in the Near East and South Asia fade away. There is no need to imagine a Near Eastern as opposed to a South Asian center. The linked and somewhat turgid notions of "diffusion" and "independent invention" also fall by the wayside, replaced with considerations of communication, the sharing of ideas and richly endowed, broad based networks of interaction of the kind discussed in the Introduction.

THE DEVELOPMENT OF FOOD PRODUCTION AND DOMESTICATION IN THE NEAR EAST

Following World War II, interest in Childe's notion of the "Neolithic" as the first great human revolution, and Braidwood's insightful thoughts about the nature of these changes, led archaeologists to develop problem oriented field programs to investigate the phenomenon. The first big project was undertaken by Braidwood in Iraqi Kurdistan, at Jarmo (Braidwood and

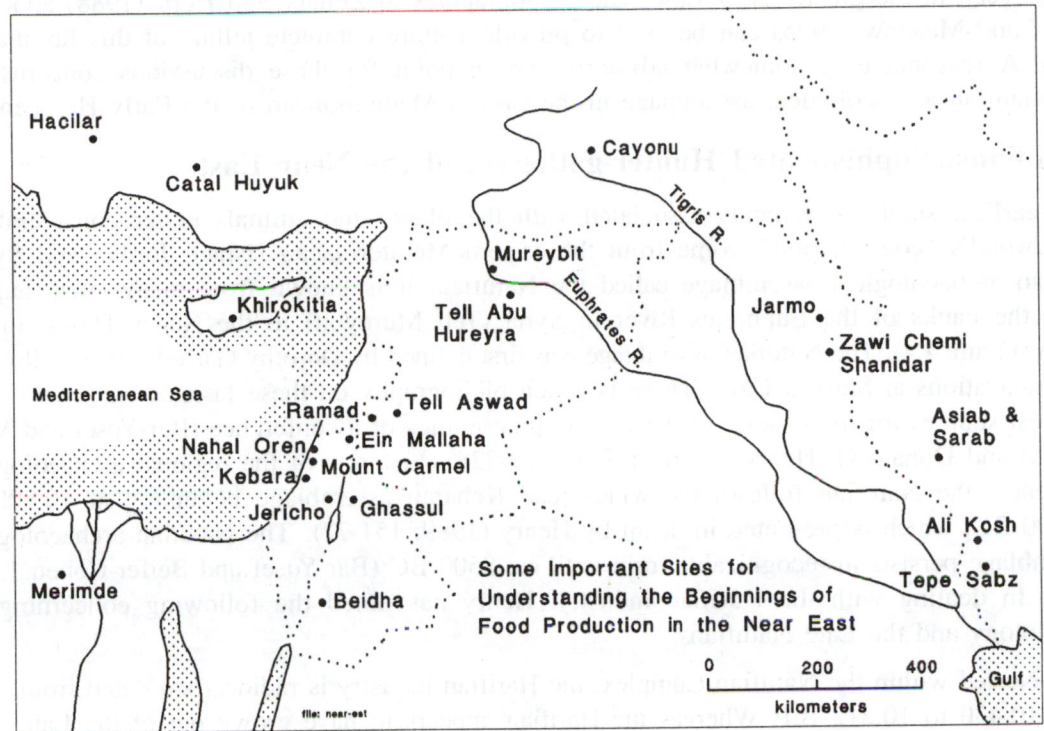

Figure 4.3. Some of the sites important to the study of the food-producing revolution in the Near East

Howe 1960; L. Braidwood et al. 1983), which was complemented by the excavation of Shanidar Cave and the nearby early village at Zawi Chemi Shanidar (Ralph Solecki 1955, 1963; Rose Solecki 1964, 1981). Since 1946, literally dozens of sites within this region have been excavated in the search for the story of the beginnings of village farming communities and pastoral camps (Figure 4.3). Although there is still a lot to be learned, the resulting data sets are significant and the broad outlines of this process, at least in this region, seem to be coming into focus. There are good surveys of this work (Mellaart 1965, 1975; Redman 1978; Purushottam Singh 1974, 1991), although these are a bit dated. Naomi Miller's reviews (1991, 1992) were especially helpful in gaining a clear picture of the palaeobotanical material as was the book-length treatment by Zohary and Hopf (1988). Gary A. Wright has written an important article on the history of this research (1971). Several recent edited works covering the development of agriculture generally can be used to contextualize the Near Eastern and South Asian materials (Renfrew 1991; van Zeist, Wasylikowa and Behre 1991; Bar-Yosef and Khazanov 1992; Gebauer and Price 1992; Cowan and Watson 1992; Price and Gebauer 1995).

The environment within which this process took place were the uplands and their adjacent plains; terrain not so different from Baluchistan and the Indus Valley. The Near Eastern environment includes the Levant, the Mediterranean coast and Jordan Valley. Pistachio, almond, oak and juniper forests are characteristic of the region. Also included along with the progenitors of the early domesticates are wild forms such as *Zizyphus* sp., prunes and onions. This is much like Baluchistan and the quote from Costantini and Biasini (1985: 16-7; see also Helbaek 1966a: 64-5) is the operative principle when dealing with the commonalities of the environment of domestication in the greater Near East and South Asia.

The following is a brief survey of the major stages of change that led to early villages and camps seen in the greater Near East. The bibliographies in Zohary and Hopf (1988) and Bar-Yosef and Meadow (1995) can be used to provide a more complete telling of this fascinating story. A reasonable, if somewhat arbitrary starting point for these discussions concerns the Natufian, an archaeological assemblage in the eastern Mediterranean of the Early Holocene.

Natufians: Sophisticated Hunter-gatherers of the Near East

The earliest stable settlements associated with the plants and animals under consideration, Braidwood's "constellation," come from the eastern Mediterranean (Israel, Jordan and Syria) and an archaeological assemblage called the Natufian. It is known from many sites ranging from the banks of the Euphrates River in Syria (Tell Mureybit) to the Negev Desert in the south (Figure 4.4). The Natufian assemblage was first defined by Dorothy Garrod (1932) following her excavations at Shukba Cave. There is a rich bibliography on these fascinating peoples, but the best sources for the general reader are the proceedings of a conference (Bar-Yosef and Valla 1991a) and Donald O. Henry's essay (1989: 179-228). In terms of the regional archaeological sequence, the Natufian follows the widespread Kebaran assemblage beginning at 10,800 or 10,500 BC, which is presented in detail by Henry (1989: 151-77). The Natufian archaeological assemblage persists in recognizable form until ca. 8500 BC (Bar-Yosef and Belfer-Cohen 1989: 467). In dealing with the Harifian industry, Henry has noted the following concerning its chronology and the Late Natufians:

> Nested within the Natufian Complex, the Harifian industry is radiocarbon dated from 10,430 to 10,212 B.P. Whereas the Harifian appears to have grown out of the Late Natufian communities that failed within the marginal habitat of the Negev, Harifian groups were coeval with those Late Natufian settlements that continued to exist within the better watered areas of northern Israel (Henry 1989: 185, see also Table 4.1).

TABLE 4.1
A Chronology for Food Production and Domestication in the Levant

PPNB		7300/7200 to ca. 5800 BC
	Sultanian	8300/100 to 7300/200 BC
PPNA		
	Khiamain	8500/8300 to 8100 BC
	Harifian	8700-8200
	Late	ca. 9000 to 8500/8300 BC
Natufian		
	Early	10,800/10,500 BC to ca. 9000 BC
Geometric Kebaran		12,000 to 10,800/10,500 BC

Donald Henry (1989: 183) makes a special point that there is apparently an absence of Early Natufian sites in the arid zone of the Negev and the Jordanian Desert. However, Harifian sites are found in this environment.

The earliest Natufians were sedentary, or semi-sedentary people who intensively exploited the oak-pistachio forest zone (Figure 4.5). In later times they also exploited the adjacent, more desertic zone. Natufians lived in caves and rockshelters, but also in the open where they built simple, small, rounded structures, using plant material for the walls and roof. Their microlithic tools, which are aesthetically attractive, included sickle blades. Ground stone tools made from limestone, basalt and sandstone are also known, some hollowed out of the living rock on which, or in which, the Natufians lived. They made and wore jewelry; shells are especially prominent. They also enjoyed carving bone and produced some very fine pieces of art (Figure 4.6, 4.7, 4.8).

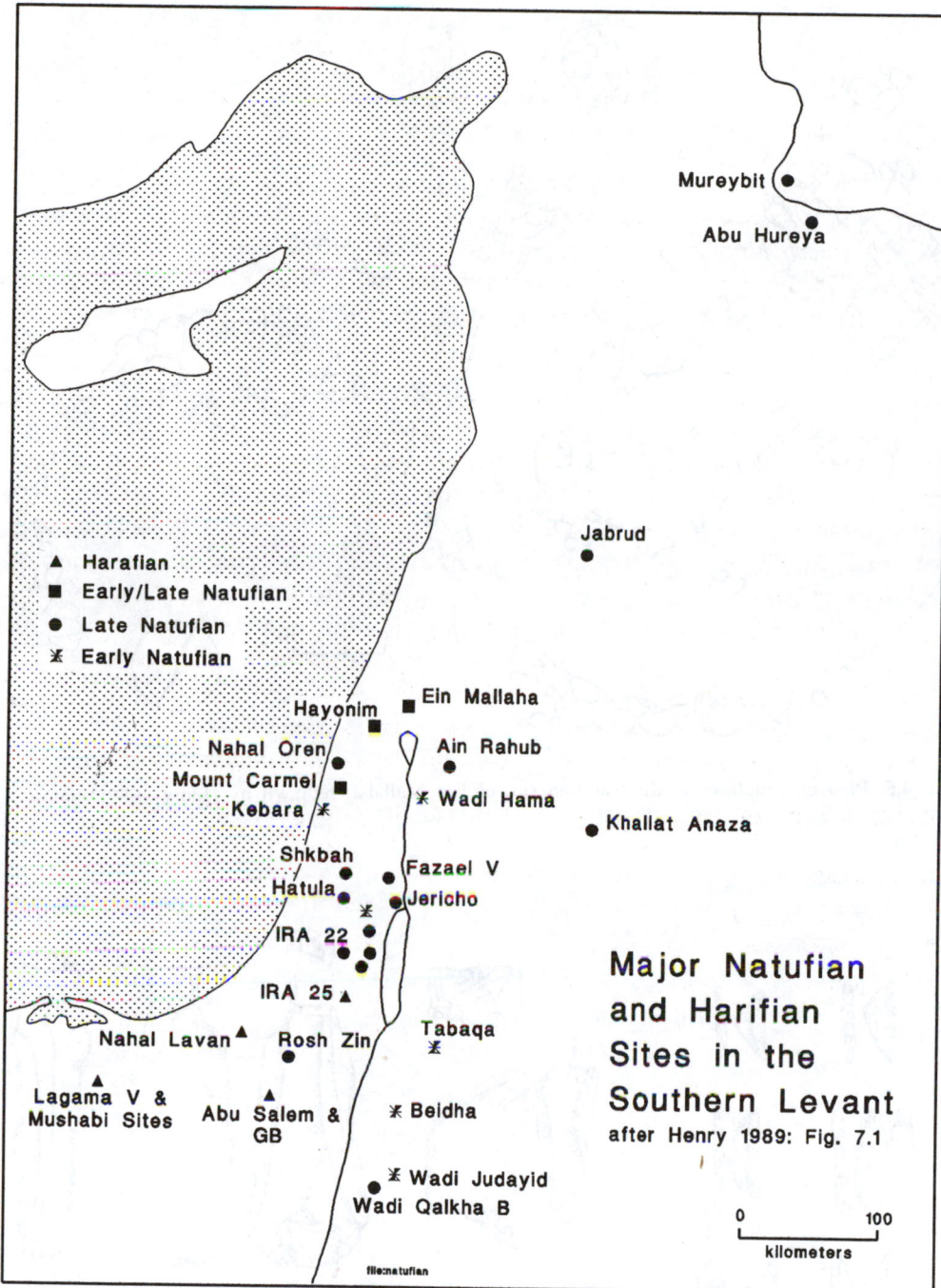

Figure 4.4. Natufian and Harifian sites, after Henry 1989: 183

The Natufians had far ranging trade relationships which brought them obsidian from Anatolia and shells from the Mediterranean, Red Sea and Nile, as in the headdress of dentalium shells on the head of a Natufian from Mount Carmel (Plate 4.1, Plate 4.2). These might have been exchanged for sulfur, salt and bitumen, all products available in the Jordan Valley. Some individual wealth may be expressed in these imported items.

The large Natufian site of Ain Mallaha exceeds 1000 square meters (0.1 hectares). The inhabitants had to level the land here. Other investments were made in the construction of

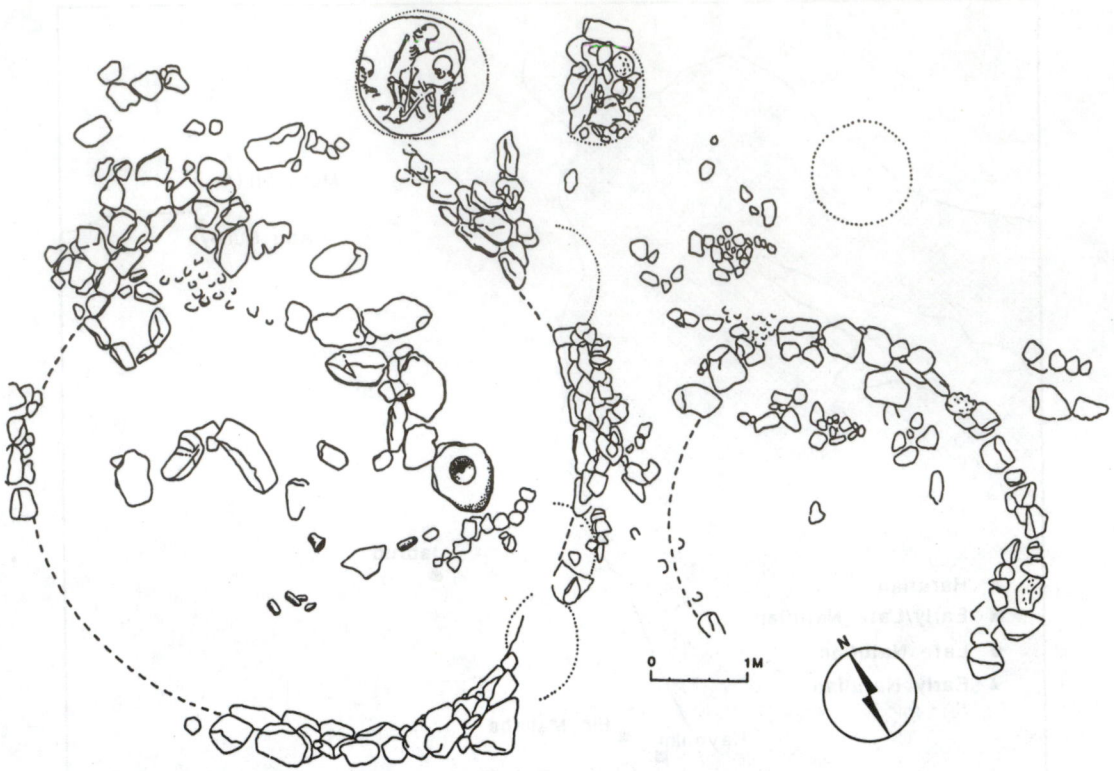

Figure 4.5. Plan of structures at the Natufian site of Ein Mallaha, redrawn by Henry 1989: Figure 7.17

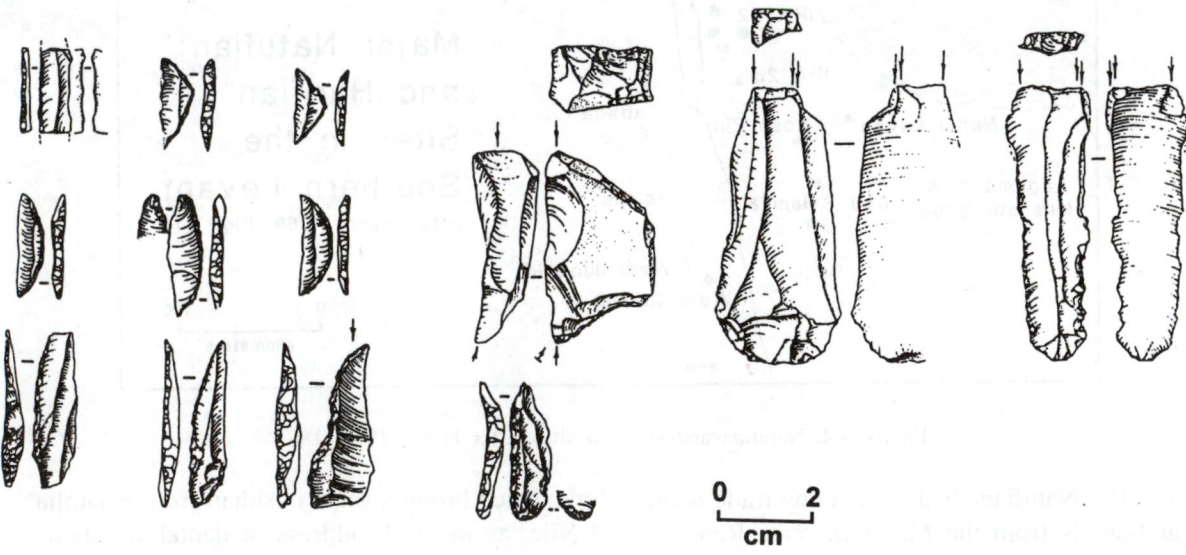

Figure 4.6. Natufian chipped stone artifacts, a sickle blade is in the upper left corner, after Henry 1989: Figures 7.3 and 7.4

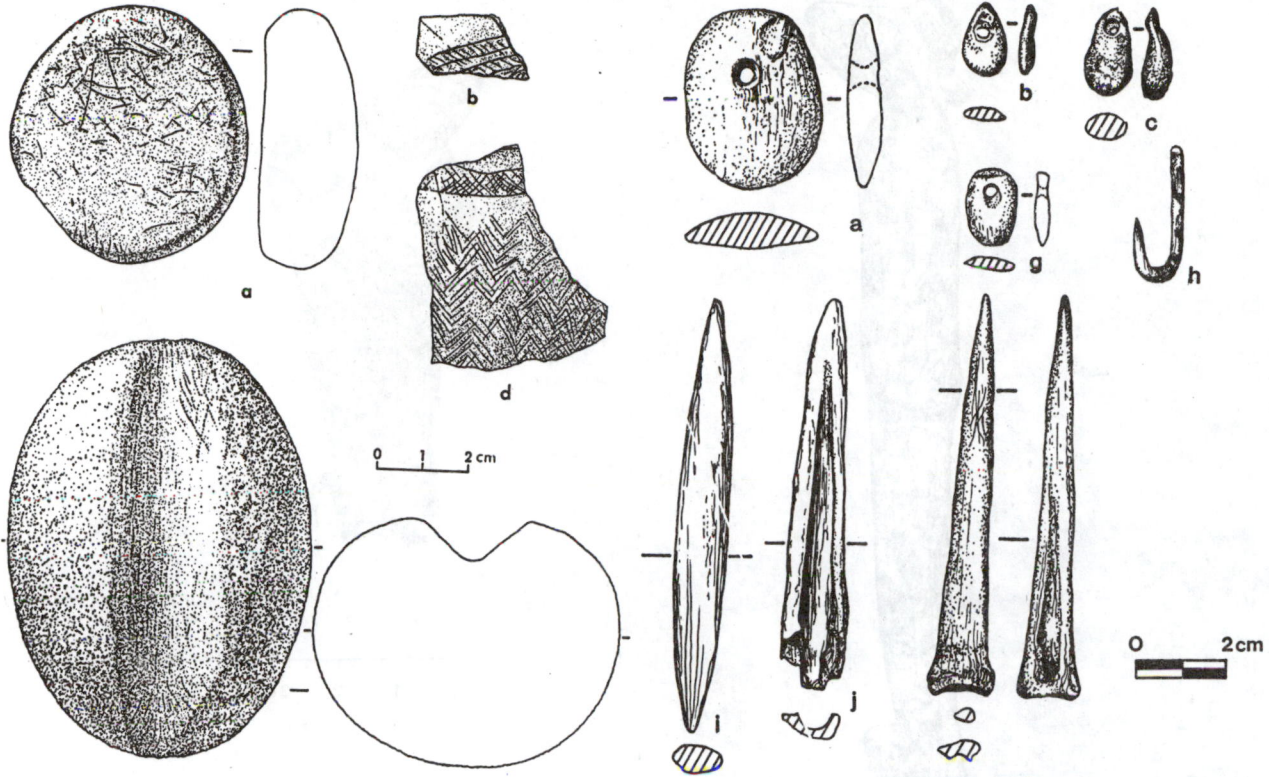

Figure 4.7. Natufian ground stone and bone tools, after Henry 1989. Figures 7.10 and 7.12

storage facilities, preparation of plastered surfaces and the transportation of heavy undressed stones. While this is important for the times, it is trivial by later standards (Mohenjo-daro is about 100 hectares) and is testimony to the truly small scale of some of these early settlements.

There is a very good typology of Natufian sites (Byrd 1989) based on location and macroenvironmental variables. It shares many features with other Natufian settlement typologies (Henry 1977; Olszewski 1988), which agree on a base camp/transitory camp dichotomy. Year-round settlement of the base camps is likely, but not fully proved, and is one of the current research interests of those studying the Natufians.

Meat was obtained through hunting: wild goat (*Capra aegagrus*), gazelle, (*Gazella* sp.), rabbits and possibly wild sheep (*Ovis vigni*). Dogs buried with humans may document their domestication (Belfer-Cohen 1991: 172), but osteological evidence is lacking. Gathering of wild barley, nuts and the like complemented these resources, as demonstrated by sickles and ground stone food processing tools.

It was originally thought that the Natufians were early agriculturalists (Garrod 1957). Others have contested this proposition (Perrot 1968; Cauvin 1978), but the idea recently has been resurrected. It is supported by some experimental data (Unger-Hamilton 1989; Hillman and Davies 1990), but remains the minority view (Bar-Yosef 1989; Bar-Yosef and Belfer-Cohen 1989; Belfer-Cohen 1991 and bibliography). The position taken here is summarized by Belfer-Cohen (1991: 173).

> Though many of the phenomena observed in the Natufian, such as the ordered burial grounds and the wealth of artistic manifestation, appear for the first time in the local prehistoric record, the Natufian is unique mainly because it constitutes the first deviation from the traditional way of prehistoric living. Instead of nomadic hunter-

420

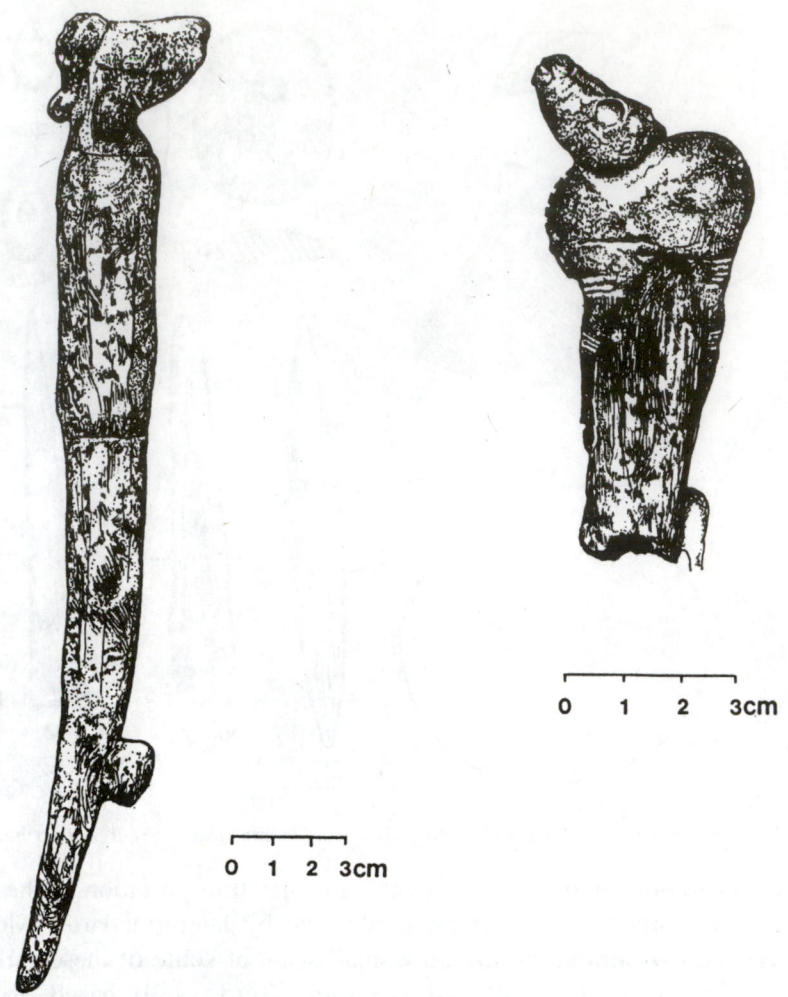

Figure 4.8. Natufian art, carved bone objects, after Henry 1989: Figure 7.13

gatherers, living in small groups (nuclear or extended families) and practicing a well-established mode of resource exploitation, we have in the Natufian indications of sedentism, of larger groups functioning at a higher level of social organization and exhibiting different patterns of resource exploitation—namely, intensive and specialized collection and possibly incipient agriculture (Hillman and Davies 1990; Unger-Hamilton 1989). This basic change occurred about 12,000 years ago, though previous more subtle changes may have occurred that are unobservable in the available archaeological evidence.

Two thoughts are prompted by this reflection. First, although the predominant view considers the Natufians to have been sophisticated hunter-gatherers, they might actually have engaged in the rudiments of cultivation (land preparation and protection of crops) and pastoralism (keeping and rearing young animals). Second, the "Higgs Hypothesis" should be kept in mind and the notion of "unobservable" stated by Belfer-Cohen is related to the way in which archaeologists go about formulating their problems and the research strategies used to address them. There is a lot to be learned about the Natufian subsistence economy, and to dismiss them as "hunter-gatherers" may well be reductionism of the worst sort.

The degree of sedentism has been difficult to index, but the appearance and change in commensal animals has been used to indicate permanence, as have studies of seasonality. This is summarized:

> Assemblages of microvertibrates from Hayonim Cave were studied by Tchernov (1984). The recently added chromosomal research (Afrey and Tchernov 1989) indicates that during the Natufian period the wild mouse, *Mus spretoides*, underwent a process of self domestication and became what is currently identified as *Mus musculus domesticus*, the house mouse. The prevalence of species within Natufian contexts of 'base camps' reflects a higher degree of human sedentism compared to the previous mode of life of Kebaran and Geometric Kebaran hunter-gatherers. Similarly, the House Sparrow (*Passer domesticus*) is a self domesticated species. An additional piece of evidence is the analysis of gazelle tooth increments (Lieberman et al. 1990) which indicates both winter and summer occupations of Hayonim Cave. It is worth mentioning that similar conclusions were reached by Davis (1982) on the basis of age analysis of Natufian gazelle samples, and comparing Epi-Palaeolithic assemblages with Natufian ones (Bar-Yosef and Valla 1991b: 5-6).

Natufians seem to have exploited their environment with sufficient skill and intensity to have been in a position to establish relatively permanent settlements, at least during the years when the environment was not too harsh. They began to process vegetable foods using ground stone tools. Not nearly enough is known about the plants that they collected and may have managed, but it seems certain that these were not yet domesticated. This observation does not rule out the possibility that crops were planted, tended and protected in some ways, as a step toward agriculture and eventual domestication evidenced in the Pre-Pottery Neolithic A which immediately follows the Natufian in time.

The investment in settlements, the presence of jewelry, bone carving and art suggests a kind of prosperity for the Natufians. They also participated in regional trading networks in non-essential objects (obsidian and shell). The obsidian was a utilitarian material, and although it makes very sharp tools it is hardly a necessity. The shells, which were used as ornaments, might even be thought of as luxury items and these people may be good representatives of an early "affluent society."

The Transition to Food Production: PPNA and PPNB

Introduction

The transition to an unmistakably food producing subsistence system in this region involves an assemblage, first defined at Jericho, known as "Pre-Pottery Neolithic A" widely abbreviated "PPNA." It has been divided recently into two phases: the Khiamain (8500/8300 to 8100 BC), that seems to have been very short, and the "Sultanian" (8300/100 to 7300/200 BC) (Bar-Yosef and Belfer-Cohen 1989: 477; Bar-Yosef 1989: 59; McCorriston and Hole 1991: 51). "A" is followed by the Pre-Pottery B assemblage, a more thoroughly developed village farming and herding complex.

PPNA and the Beginnings of Agriculture

The Khiamain is relatively simple and not as well known compared to the slightly later Sultanian, but in most respects they are similar, differences being matters of degree, not of a kind. The houses are round or oval and semi-subterranean, like those of the Natufian, but greater investment is seen in the form of the early use of mud bricks, rather than the temporary walls of the preceding time. PPNA was first defined at Jericho and there is a massive wall there from this period that is either a fortification (Kenyon 1957) or protection against flood and mud slides (Bar-Yosef 1989). An intramural tower, with a shrine(?) on the top suggests further communal involvement in this facility (Plate 4.3). PPNA sites have good storage facilities, necessary for the preservation of grain, as well as hearths and well developed grinding facilities including querns, bowls and bedrock basins. At Jericho, a site of about four hectares at this time, the houses, round or rectilinear, were made of mud plano-convex bricks. This period is usually referred to as the "Hog-back Brick Phase" because of the shape of the bricks that were used. Some houses had two rooms and were equipped with floors of pounded earth. No fewer than twenty two structural phases were documented for the PPNA occupation at Jericho (Kenyon 1957: 102).

The largest sites (Mureybit, Tell Aswad and Jericho) are in the five hectare range. Trade with Anatolia (abundant obsidian) and the Mediterranean and Red Seas (shells) is also evidenced and represents continued participation in interregional trading networks in commodities that were not necessities.

The subsistence system is still imperfectly known, but most observers are willing to concede that cultivation begins here with intensive hunting and possibly some keeping of animals; although the faunal assemblages from PPNA sites generally contain few remains of prodomestic taxa like sheep, goats and cattle. Hunting was important, especially of gazelle (Bar-Yosef and Meadow 1995: 71). However, the system is anything but "pure" or clear cut.

The economic system of the Sultanian sites in the Jordan Valley and the sites in the Damascus basin and Mureybit included the intensive collection or cultivation of cereals, mainly barley and some wheat (Kislev et al. 1986; van Zeist and Bakker-Heeres 1982, 1986; Hopf 1983) along with legumes. Wild fruits and seeds were gathered as well. Silos were found in each site, either as small stone-built bins or larger builtup mud-brick structures.

Hunting in the middle Euphrates area was mainly of gazelle, some equids and cattle and focused in the Jordan Valley predominantly on gazelle, some foxes, and fewer fallow deer, wild boar and wild cattle. Large numbers of birds, especially ducks, were trapped. Lizards and tortoises were gathered as well. The overall picture is that of a 'broad spectrum' similar to that of the Natufian (Bar-Yosef and Belfer-Cohen 1989: 482).

Thus, archaeologists seem to be closing in on one of the centers where an early development of food production and domestication took place in the Old World. Some of the evidence is clear, although it is not always certain what it means. There are also some unresolved chronological and conceptual problems:

> ...those who see a chronological or cultural Natufian 'horizon' replaced by a PPNA 'horizon' would like to terminate one when the following was established. Others would see the Late Natufian semi-arid adaptation, the Harifian, as contemporary with the earliest PPNA farming communities. Following this model, which assumes the presence of central places where cultivation of cereals and legumes was first established and later diffused into neighboring regions, we expect similar situations on other boundaries of the Levant. It should be stressed that the archaeological evidence to date indicates that the first farming communities flourished in the 'Levantine Corridor.' This sub-region of the Levant is delineated as a segmented, 10-40 km wide area which stretches from the Middle Euphrates in the north through (the) Damascus basin, the Trans-Jordanian Plateau and into the Lower Jordan Valley in the south. Hunter-gatherers carried on their traditional lifeways in the Taurus and Anatolian Plateau as well as in the Syro-Arabian desert while the agricultural revolution took place in the Levantine corridor (Bar-Yosef 1989: 58).

This view is based on a fair amount of evidence but one should not be led to believe that the full story is known. Nor was the process linear. Early food producing communities are found at an early date in Anatolia, as witnessed at places like Çayönü, and the Tigris Valley at a place called Nemrik 9, but hunting and gathering seems to have remained the predominant form of livelihood for several millennia for the inhabitants of the deserts that surrounded the more fertile zones (Bar-Yosef 1989: 58).

PPNB Pastoralism and the Development of Agriculture

There is a stratigraphic hiatus between the PPNA and PPNB levels at Jericho, where these assemblages were defined (Kenyon 1957). It is not known if this represents a discontinuity there, or whether the bridging settlement between PPNA and PPNB is located somewhere under an unexcavated portion of the huge mound. Some PPNB sites are in the 12 hectare range (e.g., Ain Ghazal, Abu Hureya), an increase in size over PPNA settlements. At Jericho the PPNB people built houses of cigar-shaped bricks marked on the top with finger made chevrons (Plate 4.4). Buildings were constructed as one large, rather commodious rectilinear room, flanked by smaller enclosures, some of which seem to have been used for storage; a general pattern for PPNB architecture. Considerable attention was paid to their floors, with polished plaster in use. At Çayönü in southeastern Turkey there is even a kind of terrazzo floor.

This floor is constructed basically of white limestone cobbles and pebbles set in concrete and varies from 5 to 20 cm in thickness. The limestone was evidently crushed for this purpose. A surface layer of primarily salmon pink pebbles 1-3 cm in diameter was set into the concrete while still wet, as were at least two sets of parallel strips of white pebbles, to make white bands 5 cm wide and over 4 m long. After the concrete had bonded, the entire surface of the floor was ground smooth and polished. Not only was the bond strong enough to support this grinding, but the concrete has remained extremely hard for over 8500 years (Braidwood, Cambel, Redman and Watson 1971: 1239).

Çayönü (Plate 4.5, Plate 4.6) is located far from Jericho, and it may or may not be a good representative of the PPNB. In the same general region, but slightly later than Çayönü is Gritille, a village on the upper Euphrates River with similar affinities to the PPNB sites. Gritille has been dated to ca. 7000-5500 BC (Voigt and Ellis 1981; Voigt 1985). The possible discontinuity of occupation at Jericho and the sense that some of the PPNB artifactual inventory is like the northern PPNA suite of artifacts has led some (i.e., Mellaart 1975: 51-3) to suggest that the origins of PPNB are in north Syria and that it spread to the south. Bar-Yosef and Belfer-Cohen express this in a cautious way.

The common cultural traits include the use of a bipolar reduction technique which resulted in proliferation of blade tools; the basic rectangular house plan; the use of either lime or gypsum plaster; the exploitation of cereals and pulses; the introduction of goats and sheep; and the frequent occurrence of female figurines. The resemblance between assemblages even led scholars to refer to Neolithic sites in Turkey as the Taurus PPNB (Cauvin 1990) (Bar-Yosef and Belfer-Cohen 1991: 192, original emphasis).

The preparation of plaster was an important technological innovation which represents the beginnings of pyrotechnology, bringing fire out of the family hearth and into the spheres of technology and industry. The next stage was pottery making, expanding human control over heat and other material skills. In fact, PPNB sites have evidence for experiments with the manufacture of containers from plaster, as humans were searching for ways to solve the container problem, without resorting to the time consuming pursuits of basket making and carving (Gourdin and Kingery 1975; Kingery, Vandiver and Prickett 1988).

Plaster was also used for the preparation of "portrait heads" (Plate 4.7). The foundation for these heads was a human skull, built up with plaster to represent the living face of a person. Some of them show great skill on the part of the sculptor, who occasionally used sea shells to represent the eyes. Twelve plastered skulls were found in PPNB levels at Tell Ramad in the Damascus suburbs (deContenson 1971) with others at Beisamoun (Lechevallier 1978) and Ain Ghazal (Rollefson 1983, 1986). Skulls modeled in asphalt were found in Nahal Hemar Cave (Bar-Yosef and Alon 1988) and rather spectacular human figurines in plaster were found at Ain Ghazal (Rollefson 1983, 1986).

Interregional exchange continues in PPNB times. In fact, there is a strong sense that it increased with large quantities of obsidian from Anatolia, jadeite from northern Syria and turquoise from the Sinai in evidence at Jericho. Commerce in Red Sea and Mediterranean shells was a part of PPNB life. Malachite, a mineral rich in copper, was traded as well and there is a fair amount of red ochre. There is also native copper from Çayönü including bracelets, pins and hooks (Braidwood, Cambel, Redman and Watson 1971).

Interesting and important changes were taking place in trade and art over the patterns seen in PPNA. This is shown in Table 4.2.

TABLE 4.2
A Comparison of Selected Aspects of PPNA and PPNB Villages

Characteristic	PPNA	PPNB
Maximum size	2.5-5 ha	12 ha
Predominant shape of structures	circular	rectangular
Variation in size of structures	5-37 sq m	7-63 sq m
Storage facilities	yes	yes
Subsistence	cultivation, hunting, herding	cultivation, gathering
Domesticated animals	no	yes
Long-distance trade	yes	yes
Obsidian	yes	yes
Greenstone	no	yes
Marien shells	yes	yes
Cultic architecture?		yes
Cultic figures	yes	yes
Plastered/modeled skulls	no	yes
Human statuary	no	yes

(after Saidel 1993: Table 2)

The evidence for animal domestication at Çayönü is interesting (Braidwood and Braidwood 1982). The materials from early deposits of Phase I were compared with those from later deposits of the same Phase (Lawrence 1982). Pigs, cattle and deer dominated the early levels with some sheep and goats. The later Phase I deposits were dominated by sheep and especially goats (Bar-Yosef and Meadow 1995: 85). This change in the faunal assemblage seems to have taken place in Late PPNB times, when faunal assemblages dominated by capraovine materials were well established, even in the lowlands, outside the natural range of these animals.

The subsistence system of PPNB times was a combination of farming and herding, mixed with a fair amount of hunting and gathering. At the important site of Beidha in Jordan (Kirkbride 1966) there is evidence for the cultivation of barley and some wheat, along with pulses, especially lentil and vetch (Helbaek 1966b: 62). Helbaek also found evidence for the weedy grasses that accompany cultivation; plants like goat-face grass (*Aegilops* sp.), ryegrass (*Lolium* sp.) and wild oat (*Avena ludoviviana*) (1966b: 63). In addition the excavators there found evidence for thousands of pistachio nuts: on the floor of a "...burnt house some five gallons of carbonized pistachio were found, obviously once contained in some kind of basket..." (Helbaek 1966b: 63). There were also acorns and they, along with the pistachios, convey the important role that gathering still played in the earliest phases of farming. At Tell Ramad there is evidence for the cultivation of barley and three different kinds of wheat (emmer, einkorn and club wheat), all on their way to full domestication, along with lentils and wild grasses (van Zeist and Bottema 1966).

The bones of wild animals, especially gazelle, are complemented by the presence of domesticated sheep, goats and pigs. "By the middle of the ninth millennium b.p., goats and sheep, possibly from the Taurus-Zagros region, were introduced into these sites, and their bones form at least half the faunal spectra" (Bar-Yosef and Belfer-Cohen 1991: 193). At Wadi Tbeik, a seasonally occupied camp of PPNB nomads most of the animals were wild, with large quantities of rabbit, wild goats and gazelle, along with birds and fish. There is evidence for rather refined culling patterns however, and these people must have been managing these wild resources in a sophisticated way (Tchernov and Bar-Yosef 1982).

A kind of bottom line on the PPNB subsistence regime is that it was mixed; these people were real farmers, who kept domesticated animals, at least the small ones. But, they were also sophisticated in their hunting and gathering. Some sites seem to indicate that this provided an important part of the diet, which probably means that there was a marked degree of regional specialization and differentiation among the peoples of the PPNB. It also probably indicates that when things got tough for them, whether from drought, plagues of locusts, or whatever, they were able to fall back on their hunting and gathering skills with considerable facility to ensure their survival. PPNB remains also display a remarkable degree of cultural cohesion, being recognizable from Turkey south to Sinai.

There were other early food producing sites to the east of this zone, and they should not be ignored as part of this story.

Important Developments in Other Regions of the Near East

While these developments were taking place in the Levant, other important sites were occupied in the hills arching around the Mesopotamian lowlands, in Turkey, Iraq and Iran. The well known site of Jarmo, to the east in Iraqi Kurdistan is an early village, but does not play the key role in the earliest domestication of plants and animals as once was thought (Robert Braidwood and Howe 1960; Linda Braidwood et al. 1983). But Shanidar Cave, and the open air site of Zawi Chemi Shanidar, are extremely important (Ralph Solecki 1955, 1963). Zawi Chemi was excavated by Rose Solecki (1964, 1981), who dug with Walter Fairservis at Kili Ghul Mohammad in 1950-51. In 1964 the late archaeozoologist Dexter Perkins proposed that an increase in the number of immature sheep in the "proto-neolithic" levels of Zawi Chemi, dated by radiocarbon to ca. 8900±300 BC (uncalibrated), was sound evidence for their domesticated state (Perkins 1964). Perkins' proposal has been generally accepted; however, a statistical analysis of the numbers of bones in his sample, using the chi square statistic, demonstrated that there was as much chance for the Middle Palaeolithic, Mousterian population at Shanidar Cave having domesticated sheep, as there was in the later "proto-neolithic" occupation (Hopkins 1967; see also Bokonyi 1969: 221-22). Thus this evidence for domesticated sheep at Shanidar has to be treated with some reservation.

Farther south in the Zagros mountains of Iraq and Iran there are many excavated early village communities and pastoral camps that have a place in the story of food production and

426

domestication. Tepe Asiab and Tepe Sarab (Braidwood, Howe and Reed 1961), Tepe Guran (Mortensen 1972) and Ganj Dareh Tepe (Smith 1976) are all important, but they do not cohere as a taxonomic set the way the data from the Levant do, and one still senses an unfinished story there, in spite of a good introduction.

Much more important and interesting are the sites excavated by Frank Hole, Kent Flannery and James Neeley on the Deh Luran Plain of southwestern Iran (Hole, Flannery and Neeley 1969). They were able to excavate a series of settlements that begin in the early village era at Ali Kosh and Tepe Sabz at ca. 7500 BC and continue in an unbroken sequence to the historical eras of their region. The well documented architectural history, along with fluctuations in the use of domesticated plants and animals are of extraordinary importance to the history of agriculture, village life and the beginnings of pastoralism.

Recent political events in the Near East have compromised much of the archaeological work in the greater Zagros area. A sound start was made in understanding the beginnings of domestication and sedentism there and it is highly likely when work resumes in the region, the story as it is now presented will be far richer than it is today, with many regional variations on the early farming and pastoral theme.

Summary

What is seen with respect to the beginnings of agriculture and domestication in the Near East is an intensive stage of "hunting and gathering," represented by the Natufian. These people may have begun the concentrated exploitation of the plants and animals that were later domesticated; although the case for plants is stronger than it is for the animals. The Natufians also used a wide range of other resources (acorns, pistachio, almonds, wild grasses, gazelle, deer and the like). We do not know for sure, but it seems probable that it is within these contexts that early experiments with the management of food resources were begun. Protecting fields of wild plants from pests, possibly watering them by redirecting spring water, for instance. Some soil preparation and weeding might have been done to ensure a slightly better yield than the one that would have come from mother nature operating on her own. Gazelle were hunted to considerable advantage, but so were other ungulates and it could be that in Natufian times some animals were captured and tamed, kept around the settlement for a time and possibly killed when there was a shortage of food. Some of them might even have reproduced in this new human environment. But, short term storage on the hoof would have been the dominant theme, not long term investment in herds. Their subsistence system was sufficiently productive and reliable that some Natufians could establish permanent village sites, and not have to pursue the usual yearly, migratory round of most hunters and gatherers. The beginnings of sedentism brought with it many implications that have already been reviewed. We should not overemphasize the Natufian village here. It was actually a tentative experiment. Most Natufians almost certainly did not have the luxury of owning their own home, living in one village all the time. But there were villages, some occupied long enough, apparently on a year-round basis, for commensal animals (mice and house sparrows) to have become the domesticates we know today.

Important technological innovations took place during Natufian times (Flannery 1969: 77-8). The use of ground stone food processing tools was one such change. These implements were used to reduce grains, seeds and nuts to powder, or flour so that they could be cooked and consumed in a convenient way. We can assume that some kind of food preparation "revolution" accompanied this innovation. The engineering of free standing architecture and preparation of village sites is also documented at this time.

PPNA represents a development of the Natufian on two important dimensions: sedentism

427

and farming. It is much more certain now that there were true villages. In contrast to the Natufian, most (perhaps only many) PPNA folk almost certainly did have the luxury of owning their own home, living in one village all, or a good deal of the time. The signs of farming and keeping the animals that were later domesticated are present, but signs of full control over them are very thin, indeed. PPNA times then seem to be a transitional period, with good evidence for sedentism. The notion that the plant and animal management strategies that bring signs of full domestication were in place is more of an implication than empirical observation; although, once again, the evidence for the plants is better than it is for animals.

The long PPNB period sees a kind of end to the early process of domestication with signs of larger village settlements as well as those that show us that wheat, barley, some pulses and sheep and goats were domesticated. The preparation of plaster was an important pyrotechnological innovation; a harbinger of pottery making and metallurgy. There are also implications of changes in social structure in PPNB times. The villages and individual structures are now large enough to accommodate large families and probably more than one biologically viable social unit. There are large, public buildings such as the Terrazzo Building at Çayönü. Bar-Yosef and Meadow (1995: 77-8) outline other architectural evidence. The plaster skulls and burials seem to be informing us of the expansion of social differentiation.

The story of the beginnings of food production and domestication in the Near East appears to be a reasonably good example of a gradualist evolutionary culture historical sequence. From about 11,000 BC, with the beginnings of the Natufian, to about 6000 BC, with the end of PPNB, we seem to have 5000 years of gradual change which takes humans from the experimental stage of agriculture and animal domestication to settled villages with the domesticates in place. The South Asian sequence is a little different from this, but it is based on only fragmentary data, so that should not come as a surprise.

With the emphasis that has to be placed on the development of the village farming community, and sedentism as a human invention, pastoral camps have been just short of ignored. They are important, however, and it is time to redress this imbalance.

The Beginnings of Pastoralism

The Traditional View

Some consideration of the beginnings of pastoralism should be made, since this form of adaptation is very much a part of the food production and domestication equation. This lifeway is also of tremendous importance to understanding the dynamics of the Indus Age. Much will be said of various forms of pastoralism in the Indus Age. There is an interesting book on the archaeology of nomads (Cribb 1991), which reviews a number of important issues, and a collection of essays on the topic (Bar-Yosef and A. Khazanov 1992). Bar-Yosef and Meadow (1995: 82-4) also have a recent statement on the subject. The prevailing view, particularly in the Near East, is that pastoral nomadism emerged within the context of agriculture (Cribb 1991: 12-5). Nomadic pastoralism in its present Near Eastern/South Asian forms is then a specialized adaptation, closely linked to irrigation and therefore the early states of the region (Spooner 1972a: 126, 1973: 40; Lees and Bates 1974; Adams 1974a; H. Wright 1977: 388). There is also a tendency for pastoral nomadism to be seen as emerging on the fringes of the agricultural zone, especially in those environments unsuitable for farming (Kohler-Rollefson 1992). The intellectual predisposition to this view may be based on a belief that hunter-gatherers have a generalized form of adaptation and that this would have carried over into the early food producing era, with a balanced dry farming/subsistence pastoralist adaptation, a view put forward by Susan Lees and Daniel Bates some years ago (1974). This is not necessarily true, since there is evidence for subsistence specialization in the early Holocene of the Near East, and it is entirely possible that pastoral specialists, even pastoral nomads, developed side by side with sedentary agriculturalists.

Some scholars view pastoral specialists, or nomadic pastoralists, as dependent on settled farming communities for their food grains: "...they do not live on animal products alone and thus are required to maintain social and/or economic ties with agricultural communities" (Bar-Yosef and Meadow 1995: 83). Two points are needed to expand and clarify this position. First, one might rephrase it with the pastoral nomads as a base and say "...they (farmers) do not live on agricultural products alone and thus are required to maintain social and/or economic ties with pastoral communities." Second, this position ignores the fact that the vast majority of pastoral nomads undertake some cultivation themselves (e.g., Barth 1961: 9 for the Basseri of Iran; Beck 1986: 29-30, 36-7 for the Qashqa'i of Iran; Pehrson 1966: 5-9 for the Marri Baluch; Spooner 1975: 171 for the Baluch generally; Forde 1963: 346 for the Khirgiz). The highly specialized form of pastoral nomadism where no cultivation is undertaken is not typical of the adaptation and may reflect the refinement of the exchange systems linking settled and pastoral peoples, as discussed in Part 3.

The village and the camp can be imagined to be on a multidimensional continuum. Village farming communities tend to rely more on agriculture and plants, than on mobility and animals. The camp tends to rely on pasture and animals to be mobile or nomadic. But, both forms of settlement and subsistence utilize both domesticated (and undomesticated) plants and animals. Very few traditional farmers in settled villages keep no animals as a part of their subsistence strategy, especially in the Near East, Iran, Central Asia and the Greater Indus Region. Farmers are generally involved in pastoralism, to some degree. The same principal applies to the camp, or pastoral nomads, most of whom undertake some agriculture themselves, while at the same time relying to a great degree on their animals for their livelihood.

A recent book on early pastoral nomadism in the Levant (Bar-Yosef and Khazanov 1992) is in some ways a step forward from the traditional view of the origins of pastoral nomadism, although it is filled with conceptual problems (noted by Meadow 1992). The work of Juris Zarins is especially important as a challenge to the view that pastoral nomadism is a relatively late adaptation in the Near East (Zarins 1989, 1992).

Whatever the theory on pastoral origins might be, Bar-Yosef and Meadow (1995: 83) are correct when they observe "In the Near East, however, where we have our earliest evidence for the domestication of food species, there is no site in which the herding of domestic animals can be shown to have taken place without the population having had access to cultivated plants." This is well documented only in the Levantine Corridor and southern Turkey, which is coincidentally the only area were anything approaching adequate research has been done. Prudence therefore dictates that this sequence of "first plant then animal domestication" be treated as an empirical observation for one region, not a demonstrated regularity of culture change. This caution is underscored by Frank Hole who has proposed that sheep-goat herding is earlier in the Zagros area, especially in southwestern Iran, where it developed in the context of seasonal mobility (Hole 1984, 1989: 98). Hole's proposal has been critically reviewed (Helmer 1989) and noted (Bar-Yosef and Meadow 1995: 83), but is not something that can be rejected.

The Inadequacy of the Traditional View of Pastoral Origins

The idea that Late Glacial hunter-gatherers were subsistence "generalists" and that this balance in their subsistence regime was carried forward into the early food producing adaptation, are both positions of uncertain validity. The Kebaran peoples of the Levant were very successful in their adaptation, and seem to have exploited a number of different environments, implying some degree of seasonal specialization in the exploitation of food resources (Hillman, Colledge and Harris 1989; see also Hillman 1989 for the Upper Palaeolithic of Egypt). The Early Natufians were able to venture out of the oak-pistachio zone, into the somewhat harsher, Irano-Turanian desertic areas. By Late Natufian times even large base camp sites were located in this second zone, with further penetration into the desert (Bar-Yosef and Belfer-Cohen 1989: 467). These remains seem to indicate an increase in specialization of resource extraction, at least as far as the seasonal exploitation of resources is concerned. It might also indicate a difference among the Natufians themselves, some of whom were more comfortable with the management of animals than their neighbors who exploited vegetal resources. Bar-Yosef's Harifian, the Late Natufian seems to have been contemporary with the earliest PPNA farming communities, but occupied the desertic lands on the periphery. There is some reason to see the Harifians as more involved with the exploitation of animals than their PPNA contemporaries in the Jordan Valley proper. By PPNB times at least one site in the Sinai, Wadi Tbeik, has "...evidence for the presence of a nomadic society with a seasonal pattern of habitation practicing a mode of hunting control" (Tchernov and Bar-Yosef 1982). There may be a pastoral camp in southwestern Iran dating as early as the seventh millennium BC (Hole 1974, 1975) (Plate 4.7, Plate 4.9).

It is in these early contexts that we sense the beginnings of subsistence diversity that in later times yields the settled village farming community and the pastoral nomadic camp and many "intermediate" or variant forms, if one wants to think typologically. Many forms of adaptation using domesticated plants and/or animals are present by the earliest historical periods of the Near East and probably appear a good deal earlier in time (Briant 1982).

Returning to the origins of pastoralism, one thing seems clear. The proposition that farming must be developed prior to specialized pastoralism (pastoral nomadism) because pastoral nomadism is dependent on the peoples with this adaptation for a significant portion of their food supply is not sound. The culture historical sequence in the Levantine Corridor and Southern Turkey may have worked out this way, but the notion that this is a universal regularity is not supported by ethnographic and historical observations. Relatively extensive dependence on pastoral resources, to the point where they lead herd owners to a nomadic existence emerges out of Late Glacial/Early Holocene specialization in hunting. It is increasingly apparent that pastoralism was at, or near, the center of the Indus subsistence and general economic adaptation.

EXPLAINING THE FOOD PRODUCING REVOLUTION IN THE NEAR EAST

A full explanation of the driving forces behind the food producing and domestication revolution in human history has yet to be offered. There have been many attempts (e.g., Childe 1936; Braidwood 1952; Binford 1968b; Flannery 1968, 1986; Meyers 1971; Harris 1972, 1977; Reed 1977a, 1977b, 1977c; M. Cohen 1977a, 1977b; Rindos 1984, Henry 1989; McCorriston and Hole 1991; Belfer-Cohen 1991, to note a few). Propinquity, overpopulation, cultural readiness, systems feedback, climatic change and stress, population pressure, even a kind of historical inevitability have all been offered, acting alone or in concert with other forces, to explain this revolution.

For the Near East, especially the Jordan Valley "core zone" (Bar-Yosef 1989: 484-89; Henry 1989; McCorriston and Hole 1991), the prevailing view stresses continuity within the Kebaran and Natufian. These people are seen to have become adept at intensifying their collecting and hunting efforts and were able to get the same amount of "produce" out of increasingly smaller territories. It brought to the food producing revolution a number of sociocultural and artifactual features that might be called "preadaptive": semi-sedentary settlements, ground stone food processing tools, the exploitation of small territories that had acquired value and would have been protected by social conventions in the same way as agricultural fields, and the possible increase in the consumption of vegetable foods (Schoninger 1981). This might have continued into PPNA times, with agriculture and pastoralism slowly being defined. In this view there was no tip point, or threshold for the achievement of food production and domestication. It was a gradual evolutionary pattern of change with culture altered in small, cumulatively important increments over a long period of time.

Lewis Binford (1968b) has perhaps the most sophisticated focus on the relationship between population size, "marginal zone" and climatic stress as a trigger for the beginnings of food production and domestication. This has survived in many variations, for example: "Abrupt climatic fluctuations in a marginal environment can force a society to recognize the urgent need for technological and social changes which will secure its survival" (Bar-Yosef 1989: 489; see also S. J. M. Davis 1982). The Natufians, especially those in marginal environments, may have been forced into highly manipulative strategies for managing their plant and animal resources when faced with short term, relatively intensive environmental change, simply to survive. The nature of this manipulation moved them over a conceptual threshold from intensive hunting and gathering to food production and domestication, a position which, in the end, was not reversible.

A recent article on the topic sees the following conditions as facilitating the shift to food production: "At the end of the Pleistocene, after a long period of climatic instability, a Mediterranean climate more strongly seasonal than any today emerged with hyper-arid summers that selected for annual species of cereals and legumes. This occurred long after people had invented tools suitable for grinding hard seeds, but the new, lengthy dry season and consequent need to use stored foods encouraged sedentism among human groups who subsequently depleted their immediate environments of wild resources. These preconditions facilitated the development of agriculture" (McCorriston and Hole 1991: 46).

A recent statement from Ofer Bar-Yosef and Richard Meadow offers the following: "In sum, we argue that the origins of agriculture must be viewed in the context of a fluctuating climatic regime that broadened and then constricted areas suitable for productive hunting and gathering and later for cultivation and pastoralism" (1995: 54).

Bar-Yosef and Meadow go on to lay out a model for an abrupt shift, or punctuated equilibrium (Gould and Eldridge 1977), in the development of food production and the domestication of plants and animals in the Near East (1995: 68-9). In this model "abrupt climatic shifts are seen as triggers."

The prominence of environmental factors, especially climatic change, is particularly unsettling in this transformation, because it places humans in such a subordinate position to the natural world and ignores, or deprecates, important cultural variables. Those who use the "short term climatic trigger" hypothesis are essentially proposing that with an adaptation like that of the Natufian, when the climate reduced resources, there was room for only one response: food production and domestication. This may have been a possibility, but there must have been other conceivable reactions to such climatic stress: e.g., migration (probably only partial) to other environments, broadening the adaptation to include plants and animals not already part of the subsistence regime,[4] population reduction, some combination or partial implementation of these solutions.

The San !Kung bushmen seem to have lived through a three year drought in Botswana and hardly noticed it. Neighboring Bantu speaking pastoralist-farmers lost 100,000 cattle and food for 200,000 farmers and herders had to be brought in as relief. In fact, the hunter-gatherers are reported to have helped Bantus who came into their area to gather. We learn from this that the human response to drought and natural adversity is difficult to predict. The hunting-gathering adaptation can be extraordinarily resilient and provide very deep, very reliable insulation against adversities of nature.

We should not imagine that the relationship between humans and the natural world involves such unsophisticated responses as those proposed by the climatic or environmental stress models. The notion that early Holocene hunting and gathering populationsin the Near East were just fine until the weather turned bad and that this caused them to domesticate plants and animals is just too simple. If the ethnographic record is to be believed, the Bantus being especially noteworthy, agriculture and herding may be a less resilient, more vulnerable form of adaptation than hunting and gathering. Moreover, placing the burden of the final shift to food production on a deteriorating climate relies on the notion that the people who "invented agriculture" were under stress, and impoverished. Carl O. Sauer objected to this many decades ago: "Agriculture did not originate from chronic food shortage. People on the brink of starvation do not have the means or time to undertake the leisurely process of domestication. Famine foods have little relationship to domesticates" (Sauer 1952: 20). There is still some wisdom in this old idea; although no one has ever demonstrated the domestication process to have been a "leisurely" one. Still, it is a thought that those who propose "stress theories" should keep in mind (P. E. L. Smith 1972b).

An approach to explaining the food production and domestication revolution that is at least a bit more multi dimensional than stress and starvation in the face of climatic change has recently been offered by Anna Belfer-Cohen:

> The success of the Natufian led to its demise. The short duration of the Natufian phenomenon and its replacement by the Neolithic cultures suggest that the unique characteristics of the Natufian created an uncontrolled momentum. Thus, Natufian populations not only did not starve, but flourished and kept growing. This population growth presumably led (at least in the Mediterranean zone) to a growing sense of proprietorship of land, especially so with the growing dependence on cultivated plants. Sedentism brought about many changes in settlement patterns, including greater investment of energy and resources in habitation structures and storage facilities. Under such conditions of population pressure, when each group defends its territory and strives to differentiate itself from its neighbors, the need for group identity increases and encourages the appearance of unique characteristics in each social group. As more and more people are forced to live in close proximity to one another, the establishment of strong institutional mechanisms becomes inevitable in order to prevent anarchy and to control emotional behavior and information exchange within the group. The strengthening of all these trends culminated in the appearance of a new cultural entity—the Neolithic Complex (Belfer-Cohen 1991: 183).

There is still a great deal of the "natural world" in this hypothesis, and one can seriously wonder what in history can be thought of as "inevitable," especially the "development of strong institutional mechanisms." There are just too many ways for culture and society to change for the domestication of plants and animals to be thought of as inescapable. It might be that this is what did happen. Strong social institutions may have developed, but this is a description of an historical happening, not its explanation.

Ultimately, it can be said that the culture historical sequence for the transition from intensive hunting and gathering to early food production and domestication in the Near East is slowly being clarified on a descriptive level. The explanation for these changes remains elusive.

The Self-fulfilling Prophesy of the Near Eastern Hearth for Early Domestication

Compared to the Near East, much less archaeological research has been done in other areas of the expanded nuclear zone interaction sphere for early domestication and food production. This is especially true for the Iranian Plateau east of the Zagros Mountains, extending into the Greater Indus Region. There are only three excavated sites in all of Pakistan that relate to this problem, Kili Ghul Mohammad (Fairservis 1956a), Gumla (Dani 1970-71: 35-53) and Mehrgarh (Jarrige and Meadow 1980; Meadow 1993a), and the first two were very small scale probings.

In spite of this discrepancy in the intensity and balance in the search for the history of food production and domestication there remains a sense in much of the archaeological literature that the Near East is, and will remain, the primary region within which this transformation took place, and that Central Asia and the Greater Indus Region should be viewed as secondary centers which received the gift of farming and herding from the Near Eastern epicenter. Some are quite explicit about this view (Zohary 1970; Zohary and Hopf 1988; Harlan 1971, 1977; P. Singh 1974, 1991; C. C. Lamberg-Karlovsky 1992, 1996: 173–74; Willcox 1992: 292; Flannery 1995: 5). At other times it seems to be implied (Binford 1968b; Zohary and Hopf 1988; Henry 1989)[5]. They can also point, with some confidence, to the early dates from Near Eastern sites and the robust archaeological data sets that backstop their position. There is no doubt that there are early dates for food producing sites in the Near East and that the substantial amount of excavation there has yielded a culture historical sequence, but it has led to a kind of self-fulfilling prophesy. Convinced that the Near East was the early center, archaeologists turned their attention to the investigation of this region, at the expense of others. Many archaeological research projects have provided the information needed to reconstruct an impressive story for the domestication of plants and animals and document the establishment of village farming communities there. But, what about other regions within which the potentially domesticable plants and animals lived? Having ignored research in virtually all of these other areas, is it surprising that the prediction that the Near East was the center of food production and domestication came true? Of course, it is not surprising; an observation that in and of itself calls for research in what is here termed the "expanded nuclear zone" in what can be thought of as Middle Asia; the region from the Mediterranean to the Indus covering the area from the Arabian Gulf into the Central Asian States. We should seek to set aside models that are dependent on "diffusion" and "independent invention." We should begin to look at interaction and the rich set of networks of many kinds that linked the peoples of the Indus Valley and its borderlands with their neighbors to the west, north and south. There is some evidence to support this model for an "expanded nuclear zone" for plant and animal domestication that needs a review of the evidence from Mehrgarh to make it clear.

THE ORIGINS AND DEVELOPMENT OF FOOD PRODUCING PEOPLES IN SOUTH ASIA

Introduction

The western borderlands of southern Asia are an excellent environment in which to conduct archaeological research on food production and domestication. The raw materials are there in the form of the wild species domesticated at an early date. Moreover, this is a region with an abundance of archaeological remains which have barely begun to be exploited. That there are thousands of unrecorded sites is a real probability.

There is a body of general reference literature on this topic. A selected bibliography listed alphabetically by author is as follows: F. R. Allchin 1969a, 1969b; Asthana 1985; Clason 1974,

1977, 1979, 1984; Conrad 1974; Dani 1983; Dupree 1989; Grigson 1985; S. P. Gupta and Dikshit 1984; Hermanns 1951; Hutchinson 1974, 1976; Jarrige and Meadow 1980; Kajale 1991; Meadow[6] 1982, 1984a, 1984b, 1987, 1989a, 1989b, 1993a, 1993b; Naseem 1982; Rissman 1989; Sahu 1988; R. P. Singh 1990; B. K. Thapar 1974, 1978, 1984, 1987; Vishnu-Mittre 1974, 1978). There are also informative sections on the subject in the best general texts on South Asian archaeology (e.g., Sankalia 1974; Fairservis 1971a, 1975; Allchin, B. and F. R. 1982; Agrawal 1982a).

Some of the earliest evidence for human intensive exploitation of sheep and goats and the wild grasses that were later domesticated comes from northern Afghanistan. Admittedly, this is somewhat removed from the Indus Valley but these sites offer important hints on the beginnings of the subsistence revolution elsewhere and cannot be ignored in this investigation.

Early Experiments with Food Production and Domestication in Afghanistan

Louis Dupree's small scale excavation at the sites of Snake Cave and Horse Cave, on the Balkh River in Afghanistan on the borders of the Greater Indus Region, (Dupree 1964, 1972a) sheds light on the potentials of this region for understanding the domestication process (Figure 4.9,

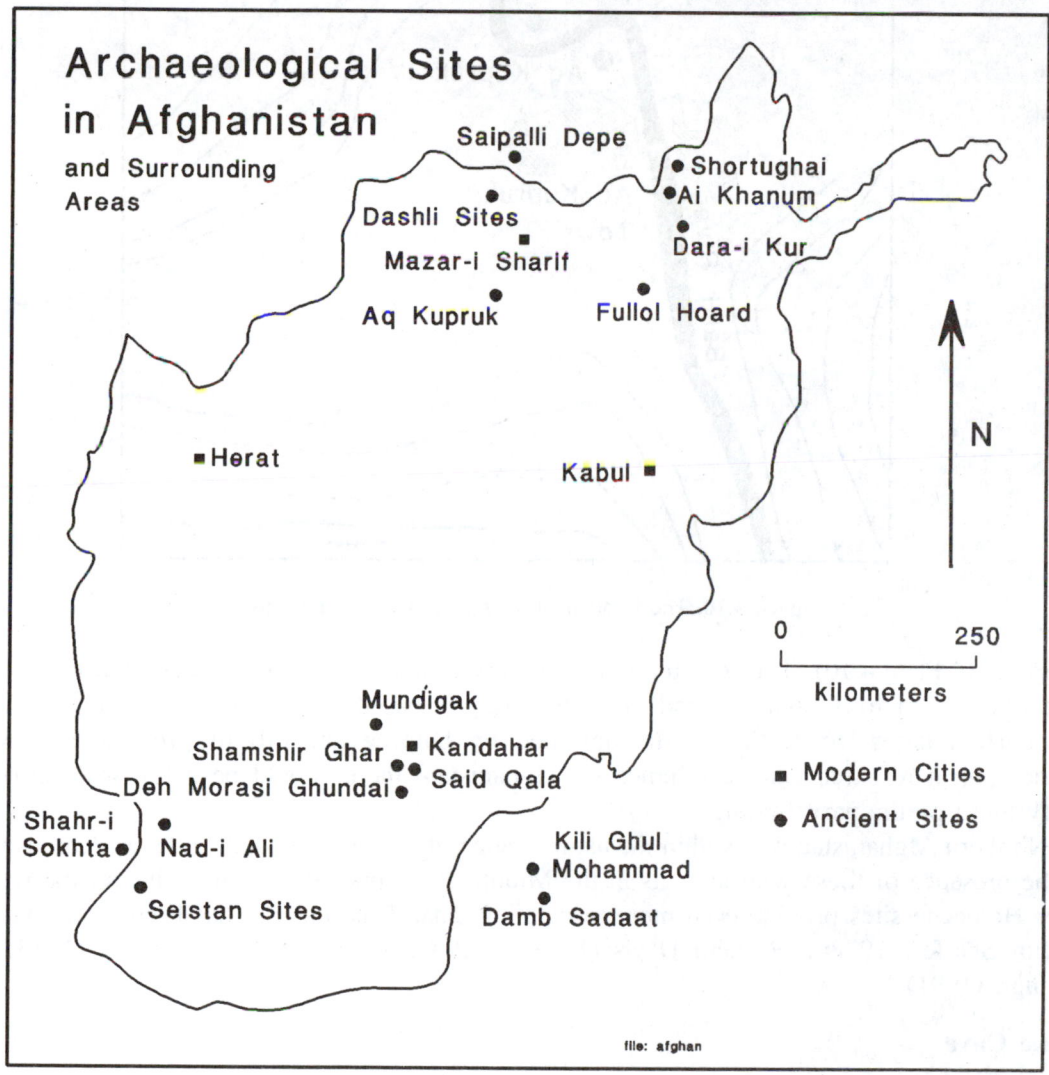

Figure 4.9. Map of sites in Afghanistan

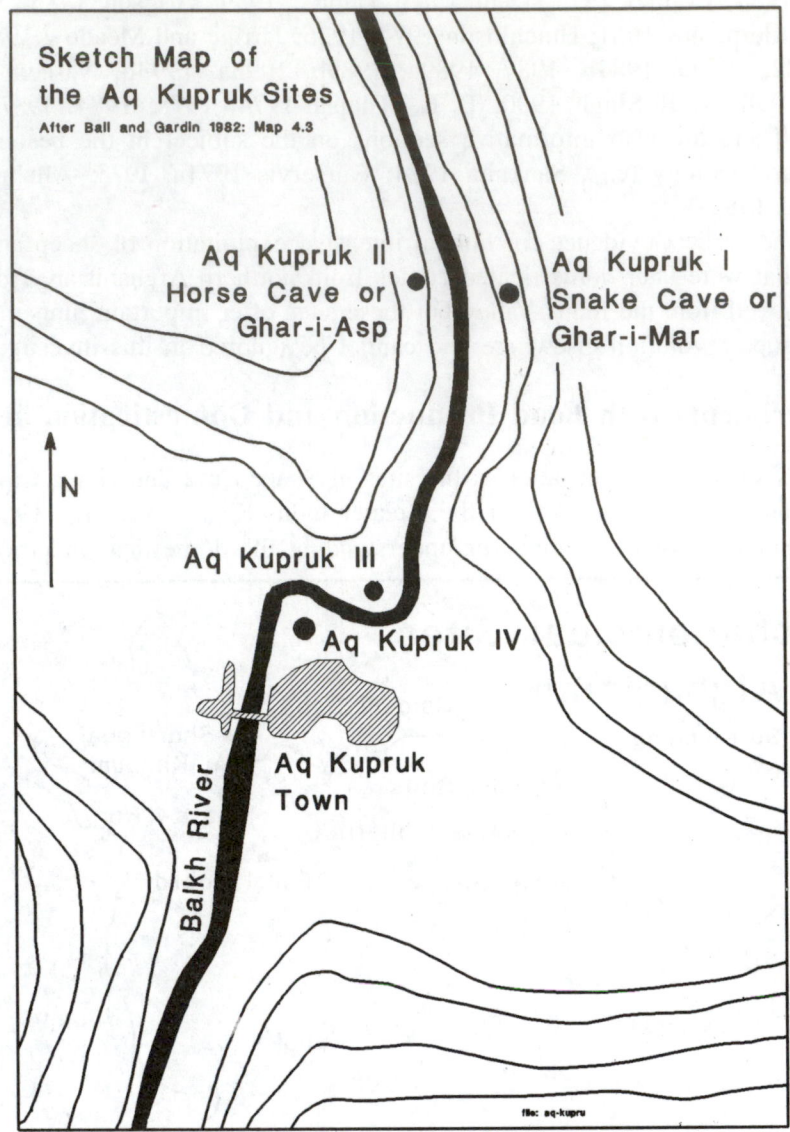

Figure 4.10. The location of sites around Aq Kupruk town

Figure 4.10, Plate 4.10). The research is preliminary in the sense that the data from these caves have never been fully analyzed and the chronology is based on a relatively small number of radiocarbon dates. Still, the results obtained by Dupree are full of promise and when archaeological research can be resumed in Afghanistan, there should be a full-scale effort to verify these preliminary findings.

Northern Afghanistan was within the natural range of sheep, goats and cattle, as demonstrated by the presence of these wild animals in the Middle and Upper Palaeolithic sites in the region. Later Holocene sites provide even more fascinating data. This material has been well reviewed by Jim Shaffer (1978a), Richard Davis (1978) S. P. Gupta and Arun Kesarwani (1983) and P. Singh (1991).

Snake Cave

Snake Cave, also known as Ghar-i-Mar or Aq Kupruk I, is a large cave on a terrace of the

Balkh River, near the town of Aq Kupruk, just south of Mazar-i-Sharif (Plate 4.11). It is a deeply stratified site with close to 10 meters (33 feet) of deposits as seen in Table 4.3.

TABLE 4.3
Snake Cave, Aq Kupruk I

Stratum	Period	Radiocarbon Dates	Pottery	Fauna
Top blackkish humus and loess, hearths	Early Islamic	None	Glazed ware	Domesticated sheep goats, cattle, horse
Reddish-brown earth	Later Iron Age Intensive habitation	Several available	Kushano-Sassanian	Domesticated sheep goats, cattle horse
Gray-brown and reddish loess over Cave Gravels I	Early Iron Age	Several available	Iron Age	Domesticated sheep goats, cattle, horse
Break in the sequence				
Upper third of Cave Gravel I	Chalcolithic	Hv-428 1Σ cal. BC 6164 (6015) 5962 HV-429 1Σ cal. BC 5972 (5929, 5916, 5863) 5732	Chaff tempered wares, hard fired wares	Domesticated sheep goat, cattle, possibly the onager
Middle third of Cave Gravels I	Ceramic Neolithic	HV-1354 1Σ cal. BC 5686 (5805) 5529 HV-1356 1Σ cal. BC 5289 (5259) 5149 HV-1357 1Σ cal. BC 5930 (5768) 5703	Undecorated soft black ware	Domesticated sheep and goats
Lower third of Cave Gravels I	Non-Ceramic Neolithic B	None	None	Domesticated sheep, goats, possibly cattle. Other wild ungulates
Sterile sands				
Upper half of Cave Gravel II	Non-Ceramic Neolithic A	HV-425 1Σ cal. BC 7881 (7586) 7540	None	Domesticated sheep and goats
Lower half of Cave Gravel II	Upper Palaeolithic Kuprukian B		None	Wild sheep, goats
Sterlle deposits	None			

It was excavated by Dupree in 1962 and again in 1965 (1964, 1972a). Stratified below historical materials are Dupree's Gravels One, with a "Ceramic Neolithic." This is a soft, limestone tempered pottery which seems to be similar to that from the site of Chust in Turkmenistan (Dupree 1964: 146), an observation congruent with three radiocarbon dates in the sixth millennium (Table 4.4).

Below the "Ceramic Neolithic" of Snake Cave is nearly a meter of sterile grey sands which cover an "Aceramic Neolithic." According to Dexter Perkins (1972: 73) these levels contain the remains of domesticated sheep and goats as well as sickle blades (Shaffer 1978a: 75). Richard Meadow has reviewed Perkins' work and believes that there is a need for caution in accepting it (1989). No reports are available on the palaeobotanical material. There is a single radiocarbon date for this level at Snake Cave, which comes to 7586 cal BC, contemporary with a PPNA site in absolute chronological terms.

TABLE 4.4
Radiocarbon Dates for Sites in Afghanistan with Evidence for Early Domestication

Lab Number	Calibrated Date
Snake Cave (Ghar-i-Mar, Aq Kupruk I): Ceramic Neolithic	
HV-1357	1Σ cal BC 5930 (5768) 5703
	2Σ cal BC 5959 (5768) 5635
HV-1354	1Σ cal BC 5686 (5605) 5529
	2Σ cal BC 5749 (5605) 5478
HV-1356	1Σ cal BC 5289 (5259) 5149
	2Σ cal BC 5422 (5259) 5071
Snake Cave (Ghar-i-Mar, Aq Kupruk I): Aceramic Neolithic A	
HV-425	1Σ cal BC 7881 (7586) 7540
	2Σ cal BC 7942 (7586) 7490
Horse Cave (Ghar-i-Asp, Aq Kupruk II): Ceramic Neolithic	
UCLA-1363F	1Σ cal BC 3343 (3297, 3237, 3173, 3168, 3107) 3043
	2Σ cal BC 3365 (3297, 3237, 3173, 3168, 3107) 2925
Horse Cave (Ghar-i-Asp, Aq Kupruk II): Aceramic Neolithic	
HV-1355	1Σ cal BC 10,416 (10,035) 9133
	2Σ cal BC 10,676 (10,035) 9014
Horse Cave (Ghar-i-Asp, Aq Kupruk II): Upper Palaeolithic	
HV-1358	1Σ cal BC 17,957 (17,620) 17,325
	2Σ cal BC 18,331 (17,620) 17,069

Horse Cave

Horse Cave, also known as Ghar-i-Asp or Aq Kupruk II, was excavated by Dupree at the same time work proceeded at Snake Cave (Plate 4.12). "Aceramic Neolithic" levels similar to those found at Snake Cave, with sheep, goats and sickles, were also present here and yielded a date which calibrates to 10,035 BC. Chronologically, this would be contemporary with the Early Natufian in the Levant as seen in Table 4.5.

Other Possible Early Food Producing Sites in Northern Afghanistan

Archaeologists from the former Soviet Union were very active in northern Afghanistan in the 1970s. In 1969, 1975 and 1976 A. V. Vinogradov conducted a survey of Balkh, Jauzjan and Faryab Provinces, all bordering the Amu Darya (Vinogradov 1979; see also Kohl 1984: 40-1; P. Singh 1991: 124-26). This work was directed, in part, to locating the sites that might have evidence for early domestication and food production. This survey produced masses of stone tools that are associated with an interesting typology of archaeological locations: "sites" that are dense surface materials 10 to 30 meters in diameter; "stations" that are simply poorer sites and "points," areas with disparate, scattered artifacts that can stretch on for two to three kilometers.

TABLE 4.5
Horse Cave, Aq Kupruk II

Stratum	Period	Radiocarbon Dates	Pottery	Fauna
Upper hurnus and loess	Early Islamic	None	Glazed ware	Domesticated sheep goats
Lower part of upper loess	Iron Age(?)	UCLA-1363E IΣ cal. AD 800 (768) 515	Painted wares, etc.	Domesticated cattle sheep, goats, dog
Loess overlying upper gravels	Ceramic Neolithic	UCLA 1363F IΣ cal. BC 3343 (3297, 3237, 3173, 3168, 3107) 3043	Chaff and sherd tempered soft ware	Domesticated cattle, sheep, goats, horse and wild ungulates
Upper cave gravels	Non-ceramic Neolithic Same stone tools as in Non-ceramic Neolithic of Aq Kupruk I, Snake cave	HV-1355 IΣ cal. BC 10416 (10035) 9133	None	Domesticated sheep, goats
Middle cave gravels	Upper Palaeolithic Kupruklan B	HV-1358 1Σ cal. BC 17957 (17620) 17325	None	Wild sheep, goats, cattle, and other ungulates, wolf
Lower Cave gravels	Upper Palaeolithic Kuprukian A	None	None	Wild sheep, goats, cattle, equid, etc.
Limestone floor of Cave	None			

As seen in Figure 4.11 the surveys took place just south of the Amu Darya. This is an area of old sediments and sand dunes, dissected by small streams flowing from south to north.

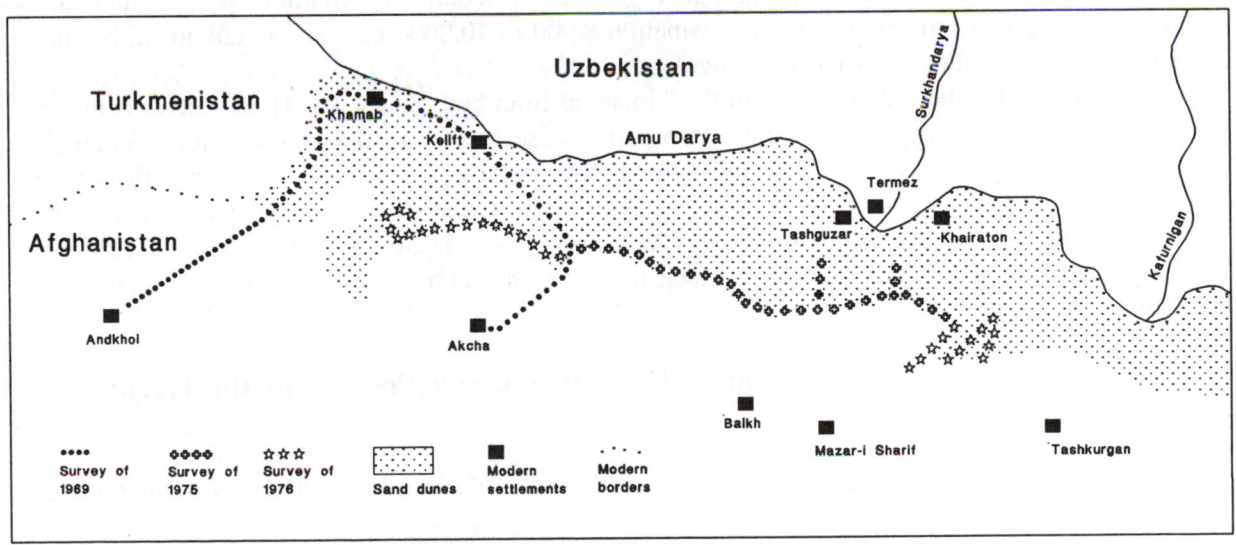

Figure 4.11. Sketch map of Vinogradov's survey in 1969, 1975 and 1976, after Kohl 1984: 40

The 1969 explorations lasted only eight days and produced ca. 700 tools from twelve "points." The explorations of 1975 lasted twenty-three days and produced eighty-one "points", including thirty-four "stations" and a collection of more than 16,000 stone tools. The final, 1976, survey lasted thirteen days and located an additional sixty-one "points" and ca. 6000 tools. This is a very rich area. Vinogradov notes: "Practically in any place in the sands in which a brief survey sweep was made flint artifacts and debitage could be found" (1979: 10; quoted from Kohl 1984: 41).

Another site which is thought to have evidence for early food production is Akli-Mami, near Shortughai, 17 kilometers from the confluence of the Kokcha River with the Amu Darya (cited in Kohl 1984: 40).

These sites are all dated by the typology of the flint tools, which carries with it a marked degree of uncertainty. Also, there is no excavation. The work is introduced here to give a sense of the potential of this region to inform us about the subsistence of early Holocene peoples. This goes well beyond the often cited excavations at Aq Kupruk, which seem to have been abodes of people with many neighbors, in a well populated region.

Purushottam Singh has given a list of some of the "sites" from Vinogradov's 1976 explorations, which are found on Table 4.6.

Summary

Jim Shaffer (1978a: 73-81) and Richard Meadow (1989) have excellent, critical overviews of the Aq Kupruk material. They agree that these finds should be seen as preliminary and that the radiocarbon dates that are available cannot be presumed to constitute the basis for a chronology. Meadow notes that "...based upon current understandings of ovicaprine zoogeography, the ibex (*Capra ibex*) and the urial (*Ovis vigni*) but neither the bezoar (*Capra aegagrus*) nor the argali (*Ovis ammon*) would be present in the Aq Kupruk region" (1989: 28). Given the genetic plasticity of sheep (Meadow 1989: 29), this may not have made much difference to their domestication because the sheep interbreed and bear fertile offspring and the same is true for the goats. In this sense they are not species and one might legitimately wonder if all of the attention given to taxonomic nomenclature, precedent and the like is anything other than an exercise in this discussion. Moreover, we are dealing here with the "modern" distribution of these animals. Whether this is a reflection of their distribution 8,000 to 10,000 years ago is unknown, but has to be held in doubt, given the time involved.

The dates for the "Aceramic Neolithic" material from both Snake and Horse Caves compare well with dates from the Near East. At present, these dates and the archaeological materials themselves, can be seen as good indications that northern Afghanistan, probably the entire western Hindu Kush, should be taken seriously as a place where early, independent experiments with agriculture and animal husbandry may have taken place. There is more "Aceramic Neolithic" material in Pakistan which is clearly much nearer to the foundations on which the Indus Age rests.

The Origins and Development of Food Producing Peoples in the Greater Indus Region

Early food producing peoples are not well documented in the western borderlands of the Greater

TABLE 4.6
Vinogradov's 1976 Exploration in Northern Afghanistan

Site	Location	Province	Material and estimated date
Chash Baba	4 km south of Khamiyab, on the Oxus	Jauzjan Province	A scatter of Neolithic tools found on top of a high isolated ridge, suggested date 8000-5000 BC
Chilik-I	22 km north of Qul Akcha	Jauzjan Province	A surface site with a large number of stone tools, 7th-6th millennium BC
Chilik-I Yaldash	22 km northeast of Akcha	Jauzjan Province	A surface site 7th-6th millennium BC
Chilik-I Yass Khan	20 km northeast of Akcha	Jauzjan Province	A surface site covering a large area. 7th-6th millennium BC
Jar Quduq	27 km south of Khamiyab	Jauzjan Province	Neolithic Date: 7th-6th millennium BC
Kauk	On the route from Khamiyab to Andkhui	Jauzjan Province	A surface site 7th-6th millennium BC
Khwaja Do Kuh	20 km northwest of Shibarghan	Faryab Province	A surface site 7th-6th millennium BC
Khwaja Do Kuh Nau	22 km northwest of Shibarghan	Faryab Province	A surface site Kuh Nau 7th-6th millennium BC
Kilift	91 km northwest of Balkh, on the Oxus	Balkh Province	An extremely rich area 7th-6th millennium BC
Qaq	7 km south of the Soviet border and 15 km southwest of Qara Tepe	Faryab Province	A surface site 7th-6th millennium BC
Qaq-I Nazar	17 km northeast of Char-Bagh	Faryab Province	An extensive surface Agha site 7th-6th millennium BC
Qara Kul	8 km northeast of Sayyidabad	Jauzjan Province	A surface site 7th-6th millennium BC
Qara Tepe	13 km southwest of Jar Quduq	Jauzjan Province	Surface scatter of stone tools on a rocky mound
Qur Quduq	13 km north of Sayyidabad	Jauzjan Province	A surface site 7th-6th millennium BC
Safarwal	23 km north of Akcha	Jauzjan Province	A surface site 7th-6th millennium BC
Sayyidabad	26 km northwest of Akcha	Jauzjan Province	A surface site 7th-6th millennium BC

(after P. Singh 1991: 124-26)

Indus Region. The earliest phase has been called "Kili Ghul Mohammad" after the site in Baluchistan where it was first identified (Fairservis 1956a). There was considerable room for doubt about the status of Kili Ghul I, but the recent excavations at Mehrgarh (Jarrige, Jarrige, Meadow and Quivron 1995) have done much to ease the situation. This is an "Aceramic Neolithic" found at Mehrgarh and possibly Gumla (Dani 1970-71: 39, 41-2). The exposure at Mehrgarh is very large and modern methods of data recovery and analysis have vastly expanded our knowledge of these times. Still many questions remain, not the least of which is the date for early food production there.

The Regions Prior to the Mature Harappan

As the story of the growth of food producing societies in the Greater Indus Region is told it will be evident that there is not always a good fit between the spatial distribution of archaeological assemblages and the Regions introduced in Part 3. This is evidence for the fact that these geographical units are both cultural and natural, admitting the probability that in some marked ways they were constructed and shaped by human activity. Notice of the Region structure will be made from time to time in the narrative that follows, indicating the good fit between archaeology and these constructs. The best fit is found during the Mature Harappan Stage, and is most useful in this context; however the Regions are also informative of the organization of life in Early Harappan times and play a role in understanding these times.

The Terminology Used for the Developmental Stages of the Indus Age

A full discussion of the terminology and chronology of the Indus Age is found in the Introduction. Most of the information on chronology comes from radiocarbon dates, the interpretation of which is not always a straightforward proposition.

Early Holocene Hunting and Gathering

A Stage of sophisticated hunting and gathering, directly antecedent to the appearance of the village farming community, has not yet been defined well in either India or Pakistan. Sites that are believed to date to the general time period ascribed to this level of hunting and gathering have been found, some with the possibility of remarkable continuity into the present (Kenoyer 1992b; Kenoyer, Clark, Pal and Sharma 1983). Almost nothing is known of the time between the late Glacial Age at ca. 15,000 BC and the beginnings of Mehrgarh at ca. 7000 BC as revealed by the following small bibliography (B. Allchin 1972, 1977; Thomas 1975). This phase might be thought of as comparable to the Kebaran Phase of the Levant. The first period at Mehrgarh has fully developed domestic architecture based on mud brick, and this settlement appears to be comparable to the PPNB settlements in the Near East. These date from 7300/ 7200 to ca. 5800 BC, in agreement with the chronology used for Mehrgarh I. So, while Mehrgarh in Kili Ghul Mohammad Phase times is undoubtedly an early village farming community, there is also a sense that the excavations there have not documented the beginnings of this tradition, or the beginnings of food production and domestication in the region. It is certainly nothing like a terminal hunting-gathering site with the intensive collection of cereals, pulses and sophisticated hunting. These people were already farmers.

A few sites with microlithic tools such as crescents, lunates, trapezoids, micro-blades and the like, have been found in Pakistan (see Table 4.7), but none has been excavated. Given the fact that the use of stone tools of this type has been documented in historical times in India, it cannot be assumed that in Pakistan all of the sites having such stone tools are necessarily early (Figure 4.12).

TABLE 4.7
Sites with Microliths in Sindh, Las Bela and Makran

Site	District	Citation
Deh Bail	Karachi	A. R. Khan 1968a: 9, A. R. Khan 1968b
Drigh Road Site	Karachi	Lambrick 1964: 50
Kara Jabal	Karachi	A. R. Khan 1968a: 7, A. R. Khan 1968b
Kotwari Buthi	Karachi	A. R. Khan 1968a: 7, A. R. Khan 1968b
Las Bela	Las Bela	A. R. Khan 1968b, A. R. Khan 1973
Lyari River	Karachi	Fairservis 1971c: 411
Mile Post 18	Karachi	A. R. Khan 1968a: 7, A. R. Khan 1968b
Mol River	Karachi	Fairservis, personal communication
Ran Pethani Nadi	Karachi	A. R. Khan 1968a: 8, A. R. Khan 1968b
Sar-i Damb	Makran	Besenval and Sanlaville 1990: 117
Tharro Hill	Hyderabad	Majumdar 1934: 20-2 Lambrick 1942a: 109-10

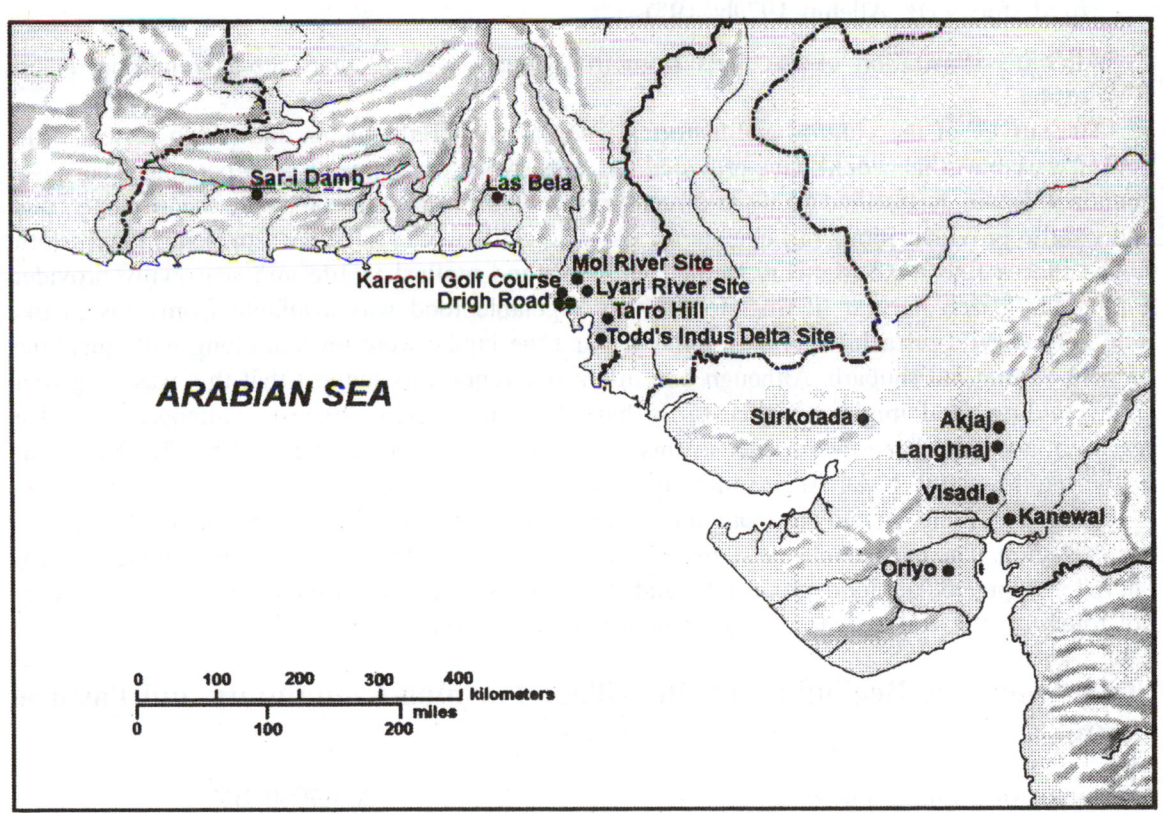

Figure 4.12. Map of sites with microliths in Sindh, Makran and Gujarat

Bridget Allchin has studied the notes and collections from K. R. U. Todd's archaeological explorations in Lower Sindh. She has an important quote from his unpublished notes in the British Museum, documenting the Karachi Golf Course microliths prior to the time the area was built up with the expansion of Karachi.

> Eight miles north of Karachi and beyond the Civil Jail is the country club. It is situated on an apparently barren waste of sand and gravel running parallel to the Hab River Hills. This expanse is sparsely covered by cactus and camel thorn bushes, and is seamed by stream beds. These stream beds reveal alternate layers of gravel and sand. The former consists of water worn pebbles of limestone, quartzite, flint and sandstone. These gullies must at some remote epoch have had water running through them in some considerable quantity, for some of them cut deeply into the underlying shales and sandstones. It is along the banks of these stream beds that implements of flint may be found. They are, generally speaking, of a putty colour, and are of Tardenois (sic) types; they consist of trapezes, lunates, cores, blade scrapers and blades. It must be emphasized that the prevailing type is the blade and blade scraper. These implements have invariably been blunted along one or both edges, and very often terminate in an end scraper reminiscent of the Magdalenian types. Burins are conspicuous by their variety, as are cores, though these latter conform to the usual microlithic types. These artefacts are found in patches a few yards in diameter, and point to the fact that here was a settlement and no passing occupation. Sometimes too among these clusters painted pottery is found, but as it is not *in situ* it might well be fairly modern. There appear to be traces of hearths, judging from clusters of fired stones (B. Allchin 1979b: 195).

Allchin's illustration of the finds from the Karachi Golf Course site is reproduced here (Figure 4.13).

The survey of the cultural and historical geography of Baluchistan and Sindh reviewed the natural variables that would have provided the subsistence economy of such peoples. There was abundant game, as testified to by 19th century accounts from hunters. Wild sheep, goats, pigs and gazelle provided forms of large game, and wild cattle would have been present in prehistoric times. Places like Lake Manchar teemed with fish and molluskan life and seasonally provided a potentially rich harvest of migratory birds. Vegetable food was available from grasses like wild barley. Wild pistachios, prunes, almonds, and the jujube were present along with quantities of wild cumin and rhubarb. Although one might not venture to suggest that this was a "garden spot," finding food might not necessarily have been mankind's greatest challenge there. The region might have been even better in this regard than the abundance found by the !Kung San in the depths of the Kalahari in southern Africa.

Almost nothing is known about the terminal era of hunting and gathering in the Greater Indus Region. The excavations at Mehrgarh have made spectacular contributions to understanding later developments in food production and domestication, but information from this site does not touch on the earliest experiments which must have preceded it.

Stage One: The Beginnings of the Village Farming Community and Pastoral Camp

Kili Ghul Mohammad Phase	7000-5000 BC
Burj Basket-marked Phase	5000-4300 BC

Documentation for the beginnings of sedentism and pastoral nomadism begins in the subcontinent

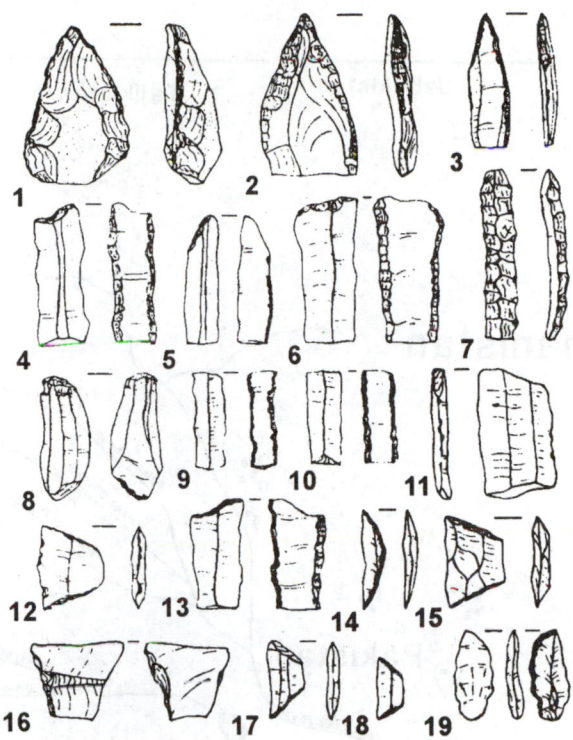

Microliths from the Karachi Golf Course Trimmed points: 1, 2, 3, 19 Reworked blades: 4, 5, 6, 9, 10, 13; Longitudinal blade trimming flake: 7; Blade core: 8; Blade fragment: 11; Transverse arrow heads: 12, 15, 16?; Lunate: 14; Trapezoids: 17, 18; After B. Allchin 1976: 196;

Figure 4.13. Karachi Golf Course site microliths, after B. Allchin 1979b: 196

in the mountains of Baluchistan, the Northwest Frontier and the adjacent plains of Sindh and the Punjab. As already noted, important and probably closely related, parallel trends in this development were taking place in the mountains and plains of northern Afghanistan (Snake Cave, Horse Cave), perhaps extending north on to the plains of Central Asia (Figure 4.14, Figure 4.15).

Two Phases, the Kili Ghul Mohammad and Burj Basket-marked are combined in this discussion of the Primary Village farming community and pastoral camp. The amount of data for these two Phases in the Subcontinent is so limited that it is simply not possible to distinguish them, except on the basis of one or two points, most notably the development of pottery.

Villages, and probably camp sites, of Stage One are found in the mountains and adjacent plains of the Greater Indus Region. It is highly likely that the piedmont areas along the Sindh Kohistan and Kirthar Ranges also have sites of this phase, possibly associated with the *nais* and springs of the region. One site, Tharro Hill, which may have been occupied during this Stage, is located near the active course of the Indus River and could indicate the early penetration of food producers into this complex environment (Figure 4.16).

Other evidence for the beginnings of agriculture in Pakistan and northwestern India comes from palynological work conducted by Gurdip Singh and his team at a series of salt lakes in Rajasthan. In the course of their investigations they found the following:

> In the salt-lake profiles of western Rajasthan one witnesses an extraordinary rise in carbonized vegetable remains (mostly wood fragments) in the sediments at about the beginning of phase III (pollen zone B) at all the sites. The phenomenon cannot be explained in terms of natural causes as the enhanced rate of the occurrence is

444

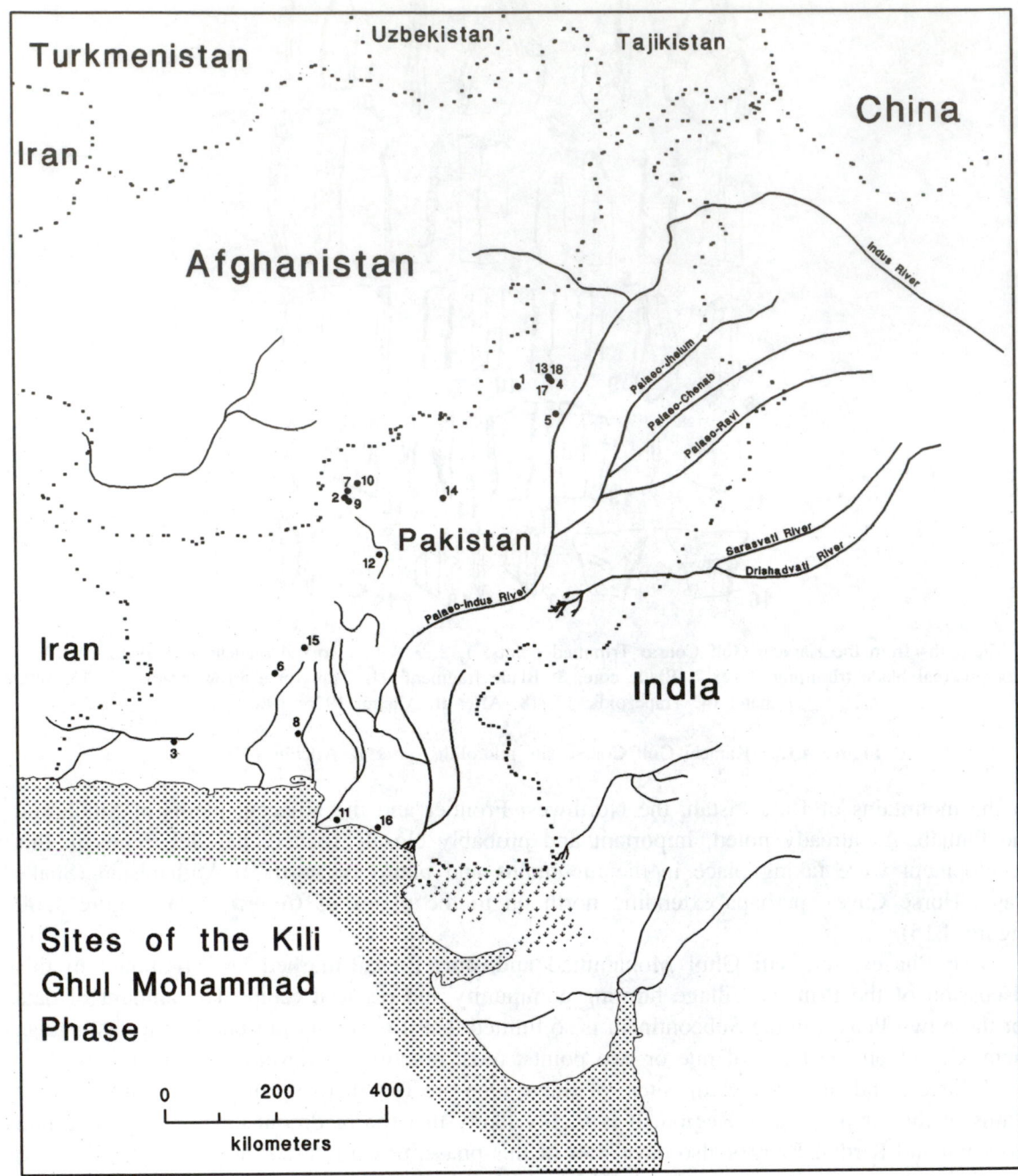

Figure 4.14. Map of sites of the Kili Ghul Mohammad Phase

Key to Figure 4.14

1 Bagh-i Kumb Damb	7 Kasiano Dozakh	13 Nakamshakh
2 Baleii	8 Khakhar Buthi	14 Rana Ghundai
3 Ghalaihak	9 Kili Ghul Mohammad	15 Shakar Khan Damb
4 Ghul Shah Tup	10 Lai Ghundai	16 Thaffo Hill
5 Gumla	11 Lyari River Area	17 Tup Takhtikhel
6 Jebri Damb Two	12 Mehrgarh	18 Yarak

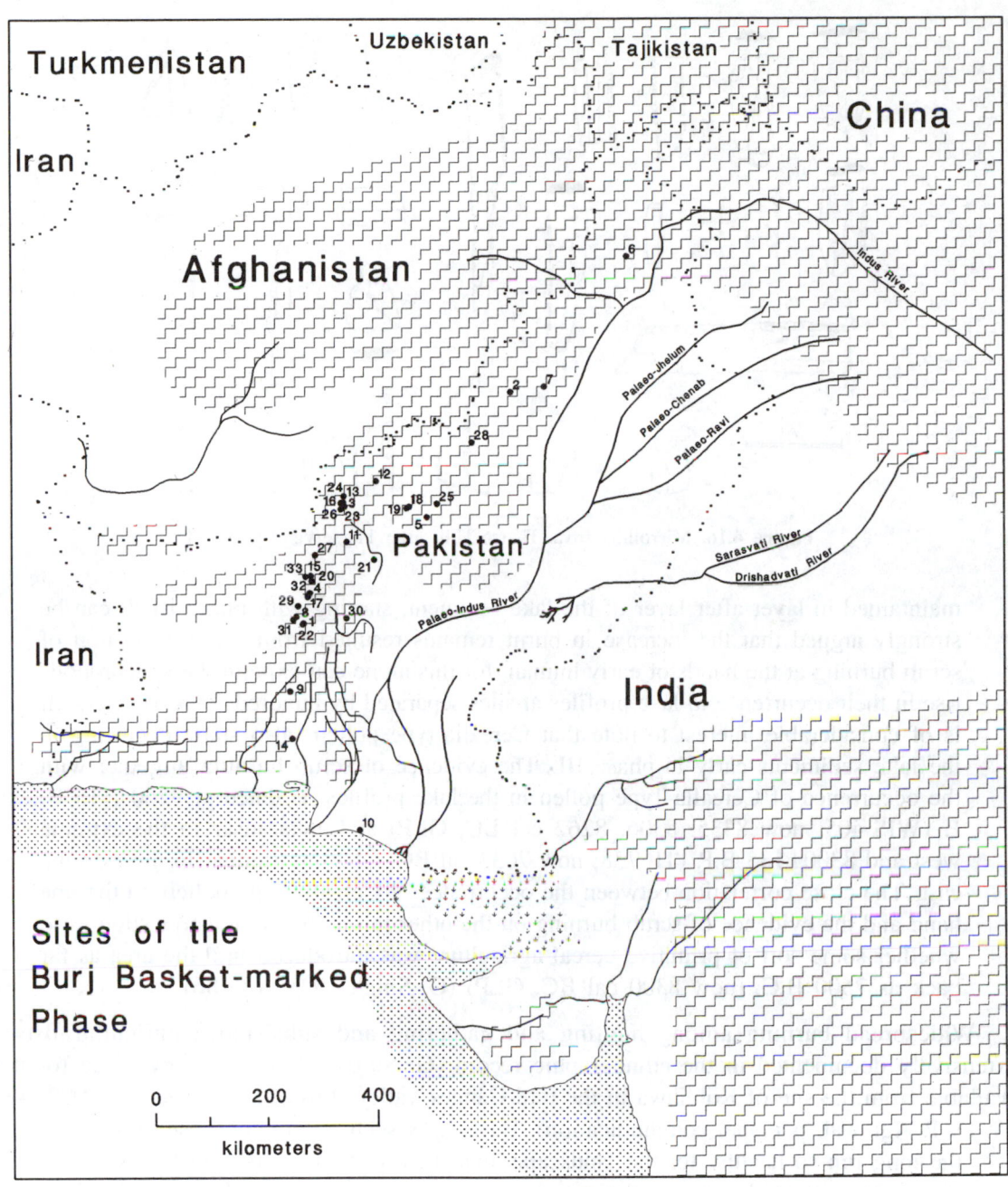

Sites of the Burj Basket-marked Phase

0   200   400

kilometers

Figure 4.15. Map of sites of the Burj Basket-marked Phase

Key to Figure 4.15

1 Anjira	9 Hurro Damb	17 Kuki Damb	25 Rana Ghundai
2 Bagh-i Kumb Damb	10 Indus Delta Site	18 L-2	26 Rizvi Karuna
3 Baleli	11 Isplinji Two	19 L-3	27 Saiyid Maurez Damb
4 Benn Chah	12 Kan Mehtarzai One	20 Malki	28 Sang
5 Duki Mound	13 Kasiano Dozakh	21 Mehrgarh	29 Siah Damb, Surab
6 Ghalegay Cave	14 Khakhar Buthi	22 Neghar Damb	30 Singen Kalat
7 Ghul Shah Tup	15 Khwaja Zabar	23 Q-17	31 Surab Valley 'A'
8 Gorpat	16 Kili Ghul Mohammad	24 Q-25	32 Thok Valley One
			33 Togau

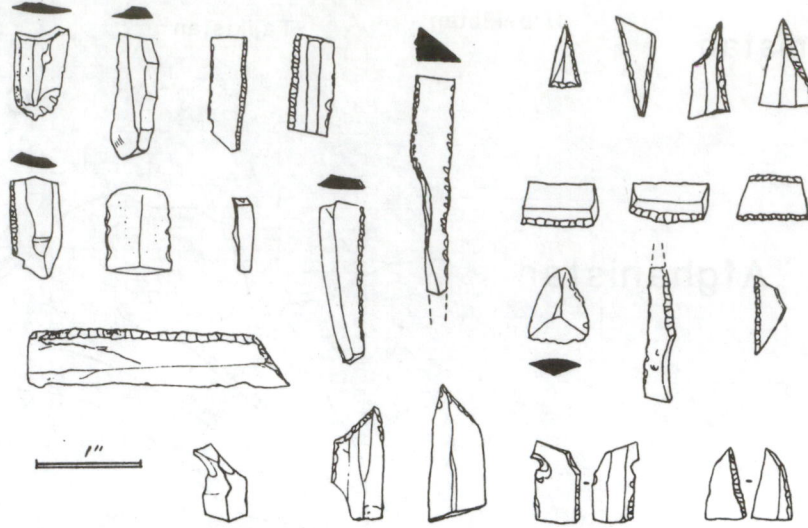

Figure 4.16. Microliths from Tharro Hill, after Fairservis 1975: 174

maintained in layer after layer of the lake sediment, starting with phase III. It can be strongly argued that the increase in burnt remains resulted from the introduction of scrub burning at the hands of early human, for this alone can explain the synchronous rise in their occurrence in lake profiles at sites separated by hundreds of kilometers...It is of considerable interest to note that Cerealia-type pollen...also starts occurring in the lake sediments early in phase III...The evidence of scrub burning, together with the occurrence of Cerealia-Type pollen in the lake profiles, is dated at 9260±115 B. P. (WIS-405; now 8335, 8306, 8262 cal BC, GLP) at Lunkaransar in the extreme west and 8300±135 B.P. (TF-738; now 7033 cal BC, GLP) at Sambar in the extreme east. The close correlation between the occurrence of Cerealia-type pollen on the one hand and the evidence of scrub burning on the other raises the obvious question as to whether some sort of primitive cereal agriculture was introduced into the area as far back as 7500 B.C. (now 8300 cal BC, GLP) (G. Singh 1971: 185-86).

Widespread burning among hunting and gathering and subsistence agriculturalists is extensively documented in the ethnographic record (G. Singh 1985). More evidence for it is available from the site of Koldihwa in the mid-Ganges Valley (Possehl and Rissman 1992: 474-75; D. P. Agrawal, personal communication). Burning is such a commonsense thing to do, and over the long run so healthy for the landscape, that there is every reason to believe that Singh is on the right track with his speculations. It is also important to note the general coincidence between his chronology and that used for Mehrgarh I.

The Kili Ghul Mohammad Phase is aceramic and has evidence for the domestication or manipulation of both plants and animals. At Mehrgarh this includes only the early portion of Period I (called "IA") since Period IB has some pottery.

The Chronology for Stage One

The chronology of the Kili Ghul Mohammad and Burj Basket-marked Phases is not yet set. The longest run of radiocarbon dates comes from Mehrgarh and is given in Table 4.8.

These dates are not entirely congruent with the summary chronology that has been proposed

TABLE 4.8

Radiocarbon dates for the Kili Ghul Mohammad Phase at Mehrgarh

Lab Number	Calibrated Date
Mehrgarh IA	
BETA-1721	1Σ cal BC 8827 (8416) 8261
	2Σ cal BC 8950 (8416) 8090
BETA-1407	1Σ cal BC 6189 (5961) 5670
	2Σ cal BC 6467 (5961) 5441
BETA-1408	1Σ cal BC 5844 (5737) 5682
	2Σ cal BC 5952 (5737) 5603
BETA-7316	1Σ cal BC 5041 (4902, 4876, 4854) 4730
	2Σ cal BC 5217 (4902, 4876, 4854) 4579
BETA-2686	1Σ cal BC 4802 (4762, 4738, 4727) 4623
	2Σ cal BC 4906 (4762, 4738, 4727) 4538
LY-1947	1Σ cal BC 4917 (4716) 4464
	2Σ cal BC 5210 (4716) 4331
LY-1948	1Σ cal BC 5420 (4540) 3777
	2Σ cal BC 5991 (4540) 2886
LY-1949	1Σ cal BC 4535 (4354) 4165
	2Σ cal BC 4780 (4354) 3973

for the Kili Ghul Mohammad Phase (7000-5000 BC). To some degree one has to look also at the chronology for the Burj basket-marked Phase to interpret the chronology. These dates are presented in Table 4.9.

Taken as a whole, the dates from Mehrgarh I and II seem to indicate that there was a settlement there at the beginning of the eighth millennium BC. The stratigraphy at the site is immensely complex. A synthesis for it emerged rather late in the excavations there and some small amount of stratigraphic contamination seems to be present. Moreover, at Kili Ghul Mohammad itself, the Period I, Kili Ghul Mohammad Aceramic occupation has three additional dates, all of which fall between ca. 5000 and 4000 BC (See Table 4.10) (Figure 4.17, Figure 4.18).

These observations do not inspire confidence that the chronology proposed here will be sustained when further chronological and cultural information is gathered for Stage One. In the end, the date for Stage One is entirely provisional at this time, in general agreement with other recent chronologies (Shaffer 1992: 426, Figure 2; Meadow 1993a: 301).

The beginnings of the Kili Ghul Mohammad Phase at ca. 7000 BC is a reasonable estimate, given the modest amount of information that is available. Ending the Burj Basket-marked Phase at ca. 4300 BC is also a reasonable proposition from the perspective of the radiocarbon dates for this Phase, and in light of the chronology for the Togau Phase. However, the internal chronology for the Kili Ghul Mohammad and Burj Basket-marked Phases has not yet been worked out and remains a project for the future.

By far the best evidence for an early South Asian village comes from Mehrgarh, the large, complex site on the Kachi Plain of the Indus Valley.

TABLE 4.9
Radiocarbon dates for the Burj Basket-marked Phase

Lab Number	Calibrated Date
Mehrgarh IB	
BETA-1719	1Σ cal BC 14192 (13994) 13789
	2Σ cal BC 14381 (13994) 13567
LY-1950	1Σ cal BC 7694 (7490) 7096
	2Σ cal BC 8008 (7490) 6719
LV-994	1Σ cal BC 5280 (5253) 5143
	2Σ cal BC 5411 (5253) 5062
LV-993	1Σ cal BC 5206 (5040, 5017, 5005) 4915
	2Σ cal BC 5253 (5040, 5017, 5005) 4798
LV-908	1Σ cal BC 5068 (4963) 4915
	2Σ cal BC 5217 (4963) 4831
LV-907	1Σ cal BC 4994 (4916) 4807
	2Σ cal BC 5198 (4916) 4726
LV-906	1Σ cal BC 4911 (4832) 4776
	2Σ cal BC 4952 (4832) 4711
LV-909	1Σ cal BC 4904 (4808) 4776
	2Σ cal BC 4938 (4808) 4714
LV-910	1Σ cal BC 4898 (4775) 4616
	2Σ cal BC 4951 (4775) 4504
Mehrgarh IIA & IIB	
BETA-1720	1Σ cal BC 6041 (5961) 5825
	2Σ cal BC 6177 (5961) 5700
BETA-7315	1Σ cal BC 4541 (4460) 4351
	2Σ cal BC 4713 (4460) 4257
BETA-2688	1Σ cal BC 4434 (4342) 4257
	2Σ cal BC 4463 (4342) 4163
BETA-7314	1Σ cal BC 4343 (4310, 4309, 4249) 4090
	2Σ cal BC 4451 (4310, 4309, 4249) 3993
LY-1945	1Σ cal BC 4497 (4228) 3804
	2Σ cal BC 4898 (4228) 3518

TABLE 4.10
Radiocarbon dates for the Kili Ghul Mohammad Phase at Kili Ghul Mohammad

Lab No.	Calibrated Date
Kili Ghul Mohammad I	
L-180A	1Σ cal BC 4904 (4344) 3781
	2Σ cal BC 5435 (4344) 3106
P-524	1Σ cal BC 4430 (4338) 4243
	2Σ cal BC 4465 (4338) 4089
UW-61	1Σ cal BC 4224 (4070, 4041) 3977
	2Σ cal BC 4320 (4070, 4041) 3828

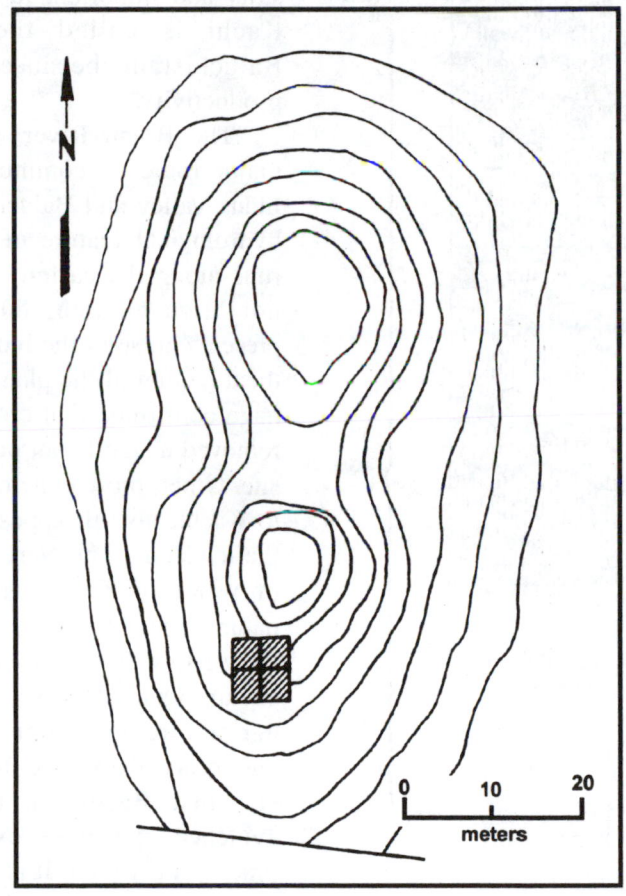

Figure 4.17. Site plan of Kili Ghul Mohammad, after Fairservis 1956a: 204

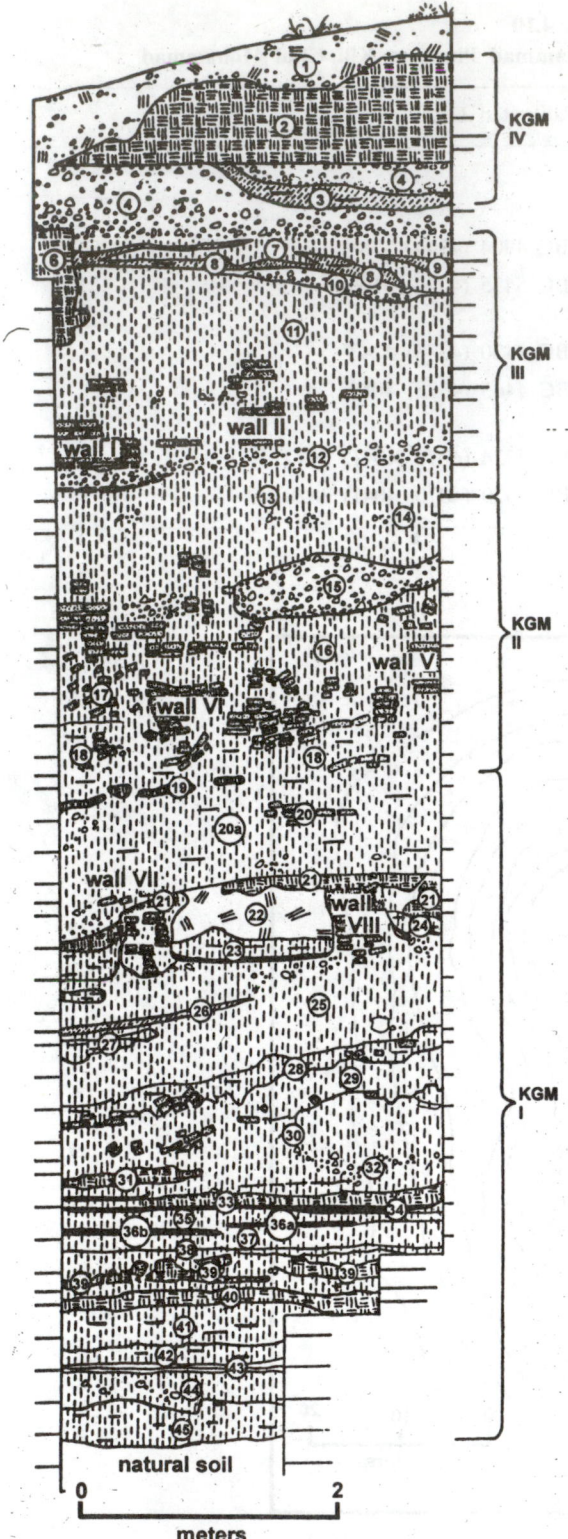

Figure 4.18. Section showing the depth of the Kili Ghul Mohammad occupation at Kili Ghul Mohammad, after Fairservis 1956a: 220

Mehrgarh: An Early Village Farming Community

The Kachi Plain

Kachi is a flat alluvial plain, an extension of the Indus Valley into an anomalous 'nick' in the eastern edge of the Iranian plateau. It is thought that the Pleistocene Indus River flowed in this area, so the alluvium is quite deep. The reconstructed course for the Indus during the Mature Harappan is just to the east of Mehrgarh (see Figure 3.123). Kachi is politically part of Baluchistan; but from a geographic perspective it is part of the Indus Valley. The politics of its capture by the Brahui Khans of Kalat is an interesting story and important to its prosperity. In fact Kachi is called the "Breadbasket of Baluchistan" because of its agricultural productivity.

The Bolan River, which flows down a major route of communication between the Indus Valley and Baluchistan, is the principal hydrological feature of the plain, and today runs along the eastern edge of the site. It is not large enough, however, to reach the present course of the Indus and disappears into the alluvium of the plain. Jarrige's excavations have confirmed that erosion by this river has removed a significant portion of the Mehrgarh site. Other, more ephemeral hill torrents drain to Kachi, also disappearing when they reach the lowlands. The Nari is a significant source of water in Kachi and the Mula River, a natural route from the hills to the plains on the western side of Kachi, is also a significant stream. One of the secrets for the success of agriculture in Kachi was the building of temporary dams and bunds on all of these streams. Based on the palaeobotanical evidence, it can be expected that this was practiced early on. It is the deep alluvium and the presence of the rivers and streams that flow into the northern and western fringes of this plain that made it an important agricultural area in prehistoric times.

The Excavation

Excavations at Mehrgarh cover eleven seasons of large-scale archaeological research (Figure 4.19). They have revealed a sizable, exceptionally complex site. The stratigraphy of Mehrgarh is difficult to understand. There is a great deal of lateral stratigraphy, with the center of habitation shifting from place to place over the mounded area, which is complemented by the fact that large portions of the settlement have been removed by the erosion of the Bolan River. Wind has also deflated some portions of the site. These factors (lateral stratigraphy and severe erosion) have meant that settlement size data have not been used from Mehrgarh for any of the periods of occupation there.

Mehrgarh is not an archaeological environment that is easily mastered and the French team that has been excavating, with their Pakistani counterparts, has done a fine job under difficult conditions of digging and synthesizing the material there.

The Bolan River has taken away what seems to have been a significant portion of the mound. This erosion did, however, offer an opportunity for the excavation team to reveal a deep section, along the river face (Plate 4.13, Figure 4.20).

The subdivision of Period I into an early aceramic and later ceramic occupation occurred after considerable excavation had been completed at Mehrgarh. Thus, it seems appropriate just to discuss Period I, since that is the term used in most of the literature. Where IA can be distinguished from IB the difference will be recognized. The same situation pertains to Periods IIA and IIB.

Mehrgarh Period I

Period I at Mehrgarh was found in an area called MR 3, in the northeastern corner of the site (Figure 4.21, Plate 4.14). It took a great deal of work to settle the stratigraphic picture for Mehrgarh Period I and its relationship to Period II. Richard Meadow has given the following synthesis:

> In Mehrgarh area MR3, the Bolan river has cut a c. 12 m deep section through the cultural deposits and alluvium. Careful study of this section in areas MR3F and MR3D-Bolan has revealed the presence of a 7-8 m thick aceramic neolithic mound (Period IA) capped and ringed by later deposits containing coarse, chaff-tempered ceramics (Periods IB and IIA) which are similar to those from the mid-sixth millennium BC in southeastern Iran (Jarrige and Lechevallier 1980; Jarrige 1987b, 1988a; Lamberg-Karlovsky and Beale 1986). The deepest levels have been reached in three locations (MR3S, MR3T, and MR3D) with the total area excavated being about 75 sq.m, a very small proportion of the at least 3-4 hectares once covered by early aceramic deposits. The precise relationships between the strata of the two soundings (MR3S and MR3T separated by about 45 m) and between the soundings and the Bolan section (MR3D, about 20 m Northeast of MR3S) have not been defined, although it appears that all deposits of M3T (levels 1-11) are aceramic while there are only seven aceramic levels in MR3S (IA.1-7) capped by seven levels of deposits with occasional sherds of a coarse, chaff-tempered ceramic (IB.1-7). This configuration can be explained by noting that Trench MR3S is located to one side of the center of the aceramic mound, which itself can best be conceptualized as a truncated cone surrounded and eventually covered by later ceramic neolithic deposits (first IB, then IIA, then IIB) interfingering with alluvial sediments. The stratigraphic situation became

452

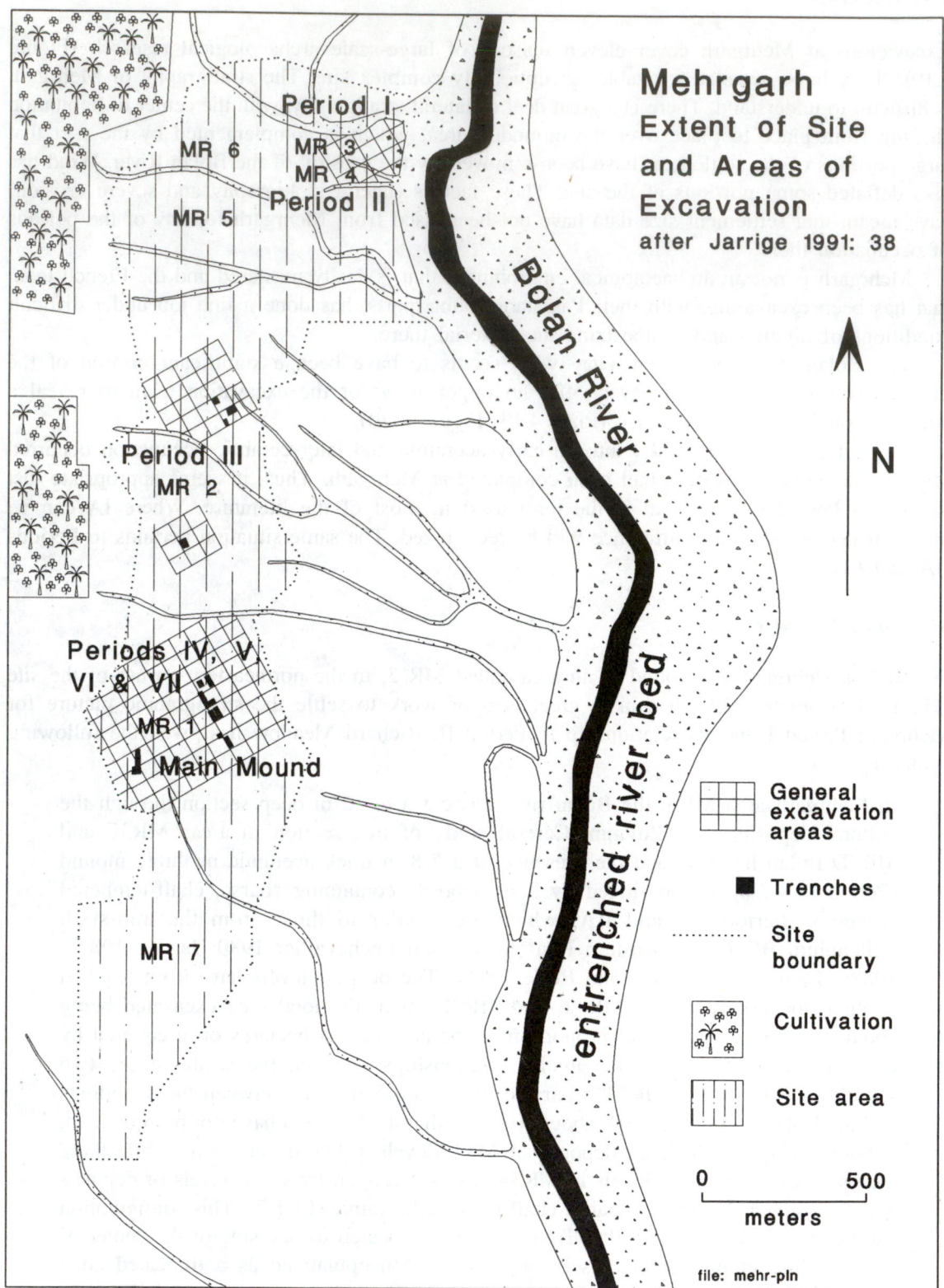

Figure 4.19. Site plan of Mehrgarh, after Jarrige, Jarrige, Meadow and Quivron 1995

Figure 4.20. Schematic section of the river section, after Lechevallier and Quivron 1985: 75

clear with the excavation of the Bolan section (MR3D) where the 10 levels of Period IA are covered on the south side by 5 steeply sloping levels of Period IB. (See Lechevallier and Quivron (1985) for sections and further discussion) (Meadow 1993a: 299).

Dwellings were found made of simple mud brick, five by four meters on the average, frequently subdivided into four or even six rooms (Quivron 1991: 59) (Figure 4.22). The floors of these houses occasionally have the impression of reeds. Ovens and hearths, sometimes simply called "fireplaces" were usually found in the corners of rooms and signs of their use can be seen as traces of smoke on the plastered walls (Figure 4.23). One circular oven was lined with bricks and had a dome, which was traced in its collapsed condition.

Bricks of regular size (33 × 14.5 × 7 cm or 28 × 14.5 × 7 cm) were used, along with other irregular sizes. They are generally bun-shaped and have finger impressions on their tops. Some walls were thin, with only one course of bricks; others were wider with two or three. Structure B is described as:

"...6.3 m by 6.7 m, is oriented north-south, and is made up of six rectangular rooms. Three rooms measure 2.25m by 1.5m and the other three 3.3m by 1.5m. No doorways between rooms were found even though there are two, three, or four preserved courses of bricks. The walls were made of two rows of bricks that are of various sizes. The floors of five of the rooms were covered with pebbles (three rooms were completely covered with them). In several rooms there were fireplaces, grinding stones, mullers, bone tools, faunal remains, and flints. A polished stone axe was found in one of the rooms and west of this building, a rectangular lapis lazuli bead was found (Jarrige, Jarrige, Meadow and Quivron 1995: 246).

These compartmented buildings can be interpreted as storage facilities (Figure 4.24). The case is clearest in Periods IB and II, but can be outlined here:

Figure 4.21. Plan of MR3, with architecture of Periods I and II, after Quivron 1991: 62

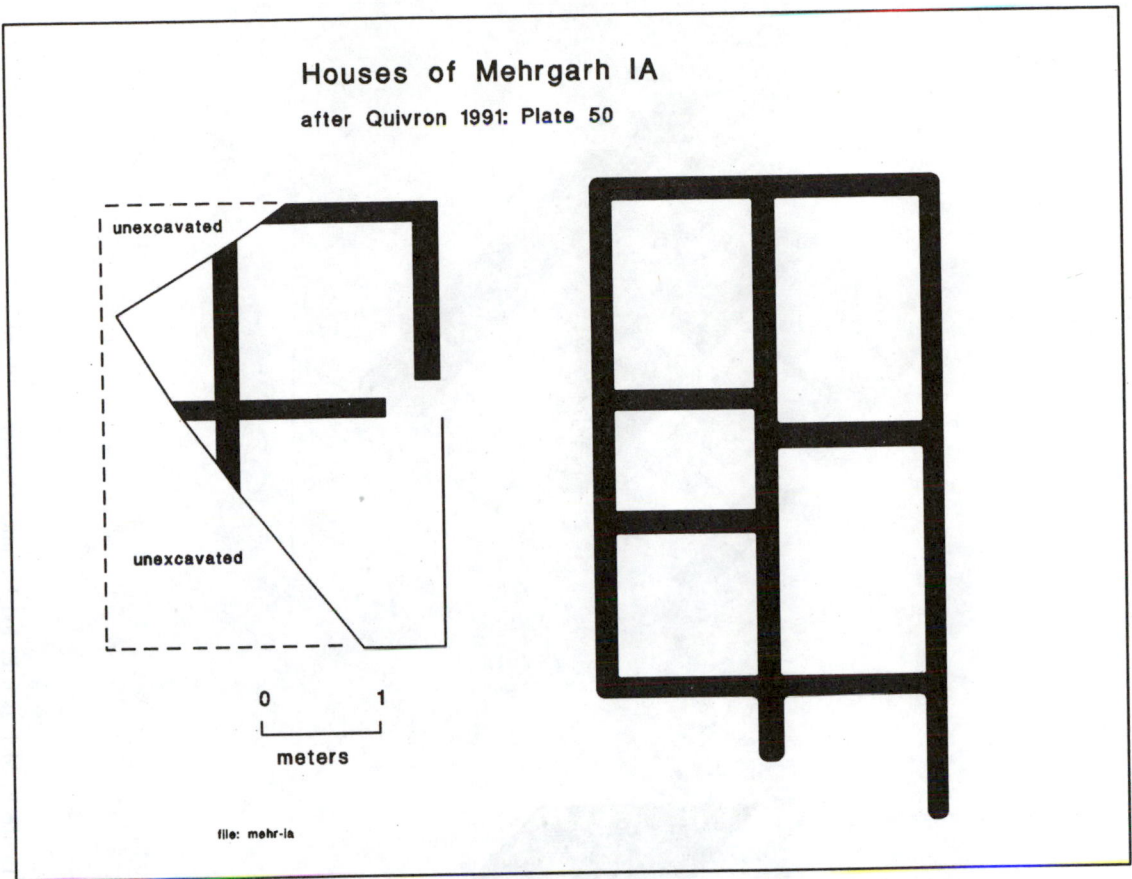

Figure 4.22. Houses of Mehrgarh IA, after Quivron 1991: Plate 50

In our previous reports we have discussed the question of the function of the compartmented buildings, and we proposed that they were large storage units. The fill of the buildings exposed so far contains no evidence to indicate that they were used as living quarters. Many of the cell-units are no larger than one square meter and movement in such a confined space would have been difficult. There is also no evidence that these structures served as a kind of foundation system on which domestic superstructures were raised. The fourth building of the complex exposed in this MR.3/ 4 AG and N sector is preserved to a height of more than fifteen courses of mud-brick and thus cannot be interpreted as a substructure. As we pointed out for the previously exposed compartmented buildings, the fill in most cases is rather homogeneous, a fact that indicates that trash was not allowed to accumulate inside the buildings during their period of use. Many of the compartments were filled with fallen bricks suggesting that several of these buildings may have been standing empty when the upper parts of the walls collapsed. We still believe that the most likely explanation for these buildings is that they formed part of a storage system (Jarrige, Jarrige, Meadow and Quivron 1995: 372).

Storage facilities of this type begin in Period I; as agricultural production increased so did their number and sophistication. Some form of communal storage, or at least a system that extended beyond the needs of a nuclear family, is suggested from the size of these facilities.

A case can be made that these buildings may have been entered through the roof. No doors

456

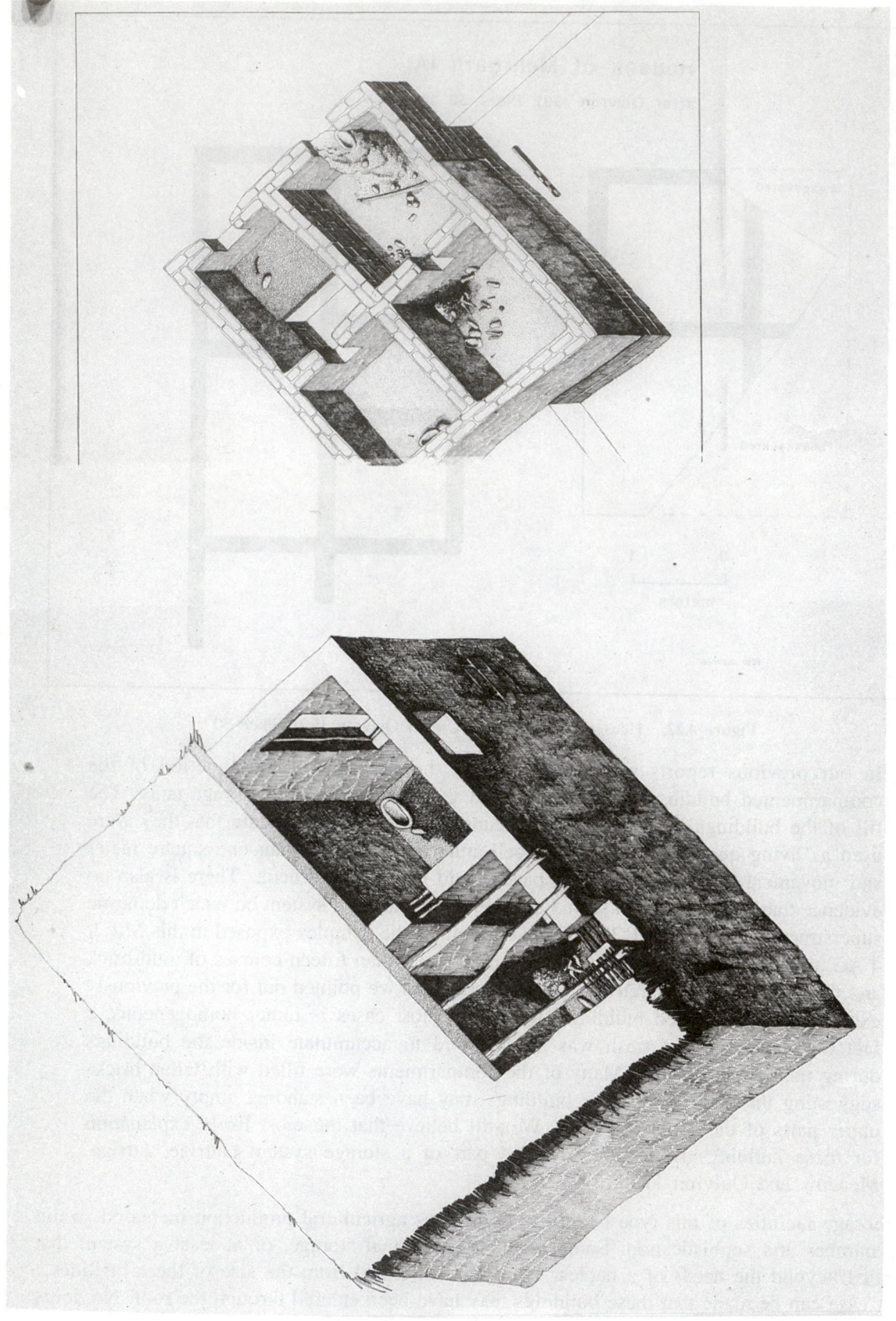

Figure 4.23. Isometric reconstruction of House E, Mehrgarh Period IA, after Quivron 1991: 65

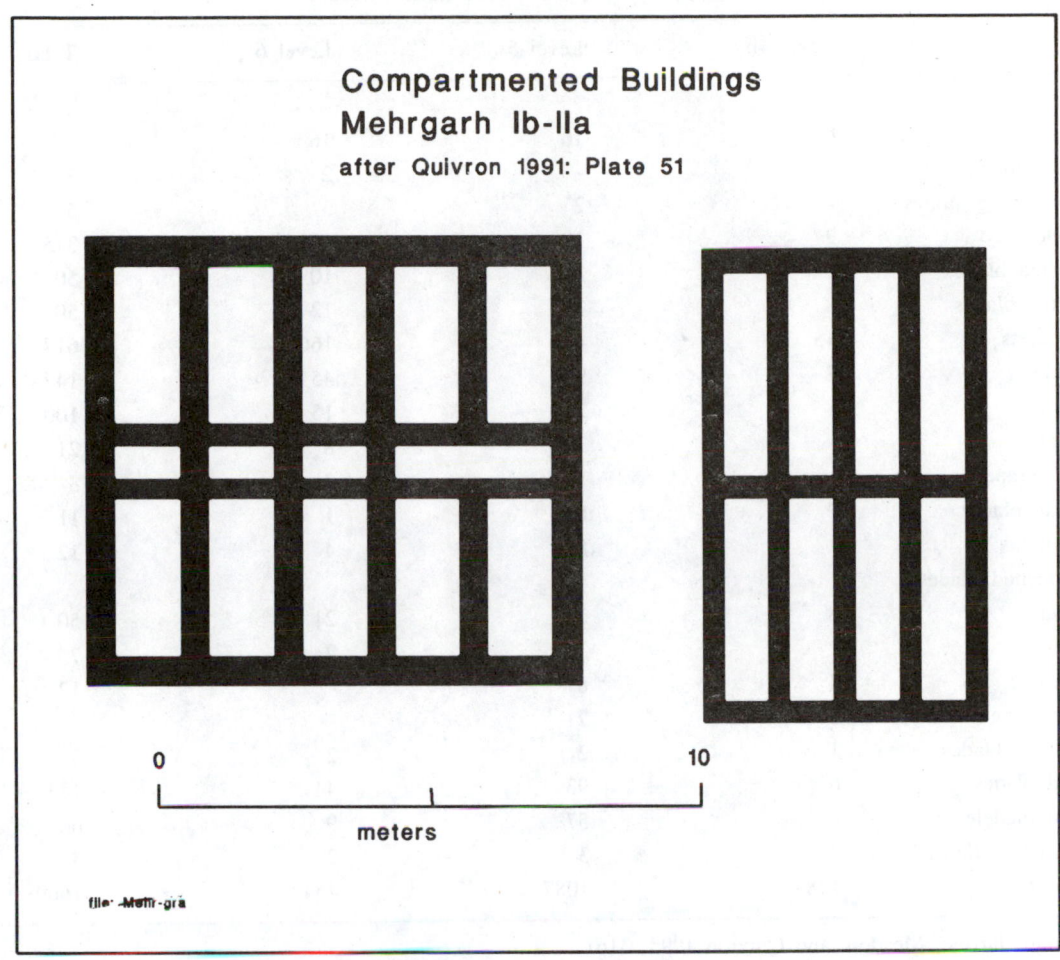

Figure 4.24. Compartmented buildings of Mehrgarh IB and IIA, after Quivron 1991: Plate 51

have been found in any of the walls and some walls are preserved to a substantial height; one (Structure F2) to a distance of three meters (Jarrige, Jarrige, Meadow and Quivron 1995: 451).

Technology in Mehrgarh I

The technology of Mehrgarh I was relatively simple. The very small amount of copper is thought to be of the native variety, not smelted. The bed of the Bolan River carries cobbles of light brown flint from which tools were fashioned: some were sickle blades which occasionally carried sheen. A profusion of ground stone food processing tools was found, including a large number of quern and grinding stone fragments, two small limestone chisels, a small bowl, and a small mortar (Jarrige, Jarrige, Meadow and Quivron 1995: 316).

In the 1980-81 season, a number of chipped stone tools was found and tabulated (Table 4.11), and is presented to give an impression of the diversity of the chipped stone tool industry (Plate 4.15, Plate 4.16). They came from Levels 4b, 5, and 6. These are tabulated below.

TABLE 4.11
Chipped Stone from Mehrgarh Period I

	Level 4b	Level 5	Level 6	Total
Cores	6	16	16	38
Core tablets	1	-	2	3
Hammering stones	-	2	3	5
Blades	27	198	90	315
Crested blades	1	39	10	50
Cortex blades	8	30	12	50
Bladelets	45	406	166	617
Flakes	7	95	45	147
Waste	8	77	15	100
Borers	-	13	8	21
End-scrapers	-	1	2	3
Sickle blades	2	8	1	11
Segments	-	8	4	12
Retouched blades:				
direct	8	21	21	50
inverse	2	3	2	7
alternate	4	8	-	12
alternating	2	7	-	9
Notched blades	1	2	2	5
Used blades	6	93	44	143
Used bladelets	-	57	9	66
Retouched flakes	-	3	2	5
TOTAL	128	1087	454	1669

(Jarrige, Jarrige, Meadow and Quivron 1995: 316)

Baskets for containers were in evidence, some of which were lined with bitumen to strengthen and waterproof them. Slabs of bitumen impressed with basket impressions are also known (Jarrige, Jarrige, Meadow and Quivron 1995: 211). A small amount of handmade pottery comes toward the end of Period I, in what is called Period .IB. Unbaked clay figurines in limited numbers were also made.

There is a rich bone industry with many awls, spatulas and a needle with an eye (Jarrige, Jarrige, Meadow and Quivron 1995: 244) (Plate 4.17). Two highly polished bone pendants with round perforations were also unearthed (Jarrige, Jarrige, Meadow and Quivron 1995: 246). It is thought that most of the bone tools were used in basket making and in the preparation of cloth. Some of the burials bore faint traces of textiles.

There is evidence for the manufacture of calcite beads at the site. Other insights into craftsmanship: "...ornaments associated with the burial of the child show the quality of bead working at this early period. Tiny disc-shaped beads in black steatite, long barrel-shaped beads in calcite, and well polished bangles of conch shell reveal the existence at the beginning of the neolithic occupation of craft traditions that lasted for a long time in the region. The quality of the belt with its two flower-shaped pendants in shell is especially worth noting" (Jarrige, Jarrige, Meadow and Quivron 1995: 277).

Subsistence Information

A great deal of information on the palaeobotany of Mehrgarh is available. Somewhat surprisingly, the collection from Period I is especially rich and complex. Most of the evidence came from thousands of impressions in the abundant mud bricks of the period. The dominant plant in the floral assemblage of Period I is naked six-row barley (*Hordeum vulgare* subspecies *vulgare* variety *nudum*). More than ninety percent of the seeds and imprints were identified as this plant. Also present is hulled six-row barley (*H. vulgare* subspecies *vulgare*), two-row barley (*H. vulgare* subspecies *spontaneum* and *H. vulgare* subspecies *distichum*), einkorn (*Triticum monococcum*), emmer (*T. turgidum* subspecies *dicoccum*), and hard wheat (*T. turgidum* cf. conv. *durum*) present in greatly reduced amounts. The non-cereals so far identified for the period include the Indian jujube (*Zizyphus* sp.) and dates (*Phoenix dactylifera*), represented by stones in an upper level of Period IB as well as Period IIB (Costantini 1984). It is interesting that the einkorn and emmer disappear from use in the region, but the bread wheat and shot wheat continue on as the eastern species of *Triticum*. Richard Meadow has observed that it seems that the free threshing wheat in the west, or Near East, was *Triticum turgidum* cf. conv. *durum* (hard wheat) and that of the east *Triticum aestivum*, bread or club wheat (Meadow 1993a: 301).

In Period IA the animal economy is dominated by "...12 species of what might be termed 'big game' " (Meadow 1984a: 35): gazelle, (*Gazella dorcas*), swamp deer (*Cervus duvaucelii*), nilgai (*Boselaphus tragocamelus*), blackbuck (*Antelope cervicapra*), onager (*Equus hemionus*), chital or spotted deer (*Axis axis*), water buffalo (*Bubalus bubalis*), wild sheep (*Ovis ?orientalis*), wild goat (*Capra ?aegagrus*), wild cattle (*Bos ?namadicus*), wild pig (*Sus scrofa*) and elephant (*Elephas maximus*). Meadow takes this to indicate that the first inhabitants of aceramic Mehrgarh I exploited the Kachi Plain itself as well as the hills that surround it. "The lack of substantial numbers of fish and bird remains suggests that the Bolan River and the lake/swampy environments associated with it were of little importance to them" (Meadow 1984a: 35). He has qualified this (personal communication 1996) with the observation that no screening was undertaken at Mehrgarh, and the recovery of fish and bird bone were therefore somewhat compromised. Screening is a part of most modern excavations, and employing it would have given us a better sense of the small mammal, bird and fish component to the faunal assemblage. But, fish vertebra are very durable, and the long bones of large birds are well preserved. Thus, the fact that so little was found might not be too far off the mark.

Meadow has made the following important points concerning the subsistence economy of early Mehrgarh:

1. Goats were kept from the time of the first occupation of the site.

2. Cattle and sheep are likely to have been domesticated from local wild stock during the course of the aceramic neolithic.

3. Size diminution in goats was largely complete by Period IB (5300 BC at the latest), in cattle by Period IIA, and in sheep perhaps not until Period III.

4. The contribution of domestic or "pro-domestic" stock to the faunal assemblages came to surpass that of other animals early in the aceramic, but not in the earliest levels.

5. The development of animal keeping by the ancient inhabitants of Mehrgarh took place in the context of cereal crop cultivation, the building of substantial mid brick structures, and the existence of social differentiation and long distance trade networks as attested by the presence of marine shells, lapis lazuli, and turquoise in even the earliest graves (after Meadow 1993a: 311).

TABLE 4.12
Wild ungulates from Mehrgarh Period IA in approximate order of abundance

Indian gazelle, chinkara (*Gazella bennettii*), most abundant

wild sheep (*Ovis vigni*)

wild goat, bezoar (*Capra aegagrus*)

swamp deer (*Cervus duvaucelii*)

nilgai (*Boselaphus tragocamelus*)

zebu (*Bos indicus*)

wild water buffalo (*Bubalus arnee*)

chital or spotted deer (*Axis axis*)

onager (*Equus hemionus*)

blackbuck (*Antelope cervicapra*)

wild pig (*Sus scrofa*)

elephant (*Elephas maximus*), one specimen

(after Meadow 1993a: 306, with some alteration of taxonomic name by GLP)

Some Additional Comments on the "Expanded Nuclear Zone"

What we see at Mehrgarh is a sequence of events that seems to document the local domestication of animals. The sheep, goats and cattle start out looking wild, and were manipulated in the way we believe people at the threshold of food production treated their animals. Over time the potential domesticates come to look like domesticated animals (smaller, with the osteological hallmarks of domesticated beasts). They also come to dominate the animals resources used by the early inhabitants of Mehrgarh; something we would expect in the early-mature stage of food production. Thus, the local domestication of sheep, goats and cattle at Mehrgarh is reasonably strong, needing confirmation from other excavations, but a very good story in and of itself.

Meadow stresses that the local domestication of animals took place within the context of fairly advanced cereal agriculture, with domesticated wheat and barley. We do not know how deep this side of the food producing economy might go in the eastern parts of the "expanded nuclear zone" but notice can be made of the cerealia pollen and early burning noted by G. Singh in the lakes of Rajasthan, as early as 7500 B.C. (G. Singh 1971: 185-86), as well as the fact that wild barley has been found in Baluchistan and Afghanistan.

The long-distance interaction called for by the notion of an "expanded nuclear zone" in Middle Asia is documented by the trade network implied by the presence of marine shells, lapis lazuli (found in Afghanistan and Baluchistan) and turquoise (Iran and Central Asia), noted by Meadow. The people of Mehrgarh IA were not isolated "home bodies" unaware of the world around them, especially the world to the north, south and west—the other parts of the "expanded nuclear zone."

Jean-Francois Jarrige has recently remarked:

> ...in the past a Mediterranean type of vegetation could have descended to the base of the Balochistan piedmont. In any case, it is clear that the vegetation cover of the Bolan Basin has evolved through time. One can now no longer eliminate the possibility that this region had an herbaceous cover in the past very different from that of today, including, in particular, the wild cereals, specimens of which we find in the deep levels of the neolithic. The existence of such a vegetation cover could have provided the milieu for mutations and spontaneous hybridizations among various cereals. The

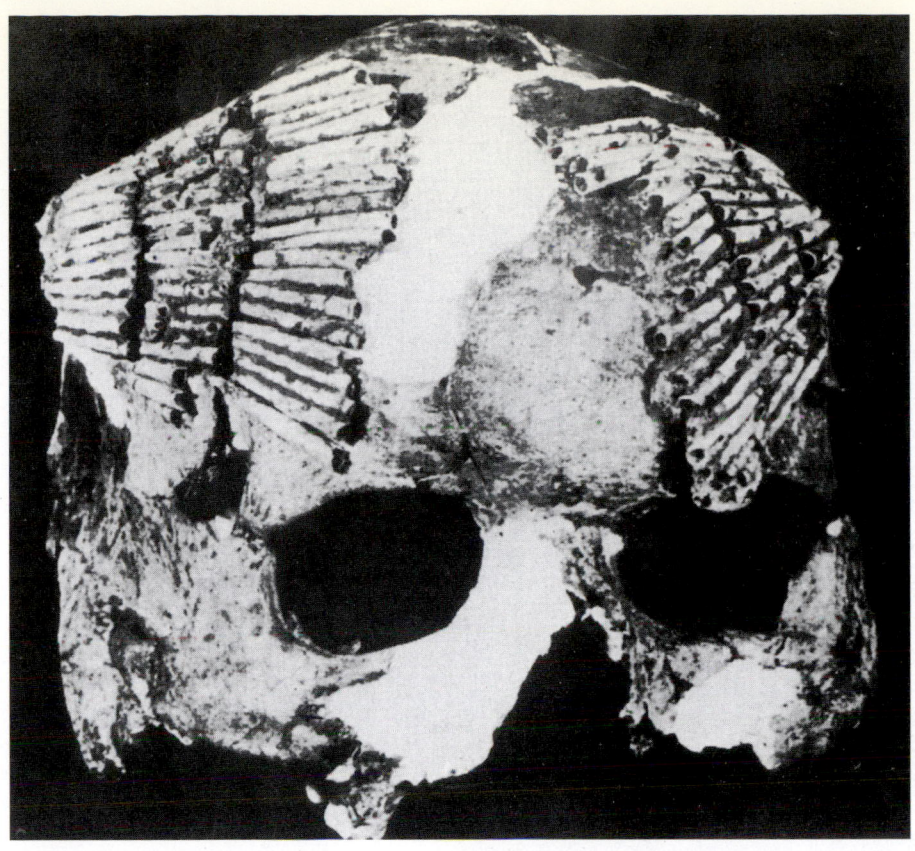

Plate 4.1. Natufian headdress from Mount Carmel, after Garrod and Bate 1937.

Plate 4.2. The caves at Mount Carmel. Courtesy of Harold Dibble.

Plate 4.3. Tower at Jericho, PPNA, from Purushottam Singh 1974: Figure 17, with acknowledgment to K. Kenyon.

Plate 4.4. Bricks from PPNB Jericho, from Purushottam Singh 1974: Figure 19, with acknowledgment to K. Kenyon.

Plate 4.5. The site of Cayonu.
Courtesy of the Joint Istanbul-Chicago Universities Prehistoric Project and Professor Robert J. Braidwood.

Plate 4.6. Cayonu, with the "terrazzo" floor near the center.
Courtesy of the Joint Istanbul-Chicago Universities Prehistoric Project and Professor Robert J. Braidwood.

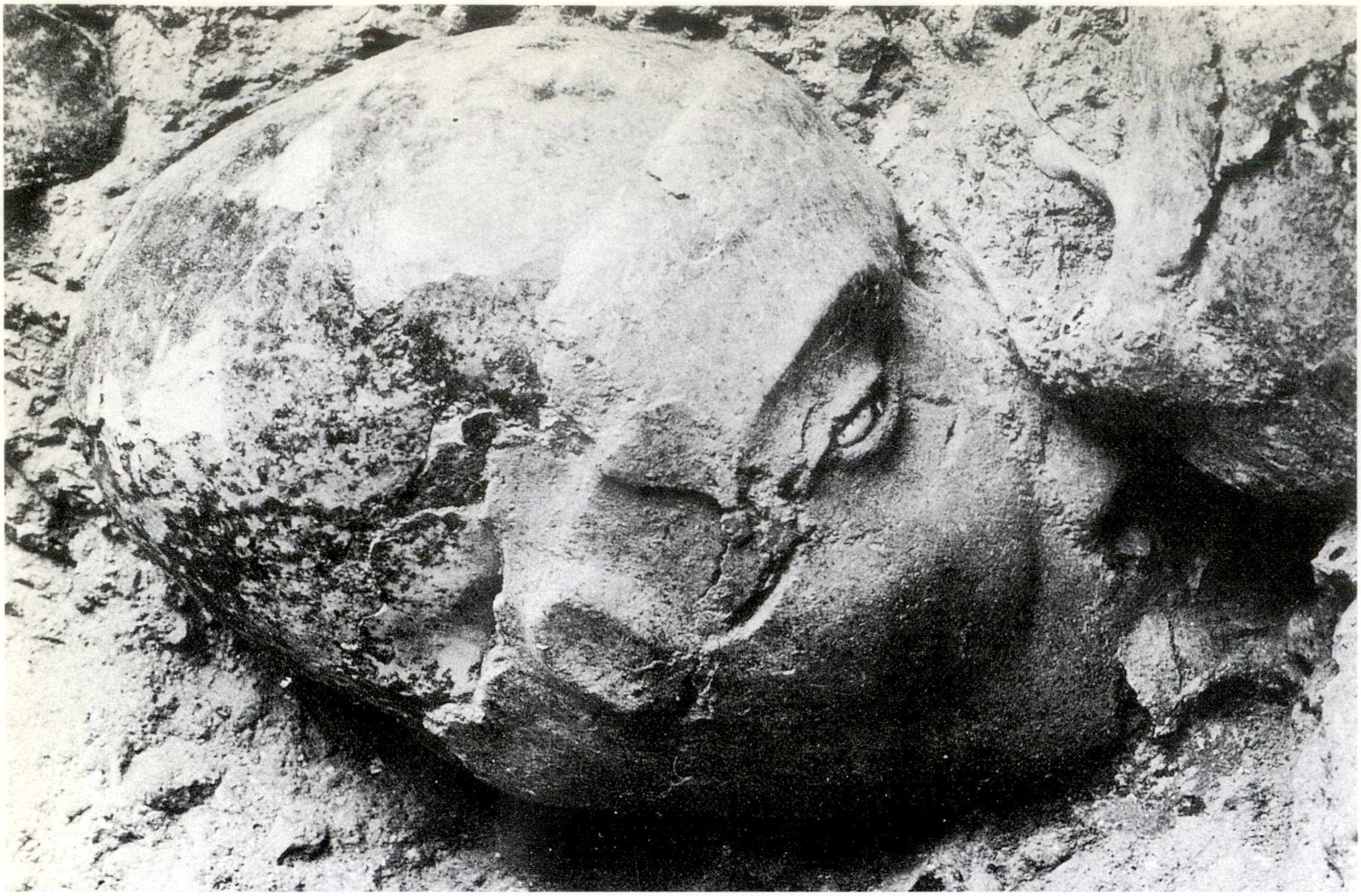

Plate 4.7. A plastered skull from PPNB Jericho, from Purushottam Singh 1974: Figure 21, with acknowledgment to K. Kenyon.

Plate 4.8. A modern pastoralist's temporary abode in Gujarat. Author's photograph.

Plate 4.9. A floor from a modern pastoralist's temporary abode in Gujarat. A fire place is near the center of the floor. A temporary structure of the kind covering the floor in the foreground is in the back. Author's photograph.

Plate 4.10. The Balk River from inside Horse Cave, looking toward Aq Kupruk town. Courtesy of Richard Davis.

Plate 4.12. Horse Cave. Courtesy of Richard Davis.

Plate 4.11. Snake Cave. Courtesy of Richard Davis.

Plate 4.13. Mehrgarh, river section for Periods Ia, Ib and IIa. Courtesy of Jean-Francois and Catherine Jarrige.

Plate 4.14. Mehrgarh IA, structures E and F. Courtesy of Jean-Francois and Catherine Jarrige.

Plate 4.15. Mehrgarh Ib, geometric microliths. Courtesy of Jean-Francois and Catherine Jarrige.

Plate 4.16. Mehrgarh IB, chipped stone borers. Courtesy of Jean-Francois and Catherine Jarrige.

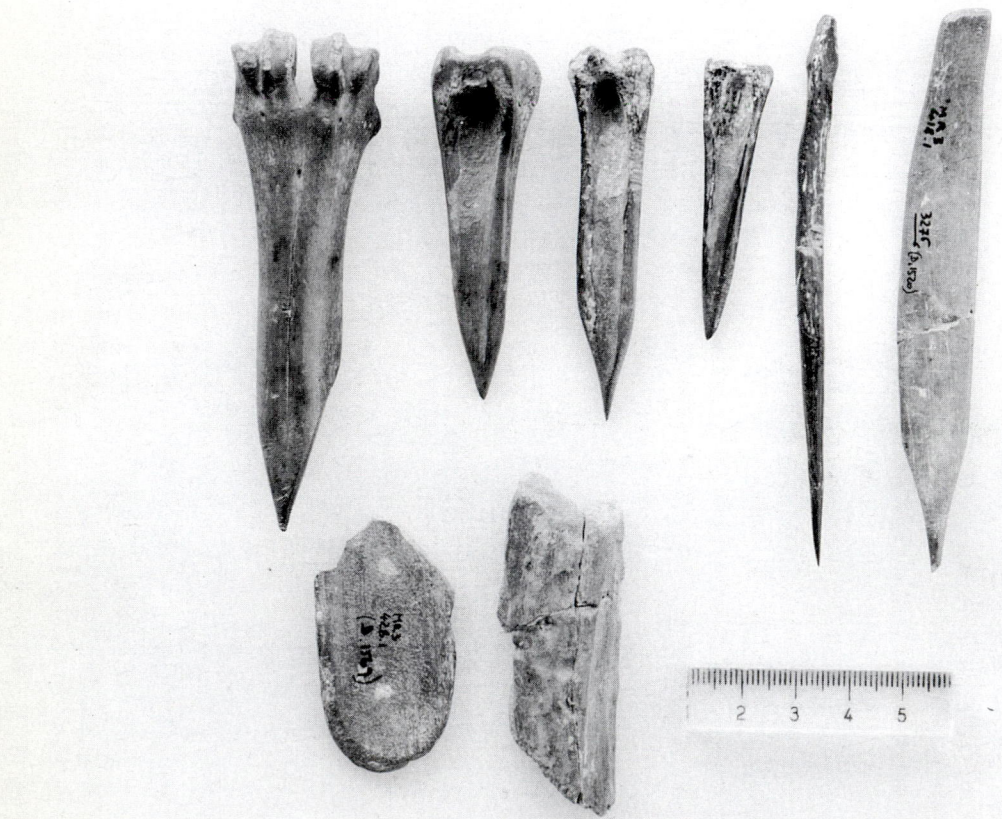

Plate 4.17. Bone tools from Mehrgarh Ib. Courtesy of Jean-Francois and Catherine Jarrige.

Plate 4.18. Mehrgarh IIa, structure LI. Courtesy of Jean-Francois and Catherine Jarrige.

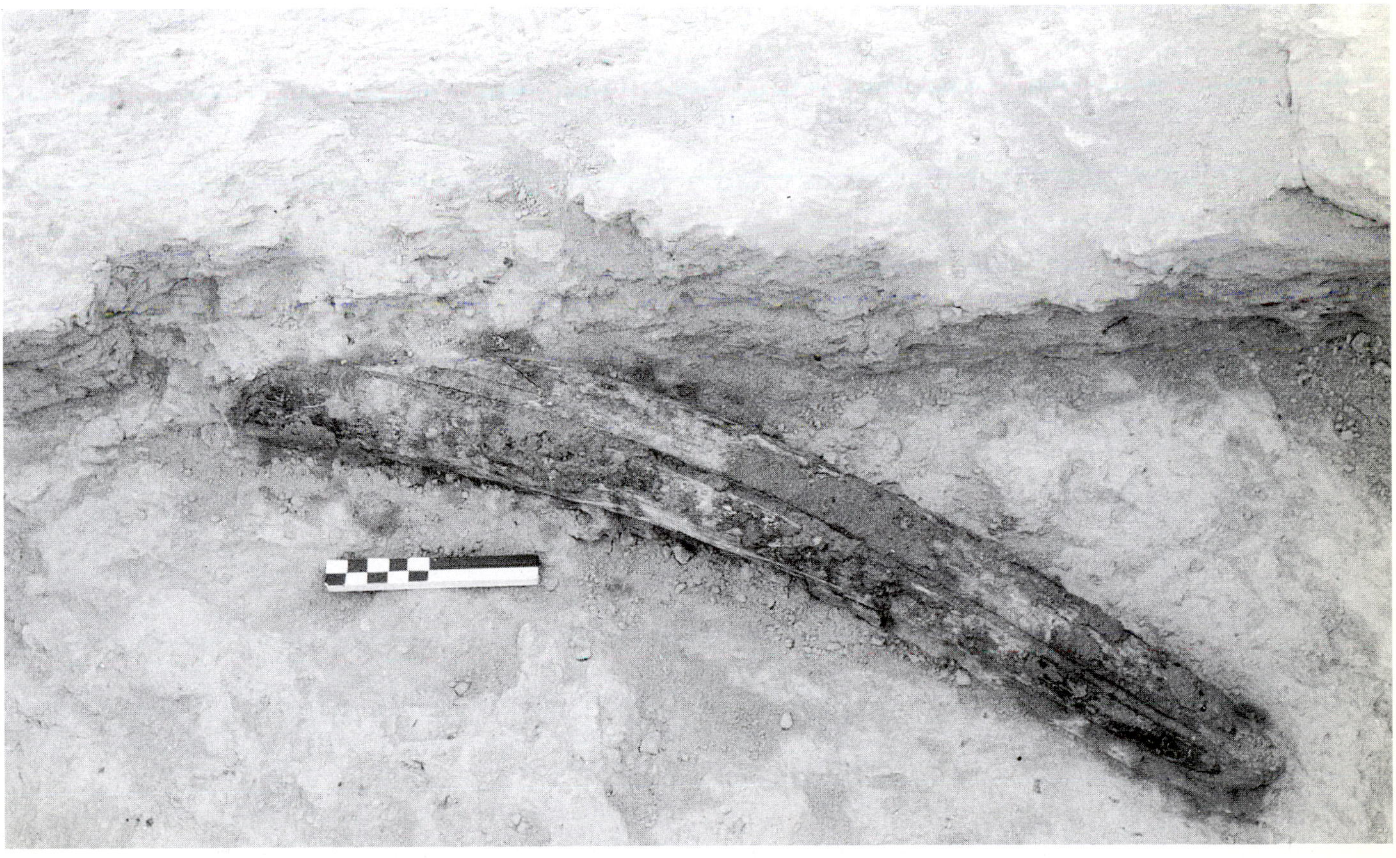

Plate 4.19. Mehrgarh IIa, incised elephant tusk. Courtesy of Jean-Francois and Catherine Jarrige.

Plate 4.20. Mehrgarh IIb, cylindrical bead and impression. Courtesy of Jean-Francois and Catherine Jarrige.

Plate 4.21. The site of Isplenji Two, that began in Burj Basket-marked times. Author's photograph.

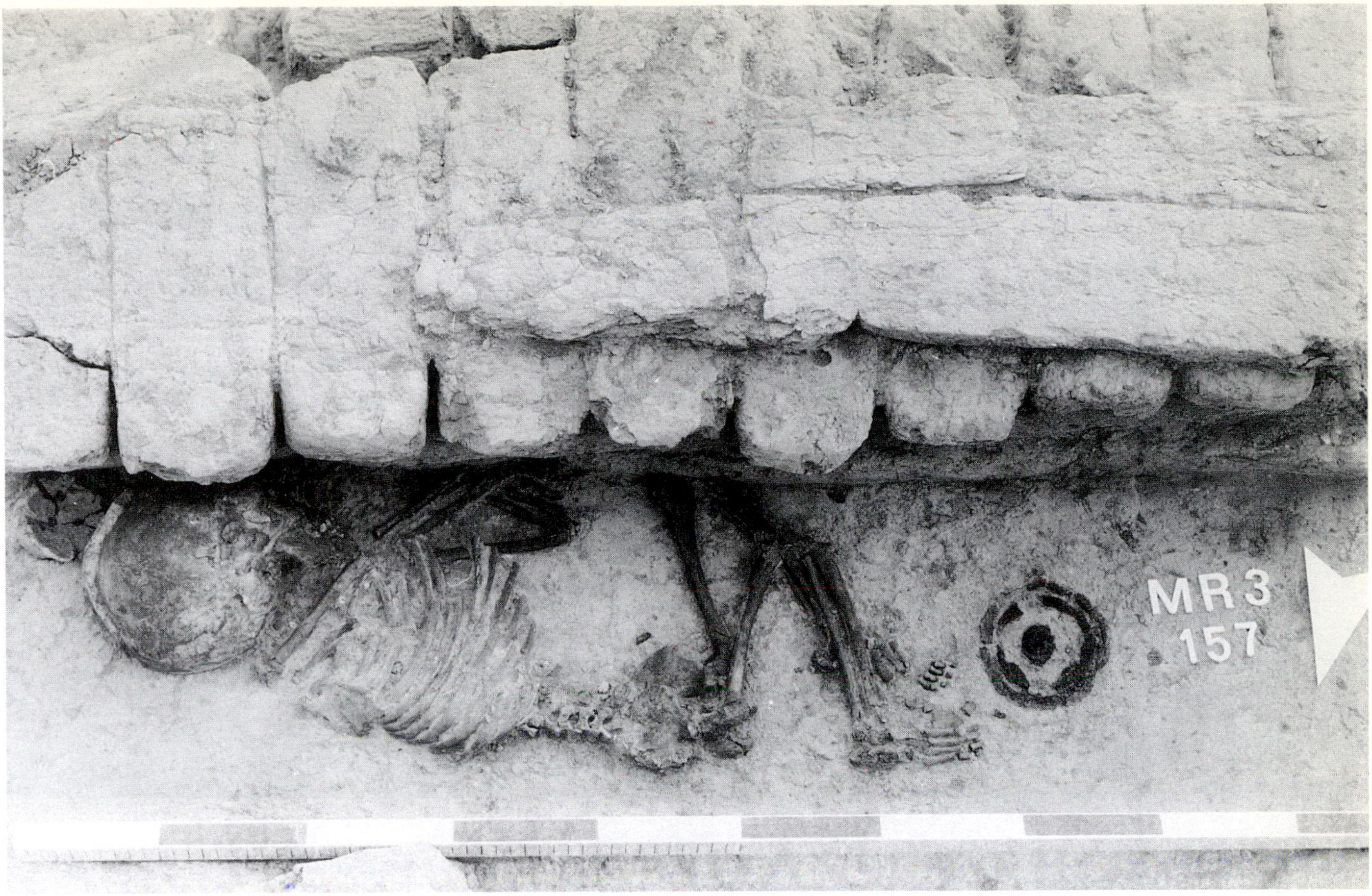

Plate 4.22. Mehrgarh Ib, western grave yard, grave 157. Courtesy of Jean-Francois and Catherine Jarrige.

Plate 4.23. Pot of Chashma Ali type. Courtesy of the Metropolitan Museum of Art.

Plate 4.24. A Mature Harappan stamp seal with the Horned Deity, after Mackay 1937-38: Plate LXXXVII, No. 235. Courtesy of the Archaeological Survey of India and Asko Parpola. Photo by Erja Lahdenpera for the Corpus of Indus Seals and Inscriptions Project of the University of Helsinki.

![Nal pottery bowl with concentric designs]

Plate 4.25. Nal pottery with concentric designs. Courtesy of the National Museum, New Delhi.

Plate 4.26. Nal pottery with concentric designs. The canister shape is characteristic of the Nal ceramic assemblage. It also occurs in the succeeding Kulli ceramic assemblage. Courtesy of the National Museum, New Delhi.

Plate 4.27. Nal pottery with concentric designs. Courtesy of the National Museum, New Delhi.

Plate 4.28. Nal pottery with a small animal. Courtesy of the National Museum, New Delhi.

Plate 4.29. Nal pottery with fish. Courtesy of the National Museum, New Delhi.

Plate 4.30. Nal pottery. Pipal leaves and the pinched vessel type to the right are characteristic of the Nal ceramic assemblage. Courtesy of the National Museum, New Delhi.

Plate 4.31. Modern Kutchee pastoralist's in Saurashtra. Author's photograph.

Plate 4.32. Modern Rajasthani itinerants in Saurashtra. Author's photograph.

Plate 4.33. Itinerant basketmakers near Rangpur in Gujarat. Author's photograph.

Plate 4.34. General view of Dholavira before excavation. Author's photograph.

Plate 4.35. A view of the high mound at Dholavira before excavations. Author's photograph.

Plate 4.36. General view of Surkotada. Author's photograph.

presence of small amounts of hare/bread wheat or of sphaerococcoid wheat and barley could be explained as their being weeds in the fields of barley with still only slightly domesticated characteristics (Costantini, personal communication) (Jarrige 1995a: 64).

There is a good case that the people of Mehrgarh were participating in the early stages of the food producing/domestication revolution. The strong evidence for local involvement in the shift of the animal economy from "hunting to herding" and the participation in interregional communication give us good reason to believe that further work in the region around Mehrgarh will tend to support the hypothesis put forth here: there was a single "expanded nuclear zone" in Middle Asia within which food production and domestication took place within a single period of time; from about 11,000 BC to 5500 BC. In the Near East this would encompass the period beginning with the Natufians through PPNB. We have no established terminology for the period in the eastern part of the "expanded nuclear zone."

Over this period of time the peoples within the "expanded nuclear zone" (at least many of them) were experimenting with their subsistence economy, seeking ways to better control the vagaries of production through the husbanding of animals and the management of plants. These experiments were many, some successful and of these successes some more successful than others. Seen in hind sight some must have been failures, possibly devastatingly so in some cases. The communication within the "expanded nuclear zone" was generally rich. This was driven in many ways. Some of these would have been 1) trade in material goods, raw materials and finished products, 2) the presence of marriage and other social networks such as systems of exchange founded in reciprocity and ecological mechanisms for spreading risk and forming alliances, 3) the maturation cycles of plants and animals, new patterns of movement and communication implied by the emergence of food production and domestication. The richness of this communication, and the diversity of these mechanisms of antiquity, are of course, poorly documented today; but there are hints, there is an underlying logic, there is enough for an hypothesis to be put forward that has sufficient substance for it to be tested, rather than dismissed.

Mehrgarh Periods IB and II

Period II at Mehrgarh is, for the most part stratified above Period I. These remains form a broad band of deposits that encircle the deposits of Period IB (Jarrige, Jarrige, Meadow and Quivron 1995: 511). There are strong signs of continuity between Periods I and II, but change is present as well. When the excavations at Mehrgarh were still in their infancy it was thought that Period I was entirely aceramic. But then a few coarse chaff ware sherds showed up in trash deposits of what can be called Period IB. The use of pottery increases in Period IIA and is now found in domestic contexts, not just refuse. Compartmented buildings are found in Periods IB and IIA (Figure 4.24).

Architecture of Mehrgarh II

The same basic kind of architecture is present in Period II as in Period I and the excavation team did a good job of exposing it. In fact twenty-three compartmented buildings were unearthed in five seasons (sixth through tenth) (Jarrige, Jarrige, Meadow and Quivron 1995: 511) (Plate 4.18).

Various retaining walls and terracing features have been found to be associated with Period II. One of the structures, designated K1, excavated in 1981-82, was part of a terrace built up in connection with the compartmented buildings in the area. "Structure K1 is a massive curving wall with buttresses that were built on the slope of earlier accumulated deposits for the purpose

462

of terracing the top of the mound during the course of Period IIA. The association of this massive and remarkable piece of architecture with the impressive complex of compartmented buildings reveals a degree of planning probably related to well developed social and community organization during the sixth millennium B.C." (Jarrige, Jarrige, Meadow and Quivron 1995: 422).

Compartmented Buildings of Mehrgarh II

One of the Period IIA compartmented buildings was designated Structure L2 (Jarrige, Jarrige, Meadow and Quivron 1995: 453). It is a large structure, 6.2 m × 7.8 m, with walls preserved to 1.3 m. It was built of finger marked bricks, coated with mud. The floor was colored with red ochre. The bricks varied in size. Most were 40 × 10 × 7cm, but bricks that were 42 × 9.5 × 6, 38 × 9 × 7, 36.5 × 8 × 7, 32 × 9 × 5.5, and 31 × 9.5 × 6.5 cm also occurred. Finger impressions were present on all of the bricks and they were made in two ways. "The most usual way was to regularly press the thumb in two rows parallel to the length of the wet brick. The second way was to link those two rows with an oblique line made with a finger" (Jarrige, Jarrige, Meadow and Quivron 1995: 453). A significant amount of charred barley was found at the bottom of the completely excavated rooms in structure L2. This tends to confirm that these were storage facilities (Jarrige, Jarrige, Meadow and Quivron 1995: 453).

Another compartmented building of Period II was completely exposed and had ten narrow compartments symmetrically aligned along each side of a central corridor, reminiscent of the much later Great Granary at Harappa (Jarrige, Jarrige, Meadow and Quivron 1995: 248). A small room had been attached to this building on the south and was raised on a small platform of compacted clay. The structure as a whole covers an area of fifty-six square meters and was constructed with what appears to be attention to symmetry. But, measurements show that this is something of an illusion. The long narrow rooms have dimensions that vary between 1.61 square meters to 2.6 square meters.

The fill in the rooms of this building had no indication of domestic debris. Moreover, there was an absence of doors between the small cellular compartments. "A connection with agricultural activities is shown by the discovery made in one of the compartments of two sickles composed of three bladelets shafted slantwise in bitumen. These almost complete sickles, lacking only the now disintegrated wooden parts of their handles, are finds of exceptional interest for our understanding of the tools used for farming activities. The function of the building as a granary is also suggested by a large number of impressions of grains in the fill of the compartments" (Jarrige, Jarrige, Meadow and Quivron 1995: 248).

Domestic Architecture of Mehrgarh II

Domestic structures are also known, and they conform to the standards of Period I. One of these buildings, known as Structure J2, is found among rows of compartmented structures. It was a rectangular building subdivided into six symmetrical rooms (Jarrige, Jarrige, Meadow and Quivron 1995: 454).

The floors in this area have yielded many bones, a relatively limited quantity of flints, and a rather larger number of potsherds (25 sherds). On the floors contemporary with the use of Building G2 and with the passageway between G2 and R2, many remains connected with daily life have been documented relating to circular fireplaces. In two circular fireplaces were noted tiny fragments of red ocher that had also colored the ground around. It can be assumed that these fireplaces were used to heat the naturally yellow ocher turning it bright red through oxidation...To the side of one of these fireplaces, a large clay human figurine colored with red ocher was found. On the same floor, two large impressions in wattle of parallel rows of reeds were exposed near two postholes. These postholes and the impressions of reeds were covered by a thick layer of sloping clay full of straw impressions. The density of straw impressions is such that it seems possible that this layer was formed by a fallen thatched roof...

We have rather good evidence showing that most of the buildings exposed in the context of Period IIA, mostly compartmented or cell-units buildings, must have been used as storage units and not as proper dwellings. The cells or compartments are too small to have been inhabited. The absence of any fireplace or remains related to domestic activities on the floors of these buildings makes it difficult to believe that they could have been used as shelters even during the few cold weeks of the year. Features related to domestic or craft activities are always found either outside the buildings often in spaces that could have been easily roofed and used as living quarters or in and around a few larger rooms... (Jarrige, Jarrige, Meadow and Quivron 1995: 513).

Craft Activities of Mehrgarh II

Among these structures of Period II are various flat, hard clay surfaces, some of which were paved with bricks, sometimes associated with fireplaces. In one of these areas there were surfaces with "...thick deposits of trash containing burnt pebbles, ashes, several hundred animal bones, about fifteen bone tools, hammer stones, polishers colored with red ocher, and a very large collection of blades, cores, and flint debitage—the debris of some kind of a workshop, possibly for leather working, basket making or weaving. Other flint tools such as borers and trapezes are represented by only a few specimens. A collection of 575 flints came from the area around Firepits 611 and 606 (above Structure I2) and from the upper fill of House J2 (that had floors heavily colored by red ocher in several spots) was studied" (Jarrige, Jarrige, Meadow and Quivron 1995: 455). One of the flint trapezes was set in bitumen as a transverse arrowhead. Two copper artifacts were found, (one bead and a ring), along with some slag (Jarrige, Jarrige, Meadow and Quivron 1995: 319).

More craft activity comes from the shell working in Period II. Conch shells (*Fascolaria trapezium* and *Turbinella pyrum*) imported from the Arabian Sea were used.

In two compartments of one building stone slabs were found covered with red ochre. One of these was rectangular and the other circular. In the central corridor of this building was a well preserved elephant tusk with three grooves cut to divide it into equal parts in preparation for splitting (Meadow 1984b: 35). (Plate 4.19). An elephant leg bone was found in Period I and this find further strengthens the case that Sindh was home to the elephant in ancient times. Ivory was an important commodity during the Mature Harappan and it played a role in international commerce as well.

A cylinder bead in terracotta was found in one of the compartmented buildings of Period II. When rolled out this bead produces an impression much like that of a cylinder seal. The motif is regular and portrays vegetation. "Bead seals and seal impressions also are known in western Iran in an early context, in particular from Tepe Sabz during the fifth millennium Bayat Phase. The bead from Mehrgarh could be considered as an early prototype of the cylinder seal" (Jarrige, Jarrige, Meadow and Quivron 1995: 319) (Plate 4.20).

Other finds include foot or violin shaped human figurines of unbaked clay colored with red ocher, animal figurines (scarce, but one zebu), grinding stones, mortars, stone bowls, a broken mace head of alabaster, chipped stone tools (in the hundreds) and drills. Many bone tools were found, most of them points with a lustrous polish that, according to preliminary examination by N. Russell, could be "consistent with use in basketry or in piercing leather" (Jarrige, Jarrige, Meadow and Quivron 1995: 422).

A study of the chipped stone tools by Patrick Vaughn, indicated that certain of these artifacts had a micropolish that results from use on animal remains, involving the preparation of hides, butchering, and the working of bone and antler. That these tools were often found in association with red ocher is an interesting observation since ochre may be used for the tanning of hides (Jarrige, Jarrige, Meadow and Quivron 1995: 455).

In another area the remains of a steatite workshop was found, with evidence for cutting the raw material and making beads.

Flint drills and flakes were associated with 334 disc-shaped beads with diameters between 3 and 4 mm including several broken during the manufacturing process. Also associated with the steatite beads were a few cut dentalia, a few beads in white talc (some colored with red ocher), and wasters in black steatite. Near this workshop, six oblong-shaped cakes of red ocher were found together. East of the building, an open space was covered with heaps of bones among which were about a hundred bone tools including awls and needles. About fifty more bone tools were found close by. This concentration could indicate that we have here an area where bone tools were used in connection with leather working (Jarrige, Jarrige, Meadow and Quivron 1995: 248).

Associated with this same building was another spectacular find:

> Against the western wall of the building a fireplace was exposed from which were collected several hundred charred seeds, some of which have been identified by L. Costantini as grains of cotton (*Gossypium* sp.). The large number of cotton seeds in this fireplace perhaps means that we are close to a ginning area for cotton, the seeds having been used as fuel. This discovery is the earliest known occurrence of cotton at an archaeological site (Jarrige, Jarrige, Meadow and Quivron 1995: 248).

Woven cotton cloth was found at Mohenjo-daro (Turner and Gulati 1929a, 1929b, Gulati and Turner 1928, 1929) and the finds at Mehrgarh may be an indication that the use of cotton, possibly its cultivation, reaches to the very beginnings of food production and domestication in Pakistan.

Ceramics of Mehrgarh IB and II

Bitumen or asphalt covered baskets were found in Period I. Some had been used in the preparation of the earliest ceramics at Mehrgarh. Further thoughts on this came to light in the course of the study of Period II remains:

> Asphalt or bitumen probably came from the tar pits that are near Gokurt, in the Bolan Pass not far from Mehrgarh. It is interesting that, in some cases, the impressions of baskets in the core of the pottery are hard and compact, a condition that suggests that asphalted baskets could have been used as molds at this experimental stage of pottery making. It appears that the first pottery at Mehrgarh is the result of a technique representing a stage between the production of asphalted baskets and true pottery even though the use of baskets as molds for pots is particularly suitable for producing solid containers. Even in the course of Period IIA, however, some sherds were made of better fabrics and represent a process of technical improvement. The link between early pottery and basketry is an interesting example of experimentation in a time of the development of both craft technologies and farming techniques (Jarrige, Jarrige, Meadow and Quivron 1995: 423).

Further diversity in the early history of South Asian ceramics is available from a pot sherd found in a compartmented building. It had a kind of framework of reeds coated inside and out with mud and then lightly baked (Jarrige, Jarrige, Meadow and Quivron 1995: 453).

The earliest pottery at Mehrgarh occurs in Period IB. It is a soft, chaff tempered ware, handmade with simple shapes. Pamela Vandiver (1995) has studied these ceramics and found that the pots were assembled from slabs and daubs of clay. The internal structure of the vessels can be seen from lines of cleavage between the "slabs" as shown in Figure 4.25. Some vessels have a red slip or daubs of red paint. Two exceptional sherds have an applique design of a stylized caprid(?). This soft ware was not found at Kili Ghul Mohammad, but has a wide distribution across the Iranian Plateau into the Zagros Mountains: (Sang-i Chaxmaq; Tepe Yahya, Belt and Hotu Caves, Tepe Sialk, Sarab, Jarmo, Hajji Firuz). In these contexts it comes in the middle of the sixth millennium BC (5500 BC), a date acceptable to the Mehrgarh sequence. The Mehrgarh pottery has been studied and it is determined that it was made by assembling slabs of clay one above the other to form a circular container. The apparent absence of this ware from Kili Ghul Mohammad could indicate a break in the

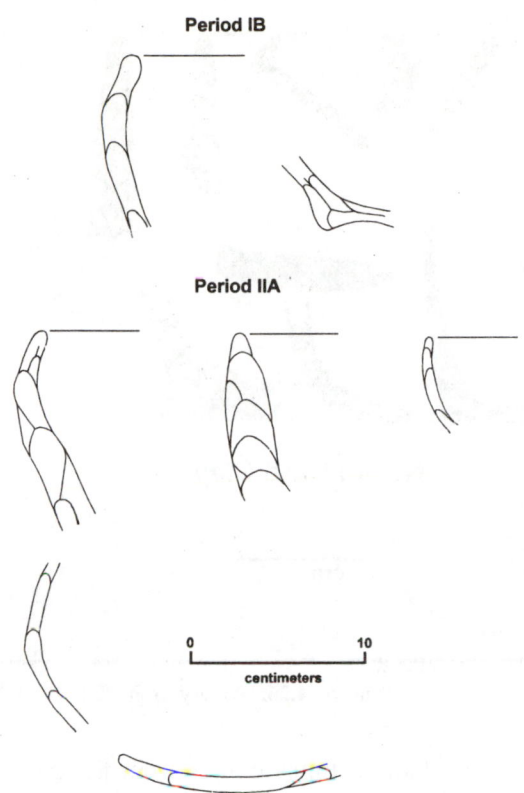

Figure 4.25. Ceramics from Mehrgarh IB and IIA, after Vandiver 1995: 654

sequence there, or simply the restricted scope of the excavation, but it is an important observation because it demonstrates that the Mehrgarh sequence is not replicated at Kili Ghul Mohammad. Containers made of plaster, a feature of early village farming communities in the Near East, are not known from Mehrgarh or other South Asian Stage One sites.

A basket marked ware occurs early in the Mehrgarh sequence. This ceramic was also found at Kili Ghul Mohammad and illustrates a fascinating way to make a pot. The potter took a basket, probably an older, used one and packed clay around the inside. It was then fired, the basket itself providing some of the fuel in a process of self-destructive creativity[7] (see Figure 4.27). The finished pot carries the impression of the basket on the outside surface and can be used in the study of ancient weaving (Bird 1956). Jarrige and his team found that the outside of these pots was sometimes covered with a thick coat of mud, to hide these impressions and smooth the surface. Kili Ghul Mohammad has no evidence of this practice (Figure 4.26, Figure 4.27).

In Period IIB the pottery becomes more sophisticated with a wheel made fine micaceous red ware. Other pots were made on a wheel and expanded by paddle and anvil (Jarrige, Jarrige, Meadow and Quivron 1995: 248). Wheel technology is vastly expanded in Period III, with beautiful, fine red wares and the Period IIB ceramics can be considered a harbinger of these developments.

Subsistence Activities of Mehrgarh II

The dependence on domesticated animals continued to grow through this period, as did the reliance on cultivated plants. An interesting observation on the subsistence

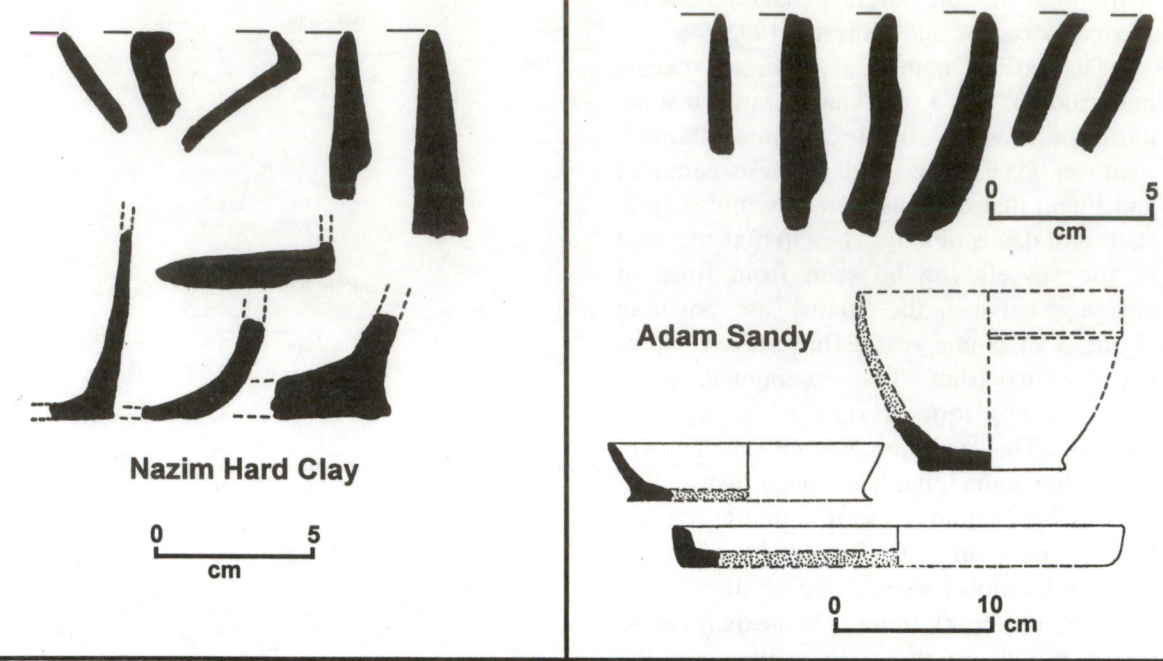

Figure 4.26. Pottery from Kili Ghul Mohammad II, after Fairservis 1956a, 248-50

regime of these times comes from the palaeobotanical remains of Period II at Mehrgarh (Burj Basket-marked times): "The charred seeds of wheat and barley belonging to the species *Triticum sphaerococcum* and *Hordeum sphaerococcum* that, according to L. Costantini, grow only on irrigated fields, also were collected from the ashy layers of Period II" (Jarrige, Jarrige, Meadow and Quivron 1995: 318). This is important documentation for the beginnings of local irrigation, not the huge, community or state sponsored works thought to have massive social impact that were used to move water between major environmental zones. The Mehrgarh evidence reflects the common sense of farmers attempting to make the best use of their soil and water resources on a local, family level.

A Very Recent Revision to the Mehrgarh Sequence

The Jarrige team returned to Mehrgarh in 1996-97 to pursue their investigation of Periods I and II, which are stratigraphically very complex. What they found in this season of work is that all of the pottery is best placed in Period IIA. The material that was assigned to Period IB, is now assigned to IIA. This ultimately simplifies the sequence, since all of Period I is now aceramic.

The Jarriges found a series of graves, without pots, that they now call Period IC. Thus, we now have a Mehrgarh Period I with three sub-divisions IA, IB and IC.

The Pottery of Period IIA is the coarse ware, already described. The hard fired red ware begins in Period IIB.

This news arrived too late in the production of this book to be integrated into the text. These paragraphs have been added to give the reader the best view of this important site.

Conclusions

Period II represents growth and continuity out of Period I and there is justification for thinking

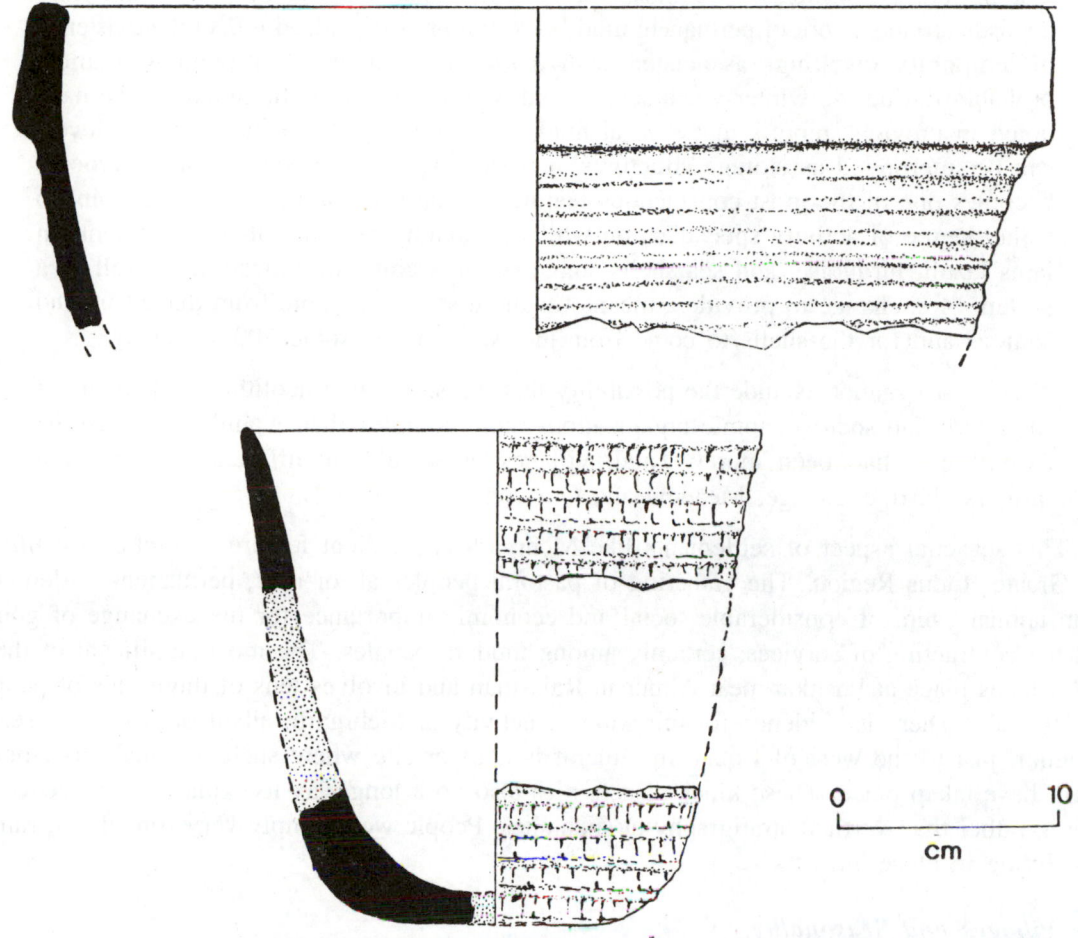

Figure 4.27. Burj Basket-marked pottery from Kili Ghul Mohammad II, after Fairservis 1956a, 260

of them as a single unit. The presence of rectangular houses subdivided into rooms that are contemporary with compartmented buildings is important to our knowledge of the South Asian village farming community. The presence of significant amounts of craft activity in and among these buildings is of consequence because of the diversity which includes flint knapping, tanning and bead making. Pottery was also probably made at the site or very close by. The presence of cotton is important, although the identification is from seeds and the exact use of this plant at Mehrgarh has yet to be determined.

Large portions of the Mehrgarh II settlement area were open and show signs of extensive use of hearths and firepits. The excavators make the following suggestion concerning the settlement:

> We have proposed that the site in the fifth and early fourth millennium could have had the function of, for instance, a marketplace or a craft center where people from the uplands gathered on a seasonal basis even as they do today around the towns on the Kachi Plain. For the aceramic period, however, it is more difficult to propose such an explanation since craft and marketing functions suppose the existence of a socioeconomic organization that does not fit our present conceptions of conditions in

that period. Nevertheless, we must entertain the idea that the fireplaces and ashy deposits around a core of permanent mud-brick buildings do indeed reflect the existence of temporary dwellings associated with a seasonal gathering of population most probably during the winter when severe cold weather pervades the uplands...We have noted in previous reports that several mud-brick buildings from the aceramic levels can be interpreted as storage structures, and by Period IIA, a system of storerooms becomes one of the most conspicuous features of the site. Grave-goods also point to some degree of activity specialization while the quality of some of the ornaments in lapis lazuli, turquoise, and sea shells suggests some craft specialization as well as a system of exchange to provide a means for these stones to come from distant upland sources and for the shells to come from the Arabian Sea some 500 km away.

In sum, we cannot exclude the possibility that the successive neolithic settlements of Mehrgarh had socioeconomic organizations more complex than would have been the case if they had been merely small villages of socially undifferentiated incipient farmers (Jarrige, Jarrige, Meadow and Quivron 1995: 366-67).

This seasonal aspect of settlements like Mehrgarh is a salient feature of prehistoric life in the Greater Indus Region. The gathering of pastoral peoples at, or near, permanent settlements is an annual event of considerable social and economic importance for the exchange of goods and the contracting of services, certainly among modern peoples. The most significant of these *melas* takes place at Pushkar, near Ajmer in Rajasthan and involves tens of thousands of people and animals. There is evidence for this kind of activity at Mehrgarh, albeit on a smaller scale. Rangpur, just to the west of Lothal in Gujarat is another site where such seasonal movements might have taken place. These kinds of activities also go a long way to explain the presence of lateral, rather than vertical stratigraphy at such sites. People were simply very spread out, rather than living in close quarters.

The Villages and Seasonality

The village settlements seem to have been inhabited year-round by some portion of the population. Some of the inhabitants of Mehrgarh may have taken to the road, moving out of Kachi in the hot season, into the cool, comfortable, mountains of Baluchistan. Kachi is today, and is likely to have been in the seventh millennium, an extremely hot, uncomfortable place in the summer. It is so uncomfortable today that people have been known to go mad from the relentless heat which, for days at a time, can be above 38° C (ca. 100° F) even at the coolest part of the day, just before sunrise.

The seasons are a great clock for farmers and herders. Their pace of life, the work they do, the kinds of food they eat, migration and opportunities to meet outsiders are all largely regulated by the season. Modern city dwellers who have never lived on a farm, or moved with a group of pastoralists, are relatively insensitive to this. There is a very nice poem on the topic, written in early nineteenth century England that attempts to capture this (Claire 1827).

Subsistence Economy

A mixed subsistence economy characterizes the initial period of village farming communities and pastoral camps. But, fully domesticated cereals were in evidence from the very beginning of Stage One with wheat seeming to be more important than barley. As noted at Mehrgarh, there is evidence that big game hunting was an important subsistence activity, but over time domesticates came to be the predominant food source. At Mehrgarh, from the end of Period IA and the beginning of Period IB, more than eighty percent of all the faunal remains come from the cattle, sheep and goats. The quantity of remains of cattle and sheep rises dramatically, with both animals better represented than goats during Periods IB/IIA. In this phase cattle bones make up well over half of the faunal remains.

At Bagor, and doubtless other pastoral camps, hunting was engaged in throughout Stage One. The role of agriculture among the pastoral peoples of this Stage is not known, but the presence of ground stone food processing tools at their settlements indicates that they either grew their own food grains or obtained them by exchange with peoples in village farming communities.

Trade

Late in the Stage, interregional trade brought raw materials from great distances. The burials of Mehrgarh Period IB have beads of seashell and turquoise. There are also objects of lapis lazuli and a bead of copper, probably the unsmelted "native" metal. The total list of raw materials that would not have been on the Kachi Plain includes lapis lazuli, turquoise, galena, copper, carnelian, steatite, calcite, dentalium shell, mother of pearl, conch shell. Clearly, the early food producing peoples of Pakistan had wide ranging contacts to secure these materials, many of which smack of luxuries and call into question the presumption that such trade is a symptom of civilization, urbanization and state organized economies. Such far reaching contacts are also characteristic of the Natufian, PPNA and PPNB Periods in the Levant.

Settlement Patterns of Stage One

Archaeological exploration in Baluchistan, the Northwest Frontier, Kachi and Sindh has revealed a total of nineteen sites that can be attributed to the Kili Ghul Mohammad Phase. These are listed in Table 4.13. Bibliography is available in Appendix A: Gazetteer of Settlements of the Indus Age. With the exception of Kili Ghul Mohammad, Mehrgarh and possibly Gumla, there is no guarantee that any of these places has been correctly assigned to either of the Phases of Stage One since this has been based on the description of surface debris (Plate 4.21). However, I have been to Baleli Damb in the Quetta Valley and it deserves the attention that problem oriented excavation would provide. It has already been excavated, unfortunately for the emplacement of artillery during World War II. The sites in Bannu that have been assigned to this phase are the object of active research by a joint team from the University of Peshawar, the British Museum and the Institute of Archaeology, London University. More will be known of them and it can be expected that Table 4.13 will be revised as explorations and excavation proceed in this region.

The sites of the Kili Ghul Mohammad Phase are small, and seem to cluster together nicely (Figure 4.28). The thirty-three Burj Basket-marked sites that have been placed on the list have either the soft, chaff-tempered ware or basket marked pottery without other ceramic associations. These are barely adequate indicators of an affinity with this Phase, and much more research, especially digging, is needed to clarify our abundant ignorance of the Burj Basket-marked Phase. For example, the basket marked ceramic seems to continue on into later periods, but with those ceramic associations. In southern Baluchistan, it may even be a part of the Kulli ceramic assemblage. For now, the best estimate for sites of this Phase is presented in Table 4.14.

TABLE 4.13
Sites of the Kili Ghul Mohammad Phase

Site Name	Province/State	District	Size in Hectares
Tharro Hill	Sindh	Nawabshah	12.5
Mehrgarh	Baluchistan	Kachi	4.0
Khakhar Buthi	Baluchistan	Las Bela	2.3
Rana Ghundai	Baluchistan	Loralai	1.4
Kasiano Dozakh	Baluchistan	Quetta-Pishin	1.3
Gumla	Northwest Frontier	Dera Ismail Khan	0.7
Baleli	Baluchistan	Quetta-Pishin	0.65
Jebri Damb Two	Baluchistan	Jhalawan	0.5
Kili Ghul Mohammad	Baluchistan	Quetta-Pishin	0.5
Bagh-i Kumb Damb	Northwest Frontier	Dera Ismail Khan	
Ghalaihak	Baluchistan	Jhalawan	
Ghul Shah Tup	Northwest Frontier	Bannu	
Lal Ghundai	Baluchistan	Quetta-Pishin	
Lyari River Area	Sindh	Karachi	
Mai Ghari	Sindh	Karachi	
Nakamshakh	Northwest Frontier	Bannu	
Shakar Khan Damb	Baluchistan	Jhalawan	
Tup Takhtikhel	Northwest Frontier	Bannu	
Yarak	Northwest Frontier	Bannu	

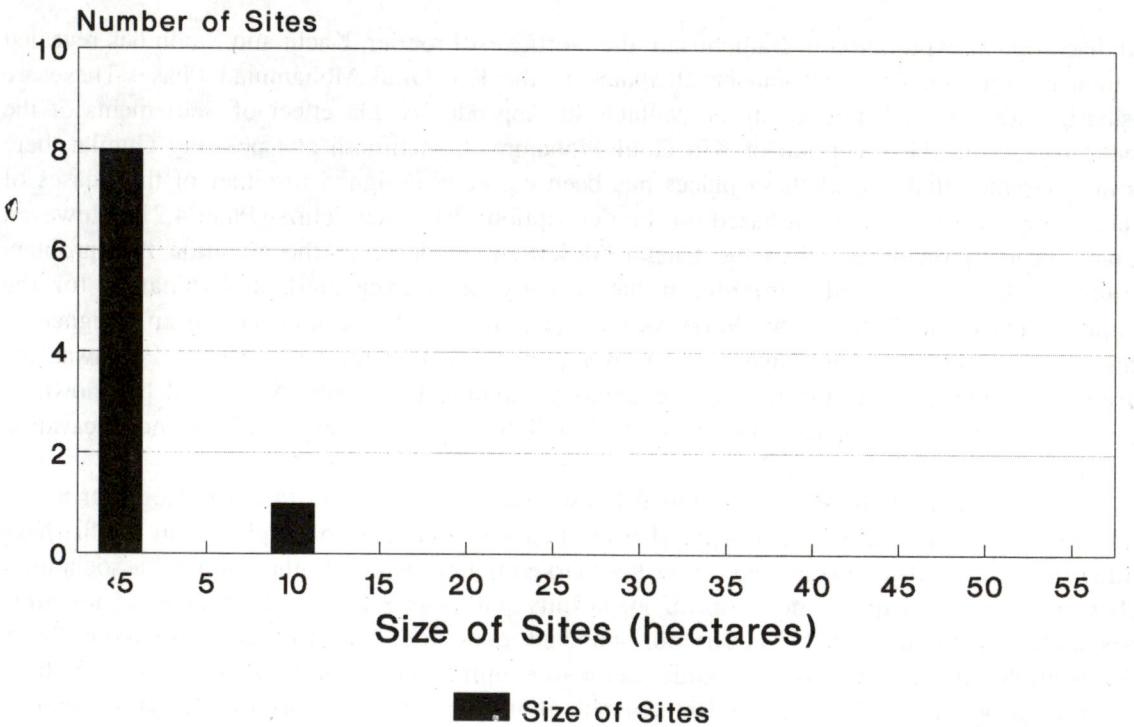

Figure 4.28. Histogram of sites of the Kili Ghul Mohammad Phase

TABLE 4.14
Sites of the Burj Basket-marked Phase

Site Name	Province/State	District	Size in Hectares
L-3	Baluchistan	Loralai	12.6
Duki Mound	Baluchistan	Loralai	6.5
Saiyid Maurez Damb	Baluchistan	Sarawan	6.3
Mehrgarh	Baluchistan	Kachi	4.0
Anjira	Baluchistan	Jhalawan	3.0
Benn Chah	Baluchistan	Jhalawan	2.5
Thok Valley One	Baluchistan	Jhalawan	2.5
Khakhar Buthi	Baluchistan	Las Bela	2.3
Q-25	Baluchistan	Quetta-Pishin	1.5
Siah Damb, Surab	Baluchistan	Jhalawan	1.5
Rana Ghundai	Baluchistan	Loralai	1.4
Kasiano Dozakh	Baluchistan	Quetta-Pishin	1.3
Isplinji Two	Baluchistan	Sarawan	0.7
Baleli	Baluchistan	Quetta-Pishin	0.65
Q-17	Baluchistan	Quetta-Pishin	0.65
L-2	Baluchistan	Loralai	0.6
Kili Ghul Mohammad	Baluchistan	Quetta-Pishin	0.5
Neghar Damb	Baluchistan	Kalat	0.35
Kuki Damb	Baluchistan	Jhalawan	0.1
Bagh-i Kumb Damb	Northwest Frontier	Dera Ismail Khan	
Ghalegay Cave	Northwest Frontier	Swat	
Ghul Shah Tup	Northwest Frontier	Bannu	
Gorpat	Baluchistan	Jhalawan	
Hurro Damb	Baluchistan	Jhalawan	
Indus Delta Site	Sindh	Tatta	
Kan Mehtarzai One	Baluchistan	Zhob	
Khwaja Zabar	Baluchistan	Sarawan	
Malki	Baluchistan	Sarawan	
Rizvi Karuna	Baluchistan	Quetta-Pishin	
Sang	Baluchistan	Zhob	
Singen Kalat	Baluchistan	Jhalawan	
Surab Valley 'A'	Baluchistan	Jhalawan	
Togau	Baluchistan	Sarawan	

There is an expansion of the number of sites in the Burj Basket-marked Phase which will continue as a trend in the data sets for Stages Two and Three, through the Mature Harappan and the third millennium BC (Figure 4.29). If food production and domestication were more or less established in the Greater Indus Region by ca. 7000 BC, then there are 2700 years from this point to the end of Stage One. The "Neolithic Revolution" in southern Asia hardly got off to a fast start! But, there is an apparent increase in the number of sites which seems to indicate population growth; a development that deserves a closer look.

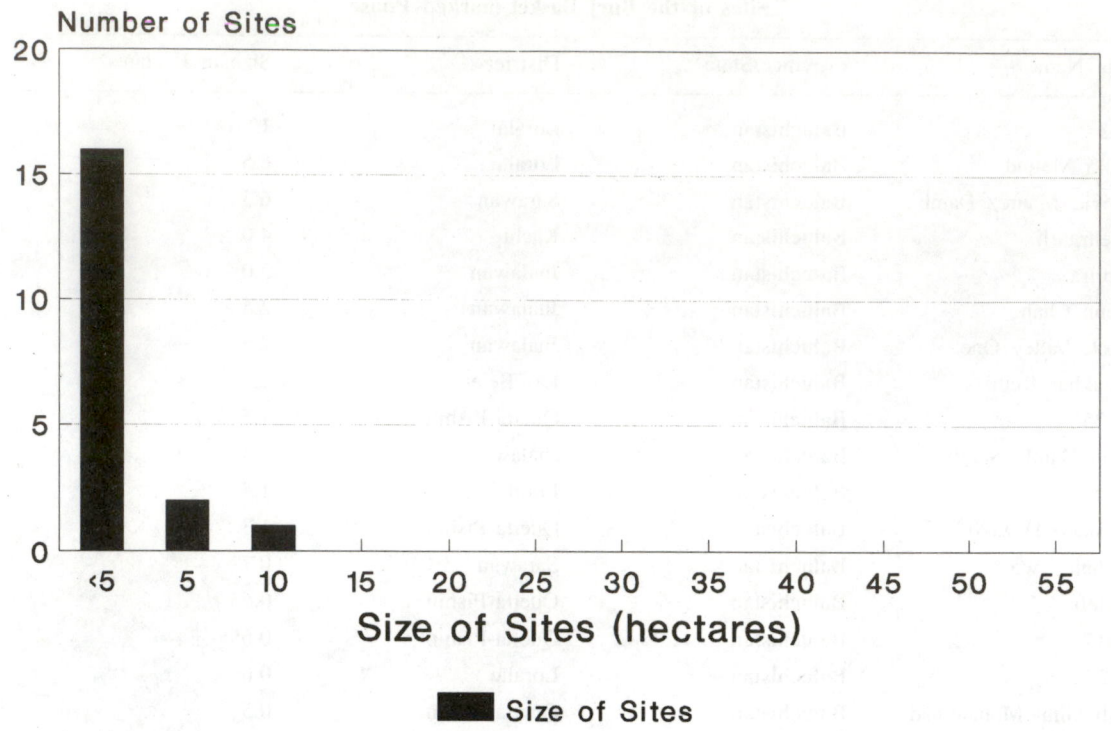

Number of Sites

Size of Sites (hectares)

■ Size of Sites

Figure 4.29. Histogram of sites of the Burj Basket-marked Phase

Estimating the Population of Stage One

It is clearly not possible for an estimate of the population of Stage One to be made with accuracy. Any approximation from archaeological data is compromised in several ways: many camps and settlements are missing from these data. Not all of the settlements in any one Phase were settled for the entire duration of that Phase; not all settlements were inhabited over their entire measured area, among other reasons. But, site size is not an irrelevant variable, even if archaeologists do not know exactly how to interpret it. The same is true for the aggregation of site sizes into a meaningful variable for a Phase. Archaeologists are not sure what it means. Preliminary investigation determined that there are trends in the total settled area of sites looked at by Phase. The average size of the sites that have been documented also seems to increase. These are internally consistent data that can be compared within the context of this study. They are not the census of the Phases of the Indus Age.

The Method for Estimating Net Settled Area

The form presented in Table 4.15 will be used for all of the Phases of the Indus Age, so the way in which the Estimated Net Settled Area for the Kili Ghul Mohammad Phase was derived will be explained in some detail. This estimate for other Phases can then be calculated by "filling in the blanks."

The net settled area for settlements of the Kili Ghul Mohammad Phase is taken from information in Appendix A, "Gazetteer of Settlements of the Indus Age." The Net Settled Area is the sum of the area for the nine sites with size data. If it is assumed that the average site size

TABLE 4.15
Estimate of Settled Area for Phases of Stage One

Kili Ghul Mohammad Phase	
Total Sites	20
Sites with Size Estimate	9
Settled Area of Sites with Known Sizes	23.85
Sites with Size Unknown	11
Average Site Site Size	2.65
Estimated Settled Area of Sites Without Size	29.15
Estimated Total Settled Area	53.00
Burj Basket-marked Phase	
Total Sites	33
Sites with Size Figures	19
Settled Area of Sites with Known Sizes	48.95
Sites with Size Unknown	14
Average Site Size	2.58
Estimated Settled area of Sites without Size	36.12
Estimated Total Settled Area	85.07

Sizes given in hectares

for the unmeasured sites is the same, or approximates that for the measured sites, the net settled area for these places can then be estimated. In the case of the Kili Ghul Mohammad Phase this is the remaining eleven sites times 2.65, the average site size, or 29.15 hectares. Adding the estimates for the measured sites to the unmeasured sites gives an Estimated Net Settled Area of 53.00.

The Estimated Net Settled Area for the Burj Basket-marked Phase was derived in precisely the same way as for the Kili Ghul Mohammad Phase. There is good growth in the settled area rising from 53.0 hectares to 85.07 hectares.

Comments on the Growth in Settled Area for Stage One

Perhaps the most striking observation concerning the Stage One estimate of net settled area is the ca. sixty percent rise in the figures between the Kili Ghul Mohammad and Burj Basket-marked Phases. This kind of growth will develop as a trend in the archaeological data set from prehistoric South Asia through Stage Four the Mature Harappan Stage. This may well be the product of real population growth, although other factors must have been involved as well, such as the acculturation of indigenous hunting and gathering peoples into a life style that leaves a more robust archaeological record than their camps.

Since the topic is people, it should also be observed that human burial and a record of human biology begins in Stage One. There are interesting and important notes that come from this data set. It is specialized material and attention is drawn to the discussion of Biological Anthropology and Archaeology available in the Introduction.

Pastoral and Camp Sites

It is apparent that pastoralism emerged as an adaptation at the very beginning of the food producing era in South Asia, a point made by S. P. Gupta and A. Kesarwani (1983). Direct evidence for Stage One camps in Baluchistan exists at Anjira, in Period I (de Cardi 1965: 100-01) and a small unexcavated site known as P-6 or Lal Ghundai (Fairservis 1956a: 201) which I visited in 1965. An example of a lowland site where pastoral nomads may have camped during the winter is Gumla I, where the first occupation was by people who did not use pottery (Dani 1970-71: 39, 41-2). Microlithic tools were in use (Dani 1970-71: 95-6) along with ground stone food processing tools. Hearths, or "community ovens" were also found, but there is no architecture, not even ephemeral floors or post holes, but the exposure was very small. Tables 8 and 9 list some very small sites like Jebri Damb 2, Baleli, Kuki Damb, Neghar Damb and L-2 that, suggest camp sites. Excavation is needed here, but there are good candidates for camps in the archaeological record.

Bagor: Another kind of camp

There is an important camp site in Rajasthan known as Bagor (25° 21' N – 74° 23' E). It is small, about 80 × 80 meters, or 0.64 hectares and is located on a sand dune on the eastern side of the Aravalli Range in southeastern Rajasthan. This is the center of the Mewar Plain, an undulating, rocky land about 500 meters above mean sea level. In 1967 a joint team from Deccan College and the University of Heidelberg found an important site on a high dune called Mahasati near Bagor village. The dune is adjacent to the Kothari River, a tributary of the Banas, the major river of the region. The significance of Bagor stems from its microlithic tool industry associated with pottery, metal artifacts and the remains of domesticated animals. One season of excavation was conducted at the site (IAR 1967-68: 41-4) by the joint team, and continued for two additional seasons by the team from Deccan College, headed by Prof. V. N. Misra (IAR 1968-69: 26-8; IAR 1969-70: 32-4). The principal report on the site is V. N. Misra (1973a) which has been useful in this review.

The Bagor Excavation

The team laid nineteen excavation trenches in all, fifteen in an area 20 by 10 meters (10, 4 × 4 meters and 5, 4 × 2 meters). In addition, four trenches of 3 × 2 meters were laid some distance from each edge in the main excavation area to test the limits of settlement at Bagor.

The excavation revealed about three meters of windblown sand, which changed color and texture in a gradual way, from bottom to top. These were divided into five "strata" (Figure 4.30), which are more or less artificial constructs, since there were no sharp breaks in the layering. Artifacts were recovered from the upper three strata, down to a depth of about 1.75 meters.

The Bagor Microlithic Tool Industry

The common element running through the Bagor sequence is the industry of several hundred thousand microlithic tools. This has been thoroughly studied by G. Khanna, in an unpublished PhD dissertation (Khanna 1988). The industry was based on the mass production of microblades from polyhedral cores of quartz and chert, both locally available. The most common types are blades, variously retouched and truncated, triangles, trapeze, transverse arrow heads, rhomboids, crescents and points (Figure 4.31). Misra speculates that this industry was well suited to hunting, which seems reasonable. (1973a: 96).

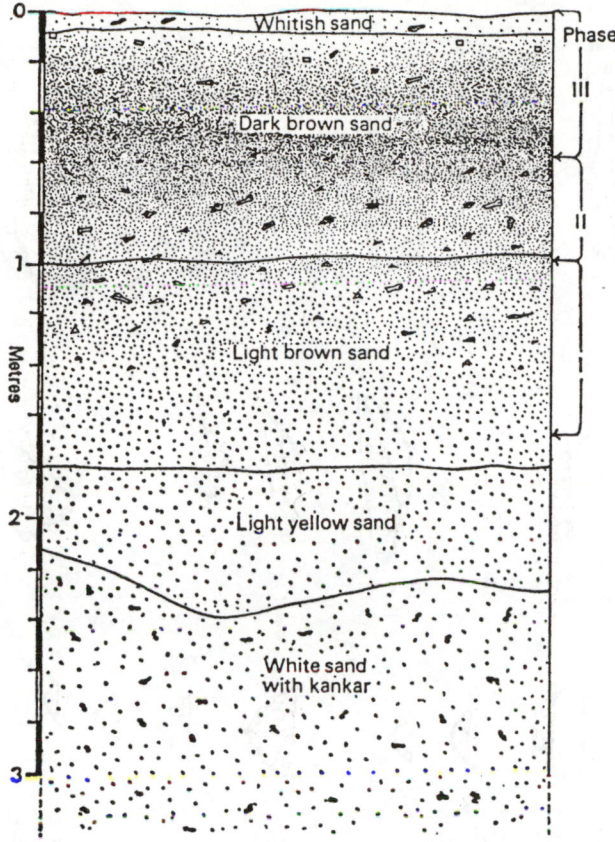

Figure 4.30. Stratigraphy at Bagor, from V. N. Misra 1974: 94

The core preparation technique employing the crested guiding ridge is absent at Bagor. This easily recognized technique was extensively used by village based, chipped stone tool makers of the Harappan cultural tradition, as well as those of the village farming communities on the Deccan Plateau. This difference in technology may prove to be one of the important ways of distinguishing the stone tool industries of hunter-gatherers from those of village based peoples.

Bagor Phase I

Large floors made of schist slabs quarried from across the Kothari River, combined with pebbles, were found in Periods I and II. The patterning of these features is not terribly strong, but there were alignments suggesting the outlines of circular shelters three to five meters in diameter. The excavator takes these to be the remains of wattle huts or wind screens. Some small areas were tightly paved. They are forty to seventy centimeters across and associated with concentrations of animal bones. No hearths were found at Bagor so these may represent butchering slabs.

One burial was found in Phase I contexts. It was extended and supine, with the left arm resting on the trunk, head to the west. No grave goods were found, but some animal bones in the vicinity may be associated with this interment.

The largest number of microlithic tools and animal bones was found in this period. There are a few stone beads in Phase I, along with rather small, shallow querns and ground stone "sling balls." The excavator does not associate pottery with period I (Misra 1973a: 100).

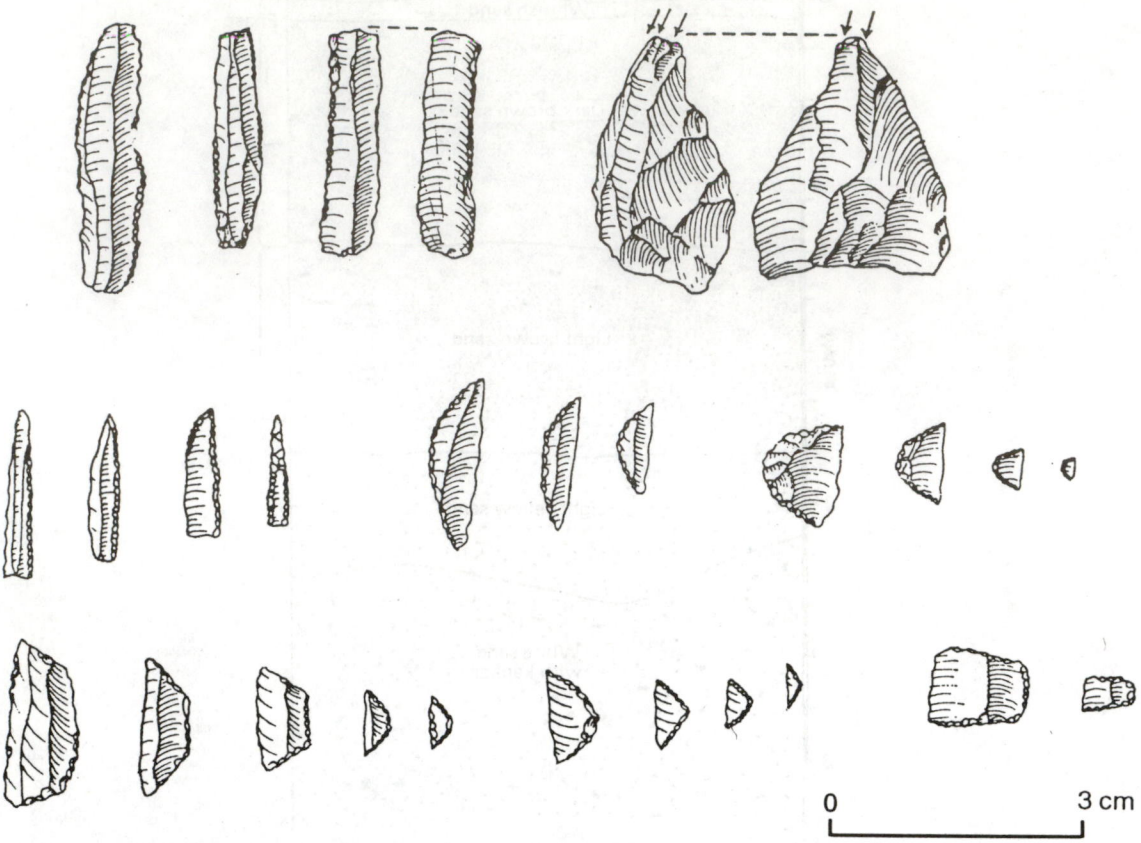

Figure 4.31. Microliths from Bagor, after Misra 1973a: Figure 22

Bagor Phase II

Phase II at Bagor is fifty to sixty centimeters thick. The number of tools and animal bones declines in this period. The architecture is the same as in Phase I. Handmade pottery with incised decoration was found, some as complete pots in burials (Figure 4.32, Figure 4.33). There are three Phase II interments, all of which were in a flexed position, with the head to the east. Phase II burials were provided with relatively lavish grave goods including the pottery, and ornaments, copper tools and joints of meat. The copper artifacts from Bagor II are all associated with two of the interments; "In one burial as many as eight pots were arranged near the head and on the left side of the body; two copper arrowheads were placed on the left side, one of them right on the lower left arm, and a large animal femur lay close to the body. In the case of another burial four pots were placed near the feet and on the left side, a spearhead and arrowhead lay near the head and an awl of antimony rod (all three objects were made of copper) was placed below the abdomen. A broken terracotta spindle whorl was kept near the feet. In addition, 36 beads, mostly of stone but some also of bone, were found strewn on the chest and around the neck..." (V. N. Misra 1973a: 104-05) (Figure 4.34). The copper arrowheads are discussed in (V. N. Misra 1970a) and are similar to those found at a number of Mature Harappan sites, but the Harappan examples are not perforated. The spearhead has a midrib, not a feature of Indus metallurgy. The beads were made of several stones, including banded agate,

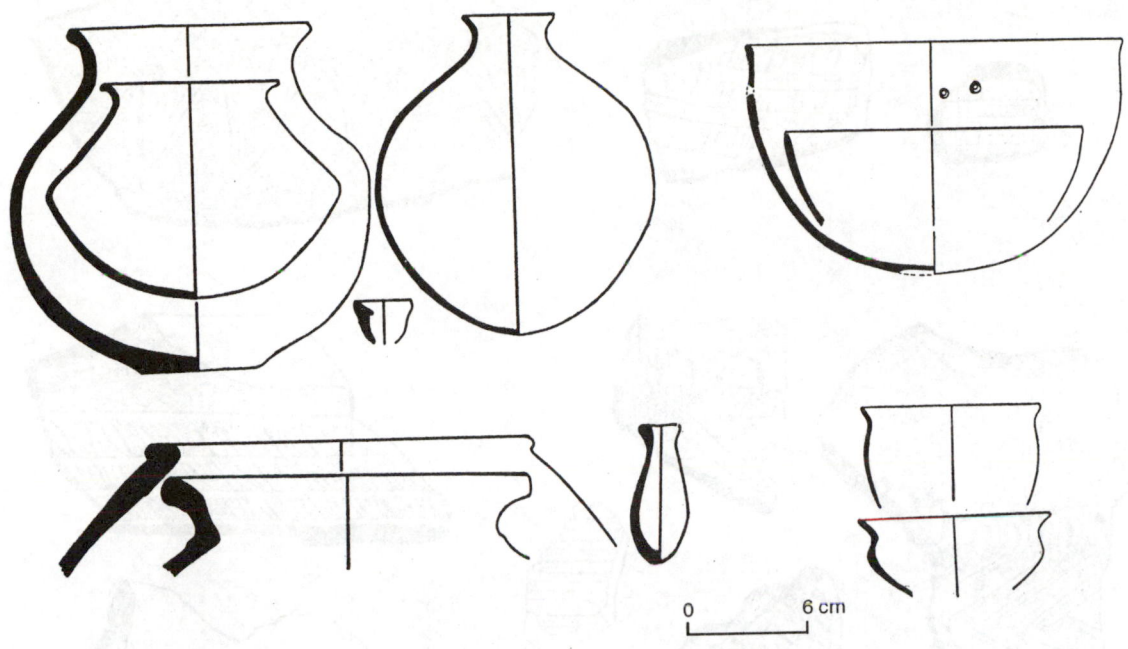

0   6 cm

Figure 4.32. Pots from Phase II at Bagor, after V. N. Misra   1970b: 87-8

carnelian and garnet. The carnelian is particularly interesting because of its special association with the Mature Harappan.

The pottery of Bagor II shares some typological connections with Ahar I (Sankalia, Deo and Ansari 1969) and the Kayatha Culture (Ansari and Dhavalikar 1975; Wakankar 1967) in that the surface treatment of the Bagor ware is like the red ware of Ahar with similar incised decorations. Ahar I shapes are also present at Bagor II. One neckless jar from Bagor has a close parallel at Kayatha I, in both fabric and shape. Misra notes other ceramic parallels between these two sites (1973a: 103, 1973b). The pottery from Ahar and Kayatha is far more diverse and technologically superior to Bagor II, but clearly Bagor was part of its region at this time and shared items of material culture with both the east (pottery) and west (metal).

Small shallow querns continued to be used in period II and two ground stone "ring-stones" or mace heads were found as well, along with "sling balls."

Bagor Phase III

Phase III was restricted to the central part of the excavation area and varied between 35 and 75 centimeters thick. This period of occupation produced the smallest number of microlithic tools and animal bones, but wheelmade pottery is present along with iron tools; two arrow heads, one socketed, the other tanged, and many amorphous lumps of iron (Figure 4.35). Glass beads and stone pendants in several shapes occur in Phase III.

The architecture is still fragmentary in Phase III, with no real houses, but baked bricks and tiles were used in construction. A Phase III wall, three meters long and one meter wide, was made of massive, partially dressed stones.

The pottery of Phase III at Bagor is different from that of Phase II (V. N. Misra 1973b). It was now entirely wheelmade, gritty, micaceous and fired at a temperature higher than the ware

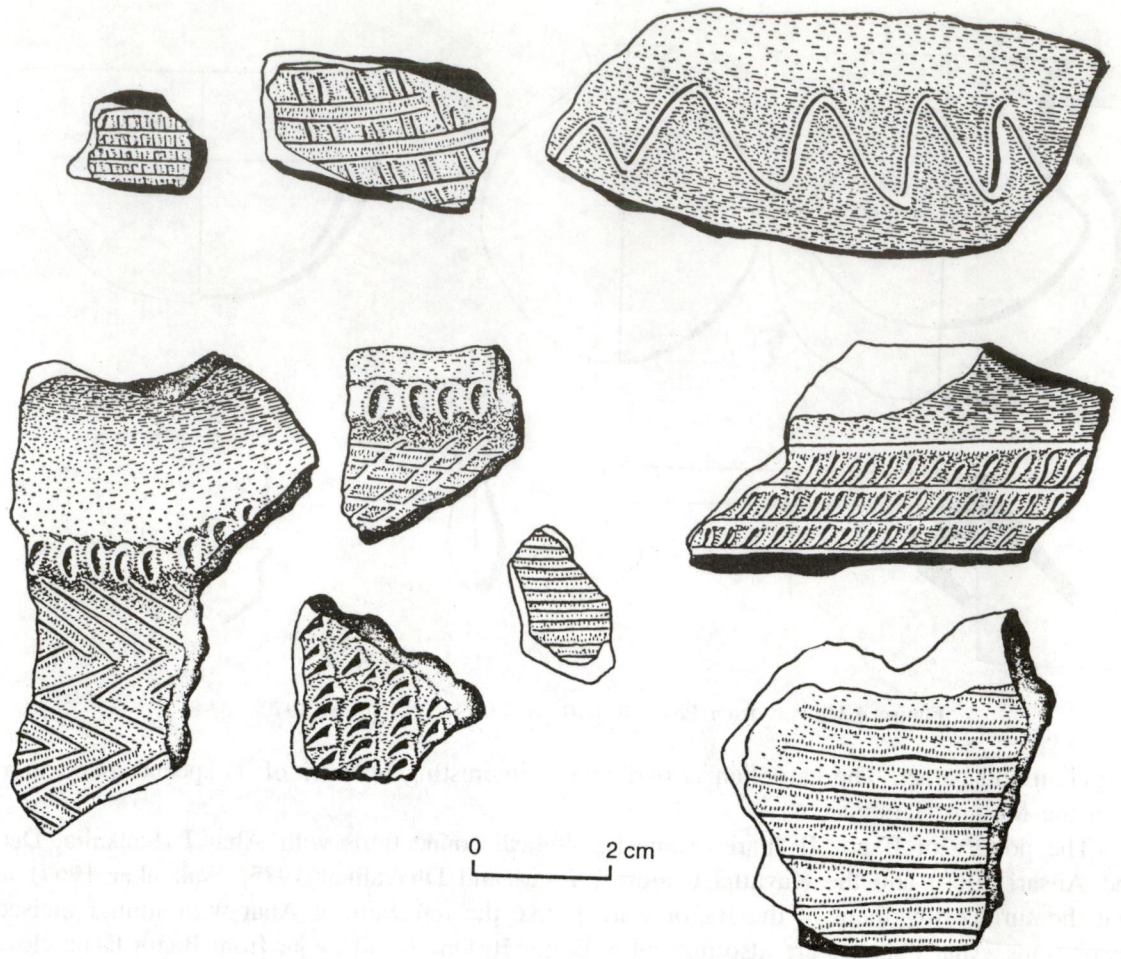

Figure 4.33. Handmade pottery from Bagor, Phase II, after V. N. Misra 1973a: 101

of Phase II. It is utilitarian pottery with little decoration or appeal. The shapes have many parallels with Early Historic sites in Rajasthan and Gujarat.

The interment associated with Phase III (V. N. Misra 1973a: 105) is now thought to be a very late burial of a Muslim and has been withdrawn from the archaeological context (V. N. Misra 1973a: 109).

Human Biology at Bagor

Five prehistoric burials were found at Bagor, one in Phase I, three in Phase II and the last in Phase III. Only the phase III interment was complete enough for full study (Lukacs, Misra and Kennedy 1982).

Subsistence Information from Bagor

The most interesting aspect of Bagor is that domesticated animals occur there from the very beginning of the settlement. The same species are basically represented in all three periods, but they vary in frequency and density, most of the faunal remains coming from the first phase (Alur 1971; Thomas 1975, 1977; Shah 1971a).

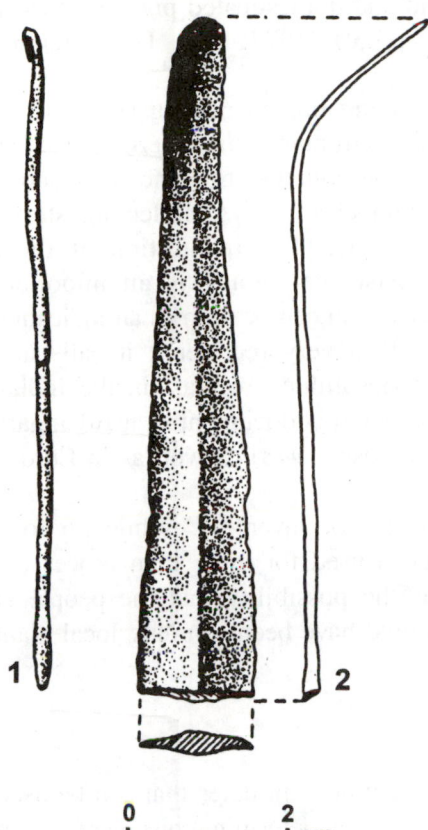

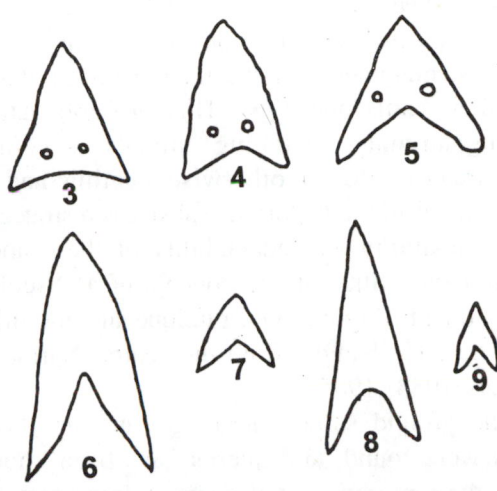

Figure 4.34. Copper artifacts from Bagor, with comparative examples from Mature Harappan sites. Nos. 1-5 Bagor, 6-7 Chanhu-daro, 8 Kot Diji, 9 Jhukar, after V. N. Misra 1973a: 98

The domesticated animals of Phase I include zebu, sheep, goat and pig. The presence of the pig might indicate a degree of sedentism at the site. The inhabitants of Bagor were also hunters and the remains of the following wild animals were found there; water buffalo, blackbuck, Indian gazelle, chital, sambar, Indian porcupine, common fox, hare, rat, along with the remains of fish, tortoise and the frog. The wild water buffalo is only present in Phase I and the minimum number of individuals represented is one (Thomas 1977: 98).

This mix of domesticated and wild animals associated with the camp of a people with a microlithic tool industry is indicative of the range of adaptations of people in protohistoric times in the Subcontinent. The most important domesticated animals were sheep and goats, with sheep more prevalent. These two animals account for more than 60 percent of the animal remains, a pattern that holds true for all three phases (Thomas 1977: 171-3). Next in order of importance are cattle: 16, 17, and seven percent of the

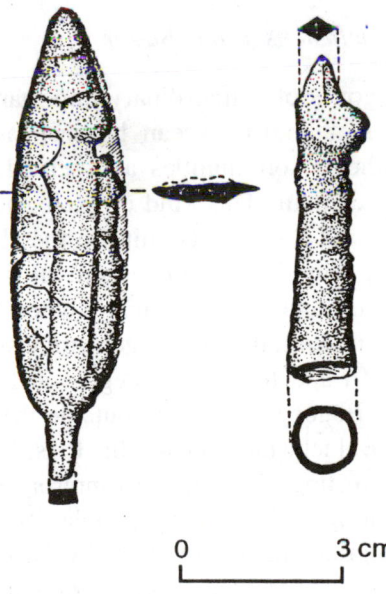

Figure 4.35. Iron arrow heads from Bagor III, after V. N. Misra 1973a: 99

remains from Phases I-III. P. K. Thomas notes that both wild and domesticated pigs are present in the following percentages from bottom to top: 3.7%; 4.2%; 3.3% (1977: 173). The chital and sambhar were the most popular of the hunted animals.

Wild sheep and goats are endemic to the eastern edge of the Iranian plateau (Baluchistan and the Northwestern Region) and are not part of the local environment in eastern Rajasthan. It can be imagined that the inhabitants of Bagor acquired these animals from the west, along with their cattle and pigs. This probably happened in a number of ways; collecting strays, stealing animals, or taking animals as compensation for work. The integration of these domesticates into an otherwise hunting and gathering subsistence regime is an important development in the history of subsistence strategies in South Asia and can be seen as an indication of the flexibility and adaptability of these ancient peoples. In a very real sense it calls into question the utility of the concept of a "Neolithic" and a "Mesolithic," at least in the Indian Subcontinent. Bagor is not a unique site and this form of adaptation is documented at Adamgarh Cave, near Hoshangabad on the central Narmada River (R. V. Joshi 1978) as well as in Europe (Geddes 1983, 1985).

The ground stone querns are an important item in the Bagor inventory. While no food grains were found, and querns have been known to have been used for more than processing grain, their presence at the site is important since it opens the possibility that the people at Bagor also had access to wheat or barley, or both. Or, they could have been grinding local plant seeds for part of their livelihood.

The Chronology for Bagor

There is a series of radiocarbon dates as well as some thermoluminescent dates that can be used to form a chronology for Bagor. Although all of the radiocarbon determinations were taken from the carbonate fraction of bone, they are internally consistent. The TL dates are also consistent, both as a series and with the material parallels in pottery and iron that date Phase III to the Early Historic. The radiometric dates are as given in Table 4.16.

Conclusions From Bagor

Bagor is of extraordinary importance. The presence of domesticated animals as well as the trade in metal artifacts can be seen as evidence that the symbiosis between South Asian hunter-gatherer communities and settled village folk around them has roots as far back as the sixth millennium. This kind of exchange on the eastern fringe of the Indus world documents that this was not a terra incognito to the Harappans and that they could easily have gained access to the vast deposits of copper ore in the region, in the so-called Khetri Belt. This information on Bagor, and doubtless many other "microlithic" sites in Rajasthan, is complemented by the finds of hunter-gatherer/village symbiosis at places like Langhnaj (Possehl 1976; Possehl and Kennedy 1979) and to a lesser degree at Kanewal (Mehta, Momin and Shah 1980).

Bagor seems to be outside the cultural traditions that gave rise to the Stage One settlements in Baluchistan and Kachi. It is, however, contemporary with some of them and presents some interesting challenges to interpretation. It is taken here as an example of the manner in which hunting and gathering people can easily find use for domesticated animals and can quite easily integrate them into their livelihoods. The source for the domesticated animals was probably strays and stolen stock, acquired by the ancient Rajasthani from the stocks of people more directly a part of the cultural traditions of Baluchistan, the Sindh pediment and Derajat.

TABLE 4.16
Radiocarbon Dates For Bagor

Period/Lab No.
Calibration

Period I
TF-786
1Σ cal BC 5418 (5221) 4936
2Σ cal BC 5570 (5221) 4721
TF-1007
1Σ cal BC 4575 (4460) 4344
2Σ cal BC 4771 (4460) 4230
TF-1011/2
1Σ cal BC 3976 (3942, 3845, 3824) 3784
2Σ cal BC 4071 (3942, 3845, 3824) 3698

Period I/II
TF-1009
1Σ cal BC 3501 (3351) 3100
2Σ cal BC 3630 (3351) 2924

Period II
TF-1005/6
1Σ cal BC 2565 (2460) 2297
2Σ cal BC 2852 (2460) 2143
The following thermoluminescence dates are available for Phase III pottery:
PRL-TL-S13, 120 BC
PRL-TL-42A, 130 BC
PRL-TL-42A, 130 BC
PRL-TL-42B, 30 BC
PRL-TL-42B, 30 BC
The chronology used by the excavator is slightly amended here based on the calibration of dates. The estimated age of the three phases at Bagor is:
Phase III ca. 600 BC-200 AD
Phase II ca. 2800-600 BC
Phase I ca. 5500-2800 BC

(based on V. N. Misra 1973a: 95)

Human Remains of Stage One

The largest number of human remains associated with the Phases prior to the Mature Harappan are found at Mehrgarh. There are scattered burials elsewhere which will be noted within the discussion of Mehrgarh itself. There is a reasonably large bibliography on the Mehrgarh burials including: Lechevallier and Quivron (1981, 1985); Lechevallier, Meadow and Quivron (1982); Lukacs (1983, 1985, 1989); Lukacs and Pastor (1988); Saizieu (1990); Samzun and Sellier (1983); Sellier (1985, 1987, 1988, 1989, 1990, 1991, 1992); Jarrige, Jarrige, Meadow and Quivron (1995).

Burials of Mehrgarh Period IA, Kili Ghul Mohammad Phase

The complex culture history of Mehrgarh has already been outlined. Burials are associated with the aceramic levels of Period IA and continue into the ceramic "neolithic" of later Period IB and then Period II.

The funerary complexes of Mehrgarh Periods I and II are also rich. There are no less than 166 graves, eighty-five from Period IA and early IB and eighty-one from later Period IB and Period IIA. Many of them were equipped with substantial amounts of grave furniture.

Two of the Period IA burials (Figure 4.36, Figure 4.37) have been described as:

> Locus 287... An adult was found lying in an ocher-stained pit dug from the Level 7 ashy layer into the compact clay below. While digging this pit, an earlier burial with a small child (Homo 290) had been disturbed. Of this burial there remained only some ribs and vertebrae and part of a dentalium necklace. The bones of Skeleton 287 were rather well preserved, and it was possible to consolidate the skull, the pelvis, and a few long bones. The ornaments consisted of one necklace of cut dentalium shells, (135 beads preserved) and another of small circles of white steatite (weathered, with diameters of 5 mm). Connected to this second necklace was a large bead of lapis lazuli. The stone varies in color from bluish-gray to sharp blue and contains impurities. It had been shaped into an irregular cylinder 27.5 mm long with one end rounded and the other square (diameters of 9 and 10 mm). The perforation is transverse, probably because of the hardness of the stone. On the chest of the skeleton there was a large, flat, shell disc (52.5 × 49 × 3 mm) perforated in the center and identical to the one found with Skeleton 283. At the back of the skull were seven small turquoise beads found together of which six were round (diameters: 4.5 mm, thickness: 2-2.5 mm). Finally, there were two anklets made of flat hexagonal calcite beads (the left anklet had 20 beads, the right one 19). The beads measure 19-25.5 × 8-12 × 5-7 mm depending upon their degree of wear, but they are much smaller than the anklets found on Skeleton 283. An offering of five goats, all aged under three months, had been laid at the feet of the deceased. Their disposition in a semi-circle corresponds to the shape of the pit.

> Locus 288...These are the bones of an adult that were badly preserved and completely crushed by the weight of the overburden. The body was flexed with legs drawn up to the pelvis. The arms were bent with the hands in contact with the face. The deceased, a tall individual, had no ornaments, but an offering of five young goats, similar to that of Tomb 287, was placed at his feet. They were laid in a semi-circle partly on top of each other (due to lack of space) and show clearly the edge of the pit (Jarrige, Jarrige, Meadow and Quivron 1995: 386; see also Lechevallier and Quivron 1985: 82-5).

These interments from the Kili Ghul Mohammad Phase at Mehrgarh are all in simple graves, without brick enclosures or other structures. The presence of caprids as food to accompany the deceased to an "after life" is a remarkably consistent feature of these interments. The burials in the Burj Basket-marked Phase are a bit different and more diverse in type.

Burials of Mehrgarh Period IB and II, Burj Basket-marked Phase

About halfway through the first period at Mehrgarh the initial settlement area was largely abandoned and erosion took place, which remodeled this human made landscape and marked the transition between subperiods IA and IB. The older area was turned into a cemetery, with

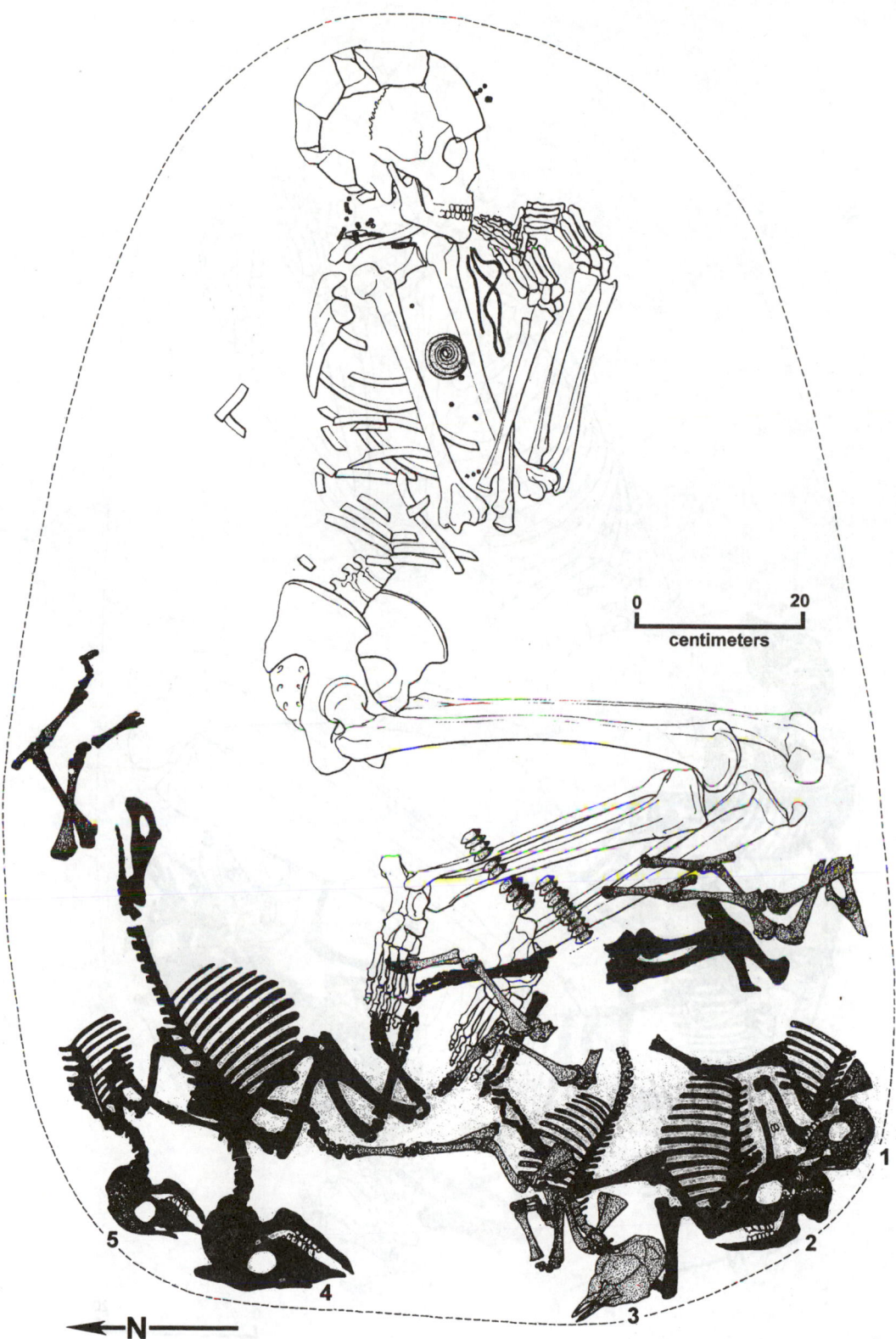

Figure 4.36. Burial 287 at Mehrgarh, Period IA, after Lechevallier and Quivron 1985: Figure 9

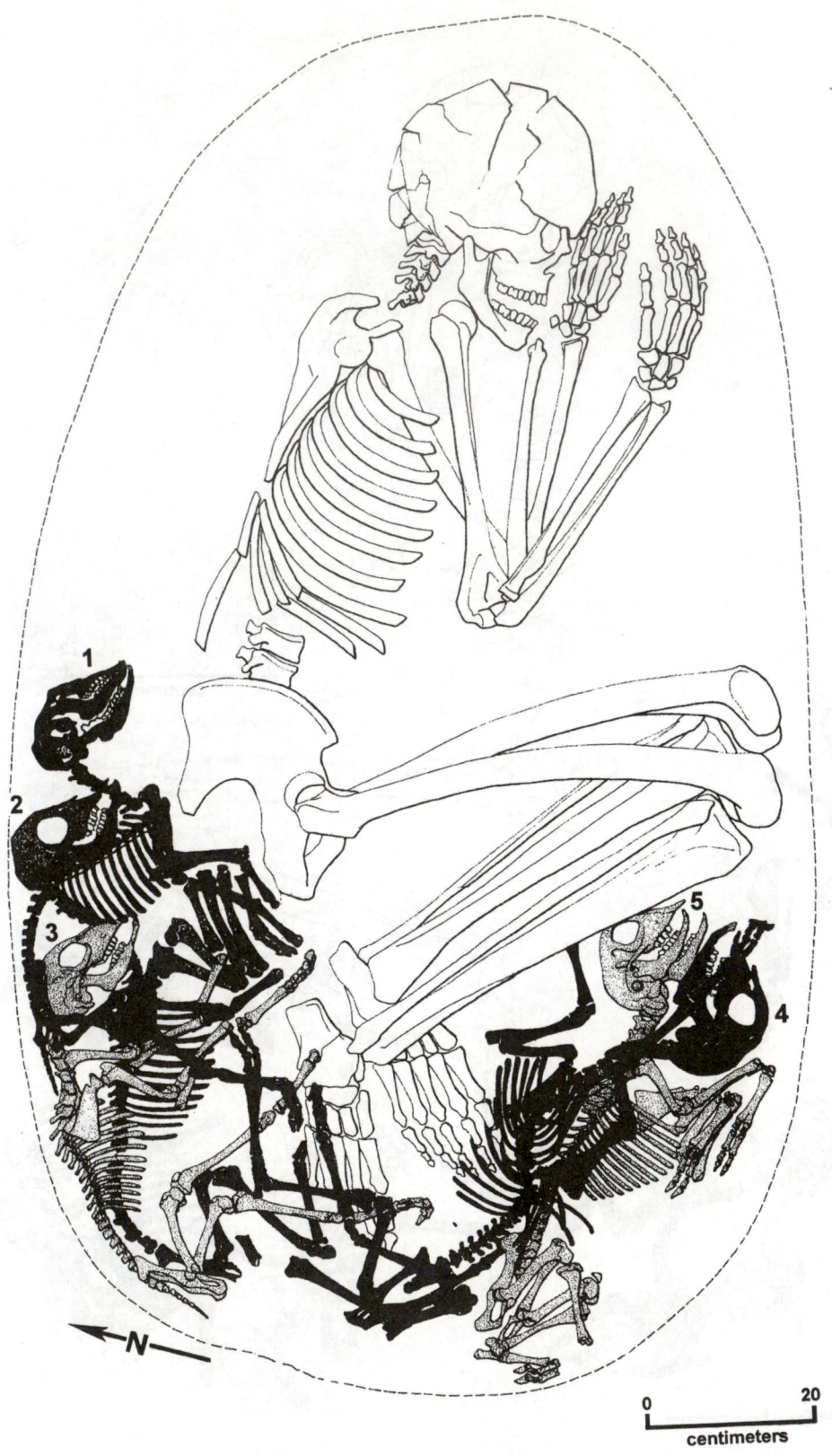

Figure 4.37. Burial 288 at Mehrgarh, Period IA, after Lechevallier and Quivron 1985: Figure 8

new style interments. The most elaborate of these have been termed "side-wall" graves with the interred in chambers sealed off from an adjoining trench by a mud brick wall (Figure 4.38). P. Sellier has a good argument for the position that the corpse was first placed in a pit and the brick work laid later. He noted, for example, that bricks are sometimes laid directly on the interred body, as in (Figure 4.39). He also found that the bricks were used to create a void in which the deceased was placed, a kind of open burial chamber as shown in (Figure 4.40). (Plate 4.22) MR3.180 is described as:

> MR3.180...an adult in standard position alongside a very eroded wall. At the feet were a polished stone axe, a large flint core, a piece of a red ocher lump, a bovine bone, and two fragments of a double-pointed bone tool, a third fragment of which lay in front of the thorax and provides evidence for intentional breaking of the tool before burial. Also associated were two turquoise beads (as a belt) and other bovine bone fragments (Jarrige, Jarrige, Meadow and Quivron 1995: 520).

Interment 114 of Mehrgarh Ib has been called the "Craftsman's Grave" (Figure 4.41). This person was evidently put to rest with the tool kit that he (possibly she?) made or used in life. It is a wonderful portrait of prehistoric life.

In general form these side-wall graves can be compared with other funerary structures in Iran and Central Asia, especially at Shahr-i Sokhta, which Sellier reviews in his text (1992:

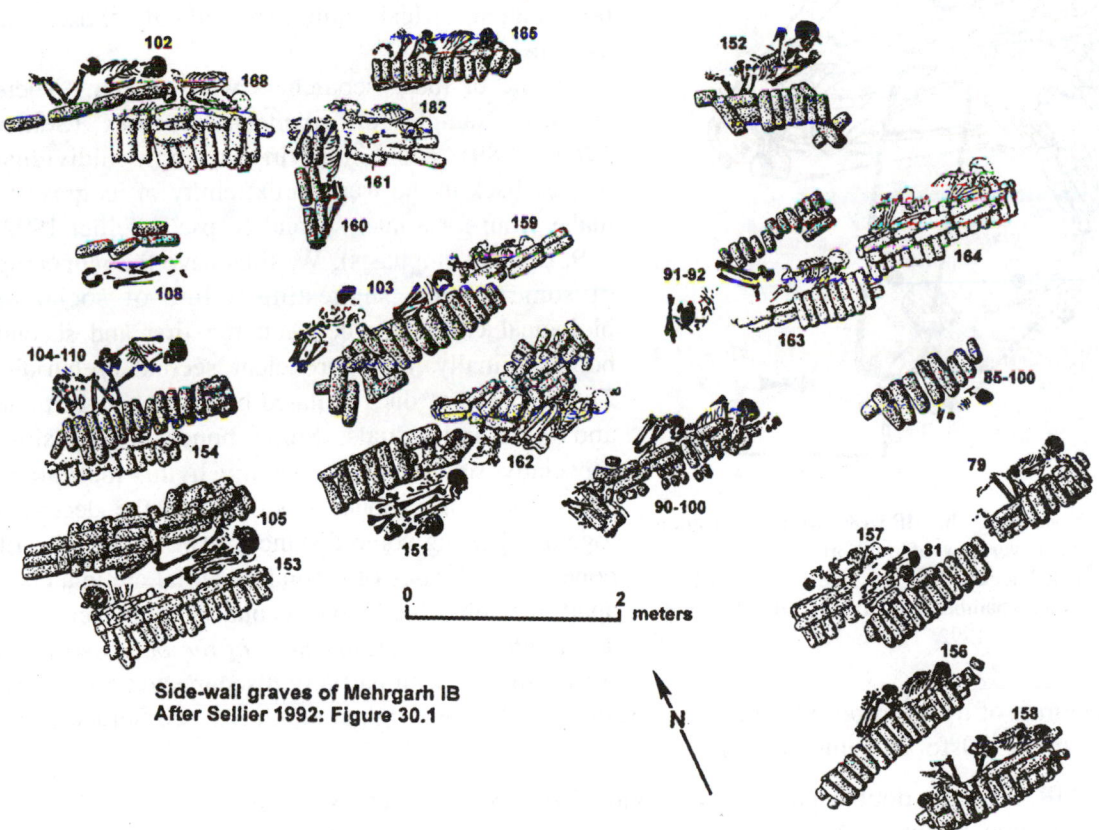

Side-wall graves of Mehrgarh IB
After Sellier 1992: Figure 30.1

Figure 4.38. Side-wall graves of Mehrgarh IB, after Sellier 1992, Figure 30.1

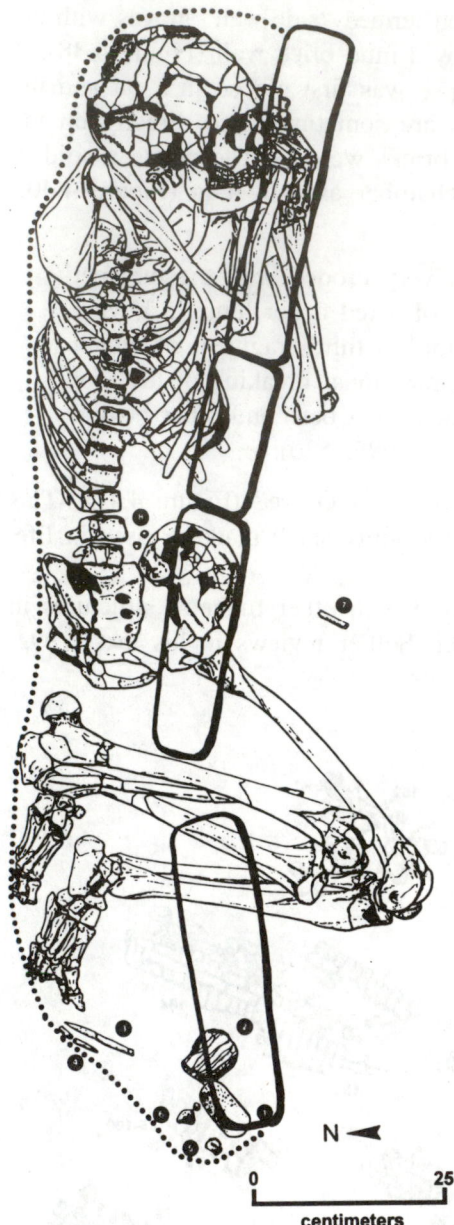

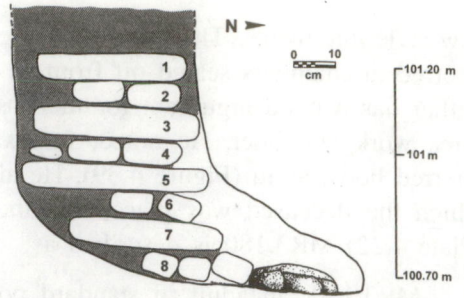

Figure 4.40. Cross-section transverse: north-south of burial MR3.167 with its eight rows of mud-bricks, viewed from the east at the level of the cranium; the limits of the access pit filled space with wall to the left and the funerary chamber unfilled space, with cranium to the right are reconstructed based on anthropological and archaeological data, after Sellier 1992, Figure 30.6

Figure 4.39. Tomb, MR3.180 with the position of the lower row of mud-bricks and reconstructed location of the side of the small funerary chamber dotted line, after Sellier 1992: Figure 30.3

263-64). Two important points complement this observation: (1) the graves at Mehrgarh Period IB are much earlier than the other examples and (2) the details of construction are also different among the exemplars and this form of interment is, at best, a general type; so general that there may be no actual historical connections among those who used it.

Some of these sepulchers were reused: "There are also examples of *compacted corpses* (Sellier 1985, 1989), each involving a single individual pushed back in the western extremity of its grave to make room for a later second corpse" (Sellier 1992: 259, original emphasis). We thus have the reopening of some graves, suggesting a line of social or biological continuity between the first and second bodies. Finally, there are clear secondary burials. These consist of disarticulated bones of between one and three individuals. Some bones are missing, especially smaller ones, but the living took some pains not to mix bones from two of the deceased together, leaving some distance between the piles of bones. "Three cases of secondary burial are in a class apart; they are exceptional secondary sepulchers with an *intentional re-arrangement of the bones* so as to 'reconstitute' (with partially disconnected bones) the appearance of a flexed primary burial..." (Sellier 1992: 259, original emphasis; see Sellier 1985, 1987 and 1990 for documentation).

MR3.166... a double burial of exceptional type with skeletons of one adult (166-A) and one infant (166-B), both incomplete and dislocated but with noticeable partial articulations and providing evidence for true secondary burial (reinhumation or

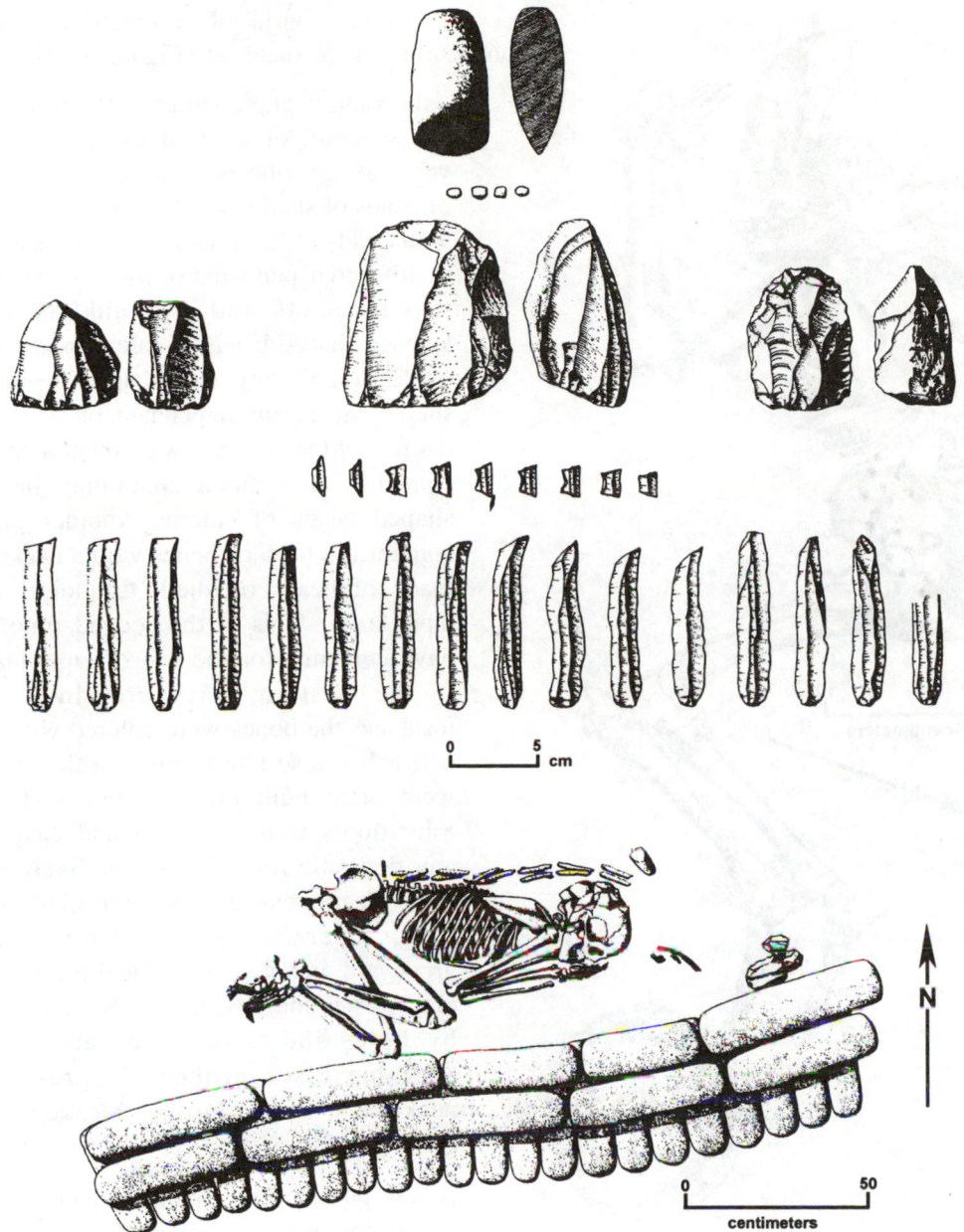

Figure 4.41. The Craftsman's Grave (114) with a polished stone axe, four turquoise beads, 3 flint cores nine geometric flint microliths and 16 flint blades, after Jarrige, Jarrige, Meadow and Quivron 1995: 261

inhumation after some body tissue decomposition). This burial revealed, for the adult, the interesting practice of an intentional arrangement of the bones in an attempt to reconstruct the skeleton in standard anatomical position (but facing north). In the process of redeposition and arrangement of the body, some important anatomical errors were made. For example, the left tibia-fibula was placed with the right femur and the lumbar vertebrae near the skull. A bitumen-coated basket was found at the western end of the grave (Jarrige, Jarrige, Meadow and Quivron 1995: 520).

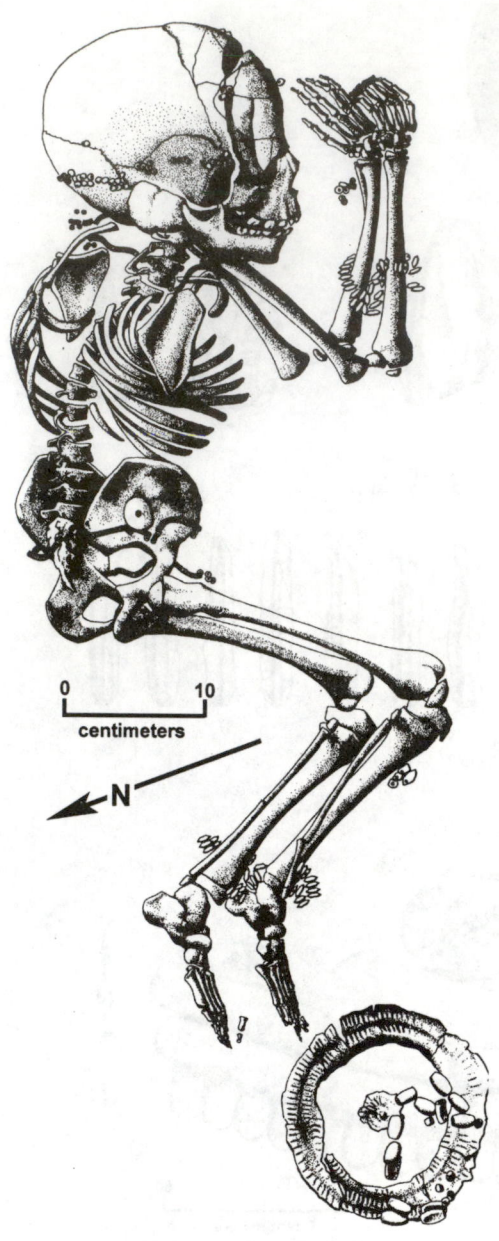

Figure 4.42. Burial of a child MR3. 121 at Mehrgarh, Period IB, after Sellier 1991: 78

And another burial of Period IB was of a child, and quite rich in material (Figure 4.42).

...the richest grave (tomb 121) contained the skeleton of a child of about seven years of age who wore a headband made of beads of shell and turquoise, a necklace with beads of turquoise and carnelian and steatite, four pendants of mother-of-pearl, two bracelets and two anklets with lozenge-shaped beads of calcite, and a belt made of 259 tiny disc-shaped beads of shell with a central pendant of shell. At the feet of the skeleton was found a basket coated with bitumen containing barrel-shaped beads of calcite. Another grave contained a heap of bones with a necklace made of beads of shell, turquoise, and lapis lazuli. This is the second time we have evidence for the use of lapis lazuli in the western graveyard. In a few instances the bones were colored with red ocher. It is also interesting that the graves were often built on ashy floors. These ashy floors were very flat and clean of any domestic refuse. It seems likely that such cleanliness can be identified with some funerary practice. Outside the graveyard area a small conical figurine in clay was found. Its upper part is pierced by holes indicating eyes and some applique discs probably represent a necklace (Jarrige, Jarrige, Meadow and Quivron 1995: 281).

A few burials were found in and among the compartmented buildings. These were generally just below the surface and some appear to have been disturbed by erosion. This, plus the paucity of associated artifacts makes dating these remains difficult, but they appear to date to Period II (Jarrige, Jarrige, Meadow and Quivron 1995: 456).

A good deal of research has been done on the teeth of the Stage One population at Mehrgarh (Lukacs 1983, 1985, 1989). These data do not distinguish Period IA from IB, but are interesting and the following can be taken to pertain to Stage One as a whole.

Lukacs found that the following pertained to the population as a whole:

1. dental fluorosis in permanent teeth of skeletal remains from MR2 and MR3 in association with a low prevalence of dental caries,

2. high frequencies of gross enamel hypoplasia and calculus formation in the MR3 permanent teeth,

3. the largest Tooth Crown Areas yet reported for permanent and deciduous dental samples (MR3) from prehistoric contexts in South Asia, justifying the use of the term megadont, and

4. a healthy deciduous dental sample (MR3) that is caries free, lacks evidence for fluorosis and gross enamel hypoplasia (Lukacs 1985: 146).

The water in the Bolan River has a good deal of fluorine in it and Lukacs concludes that this is the reason for the low rate of dental caries in this early food producing population (1985: 129). The significance of the enamel hypoplasia is not fully understood but may be related to the high amounts of fluorine, a degree of malnutrition and decreased calcium intake (1985: 128).

The shape and other morphological characteristics of the teeth of the people of Stage One at Mehrgarh are extremely interesting, as outlined in (Lukacs 1989). First they are large and have a complex micropattern with high frequencies of accessory cusps, wrinkles and stylids (1989: 85). This pattern is different from the simple teeth of the later inhabitants of Sarai Khola.

> ...it is very *unlikely* that the magnitude of difference between the Mehrgarh and Sarai Khola dentitions is explainable by evolutionary transformation. Breeding populations from different lineages are undoubtedly being sampled, and suggest that the people of Sarai Khola are genetically distinct from the Neolithic inhabitants of Mehrgarh (Lukacs 1989: 85, original emphasis).

In an interesting aside comparing the teeth of the human population of Stage One at Mehrgarh with those of Natufians Lukacs observes that there is: "...a distant genetic relationship between the Natufian and Mehrgarh samples. This finding suggests that these two groups are derived from rather different breeding populations and that gene flow between them was little and indirect" (1989: 86). This may be one more reason to argue against a simple diffusion model for the development of food production in South Asia.

Finally, Lukacs draws attention to the high frequency of shovel-shaped incisors among the inhabitants of Mehrgarh Period I (1985: 86). This is a distinctive feature of populations of eastern and southeastern Asia. He further observes that the people from Mehrgarh:

> ...contrast strongly with the European dental complex and share several dental features common with the Sundadont pattern of Turner...The Neolithic people of Mehrgarh may represent the western margin of South- Southeast Asian phenotypic dental pattern known as Sundadont (Turner 1979). The Neolithic/ Epipalaeolithic populations of Southwest Asia (Abu Gosh, Jarmo and Natufian samples) are clearly not Sundadont and belong to a different pattern with European affinities (Lukacs 1989: 86).

Lukacs presents this observation as a preliminary one; interesting but not proved. These Sundadont traits disappear from the population of Mehrgarh III (Togau Phase of Stage Two), another observation that appears to be correct, but whose significance is not well understood.

Summary

The inhabitants of Mehrgarh took some care in their burial practices and the children who died young (not necessarily infants) were obviously considered as worthy of generosity as were the adults. There may even be some glimmer of social differentiation among the interments of Mehrgarh.

Most of the evidence for long distance trade in Stage One comes from these interments, some of which seem to be comparatively rich. These far reaching contacts are indicative of the fact that the early villages of the Greater Indus Region were not small, parochial affairs, stuck in the narrow rut of their own surroundings. On the contrary, these people, and those in successive Stages, were engaged in contacts with the peoples around them and the more distant neighbors of these folk. The great "engine" of these contacts was almost certainly nomadism; pastoralists of many types, including bards, tinkers, traders and transporters. But there is room here for some touches of professionalism, even at the level of Stage One societies, especially for the harvesting of seashells and mining of some of the more exotic minerals, such as lapis lazuli and turquoise. Calcite is found in abundance in the Greater Indus Regions, especially in the black cotton soil of Saurashtra.

Stage Two: The Developed Village Farming Community and Pastoral Societies

Togau Phase	4300-3800 BC
Kechi Beg Phase	3800-3200 BC
Hakra Wares Phase	3800-3200 BC

One of the most remarkable findings of the last forty years of archaeology in the Subcontinent is the strong lines of continuity in prehistoric life there, from the very beginnings of village life to the present. The Subcontinent has been raided and invaded, conquered and colonized on many occasions throughout the 9000 years of history involved here, but the strength of the cultural traditions established there have always proved to be as powerful and as enduring as the customs brought by new peoples. Like China, the traditions of the Subcontinent have the power to absorb and alter new cultural traditions. We see with the transition from Stage One to Stage Two that this is a very old quality in Southern Asia.[8]

The Togau Phase is emerging as a key point in the culture history of the Indus Age. It was a period of significant growth in the population and settlements and had its roots deeply planted in the life and traditions of Stage One. The Togau Phase was also a time of innovation and change, with the possibility that new populations were entering the Greater Indus Region. Most of this information comes from Mehrgarh Period III, where there is a significant increase in the amount of craft activity and technological change. An analysis of the skeletons from a Togau Phase cemetery also indicates change in the biological constitution of the population. Thus, the Togau Phase is a time of both continuity and innovation, about which there is much to be learned.

Terminologically, the Kili Ghul Mohammad Phase used by Shaffer (1992: Vol. 1, 454, Vol. 2, 427) is very close to the Togau Phase employed here, which could be confusing. I have developed my scheme and terminology with the history of research in the Greater Indus Region in mind, using the paired notions of "previous and appropriate" in the selection of terms. The South Asian "Aceramic Neolithic" was discovered and defined at Kili Ghul Mohammad and it seems appropriate, to name the Phase after this site. Togau Ware is the critical ceramic in defining my Togau Phase; therefore it is the historically appropriate name for the Phase. Togau Ware was first defined by Beatrice de Cardi (1951) after her exploration of this site, which has never been excavated. Walter Fairservis' Kili Ghul Mohammad Black on Red Ware is a more broadly conceived ceramic type and fully encompasses Togau Ware (Fairservis 1956a: 256-57).

The Basis for a Chronology

Stage Two of the developmental model is composed of three chronological phases: the Togau, Kechi Beg and Hakra Wares Phase of Cholistan and adjacent parts of the Punjab. The absolute chronology for this Stage is given below. The Kechi Beg and Hakra Wares Phases are thought to be generally contemporary with one another. There has been a small amount of excavation at one Hakra Wares site, Jalilpur (Mughal 1972b, 1974b) and there are no radiocarbon dates for this Phase. All of the known Hakra Wares sites were founded on virgin soil, so there is no direct stratigraphic evidence for its relationship to the Phases of Stage One or earlier occupations. Surface collections from Azimwala Two, Dhuni, Sanukewala and Thori Wala have both Hakra Wares and Mature Harappan ceramics. Those from R. D. 89, Kuchanwala and Naharanwala have both the Hakra Wares and Early Harappan sherds. At Jalilpur, the small excavation seems to have evidence for continuity between the Hakra Wares of Period I and the overlying Kot Diji occupation (Mughal 1972b).

Radiocarbon dates for the Togau Phase are given on Table 4.17. The determinations from Mehrgarh do not seem to be very useful and may reflect the problems that this dating method has at the site. Period IV at Mehrgarh appears to fall within both the Togau and Kechi Beg Phases. The radiocarbon dates for this period do not clarify the situation and are not included in this discussion, although they are in Appendix B.

There is a short discussion of the chronology of Mehrgarh III in Samzun (1988: 127-28). It is in general agreement with the dates proposed here. The Togau Phase takes its chronology from the Rana Ghundai date; an unsatisfactory situation, but the only alternative for now. The chronology for the Kechi Beg Phase is underpinned by considerably more radiocarbon determinations, presented in Table 4.18.

TABLE 4.17
Radiocarbon dates for the Togau Phase (4300-3800 BC)

Lab Number
Calibrated Date
Mehrgarh III
BETA-2689
1Σ cal BC 5448 (5435) 5332
2Σ cal BC 5573 (5435) 5270
Rana Ghundai, Period I or Pre-Period I
P-2148
1Σ cal BC 4464 (4451, 4420, 4396, 4373, 4369) 4351
2Σ cal BC 4532 (4451, 4420, 4396, 4373, 4369) 4333
Mundigak, I,2-3
TF-1129
1Σ cal BC 3909 (3709) 3643
2Σ cal BC 3970 (3709) 3518
Mundigak, I,5
TF-1131
1Σ cal BC 3496 (3346) 3097
2Σ cal BC 3623 (3346) 2923
Mundigak, I,5
GSY-50
1Σ cal BC 2613 (2460) 2198
2Σ cal BC 2883 (2460) 1978

TABLE 4.18
Radiocarbon dates for the Kechi Beg Phase (3800-3200 BC)

Lab Number
Calibrated Date

Mundigak Period I,5 or II,1
TF-1132
1Σ cal BC 3694 (3632, 3550) 3384
2Σ cal BC 3785 (3632, 3550) 3358
Mundigak Period II,1
GSY-52
1Σ cal BC 1932 (1758) 1645
2Σ cal BC 2129 (1758) 1515
Mehrgarh Period IV
LY-1528
1Σ cal BC 2915 (2871, 2801, 2775, 2715, 2706) 2508
2Σ cal BC 3254 (2871, 2801, 2775, 2715, 2706) 2405
Mehrgarh Period IV
BETA-2690
1Σ cal BC 2019 (1926) 1789
2Σ cal BC 2130 (1926) 1748
Gumla Period II
P-1882
1Σ cal BC 2922 (2875, 2794, 2784) 2577
2Σ cal BC 3304 (2875, 2794, 2784) 2405
Gumla Period II
P-1812
1Σ cal BC 2860 (2586) 2493
2Σ cal BC 2878 (2586) 2459
Rana Ghundai Period IIIA,
P-2149
1Σ cal BC 3494 (3357) 3150
2Σ cal BC 3509 (3357) 3100
Sheri Khan Tarakai
OXA-982
1Σ cal BC 4762 (4468) 4334
2Σ cal BC 4942 (4468) 4040
OXA-1100
1Σ cal BC 4562 (4457) 4339
2Σ cal BC 4771 (4457) 4164
OXA-1003
1Σ cal BC 3934 (3709) 3639
2Σ cal BC 3982 (3709) 3385
OXA-1099
1Σ cal BC 3706 (3644) 3531
2Σ cal BC 3892 (3644) 3376
OXA-1102
1Σ cal BC 3639 (3610, 3512, 3392, 3389) 3366
2Σ cal BC 3702 (3610, 3512, 3392, 3389) 3136
OXA-1097
1Σ cal BC 3629 (3503, 3416, 3383) 3360
2Σ cal BC 3657 (3503, 3416, 3383) 3122
OXA-1098
1Σ cal BC 3629 (3501, 3424, 3381) 3353
2Σ cal BC 3664 (3501, 3424, 3381) 3103

Contd.

OXA-968
1Σ cal BC 3494 (3353) 3124
2Σ cal BC 3611 (3353) 3046
OXA-1002
1Σ cal BC 3357 (3297, 3237, 3173, 3168, 3107) 2930
2Σ cal BC 3504 (3297, 3237, 3173, 3168, 3107) 2905
OXA-1096
1Σ cal BC 3346 (3292, 3283, 3266, 3241, 3104) 3032
2Σ cal BC 3491 (3292, 3283, 3266, 3241, 3104) 2915
OXA-1101
1Σ cal BC 3346 (3292, 3283, 3266, 3241, 3104) 3032
2Σ cal BC 3491 (3292, 3283, 3266, 3241, 3104) 2915
OXA-1103
1Σ cal BC 2884 (2859, 2815, 2693, 2672, 2670) 2508
2Σ cal BC 2920 (2859, 2815, 2693, 2672, 2670) 2461

The twelve radiocarbon determinations from Sheri Khan Tarakai in Bannu include two which predate the limit of the Phase as estimated here and the latest is on the outside on the other end. The "middle" nine (75% of the samples) are within the estimate for the Kechi Beg Phase time range of 3800-3200 BC. Another date from Rana Ghundai IIIC backstops this series. The other dates are late for the chronology established here, but further study might find that this tells us of the regional non-linear chronology in the Gomal Valley. The dates from Mehrgarh and Mundigak are not congruent with the chronology proposed here.

Kapoto Damb and Kapoto Rockshelter in Baluchistan are assigned to the Kechi Beg Phase on the basis of ceramics (F. A. Khan 1959a: 189), but the radiocarbon date from the rockshelter (NZ-202) was "modern." It is a shame that the caves of Baluchistan have been almost totally ignored by archaeologists because they may be very revealing archaeological settings.

The Nature of Stage Two

The Stage of Developed Village Farming Communities and Pastoral Societies is a special time in the prelude to the Urban Stage of the Harappan Civilization. Three themes characterize this age: growth, continuity and geographical expansion. There is increasing sophistication of the potter's art and the introduction of the Togau, Kechi Beg and Hakra Wares ceramic assemblages are widespread and easily recognized. It is apparent from the study of settlement patterns that there was a vast growth of settled life in this region. The expansion is documented by an increase in the number of sites and by the spread of food producing peoples into the western deltaic regions of the ancient Sarasvati River in modern Cholistan. The Togau Phase is found in Baluchistan and adjacent regions. The Kechi Beg Phase is later in time, with the site distribution overlapping that of the Togau Phase sites. There are eighty-four Togau settlements and 256 attributed to the time period of the combined Kechi Beg-Hakra Wares Phases. This is very significant growth by Phases (thirty-three Burj Basket-marked sites, eighty-four Togau and 256 Kechi Beg-Hakra Wares). Enough exploration has been done to indicate that the figures are probably indicative of real sustained population growth over the Burj Basket-marked Phase. This should be balanced with the probability of the continued acculturation of peoples indigenous to the Greater Indus Region, to the new system of settlement and subsistence using domesticated plants and animals.

Continuity of the culture history of the Togau Phase can be illustrated in a number of ways. For example, there is continuity of settlement at a large number of sites: of the thirty-three Burj

494

Basket-marked sites, twenty-eight of them also have a Togau occupation. Of the eighty-four Togau sites, sixty-seven also have a Kechi Beg occupation indicating considerable stability in the location of villages. This type of continuity of occupation does not characterize the shift from the Early to Mature Harappan Stages, suggesting other historical concerns at this critical juncture of the Harappan Cultural Tradition.

Settlement Data for the Togau Phase

Data on settlement size are available for forty-eight of the Togau Phase sites, with a total net settled area of 168.27 hectares (Figure 4.43). This yields an average site size of 3.51 hectares. The smallest site is Rais Sher Mohammad in Jhalawan at 0.02 hectares (15 × 15 meters) almost certainly a camp site. The largest site is the Quetta Miri at twenty-three hectares, a huge mound, with many later occupations and this figure may not accurately represent the size of the Togau Phase settlement there. Moreover, the mound has been turned into a munitions storage facility by the military, which disturbed the place in a significant way. This also means that security around it prevents any kind of systematic research there.

The sites assigned to the Togau Phase are given in Table 4.19.

TABLE 4.19
Sites of the Togau Phase

Site Name	Province/State	District	Size in Hectares
Quetta Miri	Baluchistan	Quetta-Pishin	23.0
Mundigak	Kandahar	Kandahar	18.75
Q-32	Baluchistan	Quetta-Pishin	16.7
Periano Ghundai	Baluchistan	Zhob	14.4
Panju Damb	Baluchistan	Jhalawan	13.8
L-3	Baluchistan	Loralai	12.6
Phusi Damb	Baluchistan	Jhalawan	10.5
Duki Mound	Baluchistan	Loralai	6.5
Saiyid Maurez Damb	Baluchistan	Sarawan	6.3
Kashimi Damb, Wadh	Baluchistan	Jhalawan	4.0
Awaran Niabat	Baluchistan	Jhalawan	3.1
Anjira	Baluchistan	Jhalawan	3.0
Chimri	Baluchistan	Jhalawan	2.5
Benn Chah	Baluchistan	Jhalawan	2.5
Thok Valley One	Baluchistan	Jhalawan	2.5
Khakhar Buthi	Baluchistan	Las Bela	2.3
Belar Damb	Baluchistan	Jhalawan	2.25
Faiz Mohammad	Baluchistan	Quetta-Pishin	1.7
Sur Jangal	Baluchistan	Loralai	1.6
Zayak North	Baluchistan	Kharan	1.5
Siah Damb, Surab	Baluchistan	Jhalawan	1.5
Sardar Khel Damb	Baluchistan	Sarawan	1.5
Q-25	Baluchistan	Quetta-Pishin	1.5
Rana Ghundai	Baluchistan	Loralai	1.4
Kasiano Dozakh	Baluchistan	Quetta-Pishin	1.3
Kullu Kalat	Baluchistan	Sarawan	1.2
Isplinji One	Baluchistan	Sarawan	1.2
Tegak	Baluchistan	Jhalawan	1.1
Zidi	Baluchistan	Jhalawan	0.9

Contd.

Table 4.19 Contd.

Isplinji Two	Baluchistan	Sarawan	0.7
Baleli	Baluchistan	Quetta-Pishin	0.65
Q-17	Baluchistan	Quetta-Pishin	0.65
L-2	Baluchistan	Loralai	0.6
Jawarji Kalat	Baluchistan	Jhalawan	0.6
Kili Ghul Mohammad	Baluchistan	Quetta-Pishin	0.5
Old Balor	Baluchistan	Jhalawan	0.4
Sahib Khan	Baluchistan	Quetta-Pishin	0.4
Q-35	Baluchistan	Quetta-Pishin	0.4
Neghar Damb	Baluchistan	Kalat	0.35
Q-18	Baluchistan	Quetta-Pishin	0.3
Q-06	Baluchistan	Quetta-Pishin	0.3
Pir Haidar Shahr	Baluchistan	Jhalawan	0.3
Q-33	Baluchistan	Quetta-Pishin	0.3
Q-30	Baluchistan	Quetta-Pishin	0.2
Q-23	Baluchistan	Quetta-Pishin	0.2
Q-36	Baluchistan	Quetta-Pishin	0.2
Kuki Damb	Baluchistan	Jhalawan	0.1
Rais Sher Mohammad	Baluchistan	Jhalawan	0.02
Aidu Damb	Baluchistan	Jhalawan	
Ala Damb	Baluchistan	Jhalawan	
Bagh-i Kumb Damb	Northwest Frontier	Dera Ismail Khan	
Bundakhi Damb	Baluchistan	Sarawan	
Channal Kund Damb	Baluchistan	Jhalawan	
Chashma Murad	Baluchistan	Jhalawan	
Cheshma Damb One	Baluchistan	Jhalawan	
Damb Kulu	Baluchistan	Sarawan	
Damb Wali Mohammad	Baluchistan	Kalat	
Gar Mound	Baluchistan	Makran	
Ghannal Kund Damb	Baluchistan	Jhalawan	
Gorpat	Baluchistan	Jhalawan	
Hadi	Baluchistan	Jhalawan	
Jahan	Baluchistan	Jhalawan	
Kapoto Damb	Baluchistan	Jhalawan	
Kapoto Rock Shelter	Baluchistan	Jhalawan	
Kaptun Bra	Baluchistan	Sarawan	
Kasmi Damb	Baluchistan	Jhalawan	
Khoedada	Baluchistan	Zhob	
Khwaja Zabar	Baluchistan	Sarawan	
LB-13	Baluchistan	Las Bela	
Lena Singh	Baluchistan	Jhalawan	
Londo Damb	Baluchistan	Jhalawan	
Malghori Damb	Baluchistan	Sarawan	
Malki	Baluchistan	Sarawan	
Mehrgarh	Baluchistan	Kachi	
Namdai	Baluchistan	Sarawan	
Puchur Damb	Baluchistan	Jhalawan	
Rizvi Karuna	Baluchistan	Quetta-Pishin	
Sang	Baluchistan	Zhob	
Sibri Two	Baluchistan	Kachi	
Singen Kalat	Baluchistan	Jhalawan	
Singot Damb	Baluchistan	Jhalawan	
Surab Valley 'A'	Baluchistan	Jhalawan	
Togau	Baluchistan	Sarawan	
Zari Damb	Baluchistan	Jhalawan	

496

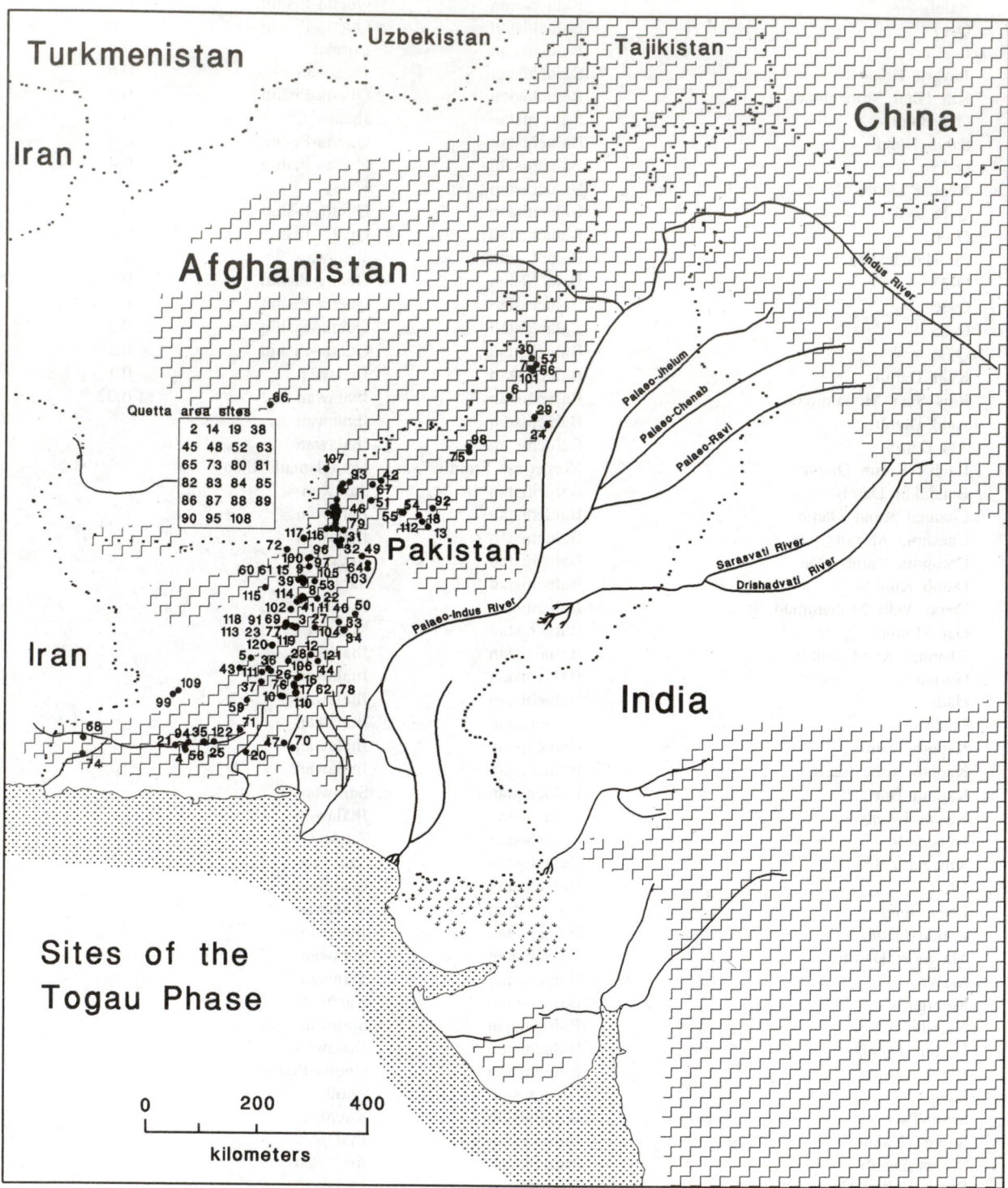

Figure 4.43. Map of Togau Phase sites

Key to Figure 4.43

1 Ahmed Khanzai North	41 Kapoto Rock Shelter	81 Q-18
2 Ahmed Khanzai South	42 Karezgai	82 Q-23
3 Anjira	43 Kargushki Damb	83 Q-25
4 Ashal	44 Kashimi Dainb, Wadh	84 Q-26
5 Badrang Damb	45 Kasiano Dozakh	85 Q-28
6 Bagh-i Kumb Damb	46 KechiBeg	86 Q-32
7 Baffai Khuarra One	47 Khakhar Buthi	87 Q-33
8 Benn Chah	48 Kili Ghul Mohammad	88 Q-35
9 Bundakhi Damb	49 Kirta	89 Q-36
10 Channal Kund Damb	50 Kotra	90 Quetta Miri
11 Chhota Kapoto	51 Kowas	91 Rais Sher Mohammad
12 Chimri	52 Kuchnai Ghundai	92 Rana Ghundai
13 Dabar Kot	53 Kuki Damb	93 Rizvi Karuna
14 Damb Sadaat	54 L-2	94 Rodkan
15 Damb Zerger	55 L-3	95 Sahib Khan
16 Dosia Khal Damb	56 Lak Largai	96 Saiyid Maurez Damb
17 Drakalo Damb	57 Lewan	97 Salu Khan
18 Duki Mound	58 Madak Kalat	98 Sang
19 Faiz Mohammad	59 Malasband	99 Serikoran Damb
20 Gajar Damb	60 Malghori Damb	100 Shahr Sardar
21 Gate Dap	61 Malki	101 Sheri Khan Tarakai
22 Ghuram Damb	62 Marki Mas	102 Siah Damb, Surab
23 Gorpat	63 Mata Ghundai	103 Sibri Two
24 Gumla	64 Mehrgarh	104 Singen Kalat
25 Gushanak	65 Mobi Damb	105 Site Near Kuki Damb
26 Gwani Kalat	66 Mundigak	106 Sorak Damb
27 Hadi	67 Murgha Mehtarzai	107 Spina Ghundai
28 Hamal Damb	68 Nazarabad	108 Sra Kala
29 Hathala	69 Neghar Damb	109 Sraduk
30 Islam Chowki	70 Niai Buthi	110 Sumer Damb
31 Isplinji One	71 Nundara	111 Suneri Damb
32 Isplinji Two	72 Nushki	112 Sur Jangal
33 Jahan	73 P-10	113 Surkh Damb
34 Jahan Northeast	74 Panodi	114 Togau
35 Jaren	75 Periano Ghundai	115 Toji Damb
36 Jawarji Kalat	76 Phusi Damb	116 Tor Ghundai
37 Jebri Damb Two	77 Pir Haidar Shahr	117 Tor Warai
38 K-1	78 Puchur Damb	118 Zari Damb
39 Kalat	79 Q-06	119 Zayak North
40 Kapoto Damb	80 Q-17	

An estimate of the population as revealed by archaeological data for the Togau Phase is given on Table 4.20.

TABLE 4.20
Estimate of Settled Area for the Togau Phase

Total Sites	84
Sites with Size Estimate	48
Settled Area of Sites with Known Sizes	168.27
Sites with Size Unknown	36
Average Site Size	3.51
Estimated Settled Area of Sites Without Size	126.36
Estimated Total Settled Area	294.63

Sizes given in hectares

When comparing settlement figures for the Togau Phase with the Burj Basket-marked Phase some very significant differences emerge. The estimate of settled area for Burj Basket-marked times was eighty-five hectares. In the Togau Phase it is 294.63, growth by a factor of 3.5. This is seen in the growth in the number of settlements, up from thirty-three to eighty-four, but also an increase of nearly a full hectare in average settlement size: 2.58 to 3.51 hectares. The Togau Phase is still a very long period 700 years, and there is room for the multiplication of net settled area due to villages shifting their settlement locations within this period of time, as well as other factors that confuse and confound the problems of estimating the size of prehistoric populations. But, even if the significance of these figures cannot be precisely defined, one thing seems reasonably clear: for whatever reason, there were more farmers and herders in Togau times than there were in Stage One.

Mehrgarh during the Togau Phase (Period III) is c. 75 hectares (Jarrige, Jarrige, Meadow and Quivron 1995: 250). This is out of line with what we know about other settlements in the region and may well reflect a process of lateral stratification at the site. Whatever the case may be, the size of Mehrgarh III has not been incorporated into the calculations for net settled area.

The distribution of sites by size is shown in (Figure 4.44).

There is also continuity in architecture, especially at Mehrgarh, where both compartmented buildings and domestic structures like those of the Burj Basket-marked occupation continued to be built, although in a new location to the south of the old village.

There is development in the potter's art, with the ascendancy of fine, hard, wheel turned, red ware ceramics that continue to dominate the assemblages of the Greater Indus Region through the second millennium BC. But, there is also continuity in types, which is best documented by the seriation diagrams prepared by Walter Fairservis for his excavations at Kili Ghul Mohammad and Damb Sadaat (1956a: 331-32).

The Site of Togau

Togau is a large mound in the Chhappar Valley of Sarawan, 12 kilometers northwest of Kalat City. It was discovered by Beatrice de Cardi in her 1948 explorations in Baluchistan. The site takes its name from a hamlet about a kilometer to the west of the settlement (de Cardi 1983: 23). At the time of discovery de Cardi found quantities of a fine, wheel made red ware; bowls usually about twenty to twenty-five cm in diameter, with a knife edge rim, slipped in red and painted in black. The designs were usually placed inside the bowl at the rim and consisted of small ungulates and stylized hooks. She saw a continuum in this and arranged the designs in four stages of evolution, designated Togau A-D (de Cardi 1951, 1965: 128-34) (Figure 4.45).

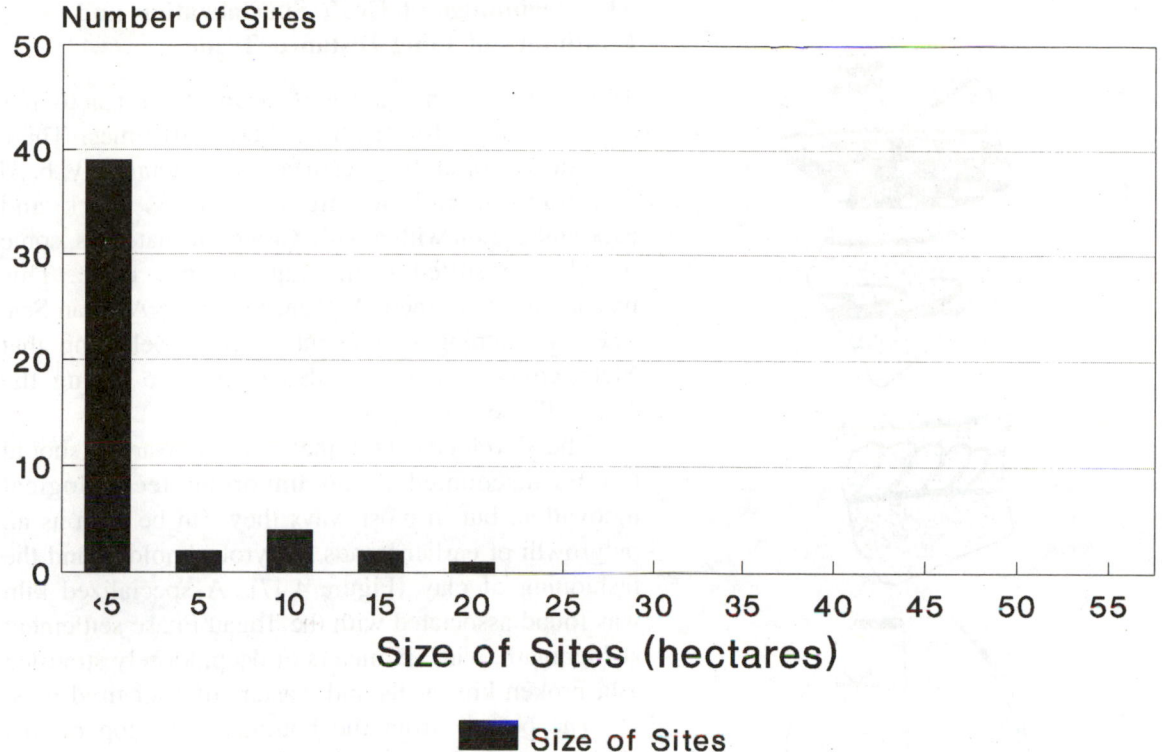

Figure 4.44. Histogram of sites of the Togau Phase

Well rendered, rather naturalistic ungulates are found in Togau A. Togau B is a slight stylization of these figures which are more curvilinear but still recognizable as animals. In Togau C, the bodies and legs of the animals disappear and all that remains are the hooks of their horns, but the execution of the design is still relatively precise. The Togau D designs are sloppy hooks around the rim. This stylistic sequence may be an artistic development through time, as indicated by de Cardi's excavated data from Siah Damb, with the realistic animals being the earliest (de Cardi 1965: 132); however, it has never been fully proven. The pottery type has been somewhat expanded by de Cardi (1965: 128-34) to include other forms and decorative motifs but it is also coincident with Kili Ghul Mohammad Black on Red Slip as defined by Walter Fairservis in the Quetta Valley (1956a: 256-57) (Figure 4.46).

Togau A

Togau B

Togau C

Togau D

Figure 4.45. Stylistic sequence for Togau A-D, after de Cardi 1951

There are some broad cultural parallels between the Togau sites and Central Asia, especially with Namazga I and II (Samzun 1988: 129-30). Some years ago Walter Fairservis also noted the similarities between the Togau Ware and the ceramics from Chashma Ali in north central Iran (Fairservis 1975: 156-57) (Plate 4.23).

500

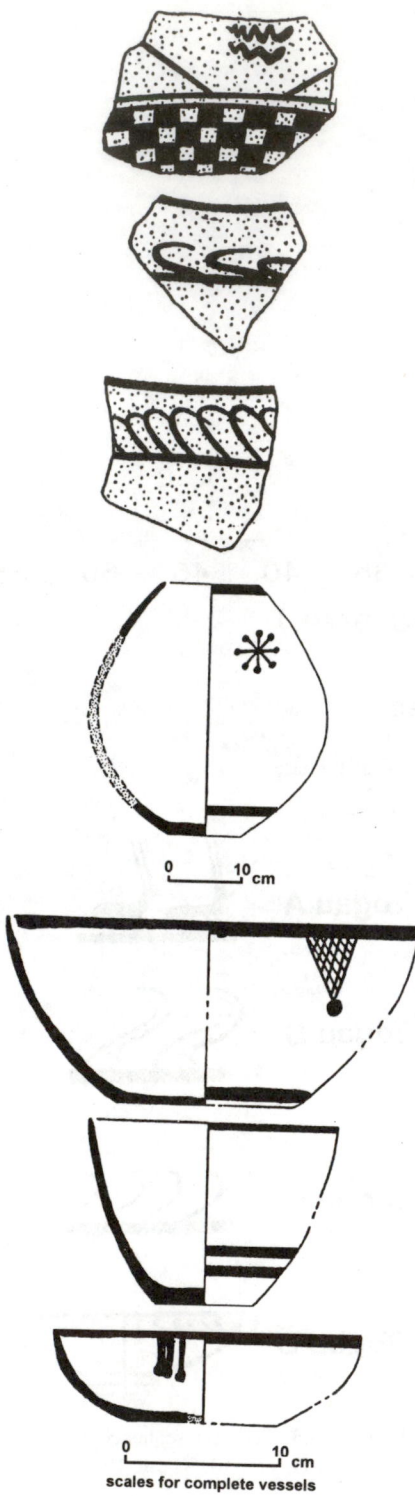

Figure 4.46. Kili Ghul Mohammad Black on Red Slip from Kili Ghul Mohammad III, Togau Phase, after Fairservis 1956a: 256-57

The Beginnings of Craft Specialization and Continuity of Long Distance Trade

There was a significant expansion of craft activities at Mehrgarh in Togau Phase, Period III times. There is evidence for craft specialization in metallurgy, bead manufacture and potting as well as work and experimentation with a wide variety of materials, some of which resulted from long distance trade. This reached from Northern Afghanistan to the Arabian Sea. There is nothing to prevent us from believing that Mehrgarh was a hub of this commerce during the Togau Phase.

The development of the "Togau Wares" should not be discounted as an important technological innovation, but in most ways they can be seen as an outgrowth of earlier trends in pyrotechnology and the fashioning of clay (Figure 4.47). A specialized kiln was found associated with the Togau Phase settlement at Mehrgarh, with six meters of deep, loosely stratified ash, broken kiln walls and wasters of over-fired pots.

The pottery from the bottom to the top of this sounding was found to be homogeneous, it is also evident that this thick deposit of stratified trash accumulated in a rather short span of time during which potters worked intensively in this area. Kilns, wasters, and ashes accumulated to form a ridge oriented north-south and rising several meters above what was then the surface of the plain...the total length of the ridge could have been more than 300 meters, all resulting from pottery manufacture (Jarrige, Jarrige, Meadow and Quivron 1995: 373).

Growth is also seen in the improvement of other crafts and technology; the development of metallurgy at Mehrgarh is one. A small amount of metal was found in Periods I and II which seem to have been native, cold worked metal, although some slag is reported from Period II (Jarrige, Jarrige, Meadow and Quivron 1995: 319). There is not much more copper in Period III but now there is evidence for melting, refining and possibly smelting copper. Testimony for this comes from a building of domestic type with three walls, and open on the western side. The floor and walls were burned, and the excavation team believes that it was used as a firing structure. This building was bordered on the south by an open area, filled with animal bones and earth, but also contained one complete and thirteen broken crucibles with

Figure 4.47. Togau Phase pottery from Mehrgarh III, after Samzun 1988: Figure 1, courtesy of Jean-Francois and Catherine Jarrige

copper dregs and stains (Jarrige, Jarrige, Meadow and Quivron 1995: 249). An important product of this new craft is an early example of a pin with a double spiral head. Three compartmented copper seals were found at Mehrgarh III along with unidentifiable fragments of the metal and one tubular gold bead is also associated with this period. Overall, copper is rare in Togau times and Mehrgarh is the only site where direct evidence for smelting, refining or melting the metal has been found.

A surface survey of the Mehrgarh III settlement area, which is huge, at ca. seventy hectares preceded excavation there. This inspection revealed considerable evidence for craft activity involving the manipulation of lapis lazuli, carnelian, calcite, garnet, turquoise, shell and bitumen. The materials on the surface were clearly waste products from workshops in the area (Jarrige, Jarrige, Meadow and Quivron 1995: 213). One of the areas had: "One micro-drill in phtanite, wasters, and fragments of lapis lazuli, carnelian, and steatite were found together with ornaments in shell, two fragments of rattle-like objects, and a few bone awls. Several stone objects such as grinding stones, pestles and flint tools also were recorded. One more exceptional find is a polished stone axe..." (Jarrige, Jarrige, Meadow and Quivron 1995: 320, see illustrations on

p. 229 and p. 266 for Mehrgarh IIB bead drills). The drills are a well-known type that have been found at other sites, including Shahr-i Sokhta, Mundigak, Amri and Ghazi Shah. This bead drilling technology was shared over a vast area, which begins in the Togau Phase and persists at least through the Mature Harappan. It might be that the spatial distribution indicates that it was a purview of a relatively small number of specialists, who travelled among sites, sometimes establishing permanent residence at one place.

Steatite "paste" was used for making beads at Mehrgarh at this time and the excavations have yielded an insight into how this material was handled. It was first heated causing the stone to become malleable. The craftsmen then squeezed it through a metal tube, slicing off a thin wafer bead (Samzun 1991: 68). A similar process for the manufacture of micro-beads was reconstructed from materials found at Zekhada, a site in North Gujarat (Hegde, Karanth and Sychanthavong 1982), although here the craftsmen used a true steatite paste of powder and water.

A shell industry using conch shells (*Fascolaria trapezium* and *Turbinella pyrum*) continues from Period II contexts. One of the bangle fragments of *Turbinella pyrum* was decorated with incised parallel lines (Jarrige, Jarrige, Meadow and Quivron 1995: 213).

Evidence for craft activity is not as impressive at Sheri Khan Tarakai in Bannu, but it was certainly there, including bead making using many of the same materials reported from Mehrgarh III as well as weaving (Farid Khan, Knox and Thomas 1991a: 58-9; see also Farid Khan, Knox and Thomas 1986, 1990a, 1990b, 1991b). Sheri Khan Tarakai, at twenty-one hectares, is also a large site for the times.

Mundigak, another excavated site of the Togau Phase, was founded at this time (Period I; Casal 1961a: 29-32). There is no particular evidence for craft activity there, but Mundigak would mature into an important settlement of the borders of the Mature Harappan.

It is also worth noting that many, even most, of the technologies that one associates with the Mature Harappan were put in place during the Togau Phase, which began 2000 years before the first emergence of urbanization in ancient India and Pakistan. There were changes and growth in this technology during the Mature Harappan, four of which were the digging of wells, the development of bronze, the manufacture of stoneware bangles and the drilling of very long carnelian beads. Much of this technology is a reflection of growth and development in existing ideas, of technologies put in place by the peoples of the Togau Phase.

Agriculture and herding were well established by the beginnings of Stage Two. Although it has not been possible to quantify food production, there is no reason to believe that subsistence surpluses were impossible. Following the lines of reasoning outlined in Marshall Sahlins' study of production in Polynesia (1958) it might be possible to see the beginnings of change in the social pyramid of settlements of this Stage, such as Mehrgarh III. This is predicated to some degree on a well institutionalized system of reciprocal exchange, but the broad regional distribution of Togau, Kechi Beg and Hakra Wares artifacts can be used as some documentation for such systems. This does not imply that we can reconstruct the social stratigraphy that would be associated with an archaic state, but some internal differentiation of the Stage Two society is entirely possible, especially given the sophistication of craft production documented at Mehrgarh.

Togau Phase Developed Village Farming Communities

Again the richness of Mehrgarh provides the best insight into the developed village farming community of early South Asia, but Sheri Khan Tarakai in Bannu is also part of the Togau Phase and represents one of the early mature forms of the village farming community. The expansion of Mehrgarh to the vicinity of seventy hectares may be significant, although there must be much lateral stratigraphy at the site and it is unlikely, but certainly not impossible, that all of the settlement was occupied at one time. Sheri Khan Tarakai is relatively large at twenty-one hectares, and there seems to be little lateral stratigraphy there.

The architecture of Mehrgarh III is based on mud brick (Figure 4.48, Figure 4.49). The same two basic kinds of buildings found in Period II, domestic structures and compartmented structures thought to be storage units, even specifically granaries, continued to be built. They were now separated from one another, however. The storage buildings had complex plans, the

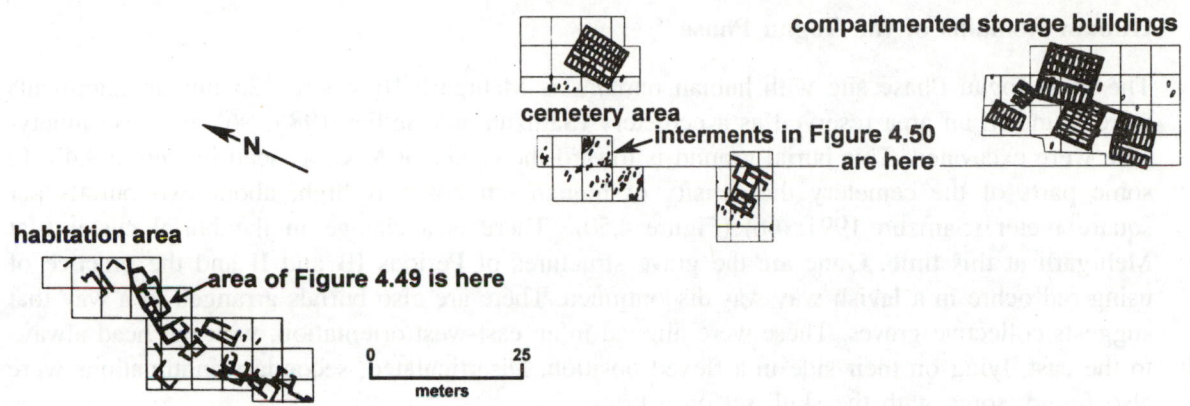

Figure 4.48. Plan of Mehrgarh III, Area MR2, after Samzun 1991: 69

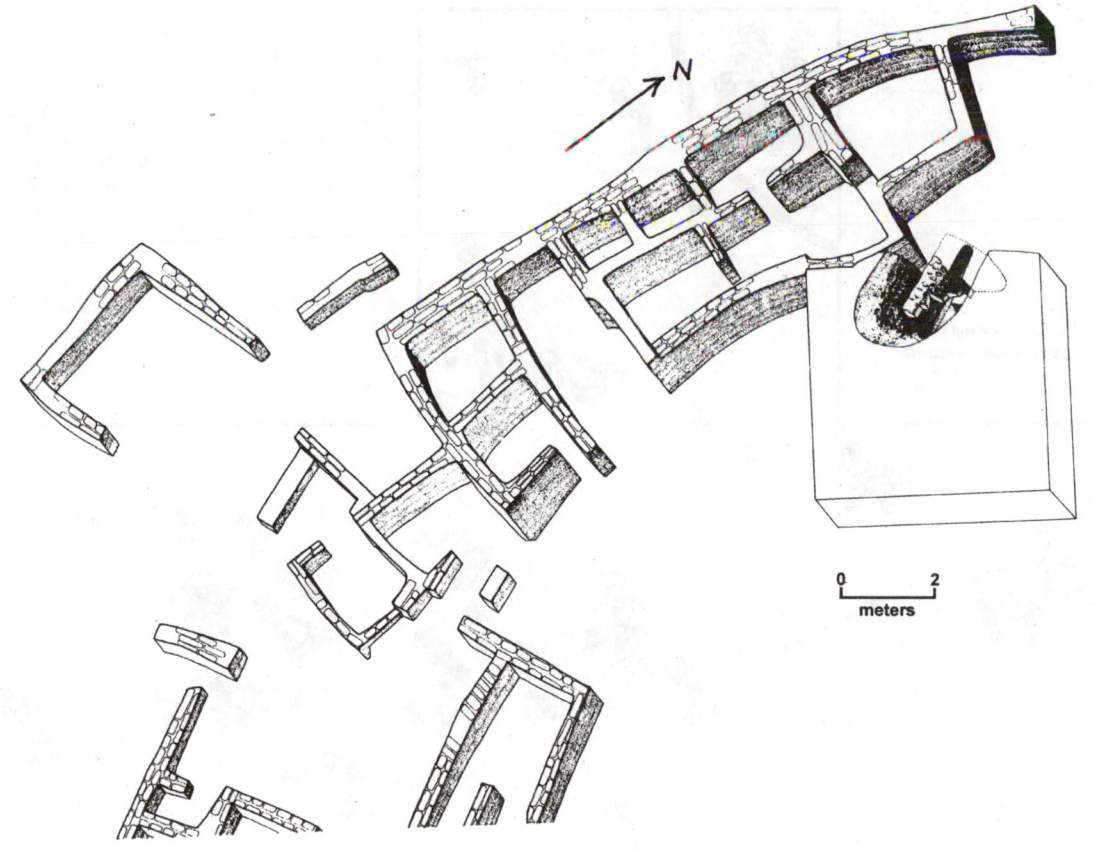

Figure 4.49. Isometric drawing of dwellings of Mehrgarh III, after Samzun 1991: 70

504

product of a community with a well developed social organization that may be indicative of a redistribution system (Jarrige, Jarrige, Meadow and Quivron 1995: 285). A relatively marked degree of social differentiation might be indicated by the scale and complexity of craft activities and long distance trade.

Architecture at other sites seems to have been less elaborate, based on mud and mud brick, often with stone foundations. Mehrgarh is the only site known, so far, that has produced a building that would have been anything other than a domestic facility.

Human Remains of the Togau Phase

The only Togau Phase site with human remains is Mehrgarh III where 125 human interments were found in an area reserved as a cemetery (Samzun and Sellier 1985: 96); of these ninety-nine were excavated. This burial ground is toward the center of MR2 as seen in Figure 4.48. In some parts of the cemetery the density of human remains was high, about two burials per square meter (Samzun 1991: 66) (Figure 4.50). There is a change in the burial customs at Mehrgarh at this time. Gone are the grave structures of Periods IB and II and the practice of using red ochre in a lavish way was discontinued. There are also burials arranged in a way that suggests collective graves. These were aligned in an east-west orientation, with the head always to the east, lying on their side in a flexed position. Disarticulated, secondary inhumations were also found, some with the skull set on a brick.

Figure 4.50. Core area of the Mehrgarh III cemetery, after Samzun 1983: 72

Dentalium shells were found in two graves, one a child's burial. A fragmentary compartmented copper seal was found with an adult and pottery found in only three graves. Other skeletons had necklaces or pendants made of lapis lazuli, turquoise, carnelian, and chrysoprase. Steatite beads were the most common ornament (Figure 4.51). The grave goods are not spectacular, but there is an indication that mature females took more with them to the grave than did mature males and immature humans of both sexes (Samzun and Sellier 1985: 113). The amount of craft activity at Mehrgarh at this time denotes a busy people, producing a great many products. They might even have been wealthy, but they apparently decided not to spend their wealth on the dead.

Samzun and Sellier (1985: 116) discuss continuities and discontinuities between the funerary records of Stage One and Stage Two at Mehrgarh. This is summarized as follows:

Continuities:

  bodies placed in the same position
  on the side
  flexed
  oriented east-west
  Similar ornaments

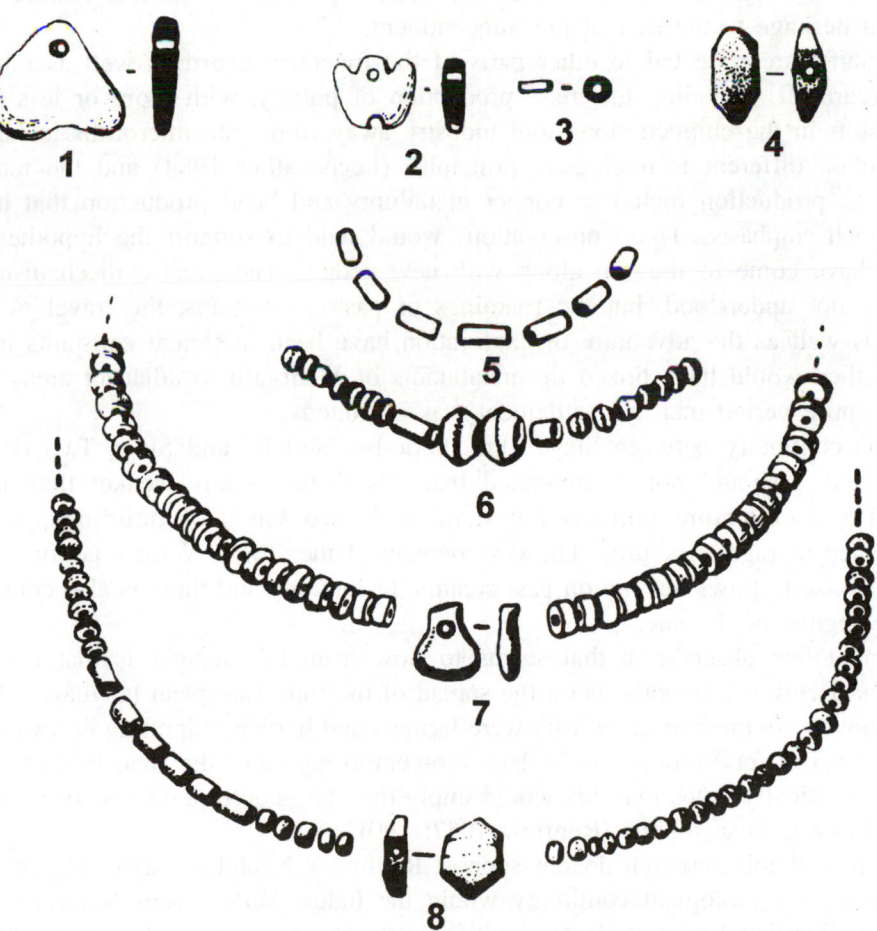

Figure 4.51. Ornaments from the Mehrgarh III Area MR2 cemetery, after Samzun and Sellier 1985: 107

Discontinuities:

Little red ochre in Stage Two interments
Wider variety of grave goods in Stage One interments
stone vessels
pottery
bitumen baskets
bone and stone tools
animal offerings
Side-wall graves in Stage One, none in Stage Two
All age classes in the Stage One burials, not true for those of Stage Two
No collective sepulcher in Stage One.

Coming at this theme of continuity and discontinuity from a slightly different data set, B. Hemphill, J. Lukacs and K. A. R. Kennedy have also found evidence for something of a discontinuity between the Stage One and Stage Two inhabitants of Mehrgarh (Hemphill, Lukacs and Kennedy 1991: 172-74). The inhabitants of the later Stage of the site share important affinities with the individuals in Mature Harappan Cemetery R-37 at Harappa, which taken together: "...bear close affinities to populations from the west, i.e., from the Iranian Plateau and the Near East" (Hemphill, Lukacs and Kennedy 1991: 174). Lukacs feels that the Stage One population at Mehrgarh shared little with this western population, but had features pointing to a biological heritage to the east of the Subcontinent.

These shifts are reflected in other parts of the funerary record as well as other evidence from Mehrgarh III, including the mass production of pottery, with more or less standardized shapes, a shift in the chipped stone tool industry away from true microliths to larger, bulkier types based on different technological principles (Lechevallier 1984) and the rather massive signs of craft production including copper metallurgy and bead production that have already received much emphasis. These observations would tend to support the hypothesis that new ideas may have come to the site along with new people. The precise mechanisms for these changes are not understood, but the roamings of pastoral nomads, the travel of traders and craftsmen as well as the adventure of exploration have been historical constants in this world region and they would have linked the inhabitants of Mehrgarh to adjacent areas on all sides during the entire period that this settlement was inhabited.

There is continuity between Stage One (Periods I and II) and Stage Two (Period III) at Mehrgarh, and it should not be imagined that this theme is any weaker than the one just outlined. The architecture remains the same with two kinds of buildings, including the compartmented storage structures. The development of the Togau Ware repertory of ceramics, while new in itself, draws heavily on past ceramic technology and there is also continuity in the subsistence regime of the site.

One immediate observation that seems to flow from this insight is that it would argue against Colin Renfrew's hypothesis on the spread of the Indo-European languages. He proposes that these moved via their speakers who were farmers and herders migrating eastwards following the development of food production in the north-central region of the Near East (Renfrew 1987, 1989). He specifically notes that this would imply that the people of Mehrgarh Periods I and II spoke an Indo-European tongue (Renfrew 1987: 190).

The results of this research do not support Renfrew's Neolithic Aryan Hypothesis. Rather than demonstrating biological continuity within the Indus Valley from Neolithic time to the dawn of the Christian Era, two discontinuities exist. The first occurs between 6000 and 4500 BC and is reflected by the strong separation between the two samples from Mehrgarh. While this discontinuity stands in marked contrast to the archaeological interpretation of Jarrige (1981, 1985; Jarrige and Lechevallier 1979) and others (Lechevallier and Quivron 1981), it accords well with archaeological evidence for increasing craft specialization, trade networks and ceramic similarities to the northwest with Kili Ghul Mohammed and Damb Sadaat (Jarrige 1982). This discontinuity also fits well with recent glottochronological studies which place the entrance of the Dravidian languages into South Asia around the 4th millennium BC (Fairservis and Southworth 1989; Gardener 1980; Southworth 1979), as well as current linguistic research that not only ascribes a common origin to the Dravidian and Elamitic languages (McAlpin 1974, 1975, 1979, 1981), but suggests that peoples of the Harappan Civilization were Dravidian Language speakers (Fairservis 1983; Mallory 1989; Parpola 1984a, 1984b, 1986). The second biological discontinuity exists between the inhabitants of Harappa, chalcolithic Mehrgarh, and post-Harappan Timargarha on the one hand and Sarai Khola on the other. This implies another discontinuity at some point after 800 BC but before 200 BC (Hemphill, Lukacs and Kennedy 1991: 173-74).

A third theme within the context of the Stage of Developed Village Farming Communities and Pastoral Societies is the expansion of the geographical horizons of these farmers and herders. During the Togau Phase, a settlement was established at Mundigak in southern Afghanistan within the drainage system of the Helmand River, but the most dramatic shift was eastwards into the drainage of the ancient, now dry, Sarasvati Valley by the peoples of the Hakra Wares. The old Sarasvati River is called the "Hakra" in Pakistan and the "Ghaggar" in India. The former Princely State of Bahawalpur was centered on the Hakra drainage, in a larger region also known as "Cholistan" or "Desert Country" in the local vernacular.

The Later Phases of the Developed Village Farming Community and Pastoral Societies

The later Phases of developmental Stage Two, the Kechi Beg and Hakra Wares Phases, represent continued ontological growth with consolidation, rather than development, of technology. These Phases also mark the beginnings of regionalism in the Indus Age. There is not an especially good fit with the Domain structure of the Mature Harappan, with sites confined to the hills and adjacent plains of the Kulli and Northwestern Regions, at least prior to Hakra Wares times. There is the first evidence for the movement of significant numbers of farmers and herders out of the old "Neolithic home land" of Baluchistan and its eastern piedmonts, across the Indus River into the western drainage of the Sarasvati River. This expansion was anticipated by the appearance of herders on the eastern fringes of the Thar Desert as early as Kili Ghul Mohammad and Burj Basket-marked times. This was noted at the site of Bagor (Misra 1973a) which seems to be of a separate tradition, but was none the less an early camp in the region. Kechi Beg settlements are found in the Kulli and Northwestern Regions as well as the plains of the Indus Valley adjacent to them. But, at the same time a large number of farmers and herders appear to have settled the eastern drainage of the ancient Sarasvati River, well away from the Kechi Beg zone. The remains of these people were first found by M. R. Mughal during his remarkable exploration of Cholistan and he has given the name "Hakra Wares" to this Phase (Mughal 1982, 1997). It is worth reiterating that none of Mughal's Hakra Wares sites in Cholistan have been excavated, but there is a small exposure of this material at Jalilpur (Mughal 1972b). Settlements of the Hakra Wares Phase extend into modern India with one site at RD 89 (Dalal 1981).

Settlements of the Kechi Beg and Hakra Wares Phases

There are 256 sites attributed to the contemporaneous Kechi Beg/Hakra Wares Phase. The Kechi Beg sites account for 153 settlements, of which twenty-four have been excavated and eighty-four have settlement size information (Figure 4.52, Figure 4.53). This totals 304.52 hectares of

508

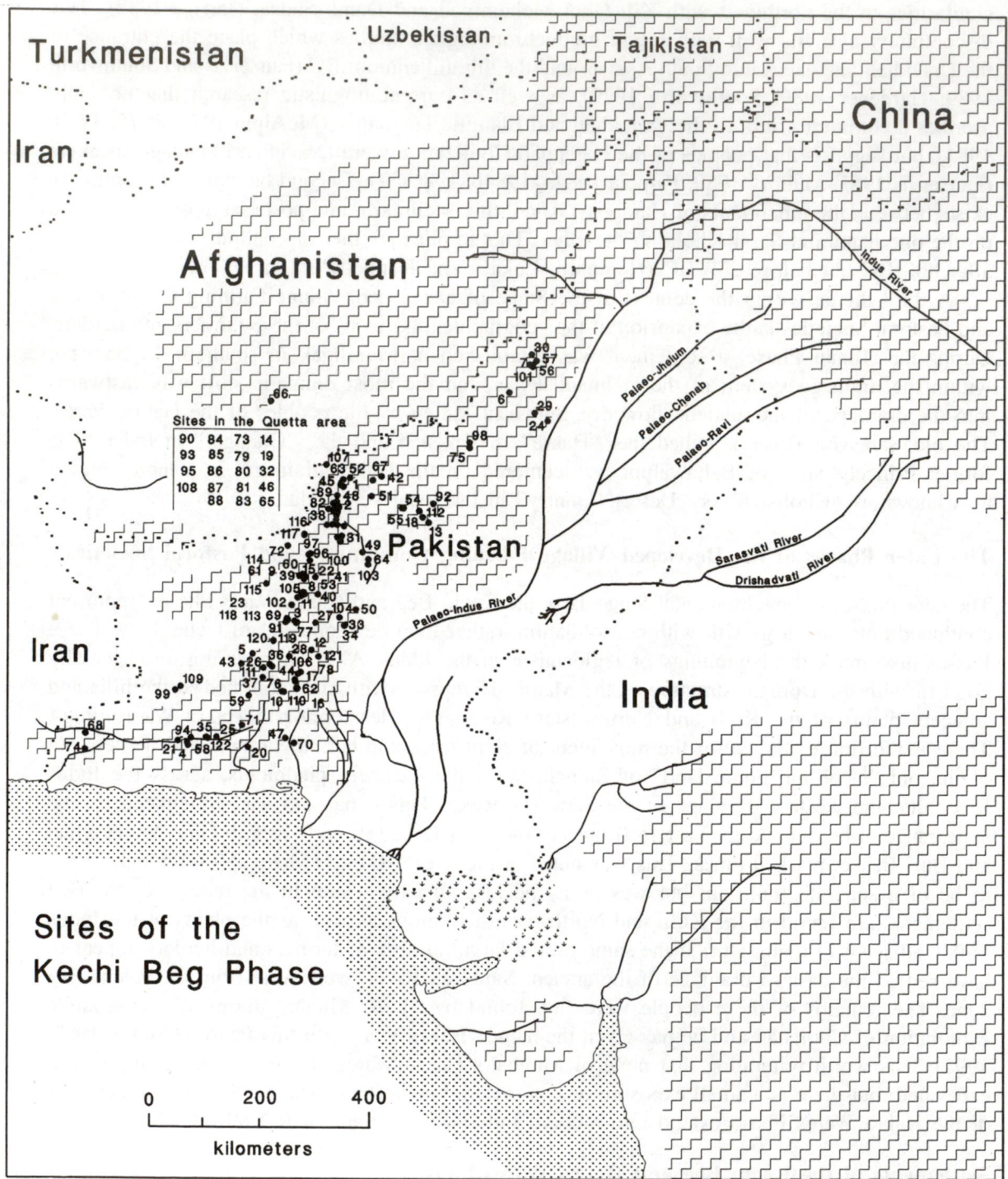

Figure 4.52. Map of Kechi Beg Phase sites

Key to Figure 4.52

1	Ahmed Khanzai North	42	Karezgai	83	Q-25
2	Ahmed Khanzai South	43	Kargushki Damb	84	Q-26
3	Anjira	44	Kashimi Damb, Wadh	85	Q-28
4	Ashal	45	Kasiano Dozakh	86	Q-32
5	Badrang Damb	46	Kechi Beg	87	Q-33
6	Bagh-i Kumb Damb	47	Khakhar Buthi	88	Q-35.
7	Barrai Khuarra One	48	Kili Ghul Mohammad	89	Q-36
8	Benn Chah	49	Kirta	90	Quetta Miri
9	Bundakhi Damb	50	Kotra	91	Rais Sher Mohammad
10	Channal Kund Damb	51	Kowas	92	Rana Ghundai
11	Chhota Kapoto	52	Kuchnai Ghundai	93	Rizvi Karuna
12	Chimri	53	Kuki Dainb	94	Rodkan
13	Dabar Kot	54	L-2	95	Sahib Khan
14	Damb Sadaat	55	L-3	96	Saiyid Maurez Damb
15	Damb Zerger	56	Lak Largai	97	Salu Khan
16	Dosia Khal Damb	57	Lewan	98	Sang
17	Drakalo Damb	58	Madak Kalat	99	Serikoran Damb
18	Duki Mound	59	Malasband	100	Shahr Sardar
19	Faiz Mohammad	60	Malghori Damb	101	Sheri Khan Tarakai
20	Gajar Damb	61	Malki	102	Siah Damb, Surab
21	Gate Dap	62	Marki Mas	103	Sibri Two
22	Ghuram Damb	63	Mata Ghundai	104	Singen-Kalat
23	Gorpat	64	Mehrgarh	105	Site Near Kuki Damb
24	Gumia	65	MobiDamb	106	Sorak Damb
25	Gushanak	66	Mundigak	107	Spina Ghundai
26	Gwani Kalat	67	Murgha Mehtarzai	108	Sra Kala
27	Hadi	68	Nazarabad	109	Sraduk
28	HamaiDamb	69	Neghar Dainb	110	Sumer Dainb
29	Hathala	70	Niai Buthi	111	Suneri Damb
30	Islam Chowki	71	Nundara	112	Sur Jangal
31	Isplinji One	72	Nushki	113	Surkh Damb
32	Isplinji Two	73	P-10	114	Togau
33	Jahan	74	Panodi	115	Toji Damb
34	Jahan Northeast	75	Periano Ghundai	116	Tor Ghundai
35	Jaren	76	Phusi Damb	117	Tor Warai
36	Jawarji Kalat	77	Pir Haidar Shahr	118	Zari Damb
37	Jebri Damb Two	78	Puchur Damb	119	Zayak North
38	K-1	79	Q-06	120	Zayak Southeast
39	Kalat	80	Q-17	121	Zidi
40	Kapoto Dainb	81	Q-18	122	Zik
41	Kapoto Rock Shelter	82	Q-23		

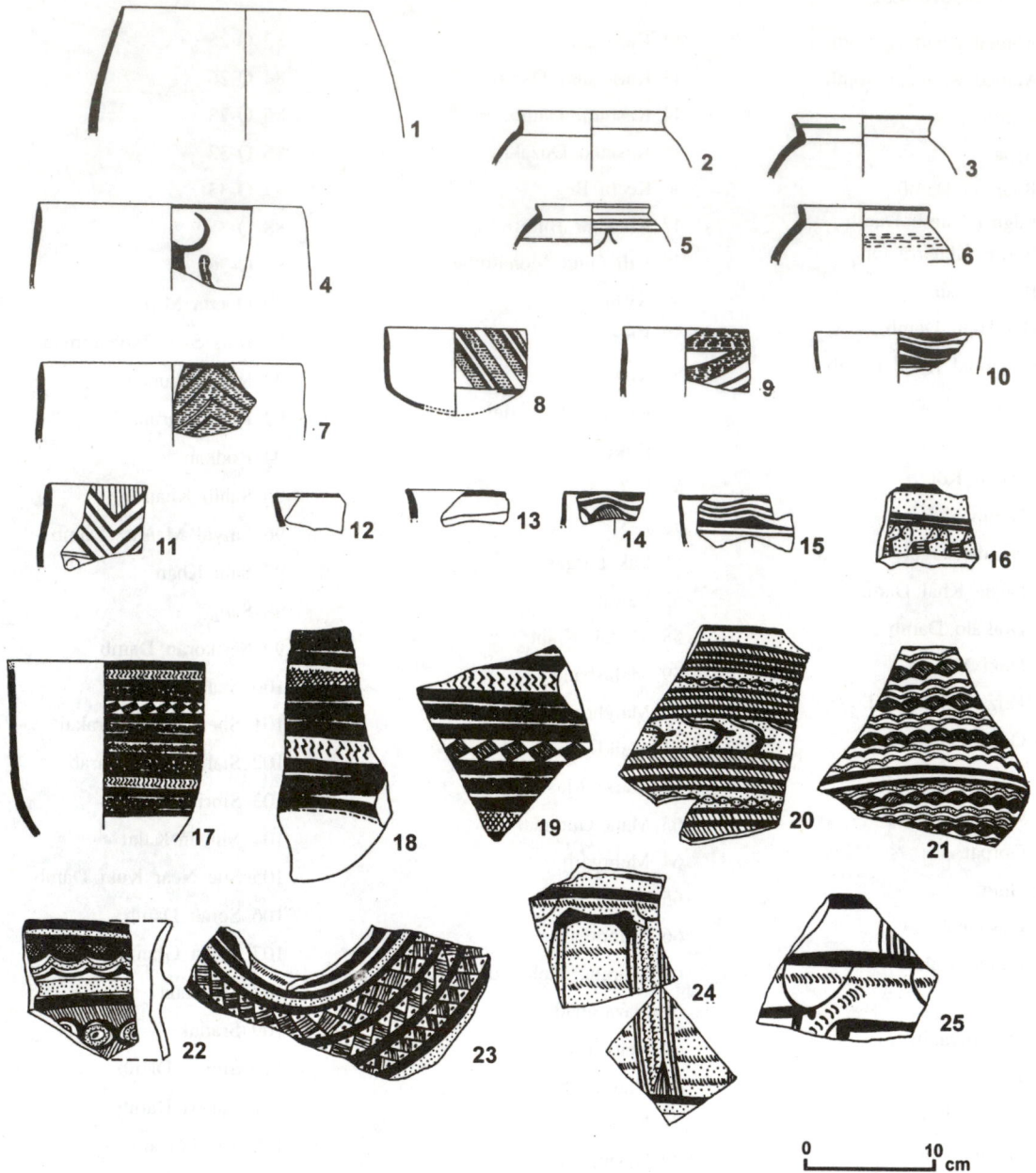

Figure 4.53. Ceramics of the Kechi Beg Phase

settled area for an average site size of 3.63 hectares, just a little larger than the Togau Phase average of 3.51 hectares. The smallest Kechi Beg site is Rais Sher Mohammad 0.02 hectares; undoubtedly a camp. The largest is Dabar Kot at 24.3 hectares, and the next is the Quetta Miri (23.0 hectares). These are both sites with several later occupations and so these dimensions might not reflect the protohistoric occupation. Thus, the largest site of the period seems to have been in the vicinity of twenty hectares, at least in the western zone.

The important theme for the Kechi Beg site data seems to be a growth in the number of settlements, not settlement size. This is especially true when the Hakra Wares Phase sites are added since there are 103 of these bringing the total known settlements to 256 from only eighty-four Togau Phase sites. This is, once again, growth by a factor of three.

Three sites of the Kechi Beg Phase have been selected for short descriptions, beginning with the type site itself.[9]

The distribution of Kechi Beg Phase sites by size is shown in (Figure 4.54).

The Site of Kechi Beg, or Q-14

Kechi Beg

Kechi Beg (Q-14) is a small, ninety by fifteen meter (0.5 hectare) low mound about half the distance between Damb Sadaat and Quetta City, just to the west of the Bolan Highway (Fairservis 1956a: 218, 219, 222). The so-called "Karez Site," Q-13 is opposite the Kechi Beg on the other side of the highway. Kechi Beg was excavated by Walter A. Fairservis, Jr. and Howard Stoudt as part of the Second Afghan Expedition from the American Museum of Natural History. The Expedition was in the field for ten months, between August 1950 and May 1951.

The site had a single period of occupation during the Kechi Beg Phase, which was also found at Kili Ghul Mohammad (Period IV) and Damb Sadaat (Period I). The excavation team sank a single trench eight by three meters. Virgin soil was reached at about minus 2.75 meters (Figure 4.55).

There were two building levels at Kechi Beg, both of which were associated with the Kechi Beg Wares and the other ceramics characteristic of the Kechi Beg Phase (Figure 4.56, Figure 4.57). Given the limited exposure, little can be said of the meaning of the architecture that was found (Fairservis 1956a: 219, Figure 13).

Kechi Beg is a good example of a small, single component settlement in the uplands of Baluchistan. It offers a contrast in settlement practices if compared to places like the Quetta Miri, Damb Sadaat and Kili Ghul Mohammad. The annual pulse of transhumant movement

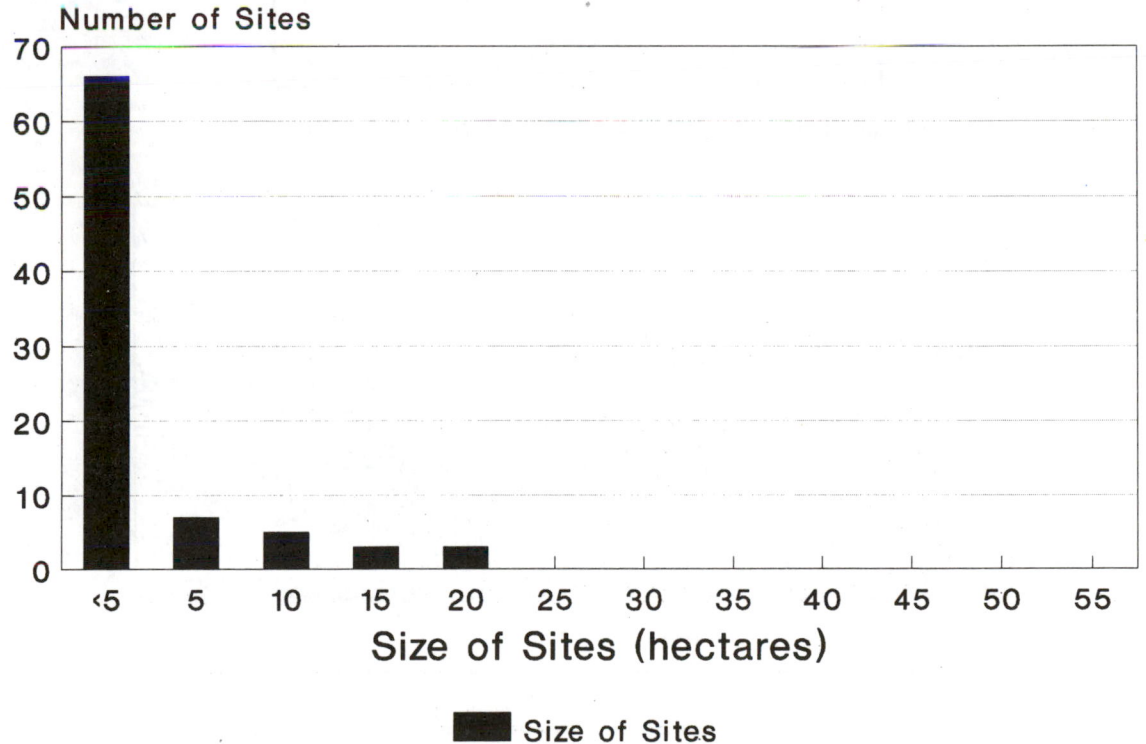

Figure 4.54. Histogram of site sizes for the Kechi Beg Phase

512

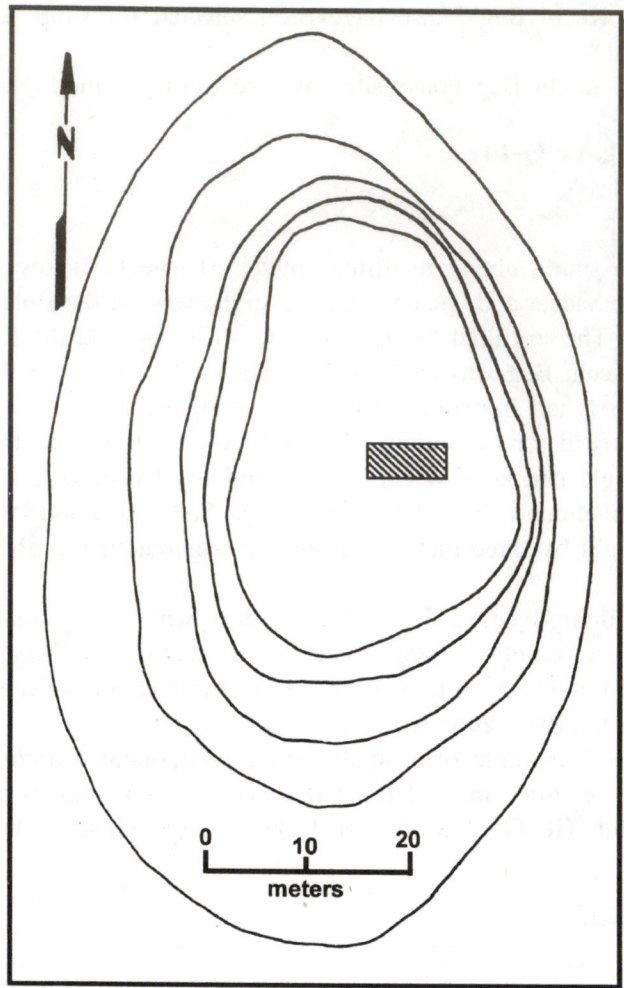

Figure 4.55. Plan of Kechi Beg, after Fairservis 1956a: 204, Q-14

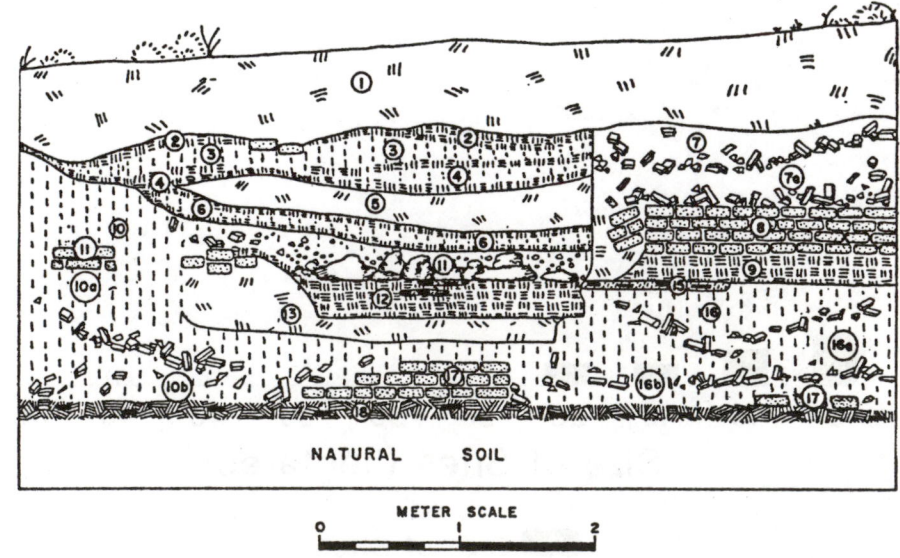

Figure 4.56. Section of Kechi Beg excavation after Fairservis 1956a: 219

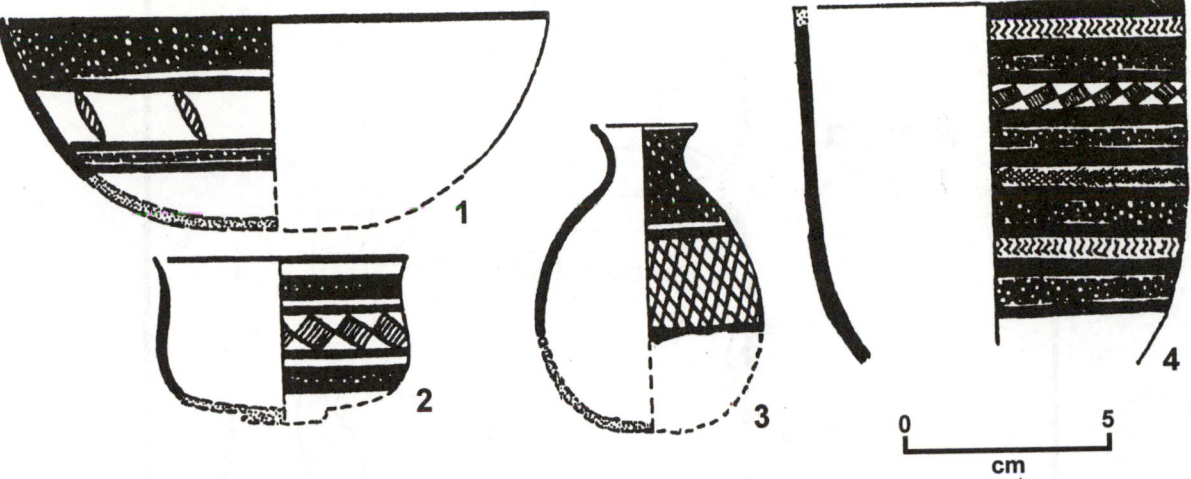

Figure 4.57. Ceramics from Kechi Beg, after Fairservis 1956a: 261

between the Indus Plains and Baluchistan is suggested by these remains and the other twenty-nine Kechi Beg sites in the Quetta/Pishin Valley.

The Site of Anjira

The mound at Anjira in the Surab area of Kalat is a three hectare mound with five periods of occupation (de Cardi 1965) (Figure 4.58). It was excavated in the summer of 1957 by Beatrice de Cardi, with the support of the Royal Asiatic Society. She discovered the site, along with Togau, during her 1947 survey in the region (de Cardi 1950, 1951, 1959, 1964, 1965, 1983, 1984). The site is low and inconspicuous, lying on the eastern bank of the Anjira River, a tributary to the Mula River which is a route onto the western Kachi Plain and the Mehrgarh area.

Three trenches were opened (de Cardi 1965: 96-9):

Trench I was a square, approximately four meters on a side. It was placed on the river side of the central part of the mound, sited to enable de Cardi to clear a room in the angle walls visible on the surface. Virgin soil was reached at ca. minus two meters.

Trenches II and III were again on the river side of the site, but in the northern section. Trench II was ca. 4.25 meters square and was dug to a depth of two meters, when sterile gravel was reached. Trench III seems to have been about the same size as number II, and was adjacent to it.

The Cultural Sequence at Anjira (de Cardi 1965: 100-03) involves three principal periods of occupation.

Period I (Burj Basket-marked Phase) is thought to have been the settlement of pastoral nomads and was located on both trenches I and II. It rested on virgin soil and consisted of ca. 70 cm. of ashy earth with a few stones that appeared to be domestic rubbish. No bricks or post holes were found. The pottery consisted of Kili Ghul Mohammad Red Ware, and well made grey and tan wares.

De Cardi notes that this deposit is, "...probably the domestic rubbish of a nomadic community" (1965: 101). This occupation is the equivalent to Kili Ghul Mohammad, Period II, as well as Period II at Mehrgarh.

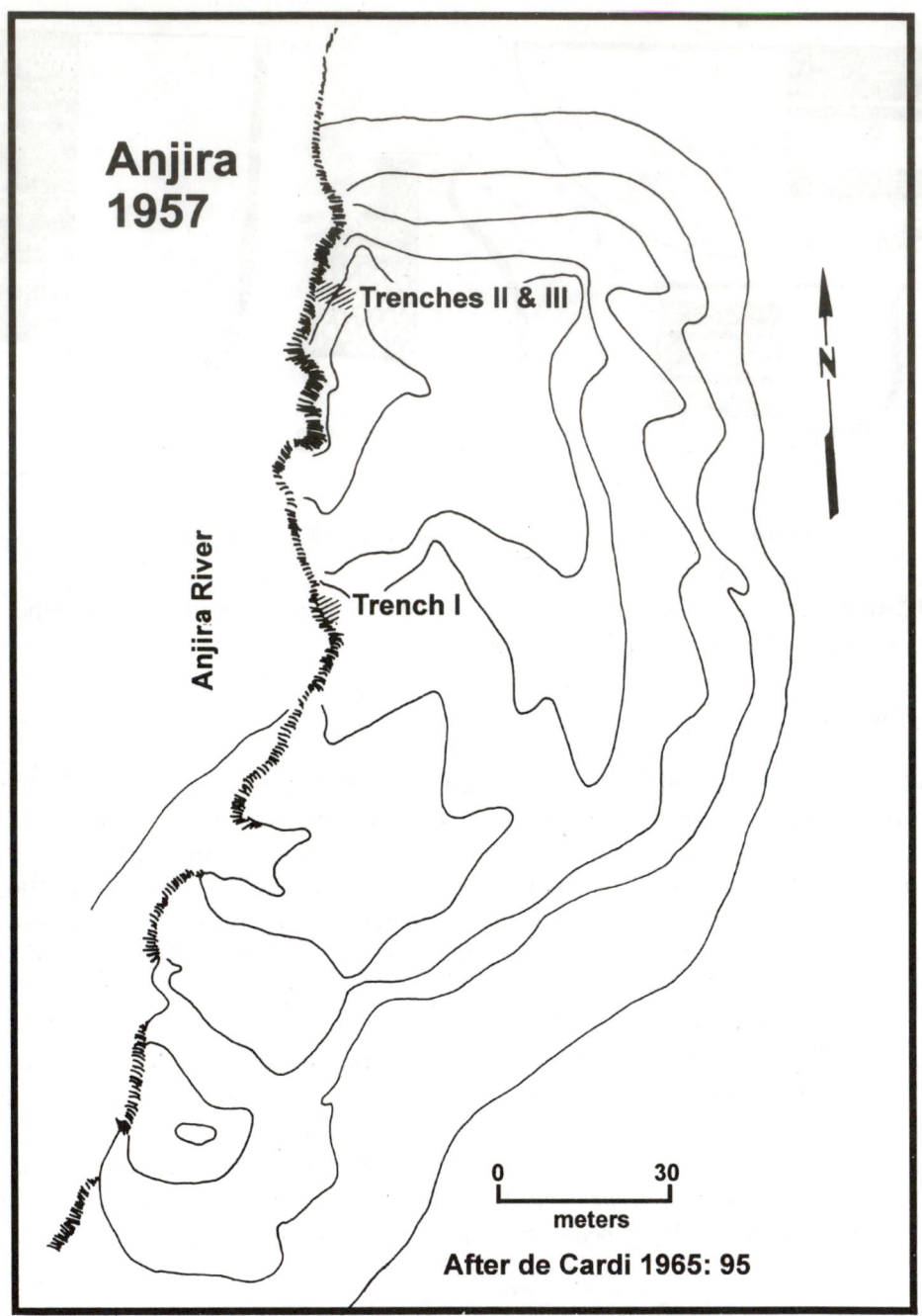

Figure 4.58. Site Plan of Anjira, after de Cardi 1956: Figure 6

Period II (Togau Phase) has the characteristic Togau or Kili Ghul Mohammad Black on Red Ware. Some suggestion of architecture comes from the use of rounded boulders for foundations and filling, possibly of mud brick. It was found in Trenches I and II and is comparable to Kili Ghul Mohammad, Period III and Siah Damb, Surab Period I.

Period III (Kechi Beg Phase) is a complex occupation with Kechi Beg ceramics, along with the related Zari Ware (de Cardi 1965: 139). Other ceramics include the continuation of the Basket-marked Ware and Togau, and the introduction of the important Nal ceramic, especially as it is

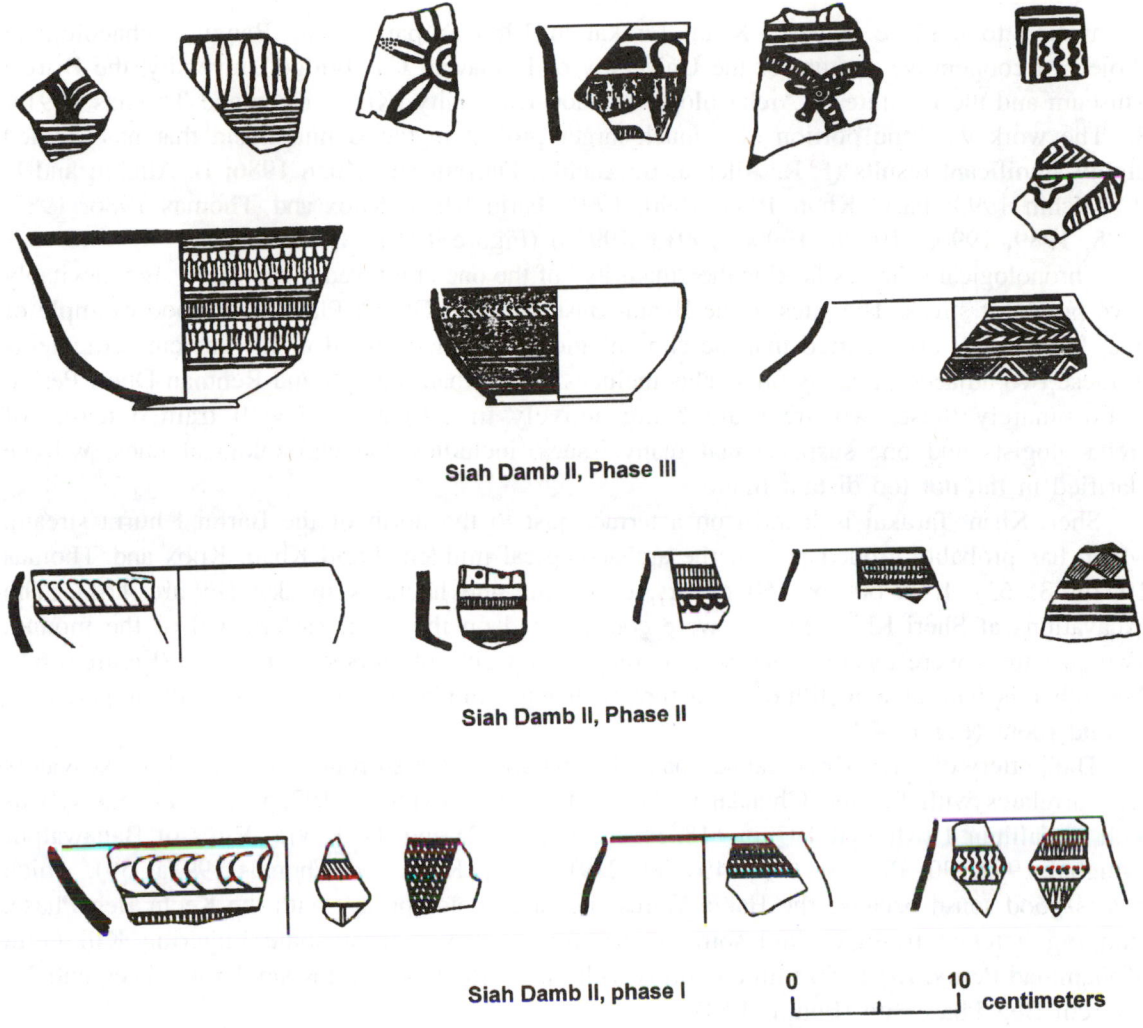

Figure 4.59. Ceramics of the Kechi Beg Phase occupation at Siah Damb, after de Cardi 1965: 145, 148

known from Siah Damb, Nundara (Stein 1931: 138-44, Pls XXV-XXVII). Anjira Ware, a new Baluchi ceramic defined at this site was also found in Period III. This is a distinct dark slipped ceramic in a gritty, buff to greenish fabric. The surface treatment ranges from raised ridges (some ending as snakes!), to comb incising and granulation. It seems "at home" in central and southern Baluchistan in the Kechi Beg and Amri-Nal Phases; although it may extend into Kulli times. The Kechi Beg Phase is also represented at Siah Damb, excavated by de Cardi (Figure 4.59).

More carefully dressed stone replaced boulders as foundations, and larger blocks were used in Period III than II. The use of mud brick can be inferred from filling.

Chert implements disappeared from the small sample gathered at Anjira and de Cardi suggests that this, plus the presence of a whet stone in Period III, could mark the introduction of metal (1965: 102). The use of copper would be perfectly reasonable in this time period.

Anjira, Period III would be comparable to Kili Ghul Mohammad, Period IV/Damb Sadaat I and Period II at Siah Damb, Surab.

516

The Site of Sheri Khan Tarakai

Excavation took place at Sheri Khan Tarakai in 1986 as part of the Bannu Archaeological Project, a cooperative venture of the University of Peshawar, Cambridge University, the British Museum and the Institute of Archaeology, London University (Khan, Knox and Thomas 1991a: 8). The work was one portion of a much larger project in the Bannu Basin that has yielded highly significant results (F. R. Allchin, B. Allchin, Durrani and Khan 1986; B. Allchin and F. R. Allchin 1993; Farid Khan 1986, 1990, 1991; Farid Khan, Knox and Thomas 1986, 1987, 1988, 1989, 1990a, 1990b, 1990c, 1991a, 1991b) (Figure 4.60).

Chronological schemes lacking the "maturity" of the one employed in the *Indus Age* inevitably have points of stress. The sites in the Bannu Basin and the Gomal Plain are a good example of this. I am not at all satisfied that the chronological placement of all of the ancient settlements in these two adjacent areas is final. This includes Sheri Khan Tarakai and Rehman Dheri Period I. Fortunately these two areas are being actively investigated by well trained teams of archaeologists and one suspects that many issues, including the chronological ones, will be clarified in the not too distant future.

Sheri Khan Tarakai is located on a terrace just to the north of the Barrai Khurra stream, which has probably eroded part of the archaeological midden (Farid Khan, Knox and Thomas 1991a: 35-63). It is 600 × 350 meters, or twenty-one hectares in size (Figure 4.61). The excavations at Sheri Khan Tarakai were concentrated on the high, eastern end of the mound. Two structures were located. One is a simple, curving line of stones set in place (Figure 4.62). The other is part of a rectilinear structure with what might be an attached wall or part of a second room (Figure 4.63).

The pottery of Sheri Khan Tarakai has a few parallels with surrounding areas. The excavators see correlates with Periano Ghundai in Waziristan citing (Mughal 1972g: 139, Pl. XXXII) as well as Jalilpur I (Mughal 1972b: 118, Pl. XXXVI A, 2) and the Hakra Wares of Bahawalpur (Mughal 1982: 90, Pl. 7.1; 1984: 499, Pl. 219) (Khan, Knox and Thomas 1991a: 39), which makes good sense because the Hakra Wares sites are contemporary with the Kechi Beg Phase. Hanging hatched triangles and some vessel forms also suggest some lingering Kili Ghul Mohammad Period II/III. This all conforms with the notion that Sheri Khan Tarakai is essentially a Kechi Beg Phase site (Figure 4.64).

Sheri Khan Tarakai produced a rich and wide range of artifacts, most in terracotta, but included bone and stone. No metal was found.

Terracotta Figurines

A large collection of terracotta figurines of both humans and cattle was found at Sheri Khan Tarakai (Khan, Knox and Thomas 1991a: 48-56). The humans are all highly stylized and are recognizable types for the region at the time. Two general types emerge from the collection. The first has no shoulders and a stem-like body, usually with a pinched face and applique breasts. The other type has a bottle like torso with shoulders and reduced arms. (Figure 4.65). One of these figurines (Figure 4.65, no. 12) has a fine rendering of the hair, suggestive of various Kulli counterparts. Another (Figure 4.65, no. 14) seems to be an hermaphroditic representation, with the female organ vastly exaggerated, accompanied by the stump of the male organ, flanked by small applique pellet testicles. Another figurine from Sheri Khan Tarakai (Figure 4.65, no. 13) appears to represent the exaggerated female sexual organ. It has a close counterpart in a figurine found by Sir Aurel Stein at Periano Ghundai (Stein 1929a: Pl. X, P.G. 17) (Figure 4.65, Periano Ghundai 17).

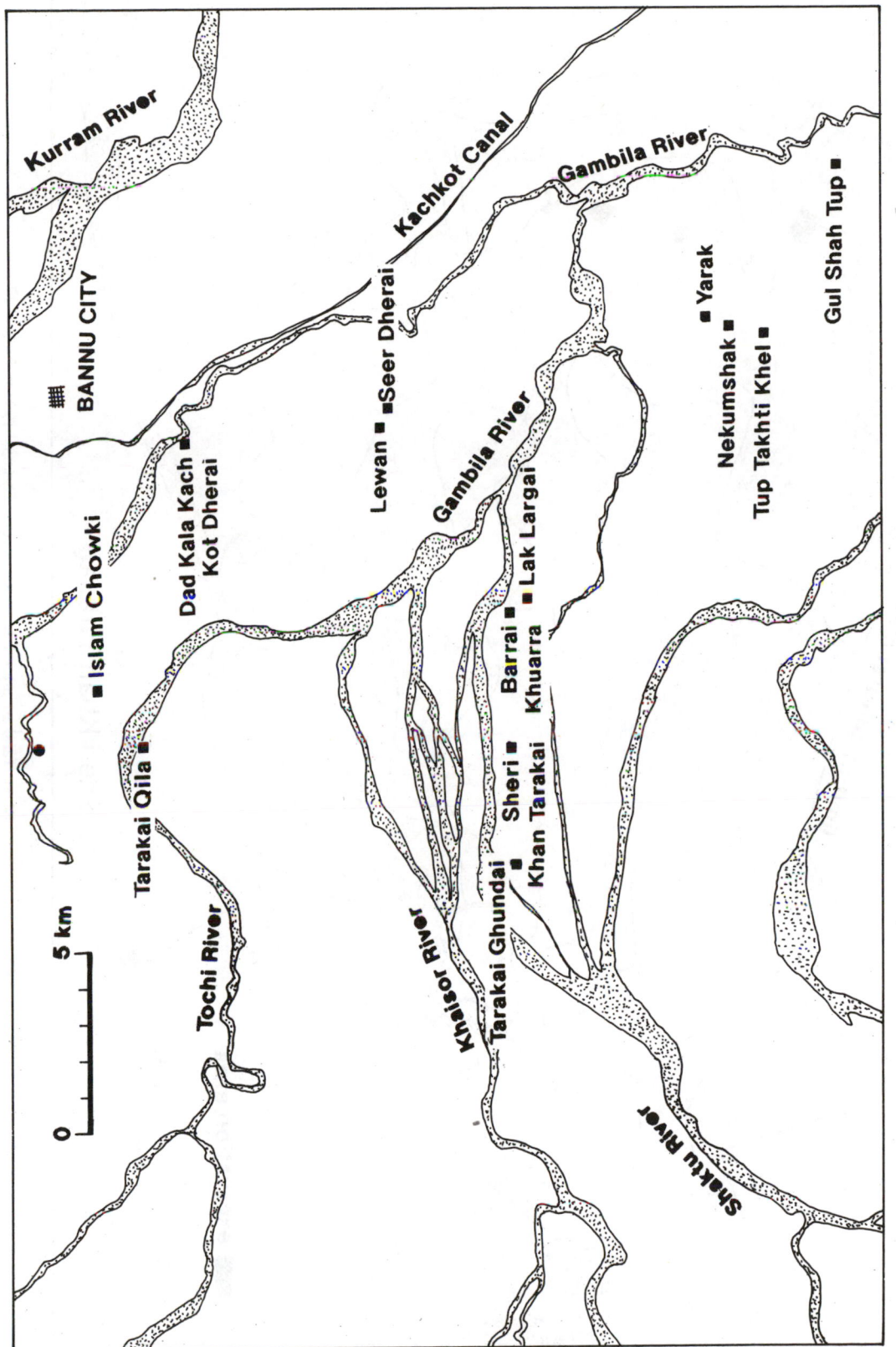

Figure 4.60. Map of sites in the Bannu Basin, after Khan, Knox and Thomas 1991a: Figure 4

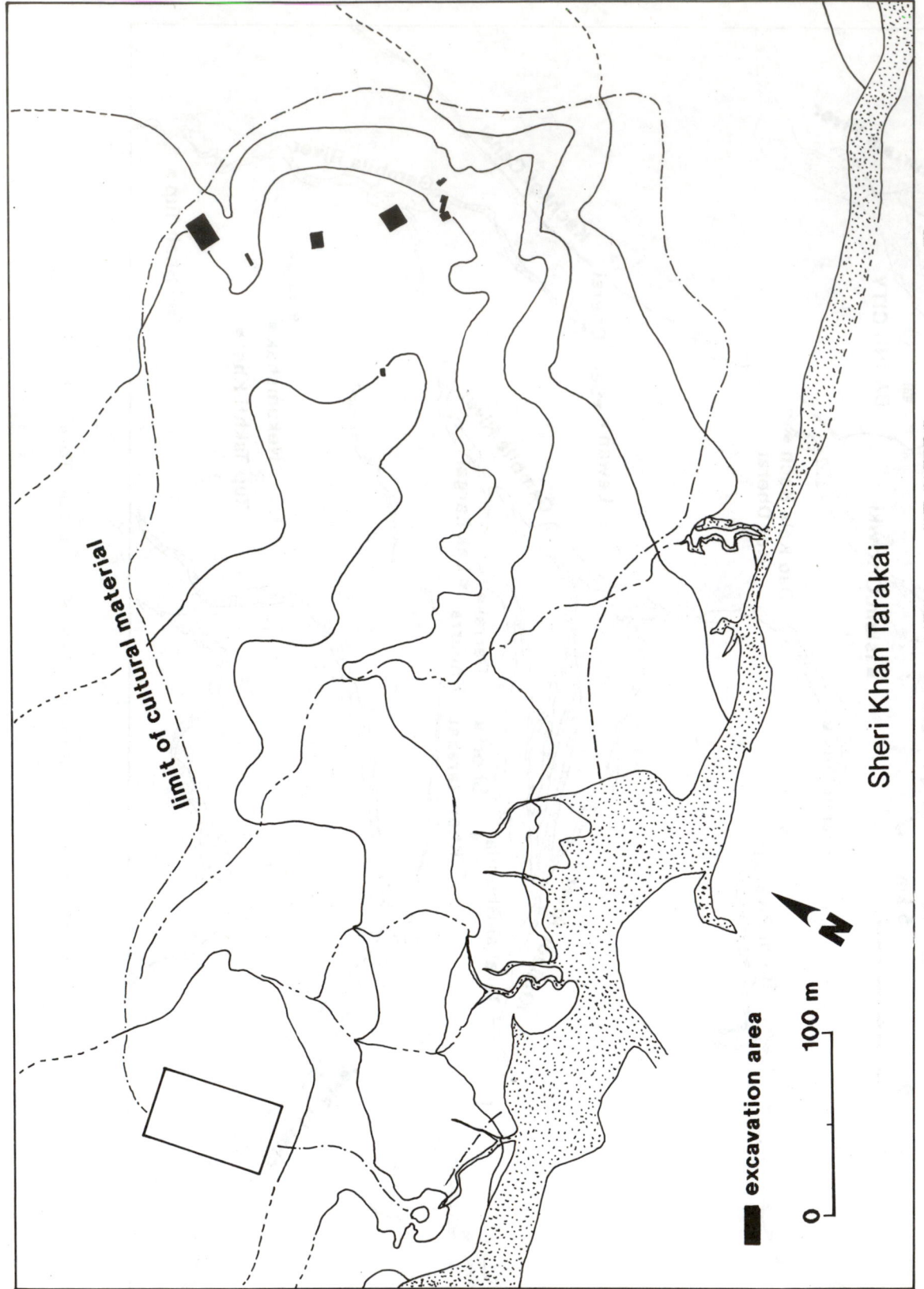

limit of cultural material

Sheri Khan Tarakai

■ excavation area

N

0   100 m

Figure 4.61. Plan of Sheri Khan Tarakai, after Khan, Knox and Thomas 1991a: Figure 27

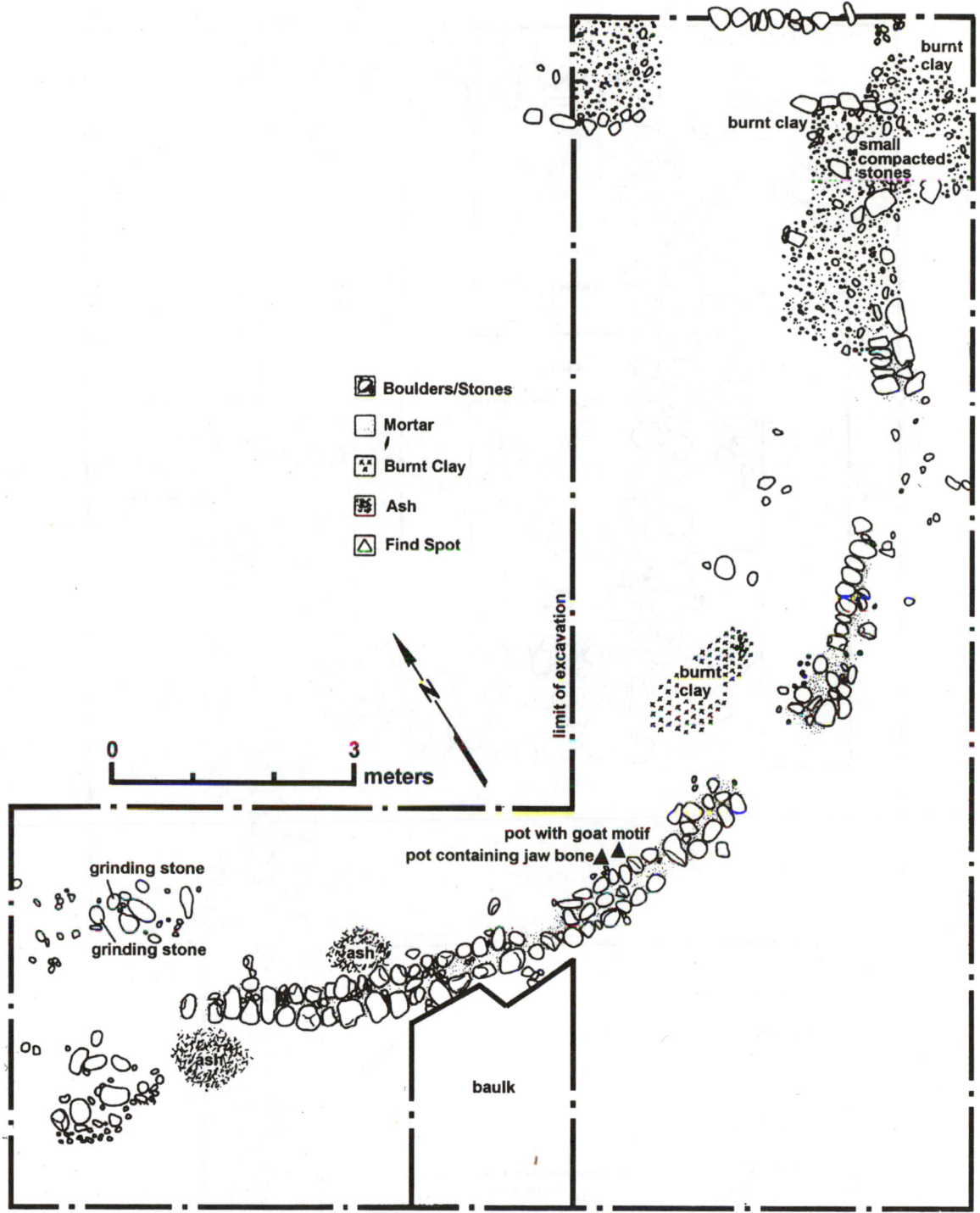

Figure 4.62. Area 5 at Sheri Khan Tarakai, after Khan, Knox and Thomas 1991a: Figure 31

The bull figurines from Sheri Khan Tarakai are not remarkable, but document the participation of the inhabitants of the site in this tradition.

Terracotta Cones and Spindle Whorls

A large number of terracotta cones with a carefully made hole in one end, which does not go

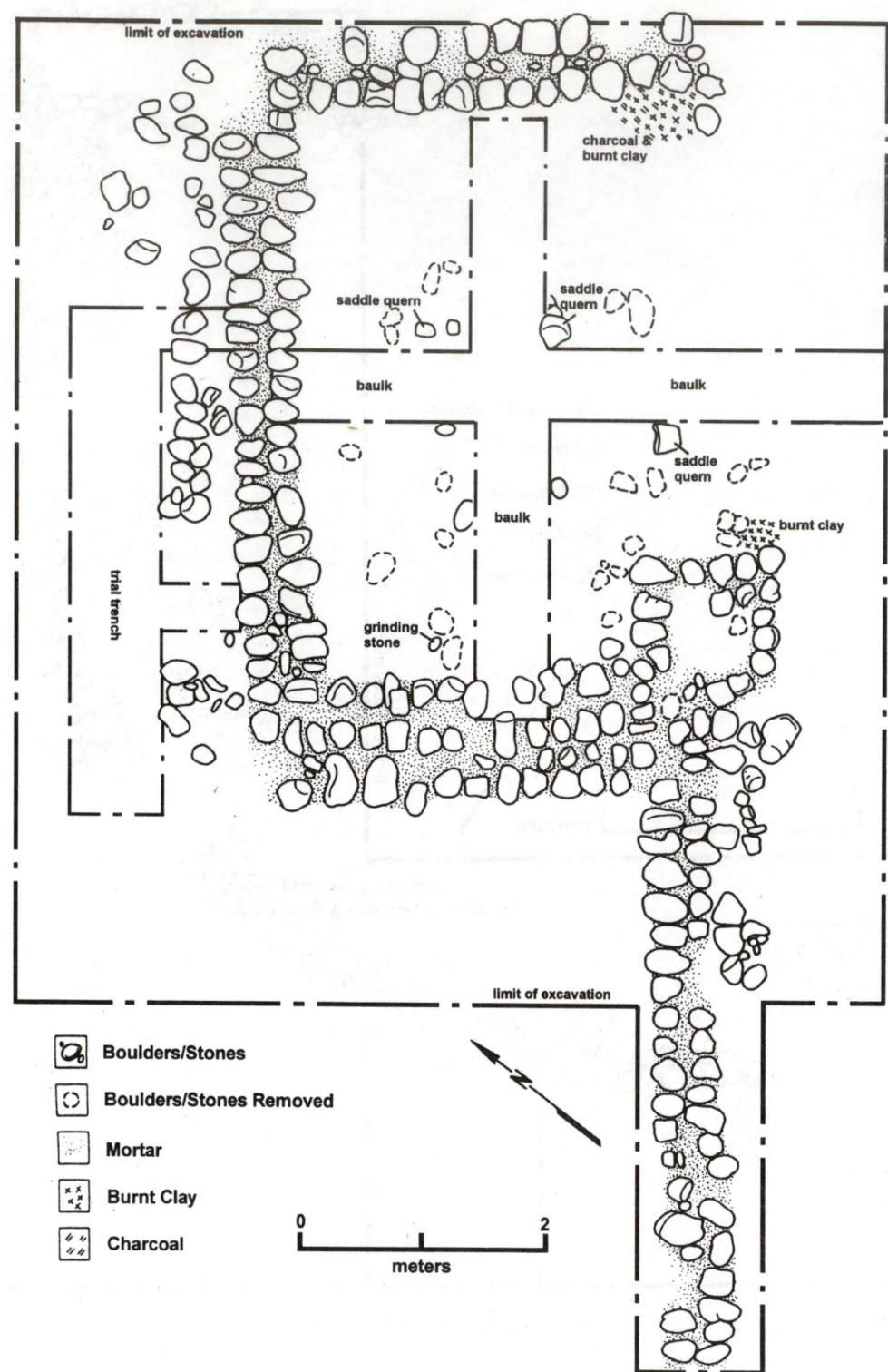

Figure 4.63. Area 7A at Sheri Khan Tarakai, after Khan, Knox and Thomas 1991a: Figure 32

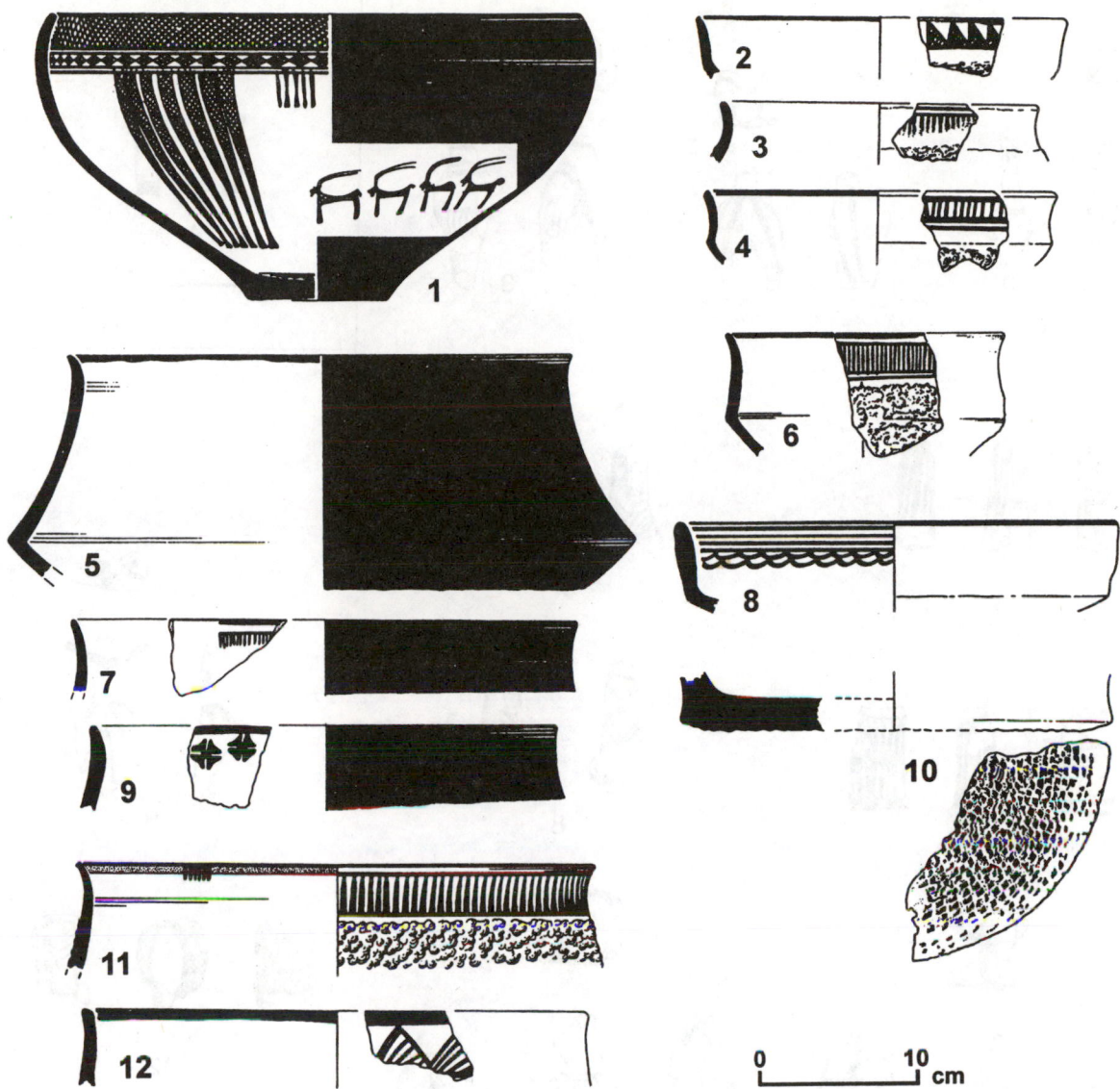

Figure 4.64. Ceramics of Sheri Khan Tarakai, after Khan, Knox and Thomas 1991a: Figures 34-46

all the way through, were recovered from Sheri Khan Tarakai (Figure 4.66). Although the function of these objects is not known, the excavators note that the semiperforated objects have parallels to the north: Kara Tepe (Masson 1960: 433, Pl. XIV); Dashliji Depe (Khlopin 1960: 219, Pl. XII) and sites in the Geoksyur Oasis (Sarianidi 1960: 316, Pl. XIII). One clear example of a spindle whorl was also found.

Terracotta "Boats"

Three small terracotta objects thought possibly to have been boat models were found (Figure 4.66, nos. 7, 8). These fall just short of being completely convincing as boat models, but are extremely interesting objects.

522

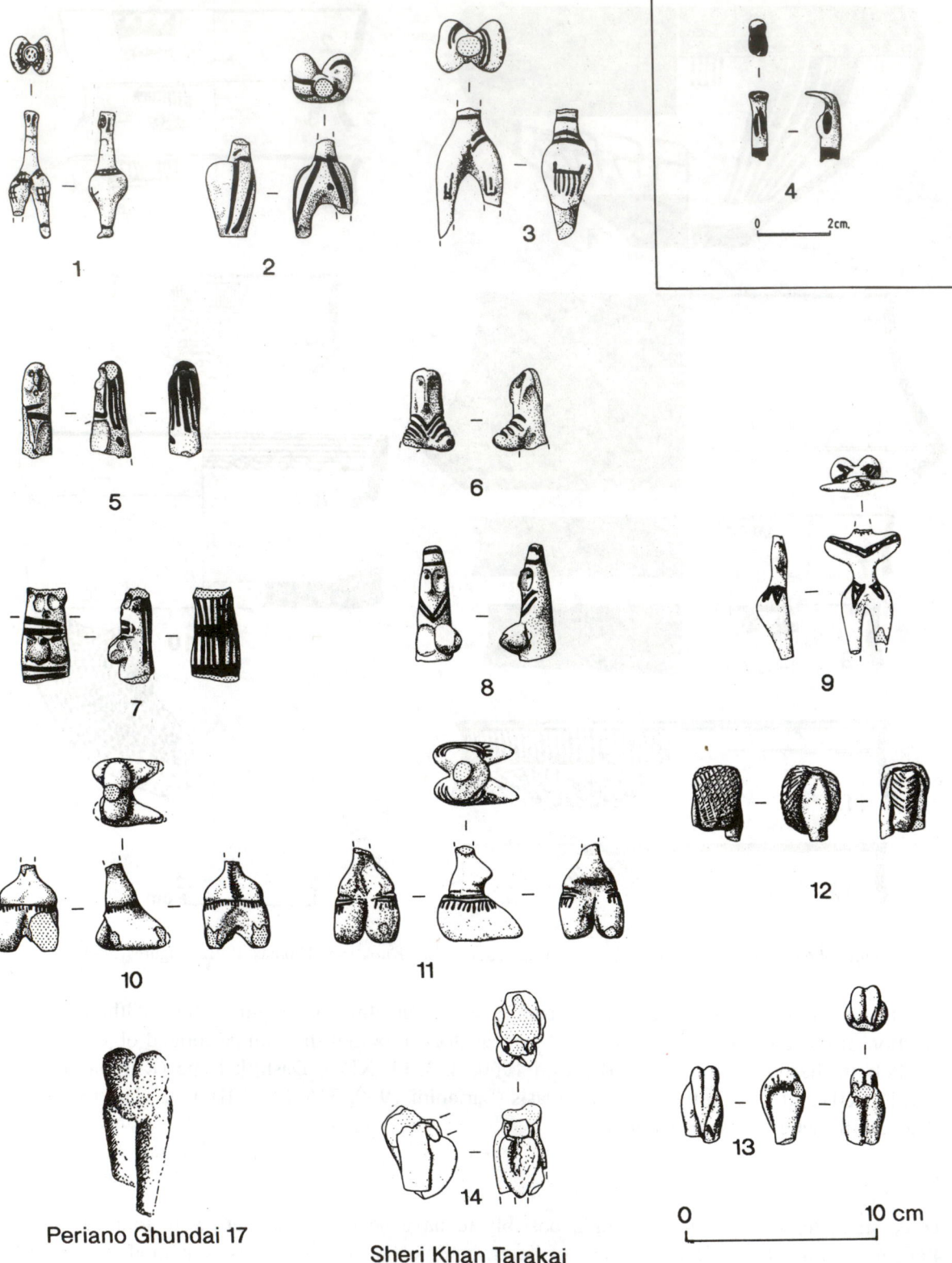

1

2

3

4

0   2cm.

5

6

7

8

9

10

11

12

Periano Ghundai 17

13

14

Sheri Khan Tarakai

0   10 cm

Figure 4.65. Anthropomorphic figurines from Sheri Khan Tarakai, after Khan, Knox and Thomas 1991a: Figures 48-58

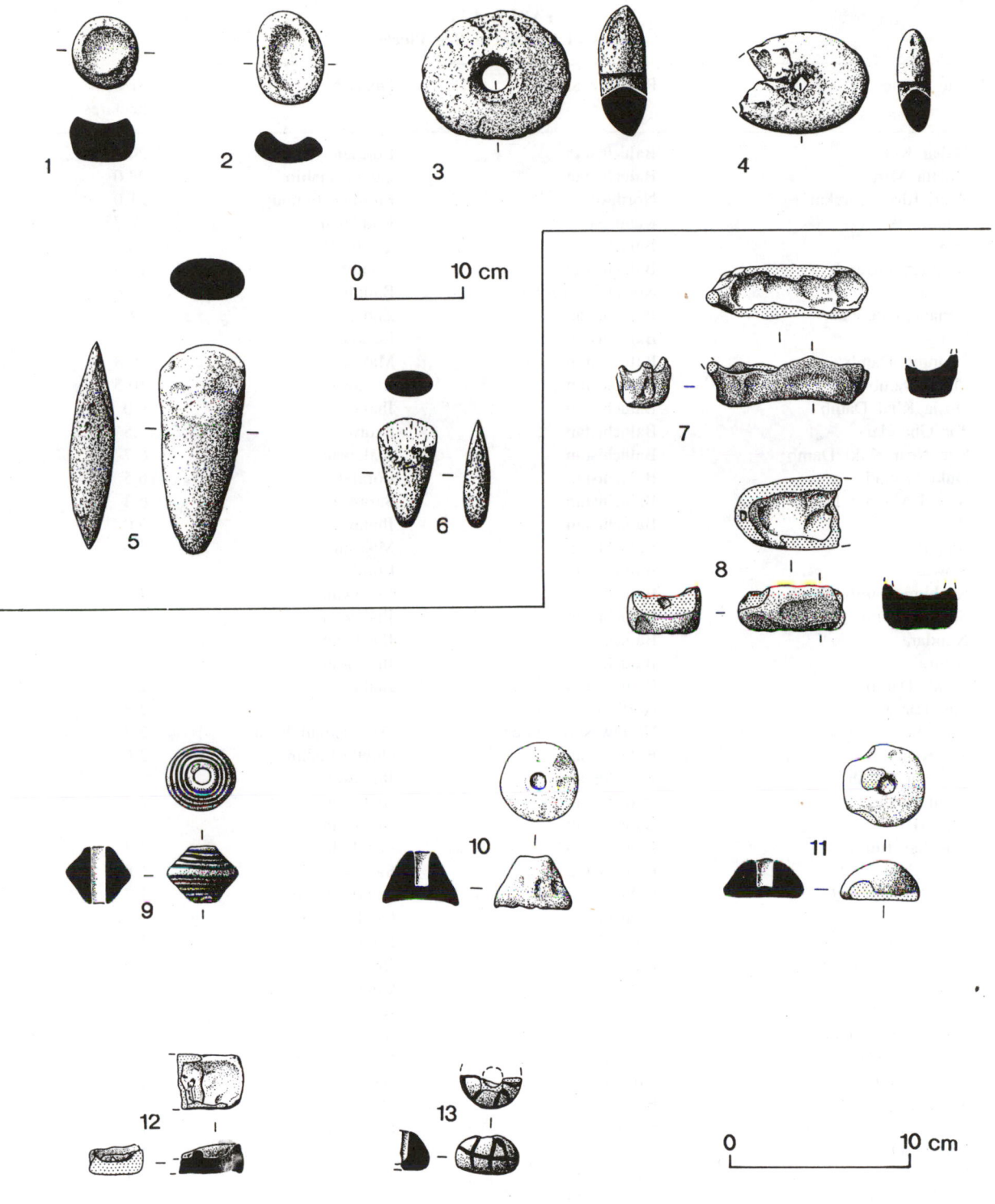

Sheri Khan Tarakai

Figure 4.66. Ground stone (Nos. 1-6) from Sheri Khan Tarakai, after Khan, Knox and Thomas 1991a: Figures 67-8, Terracotta cones and spindle whorl (Nos. 9-13) Sheri Khan Tarakai, after Khan, Knox and Thomas 1991a: Figure 60; Possible boat models (Nos. 7-8) from Sheri Khan Tarakai, after Khan, Knox and Thomas 1991a: Figure 61

TABLE 4.21
Sites of the Kechi Beg Phase

Site Name	Province/State	District	Size in hectares
Dabar Kot	Baluchistan	Loralai	24.3
Quetta Miri	Baluchistan	Quetta-Pishin	23.0
Sheri Khan Tarakai	Northwest	Frontier Bannu	21.0
Mundigak	Kandahar	Kandahar	18.75
Q-32	Baluchistan	Quetta-Pishin	16.7
Kargushki Damb	Baluchistan	Kharan	15.3
Lewan	Northwest Frontier	Bannu	14.6
Periano Ghundai	Baluchistan	Zhob	14.4
L-3	Baluchistan	Loralai	12.6
Badrang Damb	Baluchistan	Makran	10.8
Phusi Damb	Baluchistan	Jhalawan	10.5
Dosia Khal Damb	Baluchistan	Jhalawan	9.0
Tor Ghundai	Baluchistan	Sarawan	7.5
Site Near Kuki Damb	Baluchistan	Jhalawan	6.7
Duki Mound	Baluchistan	Loralai	6.5
Saiyid Maurez Damb	Baluchistan	Sarawan	6.3
Zik	Baluchistan	Jhalawan	5.0
Sraduk	Baluchistan	Makran	5.0
Kowas	Baluchistan	Loralai	4.1
Kashimi Damb, Wadh	Baluchistan	Jhalawan	4.0
Suneri Damb	Baluchistan	Jhalawan	3.5
Nundara	Baluchistan	Jhalawan	3.3
Anjira	Baluchistan	Jhalawan	3.0
Surkh Damb	Baluchistan	Jhalawan	2.9
Lak Largai	Northwest Frontier	Bannu	2.8
Hathala	Northwest Frontier	Dera Ismail Khan	2.7
Sra Kala	Baluchistan	Quetta-Pishin	2.6
Ghuram Damb	Baluchistan	Jhalawan	2.5
Benn Chah	Baluchistan	Jhalawan	2.5
Chimri	Baluchistan	Jhalawan	2.5
Khakhar Buthi	Baluchistan	Las Bela	2.3
Salu Khan	Baluchistan	Sarawan	1.8
Faiz Mohammad	Baluchistan	Quetta-Pishin	1.7
Damb Sadaat	Baluchistan	Quetta-Pishin	1.7
Sur Jangal	Baluchistan	Loralai	1.6
Siah Damb, Surab	Baluchistan	Jhalawan	1.5
Q-25	Baluchistan	Quetta-Pishin	1.5
Zayak North	Baluchistan	Kharan	1.5
Sardar Khel Damb	Baluchistan	Sarawan	1.5
Rana Ghundai	Baluchistan	Loralai	1.4
Islam Chowki	Northwest Frontier	Bannu	1.35
Kasiano Dozakh	Baluchistan	Quetta-Pishin	1.3
Niai Buthi	Baluchistan	Las Bela	1.3
Isplinji One	Baluchistan	Sarawan	1.2
Gate Dap	Baluchistan	Jhalawan	1.1
Q-26	Baluchistan	Quetta-Pishin	1.1
Zidi	Baluchistan	Jhalawan	0.9
Rodkan	Baluchistan	Jhalawan	0.9
Shahr Sardar	Baluchistan	Sarawan	0.9
Toji Damb	Baluchistan	Kharan	0.7

Contd.

Gumla	Northwest Frontier	Dera Ismail Khan	0.7
Isplinji Two	Baluchistan	Sarawan	0.7
Kirta	Baluchistan	Quetta-Pishin	0.7
Ahmed Khanzai North	Baluchistan	Quetta-Pishin	0.65
Q-17	Baluchistan	Quetta-Pishin	0.65
K-1	Baluchistan	Sarawan	0.6
L-2	Baluchistan	Loralai	0.6
Jawarji Kalat	Baluchistan	Jhalawan	0.6
Kechi Beg	Baluchistan	Quetta-Pishin	0.5
Jebri Damb Two	Baluchistan	Jhalawan	0.5
Kili Ghul Mohammad	Baluchistan	Quetta-Pishin	0.5
Ashal	Baluchistan	Jhalawan	0.5
Marki Mas	Baluchistan	Jhalawan	0.4
Ahmed Khanzai South	Baluchistan	Quetta-Pishin	0.4
Spina Ghundai	Baluchistan	Quetta-Pishin	0.4
Sahib Khan	Baluchistan	Quetta-Pishin	0.4
Q-35	Baluchistan	Quetta-Pishin	0.4
Neghar Damb	Baluchistan	Kalat	0.35
Pir Haidar Shahr	Baluchistan	Jhalawan	0.3
Sorak Damb	Baluchistan	Jhalawan	0.3
Q-18	Baluchistan	Quetta-Pishin	0.3
Q-33	Baluchistan	Quetta-Pishin	0.3
Q-28	Baluchistan	Quetta-Pishin	0.3
Q-06	Baluchistan	Quetta-Pishin	0.3
Kuchnai Ghundai	Baluchistan	Quetta-Pishin	0.25
Jaren	Baluchistan	Jhalawan	0.25
Q-36	Baluchistan	Quetta-Pishin	0.2
Karezgai	Baluchistan	Zhob	0.2
Q-23	Baluchistan	Quetta-Pishin	0.2
Sumer Damb	Baluchistan	Jhalawan	0.2
Kuki Damb	Baluchistan	Jhalawan	0.1
Drakalo Damb	Baluchistan	Jhalawan	0.1
Gwani Kalat	Baluchistan	Jhalawan	0.05
Rais Sher Mohammad	Baluchistan	Jhalawan	0.02
Ala Damb	Baluchistan	Jhalawan	
Bagh-i Kumb Damb	Northwest Frontier	Dera Ismail Khan	
Barrai Khuarra One	Northwest Frontier	Bannu	
Bundakhi Damb	Baluchistan	Sarawan	
CH-1	Baluchistan	Chagai	
Channal Kund Damb	Baluchistan	Jhalawan	
Chashma Murad	Baluchistan	Jhalawan	
Cheshma Damb One	Baluchistan	Jhalawan	
Chhota Kapoto	Baluchistan	Jhalawan	
Damb Channarozai	Baluchistan	Kalat	
Damb Ghuram	Baluchistan	Kalat	
Damb Goram	Baluchistan	Sarawan	
Damb Hasal Khanzai	Baluchistan	Kalat	
Damb Kulu	Baluchistan	Sarawan	
Damb Wali Mohammad	Baluchistan	Kalat	
Damb Zargaran	Baluchistan	Kalat	
Damb Zerger	Baluchistan	Sarawan	
Dawrao Tul Damb	Northwest Frontier	Dera Ismail Khan	
Gajar Damb	Baluchistan	Jhalawan	
Ghannal Kund Damb	Baluchistan	Jhalawan	
Ghurum	Baluchistan	Makran	
Gorpat	Baluchistan	Jhalawan	

Contd.

526

Table 4.21 Contd.

Site Name	Province/State	District	Size in hectares
Gushanak	Baluchistan	Jhalawan	
Hadi	Baluchistan	Jhalawan	
Hamal Damb	Baluchistan	Jhalawan	
Jahan	Baluchistan	Jhalawan	
Jahan Northeast	Baluchistan	Jhalawan	
Kaddour Damb	Northwest Frontier	Dera Ismail Khan	
Kafir Kot	Baluchistan	Sarawan	
Kalat	Baluchistan	Sarawan	
Kanori	Baluchistan	Loralai	
Kapoto Damb	Baluchistan	Jhalawan	
Kapoto Rock Shelter	Baluchistan	Jhalawan	
Kaptun Bra	Baluchistan	Sarawan	
Kashkai	Baluchistan	Loralai	
Kasmi Damb	Baluchistan	Jhalawan	
Khoedada	Baluchistan	Zhob	
Kotra	Baluchistan	Kachi	
Kouhlagh	Baluchistan	Quetta-Pishin	
Kulloi	Baluchistan	Sarawan	
Kuzbagh	Baluchistan	Quetta-Pishin	
Madak Kalat	Baluchistan	Jhalawan	
Majo Mill	Baluchistan	Quetta-Pishin	
Malasband	Baluchistan	Jhalawan	
Malghori Damb	Baluchistan	Sarawan	
Malki	Baluchistan	Sarawan	
Mata Ghundai	Baluchistan	Quetta-Pishin	
Mehrgarh	Baluchistan	Kachi	
Mobi Damb	Baluchistan	Sarawan	
Murgha Mehtarzai	Baluchistan	Zhob	
Namdai	Baluchistan	Sarawan	
Nazarabad	Baluchistan	Makran	
Nushki	Baluchistan	Kharan	
P-10	Baluchistan	Quetta-Pishin	
Panodi	Baluchistan	Makran	
Puchur Damb	Baluchistan	Jhalawan	
Rizvi Karuna	Baluchistan	Quetta-Pishin	
Rodinjo One	Baluchistan	Kalat	
Sang	Baluchistan	Zhob	
Serikoran Damb	Baluchistan	Makran	
Sibri Two	Baluchistan	Kachi	
Singen Kalat	Baluchistan	Jhalawan	
Togau	Baluchistan	Sarawan	
Tor Wai	Baluchistan	Sarawan	
Unnamed Damb	Northwest Frontier	Dera Ismail Khan	
Unnamed Site Five	Baluchistan	Jhalawan	
Zahrazai	Baluchistan	Sarawan	
Zari Damb	Baluchistan	Jhalawan	
Zayak Southeast	Baluchistan	Jhalawan	

Bangles

Terracotta bangles, always in a crude fabric with a red slip, were found at Sheri Khan Tarakai, but were not common. This is in contrast to other sites in this region. One *shank* bangle fragment was found. It comes from *Turbinella pyrum* (formerly *Xancus pyrum*), a maritime shell, frequently used during the Urban Phase Harappan. Fragments of this shell indicate the probability that shell bangles were made at Sheri Khan Tarakai (Khan, Knox and Thomas 1991a: 38, 559). One bone bangle was also found.

Beads

A large number of beads, in a variety of colorful stone, including lapis lazuli, turquoise and limestone, was found at Sheri Khan Tarakai. (Khan, Knox and Thomas 1991a: 58-9). These stones, and the occurrence of *Turbinella pyrum*, are indicative of the wide contacts of the ancient inhabitants of Sheri Khan Tarakai.

Bone Tools

Twenty-three bone tools have been illustrated from Sheri Khan Tarakai (Khan, Knox and Thomas 1991a: 132-33). These include awls, points, spatulas and a rectangular object that has been carefully perforated.

Ground Stone Tools

A large number of querns and other ground stone food processing tools was there. Ring stones, axes and small palettes were also found (Figure 4.66, nos. 1-6).

Chipped Stone Tools

The chipped stone tools from Sheri Khan Tarakai form a rich and varied collection. This is basically an undistinguished flake/blade tool making tradition, lacking in true microlithic types.

Subsistence Information

The faunal remains from Sheri Khan Tarakai are in a very fragile state and have not been completely analyzed. They include examples of zebu (*Bos indicus*), sheep (*Ovis aries*), goat (*Capra hircus*) and water buffalo (*Bubalus bubalis*). Samples of ashy material were taken for flotation. The preliminary analysis of this material has led to the identification of barley (*Hordeum* sp.) (Khan, Knox and Thomas 1991a: 38). Shells of freshwater gastropods were common in the deposits.

Professor Farid Khan has suggested that the modern Pathan custom of capturing cranes may go back to the era of Sheri Khan Tarakai (Farid Khan 1991). This is based on the representation of cranes on the ancient ceramics and is quite plausible. He has expanded his published thoughts on this to include the idea that some of the smaller ground ringstones from this and other Bannu Basin sites may have been parts of the bolas-like apparatus used to snare these birds (personal communication 1992).

Conclusions

Sheri Khan Tarakai represents a mature "neolithic" village in one of the rich valleys of the

Northwest Frontier. It is a large site at 21 hectares, although it is probably not as large as Dabar Kot at this time, which is the largest site of the stage. Mehrgarh III is said to cover 100 hectares (Jarrige, Jarrige, Meadow and Quivron 1995: 69), but this is almost surely inflated by lateral stratigraphy.

If we rely on the ethnographic record, and our knowledge of regional ecology, Sheri Khan Tarakai was almost certainly seasonally occupied, in part, by farming-pastoral peoples who planted wheat and/or barely, along with other rabi crops and then migrated to the Indus lowlands for the winter, returning in the spring for their harvest. This is the pattern in evidence in near historical times and fits well with the data revealed by excavation at the site.

Lifeways During the Kechi Beg Phase

We know comparatively little about the lifeways of the Kechi Beg Phase. Curiously, it is the most poorly known period at Mehrgarh, where Periods IV, V and VI have traces of this assemblage. It is clear that there was a continuity in metallurgy and some interesting changes in the subsistence regime. For example, at Mehrgarh, grape pips occur and persist through all subsequent periods until the abandonment of the site. The ascendancy of barley over wheat also seems to take place during this period, and this grain will continue to be the predominant one through the Mature Harappan. It is widely believed that this is a reflection of barley's greater tolerance of salty soils, possibly an early reflection of poor management of irrigation. An irrigation canal may date to Kechi Beg times on the Kachi Plain (Jarrige, Jarrige, Meadow and Quivron 1995: 451). Some signs of public architecture might also be found there, but this is not certain, by any means.

Hakra Wares and the Beginnings of Regionalism

It has already been noted that this Phase marks the beginnings of regional archaeological assemblages in the Greater Indus Region with the colonization of the western Sarasvati drainage (Figure 4.67). There are 103 Hakra Wares sites, only one of which has been excavated (Jalilpur). One hundred of these settlements have size data, with a total settled area of 655.65 hectares. This computes to an average site size of 6.56 hectares, considerably larger than either the Togau or Kechi Beg sites. The smallest site is R. D. 66 at 0.05 hectares. The largest is Chambrawala Ther at 34.6 hectares.

The Hakra Wares consist of an entire assemblage of different pottery types. This is best described in Mughal (1997: Figs. 3-4 and Pls. I-VI) (Figure 4.68), and Dalal (1981) (Figure 4.69) where one sees that the historical roots of the ceramics are back at Mehrgarh, Kili Ghul Mohammad and other sites. For example, there is a small amount of basket-marked pottery. "Hakra Mud Applique Ware" seems to have parallels in Amri Period IA (Casal 1964a: Fig. 40, No. 11a and Fig. 42, No. 4) as well as Harappa (Wheeler 1947a: Fig. 8, No. 1), but the example from Harappa may be a doubtful comparison. A Black Slipped Red Ware is somewhat distinctive but this technique is present at Anjira, although the forms are different there as compared to the Hakra examples. A wide shouldered vessel that is important at Kot Diji and later in the Mature Harappan (Mughal 1997: Pl. 37 and Figure 9, No. 14) (Figure 4.68, no. 5) also occurs. Some of the forms found in the Kot Diji suite of ceramic types are also found in the Hakra Wares assemblage (i.e., flanged rims). Some of the ceramics from Sheri Khan Tarakai have been compared to the Hakra Wares (Khan, Knox and Thomas 1991a: 39).

As this book was being laid out the excavation team at Harappa announced that in 1996 they had found an occupation preceeding their well defined Early Harappan (Meadow et al. 1996: 3–4, Figures 26 & 27). An illustration of some of this pottery is given in Figure 4.68a. The Field Director at Harappa, J. Mark Kenoyer has referred to this material as the "Ravi/ Hakra Assemblage." This terminology expresses the sense that there is a general resemblance of the pottery to Mughal's Hakra Wares, while recognizing the fact that there are also fabrics, shapes and decorations unique to the Harappa assemblage.

Microlithic tools are typically abundant on Hakra Wares sites, especially the camps. Mughal also collected bits and pieces of copper, beads of shell, stone mace heads or ring stones, unworked carnelian, pestles along with terracotta animal figurines, bangles and beads.

No building or room plans emerged from the limited excavations at Jalilpur, Period I, but the use of mud brick and earthen floors can be attested there (Mughal 1972b: 118). Mud "walls" were also apparently used to mark off living space on some of the Bahawalpur sites, at times with *in situ* pots (Mughal 1997: 41-2).

The Hakra Wares Phase sites are given in Table 4.22.

Hakra Wares Pastoral Camps

Of the 103 Hakra Wares sites, fifty-four can be classified as camps used by pastoralists, leaving forty-nine village farming communities (Mughal 1994, 1997). Camps are sites represented by a light scatter of pottery without a buildup of an archaeological midden. These settlements were located on the old alluvium of Cholistan as well as in stabilized sandy areas (Mughal 1997: 40-4). Mughal notes that some sites, perhaps many, may be buried under moving dunes, or have been significantly altered or erased by wind and sand erosion. The presence of these camps testifies to the importance of pastoralism in the time of the Hakra Wares in that they seem to represent the relatively long term monsoon abodes of pastoralists who came into this area to maintain their animals. Testimony from the 19th century notes: "In the rainy season the Cholistan is one stretch of grass...People take their cattle to the banks of the well-known *tobhas* (seasonal lakes) and pay the proprietors a nominal rate of *bhunga* (rent), so that the Cholistan in the rains is a vast common pasture for the Sindhians" (Din 1904: 231).

It might even have been that some of the ancient Sindhians who came there planted a food grain crop and waited for its harvest while they were in the area. At the same time they may have found employment working for farmers during one of the peaks of the agricultural season. The opportunity to travel, visit surrounding areas and meet other peoples meant that these mobile communities also brought news and gossip with them from surrounding areas. They provided social services such as maintaining contacts between relatives removed from one another and arranging for interregional marriages. They also had an opportunity to play a role as traders, bringing products not indigenous to the Sarasvati drainage to peoples there. Given that this region was largely sand, alluvium, grass and small trees, the list of such imported products could have been rather long.

The course of the ancient Sarasvati has been reconstructed, not with any particular precision, but it is probable that it flowed through Cholistan at the time of the Hakra Wares occupation (see Figure 3.140).

The distribution of Hakra Wares Phase Camp sites by size is shown in Table 4.23.

The small Hakra Wares sites are about half the size of a football field, with room for

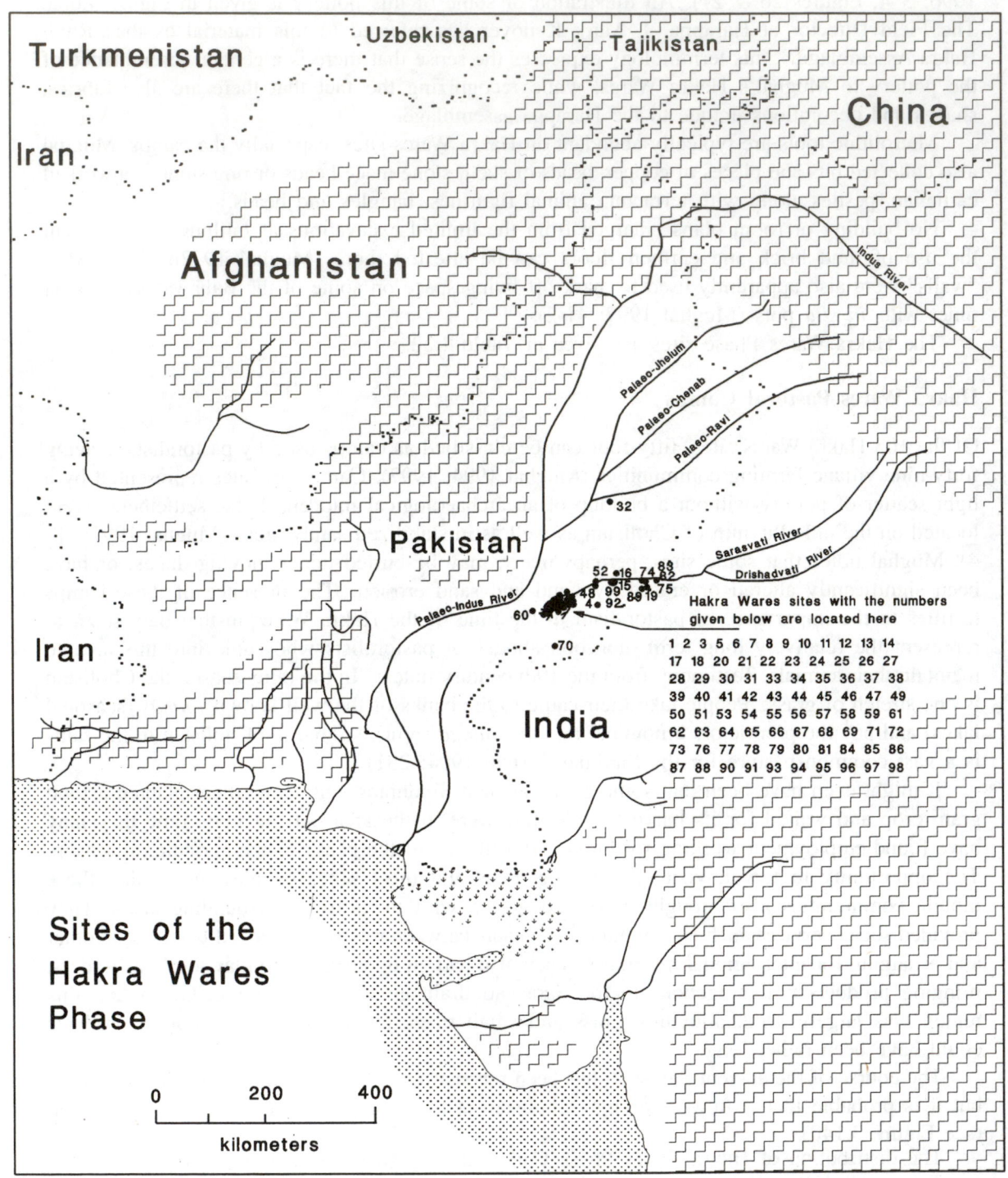

Figure 4.67. Map of sites of the Hakra Wares Phase

Key to Figure 4.67

1 Abduwali	34 Jalwali 'B'	67 Niwaniwala Three
2 Adhi One	35 Jangipar	68 Oinwala Ther
3 Akkanwali Theri	36 Jawaiwala Two	69 Parhara
4 Ambrawali	37 Jhalar	70 Parharewala 'B'**
5 Aziinwala Two	38 Jhandewala Two	71 Payunewala Bhit Three
6 Azimwali 'C'	39 Kalharwala 'B'	72 Payunewala Bhit Two
7 Badalwala Five	40 Khan Kandewala 'D'	73 Qadir Bux Their
8 Badalwala Four	41 Khanpuri Two	74 R. D. 66
9 Baggewali	42 Khiplewali	75 R. D. 89
10 Bahilawala 'B'	43 Khiplewali Three	76 Rahmanwali
11 Bahilawala 'C'	44 Khiplewali Two	77 Sadwala Kanda
12 Bandwali	45 Kikri Two	78 Saftiwala Ther
13 Bhootanwala 'C'	46 Killianwali	79 Safuwala Three
14 Bhootanwali Two	47 Killianwali 'D'	80 Safuwala Two
15 Chak 353 West	48 Kuchanwala	81 Sanukewala Two
16 Chambrawala Ther	49 Lakhman	82 Satuki West
17 Chandnewala Two	50 Lathwala Two	83 Sheruwala West
18 Changalawala 'C'	51 Litanwala	84 Sheruwala Three
19 Channawala Ther	52 Loharki Theri	85 Sheruwala Two
20 Chaudhryanwala	53 Lundewali Four	86 Shidiwala 'A'
21 Chikrala	54 Lundewali Three	87 Sohniwali
22 Chore	55 Luppewala	88 Sohniwali Two
23 Dabli East	56 Luppewala Tliiee	89 Theriwala
24 Dabli West	57 Mehwaii Two	90 Thoom Thali
25 Darkhanwala Ther	58 Merechi Kanda	91 Thoriwala
26 Dhuni South	59 Merechi Kanda Two	92 Trillar
27 Dhuni, Hakra	60 Moniwala	93 Turawewala 'B'
28 Gajjuwala Two	61 Musafarwaii	94 Turawewali 'C'
29 Hotewala Two	62 Muharnwala Two	95 Turawewali Theri
30 Jafawala Three	63 Naharnwala	96 Valwala Two
31 Jafawala Two	64 Naharwali	97 Valwali
32 Jalilpur	65 Naharwali 'B'	98 Waddenwali
33 Jalwali 'A'	66 Niwaniwala Ther West	99 Wariyal 'C'

TABLE 4.22
Sites of the Hakra Wares Phase, from Mughal 1997

Site Name	Province/State	District	Size in hectares
Chambrawala Ther	West Punjab	Bahawalpur	34.6
Musafarwali	West Punjab	Bahawalpur	27.6
Lathwala Two	West Punjab	Bahawalpur	26.3
Chandnewala Two	West Punjab	Bahawalpur	24.7
Moniwala	West Punjab	Rahimyar Khan	22.9
Luppewala	West Punjab	Bahawalpur	22.7
Sohniwali	West Punjab	Bahawalpur	22.0
Bhootanwala 'C'	West Punjab	Bahawalpur	20.6
Ambrawali	West Punjab	Bahawalpur	20.5
Adhi One	West Punjab	Bahawalpur	20.0
Chikrala	West Punjab	Bahawalpur	19.2
Chore	West Punjab	Bahawalpur	19.0
Theriwala	West Punjab	Bahawalpur	18.9
Gajjuwala Two	West Punjab	Bahawalpur	16.7
Jhalar	West Punjab	Bahawalpur	16.2
Sheruwala Two	West Punjab	Bahawalpur	15.1
Thoom Thali	West Punjab	Bahawalpur	14.1
Jalilpur	West Punjab	Sahiwal	13.0
Valwala Two	West Punjab	Bahawalpur	11.2
Merechi Kanda Two	West Punjab	Bahawalpur	10.7
Bhootanwali Two	West Punjab	Bahawalpur	10.7
Mehwali Two	West Punjab	Bahawalpur	10.6
Baggewali	West Punjab	Bahawalpur	10.0
Khiplewali Two	West Punjab	Bahawalpur	8.5
Safuwala Three	West Punjab	Bahawalpur	8.1
Darkhanwala Ther	West Punjab	Bahawalpur	8.1
Litanwala	West Punjab	Bahawalpur	7.6
Naharwali	West Punjab	Bahawalpur	7.3
Dhuni, Hakra	West Punjab	Rahimyar Khan	7.2
Abduwali	West Punjab	Bahawalpur	7.1
Jafawala Two	West Punjab	Bahawalpur	6.9
Khiplewali Three	West Punjab	Bahawalpur	6.6
Luppewala Three	West Punjab	Bahawalpur	6.3
Naharnwala	West Punjab	Bahawalpur	6.1
Sheruwala Three	West Punjab	Bahawalpur	6.0
Waddenwali	West Punjab	Bahawalpur	5.7
Sanukewala Two	West Punjab	Bahawalpur	5.4
Khiplewali	West Punjab	Bahawalpur	4.9
Azimwali 'C'	West Punjab	Bahawalpur	4.8
Channanwala Ther	West Punjab	Bahawalpur	4.7
Dabli West	West Punjab	Bahawalpur	4.7
Sadwala Kanda	West Punjab	Bahawalpur	4.5
Azimwala Two	West Punjab	Bahawalpur	4.4
Sohniwali Two	West Punjab	Bahawalpur	4.2
Badalwala Five	West Punjab	Bahawalpur	4.2
Kikri Two	West Punjab	Bahawalpur	4.1
Jalwali 'A'	West Punjab	Bahawalpur	3.7
Merechi Kanda	West Punjab	Bahawalpur	3.6

Contd.

Dabli East	West Punjab	Bahawalpur	3.6
Turawewala 'B'	West Punjab	Bahawalpur	3.5
Lundewali Four	West Punjab	Bahawalpur	3.3
Dinwala	West Punjab	Bahawalpur	3.2
Lakhman	West Punjab	Bahawalpur	3.2
Changalawala 'C'	West Punjab	Bahawalpur	3.1
Bandwali	West Punjab	Bahawalpur	3.0
Valwali	West Punjab	Bahawalpur	2.9
Akkanwali Theri	West Punjab	Bahawalpur	2.9
Trillar	West Punjab	Bahawalpur	2.9
Jangipar	West Punjab	Bahawalpur	2.8
Loharki Theri	West Punjab	Bahawalpur	2.5
Kilbaiwala	West Punjab	Bahawalpur	2.5
Oinwala Ther	West Punjab	Bahawalpur	2.4
Niwaniwala Ther West	West Punjab	Bahawalpur	2.3
Chaudhryanwala	West Punjab	Bahawalpur	2.2
Musafarwali Two	West Punjab	Bahawalpur	2.1
Lundewali Three	West Punjab	Bahawalpur	2.1
Jawaiwala Two	West Punjab	Bahawalpur	2.1
Naharwali 'B'	West Punjab	Bahawalpur	2.0
Jalwali 'B'	West Punjab	Bahawalpur	1.8
Jafawala Three	West Punjab	Bahawalpur	1.8
Bahilawala 'C'	West Punjab	Bahawalpur	1.7
Khan Kandewala 'D'	West Punjab	Bahawalpur	1.6
Chak 353 West	West Punjab	Bahawalpur	1.6
Badalwala Four	West Punjab	Bahawalpur	1.6
Parhara	West Punjab	Bahawalpur	1.5
Safuwala Ther	West Punjab	Bahawalpur	1.3
Payunewala Bhit Two	West Punjab	Bahawalpur	1.2
Bahilawala 'B'	West Punjab	Bahawalpur	1.2
Dhuni South	West Punjab	Rahimyar Khan	1.2
Hotewala Two	West Punjab	Bahawalpur	1.1
Jhandewala Two	West Punjab	Rahimyar Khan	1.1
Kalharwala 'B'	West Punjab	Bahawalpur	1.0
Turawewala 'C'	West Punjab	Bahawalpur	1.0
Turawewali Theri	West Punjab	Bahawalpur	1.0
Rahmanwali	West Punjab	Bahawalpur	1.0
Shidiwala 'A'	West Punjab	Bahawalpur	0.8
Qadir Bux Theri	West Punjab	Bahawalpur	0.7
Killianwali 'D'	West Punjab	Bahawalpur	0.6
Kuchanwala	West Punjab	Bahawalpur	0.6
Thoriwala	West Punjab	Bahawalpur	0.6
Parharewala 'B'	West Punjab	Bahawalpur	0.6
Karam Khan	West Punjab	Bahawalpur	0.5
Wariyal 'C'	West Punjab	Bahawalpur	0.4
Khanpuri Two	West Punjab	Bahawalpur	0.3
Niwaniwala Three	West Punjab	Bahawalpur	0.3
Safuwala Two	West Punjab	Bahawalpur	0.3
Killianwali	West Punjab	Bahawalpur	0.2
Dhoopsari	West Punjab	Bahawalpur	0.2
Payunewala Bhit Three	West Punjab	Bahawalpur	0.2
R. D. 66	West Punjab	Bahawalpur	0.05
Satuki East	West Punjab	Bahawalpur	
Satuki West	West Punjab	Bahawalpur	
R. D. 89	Rajasthan	Ganganagar	

534

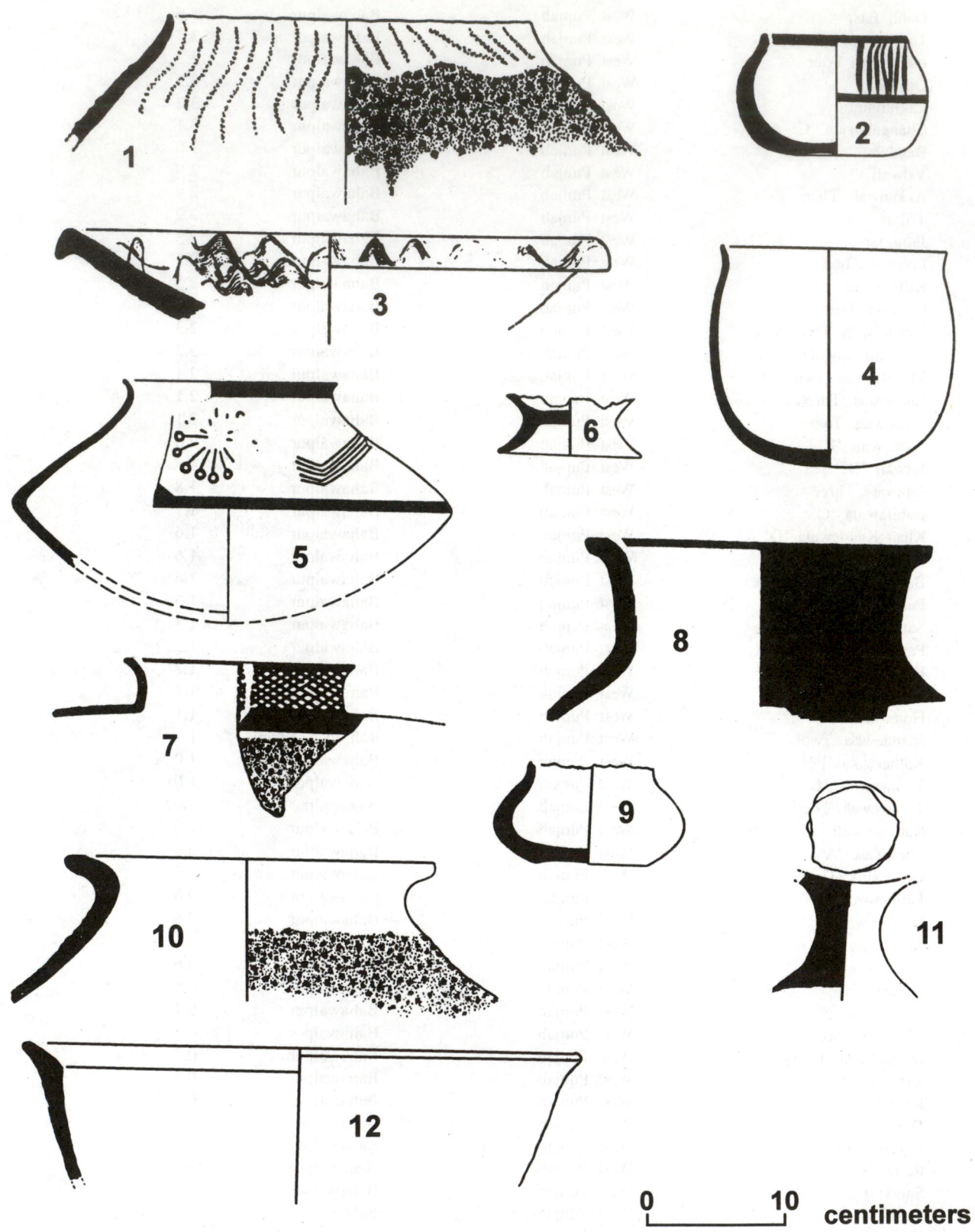

0   10 centimeters

Figure 4.68. Hakra Wares, after Mughal 1997: Figures 8-9

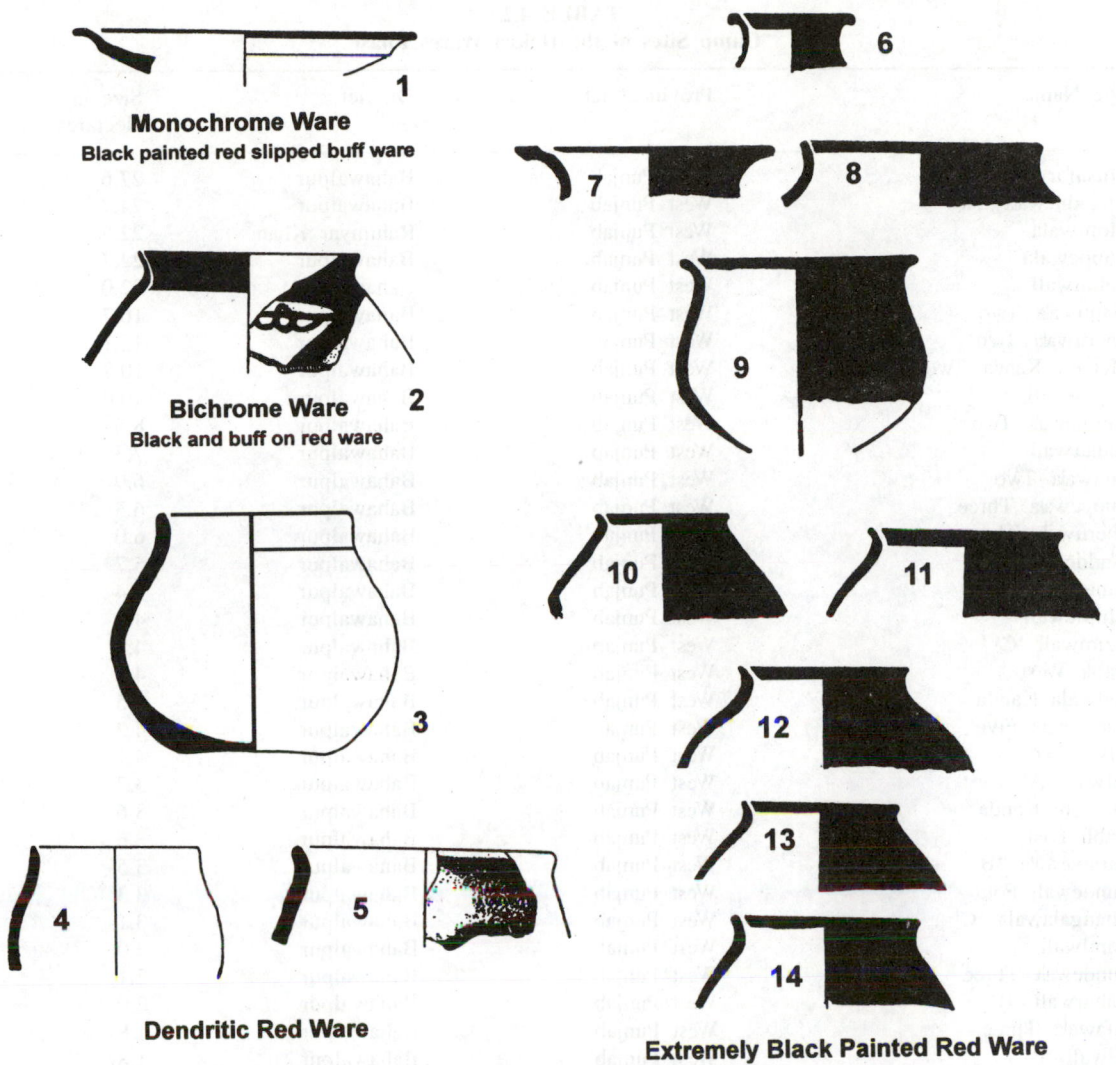

Monochrome Ware
Black painted red slipped buff ware

Bichrome Ware
Black and buff on red ware

Dendritic Red Ware

Extremely Black Painted Red Ware

Figure 4.69. Pottery from RD-89, after Dalal 1981

several families living in tents or temporary shelters. Camps total 292.8 hectares of settled area, for an average size of 5.63 hectares. The five camps that are more than twenty hectares would have been able to accommodate hundreds of people and may well represent the reuse of the same camp site over the course of a number of years—the problem of lateral stratigraphy again.

The number and size of Hakra Wares camps should be critically evaluated. There are two fundamental, unresolved, problems with this kind of settlement data. One is that with a time span of six centuries for the Phase, fifty camps could mean that one was established every twelve years. This is a very small number, too small, in fact, to be real. Moreover, it is not precisely known how to evaluate the relationship between site size and population, particularly for camps, given the problem of lateral stratigraphy.

More permanent village sites, with a buildup of stratigraphy and the formation of archaeological mounds are also present in Bahawalpur during Hakra Wares times. The existence of mounds indicates the probable presence of mud and/or mud brick buildings and a degree of sedentarism that was not apparent at the camp sites. The full stability of these kinds of villages is not known, however and it should not be assumed that everyone who lived there was a full-

TABLE 4.23
Camp Sites of the Hakra Wares Phase

Site Name	Province/State	District	Size in Hectares
Musafarwali	West Punjab	Bahawalpur	27.6
Chandnewala Two	West Punjab	Bahawalpur	24.7
Moniwala	West Punjab	Rahimyar Khan	22.9
Luppewala	West Punjab	Bahawalpur	22.7
Sohniwali	West Punjab	Bahawalpur	22.0
Gajjuwala Two	West Punjab	Bahawalpur	16.7
Sheruwala Two	West Punjab	Bahawalpur	15.1
Merechi Kanda Two	West Punjab	Bahawalpur	10.7
Baggewali	West Punjab	Bahawalpur	10.0
Khiplewali Two	West Punjab	Bahawalpur	8.5
Naharwali	West Punjab	Bahawalpur	7.3
Jafawala Two	West Punjab	Bahawalpur	6.9
Luppewala Three	West Punjab	Bahawalpur	6.3
Sheruwala Three	West Punjab	Bahawalpur	6.0
Waddenwali	West Punjab	Bahawalpur	5.7
Sanukewala Two	West Punjab	Bahawalpur	5.4
Khiplewali	West Punjab	Bahawalpur	4.9
Azimwali 'C'	West Punjab	Bahawalpur	4.8
Dabli West	West Punjab	Bahawalpur	4.7
Sadwala Kanda	West Punjab	Bahawalpur	4.5
Badalwala Five	West Punjab	Bahawalpur	4.2
Kikri Two	West Punjab	Bahawalpur	4.1
Jalwali 'A'	West Punjab	Bahawalpur	3.7
Merechi Kanda	West Punjab	Bahawalpur	3.6
Dabli East	West Punjab	Bahawalpur	3.6
Turawewala 'B'	West Punjab	Bahawalpur	3.5
Lundewali Four	West Punjab	Bahawalpur	3.3
Changalawala 'C'	West Punjab	Bahawalpur	3.1
Bandwali	West Punjab	Bahawalpur	3.0
Lundewali Three	West Punjab	Bahawalpur	2.1
Naharwali 'B'	West Punjab	Bahawalpur	2.0
Jafawala Three	West Punjab	Bahawalpur	1.8
Jalwali 'B'	West Punjab	Bahawalpur	1.8
Bahilawala 'C'	West Punjab	Bahawalpur	1.7
Parhara	West Punjab	Bahawalpur	1.5
Dhuni South	West Punjab	Rahimyar Khan	1.2
Payunewala Bhit Two	West Punjab	Bahawalpur	1.2
Bahilawala 'B'	West Punjab	Bahawalpur	1.2
Hotewala Two	West Punjab	Bahawalpur	1.1
Jhandewala Two	West Punjab	Rahimyar Khan	1.1
Turawewali Theri	West Punjab	Bahawalpur	1.0
Kalharwala 'B'	West Punjab	Bahawalpur	1.0
Turawewala 'C'	West Punjab	Bahawalpur	1.0
Qadir Bux Theri	West Punjab	Bahawalpur	0.7
Killianwali 'D'	West Punjab	Bahawalpur	0.6
Thoriwala	West Punjab	Bahawalpur	0.6
Karam Khan	West Punjab	Bahawalpur	0.5
Niwaniwala Three	West Punjab	Bahawalpur	0.3
Safuwala Two	West Punjab	Bahawalpur	0.3
Payunewala Bhit Three	West Punjab	Bahawalpur	0.2
Killianwali	West Punjab	Bahawalpur	0.2
Dhoopsari	West Punjab	Bahawalpur	0.2
Satuki East	West Punjab	Bahawalpur	
Satuki West	West Punjab	Bahawalpur	

time, year around resident. There was still room for a great deal of mobility, migration and pastoral nomadism in the region, as indicated by the archaeological and ethnographic records.

Estimate of Net Settled Area for the Kechi Beg and Hakra Wares Phases

The population estimate for the two Phases in the latter half of Stage Two are given in Tables 4.24 and 4.25.

TABLE 4.24
Estimates of Settled Area for the Kechi Beg Phase

Total Sites	153
Sites with Size Estimate	84
Settled Area of Sites with Known Sizes	304.52
Sites with Size Unknown	69
Average Site Size	3.63
Estimated Settled Area of Sites without Size	250.47
Estimated Total Settled Area	554.99

Sizes given in hectares

TABLE 4.25
Estimates of Settled Area for the Hakra Wares Phase

Total Sites	103
Sites with Size Estimate	100
Settled Area of Sites with Known Sizes	655.65
Sites with Size Unknown	3
Average Site Size	6.56
Estimated Settled Area of Sites without Size	19.68
Estimated Total Settled Area	675.33

Sizes given in hectares

The Kechi Beg and Hakra Wares Phases are approximately (exactly, according to the estimated chronology) contemporary and each represents a geographical aspect of later Stage Two, so it is legitimate to add together the figures for both Phases.

TABLE 4.26
Estimates of Settled Area for the Kechi Beg and Hakra Wares Phases

Total Sites	256
Sites with Size Estimate	184
Settled Area of Sites with Known Sizes	960.17
Sites with Size Unknown	72
Average Site Size	5.22
Estimated Settled Area of Sites without Size	375.84
Estimated Total Settled Area	1336.01

Sizes given in hectares

The two Phases combine to a total of 1336 hectares. This is an increase in settled area by a factor of four and one-half over the estimated settled area for the Togau Phase, in the first half of Stage Two. Vigorous growth is represented here, as well as geographical expansion for the Phase, which precedes the Early Harappan of Stage Three. The fundamentals in this growth must have been centered on food production and the Stage Two subsistence regime.

The size distribution of the sites of the Kechi Beg Phase, the Hakra Wares Phase and the combined Kechi Beg/Hakra Wares sites is shown in (Figure 4.70, Figure 4.71, Figure 4.72).

538

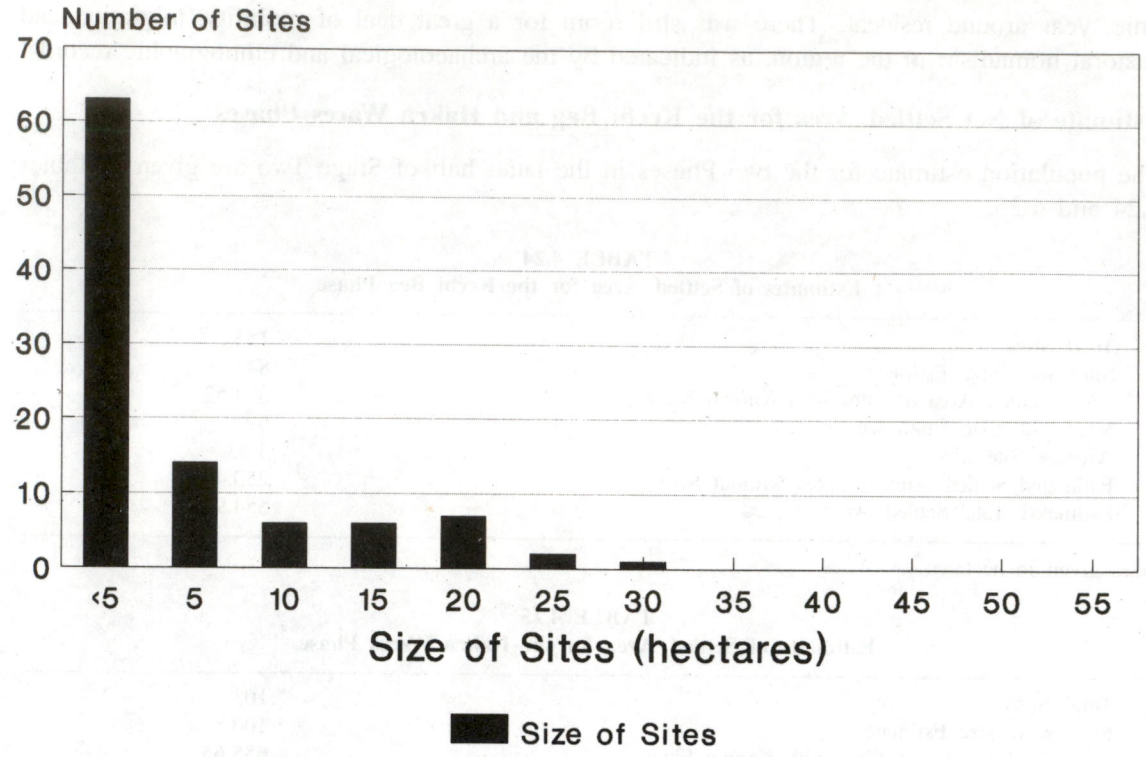

Figure 4.70. Histogram of site sizes for the Hakra Wares Phase

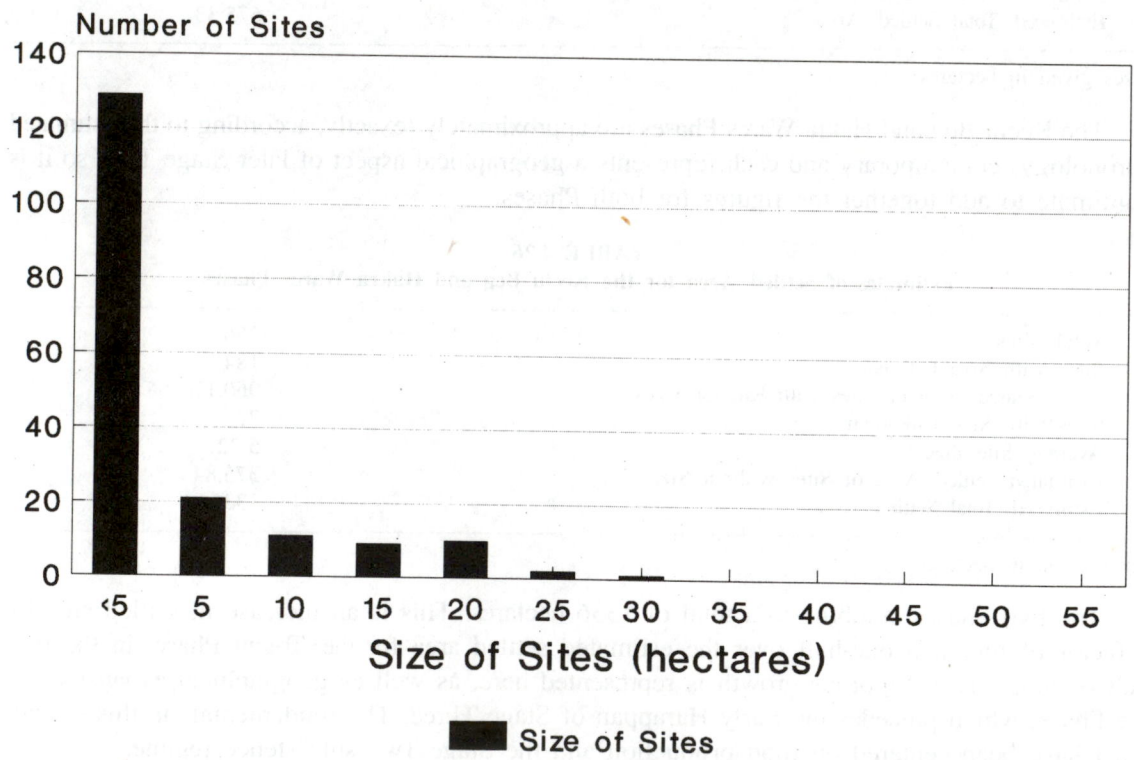

Figure 4.71. Histogram of site sizes for the combined Kechi Beg and Hakra Wares Phases

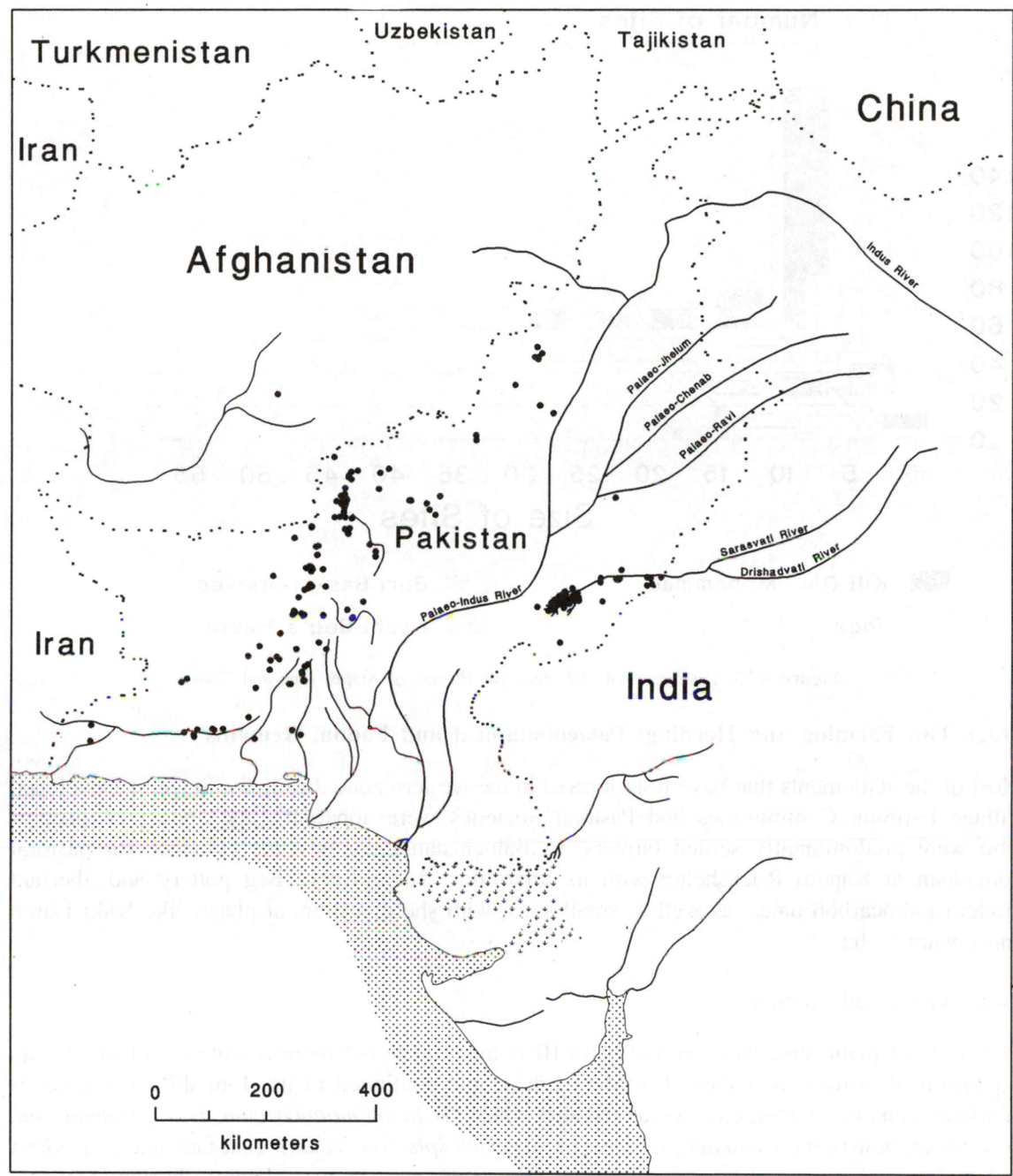

Figure 4.72. Map of sites of the combined Kechi Beg and Hakra Wares Phases

Perhaps a better illustration of these trends in settlement size and density may be gained from Figure 4.73). This illustration, along with the numerical data documents the progressive growth in the presence of the farming and pastoral peoples in the early millennia of the Indus Age. But this growth is even, with few signs of internal differentiation. The pattern of geographical expansion out of the initial "Neolithic Homeland" in and bordering the Gedrosia and Northwestern Regions sets the stage for growth in the Early Harappan.

540

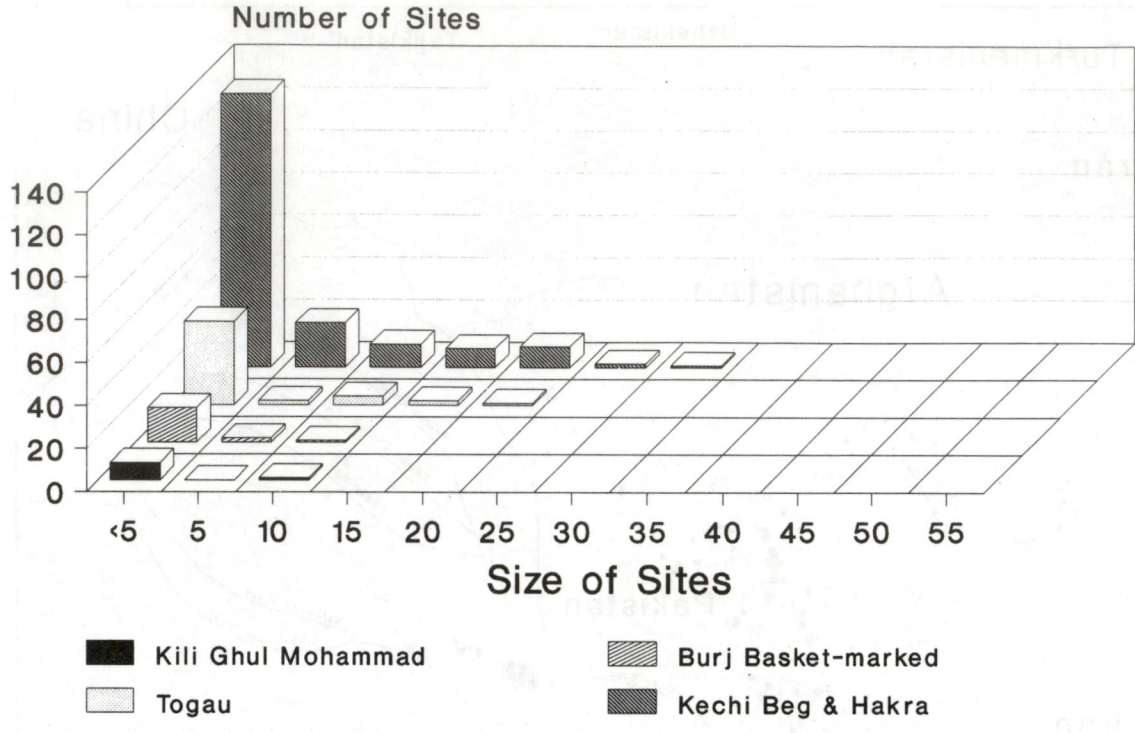

Figure 4.73. Histogram of site sizes for Phases of Stages One and Two

Stage Two Farming and Herding: Palaeobotanical and Faunal Remains

Most of the settlements that have been located in the western zone during the Stage of Developed Village Farming Communities and Pastoral Societies were apparently the abodes of peoples who were predominantly settled farmers. In Baluchistan there is some evidence for pastoral nomadism at Kapoto Rockshelter with its microliths, Togau/Kechi Beg pottery and aberrant modern radiocarbon dates, as well as small sites, with sherd scatters at places like Kuki Damb and Gwani Kalat.

Stage Two Food Grains

The study of plant remains from Mehrgarh III is incomplete but there is strong evidence for an expansion of farming activities. The Mehrgarh people continued to use four different varieties of wheat: einkorn, emmer, club wheat and shot wheat (*Triticum monococcum, Triticum dicoccum, Triticum* cf. *aestivum compactum, Triticum* cf. *aestivum sphaerococcum*), goat-face grass (*Aegilops* sp.), oats (*Avena*sp.), and two-rowed barley (*Hordeum spontaneum*) (Jarrige, Jarrige, Meadow and Quivron 1995: 250). The use of multiple varieties of wheat and barley is a reflection of a subsistence pattern that began during the Kili Ghul Mohammad and Burj Basket-marked Phases at Mehrgarh, and doubtless other early village sites in the region. By the Mature Harappan this pattern changed and barley was the single predominant food grain. But, earlier peoples used varieties of wheat that can be thought of as "eastern"; bread/club wheat (*Triticum aestivum/compactum*) and shot wheat (*Triticum sphaerococcum*). The durum wheat of the "west" was no longer used. This changeover seems to have adaptive value according to van Zeist and Bakker-Heeres: "*T. durum* is well adapted to the Mediterranean climate, whereas *T. aestivum* is a crop plant from more humid, temperate climatic conditions" (1979: 164). The Stage of the Developed Village Farming Community and Pastoral Societies seems to be the time when these changes began.

Stage Two Domesticated Animals

The animal species exploited in the Stage of the Developed Village Farming Community and Pastoral Societies remain very much as in the preceding stage. An examination of the frequency graph (Figure 4.74) showing the proportional use of species indicates that Mehrgarh Period III represents the beginning of stabilization in the animal exploitation pattern at the site that lasts to the threshold of civilization. This furthers the sense that Stage Two is a period of consolidation in the subsistence regime, and the maturation of the earlier food production into a more stable, less experimental subsistence system.

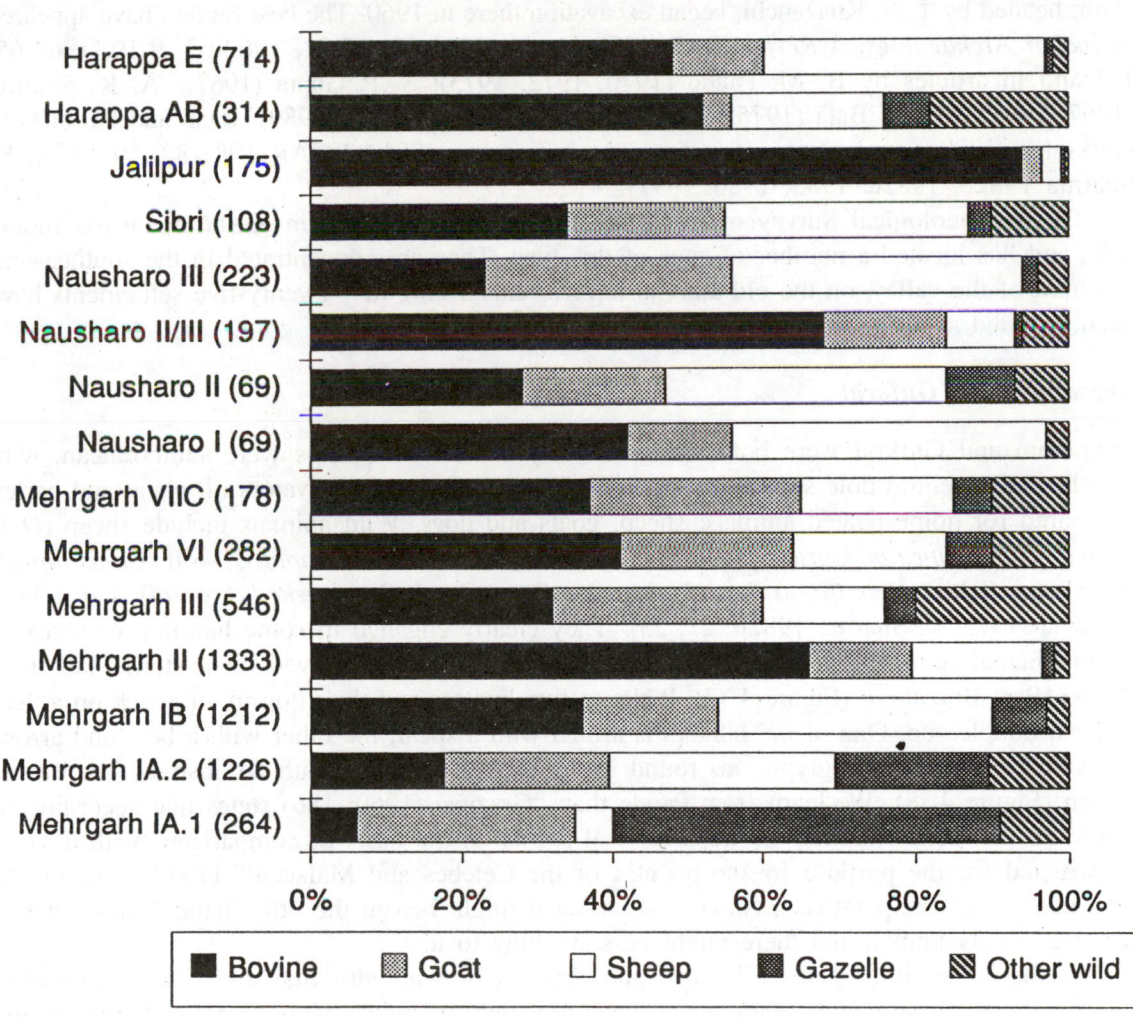

Figure 4.74. Frequency graph of animals utilized by the inhabitants of Mehrgarh and other sites, after Jarrige and Meadow 1992: 167

The Northern Neolithic: More Food Producing Communities on the Northern Border of the Indus Region

A second cultural tradition of farmers and herders has been found in the northern Subcontinent. These peoples were centered on the Vale of Kashmir, although their settlements do extend into Swat and the northern plains of the Greater Indus Valley, at places like Sarai Khola and possibly Uchali. They represent a cultural tradition whose origin is outside of South Asia. Archaeologists have come to refer to this material as the "Northern Neolithic." Sites of this affiliation begin just after the end of Stage Two.

The Northern Neolithic Tradition

The Archaeological Survey of India has conducted major excavations at two Northern Neolithic sites in the Vale of Kashmir: Burzahom and Gufkral (Figure 4.75). Burzahom lies 16 kilometers northeast of Srinagar, about 1800 meters above mean sea level, and was originally reported by H. deTerra and T. T. Paterson (1939: 233-35, Plate XXIV) (Figure 4.76). The Survey's excavation team, headed by T. N. Khazanchi, began excavation there in 1960. The best reports have appeared in *Indian Archaeology, A Review* (IAR 1960-61: 11, 1961-62: 17-21, 1962-63: 9-10, 1964-65: 13) and in articles by B. M. Pande (1970, 1972, 1973); S. P. Gupta (1967); A. K. Sharma (1967, 1968); Madhu Bala (1975); R. K. Pant (1979); Kaw (1979, 1989); Basu and Pal (1980). Gufkral was taken under excavation for only one season 1981-82 (IAR 1981-82: 19-25; A. K. Sharma 1982b, 1982c, 1983, 1986, 1991).

The Archaeological Survey of India has conducted exploration in Kashmir, on the Indian side, and has located a number of sites of this type. They are concentrated in the southeastern quadrant of the valley, on the old alluvial terraces called *karewas*. Twenty-five settlements have been reported so far. They are enumerated in Table 4.27.

Burzahom and Gufkral

Burzahom and Gufkral were both villages. Many of their dwellings were subterranean, with hearths and a central pole supporting the roof. The people were cultivators of wheat and barley and cared for domesticated animals: sheep, goats and dogs. Wild animals include sheep (*Ovis vigni*), goats (*Capra aegagrus*), cattle (*Bos* sp?), Red Deer (*Cervus elaphus*), wolf (*Canis lupus*), Himalayan Tahir (*Hemitragus jemlahicus*), the Grey Goral (*Naemorhedus goral*) and a bear (*Ursa* sp?) (A. K. Sharma 1982b: 21, 23). They clearly engaged in some hunting, as revealed by the faunal remains, as well as from an interesting scene engraved on a stone slab from Period IB at Burzahom (Figure 4.77). It shows two hunters and their dog in an attack on a deer under a double sun. One of the hunters is armed with a spear, the other with a bow and arrow. A second engraved petroglyph was found in Period IB, this time with an abstract "tectiform" design (Figure 4.78). We learn from Pande that: "Graziosi (1960: 186) states that according to Obermeir the tectiforms may be traps for evil spirits on the basis of comparison 'with devices constructed for the purpose by the peoples of the Celebes and Malacca'" (1972: 176, fn. 2). This use of the comparative method is not what it might be; on the other hand "traps" of this sort are widely known and there might be something to it.

Northern Neolithic pottery is soft, and gray to brown, with mat and cord impressions (Figure 4.79). These people made a rich bone tool industry with points, needles, harpoons and serrated points (Figure 4.80). The stone tools are mostly ground, with oval, pointed butt axes,

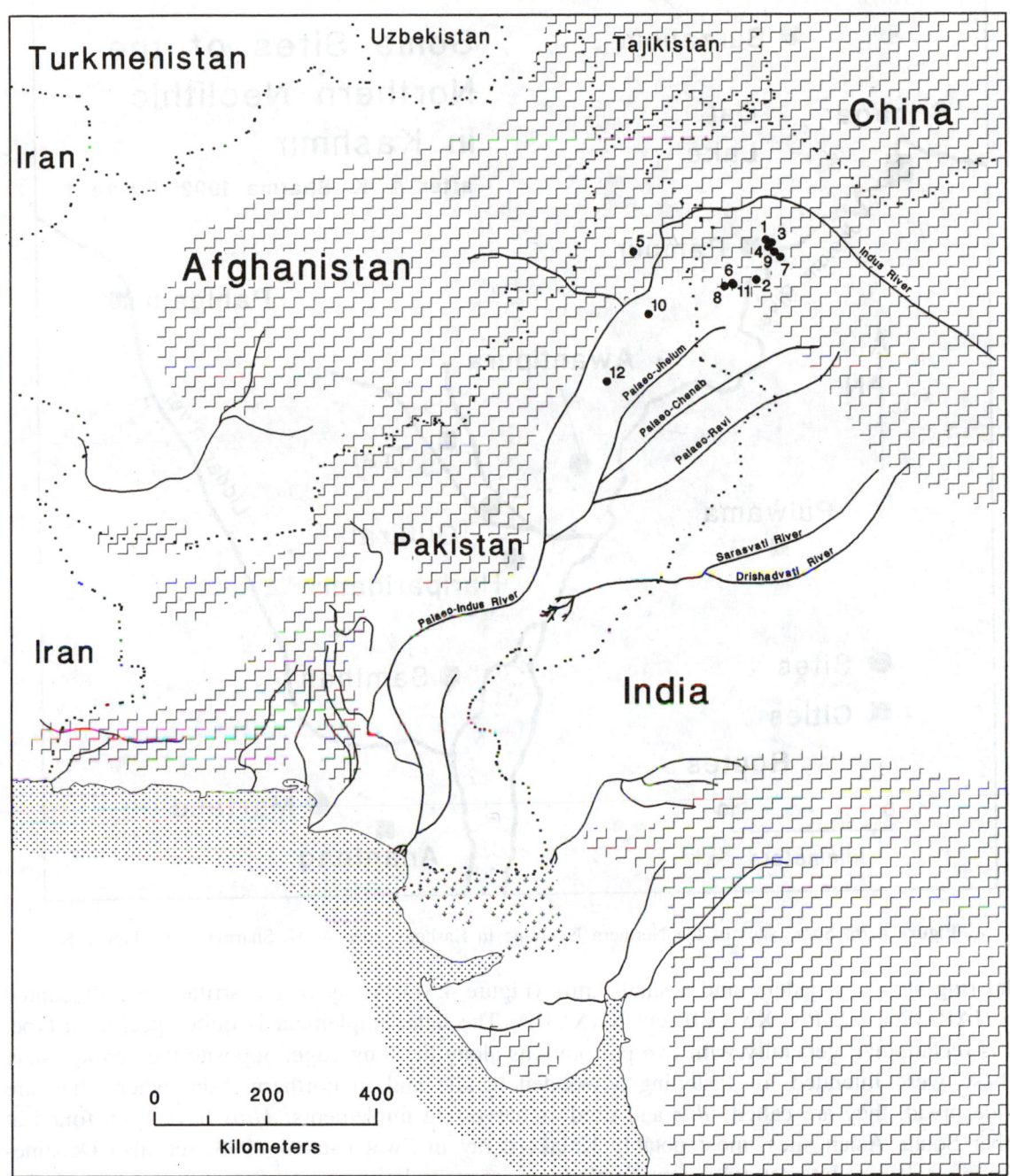

Key to Figure 4.75.

1 Awantipura
2 Burzahom
3 Gufkral
4 Hariparigom

5 Kalako Deray
6 Kanispur
7 Martand
8 Petha Gantmula

9 Samthan
10 Sarai Khola
11 Singhpur
12 Uchali

Figure 4.75. Sites of the Northern Neolithic

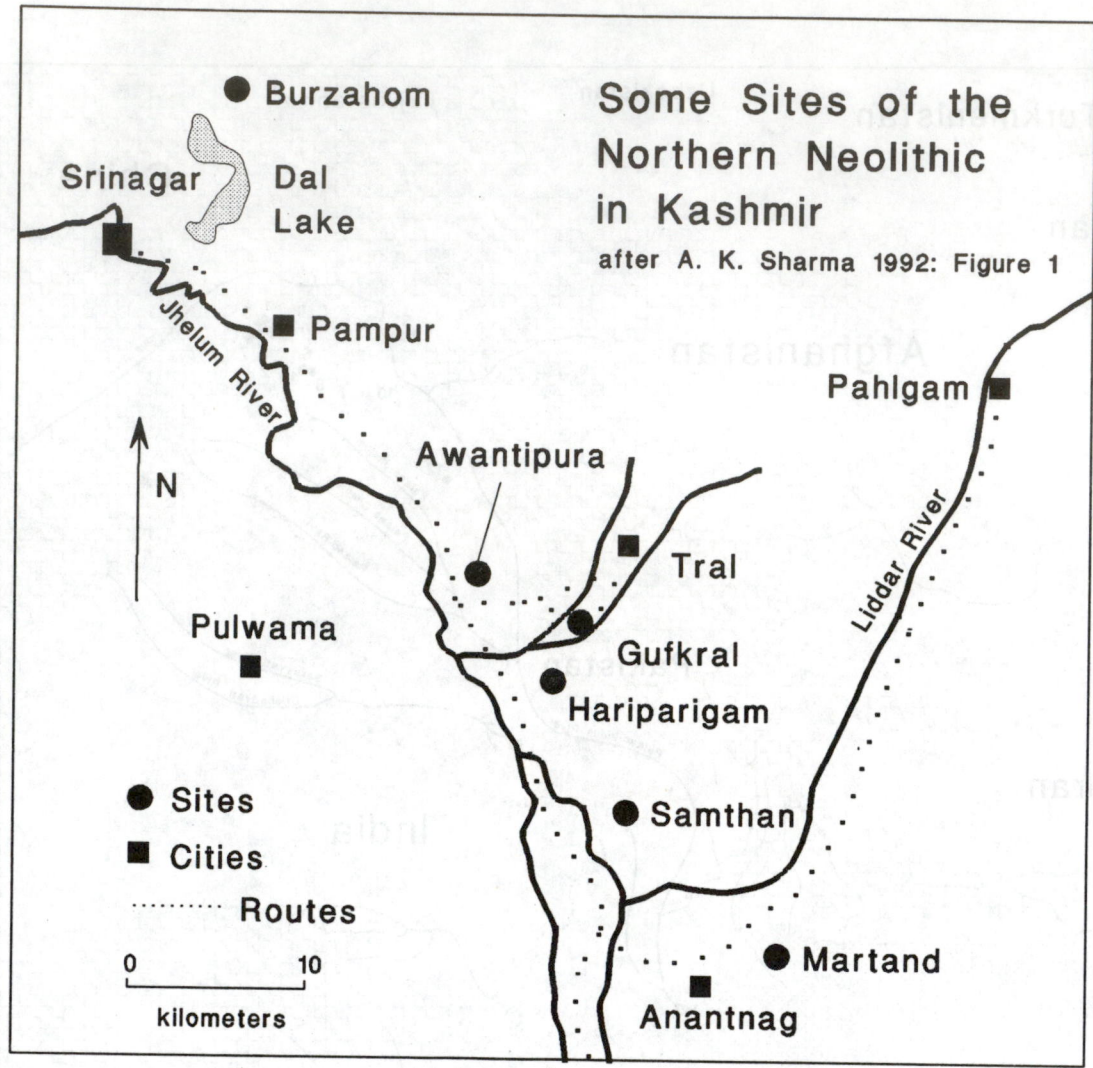

Figure 4.76. Some sites of the Northern Neolithic in Kashmir, after A. K. Sharma 1992: Figure 1

flat ring stones of jadeite and a small knife (Figure 4.81). Many of the artifacts are illustrated in (IAR 1961-62: Pls. XXXVII and XXXVIII). The latter implement is quite specific in type. It is rectangular, generally with two perforations along the long edge, opposite the cutting edge. These were intended for fastening a wooden handle and in northern Asia, where they are widespread, they are called *ulus* and used as harvesting implements. *Ulus* have been found at other South Asian sites, most notably Kalako-deray in Swat (Stacul 1993, see also Debaine-Francfort 1988). Interestingly, unperforated, square stone knives, similar to the *ulus* were found at the Mature Harappan site of Shortughai on the Amu Darya (Oxus River) (Francfort 1989b: Plate 68). Evidence for the burial of dogs and possible dog ritual or sacrifice was also obtained from Burzahom.

Two Kot Diji Phase type pots were found at Burzahom in Period IB. One of them contained ca. 950 beads of carnelian and agate (IAR 1964-65: 13) and was decorated with the "horned deity" ("Mahisha") (Figure 4.82, Figure 4.83).

The two examples of this motif on ceramics from the Sorath Harappan, one of the regional

TABLE 4.27
Camp Sites of the Northern Neolithic

Site Name	Province/State	District	Size in Hectares
Sarai Khola	West Punjab	Rawalpindi	18.6
Gufkral	Jammu & Kashmir	Pulwama	3.0
Burzahom	Jammu & Kashmir	Srinagar	2.0
Awantipura	Jammu & Kashmir	Anantang	
Begagund	Jammu & Kashmir	Anantnag	
Brah	Jammu & Kashmir		
Damodar Karewa	Jammu & Kashmir		
Gurhoma Sangri	Jammu & Kashmir		
Hariparigom	Jammu & Kashmir	Anantnag	
Jayadevi Udar	Jammu & Kashmir	Anantnag	
Kalako Deray	Northwest Frontier	Swat	
Kanispur	Jammu & Kashmir	Baramula	
Khor	Jammu & Kashmir	Baramula	
Khui Nara	West Punjab		
Martand	Jammu & Kashmir	Anantang	
Olichibag	Jammu & Kashmir	Anantnag	
Pampur	Jammu & Kashmir	Anantnag	
Panzagom	Jammu & Kashmir	Anantnag	
Pattan	Jammu & Kashmir	Baramula	
Petha Gantmula	Jammu & Kashmir	Baramula	
Samthan	Jammu & Kashmir	Anantnag	
Seru	Jammu & Kashmir	Anantnag	
Singhpur	Jammu & Kashmir	Baramula	
Sombur	Jammu & Kashmir	Anantnag	
Thajiwor	Jammu & Kashmir	Anantnag	
Uchali	West Punjab	Rawalpindi	
Waztal	Jammu & Kashmir		

Figure 4.77. Hunting scene on a stone slab from Burzahom, Period IB, after B. M. Pande 1973: 135

546

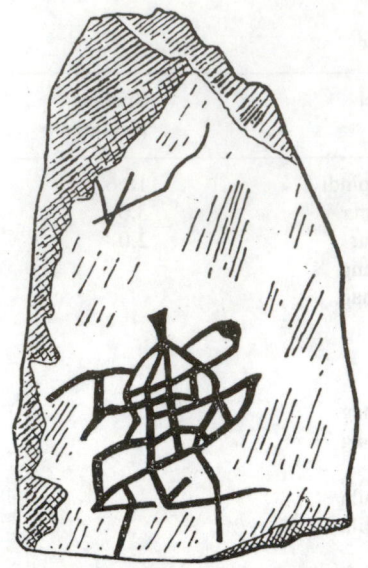

Figure 4.78. "Tectiform" design engraved on a stone slab, Burzahom, Period IB, after B. M. Pande 1972

manifestations of the Mature Harappan, are complemented by evidence from seals as in Plate 4.24. The famous "ProtoSiva" seal would be another example from Mature Harappan contexts.

A flexed human burial also had a carnelian necklace (S. P. Gupta 1972a: 85) and many other beads of this kind were found in the course of excavation. These pots and beads, along with the ecological symbiosis that is inherent to the relationship between the mountains and plains of northern India and Pakistan tell us in the most unmistakable way that there was an important set of relationships here. There is a long list of products found at Early Harappan and Mature Harappan sites on the plains which are likely to have come from the Himalaya (see Appendix D, Fentress 1976: 306-309 and "Mineral Commodity Sources for Ancient Peoples of the Lower Indus River Valley" compiled by Robert G. Schmidt and R. Williams Mathews as Open File Report of 92-519, by the U. S. Geological Survey for a tabulation of these and other products). It is quite clear that the peoples of the Northern Neolithic were at least among those that the Early and Mature Harappans dealt with when they acquired these goods.

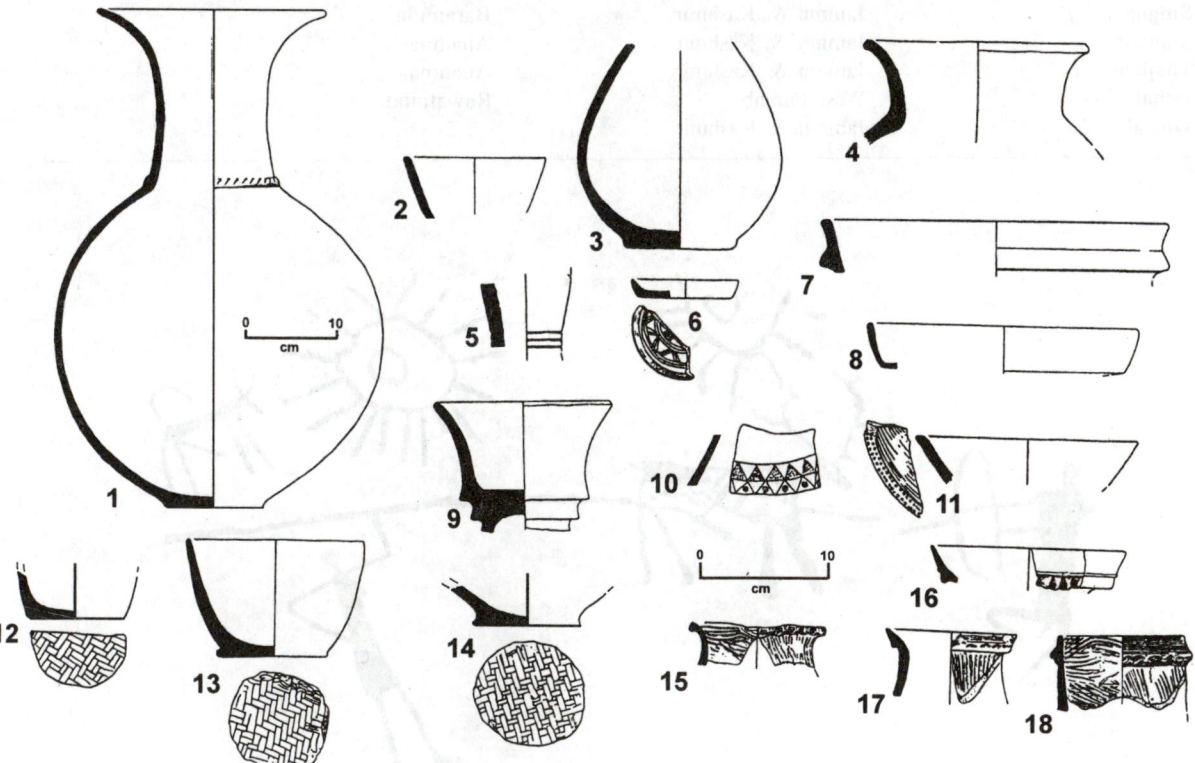

Figure 4.79. Pottery of the Northern Neolithic from Burzahom, after IAR 1961-62: 20-1

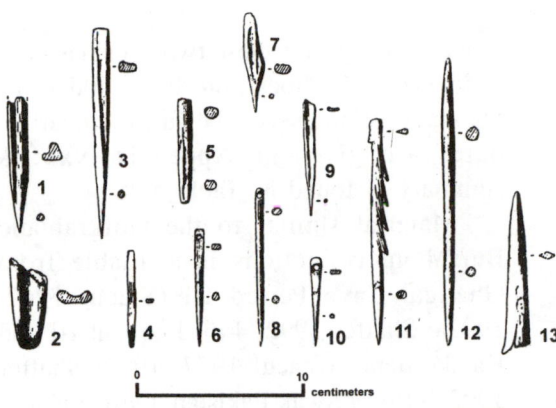

Figure 4.80. Bone artifacts of the Northern Neolithic from Burzahom, after IAR 1961-62: 21

Figure 4.81. Ground stone tools from the Northern Neolithic from Burzahom, after IAR 1961-62: Plate XXXVIII

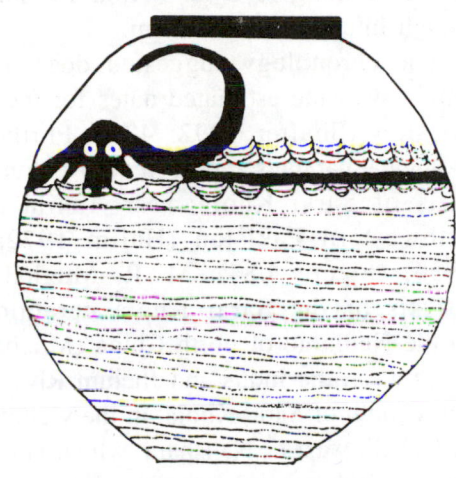

Figure 4.82. Kot Diji Phase pot from Burzahom, Period IB

Subsistence Information

The palaeobotanical finds from Gufkral include the presence of wheat (*Triticum aestivum*), barley (*Hordeum distichum*), lentil (*Lens esculenta*), field pea (*Pissum arvenae*). Towards the end of the Neolithic there is evidence for the introduction of rice (*Oryza sativa*) (A. K. Sharma 1986: 13; Buth, Khan and Lone 1986).

A. K. Sharma also informs us that at Gufkral: "The faunal assemblage (was) dominated by wild animals in the lower levels, slowly leading almost exclusively to domesticated ones in the middle and upper levels of the site" (1986: 14-4).

The Burzahom inhabitants were farming and herding peoples who also hunted. There were remains of domesticated cattle (zebu or *Bos indicus*), sheep (*Ovis aries*), goat (*Capra hircus*), pig (*Sus scrofa*), water buffalo (*Bubalus bubalis*), dog (*Canis familiaris*). Wild animals include the nilgai (*Boselaphus tragocamelus*), and Kashmir Stag (*Cervus elaphas*). There is no report on cereal cultivation, but a quern was found in Period IA contexts (Naseem 1982: 152-53). This is corroborated by some pollen data from Haigam Laka (Thapar 1974: 64).

548

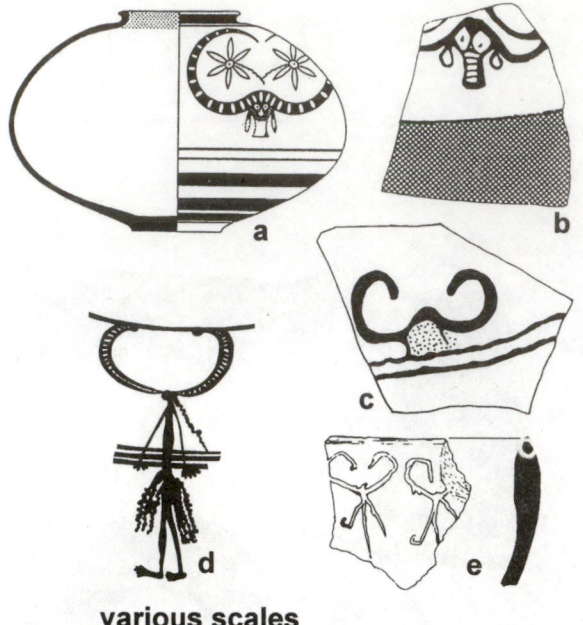

various scales

Figure 4.83. Other pots with horned deities: a, Kot Diji, Early Harappan, after F. A. Khan 1965: 58; b, Gumla III, Early Harappan, after Dani 1970-71: Plate 1a; c, Hathala, Early Harappan, after Dani 1970-71: Plate 65, No. 7; d, Padri, Sorath Harappan, after Shinde 1992a: 83 and e, Babar Kot, surface, probably Sorath Harappan, unpublished

Chronology

The chronology for these two sites has been estimated by radiocarbon dates, and some comparative analysis. The full radiocarbon dates are given in Appendix **xxx**. A summary is found in Table 4.28

Material similar to the Gufkral and Burzahom collections is available from Ghaligai Cave Period III (Stacul 1967, 1992a; Shaffer 1992: 446) Loebanr III and Kalako-deray (Stacul 1977, 1993; Shaffer 1992: 446) in Swat, Pakistan. Only Kalako-deray seems to have sufficient material to suggest that it was settled by peoples of the Northern Neolithic, the remaining material coming to Swat Period IV sites through interaction with them.

The chronology suggested does not conflict with the estimated dates for these two sites (Shaffer 1992: 429). Further typological parallels appear in the Neolithic levels of Sarai Khola, near Taxila in northwestern Pakistan (Halim 1972a, 1972b) (Figure 4.84). M. R. Mughal's analysis of the Sarai Khola ceramics contains a discussion of these ties and of parallels with the Neolithic of north China (Mughal 1972i: 36). My own travels in the Thal Desert, the doab between the Indus and Jhelum Rivers, have revealed the presence of other Northern Neolithic sites south of Sarai Khola, in the vicinity of Leiah. H. deTerra and T. T. Paterson reported a site at Uchali, west of Naushara, which is ca. 150 kilometers southwest of Rawalpindi. Their description includes the observation that "...the implement bearing layers (contained) a burial which yielded hand-made pottery, presumably of neolithic type" (1939: 277-78). There is no guarantee that this is a Northern Neolithic site, but it could be and their observation should be checked again.

TABLE 4.28
Chronological Chart for Burzahom and Gufkral

Site	Period at Site	Date	Indus Stage
Gufkral IC	Late Neolithic	2000-1500 BC	Post-urban
Burzahom IB			Harappan
Gufkral IB	Early Neolithic	2500-2000 BC	Mature Harappan
Burzahom IA			
Gufkral IA	Aceramic Neolithic	2800-2500 BC	Early Harappan

Figure 4.84. Northern Neolithic Material from Sarai Khola, after Halim 1972b: 54-9

Human Burials of the Northern Neolithic

Several burials were found at Burzahom. Period IA has no interments, but IB produced eight burials; six human and two animal (Naseem 1982: 147, 151; Sharma 1967; S. P. Gupta 1972a: 84-8). The human interments have been classified as three different types: flexed, extended and fractional. All are associated with the habitation and appear to have been placed below the floors of houses.

Burzahom Flexed Burials

Number 1. The first interment was found in the 1962-63 season and was laid with a general northeast-southwest orientation, head to the northeast. It has been well described by A. K. Sharma (1967) and S. P. Gupta (1972a: 84-5). The skull was completely covered in red ochre and had what appeared to be trepanning marks, with seven finished and four unfinished holes (IAR 1962-63: 9-10). This grave was rich in offerings, including the cranium and antlers of a deer, a soapstone object and a disk bead. An animal jaw was included and covered in red ochre, just as the human skull had been. This is the richest grave found so far at Burzahom, and it appears to be the interment of a special person from the site.

Number 2. The second interment also had a northeast-southwest orientation, resting on its left side. The arms had been raised so that the palms of the hands covered the face. A necklace of five carnelian beads was found near the neck (S. P. Gupta 1972: 85, Naseem 1982: 149).

Number 3. The third flexed burial was that of a child about two years old, oriented east-west (S. P. Gupta 1972: 85).

Burzahom Extended Burial

Number 4. There is one extended inhumation at Burzahom. It was oriented from the southwest to the northeast, and the skull was badly damaged (A. K. Sharma 1968; S. P. Gupta 1972: 85).

Burzahom Fractional Burials

Number 5. The bones of an adult who had been exposed at death and whose bones had been collected for reburial were found in a lime plaster lined pit at Burzahom. These bones were also treated with red ochre. There seems to have been a conscious effort to carefully arrange the bones in a flexed position. A single barrel shaped bead accompanied the bones to this grave. Two conical stones above the interment were arranged pointing to the feet of this individual.

Number 6. The second fractional burial was in a pit, with the skull to one side, in the northeast corner. It too, had been treated with red ochre.

TABLE 4.29
Age Distribution of the Burzahom Interments, after Basu and Pal 1980: Table 2

Category	Age Range	Number
Subadult	about 5	1
Juvenile	11-15 years	1
Young Adult	26-30 years	2
Older Adult	31-35 years	2
Middle Age	46-50 years	1
Older Adult	51-55 years	3
Total		10

It has not been possible to associate the following data with specific skeletons but it is reported that:

Five of the skeletons were male.
Three of the skeletons were female.
The sex could not be determined on two skeletons.
(Basu and Pal 1980: 8)

Animal Burials

There are two animal burials associated with the Northern Neolithic at Burzahom, both in Period IB (A. K. Sharma 1968; S. P. Gupta 1972: 87-8). The first was a simple dog burial, without grave offerings (IAR 1962-63: Plate XXVII B). The second was rather elaborate, found during the 1962-63 season (IAR 1962-63: 9-10, Plate XXVII A). The remains of several animals were reportedly interred in an oval pit, with a long axis of 1.35 meters. The pit contained the remains of five wild dogs and two antlers. All five skulls were intact and two of them could be seen to be in a position which suggested articulation with the surviving vertebral columns. The remaining dog bones were disturbed and had broken ribs, long bones and pelvic girdles.

A. K. Sharma thought of this interment as the result of some kind of ceremonial burial, with the dogs killed, stripped of their flesh and then buried. S. P. Gupta, disagreed with this notion by observing that "...the dog is hardly 'pious' enough to be 'sacrificed' as such" (1972: 87). Gupta's criticism may be a bit culture bound, since there are indications that the Northern Neolithic has its roots in a culture area where dog sacrifice is known.

The Cultural Roots of the Northern Neolithic

The cultural and historical affinities of the peoples interred at Burzahom are clearly North Asian as recognized by a number of scholars (i.e., Allchin, B. and F. R. 1968: 160, 1982: 113-16; Mughal 1972i: 36; Fairservis 1975: 316-18; D. P. Agrawal 1982a: 98-106). The principal parallels are the semi-subterranean dwellings, mat impressed pottery, rich bone industry, form of the ground stone tools, and the dog burials.

There are very good specialized studies of the East Asian and South Asian connections in the following: Anderson (1943: esp. 223, 268 and 269), W. Watson (1970: 221-6), S. P. Gupta (1979: 216-17), Debaine-Francfort (1988) and Stacul (1985, 1992a, 1993). Walter A. Fairservis has commented on the significance of the Northern Neolithic in the following way:

> Burzahom represents a movement out of Central Asia toward and into the subcontinent of a more limited kind than that out of Western Asia previously described. However, one of the surprises of the archaeological investigation of the old North-West Frontier Province and the Punjab is the absence of late prehistoric sites. It may be that future investigation of these regions will reveal a deeper penetration of the Burzahom cultural form onto the alluvial plains from its highland home. In any case Burzahom represents the southernmost expression of a widespread North Asian complex. It represents a movement that may well have started with the Mesolithic of Europe and which survived in the fertile valleys of Kashmir and perhaps Nepal, Tibet, Hunza, Baltistan and Ladakh. It is so clearly inner Asian that one finds difficulty in including it as a part of subcontinental archaeology except for the fact that it is in the river system of the subcontinent. It is also a less important but nonetheless definitive manifestation of one of the cultural streams which were through time directed toward India. In this

one is reminded of the historical travels of the Chinese monks Fa Hsien and Hsuen Tsang, who were later to travel out of inner Asia to India via High Asia. These travels were somewhat anticipated by the prehistoric cultures of the type found in Kashmir (Fairservis 1975: 317-18).

In the discussion of the Indus script it was mentioned that F. Southworth found some evidence for a language(s) of the Sino-Tibetan family in ancient South Asia (Southworth 1979, 1988, 1990, 1992). The Northern Neolithic may be a concrete archaeological expression of this hypothesis, as well as the one advanced by Bertil Tikkanen (1988) who suggested that there may be an ancient language related to modern Burushaski that goes as far back as the third millennium BC.

Other Sites with Material of Northern Neolithic Affiliation

The occurrence of a dog interred with a human in the Ropar cemetery, Burial No. 14 (Dutta, Pal, Gupta and Dutta 1987: 13) has a close parallel to this north Asian/Burzahom practice. At Chandigarh in the Punjab, sherds thought to be like the ceramics of the Northern Neolithic were found along with "...an object of animal bone with a serrated edge" recalling Burzahom (N. C. Ghosh 1989: 94). Ropar is located at the point where the Sutlej River enters the plains of the Punjab, a strategic spot, if ever there was one. This river valley is one of the oldest and easiest routes between the north Punjab and the mountains of Kashmir, and the presence of Mature Harappan and Northern Neolithic materials there documents the unsurprising fact that it was in use during the third millennium BC.

Estimate of Settled Area for the Northern Neolithic

An estimate of the settled area of the Northern Neolithic sites that have been found is possible, but given the quality of the data set it is clearly a preliminary statement on this topic. Data on site size are especially thin for these settlements.

TABLE 4.30
Estimates of Settled Area for the Northern Neolithic

Total Sites	25
Sites with Size Estimate	3
Settled Area of Sites with Known Sizes	23.6
Sites with Size Unknown	22
Average Site Size 7.87	
Estimated Settled Area of Sites without Size	173.14
Estimated Total Settled Area	196.74

Sizes given in hectares

Northern Neolithic: Summary

The Northern Neolithic is important for understanding the mechanism through which the Early and Mature Harappan peoples gained access to mountain resources: timber, stone, and possibly metal. Trade and exchange brought them into contact with truly foreign peoples, almost certainly speaking a language(s) unrelated to the different tongues of the ethnically diverse population of the plains. It is also likely that this contact genetically enriched the population through intercourse that was more than purely economic. These were people on the fringes of the Indus world. While they seem to have played an important role in the procurement of certain resources they never became a part of it.

THE PRELUDE TO THE EARLY HARAPPAN

In the Prelude to the Early Harappan the themes that have been developed in Stages One and Two will be continued: cultural continuity and change, growth, geographical expansion and regionalism. There is a minimum of technological change and the paradigm already established for the subsistence regime will be expanded, rather than modified. Archaeological data from excavated sites will be used extensively in this exploration of the Early Harappan Stage and more sophisticated use will be made of settlement data. There are strengths and weaknesses in this method which should be considered.

The following methodological points are already well known to seasoned archaeologists, but not to scholars in other disciplines, who may want to know more about the Harappan Civilization and often wonder how to evaluate archaeological data. Because the *Indus Age* is directed to this audience, as well as archaeologists, it is appropriate to take a small detour to discuss settlement archaeology, in its particular South Asian manifestation.

Settlement Patterns: An Archaeological Tool

The geographical distribution of the Early Harappan is shown in the accompanying map (Figure 4.85). Two things should be immediately apparent: (1) there is considerable growth in the number of settlements; and (2) the expansion of the Early Harappan to the east, in both Punjabs and Haryana as well as Gujarat, is significant. Cholistan actually experiences a decline in the number of settlements, but their average size increases. This may be a reflection of a decline in the number of pastoral camps and a general "settling-in" to the area.

The basic statistics on the Early Harappan settlements are as follows: the total number of sites is 479; there are 290 with size figures that total 1575.2 hectares of inhabited space. This yields an average site size of 5.43 hectares. Seventy-one Early Harappan sites have had some excavation. These raw figures are interesting in a comparative way, because they document the scale of ontological growth that seems to have characterized the Early Harappan Stage and the Togau, Kechi Beg and Hakra Wares Phases that preceded it.

Table 4.31 has been prepared as a reference to the raw site count and size data for the all phases, from Kili Ghul Mohammad, through the Mature Harappan, anticipating the discussion of that data set.

Handling these data in a critical fashion requires more than a regional perspective. The most obvious observation is that they show the location of sites where archaeologists (and others) have worked and recorded them, but do not necessarily show where all of the sites are. To understand the significance of site survey as a factor in molding perceptions of Indus settlement data, a review for the cultural geography and history of research of the Indus Age would be required on a minute basis; minimally district by district. This kind of painstaking evaluation has never been done, but the data may now be available for such a study to be attempted. It is too detailed to be included here so something less thorough and impressionistic will have to do. A version of this has already been published (Possehl 1979c: 540-46).

Other Attempts to Organize Settlement Data

Several efforts have been made to bring settlement pattern data together for the Harappan

554

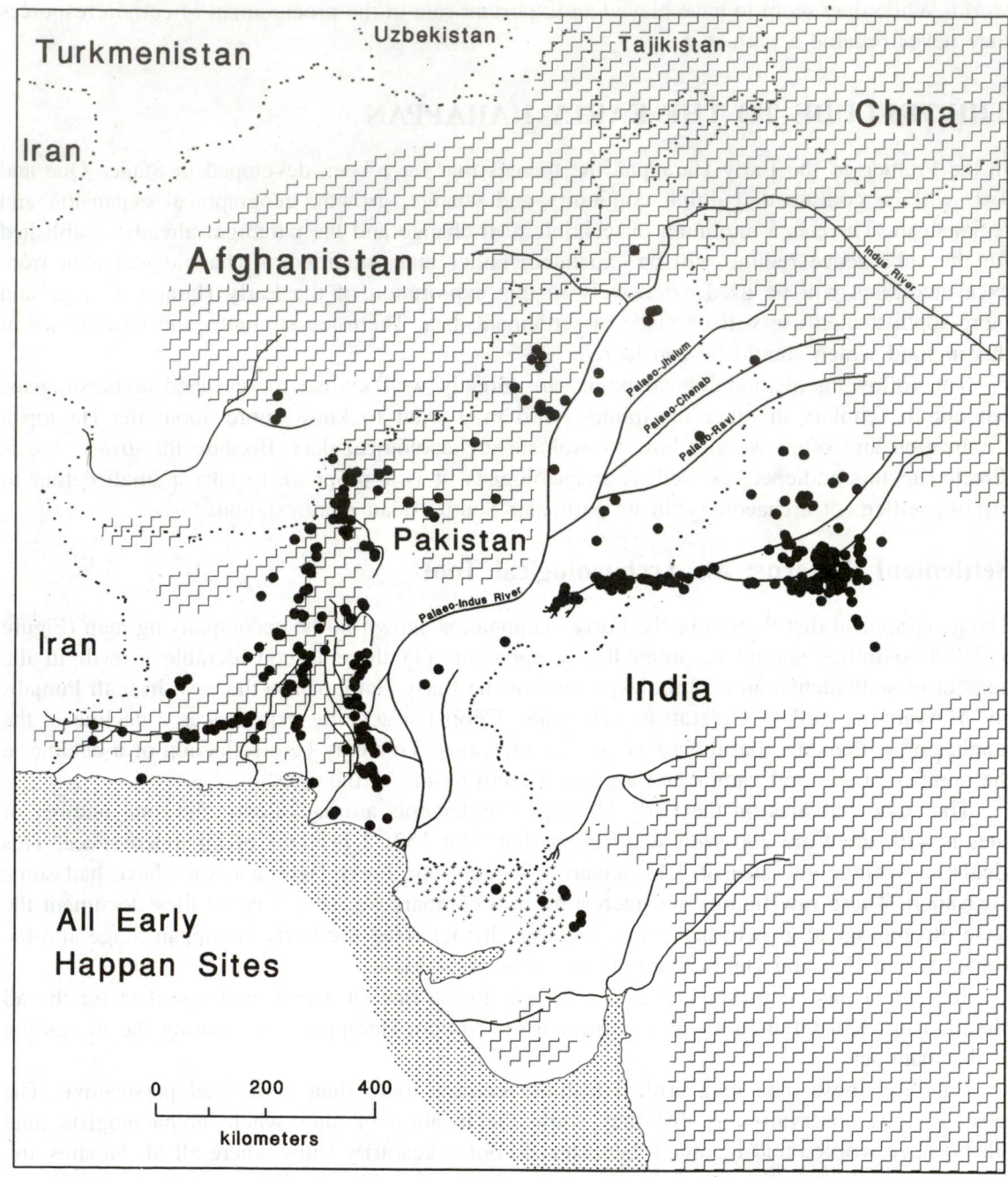

Figure 4.85. Map of Early Harappan Sites

Civilization. For Gujarat, S. R. Rao's initial list of sites (Rao, S. R. 1963a: 205-07) was expanded to a more comprehensive gazetteer by Possehl (1980: 89-119). Walter Fairservis included an Appendix of sites from the "Neolithic" to the Iron Age in Pakistan as part of his survey of South Asian Archaeology (Fairservis 1971a: 399-414). Suraj Bhan brought together much of the settlement data for the Indian Punjab and Haryana in his thesis (1972, 1975) and a list of sites for Sindh was incorporated into Louis Flam's dissertation (1981a, see also Flam 1981b). The first comprehensive list of sites of the Harappan Tradition, in both India and Pakistan, was

TABLE 4.31
Settlement Data by Early Harappan Phase

Phase/Stage	Number of Settlements	Settlements With Size	Average Size
Mature Harappan	1019	537	7.25
Early Harappan	477	281	4.51
Developed Village Farming Community and Pastoral Societies			
Kechi Beg & Hakra Wares	256	184	5.22
Togau	84	48	3.51
Primary Village Farming Community and Pastoral Camp			
Burj Basket-marked	33	19	2.58
Kili Ghul Mohammad	20	9	2.65

published by B. M. Pande and K. S. Ramachandran (1971: 37-43) as a part of their *Bibliography of the Harappan Culture*, which was expanded and updated by Michael Jansen (1981).

There is a good comprehensive list of Harappan sites in India completed by Jagat Pati Joshi, Madhu Bala and Jassu Ram (1984) in their "The Indus Civilization: A reconsideration on the basis of distribution maps." It is difficult to make an exact site count from their list because sites are listed by period (Pre-Harappan, Mature Harappan, Late Harappan) and places with more than one occupation could be enumerated twice. But, the Gazetteer of Settlements of the Indus Age (Appendix A, Part 4) lists 959 entries with a bibliographic citation to their work, which should be a very close approximation to the real total.

Volume two of A. Ghosh's *Encyclopaedia of Indian Archaeology* (1989a) has a fine coverage of sites, some of them well annotated by experts, but his book covers all periods and has not been provided with finding aids that allow one to conveniently locate sites according to their period. This encyclopaedia also shares a serious shortcoming common to many other works on South Asian archaeology, in that it contains information only on places in the modern Indian nation state, not the historical and cultural region of South Asia. Some of the studies concerning the Indus Age (e.g., Joshi, Madhu Bala and Ram 1984), deal with sites or data in either India or Pakistan, rather than taking a holistic view of the ancient cultural and political geography of the ancient world.

The Principal Survey Efforts

A survey of the principal explorations in the Greater Indus Region will help the reader to evaluate critically the settlement pattern data for the Early and Mature Harappan Stages. As a matter of convenience, the density or intensity of the survey will be divided into three levels: unobserved, surveyed, intensively surveyed. The first is self evident, but there is little ground within the Greater Indus Region that has not been looked at by someone with an archaeological interest over the past ninety years. The second is reserved for a category of exploration that has been done in haste, or by an untrained person, or from a vehicle, with little or no leg work. The

556

third is reserved for intensive ground based walking surveys, undertaken by people with some training in archaeology. There are parts of the pertinent geography where an area can be upgraded from "surveyed" to "intensively surveyed" if a significant amount of work has been done there. A map (Figure 4.86) has been prepared designating the explored areas and the intensity of the work in each zone. The very recent explorations undertaken by the Pakistan Department of Archaeology has been included here, even though most of this exploration has

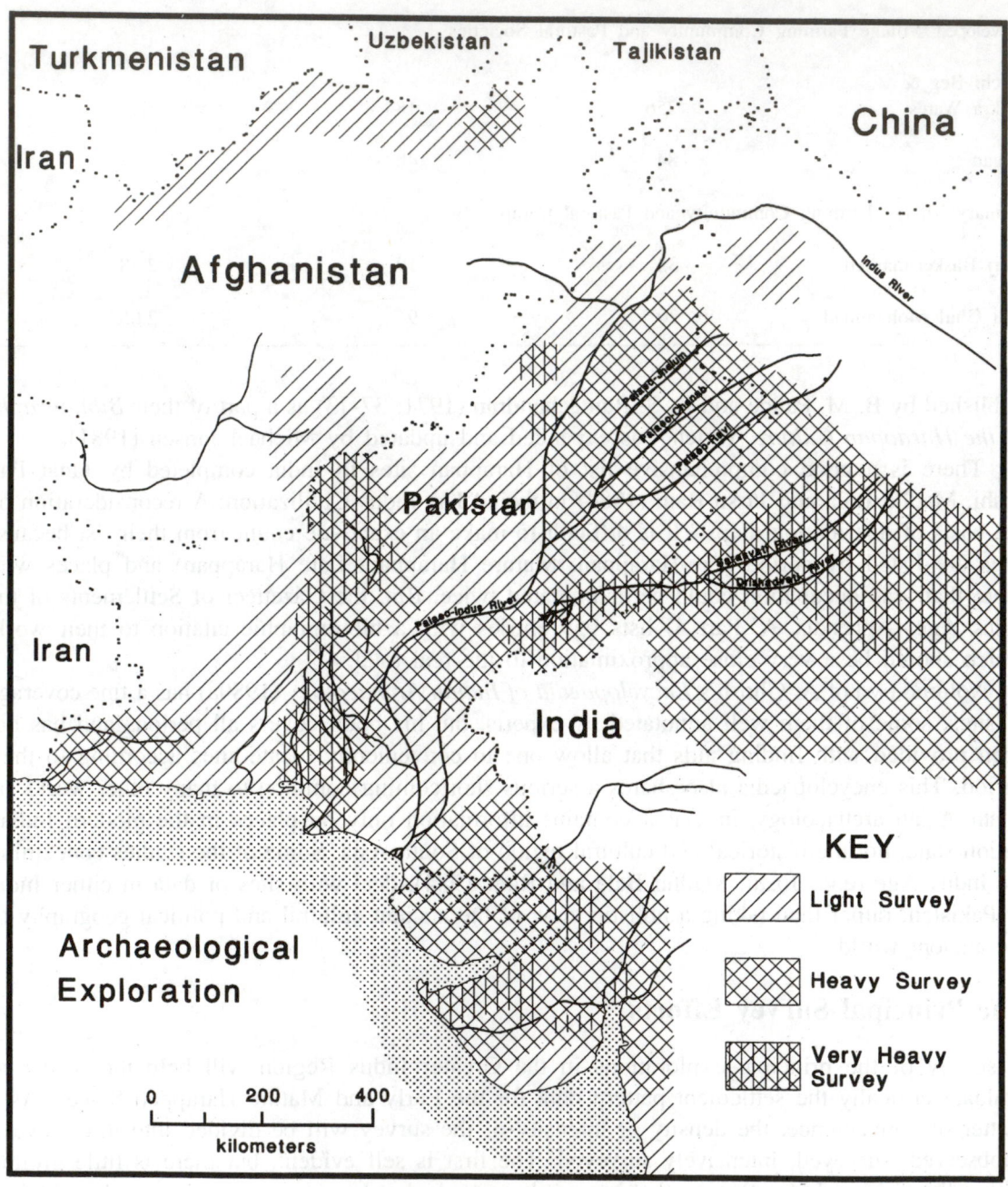

Figure 4.86. Survey in the Greater Indus Region

yet to be published. The illustration shows that a great deal of work has been done since 1977, when the first map of this type was completed (Possehl 1979b: Fig. 2).

One small, qualifying note should be made before giving an overview of the major survey efforts. No region, district, river valley or village has been so thoroughly explored that some new item of interest to the Indus Age might not be found. This is especially true for very small sites and spot finds. Thus, even when an area has been comparatively well explored, such as the state of Haryana, it is always possible that more sites will turn up, particularly small camps.

Baluchistan Survey

In Baluchistan, geographically Zhob, Loralai, Quetta, Sarawan, Jhalawan, Makran, Chagai and Kharan, survey began with Sir Aurel Stein in 1927-28, following his initial reconnaissance in 1904-05 (Stein 1905, 1929a, 1931). Beatrice de Cardi's Kalat Survey in 1948 and 1957 followed Stein (de Cardi 1965, 1984). Walter Fairservis was in Quetta/Pishin with the Second Afghan Expedition 1950-51 (Fairservis 1956a). Zhob, Loralai Quetta/Pishin and Sarawan area were reviewed by M. R. Mughal in 1972 (Mughal 1972g, 1974a). In the course of hydrological survey Robert Raikes conducted a reconnaissance of southern Baluchistan in 1955-57 and 1960-61 (Raikes 1968b). In 1955, Henry Field explored Kalat (Sarawan and Jhalawan) and Makran, retracing some of Stein's path (Field 1959). The Makran Coast was surveyed by George F. Dales in 1960 (Dales 1962a, 1962b, 1964; Dales and Lipo 1992). Work on the Makran, especially the western side is now being very competently undertaken by Roland Besenval (Besenval and Sanlaville 1990, Besenval 1992; Besenval and Marquis 1993). Las Bela was first surveyed by Sir Aurel Stein (1943b), but the most significant work there has been by Walter Fairservis in 1959-60 (1967, 1971a: 185-208). Some sites in Las Bela were also covered by Robert Raikes in his reconnaissances as well as by Professor Abdur Rauf Khan of Karachi University (1973, 1979b).

The Quetta-Pishin Valleys and Las Bela have been the most thoroughly explored in this region. Work in Kalat is less complete, but the major sites probably have been located and the same will be true of Makran when the exploration by Besenval is complete. Kharan District is not well explored, and work needs to be done there (M. Khan 1990a). Chagai is virtually an unknown. It is so dry and desolate that human habitation in any significant density will not be found there, but who really knows? Copper was plentiful there, as was lapis lazuli. Although Zhob and Loralai have been seen by archaeologists, there are immense areas which call for much more exploration, especially in Marri/Bugti and Kohlu country.[10]

The Northwest Frontier Survey

Archaeological exploration in the Northwest Frontier begins with Fritz Noetling (1898a, 1898b, 1899; Pedde 1993a, 1993b), and Stein (1905), but it was Stein's 1927 reconnaissance (Stein 1928a, 1928b, 1929a) that revealed the very substantial archaeological resources in the region. Fairservis followed on this work in 1950-51 (Fairservis 1959) and reported the new site of Duki in Zhob and Loralai. M. R. Mughal returned to the region in 1972 (Mughal 1972g, 1974a). The Bannu Archaeological Project has explored this valley in a competent way (Allchin, Allchin, Durrani and Khan 1986; Khan, Knox and Thomas 1989, 1990a, 1990b, 1991a). Many scholars have been in the Vale of Peshawar but the prehistoric record there is thin, causing one to wonder about the intensity of the work. Kohat, to the south of Peshawar and an area comparable to Bannu, is poorly known as is the much more rugged Kurram tract to the west. Swat has been extensively explored, first by Stein (1930) and then by a team from IsMEO headed by Giorgio Stacul (1966, 1970a, 1974, 1987).

558

The Derajat and Northwest Punjab

Dera Ismail Khan was first toured by Stein in 1927 (Stein 1929a), and in 1969-70 by the University of Peshawar. (Dani 1970-71). To the south, Dera Ghazi Khan is fresh territory and its archaeological potentials need to be assessed. To the north in Campbellpur and Rawalpindi Districts some exploration has been done (Mughal 1972f) but not the kind of intensive search that the region requires.

Sindh and Kachi Survey

There has been a great deal of exploration in Sindh and Kachi, beginning with the pre-modern researches of D. R. Bhandarkar (1911-12), R. D. Banerji (1918-19, 1920-21, 1922-23, 1926), Henry Cousens (1929) and G. E. L. Carter (1932). More serious work was undertaken by Rao Bahadur K. N. Dikshit (1925-26a, 1925-26b, 1925-26c). N. G. Majumdar, the "Sir Aurel Stein of Sindh," explored there from 1928 to 1931 and again in 1938 (Majumdar 1934; Krishna Deva and McCown 1949). M. S. Vats did additional work in Khairpur State in 1935-36 (Vats 1935-36). After that there is an interstice in the work, filled only with the "amateur excursions" of H. T. Lambrick (1942a, 1944, 1946). Exploration resumed in 1959-60 when Walter Fairservis investigated parts of southwestern Sindh (Fairservis 1971a: 185-208). The other side of the Indus, southeastern Sindh was explored by Mohammad Sharif of the Pakistan Department of Archaeology in 1971-72 (Mughal 1972h). Professor Abdur Rauf Khan of Karachi University conducted exploration, with varying degrees of intensity, in southeastern Sindh, Las Bela and the Karachi area (Khan, A. R. 1968a, 1968b, 1973, 1979a-g, 1981). Louis Flam has been conducting a general survey of Sindh for a number of seasons since 1975. His most intensive work has been in the Kirthar Piedmont and Sindh Kohistan (Flam 1981a, 1981b, 1984, 1986a, 1986b, 1987). In 1983, Hans Nissen of the Free University of Berlin undertook one season of exploration in the area between Lake Manchar and Sukkur (Nissen 1983, 1994). The Department of Archaeology at the Jamshero Campus of the University of Sindh also has an active field program of exploration. Qasid H. Mallah of the Shah Abdul Latif University conducted exploration in Sukkur District and located 25 sites of the Indus Age, 20 of which were newly reported (Mallah 1994). The Pakistan Department of Archaeology is currently exploring all of northern Sindh. Curiously, the deep alluvium of Sindh, the heart of the modern Indus flood plain, has received relatively little attention from archaeologists, the survey of Hans Nissen being an exception.

Kachi has been surveyed principally by the French Archaeological Mission, which has been excavating in this area since 1968, along with other scholars: (Anonymous 1964: 6, 11-2, 13-4; Enault and Jarrige 1973: 189-90; de Cardi 1983; Santoni 1980, 1984, 1988, 1989; Jarrige 1986: 67, 120, 116-17). Several prehistoric sites have been found in the Bolan pass (Fairservis 1956a: 200; Enault and Jarrige 1973).

West Punjab Survey

Exploration in the West Punjab has been somewhat patchy; something that the Pakistan Department of Archaeology is currently rectifying with a comprehensive effort to survey every district there. Archaeological work began in this area with Sir Alexander Cunningham's visits to Harappa in 1853, 1856 and 1872-73 (Cunningham 1875). Limited exploration took place during the initial period of excavation at Harappa. Sir Aurel Stein was in the vicinity of the Salt Range and Tharl desert in 1931, in the course of his search for the historical geography of Alexander the Great's last great battle (Stein 1937: 1-69). He reported no prehistoric sites in the area, in spite of a visit to Mianwali where there is at least one very prominent Kot Diji site. The same is true of Henry Field's tour of the area in 1955 (Field 1959). Sahiwal District, in which Harappa is located, has been explored by M. R. Mughal (1972e), and the area around Multan has been surveyed by Mohammad Sharif (1989). The most significant series of exploratory tours in the Punjab, probably in the history of Harappan archaeology, were undertaken by Mughal between 1974 and 1978 in Cholistan (Bahawalpur and Rahimyar Khan Districts). He found over 350 sites including ninety-nine Hakra Wares settlements, forty Early Harappan, 174 Mature Harappan, fifty Cemetery H and fourteen Painted Grey Ware sites (Mughal 1997, with amendments). Stein reported some sites in this area in 1940-41, but this was nothing compared with Mughal's results (Stein 1943a; S. P. Gupta ed., 1989).

Large areas of the West Punjab have been well explored, but there is still a lot to be done. The Pakistan Department of Archaeology has begun to address the problem. The Tharl Desert has many sites and is another area that would repay careful work, if carried out in the same way Mughal explored Bahawalpur. The Ravi/Chenab doab and the adjacent Sargoda area should also be examined in detail.

Indian Punjab and Haryana Surveys

Archaeological exploration in the Indian Punjab and Haryana begins with the work of Rai Bahadur Sahni in the 1920s, followed by M. S. Vats (1929-30, 1930-34) and the discovery of Kotla Nihang Khan. Partition in 1947 brought a renewal of work by a number of scholars, including Y. D. Sharma (1953, 1956), B. B. Lal (1954-55), and K. N. Dikshit (1969). The Archaeological Survey of India, the Punjab Department of Archaeology and Kurukshetra University have prominently contributed to the substantial exploration in the area.

Students in some of the archaeology programs in India have been offered an opportunity to explore an administrative district, as the subject of a dissertation. To complete the thesis the student is expected to visit each village in the district and report all of the archaeological and historical monuments. This is usually done by bus and on foot, if for no reason other than budgetary limitations. The work, on the whole, is sound. Several PhD dissertations and at least one MA paper have been completed on Districts or Tehsils in this region and Gujarat as well.

Other explorations of the Punjab have been done piecemeal by the Archaeological Survey of India and the State Department of Archaeology. There is no single, great Punjab Survey, with the exception of Suraj Bhan's dissertation (1972, 1975) which brought together a great deal of information up to the early 1970s. Jagat Pati Joshi and Madhu Bala, of the Archaeological Survey of India, worked in the state in the early 1980s (Madhu Bala 1981; J. P. Joshi 1986) and J. M. Thapar, also with the Archaeological Survey of India undertook a survey of the Sutlej Valley that produced a number of new sites and was particularly well reported (IAR 1980-81: 46-9).

Haryana has been impressively explored, with the most significant work as follows:

Ambala District; M. Kumar 1978
Gurgaon District; Purnia 1976
Hissar District; Ram 1972
Jind District; Safidon Tehsil; Dhattarwal 1978
Jind District; A. Singh 1981

Karnal District; A. Singh 1981
Kurukshetra District; M. Kumar 1978
Mahendragadh District; Purnia 1976
Rohtak District; Ram 1972

In addition to these documents Suraj Bhan completed a survey on the Sarasvati and Drishadvati Valleys (Suraj Bhan 1972, 1975) and northeastern Haryana with Jim Shaffer (Suraj Bhan and Shaffer 1978). Margabandhu and Sharma (1981) explored the Sabi Nadi in Gurgaon District. Datt (1980) undertook a survey of Painted Grey Ware sites in Haryana and Mohan (1988) wrote an MA thesis on prehistoric sites in Haryana while at Cambridge University. All of these efforts involve a combination of original field work and library research, resulting in one of the most thoroughly explored regions of the Harappan Civilization.

Survey in the Ganga-Yamuna Doab of Uttar Pradesh

Like the Indian Punjab, the Ganga-Yamuna Doab of Uttar Pradesh has seen reasonably intensive exploration, accomplished in piecemeal fashion with sustained, small-scale efforts. Saharanpur District is very well covered thanks largely to the efforts of Kailash Nath Dikshit (not the former Director General), who began there under the tutelage of M. N. Deshpande (Deshpande 1977; Dikshit 1977). Om Prakash Srivastava (1982) undertook a survey in Muzaffarnagar District and Makkhan Lal (1982, 1984a, 1984b) did the same in Kanpur and attempted to consolidate the settlement data for the entire Doab. R. P. Sharma conducted a survey in parts of Meerut District survey (1972).

Rajasthan Survey

Archaeological exploration in northern Rajasthan began with the work of the Italian, L. P. Tessitori (1917-18, 1918-19, 1920, 1921, n.d.), an early visitor to Kalibangan, who did a small amount of excavation there. Sir Aurel Stein, who worked there as part of his exploration of the Sarasvati Valley in 1940-41 (Stein 1943a; S. P. Gupta, ed., 1989), followed him. The geographical scope of Stein's work was extended by further exploration of the same region by A. Ghosh, then Director General of the Archaeological Survey of India, between 1950-53. It was because of this effort that the type site of Sothi was discovered, and the excavation of Kalibangan was undertaken. Ghosh published his explorations as noted in various places (Ghosh 1952, 1953b, 1956, 1959, 1989b), but there is no comprehensive list of his sites, with locational data and periods of occupation. Katie Dalal (née Frenchman) undertook a PhD dissertation devoted to recovering data on the Ghosh survey, which was partly successful (Frenchman 1972, Dalal 1980, 1981, 1987). Further efforts to systematize this body of data have been made by K. N. Dikshit (1979, 1984b, 1984c, 1987).

The northern Aravallis, especially in and around Sikar District has been explored by the Rajasthan Department of Archaeology (IAR 1979-80: 62-5; Agrawala 1981; Agrawala and Kumar 1982). As part of the study of ancient river courses and irrigation systems, a French archaeological team explored parts of the Drishadvati Valley in 1983-84, from the important site of Ganeshwar to the west (Francfort 1985a, 1985b, 1986a, 1986b, 1987, 1988a, 1988b, 1989a, 1992).

Southern Rajasthan is somewhat outside the latitude of this discussion, but exploration there has been vigorously pursued, as shown by yearly reports in *Indian Archaeology, A Review*. The Berach Basin was explored by V. N. Misra in 1963 and 1964 (V. N. Misra 1967). Exploration in this area has been continued by the Archaeological Survey of India and the

Rajasthan Department of Archaeology, as well as Dr. Rima Hooja, who conducted her own field work there in 1982-83 (Hooja 1988, especially pp. 162-67). V. N. Misra made another tour to this general region with L. Leshnik in 1967-68 (Leshnik 1968) in and around the delta of the Luni River where it drains into the Little Rann of Kutch. This is on the route from the Indus Valley that avoids crossing the Ranns, by going around the northern end of these dangerous salt flats, and then coming South into Gujarat. They found a number of traces of human habitation in this area, but none of it could be dated to the Bronze Age, or earlier. Misra and Leshnik also investigated the more central parts of the North Gujarat Plain, to the east of the borders of the Little Rann. No sites were found in this area either, but there is much more in Gujarat to be considered.

Gujarat Survey

Almost no exploration was undertaken in Gujarat until the first Director of Archaeology in the state, P. P. Pandya began a systematic program of work there in the 1950s (Pandya 1954). This was paralleled by exploration initiated by the newly formed Department of Archaeology at the Maharaja Sayajirao University of Baroda, under the leadership of B. Subbarao (1958). Yearly entries in *Indian Archaeology, A Review* complement these reports published under the principal investigator's authorship. S. R. Rao, Superintending Archaeologist of the Western Circle of the Archaeological Survey of India conducted exploration in the entire state while he was engaged in the excavation of Amreli (1952-53)[11], Rangpur (1953-56) and Lothal (1954-63). His list of sites, including those discovered by other workers, was published in 1963 (1963: 205-07). Jagat Pati Joshi conducted a systematic survey of Kutch between 1964 and 1968 (J. P. Joshi 1966, 1990b). which is being expanded by R. S. Bisht of the Archaeological Survey of India as part of the excavations at Dholavira on Kadir Island (IAR 1986-87: 29-30). The exploration by Misra and Leshnik in northern Gujarat and southern Rajasthan has been noted. Much more of North Gujarat has now been explored by teams from the Maharaja Sayajirao University of Baroda. They have found over one hundred prehistoric sites in the estuaries of the Rupen, Banas and Sarasvati[12] Rivers in Mahesana and Surendranagar Districts (Hegde and Sonawane 1986; K. K. Bhan 1994; Ajithprasad and Sonawane, in press).

District surveys in Gujarat have been completed for Banaskantha (Parikh 1978), Kheda (Momin 1979, 1984), Jamnagar (K. Bhan 1983, 1986, 1989), and the northern part of Bhavnagar (Jairath 1986). The latter area was explored earlier, first by P. D. Chudasama of the Gujarat State Department of Archaeology (IAR 1960-61: 7-9) and then Possehl (1974, 1980). Field work for a survey of Rajkot and northern Amreli Districts has been completed by Yunis M. Chitalwala and Anne Cunningham, respectively. Chitalwala has published a list of sites (1979, 1985). Cunningham's work is in progress.

S. A. Sali of the Archaeological Survey of India completed a survey of the Tapi Valley, one of the routes between the Deccan Plateau and Gujarat. He found sites with some Harappan affiliation, but their chronology is not yet clear (Sali 1970).

All of Saurashtra and most of Gujarat have been surveyed but there are some areas which need further study. The southern talukas of both Bhavnagar and Amreli Districts fall into this category as does much of Junagadh. Sabarkantha District in North Gujarat deserves further study.

Summary

The map outlining the survey activity in the Greater Indus Region testifies, better than words, to the state of exploration (Figure 4.86). It is clear that most of the Greater Indus Region has been examined to some extent, often with intensity. All of the sites have not been found, but much progress has been made in mapping the settlements of the Indus Age.

In 1979, I proposed that the settlement patterns of the Mature Harappan could be characterized by site clusters; some large, as in Cholistan, others small, as to the east of Karachi. The substantial open areas between the site clusters were not unoccupied but were utilized by pastoralists in their bountiful manifestations as land to support their animals. Additional exploration has served to reinforce this set of observations.

Critical Thoughts on Archaeological Survey

The study of settlement patterns is a well developed part of archaeology, and professionals are aware of its strengths and weaknesses. The method's strengths have already been noted as examples of the insights gained from using it. However, the method does have weaknesses. This review will be organized around three themes: (1) removal of sites from view, (2) brick robbing and the search for fertile soil, and (3) surface scatter, settlement size and population.

Removal of Sites from View

There are a number of agencies that remove sites from the natural landscape. Wind and water erosion, burial by natural alluvium, and excavation by humans seem to be the most important. The effect of these agencies on settlement archaeology is difficult (not impossible) to ascertain, but they are a factor that distorts the historical record. For Harappan archaeology, the Indus River has to be seen as a vigorous, perhaps even brawny, stream in its lower course and has changed direction many times over the millennia that separate the modern day archaeological explorer from the once lively settlements of the Indus Age. Any archaeological site in the path of a major course change would clearly experience a disturbance of some magnitude and the smaller sites could have been completely removed by erosion. The same is true for the rivers of the Punjab. The smaller settlements, situated on the lower ground within the meander entrenchment, could also have disappeared, eroded away or covered by alluvium. Even smaller rivers take their toll. It is known, for example, that the Bolan River has taken a substantial chunk out of the eastern side of Mehrgarh, especially in the northern MR.3 area. At Rojdi, in central Saurashtra, we noted that some of the river side of the settlement had been removed, but internal evidence allowed us to determine that this damage had been minimal and did not need to be factored into an estimate for the size of the original site (Possehl and Raval 1989: 37).

There was a site on the Kalubhar River in Gujarat, called Chosla, after its village, that was almost certainly not visible when P. D. Chudasama passed through this area in 1960-61, but was very apparent when I arrived there in 1970 (Possehl 1980: 158-59). Villagers told me that a flood of the Kalubhar had uncovered a concentration of pottery some years before my arrival and that they had collected and used some of the complete pots that were exposed. When I returned to reexamine Chosla in 1981 it was gone; washed away, I was told, by a great flood. Thus, for about 10 years there seems to have been a window through which Chosla could be seen by an archaeological explorer and by a remarkable coincidence I was in the valley during that time. The 1970 revelation of buried sites in the Kalubhar Valley prompted me to inspect river sections very carefully, looking for buried sites. I never found one; only some Middle Palaeolithic tools associated with a gravel horizon that is widely represented in the region.

Wind and rain take their toll of sites, too, as seen at Mehrgarh where the density of sherds on some parts of the surface indicates severe wind deflation of the earth midden (Jarrige,

Jarrige, Meadow and Quivron 1995: 69, 111). Some of the desert sites in Bahawalpur are also eroded and deflated by the wind; Satuki East, quite severely.

There seems to be at least one buried site that has been found in the Indus valley. Captain J. H. Kirby discovered it when he was in charge of the excavation of the great Indus feeder canal near Sukkur, for the rejuvenation of the Eastern Nara. Kirby's account was published by A. F. Bellasis and is given in full as follows:

> In excavating the great Nara Canal, at a distance of about two miles and a half from the town of Roree (Rohri), we occasionally came upon detached masses of brick-work and at length at a depth of about ten feet below the surface of the ground, the foundations of a very large number of houses were laid bare. These foundations consisted of stone, or of mingled stone and brick-work, and resembled those to be seen in the ruined city or Arore at the present day, where it will be observed that the foundations of the houses are generally built of stone to a height of two or three feet above the ground, and the walls which rest on this foundation are composed of mud or unburnt bricks.
>
> In one instance the earth in the centre, and also outside the walls of one of the foundations I have mentioned as having been discovered ten feet below the surface of the ground, was removed, and the walls left standing: they then appeared to be those of a house, containing one room about sixteen feet in length by ten in breadth, and two smaller ones about ten feet by six. At another place, where the canal had been excavated to a depth of about twelve feet below the surface of the ground, a circle of stone work was observed, between three and four feet in diameter. The earth was removed out of the centre to a depth of about two feet, and after taking out two or three courses of brick-work, a crowbar penetrated several feet lower down without meeting any resistance; unfortunately water immediately rose to the surface, and prevented, for the time, any further excavation.
>
> In proceeding from the direction of Roree, the first of these ruins which we came upon were those of a large wall of considerable height, about four feet in breadth, extending from one side about a hundred feet into the canal and built of extremely good and well burnt bricks. This wall has been hitherto excavated to a depth of about twelve feet. It may probably have formed a portion of the walls of the town, as I am not aware of any ruins of houses having been discovered on the northern side of it. From this point towards the south-east, the foundations of houses extend about seventeen hundred feet along the bed of the canal. Amongst these ruins were found a number of articles made of brick-clay, such as drinking cups, a *Khooza*, some water spouts, and a large number of children's toys.
>
> There were also found some round stones, which have all the appearance of having been used as weights. I did not find any which exactly correspond with the seer of the present day, but they almost all did with the chittak: for instance one stone was exactly two chittaks, another four, a third six, and so on.
>
> It appears that the town was built on the extremity of a rocky hill, and that it has been gradually covered by the mud held in suspension by the flood-waters of the Indus, which now flow over the spot; indeed its burial-ground which (according to the common custom in this part of Sind) was high up upon the rocky hill, is uncovered.

The name of the place, it appears, was Hukrah, a name still retained by a village in the neighborhood; and it is, according to the Natives of the country, mentioned by the prophet of the Manooree caste of Fakeers, who says:

When broken shall be the bund of Arore
And the water shall flow over Hukrah
Where will be the fishing of Summah?

Probably with the idea that when the bund of Arore was broken, and the waters flowed over Hukrah, the river Indus would have taken that course, and left its present bed dry. The bund of Arore, however, is not yet broken, nor is there much chance of its being so, as it has been lately repaired, partly with the bricks which were removed out of its old neighbor, the town of Hukrah, when excavating the channel for the canal Arore, 17th August 1855 J.H. Kirby Captain H. M. 86th Regiment (Bellasis 1857: 471-73; a *khooza* is a flagon or jar).

Structures of baked brick, children's toys and wells all sound Harappan. The *chittak* is an Indian weight equal to 914 grains, two ounces or 39.33 grams (Balfour 1885: Vol. I, 704). The weight system of the Indus Civilization seems to have been based on a unit of 13.625 grams. One *chittak* is close to three Indus units, 40.875, the small error coming in assessment of the ancient weights as equal to the modern one. Captain Kirby's stones could thus have been Indus weights, some of which are not square. This place has been entered into the "Gazetteer of Settlements of the Indus Age" for want of a better name, as the "Kirby Site."

We know that there is archaeological material to a depth of ca. twelve meters (thirty-nine feet) below the ground surface surrounding Mohenjo-daro (Raikes 1965a). Part of this depth is due to the accumulation of silt from annual inundations around the city, but there are other Mature Harappan sites in this same alluvial environment that are well above ground (e.g., Lohumjo-Daro, Chanhu-daro, Jhukar). Some might even be sitting on an original ground surface. It can be concluded that alluvium does not accumulate in an even way that buries all sites, nor does erosion work in a way that necessarily removes all of them. Moreover, Mohenjo-daro and the other brick settlements of the Indus, are a very dense mass of architecture and artifacts sitting in a soft, spongy, wet subsoil. Like Mexico City and Venice, they seem to be settling very slowly into the unconsolidated, well lubricated sediments on which they sit, which accounts for some, perhaps most, of the depth of the cultural deposits below ground.

In the Introduction the size of Mohenjo-daro and Harappa were discussed. It was emphasized that there are remains lying outside the mounded areas of both places which indicate that the ancient settlement is larger than the surface remains would lead us to believe.

More examples like these could be cited but they would not shed any light on the problem of how rivers, rain and wind have moulded the settlement patterns of the Indus Age. There is no precise information that would allow us to develop a kind of correction factor for mapping and for statistics to account for this distortion of settlement size and counts. Therefore, final determinations must be held in abeyance.

Brick Robbing and the Search for Fertile Soil

Archaeological sites represent one of the world's great resources, renewable in the sense that they are constantly being created; non-renewable because the remains of long dead civilizations cannot be duplicated. The value of sites extends beyond those appreciated by archaeologists, into more commercial contexts. The story of brick robbing from Harappa is well known and is a good example of the commercial value of a site. Substantial brick robbing also took place at Kalibangan and is reported from Mohenjo-daro; it apparently continues today. The soils of an archaeological site are rich in fertilizer, phosphates and nitrates, generated by humans and animals as a by product of habitation. Farmers know this and all over the world they are fast at work removing soil from sites and taking it to their fields as free fertilizer. Louis Flam has reported that the famous site of Lohumjo-daro has been completely removed by farmers and that the same is true for Deh Mari Sabra near Chanhu-daro in Nawabshah District (Flam, personal communication 1992). In Maharashtra and Gujarat sites are disappearing at a shocking rate, almost daily, certainly week by week. The great mound of Nevasa on the Pravara is no longer a mound, and although there are some pottery sherds scattered here and there, it barely qualifies as an archaeological site.

No one knows when brick robbing and the search for fertile soil seriously began to affect the archaeological record of the Indus Age. It is hard to believe that there were ever enough sites for it to have taken place at today's alarming rate. If it had, surely all of the sites would have disappeared long ago. There is a supposition, a kind of working hypothesis, that brick robbing has gone on for many centuries, but carting away entire sites is a relatively recent phenomenon, associated with the population explosion following World War II. Why else would Nevasa have been spared for so many millennia?

The Surface Scatter, Settlement Size and Population

When an archaeologist visits a site there is usually a discernible scatter of artifacts on the ground surface. This may be associated with a buildup of habitation debris into a mound, variously known as a daro, dhoro, dheri, damb, timbo, khera or ghundai in the Greater Indus Region. Not all sites have this kind of surface scatter: two that come to mind are Bisauli and Rajpur Parsu in the upper Ganga-Yamuna Doab. There is nothing there today to indicate an ancient site, nor was there when B. B. Lal excavated them in 1949 (Lal 1951: 27-8, 37). Yet, most places have an artifact scatter and by using its extent the apparent size of the ancient settlement can be estimated. It is often not easy to determine this size with any precision in the field, and sizes listed in the "Gazetteer of Settlements of the Indus Age" should probably be accompanied by a range of possible values for this number. Those who use the numbers should consider an error factor of at least 10%. Accepting this measurement is, of course, qualified by everything that has been said here about the burial and removal of sites or parts thereof.

The size of a settlement is thought to be significant since it is assumed, for good reason, that larger sites are different from small ones in the kinds of social, economic and technological processes that took place there, especially in a highly differentiated sociocultural system like the Harappan Civilization. The size of an ancient settlement is also correlated, in some complex, often indirect way, with the number of people who lived there and demographic statistics are an interesting and important aspect of history.

There is another archaeological phenomenon that complicates the use of materials which come from the surface collecting that characterizes the bulk of settlement pattern data, especially in the Eastern Region, beyond Kalibangan. In this zone, there are sites with a more or less pristine Sothi-Siswal occupation, also referred to as Siswal A or Early Siswal (Suraj Bhan 1975: 103-08). It is the kind of pottery found at Kalibangan in Period I, and its Fabrics A through F. Siswal A is followed by Siswal B (Late Siswal; Suraj Bhan 1975: 108-09) at many sites. Many Mature Harappan ceramic fabrics and types, especially the classic, heavy red wares are found in Siswal B. The assemblage also retains a basic suite of Siswal A (Sothi-Siswal) ceramics as well. In excavation it is fairly easy to separate Sothi-Siswal from Siswal B, based on stratigraphy and associated finds. But, if there is only a bagful of Sothi-Siswal (Kalibangan I) pottery and Mature Harappan red wares, it can be very difficult, sometimes impossible, to say whether the site has: (1) a Sothi-Siswal and a Siswal B occupation, or (2) only one occupation in Siswal B times.

Some Further Thoughts

The archaeological record is incomplete in many respects, which includes the total number of sites, as well as the fragmentary nature of those that have survived. The size of an archaeological site is only the *apparent* size of the ancient settlement. The relationship of site size to population is imperfect and what is achieved with site size/population ratios is a rather crude estimate of the number of people who may have lived on one of the "*daros*," "*dhoros*," "*dheris*," "*dambs*," "*ghundais*" or "*timbos*". Given the dynamics of populations, which can change rapidly, in some instances by many orders of magnitude in just a few years, it cannot be assumed that the population of any given settlement was constant for protracted periods of time. Moreover, most living village sites are never fully covered with inhabited buildings. Entire neighborhoods deteriorate and people move to another area, returning to the original location on the mound after one or two generations to "gentrify" the old district. In some settlements the stratigraphic buildup is more of a corkscrew pattern than it is a layer cake.

We should also remember that important, complex events may have taken place in small settlements and large settlements may have been relatively simple in their sociological makeup. The size of a settlement is not an infallible index of its internal complexity. Lothal, for example, is a very sophisticated small site (4.8 hectares) of the Mature Harappan Stage.

Careful monitoring of modern settlements in India, Pakistan and the Near East confirm these observations as enduring phenomena that serve to caution archaeologists. They also apply to the non-archaeologist who looks at the Harappan Civilization and studies by archaeologists with impeccable reputations, with a critical eye.

Excavation is an extremely important tool with which to establish the extent of an individual site, and the way in which it varies through time. There are techniques for intensive survey of surface remains that can help to mollify other critical points in establishing site size and complexity. But even intensive surface survey, of limited use at a deeply stratified site like Ahichchhatra or Atranjikhera, is very expensive in terms of both time and labor; excavation even more so. Only about seven percent of the sites relating to the Indus Age have been excavated and most of the work took place in an era when excavation methods that have been outmoded for many years, were used. Most of the digging was done for extremely short periods of time, a few days or weeks, more often for less than one season. All of Sir Aurel Stein's work could be characterized in this way and he dug at about fifteen sites. Moreover, a large place like Mohenjo-daro has only about seven percent of the apparent surface area exposed and the lower depths hardly have been touched. There is no point in the Lower Town of Mohenjo-daro at which virgin soil has been reached, except by a bore hole. It is not even certain whether there is an Early Harappan settlement at Mohenjo-daro. Since most of the digging was shallow, especially in the immense Moneer Area, the percentage of the volume of the site that has been observed would be much smaller than the seven percent used for the surface area; one or two percent might be a good guess. What archaeologists have created at a place like Mohenjo-daro, in spite of the immense amount of work that has been done there, is a peephole into the settlement, like the view of the world through the back end of a telescope. The hole grows wider during the late period of occupation, but it still does not let us see the broad panorama of urban life in this ancient city.

Considering the infinite amount of work that has been done, and the intensive methods of investigation that have been employed, the archaeological record of the Indus Age remains filled with incomplete, sometimes fragmentary data sets. They are certainly fraught with ambiguity and taken as a whole are impossible to evaluate precisely in terms of their potential for useful historical reconstruction. On the other hand, there are checks and balances. Simply reviewing the critical problems in dealing with settlement archaeology helps to understand and appreciate the archaeological record better. There is also a very substantial body of archaeological data that can be seen, touched and analyzed. It is not smoke and mirrors, but real, on the ground material culture that can be used in a positive way to begin to understand the life of the peoples who lived and worked in South Asia's first civilization, as well as the peoples who brought it into existence.

Back to Work

From a positive point of view, no matter how small the sample, the materials from the excavations at Mohenjo-daro and other sites are an immense resource for understanding the Indus Age. These materials can be used to compile a relative stratigraphy, absolute chronology, perceptions of daily life, history of architecture, long distance trade, commerce, more mundane day-to-day contacts, and the biological remains that have given important insights into the history of disease, subsistence and biological evolution in the region. The roughly 2600 sites documented as part of the history of the Indus Age may be imperfectly known, but they are a resource that should not be ignored just because the documentation is imperfect and full critical control over the potential meaning of the data set is not known, or possibly even knowable. The apparent size of a site may not be a perfect indicator of population size and the complexity of the ancient community, or communities, that inhabited them, but there are patterns within this record that allow interesting and potentially important insights to be made about the history of the Indus Age. They can make a cogent contribution to understanding the Harappan Civilization.

There is perhaps no part of the archaeology of the Indus Age where there is less agreement, in both terminology and concept, than the Early Harappan and beginnings of South Asian urbanization. This is in part true because the available data are sufficiently rich to allow a number of interpretations.

The Early Harappan Stage

Introduction

The period following the Kechi Beg/Hakra Wares Phase will be called the "Early Harappan." This Stage precedes urbanization and the Mature Harappan Civilization in the Greater Indus Region, with a short (100 or so years) Transitional Stage in some places separating them. The Early Harappan Stage is made up of four regional Phases that are thought to be generally contemporary with one another: The Amri-Nal Phase, the Kot Diji Phase, the Damb Sadaat Phase and the Sothi-Siswal Phase. There is pronounced geographical expansion during this phase into the Potwar Plateau and into the Indian Punjab, Haryana, northern Rajasthan and western Uttar Pradesh as well as Gujarat. The themes of cultural continuity and change, growth, geographical expansion and regionalism persist, with only hints of new technological innovation. The "growth" is, therefore, for the most part, best seen as ontological, not evolutionary. This is not to say that developmental change is absent from the Early Harappan Stage. It is there, but it is not the predominant process, as compared to ontological change. The physical expansion of cultural systems that were already in place seems to have been the predominant theme within the Greater Indus Region during the Early Harappan.

These observations are important in order to understand the Transitional Stage between the Early and Mature Harappan, since it appears that the Transitional Stage, was a period of relatively rapid culture change during which the majority of the distinctly urban features of the Harappan Civilization came into being. The Transitional Stage is thought to have been three or four generations long, anything but "instantaneous."

Jim Shaffer and Diane Lichtenstein have suggested that the Harappan Civilization is a fusion of the Bagor, Hakra and Kot Diji traditions or "ethnic groups" in the Ghaggar/Hakra Valley on the borders of India and Pakistan.

> This fusion appears to have been very rapid reinforced no doubt by its own success. The earliest set of Harappan dates are from Kalibangan, in the northern Ghaggar/ Hakra Valley at ca. 2600 B. C.; while dates from Allahdino, Balakot and sites in Saurashtra indicate Harappan settlements were established in the southern Indus Valley by ca. 2400 B. C. Possehl (1986a: 96-8; Possehl and Rissman 1992) suggests a rapid origin of 150 years for the Harappan. We suggest it was even less, or 100 years, ca. 2600-2500 B. C. Within the next 100 years, the Harappan became the largest ethnic group within the Indus Valley. This rapid distribution rate was matched only by Harappan abandonment of large sections in the Indus Valley which was under way by ca. 2000 B. C., a process intensified by later hydrological changes. Whatever the Harappan group's organizational complexity, it was a cultural system promoting rapid territorial expansion (1989: 123).

I have come to think of this short period of rapid, paroxytic change as occupying the century from about 2650 BC to 2550 BC. It must be kept in mind that such precision probably goes beyond the discriminating powers of radiocarbon dating. The Transitional Stage is a good example of a time when a major step up in the rate of culture change took place that led to the development of a new level of sociocultural complexity.

Few issues in South Asian archaeology have been debated as much as the origins of urbanization in the Indus Age. The debate involves discussion of the nature of the precursors to the Mature Harappan, the appropriateness of an "Early Harappan" versus a "Pre-Harappan," migration versus autochthonous culture processes, even the ethnic identification of the people of the Harappan Civilization.

Early Harappan or Pre-Harappan

In 1970, M. Rafique Mughal completed a PhD dissertation at the University of Pennsylvania on the Kot Diji Phase and other stratigraphic precursors of the Harappan Civilization (Mughal 1970). His dissertation was the forum in which he put forth his concept for an Early Harappan stage of cultural development in what he termed "The Greater Indus Valley and Northern Baluchistan." Mughal's efforts were directed to the organization of a large body of data from the Quetta Valley, through the Northwest Frontier and on to the plains of the Indus Valley, which would provide insights into the development of urbanization there in the second half of the third millennium BC. He consciously selected the term "Early Harappan" for this stage of cultural development:

> In my opinion the term 'pre-Harappan' is misleading because it creates the impression
> that a chronological gap exists between the 'pre-Harappan' period of the first half of

the third millennium B. C. and the 'mature' period of the Harappan culture belonging to the later half of the third millennium. The other terms, 'antecedent' and 'proto-Harappan' sometimes used in the archaeological literature are vague, remain undefined and beg questions...I feel that all of the material found stratified below the 'mature' Harappan at Kot Diji, Amri, Kalibangan and the pre-defense levels of Harappa and related material discovered at other sites belongs to an Early Harappan period assignable to the first half of the third millennium B. C. Among these separately-treated sites, having regional differences in ceramics, there are many common traits present in ceramics, stone tools and technology, terracotta objects and in architecture which also occur in the 'mature' Harappan period. The radiocarbon dates also tend to strengthen the chronological priority of Kot Dijian and related material over that of the 'mature' Harappan culture. It is therefore quite justified to call this material Early Harappan (Mughal 1970: 5-6).

Walter A. Fairservis, Jr. independently defined the Early Harappan in his writings on the origins of the ancient cities of the Indus (Fairservis 1971a: 221). He proposed that the regional mosaic formed by assemblages from sites such as Amri, Kot Diji, Kalibangan and Nal should be considered the "Early Harappan." "By this we mean the Harappan artifact form and decoration, not the civilization" (Fairservis 1971a: 221). Mughal, however, is the scholar who developed the idea, and the one who has been questioned most intensely about the appropriateness of the concept. The notion is therefore generally attributed to him, without intending to slight Fairservis' contribution to the debate.

Mughal's terminology has not been accepted universally. It is used here because I agree with the strong lines of continuity that Mughal sees in the archaeology of the region and it seems to be the best choice of terms. Many other scholars, especially in India, have been reluctant to acknowledge the usefulness of Mughal's views. The basis for this debate has a lot to do with the culture historical models that are used to grapple with the transition to urbanization. The Mughal position is anthropological and stresses continuity and internal processes of cultural change. The opposing model, or models, are more historical in nature and rely on external factors of change (diffusion, migration, even invasion) and a sense of discontinuity in the process of change, with new peoples coming into the region, interacting with the "native" population to produce a synthesis that led to urbanization. Again, it is important to emphasize that diffusion, migration and invasion can be potent historical forces for change and the Greater Indus Region was never a cultural vacuum during the Indus Age. Therefore, we need balance in our reconstructions, seeking to define and disentangle such historical forces in their totality, rather than clinging to simple explanations and monocausality or prime movers. Given the data at hand, the predominant themes in the rise of urbanization in the Greater Indus Region appear to be processes that were internal to the region, creative forces like: (1) the symbiosis between the mountains and the plains, (2) differential productivity between the inundated riverine tracts, the dry farming regions of Gujarat, the Punjab and Haryana and the desert, (3) the abundance of raw materials found in the northwestern sector of the Subcontinent, and (4) the growth of trade and culture contact between the Indus and surrounding regions.

The more historical position was stated as early as 1964 when A. Ghosh noted: "The true Harappans with all of their cultural equipment appeared on the site (Kalibangan) when the original inhabitants were still in its occupation" (Ghosh 1965a: 114, see also Ghosh 1965b). This was followed, shortly after Mughal's dissertation appeared, by an article-length appendix (S. P. Gupta 1972b) in a book on Harappan ceramics (Manchanda 1972). The critical parts of Gupta's argument deal with the chronology of the Early, or Pre-Harappan, and the relationship

570

between the diverse archaeological assemblages of the earlier era with the Mature Harappan. Some of the details of his points concerning chronology have been eclipsed by the further accumulation of dates over the past twenty years and the revolution caused by the calibration radiocarbon dates. But, he is right that Sothi style pottery persists at many sites well into the Mature Harappan in the Punjab, Haryana and northern Rajasthan, most notably at Kalibangan. Suraj Bhan's Siswal B (Late Siswal), in fact, is defined in this way. Gupta also questions the appropriateness of calling this archaeological assemblage "Early Harappan."

> Our stand is clear: none of the known pre-Harappan cultures is really parental to the Harappan culture. At present none of the theories can establish the *causal relationship* between the pre-Harappan and Harappan cultures. The pre-Mature phase of Harappa culture is really not known to us: it may be there at Mohenjo-daro or any unknown place between the Indus and the foot of the Baluchi hills but we have no clear evidence so far. The real claimant to the 'Early Harappan' seems to be still lying unexplored (Gupta 1972b: 404, original emphasis, see also Gupta 1976: 158-59).

Gupta has slightly softened his stand, but maintains his objections to use of the term "Early Harappan" (S. P. Gupta 1978: 141). B. K. Thapar joined the discussion with the following points:

> Apart from the question of interpretation there are two other factors which are relevant to the issue: (1 the occupation of the Indus Civilization at each of the above sites seems to have started quite suddenly; and (2 the ceramic industries of the preceding deposit at these sites are not homogeneous, but show instead regionalization, indicative perhaps of different "culture areas." In the light of the above considerations, the use of any of the three terms proto-Harappan, early Harappan or pre-Harappan, as a blanket term for a deposit immediately preceding that of the Harappan is obviously unsatisfactory... (Thapar 1973a: 86).

D. P. Agrawal took part in the debate with the following: "The Harappa culture, though essentially derived from the pre-Harappan cultures, continued to be coeval with the latter (Agrawal 1972-73: 40).

Some of the criticism directed toward Mughal's position involved archaeological sites that had not been excavated when he wrote his dissertation, principally the settlements in the Gomal Valley excavated by the University of Peshawar (Dani 1970-71, Durrani 1988; Durrani, Ali and Erdosy 1991) and Kalibangan (Lal and Thapar 1967, Lal 1979, Thapar 1975), which led to his most important response to his critics (1980b) in a far reaching paper. As far as the theoretical issues are concerned, Mughal sticks to his guns and makes a number of interesting points. First, he observes that everyone agrees that the archaeological assemblages under discussion precede the Mature Harappan. Mughal then asks a rhetorical question. Does this imply "...chronological priority, but not cultural? If so, some of us are perhaps expecting to find *the* site, such as Mohenjo-daro, which would give us an evolutionary sequence on unilinear scale from the early to the mature and late Harappan cultural phases. This brings up the vital and fundamental question of civilizational processes operative in the Indus Valley which led to urbanization gradually" (Mughal 1980b: 87, original emphasis). For those who propose migration into the region he asks: "Do we have any evidence of the Kot Diji related or Mature Harappan cultural stages outside the Indus Valley?" (1980b: 87). He then outlines the signs of continuity in the archaeological record and concludes that the best model to use in understanding the rise of civilization in ancient India and Pakistan is one which sees the Kot Diji Phase and Kot Diji Phase related cultural assemblages as the linear precursors to the Mature Harappan.

The issue has not been resolved as indicated by a statement from Shashi Asthana, who invokes the prestige of the Archaeological Survey of India. She asserts that the use of the term "early" "...denotes unquestionably, only the early stage of that culture" (1985: 221), with a direct, linear relationship between this stage and a later Mature Harappan. She uses a biological analogy suggesting that this relationship would resemble the one between ontological stages of childhood and adulthood in a human being. She says:

> The Survey argues that the Kot Diji-Sothi complex's relationship with the Harappa Complex is not that of childhood to adulthood, it may be that of mother and child, but obviously both existing as two separate entities, in course of time the mother dies but the child lives on with all inherited characteristics as well as many newly acquired ones. The script, weights and measures, the citadel and various other features of the Mature Harappa Culture do not find their formative stage in the Kot Diji-Sothi Complex. Hence, the use of the term Early Harappan for the Kot Diji-Sothi Complex they argue is premature, if not entirely incorrect (Asthana 1985: 221).

The title of Asthana's book, *Pre-Harappan Cultures of India and the Borderlands*, leaves little doubt on her choice of terms.

If the data were available to resolve this issue it would have been brought forward long ago, which implies that the heart of the matter is not the names that are being used but the historical modeling that is employed to understand the beginnings of ancient India's earliest cities. There are actually many models, most authors having some variation on everyone else's thoughts, but some consistent, contrasting themes do emerge from the literature regarding the notion of an Early Harappan Phase.

The Term Early Harappan is Misleading

It has been said that the term "Early" is misleading in that it "unquestionably" implies a direct relationship between the proposed Early Harappan and the Mature Harappan. Because some believe that this cannot be proved, the use of the term is premature, and might even be incorrect.

What emerges from this criticism is that the term selected as an alternative to "Early" is "Pre" as in "Pre-Harappan." The problem with the new term is that parallel critical comments leveled against "Early" can be directed toward "Pre." "Pre" implies a lack of continuity between the Pre-Harappan and the Mature Harappan. Since this has not yet been proved, it too, might also be seen as "...premature, if not entirely incorrect." Archaeologists need a term for the principal developmental Stage that precedes the Mature Harappan at least one level of abstraction above the pot sherds implied by the Kot Diji, Sothi-Siswal or Amri-Nal Phases. "Early Harappan" and "Pre-Harappan" are the predominant terms in the literature along with "Pre-Urban Stage." Alternatives such as "Proto-Harappan" or "Incipient Harappan" have similar strengths and weaknesses and their introduction solves no problems. Moreover, I have an intuitive abhorrence of the notion of "proto" cultures. Acknowledging that neither position is proved, Early Harappan has been used here because an assumption of cultural continuity between this and the Mature Harappan is more intellectually comfortable for me than an assumption of discontinuity, and there are some data to support this contention, even if it cannot be proved.

Historical Continuity versus Historical Discontinuity

The historical position generally proposes that there was a discontinuity between the Early and

Mature Harappan: that there was at best a kind of collateral relationship between the two. If the relationship is analogous to a "mother and a child" then what are the archaeological sites or assemblages that might be used to define the "mother" and the "child"?

It is widely recognized that the archaeological assemblages of the Early or Pre-Harappan are immensely different from those that characterize the Mature Harappan. But, when examined in detail there are also signs of continuity, and a Transitional Stage linking the two has been defined at Amri since 1964 (Casal 1964a). This Phase is also known from Harappa, Ghazi Shah and Nausharo. As exploration of the Greater Indus Region proceeds it is becoming increasingly clear that major surprises in terms of entirely new archaeological assemblages are less and less likely to appear. More sites will be found and there will be revelations through excavation which are immensely important and will contribute to future revisions in writings on the Indus. But, the appearance of a wholly new archaeological assemblage, while not impossible, is an increasingly remote possibility. A strong case can be made for the fact that the players in this game of urban origins are all known, imperfectly to be sure, but still discerned and if the genesis of urbanization is not a product of the Amri-Nal, Kot Diji, Damb Sadaat and Sothi-Siswal Phases then where is it?

Autochthonous versus Non-Autochthonous Culture Change

Closely related to the issue of historical continuity is the question of where an archaeologist might look for the genesis of urbanization in the Greater Indus Region. Is it to be found in the Greater Indus Valley itself? Or, is it to be found in some alien people or force, from outside the region?

That the Harappan Civilization originated through diffusion or migration is an old, well established position in the literature, not all of it by authorities whose work can be ignored (e.g., S. N. Kramer 1963, Mackay 1937-38: 668, see also Heine-Geldern 1956b, Gordon 1958: 60). A number of authorities have also derived the Indus writing system from Sumerian, implying in varying degrees an involvement with the origins of the civilization itself. The notion of intercultural borrowing between the Indus and Sumer is also prevalent (Wheeler 1968: 25), and of ideas fundamental to the definition of civilization, such as that of cities (Ghosh 1965a: 116-17).

If there was wholesale migration and colonization from another region to the Greater Indus Region one might be willing to entertain the thought that entire institutions could be integrated into a new urban system. It would be akin to the European colonization of eastern North America in the seventeenth and eighteenth centuries. But, this kind of migration could be documented archaeologically, just as it has been in North America. Even a less dramatic colonization, like that of the British in the Indian Subcontinent can be documented archaeologically.

The key to understanding the success of culture change by mass migration seems to be implied in a kind of separateness that characterizes the behavior of the migrants, certainly at the region, perhaps even within individual sites. They generally set themselves aside, either totally or to some marked degree, from the indigenous culture, and are thus able to maintain their own institutions in a foreign setting. Efforts to influence or change the institutions of the indigenous population are sometimes attempted, but are never total nor often (ever?) completely successful.

The proposition that entire institutions can be moved between cultures by stimulus diffusion is dubious. Sociocultural systems are generally too firmly integrated, too systemically complementary, for this kind of change to take place. If there was interregional "borrowing" or "influence," if the Mature Harappan began because of contact with other peoples, then it can be reasonably expected to have left evidence that archaeology could detect. But, there are no signs of such an "invasion" or "colonization" so the idea that the process of change which resulted in the beginnings of the Harappan Civilization can be found anywhere except in the Greater Indus Region can be rejected, until someone produces evidence to the contrary.

Summary of the Positions For and Against the Term Early Harappan

The term "Early Harappan" as opposed to "Pre-Harappan" has been selected for this developmental stage, recognizing that it is not likely to receive universal approval. It is a term and concept that is widely recognized in the literature on the Harappan Civilization but it carries with it a certain number of assumptions, just as the alternatives do. Principal among them are cultural and historical continuity between the Early Harappan and the Mature Harappan as well as the premise that the process of change was primarily autochthonous, involving the peoples of the Greater Indus Valley itself, without significant (out of the ordinary) external influence, such as massive migration or invasion. Neither the best, nor the worst term, Early Harappan is just better than any of the alternatives.

Regionalism During the Early Harappan

Cultural diversity is one of the principal, perhaps predominant, themes in the Early Harappan Developmental Stage. There is also continued ontological growth and an increase in the apparent size of the population in the Greater Indus Region. Regionalism during the Early Harappan is expressed in the diversity of archaeological assemblages that can be dated to ca. 3200 to 2600 BC in the Greater Indus area. The farmers and pastoralists of the Early Harappan settled in all of the regions occupied during the Mature Harappan, including Gujarat, Punjab, Haryana, reaching the Ganga/Yamuna Doab. Some of this Early Harappan expansion, such as in Gujarat and the Doab, is still poorly known, because very few settlements have been identified. In other instances site densities are considerable, as in Indian Punjab and Haryana where there are indications of a substantial village farming adaptation.

Four Regional Phases of the Early Harappan Stage

There are four regional Phases of the Early Harappan Stage. The first to be discussed is the Amri-Nal Phase in Sindh and Baluchistan, with an extension through Kutch into other parts of Gujarat. The Kot Diji Phase is generally found to the north of the Amri-Nal area, but there is a Kot Diji Phase extension as far south as the Sindh Kohistan which overlaps the Amri-Nal area. Kot Diji material is prominent in the Derajat, the northwestern districts of the West Punjab and in Cholistan. Regional variants of the Kot Diji are found in Northern Baluchistan and the Swat Valley. A Damb Sadaat Phase of the Early Harappan has been defined in the Quetta Valley and adjacent areas, including the Bolan Pass and parts of Kachi. Finally, there is the Sothi-Siswal Phase, which was first defined at the type site of Sothi (Dikshit 1984b) and includes Kalibangan in Period I. The Siswal A and Sarangpur Culture sites (Suraj Bhan 1971-72, 1975: 103-09) are included as part of a Sothi-Siswal Phase in the Eastern Region. Together these archaeological assemblages make up the Early Harappan Stage in the developmental model used here. There is a fifth assemblage on the western borderlands of the Early Harappan that will appear occasionally. This is the Dasht Assemblage recently defined by Roland Besenval on the Makran Coast of Pakistan, near the modern border with Iran (Besenval and Sanlaville 1990; Besenval 1992; Besenval and Marquis 1993) (Figure 4.87).

574

Figure 4.87. Artifacts from the Dasht assemblage, after Besenval 1992

Xu Chaolong has published a substantial study of the "Early Harappan" which he defines as a body of material culture that precedes the Mature Harappan in time (1990, see also Xu 1994). Xu handles Early Harappan regionalism in a way different from that used here, preferring to emphasize the unity of Kot Diji Phase archaeological assemblage. This view has some merit and should not be slighted. The Early Harappan Stage has a kind of internal coherence, because of a number of shared features, including a common set of subsistence practices, some architecture, figurines and, most voluminously, pottery. Xu presents two interesting illustrations, showing some of the shared vessel forms (Figure 4.88). The principal weakness of Xu's scheme

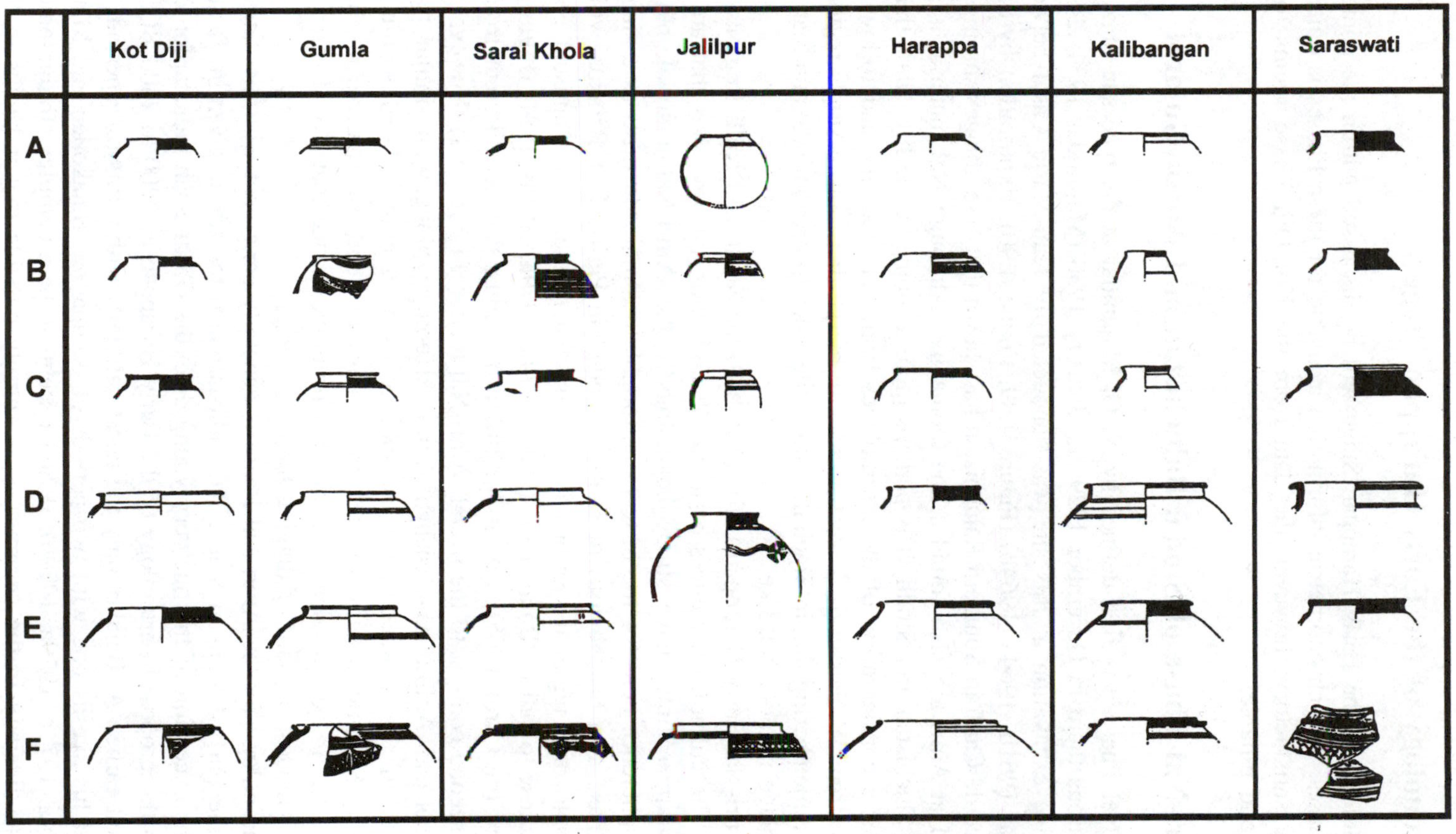

Figure 4.88. Vessel forms common to some Early Harappan Phases, after Xu 1990: Fig. 3

is its emphasis on Kot Diji ceramics and a lack of appreciation for the diversity of archaeological assemblages that precede the Mature Harappan Transition.

The Chronology of the Early Harappan Stage

The Chronology of the Early Harappan Stage will be discussed within the context of each of the four Phases. The chronometric information available for these Phases is quite different and never fully satisfactory; however, the data from the Kot Diji Phase seems to be the most consistent and reliable.

The Amri-Nal Phase of Sindh, Baluchistan and North Gujarat

The Amri-Nal Phase was first defined by N. G. Majumdar at the type site of Amri following his excavations there in December 1929 and January 1930 (Majumdar 1934: 24-33); however the definitive excavation at this site was conducted by Jean-Marie Casal between 1959 and 1962 (Casal 1961b, 1964a, 1964b) (Figure 4.89, Figure 4.90). Exploration by Sir Aurel Stein and Beatrice de Cardi in Southern Baluchistan has shown that assemblages sharing some features of Period I at Amri are also found in the mountains. Although Nal material is found in both Southern Baluchistan and Sindh, it is perhaps more at home in the highlands than the riverine plains. After a consideration of the assemblages from both regions, and following some long held advice from W. Fairservis, I have decided to merge them into a single regional Phase, the Amri-Nal, remembering that in Sindh the Amri side tends to predominate and that in Baluchistan the assemblage is more Nal-like.

The Amri-Nal Early Harappan is found in both the Sindh and Kulli Regions of the Mature Harappan. The cultural differences between the highlands and lowlands that are so evident in Mature Harappan times have strong beginnings in the Amri-Nal material, but there is still sufficient coherence here for me to feel comfortable dealing with them as a single unit.

This Phase also has obvious diversity, as found in Period I at Balakot, which presents a good example of a regional variant on the Amri-Nal theme. It was unusual enough that the excavator chose to call it "Balakotian" (Dales 1974a, 1979a, 1979b, 1981) (Figure 4.91). Period IV at Anjira (de Cardi 1965), with its profusion of Anjira Ware is different from Balakot and presents a second contrast to the overall Amri-Nal theme (Figure 4.92). However, both of these sites, Balakot and Anjira, have enough Amri-Nal pottery, along with similar figurines, beads and the rest of the archaeological assemblage to be accommodated within this regional nomenclature. So little is known of the archaeology of Southern Baluchistan, that the scheme offered here has to be considered a somewhat primitive device that would certainly be revised with even a modest amount of digging there.

The chronology for the Amri-Nal Phase is generally congruent with the dates for the other Phases of the Early Harappan Stage. The radiocarbon dates are as given in Table 4.32

With the exception of the one very young date, the Ghazi Shah radiocarbon determinations conform to the proposed chronology of the Early Harappan as 3200 to 2600 BC. TF-864 from Amri is a bit earlier. At Balakot only the latest date falls within this time period. The excavator has defined his site as one with two periods of occupation: Balakotian and Mature Harappan (Dales 1974a, 1974b, 1979a, 1979b). Period I seems to be a complex stratigraphic setting, with considerable diversity in the ceramics. It is entirely possible that it begins in the Kechi Beg Phase, as indicated by the radiocarbon dates. Balakot is not yet published and a resolution of this suggestion can be expected when the report appears.

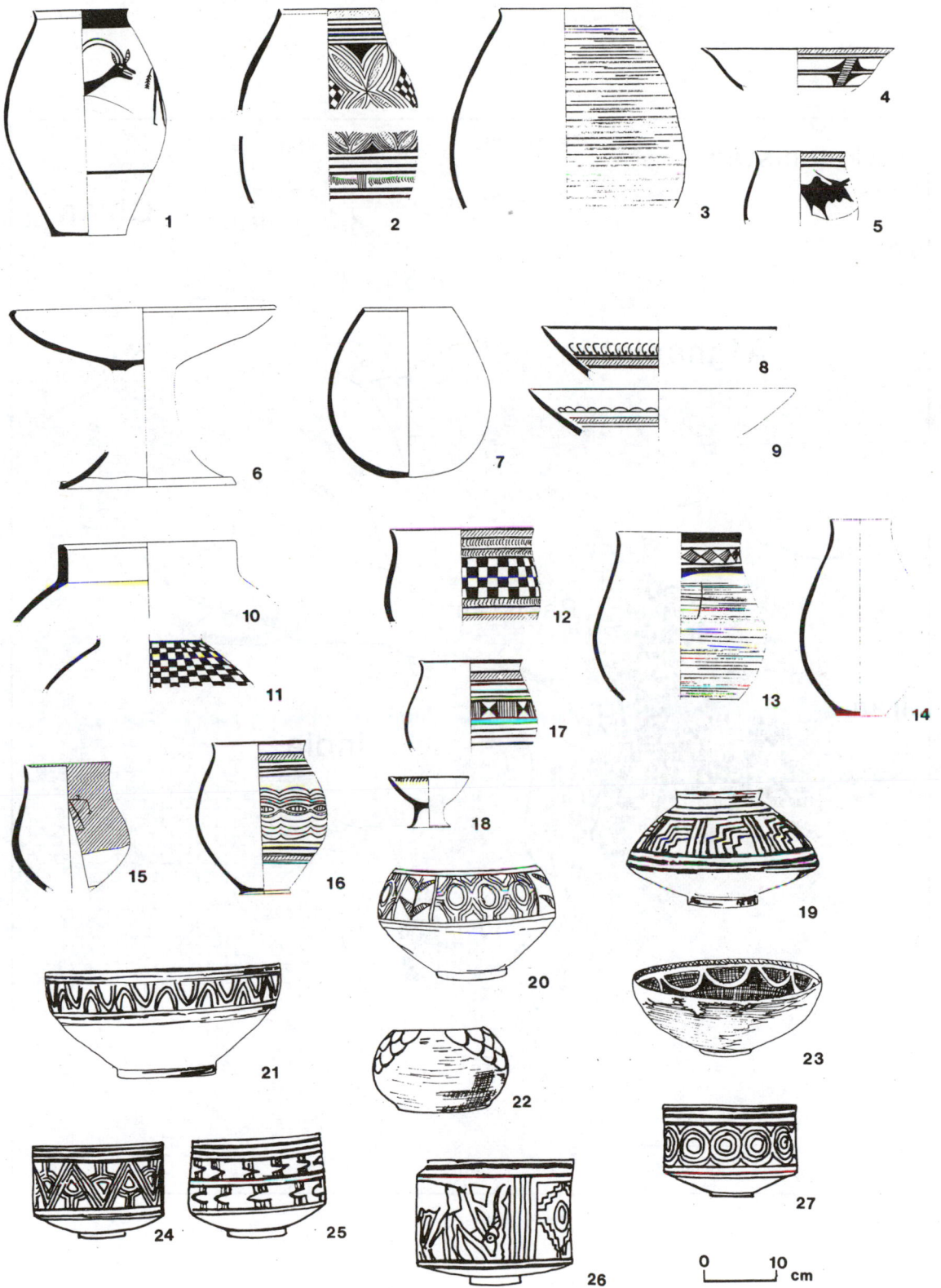

Figure 4.89. Pottery of the Amri-Nal Phase

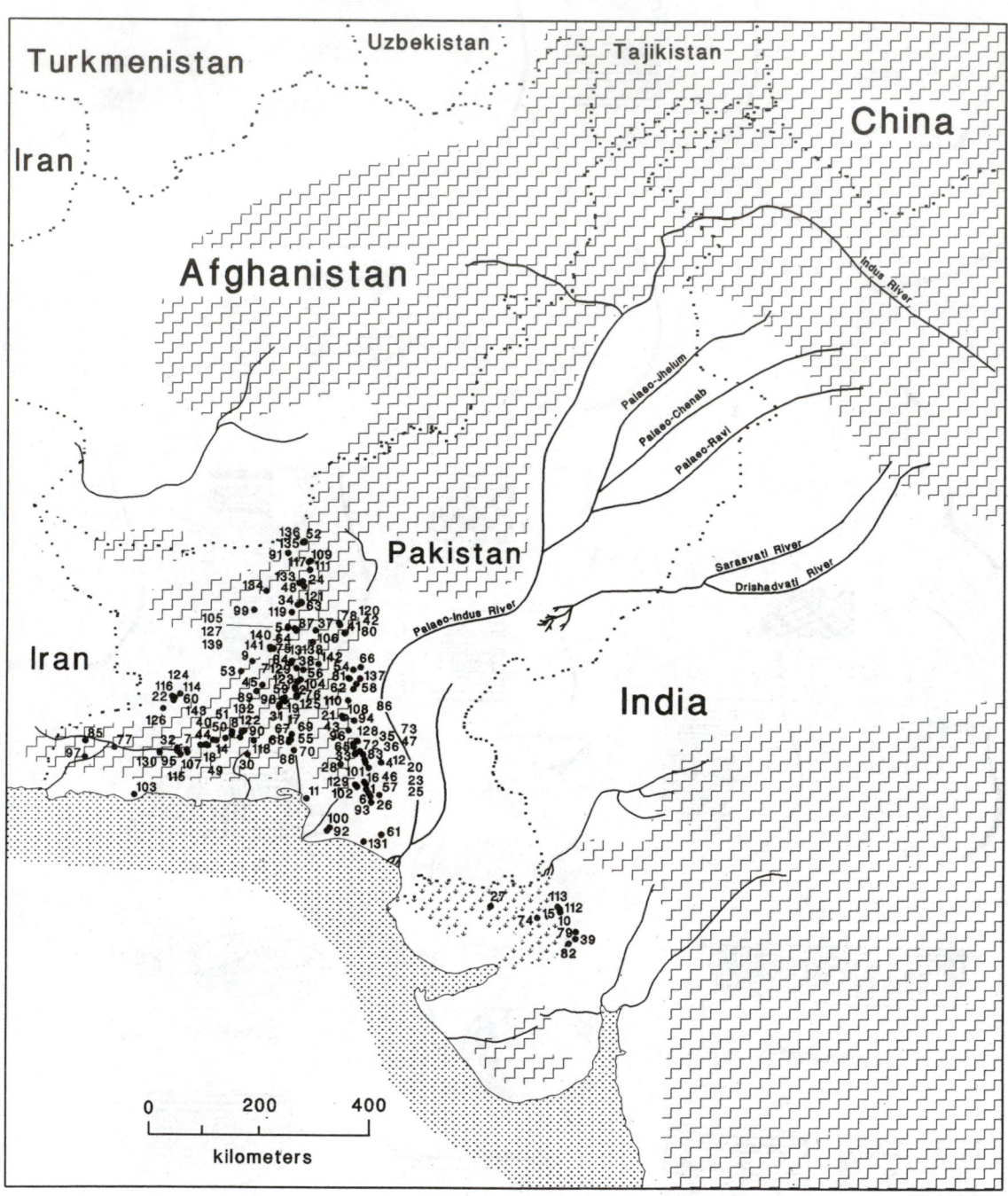

Figure 4.90. Map of sites of the Amri-Nal Phase

Key to Figure 4.90

1. Ahmed Shah
2. Aidu Damb
3. Alam Khan Shahr
4. Amri
5. Anjira
6. Arabjo Thana
7. Ashal
8. Awaran Niabat
9. Badrang Damb
10. Bajaniya-no Thumdo
11. Balakot
12. Bandhni
13. Bandu Damb
14. bazdad Kalat
15. Bhamaria Thumdo
16. Bibiji Bhit
17. Buband
18. Chahi Damb
19. Channal Kund Damb
20. Chauro
21. Chhutijo Kund
22. Chiri Damb
23. Damb Buthi
24. Damb Zerger
25. Dhal Buthi
26. Chilanijo Kot
27. Dholavira
28. Diwana
29. Dosia Khal Damb
30. Gajar Damb
31. Gaji Bhut
32. Gate Dap
33. Ghazi Shah
34. Ghuram Damb
35. Gorandi 'A'
36. Gorandi 'B'
37. Hadi
38. Hala Damb
39. Harthar-no Tirnbo
40. Hor kalat
41. Jahan
42. Jahan Northeast
43. Jarejo Kalat
44. Jaren
45. Jebri Damb One
46. Kachcho Buthi
47. Kai Buthi
48. Kalat

49. Kallag
50. Kamar Band
51. Kambar Damb
52. Kardagap
53. Kargushki Damb
54. Karo Kotiro
55. Kapras Buthi
56. Kashimi Damb, Wadh
57. Khajur
58. Khudo Pir
59. Kinneru Damb
60. Kohna
61. Kot Raja Manjhera
62. Kotiro
63. Kuki Damb
64. Kuffagi Damb
65. Lakhshmirji Mari
66. Lalanji Mari
67. LB-13
68. LB- 16 'A-B'
69. LB- 16 'C'
70. LB-17
71. Lehri
72. Lohri
73. Lundi Buthi
74. Madhvya-no Timbo
75. Mammai Damb
76. Marki Mas
77. Miri Qalat
78. Mishk
79. Moti Pipli
80. Mowari
81. Mungli Damb
82. Nagwada One
83. Naing Gar Jabal
84. Nal
85. Nazarabad
86. Nazganijo Kund
87. Neghar Damb
88. Niai Buthi
89. Nokjo Shahdinzai
90. Nundara
91. Nushki
92. Orangi
93. Othmanjo Buthi
94. Paijo Kotiro
95. Pak
96. Pandi Wahi

97. Panodi
98. Phusi Damb
99. Pir Hassan Shah
100. Pir Mango
101. Pokhran
102. Pokhran Landi
103. Prahag 'A'
104. Puchur Damb
105. Rais Sher Mohammad
106. Reko Cave
107. Rodkan
108. Roheljo Kund
109. Saiyid Maurez Damb
110. Salari
111. Salu Khan
112. Santhli Four
113. Santhli Two
114. Sari Damb
115. Segak
116. Serikoran Damb
117. Shahr Sardar
118. Siah Damb, Jhau
119. Siah Damb, Surab
120. Singen Kalat
121. Site Near Kuki Damb
122. Sohren Damb One
123. Sorak Damb
124. Sraduk
125. Sumer Damb
126. Surain Damb
127. Surkh Damb
128. Tando Rahim Khan
129. Taung
130. Thale Damb
131. Tharro Hill
132. Tikri Damb
133. Togau
134. Toji Damb
135. Tor Ghundai
136. Tor Warai
137. Tupi
138. Wahir Two
139. Zari Damb
140. Zayak North
141. Zayak Southeast
142. Zidi
143. Zik

580

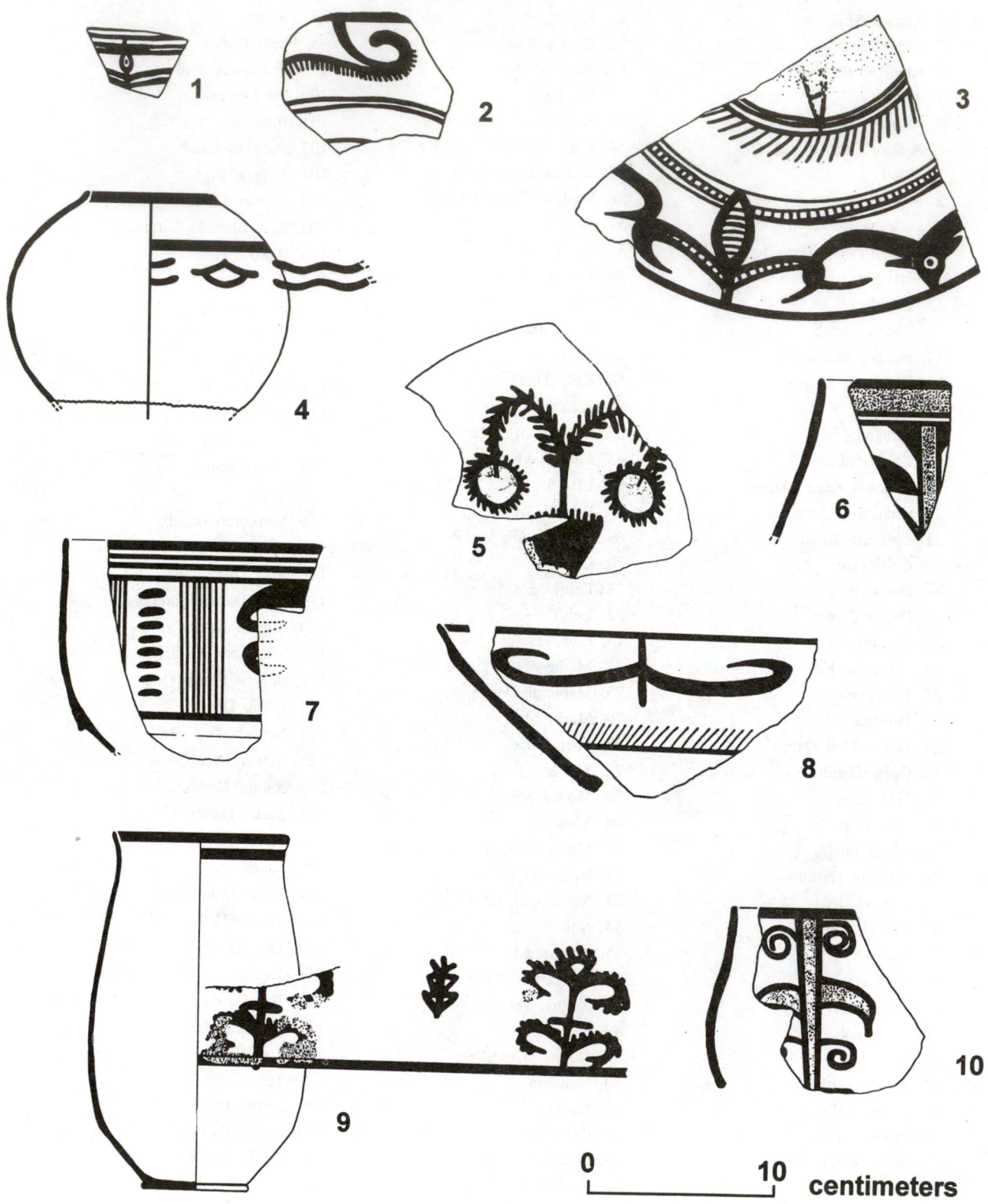

Figure 4.91. Balakotian pottery, after Dales 1979a

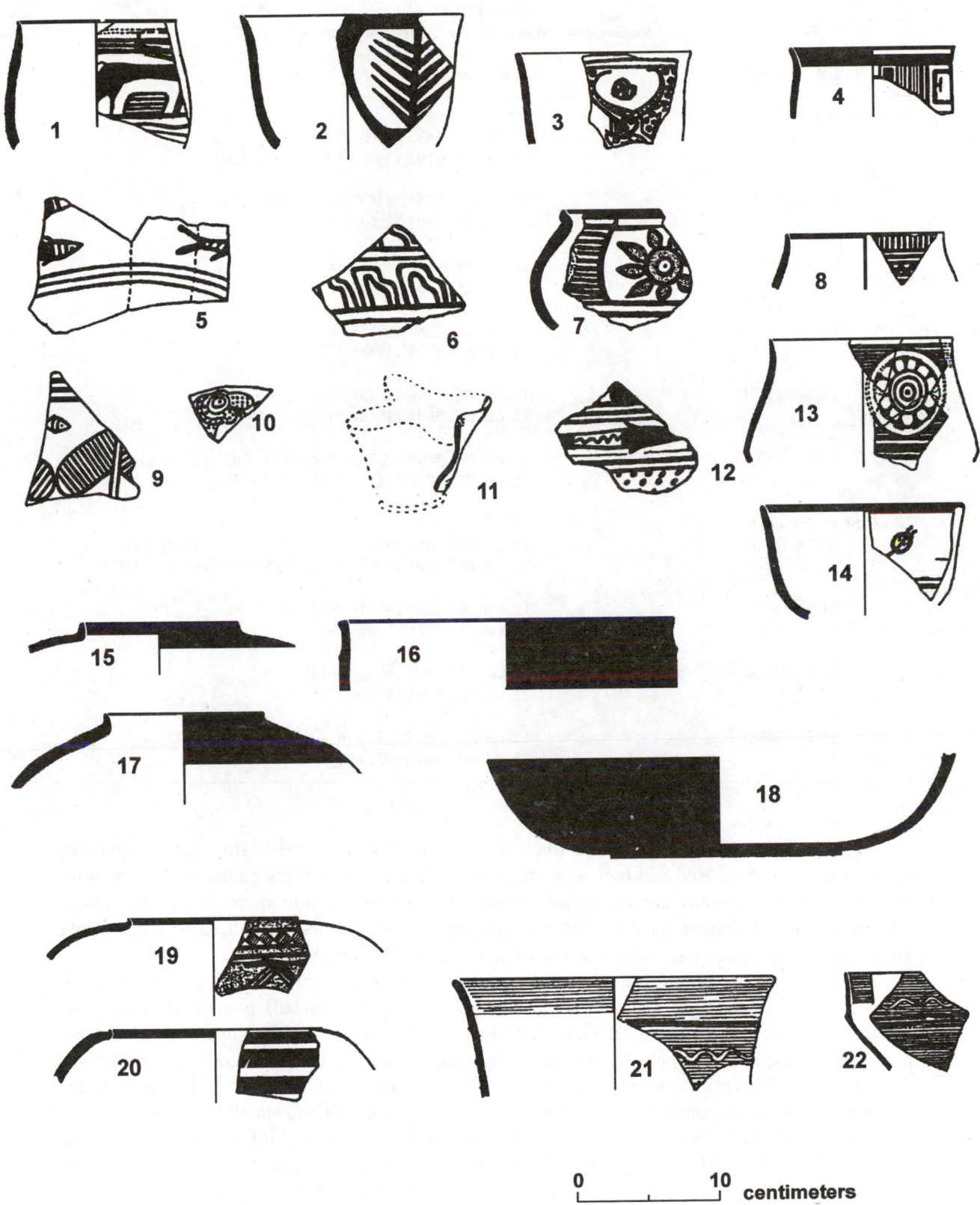

Figure 4.92. Pottery of Anjira IV, after de Cardi 1965

0   10   **centimeters**

TABLE 4.32
Radiocarbon dates for the Amri-Nal Phase

Lab Number	Calibrated Date
Amri, Period I	
TF-864	1Σ cal BC 3637 (3506, 3408, 3385) 3356
	2Σ cal BC 3702 (3506, 3408, 3385) 3103
TF-863	1Σ cal BC 3355 (3263, 3242, 3102) 2924
	2Σ cal BC 3505 (3263, 3242, 3102) 2886
Balakot, Period I	
UCLA-1923A	1Σ cal BC 4223 (3986) 3810
	2Σ cal BC 4337 (3986) 3701
UCLA-1923B	1Σ cal BC 3988 (3958) 3805
	2Σ cal BC 4212 (3958) 3771
UCLA-1923C	1Σ cal BC 3708 (3648) 3540
	2Σ cal BC 3891 (3648) 3383
UCLA-1923D	1Σ cal BC 2898 (2875, 2794, 2784) 2625
	2Σ cal BC 3010 (2875, 2794, 2784) 2507
Ghazi Shah, Period I	
BETA-18536	1Σ cal BC 3354 (3309, 3227, 3186, 3159, 3126) 3046
	2Σ cal BC 3494 (3309, 3227, 3186, 3159, 3126) 2925
BETA-18537	1Σ cal BC 3339 (3094) 2923
	2Σ cal BC 3371 (3094) 2889
BETA-32804	1Σ cal BC 3309 (3036) 2913
	2Σ cal BC 3364 (3036) 2788
BETA-32805	1Σ cal AD 604 (662) 776
	2Σ cal AD 444 (662) 891

The Amri ceramic assemblage is made up of extremely well made fine wares, generally fired light red or buff. Red and buff slips are also found, often with black paint. At the beginning of the Phase the designs are exclusively geometric, developing into more curvilinear motifs toward the end. A marker for Amri Ware is the open bowls and jars and tall vases with simple, even featureless rims. A sample of the ceramics is found in Figure 4.93.

Nal ceramics are among the best made and most attractive wares of prehistoric times in South Asia. They too, are fine wares, but tend to have been fired buff to pink (Figure 4.94), (Plate 4.26, Plate 4.27, Plate 4.28, Plate 4.29, Plate 4.30, Plate 4.31). The slips have a tendency to be very light, buff or weak red, giving a tint to the surface, rather than a dense overall color. The characteristic vessel forms are a canister and a straightsided bowl, with a simple, knife-edge rim. These were painted with black geometric designs or with realistically rendered animals: antelopes, goats, fish, scorpions, birds and felids or canids. Polychrome infilling of these designs includes the use of red, pink, blue and yellow. Painting in white over a black slip is also known, and one of the features shared with Amri. In fact, the use of white paint is a hallmark in the entire Early Harappan Stage of development in all its Phases.

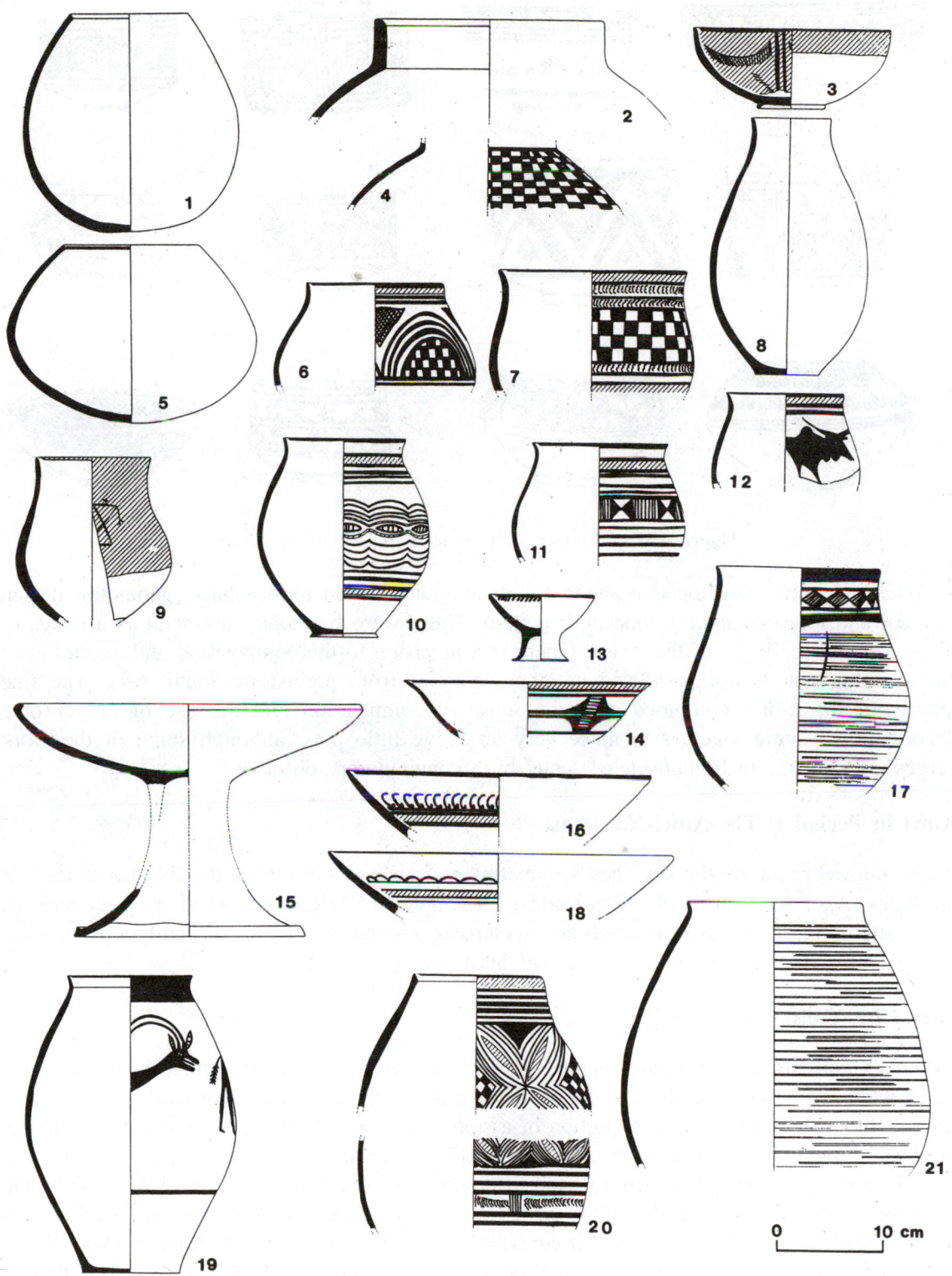

Figure 4.93. Amrian pottery, from Amri, after Casal 1964a

Figure 4.94. Nal pottery, after Hargreaves 1929: Plate XVIII

The Nal potter developed a canon for painting that often took a basic geometric design element and repeated it in a concentric pattern. These were frequently arranged as a series of panels around the body of the vessel. There is a precision to the composition and execution of Nal painting that is not paralleled in other ceramics from prehistoric South Asia. The fine quality of the fabric combined with the sense of composition and the use of polychrome decoration all come together to make very attractive little pots, although some of the work verges on what might be considered 'cute' by a contemporary observer.

Amri in Period I, The Amri-Nal Phase

Amri and Mehrgarh are the key sites for creating an image of life during the first two Stages of the Indus Age. As seen on the Amri site plan (Figure 4.95) Casal worked on both mounds there, attempting to uncover as much architecture as possible in a series of contiguous trenches in Mound A. A period by period review of his findings is as follows:

Period IA (Casal 1964a: 26-8)

Period IA consists of two separate strata. The lowest level had no architecture, but there was a small ditch on the edge of the excavation that Casal interprets as a feature used to delimit the limit of the ancient settlement. A portion of a stone wall and a rubble floor are associated with the later stratum. *In situ* pots were also found. (Figure 4.96).

The pottery is eighty-two percent hand made, the rest wheel thrown. Typical Amri bichrome painting is present along with a few examples with Togau C designs. This allows Casal to propose that his Amri IA is the rough equivalent of Mundigak Period II (Casal 1964a: 56).

Small finds include a small amount of copper, which continues in all periods, chert blades, stone sling balls and a few terracotta beads and bangles. Shell bangles are also present, although they are rare.

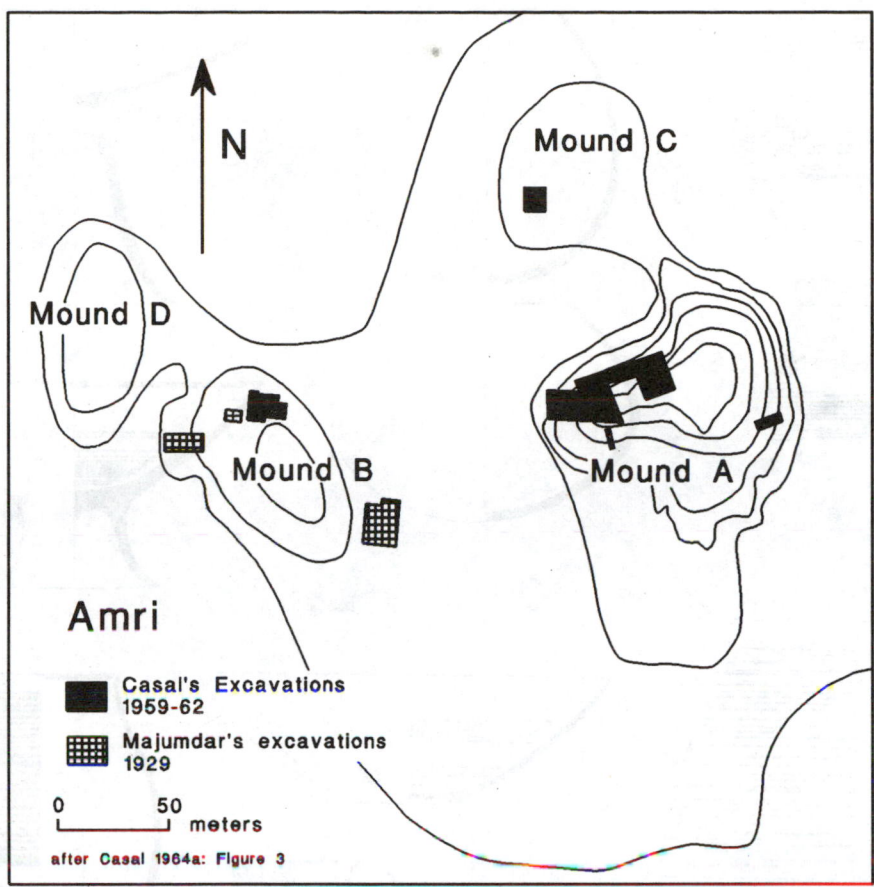

Figure 4.95. Casal's site plan of Amri

Period IB (Casal 1964a: 28-9)

Period IB also has two structural levels, both with houses made of mud bricks of irregular size. The rooms are small and rectangular, some only ca. one by one meter of interior space. The largest is about four by five meters. There is a deep foundation trench, filled with stone, crossing the excavation. Jars set in surfaces and a fireplace were also found. Togau C motifs continue, and the proportion of wheel made pottery increases. Bone tools and an abundance of chert blades are also noted.

Period IC (Casal 1964a: 29-34)

Period IC has four structural levels, all with continuity with one another. Two types of structures are present. The first is a rectangular habitation, with evidence for activities of daily life. Hearths are found associated with these buildings, but never inside them. The second type of structure is compartmented, recalling similar structures at Mehrgarh (Figure 4.97). These are too small to have afforded habitation and there is no evidence that they were occupied. Some were found filled with "rubble", others seem to have been empty. Evidence for activity outside of them was found in the form of ash and refuse; another parallel with evidence from Mehrgarh. Casal interprets these as foundation "squares" for structures raised above ground level. But evidence

586

Amri I

0   20
cm

Figure 4.96. Pottery of Amri I, after Casal 1964a

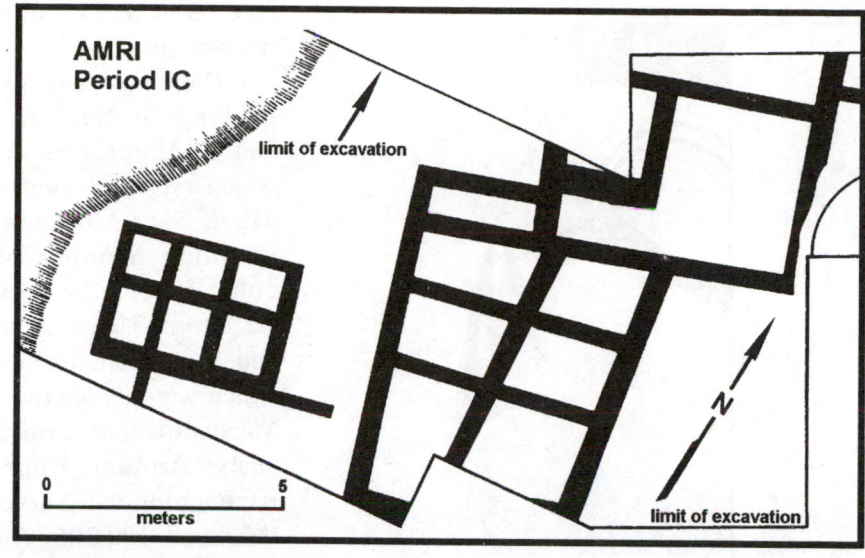

After Casal 1964: Figure 14

Figure 4.97. Possible compartmented buildings of Amri IC, after Casal 1964a: Figure 14

from Mehrgarh suggests that this may not be the case, since some of the compartmented buildings there have walls several meters high. The Jarrige team has proposed, as a working hypothesis, that their compartmented buildings were granaries, or storage facilities. Given the similarities to the Amri IC buildings this seems to be a workable hypothesis there as well.

The abundance of chert flakes and cores on Mound B during Period IC led Casal to suggest that it was a craftsmans' quarter. The pottery was fifty-five percent wheel thrown with good examples of bichrome ware, and typical Amrian jars with featureless rims.

Period ID (Casal 1964a: 34-6)

Period ID has only one structural level and has continuity with IC. The excavation area on Mound A has evidence for the leveling of the settled area and the construction of new buildings. A new compartmented building was raised on Mound A, with walls preserved to a height of 1.57 meters (Casal 1964a: Figure 21). Two of the rooms shared a doorway, which is different from the compartmented building of Period IC and those of Mehrgarh. Parts of a vase were found scattered in various rooms of this building (Figure 4.98) and in places the walls had been reddened by fire. Casal does refer to this building as a godown or store rooms, but also says that there was a superstructure that had burned; the debris from it, including the pot, falling into the compartments that were excavated.

Some of the pottery is handmade but most of it, fifty-eight percent, is wheel thrown. Some of the vessel forms can be seen as prototypes for forms in the Mature Harappan, but this is most apparent in the Transitional Period II.

The Site of Nal in Baluchistan

Nal is a prominent village c. 40 kilometers west of Khuzdar in Jhalawan. It is located at a communications node and has been a point of settlement for many millennia. There is an archaeological site c. seven kilometers to the east of the present village (27° 40' N - 66° 18' E). This is the "Sohr Damb" or Red Mound, which is a very prominent feature of the landscape. It

588

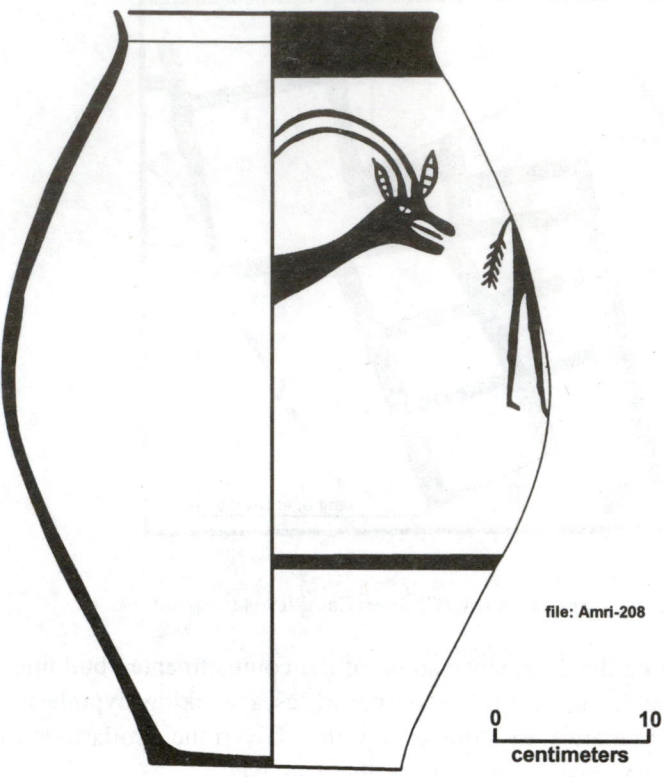

file: Amri-208

0 ⎯⎯⎯⎯ 10
centimeters

Figure 4.98. Vase from the compartmented building of Amri ID, after Casal 1964a: Figure 63, no. 208

is c. 309 × 183 meters, or 5.7 hectares in area.

There has been a good deal of digging at Nal. According to Harold Hargreaves (1929: 18) it was first excavated in 1903 by Mirza Sher Mohammad, a well-intended member of the staff compiling the Baluchistan Gazetteers. He excavated at the site and recovered 59 vessels, all of which were turned over to Sir John Marshall who described them in an early Annual Report of the Archaeological Survey of India (Marshall 1904-05) (Figure 4.99). In 1908, Colonel (later Field Marshall, Sir) Claud Jacob excavated more pottery at the site while he was commander of the Hazara Pioneers. One fifth of the ca. 250 vessels he recovered went to the McMahon Museum in Quetta. This institution, and all or most of its collections, was

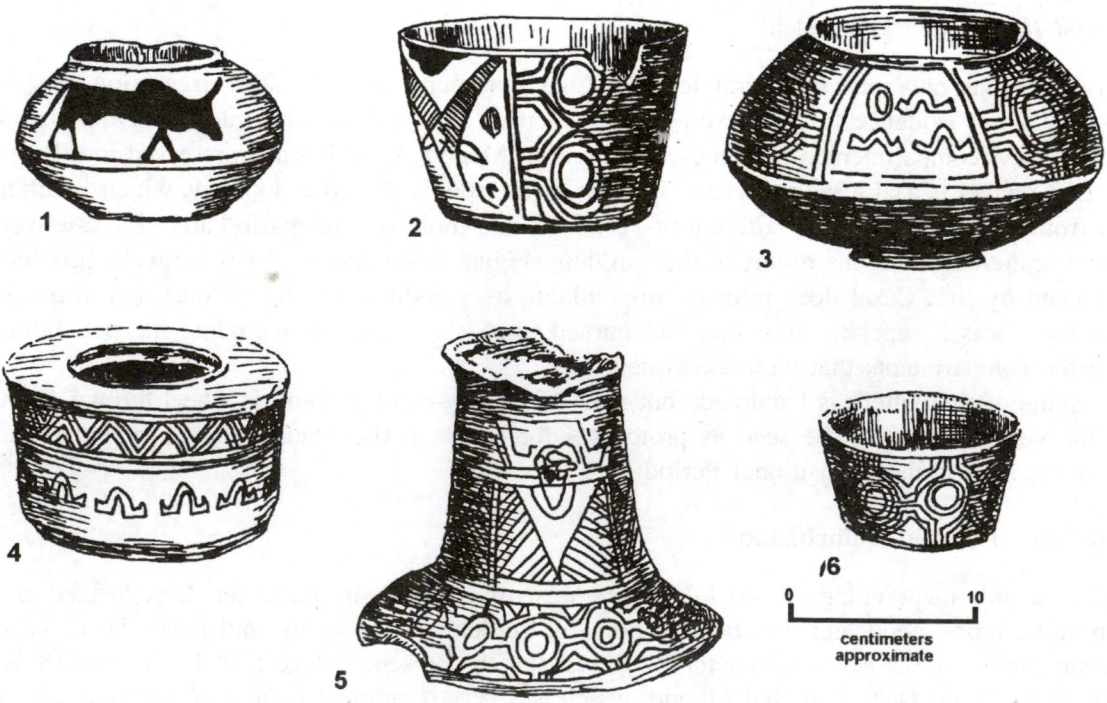

0 ⎯⎯⎯⎯ 10
centimeters
approximate

Figure 4.99. Nal pottery published by Sir John Marshall, after Marshall 1904-05: Plates XXXIII and XXXIV

destroyed in the disastrous earthquake of 1935. In 1923 or 1924 the Bizanjau Sardar of the region excavated more pottery vessels. They were broken in transport to Quetta. This led Hargreaves to conduct his more systematic excavation of the mound in 1925 (Hargreaves 1929), just before he went of to Mohenjo-daro for the big 1925-26 field season there.

Hargreaves opened seven trenches at the site, lettered A through G. Trenches A and E, which were contiguous (Figure 4.100) produced evidence for fractional burials, some of which were concentrated in association with the beautiful Nal funerary pottery (Figure 4.101). Other fractional human remains were more scattered, but they were also associated with the distinctive Nal ceramics. Three complete burials in brick lined graves were found associated with architecture and other classes of material, pottery, figurines, beads and the like, in trenches A and E.

Nal also produced a fair number of copper implements (Figure 4.102). There is also a large conical weight (Hargreaves 1929: Plate XVb, No. 78) with a parallel at Mohenjo-daro, being Mackay's Type (d) (Mackay 1937-38: 402, Plate CVI, No. 54).

The site of Sohr Damb Nal in former Kalat state of Baluchistan has been subjected to four campaigns of excavation, the first three of which were undertaken by local administrators or soldiers. But, in 1925, Harold Hargreaves of the Archaeological Survey of India went there for one season of work (Hargreaves 1929). His seven trenches, lettered A through G produced evidence for both habitation and burials, the latter found only in trenches A and E, which were contiguous operations.

There are important cultural and chronological problems that are attendant on this site (Possehl 1996b). It seems that most of the human interments can be associated with upper layers at Nal, that Hargreaves referred to as the "burial stratum" (Hargreaves 1929: 27). If this is the case, some of the interments may have been made after the settlement had been abandoned. Thus, in the area of contiguous trenches A and E, Hargreaves initially came upon a funerary area under which he found the remains of buildings. He describes the area this way:

> Whether these stone structures are the remains of deserted and ruined habitations or whether designed originally for funerary purposes cannot at present be asserted, but when excavated the whole area was found to be devoted entirely to the purpose of a necropolis and human remains and funerary pottery were found down to floor level and in a stratum nowhere more than four feet in thickness (1929: 21).

Three types of inhumations were found: (1) collective, fractional burials, (2) individual fractional burials and 3) complete burials. The greatest number of human remains at Nal are from fractional burials and a description of one of the "collective" areas can be used to represent the mass of data found in Mr. Hargreaves' report.

Collective Fractional Burials

Group B in A-6. In clearing the floor of A-6 a collection of thirty-two vessels was recovered. Part of a long bone was lying over one vase, many were scattered among the pots and long bones were lying together. The whole group of bones and vessels lay in an area 9'9" by 3'3". No skull was found with these but eight days later when removing the earth at the north-west corner of A-6 the skull of an adult was found all alone. This may have been part of Group B but was fully three feet distant from the nearest vessels. Even with this skull nothing like a complete skeleton was recovered, no pelvic bones, no shoulder blades, no vertebrae. On examination it was found that eighteen of the thirty-two vessels contained earth only. One was quite empty, having been covered by another vessel. The remaining vessels all contained bones or bone fragments mixed with earth. Two phalanges were in one vessel, parts of two small ribs in a second, three metatarsal or metacarpal bones in a third and so on. It is not clear whether

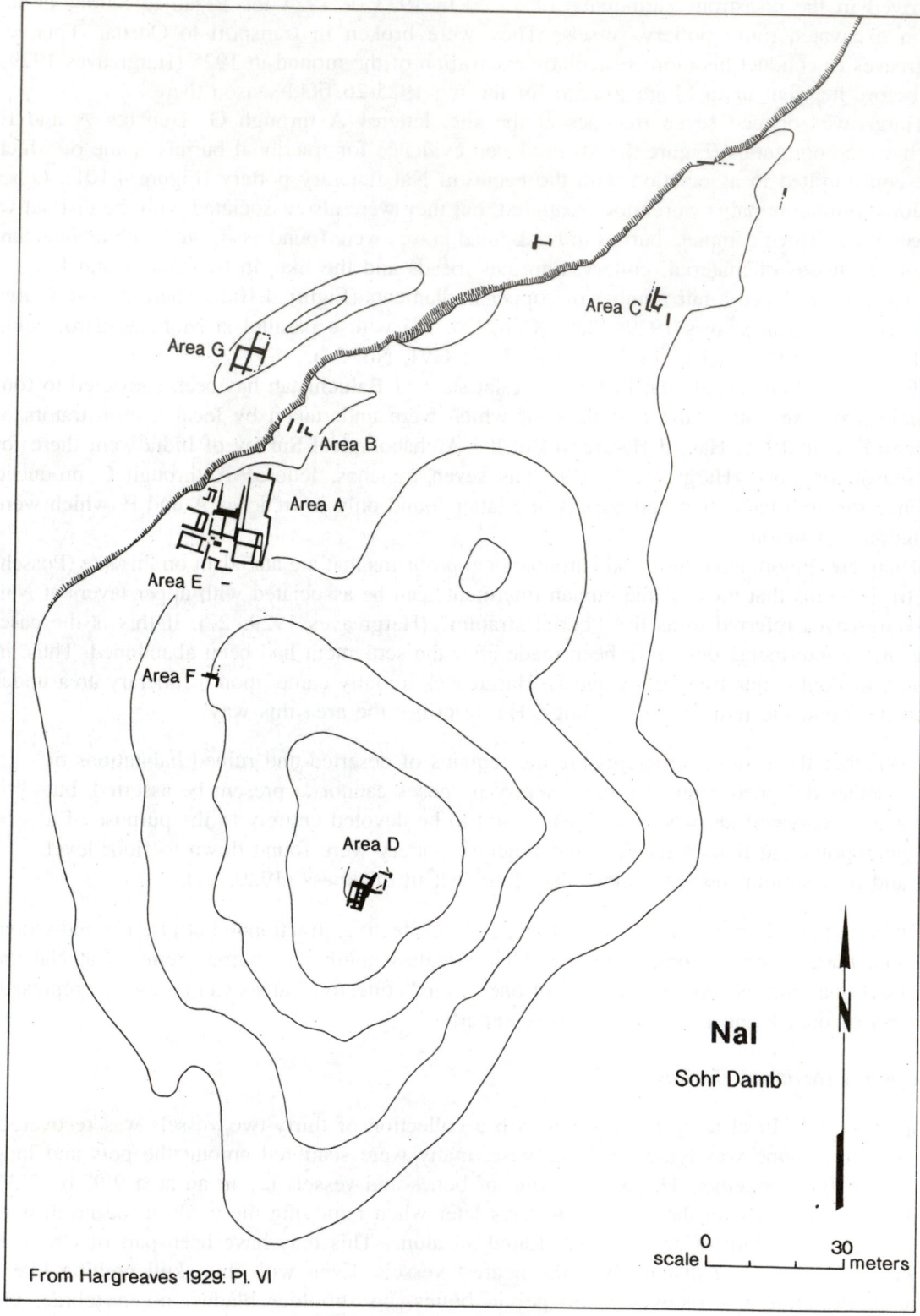

Figure 4.100. Nal site plan, after Hargreaves 1929: Plate VI omit refer to Figure 4.99, Nal painted pottery, after Hargreaves 1929: Plate XVIII

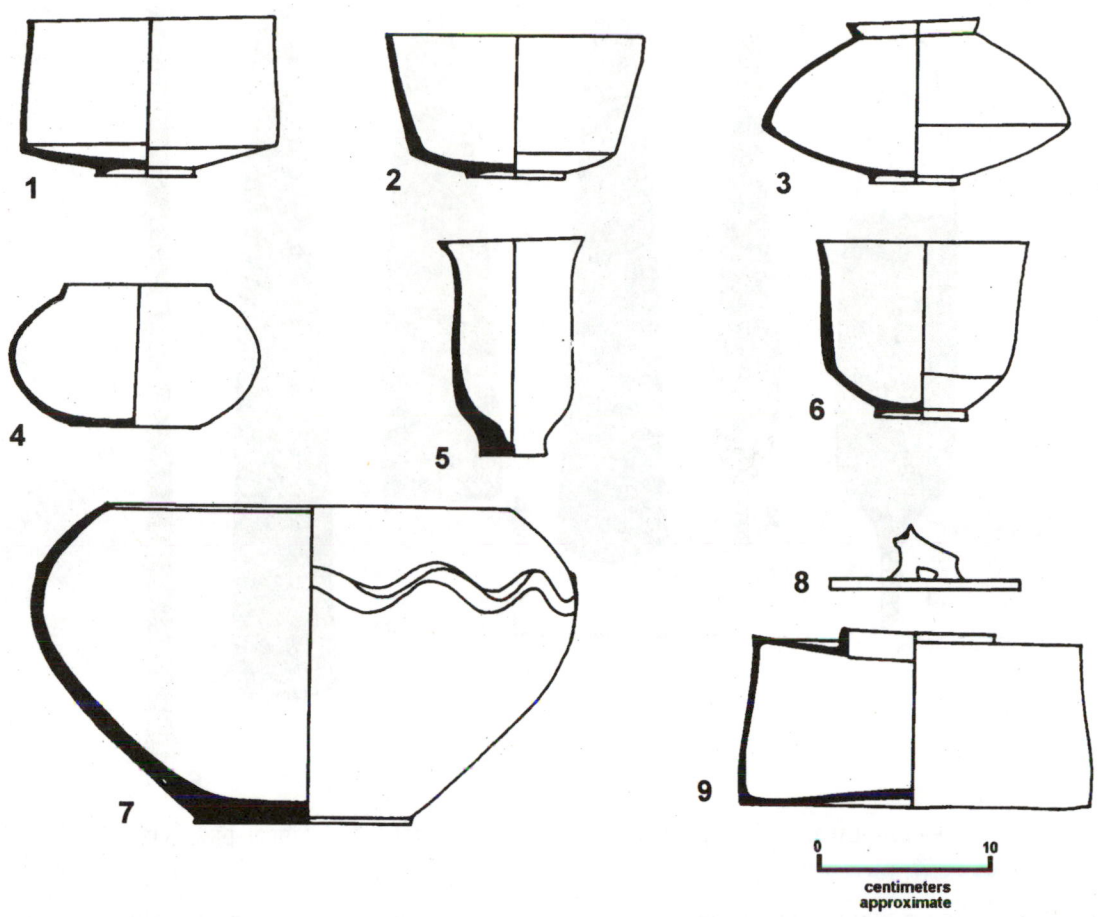

Figure 4.101. Nal, plain pottery, after Hargreaves 1929: Plate XVI

these bones were originally placed in the vessels or later found their way into them, but the latter seems the more likely in this particular case as bones were more frequently near the tops of the pots. This may be considered as typical of a form of fractional or incomplete burial of which some twenty-six examples were discovered.

Lt.-Col. Sewell and Dr. Guha report that these human remains were of four persons, namely two adults, a youth of about eighteen years, and an infant of about one year. Bones of a bird and small mammal were also recovered with this group (Hargreaves 1929: 21-2).

Fractional Burials Scattered human bones were found in trenches A and E and were considered to be parts of fractional interments as well, but they were not sufficiently concentrated for it to be suggested that they represented a collective deposit.

The fractional burials of both types were associated with the beautiful Nal ceramics as well as different kinds of beads, including agate, carnelian, lapis lazuli, shell, limestone and copper (Hargreaves 1929: 33, Pl.XV).

Complete Burials in brick-lined pits were found in trenches A and E. Two of these were infants, one in trench A and one in E, and one an adult. The latter was found lying on its left side in a slightly crouched position as shown in (Hargreaves 1929: Plate XIIa). There is no certainty that grave goods were associated with any of the complete burials (Hargreaves 1929: 27).

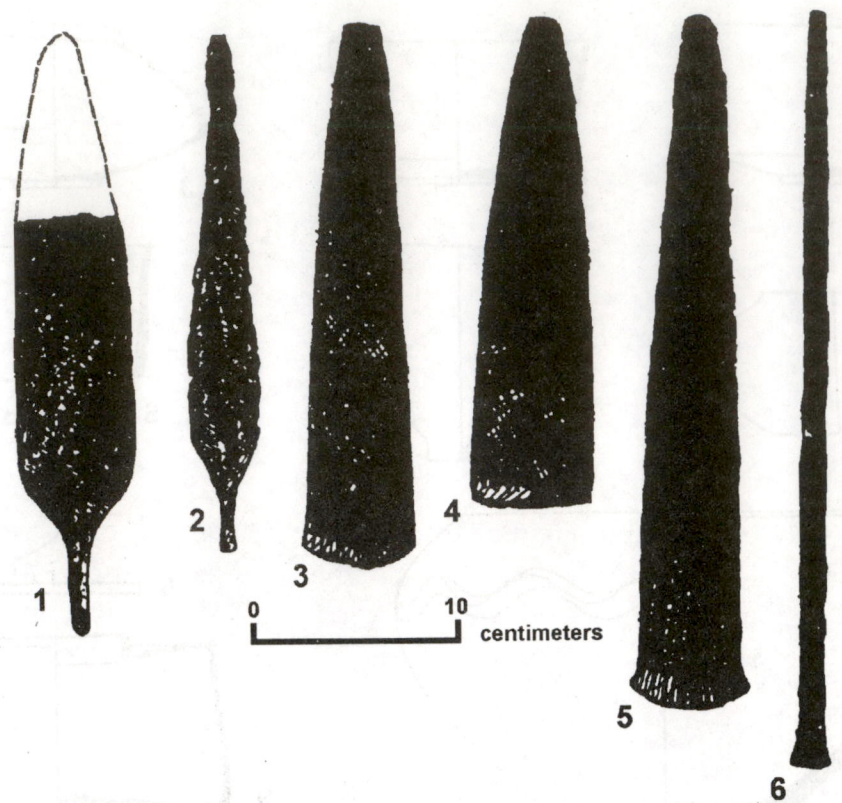

Figure 4.102. Nal, copper based implements, after Hargreaves 1929: Plate XIV

These three interments seem to be associated with the habitation layers and architecture of the Nal settlement, but since there was no funerary pottery associated with them provide no information about the important chronological issues that are apparent at this site.

Hargreaves also speaks of "complete burials without defined graves" (1929: 27-8), but the evidence that they were complete is not conclusive.

Serious difficulties arise in understanding this site because of the substantial amount of early, uncontrolled digging that took place there. Hargreaves summarizes the situation in the following way:

> How much valuable evidence was removed and destroyed by former excavators cannot be stated, but it is certain that they removed part of the burial stratum in many parts of Area A. Occasionally as in A 2-3, and in A 8-11 they had dug right down to floor level and completely through the burial stratum, but in no case do they seem to have destroyed walls. Our burials might therefore appear incomplete not because they were originally so but as a result of the removal of part of the bones in these earlier operations. While this might be possibly true in the case of Burial Group B, since these remains were in places only nine inches below the level of previous excavations, it is impossible in the case of Group F, and impossible in the case of the H burials since we ourselves found these under the A burials. All the remains in Trench E were likewise undisturbed, this trench lying outside the former diggings. From Groups A and E it is clear that in certain cases at least bones were buried and not bodies, and that antesepultural excarnation had been practiced (Hargreaves 1929: 27-8).

The Nal funerary pottery thus seems to be associated with fractional interments. These appear to have been composed of individuals who were either buried and later purposefully exhumed, or were exposed to the elements during the period of decay of the fleshy parts of the body. They were then buried at Nal, along with the pottery and some of their jewelry, without attention being paid to the integrity of the bones belonging to any particular individual.

The three burials in brick lined graves seem to belong to the habitation phase at Nal and this should be considered somewhat earlier than the later fractional interments. The habitation at Nal is considered to be Amri-Nal in affiliation, possibly early Kulli. This means that the Nal cemetery Wares are very late in the Early Harappan Phase, and may represent something that is contemporary with the early phase of Indus urbanization (Possehl 1996b).

The architecture consisted of well defined stone foundations topped with mud brick, just as at neighboring Anjira. At the summit of the mound, in Area D, room D 6, a charred beam 20 centimeters in diameter, associated with nine rafters, was found in a position that suggested that the buildings had sloping roofs (Hargreaves 1929: 31). In room D 6 and superficial debris to its north, a fragment of a copper chisel, spherical pounding stones, a piece of leaden slag, two pieces of cerusite as well as an ore consisting of cuprite and cerusite were found (Hargreaves 1929: 31; see 1929: 44 for an analysis of the ores). Together these things suggest metal working at Nal. At least one piece of silver was recovered, in addition to a quantity of copper. Copper implements are shown in Plate XIV of Hargreaves' report.

Many beads of agate, carnelian, lapis lazuli, shell, limestone and copper were recovered (Hargreaves 1929: 33, Pl.XV). Two compartmented copper seals were also found, one in the form of a pecking bird (Hargreaves 1929: Plate XV, d, f).

Subsistence Information

Animal bones, including birds have been found at Nal but there is no systematic report on these specimens.

Chronology and Cultural Affiliation

Nal is generally thought of as a single period site; however, this may not be the case and there are significant problems of chronology and cultural affiliation that remain to be resolved at this settlement. There are no radiocarbon dates from Nal.

The position of the funerary pottery in trenches A and E seems to be clear enough, and Hargreaves makes a good case for his "burial stratum" above the architectural level at the foot of the mound. There is a clear association of the classic Nal ware with these fractional burials. This pottery is one of the most distinctive and attractive of the prehistoric ceramics of the Subcontinent. It is a buff ware, sometimes slightly pink, painted in black (or dark grey) over the natural surface (at times a slip) of the vessel. Color is frequently added to the design in the form of red, yellow or blue paint. The use of yellow and blue pigments is unique to the Nal wares in prehistoric times.

Very little notice is given to the remains from the habitation itself, and the pottery from this aspect of Hargreaves' excavation is almost ignored. There is reason to believe, however, that there is a Kulli affiliation, as noted by D. H. Gordon some years ago (Gordon 1958: 39-41). This can be documented from the Hargreaves work, principally through the presence of Kulli-like figurines of bulls, a ram (with a very close parallel at Mehi; Stein 1931: Pl. XXVII, Mehi I.9.6) and one clear Kulli human figurine from trench E (Figure 4.103). Not much can be said about the pottery although Hargreaves does remark that: "...three earthen vessels found in area

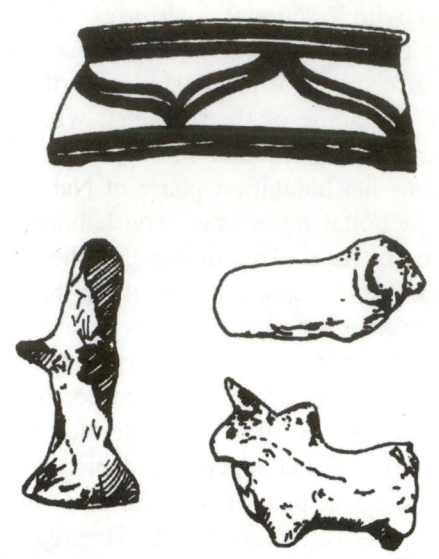

Figure 4.103. Nal, Kulli-like figurines and bracket ware, after Hargreaves 1929: Plate XXL

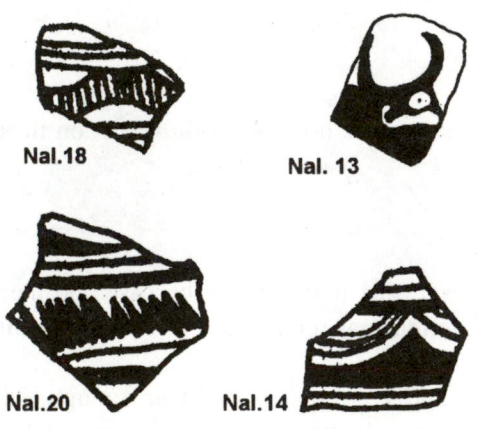

Figure 4.104. Kulli-like ceramics from Nal found by Sir Aurel Stein

D bear no resemblance in form, fabric or decoration to the funerary vessels" (1929: 31). One of these is illustrated in his Pl. XIX, 2 and it does not appear to be Kulli, but the difference is still an observation worth noting. In among the sherds of the Hargreaves report are some pieces which might be thought of as Kulli-like. Gordon mentions the pipal leaf motif (1958: 41), which might or might not be a sound clue. It should also be noted that Sir Aurel Stein visited Nal as part of his Gedrosia tour (1931: 166-68, Pl. XXXIII). His surface collection contains four sherds which are Kulli-like (certainly not the Nal ceramic), especially the wide-eyed bull (Stein 1931: Pl. XXXIII, Nal 13, Nal 14, Nal, 18, Nal 20; (Figure 4.104). The flat copper based implements from Nal (illustrated above) would fit well within the typology of tools of this type from Mature Harappan sites and in this regard have a "late" look to them.

The upper architectural levels of Nal seem then, to have a Kulli affiliation and may well be like the remains of Period I at Niai Buthi in Las Bela, that have been called "Early Kulli" here. This is an association between the Amri-Nal complex and an incipient kind of Kulli and has provisionally been assigned to the Early Harappan era. The classic Nal funerary ceramic would appear to be later than this. It may well be that both the Early Kulli occupation, once again a provisional determination for the Nal habitation, was early enough for the "burial stratum" to be accommodated within the Early Harappan era: however, it may extend into the first half of the third millennium BC, where it would be contemporary with the Mature Harappan and the Kulli Complex, also within the Kalat region.

There is no clear resolution to this issue of chronology and cultural affiliation of the habitation strata at Nal given the present data set. Only renewed digging at this fascinating site will give the information needed to answer these questions.

Architecture of the Amri-Nal Phase

Terracing and walls of stone are associated with some Amri-Nal sites. At Damb Buthi near the northeastern end of the Bado Range this is especially evident, with other examples in Baluchistan, at Toji Damb and Nundara (Figure 4.105, Figure 4.106, Figure 4.107). Stein (1931: 22-5) found the stone wall at Toji to be almost three meters thick, and it may have been a circumvallation around the site. Toji and Damb Buthi were also settled during the Mature Harappan Stage or Kulli Phases, and it may be that these features are associated with the later period than the Amri-Nal. No one really knows, but excavation would resolve the issue.

There are some large structures at Nundara, shown in (Stein 1931: Figures 49, 50, 53, 54). There is no later Kulli occupation there, but material predating the Amri-Nal occupation is available. Some of this stone work seems to be rather grand but not enough is known to say much specific about it, although one feature looks very much like a corner bastion (Figure 4.108). Thus, while there is a suggestion of some kind of a fortification at Nundara, it is just that, a suggestion; only excavation can resolve the issue.

Amri-Nal Subsistence Practices

Except for Balakot (Meadow 1979a), there are almost no remains of plants and animals that have been described from the Amri-Nal sites. The inhabitants of Balakot I were not exploiters of the nearby maritime environment, at least as documented by remains found at the site. With the exception of a few shells the faunal assemblage from this period is of terrestrial mammals, cattle, sheep, goats and gazelle (Meadow 1979a: 291).

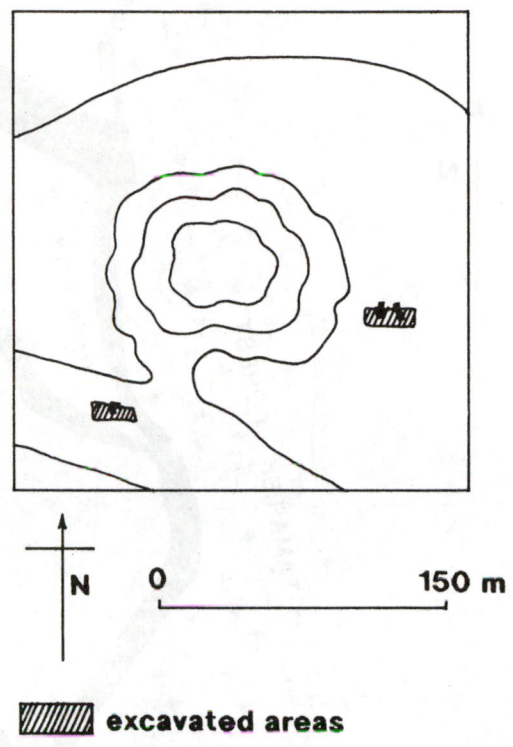

Figure 4.105. Plan of Damb Buthi, after Majumdar 1934: Plate XLV

There is a small report on the faunal remains from Amri (Poulain-Josien 1964). It documents a pattern that is recurring at other sites, with an abundance of cattle bones and some sheep and goats. It is interesting, however, that the remains of the rhinoceros appears in Period IIIC (Mature Harappan; five different skeletal elements). The gavial, or Indus crocodile, pictured on the Indus seals was also represented in the corpus of faunal remains from Period IIIB. The onager, or wild ass was also present (Periods IC and IIIC); it is not an animal that figures much in Harappan art, but it was evidently a part of the local landscape in Sindh during the Early and Mature Harappan Stages.

The Sindhi sites of the Amri-Nal Phase are closely associated with the Kirthar Range and Sindh Kohistan, not with the deep alluvium of the Indus flood plains. The settlements of this Phase are found in the mountains of Baluchistan as well. One of the keys to the subsistence regime must therefore, have involved the seasonal migration of peoples from the highlands in the winter, with a return in the summer.

The Expansion of Food Producing Peoples into Gujarat

Evidence for the early expansion of farmers and herders into Gujarat appears at a number of sites as seen in Table 4.33. (Figure 4.109, Figure 4.110).

The evidence for early occupations at these sites seems to date to the Amri-Nal Phase, with Padri and Loteshwar suggesting an even earlier movement there, possibly in Kechi Beg times. Period I at Dholavira has ceramics that have typological similarities with Amri Period II

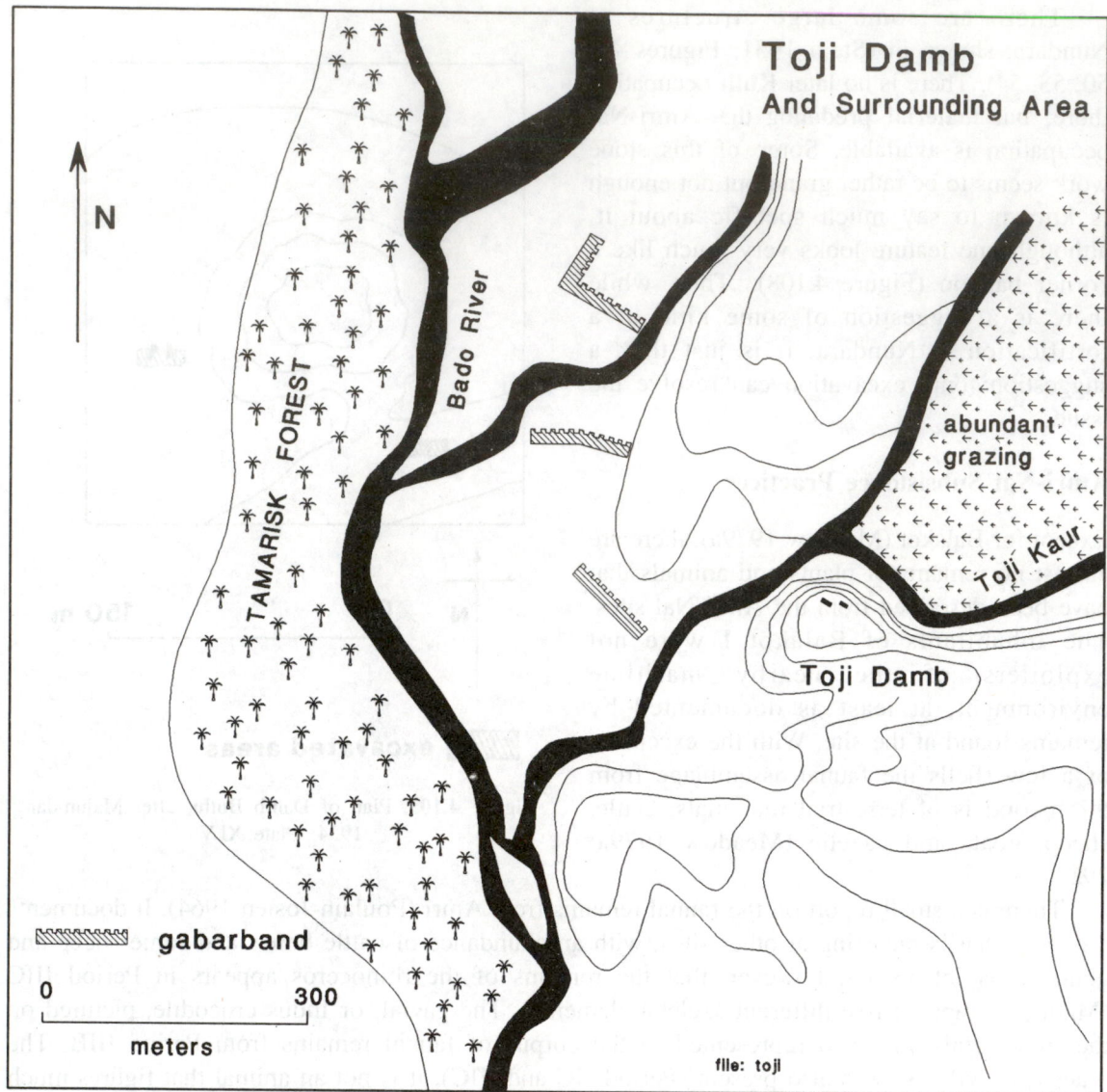

Figure 4.106. Plan of Toji Damb, after Stein 1931: Figure 1

(Transitional Stage) (R. S. Bisht 1992, personal communication). Surkotada is on this list since a reanalysis of the ceramics from the small cemetery 300 meters north of the habitation site leads on to believe that this was a place of interment for peoples associated with the Amri-Nal Complex (Possehl, in press c).[13]

There are several different bodies of material culture involved with these sites. The Arnata Chalcolithic is dominated by a Gritty Red Ware that is quite distinctive. It is accompanied by other pottery types: Fine Red Ware, Burnished Red Ware and a Burnished Grey/Black Ware. This ceramic complex is long lived, and Anarta Chalcolithic ceramics are associated with Gujarati type Mature Harappan wares and Lustrous Red Ware, a ceramic of the second millennium BC (Sonawane and Ajithprasad 1994: 134-35).

Period IA at Surkotada also has some Anarta Chalcolithic pottery, but this is associated with Mature Harappan ceramics. There is, however, one date from this period at Surkotada that

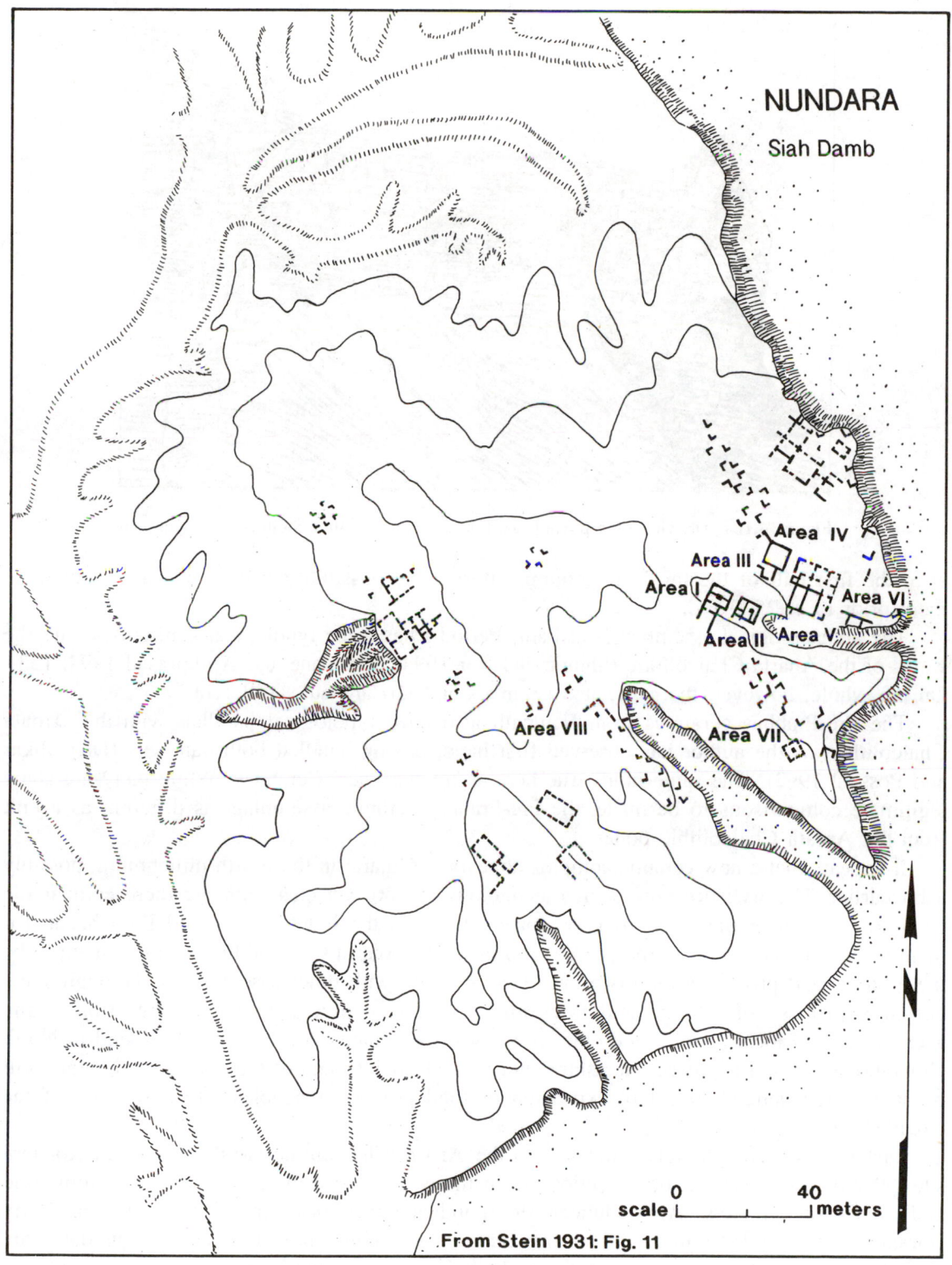

Figure 4.107. Plan of Nundara, after Stein 1931: Figure 11

598

Figure 4.108. Drawing of a possible bastion at Nundara, after Stein 1931: Figure 49

is in the first half of the third millennium, offering the possibility that there was a settlement there prior to c. 2500 BC.

The archaeological assemblages at Padri Period I has some typological similarities with the wares of the Anarta Chalcolithic (Shinde and Kar 1994; Sonawane and Ajithprasad 1994: 133). On the whole, however, the associated ceramics at Padri are quite different.

The Pre-Prabhas ceramics from Somnath also have typological parallels with the Arnata Chalcolithic, as the author has observed first hand, having handled both data sets (Dhavalikar and Possehl 1992). The same holds true here as for the Padri Ceramics. While there are some legitimate comparisons to be made, the Pre-Prabhas ceramic assemblage is different as a unit from the Arnata Chalcolithic pottery.

It appears that a new ceramic complex appears in Gujarat in the fourth millennium, possibly a bit earlier. The stylistic roots of this technology are not yet clear, nor are there comparable ceramics at sites of the Kechi Beg or Togau Phases in the Indus Valley and Baluchistan for them to be compared to. But the people who made the Anarta Chalcolithic ceramics seem to be the earliest, and provide a kind of stem of comparison with other assemblages. Through some complex process of change and integration, probably involving some migration, some acculturation of local peoples and other processes, their material culture can be found in North Gujarat, eastern and southern Saurashtra, and possibly other parts of Gujarat as well. More will be said of the general model of expansion of food producing peoples into new areas of the Greater Indus region.

Distantly related (possibly unrelated) to the Anarta Chalcolithic are the Amri-Nal Kot Diji sites. Personal observation of collections from these sites, as well as illustrations (Ajithprasad and Sonawane, in press; A. Majumdar 1994) indicate that these appear to be typical Early Harappan sites, at least in so far as the ceramics are concerned. No radiocarbon dates are available, so an absolute chronology has to be inferred by comparison with other dated places. This challenge remains for those who work with this material. These Early Harappan remains

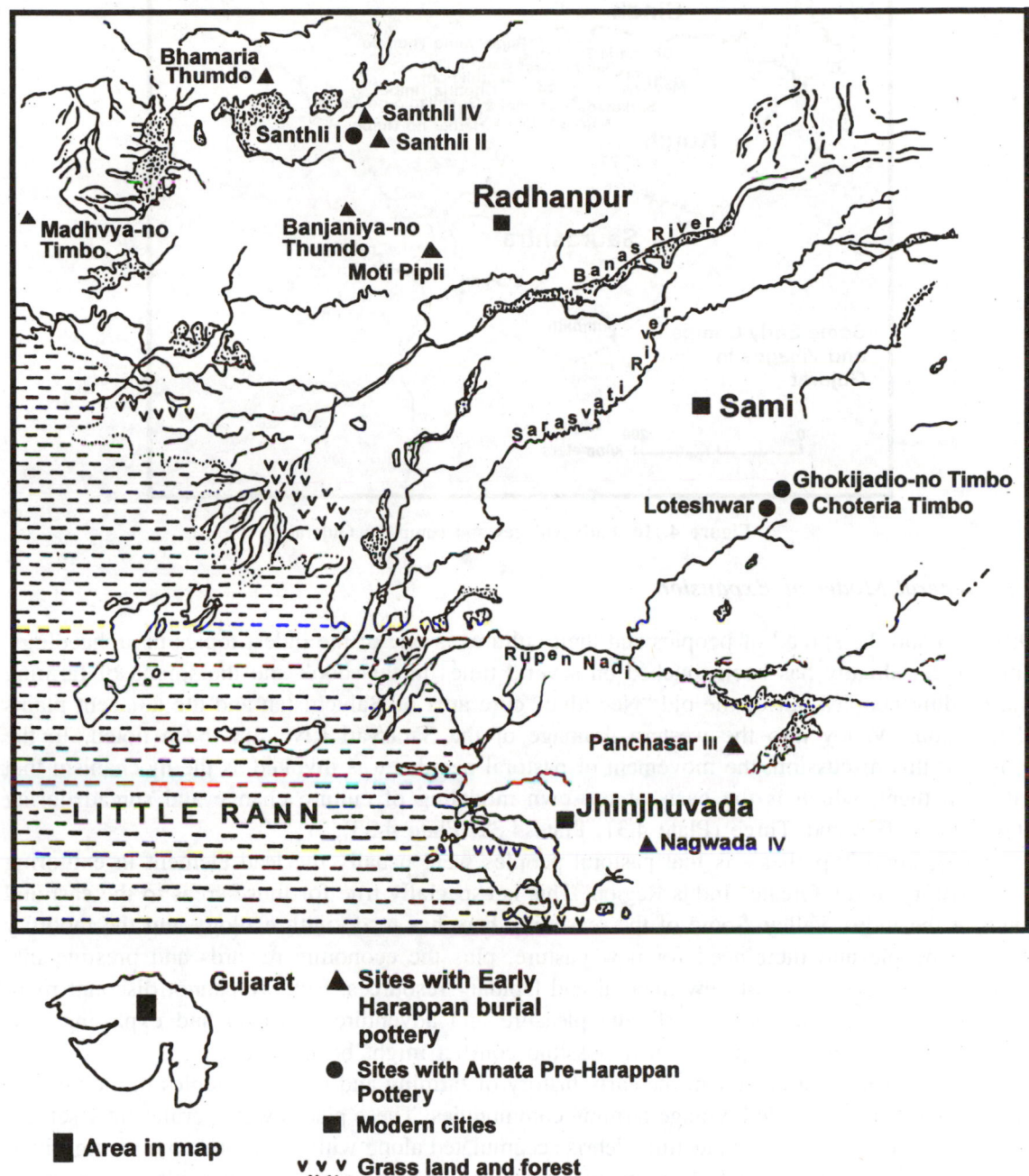

Figure 4.109. Map of Early Harappan and Arnata Pre-Harappan sites in north Gujarat

seem to represent the continuation of the cultural processes that linked Gujarat with Sindh and Baluchistan in prehistoric times. The routes involved movement into and across the Ranns, as documented at Surkotada and Dholavira. Since Surkotada is very close to the estuaries of the Beas, Rupen and Sarasvati Rivers, it might be that this was the route into north Gujarat. But, the route around the northern edge of the Ranns, via the Luni delta, represents a second possibility that may well have been a part of the process of expansion.

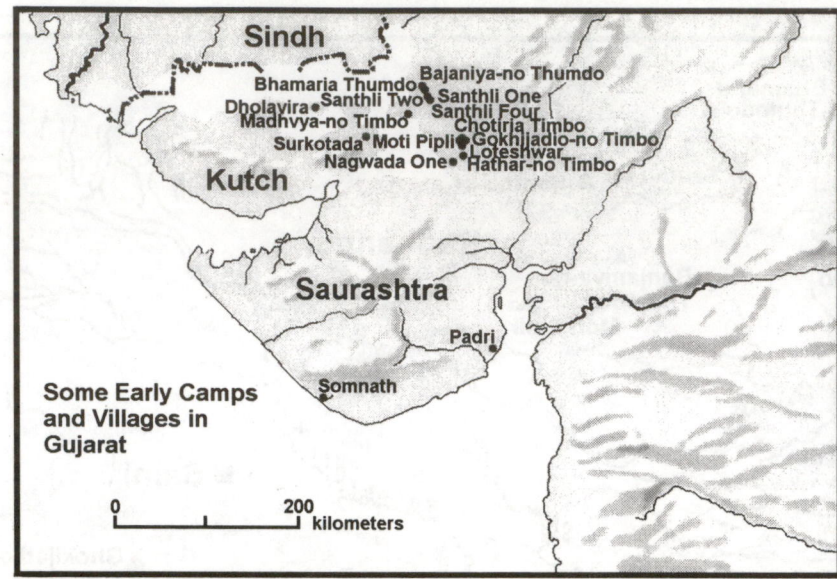

Figure 4.110. Early villages and camps in Gujarat

The General Model of Expansion

Diffusion and the spread of peoples and their cultures is one of the oldest topics in archaeology. The subject already has been touched on several times in this book and the spread of farming and herding peoples out of the old "Neolithic" core area of Baluchistan and the adjacent plains of the Indus Valley into the western drainage of the Sarasvati River has been noted. In the course of this discussion, the movement of pastoral peoples was invoked as the mechanism that led them there, which is the basis of my own modeling of culture change and spread during Stages One, Two and Three (Plate 4.31, Plate 4.32, Plate 4.33).

The general hypothesis is that pastoral peoples were usually the lead element in exploring new territory in the Greater Indus Region. This is especially true for those areas to the east and south of the Indus Valley. Some of the reasoning here has to do with ecology and the mobility of these people and their need for new pasture, plus the economic rewards and prestige that come with the discovery of new mineral and lapidary resources. But, we cannot discount more human motivations in this as well; the pleasure and adventure of travel and exploring new territory, meeting new people, even if possible conflict might be involved.

What we see most clearly in the early history of farming and herding peoples in the Greater Indus Region are the settled, village farming communities. These places were permanently settled, in a relative sense, where architectural debris accumulated along with trash: broken pots, figurines, terracotta cakes and the other flotsam and jetsam of human existence. Such places are easily identified and the artifacts allow us to give them a relative chronology. What is not seen nearly as clearly are the herders, the pastoral and other kinds of nomads, be they full time, seasonal or otherwise itinerant. Since these people travel light and are not necessarily in the same place twice, they do not leave a robust archaeological record. But, there is enough of an archaeological record, and theory is compelling here, that we can be assured that they were there and probably in large numbers, possibly even outnumbering the settled farmers. We are not in a position to estimate the size of the population of people with this adaptation with a skill approaching precision, so the latter comments are merely suggestions, but the ancient pastoral nomad is

TABLE 4.33
Sites of Early Food Producing Peoples in Gujarat with Radiocarbon Determinations

Site	District	Village
Amri-Nal Ceramics in Kutch		
Dholavira	Kutch	Dholavira
Surkotada	Kutch	Sanwa
Amri-Nal or Kot Diji Type Burial Pottery in North Gujarat		
Bajaniya-no Thumdo	Banaskantha	Koliwada
Bhamaria Thumdo	Banaskantha	Jhandada
Harthar-no Timbo	Mehsana	Panchasar
Madhvya-no Timbo	Banaskantha	Mathura
Moti Pipli	Banaskantha	Moti Pipli
Nagwada One	Surendranagar	Nagwada
Santhli Four	Banaskantha	Santhli
Santhli Two	Banaskantha	Santhli
Anarta Chalcolithic, Pre-2500 BC		
Choteria Timbo	Mehsana	Munjpur
Gokhijadio-no Timbo	Mehsana	Kukrana
Santhli One	Banaskantha	Santhli
Loteshwar	Mehsana	Loteshwar

$$\begin{array}{ll}
\text{PRL-1564} & 1\Sigma \text{ cal BC } 3346 \ (3094) \ 2919 \\
& 2\Sigma \text{ cal BC } 3499 \ (3094) \ 2881 \\
\text{PRL-1565} & 1\Sigma \text{ cal BC } 3969 \ (3905, 3880, 3804) \ 3705 \\
& 2\Sigma \text{ cal BC } 4210 \ (3905, 3880, 3804) \ 3638
\end{array}$$

Site	District	Village
Somnath, Pre-Prabhas Occupation		
Somnath	Jamnagar	Somnath

$$\begin{array}{ll}
\text{PRL-90} & 1\Sigma \text{ cal BC } 2920 \ (2881) \ 2625 \\
& 2\Sigma \text{ cal BC } 3095 \ (2881) \ 2496 \\
\text{TF-1287} & 1\Sigma \text{ cal BC } 3019 \ (2890) \ 2701 \\
& 2\Sigma \text{ cal BC } 3293 \ (2890) \ 2581
\end{array}$$

Site	District	Village
Padri, Pre-Harappan Occupation		
Padri	Bhavnagar	Padri

$$\begin{array}{ll}
\text{PRL-1785} & 1\Sigma \text{ cal BC } 3260 \ (3022, 2985, 2928) \ 2905 \\
& 2\Sigma \text{ cal BC } 3347 \ (3022, 2985, 2928) \ 2784 \\
\text{PRL-1787} & 1\Sigma \text{ cal BC } 3699 \ (3636) \ 3387 \\
& 2\Sigma \text{ cal BC } 3792 \ (3636) \ 3363
\end{array}$$

securely documented at places like Bagor in Rajasthan and in the camp sites that M. R. Mughal found associated the Hakra Wares Phase in Cholistan.

These nomadic peoples should probably be thought of in terms of more or less full-time specialists or as seasonal folk who may have been settled farmers for part of the year and pastoral nomads for the other. Even within these two norms there is great variation, with full-time pastoralists settling to be full-time agriculturalists in groups or as individuals. On the other hand, farmers might take up pastoral nomadism. These subsistence strategies have a diversity of forms, and they shift and change over time. We should imagine that there was continuity in adaptation from father to son, mother to daughter but "once a farmer always a farmer", or "once a pastoral nomad, always a pastoral nomad" simply does not hold, if we turn to the ethnohistorical record and the principles of human ecology as a guide to understanding the peoples of the Indus Age. Nor is it wise to think in terms of "typical" farmers and "typical" pastoral nomads, since there is much room for variation which seriously limits the utility of these typological categories.

People adapted to the mobile management of domesticated animals, mostly cattle in the Indus Age, were often integral, allied, symbiotic with village farming communities. But, pastoralists can also operate independently of village farming communities and it is in this mode that the resilient explorer of the Greater Indus Region is probably found. Enough is known from Gujarat and the Punjab and Haryana to believe that pastoral peoples were in these areas prior to settled farming communities, possibly by a millennium or more; witness the Anarta Chalcolithic as found at Loteshwar. This begins to document the thought that, in general, it was the pastoralists who first explored and "discovered" new lands, living there on a seasonal basis, returning there from time to time, when the needs of their animals and their own dispositions decreed. Over time this led to the pioneering of the Eastern Region and southeastern areas of the Greater Indus Region by food producing peoples.

Those pastoral communities that were relatively free from village farming communities would have had to engage in some agriculture, which implies at least a seasonal permanency of settlement, storage facilities, stable occupation of one small spot of earth—implying in turn the buildup of an archaeological midden. It also seems to be true that the inhabitants of village farming communities follow behind the nomads, slowly spreading from their bases in Baluchistan and the adjacent Indus Plains, to the east and south into areas pioneered by their more pastorally adapted "cousins." This leads to the notion that there are several interrelated processes at work here. First there is exploration by pastoralists. A second stage to this involves the settling in of some of these folk, with the beginnings of seasonal agriculture. A third stage would involve full time occupation of the newly explored lands by the pastoral *cum* farming peoples in these frontier areas, at first being quite mobile within their new lands, but some gradually settling in over time into permanent villages. There is also documentation for the progressive encroachment of village farming communities into the new areas, as more and more territory was taken under cultivation, possibly to accommodate the increasing population of the region.

These food producing peoples of the Indus Age were not the first to use the new lands to the east and south of the Indus Valley. There was an historically deep indigenous population of hunter-gatherers there, and we can expect that the explorers of the Indus Age would have come into contact with them. It would seem unlikely that all of these encounters were peaceful, happy ones, as the fortification of sites of the Indus Age in Kutch might document. But, there are signs in the archaeological record of acculturation having taken place, most notably in the archaeological record at Langhnaj and Lothal (Possehl and Kennedy 1979). Some of the encounters, at least, were sufficiently amiable for this process of cultural change to have taken place. While there is a kind of chronological sequence to this model, it is not linear and there is overlap in time between the various cultural processes.

The people who lived in village farming communities or the pastoral camps were not inalienably tied to their settlement and substance form. In fact, in most parts of the world, certainly northwestern India and Pakistan, food producing peoples are on a continuum of settlement and subsistence adaptations: some more settled, some more mobile, some more dependent on plants, fields and irrigation, some more dependent on cattle, sheep and goats, pasture land and waterholes. The pure forms or ideal types for the village farming community and pastoral camp are seldom if ever expressed in a day to day reality; everyone is somewhere "in the middle," on the continuum between the ideal types at the continuum's ends. Moreover, if we could trace the history of any one social group we would probably find that they are not stable in their adaptation. Few, if anyone stays in any one place on the continuum for too long. Shifts in adaptation should be seen as common, if viewed within the time frame of archaeological periods, with particular groups sometimes engaging in more farming than herding, becoming somewhat more sedentary, but over time taking to the road again, as a mobile pastoral people. Not all of the reasons for these shifts are known, but they are well documented. Frederick Barth told us much about this dynamic among nomads in southwestern Iran (Barth 1961), which was regulated for the most part by personal success in raising animals. Short-term climatic change, ecological disaster and political instability are also widely held to be the keys to understanding the reasons behind shifts along the village farming community-pastoral nomadic camp continuum.

The older chapters of the archaeological record inform us that by the beginning of the Early Harappan Stage all of northern India and Pakistan, outside the Kechi Beg and Hakra Wares areas, were inhabited by peoples who might be thought of as "aboriginal." In the course of exploration and land use the herder and farmer of the Indus Age would have met, engaged, even fought with these peoples, some of whom were surely quite foreign to them, not part of the peoples of the Indus Age. Others may have taken what they wanted from those of the Indus Age, such as domesticated animals, pottery and copper artifacts, but maintained their own identity, as those at Bagor seem to have done. Still other aboriginals might have ended up as refuge populations, staunchly defending their own way of life from the dreaded farmers and pastoral nomads; some were probably forced into extinction by failing to compete effectively with their new neighbors. There could, of course, be many more reasons and I leave it to the fertile mind of the reader to create the myriad possibilities of mixing and matching that a culture historical setting such as the one described here makes feasible.

This conception is a model, or image, of the forces driving the expansion of peoples during the Indus Age. There were other explorers; traders, itinerant craftsmen, tinkers, bards, travelers and the like. But the cumulative affect of all of these "others" could not have matched the impact of thousands of pastoral nomads. Thus, when one wonders who or what led the peoples of the Anarta Chalcolithic and those of the Amri-Nal/Kot Diji Phases into Kutch and Gujarat, think in terms of pastoral nomads leading the way, probably in Stage Two (Togau or Kechi Beg Phase), may be as early as Stage One, drawn to the area because of its immense value as a rich pasture land for their vast herds of cattle, sheep and goats.

Sites from the pioneering stages, prior to the appearance of villages, do exist. Some have probably been discovered, but we lack the sophistication to know them for what they are. It takes careful exploration and hard work to recognize them, but these settlements can be found and they will document the pioneering of early food producing peoples; a clear challenge for those of us who enjoy archaeological survey.

Early Harappans in Gujarat

Some new and important insights into the people of Gujarat during the Early Harappan Stage is available and a site by site review follows:

Dholavira

Dholavira is the name of a modern village on the western end of Kadir Island, just opposite the shore of the Thar Parkar area. The archaeological site, known locally as Kotada (Large Fort), lies adjacent to the village (Plate 4.34, Plate 4.35). In 1990, R. S. Bisht of the Archaeological Survey of India brought it under excavation, in the course of which he found what he has termed a "pre-Harappan" occupation (1991: 76) (Figure 4.111). It was found in a rain gully in

604

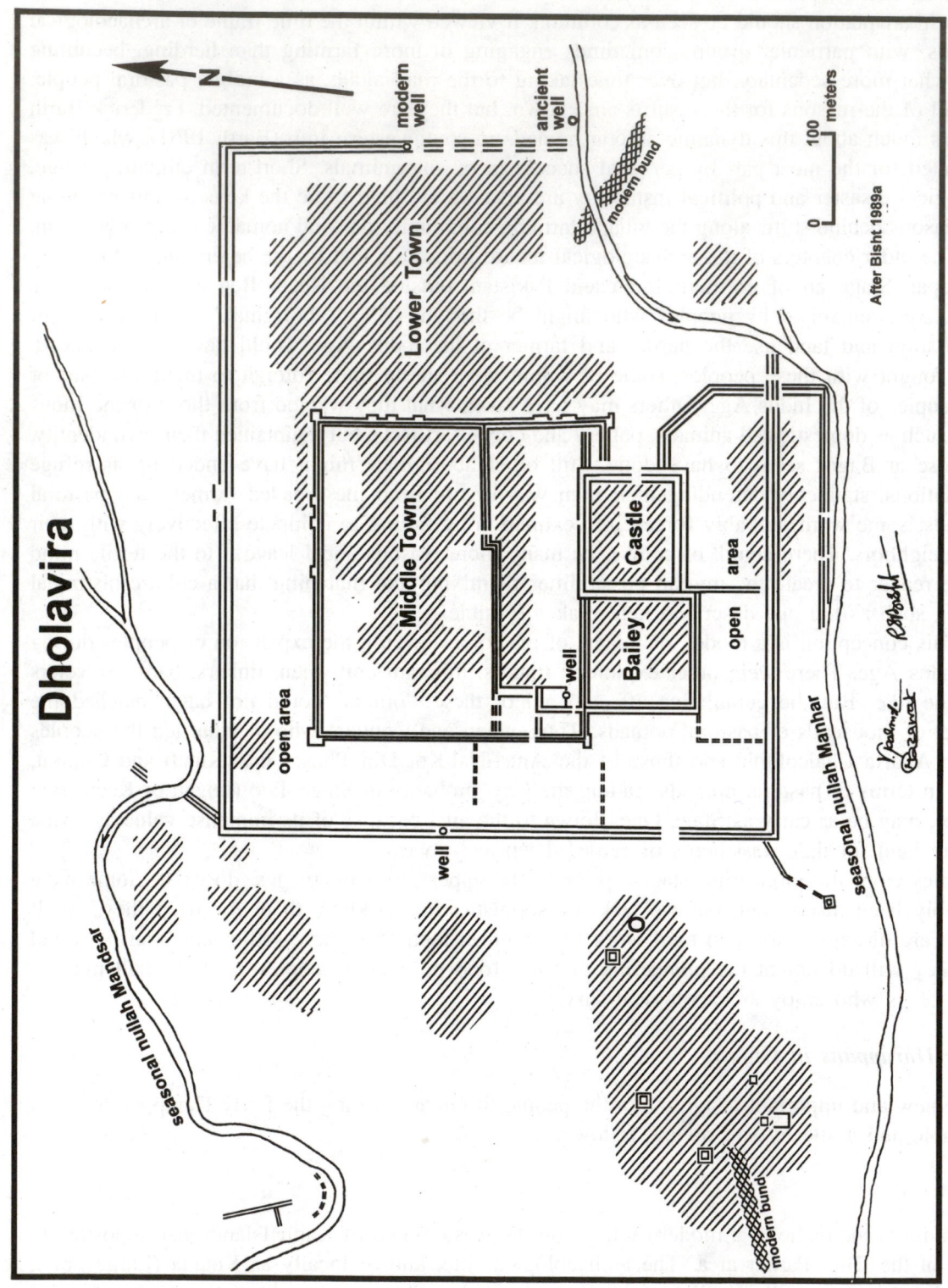

Figure 4.111. Plan of Dholavira, after Bisht 1989a: Figure 3

the southwestern quadrant of the site as part of over twelve meters of stratified habitation remains. "The first occupation of the site...pertains to a non-Harappan or pre-Harappan culture represented by an accumulation of 60 to 70 cm that lies over sterile strata made up of disintegrated rock loosely knitted with sand, which may be an artificially raised deposit" (Bisht 1991: 76).

The ceramics of Period I at Dholavira have been described only in a preliminary way, but include wheel-made red to pink wares, comb incised wares and a "reserved slip" ware. Deep dishes and jars have been reported. Slips are present in red and darker tones. Painting, also in dark colors, is sometimes highlighted in white, one of the hallmarks of the Early Harappan, occurring in all regional assemblages.

Antiquities were not abundant in Period I but Bisht notes that copper tools and other implements are found "...in good strength" (1991: 76). There are no published radiocarbon dates from Dholavira but the presence of this material, stratigraphically below the Mature Harappan should place it within the first half of the third millennium, and the description of the pottery fits the Amri-Nal pattern, or perhaps the Transitional Stage.

Surkotada

Surkotada is a prominent archaeological site in Rapar Taluka of Kutch District (J. P. Joshi 1990a) (Plate 4.36). It is a fortified place, with a very substantial wall surrounding it and bastions at the corners; although the site is not especially large at 1.4 hectares (Figure 4.112 and Figure 4.113). This is a single period site of the Mature Harappan Phase with close cultural links with the Sindhi Harappan. The occupation there was divided into three sub-periods. Using

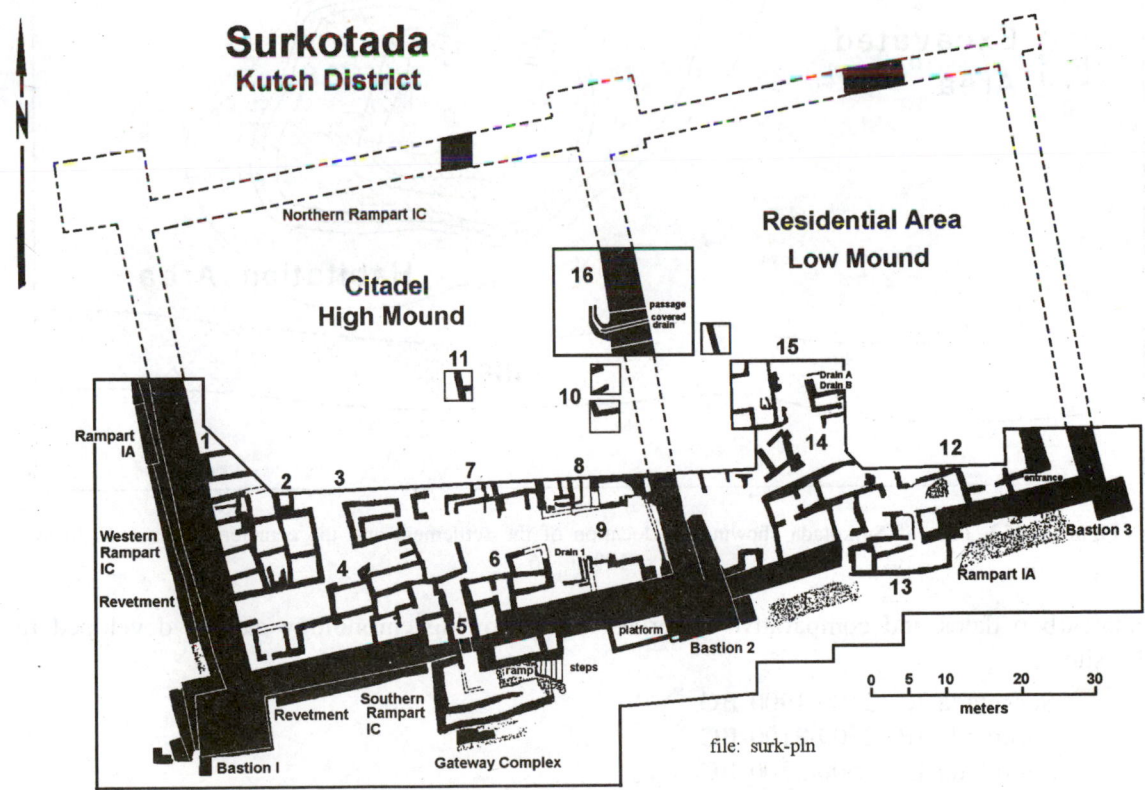

Figure 4.112. Plan of Surkotada with the fortifications, after J. P. Joshi 1990a: Plan facing page 38

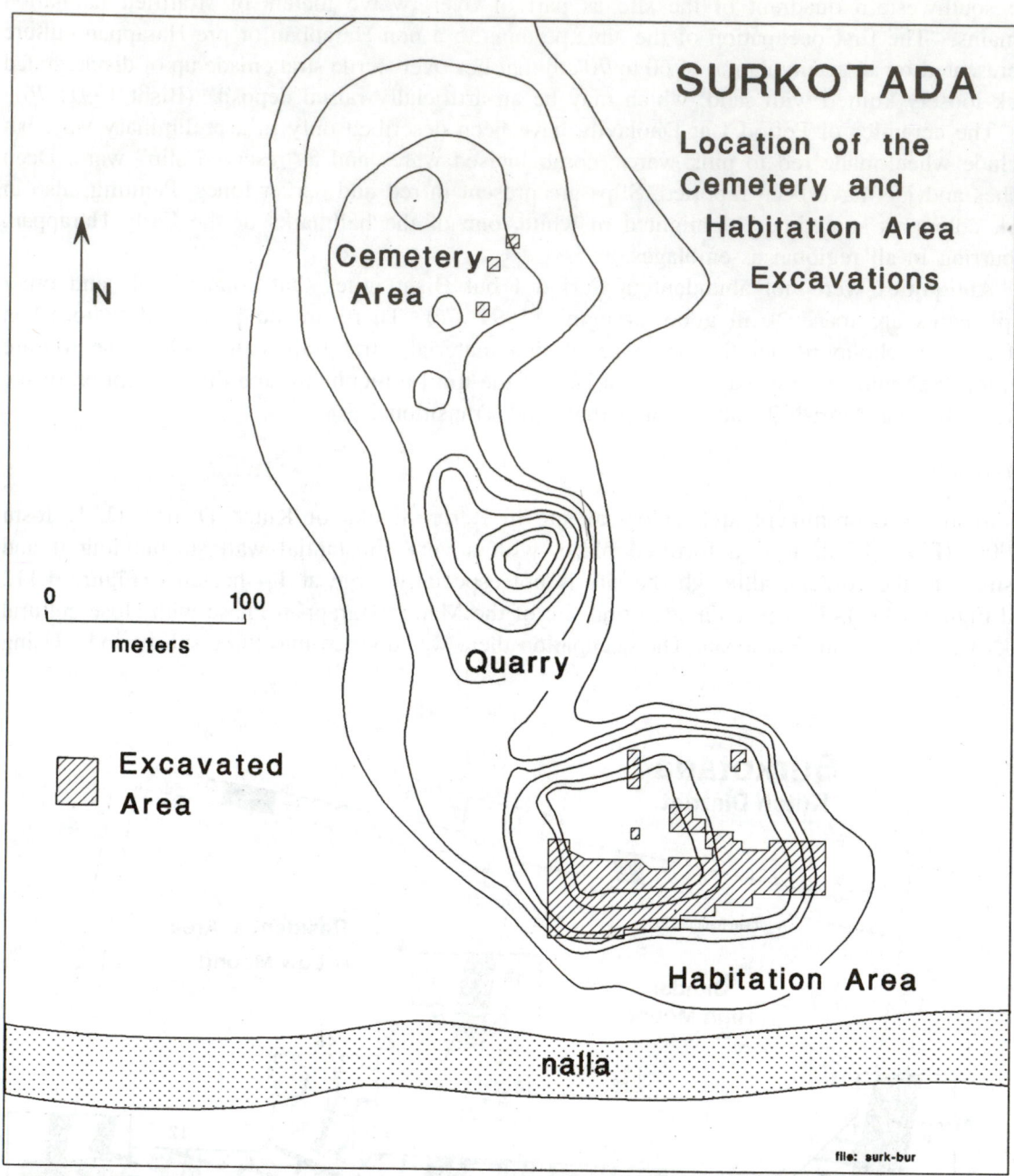

Figure 4.113. Plan of Surkotada showing the location of the settlement and the cemetery, after J. P. Joshi 1990a: 16

radiocarbon dates and comparative materials, the following chronology can be developed for the site:

Surkotada IC, 2100-1900 BC
Surkotada IB, 2300-2100 BC
Surkotada IA, 2500-2300 BC

In some ways Surkotada is a reasonably standard Sindhi Harappan site, but it has some interesting ceramics, especially the Anarta Chalcolithic, an unusual cream slipped ware and the

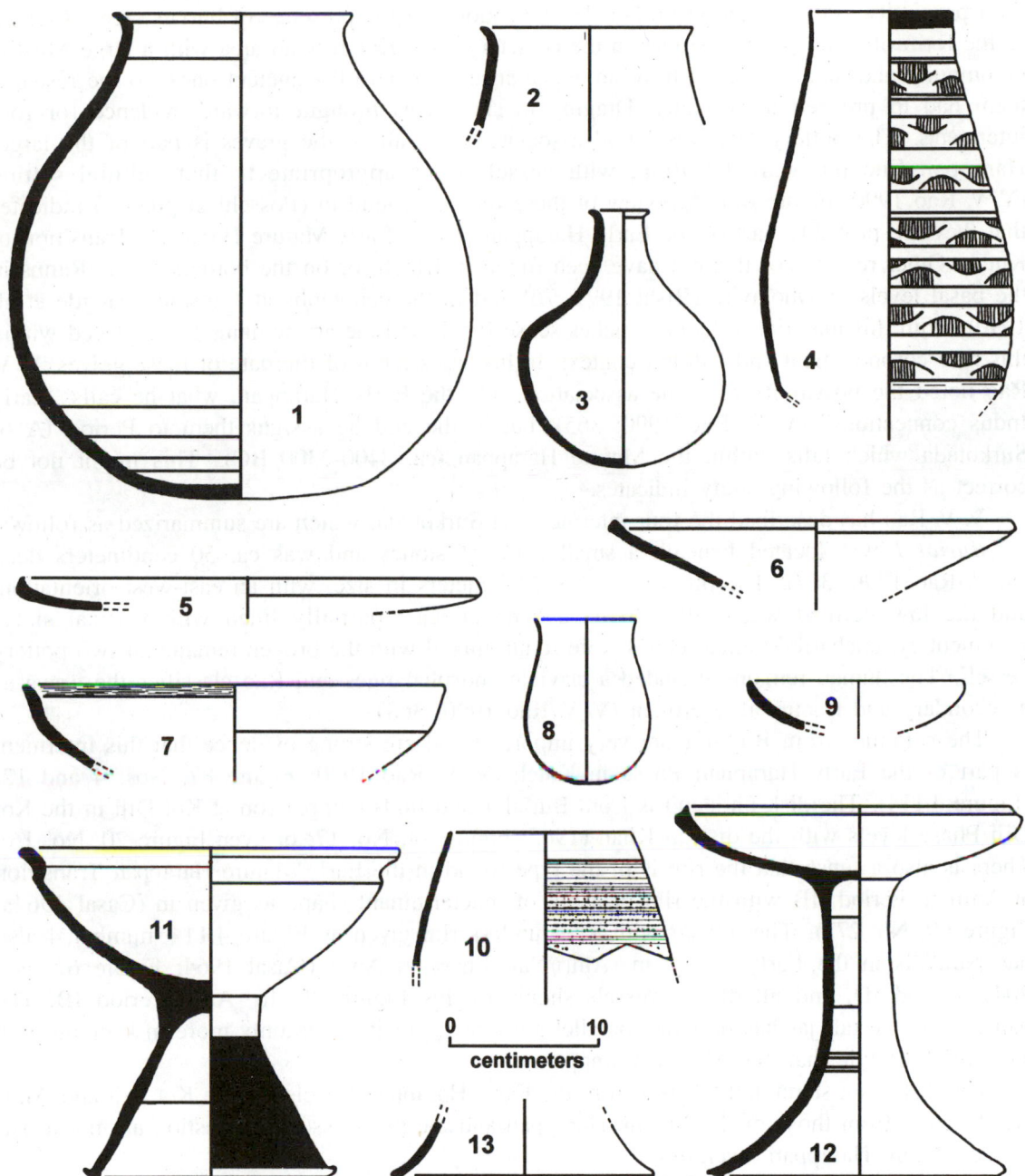

Figure 4.114. Pottery from Surkotada burials, after V. V. Rao 1990: 87

abundance of Ahar type black and red ware. There is little doubt that the habitation site is part of the Mature Harappan Stage, possibly extending over a century or two in the Late or Post-urban Harappan.

Jagat Pati Joshi found four burials near Surkotada. These four secondary interments were located in a small cemetery 300 meters northwest of the main mound and have been published as part of the final report on the site (V. V. Rao 1990) (Figure 4.114). There is no systematic report on the skeletal material which is fragmentary.

These burials are usually considered to be part of the Mature Urban Harappan because of their proximity to the mound at Surkotada. Indications for the presence of burials were observed in the form of small piles of stones in the cemetery area. Kutch is an area with a large Muslim community and modern graves have an appearance similar to the ancient ones, so the research team had to proceed respectfully. Digging in six places brought forward evidence for four interments. The pottery that was found associated with all of the graves is part of the larger Harappan fine red ware tradition, with vessel forms appropriate to that cultural setting (V. V. Rao 1990: Figure 87). A review of these remains found in (Possehl in press c) indicates that they are probably part of the Early Harappan, or the Early/Mature Harappan Transition of Kutch. Other remains of this era have been found in Kutch, or on the borders of the Ranns in the basal levels of Dholavira (Bisht 1991: 76) and in the cenotaphs at Nagwada (Hegde et al. 1990). With this material in hand it makes sense for these funerary remains to be placed within this new chronological and cultural context. In his assessment of the date of these graves, V. V. Rao noted the possibility of some association with the Early Harappan, what he calls "Early Indus connections" (V. V. Rao 1990: 365), but in the end he assigns them to Period IA of Surkotada which falls within the Mature Harappan (ca. 2400-2300 BC). This might not be correct as the following study indicates.

V. V. Rao has described the four interments at Surkotada, which are summarized as follows:

Burial 1 was located beneath a small cairn of stones and was ca. 50 centimeters deep (V. V. Rao 1990: 367). The pit was 1.48 × 2.02 meters in size, with an east-west orientation, and the low vertical walls seem to have been at least partially lined with vertical slabs. Fragmentary, uncharred human bones were found mixed with the broken remains of two pottery vessels. The human remains included a clavicle and phalanges and Rao classifies the grave as a secondary and fractional interment (V. V. Rao 1990: 368).

The ceramics from Burial 1 are very important and are strong evidence that this interment is part of the Early Harappan Phase in Kutch (V. V. Rao 1990: Figure 87: Nos. 4 and 12) (Figure 4.114). The dish on stand is from Burial 1 and finds comparison at Kot Diji in the Kot Diji Phase levels with the dish in Khan (1965: Figure 14, No. 17, or even Figure 20, No. 16). There is also a sense that the rim is of the type found in the Early/Mature Harappan Transition at Amri in Period IIB with the rim of a pot of indeterminant shape as given in (Casal 1964a: Figure 69, No. 272). The tall jar with a featureless rim given as Figure 4.114, number 4 also has parallels in the Early Harappan (Amri/Nal) Phase at Amri (Casal 1964: Figure 62, No. 204), Period ID, and all of the vessels shown on his Figure 49, for Amri Period IB. The painting on the tall jar has no exact parallel anywhere, but it is certainly more in keeping with an Amri-Nal style than the Mature Harappan.

The dishes on stand and the jars from the Early Harappan Levels at both Kot Diji and Amri are different from those of the Mature Harappan and the two vessels in question are not a part of the Mature Harappan inventory.

Burial 2 (V. V. Rao 1990: 368-69) is a cenotaph, also found under a small cairn and has a north to south orientation. This grave pit had been dug to a depth of only 35 centimeters. It was 1.95 × 1.10 meters and was unlined.

The burial pit contained no human remains but did have fragments of seven pottery vessels: two jars and four dishes, or dishes-on-stand and a base to a dish-on-stand. These particular vessel forms are all Amri-Nal and Kot Diji Phase in nature and number 6 on may be the ribbed Bhoot Ware.

Burial 3 (V. V. Rao 1990: 369) was also oriented in a north-south direction, 1.68 × 0.98 meters in size and covered by a stone slab. "At a depth of 35 cm the pit yielded a thick red ware sherd of an urn and very small charred human bone splinters or remains" (V. V. Rao 1990: 369). The sherd does not seem to deserve to have been drawn.

Burial 4 (V. V. Rao 1990: 369-70) was a second cenotaph. The oval burial pit measured 1.60 × 0.82 meters and was covered with a stone slab. It contained broken parts of four pottery vessels but no human remains. While these pots are more general in shape, they too, fit comfortably within the context of the Early Harappan.

Summary

These interments fit well within the context of the larger burial customs of the Harappan Cultural Tradition. The presence of cenotaphs, while not understood in terms of their cultural significance, is paralleled elsewhere, especially at Nagwada and in the Mature Harappan cemetery at Kalibangan. Evidence for cremation within the cultural context of the Early Harappa fits with Nal. The secondary nature of the burials is also consistent with what we know of Early Harappan practice.

Nagwada

Prof. K. T. M. Hegde and a team from the M. S. University of Baroda have found one extended and three pot "burials" at Nagwada, a site in the estuary of the Rupen River in North Gujarat (Hegde et al. 1988, 1990; Hegde 1989). The pottery from the Nagwada graves, especially the pot burials, which were in fact cenotaphs rather than burials, is very much within the Amri fold, made up of hard pink to red fabrics with shapes like those from Amri Period I, including tall vases with featureless rims (Figure 4.115, Figure 4.116).

There is also a small red slipped pot with white painting that looks for all the world like something out of a Sothi-Siswal assemblage (Hegde, Sonawane, Bhan, Prasad, and Krishnan 1990: Pl. 1). All of the interments were sealed below a stratum with Mature Harappan material, indicating that they belong to the early period at the site (Hegde et al. 1988: 58).

The second occupation at Nagwada seems to date to the Mature Harappan and has produced one beautiful impression of a square stamp seal with a bovid (Figure 4.117).

Moti Pipli

Small scale work at the site of Moti Pipli in Banaskantha District of North Gujarat has also produced Early, or Pre-Harappan ceramics (Figure 4.118). Not much is known of this work, but the pots are certainly of an Early Harappan type, especially the one with a flange rim, number 1 in Figure 4.118.

Padri

The ancient settlement at Padri village, south of Bhavnagar City, on the eastern coast of the Gulf of Cambay has produced what seems to be a new ceramic (Padri Ware) associated with early radiocarbon dates for an occupation in the first half of the third millennium BC (Shinde 1992). Not much is known of the details of this occupation, because the work is still in progress and as yet there are no reports. But it seems to document the presence of food producing villagers well into the Saurashtran Peninsula prior to Mature Harappan times.

Somnath

The ancient Nagara Mound of Somnath lies on the east bank of the Hiran (Hiranya) River on

610

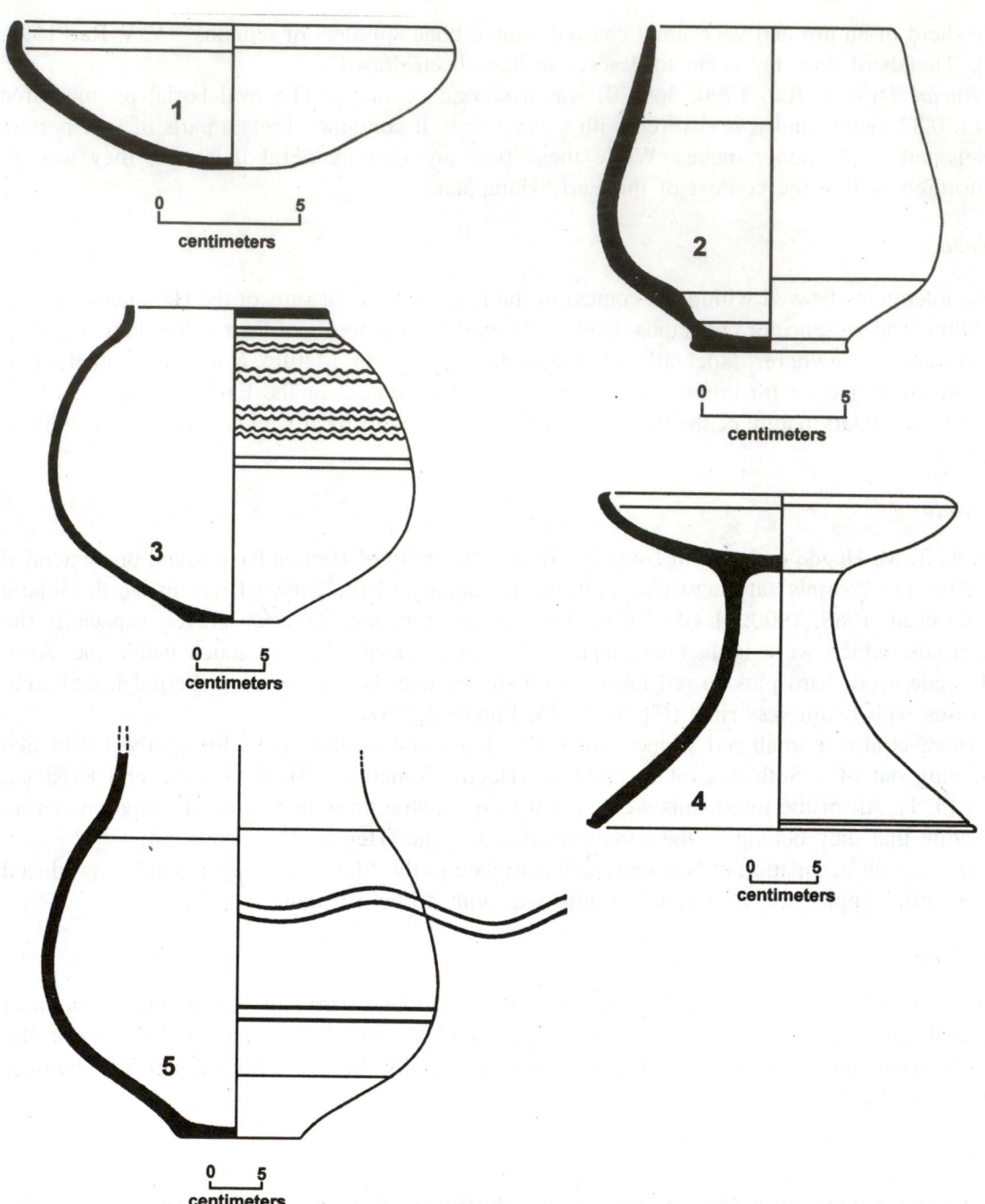

Figure 4.115. Amri pottery from Nagwada, after Hegde, et al. 1988 and A. Majumdar 1994

the southern coast of Saurashtra, just to the west of the modern town of Prabhas Patan, with its famous seaside Siva Temple (Figure 4.120, Plate 4.37, Plate 4.38). The site was first excavated under the direction of the late P. P. Pandya, with the cooperation of the Maharaja Sayajirao University of Baroda, in the 1950s (Nanavati, et al. 1971); then by Deccan College and the Gujarat State Department of Archaeology (IAR 1971-72: 12-13; IAR 1975-76: 13; IAR 1976-77: 17-18; Dhavalikar and Possehl 1992).

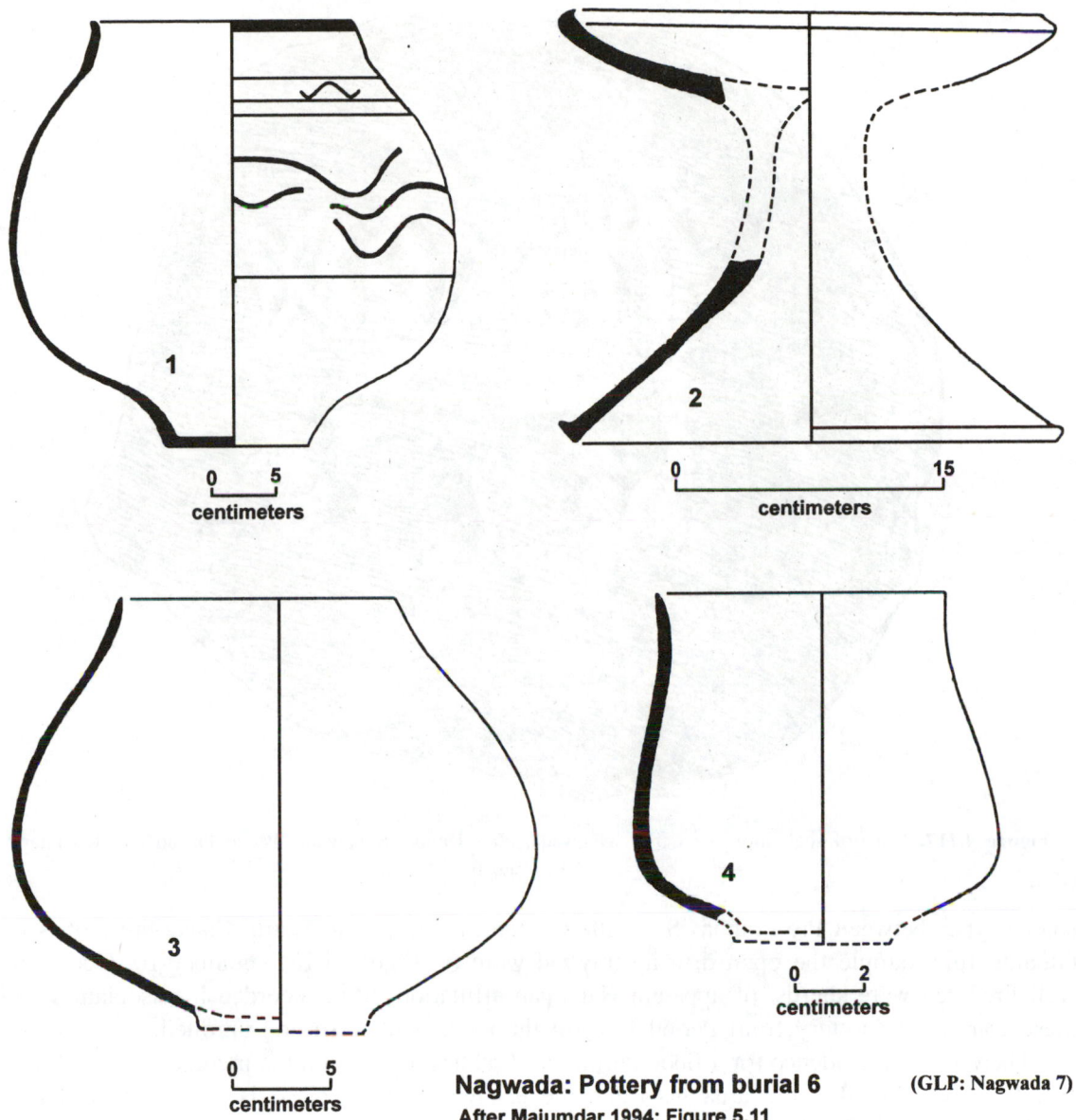

Nagwada: Pottery from burial 6   (GLP: Nagwada 7)
After Majumdar 1994: Figure 5.11

Figure 4.116. Pre-Harappan pottery from Nagwada, Burial 6, after A. Majumdar 1994: Figure 5.11

The first occupation, now referred to as the "Pre-Prabhas Period" was found in the earliest excavations (Subbarao 1958: Figure 36, 135; Dhavalikar and Possehl 1992), but their significance seems not to have been recognized. The renewed work in the 1970s re-exposed the Pre-Prabhas levels toward the end of the first season of work. They cover ca. 75 square meters and rest on a sterile deposit of marine sand about three meters below the modern ground surface. The material from the cultural levels consists of pottery, a few chalcedony blades, beads of faience and steatite, some of which are segmented. Most of the artifacts came from stratum 15, along with a fragment of wall plaster with reed impressions, suggesting simple wattle and daub architecture. The pottery includes an incised coarse gray/red ware and red slipped ware (Figure 4.121). There is a black and red ware (Figure 4.122) and a grey ware (Figure 4.123). There are

Figure 4.117. Unicorn seal impression from Nagwada, after Hegde, Sonawane, Bhan, Prasad and Krishnan
1990: Plate 6

shared types between Pre-Prabhas Somnath and the Pre-Harappan Anarta Chalcolithic of North
Gujarat, for example the open dish in gray/red ware on Figure 4.121, number 10. Occasional
well fired red ware sherds, of apparent Harappan affiliation, were recorded in association with
these wares. The pottery from Period I is, for the most part, fresh and unrolled.

There is some evidence for a flood during Pre-Prabhas times, with the presence of a yellowish
silt. It is possible that the area in which the excavation took place is a secondary deposit
resulting from this flood and that the original habitation is elsewhere under the mound. There is
a hiatus between the Pre-Prabhas and the Prabhas levels.

The date of the Pre-Prabhas settlement

The date of the first settlement at Somnath has been a source of debate, some believing that
the radiocarbon dates are too early (see Table 4.33). They would date this occupation to ca.
2000-1800 BC (Dhavalikar 1984) or ca. 2450-2150 BC on the calibrated radiocarbon time
scale. This late chronology accommodates the presence of the pottery thought to be of Sorath
Harappan affiliation, a few sherds of which were found with the Pre-Prabhas wares (Dhavalikar
and Possehl 1992). The two dates given in Table 4.33, however, are consistent with one another.
They were run at different laboratories, but with the same team managing the dating procedures.
One comes from charcoal (PRL-90) and the other from shell (TF-1287), a point that enhances
the credibility of the consistency between them.

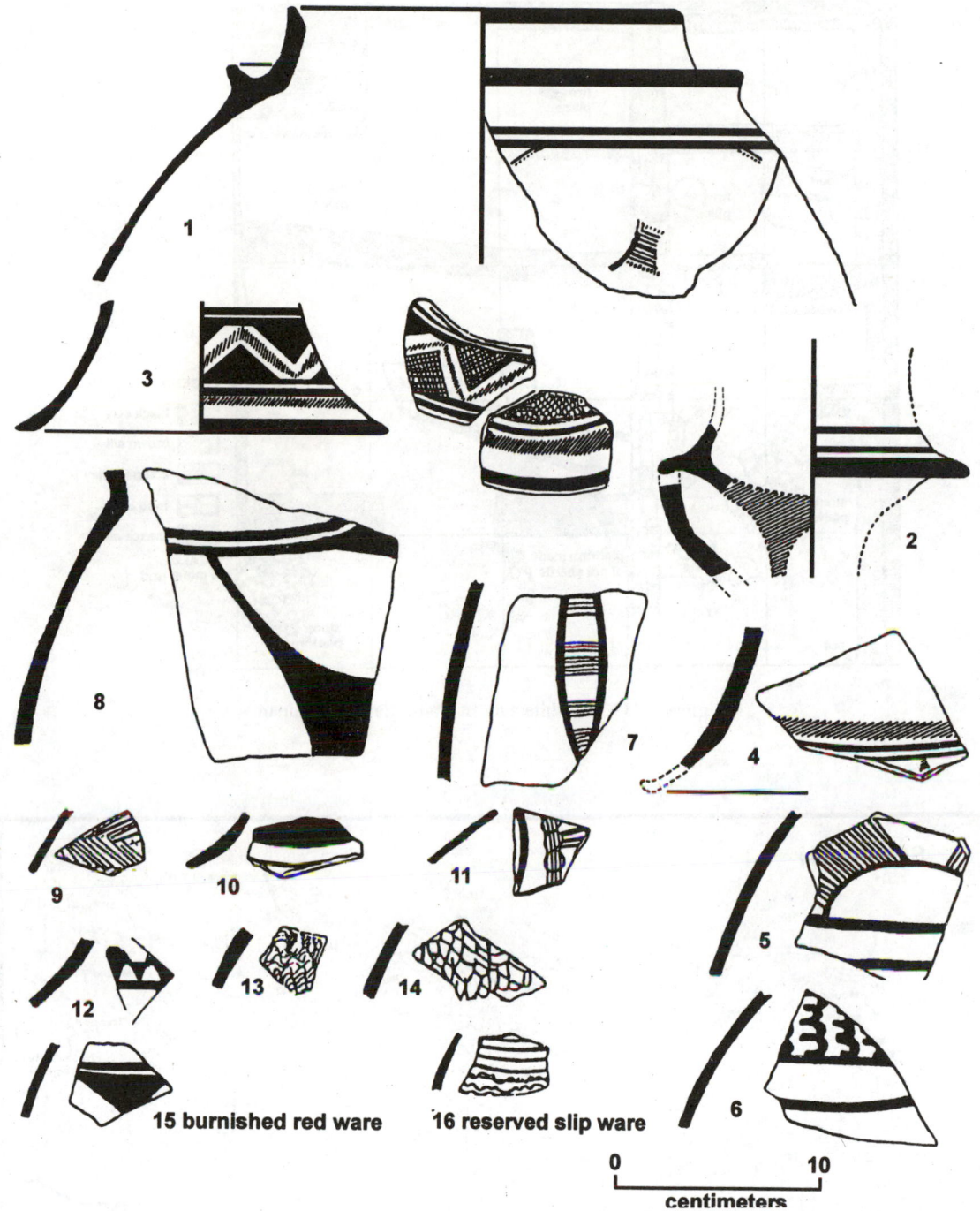

Figure 4.118. Pre-Harappan pottery from Moti Pipli, Gujarat, after Majumdar 1994: Figure 8.5

The Pre-Prabhas pottery, with the exception of the hard fired red wares, is distinctive. As things now stand, it is unique to Somnath, although the connection with some types from the Anarta Chalcolithic have been noted above. It shares nothing with the Burj Basket-marked, Togau or Kechi Beg ceramics. It is certainly not a part of the Amri-Nal assemblage. The sophistication of the Pre-Prabhas wares makes it clear that they cannot be posited as the independent beginnings of the potter's art in southern Saurashtra. There is a long history of

614

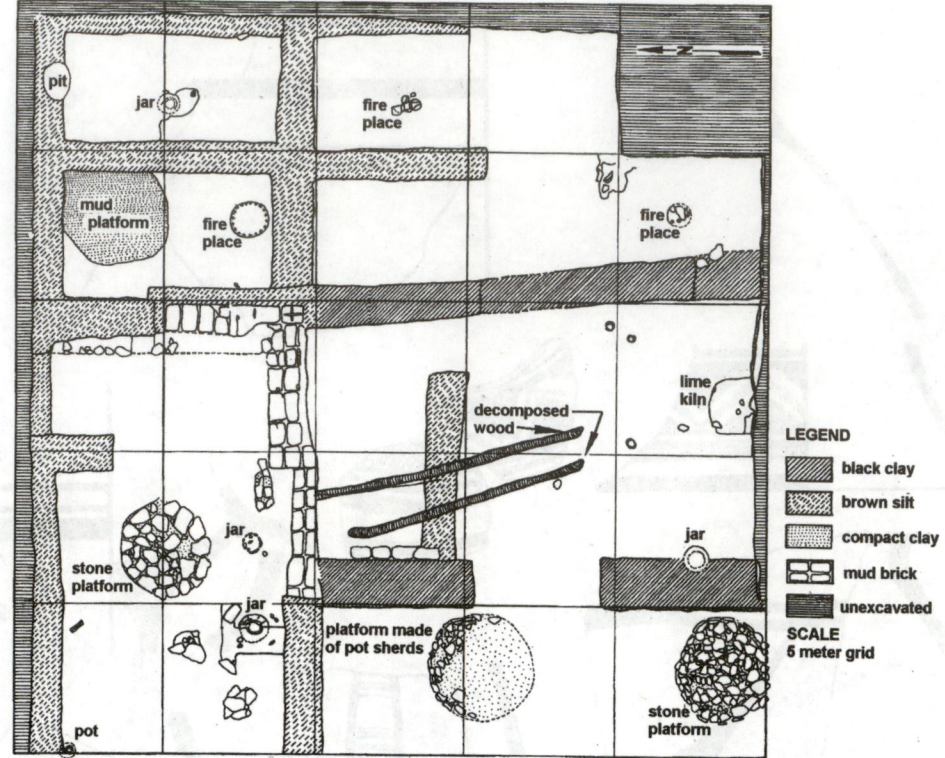

Figure 4.119. Architecture at Padri Early Harappan.

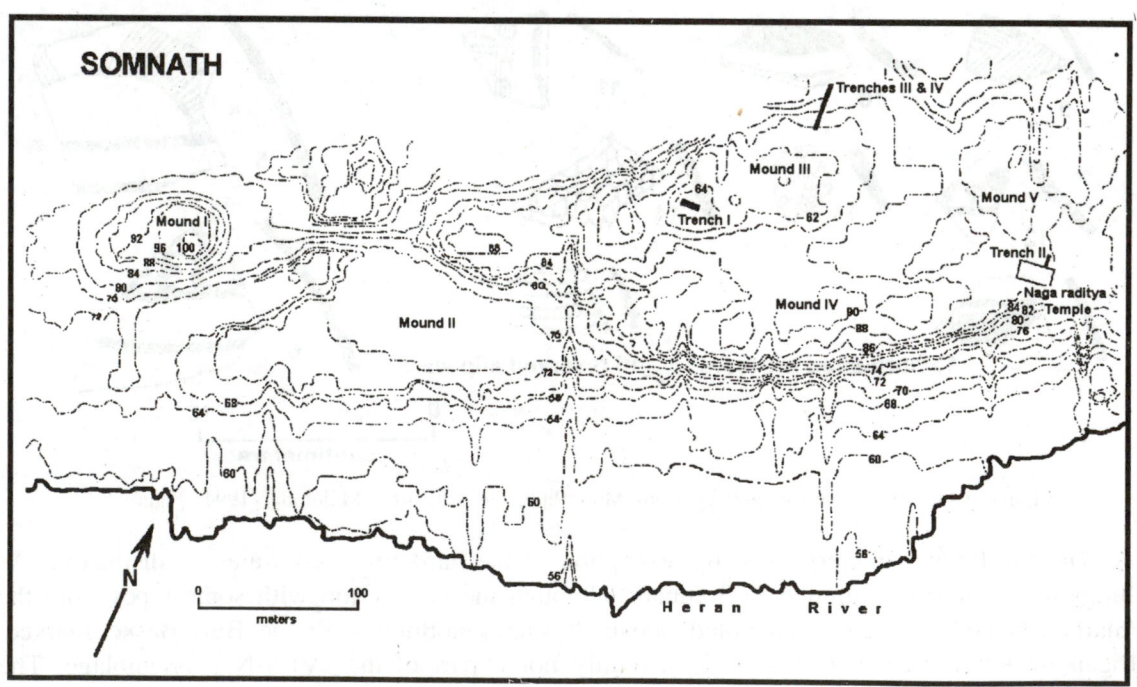

Figure 4.120. Plan of Somnath

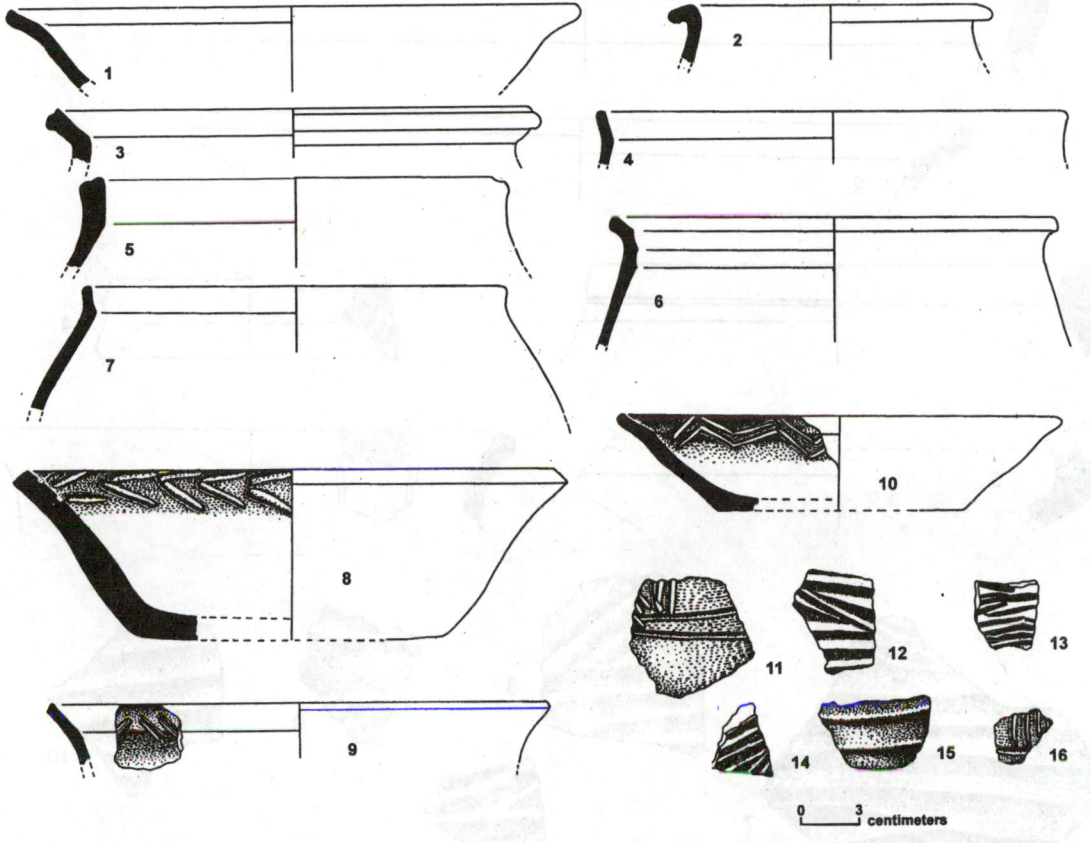

Figure 4.121. Pre-Prabhas gray/red ware and red slipped ware, after Dhavalikar and Possehl 1992: Figure 4

potting behind them indicating that there is a lot to be learned about the history of early village farming communities in Saurashtra. It seems possible that peoples of the Early Harappan Stage were not alone in this region as early cultivators and herders.

In the end, we do not know very much about the people who made and used the Pre-Prabhas ceramics. It seems clear that they are part of the early third millennium BC, and that some of their pottery lies outside the Amri-Nal tradition. It may be that their origins lie in the Arabian Gulf or Saudi Arabian Coast, but comparable material has not yet been found there. The first step in resolving some of these points should be a thorough survey of the Saurashtran coast, with the aim of locating more sites with Pre-Prabhas ceramics. An excavation at one or two of these would take us a long way in understanding this material.

More Amri-Nal Burials

There is an interesting funerary record for the Amri-Nal Phase.

Damb Buthi

Damb Buthi is an Amri-Nal and Mature Harappan site located just south of Lake Manchar in western Sindh. N. G. Majumdar conducted a small excavation there in January 1931. In the course of his excavations Majumdar exposed five rooms, outlined by stone foundations. One contained human bones, much disturbed, seemingly incomplete and definitely calcined. A bivalve

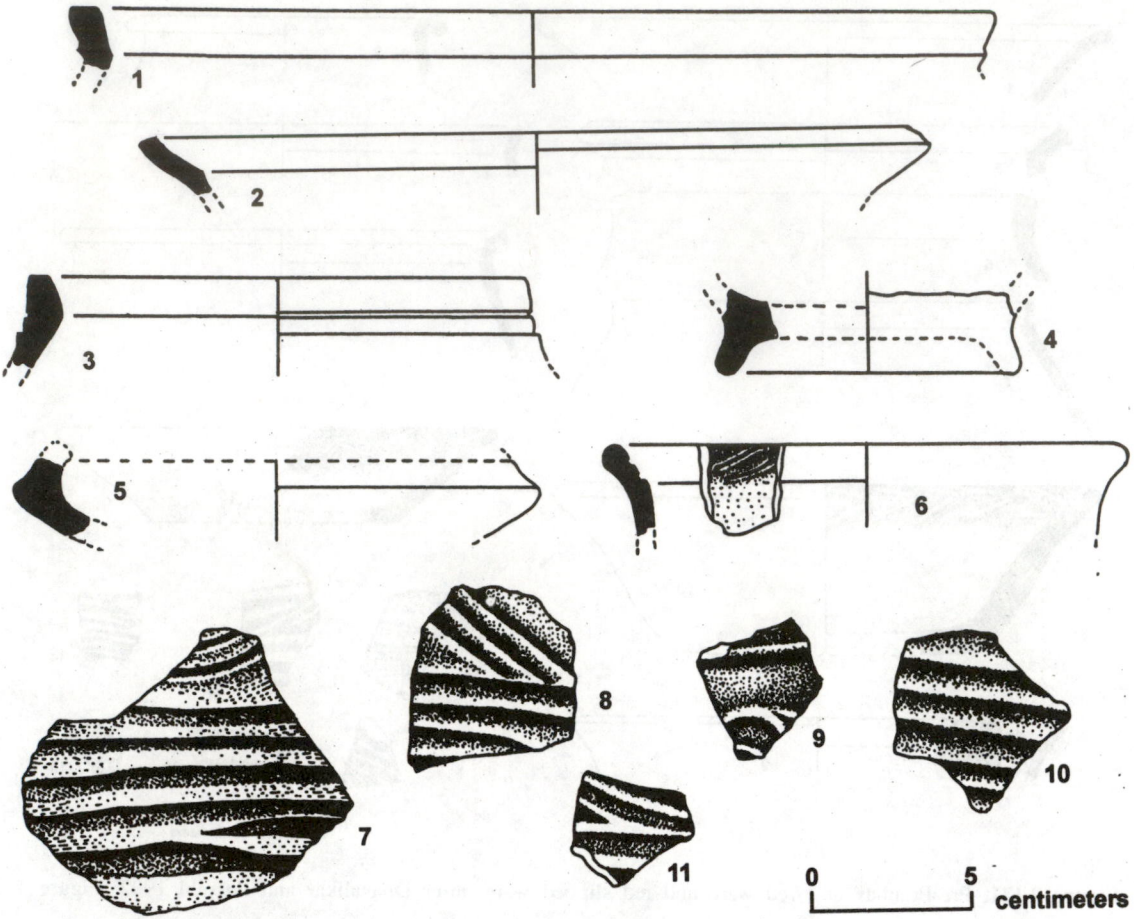

Figure 4.122. Pre-Prabhas black and red ware, after Dhavalikar and Possehl 1992: Figure 5

mussel shell contained red ochre, something Majumdar notes occurred in DK Area of Mohenjo-daro (Majumdar 1934: 115). Other burials were found in rectangular enclosures fashioned from rough-hewn stone, which Majumdar likens to similar facilities at Nal (Majumdar 1934: 116). "As stated above, no complete skeleton could be recovered, and whatever bones turned up in the course of clearance were lying pell-mell over the floor. No trace of cremation was detectable, and in all probability inhumation was practiced at Damb Buthi. The burial was probably of the class known to archaeologists as 'Fractional Burial' "(Majumdar 1934: 116). The pottery associated with the burials was all Amri-Nal in type.

It has been thought by some (e.g., S. R. Rao 1979: 141) that Damb Buthi offers evidence for the inhumation of two individuals in the same grave, a so-called "joint burial" as that found at Lothal. A close reading of Majumdar's text, and that of his physical anthropologist, B. S. Guha, does not seem to support this contention.

Other Sites

Human burials have been reported from the Kashi Qalat cemetery on the Pakistani Makran. They are not excavated and might date to a prehistoric period, possibly the Amri-Nal or Shahi Tump Phase of Besenval and Sanlaville (1990: 106).

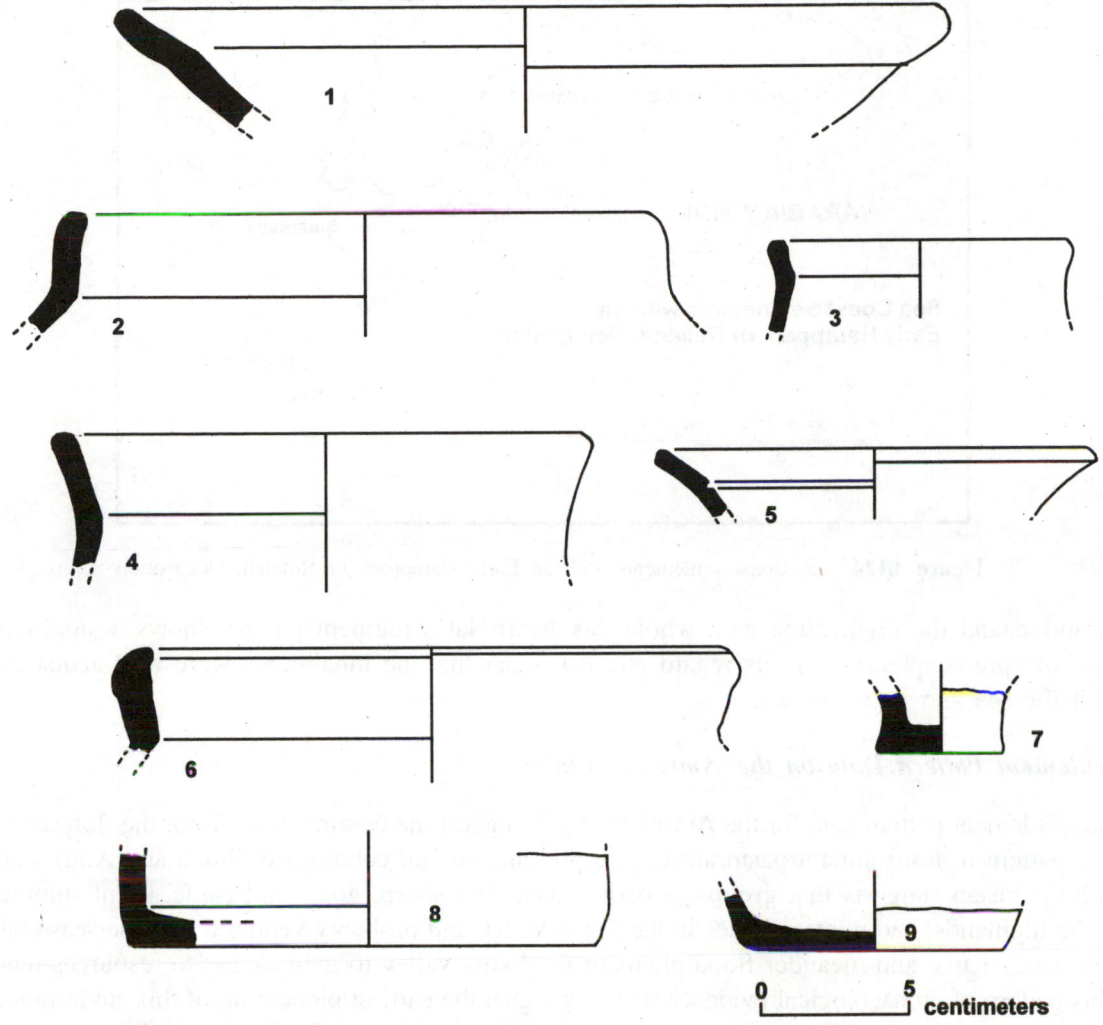

Figure 4.123. Pre-Prabhas gray ware, after Dhavalikar and Possehl 1992: Figure 5

Amri-Nal Sea Coast Settlements

We now know of a number of Amri-Nal, more generally Early Harappan sites, on the coast of the Arabian Sea and its arms in Gujarat (Figure 4.124). Balakot is on Sonmiani Bay and two little known sites to the west of Karachi, Orangi and Pir Mungo, seem to have Amri-Nal assemblages (Fairservis 1971c: 411, 412), although Pir Mungo is not well documented. Dholavira is on an island in the Great Rann of Kutch and Nagwada is virtually on the beach of Little Rann. Somnath is also a seaside settlement, and although it does not look like an Amri-Nal site, it is coeval with this Phase. In the Makran, archaeological work under the direction of Roland Besenval of C. N. R. S. has revealed sites of a "Dasht Assemblage" which seems to just pre-date the Mature Harappan. Although this is not Amri-Nal it is located in a coastal environment, demonstrating that peoples of the Early Harappan Phase were interested in the sea and lived by it, which is contrary to some recent opinions (Nilofer Shaikh 1989, Mughal 1992c: 130). In fairness, not all of this information would have been available to Shaikh and Mughal when they made their observations. Moreover, Mature Harappan maritime activity is important

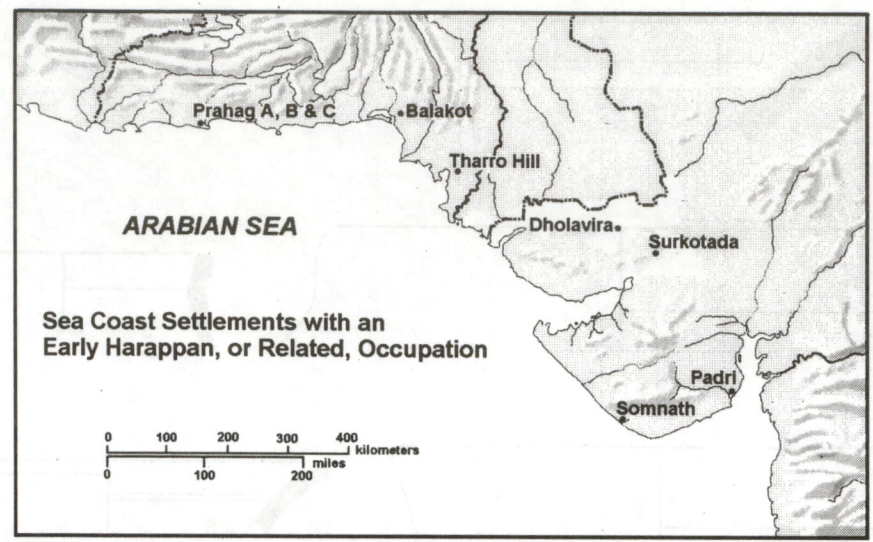

Figure 4.124. Sea Coast settlements with an Early Harappan, or Related, Occupation

to understand the civilization as a whole, but Amri-Nal settlement pattern shows a significant kind of "pre-adaptation" in this regard and it is clear that the inhabitants were well acquainted with the sea and its resources.

Settlement Pattern Data on the Amri-Nal Phase

The settlement pattern data for the Amri-Nal Phase suggest the continuation, if not the florescence, of a pattern of transhumant pastoralism. The presence of Nal ceramics in Sindh and Amri wares in Baluchistan suggests that groups of people who kept sheep, goats and cattle, spent summers in the highlands, had winter abodes in the Indus Valley and probably ventured into the seasonally quiescent, active and meander flood plains of the Indus Valley to gain access to resources there. This pattern of archaeological evidence need not signal the earliest pioneering of this environment, but it does seem to mark a time when it would have been a significant part of the subsistence pattern.

The penetration of the deeper riverine zones by pastoralists during the dry season might also mark the beginning of the process of burning, clearing, perhaps draining this landscape. The search for grass and browse, cutting wood for temporary shelter, camp fires and firing ceramics, along with the possibility of large scale burning to create a more efficient, productive landscape for humans and animals, would constitute a kind of "softening up" of this difficult terrain, preparing it for farming in Mature Harappan times. The use of fire for clearing land is not extensively documented in the archaeological record. The evidence for it in South Asia has been noted in connection with the discussion of the beginnings of agriculture (G. Singh 1971: 185-86 and above). The transport of wood and charcoal may also begin in this general time period, although it could be a Phase earlier, in the Kechi Beg. But regional, man-made landscapes almost certainly began to emerge from the millennia of intensive use by domesticated animals as well as clearing land for cultivation.

The grazing and browsing of animals and the turning of soil for cultivation are powerfully disruptive activities, but the widespread use of fire to clear land and rejuvenate grasslands, a practice documented in the ethnographic record, and the early food producing Phases of the Indus Age, along with the incessant search for building timber and firewood would all have taken their toll in the prehistoric period. The beginning of the scarcities caused by human intervention into the ecological balances of the Greater Indus Region is not a topic that is well understood or often thought about. They almost certainly predate the Mature Harappan and may have set patterns of interregional dependency that enhanced the production and distribution of natural resources, like timber and charcoal, between environmental zones.

The villages along the piedmont of Baluchistan were placed to take advantage of the hill torrents or *nais* and the natural springs that dot the outer face of the mountain front. Lake Manchar, the natural inundation basin of the Indus, was extensively utilized as an environment to be directly exploited for food (fish and shellfish, seasonally for birds) and as a huge, naturally irrigated farming tract, resulting from the seasonal expansion and contraction of the lake waters. This is documented at the site of Lohri, for example (Majumdar 1934: 65-7).

Louis Flam has suggested that extensive water control technology began in the region during Amri-Nal times. He proposes that this took three forms (1981a: 151-52). The first is very simple, using the natural flooding of a hill stream to irrigate land to either side of the *nai* with a minimum of human intervention. This is similar to a form of cultivation widely practiced on Indus flood plain known as *salaiba*. It has been described in the geography section on the Indus Plains and is documented at the site of Kohtrash Buthi. The second form, documented at the site of Kai Buthi made use of small, shallow ditches to gently guide spring water out onto a flat area that was used for cultivation. This is a useful and reliable irrigation method, and since the springs are active all year it admits the possibility of raising both a *rabi*, winter crop for food grains, and a summer *kharif* crop for other cultigens. The third form of irrigation is documented at the site of Nuka and involved an investment in some kind of bunding, either a low earthen wall, locally known as a *kach* system or a *gabarband*. This form of investment would have been useful for only the *rabi* season. *Kach* bunding and *gabarbands* are practices which are intended to provide irrigation water and conserve soil resources; a further indication that several millennia of food production, with increasing numbers of humans and animals had taken its toll on the landscape.

Twenty-five Amri-Nal sites have been excavated, the vast majority by either Sir Aurel Stein or N. G. Majumdar. All of their work was on a very small scale and the information from the work is extremely limited. For example, when Majumdar was at Arabjo Thana trouble with the local *zamindars* and rain made his work there extremely difficult. His trenches yielded only some pottery and other very minor finds (1934: 136-37). About the only thing we learn from his exercise there is that some Amri pottery was found, hardly more than would have come from a good surface collection. All of the Amri-Nal sites are listed in Table 4.34.

Amri-Nal Site Size

There are eighty-eight Amri-Nal sites with information on their size. Some sites were very small camps, such as Jebri Damb One or Kuki Damb in Kalat, at one-tenth of a hectare or Santhli Four in Gujarat at 0.01 hectares. Other camps, such as Paijo Kotiro and Roheljo Kund in the pass of the Gaj Nai through the Kirthar Mountains, where N. G. Majumdar was murdered in 1938, are a bit larger at ca. one hectare. This pass was, and remains, an important route for pastoralists and traders between the Indus Valley and the uplands of Kalat in Baluchistan. The largest Amri-Nal site in the "Gazetteer of Settlements of the Indus Age" might be Dholavira, on Kadir Island in Kutch. The size of the Mature Harappan settlement is 60 hectares. The true extent of the earlier habitation is not known. There is also some evidence that the first occupation

TABLE 4.34
Sites of the Amri-Nal Phase

Site Name	Province/State	District	Size in hectares
Dholavira	Gujarat	Kutch	30.0
LB-16 'A-B'	Baluchistan	Las Bela	22.0
Siah Damb, Jhau	Baluchistan	Jhalawan	17.6
Kargushki Damb	Baluchistan	Kharan	15.3
Pir Hassan Shah	Baluchistan	Kharan	15.0
Tharro Hill	Sindh	Nawabshah	12.5
Badrang Damb	Baluchistan	Makran	10.8
Phusi Damb	Baluchistan	Jhalawan	10.5
Damb Buthi	Sindh	Dadu	9.6
Dosia Khal Damb	Baluchistan	Jhalawan	9.0
Amri	Sindh	Dadu	8.0
Bandhni	Sindh	Dadu	7.6
Tor Ghundai	Baluchistan	Sarawan	7.5
Wahir Two	Baluchistan	Jhalawan	7.5
Nokjo Shahdinzai	Baluchistan	Jhalawan	7.5
Othmanjo Buthi	Sindh	Karachi	7.4
LB-17	Baluchistan	Las Bela	7.2
Site Near Kuki Damb	Baluchistan	Jhalawan	6.7
Saiyid Maurez Damb	Baluchistan	Sarawan	6.3
Nal	Baluchistan	Jhalawan	5.7
Bandu Damb	Baluchistan	Jhalawan	5.4
Zik	Baluchistan	Jhalawan	5.0
Sraduk	Baluchistan	Makran	5.0
Prahag 'A'	Baluchistan	Makran	5.0
Kashimi Damb, Wadh	Baluchistan	Jhalawan	4.0
Miri Qalat	Baluchistan	Makran	3.75
Nundara	Baluchistan	Jhalawan	3.3
Awaran Niabat	Baluchistan	Jhalawan	3.1
Anjira	Baluchistan	Jhalawan	3.0
Surkh Damb	Baluchistan	Jhalawan	2.9
Moti Pipli	Gujarat	Banaskantha	2.7
Balakot	Baluchistan	Las Bela	2.6
Ghuram Damb	Baluchistan	Jhalawan	2.5
Kambar Damb	Baluchistan	Jhalawan	2.4
Hala Damb	Baluchistan	Jhalawan	2.3
Harthar-no Timbo	Gujarat	Mehsana	2.25
Ghazi Shah	Sindh	Dadu	2.1
Segak	Baluchistan	Jhalawan	1.8
Salu Khan	Baluchistan	Sarawan	1.8
Chahi Damb	Baluchistan	Jhalawan	1.6
Nagwada One	Gujarat	Surendranagar	1.6
Pandi Wahi	Sindh	Dadu	1.5
Zayak North	Baluchistan	Kharan	1.5
Siah Damb, Surab	Baluchistan	Jhalawan	1.5
Surain Damb	Baluchistan	Makran	1.5
Dhal Buthi	Sindh	Dadu	1.5
Sardar Khel Damb	Baluchistan	Sarawan	1.5
Chauro	Sindh	Dadu	1.4
Kai Buthi	Sindh	Dadu	1.3
Niai Buthi	Baluchistan	Las Bela	1.3
Thale Damb	Baluchistan	Jhalawan	1.2

Contd.

Khajur	Sindh	Dadu	1.2
Gate Dap	Baluchistan	Jhalawan	1.1
Sohren Damb One	Baluchistan	Jhalawan	1.1
Roheljo Kund	Sindh	Dadu	1.0
Shahr Sardar	Baluchistan	Sarawan	0.9
Lalanji Mari	Sindh	Larkana	0.9
Rodkan	Baluchistan	Jhalawan	0.9
Kurragi Damb	Baluchistan	Kharan	0.9
Zidi	Baluchistan	Jhalawan	0.9
Pokhran	Sindh	Karachi	0.8
Bazdad Kalat	Baluchistan	Jhalawan	0.8
Arabjo Thana	Sindh	Karachi	0.8
Tando Rahim Khan	Sindh	Dadu	0.75
Pak	Baluchistan	Jhalawan	0.7
Toji Damb	Baluchistan	Kharan	0.7
Santhli Two	Gujarat	Banaskantha	0.62
Hor Kalat	Baluchistan	Jhalawan	0.6
Mammai Damb	Baluchistan	Kharan	0.6
Gorandi 'A'	Sindh	Dadu	0.6
Taung	Sindh	Dadu	0.5
Ashal	Baluchistan	Jhalawan	0.5
Kamar Band	Baluchistan	Jhalawan	0.5
Kohna Kalat	Baluchistan	Makran	0.5
Bibiji Bhit	Sindh	Dadu	0.4
Marki Mas	Baluchistan	Jhalawan	0.4
Neghar Damb	Baluchistan	Kalat	0.35
Sorak Damb	Baluchistan	Jhalawan	0.3
Nazganijo Kund	Sindh	Dadu	0.3
Jaren	Baluchistan	Jhalawan	0.25
Sumer Damb	Baluchistan	Jhalawan	0.2
Madhvya-no Timbo	Gujarat	Banaskantha	0.12
Bajaniya-no Thumdo	Gujarat	Banaskantha	0.12
Kuki Damb	Baluchistan	Jhalawan	0.1
Jarejo Kalat	Sindh	Dadu	0.1
Jebri Damb One	Baluchistan	Jhalawan	0.1
Rais Sher Mohammad	Baluchistan	Jhalawan	0.02
Santhli Four	Gujarat	Banaskantha	0.01
Adul But	Baluchistan	Jhalawam	
Ahmed Shah	Sindh	Dadu	
Aidu Damb	Baluchistan	Jhalawan	
Alam Khan Shahr	Baluchistan	Jhalawan	
Ander Damb	Baluchistan	Jhalawan	
Bhamaria Thumdo	Gujarat	Banaskantha	
Bhut Shamshi	Baluchistan	Kalat	
Buband	Baluchistan	Las Bela	
CH-1	Baluchistan	Chagai	
Channal Kund Damb	Baluchistan	Jhalawan	
Chashma Murad	Baluchistan	Jhalawan	
Cheshma Damb One	Baluchistan	Jhalawan	
Chhutijo Kund	Sindh	Dadu	
Chiri Damb	Baluchistan	Makran	
Damb Goram	Baluchistan	Sarawan	
Damb Kulu	Baluchistan	Sarawan	
Damb Shirinab	Baluchistan	Kalat	
Damb Zerger	Baluchistan	Sarawan	
Deh Bail	Sindh	Karachi	

Contd.

Table 4.34 Contd.

Site Name	Province/State	District	Size in hectares
Dhillanijo Kot	Sindh	Dadu	
Diwana	Baluchistan	Las Bela	
Gajar Damb	Baluchistan	Jhalawan	
Gaji Bhut	Baluchistan	Jhalawan	
Ghurum	Baluchistan	Makran	
Gorandi 'B'	Sindh	Dadu	
Hadi	Baluchistan	Jhalawan	
Jahan	Baluchistan	Jhalawan	
Jahan Northeast	Baluchistan	Jhalawan	
Kachcho Buthi	Sindh	Dadu	
Kafir Kot	Baluchistan	Sarawan	
Kalat	Baluchistan	Sarawan	
Kallag	Baluchistan	Jhalawan	
Kandhi Wahi Buthi	Sindh	Dadu	
Kaptun Bra	Baluchistan	Sarawan	
Kardagap	Baluchistan	Sarawan	
Karo Kotiro	Sindh	Larkana	
Karpas Buthi	Baluchistan	Las Bela	
Khudo Pir	Sindh	Larkana	
Kinneru Damb	Baluchistan	Jhalawan	
Kot Raja Manjhera	Sindh	Karachi	
Kotiro	Sindh	Larkana	
Kulloi	Baluchistan	Sarawan	
Lakhshmirji Mari	Sindh	Dadu	
LB-13	Baluchistan	Las Bela	
LB-16 'C'	Baluchistan	Las Bela	
Lehri	Baluchistan	Jhalawan	
Lohri	Sindh	Dadu	
Lundi Buthi	Sindh	Dadu	
Mai Ghari	Sindh	Karachi	
Mishk	Baluchistan	Jhalawan	
Mowari	Sindh	Larkana	
Mungli Damb	Sindh	Larkana	
Naing Gar Jabal	Sindh	Dadu	
Namdai	Baluchistan	Sarawan	
Nazarabad	Baluchistan	Makran	
Nushki	Baluchistan	Kharan	
Orangi	Sindh	Karachi	
Paijo Kotiro	Sindh	Dadu	
Panodi	Baluchistan	Makran	
Pir Mungho	Sindh	Karachi	
Pokhran Landi	Sindh	Karachi	
Puchur Damb	Baluchistan	Jhalawan	
Ran Pethani Nadi	Sindh	Karachi	
Reko Cave	Baluchistan	Jhalawan	
Salari	Sindh	Larkana	
Sari Damb	Baluchistan	Makran	
Serikoran Damb	Baluchistan	Makran	
Singen Kalat	Baluchistan	Jhalawan	
Tikri Damb	Baluchistan	Jhalawan	
Togau	Baluchistan	Sarawan	
Tor Warai	Baluchistan	Sarawan	
Tupi	Sindh	Larkana	
Unnamed Site Five	Baluchistan	Jhalawan	
Zahrazai	Baluchistan	Sarawan	
Zari Damb	Baluchistan	Jhalawan	
Zayak Southeast	Baluchistan	Jhalawan	

there took place during the Transitional Stage, not the Early Harappan and we will just have to wait to find out more about Dholavira, holding the size of the early settlement in abeyance. For the moment, it might be assumed that Dholavira about doubled in size during the Mature Harappan. This is what happened at Kalibangan. Dholavira would then be estimated at ca. 30 hectares, more comparable to the larger Amri-Nal sites such as Siah Damb, Jhau (17.6 hectares) or LB-16 "A & B" in Las Bela (22 hectares), both of which have a Kulli occupation following the Amri-Nal. The largest Amri-Nal site with the Amri-Nal as the final occupation, probably reflecting the true size of the settlement in Early Harappan times is LB-3 in Las Bela, at 12.6 hectares. There is a very fine Amri-Nal site at the Panjpai Levy Post on the Afghan Border, just southwest of Quetta called Tor Ghundai at 7.5 hectares (Plate 4.39). The distribution of Amri-Nal Phase sites by size is shown in (Figure 4.125).

TABLE 4.35
Estimate of Settled Area for the Amri-Nal Phase

Amri-Nal Phase

Total Sites	164
Sites With Size Estimate	88
Settled Area of Sites with Known Sizes	322.64
Sites with Size Unknown	76
Average Site Site Size	3.67
Estimated Settled Area of Sites Without Size	278.92
Estimated Total Settled Area	610.56

Sizes given in hectares

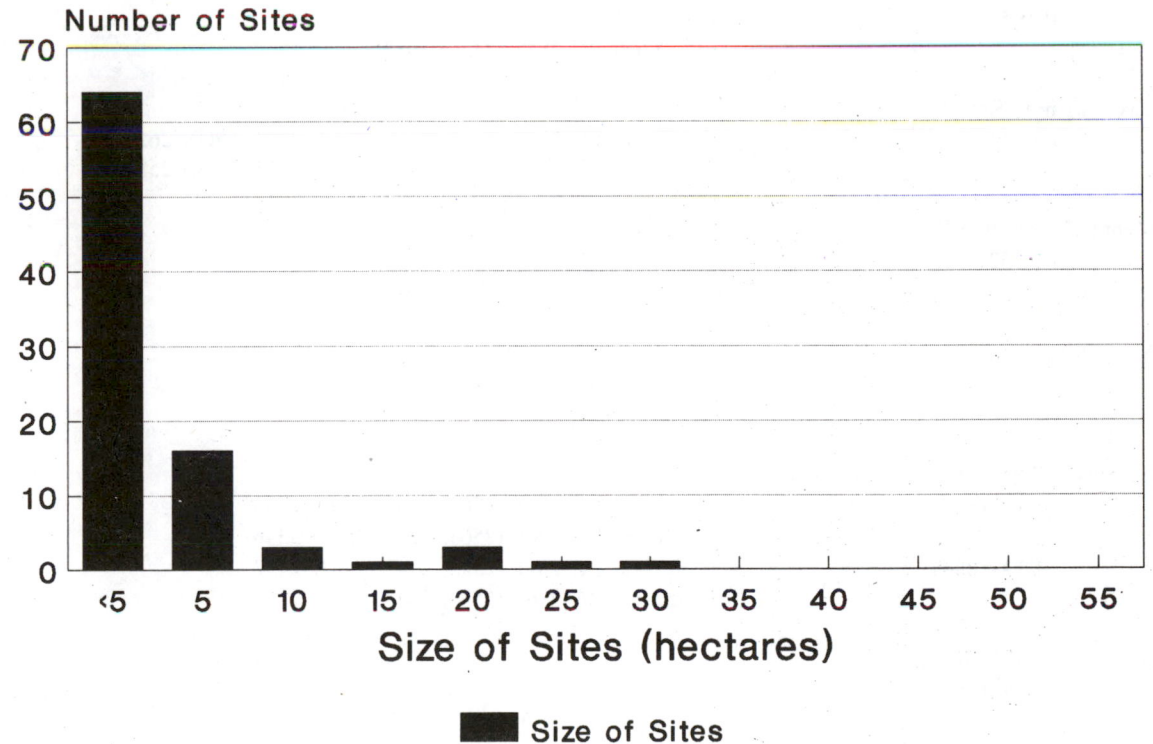

Figure 4.125. Histogram of site sizes of the Amri-Nal Phase

TABLE 4.36
Radiocarbon Dates for the Kot Diji Phase

Lab Number	Calibrated Date
Harappa, Period 1	
BETA-33873	1Σ cal BC 3366 (3336) 3048
	2Σ cal BC 3506 (3336) 2923
Hathala, Kot Diji	
P-1813	1Σ cal BC 2615 (2568, 2519, 2504) 2468
	2Σ cal BC 2863 (2568, 2519, 2504) 2408
Islam Chowki, Kot Diji	
OXA-1005	1Σ cal BC 2886 (2862, 2812, 2741, 2726, 2697) 2577
	2Σ cal BC 2922 (2862, 2812, 2741, 2726, 2697) 2463
Jhang, Kot Diji	
BM-2201R	1Σ cal BC 2924 (2886) 2669
	2Σ cal BC 3261 (2886) 2504
Kot Diji, Period I	
P-196	1Σ cal BC 3344 (3036) 2890
	2Σ cal BC 3504 (3036) 2628
P-179	1Σ cal BC 2912 (2863, 2811, 2743, 2726, 2697) 2493
	2Σ cal BC 3096 (2863, 2811, 2743, 2726, 2697) 2312
P-180	1Σ cal BC 2877 (2588) 2460
	2Σ cal BC 2921 (2588) 2203
P-195	1Σ cal BC 2577 (2456) 2197
	2Σ cal BC 2872 (2456) 1983
Lak Largai 1, Kot Diji	
BM-2402	1Σ cal BC 2878 (2865, 2808, 2755, 2723, 2700) 2621
	2Σ cal BC 2888 (2865, 2808, 2755, 2723, 2700) 2581
Mehrgarh, Period VII	
LY-1527	1Σ cal BC 2132 (1892) 1689
	2Σ cal BC 2329 (1892) 1520
Mehrgarh, Period VI	
LY-1529	1Σ cal BC 2615 (2464) 2207
	2Σ cal BC 2882 (2464) 2034
Nausharo, Period IC	
BETA-18842	1Σ cal BC 2615 (2563, 2524, 2500) 2463
	2Σ cal BC 2866 (2563, 2524, 2500) 2346
BETA-18844	1Σ cal BC 2611 (2553, 2543, 2493) 2457
	2Σ cal BC 2866 (2553, 2543, 2493) 2288
Nausharo, Period IB	
BETA-18843	1Σ cal BC 2856 (2582) 2486
	2Σ cal BC 2876 (2582) 2457

Contd.

Rehman Dheri, Period I
    PRL-676   1Σ cal BC 3367 (3309, 3227, 3186, 3159, 3126) 3032
                                             2Σ cal BC 3613 (3309, 3227, 3186, 3159, 3126) 2905
    PRL-675   1Σ cal BC 3304 (3028, 2975, 2930) 2897
                                           2Σ cal BC 3364 (3028, 2975, 2930) 2703
    WIS-1697   1Σ cal BC 2924 (2906) 2879
                                           2Σ cal BC 3087 (2906) 2696
    WIS-1698   1Σ cal BC 2886 (2871, 2801, 2775, 2715, 2706) 2621
                                         2Σ cal BC 2916 (2871, 2801, 2775, 2715, 2706) 2507

Rehman Dheri, Period II
    WIS-1699   1Σ cal BC 2884 (2868, 2805, 2770, 2719, 2703) 2618
                                         2Σ cal BC 2914 (2868, 2805, 2770, 2719, 2703) 2503

    WIS-1700   1Σ cal BC 2863 (2582) 2468
                                         2Σ cal BC 2884 (2582) 2346
    PRL-674   1Σ cal BC 2859 (2487) 2289
                                         2Σ cal BC 2907 (2487) 2041

Sarai Khola, Period IIA
    BM-1944R   1Σ cal BC 3292 (2888) 2508
                                         2Σ cal BC 3506 (2888) 2280
    BM-1942R   1Σ cal BC 2884 (2853, 2822, 2660, 2638, 2625) 2493
                                         2Σ cal BC 2924 (2853, 2822, 2660, 2638, 2625) 2347
    BM-1936R   1Σ cal BC 2924 (2850, 2825, 2655, 2645, 2622) 2327
                                         2Σ cal BC 3364 (2850, 2825, 2655, 2645, 2622) 1954
    BM-1938R   1Σ cal BC 2859 (2563, 2524, 2500) 2405
                                         2Σ cal BC 2888 (2563, 2524, 2500) 2197

Estimate of Settled Area for the Amri-Nal Phase

The discussion of population figures for this and other Phases of the Early Harappan is best done in the context of the Stage as a whole.

The Amri-Nal Phase: Summary

Sites of the Amri-Nal Phase cover the southern tier of the Indus Valley and Baluchistan. During this Phase the continued maturation of the subsistence system and a spread of farming and herding peoples to the sea coast and southeast, into Gujarat is seen. Modest attempts at fortification may also characterize some Amri-Nal settlements.

The Kot Diji Phase of Northern Sindh and Elsewhere

Kot Diji is a splendid small site on the national highway linking Karachi and Hyderabad to Sukkur. It is situated on the old alluvium of the Indus Valley, below a huge Talpur Dynasty fortress which looms over it from the escarpment of the southern Rohri Hills. This fort, or *kot* takes it name, I believe, from the Princess Diji Talpur (Figure 4.126). The Pakistan Department of Archaeology conducted an excavation there in 1955 and 1957 under the direction of F. A. Khan (F. A. Khan 1965). An analysis of the site was one of the primary foci of M. R. Mughal's PhD dissertation and he created from it the "type site" for his Early Harappan.

The Kot Diji archaeological assemblage is distinct from the Amri-Nal, although there is some overlap in ceramics, with some common vessel forms and decorative motifs, especially among the simpler pots (Figure 4.127). Both assemblages present us with extremely fine examples

626

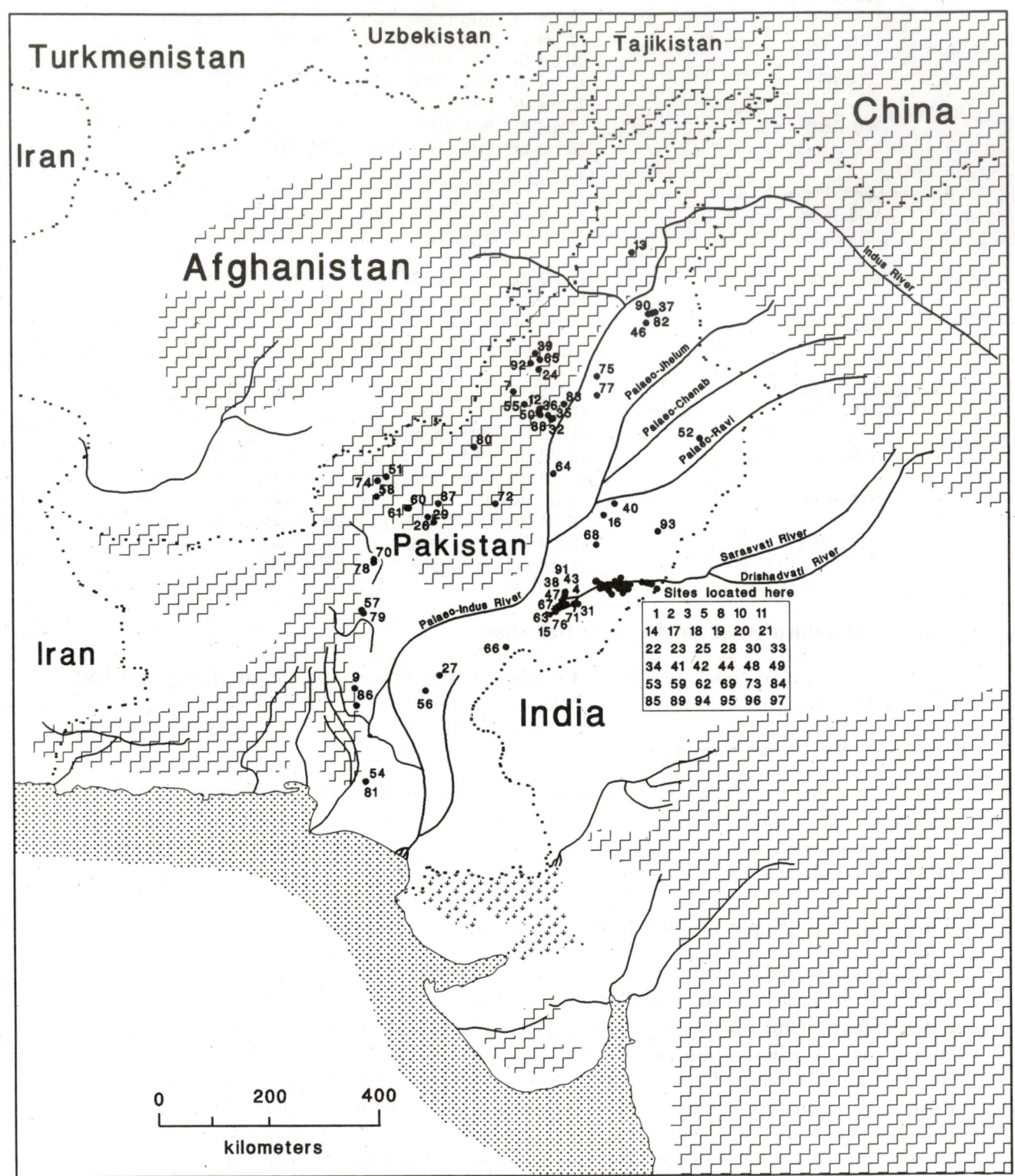

Figure 4.126. Map of sites of the Kot Diji Phase

Key to Figure 4.126

1. Ahmadwala Toba
2. Akhera
3. Ali Mohammad Wala Ther
4. Aziinwali 'B'
5. Babul Bhera
6. Badalwala Three
7. Bagh-i Kumb Damb
8. Baghanwali Theri
9. Bamba Damb
10. Bannewala Ther
11. Bokharaiwala
12. Budki Dheri
13. Butkara One
14. Chak 045
15. Chak 076
16. Chak 133/1OR
17. Chak 271 HR
18. Chak 280 HR
19. Chak 315 HR
20. Chak 337 HR
21. Chak 341
22. Chapliwala East
23. Chapliwala West
24. Chig Dheri
25. Chipwala
26. Dabar Kot
27. Diji-ji Tikri
28. Dinewali Theri
29. Duki Mound
30. Gamanwala
31. Gemuwali
32. Gomal Kalan
33. Guddal 'B'

34. Gujranwala
35. Gumla
36. Hathala
37. Hathial West
38. Hotewala Ther 'A'
39. Ialam Chowki
40. Jalilpur
41. Jalwali
42. Januwala
43. Januwali Dhar
44. Jathewali
45. Jatoiwala 'A'
46. Jhang
47. Jhumtiwala
48. Kalepar
49. Kaliwaryal
50. Karam Shah
51. Karezgai
52. Khadianwala
53. Kirarwali Ther
54. Kohtras Buthi
55. Kot Alabad
56. Kot Diji
57. Kotra
58. Kowas
59. Kuchanwala
60. L-2
61. L-3
62. Ladulai
63. Lathwala
64. Leiah
65. Lewan
66. Lundi

67. Luppewala Two
68. Mai Manoori Bhir
69. Malhalewala Ther
70. Mehrgarh
71. Merechi Kanda Three
72. Moghul Kala
73. Mojgarh Ther
74. Murgha Mehtarzai
75. Musa Khel
76. Nahamwala
77. Nammal Lake Cave
78. Nausharo
79. Pathani Damb One
80. Periano Ghundai
81. Phang
82. Pind Nausheri
83. Piplan
84. Quadarwali Theri
85. Quaraish Ther
86. Rajo-daro One
87. Rana Ghundai
88. Rehman Dheri
89. Sandhanawala Ther
90. Sarai Khola
91. Siddhuwali 'C'
92. Tarakai Ghundai
93. Vainiwal
94. Wakkarwala
95. Wariyal 'A'
96. Wariyal 'D'
97. Ziarat Bharam Shahi

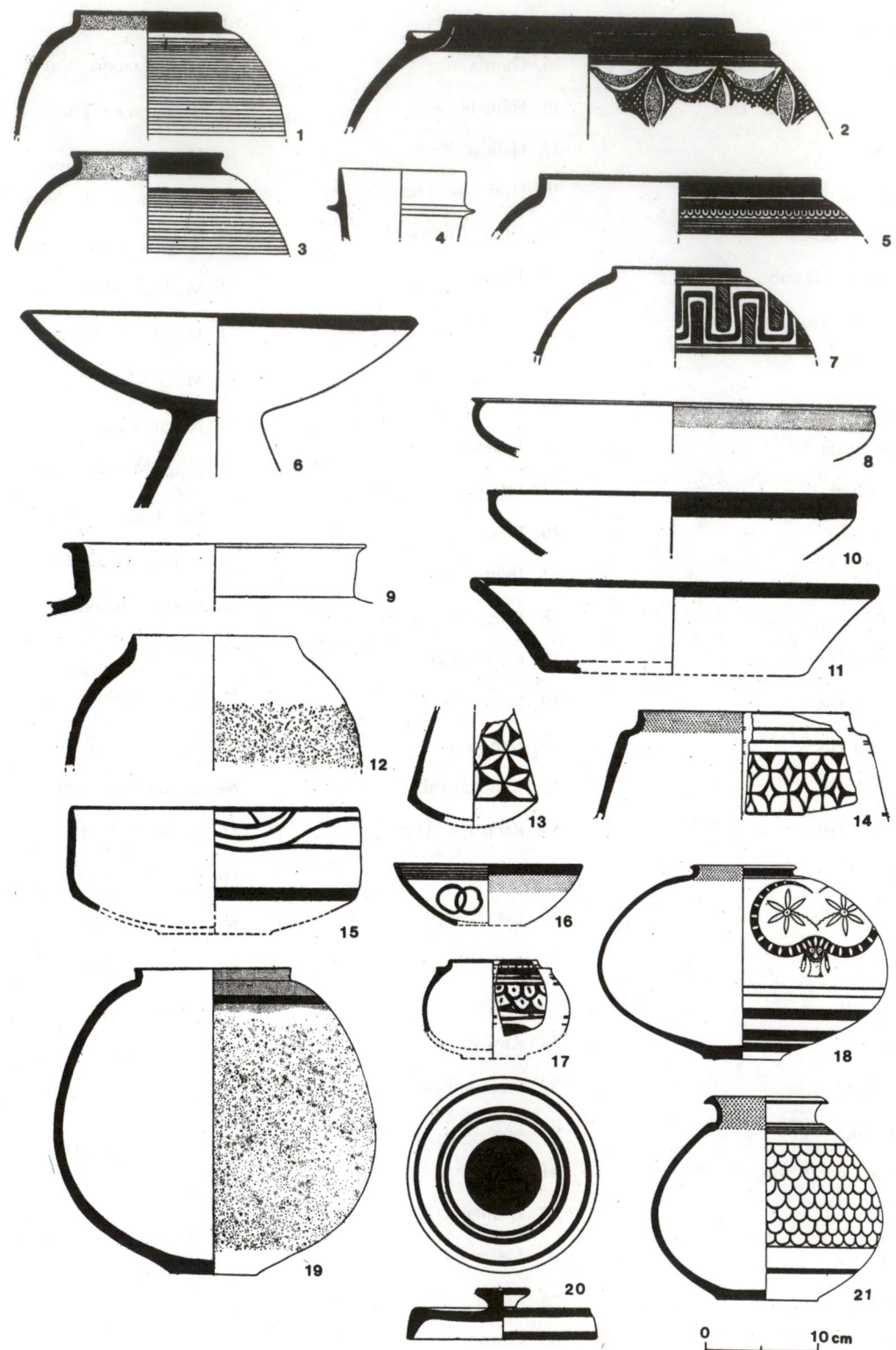

Figure 4.127. The Kot Diji ceramic assemblage

of the potter's art with well fired red and buff wares. The tall jars and vases with featureless rims of the Amri-Nal assemblage are not a part of the Kot Diji ceramic corpus and neither are the Nal canisters and fat-bodied pots. If anything like the distinctive Nal painting were found at a Kot Diji site it would be dubbed an import. The publication of the site does not indicate Nal Ware at Kot Diji, itself.

The chronology of the Kot Diji Phase is based on a remarkably coherent series of radiocarbon dates from eleven sites.

The Kot Diji Assemblage

The Kot Diji potter was committed to producing a thin lightweight ceramic with some paring of vessel walls to thin them while the pots were still wet and leathery. This was also done to the stems of vessels, but no attempt was made to carve out the fine ring bases found in the Kechi Beg assemblage. The development of the finely fashioned Kot Diji rim, often flanged is a sophisticated piece of potting, with the vertical rim, often slightly concave on the outside, shaped with a tool (Figure 4.128, Figure 4.129). In all likelihood this was either a bone or wooden spatula held to the rim during the last phases of working the pot on a wheel. A slight groove at the point where the rim meets the body of the vessel is a common, possibly universal, mark that can be used to identify this rim form, even on sherds. For the sake of clarity this groove has been slightly emphasized in Figure 4.128. The Kot Diji rim is associated with a number of vessel forms and surface treatments, but always in a red or buff fabric, never grey except for accidents in firing.

The pottery from many Kot Diji sites is well decorated. Painting is generally done with geometric designs in black over either a light slip or directly on the surface. Some animal motifs are also present, and the "horned deity" makes its first appearance. It survives into Mature Harappan times, most notably on the Mahayogi seal, thought by some to represent a "Proto-Siva." Much of the Kot Diji pottery has a fine, smoothed surface, but there are three other important surface treatments:

Bhoot Ware

Bhoot Ware has a deeply grooved surface finish, first identified at the site of Bhoot (a.k.a. Kalepar) in Cholistan (Plate 4.40). This surface treatment occurs on small globular pots, generally with the Kot Diji rim. These pots are never burnished and are quite porous. They were apparently

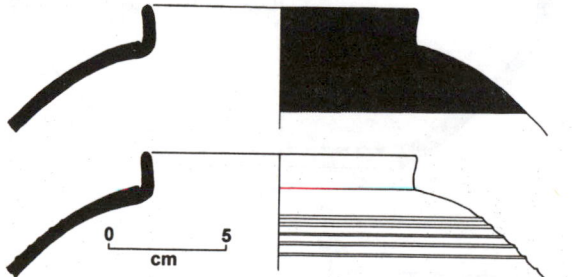

Figure 4.128. The Kot Diji Phase short neck jar, the lower example in Bhoot Ware

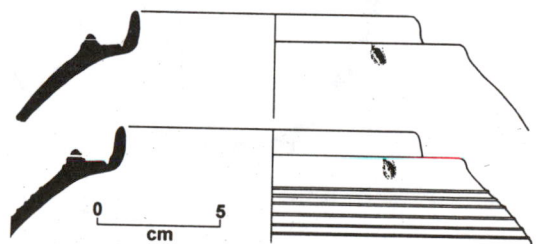

Figure 4.129. The Kot Diji Phase flange rim jar, the lower example in Bhoot Ware

630

water containers, the grooves functionally increasing the surface area of the vessel, enhancing the cooling effect achieved by the evaporation of water from the vessel surface.

Wet Ware

There are several varieties of Wet Ware, which is pottery with a crinkled surface (Figure 4.130). In the classic examples this forms a simple dendritic pattern, but more regular "geometric" patterns are also known. Wet Wares were first defined by Walter Fairservis following his excavations in the Quetta Valley (1956a: 268-70). Experiments he conducted with modern pottery showed that this surface was achieved by applying a thick slurry of viscose clay to the body of unfired, but otherwise finished pot. This pot was then covered by a wet cloth which was lifted off in a way that left the characteristic Wet Ware patterns. By varying the viscosity of the slurry and surface weave or texture of the cloth, one can manipulate the patterning on the pot surface.

Wet Ware pots are usually round or fat-bodied and the surface pattern expands the surface area of the pot for evaporation. Some, possibly most, seem to have functioned as water containers.

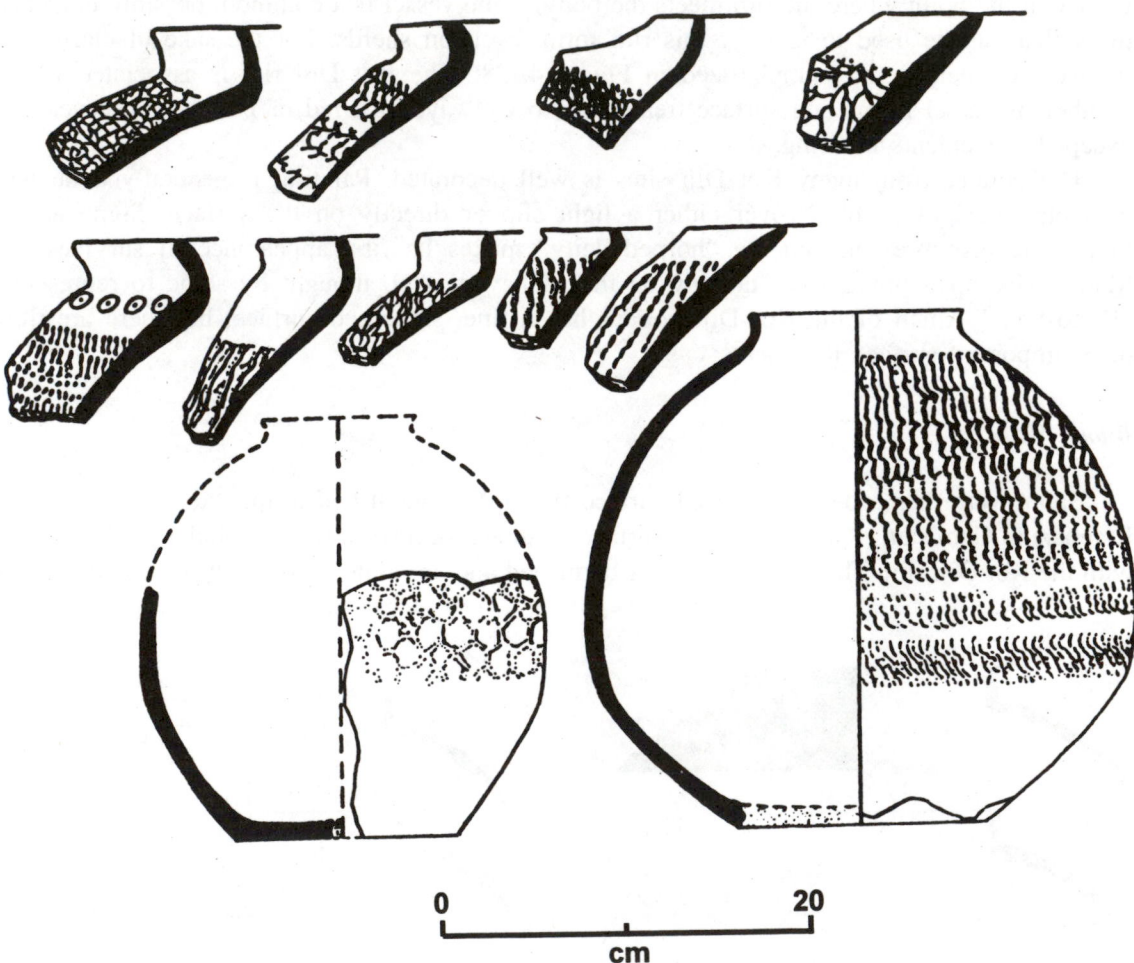

Figure 4.130. Wet Wares, after Fairservis 1956a: Figure 59

Sand Rusticated Ware

Some Kot Diji pots have a thick "slip" of sandy clay applied to the body portion of the vessel. This treatment is also found in the Amri, Damb Sadaat and Sothi-Siswal assemblages, but I have never seen it in collections of Nal pottery. In the Damb Sadaat assemblage it is called Khojak Parallel Striated. (Figure 4.131), while in Sothi-Siswal contexts it takes the name, "Fabric B" as defined at Kalibangan (IAR 1962-63: 27). The function of Rusticated Ware has not been determined.

There is certainly a measurable degree of differentiation within the Kot Diji ceramics, but on the whole there is a sense of association among many sites that made it possible to bring them together into a Phase as defined here.

The Kot Diji Phase Sites

Table 4.37 lists sites of the Kot Diji Phase.

The distribution of Kot Diji Phase sites by size is shown in (Figure 4.132).

The estimate for the settled area of the Kot Diji Phase has been computed as shown in Table 4.38.

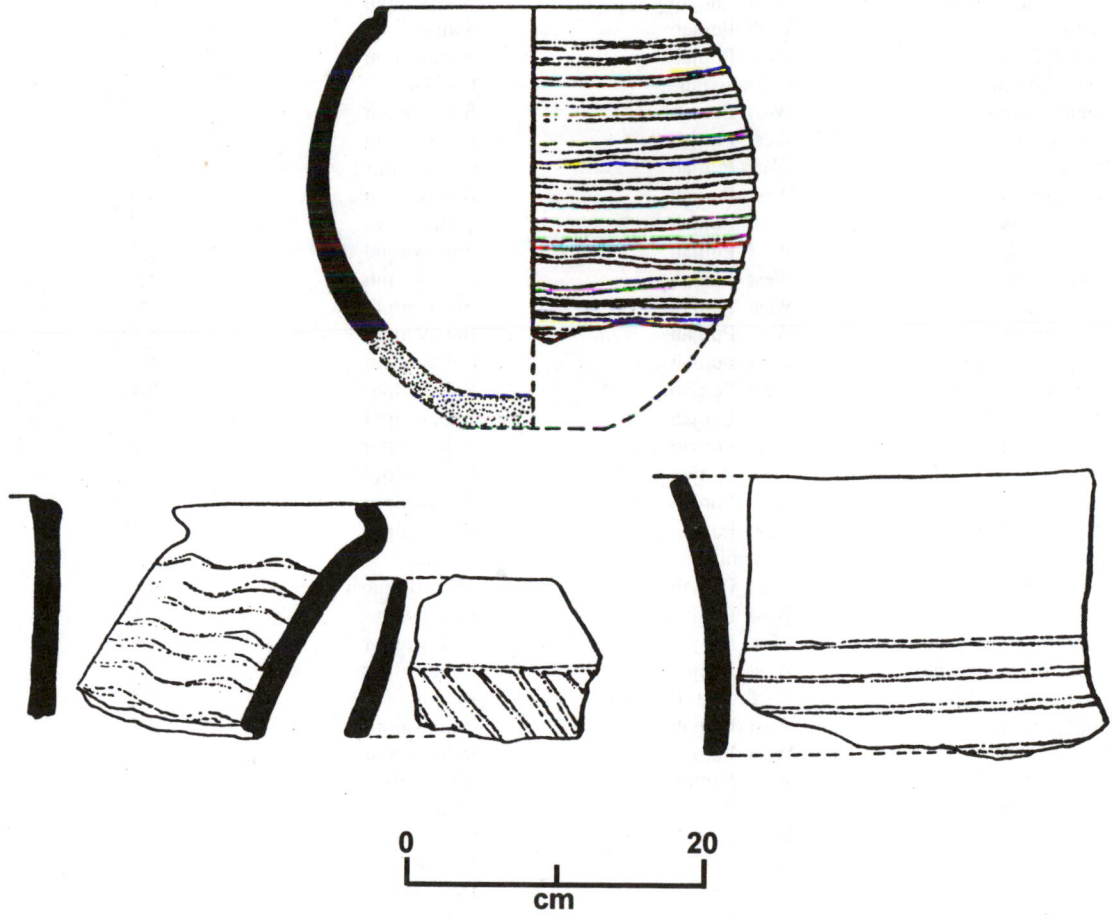

Figure 4.131. Khojak Parallel Striated pottery, after Fairservis 1956a: Figure 268

TABLE 4.37
Sites of the Kot Diji Phase

Site Name	Province/State	District	Size in hectares
Harappa	West Punjab	Sahiwal	40.0
Lathwala	West Punjab	Bahawalpur	30.5
Gamanwala	West Punjab	Bahawalpur	27.3
Dabar Kot	Baluchistan	Loralai	24.3
Jalwali	West Punjab	Bahawalpur	22.5
Chak 341	West Punjab	Bahawalpur	19.9
Malhalewala Ther	West Punjab	Bahawalpur	19.0
Rehman Dheri	Northwest Frontier	Dera Ismail Khan	19.0
Sarai Khola	West Punjab	Rawalpindi	18.6
Lewan	Northwest Frontier	Bannu	14.6
Periano Ghundai	Baluchistan	Zhob	14.4
Jalilpur	West Punjab	Sahiwal	13.0
L-3	Baluchistan	Loralai	12.6
Azimwali 'B'	West Punjab	Bahawalpur	10.9
Kohtras Buthi	Sindh	Karachi	10.2
Sandhanawala Ther	West Punjab	Bahawalpur	10.0
Bannewala Ther	West Punjab	Bahawalpur	9.9
Kalepar	West Punjab	Bahawalpur	8.6
Chapliwala West	West Punjab	Bahawalpur	8.2
Vainiwal	West Punjab	Sahiwal	7.4
Kirarwali Ther	West Punjab	Bahawalpur	6.8
Duki Mound	Baluchistan	Loralai	6.5
Babul Bhera	West Punjab	Bahawalpur	6.5
Guddal 'B'	West Punjab	Bahawalpur	6.4
Jhang	West Punjab	Campbellpur	6.4
Gujranwala	West Punjab	Bahawalpur	6.3
Wariyal 'A'	West Punjab	Bahawalpur	6.2
Naharnwala	West Punjab	Bahawalpur	6.1
Quraish Ther	West Punjab	Bahawalpur	5.9
Januwala	West Punjab	Bahawalpur	5.9
Ahmadwala Toba	West Punjab	Bahawalpur	5.9
Luppewala Two	West Punjab	Bahawalpur	5.5
Qadarwali Theri	West Punjab	Bahawalpur	5.4
Chak 315 HR	West Punjab	Bahawalpur	5.1
Chak 337 HR	West Punjab	Bahawalpur	4.6
Akhera	West Punjab	Bahawalpur	4.5
Chipwala	West Punjab	Bahawalpur	4.5
Mojgarh Ther	West Punjab	Bahawalpur	4.5
Kowas	Baluchistan	Loralai	4.1
Leiah	West Punjab	Muzaffargarh	4.0
Ladulai	West Punjab	Bahawalpur	3.9
Merechi Kanda Three	West Punjab	Bahawalpur	13.7
Ziarat Bharam Shahi	West Punjab	Bahawalpur	3.7
Tarakai Ghundai	Northwest Frontier	Bannu	3.5
Bokharaiwala	West Punjab	Bahawalpur	3.5
Jathewali	West Punjab	Bahawalpur	3.3
Musa Khel	West Punjab	Mianwali	3.1
Januwali Dhar	West Punjab	Bahawalpur	2.9
Hotewala Ther 'A'	West Punjab	Bahawalpur	2.8
Jhumtiwala	West Punjab	Bahawalpur	2.8
Hathala	Northwest Frontier	Dera Ismail Khan	2.7
Kaliwaryal	West Punjab	Bahawalpur	2.6
Loal Mari	Sindh	Sukkur	2.57

Contd.

Chak 076	West Punjab	Bahawalpur	2.5
Kot Diji	Sindh	Khairpur	2.2
Wariyal 'D'	West Punjab	Bahawalpur	2.2
Karam Shah	Northwest Frontier	Dera Ismail Khan	1.9
Nausharo	Baluchistan	Kachi	1.8
Jatoiwala 'A'	West Punjab	Bahawalpur	1.6
Diji-ji Tikri	Sindh	Khairpur	1.6
Badalwala Three	West Punjab	Bahawalpur	1.4
Rana Ghundai	Baluchistan	Loralai	1.4
Islam Chowki	Northwest Frontier	Bannu	1.35
Khannda	West Punjab	Rawalpindi	1.2
Wakkarwala	West Punjab	Bahawalpur	1.2
Chapliwala East	West Punjab	Bahawalpur	1.2
Chak 271 HR	West Punjab	Bahawalpur	1.1
Siddhuwali 'C'	West Punjab	Bahawalpur	0.9
Moghul Kala	Baluchistan	Loralai	0.9
Rajo-daro One	Sindh	Dadu	0.7
Gumla	Northwest Frontier	Dera Ismail Khan	0.7
Chak 045	West Punjab	Bahawalpur	0.7
L-2	Baluchistan	Loralai	0.6
Kuchanwala	West Punjab	Bahawalpur	0.6
Hathial West	West Punjab	Rawalpindi	0.5
Phang	Sindh	Karachi	0.4
Chak 280 HR	West Punjab	Bahawalpur	0.35
Dranjan Site	Baluchistan	Kachi	0.3
Khadianwala	West Punjab	Sheikhupura	0.3
Ali Mohammad Wala			
Thar	West Punjab	Bahawalpur	0.3
Pind Nausheri	West Punjab	Rawalpindi	0.2
Karezgai	Baluchistan	Zhob	0.2
Gemuwali	West Punjab	Bahawalpur	0.01
Bagh-i Kumb Damb	Northwest Frontier	Dera Ismail Khan	
Baghanwali Theri	West Punjab	Bahawalpur	
Bamba Damb	Sindh	Dadu	
Budki Dheri	Northwest Frontier	Dera Ismail Khan	
Butkara One	Northwest Frontier	Swat	
Chak 133/10R	West Punjab	Khanewal	
Chig Dheri	Northwest Frontier	Bannu	
Dawrao Tul Damb	Northwest Frontier	Dera Ismail Khan	
Dinewali Theri	West Punjab	Bahawalpur	
Gand Damb	Northwest Frontier	Dera Ismail Khan	
Gomal Kalan	Northwest Frontier	Dera Ismail Khan	
Kaddour Damb	Northwest Frontier	Dera Ismail Khan	
Kandai	Baluchistan	Loralai	
Kanori	Baluchistan	Loralai	
Kashkai	Baluchistan	Loralai	
Khoedada	Baluchistan	Zhob	
Kot Alabad	Northwest Frontier	Dera Ismail Khan	
Kotra	Baluchistan	Kachi	
Lahar	Baluchistan	Zhob	
Lundi Dherai	West Punjab	Rahimyar Khan	
Mai Manoori Bhir	West Punjab	Multan	
Mehrgarh	Baluchistan	Kachi	
Murgha Mehtarzai	Baluchistan	Zhob	
Nammal Lake Cave	West Punjab	Campbellpur	
Pathani Damb One	Baluchistan	Kachi	
Piplan	Northwest Frontier	Dera Ismail Khan	
Sinjawi Ghundai	Baluchistan	Loralai	
Unnamed Damb	Northwest Frontier	Dera Ismail Khan	

634

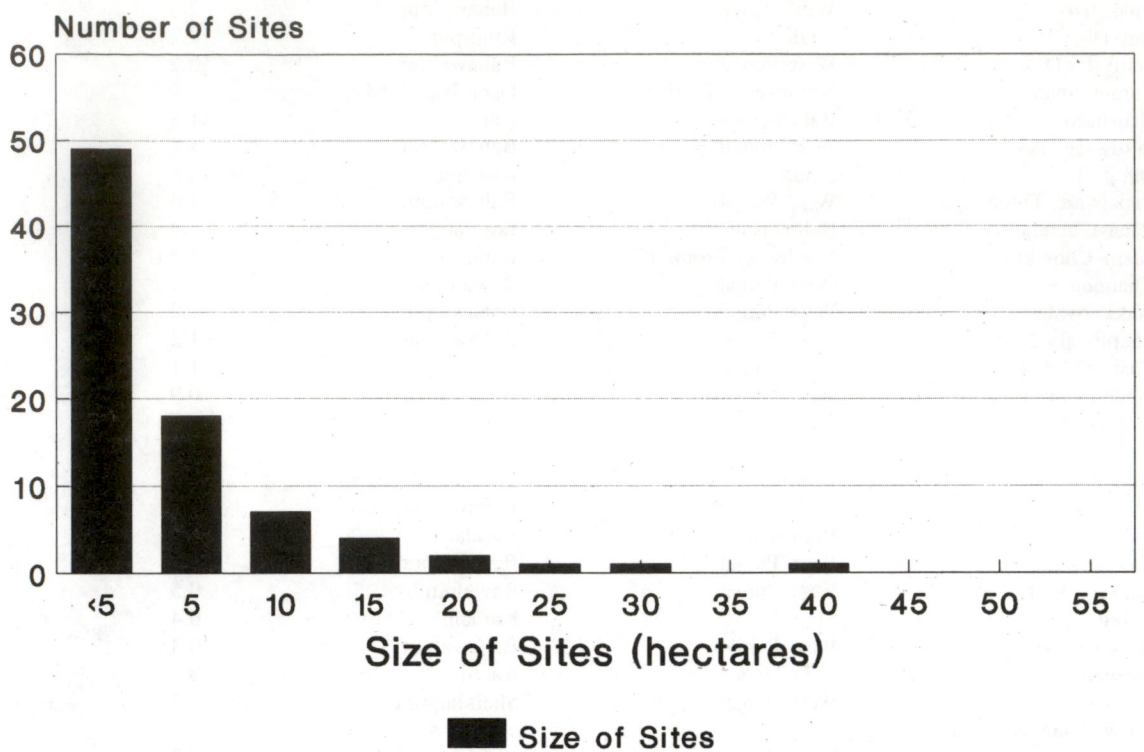

Figure 4.132. Histogram of site sizes for the Kot Diji Phase

TABLE 4.38
Estimate of Settled Area for the Kot Diji Phase

Kot Diji Phase

Total Sites	111
Sites with Size Estimate	83
Settled Area of Sites with Known Sizes	523.38
Sites with Size Unknown	28
Average Site Site Size	6.31
Estimated Settled Area of Sites without Size	176.68
Estimated Total Settled Area	700.06

Sizes given in hectares

Kot Diji Settlement Patterns

Of the 111 Kot Diji sites, eighty-three have data on their size, which averages 6.31 hectares. This average is sixty-five percent larger than that of the sites of the Amri-Nal Phase. There is also a slight increase in maximum site size when comparing the Amri-Nal with the Kot Diji, with two sites in the thirty to forty hectare range. These are site sizes that will be duplicated within the Sothi-Siswal Phase but not in the Damb Sadaat Phase. Harappa is listed as the largest of the Kot Diji Phase sites, but this is only a crude estimate of its size during these times. But there are other large, *pucca* Kot Diji sites at Lathwala (30.5 hectares; Mughal 1997: 144) and Gamanwala (27.3 hectares; Mughal 1997: 142) which give a credible indication of the high end of large site size for this Phase.

There are many Kot Diji sites to the west of the ancient Sarasvati drainage, especially in Bannu and the Gomal Valley, as well as around the Taxila Valley. The largest of these are places like Rehman Dheri (19 hectares) Sarai Khola (18.6 hectares) and Lewan (14.6 hectares), seemingly one notch below the Sarasvati sites in terms of their size.

The scatter of Kot Diji sites in Northern Baluchistan are not well known. Dabar Kot is a huge settlement and the size of the Kot Diji occupation has been suggested to have been 24.3 hectares, which would almost certainly be revised with problem oriented archaeological research at the site (Figure 4.133). The estimate of size for Periano Ghundai (14.4 hectares) carries the same observations.

There are many small Kot Diji sites that seem to have been farming homesteads of both village farming communities and nomadic camps. Some may have been used during the *kharif* growing season by these mobile peoples.

There are thirteen Kot Diji sites in the Dera Ismail Khan District, with more in the region (Figure 4.134). Rehman Dheri is the most prominent of the excavated sites. It has two occupations within the Kot Diji Phase, topped by one assigned to the Late Kot Dijian.

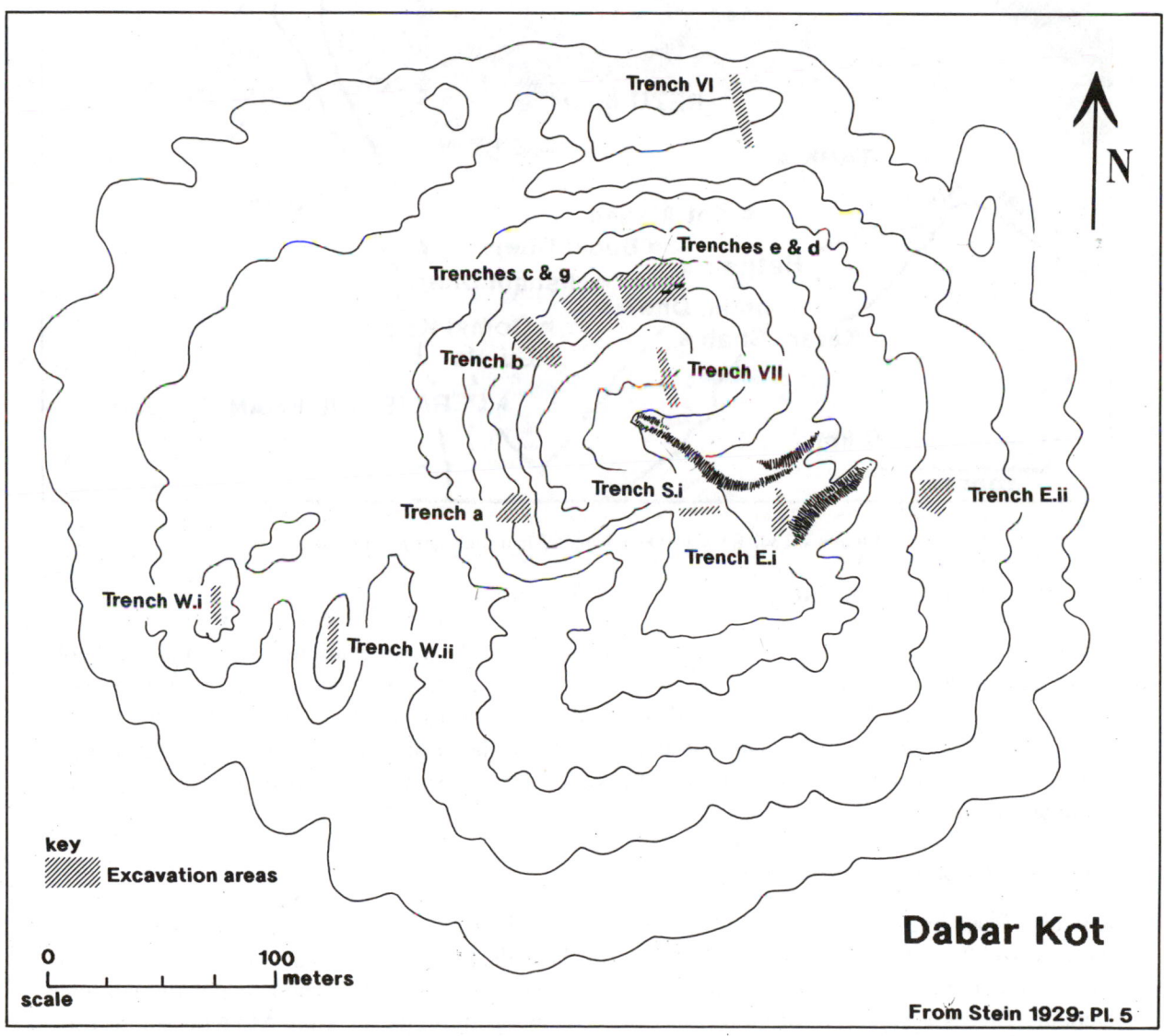

Figure 4.133. Plan of Dabar Kot, after Stein 1929a: Plan 5

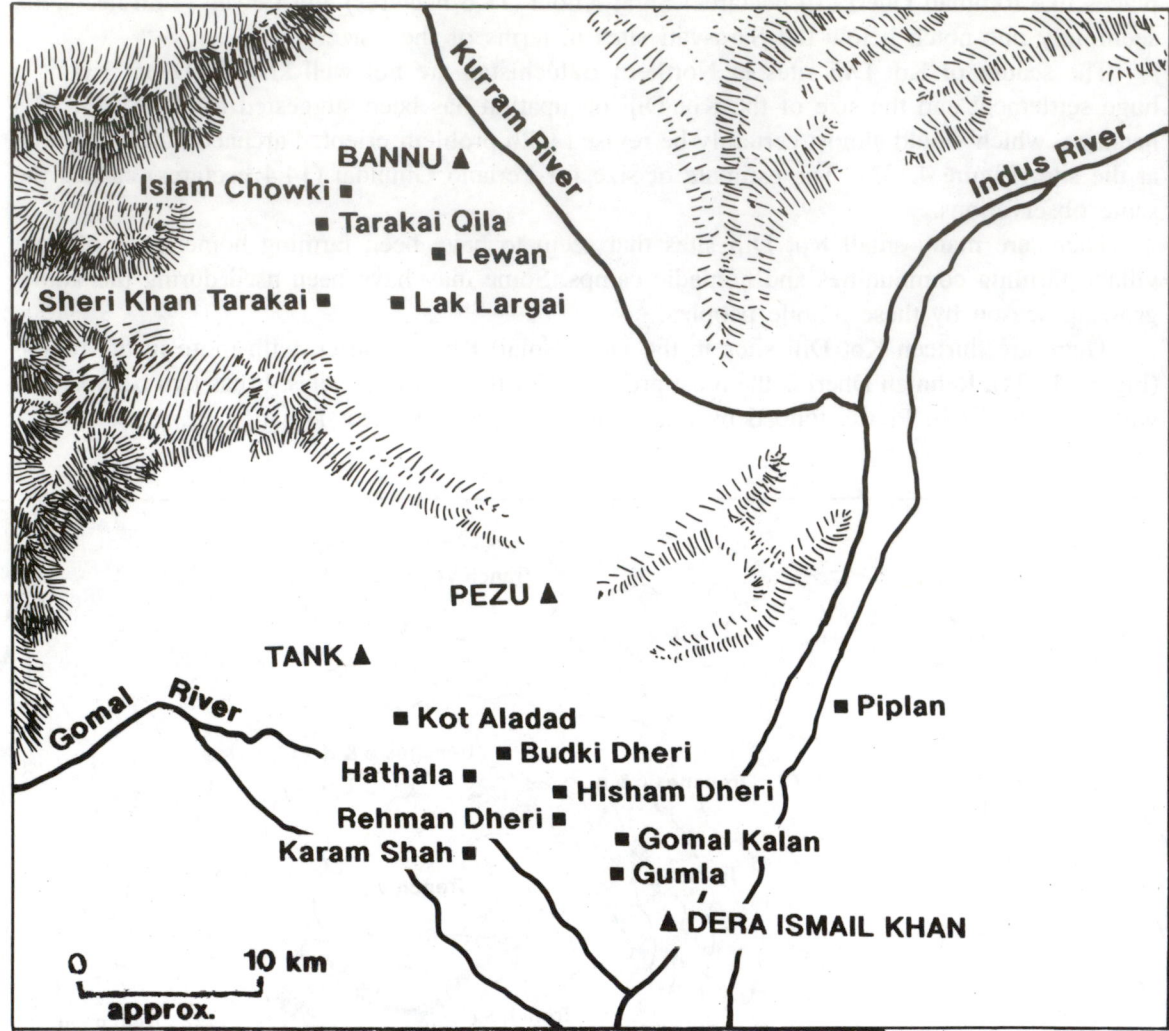

Figure 4.134. Sites in Dera Ismail Khan and surrounding areas

The Excavated Kot Diji Sites

There are twenty excavated Kot Diji sites. Since many of these excavations were done in recent years, using modern standards of data recovery, there is an improvement in the quality of this data set when compared to the Amri-Nal. Sustained digging at places like Mehrgarh, Sarai Khola and Rehman Dheri have also produced relatively large data sets and reliable results. Kot Diji itself is an extremely good example of a site of this Phase and a description of its Kot Diji occupation follows.

The Site of Kot Diji: Introduction

Kot Diji is an imposing site (Plate 4.41, Plate 4.42). It was established at the southern end of the Rohri Hills to the west, on the Indus side of the hills, on the traditional route up the eastern side of the Indus, north from Chanhu-daro to the Sukkur Gap and beyond to the Punjab and Derajat. This is a strategic location, as evidenced by the presence of a pre-Modern Sindhi fort or *kot*, built on the high escarpment of the Rohri Hills, overlooking the ancient site. The main mound of the site is twelve meters high and is an unmistakable feature of the old Indus plain.

Plate 4.37. General view of Somnath. Author's photograph.

Plate 4.38. Excavations at Somnath in 1971, Prabhas Period levels. Author's photograph.

Plate 4.39. Tor Ghundai. Author's photograph.

Plate 4.40. Bhoot Ware. Courtesy of the Pakistan Department of Archaeology.

Plate 4.41. The site of Kot Diji at the time of excavation. Courtesy of the Pakistan Department of Archaeology.

Plate 4.42. The site of Kot Diji today. Author's photograph.

Plate 4.43. Kot Diji, eastern circumvallation with northern corner bastions. Courtesy of the Pakistan Department of Archaeology.

Plate 4.44. Kot Diji, the High Mound circumvallation showing stone foundations and mud brick superstructures. Courtesy of the Pakistan Department of Archaeology.

Plate 4.45. The "Horned Deity" pot from Kot Diji, Period I. Courtesy of the Pakistan Department of Archaeology.

Plate 4.46. Stratigraphy at Jalilpur, M. R. Mughal providing scale. Courtesy of the Pakistan Department of Archaeology.

Plate 4.47. Painted pottery from Jalilpur, Period II. Courtesy of the Pakistan Department of Archaeology.

Plate 4.48. Globular vessels from Jalilpur Period II with Kot Diji type short neck rims. The vessel on the right is Bhoot Ware. Courtesy of the Pakistan Department of Archaeology.

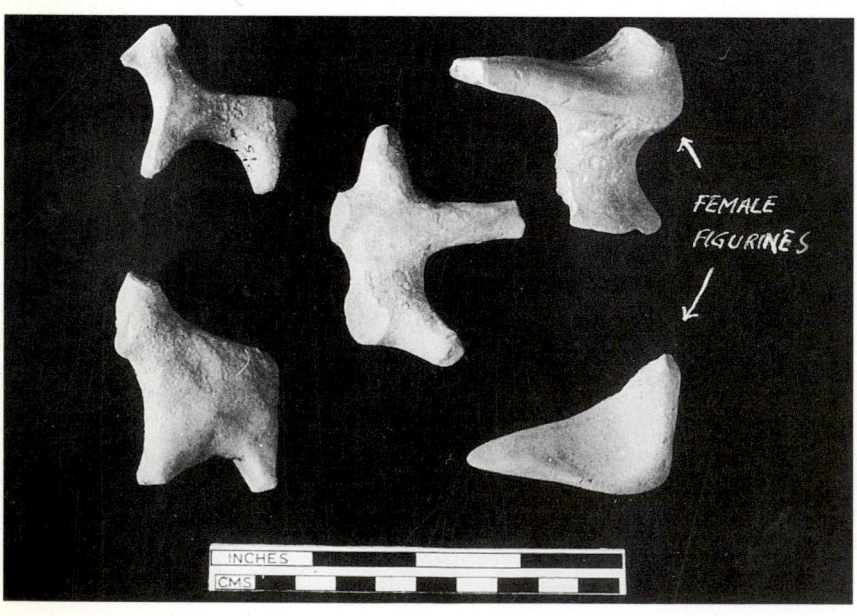

FEMALE
FIGURINES

Plate 4.49. Figurines from Jalilpur, Period II. Courtesy of the Pakistan Department of Archaeology.

Plate 4.50. The Quetta Valley from the top of Damb Sadaat. Author's photograph.

Plate 4.51. The Bull Pot in Quetta Ware from Damb Sadaat II contexts. Courtesy of the American Museum of Natural History.

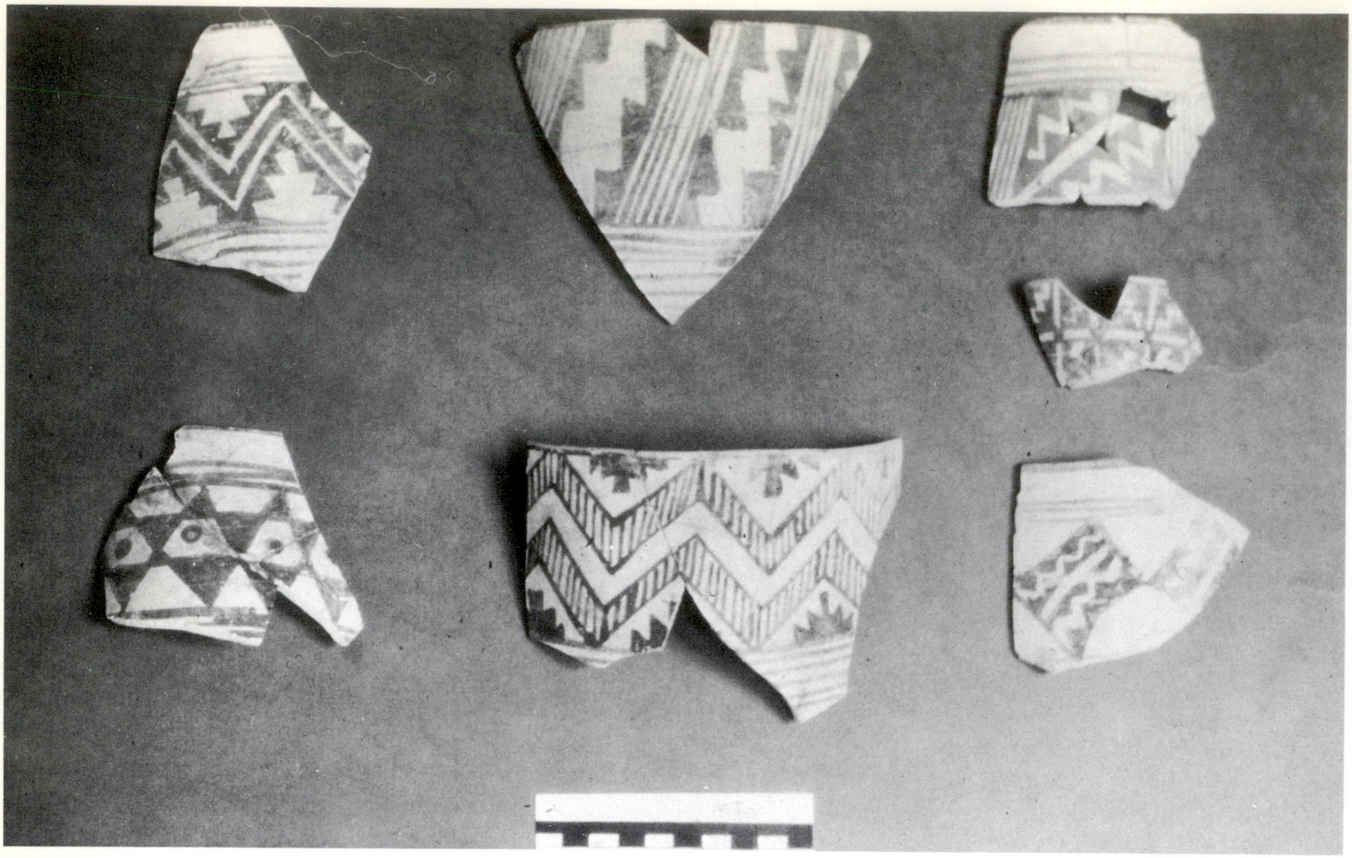

Plate 4.52. Quetta ware from the Quetta Valley. Author's photograph.

Plate 4.53. Pottery from Kalibangan Period I. Mostly Fabric A. Courtesy of the Archaeological Survey of India.

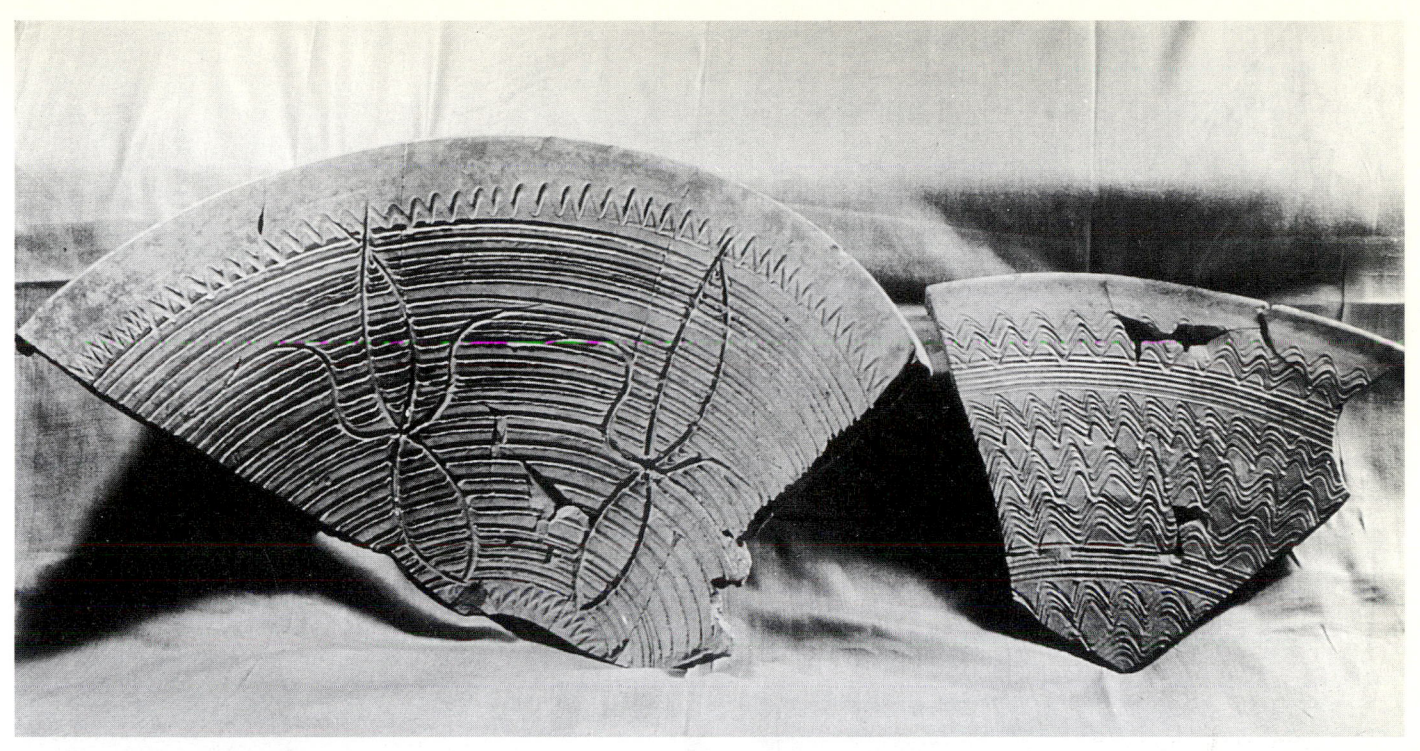

Plate 4.54. Fabric D from Kalibangan Period I. Courtesy of the Archaeological Survey of India.

Plate 4.55. The wide lane of Period I at Kalibangan. Courtesy of the Archaeological Survey of India.

Plate 4.56. Houses of Period I at Kalibangan. Courtesy of the Archaeological Survey of India.

Plate 4.57. The plowed field associated with Period I at Kalibangan. Courtesy of the Archaeological Survey of India.

Plate 4.58. Modern plowed fields in Rajasthan, with the
Archae

Plate 4.59. Kalibangan, row of "fire-altars" on the High Mound, Mature Harappan. Courtesy of the Archaeological Survey of India.

Plate 4.60. Pit with cattle bones and antlers on a platform on the High Mound at Kalibangan, Mature Harappan. Courtesy of the Archaeological Survey of India.

Spread below it is a lower habitation area, with a surface rich in pottery and stone tools. It is an unmistakable ancient settlement.

I have been to Kot Diji and one of the most striking features of the site was the huge number of cores and blades, all made of Rohri Hills flint. Clearly, ancient Kot Diji was a factory site for the making of blades and it was done on a grand scale.

Kot Diji was first recorded as an archaeological site by G. S. Ghurye (1936) in the course of his assessment of the antiquarian remains of Sindh. It was largely coincidental with M. S. Vats' explorations in Khairpur State, when he visited Naru Waro Dharo (Kotasur) and Diji-ji-Tikri (Vats 1935-36a, 1935-36b).

Ghurye did not excavate at Kot Diji, but he did make a surface collection from the site that is now in the Prince of Wales Museum, Bombay.

The Excavation

Dr. Khan has phrased his excavations in terms of two areas: Area A on the mound itself and Area B, the "Lower Town." As seen on the plan (Figure 4.135), however, there was actually one continuous area of excavation, and while it did test two distinct "districts" of the settlement, Kot Diji is a good example of horizontal excavation.

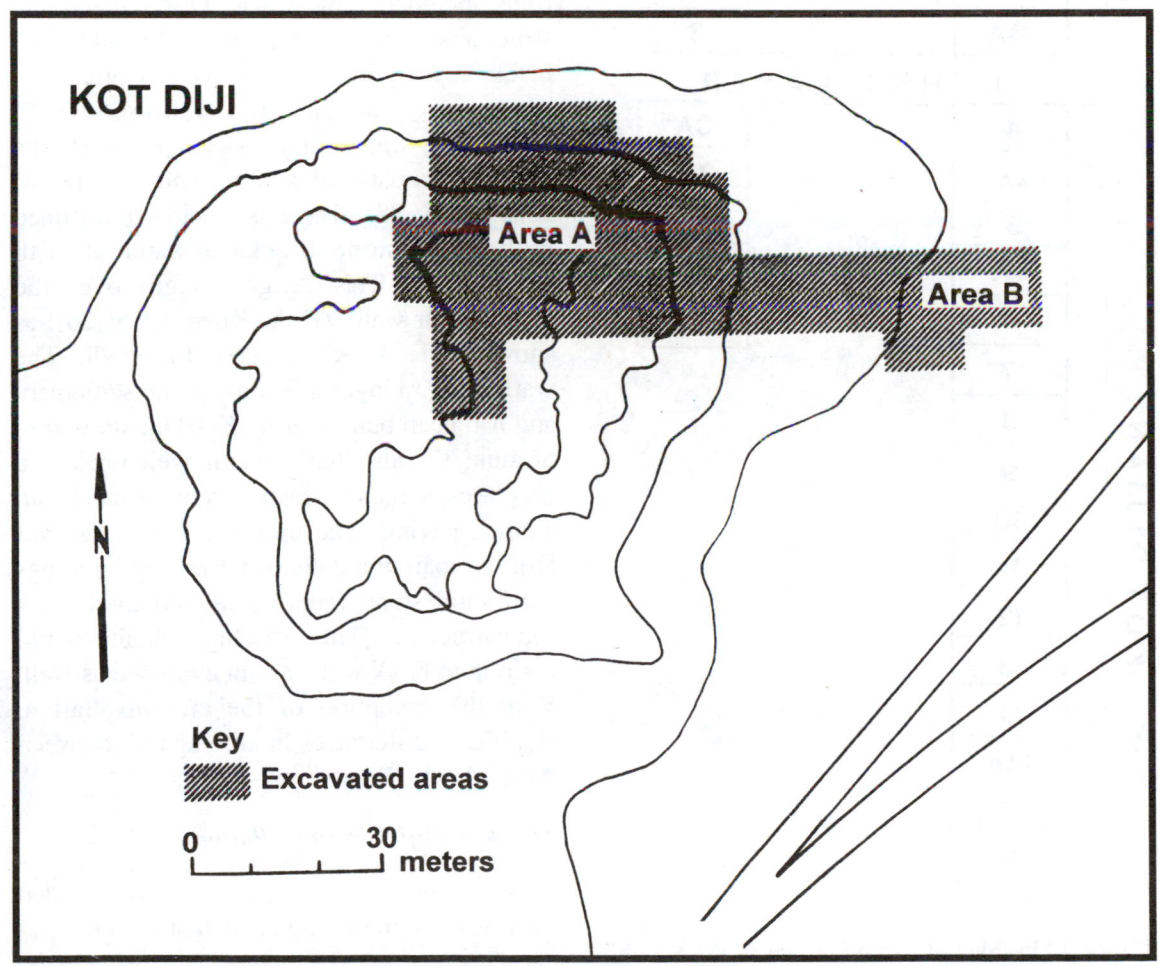

Figure 4.135. Site plan of Kot Diji, after F. A. Khan 1965: Figure 3

638

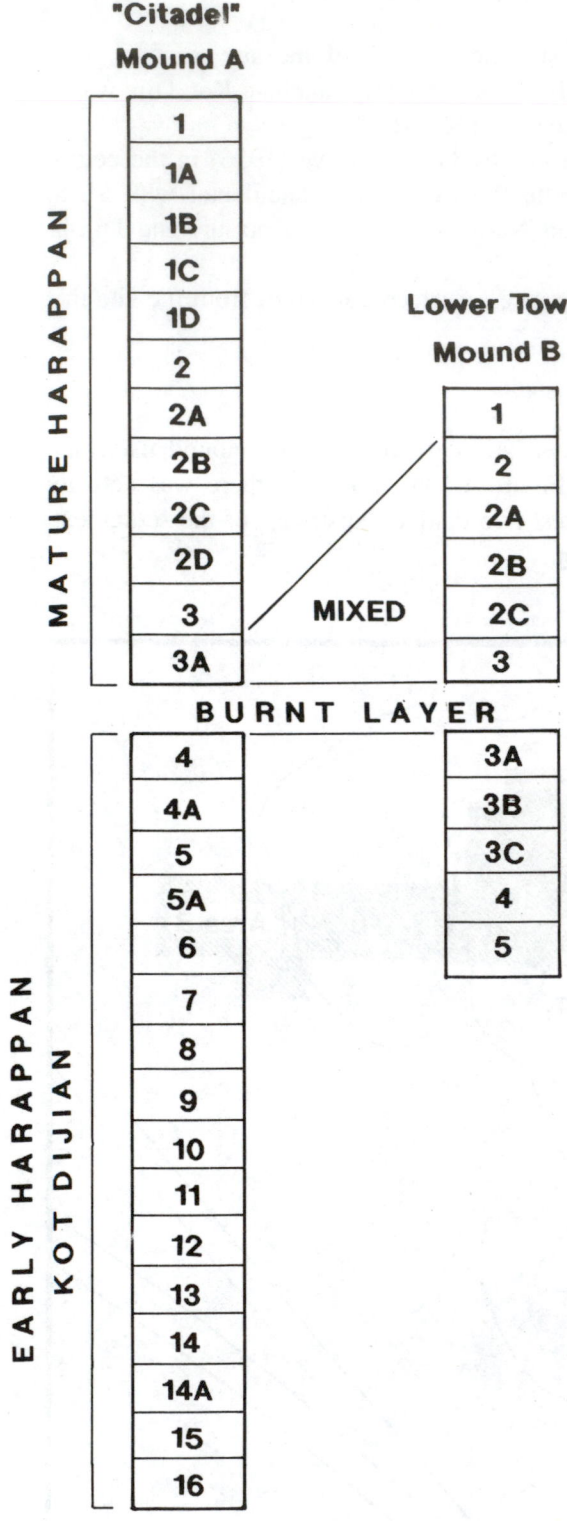

Figure 4.136. Mughal's reconciliation of the Kot Diji stratigraphy, after Mughal 1970

The stratigraphy of Kot Diji is complex and the best reconciliation of the situation is the one proposed by M. Rafique Mughal (1970: 52, Figure 4.136). There are two periods separated by a burnt level. The burning was found everywhere and represents a large scale conflagration which seems to have enveloped and destroyed the entire settlement. The "mixed levels" present another interpretative problem.

There is no information on the subsistence regime at Kot Diji.

The Kot Diji Occupation

Deep digging in a very small area on the south side of a trench in Area A reached virgin soil (F. A. Khan 1965: 28) and documents the first Kot Diji settlement at the site. The finds included typical Kot Diji pottery and structures with stone foundations and mud brick superstructures. A wall around the settlement was an early feature of the settlement, apparently associated with the second occupational stratum (no. 15) (F. A. Khan 1965: 28). There is a wide drain lined with small stone blocks associated with stratum (7). This "...goes right over the fortification wall" (F. A. Khan 1965: 26), as shown in F. A. Khan 1965, Plate VII. The wall was no longer a feature of the settlement and had been built over by Kot Diji structures. Stratum (7) also had several well preserved fireplaces, some of which were associated with a brick paving. The upper levels of the Kot Diji occupation are characterized by buildings with solid stone foundations and mud brick superstructures. This was high quality work. Plain mud brick walls are in evidence as well. With the exception of the circumvallation, significant differences in architecture between Areas A and B were not noted.

The Kot Diji Circumvallation

At least a portion of Kot Diji was surrounded by a wall for the time between strata (15) and (8). This was referred to as a "Defensive Wall" or a "fortification" in the report (F. A. Khan

1965: 26 and 29). It is a significant structure, but using this nomenclature indicates a certain predilection for the function of the feature. I prefer the more neutral term "circumvallation," leaving open the possibility that it was a fortification. (Plate 4.43, Plate 4.44).

Circumvallations are constructed around settlements for many reasons other than defense. They tend to mark the limit of settlement, and in the case of Kot Diji seemingly would have set off Area A from Area B. At Kot Diji, the circumvallation would have acted as a revetment, containing and supporting the internal habitation of the site, allowing the stratigraphy to build up inside the wall. This artificial elevation would have increased the field of view from inside the settlement. Walls of this sort are useful in regulating the comings and goings of men and animals in day-to-day business, especially securing a settlement at night, so the cows do not get out and the lions in. They are also good for show, marking the location of a special settlement. Floods at Kot Diji in the third millennium BC do not seem to be part of the regime of the Indus River, but are not impossible. These kinds of walls do not always have a single purpose and all of these functions, along with some protection from assault, may have been served by a single facility.

The Kot Diji Ceramics

The Kot Diji Phase pottery from Kot Diji is shown in Figure 4.137. The vessels from the lower levels are rather austere, but the fabrics are very fine and clean and the surfaces well finished, giving them an elegant quality. The fish scale pattern on the small pot in Figure 4.138, is significant since that motif is important during Mature Harappan times. It comes from stratum (3), Trench BV/6, one of the mixed layers of Area B. The "Horned Deity", on the pot (Plate 4.45) is one of the most famous objects from the prehistoric period in Pakistan. It too, comes from Trench BV/6, stratum (3A) just under the fish scale pot. The shape of this vessel carries over into Mature Harappan times and the Horned Headdress is one of the important themes in the iconography of those times as well.

Small Finds of the Kot Diji Occupation

The Kot Diji occupation was poor in minor antiquities (F. A. Khan 1965: 31). The most numerous were finely made flint blades, sometimes retouched into small micro-implements. Terracotta toys, plain and painted bangles, cakes, cones and beads were found (F. A. Khan 1965: 31). One copper/bronze bangle is associated with this occupation (F. A. Khan 1965: 38).

The Burned Level at Kot Diji

The end of the Kot Diji occupation is coincident with signs of massive burning at the site. F. A. Khan noted it this way: "A thick deposit of burnt and charred material, on top of layer (4) spreading over the entire site, completely sealed the lower levels from the upper ones" (F. A. Khan 1965: 22). Large scale burning has also been documented at Amri (Casal 1964a: 7) and Nausharo (Jarrige 1989: 64-5) at the historical junction of the Early Harappan/Mature Harappan Transition.

Kot Diji: Summary

Kot Diji is an extraordinary site. It occupies a strategic position on the Indus Plains, on the more lightly settled eastern side of the valley. It superbly documents the Kot Diji Phase in upper Sindh, and played an important role in the definition of the Early Harappan (Mughal 1970). There is scope for further work at the site which would offer an opportunity to gain some information on the subsistence regime.

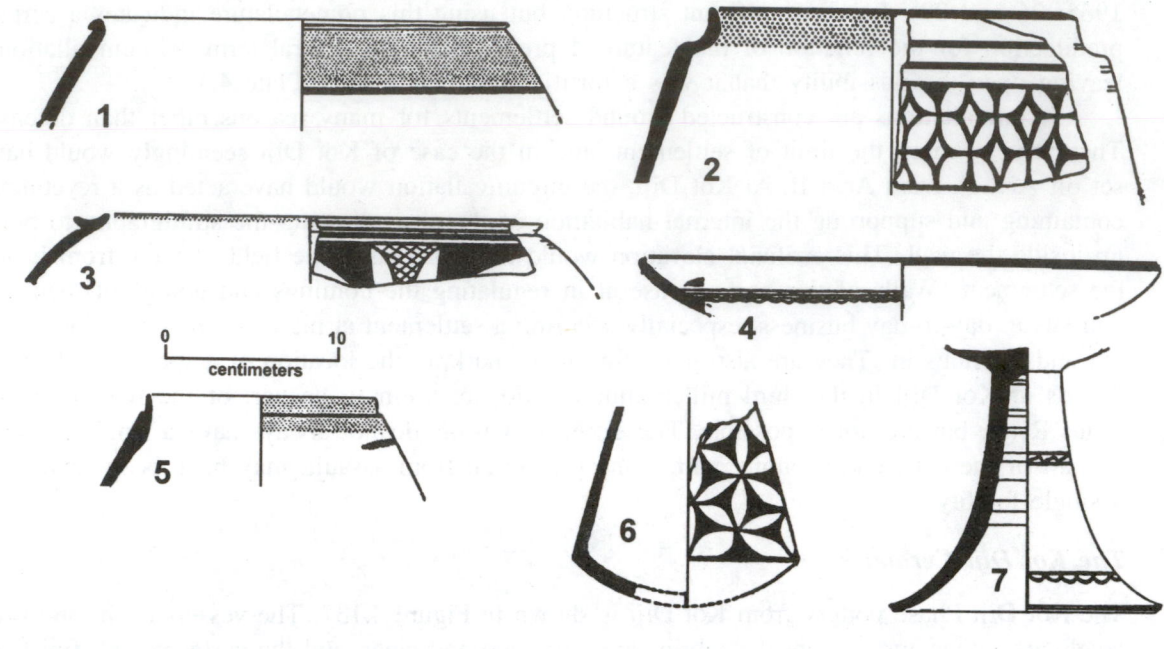

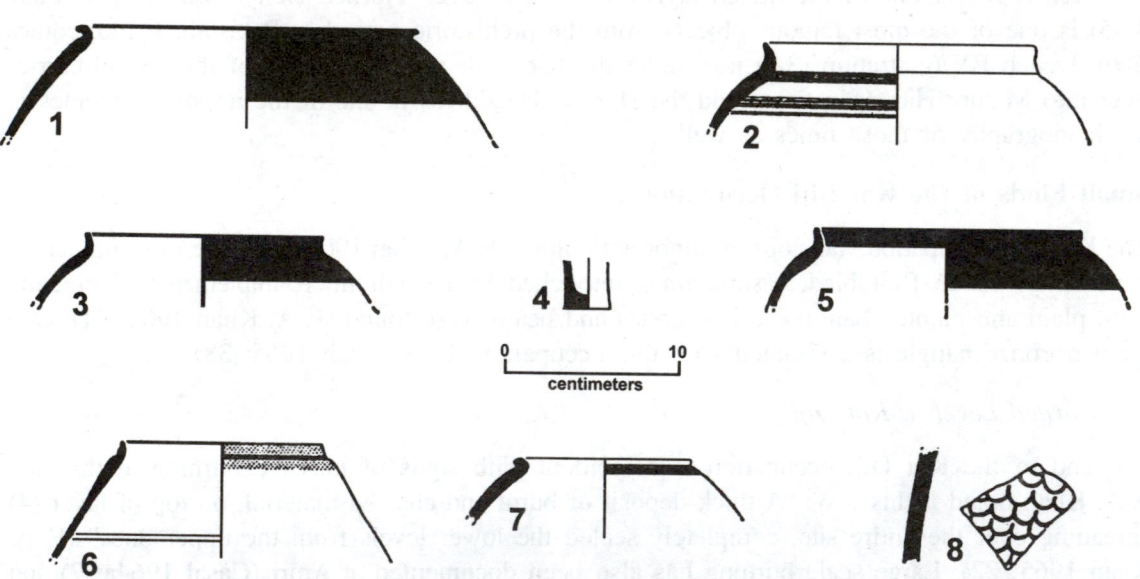

Figure 4.137. Pottery from Period I at Kot Diji, after F. A. Khan 1965.

Rehman Dheri: Introduction

The very important site of Rehman Dheri was discovered by Professor A. H. Dani in the course of his 1970-71 exploration of the Gomal Valley (Dani 1970-71: 28-31). The site is twenty-three kilometers northwest of Dera Ismail Khan, just off the main road to Bannu. Rehman Dheri was a large settlement and in a splendid state of preservation, but Dani's work at Gumla and Hathala did not allow him to undertake excavation at the time of discovery. This was left to his colleague in the University of Peshawar, Professor Farzand A. Durrani who excavated there for five

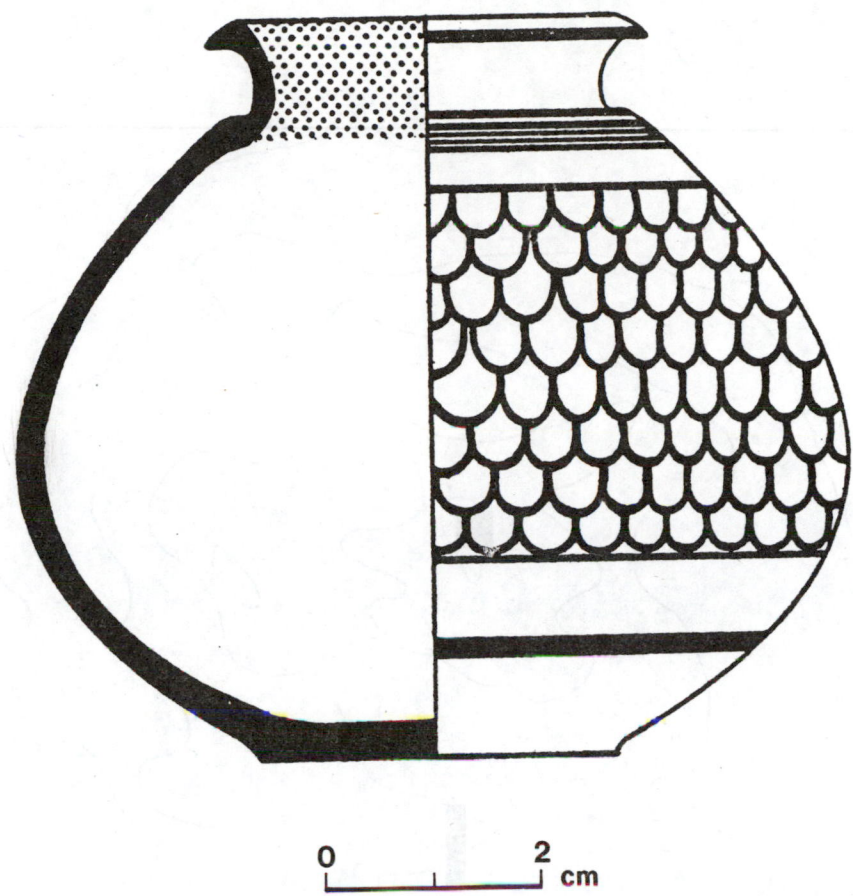

0   2
           cm

Figure 4.138. Fish scale motif from Kot Diji, after F. A. Khan 1965

consecutive seasons (1976-80). The 1976 and 1977 seasons were the largest, with the three remaining seasons confined to very limited work. Durrani was able to renew the excavations at Rehman Dheri in 1991.

The Excavation

The accompanying site plan (Figure 4.139) shows the location of Durrani's trenches at Rehman Dheri. It is useful to gain a sense of the scale of his work there.

The settlement circumvallation was found in its best state in the southernmost set of trenches, Area A. It was preserved only in the Period IB occupation, apparently having been eroded away in Periods II and III. It is four feet wide (1.2 meters) but sits on a six foot (1.8 meters) wide footing. The wall was built of large clay slabs, set in place and carefully trimmed (Durrani 1988: 26, Pl. XIVa).

Period I: Kot Diji Phase

The first two occupations of Rehman Dheri have been assigned to the Kot Diji Phase. Period I has been divided into two sub-units designated A and B (Durrani 1988: 27-8). This differentiation does not prohibit these remains from being discussed as a unit. The excavations into this period are somewhat restricted, given the overburden of the later two periods. But individual rooms were found, defined by walls formed from mud slabs. Based on ethnographic observations these slabs or blocks were taken from dried up water sources and formed into house walls

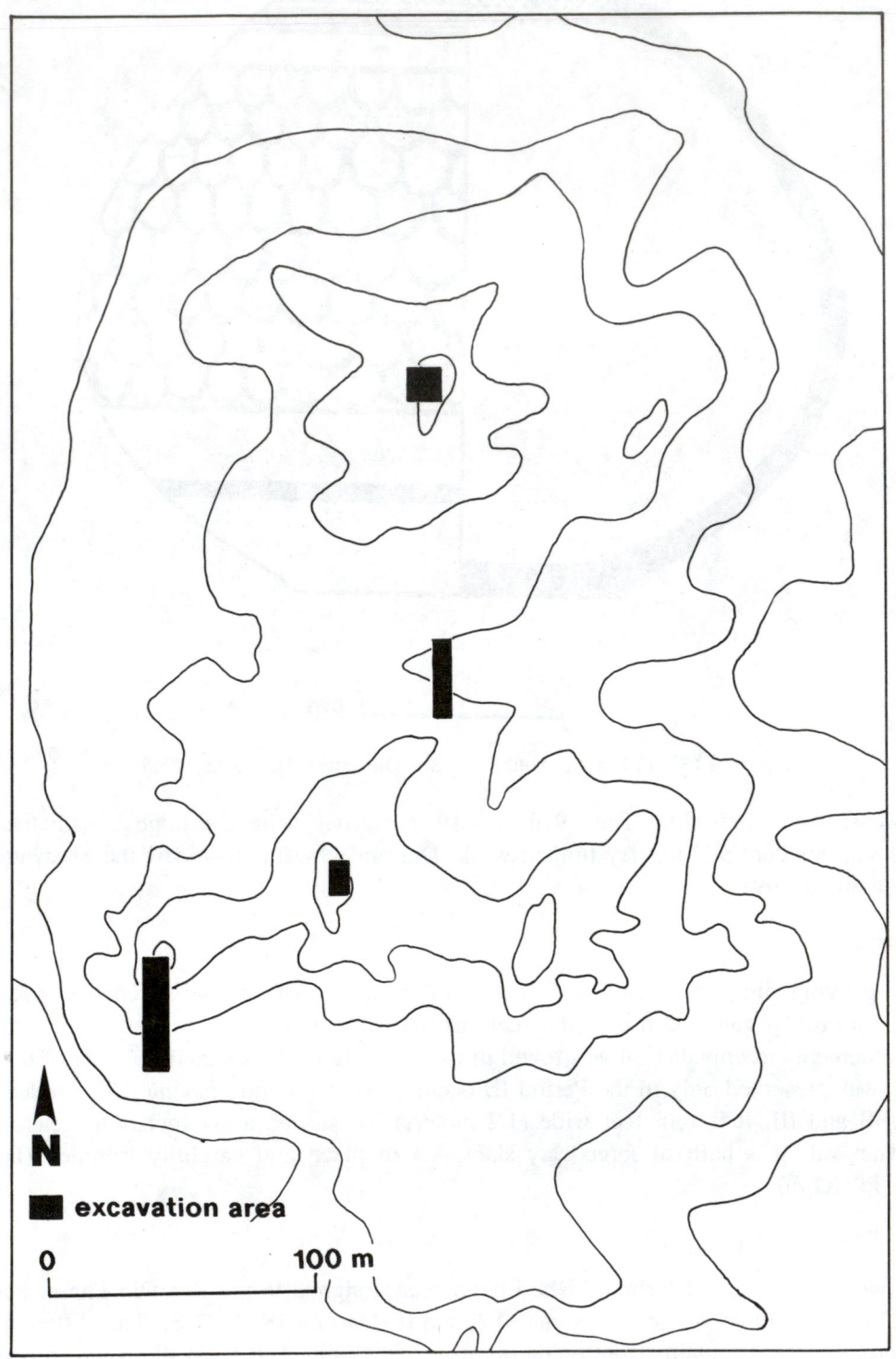

Figure 4.139. Site plan of Rehman Dheri, after Durrani 1988: Figure A

(Durrani 1988: 26). This is an unusual form of construction, not noted elsewhere in the Greater Indus Region. The walls that were found here seem to run either parallel or at right angles to the settlement wall. Both grain silos and hearths were found in these rooms. The hearths were of two types: circular and rectilinear. A unique ivory pendant (already discussed), was found in Period IB (Durrani 1988: 28).

Period II: Kot Diji Phase

The architecture of Period II shows signs of continuity out of Period I. The grain silos seem to disappear, to be replaced in function by large storage jars. Evidence for the construction of large, mud platforms is present. The ceramics could be characterized as classic Kot Diji pots.

Subsistence Information

The Peshawar team made good efforts, including the use of flotation, to collect palaeobotanical and faunal remains from Rehman Dheri. These are undergoing full analysis at the Institute of Archaeology, University of London. As a preliminary statement it can be said that wheat (*Triticum* sp.) and barley (*Hordeum* sp.) were the predominant food grains at the site. In Period IA, wheat seems to be the important grain, but in Period IIIA it was barley (Durrani 1988: 28, 30). Seeds from wild grasses are also reported in the preliminary statement (Durrani 1988: 27-30).

Cattle, sheep and goats are consistently reported for each period, which is to be expected. In addition, the remains of fish and birds are mentioned and in Period IIIB, the final occupation, they are said to have been abundant (Durrani 1988: 27-30). Some mention of wild animals is also made which, with the bird and fish remains, suggests a mixed subsistence economy that may have drawn on wild resources in a relatively consistent way.

Gumla

Professor A. H. Dani of the University of Peshawar conducted one brief season of excavation at the mound of Gumla, about eight miles northwest of Dera Ismail Khan, just to the west of the Indus River, as part of his 1970-71 exploration of the Gomal Valley. It is a very small site, 110 × 65 meters or 0.7 hectares, and about three meters high (Figure 4.140). It has a long sequence of habitation, with six occupations:

> VI: Gandhara Graves
> V: "Destruction" and Grave Circles
> IV: Late Kot Diji
> III: Kot Diji
> II: Kechi Beg
> I: Kili Ghul Mohammad

This may seem an odd place to take the reader back to the Kili Ghul Mohammad Phase, but a short review of the Gumla sequence follows. This is being done here for two reasons. First, it is always good to present materials from sites together, as a site unit. Moreover, it serves a good purpose at this point to use Gumla as an example of the depth and continuity of life in the Greater Indus Region, and Gumla offers this as a reminder to the reader. No materials from the Burj Basket-marked or Togau Phases is there, but it may be yet to come.

A good start for understanding the site has come from the Dani excavations but they have certainly not exploited its full potential, especially for the beginnings of food production and domestication in the Subcontinent.

644

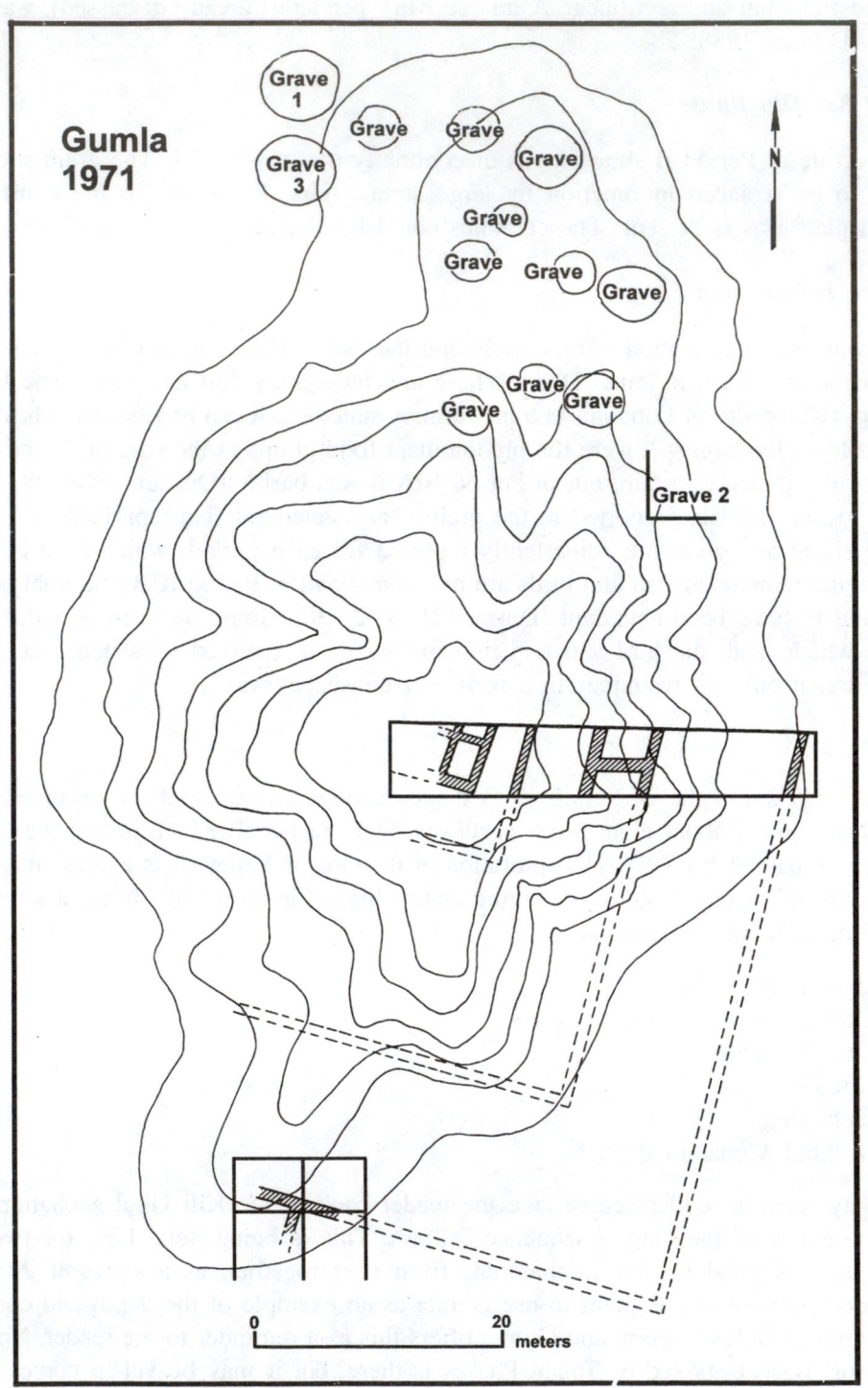

Figure 4.140. Site plan of Gumla, after Dani 1970-71: Figure 4

The Excavation

The excavation proceeded in two localities on the southern side of the mound. There was one large square of four contiguous trenches each 20 feet on a side. A second trench 20 × 80 feet was used to explore the eastern slope and in addition, two circular graves were excavated on the northern end. Dani (1970-71: 39-40) has proposed a six period occupational scheme for Gumla, with Periods V and VI being very superficial.

Gumla I: Kili Ghul Mohammad Phase

The first occupation of Gumla was made by people who did not use pottery (Dani 1970-71: 39, 41-2). Microlithic tools (Dani 1970-71: 95-6) and ground stone food processing tools are present. Hearths, or "community ovens" were also found. Animal bones are mentioned briefly in the report, but have not been identified, although one cattle bone is specifically mentioned (Dani 1970-71: 41). No radiocarbon dates are available for this occupation at Gumla. The general character of the occupation, especially the sense of semipermanent occupation and ground stone, suggests that Dani's assessment of Gumla I as "Neolithic" is probably correct.

Since this was preliminary work, and the University of Peshawar does not have specialists to deal with faunal and floral remains, Dani's discovery can be considered an important one. New excavation at Gumla needs to be done to exploit Dani's initial finds.

A preliminary assessment of the occupation at Gumla indicates that it is like those at Kili Ghul Mohammad I in the Quetta Valley and Mehrgarh I on the Kachi Plain. It is a period that is reasonably well known in some respects at Mehrgarh, but it is poorly dated. Moreover, very few sites of this Phase are known and the probable presence of a Kili Ghul Mohammad occupation at Gumla assumes some additional importance.

Gumla II: Kechi Beg Phase

No architecture was found in Period II at Gumla, but large "hearths" are present. A substantial amount of very well made ceramics was recovered. These fit into the general Kechi Beg classification (Figure 4.141). Dani also mentions the appearance of new kinds of microliths, bone tools, human figurines, bull figurines, wheels, bangles and gamesmen along with copper based metallurgy (1970-71: 42). Ground stone food processing tools are also present. The human figurines are terracotta and generally identifiable as female. They are the type with the exaggerated legs placed together and pulled to a footless point at the end.

There was a small amount of handmade pottery in stratum (11), the lowest levels assigned to this Phase, from which two radiocarbon dates were taken, but this can be seen as a part of the Kechi Beg assemblage. Dani's thought that there is therefore a break between Periods I and II is probably right (1970-71: 39) and in the scheme being used here it would have involved both the Burj Basket-marked and Togau Phases.

Gumla III: Kot Diji Phase

There is an easy, gradual transition between Periods II and III at Gumla. The ceramic inventory of Period III is clearly that of the mature Kot Diji Phase type, although the portion of the site where this period was recovered yielded a significantly smaller number of artifacts than Period II (Figure 4.142).

Fragments of mud brick (size: 11 × 5 × 2 1/2 inches) architecture were recovered, but no complete building plans are available.

A wide range of other implements is present, including three copper (bronze?) artifacts,

646

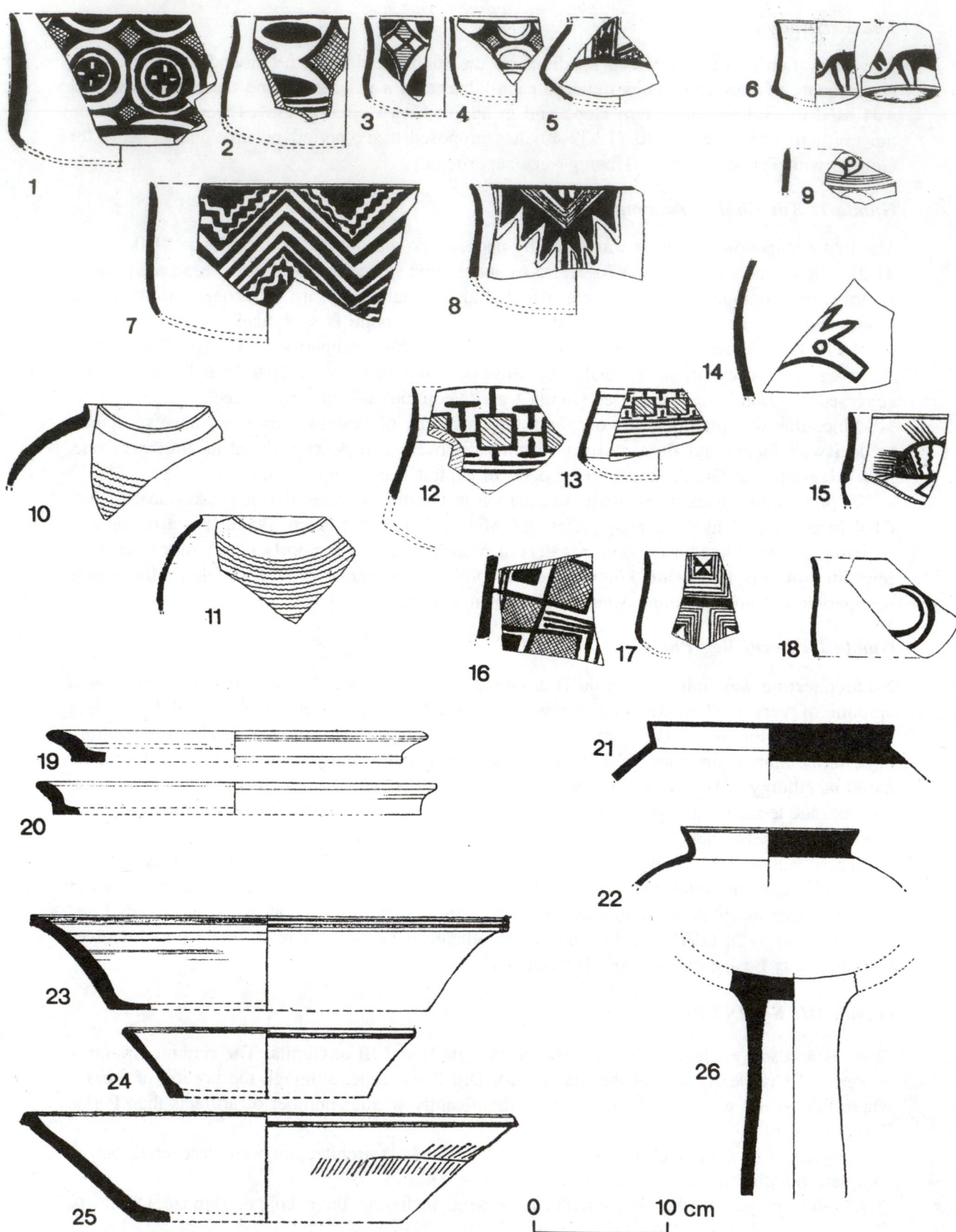

Figure 4-141. Pottery from Gumla II, Kechi Beg Phase, after Dani 1970-71: Figures 11-18

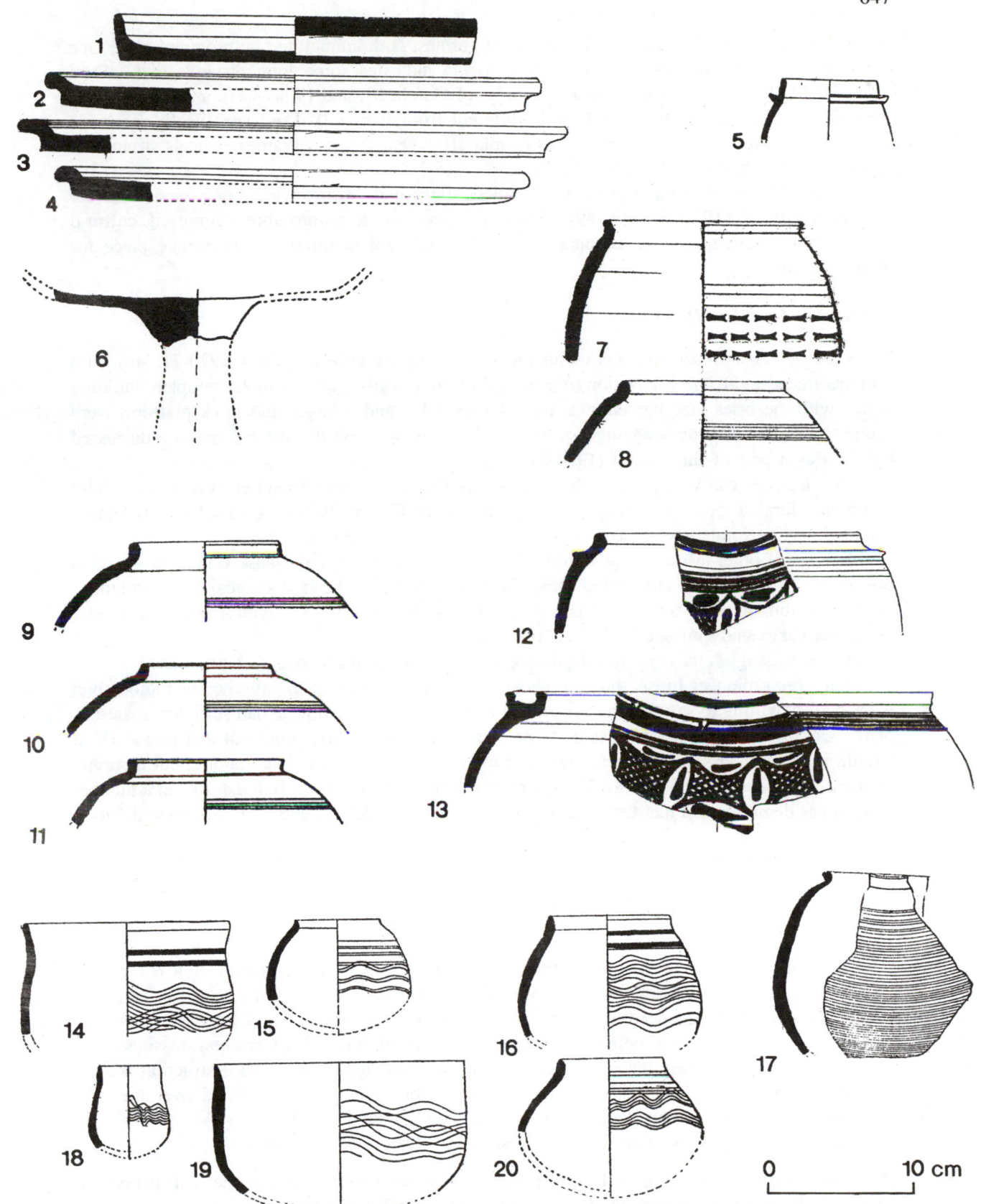

Figure 4.142. Gumla III ceramics, Kot Diji Phase, after Dani 1970-71: Figures 19-24.

beads, bangles, ground and chipped stone and figurines, both animal and anthropomorphic. One conch bangle from the sea shell *Turbinella pyrum* indicates some long distance trade (Dani 1970-71: Pl. 43, no. 11). The terracotta females of Gumla III, and IV as well, are the flat type, bent at the waist, and sitting erect; quite different from Period II. Dani specifically mentions that the following were not part of the Gumla III inventory: cart frames, wheels, triangular terracotta cakes and missiles (1970-71: 45).

Period III seems to have come to a violent, fiery end, with an ash layer separating the two occupations (1970-71: 39, 49). There is, however, a remarkable degree of cultural continuity between these two occupations and it must kept in mind that fires take place for many reasons.

Gumla IV: Late Kot Diji Phase

"This is the most flourishing period in the life of Gumla village" (Dani 1970-71: 46) with remains traced in all the excavation trenches. Mud brick walls, again without complete building plans, with the brick size the same as that of Period III, and a large mud brick platform were found. A few baked bricks, again 11 × 5 × 2 1/2 inches, were on the surface, and are discussed by Dani as a part of this period (1970-71: 47).

The ceramics can be classed with the Late Kot Diji assemblage found elsewhere, especially in Bannu (Tarakai Qila, Lewan), just to the north of the Gomal Plain (Figure 4.143). At Gumla this includes perforated ware, akin to Urban Phase Harappan types.

A range of other artifacts that would be associated with the Urban Phase Harappan was also discovered in Gumla IV. Dani notes these: an etched carnelian bead, a cubical stone weight, a faience button or seal, steatite ("paste") disk beads, toy cart frames with wheels, triangular terracotta cakes and "missiles" (1970-71: 47-8).

A conch bangle and lapis lazuli provide some information on long distance trade.

Dani was a pioneer in his thinking about this material. Even in the absence of radiocarbon dates he was willing to say that this essentially Kot Diji Phase assemblage had sufficient materials of the Urban Phase Harappan to state: "The above materials clearly point out that period IV at Gumla is more or less contemporary with the main phase of the Harappan culture, but there are regional variations" (1970-71: 48). The systematic collection of radiocarbon dates from a number of sites has demonstrated that Dani was right. (Thomas and Allchin 1986; see also Possehl 1984).

Gumla V: "Destruction" and Grave Circles

Dani asserts that the end of Period IV and the beginning of Period V was a time of great violence at Gumla:

> In Period IV the evidence of...destruction is met with all over the mound. Below the humus of the present time the top layers all over represent burning, the scatter of ash and charcoal and the destruction of walls together with the smashing of huge amounts of the material objects including pottery of all types of period IV, terracotta missiles, triangular cakes, sling balls and other various sizes of stone balls. The destruction is writ large on the surface of the mound. The debris are widely scattered over the demolished walls. Who destroyed these walls and houses? We have no evidence of any structural construction after this destruction (Dani 1970-71: 49-50).

Dani associated at least some of the circle graves at the northern end of the site with Period VI. This has allowed it to provisionally be called "Late Kot Diji II."

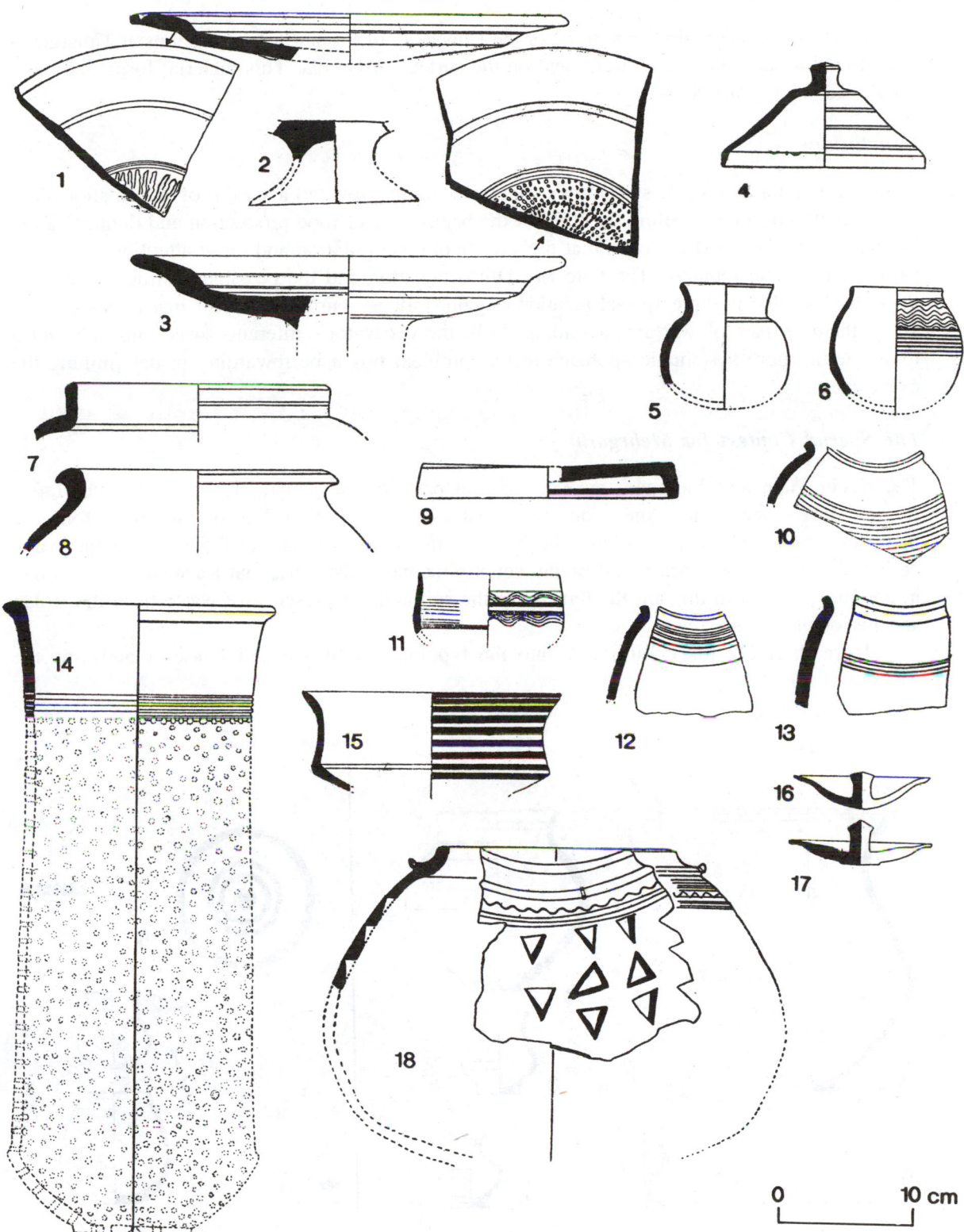

Figure 4.143. Pottery from Gumla IV, Late Kot Diji, after Dani 1970-71: Figures 25-36

0   10 cm

Gumla VI: Gandharan Grave Culture

A few sherds of pottery similar to those of the University of Peshawar's excavations at Timargarha were found around the grave circles and on the surface of Gumla. This material forms the basis for Period VI (Figure 4.144).

Conclusions

Although Gumla is a small site, Dani's trial excavations provided a wealth of information. It is clearly important in unraveling the story of the beginnings of food production and domestication in South Asia. The next excavation at the site should use flotation and close attention should be paid to the faunal remains. The Late Kot Diji occupation and the possible destruction level at the end of it also deserve special mention. Again, villages burn for a great many reasons, not all of them as part of warfare or raiding. Still, the excavator's inference was emphatic and a longer term, more systematic approach to this problem might be rewarding in determining the exact cause.

The Special Context for Mehrgarh

The Kachi Plain and Mehrgarh are very special parts of the geography of the Greater Indus Region during the Indus Age. The Bloam Pass was an extraordinarily important route in prehistoric times. Other passes, like the Mula to the west, the Nari to the east and the many defiles into what is now Marri and Bughti country increased the sense that Kachi was a crossroad in antiquity. Added to this are the fertility of the soil and the presence of water from the Bolan and the other rivers.

Mehrgarh rarely fits comfortably into the typology of Stages and Phases that forms the

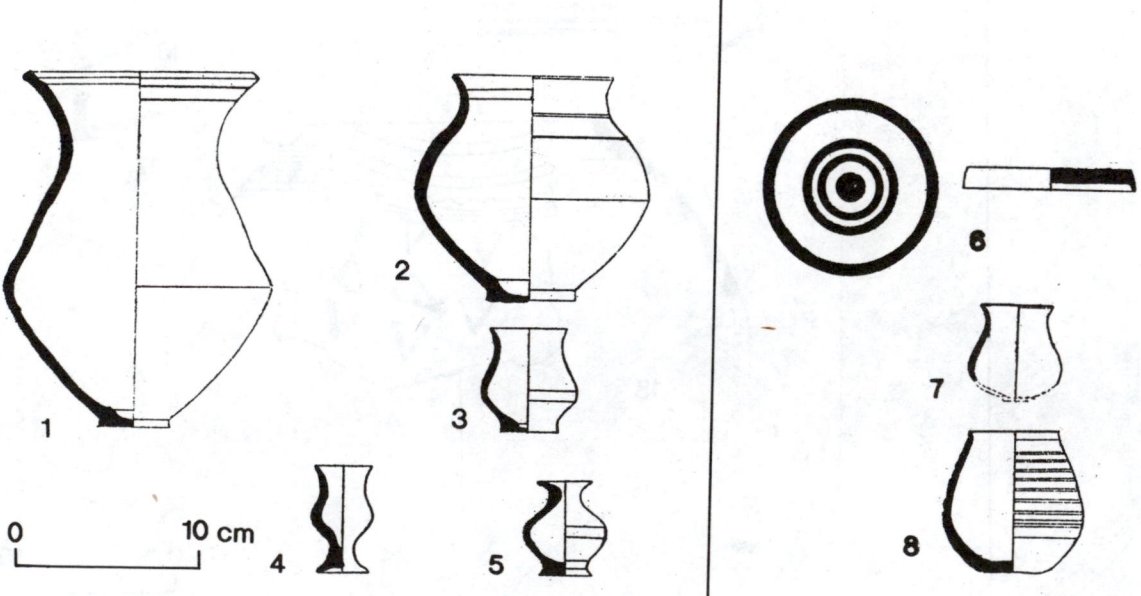

Figure 4.144. Grave pottery from Gumla, after Dani 1970-71: Figure 37

outline structure for the chronology of the Indus Age. The early Phases are certainly a better fit with the chronological scheme used in this book than are the later ones. This poorness of fit is due to the fact that Mehrgarh was always a frontier settlement of sorts, placed at the nexis of overalpping geographical, ecological and cultural spheres.

By the Early Harappan the fit with my scheme is very poor, and the notion that Mehrgarh is a Kot Dijian site, just like Kot Diji, is not a valid one. Rather than create a separate Phase for Mehrgarh alone, which may have some validity, it was decided to admit a measure of flexibility in the scheme and place Mehrgarh where it is, with this reminder that it seems to be in some ways a unique place, in others ways a blending of Phases with much material from the Damb Sadaat Phase, for example.

Jalilpur

Introduction

Jalilpur is a small Punjabi village with a large Early Harappan site. Located 75 kilometers southwest of Harappa, only five kilometers from the modern course of the Ravi River, the low, rolling mound covers an area of approximately 13 hectares (425 × 305 meters). It was excavated in 1971 by M. Rafique Mughal of the Pakistan Department of Archaeology (Mughal 1972b, 1974b). There was also a small field season in 1975 that is unpublished. Materials collected in 1963 indicated that it had Kot Diji pottery, related to the Pre-Defense levels at Harappa. Since almost nothing was known of these materials Mughal decided to excavate Jalilpur. It also turns out that Jalilpur has an earlier period which is related to the Hakra Wares Phase in Bahawalpur. Sites of this type were not defined until Mughal's survey there between 1974 and 1978, so he could not have known the significance of Jalilpur I in his preliminary report or when he was excavating the site. Jalilpur represents the only excavated site with Hakra Wares. Thus, in spite of the small scale of the work, Jalilpur has considerable importance for understanding the Early Harappan and Hakra Wares Phases.

The Excavation

In 1971 the excavation team worked for approximately two months, May and June, under what must have been trying conditions in the pre-monsoon hot weather. As can be seen from the plan (Figure 4.145), two sets of trenches were laid near the center of the mound. These were labeled Trench I & II and Trench A & B. The latter exposure was 56 × 60 feet (17 × 18 meters) and reduced to 46 × 10 feet (14 × 3 meters) as the digging progressed downward (Mughal 1972b: 118). A small trench C was also excavated, producing only Period II remains.

Period I

Period I was revealed as three strata, without architecture. Some mud brick and evidence for a floor laid on lime *kankar* did come to light, however. The pottery seems to be largely Hakra Wares, especially the so-called "Hakra Mud Applique." Many of the sherds are soft and broken into very small pieces making vessel forms difficult to reconstruct (Plate 4.46).

The material inventory included terracotta barrel shaped beads and net sinkers, chert blades (not the typical Hakra Wares microliths), a perforated gold sheet, but no copper. There was also a rich bone tool industry (Mughal 1972b: 119).

Period II

The transition from Period I to Period II at Jalilpur is not abrupt. There is a gradual change in

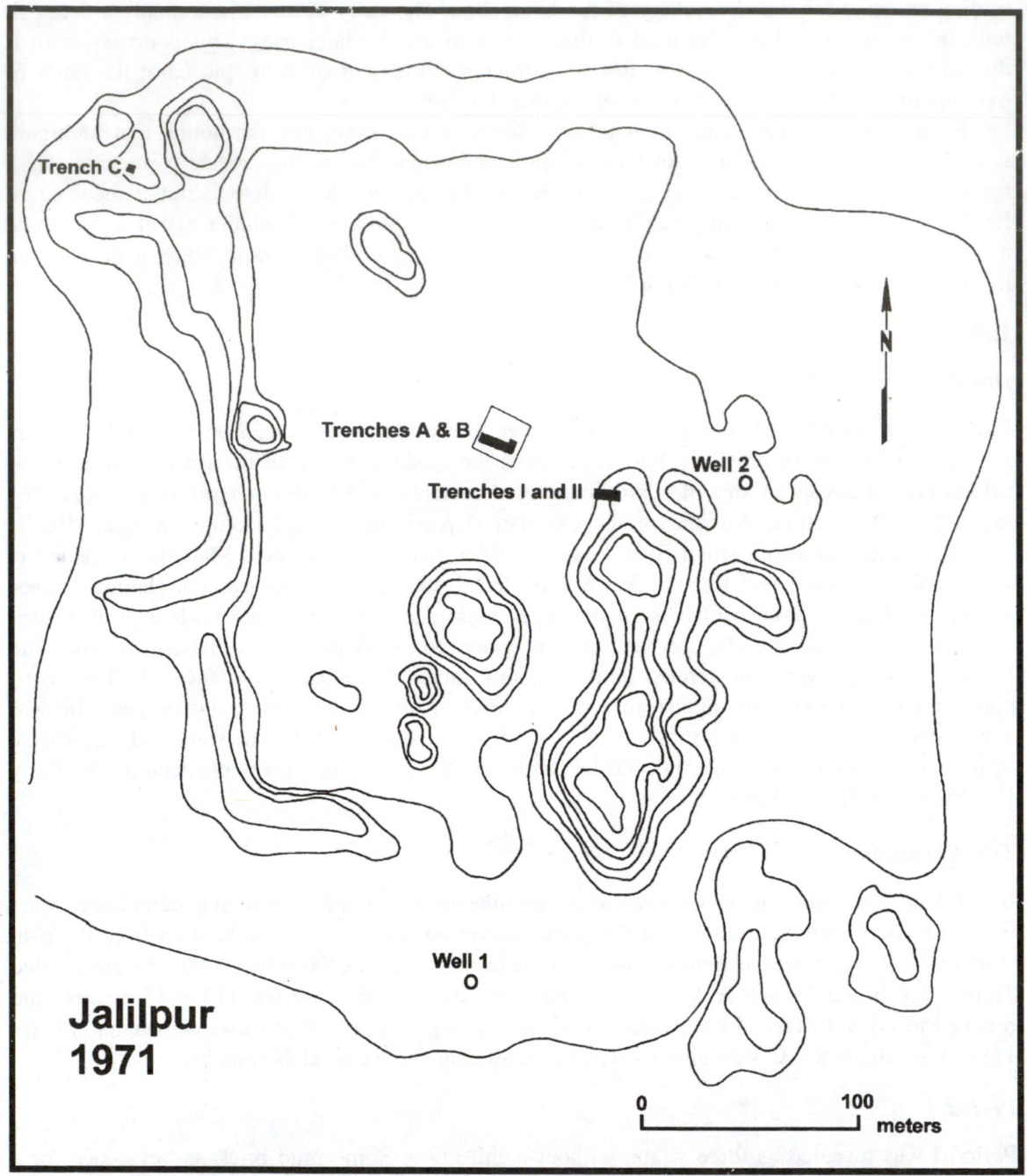

Figure 4.145. Plan of Jalilpur, after Mughal 1972b: Figure 36

the ceramic inventory. For example, there is a small amount of plain red slipped wares or those painted with black and brown or chocolate on red in Period I. These increase in number into Period II. Some Hakra Mud Applique also persists through Period II. But, the predominant ceramic in the second occupation is a fine, wheel made red ware fashioned into typical Kot Diji shapes, including those with the Kot Diji Phase Rim, flange rim jars, Bhoot Ware and the like. White in-painting of designs and bichrome wares also occur with some frequency. (Figure 4.146, Plate 4.47, Plate 4.48).

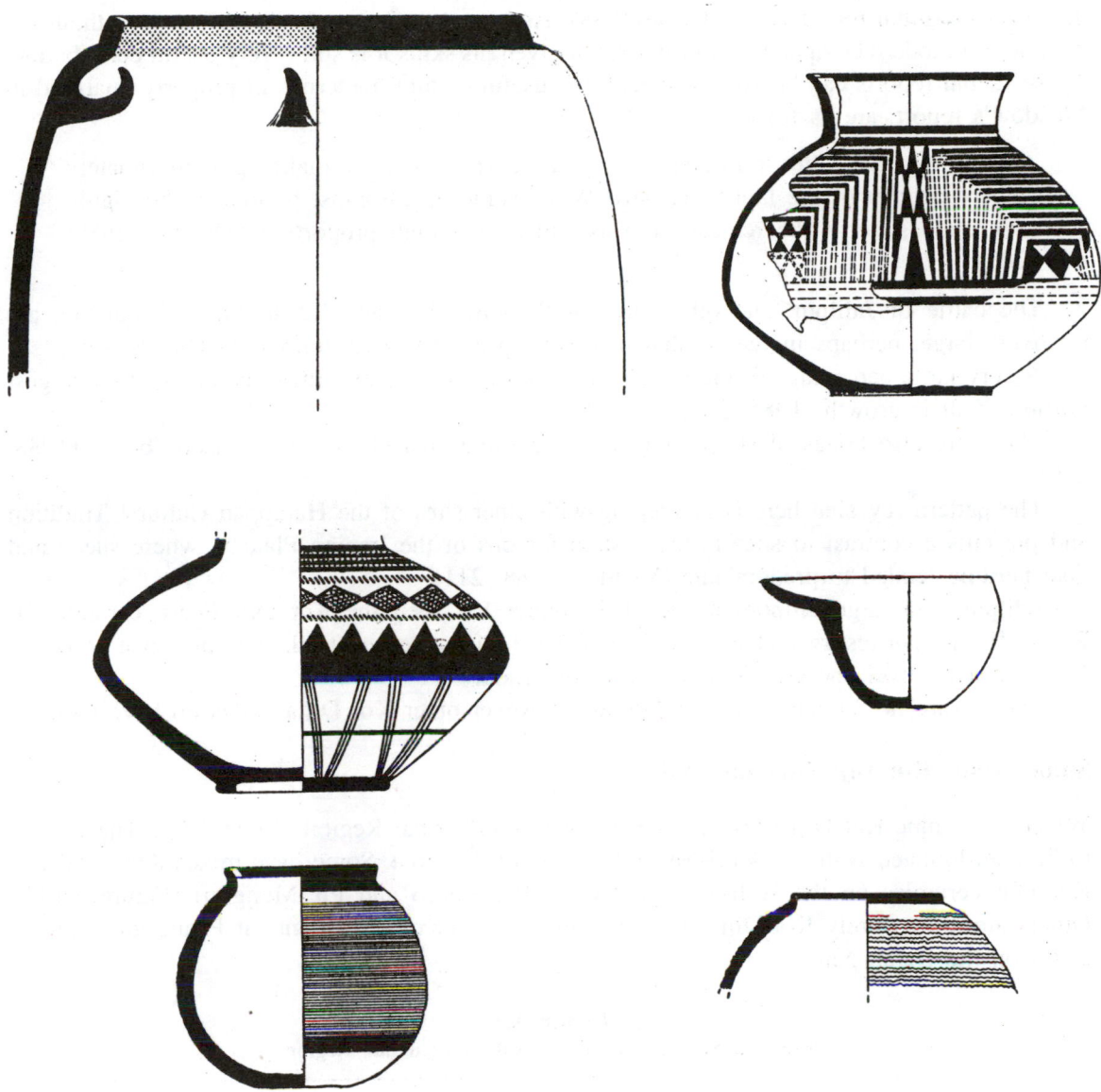

Figure 4.146. Pottery from Jalilpur II, after Mughal 1972b: Figure 37

Two structures of mud brick and mud lumps were recorded in Period II. Mughal isolated two different building periods here and speaks of Periods IIA and IIB on this basis. The material culture, is however, homogenous (1972b: 121).

The material inventory of Jalilpur II includes triangular terracotta cakes, toy cart frames, cart wheels, human figurines, bull figurines; bangles (both grey and red), other bangles of faience and shell; beads of terracotta, agate and carnelian; pestles, saddle querns, copper pieces, including a rod, and chipped stone, some with sickle sheen (?). The human figurines are comparable to those from Gumla II and III and Sarai Khola II (Mughal 1972b: 124) (Plate 4.49).

Subsistence Information

There is no palaeobotanical material reported from Jalilpur; however, Richard Meadow has given a substantial report on the fauna (1988). As he notes, this analysis was made without the benefit of a modern comparative collection, but given his skills it is still a very useful contribution. These faunal reports can be very technical; the useful cultural patterns, all properly qualified in Meadow's report, are as follows:

> Large mammals, almost all undoubtedly cattle, (*Bos indicus*), make up approximately ninety percent of the faunal remains. While some of this must be due to the highly encrusted state of the remains, this is still a very high proportion (Meadow 1988: 207).

The cattle of Jalilpur, and other sites of the Pre-urban and Urban Phase Harappan, are relatively large, perhaps indicating that they were primarily draft animals (1988: 207-08).

A very large percentage of the large mammals were killed after they had attained the largest portion of their growth (1988: 209).

There are also bones of sheep or goat (8), definite goat (1) and two gazelle bones (1988: 210).

The pattern revealed here is in keeping with other sites of the Harappan Cultural Tradition and presents a contrast to sites in the eastern regions of the Iranian Plateau, where sheep and goat herding tended to predominate (Meadow 1988: 211).

Jalilpur is a large, important site. This author has seen the Kot Diji Phase ceramics of Period II and can testify that they are finely made and quite beautiful. The presence of Hakra Wares at a relatively accessible site is also important.

There were no human burials at Jalilpur; however other Kot Dijian sites do have them.

Some Other Kot Diji Sites in Sindh

We know of nine Kot Diji sites in the Sindh Kohistan/Kirthar Region (Table 4.39). These seem to be interdigitated with the Amri-Nal settlements of this area. Some have mixed Amri-Nal and Kot Diji ceramics on the surface (e.g., Khudo Pir, Kotiro and Pir Mungho) (Figure 4.147). Others are more purely Kot Diji, as for example, the pair of settlements at Phang and Kohtras Buthi on the Baran Nai.

TABLE 4.39
Kot Diji Sites in the Sindh Kohistan/Kirthar Region

Site	District
Bamba Damb	Dadu
Diji-ji Tikri	Khairpur
Khudo Pir	Larkana
Kohtras Buthi	Dadu
Kotiro	Larkana
Mungli Damb	Larkana
Phang	Dadu
Rajo-daro One	Dadu
Tupi	Larkana

Kohtras Buthi

Kohtras Buthi is a marvelous settlement, which merits full excavation. It appears to be a single occupation site, without later occupations and it can reasonably be assumed that the architecture

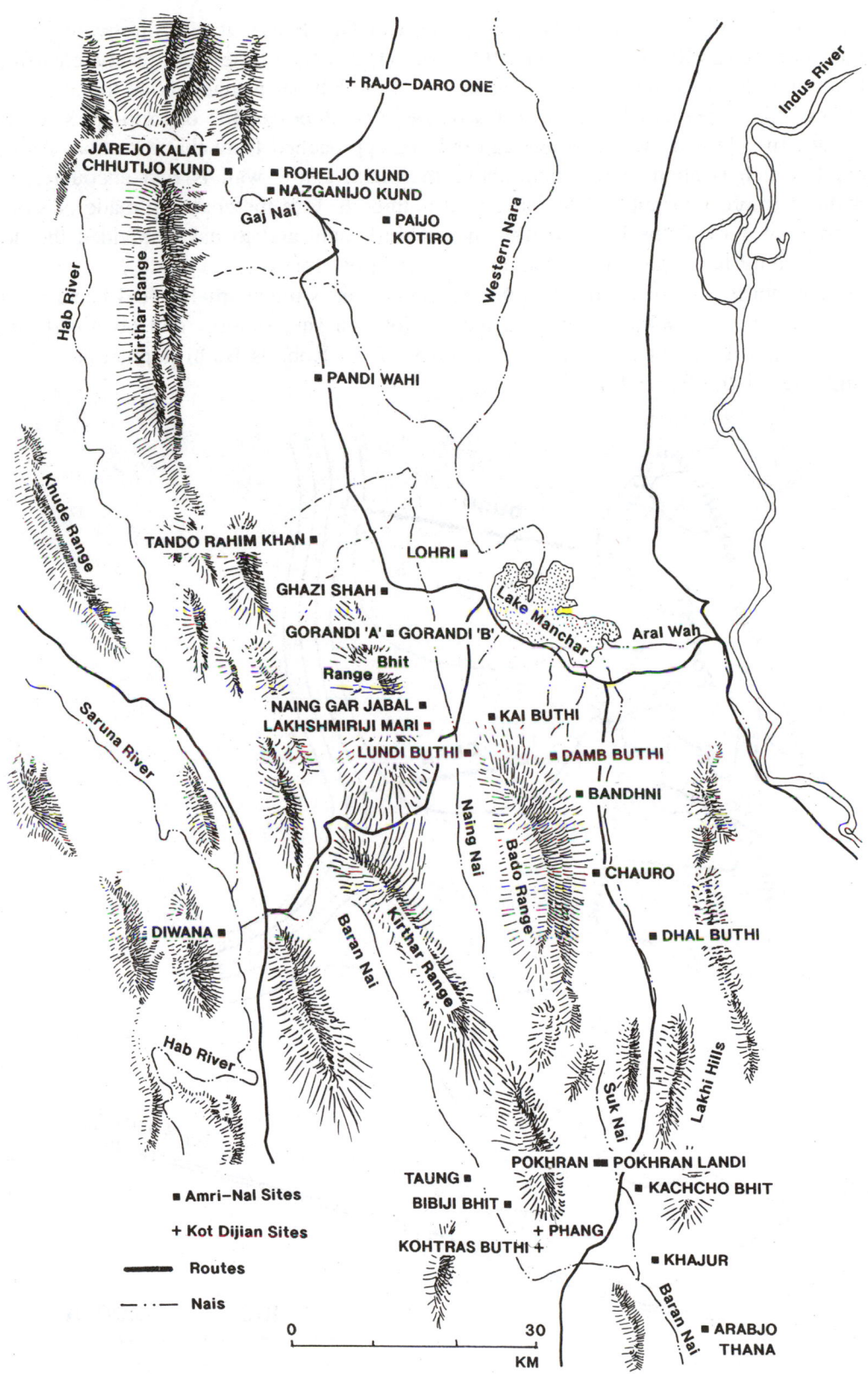

Figure 4.147. Map of the overlap area between Amri-Nal Phase and Kot Diji Phase sites in Sindh

which is still well preserved there belongs to the Kot Diji Phase. It was discovered by N. G. Majumdar in February 1931 (Majumdar 1934: 132-34) at which time he did some clearing. The site sits on an outcrop at the southern-most extent of the Kirthar Range, above the alluvial plain of the Baran Nai, a perennial stream in this region. The slopes of the outcrop are steep except on the southern side and the settlement can only be approached from that direction. Ascending this height, which is about 300 meters above the plain, a low wall is first encountered, then another that is more substantial. The latter wall is three to four meters high, made of stone and appears to have marked the limits of the ancient settlement and to have provided the defense for what can only have been a substantial (10.2 hectares) fort (Figure 4.148).

The neighboring site of Phang, also on the Baran Nai, is much smaller (0.4 hectares) and is associated with a *gabarband*. It too, is a purely Kot Diji site, shallow and obviously of short duration. It could represent a subsidiary settlement of the Kohtras Buthi population, essentially a farming site for the larger fort.

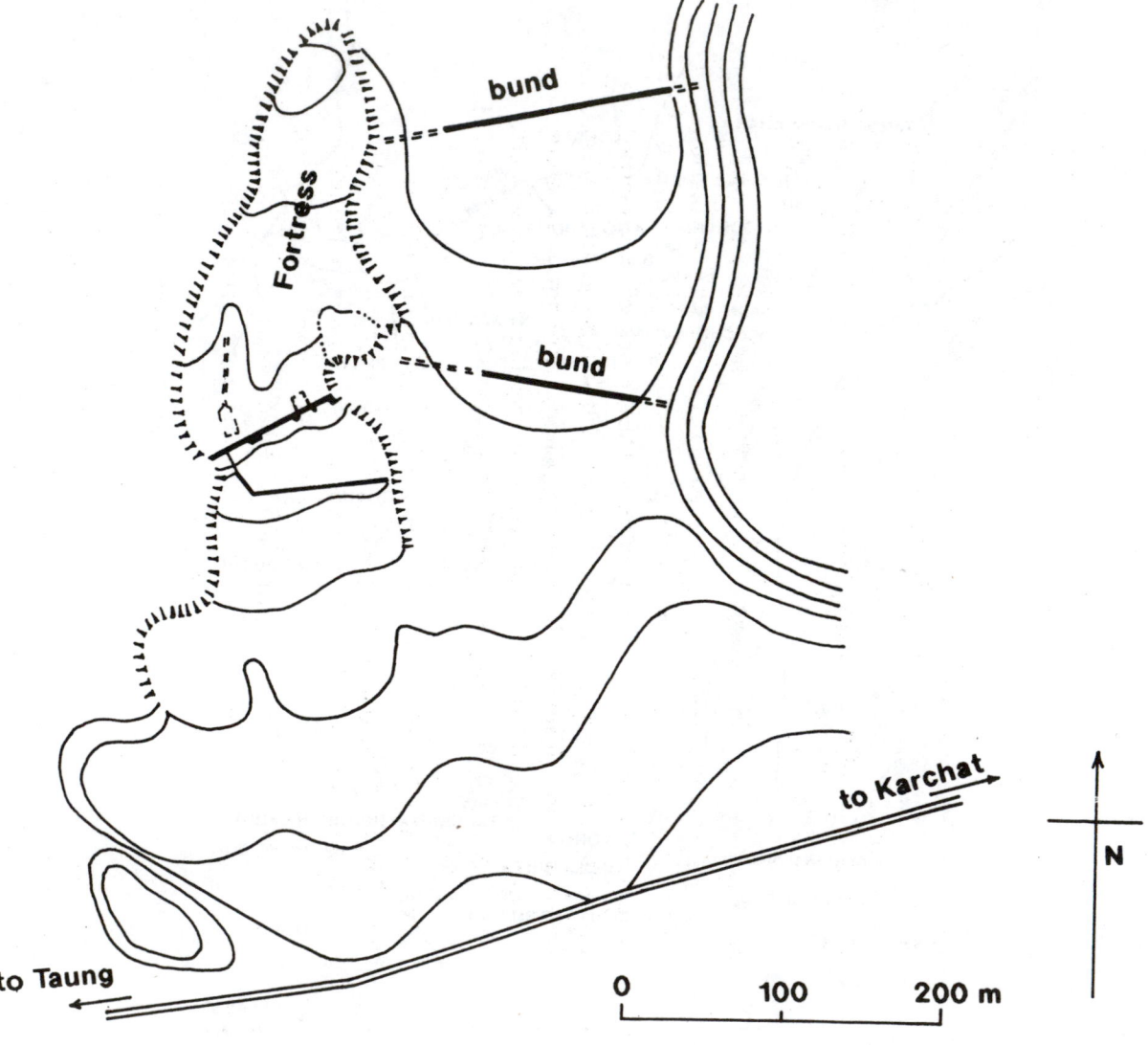

Figure 4.148. Plan of Kohtras Buthi, after Majumdar 1934: Plate XLVI

The historical significance of Kohtras Buthi and Phang are not known, and there is little archaeological midden at either place. It does not seem that either of them had a long period of occupation and they seem to be closely linked in time. Thus, they may well represent a temporary incursion of the peoples of the Kot Diji Phase into the region otherwise occupied by Amri-Nal folk.

The other sites, with the mixed Amri-Nal and Kot Diji pottery on the surface are more likely to have seen day-to-day interaction between the peoples who made and used these ceramics. In some ways the interaction was mundane but it was also a catalyst for trade and exchange; the exchange of young people as spouses, the movement of goods in pots, relevant observations that can be used to explain these mixed archaeological assemblages. The sites are generally so small and shallow that it does not seem likely that there was one relatively "pure" Amri-Nal occupation followed by that of the Kot Diji ceramic users, with everything mixed together on the surface of the modern mound.

Kot Diji Sites in the North

To the north, in the Gomal Valley, Bannu, northern Baluchistan, Waziristan and the northwest Punjab, there are a number of Kot Diji sites: twelve or thirteen in Dera Ismail Khan, four in Bannu, five in Zhob, ten in Loralai and four in the Taxila Valley (Figure 4.149, Figure 4.150). This is the region within which the transhumant symbiosis of the mountains and plains is best expressed in the Kot Diji Region. The largest of these sites is Rehman Dheri at nineteen hectares. It is surrounded by a number of smaller places on the Gomal Plain, all concentrated to the west

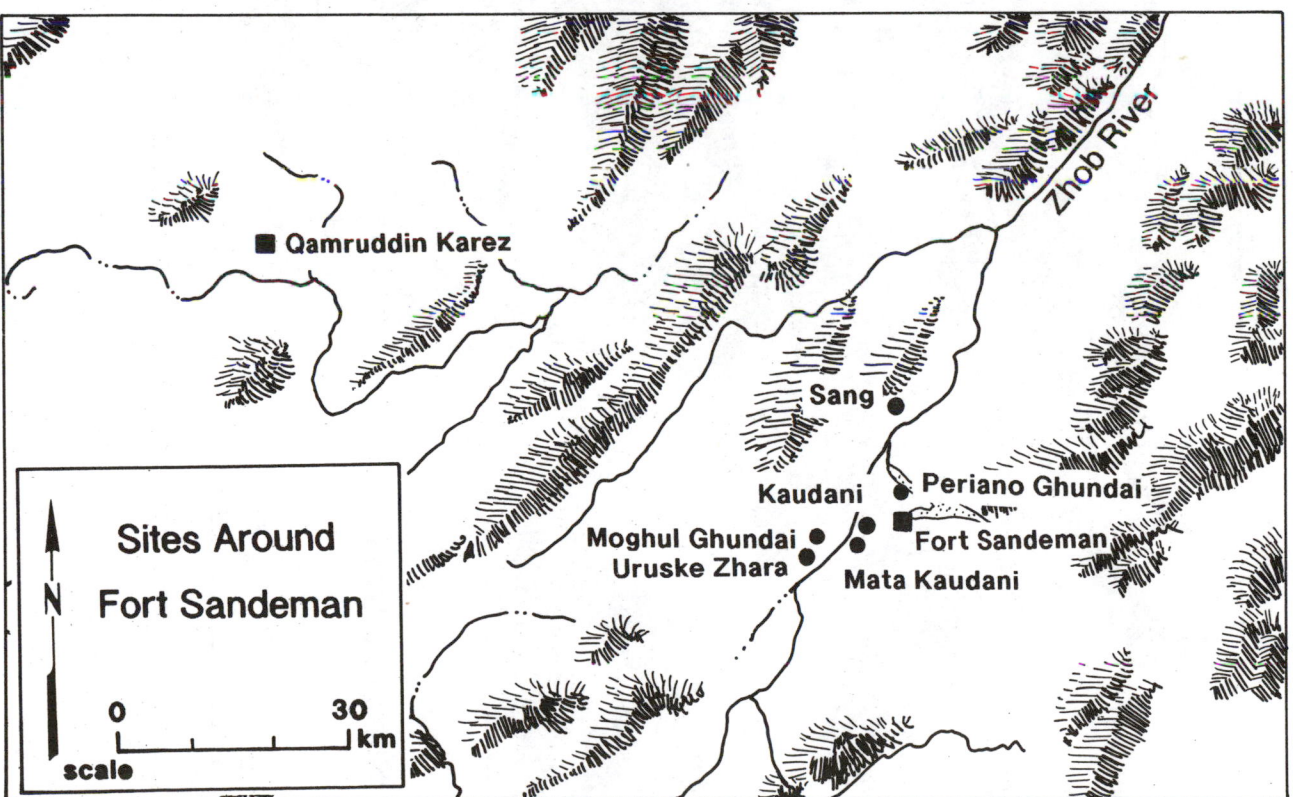

Figure 4.149. Map of sites around Fort Sandeman

658

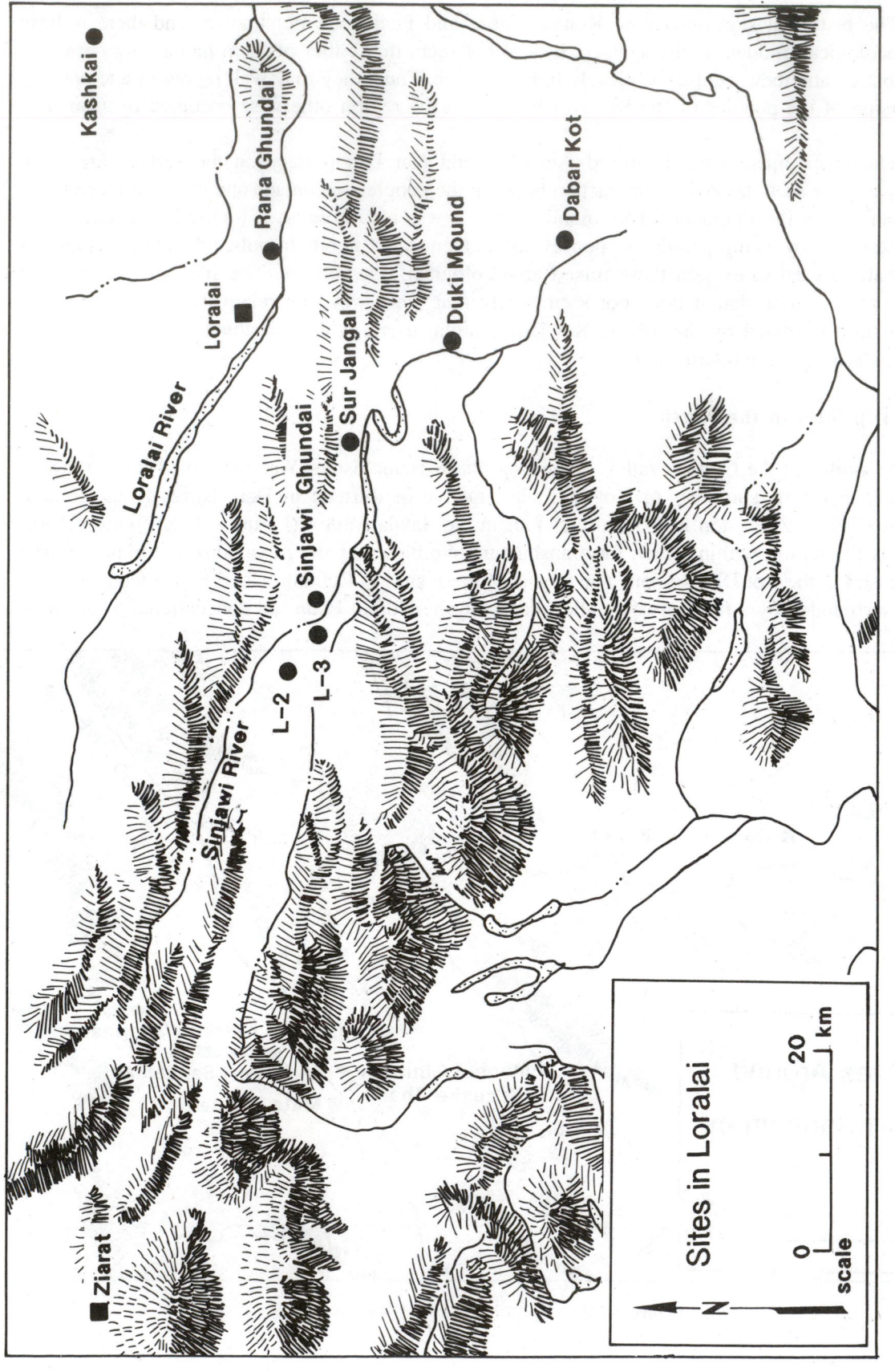

Figure 4.150. Map of sites in Loralai

Kashkai

Rana Ghundai

Loralai

Loralai River

Sur Jangal

Sinjawi Ghundai

Duki Mound

Dabar Kot

Sinjawi River

L-2

L-3

Ziarat

Sites in Loralai

N

0   20   km

scale

of the Indus River, which may have flowed closer to these settlements in the past than it does today.

In the uplands, Periano Ghundai is located near the junction of the Zhob River and the Saliazo torrent bed, four miles west of Fort Sandeman (Figure 4.151). This is the largest site in the region and the Zhob Valley is a communication route of some note, connecting north-

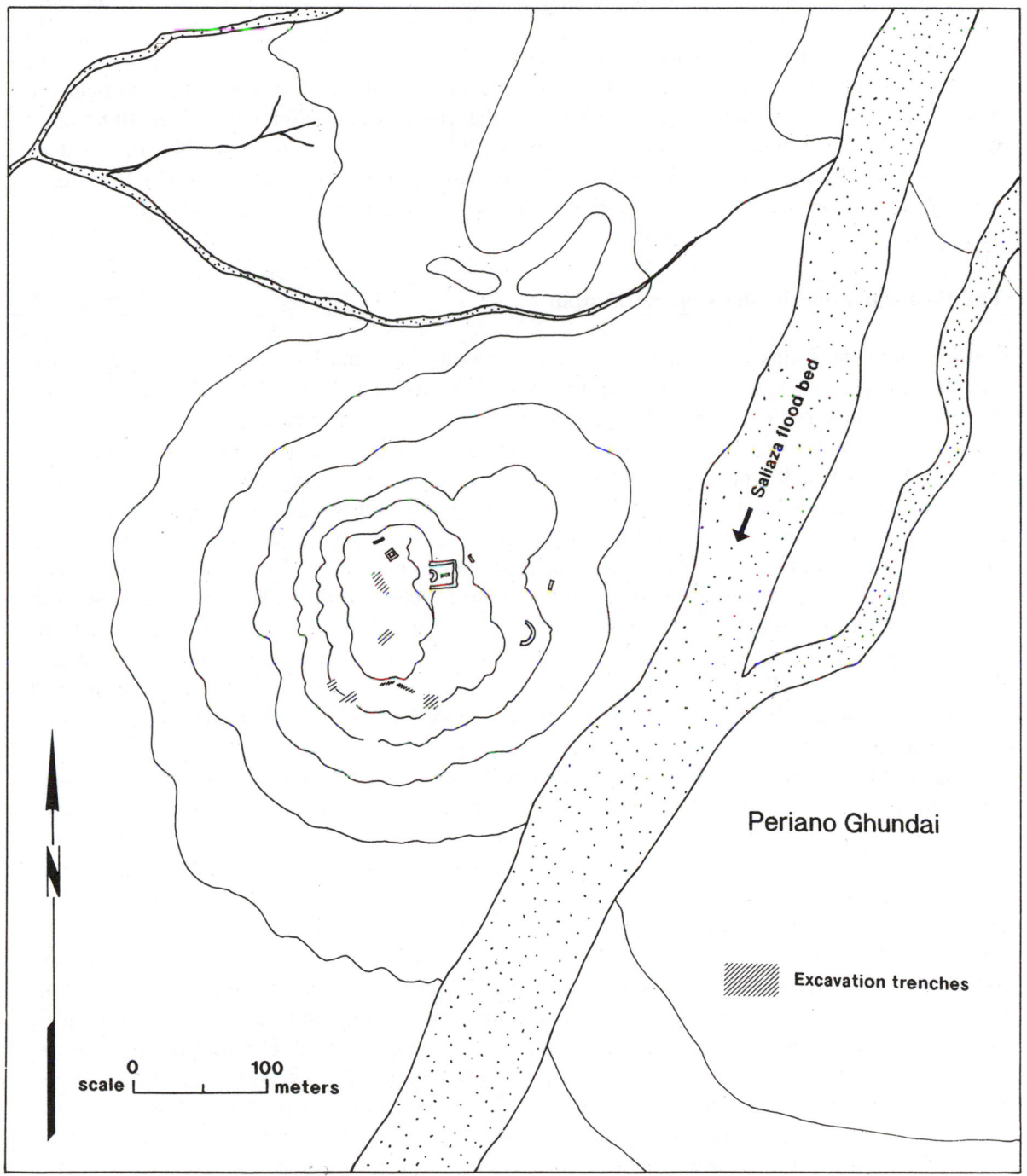

Figure 4.151. Site plan of Periano Ghundai, after Stein 1929a: Figure 2

central Baluchistan with northeastern Iran on one side and the north Punjab on the other. Periano Ghundai is one of the most important sites in Baluchistan, and what we know about it is mostly confusing. Fritz Noetling was at the site in the late nineteenth century (1898). His collections have recently been found in the Museum fur Indische Kunst, Berlin and have been published (Pedde 1993a, 1993b). The Northern Baluchistan "Waziristan Kot Diji" is somewhat different from the rest; not so different that it need be called a separate Phase, but different nonetheless.

To the east of the Indus River, in the Indus-Jhelum Doab, there are a number of Kot Diji sites, only three of which have been published (Leiah, Piplan and Musa Khel). But, there are others that have been informally reported, and the entire Thar Desert should be thoroughly surveyed. There are indications of the Northern Neolithic extending south into this zone as does the later Late Bronze-Iron Age Gandharan Grave Culture. There is neither a Kechi Beg Phase nor a Mature Harappan here, although digging at Leiah and Musa Khel might change this judgment.

The Pastoral Zone in the Central Punjab

Starting from the Indus River at Leiah and moving east, one must traverse the Punjab all the way to Harappa to reach the next known Kot Diji site. This will change with additional exploration, which has been begun by the Pakistan Department of Archaeology. But, vast stretches of the central portion of the modern West Punjab seem to have been open grazing land. The rivers Jhelum, Chenab and Ravi are entrenched to some degree, except near the Panchnad. The bars between the entrenched rivers were vast pastures in prehistoric times, in fact up to the nineteenth century when huge, modern irrigation works changed the landscape. In prehistoric times this area would have been a savanna grassland, with gallery forests in the entrenched beds of the rivers; a splendid environment for mobile, specialized, cattle keeping people with its abundant pasture, reliable water in perennial rivers and easy terrain. Villages of sedentary, or semi-sedentary farmers, would have been found in the entrenchments, near the rivers, where there was both fertile alluvium and natural irrigation. Much of this was discussed, and documented in Part Three of this book where "Landforms and More Rivers" are covered in the discussion of the Harappa Region.

The notion of the Punjabi village, filled with families of farmers tilling their irrigated fields, keeping a few cattle, sheep, goats and water buffalo, is a contemporary one, that does not reflect the deeper historical traditions of this part of the region. In pre-modern times, before the 19th century, the region was home to numerous cattle keeping "tribes" and farmers along the rivers. In fact, none of the copper land grant tablets of the historical eras that deal with the gift or transfer of farming land, not pasture, has ever been found in this area.

In the discussion of pastoral nomadism in Part 3 of this book notice was taken of the importance of this form of subsistence adaptation in the eras prior to the massive irrigation systems developed by the British in the nineteenth century. Gujranwala District was divided into two portions: *des*, the cultivated land and *bar* the grazing land. The former *des* was the land on the banks of the rivers and *bar* the large, uncultivated tract down the center of the Doab. The system of production differs in each area, with agriculture predominating in *des* and pastoralism in *bar* (Government of India 1884c: 3-4). The Montgomery District Gazetteer described a tribe there whose principal occupation was the breeding and grazing of cattle. These nomadic Jats were contrasted to settled peoples called ryots (Government of India 1884g: 51). These citations, and many other like them in the District Gazetteers, are the best evidence for the form of subsistence adaptation in the western Punjab prior to large scale irrigation. There were farmers near the rivers and pastoralists, some of whom were nomadic, in the Doabs.

It does not make much sense, at least in the opinion of the author, to think of a rich environment such as the one under discussion as being empty and not utilized by humans during the Indus Age. Since village farming sites do not seem to be present in significant numbers, the alternative is to look to the other end of the subsistence continuum and one of the many forms of pastoral nomadism as a prominent form of adaptation in the region and the central West Punjab can be thought of as a great pasture land right through prehistoric times, with village farming communities in the riverine entrenchments.

There will be an archaeological record of the prehistoric cattle keepers who lived in the central Punjab, but the record will be encapsulated in sites that are stratigraphically thin and scattered. Most of them will be small, but there is also the chance for larger places to be found where camps were established many times over several centuries. Certain points on the landscape might have been returned to, time after time, for seasonal "fairs" or because of their advantageous location for pasture, water and travel. Monsoon season camps would have been more stable, occupied on a longer term, with the possibility that a shallow archaeological midden would accumulate.

Kot Diji Sites in Cholistan

There are fifty-one Kot Diji sites in the western Sarasvati, forty of which are reported by M. R. Mughal (1997: Table 3), the balance are part of the results of Sir Aurel Stein's research there in 1941 (Stein 1943a; see Figure 3.141). There may be a duplication of sites on these two lists, but the overlap has not yet been eliminated. The preceding Hakra Wares Phase documented the presence of nomadic and semi-sedentary peoples, but by the Early Harappan this changed. Village farming communities predominate, and while site counts drop in this area, the presence of Kot Diji occupations is strong and deep.

The Sarasvati River would have flooded seasonally, probably quite a marked phenomenon. The history of the Sarasvati River shows that its terminus in modern Cholistan seems to have been an inland delta. The surrounding terrain is flat which may have caused great sheets of water to spread new alluvium across the landscape. No one is sure of the magnitude of such floods, but the Sarasvati judged by the width of the now dry bed seems to have been a substantial river, on the scale of the Yamuna or the upper Ganges. The local farming population would have had to adjust to this in order to master life in close proximity to the river, but the productivity of the land would have been very high. This prosperity is something that is born out by the archaeology, especially during the Mature Harappan.

Flooding would have renewed grasslands as well as agricultural fields and the apparent increase in village farming communities should not mask the fact that vast reaches of this environment would have been prime land for cattle keeping peoples, living in symbiosis with agriculturalists. Thus, there is some reason to believe that the drop in site counts from about one hundred to about fifty, between the Hakra Wares and the Kot Diji Phases, should not be seen an in indication that the population of the area actually decreased. This could have happened, of course, but it should not be assumed based on the site counts alone.

One day some of the extraordinary Kot Diji sites in Cholistan will be excavated, perhaps even on a scale comparable to Kalibangan. Sir Aurel Stein made a good start with his brief work at Bhoot (a.k.a. Kalepar). What is needed is a horizontal excavation of a site, with adequate attention given to the palaeobotanical and faunal remains, with complementary studies of the ancient environment and the nature of the Sarasvati River. Until that becomes a reality there is not much more that can be said about these remains.

Kot Diji Phase Funerary Practices

Mehrgarh

Mehrgarh has produced evidence for funerary practices during the Early Harappan. A cemetery with infant burials was found in the central part of MR.1.

Nineteen little box-like chambers made of mud bricks set on edge were found, the size of the boxes being about 60 cm in length, 45 cm in width, and between 15 and 25 cm deep. They were oriented roughly southeast to northwest. In thirteen of these graves were found skeletons of babies from birth to three years of age. All of the skeletons were laid out in fetal position, their faces looking north; in seven cases, the body was turned toward the east, the six other skeletons being turned toward the west. In one grave, two skulls were found among disturbed bones, and from near the neck of one of the infants, two disc-shaped beads were recovered. An identical bead was also found in another grave. Since these graves were below the surface, we have no stratigraphic means to date them. We merely know that they were built above the deposits of the upper levels of the occupation. The only other example of a box-grave of mud bricks from Baluchistan is the grave of an infant found at Nal. The grave from Nal has the same shape and is almost exactly the same size as the ones from Mehrgarh, but this is not enough to chronologically place our graves since they could also be of a later date (Jarrige, Jarrige, Meadow and Quivron 1995: 111).

Since the Period VII deposits are the latest at the site it seems reasonable to assume that these interments can be dated to this era; however, the excavation team's caution is appropriate.

Periano Ghundai

Sir Aurel Stein's excavation at Periano Ghundai near Fort Sandeman in the Zhob Valley of Northern Baluchistan, in early 1927 produced evidence for the cremation of human remains (Figure 4.151). Stein's digging here was almost perfunctory and the report is inadequate; however, relying on Stein's own words, the work carried out by Walter Fairservis (1959: 330-33) and that by M. R. Mughal (1972g) we can now associate these urns with the Early Harappan, Kot Diji Phase occupation of the site, or Mughal's Periano Ghundai C. One of the two vessels shown in Stein's report (1929a: Figure 8) appears to be a good example of ribbed, Bhoot Ware. A third pot with cremated human remains was found in this vicinity "...broken, amidst refuse of animal bones and pottery debris..." (Stein 1929a: 37). A fourth "cinerary pot" was also recorded in such a position that it allowed Stein to suggest that: "These finds made it clear that burial of human remains after burning was practiced by the occupants of the site when their dwellings stood approximately on the level indicated and that the customary position chosen for such deposits was probably intramural" (1929a: 37).

Moghul Ghundai

Stein's work at Moghul Ghundai was even more cursory than at Periano Ghundai, but he did find another "cinerary pot" containing cremated human remains. Moghul Ghundai is also in the Zhob valley ca. 20 kilometers southwest of Periano Ghundai (Figure 4.152). This was found approximately 1.2 meters below the surface close to a wall in his north trench (1929a: 45). Fairservis (1959: 359) suggests that the pot was buried in the floor of a room, along with the two smaller jars it contained. One of the jars had the remains of some foodstuff. The large pot and one of the two found within it are a local type called "Periano Painted" (Fairservis 1959: 359). This and other evidence suggest that this interment should also be associated with the Early Harappan Phase. The similarity between the mortuary practices at Periano Ghundai and Moghul Ghundai at this time is a meaningful observation.

The Damb Sadaat Phase of Central Baluchistan

Contemporary with the Kot Diji and Amri-Nal Phases is a smaller, more localized cultural phase of the Early Harappan in Central Baluchistan, centered on the Quetta Valley (Figure 4.153). It rests on a long history of occupation in this fertile, well watered valley. Quetta-Pishin is blessed with substantial subsurface water resources, available even to relatively primitive

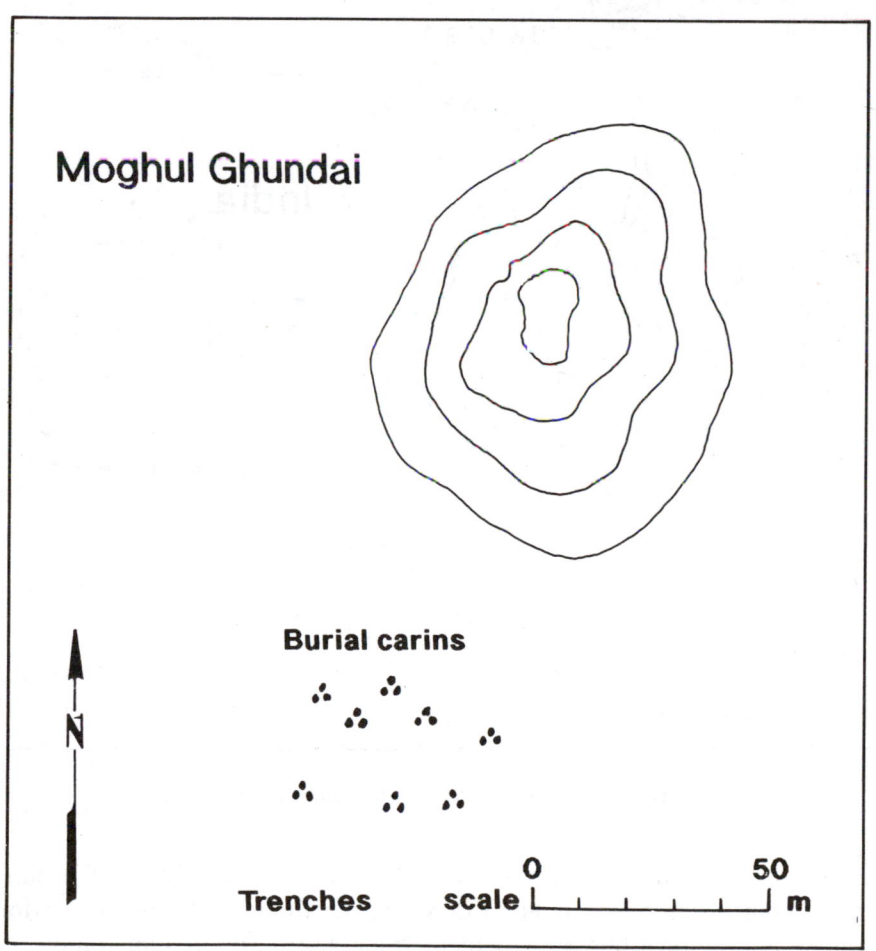

Figure 4.152. Site plan of Moghul Ghundai, after Stein 1929a: Figure 4

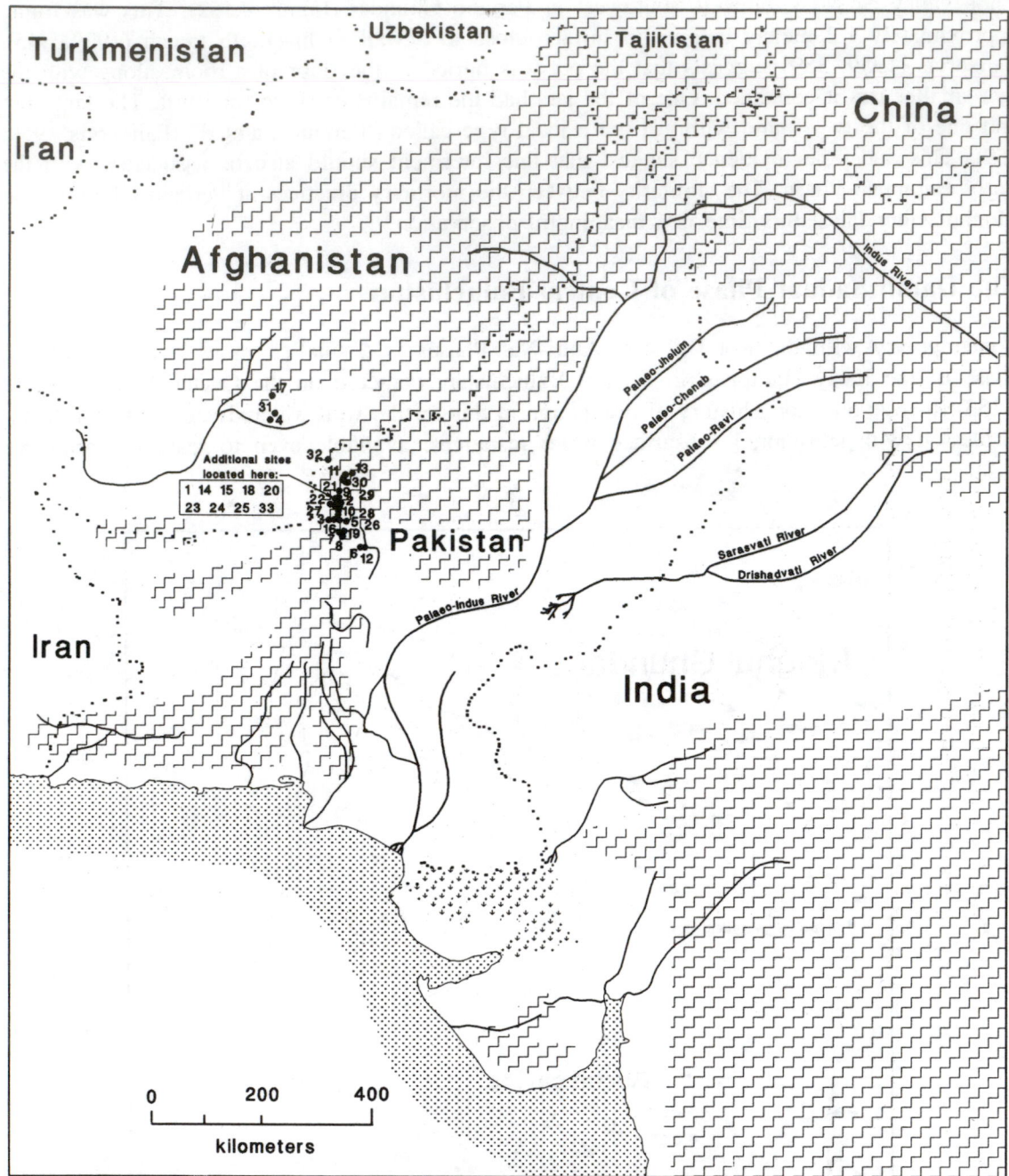

Figure 4.153. Map of sites of the Damb Sadaat Phase

cultivators in the form of artesian springs. This valley is also the center of a natural corridor linking southern Afghanistan to the Indus Valley, via the Bolan and Khojak. Historically these factors have made it a regional hub of settlement, trade, travel and administration. In prehistoric times a distinctive set of archaeological assemblages developed in Quetta-Pishin and the valleys to the immediate north, south and beyond into Afghanistan as at the famous site of Mundigak, even reaching Shahr-i Sokhta in Seistan.

Chronology of the Damb Sadaat Phase

There are fifteen radiocarbon dates that give a chronology for the Damb Sadaat Phase. They are given in Table 4.40.

TABLE 4.40
Radiocarbon Dates for the Damb Sadaat Phase

Lab Number	Calibrated Date
Damb Sadaat Period II	
L-180C	1Σ cal BC 3627 (3012, 3005, 2925) 2464
	2Σ cal BC 3985 (3012, 3005, 2925) 1885
P-522	1Σ cal BC 3348 (3014, 3001, 2925) 2704
	2Σ cal BC 3622 (3014, 3001, 2925) 2469
L-180E	1Σ cal BC 3511 (2923) 2491
	2Σ cal BC 3942 (2923) 1979
P-523	1Σ cal BC 2616 (2562, 2525, 2500) 2462
	2Σ cal BC 2868 (2562, 2525, 2500) 2337
Deh Morasi Ghundai, Period IIb and IIc	
P-2292	1Σ cal BC 4898 (4507) 4237
	2Σ cal BC 5247 (4507) 3818
P-2291	1Σ cal BC 3346 (3297, 3237, 3173, 3168, 3107) 3039
	2Σ cal BC 3371 (3297, 3237, 3173, 3168, 3107) 2921
P-2289	1Σ cal BC 3503 (3085, 3061, 3043) 2703
	2Σ cal BC 3755 (3085, 3061, 3043) 2409
P-1493	1Σ cal BC 3251 (3034) 2922
	2Σ cal BC 3308 (3034) 2911
P-2290	1Σ cal BC 2911 (2611) 2327
	2Σ cal BC 3332 (2611) 1981
P-2288	1Σ cal BC 2558 (2193, 2155, 2148) 1881
	2Σ cal BC 2886 (2193, 2155, 2148) 1527
Mundigak Period III	
GSY-53	1Σ cal BC 2916 (2870, 2803, 2773, 2717, 2705) 2502
	2Σ cal BC 3264 (2870, 2803, 2773, 2717, 2705) 2342
GSY-51	1Σ cal BC 1394 (1255, 1240, 1216) 1028
	2Σ cal BC 1501 (1255, 1240, 1216) 908
Said Qala Periods I, II and III	
DIC-18	1Σ cal BC 2558 (2200) 1911
	2Σ cal BC 2882 (2200) 1635
DIC-20	1Σ cal BC 2200 (2128, 2080, 2045) 1953
	2Σ cal BC 2397 (2128, 2080, 2045) 1789
DIC-22	1Σ cal BC 2285 (1957) 1683
	2Σ cal BC 2577 (1957) 1429

With the exception of Mundigak GSY-51, and the dates from Said Qala, this series corresponds well with the chronology for the Damb Sadaat Phase that has been used here. Said Qala presents something of a problem, since the radiocarbon dates indicate that it is contemporary with the Mature Harappan, as noted by Shaffer (1978b: 95). Shaffer has made a strong argument that the ceramics compare well with other Damb Sadaat Phase sites, especially Mundigak III-IV (Shaffer 1978b: 78-95, 1992: 462-63). Said Qala has been provisionally left in the Damb Sadaat Phase out of respect for Shaffer's archaeological skills, especially in chronology; however this might change. Said Qala may well represent a kind of "Late Damb Sadaat" phenomenon, akin to the Late Kot Diji of the Derajat. Employing such a construct would bring together the comparative stratigraphy using ceramics and the radiocarbon dates.

Damb Sadaat Phase Sites

There are thirty-seven Damb Sadaat sites, twenty-nine of which have data on size (Table 4.41). They average 2.64 hectares. The largest site is the Quetta Miri (twenty-three hectares), located at the one spot in the valley which has been occupied continuously from prehistoric to modern times. It is a huge mound and there are many problems with an accurate estimate of its size. If the size of the Quetta Miri cannot be estimated accurately it would still seem reasonable to suggest that it may have been the largest site during the Damb Sadaat Phase, since it is blessed with reliable water from the Hana River and other sources. The area covered by the modern city has been the central place of the joined Quetta-Pishin Valleys, and the other sites are outliers to this focus of settlement. The next largest site, Mundigak, at 18.75 hectares, is in the Kushk-i Nakhud Valley of the Helmand River drainage over 200 kilometers to the northwest of the Miri. Mundigak was a town during Early Harappan times, here seen as the end of Mundigak Period III and the beginning of Mundigak Period IV. It is entirely possible that the settlement was smaller than the eighteen plus hectares estimated here.

The ceramics and other finds at Mundigak III/IV have wide ranging parallels with surrounding regions, including Central Asia. But, from the beginning the closest relationships are clearly with the Quetta Valley and Central Baluchistan, with Togau/Kili Ghul Mohammad Black on Red Ware being a prominent type, along with Kechi Beg Polychrome. The site marks the western limit of settlements with the Baluchi archaeological assemblages. Shahr-i Sokhta is outside this fold in spite of many parallels in material culture with Baluchistan.

The distribution of Damb Sadaat Phase sites by size is shown in Figure 4.154.

Estimate of Settled Area for the Damb Sadaat Phase

Table 4.42 presents the estimate of settled area for the Damb Sadaat Phase:

The Excavated Sites

There are eight excavated Damb Sadaat Phase sites. The Quetta Miri is included in the list for historical reasons, to recall the early history of archaeology in this region. From these sites it is learned that the Damb Sadaat peoples were farmers and herders, for the most part living in mud houses, which seem to have had flat roofs. They knew copper metallurgy and carried on trade and commerce with surrounding regions, just as their early food producing forebears did.

Damb Sadaat in the Quetta Valley is a good example of the Damb Sadaat Phase site.

TABLE 4.41
Sites of the Damb Sadaat Phase

Site Name	Province/State	District	Size in Hectares
Quetta Miri	Baluchistan	Quetta-Pishin	23.0
Mundigak	Kandahar	Kandahar	18.75
Kranai Hill	Baluchistan	Quetta-Pishin	10.7
Said Qala Tepe	Kandahar	Kandahar	3.5
Sra Kala	Baluchistan	Quetta-Pishin	2.6
Faiz Mohammad	Baluchistan	Quetta-Pishin	1.7
Damb Sadaat	Baluchistan	Quetta-Pishin	1.7
Gurdi Mound	Baluchistan	Bolan Pass	1.7
Q-25	Baluchistan	Quetta-Pishin	1.5
Kasiano Dozakh	Baluchistan	Quetta-Pishin	1.3
Isplinji One	Baluchistan	Sarawan	1.2
Deh Morasi Ghundai	Kandahar	Kandahar	1.1
Q-26	Baluchistan	Quetta-Pishin	1.1
Isplinji Two	Baluchistan	Sarawan	0.7
Kirta	Baluchistan	Bolan Pass	0.7
Ahmed Khanzai North	Baluchistan	Quetta-Pishin	0.65
Q-17	Baluchistan	Quetta-Pishin	0.65
K-1	Baluchistan	Sarawan	0.6
Q-35	Baluchistan	Quetta-Pishin	0.4
Spina Ghundai	Baluchistan	Quetta-Pishin	0.4
Ahmed Khanzai South	Baluchistan	Quetta-Pishin	0.4
Sahib Khan	Baluchistan	Quetta-Pishin	0.4
Q-06	Baluchistan	Quetta-Pishin	0.3
Q-28	Baluchistan	Quetta-Pishin	0.3
Q-18	Baluchistan	Quetta-Pishin	0.3
Q-33	Baluchistan	Quetta-Pishin	0.3
Kuchnai Ghundai	Baluchistan	Quetta-Pishin	0.25
Q-36	Baluchistan	Quetta-Pishin	0.2
Karez Site	Baluchistan	Quetta-Pishin	0.02
Jagjai	Baluchistan	Quetta-Pishin	
Kouhlagh	Baluchistan	Quetta-Pishin	
Kuzbagh	Baluchistan	Quetta-Pishin	
Majo Mill	Baluchistan	Quetta-Pishin	
Mata Ghundai	Baluchistan	Quetta-Pishin	
Mobi Damb	Baluchistan	Sarawan	
P-10	Baluchistan	Quetta-Pishin	
Q-20	Baluchistan	Quetta-Pishin	

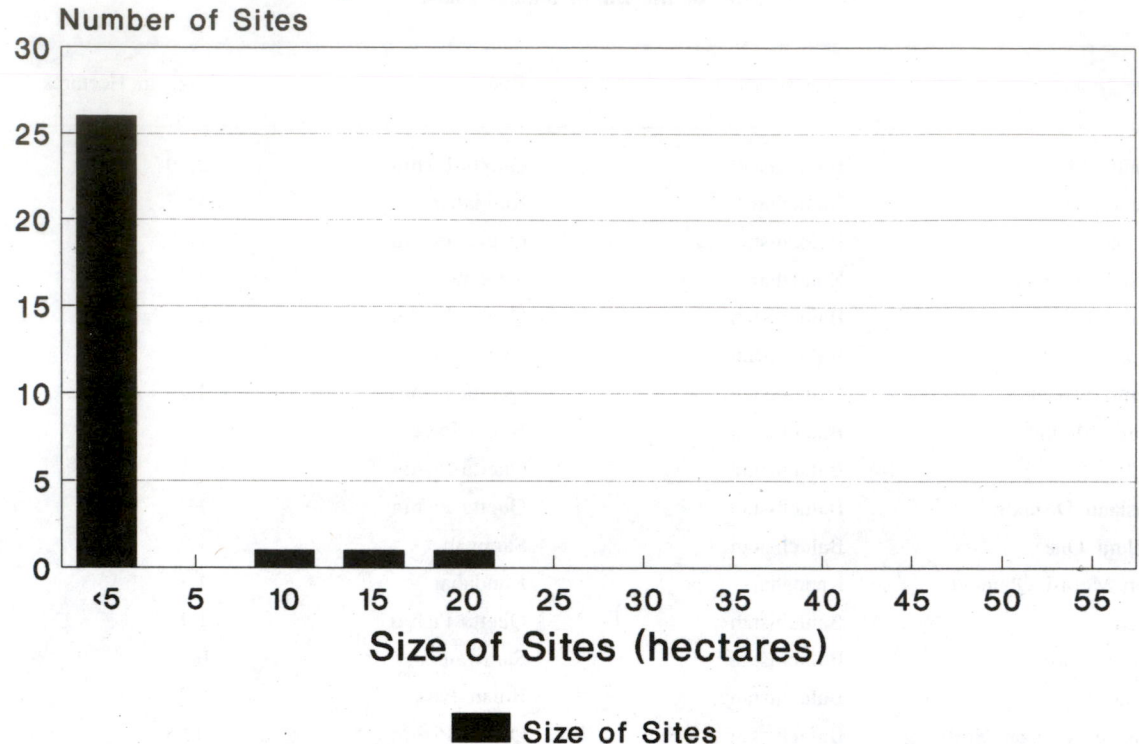

Figure 4.154. Histogram of site sizes of the Damb Sadaat Phase

TABLE 4.42

Estimate of Settled Area for the Damb Sadaat Phase

Damb Sadaat Phase	
Total Sites	37
Sites with Size Estimate	29
Settled Area of Sites with Known Sizes	76.42
Sites with Size Unknown	8
Average Site Site Size	2.64
Estimated Settled Area of Sites without Size	21.12
Estimated Total Settled Area	97.54

Sizes given in hectares

Damb Sadaat: Introduction

Damb Sadaat, or Mian Ghundai in Brahui, is one of the most important archaeological sites in the Indo-Iranian Borderlands (Figure 4.155, Figure 4.156, Figure 4.157, Plate 4.50). It was first investigated as part of the program of the Second Afghan Expedition from the American Museum of Natural History under the direction of Walter A. Fairservis, Jr. The bulk of the actual excavation of Damb Sadaat was undertaken by Mr. Howard Stoudt and Mr. and Mrs. Leslie Alcock. However, Fairservis had overall charge and directed the excavation strategy.

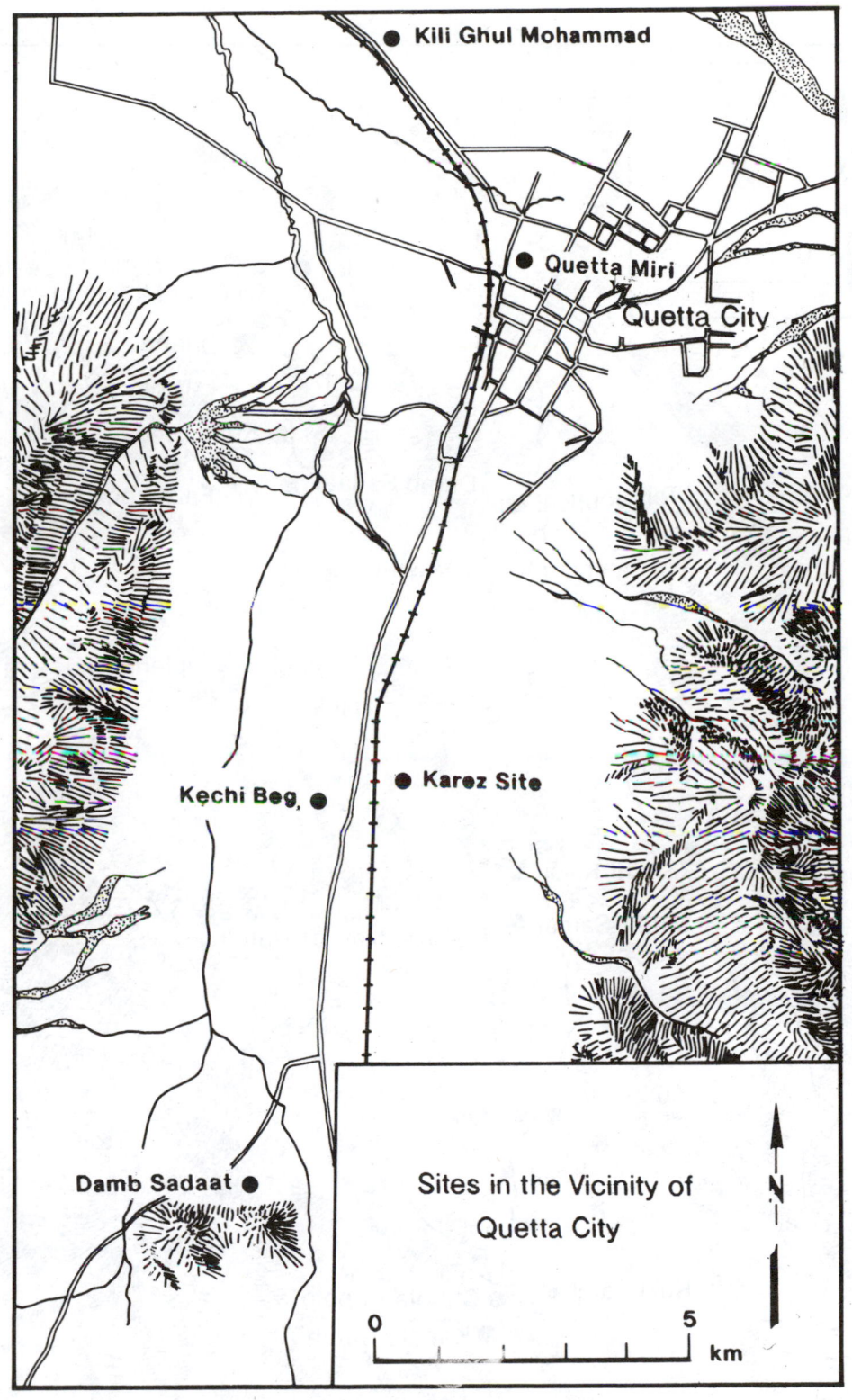

Figure 4.155. Map of sites in the vicinity of Quetta City

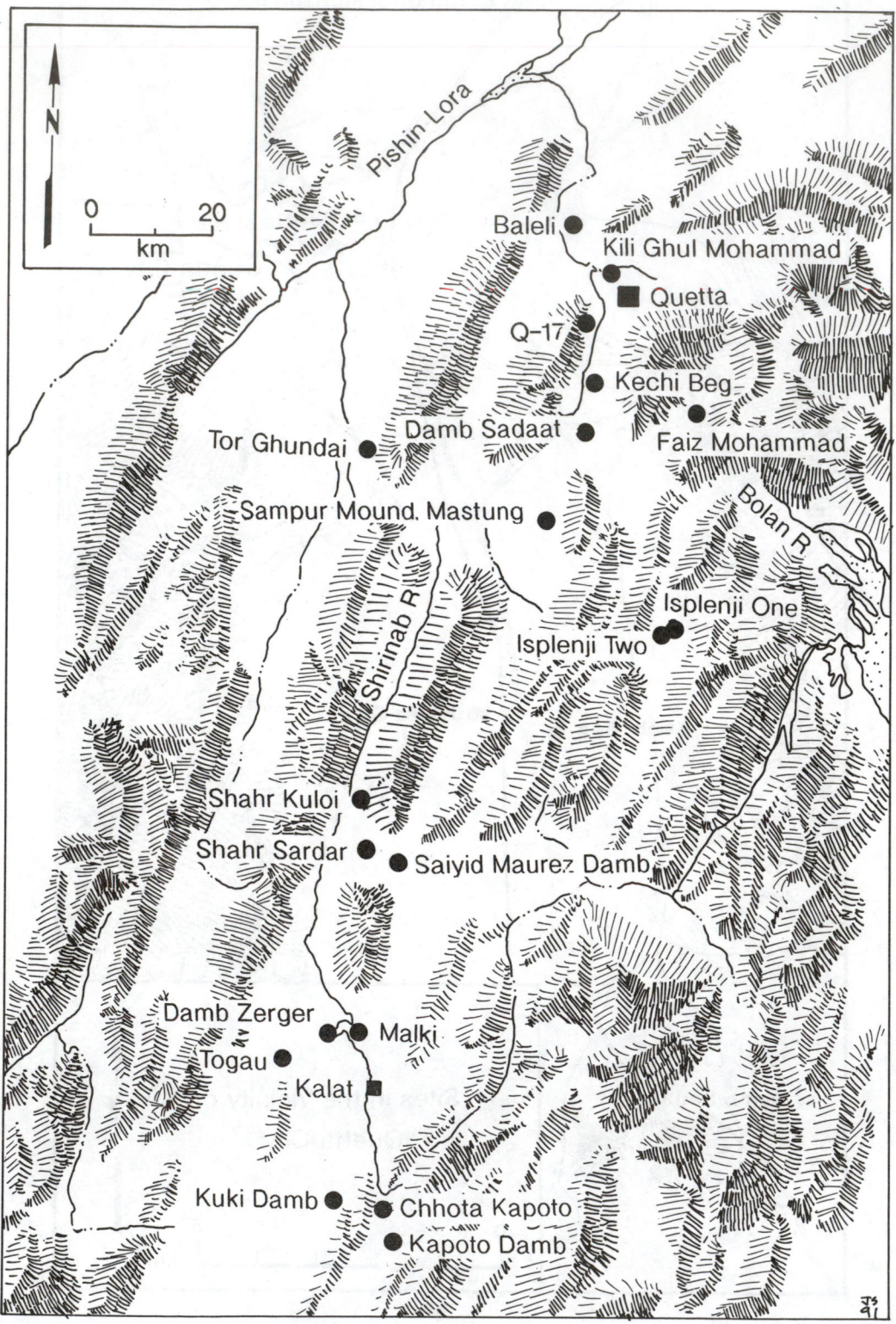

Figure 4.156. Map of sites in the Quetta Valley and surrounding valleys

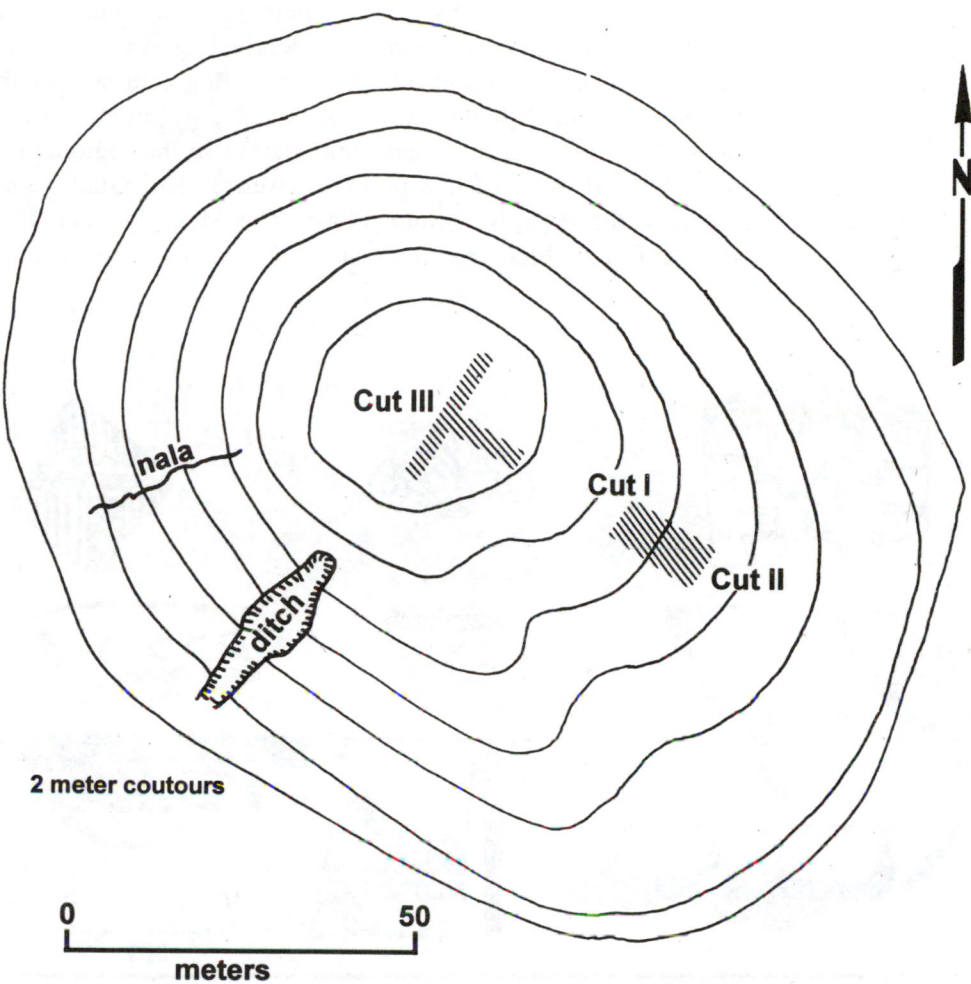

Figure 4.157. Site plan of Damb Sadaat, after Fairservis 1956a: 204 Q-8

Damb Sadaat is important for two reasons. Just as at Kili Ghul Mohammad, it documents the continuity of occupation in this region of Baluchistan, the top of the Bolan Pass, one of the most important gateways to the plains of the Subcontinent. Damb Sadaat also documents significant culture historical interactions between the Subcontinent, northern Afghanistan and Central Asia during the Indus Age. Damb Sadaat III, the Sibri Cemetery and Mehrgarh VII, along with Indus sites themselves, trace the participation of the Harappan Civilization in the Middle Asian Interaction Sphere which are discussed in the context of the *Indus Age: The Mature Harappan.*

Three trenches were sunk at Damb Sadaat, called Cuts 1, 2 and 3 in the excavation report. As can be seen on the sketch plan of the mound, contiguous Cuts 1 and 2, under the supervision of Mr. Stoudt, were placed on the southeastern slope of the mound and Cut 3, under the supervision of the Alcocks, was a 'T-shaped' trench at the summit.

There is a Kechi Beg occupation there which needs to be described to place the Period II, Damb Sadaat Phase occupation in proper perspective.

Damb Sadaat I: The Kechi Beg Phase

The initial occupation of Damb Sadaat is marked by the presence of the same suite of ceramics

672

which characterized the final occupation of Kili Ghul Mohammad; Nazim Hard Clay, Adam Sandy, Mian Ghundai Fine Buff Plain Ware and especially the Kechi Beg Wares, an extremely fine, usually buff ceramic, which can be very beautiful. One Kechi Beg ceramic not found at Kili Ghul Mohammad, but present in Damb Sadaat I, is the signal polychrome variety. That this is confined to Damb Sadaat I makes it an important time marker in the regional sequence (Figure 4.158). Khojak Parallel Striated Ware of this period as well as Kili Ghul Mohammad IV, may have ties to Kalibangan I, the Pre-urban, Sothi Phase. The Mian Ghundai Dark Rim Wares of Damb Sadaat I and Kili Ghul Mohammad IV have wide parallels in the Kot Diji

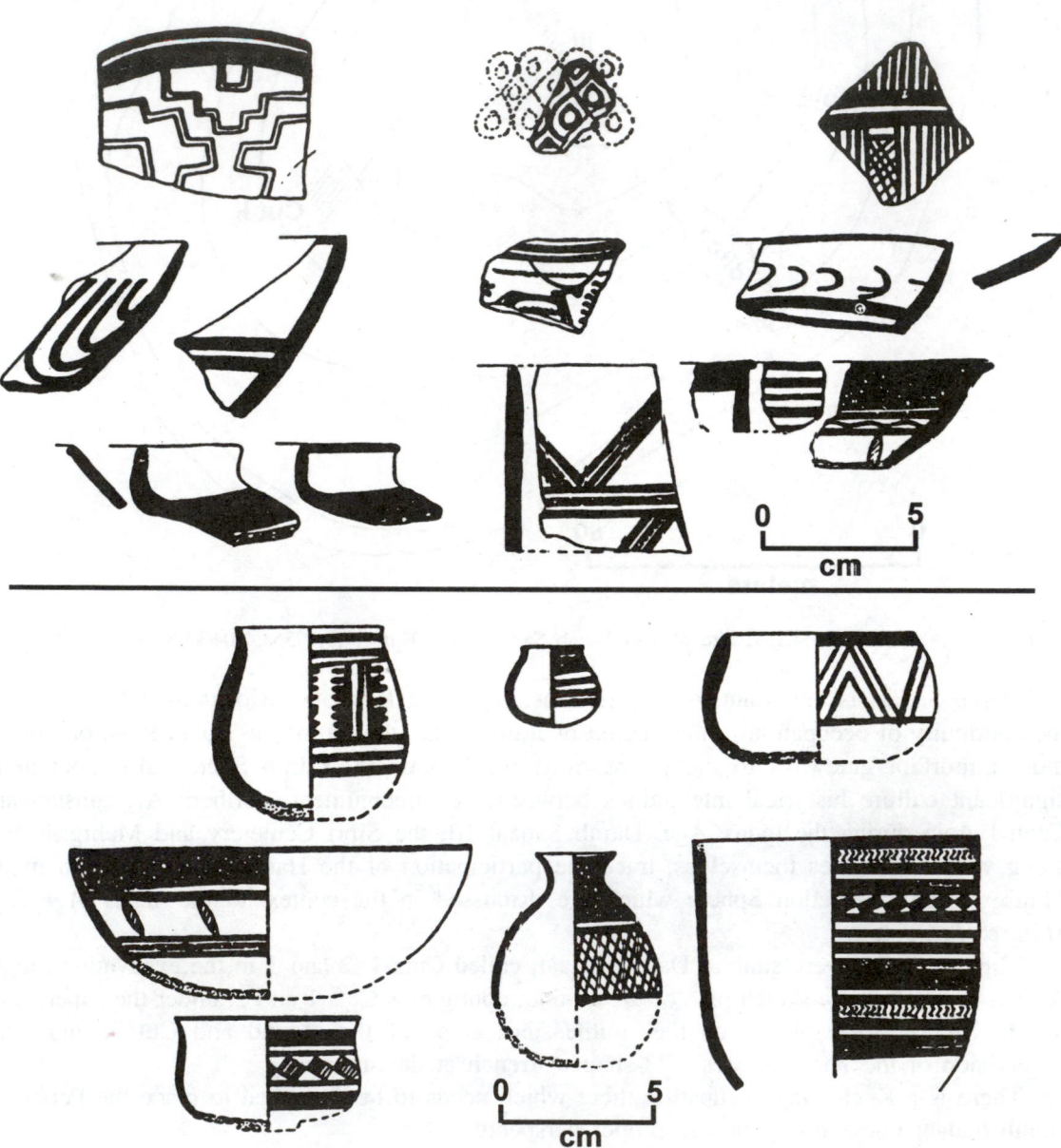

Figure 4.158. Ceramics of the Kechi Beg Phase in the Quetta Valley, Damb Sadaat and other sites, after Fairservis 1956a

Phase of M. R. Mughal's Early Harappan (Mughal 1970). Damb Sadaat I was found only in Cuts 1 and 2, not associated with substantial architecture.

Damb Sadaat II: The Damb Sadaat Phase

There is considerable continuity in the ceramics between Damb Sadaat I and II and also from II to III. For details refer to Fairservis (1956a: 331-32) for the ceramic frequency charts. The ceramics of Damb Sadaat II and III are characterized by the predominance of the Quetta Wares, Faiz Mohammad Grey Ware, Mian Ghundai Fine Plain and the Wet Wares (Figure 4.159). Quetta Black on Buff Slip Ware and Black on Surface Ware tend to be painted with more organic designs, plant and animal designs in Period II and more geometric designs in Period III, especially the so-called "Sadaat motif."

There is some architecture in Damb Sadaat II amounting to a domestic oven built of regularly coursed bricks along with mud and fragments of bricks. This may be a *tandoor*. It is associated with what appear to be domestic structures with ground stone food processing implements.

Female figurines, some with elaborate dress and adornment make their appearance in the Quetta Valley at this time along with compartmented stamp seals. Both of these classes of artifacts carry over into Damb Sadaat III. They have parallels at Mehrgarh, in the Zhob sites as well as sites in Central Asia.

Much of the Damb Sadaat pottery is a buff ware, occasionally slightly pink. The best wares were made of finely levigated clay and wheel thrown (Plate 4.51).

Damb Sadaat Phase Ceramics

Pottery of the Damb Sadaat Phase was often slipped to create a uniform surface, even if it was not painted. Paring was often done to thin the walls of vessels and the stems of goblets. A painted ceramic, called Quetta Ware, is the most characteristic type of pottery. Wet Wares are also a part of this assemblage, and the Kot Diji rim occurs on short neck, globular jars. A ceramic known as Faiz Mohammad Gray Ware was also manufactured. It is a fine ware ceramic, generally rendered as a plate, a form also used for Quetta Ware. The technology used in its manufacture is somewhat complicated since it took place in two stages of firing; first baked as a red-buff ware in an oxidizing atmosphere, then refired under reducing conditions to obtain the finished grey color (R. Wright 1985). The designs in black paint (sometimes red) are closely paralleled in the Quetta Ware repertory of motifs.

Faiz Mohammad Gray Ware shares a number of important features with a ceramic in eastern Iran, called Emir Gray Ware. This ceramic was manufactured in the same way, with two stages of firing and black on grey decoration. The vessel forms for Faiz Mohammad Gray Ware and Emir Grey Ware are different, however, and they share few painted designs. Rita Wright has hypothesized that in spite of these differences the technology for the manufacture of these two pottery types is too specific, and complex, for it to have been independently invented. She proposes that in spite of the stylistic differences between the Faiz Mohammad and Emir Grey Wares, there was one center for the invention of the technology behind them (R. Wright 1984, 1987, 1989).

Burials

Isplenji Two

Isplenji is a broad valley to the south of Quetta. It connects to the Gwandin Valley, a part of

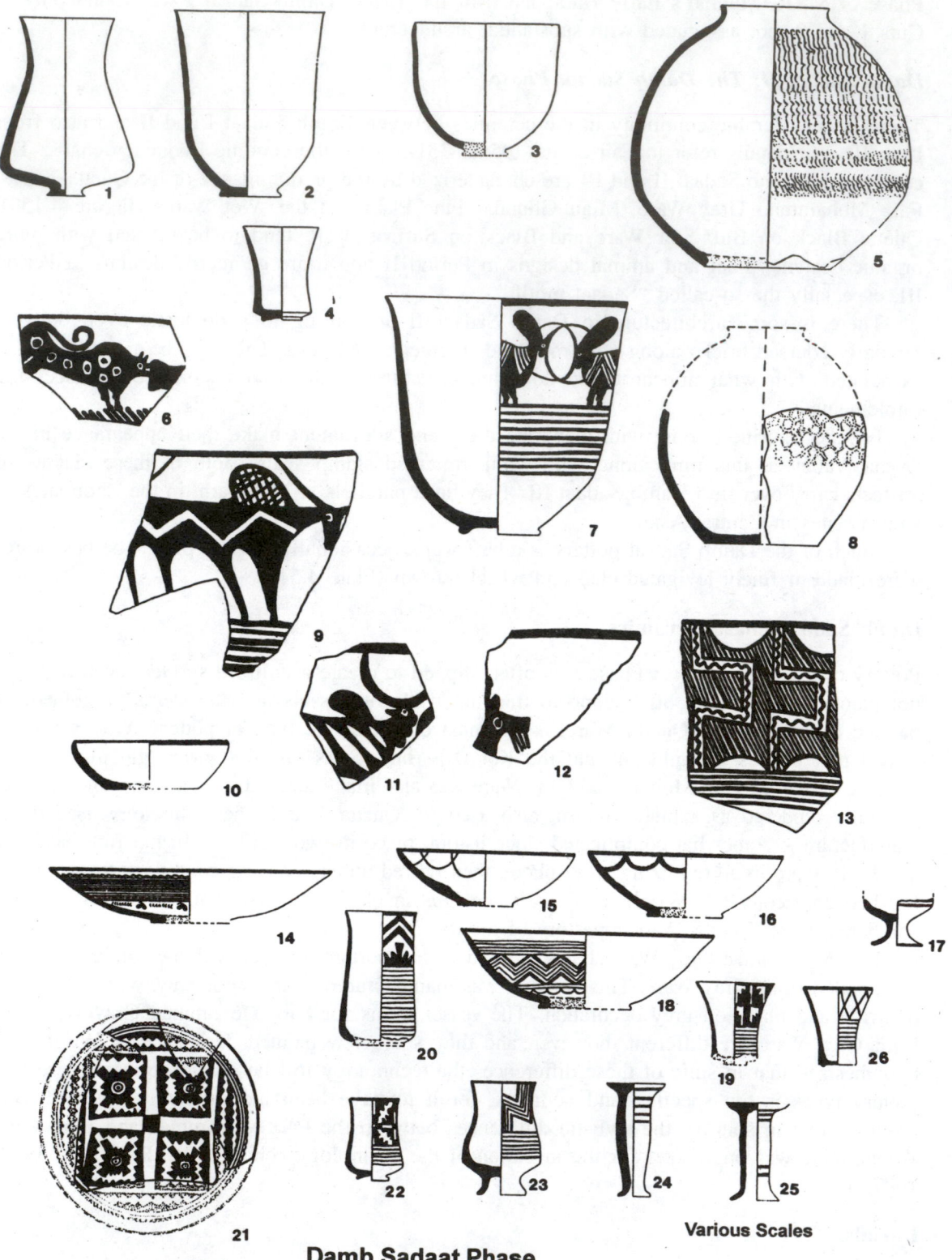

Damb Sadaat Phase

Figure 4.159. Ceramics of the Damb Sadaat Phase in the Quetta Valley, Damb Sadaat and other sites, after Fairservis 1956a

the Quetta region, by a steep, but short pass. There are two prehistoric mounds in Isplenji, labeled "one" and "two". Both sites have several occupations and dating the cemetery found at Isplenji Two will have to await formal excavation. What we know of this cemetery is given here:

Mound II is evidently a cemetery site. Slight clearance of debris at the eroded portion partially exposed three skeletons—two adults and one of a child—in the same grave. The skeleton of the child, lying on its left side, slightly bent, was found in somewhat better preserved condition. They were all buried roughly in the east-west direction, heads being on the eastern side (Anonymous 1964: 16-7).

While this report goes on to suggest that these interments might be associated with the Togau or Amri-Nal occupations of the valley, this is not established and they could date as late as the Quetta Phase, largely contemporary with the Mature Harappan.

Quetta Ware

It has long been recognized that the Quetta Valley sites share important and broad parallels in ceramics and some small finds, especially figurines, with parts of Central Asia, particularly Turkmenistan, Uzbekistan, Tadjikistan and Bactria. These interconnections probably have historically deep roots, which become apparent with the appearance of the black painted Quetta Wares in Damb Sadaat II, Mundigak III and Mehrgarh VI and VII, which can be broadly correlated with the Namazga III sites to the north (S. P. Gupta 1979: Vol. 2, 122-24). Depending on the exact site, or portion of a period that is being addressed, these are all occupations of the first half of the third millennium BC. (Plate 4.52).

Quetta Ware was first defined by Stuart Piggott (1947). His description was substantially expanded by Walter Fairservis following the excavation of Damb Sadaat (1956a: 254-56) as well as by Jean-Marie Casal's excavations at Mundigak (1961a) and Jim Shaffer's work at Said Qala (1978b). There is a lot yet to be learned about the development of Quetta Ware, but a case can be made for its beginning as a set of geometric motifs executed on fine buff cups and beakers which then develop into a more organic set of designs, including plant and animal motifs on an expanded repertory of vessel forms made of the same fabric. The most highly developed Quetta Ware is found in Damb Sadaat II and III, reaching a peak in the upper levels of Damb Sadaat III as described by Leslie Alcock (1956) with elegant, simple designs including the so called "bracket" motif (Figure 4.160).

One of the unresolved problems in the relative stratigraphy of central Baluchistan and Kachi centers on Bracket Ware. This ceramic is characteristic of Damb Sadaat III, which is contemporary with the Mature Harappan, as used here. In Kachi it is associated with Mehrgarh VIIC and Nausharo IC and ID. These occupations at Nausharo are placed in the Transitional Stage (c. 2650-2550). It seems that Bracket Ware continued to be made in the Quetta Valley in Damb Sadaat III, when the inhabitants of Nausharo used the Mature Harappan fine red wares.

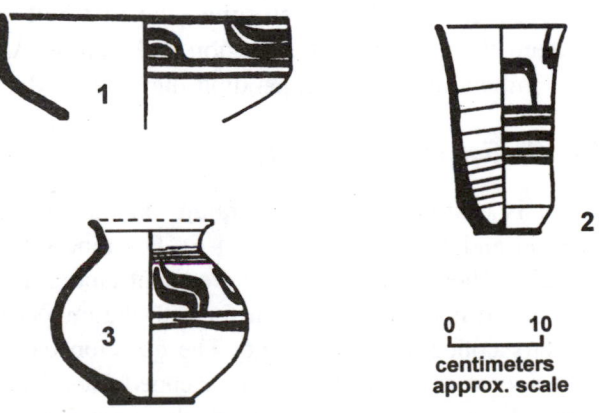

Figure 4.160. The bracket motif, or Bracket Ware

One of the most common motifs on Quetta Ware is the stepped square, which was first noticed on Nal Ware. The Quetta versions are more angular than those of Nal and occur in a large number of variations, including concentric renderings. Other designs occur as well; squares, diamonds and zigzags, some of which look like lightning bolts, but the stepped cross is the distinctive motif.

Close parallels to the Quetta Ware motifs occur at many sites. They are found at Mehrgarh, Mundigak and Said Qala as well as Damb Sadaat. They are also at Shahr-i Sokhta and other sites in Seistan and interestingly enough in Central Asia at places like Altyn Depe and the Geoksyur Oasis. It is important to note that these are *versions* of Quetta Ware and its motifs, as originally proposed by Piggott and refined by Fairservis. The Mehrgarh, Mundigak and Said Qala wares are very close to those in Quetta. But, the Quetta Ware at Shahr-i Sokhta and the Central Asian sites is definitely different and in some important ways (Figure 4.161).

There are many ways to compare ceramics, but three of the most important dimensions are: (1) ware or fabric (forming technique, color, fineness, etc.), (2) vessel form, and (3) decoration. The Pakistani and Afghan sites compare well on all three dimensions for Quetta Ware: wheel thrown buff wares, on similar vessel forms with closely related motifs. But the Central Asian "Quetta Ware" compares well only in terms of painted motifs. Most of the pots with these motifs from Central Asian places are hand made of a rather coarse fabric and the vessel forms on which the motifs are executed are different from those in the Quetta Valley. Moreover the Central Asian "Quetta Ware" makes use of polychrome painting, unlike the black on buff ware in Pakistan. But, the correspondence between designs in the two regions is striking and counts for something since it is not the only important comparable body of material. The figurines and compartmented stamp seals from Baluchistan and Central Asia are also alike (Figure 4.162).

The role played by the terracotta figurines in the lives of the people of the Damb Sadaat Phase is not known. Indeed, they may have played more than one role in these societies; some types having been used in one way and others employed quite differently. Some of them may have been toys, some may have played a role in the system of belief. One thing is certain, both males and females are present and the notion that they were all "mother goddesses" is untenable. The compartmented stamp seals, widespread on the Iranian Plateau and in Central Asia, a substantial number of which also employ the stepped square motif, are also enigmatic in their use since impressions are lacking. They do, however, seem to have been identifiers of some kind, and cannot be dismissed as trivial in their occurrence in both Central Baluchistan and Central Asia, as well as Seistan and Afghanistan.

Even in Early Harappan times, the first half of the third millennium, there are strong links between the Greater Indus Region and Central Asia. These continue into the remainder of the third millennium, even expanding during the Mature Harappan.

The Origins of Quetta Ware

There is a small body of literature on the origins of the Quetta Ware: Tosi (1969: 283-86), Masson and Sarianidi (1972: 94-6), Biscione (1973), Jarrige (1988b) and Gupta (1979: Vol. 2, 122-23). There is unanimous agreement among them that this pottery had its origins in Central Asia and it is a rare treat to differ with the impeccable authority represented by these established scholars concerning this point. The question cannot be resolved on available data, although it does appear that the important "stepped cross" motif is Central Asian in origin. For the larger body of ceramics, there is as much reason to propose that the ware (or wares) originated in Central Baluchistan as there is to support their hypothesis. Masson and Sarianidi note that the

677

Figure 4.161. Ceramics resembling Quetta Ware from Altyn Depe, after Masson 1988: Plate XXV

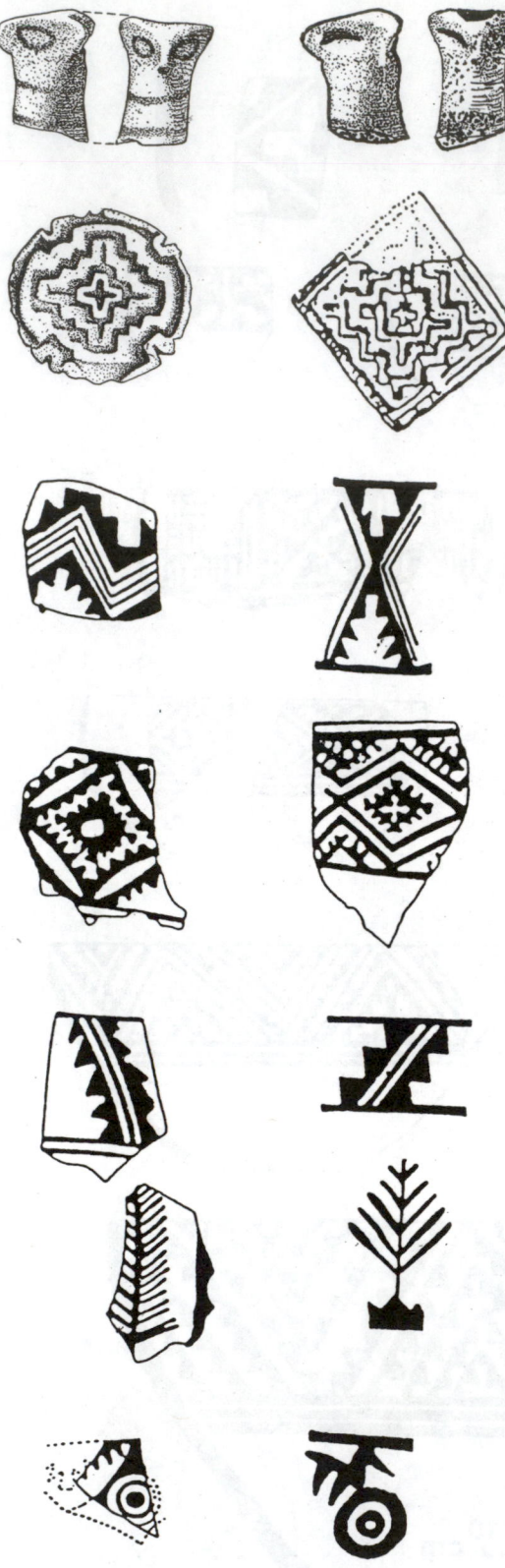

Figure 4.162. Pottery motifs, figurines and compartmented stamp seals from Baluchistan and Central Asia

formal comparisons of the Quetta Ware from Central Asia and Baluchistan are very close, sometimes identical, particularly for the painted motifs.

These analogies are not limited to painted pottery, but are also found in the small anthropomorphic figurines, certain metal artifacts, stamp seals and finally in similar types of burials.

In addition we find collective burials in rectangular chambers, similar to those found in Geoksyur II, Altyn-depe and Ulug-depe. It is worth noting that collective burials in *tholi* in southern Turkmenia date back to the fourth-third millennia BC, which means that they carry much older traditions than their equivalent in southern Afghanistan. In other words, there are clear-cut analogies in such conservative and lasting traditions as funeral rites, which can hardly be dismissed as accidental.

All this provides evidence to support the hypothesis that the Quettan complex formed under the influence of south-east Turkmenian cultures (1972: 94-5).

Since there is no information on prehistoric burials in the Quetta Valley, or Central Baluchistan, hanging the principal element of their position on this data set places Masson's and Sarianidi's argument in serious jeopardy because it is not known whether the burials in Baluchistan would support, or deny their position.

Raffaele Biscione (1973) has stated his position in the following way:

> ...Soviet scholars, chiefly Professor Masson, Dr. Sarianidi and Dr. Hlopin, succeeded in showing the continuity of the pottery tradition throughout the Chalcolithic period (Sarianidi 1965: 28-9; Hlopin 1963: 22, 1969: 49-50). They have clearly demonstrated that the Quetta Ware was the logical continuation of ceramic styles of periods Namazga I and II, Early and Middle Chalcolithic (Sarianidi

1965: 28-9). We must therefore conclude that the birthplace of Quetta Ware was Southern Turkmenia, and that its spreading over so wide an area was a later phenomenon (Masson 1961a: 213; 1964: 437-39; Sarianidi 1965: 50) (Biscione 1973: 105).

Biscione's observations are correct and the Soviet's study of their ceramics do indicate continuity in vessel form, decoration and ceramic technology. But the same is true for the ceramics of the Quetta Valley, based on Walter Fairservis' original study (1956a) and my own work with this body of material. It can be concluded, to paraphrase Biscione, that Quetta Ware was the logical outgrowth of ceramic development from Kili Ghul Mohammad III to Damb Sadaat II.

The idea that both Central Baluchistan and Central Asia have data to support the positions just stated is viable. There is sound internal evidence for the development of the Quetta Ware in both regions, the burial data being moot. If this is the case it suggests that the problem may have been incorrectly formulated or misunderstood. There is an implicit assumption that there must have been a "donor-receptor" relationship between Central Baluchistan and Central Asia and that diffusion from one region or the other must have been the mechanism for the transfer of Quetta Ware, the figurines and the rest.

The alternative to this model, and one which satisfies the evidence for the development of Quetta Ware, is to rid it of the donor-receptor relationship and restate it in terms of mutual interaction, as in an interaction sphere proposed by Joseph Caldwell many years ago (Caldwell 1964). The peoples of Central Baluchistan, Central Asia and the intervening areas as well, established an enduring relationship, probably a series of them, and part of this involved the manufacture of ceramics, figurines and seals, which developed side by side in the area encompassed by the interaction sphere.

The mechanisms that fueled the interaction were probably based on the physical movement of peoples within the sphere: a shared set of activities, with some peoples from all or most of the settlements participating. The movement itself was based in part on ecology and the diverse activities of pastoral nomads in their own diversity of form, but other motives would have propelled it, too; trade, systems of exchange and gift giving, even the human propensity for travel and adventure should be considered a part of the instrumentality. This set of relationships linking Central Asia to Central Baluchistan, extending down on to the Kachi Plain, reaching Mundigak and Shahr-i Sokhta, also seems to have been based more on peaceful processes than on war and antagonism. The durability of the interaction sphere, and a lack of signs of large scale conflict in the archaeological record suggest this. It does not mean that these peoples were all happy, eager to please and help their neighbors. There must have been a variety of human values and feelings, some of which may have been antagonistic, even resulting in outbreaks of violence. Yet these emotions seem to have been held in check, or compromised by mechanisms such as mutual self-interest so that the strength of the interaction sphere had an enduring quality. Since the interaction lasted well into the second millennium, a period exceeding a thousand years, one has to believe that the social and cultural mechanisms on which it rested were strong and positive. There would have been, for example, marriages and an exchange of people among these communities.

More on the Distribution of Quetta Ware Sites

The distribution of Quetta Ware sites is interesting. There is a cluster of them in Quetta-Pishin and more settlements down the Bolan Pass to Kachi. They are found in the valleys adjacent to

Quetta-Pishin. One such place is Isplenji, where there is a fine Quetta Ware site on the edge of a playa, so large and flat that a Land Rover can be driven across it at 150 kilometers an hour. Beyond this the Quetta Ware in Baluchistan occurs only in small quantities. Across the Khojak Pass, on to the Registan Desert it is found at Said Qala and Deh Morasi Ghundai and then Mundigak. A variety occurs in Seistan, principally at Shahr-i Sokhta, with another closely related type in Central Asia.

This distribution has an interesting funnel-like shape, with Quetta-Pishin at the base and the narrow neck projecting down the Bolan Pass to Kachi and the Indus Plains. The cup of the funnel holds Seistan, the Kandahar region and extends north to Turkestan.

There are many routes within this vast area (Figure 3.3) but there is a relatively direct one, connecting Kachi to the vicinity of Altyn Depe. It follows the Bolan and Khojak Passes to Kandahar, then skirts the western foothills of the Hindu Kush, the central massif of Afghanistan, to Herat and north to Central Asia. The modern highway from Sibi to Quetta, Kandahar, Herat and Merv approximates this track which was direct, lacked serious impediments to travel and had ample sources of water along its entire course and should be considered one of the great, reliable, expressways of antiquity.

Long Distance Trade

One of the distinguishing accomplishments of the Damb Sadaat Phase was the growth in connections between the Greater Indus Region and surrounding tracts. Even in Mehrgarh I, the Aceramic Period, there were abundant signs of long distance trade in luxury items such as lapis lazuli, turquoise and sea shells. The ability of peoples in the Subcontinent to reach out and capture such goods, apparently on such a scale that it stands out in the archaeological record, starts at the very beginning of the Indus Age and persists through the Mature Harappan Stage. It is not something that builds slowly, or comes in fits and starts. Long distance trade begins with the development of villages and pastoral camps and persists right into the Mature Harappan. In the Indus case it is not necessarily a distinctive marker of urbanization as suggested by V. Gordon Childe when he included this feature as one of his so-called "ten criteria for civilization" (Childe 1950).

The Baluchistan-Central Asia interaction sphere emerges in the archaeological record as one based on durable goods, mostly stone and metal. With the exception of turquoise there are few durable products from Central Asia that might have been desired by the inhabitants of the Greater Indus Region. For its part, Baluchistan might have supplied copper, and Afghan tin. The recently reported source of lapis lazuli in the Chagai Hills of Baluchistan (Delmas and Casanova 1990, Casanova 1992, 1994) would also have been important, as might have been the Badakshan source. But, viewed from an historical perspective it was not necessarily durables like these that played the predominant role in trade and exchange here. When we have written sources we learn that this kind of interaction is generally based on perishables, especially grain and textiles. These important commodities should not be neglected in our thought, in spite of the fact that there is virtually no archaeological record for these in the Indus Age. See Irene Good (1995) and Janaway and Coningham (1995) for recent reviews of the textile evidence.

The Early Harappan, Damb Sadaat Phase seems to mark a growth in interregional connections on the western side of the Indus area. This seems to have been on a large scale, involved long distance travel and was enduring. It was also an important harbinger of developments that took place during the Mature Harappan, which build on the foundation laid in Damb Sadaat and earlier interaction.

The Sothi-Siswal Phase of the Eastern Region

To the east, on the other side of the Greater Indus Region, there were also important developments taking place during the Early Harappan Stage (Figure 4.163, Figure 4.164). These began along the natural route of the Sarasvati and its Indian tributaries, especially the Drishadvati or Chautung but it spread into Punjab, Haryana, with one lone site (Nawanbans) in the Ganga-Yamuna Doab of western Uttar Pradesh.

The Excavated Sites of the Sothi-Siswal Phase

There are sixteen excavated Sothi-Siswal sites. These range from large scale, long term excavations at places like Kalibangan and Banawali, to little more than tests at Sothi, Nohar, Siswal, Sarangpur and Tarkhanewala Dera. This Phase takes its name from two of the excavated sites in this region: Sothi and Siswal.

Kalibangan and Banawali are the most extensively and best reported excavated sites of the Sothi-Siswal Phase. Banawali is reported to have been 16 hectares in size, but these are only the apparent dimensions of the mound. The exact size of the Sothi-Siswal settlement is not yet known. In some ways these sites are unremarkable as harbingers of urbanization. There is no sense of the beginning of monumental architecture, although Kalibangan and Banawali are both surrounded by a wall which *is possibly a fortification*. But Kalibangan at the time was small, 4.5 hectares, and this has been determined with some accuracy. It was not a town at the time, if judged by size or internal complexity. Neither are the craft activities implied by finds from these sites especially interesting: pottery making, metallurgy (copper at both sites, a bit of gold from Banawali). Faience, steatite are both present and will grow to become very important materials during the Mature, Urban Harappan. There is some indication of long distance trade with sea shells and lapis lazuli at Kalibangan and Banawali and other Sothi-Siswal sites.

The Site of Sothi

Sothi, a small site in the Drishadvati Valley eight kilometers east of Nohar, was discovered by A. Ghosh of the Archaeological Survey of India. This is the first place that pottery characteristic of Kalibangan Period I was found in stratigraphic context. Sothi is a small mound about 200 by 200 meters or four hectares in size and about three meters high. There is both a Sothi-Siswal and Mature Harappan occupation there.

Ghosh placed six trenches at Sothi in 1950-51 (Dikshit 1984b: 532). The results of this excavation were never published, but in 1978 K. N. Dikshit, also of the Archaeological Survey of India, returned to Sothi and put in one small trial trench, two by two meters, to assess the stratigraphy (Dikshit 1980, 1984b).

Dikshit found two cultural levels in 3.4 meters of deposit. The excavation was too small to have unearthed any significant architecture. The upper cultural level (Period I) consisted of Mature, Urban Phase Harappan ceramics mixed with Sothi Wares, triangular terracotta cakes, cart frames and bangles. The lower level consisted only of Sothi ceramics. Stratigraphic sections are published in Dikshit (1984b: 533). Dikshit takes pains to note that there is apparent continuity between Periods I and II at Sothi, and neighboring Nohar as well, but there are signs of discontinuity at Kalibangan and Sandhanawala (1984b: 533, 537).

The ceramics of both Sothi and Siswal have been described in terms of the fabrics found at Kalibangan in Period I. These were originally laid out by B. K. Thapar, who identified six fabrics, which are designated A through F.

682

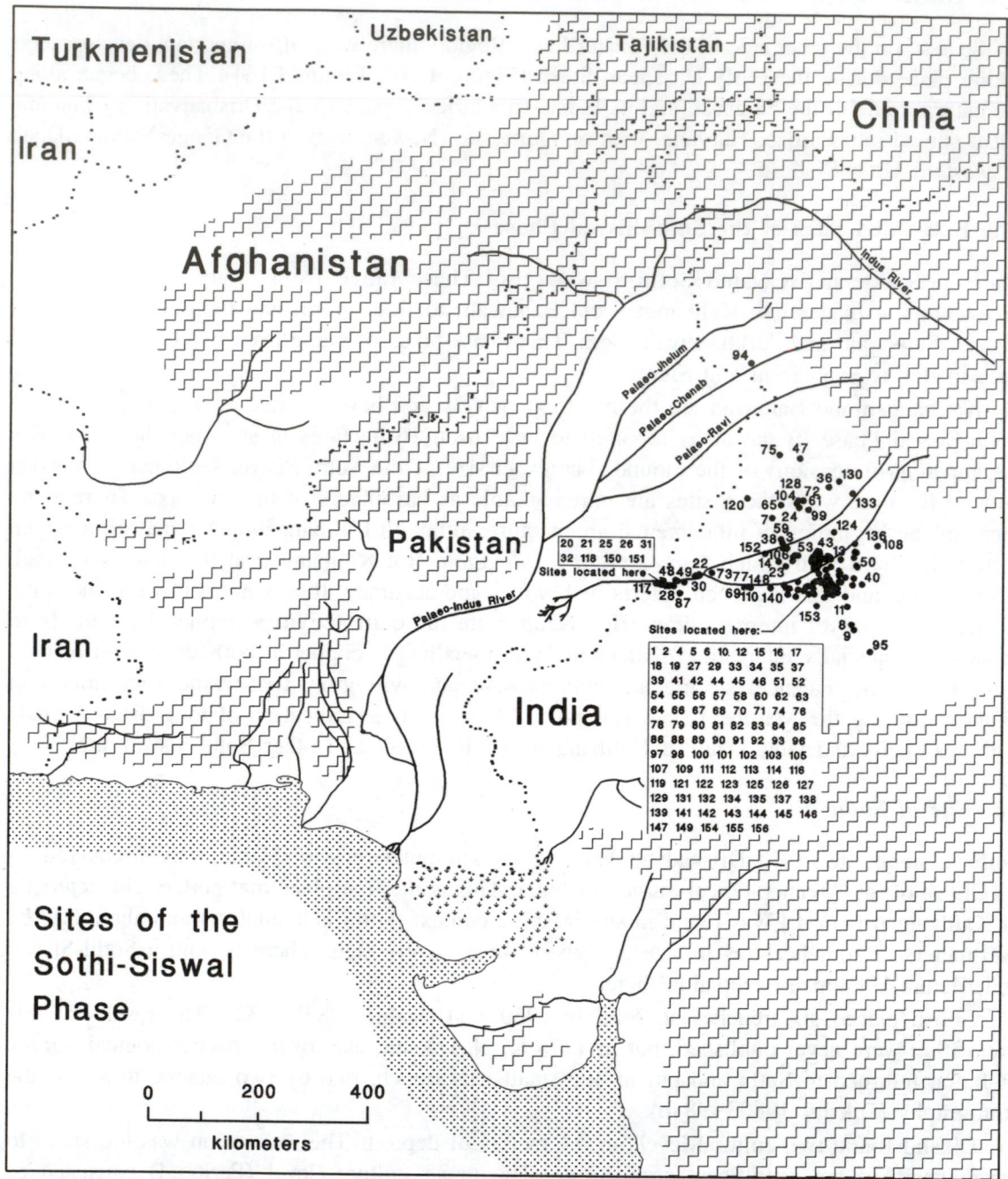

Figure 4.163. Map of sites of the Sothi-Siswal Phase

Key to Figure 4.163

1. Alipur Kharar Three
2. Alipur Kharar Two
3. Alipur Mandran
4. Amargarh One
5. Amarheri One

6. Arada
7. Amiwala Theh
8. Badli, Rohtak
9. Badsa
10. Baghru Khurd

11. Baliana
12. Balu
13. Balu Two
14. Banawali
15. Bare

683

16. Barki
17. Baroli
18. Barsana, Kurukshetra
19. Bata One
20. Berore
21. Bhagwansar Four
22. Bhaironpura
23. Bhirrana
24. Bhudan
25. Binjor One
26. Binjor three
27. Budha Khera Three
28. Bugia
29. Buwana Two
30 Chak 01 1
31. Chak 072/3
32. Chak 075, India
33. Chanat One
34. Chanat Three
35. Chanat Two
36. Chandiala
37. Chhapra
38. Chhoti Mansa
39. Daroli Khera
40. Datta
41. Deverar
42. Dhakal One
43. Dhanouri
44. Dharodi
45. Dhingana
46. Dhur-fnarkha Kalan One
47. Domeli
48. G. B. 12
49. G. B. 16
50. Gansina
51. Garhi
52. Garhwal, Sonepat
53. Ghaswa
54. Ghatauli
55. Ghimana One
56. Gossain
57. Gularwala
58. Gunkali
59. Gumikalan Two
60. Hamalpur
61. Handali
62. Hansdhera

63. Hansi
64. Hatho Two
65. Inewala Theh
66. Jhamola
67. Jind Five
68. Jind Two
69. Jogiasson
70. Kachrana Kalan
71. Kalait One
72. Kalian
73. Kalibangan
74. Kandala Two
75. Karalan
76. Karela Two
77. Karoti
78. Karsola One
79. Karsola Two
80. Kathana Two
81. Khapran
82. Kharak Pandwan
83. Kharal One
84. Kharal Three
85. Kharal Two
86. Kharar
87. Kharuwala Ther
88. Khema Kheri
89. Koel
90. Kunal
91. Laun
92. Lohar Raghu
93. Lohari
94. Manda
95. Mandkaula
96. Mangali One
97. Mangali Two
98. Mangalpur
99. Manorana
100. Masaudpur
101. Matar Sham
102. Mirchpur
103. Moana
104. Moholi
105. Morkhi
106. Naiwala Theh
107. Nandgarh One
108. Nawanbans
109. Nidani

110. Nohar
111. Pahlwan
112. Pali
113. Paoli
114. Pindara
115. Pinjupura
116. Pipaltha One
117. R. D. 89
118. R. D. 92
119. Radhana
120. Raja Sirkap
121. Rajpura Sirkap
121. Rajpura Two
122. Rakhighari
123. RaniRan
124. Ratta Khera Khuram
125. Ratta Theh
126. Rawalwas Kalan
127. Rindhana
128. Rohira
129. Rookhi
130. Ropar
131. Sadha Majra
132. Salimarh
133. Sarangpur
134. Satrod Khurd One
135. Satrod Khurd Three
136. Saunkhr Three
137. Saunkhra Three
138. Saunkhra Two
139. Shahpur, Hissar
140. Sherpura
141. Shshpur, Kamal
142. SiamloKalan One
143. Siamlo Kalan Two
144. Singhra
145. Singhwa
146. Sisana
147. Siswal
148. Sothi
149. Surbra
150. Suwaiki
151. Tarkhanwala Dera
152. Theraj
153. Tigrana
154. Ujhana Two
155. Urdana
156. Urlana Khurd Two

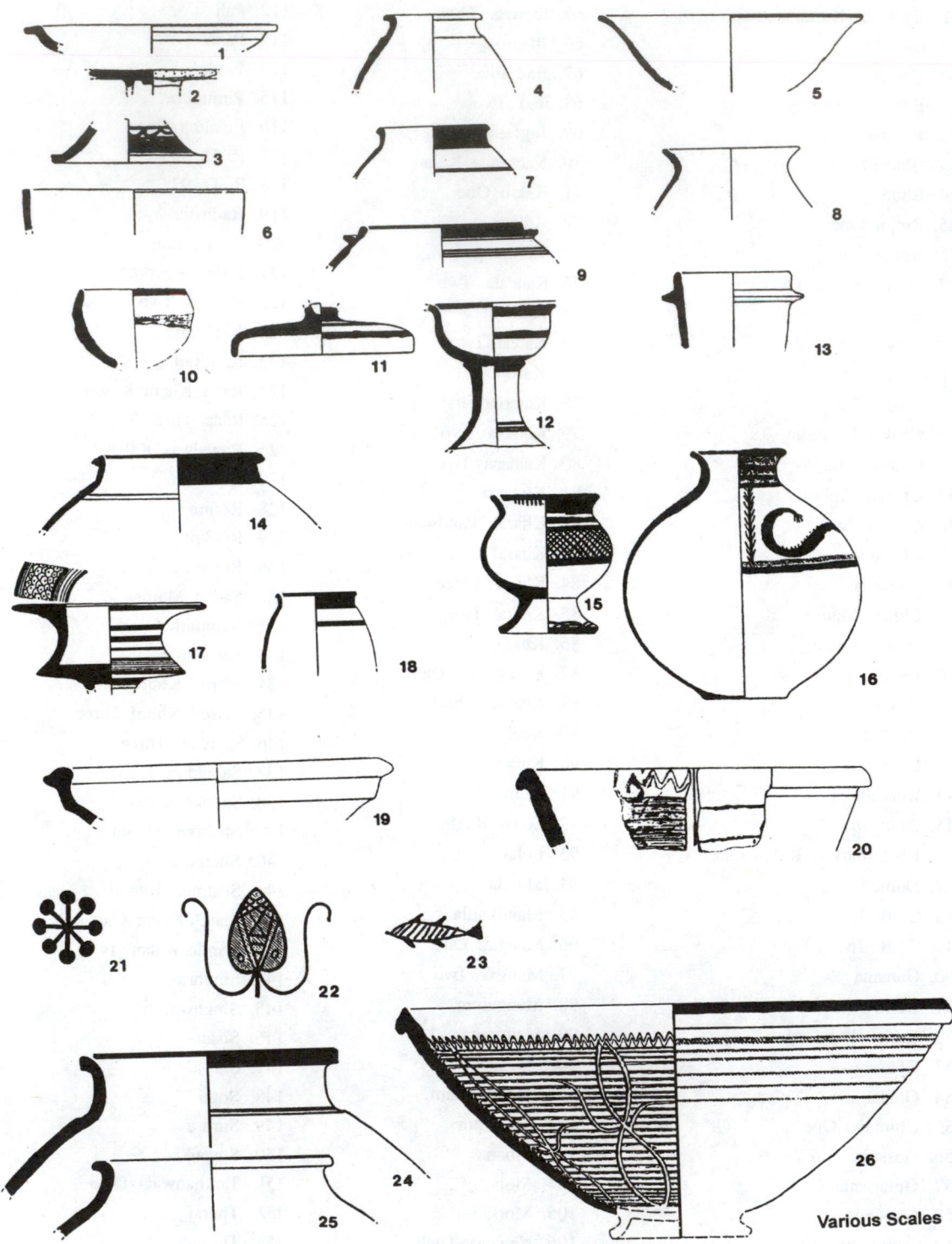

Figure 4.164. Ceramics of the Sothi-Siswal Phase.

Fabric A: poorly potted with painted designs in faint black, at times white was added. Kot Diji short necked jars with a black band at the neck. The grooved ceramic already defined called Bhoot Ware (Plate 4.53).

Fabric B: rusticated lower portion and smooth upper portion. This ware closely resembles a ceramic type from the Quetta Valley known as Khojak Parallel Striated (Fairservis 1956a: 268; IAR 1962-63: 27) (see Figure 4.131). Kot Diji short necked jars with a black band at the neck; Periano Wet Ware.

Fabric C: fine ware pottery with smooth outer surfaces. Slips in red, purple and plum red are present.

Fabric D: thick sturdy ware used for storage jars, troughs and basins. The interior of Fabric D basins may be comb incised; Bhoot Ware (Plate 4.54).

Fabric E: buff ware

Fabric F: grey ware (IAR 1962-63: 20-7)

The pottery assemblage of Sothi was dominated by Fabrics C and D of Kalibangan. Fabric A was rare (Figure 4.165).

The Site of Siswal

Siswal, in Hissar District of Haryana, has the same basic ceramics and small finds as those found at Sothi. It was also briefly excavated in 1970 by Suraj Bhan, the man who found the site (1975: 103-09). His trench was only two by two meters, and at -1.25 meters virgin soil was reached. Suraj Bhan describes the pottery that he found there (1975: 103-09) in terms of their close relationship to the Fabrics of Kalibangan I. All six (A-F) are present, with an overlap between them and the Mature Harappan occupation of Period II.

No small finds were recovered in excavation, however some did come from surface prospecting. These included a fragment of a crucible that has been used in the processing of copper (Suraj Bhan 1975: 109).

Both Sothi and Siswal have been retained for this Phase of the Early Harappan since they frequently occur in the literature and both of them are appropriate. Rather than choosing between them, I decided to use both.

The Site of Kalibangan

Kalibangan is one of the most famous of the Indus sites. It was first discovered by L. P. Tessitori of the Archaeological Survey of India in 1917 and test excavated by him in 1918. He had no idea of the importance of the place and called it "Kali Banga" or "Kali Vangu." Sir Aurel Stein visited there in 1941 as part of his Sarasvati tour as did A. Ghosh in 1950 as part of his exploration of the same area. This led to nine seasons of excavation by the Archaeological Survey of India from 1960-61 to 1968-69 (IAR 1962-63, 1964-65, 1968-69; B. B. Lal 1979; B. K. Thapar 1973a, 1973b, 1975).

Kalibangan is strategically located at the point where the Sarasvati and Drishadvati Rivers meet. The mounds there are high, with ten meters of relief. In Period I (Sothi-Siswal) it was a single mound c. 250 × 180 meters or 4.5 hectares. The remodeling of Period II (Mature Harappan) created two mounds and expanded the area to c. 240 by 120 meters plus c. 360 by 240 meters for a total of 11.5 hectares (Figure 4.166, Figure 4.167). It appears that Kalibangan may have been fortified from its very beginning, reinforcing the notion that it sits at a strategic location at the confluence of two rivers, and perhaps on an ancient frontier as well. From an environmental perspective Kalibangan was located outside the active flood plain of its riverine system, but

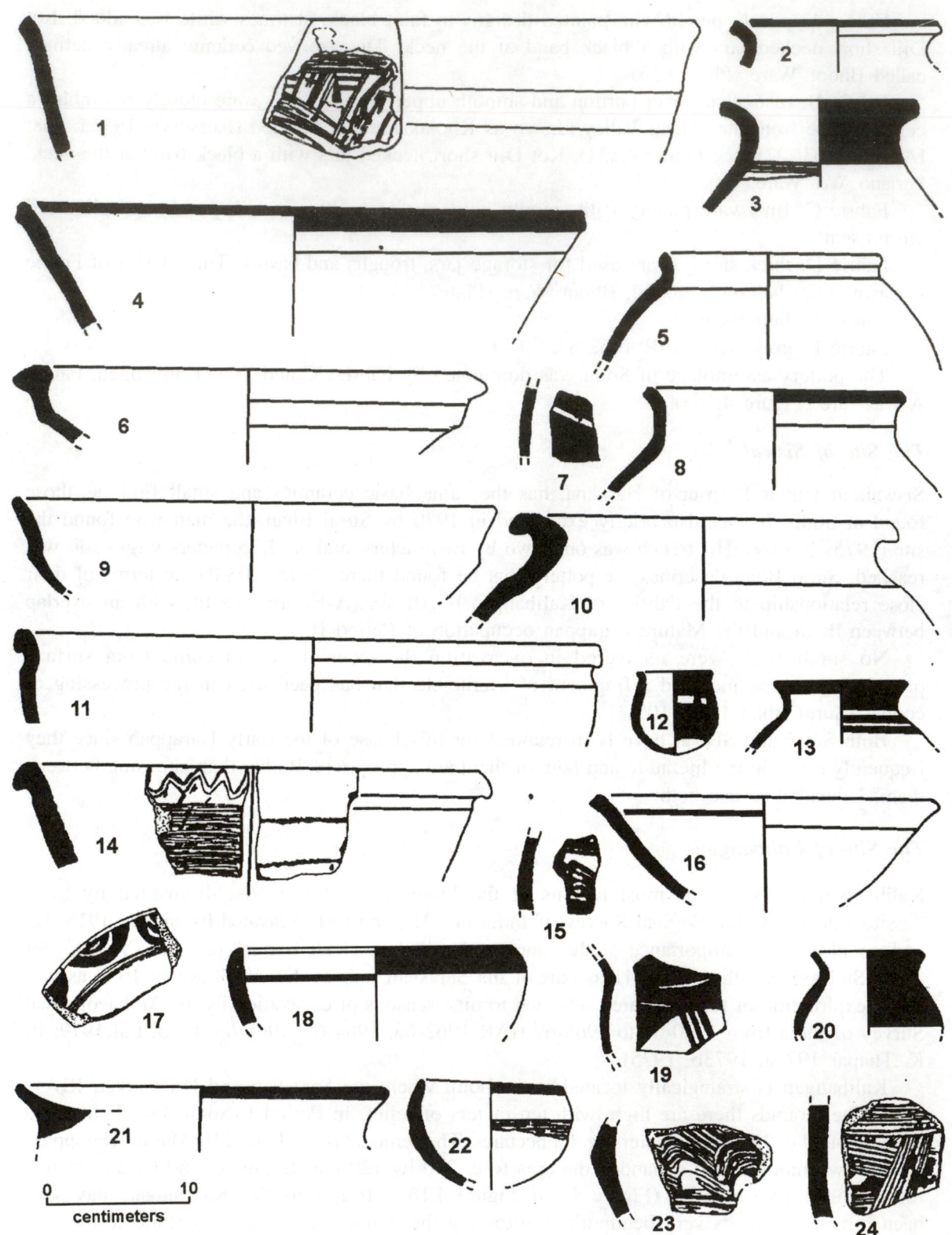

Figure 4.165. Pottery from Sothi, after K. N. Dikshit 1980

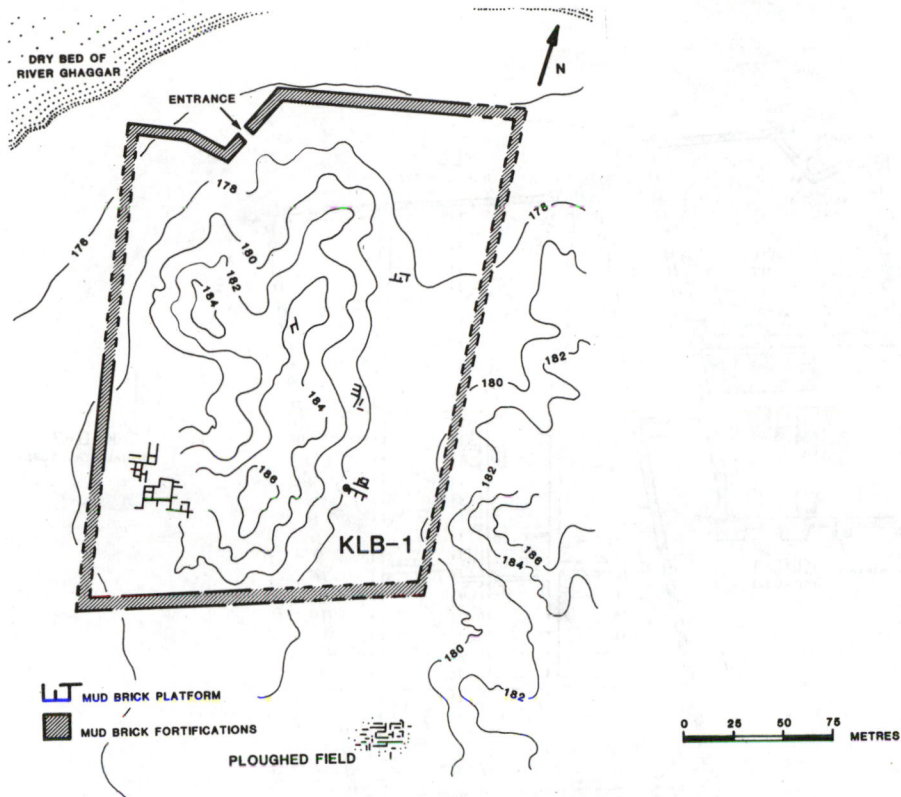

Figure 4.166. Site plan of Kalibangan, Period I, Sothi-Siswal Phase

was sufficiently close for it to be an important source of water. Agriculture and pastoralism would have been possible in close proximity to the site.

The Sothi-Siswal, Early Harappan Settlement

The Sothi-Siswal Phase settlement at Kalibangan is surrounded by a fortification wall in the shape of a parallelogram ca. 250 by 170 meters in extent. The first phase of the wall was made of mud bricks (30 × 20 × 10 cm) laid to a thickness of ca. 1.90 meters. A second phase of construction brought the thickness of this fortification up to three or four meters, varying from place to place. The inner and outer faces of the fortifications were plastered with mud. Only one entrance, at the northwest corner, was excavated; other entrances were probably obscured by later Mature Harappan material. This opening has an interesting configuration as seen on the site plan and is cunningly designed for the protection of this vulnerable point. One lane, ca. 1.50 meters wide, was found for this period, the other streets eclipsed by the overburden of Mature Harappan remains (Plate 4.55).

The Sothi-Siswal Phase inhabitants of Kalibangan lived in well made houses, oriented to the cardinal directions and made of the same small mud bricks used for their fortifications (Plate 4.56). The bricks were laid in English bond, with alternating rows of headers and stretchers. One house of the period had a drain made of baked bricks, a harbinger of later times. Baked bricks were never used in abundance at Kalibangan, as they were at Mohenjo-daro. The rooms of the houses were arranged around a courtyard and had domestic facilities including ovens.

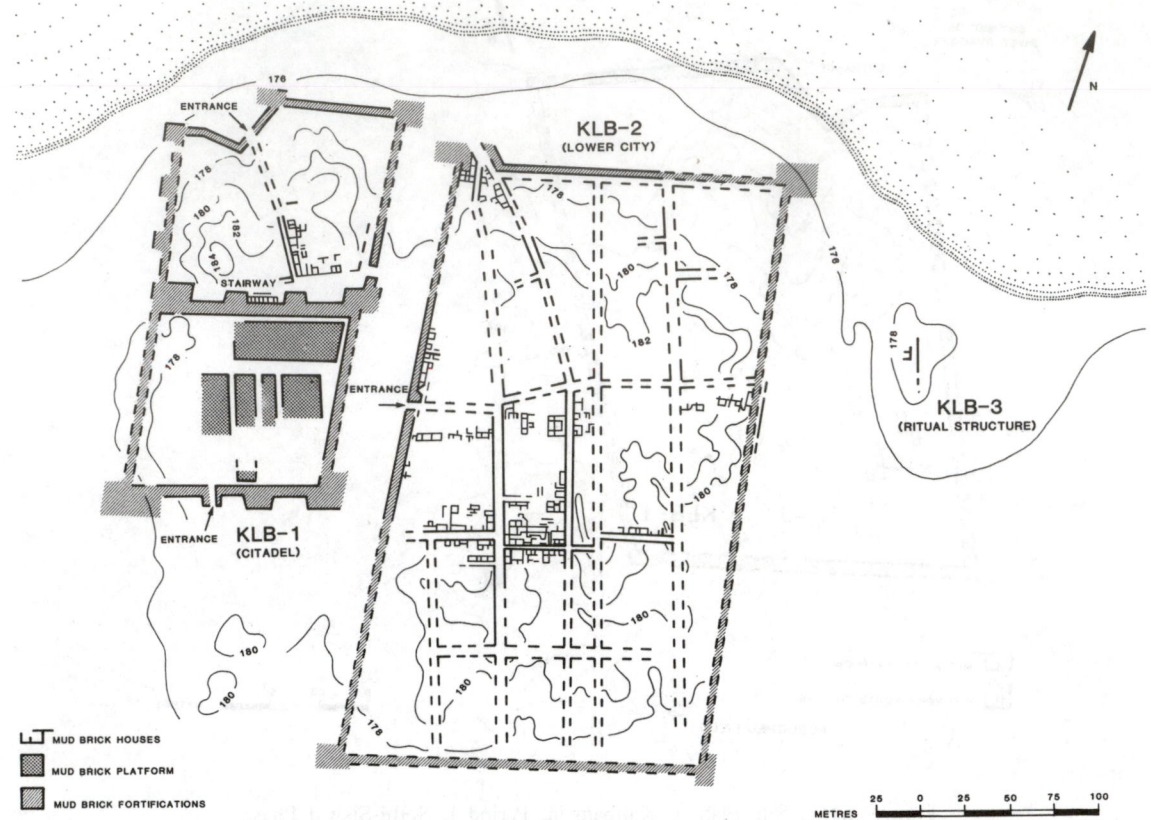

Figure 4.167. Site plan of Kalibangan, Period II, Mature Harappan

Above ground, closed ovens and the subterranean *tandoor* were found. The evidence for bread making is complemented by the presence of querns and milling stones.

Direct and important evidence for cultivation was found in the form of a preserved plowed field, about 100 meters to the south of the Period I settlement. It was covered by slump from the Sothi-Siswal Phase occupation and consisted of alternating furrows and hummocks in the earth (Plate 4.57, Plate 4.58). These were oriented to the cardinal directions and have a close ethnographic parallel in modern Rajasthani agricultural practice (Lal 1970-71).

Some copper was in use. Of some importance is a knife of a style now called a *parsu* with parallels at Mitathal (Suraj Bhan 1975: Fig. 14a, 7) and Rojdi (Possehl and Raval 1989: 162).

Copper was used to make bangles, beads and other objects. Bangles were also made of terracotta and shell. Beads of agate, carnelian and shell also occur in Period I.

The Shift from Periods I to II

There is an interesting and important shift between Periods I and II at Kalibangan. First, the excavators noticed cleavage and/or displacement of strata in the Period I levels. They have interpreted this as indicative of an earthquake (Lal 1979: 75) which may have led to the abandonment of the settlement. B. K. Thapar expresses it this way: "This occupation continued through five structural phases, rising to a height of some 1.6 m, when it was brought to a close by a catastrophe (perhaps seismic), as evidenced by the occurrence of displaced (faulted?) deposits and subsided walls in different parts of the excavated area. Thereafter the site seems to have been abandoned, though only temporarily and a thin layer of sand, largely infertile, accumulated over the ruins" (Thapar 1973a: 87). The upper levels of the Period I settlement were also eroded in some places. Whatever the reason for abandonment, and an earthquake is a good hypothesis, it was apparently complete and the presence of the infertile, windblown sand indicates this.

The Mature Harappan is not the subject of this book, but it will be useful to describe some of what was found at Kalibangan during this period, if only to introduce the Mature Harappan Stage and give a sense of the history of this extraordinary site.

The Mature Harappan Settlement

When the Mature Harappans reoccupied Kalibangan their ceramics included many of the shapes and fabrics of the Period I occupation. This lasted for about one-half of Period II when it gave way to a more purely Harappan ceramic corpus (Thapar 1989: 196). Other sites in the northeastern region of the Indus Civilization share this mixture of ceramics as seen at Kalibangan.

The Mature Harappan settlement plan of Kalibangan is significantly different from the original. There are two parts: the High Mound, designated KLB-1, is situated to the west, covering most of the abandoned Sothi-Siswal Phase settlement and to the east is the Lower Town, designated KLB-2, most of it on virgin soil. The old entrance in the northwestern corner of the High Mound was once again in use. The Harappan settlers did another interesting thing; they used the old eastern wall of the original settlement (the Sothi-Siswal Phase site) as the northern part of the western wall of the new Lower Town. This reduced the width of the High Mound by about sixty meters but created a High Mound that was exactly twice as long as it was wide, the same proportions employed at the Mound of the Great Bath at Mohenjo-daro. They also made good use of older building material, typical of our efficient Harappans.

The High Mound of Period II

During Period II the High Mound was well fortified, although the southern half was stronger than the north. There were two phases of construction and the wall is three to seven meters in thickness. In the earlier phase the Harappans used large bricks (40 × 20 × 10 cm), in the later phase they used smaller bricks (30 × 15 × 7.5 cm). Interestingly, the smaller size bricks were used throughout Period II for the construction of buildings.

The southern half of the High Mound, sometimes called the "southern rhomb" (Lal 1979: 77), was equipped during Harappan times with a series of mud brick platforms on which ritual structures, connected with the use of fire and possibly animal remains, were located. These have been called "fire-altars." They are oval in plan, sunk in the ground and lined with clay.

The southern rhomb contained several mud-brick platforms, oriented along the cardinal directions, on each of which there stood a special structure. Although in most cases the details of these structures have disappeared owing to subsequent spoliation, there is reasonable evidence about their likely use. Thus, atop one of the platforms there lay a series of seven "fire-altars" in a row (Plate 4.59). Behind these fire altars ran a wall in a north-south direction, which shows that the people had to face east while performing rituals at these altars. The altars were oblong on plan, sunk into the ground and lined with clay. They contained ash and charcoal, besides a cylindrical or faceted clay (burnt or unburnt) stele standing up near the centre. Though in the series under discussion only fragments of what are called "terracotta cakes" were obtained, elsewhere these were found in sufficient numbers showing that they formed some kind of an "offering." To the west of these fire-altars lay embedded the lower half of a jar. It contained ash and charcoal and was evidently connected with the use of the fire-altars. Within a few meters of these altars were a well and a few bath-pavements suggesting ablutions before the performance of the ritual—a tradition still in vogue in India, amongst the Hindus (Lal 1979: 77).

One of the platforms contained a well, a fire-altar and a rectangular pit lined with burnt bricks in which cattle bones and antlers were found (Plate 4.60). Professor B. B. Lal has suggested that this might indicate animal sacrifice (Lal 1979: 78).

The platforms on which the fire-altars were found were freestanding structures, not integrated into the brick work of the fortifications. They were elevated and access was by means of stairs placed in passage ways between them. The orientation of these "fire alters" tells us that the Harappans faced east when they were used. The northern half of the High Mound is covered with houses, seemingly those of an elite population, somehow differentiated from the inhabitants of the Lower Town. It makes good sense to think of the inhabitants of these buildings as the users and/or "managers" of the "fire alters." There were two entrances to the southern half of the High Mound and three to the northern half.

There is no agreement about the function of these "fire altars." Discussion of these features with Richard Meadow has been instructive. He notes that the most typical hearth at Harappa is oblong or key-hole shaped with a pillar in the center.

All that have been found during the recent excavations there are in domestic contexts, with up to three in one room. This seems to be a standard type Harappan hearth, at least in the north (R. Meadow, personal communication 1996).

The Lower Town of the Mature Harappan

There is no Harappan settlement more like Mohenjo-daro than Kalibangan. They are both composed of a western high mound and a lower town. The abundant use of baked brick preserved structures of some similarity. The grid town plan, street drains and the like all add to this sense of similarity. Most of the people lived in the Lower Town of the Mature Harappan at Kalibangan. It was surrounded by a fortification wall that ranged in thickness between three and a half and nine meters and had three or four phases of construction. This construction, just as with that of the High Mound, was plastered with mud and tapered from bottom to top. The fortifications protected a town laid out in a gridiron plan separating blocks of habitations. There were four streets running the full north-south distance of the settlement and three (possibly four) oriented east-west. It is interesting that the north-south streets do not run parallel to the fortifications, and two of them converge on the principal entrance to the Lower Town in the northwest corner of the settlement. Buildings at some intersections of these streets were equipped with wooden fenders to limit damage to, and done by, vehicular traffic. Lanes within the community blocks were ca. 1.80 meters wide and the other streets were multiples of this standard: 3.60, 5.40 and 7.20 meters. There is some indication of habitation extending outside the fortifications in the protected area to the south of the High Mound and to the west of the Lower Town.

Kalibangan Harappan houses were of mud brick and consisted of rooms set around courtyards, many of which had their own wells. Roofs were flat, with wooden rafters supporting a covering of reeds and mud. There is only one building with stairs suggesting a second story. Floors were of rammed earth, although there was some paving. Cooking was done in the open, generally in a corner of the courtyard. "Most of the rooms were used for living purposes, which include their use as bedrooms, but some also served as stores. In one of the rooms many large jars were found embedded in the ground. These seem to have been used for the storage of grains. It further appears that in almost every house a room was reserved for the 'fire-altars' which had their characteristic shape and other features including the central stele. In a few cases these were lined with mud bricks" (Lal 1979: 85).

Some houses had narrow platforms along their exterior walls, on lanes and streets. These seem to be seating areas, similar to those in modern villages of the northwestern Subcontinent, used by the inhabitants to meet friends, exchange information and keep up with the day-to-day life of their community.

A few baked bricks were used at Kalibangan in the Harappan period. They were pretty much reserved for use in ritual structures, drains, wells, bathing platforms and thresholds. Unlike Mohenjo-daro the drainage system was localized and discharged into large pots set in the ground.

KLB-3, The Ritual Structure

There is a small mound about 75 meters to the east of the Lower Town at Kalibangan. This has been designated KLB-3 and is called a "ritual structure." It was excavated during the 1968-69 field season (IAR 1968-69: 31). A set of trenches covering an area twenty by thirty meters was laid over the area.

The excavation at KLB-3 brought to light a mud-brick structure enclosing "fire altars" with the usual contents—viz. terracotta cakes, ash and the cylindrical blocks. On the eastern side of the structure was a 1.65 m thick mud-brick wall, of which a length of 12 meters was available. As the site did not show any remains of residential buildings, the existence of a structure with "fire altars" may perhaps suggest its use exclusively for religious purposes. Its location outside the city on the east may also probably be of some significance. The pottery obtained from the associated levels revealed that the structure was in use during the Harappan Period (IAR 1968-69: 31).

The ritual structure consists of an impressive mud brick wall that seems to have completely surrounded a room with four or five "fire altars" of standard Kalibangan type. The bricks were 30 × 15 × 7.5 cm, the smaller size usually employed at Kalibangan, but this small mound was badly eroded and a complete outline of the facility could not be obtained.

Mature Harappan Finds

Finds from the Mature Harappan include an abundance of copper based metal objects, three of which could be classed as low tin bronzes. Copper objects include beads, bangles, axes, at least one of the miniature hatchets, and points. There is also a very finely crafted bull figurine in copper. Interestingly, it is not a zebu. There is a wide range of typical Harappan cubical stone weights and a graduated measuring scale in terracotta. An ivory comb with tube drill decoration is present as well.

A significant number of seals and sealings were found at Kalibangan. These are fully illustrated in J. P. Joshi and Parpola (1987: 298-326) and include examples of both unicorn and zebu motifs along with other varieties. Two seals are worth particular notice; a flat, stamp seal with a human/animal device, including Indus script and a cylinder seal. The human/animal motif is repeated on the cylinder seal: however, on the flat seal the rear feet of the animal are clawed, not cloven. The front feet seem to be human. The cylinder seal has two scenes. To the left are three human figures. The central figure is covered by two arching "thorned branches," seemingly held by the flanking figures, who face one another. This scene may be related to the "human in pipal tree" motif from Mohenjo-daro. To the right is a human/animal motif, with human front feet and cloven hind feet. The human arms are covered in bangles, Harappan style. The head bears a three part, Harappan style, head dress. The hairdo of this figure and the central figure of the scene to the left may be the same. The cylinder seal has no script, except for the possibility that three vertical strokes in the area separating two scenes represent numbers.

There are small bar sealings with a scene involving what appears to be one of the "braziers" associated with a standard unicorn motif. In the center are 26 vertical strokes arranged in six groups of four and one of two to the left of two script stick figures.

Finally, there is a large Harappan style terracotta cake that is broken, but scenes incised on both sides are visible. On one side is a "human" figure with horns and a plant growing out of the top of its head. Plants growing out of the head of "human" figures are well known in Harappan iconography. On the other side is a human figure which seems to be pulling on another object, or animal, with a rope.

The Kalibangan Cemetery

A cemetery is located about 300 meters west southwest of the habitation area. This is both down wind and down river from the settlement itself. The cemetery is devoid of obvious surface markings and was located originally after a rainfall brought out an efflorescence of salt in a pattern suggesting possible inhumations; a suggestion confirmed by excavation.

There are two types of burials at Kalibangan and they all belong to the Mature Harappan of the habitation mounds. The first is an extended inhumation in a rectangular or oval pit. There are also cenotaphs, circular and rectilinear, including pottery but without skeletons. The cenotaphs were scattered through the area used for the extended inhumations. It is further apparent that the extended inhumations were found in groups, suggesting family burial areas to A. K. Sharma (1982a: 298).

The Kalibangan cemetery has evidence for: (1) trepanning of a child, (2) a serious, unhealed axe wound to the knee, 3) the remains of an individual with serious body deformation, (4) both sumptuous and plain burials.

Palaeobotany

The palaeobotanical finds from Kalibangan have been discussed in Weber (1989: 78-9). Wheat (*Triticum sphaerococcum*) and barley (*Hordeum vulgare*) have been documented in both Periods I and II at the site. Barley appears, from the sample obtained, to have been the more common grain at Kalibangan. Other food plants include the chick pea (*Cicer arietinum*) and the field pea(?) (*Pisum arvenae*), all from Period II, Mature Harappan. The report of rice from Kalibangan is not correct, as discussed by Vishnu-Mittre and Savithri (1973). These continue to be staples in the area today, indicating long term continuity in this aspect of the subsistence regime.

There are some interesting charcoal samples that have been identified. Period I charcoal included samples from: *Acacia* sp., teak (*Tectona grandis*), heartwood (*Dalbergia* sp.) and axelwood (*Anogeissus* sp.). Mature Harappan charcoal included: *Acacia* sp., teak (*Tectona grandis*) and heartwood (*Dalbergia* sp), axelwood (*Anogeissus* sp.), siris (*Albizzia* sp.), materials from the genus *Terminalia*, salt-cedar (*Tamarix diaca*), mulberry (*Morus alba*), the Indian olibanum tree (*Boswellia serrata*), saltbush (*Salvadora persica*), phog (*Calligonum* sp.), and the fig (*Ficus* sp.). These are mostly trees that would have been along the ancient Sarasvati River, in gallery forests, spreading into the desert. The teak is an exception to this and it may have been brought to Kalibangan from forests at a higher elevation. The olibanum tree produces a fragrant resin.

Archaeozoology

There is a brief report on animal bones from Kalibangan in (IAR 1964-65: 38). They include: zebu (*Bos indicus*), water buffalo (*Bubalus bubalis*), sheep (*Ovis aries*), goat (*Capra hircus*), pig (*Sus scrofa*), onager (*Equus hemionus*), camel (*Camelus dromedirus*, possibly *C. bactrianius*), elephant (*Elephas maximus*), rhinoceros, (*Rhinoceros unicornis*), chital or spotted deer (*Axis axis*), swamp deer (*Cervus duvauceli*) and turtles. A gaur (*Bos gaurus*) is reported by Mukherjee and Saha (1988).

The Final Abandonment of Kalibangan

The final abandonment of Kalibangan has been the subject of some discussion. Robert Raikes carried out a brief environmental survey there in 1968 with R. K. Karanth of the Geological Survey of India and the Archaeological Survey of India (Raikes 1968a). Four bore holes were excavated in the bed of the Sarasvati due north of Kalibangan. An analysis of the materials they recovered suggests that "The general hypothesis, which emerges from the calculations..., is of alternating capture of the Yamuna by the Indus and Ganges systems respectively. That the low and almost indiscernible watershed between the two systems and the slow migration of the Yamuna across its flood-plain under the influence of *coriolis* force (or deflection force due to the earth's rotation) would result inevitably in a right-bank avulsion somewhere near where Indri now stands" (Raikes 1968: 289). The Table 4.43 gives the stages and dates:

The notion that the abandonment of Kalibangan, and many other Mature Harappan sites in its region, was due to changes in the flow of the Sarasvati is widely accepted. Whether or not the system switched back and forth according to Raikes' model is somewhat more in doubt, but is the topic of active geological and hydrological research.

The chronology of the Sothi-Siswal Phase is taken from a series of thirteen radiocarbon dates from Kalibangan I. These are given in Table 4.44.

TABLE 4.43

The Changes in the Sarasvati River at Kalibangan, after Raikes 1968: 290

Westward diversion to Indus 2500-1700 BC (coinciding with Harappan occupation)	750 years
Eastward diversion to Ganga 1750-1100 BC (coinciding with abandonment)	650 years
Westward diversion to Indus 1100-500 BC (coinciding with Painted Gray Ware sites)	600 years
Eastward diversion to Ganga 500-100 BC (coinciding with abandonment)	400 years
Westward diversion to Indus 100 BC-500 AD (coinciding with Early Historic)	600 years
Eastward diversion to Ganga in about 500 AD (coinciding with abandonment)	

TABLE 4.44

Radiocarbon Dates for the Sothi-Siswal Phase

Lab Number	Calibrated Date
Kalibangan Period I	
TF-439 (BS)	1Σ cal BC 5566 (5436) 5289
	2Σ cal BC 5600 (5436) 5224
TF-439	1Σ cal BC 5566 (5436) 5289
	2Σ cal BC 5600 (5436) 5224
TF-155	1Σ cal BC 2911 (2872, 2799, 2777, 2713, 2708) 2586
	2Σ cal BC 3072 (2872, 2799, 2777, 2713, 2708) 2465
TF-157	1Σ cal BC 2880 (2850, 2825, 2655, 2645, 2622) 2493
	2Σ cal BC 2918 (2850, 2825, 2655, 2645, 2622) 2362
TF-241	1Σ cal BC 2869 (2611) 2486
	2Σ cal BC 2888 (2611) 2404
TF-156 (BS)	1Σ cal BC 2867 (2553, 2543, 2493) 2287
	2Σ cal BC 2917 (2553, 2543, 2493) 2034
TF-162	1Σ cal BC 2568 (2459) 2284
	2Σ cal BC 2857 (2459) 2137
TF-161	1Σ cal BC 2563 (2457) 2280
	2Σ cal BC 2853 (2457) 2059
TF-165	1Σ cal BC 2450 (2200) 2041
	2Σ cal BC 2489 (2200) 1934
TF-156	1Σ cal BC 2287 (2137) 1974
	2Σ cal BC 2462 (2137) 1789
TF-154	1Σ cal BC 2192 (2029, 1994, 1987) 1886
	2Σ cal BC 2395 (2029, 1994, 1987) 1741
TF-240	1Σ cal BC 2132 (1944) 1776
	2Σ cal BC 2281 (1944) 1680
TF-957	1Σ cal BC 782 (398) 185
	2Σ cal BC 900 (398) cal AD 70

This is not a coherent data set and is of very little assistance in dating the Sothi-Siswal Phase. It is curious that in spite of the fact that there are a number of other excavated Sothi-Siswal sites (e.g., Sothi, Siswal, Nohar, Mitathal, Banawali) there are no radiocarbon dates available from them to date this Phase. It takes an act of faith to suggest that the Sothi-Siswal Phase conforms to the chronology of the Early Harappan Stage generally. Much more work is needed in this key area to establish the outlines of the chronology for the Early Harappan in the northeastern area of the Early Harappan Stage.

Sothi-Siswal Phase Subsistence

The Sothi-Siswal area was one with mixed farming and herding. Some of the sites are very small and their transitory nature assures us that they were the locales of temporary encampments. Perhaps the most interesting observation concerning the subsistence regime here was made by Walter Fairservis (1961b: 5, 28), when he noted that with the Early Harappan expansion into this area they reached the limits of practical wheat/barley cultivation, if the modern distribution of this practice is any guide.

Sothi-Siswal Settlement Patterns

There are 165 Sothi-Siswal sites, ninety-one of which have information on site size (Table 4.45). The average settlement size is 4.28 hectares. There are two Sothi-Siswal settlements larger than twenty hectares.

The distribution of Sothi-Siswal Phase sites by size is shown in Figure 4.168.

A Comparison of Sothi-Siswal and the Kot Diji Ceramics

All of the Sothi-Siswal fabrics seem to be found in the Cholistan Kot Diji, as far as can be seen from M. R. Mughal's illustrations (Mughal 1997: Figs. 10-2, Plates 45-8). But, the fit is not perfect and there is a need for a full, qualitative and quantitative study of the relationships between the Kot Diji and Sothi-Siswal ceramic assemblages. For the moment the following appear to hold. The Fabric D comb incised wares appear to grow scarcer as one moves west and south out of the Sarasvati area. They are absent at Kot Diji. The important and frequently noted grooved "Bhoot Ware" is more a part of the Kot Diji than it is of the Sothi-Siswal, where it is quite rare. The relationship between Fabric B and Khojak Parallel Striated needs to be clarified.

M. R. Mughal had an opportunity to study the Kalibangan Fabrics in New Delhi in January 1986. The typological system developed by B. K. Thapar as compared to the one used by Mughal is quite different and it is not easy to reconcile the two systems, each of which has its own validity. But Mughal has made the following observations:

> Important points emerging out of this study are that 'Fabric C' *contains* diagnostic short-necked Kot Diji globular vessels with a wide painted band on the neck. A similar type is also *included* in 'Fabric A.' Fabric D includes Kot Diji grooved ware, and 'E' cups and dishes on stands. Fabric 'B,' includes specimens of Kot Diji forms but the external surface is plain and sand-slipped ('rusticated') and is also treated with multiple wavy lines in relief, otherwise known as 'Periano Wet' in Baluchistan (Mughal 1972b). In the assemblage are certain types which have precise parallels with those from Early Harappan sites in Cholistan, Jalilpur, Harappa and the Gomal Valley. Buff ware specimens of typical 'Quetta Wet' wares are also included in the "Fabrics" of Kalibangan which are reported only from the water-logged levels at Mohenjo-daro during the excavations in 1950, and earlier by Mackay (1937-38: Pl. LXVI, 1-4), but otherwise found at the Gomal Valley sites in association with the Early Harappan pottery (Mughal 1990a: 184).

Some other differences in the ceramics among Sothi-Siswal sites have been noted by K. N. Dikshit (1980, 1984b).

The Siswal Phase Terminology

Professor Suraj Bhan of Kurukshetra University has proven to be one of the most vigorous field archaeologists who has worked on the Harappan Civilization in north India. His explorations in Haryana and the Punjab, as well as excavations at Siswal, Mitathal, Balu and other places, some of which were undertaken with his colleague Professor Udai Vir Singh, have added much to our knowledge of this important region.

TABLE 4.45
Sites of the Sothi-Siswal Phase

Site Name	Province/State	District	Size in Hectares
Rakhighari	Haryana	Hissar	40.0
Ratta Theh	Haryana	Hissar	24.0
Banawali	Haryana	Hissar	16.0
Gurnikalan Two	Punjab	Bhatinda	16.0
Naiwala Theh	Punjab	Bhatinda	16.0
Chanat Three	Haryana	Hissar	11.5
Pali	Haryana	Hissar	10.0
Arada	Haryana	Hissar	9.0
Chhoti Mansa	Punjab	Bhatinda	9.0
Shahpur, Hissar	Haryana	Hissar	9.0
Rohira	Punjab	Sangrur	9.0
Paoli	Haryana	Jind	8.5
Ropar	Punjab	Ropar	8.0
Masaudpur	Haryana	Hissar	7.8
Baghru Khurd	Haryana	Jind	7.1
Ghaswa	Haryana	Hissar	6.9
Siswal	Haryana	Hissar	6.0
Chanat One	Haryana	Hissar	6.0
Tigrana	Haryana	Bhiwani	5.0
Pindara	Haryana	Jind	5.0
Barsana, Kurukshetra	Haryana	Kurukshetra	5.0
Laun	Haryana	Jind	4.9
Mirchpur	Haryana	Hissar	4.5
Kalibangan	Rajasthan	Ganganagar	4.5
Chanat Two	Haryana	Hissar	4.5
Berore	Rajasthan	Ganganagar	4.4
Dhakal One	Haryana	Jind	4.3
Sothi	Rajasthan	Ganganagar	4.0
Kathana Two	Haryana	Jind	4.0
Satrod Khurd One	Haryana	Hissar	4.0
Morkhi	Haryana	Jind	4.0
Kandala Two	Haryana	Jind	4.0
Gossain	Haryana	Jind	3.8
Hansdhera	Haryana	Jind	3.8
Balu	Haryana	Jind	3.8
Kharuwala Ther	Rajasthan	Ganganagar	3.7
Gagsina	Haryana	Karnal	3.5
Salimgarh	Haryana	Hissar	3.25
Rajpura Two	Haryana	Jind	3.0
Budha Khera Three	Haryana	Jind	3.0
Kunal	Haryana	Hissar	2.9
Baroli	Haryana	Jind	2.8
Binjor Three	Rajasthan	Ganganagar	2.6
Kachrana Kalan	Haryana	Jind	2.6
Dhingana	Haryana	Jind	2.55
Urlana Khurd Two	Haryana	Karnal	2.5
Ghimana One	Haryana	Jind	2.3
Pahlwan	Haryana	Jind	2.3
Kharal Two	Haryana	Jind	2.25
Daroli Khera	Haryana	Jind	2.25
Khapran	Haryana	Jind	2.25
Jhamola	Haryana	Jind	2.2
Hatho Two	Haryana	Jind	2.2

Contd.

Nidani	Haryana	Jind	2.15
Siamlo Kalan Two	Haryana	Jind	2.1
Garhi	Haryana	Hissar	2.0
Siamlo Kalan One	Haryana	Jind	2.0
Rani Ran	Haryana	Jind	2.0
Nohar	Rajasthan	Ganganagar	2.0
Sherpura	Rajasthan	Ganganagar	2.0
Khema Kheri	Haryana	Jind	1.95
Nandgarh One	Haryana	Jind	1.9
Radhana	Haryana	Jind	1.8
Binjor One	Rajasthan	Ganganagar	1.8
Moana	Haryana	Jind	1.8
Kharar	Haryana	Hissar	1.75
Deverar	Haryana	Jind	1.5
Pinjupura	Haryana	Jind	1.45
Surbra	Haryana	Jind	1.4
Bahni Theh	Haryana	Kurukshetra	1.2
Ujhana Two	Haryana	Jind	1.15
Amargarh One	Haryana	Jind	1.15
Dhurmarkha Kalan One	Haryana	Jind	1.15
Karsola Two	Haryana	Jind	1.1
Lohari	Haryana	Karnal	1.1
Amarheri One	Haryana	Jind	1.0
Kharal One	Haryana	Jind	1.0
Kharal Three	Haryana	Jind	1.0
Ghatauli	Haryana	Jind	0.95
Mangalpur	Haryana	Jind	0.9
Datta	Haryana	Hissar	0.85
Kalait One	Haryana	Jind	0.75
Singhra	Haryana	Karnal	0.7
Shishpur, Karnal	Haryana	Karnal	0.7
Saunkhra Three	Haryana	Karnal	0.7
Gunkali	Haryana	Jind	0.55
Buwana Two	Haryana	Jind	0.55
Pipaltha One	Haryana	Jind	0.5
Balu Two	Haryana	Jind	0.45
Dhanouri	Haryana	Jind	0.45
Koel	Haryana	Jind	0.2
Alipur Kharar Three	Haryana	Hissar	
Alipur Kharar Two	Haryana	Hissar	
Alipur Mandran	Punjab	Bhatinda	
Arniwala Theh	Punjab	Ferozpur	
Badli, Rohtak	Haryana	Rohtak	
Badsa	Haryana	Rohtak	
Baliana	Haryana	Rohtak	
Bare	Punjab	Bhatinda	
Barki	Haryana	Hissar	
Bata One	Haryana	Jind	
Bhagwansar Four	Rajasthan	Ganganagar	
Bhaironpura	Rajasthan	Ganganagar	
Bhirrana	Haryana	Hissar	
Bhudan	Punjab	Sangrur	
Bugia	Rajasthan	Ganganagar	
Chak 011	Rajasthan	Ganganagar	
Chak 040	Rajasthan	Ganganagar	
Chak 058/1	Rajasthan	Ganganagar	
Chak 059	Rajasthan	Ganganagar	

Contd.

Table 4.45 Contd.

Site Name	Province/State	District	Size in Hectares
Chak 072/3	Rajasthan	Ganganagar	
Chak 075, India	Rajasthan	Ganganagar	
Chandiala	Punjab	Ludhiana	
Chhapra	Haryana	Sonepat	
Dharodi	Haryana	Jind	
Domeli	Punjab	Kapurthala	
Farmana One	Haryana	Sonepat	
G. B. 12	Rajasthan	Ganganagar	
G. B. 16	Rajasthan	Ganganagar	
Gadhwal Two	Punjab	Rohtak	
Garhwal, Sonepat	Haryana	Sonepat	
Ghaswa Three	Haryana	Jind	
Gularwala	Haryana	Hissar	
Hamalpur	Haryana	Karnal	
Handali	Punjab	Sangrur	
Hansi	Haryana	Hissar	
Inewala Theh	Punjab	Faridkot	
Jind Five	Haryana	Jind	
Jind Two	Haryana	Jind	
Jogiasson	Rajasthan	Ganganagar	
Kalian	Punjab	Sangrur	
Karalan	Punjab	Kapurthala	
Karela Two	Haryana	Jind	
Karoti	Rajasthan	Ganganagar	
Karsola One	Haryana	Jind	
Kharak Pandwan	Haryana	Jind	
Kunal One	Haryana	Hissar	
Lohar Raghu	Haryana	Hissar	
Manda	Jammu & Kashmir	Jammu Kashmir	
Mandkaula	Haryana	Gurgaon	
Mangali One	Haryana	Hissar	
Mangali Two	Haryana	Hissar	
Manorana	Punjab	Sangrur	
Matar Sham	Haryana	Hissar	
Moholi	Punjab	Sangrur	
Nawanbans	Uttar Pradesh	Saharanpur	
R. D. 89	Rajasthan	Ganganagar	
R. D. 92	Rajasthan	Ganganagar	
Raja Sirkap	Punjab	Faridkot	
Ratta Khera Khuram	Haryana	Kurukshetra	
Rawalwas Kalan	Haryana	Hissar	
Rindhana	Haryana	Sonepat	
Rookhi	Haryana	Sonepat	
Sadha Majra	Haryana	Jind	
Sarangpur	Punjab	Ropar	
Satrod Khurd Three	Haryana	Hissar	
Saunkhra Three	Haryana	Karnal	
Saunkhra Two	Haryana	Karnal	
Singhwa	Haryana	Hissar	
Sisana	Haryana	Rohtak	
Sulla West	Punjab	Bahawalpur	
Suwaiki	Rajasthan	Ganganagar	
Tarkhanwala Dera	Rajasthan	Ganganagar	
Theraj	Haryana	Hissar	
Urdana	Haryana	Jind	

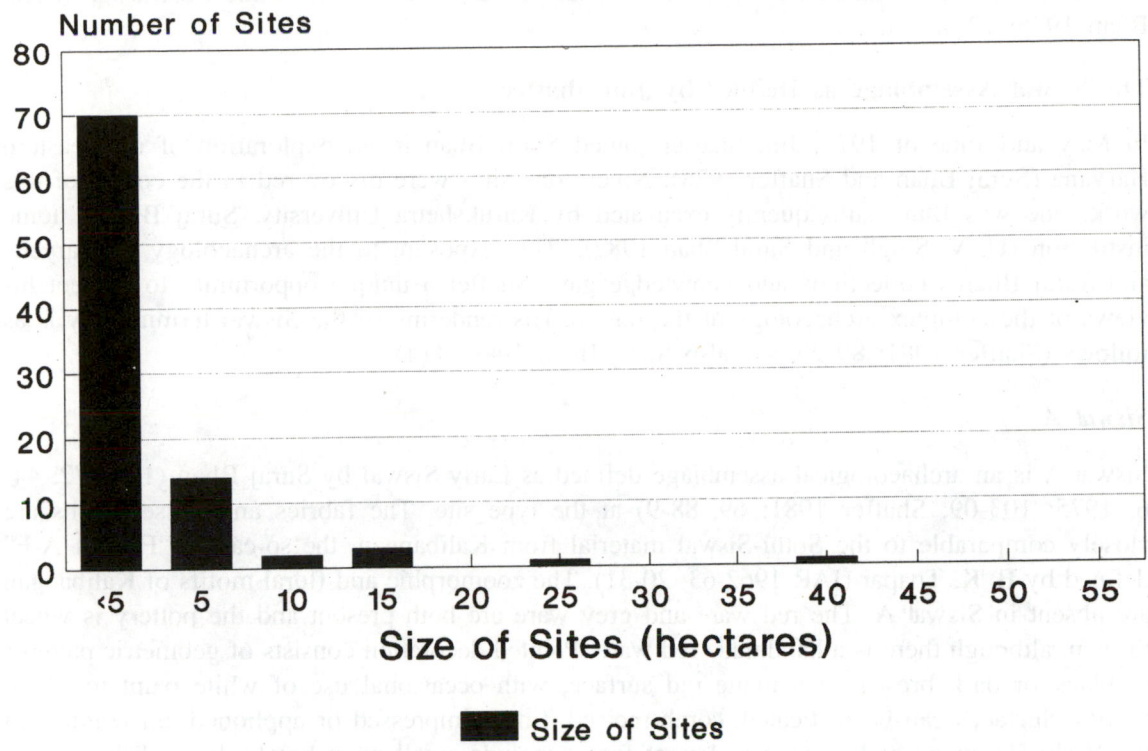

Figure 4.168. Histogram of site sizes of the Sothi-Siswal Phase

Estimate of Settled Area for the Sothi-Siswal Phase

TABLE 4.46
Estimate of Settled Area for the Sothi-Siswal Phase

Sothi-Siswal Phase	
Total Sites	165
Sites with Size Estimate	91
Settled Area of Sites with Known Sizes	389.15
Sites with Size Unknown	74
Average Site Site Size	4.28
Estimated Settled Area of Sites without Size	316.72
Estimated Total Settled Area	705.87

Sizes given in hectares

Suraj Bhan[14] developed a terminology to handle the cultural and chronological organizing of the sites he has found. This terminology is based on his excavations at Siswal (Suraj Bhan 1975: 103-09). The terms and their brief definition are as follows:

Early Siswal	Sothi-Siswal Phase (Kalibangan I)
Late Siswal	Mature Harappan Stage
Degenerate Siswal	Post-urban Stage
(Suraj Bhan 1975: 121)	

He also has a "Sarangpur Culture" found only on three sites (Suraj Bhan 1975: 117, 122), but has pottery of Sothi-Siswal type. His "Mitathal IIB" is a variant of the Post-urban (Suraj Bhan 1975: 121).

The Siswal Assemblage as Defined by Jim Shaffer

In May and June of 1977, Jim Shaffer joined Suraj Bhan in an exploration of northeastern Haryana (Suraj Bhan and Shaffer 1978). Ninety-one sites were discovered in the course of this work, one was Balu, subsequently excavated by Kurukshetra University, Suraj Bhan's home institution (U. V. Singh and Suraj Bhan 1982). This exposure to the archaeology of Haryana and Suraj Bhan's collections and knowledge gave Shaffer a unique opportunity to present his views of the complex archaeology of the region. His rendering of the Siswal terminology is as follows (Shaffer 1981: 89-90, see also Suraj Bhan 1989: 414):

Siswal A

Siswal A is an archaeological assemblage defined as Early Siswal by Suraj Bhan (1971-72: 44-6; 1975: 103-09; Shaffer 1981: 69, 88-9) at the type site. The fabrics and vessel forms are closely comparable to the Sothi-Siswal material from Kalibangan, the so-called "Fabrics A-F" defined by B. K. Thapar (IAR 1962-63: 20-31). The zoomorphic and floral motifs of Kalibangan are absent in Siswal A. The red ware and grey ware are both present and the pottery is wheel thrown, although there is a handmade red ware. Painted decoration consists of geometric patterns in black or dark brown on a matte red surface, with occasional use of white paint to fill in motifs. Surfaces can be rusticated, comb-incised, finger impressed or appliqued, all features of the Early Harappan at Kalibangan. Vessel forms include small open bowls, large dishes, some on stands, as well as a wide range of jars with restricted mouths. A small amount of black and red ware may be found.

Siswal B

Siswal B is defined as Late Siswal by Suraj Bhan at the type site (Suraj Bhan 1971-72: 44-6; 1975: 103-09; Shaffer 1981: 69, 89). The principal features of Siswal B are the continuity of the Siswal A fabrics and the addition of Mature Harappan ceramics, including a regional variation on the black-on-red painting style using intersecting circles, pipal leaves and the fish-scale motif. Harappan vessel forms include the dish-on-stand, perforated ware and jars, and rarely the classic flanged-rim 'S' form. Mature Harappan pottery does not occur with much frequency at sites in the northeast.

The non-Harappan aspect of this ceramic assemblage shows significant continuity from Siswal A. The red and gray wares continue, although the use of white paint disappears. Large open-mouth storage jars are added to the vessel form repertoire and the rims of smaller jars are modified. More dark painted rims seem to be included on many forms. There is no black and red ware associated with Siswal B.

Small finds from the surface that Suraj Bhan assigned to Siswal B include terracotta bangles, triangular terracotta cakes, oblong cakes with finger impressions, biconical beads and a crucible with copper oxide on the inside.

The topic has been broached and so it seems reasonable to continue with the definitions of Siswal C and D, although they go beyond the scope of this work.

Siswal C

The predominant characteristic of Siswal C, as defined by Shaffer (1981: 90), is the disappearance of Mature Harappan ceramics with a continuity in the remainder of the Siswal B ceramic assemblage. New forms include a carinated bowl with a "*handi*"-like shape, a tall, thin-waisted vase, and a jar with a tall neck. Dishes and dishes-on-stand with large, drooping rims are present and unusually distinctive. At several sites the excavators draw attention to vessel forms recalling Cemetery H and the eastern "Late Harappan."

Siswal D

Two characteristics distinguish Siswal D from C: (1) the addition of Painted Grey Ware, and its associated ceramics, to the assemblage and (2) the occurrence of Siswal C vessel forms in new grey ware fabrics (Shaffer 1981: 90). Siswal D represents Jagat Pati Joshi's important "Harappan/PGW Overlap" (Joshi 1976, 1977, 1978a, 1978b, 1993).

Shaffer introduces his discussion of these terms with the following: "These units DO NOT have any specific chronological connotations, nor are they meant to imply specific cultural affinities. They are instead used as a heuristic device to arrange a large and varied amount of data" (Shaffer 1981: 88, original emphasis).

Not all of this information is pertinent to the present discussion but the terms Siswal A, Siswal B and Siswal C will crop up from time to time and it is better to clarify them now, than to deal with them as they enter the vocabulary of the Harappan Civilization.

The Giant Sites: Lakhmirwala, Gurnikalan One and Hasanpur Two

Lakhmirwala, Gurnikalan One and Hasanpur Two in Mansa Tahsil of Bhatinda District are all extremely large. The raw data on their size indicate that they are 225 hectares, 144 hectares, and 100 hectares, respectively. These sites were first reported by Jagat Pati Joshi and his team (Joshi 1986, Madhu Bala 1992: 43-5) following exploration in the southwest Punjab. Lakhmirwala is currently the largest site of the Indus Age. All three settlements are reported to have both a Sothi-Siswal occupation followed by the Mature Harappan. Gurnikalan One and Hasanpur Two have Early Historical occupations.

These sites are not considered to be a part of the Early Harappan, and some explanation is called for since there is Sothi-Siswal material there. Dr. Joshi and his team have a great deal of archaeological field experience and these site sizes should be considered accurate, at least in so far as a sherd scatter and spread of an archaeological midden are concerned. However, three Sothi-Siswal sites all in excess of 100 hectares closely spaced in Bhatinda District, would have a significant impact on the interpretation of the development of Harappan urbanization. They are certainly within the size range for the cities of the Indus Age. (Figure 4.169). This area would therefore qualify for the most highly urbanized locality of the entire civilization, beginning in the first half of the third millennium, not the second. Moreover, the demonstrated presence of a 225 hectare site at Lakhmirwala in the Early Harappan Stage would demand a thorough rethinking of the culture history of the Early Harappan. No one should believe that there is so much known about Indus culture history, or the urbanization process that took place there in the third millennium, that it would be impossible for a new discovery like this to be ruled out simply because it does not fit present theory. Many points that run counter to present theory are possible, a 200 hectare Sothi-Siswal settlement in Bhatinda District among them. But, the size of these settlements has important implications that cannot be resolved without excavation. Unfortunately, there is no prospect for this in the immediate future; so this evaluation will have to proceed with the limited information at hand. There are three points that may bring the apparent size of these sites into better conformity with present thoughts on the development of Indus cities.

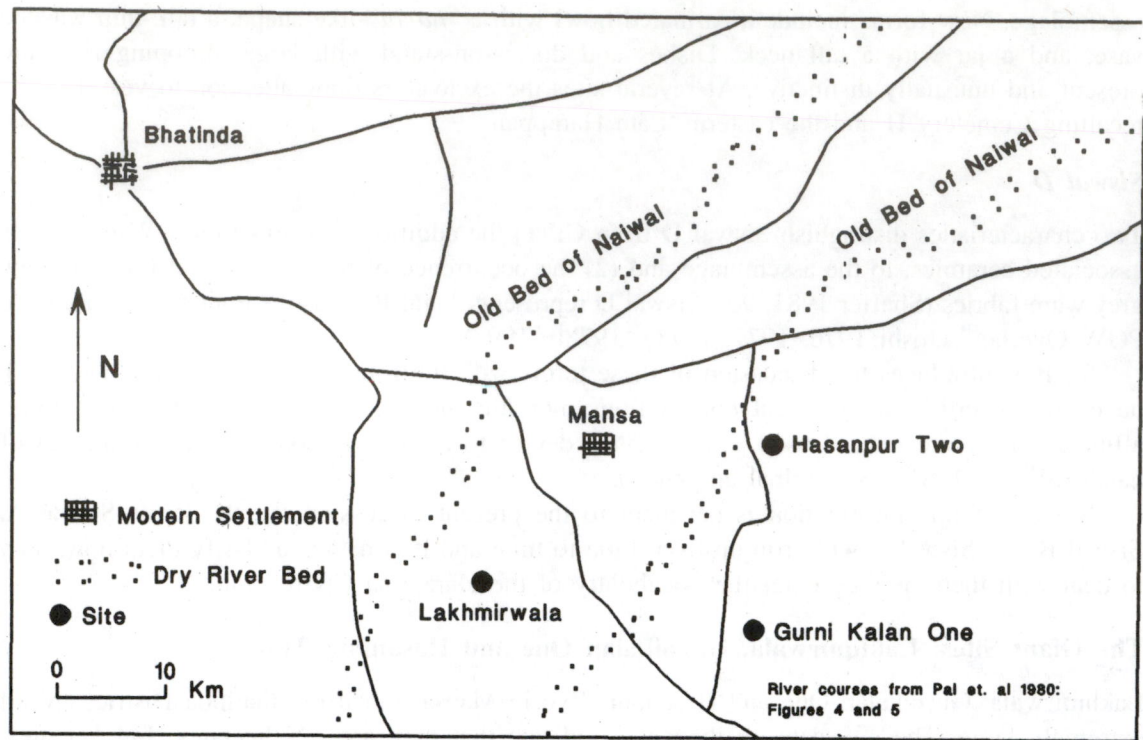

Figure 4.169. Sketch map showing the location of Lakhmirwala, Gurnikalan One and Hasanpur Two

Historic Period Occupations: Since there has been no excavation the effect of the historic occupations at Gurnikalan One and Hasanpur Two on the apparent size of these places is not known. Later occupation could easily have inflated the size of the mounds, which could be misleading in the absence of excavation or systematic surface survey.

Lateral Stratigraphy: The effect of lateral stratigraphy, so important at places like Mehrgarh and Rangpur, has not yet been assessed at Lakhmirwala, Gurnikalan One and Hasanpur Two. Rangpur, for example, would be over 100 hectares if we did not know that lateral stratigraphy had vastly expanded the apparent size of that site.

Accurate Dating: The fact that there is both a Sothi-Siswal and a Mature Harappan settlement at all three sites brings up the point that Sothi-Siswal ceramics are found in both of these Phases, as is very well documented at Kalibangan. As already noted, this makes it extremely difficult to ascertain whether any given site has a Mature Harappan occupation alone, or whether it is preceded by a Sothi-Siswal component. Many archaeologists believe that there is a sloping horizon of Sothi-Siswal and Mature Harappan remains as one moves east beyond Kalibangan and these three sites might be somewhat later than they appear at first glance. Excavation is needed to determine this.

There are some suggestions on how the Early Harappan Sothi-Siswal ceramics can be separated from their Mature Harappan cousin (Siswal B). Suraj Bhan has noted that in the Late Sothi-Siswal (Siswal B), white painting disappears, the vessel forms are "evolved" and there is "austerity" in shapes and painted designs. The vessels are also sturdier than those in the earlier phase and they may be better potted (1975: 108). These observations are fine as a starting point, but they cannot be used to judge the collections in question, at this point in time, anyway. Moreover, what do the terms "evolved vessel forms" and "austerity" in design and vessel form really mean without concrete, illustrated examples? We can be reasonably assured that the Sothi-Siswal ceramics of Siswal A and Siswal B are different. What is needed is a published, definitive study of these two bodies of ceramics so that the vague notions current today are replaced by something much more concrete. — Another reasonable dissertation problem in Harappan archaeology?

The Lack of a Hinterland: Three cities, all contemporary with each other, functioning at the same time, closely spaced in the Punjab, only twenty to thirty kilometers from one another? The distance between the other Harappan cities, Mohenjo-daro, Ganweriwala and Harappa, is in excess of 300 kilometers. This close spacing and the lack of a hinterland to support such population concentrations for the large sites in Bhatinda District needs some kind of explanation.

It could be that there is the serial occupation of three different civic settings here, and that only one real settlement was present at any given time. Some support for this proposal comes from the fact that the now largely dry Naiwal Nadi flows in the area of these sites, and seems to have made its way to the west, occupying a succession of channels as it migrated away from the Sarasvati toward the Sutlej. This shift in course could have mandated the shift of the settlement site around Lakhmirwala, Gurnikalan One and Hasanpur Two.

These points have not been made to challenge the veracity of these data on three ancient settlements that are obviously very important. Jagat Pati Joshi is a former Director General of the Archaeological Survey of India, an archaeologist with a fine reputation for producing data that are both accurate and complete, as in his excavations at Surkotada. But, these Bhatinda District sites are larger than one might expect in this region, especially during the Sothi-Siswal Phase, and to accept them at face value, without considering a variety of factors to account for their apparent dimensions does not seem appropriate.

Some kind of temporary expedient is needed to accommodate these extraordinarily interesting sites. Since it has not been demonstrated that any of these very large sites has an occupation during the Sothi-Siswal Phase I am, for the moment, going to consider them all Mature Harappan. Their cultural inventory would then be like that of Kalibangan II, with ceramics of both the Sothi-Siswal Phase and the Mature Harappan together in one occupation. This is decidedly a "patch" on the existing data set that begs important questions, is somewhat highhanded and therefore probably undesirable. I see no alternative at this point and am perfectly happy to admit the inadequacies of the proposal. In fact, I stand a very good chance of being shown wrong on any number of points that would follow real research in archaeology of the Indus Age Bhatinda District.

The Site at Ropar

A similar ambiguity pertains to the important site of Ropar. Most reviews of the stratigraphy of the site conclude that settlement there began with the Mature Harappan (e.g., Madhu Bala 1992: 26-31). But there is clearly Sothi-Siswal material there, referred to as "pre-Harappan" by the excavator (Y. D. Sharma 1982a: 151-75, 1982b) (Figure 4.170). Sharma laid some thirty trenches at the site, first investigating the main mound and then the cemetery. The digging was mainly vertical: however, some horizontal coverage was achieved in the south-central and north-central parts of the main mound. Period I has been variously divided into two or three sub-periods (Y. D. Sharma 1976, 1982a: 151).

Period Ia, the earliest settlement at Ropar, was found on alluvium and is best defined in trench RPR-1, a large cutting on the north-central side of the main mound. Sharma reports a ceramic assemblage dominated by the fabrics of Kalibangan Period I, with some Mature Harappan material in association. There is also some pottery which could be seen as Mature Harappan

704

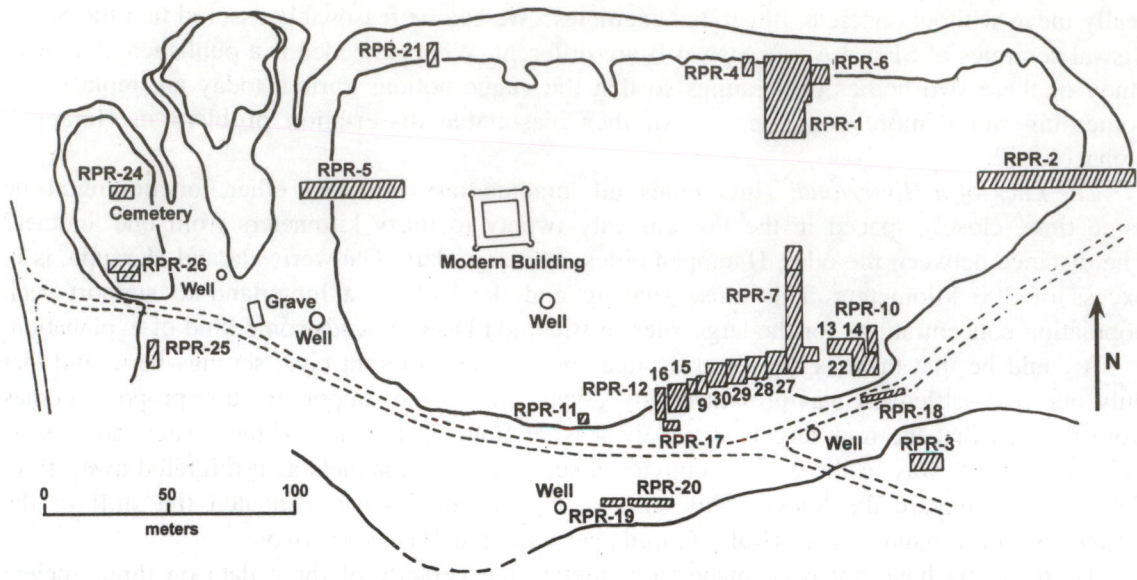

Figure 4.170. Plan of Ropar, after Y. D. Sharma 1982a: Figure 13-11

vessels. Other Mature Harappan artifacts include a bronze jar, broken celt, terracotta bangles and beads of steatite, faience and carnelian (Y. D. Sharma 1989: 377). It is thus not clear whether this level offers evidence for the local development of the Mature Harappan style in the northern Punjab, or if it speaks for the later association between Sothi-Siswal ceramics within the context of a fully developed Mature Harappan. This is essentially a problem in time/space systematics, but it has not been settled since the Sothi-Siswal ceramics continued to be used side by side with Mature Harappan sturdy red wares during Period II at both Kalibangan and Banawali.

The Date of Sothi-Siswal Sites and the Relationship to the Mature Harappan

Clearly, some of the Sothi-Siswal sites were quite large. It has been suggested that this is because they are late in the history of the Harappan Civilization. K. N. Dikshit has observed:

> In India the Sothi Ware may not represent the 'Early' Harappan phase. The bichrome Sothi fabric and brick ratio (1:2:3) did not find any place in the Harappan complex. At Kot Diji, it may, however, be noted that the pre-Harappan and Harappan brick ratio are the same (1:2:4). Moreover, being late in the hierarchy of development of Harappan cultures, Sothi cannot be placed in the group of Early Harappan culture, Sothi Ware has been reported in the late levels of Kot Diji at Sarai Khola. Further, Fabric C and E of Kalibangan and Sothi are found at 'mature' Harappan sites. Similarly, Fabric F, the grey ware, is nearer to the Harappan grey ware (Lal 1979). Sothi, therefore, appears to be contemporary of the 'mature' Harappan in the Indus Valley as was long ago clearly demonstrated by Gupta (1970)[15] on the basis of stratigraphy and chronology (K. N. Dikshit 1984b: 537).

S. P. Gupta has proposed a six stage model for the development of urbanization in the Greater Indus Valley (1972-73). This is an interesting paper with many aspects, which proposes, in part, much the same thing that Dikshit has put forth. In Gupta's Stage III, "Efflorescence" he proposes the following synchronisms: "Kalibangan late I; Early Phase of Harappa; and early phase of the known levels of Mohenjo-daro; Sutkagen-dor, etc" (1972-73: 47).

Finally, B. K. Thapar (1982; see also Xu 1990: 193) sees a double sloping horizon, emanating from Mohenjo-daro, or central Sindh, with the dates for Mature Harappan sites becoming progressively later as one moves southeast into Gujarat as well as northeast into northern Rajasthan, Punjab, Haryana, and western Uttar Pradesh (Thapar 1982: Figure 1; Figure 4.171).

The proposal made by Dikshit, Gupta and Thapar is not based on strong chronological data. In fact, the radiocarbon dates that are available argue against it. For example, the two dates for the Mature Harappan at Mitathal (PRL-290 and PRL-291) calibrate to 2288 cal. BC and 1961 cal. BC. These are not so different from dates for the Mature Harappan Mohenjo-daro and Harappa (see table 4.47).

The radiocarbon dates for Kalibangan Period II are given in Table 4.48.

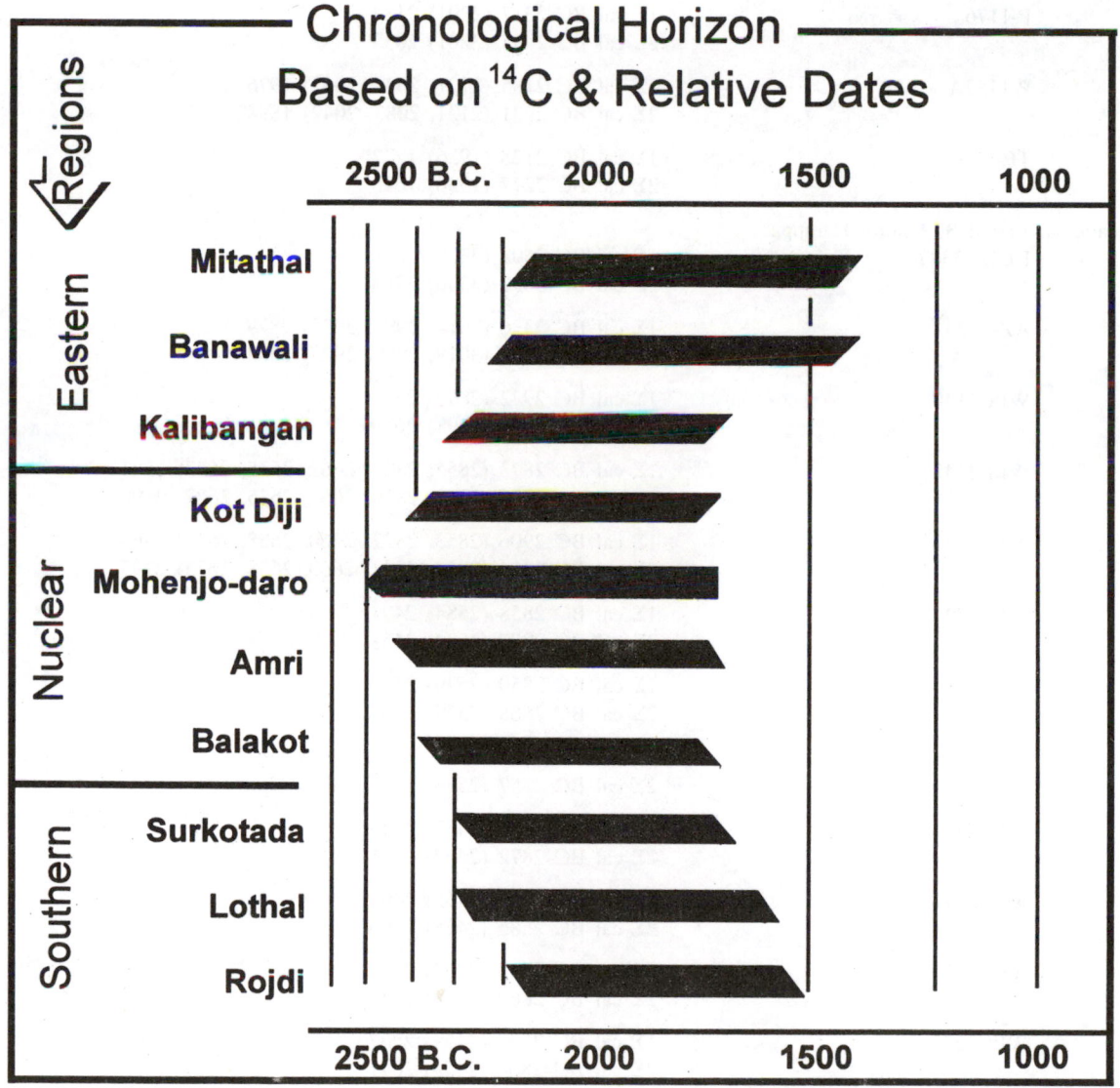

Figure 4.171. B. K. Thapar's illustration of the double sloping horizon, after Thapar 1982: Figure 1

TABLE 4.47

Radiocarbon Dates from the Mature Harappan at Mohenjo-daro and Harappa

Lab Number	Calibrated Date
Mohenjo-daro	
P-1177	1Σ cal BC 2572 (2469) 2409
	2Σ cal BC 2842 (2469) 2299
P-1179	1Σ cal BC 2468 (2453, 2420, 2406) 2288
	2Σ cal BC 2569 (2453, 2420, 2406) 2149
P-1180	1Σ cal BC 2397 (2280, 2212, 2210) 2144
	2Σ cal BC 2462 (2280, 2212, 2210) 2043
P-1178A	1Σ cal BC 2318 (2201) 2138
	2Σ cal BC 2455 (2201) 2035
P-1176	1Σ cal BC 2317 (2201) 2137
	2Σ cal BC 2455 (2201) 2035
P-1182A	1Σ cal BC 2185 (2121, 2083, 2042) 1976
	2Σ cal BC 2281 (2121, 2083, 2042) 1898
TF-75	1Σ cal BC 2128 (1936) 1772
	2Σ cal BC 2277 (1936) 1676
Harappa, Period 3, Mature Harappa	
BETA-33874	1Σ cal BC 3508 (3336) 2921
	2Σ cal BC 3692 (3336) 2703
AZ-7524	1Σ cal BC 3336 (3018, 2990, 2927) 2879
	2Σ cal BC 3502 (3018, 2990, 2927) 2584
WIS-2140	1Σ cal BC 2922 (2898) 2789
	2Σ cal BC 3078 (2898) 2669
WIS-2142	1Σ cal BC 2873 (2855, 2820, 2662, 2635, 2627) 2581
	2Σ cal BC 2887 (2855, 2820, 2662, 2635, 2627) 2490
AZ-8046	1Σ cal BC 2906 (2853, 2822, 2660, 2638, 2625) 2464
	2Σ cal BC 3254 (2853, 2822, 2660, 2638, 2625) 2197
AZ-8052	1Σ cal BC 2858 (2584) 2491
	2Σ cal BC 2877 (2584) 2458
AZ-8051	1Σ cal BC 2850 (2579) 2493
	2Σ cal BC 2868 (2579) 2462
WIS-2145	1Σ cal BC 2587 (2558, 2530, 2497) 2463
	2Σ cal BC 2857 (2558, 2530, 2497) 2360
AZ-8048	1Σ cal BC 2589 (2467) 2320
	2Σ cal BC 2872 (2467) 2141
AZ-8047	1Σ cal BC 2558 (2465) 2404
	2Σ cal BC 2585 (2465) 2290
AZ-7527	1Σ cal BC 2575 (2464) 2320
	2Σ cal BC 2860 (2464) 2145
WIS-2221	1Σ cal BC 2577 (2459) 2207
	2Σ cal BC 2869 (2459) 2041

Contd.

Table 4.47 Contd.

Lab Number	Calibrated Date
WIS-2141	1Σ cal BC 2474 (2455, 2412, 2409) 2288 2Σ cal BC 2578 (2455, 2412, 2409) 2147
WIS-2053	1Σ cal BC 2853 (2455, 2412, 2409) 2045 2Σ cal BC 2917 (2455, 2412, 2409) 1776
WIS-2219	1Σ cal BC 2467 (2452, 2423, 2405) 2286 2Σ cal BC 2568 (2452, 2423, 2405) 2147
AZ-7529	1Σ cal BC 2468 (2451, 2429, 2403) 2280 2Σ cal BC 2575 (2451, 2429, 2403) 2141
QL-4730	1Σ cal BC 2457 (2450, 2446, 2401, 2372, 2365) 2325 2Σ cal BC 2465 (2450, 2446, 2401, 2372, 2365) 2282
AZ-7521	1Σ cal BC 2465 (2399, 2376, 2355) 2208 2Σ cal BC 2566 (2399, 2376, 2355) 2141
AZ-8050	1Σ cal BC 2565 (2399, 2376, 2355) 2141 2Σ cal BC 2867 (2399, 2376, 2355) 1947
QL-4732	1Σ cal BC 2453 (2397, 2379, 2348) 2323 2Σ cal BC 2458 (2397, 2379, 2348) 2286
QL-4731	1Σ cal BC 2455 (2393, 2386, 2338) 2284 2Σ cal BC 2464 (2393, 2386, 2338) 2199
AZ-7522	1Σ cal BC 2457 (2390, 2389, 2333) 2207 2Σ cal BC 2470 (2390, 2389, 2333) 2143
QL-4485	1Σ cal BC 2452 (2319) 2206 2Σ cal BC 2463 (2319) 2145
WIS-2217	1Σ cal BC 2455 (2315) 2200 2Σ cal BC 2469 (2315) 2136
QL-4777	1Σ cal BC 2451 (2315) 2206 2Σ cal BC 2460 (2315) 2147
QL-4378	1Σ cal BC 2451 (2289) 2200 2Σ cal BC 2462 (2289) 2139
QL-4733	1Σ cal BC 2320 (2285) 2206 2Σ cal BC 2395 (2285) 2199
AZ-7523	1Σ cal BC 2395 (2283) 2149 2Σ cal BC 2459 (2283) 2067
WIS-2075	1Σ cal BC 2397 (2281) 2145 2Σ cal BC 2462 (2281) 2044
WIS-2143	1Σ cal BC 2395 (2279, 2217, 2209) 2144 2Σ cal BC 2461 (2279, 2217, 2209) 2042
QL-4734	1Σ cal BC 2393 (2277, 2225, 2207) 2142 2Σ cal BC 2460 (2277, 2225, 2207) 2041

Contd.

708

Table 4.47 Contd.

Lab Number	Calibrated Date
QL-4778	1Σ cal BC 2393 (2277, 2225, 2207) 2142 2Σ cal BC 2460 (2277, 2225, 2207) 2041
WIS-2053	1Σ cal BC 2393 (2277, 2225, 2207) 2142 2Σ cal BC 2460 (2277, 2225, 2207) 2041
QL-4487	1Σ cal BC 2286 (2275, 2237, 2206) 2197 2Σ cal BC 2329 (2275, 2237, 2206) 2143
WIS-2220	1Σ cal BC 2391 (2274,2243,2205) 2141 2Σ cal BC 2459 (2274,2243,2205) 2039
QL-4376	1Σ cal BC 2317 (2272, 2258, 2204) 2142 2Σ cal BC 2453 (2272, 2258, 2204) 2044
QL-4374	1Σ cal BC 2289 (2200) 2139 2Σ cal BC 2451 (2200) 2041
AZ-7525	1Σ cal BC 2391 (2197) 2043 2Σ cal BC 2464 (2197) 1950
QL-4486	1Σ cal BC 2281 (2195, 2152, 2149) 2137 2Σ cal BC 2392 (2195, 2152, 2149) 2039
AZ-8049	1Σ cal BC 2457 (2195, 2152, 2149) 1976 2Σ cal BC 2584 (2195, 2152, 2149) 1774
QL-4483	1Σ cal BC 2275 (2195, 2152, 2149) 2140 2Σ cal BC 2288 (2195, 2152, 2149) 2048
QL-4776	1Σ cal BC 2285 (2193, 2155, 2148) 2048 2Σ cal BC 2451 (2193, 2155, 2148) 1984
WIS-2043	1Σ cal BC 2285 (2190, 2160, 2145) 2041 2Σ cal BC 2453 (2190, 2160, 2145) 1971
QL-4488	1Σ cal BC 2197 (2140) 2044 2Σ cal BC 2282 (2140) 1988
AZ-7526	1Σ cal BC 2450 (2140) 1935 2Σ cal BC 2573 (2140) 1742
QL-4775	1Σ cal BC 2281 (2137) 1980 2Σ cal BC 2455 (2137) 1887
QL-4484	1Σ cal BC 2181 (2135, 2071, 2063) 2041 2Σ cal BC 2198 (2135, 2071, 2063) 1987
QL-4729	1Σ cal BC 2180 (2132, 2076, 2048) 2034 2Σ cal BC 2271 (2132, 2076, 2048) 1975
WIS-2144	1Σ cal BC 2277 (2132, 2076, 2048) 1954 2Σ cal BC 2455 (2132, 2076, 2048) 1785
AZ-8053	1Σ cal BC 2180 (2124, 2082, 2043) 1980 2Σ cal BC 2276 (2124, 2082, 2043) 1929
WIS-2074	1Σ cal BC 2179 (2120, 2084, 2042) 1976 2Σ cal BC 2278 (2120, 2084, 2042) 1905
AZ-7528	1Σ cal BC 1629 (1422) 1168 2Σ cal BC 1883 (1422) 913

TABLE 4.48
Radiocarbon Dates from Kalibangan Period II

Lab Number	Calibrated date
TF-160	1Σ cal BC 2863 (2577) 2464
	2Σ cal BC 2886 (2577) 2313
TF-942	1Σ cal BC 2864 (2575, 2511, 2510) 2460
	2Σ cal BC 2889 (2575, 2511, 2510) 2282
TF-607	1Σ cal BC 2573 (2457) 2203
	2Σ cal BC 2866 (2457) 2038
TF-25	1Σ cal BC 2568 (2457) 2207
	2Σ cal BC 2860 (2457) 2045
TF-163(BS)	1Σ cal BC 2573 (2456) 2200
	2Σ cal BC 2867 (2456) 2033
TF-153	1Σ cal BC 2558 (2452, 2423, 2405) 2200
	2Σ cal BC 2853 (2452, 2423, 2405) 2038
TF-608	1Σ cal BC 2558 (2452, 2423, 2405) 2200
	2Σ cal BC 2853 (2452, 2423, 2405) 2038
TF-163	1Σ cal BC 2553 (2452, 2423, 2405) 2203
	2Σ cal BC 2837 (2452, 2423, 2405) 2044
TF-145	1Σ cal BC 2481 (2399, 2376, 2355) 2198
	2Σ cal BC 2613 (2399, 2376, 2355) 2039
P-481	1Σ cal BC 2462 (2392, 2387, 2337) 2202
	2Σ cal BC 2560 (2392, 2387, 2337) 2069
TF-147	1Σ cal BC 2465 (2321) 2144
	2Σ cal BC 2580 (2321) 1987
TF-948	1Σ cal BC 2454 (2274, 2243, 2205) 2046
	2Σ cal BC 2556 (2274, 2243, 2205) 1946
TF-605	1Σ cal BC 2454 (2272, 2258, 2204) 2043
	2Σ cal BC 2558 (2272, 2258, 2204) 1934
TF-151	1Σ cal BC 2450 (2200) 2041
	2Σ cal BC 2489 (2200) 1934
TF-139	1Σ cal BC 2391 (2192, 2157, 2147) 2033
	2Σ cal BC 2467 (2192, 2157, 2147) 1898
TF-947	1Σ cal BC 2289 (2184, 2163, 2144) 2034
	2Σ cal BC 2458 (2184, 2163, 2144) 1930
TF-150	1Σ cal BC 2285 (2137) 1976
	2Σ cal BC 2460 (2137) 1881

Contd.

710

Table 4.48 Contd.

Lab Number	Calibrated date
TF-141	1Σ cal BC 2275 (2124, 2082, 2043) 1931 2Σ cal BC 2456 (2124, 2082, 2043) 1766
TF-149	1Σ cal BC 2275 (2033) 1828 2Σ cal BC 2463 (2033) 1681
TF-142	1Σ cal BC 2136 (1975) 1828 2Σ cal BC 2283 (1975) 1705
TF-152	1Σ cal BC 2121 (1948) 1789 2Σ cal BC 2195 (1948) 1741
TF-946	1Σ cal BC 2124 (1940) 1778 2Σ cal BC 2271 (1940) 1684
TF-149(BS)	1Σ cal BC 2124 (1919) 1747 2Σ cal BC 2279 (1919) 1621
TF-152(BS)	1Σ cal BC 2116 (1892) 1741 2Σ cal BC 2277 (1892) 1538
TF-143	1Σ cal BC 1959 (1872, 1840, 1811, 1808, 1781) 1683 2Σ cal BC 2135 (1872, 1840, 1811, 1808, 1781) 1524
TF-244	1Σ cal BC 1620 (1516) 1419 2Σ cal BC 1737 (1516) 1316
TF-138	1Σ cal BC 1427 (1378, 1345, 1319) 1168 2Σ cal BC 1522 (1378, 1345, 1319) 1014

*Dates with BS as a lab are those determinations that were first run by the Tata Institute of Fundamental Research and then additional portions of the original charcoal were run at the Radiocarbon Laboratory at the Birbal Sahni Institute of Palaeobotany.

There is something of a spread here, but it does not suggest that the Mature Harappan occupation at Kalibangan is particularly late, as compared to that at Mohenjo-daro. While there are some dates from the first half of the third millennium for the Mature Harappan at Harappa, they may not be reliable.

There are also four radiocarbon dates from Period II at Banawali, the Mature Harappan occupation (see table 4.49).

These dates give an equivocal result because they are sharply divided between "late" dates for the Mature Harappan and two that fit comfortably within the series from Mohenjo-daro, Harappa, or Allahdino. Since there is a Post-urban occupation at Banawali, the two "late" dates might be explained in light of this point. In any event, the radiocarbon determinations from Banawali do not offer support for the sloping horizon.

TABLE 4.49
Radiocarbon Dates from Banawali

Lab Number	Calibrated date
PRL-205	1Σ cal BC 2473 (2272, 2258, 2204) 1972
	2Σ cal BC 2866 (2272, 2258, 2204) 1742
PRL-203	1Σ cal BC 2462 (2200) 1981
	2Σ cal BC 2615 (2200) 1776
PRL-204	1Σ cal BC 1677 (1518) 1409
	2Σ cal BC 1869 (1518) 1262
PRL-207	1Σ cal BC 1443 (1392, 1332, 1329) 1219
	2Σ cal BC 1590 (1392, 1332, 1329) 1044

The result is that radiocarbon dates do not seem to support the proposition that the Sothi-Siswal Phase or the Mature Harappan in Punjab, Haryana, northern Rajasthan and western Uttar Pradesh is any later than it is in central Sindh or at Harappa. There is, however, some chance that the radiocarbon determinations that are now available do not have the statistical robustness to substantiate this point. More dates may be needed, especially from sites of the Sothi-Siswal Phase, to test the hypothesis proposed by S. P. Gupta, K. N. Dikshit, B. K. Thapar and others.

The Late Kot Diji: A contrast to Siswal B

The Kot Diji ceramic assemblage also has a late stage in the Derajat and surrounding areas (e.g., Gumla, Rehman Dheri, Lewan, Tarakai Qila) (Figure 4.172). This was first suggested by A. H. Dani (1970-71: 48), and later confirmed by a series of radiocarbon dates (Thomas and Allchin 1986; see also Possehl 1993b). Unlike the Sothi-Siswal Phase there is an adequate description of the Late Kot Diji which allows it to be separated from the Early Harappan assemblage. This is given by F. R. Allchin and J. Robert Knox in their report on the excavations at Lewan in Bannu District (1981: 106-08).

A significant contrast offered by the Late Kot Diji is that it has yet to be found in association with Mature Harappan ceramics. Some Mature painted motifs such as the pipal leaf, fish scale, intersecting circle and peacock have been found, as at Rehman Dheri III (Durrani 1988: 30), but they are not necessarily executed in the Harappan style. Perforated Ware, akin to Mature Harappan type, occurs at Gumla IV.

It has also been observed that Mature Harappan artifacts occur in the Late Kot Diji. For example, Gumla IV produced an etched carnelian bead, a cubical stone weight, a faience button or seal, steatite ("paste") disk beads, toy cart frames with wheels, triangular terracotta cakes and "missiles" (Dani 1970-71: 47-8).

Manda

A small scale excavation at Manda, in Akhnoor city of Jammu and Kashmir has evidence for an association between Early and Mature Harappan ceramics in the lowest Period IA (Joshi and Madhu Bala 1982). This assemblage could be classified as either Late Kot Diji or Transitional Stage based on the available information. The short necked Kot Diji jar is present in quantity, along with grooved Bhoot Ware (Joshi and Madhu Bala 1982: 188). The Early Harappan pottery

712

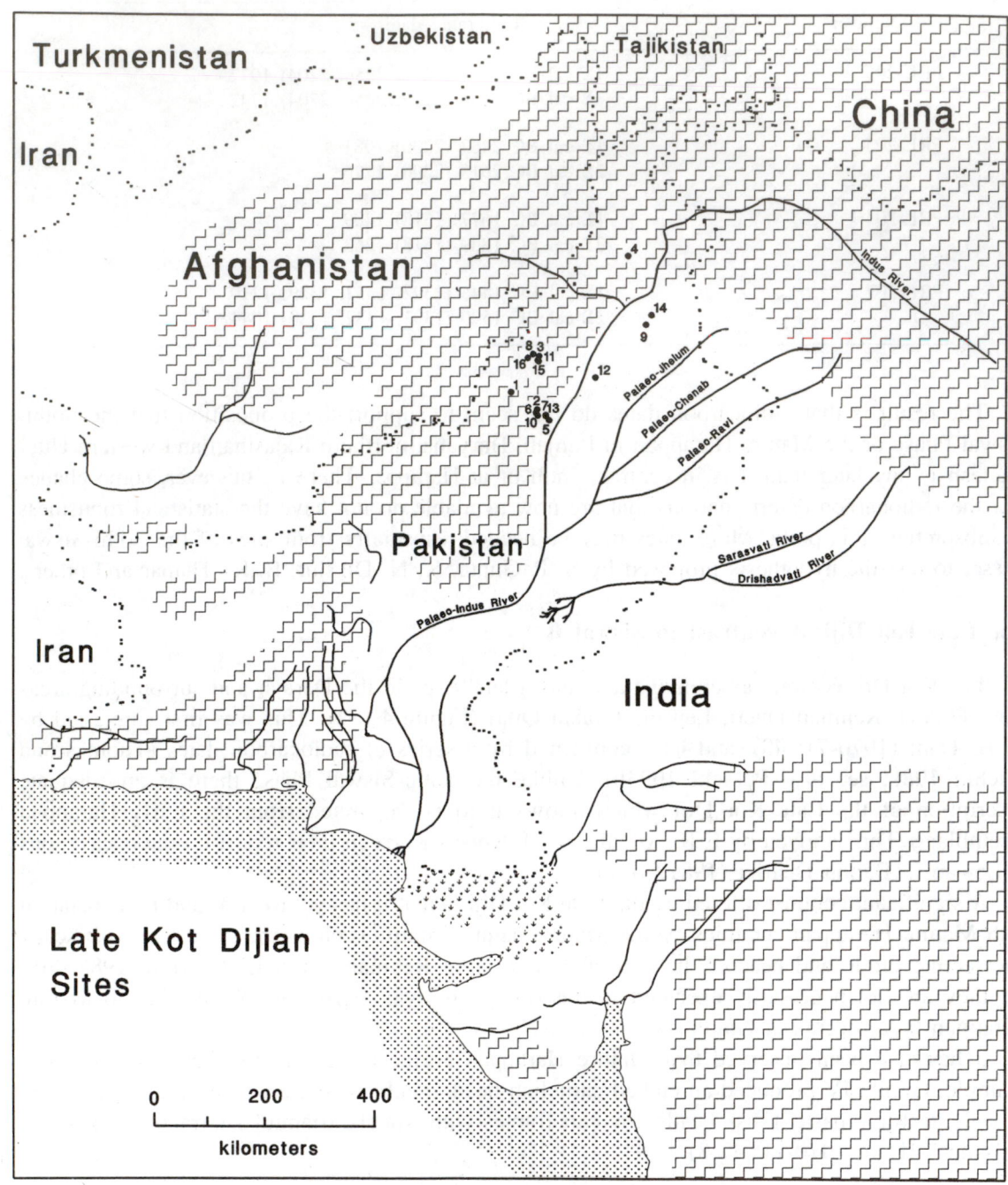

Key to Figure 4.172

1 Bagh-i Kumb Damb	5 Gumla	9 Jhang	13 Rehman Dheri
2 Budki Dheri	6 Hathala	10 Karam shah	14 Sarai Khola
3 Dad Kala Kach Kot Dherai	7 Hisham Dheri	11 Lewan	15 Seer Dheri
4 Ghalegay Cave	8 Islam Chowki	12 Musa Khel	16 Tarakai Qila

Figure 4.172. Map of sites of the Late Kot Diji Phase

is approximately twenty-five percent of the total assemblage in Period IA, the remaining seventy-five percent is the sturdy red wares of the Mature Harappan.

There is no doubt that the pottery is both Early and Mature Harappan. But, given the small scale of the excavation and the fact that this material was at the bottom of a trench 9.22 meters deep it cannot be said with certainty that the association is valid in culture historical terms. The mixture could have happened in the context of a dump, or as a secondary or tertiary deposit created during the Mature Harappan (or later) that artificially brought the sherds into the same stratum as a mixture of different, older strata.

There are some archaeological observations that cannot be resolved with the data that are presently available, and this is one of them. We simply do not know where to place Manda within the time-space systematics of the region.

Sothi-Siswal Phase: Concluding Remarks

Perhaps the most striking feature of the Sothi-Siswal Phase is the ambiguity surrounding it. There are important issues of chronology and cultural affiliation yet to be resolved that are straightforward empirical problems that can be settled with data, not armchair thought. Do the Sothi-Siswal sites grow progressively older as one moves east beyond Kalibangan? Does the transition to urbanism follow the same or a similar sloping horizon?

There is a growing sense among the archaeologists involved with the Indus Civilization that the Harappan world in the east, beyond Kalibangan is a separate, different place from the Harappan world of Sindh and the West Punjab. It is of the Mature Harappan, of course, but the Sothi-Siswal heritage in this region may well be quite different from the Early Harappan elsewhere. Ultimately the question arises - in what way were these people Harappan? Artifacts and architecture strongly suggest that they were part of the Harappan Civilization, but were a distinctive regional manifestation or "sub-culture," just as the Harappans of Saurashtra seem to have been.

CONCLUSIONS: The Early Harappan Stage, A Prelude to Civilization?

The Early Harappan Stage is one of the most interesting aspects of the Indus Age. Based on a reasonably sound chronology, both comparative and absolute, the four regional Phases of the Early Harappan immediately precede the Mature Harappan and bring the culture historical sequence to the onset of urbanization. Gradualist evolutionary theory suggests that the Early Harappan Stage, especially the latter parts of it, should have clear signs of significant development of the traits of urbanization and sociocultural complexity. The late Early Harappan and the earliest Mature Harappan should resemble one another in terms of their level of sociocultural complexity. But, it does not appear that the Early Harappan Stage fits this model (Possehl 1986a: 96-7, 1990b).

There are some new thoughts on my original assessment of this topic and a reexamination of the level of sociocultural differentiation apparent in the Early Harappan.[16] Since archaeology, in the absence of written texts, cannot readily observe this level directly, we have developed a series of proxies that stand for, or represent, the sociocultural features we seek to understand.

They include: 1) settlement patterns and the growth of urban centers, 2) the development of public architecture, 3) evidence for social stratification, 4) the evolution of writing and the system of weights and measures 5) the ethnic diversity of the Early Harappan and 6) political units in the Early Harappan.

Settlement Patterns: the Early Harappan Stage

Settlement during the Early Harappan is somewhat undifferentiated with respect to settlement size. The "Gazetteer of Settlements of the Indus Age" (Appendix A) currently has 477 sites listed as having been occupied during the Early Harappan. Of these 477 sites there are 291 with reliable estimates of their size, which average 4.54 hectares in extent. Two hundred and fifty-seven of these 277 sites (ninty-three percent) are smaller than ten hectares.

TABLE 4.50
Size Distribution of Early Harappan Sites

Smaller than 10 hectares	257
Smaller than 5 hectares	209
Smaller than 3 hectares	171
Smaller than 2 hectares	133
Smaller than 1 hectare	78
Smaller than 0.5 hectares	36

Some sites are very small (e.g., 0.01 hectares); although in Bahawalpur there are three Early Harappan sites in the twenty-two to thirty hectare range. Of the three Mature Harappan cities (Harappa, Mohenjo-daro and Ganweriwala) only Harappa has a documented Early Harappan occupation, the giant sites of Bhatinda District notwithstanding.

Enough has been said of the giant sites in Bhatinda District to conclude that we just do not know how they will figure in this assessment. It may well be that they are not of the Early Harappan at all. A graph comparing the size distribution of sites in all four Phases of the Early Harappan is shown as (Figure 4.173).

Settlement Patterns: the Mature Harappan Stage

The emergence of the Mature Harappan brings change. First, there is a significant increase in the number of sites. The "Gazetteer of Settlements of the Indus Age" lists 976 Mature Harappan settlements. Some of this increase comes from the expanded Harappan settlement of Gujarat, both Kutch and Saurashtra (Possehl 1980) as well as the integration of the Kulli Complex of Baluchistan into the greater Harappan urbanization process (Possehl 1986a). But in Cholistan, already well settled with forty sites during the Early Harappan, there is a jump to 174 in the Mature Harappan (Mughal 1982: 87).

There seems to be a gap in settlement size between the three cities (Mohenjo-Daro, Harappa and Ganweriwala) with the next largest settlement being the Kulli site of Nindowari at fifty hectares. The three large settlements are also nicely spaced within the Harappan Region, with Ganweriwala almost exactly centered between Mohenjo-daro and Harappa (Possehl 1982b: 19, Figure 2).

M. R. Mughal has attempted to demonstrate that there is a four tiered settlement hierarchy in Early Harappan times in Cholistan (Mughal 1990a: 190-94). An examination of his graphs (1990a: Figures 6 and 7) indicates that this contention might simply reflect the fact that he created four size categories and that as site size grows larger, the number of settlements grows smaller. This happens in a smooth, regular way, without the expected "blip" for the appearance of towns.[17]

None of the statistical tests I have performed on these data for either the Early or Mature Harappan gives a clear indication of clustering within what would be called a tiered hierarchy

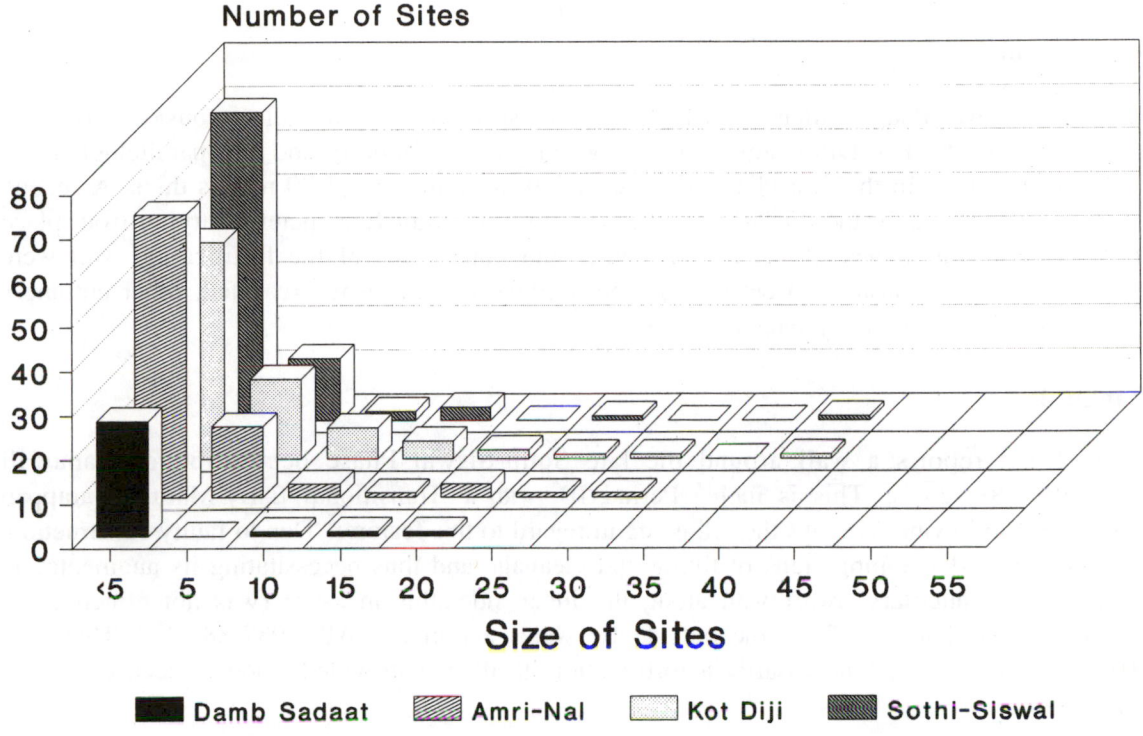

Figure 4.173. Histogram of the site size distribution of settlements in all four Phases of the Early Harappan

of settlement patterns, a conclusion also reached by Jim Shaffer (1989, personal communication) and Maurizio Tosi (1989, personal communication). Work on this problem is part of my current research effort and it is possible that this conclusion could be revised.

The working postulate that rises out of this discussion is, that when compared to Mature Harappan settlements, those of the Early Harappan are small and not strongly organized as an emerging tiered settlement hierarchy.

The Development of Public Architecture

A survey of the Early Harappan Stage has found seven sites with buildings thought to have been "public architecture:"

Kot Diji

There may be a circumvallation around Kot Diji which can be dated to the Kot Diji occupation. No one is certain that this wall ever surrounded the entire high mound at the site (F. A. Khan 1965: Figure 4). This feature seems to have been constructed just after the founding of the settlement, but went out of use in stratum eight times, well before the end of the Early Harappan settlement there. At its widest point the stone work of this wall is only three feet (ninety-one centimeters), but most of the wall is only about one foot wide (thirty centimeters) (F. A. Khan 1965: 29-30). A brick revetment is of a later structural stage. These are not the dimensions of a wall intended to stop an enemy intent on even a desultory attack and the inhabitants of Kot Diji would have been foolish indeed if they had built such a structure with defense as the intent. Thus, even if this wall did surround the entire site, which has to remain in doubt, it was not much of a feature.

Kalibangan

The Sothi-Siswal Phase settlement at Kalibangan is surrounded by a wall of considerably more substance than the Kot Diji example. It can be traced in its entirety and is a parallelogram ca. 250 × 170 meters. In the first phase of construction the wall is ca. 1.90 meters thick. A second building phase brought the thickness of the wall up to three or four meters, varying from place to place. Excavation has shown that the inner and outer faces of the fortification wall were covered with mud plaster. An entrance in the northwest corner was excavated, other entrances were probably obscured by later building.

Banawali

R. S. Bisht reports a wall around the late Sothi-Siswal Phase occupation of Banawali (IAR 1987-88: 23-4). This is in his Period IB, with a Transitional Early-Mature Harappan Period (IC) following. He says the following in regard to this feature: "Due to faulty construction, it soon started developing signs of tilting and cleavage and thus necessitating its augmentation by raising an ancillary dwarf wall along the inner side...this measure (was not effective) as it was further damaged from the outside by water action..." (IAR 1987-88: 23). Thus, the Banawali wall was not necessarily a fortification at all, but provided flood protection for the settlement.

Kohtras Buthi

Kohtras Buthi is one of the Kot Diji settlements in the Sindh Kohistan. Located on the Baran Nai, the site sits on a natural ridge. Only a small amount of clearance has been done there (Majumdar 1934: 132-34; see also Lambrick 1944: 60-1) but the stone masonry appears to be substantial. The outcrop rises thirty meters above the surrounding plain with a steep escarpment on the northern side. It slopes to the south and is approached from this direction. According to Louis Flam, who has visited the site (1981a: 331-33), as the settlement is approached from this direction one first encounters a small, low stone wall about one meter high. A second wall, now standing between three and four meters in height is found slightly higher on the slope and is the principal wall protecting the settlement. The extremities of this wall, each turning north-south, were integrated with the natural terrain in such a way as to protect the entire settled area. Like Kalibangan, the remains at Kohtras Buthi seem to document the presence of a fortification for the Early Harappan Stage.

Rehman Dheri

A wall may have surrounded the settled area at Rehman Dheri. It was found only in the southern-most set of trenches at the site and then only in the Period IB occupation. It measures 1.2 meters (four feet) wide but sits on a 1.8 meter (six feet) wide footing. The wall was built of large clay slabs, set in place and carefully trimmed (Durrani 1988: 26, Pl. XIVa).

Durrani forcefully states his case for the existence of a circumvallation: "Since the earliest occupation, except for the extension outside the city in the south, the entire habitation area of Rehman Dheri was enclosed by a massive wall. It has now been exposed in the IB phase, in the south-west excavation Unit A, trenches BIV/24 and 25. Unfortunately the wall did not survive in the intermediate, RHD II, and the last occupation, RHD III" (Durrani 1988: 26).

This means that there is only evidence for a wall along the southern part of the site during Period IB and the rest is assumed. Until someone finds some "bricks and mortar" for this wall on all four sides of the settlement the only reasonable conclusion is that Rehman Dheri, like so many other Early Harappan sites, was an open settlement, not surrounded by a wall.

Tharro Hill

The so-called "fortifications" at Tharro Hill (Majumdar 1934: 77-8) in Sindh cannot be confirmed.

Mehrgarh VIIA

A large platform, fronted by a buttressed wall was found in the first phase of Period VII at Mehrgarh. More than 300 square meters of this structure were exposed but the function of the platform, and the nature of the relationship between it and the large wall has not yet been determined (Jarrige and Lechevallier 1979: 509-11). Jarrige and Lechevallier refer to the platform as "monumental" which may or may not be the case. The wall could be traced for approximately thirty meters, but it is less than one-half a meter thick, not counting the buttresses. These are not the dimensions of a fortification. The platform is large, and it must have taken a great deal of work to complete, but not enough is known of it for much more to be said.

Other than these references to "fortifications" and a platform, I know of no other possible public architecture in the Greater Indus Region during the Early Harappan Stage. There is a massive wall exposed around the northern end of Nausharo that is attributed to Period IC. The excavators place this occupation in what is being termed the "Transitional Stage" in the Indus Age, so this feature is not a part of the Early Harappan.

Of the 477 sites there are three which have a circumvallation substantial enough to suggest fortifications and the protection of community interests. Even admitting Kot Diji, Rehman Dheri and Mehrgarh to this class we are hardly left with an impressive statistic and Piggott's 1950 observation for the Amri sites still holds as a generalization for the Early Harappan: "...villages appear to have been undefended by walls or ramparts" (1950: 78).

Evidence for Social Stratification and Differentiation

The Early Harappan has little evidence for any degree of social differentiation. Full scale excavations within this period have been undertaken at Amri (Casal 1964a), Kot Diji (Khan 1965), Kalibangan (Thapar 1973a, 1973b, 1975; Lal 1979) and Bala Kot (Dales 1974a, 1974b, 1979a, 1979b). In addition, A. H. Dani worked at two Early Harappan Phase sites in the Gomal Valley (Gumla and Hathala 1970-71) and the University of Peshawar continues it excavations at Rehman Dheri (Durrani 1988). Additional horizontal excavation is certainly called for at Early Harappan Phase sites, but what we see as a result the work that has been done is a remarkably uniform inventory of material culture couched within a village structure. There are, of course, differences in the stylistic attributes of these Early Harappan settlements. The ceramics, for example, can be organized into stylistic regions. There might be some differences in other artifact classes as well. But this stylistic variation in artifacts does not change the underlying uniformity, and the minimal level of sociocultural differentiation. There is little evidence to suggest that the Early Harappan is a period within which we can see the unmistakable beginnings of the Mature, Urban Harappan elite class or classes.

The Mature Harappan has unambiguous evidence for social differentiation. The presence of substantial architectural features, such as the Great Bath and Warehouse at Mohenjo-daro, suggests patterns of use that are not open to the bulk of the city's population. The limited number of stamp seals seems to indicate that not everyone possessed these splendidly crafted, probably "expensive," items of personal identification. Evidence for large scale craft specialization at Mohenjo-daro, Harappa, Chanhu-daro and Lothal, sometimes set within their own "districts," further suggests a degree of job differentiation of the population not seen in the Early Harappan Phase. Social differentiation is also shown by contrasts of big house/little house, baked brick house/mud brick house, city dweller/village dweller which are clearly present in the Mature Harappan and can only be noted here. Finally, the presence during the Mature Harappan of truly sumptuous items of personal adornment such as the necklaces found at Mohenjo-daro (Marshall 1931a: Vol. III, Pl. CXLIX) and Allahdino (Fairservis 1985, personal communication), as well as a growth in the use of precious metals and beads, are all indicative of differential access to wealth, productivity and abundance.

The Development of Writing and the System of Weights and Measures

Writing has been used as an index of sociocultural complexity and deserves special mention. It is widely known that there is no evidence for the gradual, logical evolution of the Harappan script or of their unified system of weights and measures. Prototypes for the square Indus stamp seal seem to been found at the site of Kunal in Hisar District of Haryana (Khatri and Acharya 1995, in press). These are not yet published. There are six seals, all of a soft grey stone. Five are white and appear to have been baked. They are small, about one to one and one-half centimeters on a side and approximately square. The face is carved with geometric designs and there is a very clear, small boss on the back. The sixth seal is unbaked, with a square face and a high back, with a perforation. The "proto-seals" come from Period Ic at the site, which may belong to the Transitional Stage (Khatri and Acharya 1995: 86). Tiny, cubical stone weights were associated with these "protoseals" at Kunal.

Farzand Durrani has made a claim that the potter's marks from Rehman Dheri are symbols from which the signs of the Indus script have been taken (Figure 4.174). It is a reasonable idea, one that Professor B. B. Lal has been pursuing for the Early Harappan Stage (Lal 1992). But at Rehman Dheri the chronology of the site cannot be forgotten when evaluating Durrani's suggestion. Period III is a Late Kot Diji occupation, contemporary with the Mature Harappan. Since Durrani does not say which signs come from each of the three periods at Rehman Dheri the coincidence may be a case of those at Rehman Dheri borrowing signs, rather than contributing to the evolution of the Indus script.

Durrani also draws attention to an ivory object found in Period I at Rehman Dheri (Figure 4.175; see also Shah and Parpola 1991: 352). He believes that this is both a seal and a prototype for the Mature Harappan seals (1984: 509). The two circular marks at the top of the object are perforations and it may well be a pendant, or something made to be worn on clothing. It is not a seal, as demonstrated by the absence of a boss, or a handle of some kind, as well as the designs on both sides.

It is common practice to call many objects from the archaeological record "seals" without full confirmation of this function, and that is a critical point in the present discussion. My attention has been drawn to carved or inscribed objects from Tepe Gawra that fit this description (Tobler 1950: Plate CLXXII) (Figure 4.176). It is interesting that in the Tepe Gawra examples, Tobler labeled his plate "Tanged pendants," closer, it seems to me, to their probable function.

719

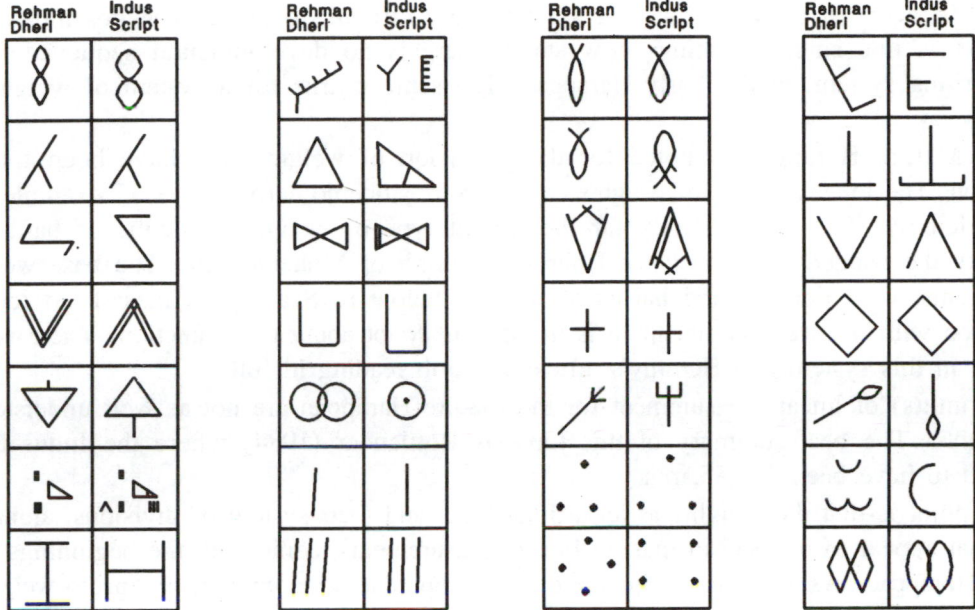

Figure 4.174. Durrani's chart of potter's marks from Rehman Dheri, after Durrani 1984: 509-10

Figure 4.175. The carved ivory object from Rehman Dheri, after Durrani 1984

Figure 4.176. Objects from Tepe Gawra sometimes called "seals," after Tobler 1950: Plate CLXXII

The fact that the Rehman Dheri pendant comes from Period I, a Kechi Beg Phase occupation, without a similar object in the Period II, Kot Diji occupation, means that there is a gap of at least 500 years between the Rehman Dheri pendant and the Late Kot Diji occupation of Period III. To think of this piece in terms of a "prototype" for anything in the second half of the third millennium is stretching things quite a bit.

A number of scholars have remarked on the similarities between the Indus script and the Proto-Elamite writing system of the Iranian Plateau (e.g., Pran Nath 1932, 1986; G. R. Hunter 1932: 483; G. de Hevesy 1933a, 1933b; Walter Fairservis 1976: 46-7). Fairservis has even transliterated the Harappan script into Proto-Elamite. There can be little doubt that some very striking similarities are present, but then, *all* pictorgaphic scripts have some similarities, simply because they are pictographic. Squares, circles, triangles hatched, unhatched, and set at various angles, with circles intersecting, and/or grading into ovals are generally present. A fish sign, birds, body parts, objects of daily life are all likely to be present in some simplified, easy to write, easy to compare way. This kind of convergence makes an assessment of the historical relationship between these two writing systems very difficult to judge. The possibility exists that there is one since, as things now stand, there is no developmental sequence for the Indus writing system, in the Early Harappan. The same is true for a system of weights and measures.

The Mature Harappan is noted for the profusion of weights that have been found in excavation. The longest series of weights comes from Mohenjo-daro where 377 examples were found (Hemmy 1937-38: 601). By far the largest type of weight is a cube of hard stone, frequently the banded chert from the Rohri Hills north of Mohenjo-daro. The base weight is 13.66 grams, with doubles and halves above and below it. Scale pans have been found in association with the weights and there is no serious doubt about their function. There is more variation in this system and Hemmy's article is worth reading in full.

The unit(s) of linear measurement for the Mature Harappan are not as well understood as the weights. The best summary of this topic is Rottlander (1984) where the Indus foot is estimated to have been 345.55 mm.

The point is that the weights as an artifact type, and their system of divisions, along with things that appear to be used in making linear measurements, come with the beginnings of the Mature Harappan. As with the script there is no apparent development, or "proto-weight" or "proto-ruler" in the Early Harappan, no pun intended.

The Ethnic Diversity of the Early Harappan

It has been claimed that the Indus Civilization was a unified, homogeneous sociocultural system. This is a controversial topic, in part because it has been so emphasized, possibly to the point of abuse and misunderstanding. Sir Mortimer Wheeler observed: "Behind so vast a uniformity must lie an administrative and economic discipline, however exercised, of an impressive kind" (1968: 4). The mosaic of the Early Harappan, with its four Phases, or regional aspects, is in contrast to this "unity" of style and sets this Stage apart from the Mature Harappan.

The diversity in the artifacts of the Early Harappan Stage is clearly an important part of the archaeological record of the Indus Age. While it is true that "pots aren't people" it is also true that most societies use material culture as a marker of self identity, as a contrast to the different kinds of people around them as well as social differentiation within them. Dress, especially hats or head gear, seem to be widely resorted to in this regard—only a king wears a crown. Pots, figurines and objects of personal adornment are also used in this symbolic way. But, ethnicity and self-identification are not always items free of ambiguity, change, switching, passing and their own social processes (Leach 1964; Barth 1956, 1969). These sources of ambiguity in ethnicity are reflected in the material record of self-identification by overlaps in material culture and fuzzy, indistinct boundaries between groups; something that fits perfectly with the archaeological record of the Early Harappan Stage. Moreover, Barth (1969: 9-38) says that while ethnicity is abundantly displayed in material culture of virtually all peoples, only a limited number of articles from the wide spectrum of available objects will act as this marker, or be used in this way. This is an important cautionary statement, and archaeologists should not simply assume that ceramics were the elements in the total inventory of material culture that carried an ethnic marker. On the other hand, the Early Harappan Phases have ceramics that are historically deep and stylistically identifiable.

There is no guarantee in this, but I find it comfortable, in a provisional way, to see the four Phases of the Early Harappan Stage as proxies for four large divisions of people within the Greater Indus Region. None of these divisions was fully distinct from the others, admitting the expected overlap and fuzzy edges in self-identification. There is also an overall style for the Early Harappan Stage, and I would suggest that the people of the four Phases may have recognized this as well, possibly as a "super-ethnic" identity for the Greater Indus Region. Since the four Phases of the Early Harappan are also quite large, except perhaps for the Damb Sadaat assemblage, there must have been social subdivisions within and among the Phases as well.

It is not known if the Phases of the Early Harappan are linguistic, although given the complexity of the archaeological record and the huge area we are dealing with in the Early Harappan Stage, it would border on the foolish to imagine that there was only one language there, even admitting the possibility of dialectal proliferation. But we do not know the sociocultural basis for the divisions.

Others have been studying the problem of ethnicity in the prehistory of the greater Indus region. In 1989 Jim Shaffer and his wife, Diane Lichtenstein, a cultural anthropologist, published a paper concerning the cultural diversity and change there (Shaffer and Lichtenstein 1989). Their essay begins with a critique of linear models for understanding cultural development and then focuses on the Indus Civilization. They observe that the assumption that cultures are closed systems that move through prescribed sequences of cultural integration is unwarranted. Rather, sociocultural systems are always reacting independently to forces of change from both within and outside their boundaries (Shaffer and Lichtenstein 1989: 117). They then examine the diversity of archaeological assemblages in the greater Indus region from the beginnings of agriculture to the eclipse of the Mature Harappan. This is organized as a developmental scheme for the archaeology of this region. Their scheme shares many features with the one employed here, which can be taken as an intellectual debt on my part to their work. The Shaffer-Lichtenstein scheme is worth presenting in full, since it is another way of looking at the Indus world:

Taken together these archaeological complexes form what Shaffer and Lichtenstein call the "Indus Valley Cultural Tradition."

> These patterned sets are designated here as ethnic groups. An ethnic group is an analytical unit composed of archaeological assemblages with one or more traits sufficiently characteristic to distinguish it from other similarly conceived units. The ethnic group is similar to the traditional archaeological "phase" concept, but no chronological limits are implied. As used here, the ethnic group is similar to Barth's (1969) "ethnic group" concept. According to Barth (1969: 13) the critical feature of an ethnic group is that it "...has membership which identifies itself, and is identified by others, as constituting a category distinguishable from other categories of the same order". In other words (Barth 1969:14), an ethnic group is an ascriptive and exclusive social unit which depends upon the maintenance of recognizable boundaries. The definition of such boundaries may involve diverse cultural factors, but in an archaeological context such salient cultural traits are material cultural symbols, such as distinctive ceramic styles, used to indicate membership in cooperative social units, organized to facilitate access to sources of production and reproduction (Hodder 1979: 447-50). Since any ethnic group's organization reflects response to the social and natural environments, cultural stability as well as rapid cultural change may be the day-to-day adjustments to survive (Shaffer and Lichtenstein 1989: 119).

TABLE 4.51
Ethnic Diversity Proposed by Shaffer and Lichtenstein

Complex/Group	Representative Sites
Mehrgarh	Mehrgarh I/II
Bagor	Bagor I
Kili Ghul Mohammad	Mehrgarh III
Nal	Anjira IV, Siah Damb II, phase 3
Hakra	Jalilpur I, Bahawalpur Hakra Wares sites
Hakra-Northern	Sarai Khola I, Swat Valley Periods I, III-IV
Balakot	Balakot I
Amri	Amri IA-D
Kechi Beg	Mehrgarh IV-V
Kot Diji	Kot Diji Levels 4-16, Jalilpur II, Gumla II-IV, Kalibangan I, Sarai Khola IB, II, Rehman Dheri I-III
Damb Sadaat	Mehrgarh VI-VII
Harappan	Mature occupations at Harappa, Mohenjo-daro, Chanhu-daro, Allahdino, Balakot, Kalibangan II, Lothal A, Surkotada, etc.
Punjab	Cemetery H at Harappa, Mitathal IIB Bhagwanpura IA-B
Jhukar	Jhukar, Late levels at Mohenjo-daro and Chanhu Daro
Rangpur	Rangpur IIB-III
Pirak	Pirak I-II
Langhnaj	Langhnaj
Ganeshwar	Ganeshwar, Jodhpura
Ahar	Ahar I, Kayatha I-II

(Shaffer and Lichtenstein 1989: 118).

This is an interesting set of ideas, but brings us face to face with the "pots aren't people" problem. How can we possibly know that the Shaffer and Lichtenstein archaeological complexes were "ascriptive and exclusive social units?" The answer is that we cannot. Still, I am drawn to this notion as a potentially important theoretical construct for the Early Harappan Stage for the understanding of the development of Harappan urbanization.

On the positive side, the assumption that the Early and Mature Harappan Stages were characterized by ethnic diversity is supported by two observations from the early history of South Asia; one is linguistic, the other more purely historical. Historical linguists know that Vedic Sanskrit was not a language unaffected by borrowings. Dravidian words are certainly present (Southworth 1976: 74). Southworth (1979, 1988, 1990, 1992) has done a great deal of work on this topic and found some indications that there might even have been one or more Sino-Tibetan languages in the region. As already noted, this would correlate very well with the Neolithic archaeological materials from Kashmir as found at Burzahom, Gufkral, as well as Sarai Khola near Taxila (Agrawal 1982a: 94-106). Bertil Tikkanen (1988) suggests that an ancient language related to modern Burushaski may also have been a part of this linguistic environment. The Dravidian component may have been the "Proto-Elamo-Dravidian" proposed by David McAlpin (1981). This itself would have been a large, diverse linguistic family made up of several or even many individual languages. Finally, Vedic Sanskrit is just the earliest documented Indo-European language in the Subcontinent. There is also a possibility that older Indo-European speakers were there prior to these folk. The second point relates to the ethnic diversity that comes from ancient texts. The Vedas mention many different kinds of people in the Punjab and surrounding regions. There is also the testimony of Herodotus: "There are many Indian nations, none speaking the same language..." (Book III, 98, Godley 1926). Herodotus told us many things about India, not all of which were important, but, this particular one may be evidence for the ethnic diversity of the early Stages of the Indus Age.

Archaeologists do not know who made these pottery assemblages; men, women or both, or whether it was a profession or a universal household activity. But, whoever fashioned the pottery did so in a way that had clear definition, which almost certainly has some relationship to social domains other than pots. The thought that they were somehow involved with the identity of different kinds of people, or ethnic groups, is perfectly reasonable. This is simply the observation of a possibility, not the assertion of proof.

The speculation that Shaffer, Lichtenstein and I choose to indulge in is not all "smoke and mirrors" or the creation of our imagination. There are good reasons to propose ethnic diversity in the Greater Indus Region during the Early Harappan Stage and the four Phases that I have defined are perfectly good candidates to account for some of this diversity.

Political Units in the Early Harappan

We are not certain about the way in which political organization should be meshed with the four Early Harappan Phases. Again, the diversity of the archaeological record and the enormity of the area probably precludes the notion that it was a single polity. One thing is apparent in the archaeological record: there are no clear candidates for the "capitals" of the four regional Phases. In the Amri-Nal Phase, no site stands out as the predominant settlement of the region. Kot Diji is not likely to be the capital for that Phase. We do not know enough about the Sothi-Siswal sites to say anything about "capitals" there and it would only be guessing to suggest that the big sites in Bhatinda District functioned in this fashion. There is certainly no settlement that could be associated with the hypothesized "superethnic" entity mentioned above.

There are signs of only minimal social differentiation in the Early Harappan Stage, and nothing in the settlement archaeology to suggest that the polities of the times in the Greater Indus Region were dominant, or even strong. Therefore, there is little reason to think that the four Phases represent effective, powerful political units. More than likely, the political units of the Early Harappan were at a level lower than the Phase, something quite small, probably centered on social units like clans or lineages: the notion of a "tribe" might fit here.

Population Trends for the Early Harappan and Earlier Stages

Some effort has been made to make an estimate of the settled area for the Phases and Stages preceding the Mature Harappan. The results of these computations are given in Table 4.52.

Several things are apparent in these figures. In terms of percentage of change the most important time seems to be quite early, in the Burj Basket-marked and Togau Phases, when the settled area changes by three and one-half times: 85.07 to 294.63 hectares. Then from Togau to the Kechi Beg-Hakra Wares Phase: 294.63 to 1230.32; when there was a fourfold increase. The Togau Phase is centered on Mehrgarh Period III, when there was a sudden and important increase in craft activity, including the development of copper metallurgy and the perfection of a technique for bead drilling. The physical anthropologists have also suggested that this was a time during which new biological traits are present in the population at Mehrgarh. These population figures add yet another important cultural and historical dynamic to this time period, which is clearly an extraordinarily important one in the history of the Indus Civilization.

The second observation is a rather simple one. There seems to have been a fair number of

TABLE 4.52
Summary of Estimates of Settled Area by Stage and Phase

Stage	Phase	Total Area
Stage Three		2114.03
	Amri-Nal Phase	610.56
	Kot Diji Phase	700.06
	Damb Sadaat Phase	97.54
	Sothi-Siswal Phase	705.87
Stage Two		1524.95
	Kechi Beg & Hakra Wares Phases	1230.32
	Togau Phase	294.63
Stage One		138.07
	Burj Basket-marked Phase	85.07
	Kili Ghul Mohammad Phase	53.00

Settled areas are given in hectares

people around the Greater Indus Region during the Early Harappan Stage, estimated to have been about half a million people. This is, of course, the archaeologically apparent population, not the true census population which was probably much larger.

There is an impressive relative density of people in the Eastern Region, during the early history of food production there and it is the area with the biggest sites, estimated to have been in the fifty hectare range. While the Damb Sadaat area is small, the other areas for these Phases are comparable in size, so that factor cannot be used to explain the sizable difference between the population estimate for the Amri-Nal Phase as compared to the Sothi-Siswal.

By looking at all of the data from the Early Harappan Stage it can be seen how weakly developed it is as a threshold to the Mature Harappan. There seems to have been a minimum of development of social differentiation, craft and career specialization, and little evolution of the political and ideological institutions that produce public architecture. These sociocultural features are in marked contrast to levels of developments inferred for the Mature Harappan and must be used to shape perceptions of the nature of Mature Harappan society, its institutions and the historical, developmental process that took it from the Early Harappan Stage to urbanization.

NOTES

1. There is a long and interesting history of ideas on the domestication of plants and animals. Gary Wright (1971) is an excellent source for this story.

2. I realize that it is no longer fashionable for the tower at Jericho to be viewed as a "fortification." The critiques of this interpretation are, in my opinion less than compelling, and the possibility still exists that one of the functions of this early example of public architecture on a large scale was the protection of the village.

3. These matters are somewhat specialized and methodological. Those interested in following up on them could start with (Bokonyi 1969; Hasdorf and Popper 1988; Klein and Cruz-Uribe 1984). The identification of biological remains from archaeological sites has grown to be important, specialized work in archaeology. Separate positions for palaeobotany and archaeozoology are parts of most excavation projects.

4. There are always perfectly edible plants and animals in the environment that are not

selected to be included in the subsistence regime of a people. Think of the American abhorrence of eating insects. Even the !Kung San are selective in their desert environment. They have named 223 species of animals, but only 54 of these are classed as edible, and of these only seventeen are hunted more or less regularly. The !Kung also have identified 85 species of food plants, including 29 fruits, berries and melons and 30 or so roots and bulbs, but 90 percent of the vegetable food intake comes from only 23 species (Lee and DeVore 1968).

5. There is also some fence sitting on this issue, as in Cowan and Watson (1992: 211,) or Meadow (1993a: 311 and 1996.)

6. The key work on this topic is by Meadow, who has access to the important collections from Mehrgarh.

7. The thought that the clay pot would shrink enough for it to have been extracted from the basket has been raised. While clay shrinks when it dries, my experience suggests that this would not work. But, no one has carried out an experiment, and that might settle the issue.

8. This is not to suggest that the Subcontinent is free of important innovations introduced from the outside world. The apparent ascension of Indo-European languages in the first millennium BC is one important innovation from the "outside." But so is the acceptance of Islam by hundreds of millions of people in the Subcontinent. The bicameral parliamentary form of government in India and Pakistan with a Prime Minister, is later yet and clearly based on a British model, brought by their colonial domination. Still there is an enduring quality to South Asian life and each of these innovations has been shaped by life there. The parliamentary systems of India and Pakistan are different from one another, and they in turn could hardly be considered a direct copy of the British system.

9. The Kechi Beg occupation of Damb Sadaat is also described below.

10. Sylvia Matheson, someone with an interest in archaeology, has done some travel in these areas.

11. Amreli is a site of the Western Kshatrapas, associated with the well known Red Polished Ware. There is an earlier occupation there, that needs to be better understood, which may well relate to the Harappan occupation of Saurashtra.

12. This is a second river with the name "Sarasvati." It flows across the north Gujarat plain, not northern Rajasthan.

13. The Micaceous Red Ware found at Lothal will not be discussed since this ware has never been properly defined and documented. Moreover, there is no reason for it to be seriously considered to have been a separate phase at the site prior to the Mature Harappan.

14. Professor Suraj Bhan should be considered to have one name and is properly alphabeticized under "S" not "B."

15. This refers to Gupta 1972-73 in my bibliography.

16. This presentation is based on the text and structure of that in Possehl 1990b.

17. There are some technical questions that emerge with Mughal's graphs, that should be noted as well. He begins with a plot of settlements in the range 0-5 hectares and then 5-10. But then he shifts to 10 hectare increments: 10-20, 20-30, 30-40, following which he has a category of >80 hectares. There are two small problems with this: 1) he never explains why he begins with one unit and then shifts to another, and 2) we do not know which category receives the count for sites of exactly 5, 10, 20... hectares since they are listed in two places.

APPENDIX-A

Gazetteer of Sites of the Indus Age

SITE	DISTRICT	COORDINATES	PERIODS	BIBLIOGRAPHY	SIZE
Abdui	Makran	26° 20' 00" N - 62° 19' 00" E	Shahi Tump Dasht	Besenval and Sanlaville 1990: 122	0.05
Abdul But	Jhalawan	27° 20' 00" N - 66° 25' 30" E	Kulli?	Stein 1931: 175	1.00
Abduwali	Bahawalpur	28° 45' 20" N - 71° 20' 38" E	Hakra Wares	Mughal 1997: 42	7.10
Abha	Saharanpur	29° 55' 00" N - 77° 44' 00" E	Post-urban Harappan	Joshi et al. 1984: 522	
Achhal Sahib	Gurdaspur	32° 00' 00" N - 75° 18' 00" E	Post-urban Harappan	Joshi et al. 1984: 526	
Achharwala	Bahawalpur	28° 50' 25" N - 71° 24' 26" E	Mature Harappan	Mughal 1997: 47	2.30
Adasta Damb	Jhalawan	26° 27' 00" N - 65° 39' 00" E	Kulli-Harappan	Stein 1931: 138	1.10
Adatala	Bhavnagar	21° 58' 05" N - 71° 37' 06" E	Late Historic Late Sorath Harappan Sorath Harappan	Possehl 1980: 89 Joshi et al. 1984: 528	7.00
Adatjo-daro	Larkana	27° 19' 00" N - 68° 01' 00" E	Jhukar Mature Harappan	Majumdar 1934: 47-8 Flam 1981a: 216	0.05
Adeva	Kheda	22° 36' 00" N - 72° 33' 00" E	Sorath Harappan	IAR 1972-73: 10 Momin 1979: 126-27	8.00
Adhi One	Bahawalpur	28° 46' 04" N - 71° 05' 03" E	Hakra Wares	Mughal 1997: 42	20.00
Adhi Three	Bahawalpur	28° 45' 10" N - 71° 05' 26" E	Mature Harappan	Mughal 1997: 47	4.80
Adhi Two	Bahawalpur	28° 46' 12" N - 71° 05' 25" E	Mature Harappan	Mughal 1997: 47	6.70
Adinga	Mathura		Sunga-Kushan PGW OCP	IAR 1982-83: 99	
Agavibani	Midnapur		Copper Hoard	Makkhan Lal 1984a: 40-1	
Aghiana	Saharanpur	29° 54' 00" N - 77° 17' 00" E	OCP	Joshi et al. 1984: 522 IAR 1965-66: 54	
Ahar	Bulandshahr	28° 25' 00" N - 78° 15' 00" E	OCP	IAR 1970-71:	

Ahichchhatra	Bareilly	28° 22' 00" N 79° 07' 00" E	-	Kushan-Gupta NBP PGW OCP	IAR 1964-65: 39-42	
Ahmad Khan Dheri	Jaisalmer	27° 54' 00" N 70° 24' 00" E	-	Mature Harappan	Stein 1943a: 97	2.10
Ahmad Khan's Dheri	Jaisalmer	27° 54' 30" N 70° 24' 00" E	-	Mature Harappan	Stein 1943a: 98	16.80
Ahmadwala Ther	Bahawalpur	29° 06' 07" N 71° 53' 46" E	-	Mature Harappan	Stein 1943a: 115-16 Mughal 1997: 47	7.70
Ahmadwala Toba	Bahawalpur	29° 08' 48" N 72° 59' 56" E	-	Kot Diji	Mughal 1997: 44	5.90
Ahmed Khanzai North	Quetta-Pishin	30° 11' 00" N 66° 58' 00" E	-	Iron Age Quetta Damb Sadaat Kechi Beg	Fairservis 1956a: 197 de Cardi 1983: 19	0.60
Ahmed Khanzai South	Quetta-Pishin	30° 09' 00" N 66° 57' 00" E	-	Damb Sadaat Kechi Beg	Fairservis 1956a: 197 de Cardi 1983: 19	0.40
Ahmed Shah	Dadu	25° 35' 00" N 67° 52' 00" E	-	Amri-Nal	Fairservis 1971c: 409 Flam 1981a: 344	
Ahulana	Sonepat	29° 07' 00" N 76° 38' 00" E	-	Post-urban Harappan	Joshi et al. 1984: 525	
Aidu Damb	Jhalawan	27° 08' 00" N 66° 25' 00" E	-	Londo Kulli Amri-Nal Togau	Stein 1931: 177 Raikes 1968a: 151	
Ajmer	Rajkot	22° 40' 00" N 70° 50' 00" E	-	Late Sorath Harappan	Rao 1963a: 205 Possehl 1980: 89	
Ajmeri	Sikar			OCP and Microliths	IAR 1981-82: 62	
Akalgarh	Jind	29° 07' 13" N 76° 27' 45" E	-	Post-urban Harappan	Joshi et al. 1984: 525	0.80
Akhera	Bahawalpur	29° 10' 43" N 72° 11' 25" E	-	Kot Diji	Mughal 1997: 44	4.50
Akkanwali Theri	Bahawalpur	28° 50' 04" N 71° 24' 26" E	-	Hakra Wares	Mughal 1997: 42	2.90
Akrabas	Bulandshahr			Medieval Sunga-Kushan OCP	IAR 1970-71:	
Akru	Ahmedabad	22° 15' 00" N 71° 55' 00" E	-	Late Sorath Harappan Sorath Harappan	Possehl 1980: 89 Joshi et al. 1984: 529	4.10
Akvada	Bhavnagar			Sorath Harappan Microliths	IAR 1980-81: 12	
Ala Damb	Jhalawan			Early Historic Londo Kechi Beg Togau	Fairservis 1971c: 405	
Alam Khan Shahr	Jhalawan	26° 57' 00" N 66° 05' 00" E	-	Early Kulli Amri-Nal	Fairservis 1971c: 405 Raikes 1964	
Alamgirpur	Meerut	29° 00" 00" N 77° 22' 00" E	-	Late Medieval Early Historic PGW Post-urban Harappan Mature Harappan	IAR 1958-59: 50-5 Joshi et al. 1984: 521	0.30

Alau	Ahmedabad	22° 15' 00" N - 71° 30' 00" E		Late Sorath Harappan Sorath Harappan	Possehl 1980: 89 Joshi et al. 1984: 529	
Alav				Sorath Harappan	Chitalwala 1985: key Figure 8	
Alduka	Gurgaon	28° 06' 00" N - 77° 06' 00" E		Post-urban Harappan	Suraj Bhan 1975: 112, 126 Joshi et al. 1984: 519	
Ali Mohammad Wala Ther	Bahawalpur	29° 13' 36" N - 71° 50' 15" E		Kot Diji	Mughal 1997: 44	0.30
Ali Murad	Dadu	26° 32' 00" N - 67° 27' 00" E		Mature Harappan	Majumdar 1934: 89-91 Flam 1981a: 274-75	10.20
Alia Bada	Jamnagar	22° 08' 00" N - 69° 07' 00" E		Late Sorath Harappan Sorath Harappan	Rao 1963a: 205 Possehl 1980: 89 K. K. Bhan 1986: 17	
Alida Theh	Bhatinda	30° 20' 00" N - 75° 20' 00" E		Post-urban Harappan Mature Harappan	Joshi et al. 1984: 522	
Aligrama	Swat	34° 47' 00" N - 72° 18' 00" E		Swat Proto-Historic	Stacul 1987: 63	
Alike	Bhatinda	29° 45' 00" N - 75° 20' 00" E		Post-urban Harappan	Joshi 1986: 139	4.00
Alipur Kharar One	Hissar	29° 08' 00" N - 75° 53' 00" E		Post-urban Harappan Mature Harappan	Joshi et al. 1984: 519, 526	
Alipur Kharar Three	Hissar	29° 08' 00" N - 75° 53' 00" E		Sothi-Siswal	Joshi et al. 1984: 519	
Alipur Kharar Two	Hissar	29° 08' 00" N - 75° 53' 00" E		Sothi-Siswal	Joshi et al. 1984: 519, 526	
Alipur Mandran	Bhatinda	29° 50' 00" N - 75° 28' 00" E		Post-urban Harappan Mature Harappan Sothi-Siswal	Joshi et al. 1984: 520	
Alipur, Uttar Pradesh	Saharanpur	29° 59' 00" N - 77° 27' 00" E		Post-urban Harappan	Joshi et al. 1984: 522	
Alipura	Saharanpur			OCP	IAR 1967-68	
Alipura	Muzaffarnagar			OCP	Srivastava 1982:54-5	
Alipura One	Jind	29° 30' 49" N - 76° 15' 55" E		Post-urban Harappan	Joshi et al. 1984: 525	
Alipura Two	Jind	29° 31' 25" N - 76° 16' 30" E		Post-urban Harappan	Singh 1981: 96	
Allahdino	Karachi	24° 57' 00" N - 67° 18' 00" E		Mature Harappan	Fairservis 1973: 95-102 Flam 1981a: 350-51	1.40
Amai	Jaipur			OCP	IAR 1973-74: 24	
Amarali Khera	Jind	29° 22' 00" N - 76° 29' 00" E		Post-urban Harappan	Joshi et al. 1984: 525	
Amargarh One	Jind	29° 37' 05" N - 76° 01' 10" E		Post-urban Harappan Sothi-Siswal	Joshi et al. 1984: 519, 525 Singh 1981: 97	1.10
Amarheri One	Jind	29° 21' 40" N - 76° 18' 45" E		Sothi-Siswal	Joshi et al. 1984: 525 Singh 1981: 75	1.00
Amarheri Two	Jind	29° 20' 55" N - 76° 18' 20" E		Post-urban Harappan	Joshi et al. 1984: 525	2.00
Ambaliala	Jamnagar	22° 12' 00" N - 69° 44' 00" E		Sorath Harappan	Joshi et al. 1984: 529	
Ambaradi	Rajkot			Lustrous Red Ware	IAR 1978-79: 5	
Ambardi				Sorath Harappan	Chitalwala 1985: key Figure 8	
Ambhliyar	Jamnagar	21° 59' 00" N - 69° 42' 00" E		Late Sorath Harappan Sorath Harappan	K. K. Bhan 1986: 16	
Ambkheri	Saharanpur	29° 44' 00" N - 77° 46' 00" E		OCP	IAR 1963-64: 56 Joshi et al. 1984: 522	

Ambliana	Jamnagar			Sorath Harappan	IAR 1978-79: 7	
Ambrawala Ther	Rahimyar Khan	28° 47' 15" N 70° 59' 17" E	-	Mature Harappan	Mughal 1997: 43	11.20
Ambrawali	Bahawalpur	28° 47' 27" N 71° 58' 05" E	-	Hakra Wares	Mughal 1997: 42	20.50
Amilano	Karachi	25° 02' 00" N 67° 27' 00" E	-	Mature Harappan	Majumdar 1934: 143	0.50
Amra	Jamnagar	22° 16' 00" N 69° 56' 00" E	-	Medieval Red Polished Ware Lustrous Red Ware Sorath Harappan	Rao 1963a: 183, 205 Possehl 1980a: 90 Joshi et al. 1984: 528 K. K. Bhan 1986: 236	1.20
Amri	Dadu	26° 10' 00" N 68° 01' 00" E	-	Jhangar Jhukar Mature Harappan Early to Mature Harappan Amri-Nal	Majumdar 1934: 24-33 Casal 1964a Flam 1981a: 313-15	8.00
Ander Damb	Jhalawan			Kulli Amri-Nal	Fairservis 1971c: 405 Possehl 1986a: 148	
Andheri	Ropar	30° 23' 00" N 77° 07' 00" E	-	Post-urban Harappan	Joshi et al. 1984: 523	
Andheri	Ambala			Post-urban Harappan	Joshi et al. 1984: 523	3.00
Andheri Hoard	Singhbhum			Copper Hoard	Makkhan Lal 1984a: 38-9	
Andhi	Surat	21° 23' 00" N 72° 47' 00" E	-	Post-urban Harappan	IAR 1961-62: 14, 16	
Aneki Five	Saharanpur	29° 59' 00" N 78° 01' 00" E	-	Post-urban Harappan	Joshi et al. 1984: 522	
Angaikhera	Hardoi			Copper Hoard	A. Ghosh 1989a: 20	
Anjira	Jhalawan	28° 17' 00" N 66° 19' 00" E	-	Anjira Amri-Nal Kechi Beg Togau Burj Basket-marked	deCardi 1965: 86-103 deCardi 1983: 31	3.00
Anupgarh	Jind	29° 15' 26" N 76° 21' 08" E	-	Post-urban Harappan	Joshi et al. 1984: 525 Mohan 1988: 63	1.90
Anwarpur Baroli	Saharanpur	30° 08' 00" N 77° 40' 00" E	-	Sunga-Kushan OCP	IAR 1964-65: 44 Joshi et al. 1984: 522	
Apara	Jullunder	31° 05' 00" N 75° 52' 00" E	-	Post-urban Harappan	Joshi et al. 1984: 526	
Arabjo Thana	Karachi	25° 38' 00" N 67° 50' 00" E	-	Amri-Nal	Majumdar 1934: 136-37 Flam 1981a: 342-43	0.80
Aralee	Jamnagar			Sorath Harappan	IAR 1980-81: 13	
Aranauli	Ropar			Post-urban Harappan Mature Harappan	IAR 1962-63: 17	
Ardoi	Rajkot	22° 05' 00" N 70° 47' 00" E	-	Late Sorath Harappan	IAR 1957-58: 19 Rao 1963a: 205 Possehl 1980: 90 Joshi et al. 1984: 528	
Areenono Timbo	Amreli			Late Sorath Harappan Sorath Harappan	A. F. Cunningham, unpublished	0.80
Arikhan One	Jamnagar	22° 05' 00" N 70° 01' 00" E	-	Sorath or Late Sorath Har	K. K. Bhan 1986: 20	
Arnauli	Ropar	30° 14' 00" N 77° 16' 00" E	-	PGW Post-urban Harappan Mature Harappan	IAR 1962-63: 17 Joshi et al. 1984: 523	

Arniwala Theh	Ferozpur	30° 20' 00" N - 75° 15' 00" E	Mature Harappan Sothi-Siswal	Joshi et al. 1984: 520, 522	
Asan	Rohtak	28° 54' 00" N - 76° 46' 00" E	Post-urban Harappan	Joshi et al. 1984: 525	
Asanwali	Saharanpur	30° 02' 00" N - 77° 36' 00" E	OCP Mature Harappan	IAR 1966-67: 43 Joshi et al. 1984: 521, 522	
Ashal	Makran	26° 03' 30" N - 64° 25' 00" E	Amri-Nal Kechi Beg	Stein 1931: 110-111	0.50
Ashrafgarh	Jind	29° 17' 43" N - 76° 21' 50" E	Medieval PGW Post-urban Harappan	Joshi et al. 1984: 525 Mohan 1988: 64	3.60
Atariyano Timbo	Mehsana	23° 39' 30" N - 71° 55' 30" E	Lustrous Red Ware	IAR 1982-83: 28 Hegde and Sonawane 1986: 30 K. K. Bhan 1994: 86-7	0.40
Ati Kund	Saharanpur	29° 54' 00" N - 78° 09' 00" E	Post-urban Harappan	Joshi et al. 1984: 523	
Atkot	Rajkot	22° 00" 00" N - 71° 05' 00" E	Sorath Harappan	IAR 1957-58: 18-9 Rao 1963a: 186, 205 Possehl 1980: 89 Joshi et al. 1984: 528	
Atkot Bus Stand	Rajkot	22° 00" 42" N - 71° 08' 46" E	Late Sorath Harappan Sorath Harappan	IAR 1957a-58: 18-9 Rao 1963a: 186, 205 Possehl 1980: 89 Joshi et al. 1984: 528	1.50
Atranjikhera	Etah	27° 42' 00" N - 78° 44' 00" E	Islamic Gupta-Medieval Early Historic NBP PGW Black and Red ware OCP	Gaur 1983 Joshi et al. 1984: 523	1.50
Au	Bharatpur		Black and Red Ware PGW OCP	IAR 1965-66:	
Augand	Karnal	29° 41' 00" N - 76° 47' 00" E	Post-urban Harappan	Suraj Bhan & Shaffer 1978: 65-6 Joshi et al. 1984: 524	1.60
Aurangapur			Post-urban Harappan	IAR 1981-82: 15	
Awaran Niabat	Makran	26° 25' 00" N - 65° 14' 00" E	Medieval Londo Kulli Amri-Nal Togau	Stein 1931: 128-129 Possehl 1986a: 148	3.10
Azimwala Two	Bahawalpur	28° 47' 33" N - 71° 11' 40" E	Mature Harappan Hakra Wares	Mughal 1997: 42	4.40
Azimwali	Bahawalpur	28° 47' 18" N - 71° 12' 03" E	Mature Harappan	Mughal 1997: 47	2.10
Azimwali 'A'	Bahawalpur	28° 46' 37" N - 71° 10' 55" E	Mature Harappan	Mughal 1997: 47	17.70
Azimwali 'B'	Bahawalpur	28° 46' 44" N - 71° 11' 57" E	Kot Diji	Mughal 1997: 44	10.90
Azimwali 'C'	Bahawalpur	28° 46' 54" N - 71° 12' 53" E	Hakra Wares	Mughal 1997: 42	4.80

Babar Kot	Bhavnagar	22° 16' 04" N	-	Sorath Harappan	IAR 1955-56: 70	2.70
		71° 34' 15" E			Rao 1963a: 184, 205	
					Possehl 1980: 90	
					Joshi et al. 1984: 529	
Babra	Rajkot			Sorath Harappan	IAR 1965-66: 12	
Babul Bhera	Bahawalpur	29° 10' 00" N	-	Kot Diji	Stein 1943a: 123	6.50
		72° 12' 00" E				
Bachani	Dadu	25° 32' 00" N	-	Mature Harappan	Majumdar 1934: 141	
		67° 50' 00" E			Flam 1981a: 346	
Bachari	Sikar			OCP and Microliths	IAR 1981-82: 62	
Bada Samana	Ropar			Mature Harappan	IAR 1964-65: 33	
Badal Kaithwada	Meerut			OCP	IAR 1978-79: 24	
Badalwala	Bahawalpur	28° 40' 30" N	-	Mature Harappan	Mughal 1997: 47	4.10
		71° 04' 23" E				
Badalwala Five	Bahawalpur	28° 41' 18" N	-	Hakra Wares	Mughal 1997: 42	4.20
		71° 04' 59" E				
Badalwala Four	Bahawalpur	28° 41' 28" N	-	Hakra Wares	Mughal 1997: 42	1.60
		71° 05' 17" E				
Badalwala Three	Bahawalpur	28° 41' 11" N	-	Kot Diji	Mughal 1997: 44	1.40
		71° 04' 32" E				
Badalwala Two	Bahawalpur	28° 40' 30" N	-	Mature Harappan	Mughal 1997: 47	6.10
		71° 04' 40" E				
Baddowal	Ludhiana	30° 52' 00" N	-	Post-urban Harappan	Joshi et al. 1984: 527	
		75° 46' 00" E				
Badgam	Saharanpur	30° 06' 00" N	-	Post-urban Harappan	Joshi et al. 1984: 521, 522	
		77° 32' 00" E		Mature Harappan		
Badhaikalan	Muzaffarnagar			Medieval	Srivastava 1982: 57-8	
				Kushan		
				OCP		
Badhana	Jaipur			OCP	IAR 1972-73: 28	
Badhauli One	Ambala	30° 20' 00" N	-	Post-urban Harappan	IAR 1963-64: 27	
		77° 00' 00" E			Suraj Bhan 1975: 123	
Badhera	Karnal	29° 53' 00" N	-	Medieval	B. Datt 1980: 134	
		76° 40' 00" E		Early Historic	Singh 1981: 335	
				Post-urban Harappan	Joshi et al. 1984: 524	
Badhsa	Mahendragarh			Post-urban Harappan	Suraj Bhan 1975: 126	
Badla	Ludhiana	30° 45' 00" N	-	Post-urban Harappan	IAR 1976-77: 43	
		76° 28' 00" E			Joshi et al. 1984: 527	
Badla Nicha	Ludhiana	30° 46' 00" N	-	Post-urban Harappan	Joshi et al. 1984: 527	
		76° 17' 00" E				
Badli, Mahendragarh	Mahendragarh			Post-urban Harappan	Suraj Bhan 1975: 126	
Badli, Rohtak	Rohtak	28° 35' 00" N	-	Sothi-Siswal	Suraj Bhan 1975: 112	
		76° 48' 00" E			Joshi et al. 1984: 519	
Badoli	Ropar	30° 21' 00" N	-	Post-urban Harappan	Joshi et al. 1984: 523	
		77° 02' 00" E				
Badrang Damb	Makran	27° 40' 00" N	-	Kulli	Stein 1931: 35-36	10.80
		65° 31' 00" E		Amri-Nal	Possehl 1986a: 150	
				Kechi Beg		
Badsa	Rohtak	28° 30' 00" N	-	Sothi-Siswal	Suraj Bhan 1975: 112	
		76° 51' 00" E			Joshi et al. 1984: 519	
Badsikri Kalan One	Jind	29° 36' 21" N	-	PGW	Datt 1980: 139	
		76° 19' 04" E		Post-urban Harappan	Singh 1981: 97	

Site	District	Coordinates		Period	Reference	Area
Badsikri Khurd	Jind	29° 36' 23" N 76° 19' 47" E	-	Post-urban Harappan	Singh 1981: 98 Joshi et al. 1984: 525	
Bagasara	Rajkot	22° 50' 00" N 70° 41' 00" E	-	Sorath Harappan	Meadow, personal communication	
Bagaya-no Timbo	Mehsana	23° 25' 30" N 71° 49' 30" E	-	Lustrous Red Ware Anarta Microliths	Hegde and Sonawane 1986: 31 K. K. Bhan 1994: 86-7	0.20
Baggapura Ther	Rahimyar Khan	28° 23' 35" N 70° 34' 17" E	-	Mature Harappan	Mughal 1997: 47	2.60
Baggapura Two	Rahimyar Khan	28° 22' 55" N 70° 33' 30" E	-	Mature Harappan	Mughal 1997: 47	11.20
Baggewali	Bahawalpur	28° 50' 02" N 71° 09' 10" E	-	Hakra Wares	Mughal 1997: 42	10.00
Bagh-i Kumb Damb	Dera Ismail Khan	32° 20' 00" N 70° 05' 00" E	-	Late Kot Diji Kot Diji Kechi Beg Togau Burj Basket-marked Kili Ghul Mohammad	Fairservis 1971c: 413	
Baghada	Mayurbhanj			Copper Hoard	Mohapatra 1964: 45-7 Makkhan Lal 1984a: 40-1	
Baghanwali Theri	Bahawalpur	29° 07' 00" N 72° 27' 00" E	-	Kot Diji	Stein 1943a: 132 Dalal 1980: 11	
Baghru	Sonepat			Mature Harappan	Suraj Bhan 1975: 125	
Baghru Kalan	Jind	29° 18' 45" N 76° 36' 00" E	-	Post-urban Harappan	Joshi et al. 1984: 519 Mohan 1988: 65	4.00
Baghru Khurd	Jind	29° 17' 28" N 76° 35' 55" E	-	Historic Post-urban Harappan Sothi-Siswal	Mohan 1988: 64	7.10
Baghwala Ther	Bahawalpur			Mature Harappan	Mughal 1997: 47	3.30
Baglianda Theh	Bhatinda	29° 56' 00" N 75° 29' 00" E	-	Medieval Rang Mahal Mature Harappan	Joshi et al. 1984: 520 Joshi 1986: 139	30.00
Bagrauwala Ther	Bahawalpur	28° 56' 52" N 71° 37' 43" E	-	Mature Harappan	Mughal 1997: 47	0.40
Bahadarpur	Jind	29° 22' 42" N 76° 40' 08" E	-	Post-urban Harappan	Mohan 1988: 65	3.20
Bahadrabad	Saharanpur	29° 56' 00" N 78° 03' 00" E	-	OCP & Copper Hoard	Y. D. Sharma 1971-72: 39-42 Makkhan Lal 1984a: 34-5 Joshi et al. 1984: 522	
Baharia	Saharanpur	27° 30' 00" N 79° 32' 00" E	-	OCP & Copper Hoard	IAR 1966-67: 43-4 G. R. Sharma 1971-72: 42-3 Makkhan Lal 1984a: 34-5	
Bahawa	Sangrur	30° 29' 00" N 75° 48' 00" E	-	Post-urban Harappan	Joshi et al. 1984: 527	
Baherakhurd	Saharanpur	30° 03' 00" N 77° 40' 00" E	-	Post-urban Harappan	IAR 1967-68: Joshi et al. 1984: 522	
Bahilawala Ther	Bahawalpur	28° 51' 10" N 71° 28' 55" E	-	Mature Harappan	Mughal 1997: 47	1.30
Bahilawala 'B'	Bahawalpur	28° 51' 11" N 71° 28' 47" E	-	Hakra Wares	Mughal 1997: 42	1.20
Bahilawala 'C'	Bahawalpur	28° 51' 55" N 71° 28' 00" E	-	Hakra Wares	Mughal 1997: 42	1.70

Site	District	Coordinates		Period	Reference	Size
Bahini Raiyan	Ludhiana	30° 56' 00" N	-	Medieval	IAR 1980-81: 48	0.50
		75° 32' 00" E		Kushan		
				Post-urban Harappan		
				(Bara)		
Bahloli	Ropar	30° 25' 00" N	-	Post-urban Harappan	Joshi et al. 1984: 523	
		76° 57' 00" E				
Bahloli One	Ambala			PGW	Kumar 1978: 46	5.00
				Post-urban Harappan		
Bahloli Two	Ambala			Post-urban Harappan	Kumar 1978: 46	1.00
Bahlolpur	Karnal	29° 43' 40" N	-	Medieval	Singh 1981: 50	8.00
Mustarka		76° 50' 42" E		Early Historic	Joshi et al. 1984: 524	
				Post-urban Harappan		
Bahni Theh	Kurukshetra			Mature Harappan	Suraj Bhan & Shaffer 1978: 62	1.20
				Sothi-Siswal		
Bahola	Karnal	29° 48' 00" N	-	PGW	Suraj Bhan 1975: 125	
		76° 46' 00" E		Post-urban Harappan	Joshi et al. 1984: 521	
Baholi Two	Karnal	29° 28' 00" N	-	Early Historic	B. Datt 1980: 42	
		76° 53' 00" E		PGW	Joshi et al. 1984: 524	
				Post-urban Harappan		
Bahrah Khurd	Jind			Post-urban Harappan	Suraj Bhan & Shaffer 1978: 62	1.20
Bahrampur	Ludhiana	30° 43' 00" N	-	Post-urban Harappan	Joshi et al. 1984: 527	
		76° 25' 00" E				
Bahupura	Saharanpur	30° 00" 00" N	-	Post-urban Harappan	IAR 1964-65: 43	
		77° 30' 00" E			Dikshit 1982a: 114	
					Joshi et al. 1984: 522	
Bajaniya-no	Banaskantha	23° 49' 40" N	-	Microliths with	Ajithprasad and Sonawane, in	0.10
Thumdo		71° 29' 30" E		Amri-Nal Burial	press	
				Pottery		
Bakana	Kurukshetra	30° 06' 14" N	-	Early Historic	Kumar 1978: 63	5.00
		76° 55' 30" E		Post-urban Harappan	Joshi et al. 1984: 524	
Bakaraka Mound	Saharanpur	30° 00" 00" N	-	PGW	IAR 1963-64:	
		77° 27' 00" E		OCP	Joshi et al. 1984: 522	
Bala One	Karnal	29° 30' 22" N	-	Early Historic	Singh 1981: 49-50	0.80
		76° 47' 51" E		Post-urban Harappan	Joshi et al. 1984: 524	
Bala Two	Karnal	29° 30' 00" N	-	Medieval	Singh 1981: 50	1.90
		76° 47' 00" E		Early Historic	Joshi et al. 1984: 524	
				Post-urban Harappan		
Balakot	Las Bela	25° 28' 30" N	-	Mature Harappan	Raikes 1968b: 159-60	2.60
		66° 43' 30" E		Amri-Nal	Dales 1974a, 1979a, 1979b	
Balamba	Jamnagar	22° 40' 00" N	-	Late Sorath Harappan	K. K. Bhan 1986: 17	
		70° 20' 00" E		Sorath Harappan		
Balamdi	Jamnagar	22° 08' 00" N	-	Late Sorath Harappan	K. K. Bhan 1986: 18	
		70° 25' 00" E		Sorath Harappan		
Balana	Ambala	30° 20' 00" N	-	PGW	IAR 1963-64: 27	
		76° 44' 00" E		Post-urban Harappan	Suraj Bhan 1975: 123	
					Joshi et al. 1984: 523	
Baleli	Quetta-Pishin	30° 20' 00" N	-	British	Stein 1929a: 89	0.60
		66° 53' 00" E		Togau	Fairservis 1956a: 199	
				Burj Basket-marked	de Cardi 1983: 19	
				Kili Ghul Mohammad		
Baliana	Rohtak	28° 53' 00" N	-	PGW	Suraj Bhan 1975: 125	
		76° 43' 00" E		Post-urban Harappan	Joshi et al. 1984: 519, 521,	
				Mature Harappan	525	
				Sothi-Siswal		

Site	District	Coordinates	Period	References	Area
Baliji	Jaipur		OCP	IAR 1973-74: 24	
Balpur	Bilaspur		Copper Hoard	Gordon 1958: 142	
				Makkhan Lal 1984a: 36-7	
Balu	Jind	29° 40' 15" N - 76° 23' 16" E	Post-urban Harappan Mature Harappan Sothi-Siswal	Suraj Bhan & Shaffer 1978: 65 Mohan 1988: 66 Joshi et al. 1984: 519, 521, 525	3.80
Balu Two	Jind	29° 41' 15" N - 76° 23' 16" E	Post-urban Harappan Mature Harappan Sothi-Siswal	Singh 1981: 98-9	0.40
Balua	Varanasi		Copper Hoard	Dikshit 1968: 50 Makkhan Lal 1984a: 34-5	
Bamba Damb	Dadu	27° 15' 00" N - 67° 20' 00" E	Mature Harappan Kot Diji	deCardi 1964: 28 de Cardi 1983: 40 Flam 1981a: 257	
Banali	Ludhiana		Post-urban Harappan	Joshi et al. 1984: 527	
Banawali	Hissar	29° 36' 25" N - 75° 23' 55" E	Post-urban Harappan Mature Harappan Early/Mature Trans. Sothi-Siswal	Suraj Bhan 1975: 123 Bisht 1982 Joshi et al. 1984: 519, 521, 526	16.00
Bandhni	Dadu	26° 12' 00" N - 67° 42' 00" E	Amri-Nal	Majumdar 1934: 120-22 Flam 1981a: 301	7.60
Bandhri	Dadu	26° 13' 00" N - 67° 42' 00" E	Mature Harappan	Majumdar 1934: 120-22 Flam 1981a: 302	0.60
Bandrala	Karnal	29° 29' 28" N - 76° 34' 45" E	Post-urban Harappan	Joshi et al. 1984: 521 Singh 1981: 50-51	1.30
Bandu Damb	Jhalawan	27° 23' 00" N - 66° 24' 00" E	Kulli Amri-Nal	Stein 1931: 176 Raikes 1968b: 112, 147	5.4
Bandua	Ranchi		Copper Hoard	Makkhan Lal 1984a: 38-9	
Bandwali	Bahawalpur	28° 52' 27" N - 71° 25' 38" E	Hakra Wares	Mughal 1997: 42	3.00
Banehra One	Kurukshetra	30° 02' 00" N - 76° 25' 00" E	Post-urban Harappan	Suraj Bhan 1975: 124 Joshi et al. 1984: 524	
Banehra Two	Kurukshetra	30° 02' 20" N - 76° 25' 20" E	Post-urban Harappan	Suraj Bhan 1975: 124	
Banhera	Patiala	30° 20' 00" N - 76° 13' 00" E	Post-urban Harappan	Joshi et al. 1984: 527	
Bani	Hissar	29° 35' 00" N - 74° 35' 00" E	PGW Mature Harappan	Suraj Bhan 1975: 123 Joshi et al. 1984: 519, 526	
Bannewala Ther	Bahawalpur	29° 18' 00" N - 72° 18' 00" E	Kot Diji	Stein 1943a: 124 Dalal 1980: 10	9.90
Banti Khera One	Muzaffarnagar	29° 30' 00" N - 77° 26' 00" E	Post-urban Harappan	Dikshit 1981: 72 Joshi et al. 1984: 523	
Banti Khera Two	Muzaffarnagar	29° 30' 00" N - 77° 27' 30" E	Post-urban Harappan	Dikshit 1981: 72 Joshi et al. 1984: 523	
Bara	Ropar	30° 54' 00" N - 76° 30' 00" E	PGW Mature Harappan	IAR 1953-54: 38 Suraj Bhan 1975: 122 Y. D. Sharma 1982a: 143 Joshi et al. 1984: 526	16.50
Bara Samana	Ropar		Post-urban Harappan	IAR 1962-63: 17 Suraj Bhan 1975: 122	
Bara Ther	Bahawalpur	28° 57' 00" N - 71° 38' 42" E	Mature Harappan	Mughal 1997: 47	1.00
Barah Khurd	Jind	29° 18' 10" N - 76° 23' 05" E	Post-urban Harappan	Joshi et al. 1984: 525 Mohan 1988: 69	3.80

Barah-Ki Dhani	Sikar		OCP and Microliths	IAR 1981-82: 62	
Barama	Swat	34° 46' 00" N - 72° 22' 00" E	Swat Proto-Historic	Stacul 1987: 63	
Barasana	Kurukshetra	29° 40' 00" N - 76° 65' 00" E	Post-urban Harappan	Joshi et al. 1984: 524	
Bare	Bhatinda	29° 55' 00" N - 75° 28' 00" E	Sothi-Siswal	Joshi et al. 1984: 520	
Bare Two	Bhatinda	29° 55' 00" N - 75° 28' 00" E	Post-urban Harappan	Joshi et al. 1984: 527 Joshi 1986: 139	25.00
Bargaon	Saharanpur	30° 12' 00" N - 77° 32' 00" E	OCP & Copper Hoard Mature Harappan	IAR 1963-64: 56-7 Makkhan Lal 1984a: 34-5	0.80
Bari Bhaini One	Karnal	29° 45' 00" N - 76° 56' 00" E	Post-urban Harappan	Suraj Bhan 1975: 125 Singh 1981: 335 Joshi et al. 1984: 524	
Bari Bhaini Two	Karnal	29° 45' 00" N - 76° 56' 00" E	Post-urban Harappan	Suraj Bhan 1975: 125 Joshi et al. 1984: 54	
Barki	Hissar	29° 17' 00" N - 75° 46' 00" E	Mature Harappan Sothi-Siswal	Joshi et al. 1984: 519, 521	
Baroda One	Jind	29° 26' 19" N - 76° 12' 30" E	Early Historic Post-urban Harappan	Singh 1981: 99 Joshi et al. 1984: 525	1.40
Baroda Two	Jind	29° 25' 40" N - 76° 11' 40" E	Early Historic Post-urban Harappan	Singh 1981: 99 Joshi et al. 1984: 525	0.60
Barodi	Jind	29° 23' 20" N - 76° 17' 06" E	Post-urban Harappan	Singh 1981: 77 Joshi et al. 1984: 525	1.50
Baroli	Jind	29° 16' 16" N - 76° 21' 29" E	PGW Post-urban Harappan Sothi-Siswal	Singh 1981: 77 Joshi et al. 1984: 525 Mohan 1988: 69	2.80
Barot One	Kurukshetra	29° 51' 00" N - 76° 31' 00" E	Post-urban Harappan	Joshi et al. 1984: 524	
Barot Three	Kurukshetra	29° 52' 20" N - 76° 32' 20" E	Post-urban Harappan	Kumar 1978: 56	3.70
Barot Two	Kurukshetra	29° 52' 40" N - 76° 31' 00" E	Post-urban Harappan	Kumar 1978: 56 Joshi et al. 1984: 524	
Barota	Karnal	29° 38' 00" N - 76° 56' 00" E	Medieval Early Historic PGW Post-urban Harappan	B. Datt 1980: 41-2 Singh 1981: 335 Joshi et al. 1984: 524	
Barrai Khuarra One	Bannu	32° 47' 00" N - 70° 31' 00" E	Kechi Beg	Khan, Knox and Thomas 1988 Khan, Knox and Thomas 1991a: 64-5	
Barriwala Ther	Bahawalpur	28° 39' 00" N - 71° 12' 21" E	Mature Harappan	Mughal 1997: 47	3.80
Barsana Two	Jind	29° 22' 00" N - 76° 25' 00" E	Post-urban Harappan	Suraj Bhan 1975: 124 Joshi et al. 1984: 519	
Barsana, Jind	Jind	29° 22' 00" N - 76° 25' 00" E	Post-urban Harappan	Joshi et al. 1984: 525	
Barsana, Kurukshetra	Kurukshetra	29° 40' 00" N - 76° 35' 00" E	Sothi-Siswal	Kumar 1978: 56 Joshi et al. 1984: 519	5.00
Barsi	Saharanpur	29° 43' 00" N - 77° 22' 00" E	Post-urban Harappan	Joshi et al. 1984: 522	
Bartola	Ranchi		Copper Hoard	Coggin-Brown 1915b Makkhan Lal 1984a: 38-9	
Barula One	Bahawalpur	28° 36' 27" N - 71° 09' 43" E	Mature Harappan	Mughal 1997: 47	0.60

Barula Two	Bahawalpur	28° 36' 45" N	-	Mature Harappan	Mughal 1997: 47	0.80
		71° 09' 48" E				
Barwali	Ludhiana	30° 47' 00" N	-	Post-urban Harappan	IAR 1976-77: 43	
		76° 17' 00" E			Joshi et al. 1984: 527	
Basami	Ludhiana	30° 55' 00" N	-	Medieval	IAR 1980-81: 46	4.00
		75° 43' 00" E		Kushan		
				Post-urban Harappan		
				Mature Harappan(?)		
Basanda	Gurgaon	28° 23' 00" N	-	Post-urban Harappan	Joshi et al. 1984: 526	
		76° 46' 00" E				
Basi Gujran	Ludhiana	30° 53' 00" N	-	Post-urban Harappan	Joshi et al. 1984: 527	
		76° 21' 00" E				
Bassi	Gurgaon	28° 28' 00" N	-	Post-urban Harappan	Suraj Bhan 1975: 112, 126	
		77° 00' 00" E			Joshi et al. 1984: 526	
Bassi, Patiala	Patiala			Post-urban Harappan	Suraj Bhan 1975: 123	
Bata Four	Jind	29° 41' 39" N	-	Post-urban Harappan	Singh 1981: 101	1.30
		76° 18' 00" E			Joshi et al. 1984: 525	
Bata One	Jind	29° 42' 49" N	-	Post-urban Harappan	Singh 1981: 100, 339	
		76° 19' 31" E		Sothi-Siswal		
Bata Three	Jind	29° 42' 49" N	-	Early Historic	Singh 1981: 100	3.00
		76° 18' 30" E		Post-urban Harappan	Joshi et al. 1984: 525	
Bata Two	Jind	29° 43' 50" N	-	Post-urban Harappan	Singh 1981: 100	1.90
		76° 18' 30" E			Joshi et al. 1984: 525	
Bathan Mathan	Ludhiana	30° 47' 00" N	-	Post-urban Harappan	Joshi et al. 1984: 527	
		76° 23' 00" E				
Batoorwala	Bahawalpur	28° 45' 35" N	-	Mature Harappan	Mughal 1997: 47	2.20
		71° 14' 58" E				
Bauli	Kurukshetra	29° 59' 00" N	-	Post-urban Harappan	Kumar 1978: 64	1.60
		76° 54' 00" E			Joshi et al. 1984: 524	
Baundki	Saharanpur	30° 04' 00" N	-	OCP	IAR 1966-67: 43	
		77° 37' 00" E		Mature Harappan	Joshi et al. 1984: 522	
Baursham One	Karnal	29° 53' 00" N	-	PGW	Kumar 1978: 76	3.00
		76° 47' 00" E		Post-urban Harappan	Singh 1981: 335	
					Joshi et al. 1984: 524	
Baursham Two	Karnal	29° 53' 00" N	-	Post-urban Harappan	Singh 1981: 335	
		76° 47' 00" E			Joshi et al. 1984: 524	
Bava Khakaria One	Jamnagar	22° 14' 00" N	-	Late Sorath Harappan	K. K. Bhan 1986: 18	
		70° 24' 00" E		Sorath Harappan		
Bazariwala	Bahawalpur	29° 07' 02" N	-	Mature Harappan	Mughal 1997: 47	8.90
		71° 56' 15" E				
Bazariwali 'A'	Bahawalpur	28° 47' 54" N	-	Cemetery H	Mughal 1997: 51	0.05
		71° 20' 38" E				
Bazariwali 'B'	Bahawalpur	28° 47' 56" N	-	Cemetery H	Mughal 1997: 51	0.01
		71° 20' 45" E				
Bazariwali 'C'	Bahawalpur	28° 47' 59" N	-	Cemetery H	Mughal 1997: 51	0.05
		71° 20' 50" E				
Bazdad Kalat	Makran	26° 21' 00" N	-	Kulli	Stein 1931: 1271-28	0.80
		65° 07' 00" E		Amri-Nal	Possehl 1986a: 148	
Bazidpur	Saharanpur	30° 03' 00" N	-	OCP	IAR 1966-67: 43	
		77° 36' 00" E		Mature Harappan	Joshi et al. 1984: 522	
Bed	Jamnagar	22° 26' 00" N	-	Late Sorath Harappan	Rao 1963a: 205	1.20
		69° 57' 00" E			Possehl 1980: 90	
					Joshi et al. 1984: 528	
					K. K. Bhan 1986: 236	

Site	District	Coordinates	Period	Reference	Size
Bedi	Jamnagar	22° 27' 00" N – 69° 57' 00" E	Late Sorath Harappan Sorath Harappan	K. K. Bhan 1986: 17	
Belar Damb	Jhalawan	27° 07' 00" N – 66° 27' 00" E	Kulli? Togau?	Stein 1931: 177 Raikes 1968b: 151	2.20
Belarkha	Jind	29° 39' 00" N – 76° 07' 00" E	Post-urban Harappan	Joshi et al. 1984: 525	
Belora	Rajkot	21° 47' 00" N – 70° 46' 00" E	Late Sorath Harappan Sorath Harappan	IAR 1957-58: 19 Rao 1963a: 205 Possehl 1980: 90 Joshi et al. 1984: 528	0.60
Benn Chah	Jhalawan	28° 48' 00" N – 66° 23' 00" E	Kechi Beg Togau Burj Basket-marked	Stein 1931: 18	2.50
Berajano Timbo	Jamnagar	22° 20' 00" N – 69° 44' 00" E	Late Sorath Harappan Sorath Harappan	K. K. Bhan 1986: 20 K. K. Bhan 1989: 236	1.00
Beri Khera	Jind	29° 23' 40" N – 76° 31' 50" E	PGW Post-urban Harappan	Suraj Bhan 1975: 125 Singh 1981: 341 Joshi et al. 1984: 525 Mohan 1988: 70	1.60
Berore	Ganganagar	29° 09' 55" N – 73° 14' 30" E	Rang Mahal PGW Mature Harappan Sothi-Siswal	Stein 1943a: 71 Dalal 1980: 25 Joshi et al. 1984: 522	4.40
Besham Damb	Makran	27° 00' 00" N – 64° 10' 00" E	Islamic Buddhist Kulli	Stein 1931: 45 Possehl 1986a: 150	
Beyt Dwarka	Jamnagar	22° 20' 00" N – 69° 05' 00" E	Lustrous Red Ware	IAR 1969-70: 59 Joshi et al. 1984: 529 K. K. Bhan 1986: 20	
Bhabri	Saharanpur	29° 57' 00" N – 77° 38' 00" E	Post-urban Harappan	Joshi et al. 1984: 522	
Bhabru	Jaipur		OCP	IAR 1973-74: 24	
Bhachau	Kutch		Medieval Mature Harappan	IAR 1985-86: 17	
Bhadas Khera	Gurgaon		Post-urban Harappan	Purnia 1976	
Bhaderi	Ambala	30° 14' 20" N – 77° 10' 30" E	Early Historic Post-urban Harappan	Joshi et al. 1984: 523	3.00
Bhadriwala	Bahawalpur	28° 42' 37" N – 71° 20' 38" E	Mature Harappan	Mughal 1997: 47	4.40
Bhagatrav	Broach	21° 29' 00" N – 72° 42' 00" E	Late Sorath Harappan Sorath Harappan	IAR 1957-58: 15-7 Rao 1963a: 190, 205 Possehl 1980: 90 Joshi et al. 1984: 529	16.00
Bhagwanpura	Kurukshetra	30° 04' 00" N – 76° 57' 00" E	PGW Harappan/PGW Overlap Post-urban Harappan	Suraj Bhan & Shaffer 1978: 62 Joshi et al. 1984: 524	1.00
Bhagwansar Four	Ganganagar	29° 22' 00" N – 73° 53' 00" E	Cemetery H Mature Harappan Sothi-Siswal	Dalal 1980: 25 A. Ghosh 1989a: Vol II, 64	
Bhagwansar Three	Ganganagar	29° 23' 00" N – 73° 53' 00" E	Mature Harappan	Dalal 1980: 25 A. Ghosh 1989a: Vol. II, 64	
Bhaini	Kurukshetra	30° 02' 00" N – 77° 00' 00" E	Post-urban Harappan	Kumar 1978: 63 Joshi et al. 1984: 524	3.00
Bhainkio Wandh	Sukkur		Mature Harappan	Mallah 1994: 169-70	0.50

Bhainsawal	Jaipur		PGW OCP	IAR 1972-73: 29	
Bhaironpura	Ganganagar	29° 21' 00" N - 73° 49' 00" E	Mature Harappan Sothi-Siswal	Stein 1943a: 47 Dalal 1980: 8, 34	
Bhaishlana	Jaipur		OCP	IAR 1973-74: 24	
Bhaktabandh	Bankura		Copper Hoard	Nag and Chakrabarti 1980: 97-100 Makkhan Lal 1984a: 40-1	
Bhalari	Kurukshetra	30° 01' 24" N - 77° 02' 00" E	Post-urban Harappan (OCP)	Kumar 1978:64	4.00
Bhalari	Kurukshetra	30° 01' 00" N - 77° 00' 00" E	Post-urban Harappan	Joshi et al. 1984: 524	
Bhalbhai-no Timbo	Mehsana	23° 27' 00" N - 71° 46' 00" E	Lustrous Red Ware	IAR 1978-79: 5 Joshi et al. 1984: 529 K. K. Bhan 1994: 86-7	1.40
Bhalgam	Rajkot	22° 02' 00" N - 71° 05' 00" E	Sorath Harappan	Rao 1963a: 205 Possehl 1980: 90 Joshi et al. 1984: 528	
Bhamakdal	Amreli	21° 45' 00" N - 70° 50' 00" E	Sorath Harappan	IAR 1957-58: 19 Rao 1963a: 205 Possehl 1980: 90 Joshi et al. 1984: 528	
Bhamal	Ludhiana	30° 56' 00" N - 75° 31' 00" E	Rang Mahal Post-urban Harappan	IAR 1980-81: 48	7.00
Bhamaria Thumdo	Banaskantha	23° 54' 00" N - 71° 27' 00" E	Anarta-Rangpur IIC Amri-Nal Burial Pottery	Ajithprasad and Sonawane, in press	
Bhangarapir	Mayurbhanj		Copper Hoard	Coggin-Brown 1916 Makkhan Lal 1984a: 40-1	
Bhangor	Jamnagar	22° 05' 00" N - 69° 22' 00" E	Lustrous Red Ware Late Sorath Harappan	Rao 1963a: 205 Possehl 1980: 90 Joshi et al. 1984: 528	
Bhangor One	Jamnagar	22° 05' 00" N - 69° 49' 00" E	Sorath or Late Sorath Har	K. K. Bhan 1986: 16	
Bhani Theh	Kurukshetra	29° 45' 00" N - 76° 30' 00" E	Post-urban Harappan	Joshi et al. 1984: 524	
Bhankri	Jaipur		OCP	IAR 1975-76: 77	
Bhasmara	Karnal		Post-urban Harappan	IAR 1975-76: 38	
Bhassaur	Sangrur	30° 26' 00" N - 75° 55' 00" E	Post-urban Harappan	Joshi et al. 1984: 527	
Bhatiwadi	Amreli	21° 45' 00" N - 70° 50' 00" E	Lustrous Red Ware Late Sorath Harappan Sorath Harappan	IAR 1957-58: 19 Possehl 1980: 91 Joshi et al. 1984: 530, 5	0.90
Bhatnura	Kapurthala	31° 01' 00" N - 75° 31' 00" E	Mature Harappan	Joshi et al. 1984: 522	
Bhatpura	Bulandshahr	28° 32' 00" N - 78° 03' 00" E	OCP/Post-urban Harappan	IAR 1960-61: 66 Joshi et al. 1984: 523	
Bhawani Khera	Kurukshetra	29° 59' 00" N - 76° 50' 00" E	PGW Post-urban Harappan	U. V. Singh 1976: 29 Joshi et al. 1984: 524	
Bhawar	Sonepat	29° 13' 00" N - 76° 30' 00" E	Post-urban Harappan	Joshi et al. 1984: 525	
Bhayakha Kharia	Ganganagar		Mature Harappan	Pande & Ramachandran 1971: 37	

Bhayakhakharia	Jamnagar	22° 10' 00" N	-	Sorath Harappan	IAR 1957-58: 19	
		71° 50' 00" E			Possehl 1980: 91	
					Joshi et al. 1984: 529	
Bhbhuro Dhoro	Amreli			Red Polished Ware	A. F. Cunningham, unpublished	2.70
				Lustrous Red Ware		
				Late Sorath Harappan		
				Sorath Harappan		
Bhedki	Saharanpur	29° 57' 00" N	-	OCP/Post-urban	IAR 1967-68	
		77° 36' 00" E		Harappan	Joshi et al. 1984: 522	
Bhikhi	Bhatinda	30° 04' 00" N	-	Post-urban Harappan	Joshi et al. 1984: 527	9.00
		75° 31' 00" E			Joshi 1986: 139	
Bhilwara	Bhilwara			Chalcolithic	IAR 1983-84: 71	
Bhimnath	Ahmedabad	22° 15' 00" N	-	Sorath Harappan	IAR 1978-79: 94	1.30
		71° 55' 00" E			Joshi et al. 1984: 530	
					K. K. Bhan 1986: 236	
Bhimpatal	Ahmedabad	22° 15' 00" N	-	Late Sorath Harappan	IAR 1956-57: 70	1.30
		71° 30' 00" E		Sorath Harappan	Rao 1963a: 185	
					Possehl 1980: 91	
Bhirrana	Hissar	29° 32' 00" N	-	Historic	Joshi et al. 1984: 526, 519,	
		75° 32' 00" E		Post-urban Harappan	521	
				Mature Harappan	IAR 1985-86: 26	
				Sothi-Siswal		
Bhojavadar	Bhavnagar	21° 50' 59" N	-	Red Polished Ware	Possehl 1980: 91	3.40
Three		71° 42' 49" E		Late Sorath Harappan	Joshi et al. 1984: 528	
				Sorath Harappan		
Bhoklidhar	Bhavnagar	21° 58' 00" N	-	Lustrous Red Ware	Possehl 1980: 92	5.60
		71° 38' 00" E		Late Sorath Harappan	Joshi et al. 1984: 528	
				Sorath Harappan		
Bholni	Saharanpur	30° 07' 00" N	-	OCP	IAR 1964-65: 44	
		77° 41' 00" E			Joshi et al. 1984: 522	
Bhomya-Ka Tiba	Jaipur			OCP	IAR 1973-74: 24	
Bhongra	Jind	29° 26' 11" N	-	PGW	Singh 1981: 102	2.40
		76° 09' 12" E		Post-urban Harappan	Joshi et al. 1984: 525	
Bhootanwala	Bahawalpur	28° 46' 14" N	-	Mature Harappan	Mughal 1997: 47	7.00
'A' & 'B'		71° 02' 54" E				
Bhootanwala	Bahawalpur	28° 46' 45" N	-	Hakra Wares	Mughal 1997: 42	20.60
'C'		71° 03' 10" E				
Bhootanwali	Bahawalpur	28° 46' 05" N	-	Cemetery H	Mughal 1997: 51	4.80
		71° 02' 06" E				
Bhootanwali	Bahawalpur	28° 46' 09" N	-	Hakra Wares	Mughal 1997: 42	10.70
Two		71° 02' 14" E				
Bhorgarh		28° 05' 00" N	-	Kushan	Babu 1995	1.30
		77° 05' 00" E		PGW		
				Post-urban Harappan		
Bhudan	Sangrur	30° 31' 00" N	-	Post-urban Harappan	Suraj Bhan 1975: 122	
		75° 46' 00" E		Mature Harappan	Shaffer 1981: Fig. 2	
				Sothi-Siswal	Suraj Bhan & Shaffer 1978	
					Joshi et al. 1984: 520. 527	
Bhudha Khera	Saharanpur	30° 03' 00" N	-	Post-urban Harappan	Joshi et al. 1984: 522	
		77° 31' 00" E				
Bhukari	Ropar	30° 11' 00" N	-	PGW	Suraj Bhan & Shaffer 1978: 66	12.20
		77° 21' 00" E		Post-urban Harappan	Joshi et al. 1984: 523	
Bhura,	Muzaffarnagar	29° 25' 00" N	-	Post-urban Harappan	Dikshit 1982a: 115	4.00
Muzaffarnagar		77° 14' 00" E			Joshi et al. 1984: 523	

Bhura, Patiala	Patiala	30° 28' 00" N	-	Post-urban Harappan	Joshi et al. 1984: 527	
		76° 10' 00" E				
Bhurtana	Bhiwani	28° 55' 00" N	-	Mature Harappan	IAR 1986-87: 21	
		76° 58' 00" E				
Bhut Kotada	Rajkot	22° 35' 00" N	-	Sorath Harappan	Joshi et al. 1984: 529	
		70° 45' 00" E				
Bhut Shamshi	Sarawan	29° 56' 00" N	-	Quetta	Mughal 1972a: 147	
		66° 44' 00" E		Amri-Nal		
Bhutakotda	Surendranagar			Sorath Harappan	IAR 1962-63: 8	
					Possehl 1980: 92	
Bhutana	Sonepat	29° 11' 00" N	-	Post-urban Harappan	Joshi et al. 1984: 525	
		76° 37' 00" E				
Bhutawed-no Godh	Banaskantha	23° 51' 00" N	-	Anarta-Lustrous Red Ware	Ajithprasad and Sonawane, in press	0.30
		71° 23' 00" E				
Bibiji Bhit	Dadu	25° 44' 00" N	-	Mature Harappan	Lambrick 1941: 99	0.40
		67° 36' 00" E		Amri-Nal	Flam 1981a: 330	
Bibipur	Kurukshetra	29° 59' 00" N	-	PGW	Suraj Bhan 1975: 123	
		76° 40' 00" E		Post-urban Harappan	Joshi et al. 1984: 524	
Bichana	Ranchi			Copper Hoard	S. C. Roy 1915	
					Makkhan Lal 1984a: 38-9	
Bichpari	Sonepat	29° 12' 00" N	-	Post-urban Harappan	Suraj Bhan 1975: 125	
		76° 40' 00" E			Joshi et al. 1984: 525	
Bijna	Karnal	29° 35' 56" N	-	Post-urban Harappan	Singh 1981: 51	
		76° 55' 54" E			Joshi et al. 1984: 524	
Bikkum	Solan	31° 05' 00" N	-	Post-urban Harappan	Joshi et al. 1984: 528	
		76° 38' 00" E				
Bikkunor	Ropar			Mature Harappan	Pande & Ramachandran 1971: 32	
Bilaspur	Saharanpur	29° 44' 00" N	-	Post-urban Harappan	Joshi et al. 1984: 522	
		77° 13' 00" E				
Bilewali	Bahawalpur	28° 35' 49" N	-	Mature Harappan	Mughal 1997: 47	0.60
		71° 07' 11" E				
Binanagari	Jamnagar	22° 43' 00" N	-	Lustrous Red Ware	Rao 1963a: 205	0.90
		70° 22' 00" E		Late Sorath Harappan	Possehl 1980: 92	
					Joshi et al. 1984: 528	
Bingee	Ganganagar	29° 11' 00" N	-	Historic	IAR 1977-78: 47	
		73° 07' 00" E		PGW	Dikshit 1984b: 70	
				Mature Harappan		
Binjor Four	Ganganagar	29° 10' 00" N	-	Rang Mahal	Dalal 1980: 34, 37	
		73° 08' 00" E		Mature Harappan		
Binjor One	Ganganagar	29° 11' 00" N	-	Mature Harappan	Stein 1943a: 72	1.80
		73° 10' 00" E		Sothi-Siswal	Dalal 1980: 8, 25	
					Frenchman 1972: 276-311	
					Joshi et al. 1984: 522	
Binjor Three	Ganganagar	29° 12' 00" N	-	Mature Harappan	Stein 1943a: 72	2.60
		73° 06' 00" E		Sothi-Siswal	Ghosh 1962: 3	
				Microliths	Dalal 1980: 34, 37	
					Joshi et al. 1984: 522	
Binjor Two	Ganganagar	29° 13' 00" N	-	Modern	Dalal 1980: 34	
		73° 05' 00" E		Rang Mahal		
				PGW		
				Mature Harappan		
Birkot Ghwandai	Swat	34° 41' 00" N	-	Swat Proto-Historic	Stacul 1987: 60-63	0.05
		72° 12' 00" E				

Birmi	Ludhiana	30° 55' 00" N - 74° 45' 00" E	Medieval Post-urban Harappan	IAR 1980-81: 46	10.00
Bisauli	Budaun	28° 18' 00" N - 78° 56' 00" E	OCP & Copper Hoard	B. B. Lal 1951: 24-6 B. B. Lal 1954-55: 146 Makkhan Lal 1984a: 34-5	
Bithur	Kanpur		Copper Hoard	V. Smith 1905: 232 B. B. Lal 1951: 24 Makkhan Lal 1984a: 34-5	
Bizinjau Kasar	Makran	25° 49' 15" N - 62° 42' 45" E	Zangian Kulli Dasht	Besenval and Sanlaville 1990: 102	
Bodaka			Sorath Harappan	Chitalwala 1985: key Figure 8	
Bodaka	Jamnagar	22° 20' 00" N - 70° 30' 00" E	Late Sorath Harappan Sorath Harappan	Bhan 1986:17	
Bodha	Ambala	30° 04' 00" N - 76° 35' 00" E	Post-urban Harappan	Suraj Bhan 1975: 123 Joshi et al. 1984: 524	
Bodiono Dhoro	Amreli		Red Polished Ware Late Sorath Harappan Sorath Harappan	A. F. Cunningham, unpublished	2.80
Bodiyo, Amreli	Amreli	21° 49' 00" N - 71° 06' 00" E	Late Sorath Harappan Sorath Harappan	IAR 1958-59: 19 Rao 1963a: 205 Possehl 1980: 93 Joshi et al. 1984: 528	1.90
Bodiyo, Rajkot	Rajkot		Sorath Harappan	IAR 1958-59:	
Boharwala Ther	Bahawalpur	29° 12' 48" N - 71° 42' 55" E	Cemetery H	Mughal 1997: 51	3.20
Bokharaiwala	Bahawalpur	29° 10' 39" N - 72° 07' 44" E	Kot Diji	Mughal 1997: 44	3.50
Bokhariyanwala	Bahawalpur	29° 07' 40" N - 71° 56' 50" E	Mature Harappan	Mughal 1997: 47	1.90
Bokhariyanwala 'A'	Bahawalpur	29° 07' 38" N - 71° 56' 30" E	Cemetery H	Mughal 1997: 51	0.40
Bondhansinghka Tila	Jaipur		OCP	IAR 1975-76: 77	
Bootewala Ther 'A'	Bahawalpur		Mature Harappan	Mughal 1997: 47	2.80
Bootewala Ther 'B'	Bahawalpur		Cemetery H	Mughal 1997: 51	4.10
Bootewali	Bahawalpur	28° 42' 08" N - 71° 02' 04" E	Mature Harappan	Mughal 1997: 47	3.40
Bootgarh	Ambala		Post-urban Harappan	Kumar 1978: 41	2.20
Borawalo Khetra	Mehsana	23° 42' 00" N - 71° 51' 00" E	Lustrous Red Ware	IAR 1982-83: 28 Hegde and Sonawane 1986: 31 K. K. Bhan 1994: 86-7	1.00
Bordogaon	Singhbhum		Copper Hoard	S. P. Gupta 1965 K. N. Dikshit 1968: 50 Makkhan Lal 1984a: 38-9	
Boriya	Jamnagar		Sorath Harappan	IAR 1980-81: 14	
Brass	Patiala	30° 35' 00" N - 76° 32' 00" E	Post-urban Harappan	Joshi et al. 1984: 527	
Broach College	Broach	21° 48' 00" N - 72° 58' 00" E	Late Sorath Harappan Sorath Harappan	IAR 1969-70: 6-7	
Buband	Las Bela	26° 22' 30" N - 66° 19' 30" E	Kulli Amri-Nal	Stein 1943b Khan 1979b: 63, 73-4	

Site	District	Coordinates	Culture	Reference	Size
Buchahar	Sikar		OCP and Microliths	IAR 1981-82: 62	
Budan	Sangrur	30° 31' 00" N - 75° 46' 00" E	Mature Harappan	Joshi et al. 1984: 522	
Budanpur	Kurukshetra		Post-urban Harappan	Kumar 1978: 51	
Budanpur	Karnal	29° 42' 00" N - 76° 04' 00" E	Post-urban Harappan	Joshi et al 1984:524	
Budanpura	Kurukshetra	30° 05' 00" N - 76° 25' 00" E	Post-urban Harappan	Joshi et al. 1984: 524	
Buddkern Pin	Karnal	29° 44' 00" N - 76° 56' 00" E	Post-urban Harappan	Suraj Bhan & Shaffer 1978: 62 Joshi et al. 1984: 524	
Budha Khera	Ambala	30° 21' 40" N - 77° 04' 00" E	Post-urban Harappan	Kumar 1978: 47	
Budha Khera Ahir	Saharanpur	29° 58' 00" N - 77° 42' 00" E	OCP	IAR 1964-65: 44 Joshi et al. 1984: 522	
Budha Khera Three	Jind	29° 23' 55" N - 76° 33' 10" E	Post-urban Harappan Sothi-Siswal	Mohan 1988: 73 Joshi et al. 1984: 525	3.00
Budha Khera, Kurukshetra	Kurukshetra	29° 50' 00" N - 76° 15' 00" E	Post-urban Harappan	Joshi et al. 1984: 524	
Budha Khere Two	Jind	29° 23' 55" N - 76° 33' 10" E	PGW Post-urban Harappan	B. Datt 1980: 76 Singh 1981: 341	
Budhej	Kheda	22° 26' 00" N - 72° 36' 00" E	Sorath Harappan	IAR 1971-72: 10 Momin 1976: 51-4 Momin 1979: 103	1.00
Budhel	Bhavnagar	21° 45' 00" N - 72° 09' 00" E	Late Sorath Harappan Sorath Harappan	Possehl 1980: 93 IAR 1980-81: 12 Joshi et al. 1984: 528	23.90
Budki Dheri	Dera Ismail Khan	32° 04' 00" N - 70° 37' 00" E	Late Kot Diji Kot Diji	Dani 1970-71: 32	
Bugia	Ganganagar	29° 10' 00" N - 73° 24' 00" E	Mature Harappan Sothi-Siswal	IAR 1977-78: 47 Dikshit 1980: 35 Joshi et al. 1984: 520, 522	
Bulbaliwala	Bahawalpur		Mature Harappan	Mughal 1997: 47	3.80
Bulloji Buthi	Dadu	26° 16' 00" N - 67° 42' 00" E	Mature Harappan	Nissen 1983: 8	2.00
Bundakhi Damb	Sarawan	29° 04' 00" N - 66° 37' 00" E	Kechi Beg Togau	Stein 1931: 184-185	
Burhanewala Ther	Rahimyar Khan	28° 43' 25" N - 70° 56' 30" E	Mature Harappan	Mughal 1997: 47	4.40
Burj, Hissar	Hissar	29° 38' 00" N - 75° 40' 00" E	Historic PGW Post-urban Harappan	Joshi et al. 1984: 526 Suraj Bhan 1975: 123 IAR 1985-86: 26	
Burj, Patiala	Patiala	30° 09' 00" N - 76° 29' 00" E	Post-urban Harappan (OCP)	Kumar 1978: 77, 87-8 Joshi et al. 1984: 527	2.20
Burkhara	Ludhiana	30° 35' 00" N - 75° 55' 00" E	Post-urban Harappan	IAR 1980-81: 45 Joshi et al. 1984: 527	4.00
Butewala	Bahawalpur	28° 55' 10" N - 71° 05' 56" E	Mature Harappan	Mughal 1997: 47	31.10
Butkara One	Swat	34° 44' 00" N - 72° 20' 00" E	Kot Diji, Swat III	Stacul 1987: 30	
Buwana One	Jind	29° 12' 48" N - 76° 17' 45" E	Post-urban Harappan	Singh 1981:78 Joshi et al. 1984: 525 Mohan 1988: 73	1.00

Buwana Two	Jind	29° 12' 48" N - 76° 18' 27" E	Post-urban Harappan Sothi-Siswal	Singh 1981: 78 Joshi et al. 1984: 525 Mohan 1988: 73	0.50
Chabbuwala	Bahawalpur	29° 09' 00" N - 71° 54' 00" E	Mature Harappan	Stein 1943a: 117	41.60
Chabbuwala Ther			Mature Harappan	Stein 1943a: 117 Dalal 1980: 9	4.1
Chachana	Surendranagar	22° 25' 00" N - 71° 50' 00" E	Lustrous Red Ware Late Sorath Harappan Sorath Harappan	Rao 1963a: 184, 205 Possehl 1980: 93 Joshi et al. 1984: 529	
Chachro	Sukkur		Mature Harappan	Mallah 1994: 130-31	3.20
Chadsai	Santal Parganas		Copper Hoard	Makkhan Lal 1984a: 38-9	
Chahi Damb	Makran	26° 18' 00" N - 64° 57' 00" E	Kulli Amri-Nal	Stein 1931: 115-16 Possehl 1986a: 148	1.60
Chak 011	Ganganagar	29° 14' 00" N - 73° 36' 00" E	Mature Harappan Sothi-Siswal	Dalal 1980: 25 Joshi et al. 1984: 522	
Chak 015/3	Ganganagar	29° 14' 00" N - 73° 36' 00" E	Mature Harappan	Dalal 1980: 25 Joshi et al. 1984: 522	
Chak 021	Ganganagar	29° 13' 00" N - 73° 34' 00" E	Mature Harappan	Dalal 1980: 25 Joshi et al. 1984: 522	
Chak 040	Ganganagar		PGW Sothi-Siswal	Dalal 1980: 25	
Chak 043	Ganganagar	29° 10' 00" N - 73° 29' 00" E	Mature Harappan	Dalal 1980: 25 Joshi et al. 1984: 522	
Chak 044	Bahawalpur	29° 13' 55" N - 71° 46' 15" E	Mature Harappan	Mughal 1997: 47	0.80
Chak 045	Bahawalpur	29° 13' 15" N - 71° 48' 48" E	Kot Diji	Mughal 1997: 44	0.70
Chak 045 'A', South	Bahawalpur	29° 11' 50" N - 71° 47' 27" E	Mature Harappan	Mughal 1997: 47	1.50
Chak 045 'B', North	Bahawalpur	29° 13' 25" N - 71° 48' 00" E	Mature Harappan	Mughal 1997: 47	
Chak 050	Ganganagar	29° 10' 00" N - 73° 29' 00" E	Mature Harappan	Dalal 1980: 25 Joshi et al. 1984: 522	
Chak 051	Bahawalpur	29° 11' 05" N - 71° 43' 50" E	Cemetery H	Mughal 1997: 51	0.50
Chak 058/1	Ganganagar		PGW Sothi-Siswal	Dalal 1980: 25	
Chak 058/2	Ganganagar		Mature Harappan	Dalal 1980: 25	
Chak 059	Ganganagar		PGW Sothi-Siswal	Dalal 1980: 25	
Chak 061 East	Bahawalpur	29° 06' 30" N - 71° 37' 38" E	Cemetery H	Mughal 1997: 51	0.70
Chak 061 West	Bahawalpur	29° 06' 27" N - 71° 37' 30" E	Mature Harappan	Mughal 1997: 47	
Chak 069	Bahawalpur	29° 09' 32" N - 71° 51' 13" E	Cemetery H	Mughal 1997: 51	5.00
Chak 071/1	Ganganagar	29° 14' 00" N - 73° 17' 00" E	Mature Harappan	Dalal 1980: 26 Joshi et al. 1984: 522	
Chak 072/3	Ganganagar	29° 10' 00" N - 73° 19' 00" E	Mature Harappan Sothi-Siswal	Dalal 1980: 26 Joshi et al. 1984: 522	
Chak 075, India	Ganganagar	29° 10' 00" N - 73° 18' 00" E	Mature Harappan Sothi-Siswal	Dalal 1980: 26 Joshi et al. 1984: 522	

Chak 075, Pakistan	Bahawalpur	29° 01' 33" N 71° 14' 58" E	-	Mature Harappan	Mughal 1997: 47	0.40
Chak 076	Bahawalpur	29° 01' 25" N 71° 14' 38" E	-	Mature Harappan Kot Diji	Mughal 1997: 44, 47	2.50
Chak 077	Ganganagar			Mature Harappan	Dalal 1980: 26	
Chak 080	Ganganagar	29° 12' 00" N 73° 15' 00" E	-	Mature Harappan	Dalal 1980: 26 Joshi et al. 1984: 522	
Chak 087	Ganganagar	29° 13' 15" N 73° 15' 00" E	-	Rang Mahal Mature Harappan	Dalal 1980: 34	
Chak 088 'A' West	Bahawalpur	29° 06' 51" N 71° 47' 30" E	-	Cemetery H	Mughal 1997: 51	8.10
Chak 088, India	Ganganagar			Mature Harappan	Dalal 1980: 26	
Chak 088, Pakistan	Bahawalpur	29° 06' 53" N 71° 47' 50" E	-	Cemetery H	Mughal 1997: 51	4.20
Chak 097	Bahawalpur	29° 00' 35" N 71° 14' 34" E	-	Mature Harappan	Mughal 1997: 47	3.80
Chak 107	Bahawalpur	29° 06' 24" N 71° 40' 20" E	-	Cemetery H	Mughal 1997: 51	0.05
Chak 112 'P'	Rahimyar Khan	28° 22' 08" N 70° 29' 01" E	-	Mature Harappan	Mughal 1997: 47	0.80
Chak 113/10R	Khanewal	30° 03' 00" N 71° 48' 00" E	-	Mature Harappan	Siddique 1992: 34-5	0.60
Chak 121 'A'	Rahimyar Khan	28° 24' 40" N 70° 36' 10" E	-	Mature Harappan	Mughal 1997: 47	19.30
Chak 124	Rahimyar Khan	28° 25' 40" N 70° 37' 45" E	-	Mature Harappan	Mughal 1997: 47	4.90
Chak 133/10R	Khanewal	30° 20' 00" N 71° 55' 00" E	-	Mature Harappan Kot Diji	A. N. Khan 1988b: 85	
Chak 271 HR	Bahawalpur	29° 13' 10" N 72° 53' 34" E	-	Kot Diji	Mughal 1997: 44	1.10
Chak 280 HR	Bahawalpur	29° 14' 19" N 72° 47' 37" E	-	Kot Diji	Mughal 1997: 44	0.30
Chak 315 HR	Bahawalpur	29° 12' 07" N 72° 24' 42" E	-	Kot Diji	Mughal 1997: 44	5.10
Chak 337 HR	Bahawalpur	29° 07' 40" N 72° 20' 10" E	-	Kot Diji	Mughal 1997: 44	4.60
Chak 341	Bahawalpur	29° 10' 27" N 72° 17' 53" E	-	Kot Diji	Mughal 1997: 44	19.90
Chak 353 West	Bahawalpur	29° 11' 06" N 72° 16' 19" E	-	Hakra Wares	Mughal 1997: 42	1.60
Chak Purbane Syal	Sahiwal	30° 24' 00" N 72° 59' 00" E	-	Mature Harappan	Vats 1940: 475-76	2.00
Chakwali	Bahawalpur	28° 39' 42" N 71° 07' 54" E	-	Mature Harappan	Mughal 1997: 47	1.90
Chambrawala Ther	Bahawalpur	29° 20' 00" N 72° 18' 00" E	-	Hakra Wares?	Mughal 1997: 42	34.60
Chamkaur	Ropar	30° 54' 00" N 76° 25' 00" E	-	PGW Post-urban Harappan	IAR 1953-54: 38 Suraj Bhan 1975: 122 Joshi et al. 1984: 526	
Chanarthal Kalan	Patiala	30° 31' 00" N 76° 21' 00" E	-	Post-urban Harappan	Joshi et al. 1984: 527	

Chanat One	Hissar	29° 12' 00" N - 75° 56' 00" E	Mature Harappan Sothi-Siswal	IAR 1980-81: 16 Joshi et al. 1984: 519, 521 Mohan 1988: 76	6.00
Chanat Three	Hissar	29° 11' 52" N - 75° 55' 40" E	Mature Harappan Sothi-Siswal	Joshi et al. 1984: 519, 521 Mohan 1988: 77	11.50
Chanat Two	Hissar	29° 12' 20" N - 75° 56' 23" E	Mature Harappan Sothi-Siswal	Joshi et al. 1984: 519, 521 Mohan 1988: 77	4.50
Chandan	Muzaffarnagar		OCP	Srivastava 1982: 133-5	2.00
Chandausi	Moradabad		Copper Hoard	IAR 1966-67: 81 K. N. Dikshit 1968: 50 Makkhan Lal 1984a: 34-5	
Chandiala	Ludhiana	30° 52' 00" N - 76° 20' 00" E	Post-urban Harappan Sothi-Siswal	Joshi et al. 1984: 520, 527	
Chandigarh	Chandigarh	30° 45' 00" N - 76° 47' 00" E	Post-urban Harappan Mature Harappan	IAR 1970-71: 7-8 Suraj Bhan 1975: 123 Joshi et al. 1984: 527 IAR 1985-86: 15	
Chandigarh One	Chandigarh	30° 45' 00" N - 76° 47' 20" E	Post-urban Harappan	Suraj Bhan 1975: 123	
Chandlana	Kurukshetra	29° 57' 00" N - 76° 40' 00" E	Post-urban Harappan	Joshi et al. 1984: 524	
Chandnewala Ther	Bahawalpur	28° 43' 53" N - 71° 12' 11" E	Mature Harappan	Mughal 1997: 47	12.60
Chandnewala Three	Bahawalpur	28° 42' 25" N - 71° 10' 36" E	Mature Harappan	Mughal 1997: 47	3.40
Chandnewala Two	Bahawalpur	28° 44' 10" N - 71° 12' 25" E	Hakra Wares	Mughal 1997: 42	24.70
Chandpur	Bulandshahr	28° 37' 00" N - 78° 04' 00" E	Post-urban Harappan	Joshi et al. 1984: 523	
Chandpur	Ropar		Early Medieval PGW Mature Harappan	IAR 1975-76: 38	
Chandrawara One	Jamnagar	21° 50' 00" N - 69° 25' 00" E	Lustrous Red Ware	IAR 1957-58: 19 Possehl 1980: 94 K. K. Bhan 1986: 19	2.00
Chandrawara Two	Jamnagar	21° 50' 00" N - 69° 25' 00" E	Lustrous Red Ware	IAR 1957-58: 19 Possehl 1980: 94 K. K. Bhan 1986: 19	
Chang	Bhiwani	28° 53' 00" N - 76° 13' 23" E	Post-urban Harappan Mature Harappan	Suraj Bhan 1975: 125 Joshi et al. 1984: 526 Mohan 1988: 78	3.00
Changalawala Ther	Bahawalpur	28° 51' 00" N - 71° 22' 38" E	Mature Harappan	Mughal 1997: 47	6.10
Changalawala 'B'	Bahawalpur	28° 50' 55" N - 71° 22' 45" E	Mature Harappan	Mughal 1997: 47	0.01
Changalawala 'C'	Bahawalpur	28° 51' 07" N - 71° 22' 55" E	Hakra Wares	Mughal 1997: 42	3.10
Changda	Kheda	22° 32' 00" N - 72° 33' 00" E	Sorath Harappan Microliths	IAR 1972-73: 10 IAR 1974-75: 13 Momin 1979: 103-04	1.00
Chanhu-daro	Nawabshah	26° 11' 00" N - 68° 19' 00" E	Jhangar Trihni Jhukar Mature Harappan	Majumdar 1934: 35-44 Mackay 1943 Flam 1981a: 217-18	4.70

Chanidhar	Jamnagar	22° 16' 00" N 70° 01' 00" E	-	Lustrous Red Ware	K. K. Bhan 1983: 245-46	3.60
Chaniyathar-no Timbo	Banaskantha	23° 31' 00" N 71° 44' 00" E	-	Lustrous Red Ware	K. K. Bhan 1994: 86-7	1.30
Channal Kund Damb	Jhalawan	27° 05' 00" N 66° 09' 00" E	-	Kulli Amri-Nal Kechi Beg Togau	Raikes 1968b: 154-55	
Channanwala Ther	Bahawalpur	29° 07' 30" N 72° 54' 10" E	-	Hakra Wares	Mughal 1997: 42	4.70
Chapliwala East	Bahawalpur	29° 08' 00" N 72° 17' 43" E	-	Kot Diji	Mughal 1997: 44 Stein 1943a: 125 Dalal 1980: 10	1.20
Chapliwala West	Bahawalpur	29° 07' 20" N 72° 16' 00" E	-	Kot Diji	Mughal 1997: 44 Stein 1943a: 125 Dalal 1980: 10	8.20
Chapuwala	Bahawalpur	29° 08' 52" N 72° 16' 32" E	-	Mature Harappan	Mughal 1997: 47	12.20
Charaiwala Ther	Bahawalpur	28° 48' 00" N 71° 19' 00" E	-	Mature Harappan	Stein 1943a: 166	11.60
Charanio	Bhavnagar	21° 52' 00" N 71° 38' 00" E	-	Red Polished Ware Late Sorath Harappan Sorath Harappan	IAR 1960-61: 8 Rao 1963a: 205 Possehl 1980: 93 Joshi et al. 1984: 528	7.50
Charhoyanwala	Bahawalpur	28° 48' 22" N 71° 16' 14" E	-	Mature Harappan	Mughal 1997: 47	6.20
Chashiana	Surendranagar	22° 25' 00" N 71° 50' 00" E	-	Sorath Harappan	IAR 1954-55: 59 Possehl 1980: 94 Joshi et al. 1984: 530	
Chashma Murad	Jhalawan			Complex B Pirak? Early Kulli Amri-Nal Kechi Beg Togau	Stein 1931: 174 Raikes 1968b Possehl 1986a: 149	
Chatla	Midnapur			Copper Hoard	IAR 1965-66: 68 Makkhan Lal 1984a: 38-9	
Chaudhryanwala	Bahawalpur	28° 47' 37" N 71° 16' 24" E	-	Hakra Wares	Mughal 1997: 42	2.20
Chaurdeo	Saharanpur	29° 57' 00" N 77° 44' 00" E	-	Post-urban Harappan	Joshi et al. 1984: 522	
Chauro	Dadu	26° 09' 00" N 67° 43' 00" E	-	Amri-Nal	Majumdar 1934: 123-25 Flam 1981a: 305	1.40
Chava Sri	Jhunjhunu			Mature Harappan	IAR 1980-81: 56	
Chavaneshwar	Broach	21° 41' 00" N 72° 48' 00" E	-	Late Sorath Harappan Sorath Harappan	IAR 1966-67: 9 Allchin and Joshi 1970: 21 Possehl 1980: 94 Joshi et al. 1984: 529	
Cheeka	Kurukshetra	30° 03' 00" N 76° 21' 00" E	-	PGW Post-urban Harappan	Kumar 1978: 51-2 Joshi et al. 1984: 524	5.00
Cheelanwali	Bahawalpur	28° 53' 32" N 71° 28' 00" E	-	Cemetery H	Mughal 1997: 51	0.50
Cheelanwali 'B'	Bahawalpur	28° 53' 15" N 71° 27' 47" E	-	Cemetery H	Mughal 1997: 51	0.50

Cheshma Damb One	Jhalawan			Complex B Kulli Amri-Nal Kechi Beg Togau	Fairservis 1971c: 405 Possehl 1986a: 147	
Chhabasr	Ahmedabad	22° 46' 00" N 72° 16' 00" E	-	Sorath Harappan	Joshi et al. 1984: 530	
Chhajpura	Saharanpur	29° 59' 00" N 77° 37' 00" E	-	OCP Mature Harappan	IAR 1966-67: 43 Joshi et al. 1984: 521, 522	
Chhalgari	Kachi	28° 50' 00" N 67° 50' 00" E	-	Early to Mature Harappan	Stein 1905: 54-5 Jarrige 1986: 117	
Chhapar Heri	Saharanpur	29° 54' 00" N 77° 30' 00" E	-	OCP Mature Harappan	IAR 1966-67: 43 Joshi et al. 1984: 521, 522	
Chhapra	Sonepat	29° 07' 00" N 76° 32' 00" E	-	Post-urban Harappan Mature Harappan Sothi-Siswal	Joshi et al. 1984: 519, 521, 525	
Chhina	Amritsar	31° 45' 00" N 74° 45' 00" E	-	Post-urban Harappan	Joshi et al. 1984: 526	
Chhota Kapoto	Jhalawan	28° 46' 00" N 66° 25' 00" E	-	Kechi Beg	de Cardi 1983: 25	
Chhoti Mansa	Bhatinda	29° 59' 00" N 75° 26' 00" E	-	Post-urban Harappan Mature Harappan Sothi-Siswal	IAR 1980-81: 45 Joshi et al. 1984: 522, 527 Joshi 1986: 139	9.00
Chhutijo Kund	Dadu	26° 52' 00" N 67° 15' 00" E	-	Amri-Nal	Krishna Deva and McCown 1949: 27 Flam 1981a: 261	
Chig Dheri	Bannu	32° 43' 00" N 70° 34' 00" E	-	Historic Kot Diji	Allchin, Allchin, Durrani and Khan 1985: 9, 186	
Chiheywali	Bahawalpur	28° 48' 52" N 71° 11' 40" E	-	Mature Harappan	Mughal 1997: 47	2.70
Chikrala	Bahawalpur	28° 45' 05" N 71° 12' 02" E	-	Hakra Wares	Mughal 1997: 42	19.20
Chilhera	Saharanpur	30° 02' 00" N 77° 39' 00" E	-	OCP Mature Harappan	IAR 1966-67: 43 Dikshit 1982a: 114 Joshi et al. 1984: 521, 522	3.00
Chimarheri	Kurukshetra			Post-urban Harappan	Suraj Bhan 1975: 124	
Chimri	Jhalawan	27° 49' 00" N 66° 38' 00" E	-	Kechi Beg Togau	Stein 1931: 171 de Cardi 1983: 37	2.50
Chimun	Hissar	29° 40' 13" N 75° 39' 45" E	-	Post-urban Harappan	Suraj Bhan 1975: 123 Joshi et al. 1984: 519, 521, 526	3.20
Chimun Two	Hissar	29° 40' 50" N 75° 39' 52" E	-	Post-urban Harappan	Mohan 1988: 79	2.00
Chinchroli	Jhunjhunu			OCP	IAR 1980-81: 56	
Chinikangrida Theh	Jullunder	31° 23' 00" N 75° 47' 00" E	-	Post-urban Harappan	Joshi et al. 1984: 526	
Chipa-no Godh	Banaskantha	23° 45' 00" N 71° 16' 30" E	-	Lustrous Red Ware	Ajithprasad and Sonawane, in press	1.20
Chipwala	Bahawalpur	29° 04' 53" N 72° 04' 55" E	-	Kot Diji	Mughal 1997: 44	4.50
Chiri Damb	Makran	26° 58' 00" N 64° 02' 00" E	-	Islamic Kulli-Harappan Amri-Nal	Stein 1931: 44 Possehl 1986a: 150	
Chitauli	Ropar	30° 51' 00" N 76° 35' 00" E	-	Post-urban Harappan	Joshi et al. 1984: 527	

Chitrod	Kutch	23° 24' 00" N	-	Mature Harappan	IAR 1977-78: 20	
		70° 40' 00" E			Joshi et al. 1984: 529	
Chore	Bahawalpur	28° 45' 36" N	-	Hakra Wares	Mughal 1997: 42	19.00
		71° 09' 30" E				
Chorewala	Bahawalpur	28° 44' 05" N	-	Mature Harappan	Mughal 1997: 47	8.10
		71° 08' 46" E				
Chosla	Bhavnagar	21° 53' 00" N	-	Late Sorath Harappan	Possehl 1980: 93	4.80
		71° 34' 00" E		Sorath Harappan	Joshi et al. 1984: 528	
Chota Isvaria	Bhavnagar	21° 58' 00" N	-	Lustrous Red Ware	Possehl 1980: 94	0.80
		71° 42' 00" E			Joshi et al. 1984: 528	
Choteria Timbo	Mehsana	23° 36' 00" N	-	Anarta	K. K. Bhan 1994: 86-7	0.20
		71° 51' 00" E		(Pre-Harappan)		
Chouradeo	Saharanpur			Mature Harappan	Pande & Ramachandran 1971: 38	
Chowala	Ambala			Post-urban Harappan	Kumar 1978: 41	2.00
Chowala	Ropar	30° 15' 00" N	-	Post-urban Harappan	Joshi et al. 1984: 523	
		77° 17' 00" E				
Chunehti Shekh	Saharanpur	29° 54' 00" N	-	OCP	IAR 1966-67: 43	
		77° 43' 00" E		Mature Harappan	Joshi et al. 1984: 521, 522	
Churbuk	Makran	26° 04' 15" N	-	Dasht	Besenval and Sanlaville 1990:	
		62° 40' 30" E			111-12	
Dabakia	Jabalpur			Copper Hoard	IAR 1961-62: 99	
					Makkhan Lal 1984a: 36-7	
Dabar Kot	Loralai	30° 05' 00" N	-	Partho/Sassanian	Noetling 1898: 102, 104	24.30
		68° 41' 00" E		Buddhist	Stein 1929a: 55-64	
				Iron Age	Fairservis 1959: 289	
				Mature Harappan		
				Kot Diji		
				Kechi Beg		
Dabli East	Bahawalpur	28° 54' 10" N	-	Hakra Wares	Mughal 1997: 42	3.60
		71° 28' 13" E				
Dabli Theri	Bahawalpur	29° 00' 59" N	-	Cemetery H	Mughal 1997: 51	0.70
		71° 12' 43" E				
Dabli West	Bahawalpur	28° 54' 20" N	-	Hakra Wares	Mughal 1997: 42	4.70
		71° 28' 10" E				
Dachor	Karnal	29° 40' 00" N	-	Post-urban Harappan	Suraj Bhan 1975: 125	
		76° 42' 00" E			Joshi et al. 1984: 519, 524	
Dad	Rajkot	22° 50' 00" N	-	Sorath Harappan	IAR 1957-58: 19	2.60
		70° 55' 00" E			Possehl 1980: 94	
					Joshi et al. 1984: 529	
Dad Kala Kach	Bannu	32° 57' 20" N	-	Late Kot Diji	Allchin, Allchin, Durrani and	
Kot Dherai		70° 36' 15" E			Khan 1985: 9, 186	
Dadhera	Patiala	30° 20' 00" N	-	Post-urban Harappan	Joshi et al. 1984: 527	
		76° 21' 00" E				
Dadheri	Ludhiana	30° 40' 00" N	-	Harappan/PGW Overlap	Suraj Bhan 1975: 122	
		76° 19' 00" E		Post-urban Harappan	IAR 1976-77: 43-4	
					Joshi et al. 1984: 527	
Dadiya	Sikar			Mature Harappan(?)	IAR 1981-82: 62	
Pajyalli				and Microliths		
Dadri	Mahendragarh	28° 35' 00" N	-	Copper Hoard	Suraj Bhan 1975: 126	
		76° 16' 00" E		Mature Harappan	Joshi et al. 1984: 519, 526	
					Makkhan Lal 1984a: 34-35	
Daduka	Jaipur			PGW	IAR 1973-74: 24	
				OCP		

Dadwala Ther	Bahawalpur	28° 43' 15" N - 71° 18' 09" E		Mature Harappan	Mughal 1997: 47	1.90
Dadwala Two	Bahawalpur	28° 43' 13" N - 71° 18' 31" E		Mature Harappan	Mughal 1997: 47	0.01
Dagru	Faridkot			Mature Harappan	Suraj Bhan 1975: 122	
Daheru	Ludhiana	30° 45' 00" N - 76° 09' 00" E		Post-urban Harappan	Suraj Bhan 1975: 122 Joshi et al. 1984: 527	
Daidungri	Rajkot	22° 00' 00" N - 71° 05' 00" E		Lustrous Red Ware Late Sorath Harappan	Rao 1963a: 205 Possehl 1980: 95 Joshi et al. 1984: 528	
Daimabad	Ahmednagar	19° 31' 00" N - 74° 42' 00" E		Jorwe Malwa Daimabad Culture Post-urban Harappan Savalda	Sali 1986: 11	50.00
Daiwala	Bahawalpur	28° 54' 23" N - 71° 20' 00" E		Cemetery H	Stein 1943a: 161-62 Mughal 1997: 51 Dalal 1980: 11	8.40
Dalamwala	Jind	29° 23' 08" N - 76° 23' 02" E		Post-urban Harappan	Singh 1981: 79 Joshi et al. 1984: 525	0.90
Dalheri	Saharanpur			Post-urban Harappan	IAR 1985-86: 85	
Dalliwala One	Bhatinda	29° 49' 00" N - 75° 25' 00" E		Mature Harappan	Joshi 1986: 139	25.00
Dalliwala Two	Bhatinda	29° 50' 00" N - 75° 25' 00" E		Mature Harappan	Joshi 1986: 139	25.00
Damb Buthi	Dadu	26° 17' 00" N - 67° 40' 00" E		Mature Harappan Amri-Nal	Majumdar 1934: 114-17 Flam 1981a: 298-301	9.60
Damb Channarozai	Kalat			Kechi Beg	Mughal 1972a: 147	
Damb Ghuram	Kalat			Kechi Beg	Mughal 1972a: 147	
Damb Goram	Sarawan			Quetta Amri-Nal Kechi Beg	Fairservis 1971c: 402	
Damb Hasal Khanzai	Kalat			Islamic? Kechi Beg	Mughal 1972a: 147	
Damb Kulu	Sarawan			Quetta Amri-Nal Kechi Beg Togau	Fairservis 1971c: 402	
Damb Sadaat	Quetta-Pishin	30° 03' 00" N - 66° 57' 00" E		Quetta Damb Sadaat Kechi Beg	Fairservis 1956a: 204 de Cardi 1983: 20	1.70
Damb Shirinab	Sarawan	29° 55' 00" N - 66° 40' 00" E		Quetta Amri-Nal	Mughal 1972a: 147	
Damb Wali Mohammad	Kalat			Kechi Beg Togau	Mughal 1972a: 147	
Damb Zargaran	Kalat	29° 06' 00" N - 66° 23' 00" E		Kechi Beg	Mughal 1972a: 148	
Damb Zerger	Sarawan	29° 06' 00" N - 66° 22' 00" E		Kulli-Harappan Amri-Nal Kechi Beg	de Cardi 1983: 24	
Damb-i Bambi	Makran	26° 57' 20" N - 64° 09' 00" E		Kulli	Stein 1931: 44,45 Possehl 1986a: 150	

Site	District	Coordinates		Period	Reference	Size
Damboli	Kachi	29° 21' 00" N 67° 36' 00" E	-	BMAC (Mehrgarh VIII)	Santoni 1984: 58 Jarrige, Jarrige, Meadow and Quivron 1995: 328	
Damkot	Swat	34° 40' 00" N 72° 00' 00" E	-	Swat Proto-Historic	Stacul 1987: 63-4	
Dandar	Makran	25° 44' 00" N 62° 27' 30" E	-	Dasht	Besenval and Sanlaville 1990: 104	
Dandhi	Sukkur			Mature Harappan	Mallah 1994: 171-74	2.80
Dandra	Ludhiana	30° 51' 00" N 75° 48' 00" E	-	Post-urban Harappan	Joshi et al. 1984: 527	
Dandrala	Patiala	30° 28' 00" N 76° 18' 00" E	-	Post-urban Harappan	Joshi et al. 1984: 527	
Danewala One	Bhatinda	29° 50' 00" N 75° 25' 00" E	-	Post-urban Harappan Mature Harappan	Joshi et al. 1984: 522, 527 Joshi 1986: 139	4.00
Danewala Two	Bhatinda	29° 49' 00" N 75° 24' 00" E	-	Post-urban Harappan Mature Harappan	Joshi et al. 1984: 522 Joshi 1986: 139	4.00
Dantrad				Sorath Harappan	Chitalwala 1985: key Figure 8	
Dared				Sorath Harappan	Chitalwala 1985: key Figure 8	
Dared Two	Bhavnagar	21° 58' 00" N 71° 46' 00" E	-	Lustrous Red Ware	Possehl notes 12 October 1980	2.10
Dargama	Ranchi			Copper Hoard	S. C. Roy 1915: 239 Makkhan Lal 1984a: 38-9	
Darkhanwala Ther	Bahawalpur	28° 43' 20" N 71° 13' 38" E	-	Hakra Wares	Mughal 1997: 42	8.10
Darkhanwala Two	Bahawalpur	28° 43' 37" N 71° 13' 37" E	-	Mature Harappan	Mughal 1997: 47	0.50
Daroli Khera	Jind	29° 29' 24" N 76° 06' 33" E	-	PGW Sothi-Siswal	Singh 1981: 103 Joshi et al. 1984: 519	2.20
Datrana Eight	Banaskantha	23° 46' 00" N 71° 06' 45" E	-	Anarta Blade Making Microlith Blade Making	Ajithprasad and Sonawane, in press	35.00
Datrana Five	Banaskantha	23° 46' 15" N 71° 07' 00" E	-	Anarta-Rangpur IIC	Ajithprasad and Sonawane, in press	0.10
Datrana Four	Banaskantha	23° 46' 00" N 71° 06' 50" E	-	Anarta Chalcolithic	Ajithprasad and Sonawane, in press	0.03
Datrana One	Banaskantha	23° 46' 10" N 71° 07' 00" E	-	Lustrous Red Ware	Ajithprasad and Sonawane, in press	0.60
Datrana Seven	Banaskantha	23° 46' 40" N 71° 07' 00" E	-	Anarta Blade Making	Ajithprasad and Sonawane, in press	0.70
Datrana Six	Banaskantha	23° 47' 00" N 71° 07' 15" E	-	Lustrous Red Ware	Ajithprasad and Sonawane, in press	0.60
Datrana Three	Banaskantha	23° 45' 50" N 71° 07' 00" E	-	Rangpur IIC	Ajithprasad and Sonawane, in press	0.01
Datrana Two	Banaskantha	23° 46' 00" N 71° 07' 10" E	-	Lustrous Red Ware	Ajithprasad and Sonawane, in press	0.04
Datta	Hissar	29° 15' 25" N 76° 59' 50" E	-	Post-urban Harappan Sothi-Siswal	Suraj Bhan 1975: 124 Joshi et al. 1984: 519, 526 Mohan 1988: 80	0.80
Daudpur	Saharanpur	30° 05' 00" N 77° 36' 00" E	-	OCP Mature Harappan	IAR 1966-67: 43 Joshi et al. 1984: 521, 522	
Daulatpur	Kurukshetra	29° 57' 00" N 76° 57' 00" E	-	Late Medieval Early Historic PGW Post-urban Harappan	IAR 1977-78: 23	5.70

Daulatpur	Bulandshahr	28° 14' 00" N - 78° 11' 00" E	OCP/Post-Urban Harappan	IAR 1984-85: 86-8 Gaur 1995: 215-19	4.60
Dawrao Tul Damb	Dera Ismail Khan		Kot Diji Kechi Beg	Fairservis 1971c: 413	
Deariro One	Sukkur		Mature Harappan	Mallah 1994: 132-36	0.60
Deh Bail	Karachi		Amri-Nal Microliths	A. R. Khan 1968a: 9	
Deh Mari Sabra	Nawabshah	26° 12' 00" N - 68° 26' 00" E	Mature Harappan	Anonymous 1964b: 10 Flam 1981a: 219	0.60
Deh Morasi Ghundai	Kandahar	31° 31' 00" N - 65° 30' 00" E	Post-urban Phase Damb Sadaat	Dupree 1963 Ball 1982: 90	1.10
Dehada	Kheda	22° 23' 00" N - 72° 33' 00" E	Sorath Harappan Microliths	Momin 1976: 53 Momin 1979: 104-05 Momin 1984	
Dehra	Karnal	29° 12' 22" N - 77° 04' 20" E	Post-urban Harappan	Singh 1981: 66 Joshi et al. 1984: 524	1.10
Deorar	Jind	29° 05' 57" N - 76° 23' 38" E	Post-urban Harappan	Mohan 1988: 80	8.00
Deoti	Lucknow		OCP & Copper Hoard	B. B. Lal 1951: 29 IAR 1978-79: 101 Makkhan Lal 1984a: 34-5	
Derawar Ther	Bahawalpur	28° 46' 15" N - 71° 19' 40" E	Mature Harappan	Stein 1943a: 173-79 Mughal 1997: 47	35.20
Deriwalokhetra One	Mehsana	23° 30' 20" N - 71° 55' 30" E	Lustrous Red Ware	Joshi et al. 1984: 529 K. K. Bhan 1994: 86-7	2.20
Desalpur	Kutch	23° 37' 00" N - 69° 08' 00" E	Early Historic Mature Harappan	IAR 1955-56: 69-70 Rao 1963a: 188, 205 Possehl 1980: 95	1.30
Deudhar	Rajkot		Sorath Harappan	IAR 1957-58: 19	
Devagana	Ahmedabad		Sorath Harappan	IAR 1966-67: 8	
Deval Khera	Bulandshahr	28° 20' 00" N - 78° 15' 00" E	Post-urban Harappan	Joshi et al. 1984: 523	
Devalio, Amreli	Amreli	21° 53' 00" N - 71° 23' 00" E	Lustrous Red Ware Late Sorath Harappan	IAR 1955-56: 70 Rao 1963a: 184, 205 Possehl 1980: 95 Joshi et al. 1984: 528	2.90
Devalio, Surendranagar	Surendranagar	22° 25' 00" N - 71° 55' 00" E	Sorath Harappan	Possehl 1980: 96 Joshi et al. 1984: 529	31.90
Devalkano Doro	Rajkot		Lustrous Red Ware	Chitalwala 1979: 115	0.10
Devalkano Timbo	Rajkot		Lustrous Red Ware Sorath Harappan	Chitalwala 1979: 115	0.10
Devdhar	Rajkot	22° 07' 00" N - 71° 09' 00" E	Late Sorath Harappan Sorath Harappan	IAR 1957-58: 19 Rao 1963a: 205 Possehl 1980: 96 Joshi et al. 1984: 528	
Develiwala Ther	Bahawalpur	28° 40' 45" N - 71° 02' 00" E	Mature Harappan	Mughal 1997: 47	23.10
Develiwala Two	Bahawalpur	28° 40' 40" N - 71° 02' 40" E	Mature Harappan	Mughal 1997: 47	3.60
Deverar	Jind	29° 05' 18" N - 76° 22' 55" E	Post-urban Harappan Sothi-Siswal	Singh 1981: 79 Joshi et al. 1984: 519, 525	1.50

Devganga	Ahmedabad	22° 18' 00" N - 71° 50' 00" E	Sorath Harappan	Joshi et al. 1984: 530	
Devidaspur	Kurukshetra	29° 58' 00" N - 76° 58' 00" E	Post-urban Harappan	Kumar 1978: 64 Joshi et al. 1984: 524	3.00
Dewaliana Ther	Bahawalpur	28° 45' 00" N - 71° 26' 00" E	Mature Harappan	Stein 1943a: 168 Mughal 1970: 158	21.50
Dhablan	Patiala	30° 20' 00" N - 76° 15' 00" E	Post-urban Harappan	Joshi et al. 1984: 527	
Dhaka	Shahjahanpur		Copper Hoard	B. B. Lal 1951: 27-8 Makkhan Lal 1984a: 34-5	
Dhakal One	Jind	29° 34' 45" N - 76° 09' 42" E	PGW Post-urban Harappan Mature Harappan Sothi-Siswal	Suraj Bhan & Shaffer 1978: 62 Joshi et al. 1984: 519, 521, 525 Mohan 1988: 81	4.30
Dhakal Two	Jind	29° 31' 09" N - 76° 10' 25" E	Post-urban Harappan	Suraj Bhan & Shaffer 1978: 62 Joshi et al. 1984: 525 Mohan 1988: 81	3.80
Dhal Buthi	Dadu	26° 04' 00" N - 67° 47' 00" E	Mature Harappan Amri-Nal	Majumdar 1934: 125-27 Flam 1981a: 308	1.50
Dhalewan	Bhatinda	30° 02' 00" N - 75° 33' 00" E	Rang Mahal Post-urban Harappan Mature Harappan	Joshi et al. 1984: 520, 522 Joshi 1986: 139	40.00
Dhama	Surendranagar	23° 23' 00" N - 71° 39' 00" E	Rangpur IIC Anarta	K. K. Bhan 1994: 86-7	0.01
Dhammo Majra	Patiala	30° 20' 00" N - 76° 22' 00" E	Post-urban Harappan	Joshi et al. 1984: 527	
Dhamola	Saharanpur	30° 00' 00" N - 77° 35' 00" E	Post-urban Harappan	Joshi et al. 1984: 522	
Dhamraho	Larkana		Mature Harappan	Banerji 1920-21 Dikshit 1925-26a: 99	
Dhanana	Jind	28° 54' 50" N - 76° 09' 08" E	Post-urban Harappan Mature Harappan	Mohan 1988: 82	4.00
Dhang, Himachal Pradesh	Solan	31° 05' 00" N - 76° 40' 00" E	Post-urban Harappan	Suraj Bhan 1975: 122 Joshi et al. 1984: 528	
Dhang, Punjab			Mature Harappan	IAR 1954-55: 59	
Dhangerian	Patiala	30° 37' 00" N - 76° 30' 00" E	Post-urban Harappan	Joshi et al. 1984: 527	
Dhankanio	Amreli	21° 45' 00" N - 70° 55' 00" E	Sorath Harappan	IAR 1957a-58: 19 Rao 1963a: 205 Possehl 1980: 96 Joshi et al. 1984: 528	
Dhankanio Two	Amreli	21° 47' 00" N - 70° 55' 00" E	Sorath Harappan	IAR 1958-59: 19 Possehl 1980: 96 Joshi et al. 1984: 530	
Dhanora	Kurukshetra		Post-urban Harappan	Kumar 1978: 65	4.00
Dhanouri	Jind	29° 47' 20" N - 76° 10' 30" E	Early Medieval Sothi-Siswal	Singh 1981: 105 Joshi et al. 1984: 519 Mohan 1988: 82	0.40
Dhansa	Delhi	28° 31' 00" N - 76° 56' 00" E	OCP and Post-urban Mature Harappan	Suraj Bhan 1975: 112,126 Suraj Bhan & Shaffer 1978: 67 Joshi et al. 1984: 528	
Dhansa Three	Delhi		Post-urban Harappan	Suraj Bhan 1975: 126	
Dhansa Two	Delhi		Post-urban Harappan	Suraj Bhan 1975: 126	

Dhantor One	Kurukshetra	30° 04' 28" N 76° 53' 02" E	-	Post-urban Harappan	Kumar 1978: 65 Joshi et al. 1984: 524	4.50
Dhar	Jaipur			OCP	IAR 1973-74: 24	
Dharam Garh	Jind	29° 25' 00" N 76° 40' 00" E	-	Post-urban Harappan	Joshi et al. 1984: 525	
Dharamgarh	Karnal	29° 27' 42" N 76° 49' 10" E	-	Post-urban Harappan	Singh 1981: 66 Joshi et al. 1984: 524	0.80
Dharmheri One	Patiala			Post-urban Harappan	Suraj Bhan 1975: 122	
Dharmheri Two	Patiala	30° 07' 00" N 76° 19' 00" E	-	Post-urban Harappan Mature Harappan	Suraj Bhan 1975: 122 Joshi et al. 1984: 522, 527	
Dharodi	Jind	29° 38' 22" N 76° 04' 03" E	-	PGW Post-urban Harappan Sothi-Siswal	Singh 1981: 105 Joshi et al. 1984: 525	
Dharovadno Timbo	Surendranagar	23° 23' 30" N 71° 48' 00" E		Lustrous Red Ware	IAR 1984-85: 19 K. K. Bhan 1994: 86-7	3.00
Dhatva	Surat	21° 09' 00" N 72° 46' 00" E	-	Early Historic Late Sorath Harappan-Malwa	Mehta, Chowdhary, Hegde and Shah 1975 K. K. Bhan 1989: 240	1.70
Dhedeniwala Ther	Bahawalpur			Mature Harappan	Mughal 1997: 47	8.40
Dher Majra	Ropar	31° 02' 00" N 76° 33' 00" E	-	Post-urban Harappan Mature Harappan	Prüfer 1952 IAR 1953-54: 38 Joshi et al. 1984: 528	0.90
Dhillanijo Kot	Dadu	25° 37' 00" N 68° 02' 00" E	-	Amri-Nal	Majumdar 1934: 145 Flam 1981a: 348	
Dhingana	Jind	29° 13' 30" N 76° 26' 33" E	-	Post-urban Harappan Sothi-Siswal	Singh 1981: 79-80 Joshi et al. 1984: 519, 525	2.50
Dhingi	Patiala	30° 25' 00" N 76° 07' 00" E	-	Post-urban Harappan	Joshi et al. 1984: 527	
Dhogri	Jullunder	31° 23' 00" N 75° 40' 00" E	-	Post-urban Harappan Mature Harappan	IAR 1956-57: 79 Joshi et al. 1984: 522, 526	
Dholavira	Kutch	23° 53' 10" N 70° 13' 00" E	-	Mature Harappan Amri-Nal	IAR 1967-68: 17 Possehl 1980: 97 Joshi et al. 1984: 529 Bisht 1989, 1991	60.00
Dhonderi	Jullunder	31° 22' 00" N 75° 40' 00" E	-	Post-urban Harappan	Joshi et al. 1984: 526	
Dhoopsari	Bahawalpur			Hakra Wares	Mughal 1997: 42	0.20
Dhoraji	Rajkot			Lustrous Red Ware	IAR 1978-79: 5	
Dhrosan	Amreli	20° 50' 00" N 70° 40' 00" E	-	Sorath Harappan	IAR 1957-58: 19 Rao 1963a: 205 Possehl 1980: 96 Joshi et al. 1984: 528	
Dhrufaniya	Rajkot			Lustrous Red Ware	IAR 1982-83: 27	
Dhuapino	Amreli	21° 27' 00" N 71° 49' 00" E	-	Sorath Harappan	IAR 1960-61: 7 Possehl 1980: 97 Joshi et al. 1984: 530	
Dhudasia	Rajkot			Sorath Harappan	IAR 1957-58: 19	
Dhuhinwala Ther	Rahimyar Khan	28° 36' 00" N 70° 55' 50" E	-	Mature Harappan	Mughal 1997: 47	1.30
Dhulkot	Jamnagar	20° 50' 00" N 71° 02' 00" E	-	Late Sorath Harappan Sorath Harappan	Rao 1963: 205 Possehl 1980: 97 Joshi et al. 1984: 528	

Name	District	Coordinates		Period	Reference	Size
Dhumarkha Kalan Two	Jind	29° 32' 27" N 76° 08' 42" E	-	Post-urban Harappan	Singh 1981: 106-07 Joshi et al. 1984: 525 Mohan 1988: 83	1.20
Dhundwa	Jind	29° 42' 48" N 76° 11' 19" E	-	Post-urban Harappan	Singh 1981: 106 Joshi et al. 1984: 525	1.10
Dhunga-Ka Nagala	Sikar			OCP	IAR 1973-74: 24	
Dhuni	Rahimyar Khan	28° 35' 25" N 70° 55' 57" E	-	Mature Harappan	Mughal 1997: 47	2.60
Dhuni South	Rahimyar Khan	28° 35' 00" N 70° 56' 13" E	-	Hakra Wares	Mughal 1997: 42	1.20
Dhuni, Hakra	Rahimyar Khan	28° 35' 25" N 70° 55' 57" E	-	Mature Harappan Hakra Wares	Mughal 1997: 42, 47	7.20
Dhurala	Kurukshetra	30° 16' 00" N 76° 55' 00" E	-	Post-urban Harappan	U. V. Singh 1976: 29 Joshi et al. 1984: 524	
Dhurasiano Timbo	Rajkot			Lustrous Red Ware Sorath Harappan	Chitalwala 1979: 115	2.00
Dhurmarkha Kalan One	Jind	29° 33' 24" N 76° 09' 40" E	-	Post-urban Harappan Sothi-Siswal	Singh 1981: 106-07 Joshi et al. 1984: 525	1.10
Dhurmarkha Kalan Two	Jind	29° 32' 24" N 76° 08' 40" E	-	PGW Post-urban Harappan	Singh 1981: 106-07 Joshi et al. 1984: 525	0.90
Dhutarpur	Rajkot	21° 50' 00" N 71° 00' 00" E	-	Sorath Harappan	IAR 1958-59: 19 Possehl 1980: 97 Joshi et al. 1984: 529	
Diji-ji Tikri	Khairpur	27° 32' 00" N 68° 55' 00" E	-	Kot Diji	Vats 1935-36a: 36-7 Flam 1981a: 220	1.60
Dikadla	Karnal	29° 13' 50" N 77° 04' 13" E	-	Post-urban Harappan Mature Harappan	Singh 1981: 66-7 Joshi et al. 1984: 521, 524	0.40
Dilwashwala	Bahawalpur	28° 49' 20" N 71° 22' 10" E	-	Mature Harappan	Mughal 1997: 47	3.50
Dinewali Theri	Bahawalpur	29° 10' 00" N 72° 06' 00" E	-	Kot Diji	Stein 1943a: 123 Dalal 1980: 9	
Dinwala	Bahawalpur			Hakra Wares	Mughal 1997: 42	3.20
Disoi	Dadu	25° 23' 00" N 67° 54' 00" E	-	Mature Harappan	Majumdar 1934: 142 Lambrick 1964: 86 Flam 1981a: 347	2.50
Diwana	Las Bela	26° 06' 00" N 67° 15' 00" E	-	Amri-Nal	Fairservis 1961b: 6	
Diz Parom Mound East	Makran	26° 38' 00" N 63° 32' 01" E	-	Londo Kulli	Stein 1931: 49 Possehl 1986a: 150	0.20
Dodwan	Gurdaspur	32° 08' 00" N 75° 25' 00" E	-	Post-urban Harappan	Joshi et al. 1984: 526	
Dogru	Faridkot	30° 50' 00" N 75° 03' 00" E	-	Post-urban Harappan	Joshi et al. 1984: 527	
Domeli	Kapurthala	31° 20' 00" N 75° 46' 00" E	-	Post-urban Harappan Mature Harappan Sothi-Siswal	Joshi et al.1984: 520, 522, 526	
Doraha	Ludhiana	30° 48' 00" N 76° 01' 00" E	-	Early Historic Post-urban Harappan	IAR 1975-76: 38 Joshi et al. 1984: 527	
Dosia Khal Damb	Jhalawan	27° 18' 00" N 66° 22' 00" E	-	Kulli Amri-Nal Kechi Beg	Raikes 1968b: 149	9.00
Drakalo Damb	Jhalawan	27° 09' 00" N 66° 25' 00" E	-	Early Historic Iron Age Kechi Beg	Stein 1931: 177	0.10

Dranjan Site	Kachi			Mature Harappan Kot Diji	Anonymous 1964b: 13-4	0.30
Drigwala	Bahawalpur	28° 52' 28" N 71° 13' 20" E	-	Mature Harappan	Mughal 1997: 47	10.80
Dudakheri	Kurukshetra	29° 46' 00" N 76° 27' 00" E	-	PGW Post-urban Harappan	U. V. Singh 1976: 28 Joshi et al. 1984: 524	
Dudhala	Jamnagar	22° 14' 00" N 70° 17' 00" E	-	Late Sorath Harappan Sorath Harappan	K. K. Bhan 1986: 18	
Dudheriya Timbo	Mehsana	23° 27' 00" N 71° 48' 00" E	-	Rangpur IIC Anarta	Hegde and Sonawane 1986: 31 K. K. Bhan 1994: 86-7	0.40
Dudli Bukhara	Saharanpur	29° 56' 00" N 77° 36' 00" E	-	Post-urban Harappan	Joshi et al.1984: 522	
Dugchari	Saharanpur			Post-urban Harappan	IAR 1985-86: 85	
Dugri	Ropar	30° 54' 00" N 76° 28' 00" E	-	Post-urban Harappan	Joshi et al. 1984: 527	
Dukheri One	Ambala	30° 16' 00" N 76° 53' 00" E	-	Post-urban Harappan	IAR 1963-64: 27 Suraj Bhan 1975: 123 Joshi et al. 1984: 521, 523	
Dukheri Two	Ambala	30° 15' 20" N 76° 53' 00" E	-	Post-urban Harappan	Suraj Bhan 1975: 123	
Duki Mound	Loralai	30° 10' 00" N 68° 34' 00" E	-	Waziri Kot Diji Kechi Beg Togau Burj Basket-marked	Fairservis 1959: 289	6.50
Dulakot				Sorath Harappan	Chitalwala 1985: key Figure 8	
Dumas				Sorath Harappan	Chitalwala 1985: key Figure 8	
Dumiani	Rajkot	21° 45' 00" N 70° 20' 00" E	-	Sorath Harappan	IAR 1958-59: 19 Possehl 1980: 97 Joshi et al. 1984: 530	
Dundkianwali	Bahawalpur	29° 01' 07" N 71° 12' 50" E	-	Mature Harappan	Mughal 1997: 47	3.20
Dungar	Muzaffarnagar	29° 15' 00" N 77° 22' 00" E	-	OCP/Post-urban Harappan	IAR 1986-87: 80	
Dungarpur	Rajkot	22° 03' 00" N 71° 31' 00" E	-	Late Sorath Harappan	IAR 1957-58: 19 Rao 1963a: 205 Possehl 1980: 97 Joshi et al. 1984: 530	
Dunkkian	Bahawalpur	29° 02' 13" N 71° 30' 06" E		Mature Harappan	F. A. Khan 1959a: 191 Mughal 1997: 47	9.40
Dunria	Pal Lahara			Copper Hoard	B. B. Lal 1951: 29 Makkhan Lal 1984a: 40-1	
Durad	Karnal			PGW Post-urban Harappan	IAR 1975-76:38	
Durad	Patiala	30° 10' 00" N 76° 27' 00" E	-	PGW Post-urban Harappan	Joshi et al. 1984: 527 Kumar 1978: 78	3.00
Durrah-i Bast	Makran	25° 45' 00" N 62° 30' 30" E	-	Dasht	Besenval and Sanlaville 1990: 105	
Dwarka	Jamnagar	22° 13' 00" N 69° 00' 00" E	-	Post 1500 A.D. 13-15th Century 12-13th Century Early Historic-Medieval 900-500 B.C.(?) Lustrous Red Ware	IAR 1979-80: 25-9 K. K. Bhan 1986: 20	
Edith Shahr	Las Bela	26° 23' 00" N 66° 20' 00" E	-	Kulli	Fairservis 1971a: 195-201 Possehl 1986a: 151	20.00
Elana	Unknown			Copper Hoard	R. C. Agrawala 1979 Makkhan Lal 1984a: 36-7	

Faiz Mohammad	Quetta-Pishin	29° 57' 00" N 67° 06' 00" E	·	Quetta Damb Sadaat Kechi Beg Togau	Fairservis 1956a: 196	1.70
Fala	Jamnagar			Sorath Harappan	Chitalwala 1985: key Figure 8	
Faridpur	Saharanpur	30° 06' 00" N 77° 45' 00" E		Post-urban Harappan	Joshi et al. 1984: 522	
Fariyadka	Bhavnagar			Sorath Harappan	IAR 1980-81: 12	
Farmana One	Sonepat			Sothi-Siswal	Suraj Bhan 1975: 125	
Farmana Two	Sonepat			Post-urban Harappan	Suraj Bhan 1975: 125	
Fatehgarh	Farrukhabad			Copper Hoard	Anderson 1883: 405-08	
					Makkhan Lal 1984a: 34-5	
Fatehpur	Muzaffarnagar	29° 27' 45" N 77° 22' 50" E	-	PGW OCP/Post-urban Harappan	Gaur and Lal 1992: 378	
Fatehpur Jat	Saharanpur	29° 56' 00" N 77° 31' 00" E	-	OCP Mature Harappan	IAR 1966-67: 43 Joshi et al. 1984: 521, 522	
Fatehpur, Saharanpur	Saharanpur	29° 53' 00" N 77° 32' 00" E	-	OCP Mature Harappan	IAR 1966-67: 43 Dikshit 1982a: 115 Joshi et al. 1984: 521, 522	
Firoz Kahn Damb	Makran	26° 30' 00" N 65° 16' 00" E	-	Londo Kulli	Stein 1931: 130-31	2.90
Footariya	Mehsana	23° 37' 00" N 71° 43' 00" E	-	Anarta	K. K. Bhan 1994:	0.03
G. B. 11	Ganganagar	29° 15' 00" N 73° 28' 00" E	-	Mature Harappan	Dikshit 1984b: 67	
G. B. 12	Ganganagar	29° 16' 00" N 73° 26' 00" E	-	Sothi-Siswal	Stein 1943a: 75	
G. B. 16	Ganganagar	29° 15' 00" N 73° 28' 00" E	-	Sothi-Siswal	Stein 1943a: 75	
G. B. 72	Ganganagar			Mature Harappan	IAR 1977-78: 47	
G. B. 80	Ganganagar			Mature Harappan	IAR 1977-78: 47	
Gaddiawala Ther	Rahimyar Khan	28° 34' 09" N 70° 46' 32" E	-	Mature Harappan	Mughal 1997: 47	3.30
Gadhada	Bhavnagar	21° 58' 20" N 71° 33' 45" E	-	Sorath Harappan	Chitalwala 1985: key Figure 8	
Gadhada One	Rajkot	22° 26' 00" N 70° 36' 00" E	-	Sorath Harappan	IAR 1960-61: 8 Possehl 1980: 97 Joshi et al. 1984: 530	
Gadhada Three	Rajkot	22° 26' 00" N 70° 36' 00" E	-	Sorath Harappan	IAR 1960-61: 8 Possehl 1980: 98 Joshi et el. 1984: 530	
Gadhada Two	Rajkot	22° 26' 00" N 70° 36' 00" E	-	Sorath Harappan	IAR 1960-61: 8 Possehl 1980: 98 Joshi et al. 1984: 530	
Gadharia				Sorath Harappan	Chitalwala 1985: key Figure 8	
Gadhiyano Timbo	Mehsana	23° 31' 00" N 71° 53' 00" E	-	Lustrous Red Ware	Joshi et al. 1984: 529 K. K. Bhan 1994: 86-7	
Gadhrona	Saharanpur	29° 46' 00" N 77° 58' 00" E	-	Post-urban Harappan	Joshi et al. 1984: 522	
Gadhwal Two	Rohtak			Early Historic PGW Sothi-Siswal	A.Ghosh 1989a: Vol. II, 144	
Gadhwaliwadi	Kutch	23° 30' 00" N 69° 08' 00" E	-	Mature Harappan	IAR 1976-77: 74 IAR 1978-79: 94 Joshi et al. 1984: 529	

758

Gadia	Jamnagar	22° 15' 00" N 70° 65' 00" E	-	Late Sorath Harappan Sorath Harappan	K. K. Bhan 1989: 236	1.00
Gadiwali	Bahawalpur	28° 47' 25" N 71° 20' 25" E	-	Mature Harappan	Mughal 1997: 47	0.10
Gagsina	Karnal	29° 34' 00" N 76° 53' 00" E	-	Post-urban Harappan Sothi-Siswal	Suraj Bhan 1975: 125 Suraj Bhan & Shaffer 1978: 62 Joshi et al. 1984: 519, 524	3.50
Gajar Damb	Jhalawan	26° 06' 50" N 65° 34' 00" E	-	Kulli Amri-Nal Kechi Beg	Stein 1931: 151	
Gaji Bhut	Jhalawan	26° 59' 00" N 66° 05' 00" E	-	Partho-Sassanian Londo Nal	Raikes 1968b: 152-53	
Gajju Khera	Patiala	30° 35' 00" N 76° 28' 00" E	-	Post-urban Harappan	Joshi et al. 1984: 527	
Gajjuwala Ther	Bahawalpur	28° 50' 13" N 71° 06' 56" E	-	Mature Harappan	Mughal 1997: 47	12.90
Gajjuwala Two	Bahawalpur	28° 50' 20" N 71° 07' 06" E	-	Hakra Wares	Mughal 1997: 42	16.70
Galarian	Hoshiarpur	31° 57' 00" N 75° 39' 00" E	-	Post-urban Harappan	Joshi et al. 1984: 526	
Galunda-i Dur	Jhunjhunu			OCP	IAR 1980-81: 56	
Galwadhi	Patiala	30° 42' 00" N 76° 14' 00" E	-	Post-urban Harappan	Joshi et al. 1984: 527	
Gamanwala	Bahawalpur	29° 11' 09" N 72° 22' 56" E	-	Kot Diji	Mughal 1997: 44	27.30
Gamapipalia				Sorath Harappan	Chitalwala 1985: key Figure 8	
Gameri	Kutch			Medieval Post-urban Harappan	IAR 1985-86: 17	
Gamuwala Ther	Bahawalpur	28° 47' 13" N 71° 06' 44" E	-	Cemetery H	Mughal 1997: 51	19.20
Gamuwali	Bahawalpur			Mature Harappan	Mughal 1997: 47	2.70
Ganario-no Thumdo	Banaskantha	23° 56' 10" N 71° 31' 00" E	-	Anarta with Microliths	Ajithprasad and Sonawane, in press	0.20
Gand Damb	Dera Ismail Khan			Late Kot Diji Kot Diji	Fairservis 1971c: 414	
Gandhara	Rohtak	28° 50' 00" N 76° 44' 00" E	-	Post-urban Harappan	Joshi et al. 1984: 525	
Gandhauli	Sitapur			Copper Hoard	IAR 1956-57: 74 IAR 1969-70: 38 Makkhan Lal 1984a: 34-5	
Gangana	Sonepat	29° 15' 00" N 76° 37' 00" E	-	Post-urban Harappan	Suraj Bhan 1975: 125 Joshi et al. 1984: 525	
Ganweriwala	Bahawalpur	28° 35' 56" N 71° 09' 00" E	-	Mature Harappan	Mughal 1997: 47	81.50
Gar Mound	Makran	26° 52' 00" N 63° 33' 00" E	-	Togau	Stein 1931: 47	
Garakwala	Bahawalpur	28° 54' 54" N 71° 14' 25" E	-	Mature Harappan	Stein 1943a: 170 Mughal 1997: 47 Dalal 1980: 12	8.10
Garani				Sorath Harappan	Chitalwala 1985: key Figure 8	
Garasya-no Thumdo	Banaskantha	24° 00' 30" N 71° 30' 00" E	-	Rangpur IIC Rangpur IIB	Ajithprasad and Sonawane, in press	0.10

Site	District	Coordinates		Period	Reference	Area
Garewala	Bahawalpur	28° 50' 20" N 71° 14' 52" E	-	Mature Harappan	Mughal 1997: 47	12.70
Garh	Saharanpur	29° 57' 00" N 77° 58' 00" E	-	Post-urban Harappan	Joshi et al. 1984: 523	
Garhi	Hissar	29° 04' 44" N 76° 05' 20" E	-	Post-urban Harappan Mature Harappan Sothi-Siswal	IAR 1980-81: 16 Joshi et al. 1984: 519, 521, 526 Mohan 1988: 84	2.00
Garhi Rodan	Kurukshetra	29° 57' 30" N 76° 43' 44" E	-	PGW Post-urban Harappan	Kumar 1978: 66	4.00
Garhi Sardaran	Kurukshetra	29° 57' 10" N 76° 41' 10" E	-	Post-urban Harappan	Joshi et al. 1984: 524	5.00
Garhwal, Sonepat	Sonepat	29° 11' 00" N 76° 32' 00" E	-	Post-urban Harappan Mature Harappan Sothi-Siswal	Joshi et al. 1984: 519, 521, 525	
Gate Dap	Makran	26° 07' 00" N 64° 13' 00" E	-	Islamic-British Nal Kechi Beg	Stein 1931: 108-09	1.10
Gathera	Saharanpur	30° 04' 00" N 77° 30' 00" E	-	Post-urban Harappan	Joshi et al. 1984: 523	
Gaunspur	Ludhiana	30° 57' 00" N 75° 42' 00" E	-	Medieval Kushan-Rang Mahal Post-urban Harappan	IAR 1980-81: 47	12.00
Gemuwala Dehar	Bahawalpur	28° 46' 55" N 71° 06' 32" E	-	Mature Harappan	Mughal 1997: 47	0.10
Gemuwali	Bahawalpur	28° 46' 44" N 71° 06' 45" E	-	Kot Diji	Mughal 1997: 44	0.01
Genghda Thumdo	Banaskantha	23° 50' 00" N 71° 22' 00" E	-	Anarta-Rangpur IIC	Ajithprasad and Sonawane, in press	0.10
Ghachi-no Bor	Mehsana	23° 36' 00" N 71° 53' 00" E	-	Mature Harappan(?) Anarta	K. K. Bhan 1994: 86-7	0.02
Ghadrona	Saharanpur	29° 46' 00" N 77° 58' 00" E	-	Post-urban Harappan	Joshi et al. 1984: 522	
Ghadwal One	Rohtak			Mature Harappan	A. Ghosh 1989a: Vol. II, 144	
Ghalaihak	Makran	26° 01' 00" N 63° 56' 00" E	-	Kili Ghul Mohammad	Stein 1931: 104	
Ghalegay Cave	Swat	34° 42' 00" N 72° 16' 00" E	-	Swat Proto-Historic Late Kot Diji Neolithic (Burj Basket-marked)	Stacul 1967 Stacul 1987: 29-49	
Ghamur Kheri	Kurukshetra	30° 00' 00" N 76° 48' 00" E	-	Post-urban Harappan	U. V. Singh 1976: 29 Joshi et al. 1984: 524	
Ghana Khandi	Saharanpur	30° 04' 00" N 77° 36' 00" E	-	OCP Mature Harappan	IAR 1966-67: 43 Joshi et al. 1984: 521, 523	
Ghannal Kund Damb	Jhalawan			Early Historic Iron Age Kechi Beg Togau	Fairservis 1971c: 405	
Gharaiyanwala	Bahawalpur	29° 12' 17" N 71° 51' 30" E	-	Mature Harappan	Mughal 1997: 47	1.10
Gharaunda	Karnal	29° 32' 02" N 76° 58' 13" E	-	Post-urban Harappan	Singh 1981: 53 Joshi et al. 1984: 524	1.00
Gharinda	Amritsar	31° 35' 00" N 74° 35' 00" E	-	Post-urban Harappan	Joshi et al. 1984: 526	

Site	District	Coordinates	Periods	References	Size
Gharo Bhiro	Thar Parkar	24° 58' 05" N – 69° 32' 00" E	Buddhist, Mature Harappan	Lambrick 1946: 59-60, Lambrick 1964: 89, Flam 1981a: 221	0.50
Gharwali	Jind	29° 10' 06" N – 76° 20' 31" E	PGW, Post-urban Harappan	Singh 1981: 80, Joshi et al. 1984: 525	1.20
Ghaswa	Hissar	29° 41' 29" N – 75° 40' 20" E	Post-urban Harappan, Sothi-Siswal	Joshi et al. 1984: 519, 526	6.90
Ghaswa One	Jind		Post-urban Harappan	Suraj Bhan 1975: 124	
Ghaswa Three	Jind		Sothi-Siswal	Suraj Bhan 1975: 124	
Ghatauli	Jind	29° 11' 07" N – 76° 21' 38" E	Mature Harappan, Sothi-Siswal	Singh 1981: 80, Joshi et al. 1984: 519, 521	0.90
Ghatoro	Rahimyar Khan	28° 20' 05" N – 70° 28' 13" E	Mature Harappan	Mughal 1997: 47	5.50
Ghatti	Sukkur		Mature Harappan	Mallah 1994: 175-77	·1.70
Ghazi Shah	Dadu	26° 27' 00" N – 67° 28' 00" E	Mature Harappan, Early to Mature Harappan Amri-Nal	Majumdar 1934: 79-86, Flam 1981a: 281	2.10
Ghaziwala Ther	Rahimyar Khan	28° 47' 33" N – 70° 55' 25" E	Mature Harappan	Mughal 1997: 47	0.30
Ghelo Bund	Bhavnagar	21° 58' 00" N – 71° 27' 00" E	Red Polished Ware, Late Sorath Harappan, Sorath Harappan	Possehl 1980: 98, Joshi et al. 1984: 530	4.20
Gheora	Patiala	30° 07' 00" N – 76° 16' 00" E	Post-urban Harappan, Mature Harappan	Suraj Bhan 1975: 123, Joshi et al. 1984: 522, 527	
Ghimana One	Jind	29° 15' 32" N – 76° 17' 16" E	Post-urban Harappan, Sothi-Siswal	Singh 1981: 80, Joshi et al. 1984: 519, 525	2.30
Ghodhapadar	Rajkot		Late Sorath Harappan	Joshi et al. 1984: 528	
Ghorwada	Rajkot	21° 57' 00" N – 71° 00' 00" E	Late Sorath Harappan, Sorath Harappan	IAR 1958-59: 19, Rao 1963a: 205, Possehl 1980: 98, Joshi et al. 1984: 528	
Ghul Shah Tup	Bannu	32° 27' 00" N – 70° 45' 00" E	Burj Basket-marked?, Kili Ghul Mohammad?	Khan, Knox and Thomas 1989: 288	
Ghumharianwala	Bhawalnagar	28° 47' 35" N – 71° 16' 24" E	Cemetery H	Mughal 1997: 51	2.00
Ghuram	Patiala	30° 07' 00" N – 76° 23' 00" E	Islamic, Medieval, Early Historic, PGW, Post-urban Harappan	Kumar 1978: 78, 81-7, Joshi et al. 1984: 527	
Ghuram Damb	Jhalawan	28° 42' 00" N – 66° 17' 00" E	Kulli, Amri-Nal, Kechi Beg	Stein 1931: 18, de Cardi 1983: 27, Possehl 1986a: 148	2.50
Ghurum	Makran		Amri-Nal, Kechi Beg	Fairservis 1971c: 408	
Gidar Windi	Ludhiana	30° 56' 00" N – 75° 25' 00" E	Medieval, Post-urban Harappan	IAR 1980-81: 48	4.00
Gilli Reg	Makran	26° 17' 15" N – 63° 55' 15" E	Zangian, Dasht	Besenval and Sanlaville 1990: 120-21	
Gitalpur	Karnal	29° 53' 00" N – 76° 49' 00" E	Medieval, Post-urban Harappan	Singh 1981: 54, Joshi et al. 1984: 524	
Godavari One	Jamnagar	22° 12' 00" N – 69° 55' 00" E	Late Sorath Harappan, Sorath Harappan, Microliths	K. K. Bhan 1989: 236	4.00

Godha	Banaskantha	23° 36' 00" N 71° 28' 00" E	-	Lustrous Red Ware Rangpur IIB-C	K. K. Bhan 1994: 86-7	0.40
Godha	Mehsana	23° 40' 00" N 71° 36' 00" E	-	Lustrous Red Ware	K. K. Bhan 1994: 86-7	0.40
Godhapadar	Rajkot	22° 15' 00" N 71° 03' 00" E	-	Late Sorath Harappan Sorath Harappan	IAR 1957-58: 19 Rao 1963a: 205 Possehl 1980: 98	
Godhiya-no Timbo	Mehsana	23° 30' 10" N 71° 53' 30" E	-	Lustrous Red Ware	Ajithprasad and Sonawane, in press	1.00
Gogrian One	Jind	29° 27' 46" N 76° 16' 20" E	-	Early Historic Post-urban Harappan	Singh 1981: 107 Joshi et al. 1984: 525	0.70
Gogrian Three	Jind	29° 27' 46" N 76° 15' 10" E	-	Post-urban Harappan	Singh 1981: 108 Joshi et al. 1984: 525	2.60
Gogrian Two	Jind	29° 27' 36" N 76° 15' 50" E	-	Medieval Early Historic Post-urban Harappan	Singh 1981: 107 Joshi et al. 1984: 525	1.90
Gokhijadio-no Timbo	Mehsana	23° 37' 00" N 71° 52' 30" E	-	Anarta (Pre-Harappan)	K. K. Bhan 1994: 86-7	0.50
Gokulpur	Gurgaon	27° 48' 00" N 77° 07' 00" E	-	Post-urban Harappan	Suraj Bhan 1975: 112 Joshi et al. 1984: 519, 526	
Gomal Kalan	Dera Ismail Khan	31° 54' 00" N 70° 52' 00" E	-	Kot Diji	Dani 1970-71: Fig. 1	
Gomsar-no Timbo	Surendranagar	23° 16' 20" N 71° 41' 25" E	-	Rangpur IIB-C Anarta	K. K. Bhan 1994: 86-7	5.00
Goni Timbo	Surendranagar	22° 27' 00" N 71° 55' 00" E	-	Sorath Harappan	IAR 1954-55: 59 Possehl 1980: 98 Joshi et al. 1984: 530	
Goongal Mar	Bahawalnagar	28° 47' 48" N 71° 21' 28" E	-	Cemetery H	Mughal 1997: 51	
Gop	Jamnagar	22° 01' 00" N 69° 56' 00" E	-	Late Sorath Harappan Sorath Harappan	IAR 1953-54: 38 Rao 1963a: 187, 205 Possehl 1980: 98 Joshi et al. 1984: 528	
Gopawala	Bahawalnagar	28° 53' 55" N 71° 17' 52" E	-	Cemetery H	Mughal 1997: 51	19.80
Gorandi 'A'	Dadu	26° 24' 00" N 67° 29' 00" E	-	Amri-Nal	Majumdar 1934: 87-91 Flam 1981a: 282-83	0.60
Gorandi 'B'	Dadu	26° 24' 00" N 67° 29' 00" E	-	Mature Harappan Amri-Nal	Majumdar 1934: 87-91 Flam 1981a: 284	
Gordhaniya Timbo	Surendranagar	23° 28' 00" N 71° 54' 00" E	-	Rangpur IIC Anarta	Ajithprasad and Sonawane in press K. K. Bhan 1994: 86-7	
Gorivata-no Timbo	Mehsana	23° 29' 20" N 71° 46' 00" E	-	Lustrous Red Ware	Hegde and Sonawane 1986: 30 K. K. Bhan 1989: 240 K. K. Bhan 1994: 86-7	0.60
Goriya	Jamnagar			Sorath or Late Sorath Harappan	IAR 1958-59: 69	
Gorpat	Jhalawan	28° 20' 00" N 66° 07' 00" E	-	Modern Islamic-British Kechi Beg Togau Burj Basket-marked	de Cardi 1983: 29	
Gorsian Qadir	Ludhiana	30° 57' 00" N 75° 33' 00" E	-	Early Medieval Kushan Post-urban Harappan	IAR 1980-81: 48	4.50

Gossain	Jind	29° 12' 50" N - 76° 22' 28" E	Post-urban Harappan Mature Harappan Sothi-Siswal	Mohan 1988: 86	3.80
Guddal 'B'	Bahawalpur	29° 07' 10" N - 71° 58' 20" E	Kot Diji	Mughal 1997: 44	6.40
Guddal Ther	Bahawalpur	29° 07' 15" N - 71° 57' 23" E	Mature Harappan	Mughal 1997: 47	1.70
Guddal 'A'	Bahawalpur	29° 07' 14" N - 71° 57' 05" E	Mature Harappan	Mughal 1997: 47	1.90
Gudel	Kheda	22° 44' 00" N - 72° 31' 00" E	Sorath Harappan Microliths	Momin 1976: 53 Momin 1979: 106 Momin 1984	3.00
Gudri Mound	Sibi	29° 32' 00" N - 67° 23' 00" E	Early Historic Partho/Sassanian Iron Age Quetta Damb Sadaat	Fairservis 1956a: 200 Enault and Jarrige 1973: 193-94	1.70
Gujranwala	Bahawalpur	29° 08' 17" N - 72° 21' 02" E	Kot Diji	Mughal 1997: 44 Stein 1943a: 127 Dalal 1980: 10	6.30
Gulab Garh	Kurukshetra	29° 57' 00" N - 76° 47' 00" E	Post-urban Harappan	Joshi et al. 1984: 524	
Gulabgarh	Kurukshetra	29° 57' 45" N - 76° 47' 30" E	Post-urban Harappan	Kumar 1978: 67	1.50
Gulariya	Budaun		Medieval Early Historic PGW OCP	IAR 1978-79: 21	
Gularwala	Hissar	29° 43' 00" N - 75° 46' 00" E	Post-urban Harappan Mature Harappan Sothi-Siswal	IAR 1980-81: 16 Joshi et al. 1984: 519, 521, 526	
Gulistanpur, Bulandshahar	Bulandshahr	28° 30' 00" N - 77° 30' 00" E	PGW Post-urban Harappan	IAR 1963-64: 91 Joshi et al. 1984: 523	
Gulistanpur, Meerut	Meerut	28° 30' 00" N - 77° 30' 00" E	Mature Harappan	IAR 1963-64: 91 Joshi et al. 1984: 521	
Gumla	Dera Ismail Khan	31° 53' 00" N - 70° 50' 00" E	Gandhara Graves? Late Kot Diji Kot Diji Kechi Beg Kili Ghul Mohammad	Dani 1970-71: 22, 35-53	0.70
Gungeria	Balaghat		Copper Hoard	Anderson 1883: 414-15 V. Smith 1905: 233 Makkhan Lal 1984a: 36-7	
Gunkali	Jind	29° 16' 50" N - 76° 12' 34" E	Sothi-Siswal	Singh 1981: 82 Joshi et al. 1984: 519	0.50
Guntarighadh			Sorath Harappan	Chitalwala 1985: key Figure 8	
Gunthai	Kutch	23° 28' 00" N - 69° 09' 00" E	Mature Harappan	Possehl 1980: 98 Joshi et al. 1984: 529	
Gurah	Ludhiana	30° 50' 00" N - 75° 34' 00" E	Medieval Rang Mahal Post-urban Harappan (Bara)	IAR 1980-81: 48	6.00
Gurdas Nangalda Theh	Gurdaspur	32° 00' 00" N - 75° 22' 00" E	Post-urban Harappan	Joshi et al. 1984: 526	

Gurnikalan One	Bhatinda	29° 50' 00" N - 75° 33' 00" E	Rang Mahal Mature Harappan	Joshi et al. 1984: 520, 522 Joshi 1986: 139	144.00
Gurnikalan Two	Bhatinda	29° 50' 00" N - 75° 33' 00" E	Early Historic Mature Harappan Sothi-Siswal	Joshi et al. 1984: 520 Joshi 1986: 139	16.00
Gushanak	Makran	26° 14' 00" N - 64° 57' 00" E	Early Historic Iron Age Kechi Beg	Stein 1931: 117-118	
Gwani Kalat	Jhalawan	27° 29' 00" N - 65° 55' 00" E	Islamic-British Early Islamic Partho-Sassanian Early Historic Kechi Beg	Stein 1931: 164-165	0.05
Hadi	Jhalawan	28° 18' 00" N - 66° 40' 00" E	Londo Anjira Amri-Nal Kechi Beg Togau	Mughal 1972a: 148 de Cardi 1983: 30	
Hadi Bux-jee-Wandh	Sukkur		Mature Harappan	Mallah 1994: 139-40	7.50
Hadi Bux-jee-Wandh Two	Sukkur		Mature Harappan	Mallah 1994: 178-79	2.70
Hadiyana One	Jamnagar	22° 35' 00" N - 70° 15' 00" E	Late Sorath Harappan Sorath Harappan	K. K. Bhan 1989: 236	0.40
Hadmatala	Ahmedabad	22° 30' 00" N - 72° 08' 00" E	Sorath Harappan	IAR 1978-79: 4 Joshi et al. 1984: 530	
Hadwa	Jind		Medieval Historic Post-urban Harappan	Singh 1981: 341	
Hadwa			Post-urban Harappan	Mohan 1988: 86	2.90
Haiduk-no Thumdo Two	Banaskantha	23° 56' 00" N - 71° 31' 00" E	Lustrous Red Ware	Ajithprasad and Sonawane, in press	0.20
Hajanbi	Rajkot	22° 50' 00" N - 70° 35' 00" E	Sorath Harappan	IAR 1959-60: 68 Possehl 1980: 98	
Hakim Ali Ther	Bahawalpur	29° 07' 13" N - 71° 48' 28" E	Mature Harappan	Mughal 1997: 47	1.40
Hala Damb	Jhalawan	27° 37' 00" N - 66° 22' 00" E	Kulli Amri-Nal	Stein 1931: 169	2.30
Halenda			Sorath Harappan	Chitalwala 1985: key Figure 8	
Hamal Damb	Jhalawan	27° 40' 30" N - 66° 13' 30" E	Londo Kechi Beg	Stein 1931: 169	
Hamalpur	Karnal	29° 33' 00" N - 76° 54' 00" E	Sothi-Siswal	Joshi et al. 1984: 519	
Hami	Palamau		Copper Hoard	S. C. Roy 1916: 482-83 Makkhan Lal 1984a: 38-9	
Hanaswala	Bahawalpur	29° 07' 45" N - 71° 58' 05" E	Mature Harappan	Mughal 1997: 47	3.60
Handali	Sangrur	30° 38' 00" N - 75° 51' 00" E	Post-urban Harappan Mature Harappan Sothi-Siswal	Joshi et al. 1984: 520, 522, 527	
Hansali	Patiala	30° 36' 00" N - 76° 29' 00" E	Post-urban Harappan	Joshi et al. 1984: 527	

Site	District	Coordinates		Period	Reference	Size
Hansdhera	Jind	29° 48' 03" N 76° 08' 30" E	-	Post-urban Harappan Sothi-Siswal	Mohan 1988: 88	3.80
Hansi	Hissar	29° 05' 00" N 75° 59' 00" E	-	Mature Harappan Sothi-Siswal	Joshi et al. 1984: 519, 521	
Hansyala	Kurukshetra	30° 01' 34" N 76° 47' 30" E	-	PGW Post-urban Harappan	Kumar 1978: 67 Joshi et al. 1984: 524	
Hanumanno Timbo	Bhavnagar	21° 57' 43" N 71° 34' 44" E	-	Recent Late Historic Red Polished Ware Late Sorath Harappan Sorath Harappan	Possehl 1980: 99 Joshi et al. 1984: 528	11.90
Harappa	Sahiwal	30° 38' 00" N 72° 52' 00" E	-	Cemetery H Transitional Mature Harappan Transitional Kot Diji Hakra/Ravi	Vats 1940 Meadow 1991a	100.00
Harda Kheri	Saharanpur	30° 02' 00" N 77° 28' 00" E	-	Post-urban Harappan	Joshi et al. 1984: 523	
Hardi	Sitapur			Copper Hoard	B. B. Lal 1951: 27 Makkhan Lal 1984a: 34-5	
Hardo Raval Khurd	Gurdaspur	31° 55' 00" N 74° 57' 00" E	-	Post-urban Harappan	Joshi et al. 1984: 526	
Harhari-no Thumdo	Banaskantha	23° 53' 00" N 71° 23' 30" E	-	Anarta-Rangpur IIC Microliths	Ajithprasad and Sonawane, in press	0.60
Hariana	Jamnagar	22° 36' 00" N 70° 15' 00" E	-	Sorath Harappan	Rao 1963a: 205 Possehl 1980: 99 Joshi et al. 1984: 528	0.50
Haribas	Saharanpur	29° 57' 00" N 77° 40' 00" E	-	Post-urban Harappan	Joshi et al. 1984: 523	
Haripur One	Jamnagar	22° 16' 00" N 70° 01' 00" E	-	Lustrous Red Ware	K. K. Bhan 1986: 20	
Haripur, Gurdaspur	Gurdaspur	31° 55' 00" N 74° 55' 00" E	-	Post-urban Harappan	Joshi et al. 1984: 526	
Haripur, Jullundur	Jullunder	31° 22' 00" N 75° 44' 00" E	-	Post-urban Harappan	Joshi et al. 1984: 526	
Harnauli	Ropar			Post-urban Harappan	Suraj Bhan 1975: 122	
Hartari	Karnal	29° 18' 52" N 76° 56' 07" E	-	Post-urban Harappan	Singh 1981: 67 Joshi et al. 1984: 524	0.20
Harthar-no Timbo	Mehsana	23° 26' 00" N 71° 49' 00" E	-	Lustrous Red Ware Amri-Nal Burial Pottery	Hegde and Sonawane 1986: 31 K. K. Bhan 1994: 86-7	2.20
Hasan Wali	Karachi	25° 00' 00" N 67° 19' 00" E	-	Mature Harappan	A.R.Khan 1968a: 4 Flam 1981a: 349	1.00
Hasanpur	Ropar	30° 21' 00" N 77° 07' 00" E	-	Post-urban Harappan	Joshi et al. 1984: 524	
Hasanpur	Surat	21° 25' 00" N 72° 46' 00" E	-	Lustrous Red Ware Late Sorath Harappan	Joshi et al. 1984: 524	
Hasanpur Two	Bhatinda	29° 59' 00" N 75° 33' 00" E	-	Early Historic Mature Harappan	Joshi et al. 1984: 529 Joshi 1986: 139	100.00
Hasilwala Ther	Bahawalpur	28° 48' 25" N 71° 07' 33" E	-	Mature Harappan	Mughal 1997: 47	8.30
Hassanpur	Ambala			Post-urban Harappan	Kumar 1978: 47	2.20

Hastinapura	Meerut	29° 09' 00" N	-	Medieval	Lal 1954-55: 5-151	
		78° 03' 00" E		Sunga-Kushan	Joshi et al. 1984: 523	
				NBP		
				PGW		
				OCP		
Hatampur	Saharanpur	29° 57' 00" N	-	Post-urban Harappan	Joshi et al. 1984: 522	
		78° 01' 00" E				
Hatchhoya One	Muzaffarnagar	29° 37' 00" N	-	Post-urban Harappan	Dikshit 1981: 72	
		77° 18' 00" E			Joshi et al. 1984: 523	
Hatchhoya Two	Muzaffarnagar	29° 36' 00" N	-	Post-urban Harappan	Dikshit 1981: 72	
		77° 18' 00" E			Joshi et al. 1984: 523	
Hathab	Bhavnagar			Sorath Harappan	IAR 1980-81: 12	
Hathala	Dera Ismail	32° 01' 00" N	-	Gandhara Graves	Dani 1970-71: 54-63	2.70
	Khan	70° 35' 50" E		Late Kot Diji		
				Kot Diji		
				Kechi Beg		
Hathial West	Rawalpindi	33° 45' 00" N	-	Kot Diji	F. R. Allchin 1982	0.50
		72° 50' 00" E				
Hathnaur 'A'	Ropar			Mature Harappan	IAR 1975-76: 38	
Hathnaur 'B'	Ropar			Mature Harappan	IAR 1975-76: 38	
Hatho One	Jind	29° 36' 35" N	-	Post-urban Harappan	Joshi et al. 1984: 519, 525	6.00
		76° 11' 18" E				
Hatho Two	Jind	29° 38' 00" N	-	Post-urban Harappan	Suraj Bhan & Shaffer 1978: 62	2.20
		76° 11' 00" E		Sothi-Siswal	Joshi et al. 1984: 519, 525	
Hathwala	Jind	29° 06' 18" N	-	Post-urban Harappan	Joshi et al. 1984: 525	3.20
		76° 27' 50" E				
Hawara	Ropar	30° 50' 00" N	-	Post-urban Harappan	Joshi et al. 1984: 527	
		76° 24' 00" E			IAR 1953-54: 38	
					Suraj Bhan 1975: 122	
Hazaribagh	Hazaribagh			Copper Hoard	Foote 1916: 164	
					Makkhan Lal 1984a: 38-9	
Helmana Khurd	Alwar			OCP	IAR 1980-81: 55	
Hemadra	Rajkot			Lustrous Red Ware	Chitalwala 1979: 115	0.20
Her	Amritsar	31° 40' 00" N	-	Post-urban Harappan	Joshi et al. 1984: 526	
		74° 48' 00" E				
Hirke	Bhatinda	29° 44' 00" N	-	Post-urban Harappan	IAR 1980-81: 45	25.00
		75° 22' 00" E		Mature Harappan	Joshi et al. 1984: 520	
					Joshi 1986: 139	
Hirke, Hissar	Hissar			Post-urban Harappan	Suraj Bhan 1975: 122	
Hisham Dheri	Dera Ismail	31° 58' 00" N	-	Late Kot Diji	Dani 1970-71: 31	
	Khan	70° 46' 00" E				
Hodthali				Sorath Harappan	Chitalwala 1985: key Figure 8	
Holivalo	Bhavnagar	21° 57' 00" N	-	Lustrous Red Ware	IAR 1960-61: 8	
		71° 40' 00" E			Rao 1963a: 205	
					Possehl 1980: 99	
					Joshi et al. 1984: 528	
Hor Kalat	Makran	26° 12' 00" N	-	Kulli	Stein 1931: 111-12	0.60
		64° 39' 00" E		Amri-Nal	Possehl 1986a: 148	
Hotewala Ther 'A'	Bahawalpur	28° 55' 30" N	-	Kot Diji	Mughal 1997: 44	2.80
		71° 13' 26" E				
Hotewala Ther 'B'	Bahawalpur	28° 55' 23" N	-	Mature Harappan	Mughal 1997: 47	3.00
		71° 13' 20" E				

Hotewala Two	Bahawalpur	28° 55' 28" N 71° 13' 35" E	-	Hakra Wares	Mughal 1997: 42	1.10
Hudia Two	Kurukshetra	30° 08' 00" N 77° 07' 00" E	-	Post-urban Harappan	Kumar 1978: 68-9 Joshi et al. 1984: 524	1.60
Hulas	Saharanpur	29° 42' 00" N 77° 22' 00" E	-	Kushan PGW Post-urban Harappan	IAR 1980-81: 73-6 Joshi et al. 1984: 523	0.20
Hulas Khera	Saharanpur	29° 42' 00" N 77° 22' 00" E	-	Mature Harappan	Joshi et al. 1984: 521	
Hurro Damb	Jhalawan	27° 06' 00" N 66° 10' 00" E	-	Burj Basket-marked	Raikes 1968b: 155	
Hussainpur Bopada	Muzaffarnagar	29° 21' 10" N 77° 42' 20" E	-	NBP OCP/Post-urban Harappan	Gaur and Lal 1992: 378	
Huzur Nagar	Muzaffarnagar	29° 19' 00" N 77° 40' 00" E	-	PGW OCP/Post-urban Harappan	Gaur and Lal 1992: 378	
Inderwa-no Timbo One	Banaskantha	24° 01' 10" N 71° 28' 00" E	-	Lustrous Red Ware	Ajithprasad and Sonawane, in press	0.40
Inderwa-no Timbo Two	Banaskantha	24° 01' 00" N 71° 29' 00" E	-	Microliths-Rangpur IIC	Ajithprasad and Sonawane, in press	0.10
Indilapur	Saharanpur			Copper Hoard	B. B. Lal 1951: 29 Makkhan Lal 1984a: 34-5	
Indo-Pak Boundary Site	Ganganagar	29° 12' 30" N 73° 03' 00" E	-	Rang Mahal Mature Harappan	Dalal 1980: 34	
Indranagar-no Thumdo	Banaskantha	23° 53' 00" N 71° 35' 00" E	-	Rangpur IIC Rangpur IIB	Ajithprasad and Sonawane, in press	0.02
Indranaj	Kheda	22° 30' 00" N 72° 33' 00" E	-	Late Sorath Harappan Sorath Harappan Microliths	Momin 1976: 51-2 Momin 1979: 107-08	
Indus Delta Site	Tatta	24° 52' 00" N 67° 36' 00" E	-	Burj Basket-marked?	B. Allchin 1966: 94-5	
Inewala Theh	Faridkot	30° 33' 00" N 75° 25' 00" E	-	Post-urban Harappan Mature Harappan Sothi-Siswal	Joshi et al. 1984: 520, 522, 527	
Iserhel	Patiala	30° 38' 00" N 76° 31' 00" E	-	Post-urban Harappan	Joshi et al. 1984: 527	
Ishwar Godh	Banaskantha	23° 46' 00" N 71° 18' 00" E	-	Rangpur IIC	Ajithprasad and Sonawane, in press	0.10
Islam Chowki	Bannu	32° 59' 00" N 70° 29' 00" E	-	Late Kot Diji Kot Diji Kechi Beg	Allchin, Allchin, Durrani and Khan 1985: 9, 108 Khan, Knox and Thomas 1991a: 7-18	1.30
Isplinji One	Sarawan	29° 41' 30" N 67° 03' 00" E	-	Quetta Damb Sadaat Kechi Beg Togau	Anonymous 1964b: 15-6 de Cardi 1983: 20 Possehl 1986a: 147	1.20
Isplinji Two	Sarawan	29° 41' 30" N 67° 02' 30" E	-	Quetta Damb Sadaat Kechi Beg Togau Burj Basket-marked	Anonymous 1964b: 16-7 de Cardi 1983: 20	0.70
Isvaria	Bhavnagar	21° 58' 00" N 71° 42' 00" E	-	Late Sorath Harappan	Joshi et al. 1984: 528	

Itaria	Bhavnagar	21° 58' 00" N	-	Sorath or Late	Possehl 1980: 99	3.20
		71° 27' 00" E		Sorath Har	Joshi et al. 1984: 528	
Jafawala Three	Bahawalpur	28° 42' 30" N	-	Hakra Wares	Mughal 1997: 42	1.80
		71° 08' 20" E				
Jafawala Two	Bahawalpur	28° 42' 14" N	-	Hakra Wares	Mughal 1997: 42	6.90
		71° 07' 43" E				
Jafewala	Bahawalpur	28° 42' 30" N	-	Mature Harappan	Mughal 1997: 47	4.10
		71° 07' 29" E				
Jafewala Theri	Bahawalpur	28° 42' 30" N	-	Mature Harappan	Mughal 1997: 47	0.70
		71° 09' 05" E				
Jafrabad	Kheda	22° 25' 00" N	-	Sorath Harappan	Momin 1976: 52-3	8.00
		72° 32' 00" E			Momin 1979: 109	
Jagaroh	Kutch	23° 21' 00" N	-	Medieval	IAR 1986-87: 29	
		70° 11' 00" E		Post-urban Harappan		
Jagjai	Quetta-Pishin			Quetta	Mughal 1972a: 148	
				Damb Sadaat		
Jagria	Gurdaspur	32° 05' 00" N	-	Post-urban Harappan	Joshi et al. 1984: 526	
		75° 29' 00" E				
Jagtapirno Dhoro	Rajkot			Lustrous Red Ware	Chitalwala 1979: 115	0.70
Jahan	Jhalawan	28° 17' 00" N	-	Kulli	de Cardi 1983: 34	
		67° 12' 00" E		Amri-Nal		
				Kechi Beg		
				Togau		
Jahan Northeast	Jhalawan	28° 18' 00" N	-	Kulli-Harappan-Quetta	de Cardi 1964	
		67° 13' 00" E		Amri-Nal	de Cardi 1983: 34	
				Kechi Beg	Possehl 1986a: 148	
Jai Damb	Makran	26° 39' 00" N	-	Kulli	Stein 1931: 49-50	
		63° 24' 00" E			Possehl 1986a: 150	
Jaidak	Jamnagar	22° 40' 00" N	-	Late Sorath Harappan	Rao 1963a: 205	
		70° 35' 00" E		Sorath Harappan	IAR 1979-80: 25	
					Possehl 1980: 100	
					Joshi et al. 1984: 528	
Jainer	Saharanpur	30° 02' 00" N	-	Post-urban Harappan	Joshi et al. 1984: 523	
		77° 43' 00" E				
Jainpur	Saharanpur			OCP	IAR 1964-65: 44	
Jakhera	Etah	27° 51' 00" N	-	NBP	S. B. Singh 1976: 8-9	8.00
		78° 41' 00" E		PGW & NBP	IAR 1985-86: 79-81	
				PGW	Sahi 1990: 217	
				Proto-PGW		
				Black and Red Ware		
				OCP		
Jakhrapir-no Thumdo	Mehsana	24° 07' 00" N	-	Anarta-Rangpur IIC	Ajithprasad and Sonawane, in press	0.70
		71° 20' 00" E				
Jalharwala Ther	Bahawalpur	28° 50' 00" N	-	Mature Harappan	Stein 1943a: 167	2.30
		71° 25' 00" E			Dalal 1980: 12	
Jalilpur	Sahiwal	30° 32' 00" N	-	Kot Diji		13.00
		72° 07' 00" E		Hakra Wares	Mughal 1970: 88-9	
				(overlap)	Mughal 1972: 117-24	
Jalmana One	Karnal	29° 35' 00" N	-	Post-urban Harappan	Singh 1981: 55	1.50
		76° 44' 30" E		Mature Harappan	Joshi et al. 1984: 524	
Jalmana Two	Karnal	29° 35' 00" N	-	Post-urban Harappan	Singh 1981: 55	9.00
		76° 44' 00" E			Joshi et al. 1984: 521, 524	

Jalwali	Bahawalpur	29° 14' 21" N 72° 11' 39" E	-	Kot Diji	Mughal 1997: 44	22.50
Jalwali 'A'	Bahawalpur	28° 51' 22" N 71° 23' 00" E	-	Hakra Wares	Mughal 1997: 42	3.70
Jalwali 'B'	Bahawalpur	28° 51' 23" N 71° 22' 52" E	-	Hakra Wares	Mughal 1997: 42	1.80
Jamathar-no Thumdo	Banaskantha	23° 45' 00" N 71° 14' 00" E	-	Rangpur IIC Rangpur IIB	Ajithprasad and Sonawane, in press	1.00
Jambalpur	Sikar			OCP and Microliths	IAR 1981-82: 62	
Jamuwali 'A'	Bahawalpur	28° 55' 54" N 71° 10' 08" E	-	Mature Harappan	Mughal 1997: 47	4.20
Jamuwali 'B'	Bahawalpur	28° 55' 17" N 71° 10' 23" E	-	Mature Harappan	Mughal 1997: 47	2.80
Jandheri	Muzaffarnagar	29° 40' 00" N 77° 26' 00" E	-	Post-urban Harappan	Dikshit 1981: 72 Joshi et al. 1984: 523	
Jangipar	Bahawalpur	28° 40' 47" N 71° 04' 43" E	-	Hakra Wares	Mughal 1997: 42	2.80
Janiwali	Bahawalpur	28° 41' 52" N 71° 17' 47" E	-	Mature Harappan	Mughal 1997: 48	4.20
Januwala	Bahawalpur	29° 08' 00" N 71° 59' 00" E	-	Kot Diji	Stein 1943a: 121	5.90
Januwali Dhar	Bahawalpur	28° 50' 00" N 71° 25' 00" E	-	Kot Diji	Stein 1943a: 122 Dalal 1980: 9	2.90
Jarejo Kalat 0.10	Dadu	26° 54' 00" N	-	Mature Harappan	Krishna Deva and McCown 1949: 27-8	
		67° 14' 00" E		Amri-Nal	Flam 1981a: 260	
Jaren	Makran	26° 13' 00" N 64° 45' 00" E	-	Kulli Amri-Nal Kechi Beg	Stein 1931: 112 Possehl 1986a: 148	0.20
Jaroji	Las Bela			Kulli Early Kulli	Fairservis 1961b & c	
Jasal	Muzaffarnagar	29° 21' 00" N 77° 17' 00" E	-	Post-urban Harappan	Dikshit 1981: 72 Joshi et al. 1984: 523	
Jasapar	Jamnagar	22° 12' 00" N 70° 25' 00" E	-	Lustrous Red Ware	K. K. Bhan 1986: 18	
Jasat	Gurgaon	28° 18' 00" N 76° 38' 00" E	-	Post-urban Harappan	Joshi et al. 1984: 526	
Jasvantgadh	Amreli			Late Sorath Harappan Sorath Harappan	A. F. Cunningham, unpublished	2.00
Jatavadar	Kutch	23° 45' 00" N 70° 40' 00" E	-	Mature Harappan	Joshi et al. 1984: 529	
Jatheri	Kurukshetra	29° 44' 00" N 76° 33' 00" E	-	PGW Post-urban Harappan	Suraj Bhan 1975: 125 Joshi et al. 1984: 524	
Jathewali	Bahawalpur	29° 10' 42" N 72° 17' 26" E	-	Kot Diji	Mughal 1997: 44	3.30
Jatoiwala Ther	Bahawalpur	29° 06' 55" N 71° 52' 15" E	-	Mature Harappan	Mughal 1997: 48	1.90
Jatoiwala 'A'	Bahawalpur	29° 07' 20" N 71° 56' 51" E	-	Kot Diji	Mughal 1997: 44	1.60
Jatoiwala 'B'	Bahawalnagar	29° 07' 10" N 71° 56' 50" E	-	Cemetery H	Mughal 1997: 51	1.60
Jaula	Muzaffarnagar	29° 16' 45" N 77° 25' 00" E	-	PGW OCP/Post-urban	Gaur and Lal 1992: 378	

Jaurasi Khas	Karnal	29° 15' 06" N 77° 02' 58" E	-	Harappan Medieval Early Historic PGW Post-urban Harappan	Joshi et al. 1984: 524	2.20
Javantri	Banaskantha	23° 54' 00" N 71° 33' 00" E	-	Anarta-Rangpur IIC	Ajithprasad and Sonawane, in press	0.02
Jawaiwala Ther	Bahawalpur	28° 43' 43" N 71° 04' 03" E	-	Mature Harappan	Mughal 1997: 48	5.40
Jawaiwala Two	Bahawalpur	28° 43' 54" N 71° 04' 22" E	-	Hakra Wares	Mughal 1997: 42	2.10
Jawanpura	Panch Mahals			Sorath or Late Sorath Harappan	IAR 1959-60: 68	
Jawarji Kalat	Jhalawan	27° 31' 00" N 65° 52' 00" E	-	Modern Islamic-British Early Islamic Partho-Sassanian Early Historic Kechi Beg Togau	Stein 1931: 165	0.60
Jebri Damb One	Jhalawan	27° 17' 20" N 65° 45' 00" E	-	Amri-Nal	Stein 1931: 153,163	0.10
Jebri Damb Two	Jhalawan	27° 17' 20" N 65° 45' 10" E	-	Kechi Beg Kili Ghul Mohammad	Stein 1931: 153,163	0.50
Jejalam	Rahimyar Khan	28° 31' 47" N 70° 51' 00" E	-	Mature Harappan	Mughal 1997: 48	0.01
Jhakar	Jamnagar	22° 14' 00" N 69° 41' 00" E	-	Sorath or Late Sorath Har	K. K. Bhan 1986: 20	
Jhal	Muzaffarnagar	29° 16' 15" N 77° 20' 50" E	-	NBP PGW OCP/Post-urban Harappan	Gaur and Lal 1992: 378	
Jhalar	Bahawalpur	28° 42' 45" N 71° 07' 10" E	-	Hakra Wares	Mughal 1997: 42	16.20
Jhaloriano Tekro	Ahmedabad			Sorath Harappan	IAR 1976-77: 74	
Jhamola	Jind	29° 08' 50" N 76° 20' 30" E	-	Post-urban Harappan Sothi-Siswal	Singh 1981: 83 Joshi et al. 1984: 519, 525	2.20
Jhandada-no Thumdo One	Banaskantha	23° 54' 20" N 71° 27' 00" E	-	Anarta-Lustrous Red Ware	Ajithprasad and Sonawane, in press	0.80
Jhandada-no Thumdo Two	Banaskantha	23° 54' 10" N 71° 27' 00" E	-	Anarta-Rangpur IIC	Ajithprasad and Sonawane, in press	0.01
Jhandewala Ther	Rahimyar Khan	28° 43' 15" N 70° 58' 29" E	-	Mature Harappan	Mughal 1997: 48	3.50
Jhandewala Two	Rahimyar Khan	28° 43' 05" N 70° 59' 02" E	-	Hakra Wares	Mughal 1997: 42	1.10
Jhang	Campbellpur	33° 34' 00" N 72° 40' 00" E	-	Late Kot Diji Kot Diji	Mughal 1972a: 131 Thomas and Allchin 1986	6.40
Jhangar	Dadu	26° 21' 00" N 67° 43' 30" E	-	Jhangar	Majumdar 1934: 68-70	2.50
Jhangar, Anjar	Kutch	23° 19' 00" N 70° 05' 00" E	-	Mature Harappan	IAR 1965-66: 14 Possehl 1980: 100 Joshi et al. 1984: 528 Joshi 1990b: 418	8.00

Jhangar, Khavada	Kutch	23° 53' 00" N 69° 44' 00" E	-	Mature Harappan	Chitalwala 1985: key Figure 8	
Jhanjari	Karnal	29° 45' 00" N 76° 59' 00" E	-	Post-urban Harappan	Suraj Bhan 1975: 125 Joshi et al. 1984: 524	
Jhansal	Ganganagar	29° 16' 00" N 75° 00' 00" E	-	Mature Harappan	Dikshit 1984b: 61	
Jhikri	Rajkot	21° 55' 00" N 70° 50' 00" E	-	Sorath Harappan	IAR 1959-60: 68 Possehl 1980: 100 Joshi et al. 1984: 530	
Jhinjar	Mahendragarh	28° 40' 00" N 76° 20' 00" E	-	Post-urban Harappan	Suraj Bhan 1975: 126 Joshi et al. 1984: 526	
Jhinjhana	Muzaffarnagar	29° 30' 00" N 77° 15' 00" E	-	PGW OCP	Joshi et al. 1984: 523	
Jhogrodi	Ludhiana	30° 50' 00" N 76° 10' 00" E	-	Post-urban Harappan	Joshi et al. 1984: 527	
Jhukar	Larkana	27° 34' 00" N 68° 07' 00" E	-	Jhukar Mature Harappan	Banerji: 1918-19: 58 Majumdar 1934: 5-18 Mughal 1992a Flam 1981a: 222	10.30
Jhumtiwala	Bahawalpur	28° 49' 04" N 71° 16' 40" E	-	Kot Diji	Mughal 1997: 44	2.80
Jinaj	Kheda	22° 24' 00" N 72° 36' 00" E	-	Sorath Harappan	Momin 1979: 110 Momin 1984	
Jind Five	Jind	29° 19' 00" N 76° 19' 00" E	-	Medieval Early Historic Mature Harappan Sothi-Siswal	Singh 1981: 83 Joshi et al. 1984: 519, 521	
Jind Four	Jind	29° 19' 00" N 76° 21' 45" E	-	Post-urban Harappan	Singh 1981: 84 Joshi et al. 1984: 519, 521	0.90
Jind Two	Jind	29° 19' 30" N 76° 19' 00" E	-	Early Historic Mature Harappan Sothi-Siswal	Singh 1981: 338	
Jivanino Dhoro	Bhavnagar	21° 50' 29" N 71° 45' 34" E	-	Red Polished Ware Late Sorath Harappan Sorath Harappan	IAR 1960-61: 8 Rao 1963a: 205 Possehl 1980: 100 Joshi et al. 1984: 528	6.70
Jivapar	Jamnagar	22° 12' 00" N 70° 22' 00" E	-	Late Sorath Harappan Sorath Harappan	K. K. Bhan 1989: 237	0.30
Jivapur	Jamnagar			Late Sorath Harappan Sorath Harappan	K. K. Bhan 1986: 17	
Jiwaiwali	Bahawalpur	28° 52' 10" N 71° 26' 12" E	-	Mature Harappan	Mughal 1997: 48	1.90
Jiwan Khera	Jind	29° 24' 00" N 76° 23' 00" E	-	Post-urban Harappan	Suraj Bhan 1975: 125 Joshi et al. 1984: 525	
Jobalanesno Timbo	Ahmedabad			Sorath Harappan	IAR 1966-67: 8	
Jodhakann	Sirsa			Historic PGW Mature Harappan	IAR 1983-84: 31 IAR 1985-86: 32	
Jodhpur	Jhunjhunu			OCP	IAR 1980-81: 56	
Jodhpur	Rajkot	22° 40' 00" N 70° 53' 00" E	-	Sorath Harappan	IAR 1980-81: 56	
Jogiason Chak One	Ganganagar	29° 10' 00" N 74° 45' 00" E	-	Mature Harappan	Joshi et al. 1984: 522	

Jogiasson	Ganganagar	29° 10' 00" N	-	Sothi-Siswal	Joshi et al. 1984: 520	
		74° 45' 00" E				
Jogna Khera One	Kurukshetra	29° 59' 00" N	-	PGW	U. V. Singh 1976: 29	
		76° 48' 00" E		Post-urban Harappan	Joshi et al. 1984: 524	
Jogna Khera Two	Kurukshetra	29° 59' 20" N	-	Post-urban Harappan	Kumar 1978: 305	
		76° 48' 20" E				
Jokha	Surat	21° 17' 00" N	-	E. Hist-Medieval	Mehta, Chowdhary, Hegde and	2.00
		73° 00' 00" E		Black and red Ware	Shah 1971	
				L. Sorath Har-Malwa	IAR 1966-67: 10	
Janoya-no Timbo	Surendranagar	23° 25' 00" N	-	Lustrous Red Ware	IAR 1982-83: 28	0.50
		71° 51' 20" E		Microliths	Hegde and Sonawane 1986: 31	
					K. K. Bhan 1994: 86-7	
Joshi	Karnal	29° 25' 08" N	-	Medieval	Singh 1981: 68	0.20
		76° 45' 28" E		Early Historic	Joshi et al. 1984: 524	
				Post-urban Harappan		
Judeirjo-daro	Kachi	28° 28' 00" N	-	Mature Harappan	Anonymous 1964b: 11-2	25.00
		68° 15' 00" E			Flam 1981a: 251-53	
Julani Khera	Jind	29° 38' 30" N	-	Post-urban Harappan	Singh 1981: 108	1.00
		76° 18' 51" E			Joshi et al. 1984: 525	
					Mohan 1988: 90	
Juna Chopadwa	Kutch	23° 16' 00" N	-	Mature Harappan	IAR 1986-87: 29	
		70° 15' 00" E				
Juna Rampur	Bhavnagar			Sorath Harappan	IAR 1980-81: 12	
				Microliths		
Jungla Populzai	Quetta-Pishin	30° 51' 00" N	-	Modern	Fairservis 1956a: 200	0.50
		66° 45' 00" E		Quetta		
Juni Timbo	Jamnagar	22° 09' 00" N	-	Sorath Harappan	IAR 1980-81: 13	1.50
		70° 22' 00" E			K. K. Bhan 1989: 241	
K-1	Sarawan	29° 57' 50" N	-	Quetta	Fairservis 1956a: 199	0.60
		66° 51' 00" E		Damb Sadaat		
				Kechi Beg		
Kabirpur	Saharanpur	30° 05' 00" N	-	OCP	IAR 1966-67: 43	
		77° 38' 00" E		Mature Harappan	Joshi et al. 1984: 523	
Kabracha	Jind	29° 33' 30" N	-	Post-urban Harappan	Singh 1981: 108-09	0.80
		76° 13' 20" E			Joshi et al. 1984: 525	
					Mohan 1988: 91	
Kachcho Buthi	Dadu	25° 47' 00" N	-	Amri-Nal?	Majumdar 1934: 129	
		67° 46' 00" E			Flam 1981a: 322	
Kachha-no Thumdo	Banaskantha	23° 53' 00" N	-	Lustrous Red Ware	Ajithprasad and Sonawane, in	0.01
		71° 24' 30" E			press	
Kachha-no Timbo	Banaskantha	23° 59' 00" N	-	Lustrous Red Ware	Ajithprasad and Sonawane, in	0.01
		71° 20' 00" E			press	
Kachhwa One	Karnal	29° 43' 40" N	-	Post-urban Harappan	Suraj Bhan 1975: 125	
		76° 53' 21" E			Singh 1981: 55, 336	
Kachhwa Two	Karnal	29° 44' 00" N	-	Post-urban Harappan	Singh 1981: 56	0.60
		76° 53' 00" E			Joshi et al. 1984: 524	
Kacho Timbo	Mehsana	23° 25' 00" N	-	Lustrous Red Ware	IAR 1978-79: 7	1.60
		71° 45' 00" E			Joshi et al. 1984: 529	
					K. K. Bhan 1994: 86-7	
Kachrana Kalan	Jind	29° 29' 32" N	-	Post-urban Harappan	Singh 1981: 85	2.60
		76° 18' 07" E		Sothi-Siswal	Joshi et al. 1984: 519, 525	
Kaddon	Ludhiana	30° 46' 00" N	-	Post-urban Harappan	Joshi et al. 1984: 527	
		76° 02' 00" E				

Kaddour Damb	Dera Ismail Khan			Kot Diji Kechi Beg	Fairservis 1971c: 413	
Kaero Timbo	Surendranagar	22° 24' 00" N 71° 55' 00" E	-	Sorath Harappan	IAR 1954-55: 59 Possehl 1980: 101 Joshi et al. 1984: 530	
Kafir Kot	Sarawan			Quetta Amri-Nal Kechi Beg	Fairservis 1971c: 401	
Kagvadar				Sorath Harappan	Chitalwala 1985: key to Figure 8	
Kaharbari	Hazaribagh			Copper Hoard	Makkhan Lal 1984a: 38-9	
Kai Buthi	Dadu	26° 20' 00" N 67° 36' 00" E	-	Amri-Nal	Lambrick 1944: 67-8 Flam 1981a: 292	1.30
Kailapur	Muzaffarnagar	29° 20' 00" N 77° 59' 00" E	-	Post-urban Harappan	Joshi et al. 1984: 523	
Kailaspur	Saharanpur	29° 59' 00" N 77° 39' 00" E	-	OCP Mature Harappan	IAR 1966-67: 43 Joshi et al. 1984: 521, 523	
Kainnaur	Ropar			Mature Harappan	IAR 1964-65: 33	
Kainor	Ropar			Post-urban Harappan	IAR 1962-63: 17 Suraj Bhan 1975: 122	
Kainur	Ropar	30° 50' 00" N 76° 30' 00" E	-	Post-urban Harappan	IAR 1964-65: 28 Joshi et al. 1984: 527	
Kaiyanwala One	Bahawalpur	28° 49' 35" N 71° 18' 05" E	-	Mature Harappan	Mughal 1997: 48	5.50
Kaiyanwala Two	Bahawalnagar	28° 48' 50" N 71° 18' 17" E	-	Cemetery H	Mughal 1997:51	6.0
Kaj	Amreli	20° 44' 00" N 70° 51' 00" E	-	Sorath Harappan	IAR 1957-58: 19 Rao 1963a: 205 Possehl 1980: 101 Joshi et al. 1984: 528	11.70
Kala Garh	Kurukshetra	29° 47' 00" N 76° 30' 00" E	-	Post-urban Harappan	Joshi et al. 1984: 524 Suraj Bhan & Shaffer 1978: 62 Joshi et al. 1984: 524	
Kalahetti	Saharanpur	29° 42' 00" N 77° 13' 00" E	-	Post-urban Harappan	Dikshit 1982a: 115 Joshi et al. 1984: 523	3.10
Kalait One	Jind	29° 40' 38" N 76° 15' 23" E	-	Islamic NBP PGW Post-urban Harappan Mature Harappan Sothi-Siswal	Suraj Bhan 1975: 124 Singh 1981: 109, 340 Joshi et al. 1984: 519, 521, 525	0.70
Kalait Three	Jind	29° 41' 38" N 76° 15' 53" E	-	Post-urban Harappan	Singh 1981: 109	2.20
Kalait Two	Jind	29° 40' 48" N 76° 15' 23" E	-	Early Historic Post-urban Harappan	Singh 1981: 109, 340 Datt 1980: 139	
Kalako Deray	Swat	34° 45' 30" N 72° 24' 30" E	-	Northern Neolithic Swat Proto-Historic	Stacul 1987: 53-127	
Kalapan	Rajkot	21° 55' 00" N 70° 20' 00" E	-	Late Sorath Harappan Sorath Harappan	IAR 1957-58: 19 Rao 1963a: 205 Possehl 1980: 101 Joshi et al. 1984: 528	
Kalarino Timbo	Mehsana	23° 30' 10" N 71° 45' 00" E	-	Lustrous Red Ware	Hegde and Sonawane 1986: 30 K. K. Bhan 1994: 86-7	2.00
Kalaro Damb	Jhalawan	27° 05' 00" N	-	Kulli	Stein 1931: 150	

		65° 34' 30" E			Possehl 1986a: 147	
Kalat	Sarawan	29° 01' 00" N	-	Amri-Nal	de Cardi 1983: 25	
		66° 24' 00" E		Kechi Beg		
Kalat Damb	Makran			Kulli	Field 1959	
					Possehl 1986a: 150	
Kalatuk Bund	Makran	26° 08' 00" N	-	Islamic	Besenval and Sanlaville 1990:	0.05
		62° 01' 30" E		Shahi Tump	109	
				Dasht		
Kalatuk Damb	Makran	27° 22' 45" N	-	Kulli	Stein 1931: 36-7	14.70
		65° 09' 00" E			Possehl 1986a: 150	
Kalavad Four	Jamnagar	22° 12' 00" N	-	Late Sorath Harappan	IAR 1957-58: 19	0.20
		70° 22' 00" E		Sorath Harappan	K. K. Bhan 1989: 237	
Kalavad Three	Jamnagar	22° 12' 00" N	-	Late Sorath Harappan	IAR 1957-58: 19	0.10
		70° 22' 00" E		Sorath Harappan	K. K. Bhan 1989: 237	
Kalavad Two	Jamnagar	22° 12' 00" N	-	Late Sorath Harappan	IAR 1957-58: 19	1.00
		70° 22' 00" E		Sorath Harappan	K. K. Bhan 1989: 237	
Kalawati	Jind	29° 20' 20" N	-	Post-urban Harappan	Joshi et al. 1984: 525	2.50
		76° 32' 34" E			Mohan 1988: 91	
Kalbeto	Saharanpur			Mature Harappan	IAR 1965-66: 54	
Kalepar	Bahawalpur	29° 10' 15" N	-	Kot Diji	Mughal 1997: 43	8.60
		72° 03' 35" E			Dalal 1980: 9	
Kalharwala	Bahawalpur	28° 52' 25" N	-	Mature Harappan	Mughal 1997: 48	6.60
		71° 15' 02" E				
Kalharwala 'B'	Bahawalpur	28° 52' 12" N	-	Hakra Wares	Mughal 1997: 42	1.00
		71° 15' 00" E				
Kalian	Sangrur	30° 35' 00" N	-	Post-urban Harappan	IAR 1982-83: 65	
		75° 43' 00" E		Mature Harappan	Joshi et al. 1984: 520, 522,	
				Sothi-Siswal	527	
Kalianpur	Jamnagar	21° 50' 00" N	-	Late Sorath Harappan	Rao 1963a: 205	
		69° 25' 00" E		Sorath Harappan	Possehl 1980: 101	
					Joshi et al. 1984: 528	
Kalibangan	Ganganagar	29° 25' 00" N	-	Mature Harappan	Tessitori 1918-19: 23	11.50
		74° 05' 00" E		Sothi-Siswal	Stein 1943a: 49-52	
					Joshi et al. 1984: 520	
Kalipat	Rajkot			Sorath Harappan	IAR 1957-58: 19	
					Possehl 1980: 101	
Kaliwaryal	Bahawalpur	29° 10' 00" N	-	Kot Diji	Stein 1943a: 117-18	2.60
		71° 58' 00" E			Dalal 1980: 9	
Kaliyar	Bahawalpur	29° 09' 48" N	-	Mature Harappan	Mughal 1997: 48	2.60
		71° 43' 44" E				
Kallag	Makran	26° 18' 00" N	-	Kulli-Harappan	Stein 1931: 114-15	
		64° 53' 00" E		Amri-Nal	Possehl 1986a: 148	
Kallur	Raichur			Copper Hoard	Makkhan Lal 1984a: 40-1	
Kalram	Jind	29° 42' 44" N	-	Medieval	Singh 1981: 109	1.20
		76° 21' 52" E		Post-urban Harappan		
Kalvad One	Jamnagar			Sorath Harappan	IAR 1980-81: 13	
Kalvad Two	Jamnagar			Sorath Harappan	IAR 1980-81: 13	
Kalvad Three	Jamnagar			Sorath Harappan	IAR 1980-81: 13	
Kalwa One	Jind	29° 20' 07" N	-	Post-urban Harappan	Singh 1981: 110	1.60
		76° 31' 00" E			Mohan 1988: 92	
Kalwa Two	Jind	29° 21' 38" N	-	Post-urban Harappan	Mohan 1988: 94	3.80
		76° 31' 30" E				
Kalwa, Kurukshetra	Kurukshetra	30° 07' 00" N	-	Post-urban Harappan	Joshi et al. 1984: 524	
		76° 58' 00" E				

Kalwa, Patiala	Patiala	30° 25' 00" N 76° 26' 00" E	-	Post-urban Harappan	Joshi et al. 1984: 527	
Kalwah	Kurukshetra	30° 07' 00" N 76° 58' 58" E	-	Post-urban Harappan	Kumar 1978: 69	3.00
Kalwan Two	Jind	29° 42' 16" N 75° 58' 17" E	-	Post-urban Harappan	Singh 1981: 110 Joshi et al. 1984: 525	0.50
Kalyanpur Three	Jamnagar	21° 41' 00" N 69° 37' 00" E	-	Lustrous Red Ware	K. K. Bhan 1986: 19	
Kamalapur	Hardoi			OCP & Copper Hoard	IAR 1978-79: 101	
Kamalpur, Hardoi	Hardoi			Copper Hoard	Shastri 1915: 4 Makkhan Lal 1984a: 34-5	
Kamalpur, Jind	Jind	29° 36' 01" N 76° 20' 03" E	-	Early Historic Post-urban Harappan	Singh 1981: 111 Joshi et al. 1984: 525 Mohan 1988: 94	1.00
Kamar Band	Makran	26° 18' 00" N 64° 56' 30" E	-	Kulli Amri-Nal	Stein 1931: 115 Possehl 1986: 148	0.50
Kambar Damb	Makran	26° 28' 00" N 65° 14' 00" E	-	Londo Kulli Amri-Nal	Stein 1931: 129-130 Possehl 1986: 148	2.40
Kambaro Damb	Makran	26° 26' 30" N 65° 25' 30" E	-	Kulli	Stein 1931: 131 Possehl 1986: 148	
Kamdera	Ranchi			Copper Hoard	Makkhan Lal 1984a: 38-9	
Kan Mehtarzai One	Zhob	30° 43' 30" N 67° 33' 00" E	-	Burj Basket-marked	Stein 1929a: 80 Mughal 1972a: 148	
Kanadia Thumdo	Rajkot	24° 01' 00" N 71° 28' 50" E		Anarta-Rangpur IIB-C	Ajithprasad and Sonawane, in press	0.30
Kanasutaria	Ahmedabad	22° 47' 00" N 72° 16' 00" E	-	Lustrous Red Ware Late Sorath Harappan	IAR 1954-55: 59 Rao 1963a: 188, 206 Possehl 1980: 102 Joshi et al. 1984: 530	
Kandai	Loralai			Waziri Kot Diji	Mughal 1972a: 148	
Kanadai One	Jind	29° 23' 02" N 76° 20' 23" E	-	Post-urban Harappan	Singh 1981: 85 Joshi et al. 1984: 525	0.80
Kanadala Two	Jind	29° 23' 30" N 76° 19' 30" E	-	Medieval PGW Post-urban Harappan Sothi-Siswal	Singh 1981: 85-6 Joshi et al. 1984: 519, 525	4.00
Kander Bhit	Sukkur	27° 25' 00" N 69° 01' 00" E	-	Mature Harappan	Lambrick 1946: 52 Flam 1981a: 223	1.10
Kandera Fort	Rahimyar Khan	28° 05' 00" N 70° 12' 00" E	-	Mature Harappan	Stein 1943a: 100-01 Dalal 1980: 8	0.20
Kandhi Wahi Buthi	Dadu			Amri-Nal	Lambrick 1944: 63 Flam 1981a: 288	
Kandholi	Kurukshetra	30° 05' 00" N 77° 00' 00" E	-	Post-urban Harappan	Joshi et al. 1984: 524	
Kanewal, Keseri Sing No Timbo	Kheda	22° 28' 00" N 72° 30' 00" E	-	Lustrous Red Ware	IAR 1972-73: 10 IAR 1974-75: 13 IAR 1977-78: 21 Momin 1979: 110-11 Momin 1984	5.00
Kanewal, Sai No Tekro	Kheda	22° 27' 00" N 72° 30' 00" E	-	Lustrous Red Ware Microliths	IAR 1972-73: 10 IAR 1974-75: 13	6.00

				IAR 1977-78: 21	
				Momin 1979: 110-11	
				Mehta, Momin and Shah 1980	
				Momin 1982	
				Momin 1984	
Kanganwal	Ludhiana	30° 51' 00" N - 75° 56' 00" E	Post-urban Harappan Mature Harappan	IAR 1980-81: 47 Joshi et al. 1984: 522, 527	0.50
Kanjetar	Amreli	20° 45' 00" N - 70° 40' 00" E	Late Sorath Harappan Sorath Harappan	IAR 1956-57: 70 Rao 1963a: 181, 205 Possehl 1980: 102 Joshi et al. 1984: 528	2.30
Kanmer	Kutch		Medieval Mature Harappan	IAR 1985-86: 19	
Kannauj	Farrukhabad		OCP	IAR 1978-79: 101	0.80
Kanoli	Kurukshetra	30° 05' 00" N - 76° 58' 00" E	Post-urban Harappan	Kumar 1978: 70 Joshi et al. 1984: 524	4.00
Kanori	Loralai		Early Historic Mature Harappan Kot Diji Kechi Beg	Mughal 1972a: 148	
Kansala	Rohtak	28° 53' 00" N - 76° 46' 00" E	Post-urban Harappan	Suraj Bhan 1975: 125 Joshi et al. 1984: 526	
Kanthkot	Kutch	23° 29' 00" N - 70° 29' 00" E	Mature Harappan	IAR 1967-68: 17 Possehl 1980: 102 Joshi et al. 1984: 529	
Kanwa	Gurdaspur	32° 10' 00" N - 75° 30' 00" E	Post-urban Harappan	Joshi et al. 1984: 526	
Kapoto Damb	Jhalawan	28° 47' 00" N - 66° 40' 00" E	Kechi Beg Togau	Fairservis 1971c: 405	
Kapoto Rock Shelter	Jhalawan	28° 47' 00" N - 66° 40' 00" E	Kechi Beg Togau	Field 1959: 97-8, 189	
Kaptun Bra	Sarawan		Pathro-Sassanian Quetta Amri-Nal Kechi Beg Togau	Fairservis 1971c: 402	
Karahyo Pir	Thar Parkar	24° 24' 00" N - 68° 50' 00" E	Mature Harappan	A. R. Khan 1979 Baloch 1973 Baloch 1975 Flam 1981a: 224	
Karalan	Kapurthala	31° 23' 00" N - 75° 22' 00" E	Post-urban Harappan Sothi-Siswal	Joshi et al. 1984: 520, 526	
Karam Khan	Bahawalpur		Hakra Wares	Mughal 1997: 42	0.50
Karam Shah	Dera Ismail Khan	31° 57' 00" N - 70° 36' 50" E	Late Kot Diji Kot Diji	Dani 1970-71: 23-4	1.90
Karamgarh	Jind	29° 38' 00" N - 76° 03' 00" E	Early Historic Post-urban Harappan	Singh 1981: 111 Joshi et al. 1984: 525	2.60
Karan Khan Two	Bahawalnagar		Cemetery H	Mughal 1997: 51	1.90
Karandji Bhit	Sukkur		Mature Harappan	Lambrick 1946: 51 Flam 1981a: 225	
Karanpura	Bhatinda	29° 52' 00" N - 75° 23' 00" E	Mature Harappan	Joshi et al. 1984: 522 Joshi 1986: 139	25.00
Karchat	Dadu	25° 45' 00" N - 67° 44' 00" E	Mature Harappan	Majumdar 1934: 129-31 Flam 1981a: 323-24	4.70

Kardagap	Sarawan	29° 45' 00" N - 66° 18' 00" E	Quetta Amri-Nal	de Cardi 1983: 21	
Karela One	Jind	29° 08' 08" N - 76° 19' 56" E	Post-urban Harappan	Singh 1981: 86 Joshi et al. 1984: 525 Mohan 1988: 97	1.10
Karela Two	Jind	29° 08' 03" N - 76° 19' 27" E	Sothi-Siswal	Singh 1981: 86 Joshi et al. 1984: 519	
Karez Damb	Jhalawan	27° 05' 00" N - 66° 11' 00" E	Complex B Kulli	Raikes 1968b: 153-54 Possehl 1986a: 149 de Cardi 1983: 39	
Karez Site	Quetta-Pishin	30° 07' 00" N - 66° 57' 00" E	Damb Sadaat	Fairservis 1956a: 197	0.02
Karezgai	Zhob	30° 48' 30" N - 67° 45' 00" E	Partho-Sassanian Waziri Kot Diji Kechi Beg	Stein 1929a: 79-80	0.20
Kargushki Damb	Kharan	27° 29' 00" N - 65° 19' 00" E	Early Kulli Amri-Nal Kechi Beg	Stein 1931: 38-41 Possehl 1986a: 150	15.30
Karinkot	Alwar		OCP	IAR 1980-81: 55	
Kariyana	Muzaffarnagar	29° 23' 00" N - 77° 15' 00" E	Post-urban Harappan	Joshi et al. 1984: 523	
Karkak	Makran	25° 45' 00" N - 62° 20' 00" E	Dasht	Besenval and Sanlaville 1990: 106-07	
Karmalkota	Rajkot	21° 56' 01" N - 71° 00' 09" E	Sorath Harappan	Chitalwala 1985: key to Figure 8	3.40
Karmar	Rajkot	21° 50' 00" N - 70° 53' 00" E	Sorath Harappan	IAR 1977-78: 20 Joshi et al. 1984: 530	
Karo Kotiro	Larkana	27° 32' 00" N - 67° 20' 00" E	Mature Harappan Amri-Nal	Flam, unpublished	
Karohar Mound	Larkana	27° 30' 00" N - 67° 44' 00" E	Mature Harappan	Nissen 1983: 17	0.80
Karoti	Ganganagar	29° 10' 00" N - 74° 52' 00" E	Mature Harappan Sothi-Siswal	Joshi et al. 1984: 520, 522	
Karowala	Bahawalpur	28° 28' 35" N - 70° 58' 15" E	Mature Harappan	Mughal 1997: 48	1.10
Karowala Ther Two	Bahawalpur		Mature Harappan	Mughal 1997: 48	2.10
Karpas Buthi	Las Bela	26° 24' 30" N - 66° 20' 30" E	Kulli Early Kulli Amri-Nal	Fairservis 1961b & c Raikes 1968b Possehl 1986a: 151	
Karsa	Karnal	29° 38' 00" N - 76° 40' 00" E	Medieval Early Historic PGW Post-urban Harappan	B. Datt 1980: 80 Singh 1981: 336 Joshi et al. 1984: 524	
Karsola One	Jind	29° 09' 00" N - 76° 26' 00" E	Sothi-Siswal	Suraj Bhan 1975: 125 Singh 1981: 338	
Karsola Two	Jind	29° 09' 30" N - 76° 26' 00" E	Sothi-Siswal	Singh 1981: 86-7 Joshi et al. 1984: 519	1.10
Karsola, Sonepat	Sonepat		Post-urban Harappan	Suraj Bhan 1975: 125	

Kartarpur	Jullunder	31° 25' 00" N	-	Post-urban Harappan	Joshi et al. 1984: 526	
		75° 30' 00" E				
Kasano Relo	Surendranagar	23° 27' 00" N	-	Lustrous Red Ware		2.80
		71° 29' 20" E			K. K. Bhan 1994: 86-7	
Kasaur	Kurukshetra	30° 00' 00" N	-	Post-urban Harappan	Joshi et al. 1984: 524	
		76° 15' 00" E				
Kaseri	Meerut	28° 44' 00" N	-	Post-urban Harappan	Joshi et al. 1984: 523	
		77° 22' 00" E				
Kashi Qalat	Makran	25° 45' 10" N	-	Shahi Tump	Besenval and Sanlaville 1990:	
		62° 15' 30" E		Dasht	105-06	
Kashi Qalat	Makran	25° 45' 10" N	-	Shahi Tump?	Besenval and Sanlaville 1990:	
Cemetery		62° 15' 30" E		Dasht?	106	
Kashimi Damb,	Jhalawan	27° 24' 00" N	-	Medieval	Stein 1931: 176	4.00
				Kulli?		
Wadh		66° 25' 00" E		Amri-Nal	Raikes 1968b: 112, 146	
				Kechi Beg		
				Togau		
Kashimpur	Meerut	28° 50' 00" N	-	Post-urban Harappan	Joshi et al. 1984: 523	
		76° 40' 00" E				
Kashkai	Loralai			Waziri	Mughal 1972a: 148	
				Kot Diji		
				Kechi Beg		
Kasiano Dozakh	Quetta-Pishin	30° 27' 00" N	-	Damb Sadaat	Stein 1929a: 88	1.30
		66° 56' 00" E		Kechi Beg	Fairservis 1956a: 199	
				Togau		
				Burj Basket-marked		
				Kili Ghul Mohammad		
Kasmi Damb	Jhalawan			Modern	Fairservis 1971c: 405	
				Islamic-British		
				Kechi Beg		
				Togau		
Kasnati	Rohtak	28° 53' 00" N	-	Post-urban Harappan	Joshi et al. 1984: 526	
		76° 46' 00" E				
Kasor	Kurukshetra			PGW	Kumar 1978: 52	
				Post-urban Harappan		
Kasuna Three	Jind	29° 27' 00" N	-	Post-urban Harappan	Singh 1981: 112	1.10
		76° 15' 00" E			Joshi et al. 1984: 525	
Kasuna Two	Jind	29° 26' 00" N	-	Post-urban Harappan	Singh 1981: 111-12	2.20
		76° 16' 00" E			Joshi et al. 1984: 525	
Katadia-no	Banaskantha	23° 55' 10" N	-	Rangpur IIC	Ajithprasad and Sonawane, in	0.04
Thumdo		71° 20' 00" E			press	
Katana	Ludhiana	30° 50' 00" N	-	Post-urban Harappan	Joshi et al. 1984: 527	
		76° 04' 00" E				
Katasar	Kutch	23° 34' 00" N	-	Late Sorath Harappan	Rao 1963a: 188	
		70° 29' 00" E			Possehl 1980: 102	
					Joshi et al. 1984: 528	
Kathana Four	Jind	29° 32' 45" N	-	Post-urban Harappan	Singh 1981: 88	
		76° 22' 58" E			Joshi et al. 1984: 525	
Kathana One	Jind	29° 33' 04" N	-	Post-urban Harappan	Singh 1981: 87	1.90
		76° 22' 58" E			Joshi et al. 1984: 525	
Kathana Three	Jind	29° 32' 00" N	-	Post-urban Harappan	Singh 1981: 87-8	1.00
		76° 22' 00" E			Joshi et al. 1984: 525	

Kathana Two	Jind	29° 32' 23" N - 76° 23' 30" E		Post-urban Harappan Sothi-Siswal	Singh 1981 Joshi et al. 1984: 519, 525 Mohan 1988: 98	4.00
Kathpalon	Jullunder	31° 02' 00" N - 75° 51' 00" E		Post-urban Harappan-PGW Overlap	IAR 1963-64: 28 Suraj Bhan 1975: 122 Joshi et al. 1984: 526	
Kaudani	Zhob	31° 26' 00" N - 69° 18' 00" E		Partho-Sassanian Buddhist Waziri	Stein 1929a: 41-3 Fairservis 1959: 360	3.60
Kaul Heri	Saharanpur	29° 53' 00" N - 77° 17' 00" E		Post-urban Harappan	Joshi et al. 1984: 523	
Kaula Kheri	Saharanpur	29° 41' 00" N - 77° 18' 00" E		Post-urban Harappan Mature Harappan	Joshi et al. 1984: 523	
Kauriaganj	Aligarh			OCP	IAR 1965-66: 84	
Kausambi	Allahabad			Copper Hoard	V. Smith 1905: 232 Makkhan Lal 1984a: 36-7	
Kaushaya	Monghyr			Copper Hoard	Mukharjee 1935: 517 Makkhan Lal 1984a: 38-9	
Kazipur	Saharanpur	29° 58' 00" N - 77° 27' 00" E		Post-urban Harappan	Joshi et al. 1984: 523	
Kechi Beg	Quetta-Pishin	30° 07' 00" N - 66° 57' 00" E		Kechi Beg	Fairservis 1956a: 197, 218, 222 Mughal 1972a: 148 de Cardi 1983: 20	0.50
Kehiwali	Bahawalpur			Mature Harappan	Mughal 1997: 48	1.70
Kelbanwali	Bahawalpur			Mature Harappan	Mughal 1997: 48	0.90
Kelsi	Sagar			Copper Hoard	Makkhan Lal 1984: 38-9	
Kera	Singhbhum			Copper Hoard	Makkhan Lal 1984: 38-9	
Kerali	Rajkot	22° 00' 00" N - 70° 20' 00" E		Late Sorath Harappan	IAR 1958-59: 19 Rao 1963a: 205 Chitalwala 1979: 115 Possehl 1980: 102	0.80
Kerasi	Kutch	23° 40' 00" N - 70° 44' 00" E		Mature Harappan	IAR 1965-66: 12 Possehl 1980: 102 Joshi et al. 1984: 529 Joshi 1990: 412	30.50
Kerisimano Timbo	Kheda	22° 28' 00" N - 72° 31' 00" E		Sorath Harappan	Joshi et al. 1984: 530	
Kerlavlo	Bhavnagar	21° 51' 24" N - 71° 39' 32" E		Late Historic Late Sorath Harappan Sorath Harappan	IAR 1960-61: 8 Rao 1963a: 205 Possehl 1980: 103 Joshi et al. 1984: 528	1.40
Ket Ram	Jind	29° 41' 32" N - 76° 22' 00" E		Post-urban Harappan	Singh 1981: 109 Joshi et al. 1984: 525 Mohan 1988: 99	0.20
Khadianwala	Sheikhupura	31° 37' 00" N - 73° 44' 00" E		Kot Diji	Dar 1983	0.30
Khairgarh Ther	Rahimyar Khan	28° 28' 00" N - 70° 50' 46" E		Mature Harappan	Mughal 1997: 48	2.00
Khaja Ahmadpur	Karnal	29° 51' 00" N - 76° 55' 00" E		Post-urban Harappan	Singh 1981: 56-7 Joshi et al. 1984: 524	
Khajur	Dadu	25° 42' 00" N - 67° 47' 00" E		Amri-Nal	Majumdar 1934: 134-35	1.20
Khakhar	Kheda	22° 27' 00" N - 72° 30' 00" E		Lustrous Red Ware	Momin 1979: 114	

Khakhar Buthi	Las Bela	26° 19' 00" N 66° 16' 00" E	-	Kechi Beg Togau Burj Basket-marked Kili Ghul Mohammad	Fairservis 1961b & c Raikes 1968b: 157 A. R. Khan 1979: 67-71	2.30
Khakhara Bela One	Rajkot	22° 29' 00" N 70° 35' 00" E	-	Sorath Harappan	IAR 1960-61: 9	
Khakhara Bela Three	Rajkot	22° 29' 00" N 70° 35' 00" E	-	Sorath Harappan	IAR 1960-61: 9 Possehl 1980: 103	
Khakhra Dera	Kutch	23° 34' 00" N 70° 29' 00" E	-	Mature Harappan	IAR 1960-61: 8 Possehl 1980: 103 Joshi et al. 1984: 529	
Khaksar	Kheda	22° 27' 00" N 72° 30' 00" E	-	Sorath Harappan	Momin 1976: 53 Momin 1979: 114-15 Momin 1984	12.00
Khamba Hera	Kurukshetra	30° 06' 00" N 76° 20' 00" E	-	Post-urban Harappan	Joshi et al. 1984: 524	
Khambahera	Kurukshetra			Post-urban Harappan (OCP)	Kumar 1978: 52	1.50
Khambalano Dhore	Amreli			Late Sorath Harappan Sorath Harappan	A. F. Cunningham, unpublished	2.00
Khambhodhar	Jamnagar	21° 45' 00" N 69° 35' 00" E	-	Late Sorath Harappan Sorath Harappan	IAR 1957-58: 19 Rao 1963a: 205 Possehl 1980: 103 Joshi et al. 1984: 528	7.50
Khan Kandewala 'A'	Bahawalpur	28° 50' 00" N 71° 24' 10" E	-	Mature Harappan	Mughal 1997: 48	11.10
Khan Kandewala 'B'	Bahawalpur	28° 50' 04" N 71° 24' 15" E	-	Mature Harappan	Mughal 1997: 48	4.5
Khan Kandewala 'C'	Bahawalpur	28° 50' 17" N 71° 24' 22" E	-	Mature Harappan	Mughal 1997: 48	3.00
Khan Kandewala 'D'	Bahawalpur	28° 50' 10" N 71° 24' 22" E	-	Hakra Wares	Mughal 1997: 42	1.60
Khan Kandewali 'E'	Bahawalnagar	28° 50' 02" N 71° 24' 20" E	-	Cemetery H	Mughal 1997: 51	0.60
Khandadhar				Sorath Harappan	Chitalwala 1985: key to Figure 8	
Khandariya	Kutch			Late Medieval Mature Harappan(?)	IAR 1985-86: 19	
Khanderio One	Bhavnagar	21° 58' 00" N 71° 29' 00" E	-	Modern Red Polished Ware Sorath or Late Sorath Harappan	IAR 1960-61: 8 Possehl 1980: 192 Joshi et al. 1984: 528	2.60
Khanderio Two	Bhavnagar	21° 58' 00" N 71° 30' 00" E	-	Late Sorath Harappan Sorath Harappan	Possehl 1980: 104 Joshi et al. 1984: 528	5.70
Khandewal	Gurgaon	27° 43' 00" N 77° 03' 00" E	-	Post-urban Harappan	Joshi et al. 1984: 526	
Khanjahanpur	Muzaffarnagar			Medieval PGW OCP	Srivastava 1982: 70-3	2.20
Khannda	Rawalpindi			Kot Diji	Mughal 1972a: 132	1.20
Khanpar	Rajkot			Sorath Harappan	Chitalwala 1979: 115	5.00
Khanpur, Bulandshahar	Bulandshahr	28° 25' 00" N 77° 34' 00" E	-	Post-urban Harappan	Joshi et al. 1984: 523	
Khanpur, Kaira	Kheda	22° 29' 00" N	-	Sorath Harappan	IAR 1972-73: 10	

		72° 23' 00" E		IAR 1974-75: 13	
				Momin 1979: 115-16	
				Momin 1984	
Khanpur, Rajkot	Rajkot		Sorath Harappan	Chitalwala and Thomas 1978	
Khanpur, Surendranagar	Surendranagar	22° 32' 00" N - 71° 58' 00" E	Sorath Harappan	IAR 1962-63: 8 Possehl 1980: 104 Joshi et al. 1984: 530	
Khanpuri	Bahawalpur	28° 45' 05" N - 71° 17' 15" E	Mature Harappan	Stein 1943a: 168-69 Mughal 1997: 48 Dalal 1980: 12	27.50
Khanpuri Two	Bahawalpur	28° 45' 10" N - 71° 16' 25" E	Hakra Wares	Mughal 1997: 42	0.30
Khapran	Jind	29° 25' 14" N - 76° 10' 18" E	Medieval Post-urban Harappan Sothi-Siswal	Singh 1981: 113 Joshi et al. 1984: 525	2.20
Khar Khoda	Meerut	28° 50' 00" N - 76° 45' 00" E	Post-urban Harappan	Joshi et al. 1984: 523	
Kharak Pandwan	Jind	29° 40' 00" N - 76° 17' 00" E	Early Historic NBP PGW Post-urban Harappan Sothi-Siswal	Joshi et al. 1984: 519, 525	
Kharal One	Jind	29° 42' 10" N - 76° 04' 30" E	Post-urban Harappan Sothi-Siswal	Singh 1981: 99, 113 Joshi et al. 1984: 519, 525	1.00
Kharal Three	Jind	29° 42' 00" N - 76° 03' 00" E	Mature Harappan Sothi-Siswal	Singh 1981: 114 Joshi et al. 1984: 521	1.00
Kharal Two	Jind	29° 41' 48" N - 76° 04' 52" E	Sothi-Siswal	Singh 1981: 114 Joshi et al. 1984: 519 Mohan 1988: 100	2.20
Kharanti	Jind	29° 10' 07" N - 76° 19' 10" E	PGW Post-urban Harappan	Singh 1981: 88-9 Joshi et al. 1984: 525	1.90
Kharar	Hissar	29° 08' 57" N - 75° 53' 42" E	Sothi-Siswal	Suraj Bhan 1975: 123 IAR 1980-81: 16 Joshi et al. 1984: 521 Mohan 1988: 100	1.70
Khared			Sorath Harappan	Chitalwala 1985: key to Figure 8	
Khareda			Sorath Harappan	Chitalwala 1985: key to Figure 8	
Kharedano Timbo	Rajkot	22° 05' 00" N - 70° 48' 00" E	Sorath Harappan	IAR 1967-68: 9 Possehl 1980: 104 Joshi et al. 1984: 530	
Khari-nu Khetar	Banaskantha	23° 59' 10" N - 71° 26' 00" E	Chalcolithic Blade Manufacturing	Ajithprasad and Sonawane, in press	0.30
Kharika Khanda	Kutch	23° 27' 00" N - 70° 19' 00" E	Mature Harappan	IAR 1965-66: 14 Possehl 1980: 105 Joshi et al. 1984: 529	
Kharuwala Ther	Ganganagar	29° 03' 00" N - 73° 31' 00" E	Sothi-Siswal	Stein 1943a: 73	3.70
Kharwan	Ropar	30° 12' 00" N - 77° 22' 00" E	OCP	Suraj Bhan & Shaffer 1978: 62 Joshi et al. 1984: 524	
Khatariya-no Timbo	Mehsana	23° 42' 00" N - 71° 51' 00" E	Late Sorath Harappan Sorath Harappan	K. K. Bhan 1994: 86-7	1.50

Khatauli	Saharanpur	30° 00' 00" N -	OCP	IAR 1964-65: 44	
		77° 40' 00" E	Mature Harappan	IAR 1966-67: 43	
				Joshi et al. 1984: 523	
Khatkar One	Jind	29° 24' 08" N -	Early Historic	Singh 1981: 114	1.00
		76° 15' 46" E	Post-urban Harappan	Joshi et al. 1984: 525	
Khatli			Sorath Harappan	Chitalwala 1985: key to Figure 8	
Khatoli	Mahendragarh	28° 05' 00" N -	Post-urban Harappan	R. P. Sharma 1982: 123-25	0.10
		76° 15' 00" E			
Khavda	Kutch		Mature Harappan	IAR 1977-78: 20	
Khayali Vero	Sukkur		Mature Harappan	Mallah 1994: 180-81	1.10
Kheda Jat	Saharanpur		OCP/Post-Urban	IAR 1984-85: 92	
			Harappan		
Khedoi	Kutch	23° 03' 00" N -	Mature Harappan	IAR 1970-71: 13	
		69° 57' 00" E	Microliths	IAR 1976-77: 15	
				Joshi et al. 1984: 529	
Khedwala	Jaipur		OCP	IAR 1972-73: 29	
Khema Kheri	Jind	29° 14' 00" N -	Post-urban Harappan	Singh 1981: 89	1.90
		76° 23' 12" E	Sothi-Siswal	Joshi et al. 1984: 519, 525	
				Mohan 1988: 102	
Khera	Ludhiana		OCP	IAR 1973-74: 23	
			Post-urban Harappan		
Khera, Haryana	Jind	29° 20' 00" N -	Post-urban Harappan	Joshi et al. 1984: 525	
		76° 30' 00" E			
Khera, Punjab	Patiala	30° 36' 00" N -	Post-urban Harappan	Joshi et al. 1984: 527	
		76° 29' 00" E			
Kheradano			Sorath Harappan	Pande & Ramachandran 1971: 39	
Timbo					
Kherai	Swat	34° 54' 00" N -	Swat Proto-Historic	Stacul 1987: 53-127	
Graveyard		72° 49' 00" E			
Kheri Barki	Hissar	29° 17' 00" N -	Post-urban Harappan	IAR 1980-81: 16	
		75° 46' 00" E		Joshi et al. 1984: 526	
Kheri Gaurian	Patiala	30° 23' 00" N -	PGW	IAR 1976-77: 43	
		76° 15' 00" E	Post-urban Harappan	Joshi et al. 1984: 527	
Kheri Man	Karnal	29° 50' 00" N -	Post-urban Harappan	Suraj Bhan 1975: 125	
Singh		77° 00' 00" E		Joshi et al. 1984: 524	
Kheri Nudh	Ludhiana	30° 44' 00" N -	Post-urban Harappan	IAR 1961-62: 103	
Singh		76° 22' 00" E		Suraj Bhan 1975: 122	
				Joshi et al. 1984: 527	
Kheri Raiwali	Kurukshetra	29° 52' 00" N -	Post-urban Harappan	Kumar 1978: 59-60	3.00
		76° 33' 00" E		Joshi et al. 1984: 524	
Kheri Safa	Jind	29° 31' 10" N -	Early Historic	Singh 1981: 114-15	1.10
		76° 10' 01" E	Post-urban Harappan	Joshi et al. 1984: 525	
				Mohan 1988: 102	
Kheri Sherkhan	Jind	29° 33' 57" N -	Post-urban Harappan	Singh 1981: 115	0.80
		76° 10' 02" E		Joshi et al. 1984: 525	
Khetarvalo	Bhavnagar	21° 48' 00" N -	Lustrous Red Ware	IAR 1960-61: 7	3.40
		71° 37' 00" E		Rao 1963a: 206	
				Possehl 1980: 105	
				Joshi et al. 1984: 528	
Kheth Talvadi	Mehsana	23° 39' 30" N -	Lustrous Red Ware	IAR 1982-83: 28	0.20
		71° 45' 10" E		Joshi et al. 1984: 529	
				K. K. Bhan 1994: 86-7	

Khetranwali One	Bahawalpur	28° 57' 34" N 71° 16' 30" E	-	Mature Harappan	Mughal 1997: 48	3.30
Khetranwali Two	Bahawalpur	28° 57' 34" N 71° 16' 15" E	-	Mature Harappan	Mughal 1997: 48	2.40
Khetwal Ther	Bahawalpur	29° 10' 00" N 72° 01' 00" E	-	Cemetery H	Stein 1943a: 118 Dalal 1980: 9	5.90
Khewtal	Bahawalnagar	29° 10' 22" N 71° 58' 43" E	-	Cemetery H	Mughal 1997: 51	6.60
Khiching	Mayurbhanj			Copper Hoard	Mohapatra 1964: 45-7 Makkhan Lal 1984a: 40-1	
Khingarwali	Bahawalpur	28° 49' 28" N 71° 23' 50" E	-	Mature Harappan	Mughal 1997: 48	0.50
Khiplewala	Bahawalpur	28° 44' 00" N 71° 01' 05" E	-	Mature Harappan	Mughal 1997: 48	0.50
Khiplewala Ther	Bahawalpur			Mature Harappan	Mughal 1997: 48	12.70
Khiplewala Two	Bahawalpur	28° 44' 25" N 71° 01' 55" E	-	Mature Harappan	Mughal 1997: 48	3.90
Khiplewali	Bahawalpur	28° 43' 32" N 71° 01' 00" E	-	Hakra Wares	Mughal 1997: 42	4.90
Khiplewali Three	Bahawalpur	28° 43' 00" N 71° 01' 33" E	-	Hakra Wares	Mughal 1997: 42	6.60
Khiplewali Two	Bahawalpur	28° 43' 22" N 71° 01' 13" E	-	Hakra Wares	Mughal 1997: 42	8.50
Khirasara				Sorath Harappan	Chitalwala 1985: key to Figure 8	
Khodiyar, Talaja	Bhavnagar	21° 24' 05" N 71° 59' 24" E	-	Late Sorath Harappan Sorath Harappan	Rao 1963a: 206 Possehl 1980: 105 Joshi et al. 1984: 528	0.50
Khodiyar, Valabhipur	Bhavnagar	21° 58' 00" N 71° 57' 00" E	-	Sorath Harappan	Possehl 1980: 105	
Khoedada	Zhob			Kot Diji Kechi Beg Togau	Mughal 1972a: 148	
Khohi Siddhuwali	Bahawalpur	28° 57' 13" N 71° 13' 25" E	-	Mature Harappan	Mughal 1997: 48	1.80
Khokhari One	Jind	29° 20' 00" N 76° 20' 00" E	-	PGW Post-urban Harappan	Suraj Bhan 1975: 124 Joshi et al. 1984: 525	
Khokhari Two	Jind	29° 20' 00" N 76° 20' 00" E	-	PGW Post-urban Harappan	Suraj Bhan 1975: 124 Joshi et al. 1984: 525	
Khopala				Sorath Harappan	Chitalwala 1985: key to Figure 8	
Khorana				Sorath Harappan	Chitalwala 1985: key to Figure 8	
Khosa-daro	Sukkur	25° 44' 00" N 69° 35' 00" E	-	Mature Harappan	Lambrick 1946: 52 Flam 1981a: 226	
Khudo Pir	Larkana	27° 27' 00" N 67° 28' 00" E	-	Mature Harappan Amri-Nal (w/ Kot Diji)	Flam, unpublished	
Khurdi	Nagaur			Copper Hoard	IAR 1960-61: 66 Makkhan Lal 1984a: 36-7	
Khwaja Zabar	Sarawan	29° 00' 00" N 66° 24' 00" E	-	Islamic Londo Togau Burj Basket-marked	Stein 1931: 185 Mughal 1972a: 148 deCardi 1983: 25	
Kikri	Bahawalpur	28° 43' 45" N 71° 19' 57" E	-	Mature Harappan	Mughal 1997: 48	1.20

Kikri Two	Bahawalpur	28° 43' 07" N 71° 19' 30" E	-	Hakra Wares	Mughal 1997: 42	4.10
Kikriwala Ther	Bahawalpur	28° 44' 55" N 71° 18' 57" E	-	Mature Harappan	Mughal 1997: 48	1.30
Kilayanpura 'B'	Jaipur			OCP	IAR 1973-74: 24	
Kilbaiwala	Bahawalpur			Hakra Wares	Mughal 1997: 42	2.50
Kili Ghul Mohammad	Quetta-Pishin	30° 17' 00" N 66° 58' 00" E	-	Kechi Beg Togau Burj Basket-marked Kili Ghul Mohammad	Fairservis 1956a: 198 de Cardi 1983: 19	0.50
Killianwali	Bahawalpur	28° 53' 25" N 71° 25' 44" E	-	Hakra Wares	Mughal 1997: 42	0.20
Killianwali 'B'	Bahawalpur	28° 53' 33" N 71° 25' 57" E	-	Mature Harappan	Mughal 1997: 48	1.40
Killianwali 'C'	Bahawalpur	28° 53' 05" N 71° 26' 18" E	-	Mature Harappan	Mughal 1997: 48	1.3
Killianwali 'D'	Bahawalpur	28° 52' 40" N 71° 26' 47" E	-	Hakra Wares	Mughal 1997: 42	0.60
Kindarkhera	Jamnagar	21° 48' 00" N 69° 33' 00" E	-	Late Sorath Harappan Sorath Harappan	Rao 1963a: 183, 206 Possehl 1980: 105 Joshi et al. 1984: 528	0.80
Kinner Kheda	Jamnagar			Sorath Harappan	IAR 1955-56: 70	
Kinneru Damb	Jhalawan	27° 03' 00" N 66° 12' 00" E	-	Burnished Red & Grey Complex B Londo Kulli-Harappan Amri-Nal	de Cardi 1964 Raikes 1968b: 154 de Cardi 1983: 38 Possehl 1986a: 149	
Kippianwala	Bahawalpur	28° 43' 10" N 71° 04' 20" E	-	Mature Harappan	Mughal 1997: 48	20.10
Kirarwali Ther	Bahawalpur	29° 10' 00" N 72° 21' 00" E	-	Kot Diji	Stein 1943a: 125 Dalal 1980: 10	6.80
Kiratapur	Bulandshahr	28° 31' 40" N 78° 15' 00" E	-	Copper Hoard	IAR 1969-70: 38 Makkhan Lal 1984a: 34-5	
Kiratpura	Jaipur			OCP	IAR 1973-74: 24	
Kirby Site	Sukkur	27° 38' 00" N 68° 55' 30" E	-	Mature Harappan	Bellasis 1857: 471-73 Lambrick 1964: 88 Mallah 1994: 137-38	
Kiri	Ludhiana	30° 56' 00" N 75° 41' 00" E	-	Post-urban Harappan	IAR 1980-81: 49 Joshi et al. 1984: 527	
Kirta	Sibi	29° 32' 00" N 67° 28' 00" E	-	Quetta-Harappan Damb Sadaat Kechi Beg	Fairservis 1956a: 200 Enault and Jarrige 1973: 190-92	0.70
Kirtan	Hissar	29° 08' 44" N 75° 32' 08" E	-	Mature Harappan	IAR 1980-81: 16 Joshi et al. 1984: 521	0.70
Koba	Rajkot	21° 45' 00" N 70° 50' 00" E	-	Late Sorath Harappan	Rao 1963a: 206 Possehl 1980: 105 Joshi et al. 1984: 528	
Koel	Jind	29° 44' 58" N 76° 10' 50" E	-	Early Medieval Post-urban Harappan Sothi-Siswal	Singh 1981: 115 Joshi et al. 1984: 519, 525 Mohan 1988: 103	0.20
Koh Mundri	Sikar			OCP and Microliths	IAR 1981-82: 62	
Kohada	Ludhiana	30° 52' 00" N 76° 00' 00" E	-	Post-urban Harappan	Joshi et al. 1984: 527	

Kohara	Ludhiana		Early Historic PGW Post-urban Harappan	IAR 1975-76: 38	
Kohna Kalat	Makran	26° 54' 00" N - 64° 04' 00" E	Islamic Kulli? Amri-Nal	Stein 1931: 43-44 Possehl 1986a: 150	0.50
Kohtras Buthi	Karachi	25° 42' 00" N - 67° 38' 00" E	Kot Diji	Majumdar 1934: 132-34 Lambrick 1944: 60-1 Flam 1981a: 331-33	10.20
Kojar	Jhunjhunu		OCP	IAR 1980-81: 56	
Kolabarty	Dhandabad		Copper Hoard	Mukharjee 1935: 517 ff. Makkhan Lal 1984a: 38-9	
Kolkikalan	Saharanpur		Mature Harappan	Pande & Ramachandran 1971: 39	
Koonj Sor	Thar Parkar	24° 22' 00" N - 68° 39' 00" E	Mature Harappan	Baloch 1973 Baloch 1975 Khan 1979b: map Flam 1981a: 227	
Koor	Sukkur		Mature Harappan	Mallah 1994: 141-49	0.40
Kot	Kachi	29° 30' 00" N - 67° 26' 00" E	Quetta	Enault and Jarrige 1973: 189-90	
Kot Alabad	Dera Ismail Khan	32° 08' 00" N - 70° 18' 50" E	Kot Diji	Dani 1970-71: Fig. 1	
Kot Diji	Khairpur	27° 16' 00" N - 68° 40' 00" E	Mature Harappan Kot Diji	F. A. Khan 1965 Flam 1981a: 229-30	2.20
Kot Kori	Thar Parkar	24° 25' 00" N - 69° 02' 00" E	Mature Harappan	Khan 1979b: 84	
Kot Mandial	Ludhiana	30° 47' 00" N - 76° 03' 00" E	Post-urban Harappan	Joshi et al. 1984: 527	
Kot Raja Manjhera	Karachi	24° 58' 00" N - 68° 08' 00" E	Amri-Nal	A. R. Khan 1968a: 5 A. R. Khan 1979a: 71-2	
Kot Waro Daro	Sukkur		Mature Harappan	Mallah 1994: 182-84	0.60
Kota	Jamnagar	22° 10' 00" N - 69° 42' 00" E	Sorath Harappan Microliths	Joshi et al. 1984: 523	0.80
Kota	Saharanpur	29° 54' 00" N - 77° 38' 00" E	Post-urban Harappan	Joshi et al. 1984: 523	
Kota One	Jamnagar	22° 10' 00" N - 69° 42' 00" E	Late Sorath Harappan Sorath Harappan	IAR 1954-55: 59 Rao 1963a: 206 Possehl 1980: 105 K. K. Bhan 1986: 19	0.50
Kotada Bhadli One	Kutch	23° 22' 00" N - 69° 26' 00" E	Lustrous Red Ware Mature Harappan	IAR 1965-66: 14-6 Possehl 1980: 105 Joshi et al. 1984: 529	3.00
Kotada Bhadli Three	Kutch	23° 22' 00" N - 69° 26' 00" E	Mature Harappan	IAR 1965-66: 14, 16 Possehl 1980: 106	
Kotada Bhadli Two	Kutch	23° 22' 00" N - 69° 26' 00" E	Mature Harappan	IAR 1965-66: 14-6 Possehl 1980: 106 Joshi et al. 1984: 529	8.00
Kotada, Jamnagar	Jamnagar	22° 12' 00" N - 70° 22' 00" E	Sorath Harappan Microliths	Rao 1963a: 206 Possehl 1980: 106 Joshi et al. 1984: 528 K. K. Bhan 1989: 237	72.00
Kotada, Kutch	Kutch	23° 18' 00" N - 70° 06' 00" E	Lustrous Red Ware Mature Harappan	Possehl 1980: 106 Joshi et al. 1984: 529	
Kotahra	Kutch		Mature Harappan	IAR 1977-78: 20	

Kotar Khana	Ropar	30° 13' 00" N	-	Post-urban Harappan	Joshi et al. 1984: 524	
		77° 13' 00" E				
Kotara	Kutch	23° 58' 00" N	-	Mature Harappan	IAR 1967-68: 17	
		69° 47' 00" E			Possehl 1980: 106	
					Joshi et al. 1984: 529	
Kotarkhana	Ambala	30° 13' 35" N	-	Post-urban Harappan	Kumar 1978: 43	3.00
		77° 13' 16" E				
Kotda	Jamnagar	23° 14' 00" N	-	Sorath Harappan	Possehl 1980: 107	
		70° 21' 00" E			Joshi et al. 1984: 529	
Koth	Ahmedabad	22° 38' 00" N	-	Late Sorath Harappan	Rao 1963a: 206	
		72° 18' 00" E		Mature Harappan	Possehl 1980: 107	
					Joshi et al. 1984: 529	
Kotiro	Larkana	27° 21' 30" N	-	Amri-Nal (w/ Kot	Flam, unpublished	
		67° 25' 00" E		Diji)		
Kotla Nihang Khan	Ropar	30° 56' 00" N	-	Mature Harappan	Vats 1940: 203	2.60
		76° 34' 00" E			Suraj Bhan 1975: 122	
					Y. D. Sharma 1982a: 141	
					Joshi et al. 1984: 520	
Kotli	Ropar	30° 53' 00" N	-	Post-urban Harappan	IAR 1953-54: 38	
		76° 29' 00" E		Mature Harappan	Suraj Bhan 1975: 122	
					Joshi et al. 1984: 522	
Kotra	Kachi	28° 34' 00" N	-	Quetta-Mature	de Cardi 1983: 35	
		67° 24' 00" E		Harappan Kot Diji		
				Kechi Beg		
Kouhlagh	Quetta-Pishin			Quetta	Mughal 1972a: 148	
				Damb Sadaat		
				Kechi Beg		
Kowas	Loralai	30° 28' 00" N	-	Iron Age	Fairservis 1959: 287	4.10
		67° 35' 00" E		Kot Diji		
				Kechi Beg		
Kranai Hill	Quetta-Pishin	30° 35' 30" N	-	Quetta	Stein 1929a: 85-86	10.70
		67° 05' 30" E		Damb Sadaat		
Kridhni	Saharanpur	29° 55' 00" N	-	OCP	IAR 1966-67: 43	
		77° 30' 00" E		Mature Harappan	Dikshit 1982a: 114	
					Joshi et al. 1984: 521, 523	
Kshetra	Mayurbhanj			Copper Hoard	Mohapatra 1964: 45-7	
					Makkhan Lal 1984a: 40-1	
Kubaheri	Ropar	30° 52' 00" N	-	Early Historic	IAR 1975-76: 38	
		76° 40' 00" E		PGW	IAR 1976-77: 43	
				Post-urban Harappan	Joshi et al. 1984: 527	
Kuchanwala	Bahawalpur	29° 06' 30" N	-	Kot Diji	Mughal 1997: 42, 44	0.60
		71° 54' 41" E		Hakra Wares		
Kuchanwala	Bahawalpur	29° 06' 30" N	-	Kot Diji	Mughal 1997: 42	0.60
		71° 54' 41" E		Hakra Wares		
Kuchnai Ghundai	Quetta-Pishin	30° 43' 20" N	-	Partho-Sassanian?	Mughal 1972a: 148	0.20
		67° 02' 30" E		Quetta		
				Damb Sadaat		
				Kechi Beg		
Kudana	Muzaffarnagar	29° 25' 45" N	-	PGW	Gaur and Lal 1992: 378	
		77° 22' 20" E		OCP/Post-urban		
				Harappan		
Kudwala Ther	Bahawalpur	29° 11' 30" N	-	Cemetery H	Mughal 1997: 51	38.10
		71° 53' 00" E		Mature Harappan	Stein 1943a: 113-14	
					Khan 1959a: 190	

Kuki Damb	Jhalawan	28° 45' 00" N - 66° 21' 00" E	Amri-Nal Kechi Beg Togau Burj Basket-marked	Stein 1931: 17-18 de Cardi 1983: 26	0.10
Kulghera	Purulia		Copper Hoard	IAR 1971-72: 51 Makkhan Lal 1984a: 338-9	
Kulheri	Muzaffarnagar		Medieval NBP PGW OCP	O. P. Srivastava 1982: 66-70	
Kulki Kalan	Saharanpur	29° 56' 00" N - 77° 39' 00" E	Post-urban Harappan	Joshi et al. 1984: 523	
Kulli	Makran	26° 15' 00" N - 65° 00' 00" E	Kulli	Stein 1931: 118-27 Raikes 1968b: 152 Possehl 1986a	10.80
Kulloi	Sarawan		Quetta Amri-Nal Kechi Beg	Fairservis 1971c: 401	
Kullu Kalat	Sarawan	29° 04' 00" N - 66° 22' 00" E	Early Historic Iron Age Togau	Stein 1931: 186 de Cardi 1983: 23-4	1.20
Kumar	Mehsana	23° 27' 00" N - 71° 46' 00" E	Lustrous Red Ware	IAR 1978-79: 7	
Kumhara	Patiala	30° 38' 00" N - 76° 18' 00" E	Post-urban Harappan	Joshi et al. 1984: 527	
Kumkalan	Ludhiana	30° 55' 00" N - 76° 05' 00" E	OCP Post-urban Harappan	IAR 1976-77: 78 IAR 1980-81: 47	3.00
Kunal	Hissar	29° 37' 35" N - 75° 39' 30" E	PGW Mature Harappan Early/Mature Trans. Sothi-Siswal Hakra Wares Early	Joshi et al. 1984: 521, 526 IAR 1985-86: 23-4 Mohan 1988: 104 Khatri and Acharya 1995	2.90
Kundanpur	Rajkot	22° 05' 00" N - 71° 10' 00" E	Late Sorath Harappan Sorath Harappan	IAR 1957-58: 19 Rao 1963a: 205 Possehl 1980: 107 Joshi et al. 1984: 528	
Kuntasi	Rajkot	22° 50' 40" N - 70° 37' 30" E	Late Sorath Harappan Sorath Harappan	IAR 1977-78: 200 IAR 1987-88: 17-9 Dhavalikar 1993	3.30
Kurda	Ropar		Post-urban Harappan	Suraj Bhan 1975: 123	
Kurdi	Ropar		Post-urban Harappan	Suraj Bhan 1975: 123	
Kurragi Damb	Kharan	27° 54' 00" N - 65° 50' 30" E	Kulli? Amri-Nal	Stein 1931: 30-1	0.90
Kurrara	Ropar	30° 39' 00" N - 76° 46' 00" E	Mature Harappan	IAR 1962-63: 17 IAR 1964-65: 33 Joshi et al. 1984: 527	
Kurrari	Ropar		Mature Harappan	IAR 1964-65: 33 Joshi et al. 1984: 527	
Kurukshetra Two	Kurukshetra	29° 58' 10" N - 76° 51' 40" E	Early Historic Post-urban Harappan	Kumar 1978: 71 Joshi et al. 1984: 524	2.20
Kuruwala	Bahawalpur	29° 02' 05" N - 71° 25' 25" E	Mature Harappan	Mughal 1997: 48	3.10

Kuruzkol	Makran	26° 39' 00" N	-	Kulli	Stein 1931: 50-51	0.20
		63° 23' 00" E				
Kutharivad	Jamnagar			Sorath Harappan	IAR 1980-81: 13	
				Microliths		
Kuzbagh	Quetta-Pishin			Damb Sadaat	Mughal 1972a: 148	
				Kechi Beg		
L-2	Loralai	30° 18' 00" N	-	Kot Diji	Fairservis 1959: 287	0.60
		68° 10' 00" E		Kechi Beg		
				Togau		
				Burj Basket-marked		
L-3	Loralai	30° 18' 00" N	-	Kot Diji	Fairservis 1959: 287	12.60
		68° 12' 00" E		Kechi Beg		
				Togau		
				Burj Basket-marked		
Lachkane	Patiala	30° 25' 00" N	-	Post-urban Harappan	Joshi et al. 1984: 527	
		76° 21' 00" E				
Ladai	Kutch			Mature or Post-urban	IAR 1955-56: 69	
				Harappan		
Ladana Chaku	Kurukshetra	29° 59' 40" N	-	Post-urban Harappan	Kumar 1978: 52-3	
		76° 15' 38" E		(OCP)		
Ladava	Muzaffarnagar			PGW	Srivastava 1982: 104-07	
				OCP		
Ladulai	Bahawalpur	29° 08' 51" N	-	Kot Diji	Mughal 1997: 44	3.90
		72° 21' 12" E			Stein 1943a: 126	
					Dalal 1980: 10	
Lahar	Zhob			Kot Diji	Mughal 1972a: 148	
Lahboli	Saharanpur			Sunga-Kushan	IAR 1984-85: 92	
				Post-urban Harappan		
Lajwan Kalan	Jind	29° 08' 45" N	-	Post-urban Harappan	Mohan 1988: 105	2.50
		76° 27' 30" E				
Lak Largai	Bannu	32° 49' 00" N	-	Kechi Beg	Allchin, Allchin, Durrani and	2.80
		70° 31' 00" E			Khan 1985: 9, 190	
					Khan, Knox and Thomas 1991a:	
					26-31	
Lak Plateau	Makran	25° 04' 15" N	-	Zangian	Stein 1931: 77-82	
		61° 44' 45" E		Dasht	Besenval and Sanlaville 1990:	
					98-9	
Lakhabawal	Jamnagar	22° 24' 00" N	-	Early Historic	IAR 1955-56: 7	1.50
		70° 00' 00" E		Red Polished Ware	Rao 1963a: 206	
				Lustrous Red Ware	Possehl 1980: 107	
				Sorath Harappan	Joshi et al. 1984: 528	
					K. K. Bhan 1989: 238	
Lakhan Timbo	Jamnagar	22° 29' 00" N	-	Sorath Harappan	IAR 1960-61: 8	
		70° 36' 00" E			Possehl 1980: 107	
					Joshi et al. 1984: 529	
Lakhanka	Bhavnagar	21° 48' 00" N	-	Sorath or Late	Possehl 1980: 107	0.60
		71° 38' 00" E		Sorath Harappan	Joshi et al. 1984: 528	
Lakhasar One	Kutch	23° 14' 00" N	-	Mature Harappan	IAR 1986-87: 29	
		70° 41' 00" E				
Lakhasar Two	Kutch	23° 14' 00" N	-	Mature Harappan	IAR 1986-87: 29	
		70° 41' 00" E				
Lakhavad	Ahmedabad			Sorath Harappan	IAR 1978-79: 94	
Lakhavan	Amreli			Sorath Harappan	Pande & Ramachandran 1971: 40	

Lakhavan Lathi		21° 51' 00" N 71° 27' 00" E	-	Sorath Harappan	Jansen 1981: 265	
Lakhavarno Dhoro	Amreli			Late Sorath Harappan Sorath Harappan	A. F. Cunningham, unpublished	5.30
Lakhavav, Amreli	Amreli	21° 51' 00" N 71° 27' 00" E	-	Lustrous Red Ware Late Sorath Harappan	IAR 1960-61: 8 Rao 1963a: 206 Possehl 1980: 108	
Lakhavav, Bhavnagar	Bhavnagar	21° 30' 00" N 71° 55' 00" E	-	Sorath Harappan	Joshi et al. 1984: 530	
Lakhetra-no Timbo	Surendranagar	23° 27' 00" N 71° 33' 00" E	-	Lustrous Red Ware	Sone K. K. Bhan 1994: 86-7	3.30
Lakhiyo	Dadu	26° 31' 00" N 67° 35' 00" E	-	Mature Harappan	Majumdar 1934: 67-8 Flam 1981a: 231	
Lakhman	Bahawalpur	28° 43' 20" N 71° 10' 23" E	-	Hakra Wares	Mughal 1997: 42	3.20
Lakhmanti Kalan	Saharanpur	30° 03' 00" N 77° 38' 00" E	-	OCP	IAR 1966-67: 43 Joshi et al. 1984: 523	
Lakhmirwala	Bhatinda	29° 52' 00" N 75° 22' 00" E	-	Mature Harappan	Joshi et al. 1984: 520, 522 Joshi 1986: 139	225.00
Lakhneyani Thumdo One	Mehsana	23° 39' 00" N 71° 34' 00" E	-	Lustrous Red Ware	Ajithprasad and Sonawane, in press K. K. Bhan 1994: 86-7	0.10
Lakhpar	Kutch	23° 33' 00" N 70° 28' 00" E	-	Mature Harappan	IAR 1965-66: 16 Possehl 1980: 107 Joshi et al. 1984: 529 Joshi 1990b: 418	8.00
Lakhpat	Kutch	23° 50' 00" N 68° 47' 00" E	-	Mature Harappan	IAR 1960-61: 8 Possehl 1980: 108 Joshi et al. 1984: 529	
Lakhshmirji Mari	Dadu	26° 17' 00" N 67° 31' 00" E	-	Amri-Nal	Frere 1853: 351-52 Lambrick 1944: 64-6 Flam 1981a: 285-86	
Lakhueenjo-daro	Sukkur	27° 43' 00" N 68° 50' 00" E	-	Mature Harappan	Kazi 1989: 89-106 Qasim 1990 Mallah 1994: 150-51	50.00
Lal Ghundai	Quetta-Pishin	30° 35' 00" N 67° 07' 00" E	-	Kili Ghul Mohammad	Fairservis 1956a: 201	
Lal Patel	Bahawalpur	29° 04' 30" N 71° 52' 27" E	-	Mature Harappan	Mughal 1997: 48	0.80
Lal Qila	Bulandshahr	28° 30' 00" N 78° 15' 00" E	-	OCP	IAR 1971-72: 45-6 Joshi et al. 1984: 523 Gaur 1989: Gaur 1995	
Lal Shah	Kachi	29° 25' 00" N 67° 33' 30" E	-	Mehrgarh VIIC	Jarrige 1986: 116-17	
Lalanji Mari	Larkana	27° 41' 00" N 67° 24' 00" E	-	Mature Harappan Amri-Nal	Lambrick 1941: 93 Flam 1981a: 258	0.90
Lalauda	Patiala	30° 22' 00" N 76° 17' 00" E	-	Post-urban Harappan	Joshi et al. 1984: 527	
Lalbaba	Jaipur			OCP	IAR 1973-74: 24	
Lalianwali	Bhatinda	29° 52' 00" N 75° 20' 00" E	-	Mature Harappan	Joshi et al. 1984: 522 Joshi, 1986: 139	4.00
Laloino Timbo	Jamnagar	22° 12' 00" N 70° 14' 00" E	-	Sorath or Late Sorath Har	IAR 1980-81: 13 K. K. Bhan 1989: 238	3.00

Lalu Wala	Bhatinda	29° 59' 00" N 75° 27' 00" E	-	Mature Harappan	IAR 1980-81: 45 Joshi et al. 1984: 522 Joshi 1986: 139	4.00
Laluwala Ther	Rahimyar Khan	28° 47' 01" N 70° 52' 48" E	-	Mature Harappan	Mughal 1997: 48	1.20
Landhaur Gujar	Saharanpur	29° 53' 00" N 77° 31' 00" E	-	Post-urban Harappan	Joshi et al. 1984: 523	
Lataur	Patiala	30° 32' 00" N 76° 25' 00" E	-	Post-urban Harappan	Joshi et al. 1984: 527	
Lathwala	Bahawalpur	28° 50' 20" N 71° 11' 58" E	-	Kot Diji	Mughal 1997: 44	30.50
Lathwala Two	Bahawalpur	28° 50' 00" N 71° 11' 57" E	-	Hakra Wares	Mughal 1997: 42	26.30
Laun	Jind	29° 40' 04" N 76° 02' 00" E	-	Early Historic Post-urban Harappan Sothi-Siswal	Singh 1981: 115-16 Joshi et al. 1984: 519, 525 Mohan 1988: 105	4.90
Lavana-no Godh	Banaskantha	23° 49' 00" N 71° 35' 00" E	-	Anarta-Rangpur IIC	Ajithprasad and Sonawane, in press	0.40
LB-13	Las Bela	26° 25' 30" N 66° 20' 00" E	-	Kulli Early Kulli Nal Togau	Fairservis 1961b & c Possehl 1986a: 151	
LB-16 'A-B'	Las Bela	26° 25' 00" N 66° 21' 30" E	-	Early Historic Iron Age Kulli Amri-Nal	Fairservis 1961b & c Possehl 1986a: 151	22.00
LB-16 'C'	Las Bela	26° 30' 30" N 66° 22' 00" E	-	Kulli Amri-Nal	Fairservis 1961b & c	
LB-17	Las Bela	26° 26' 00" N 66° 21' 00" E	-	Early Historic Iron Age Kulli Amri-Nal	Fairservis 1961b & c Possehl 1986a: 151	7.20
LB-9	Las Bela	26° 25' 30" N 66° 18' 30" E	-	Early Historic Londo Kulli	Fairservis 1961b & c Raikes 1968b: 157	
Lehri	Jhalawan	27° 41' 30" N 66° 15' 30" E	-	Nal	Hargreaves 1925-26a: 61 Stein 1931: 168-69	
Leiah	Muzaffargarh	30° 59' 00" N 70° 55' 00" E	-	Kot Diji	Dani 1970-71: Fig. 1	4.00
Lena Singh	Jhalawan	28° 17' 00" N 66° 18' 00" E	-	Early Historic Iron Age Kulli-Harappan Togau	de Cardi 1983: 27	
Lewan	Bannu	32° 53' 00" N 70° 35' 00" E	-	Late Kot Diji Kot Diji Kechi Beg	Allchin, Allchin, Durrani and Khan 1985: 9, 190-1	14.60
Limbadka-no Thumdo	Banaskantha	23° 54' 00" N 71° 31' 00" E	-	Anarta-Rangpur IIC	Ajithprasad and Sonawane, in press	0.30
Limbuni-no Godh	Banaskantha	24° 09' 00" N 71° 20' 00" E	-	Lustrous Red Ware	Ajithprasad and Sonawane, in press	0.10
Limdavalo Timbo	Mehsana	23° 39' 30" N 71° 45' 10" E	-	Lustrous Red Ware	Ajithprasad and Sonawane, in press	1.00
Limejo-daro	Larkana	27° 58' 00" N 68° 04' 00" E	-	Mature Harappan	Dikshit 1925-26a: 99 Majumdar 1934: ii Flam 1981a: 254	3.80

Linedoriwalo Khetra	Surendranagar	23° 27' 00" N 71° 34' 00" E	-	Lustrous Red Ware	K. K. Bhan 1994: 86-7	0.40
Litanwala	Bahawalpur	28° 46' 34" N 71° 22' 35" E	-	Hakra Wares	Mughal 1997: 42	7.60
Loal Mari	Sukkur			Mature Harappan Kot Dijian	Mallah 1994: 123-27	2.60
Loebanr 3	Swat	34° 45' 00" N 72° 23' 00" E	-	Swat Proto-Historic	Stacul 1980b Stacul 1987: 55-59	1.20
Lohar Majra	Ludhiana	30° 42' 00" N 76° 19' 00" E	-	Post-urban Harappan	Joshi et al. 1984: 527	
Lohar Raghu	Hissar	29° 16' 00" N 76° 04' 00" E	-	Post-urban Harappan Sothi-Siswal	IAR 1980-81: 16 Joshi et al. 1984: 519, 526	
Lohari	Karnal	29° 21' 30" N 76° 50' 19" E	-	Sothi-Siswal	Singh 1981: 69 Joshi et al. 1984: 519	1.10
Loharki Theri	Bahawalpur	29° 10' 00" N 72° 15' 00" E	-	Hakra Wares?	Mughal 1997: 4211	2.50
Lohat, Mahendragarh	Mahendragarh			Post-urban Harappan	Suraj Bhan 1975: 126	
Lohat, Rohtak	Rohtak	28° 32' 00" N 76° 50' 00" E	-	Mature Harappan	Suraj Bhan 1975: 112 Joshi et al. 1984: 521	
Lohgarh	Gurdaspur	32° 14' 00" N 75° 30' 00" E	-	Post-urban Harappan	Joshi et al. 1984: 526	
Lohri	Dadu	26° 30' 00" N 67° 32' 00" E	-	Mature Harappan Early to Mature Harappan Transition Amri-Nal	Majumdar 1934: 65-7 Flam 1981a: 232	
Lohumjo-daro	Larkana	26° 58' 00" N 67° 51' 00" E	-	Jhukar Mature Harappan	Dikshit 1925-26a: 99-100 Majumdar 1934: 48-58 Flam 1981a: 233	5.00
Lolada	Mehsana	23° 33' 00" N 71° 41' 00" E	-	Rangpur IIC Anarta	IAR 1978-79: 7 K. K. Bhan 1994: 86-7	
Lolai	Jamnagar	22° 12' 00" N 70° 14' 00" E	-	Late Sorath Harappan Sorath Harappan	K. K. Bhan 1986: 18	
Loliana	Bhavnagar	21° 54' 00" N 71° 48' 20" E	-	Sorath Harappan	Momin 1980	5.00
Lomriwala	Bahawalpur	28° 53' 00" N 71° 28' 00" E	-	Cemetery H	Stein 1943a: 169-70 Dalal 1980: 13	2.10
Londo Damb	Jhalawan	27° 58' 00" N 66° 33' 00" E	-	Londo Togau	Stein 1931: 181 de Cardi 1983: 37	
Lopen	Patiala	30° 28' 00" N 76° 11' 00" E	-	Post-urban Harappan	Joshi et al. 1984: 527	
Loteshwar	Mehsana	23° 36' 00" N 71° 50' 20" E	-	Anarta (Pre-Harappan) Microliths	Hegde and Sonawane 1986: 30 K. K. Bhan 1994: 86-7	1.10
Lothal	Ahmedabad	22° 31' 25" N 72° 14' 59" E	-	Late Sorath Harappan Mature Harappan	Rao 1963a: 206 Rao 1979 & 1985 Possehl 1980: 108 Joshi et al. 1984: 530, 535	4.80
Ludana	Jind	29° 14' 22" N 76° 30' 35" E	-	Early Historic Post-urban Harappan	Singh 1981: 123 Joshi et al. 1984: 525	2.70
Luhinga Kalan	Gurgaon	27° 50' 00" N 77° 08' 00" E	-	Post-urban Harappan	Suraj Bhan 1975: 112, 126 Joshi et al. 1984: 519, 526	
Lukhela	Rajkot	21° 50' 00" N 70° 00' 00" E	-	Lustrous Red Ware Sorath Harappan	IAR 1958-59: 19 Chitalwala 1979: 115 Possehl 1980: 108	0.40

Lukhi	Kurukshetra	30° 02' 00" N - 76° 44' 00" E	PGW Post-urban Harappan	Suraj Bhan 1975: 123 Joshi et al. 1984: 524	
Luna	Kutch	23° 40' 00" N - 69° 15' 00" E	Mature Harappan	Rao 1963a: 206 Possehl 1980: 108 Joshi et al. 1984: 528	
Luna Mandvi	Kutch	22° 50' 00" N - 69° 24' 00" E	Mature Harappan	Possehl 1980: 108 Joshi et al. 1984: 528	
Lundewali Four	Bahawalpur	28° 53' 08" N - 71° 24' 30" E	Hakra Wares	Mughal 1997: 42	3.30
Lundewali Ther	Bahawalpur	28° 51' 50" N - 71° 23' 40" E	Mature Harappan	Mughal 1997: 48	7.10
Lundewali Three	Bahawalpur	28° 53' 17" N - 71° 24' 38" E	Hakra Wares	Mughal 1997: 42	2.10
Lundewali Two	Bahawalpur	28° 52' 40" N - 71° 24' 15" E	Cemetery H	Mughal 1997: 51	16.70
Lundi Buthi	Dadu	26° 17' 00" N - 67° 30' 30" E	Mature Harappan Amri-Nal	Lambrick 1944: 64-5 Flam 1981a: 289	
Lundi Dherai	Rahimyar Khan	28° 03' 30" N - 70° 09' 00" E	Kot Diji	Stein 1943a: 101 Dalal 1980: 8	
Lundi Thori	Sukkur	27° 30' 00" N - 69° 01' 00" E	Mature Harappan	Lambrick 1946: 52 Flam 1981a: 234	1.20
Lunida One	Bahawalpur	28° 53' 15" N - 71° 06' 43" E	Mature Harappan	Mughal 1997: 48	23.30
Lunida Two	Bahawalpur	28° 53' 20" N - 71° 06' 38" E	Mature Harappan	Mughal 1997: 48	1.00
Luppewala	Bahawalpur	28° 49' 07" N - 71° 12' 20" E	Hakra Wares	Mughal 1997: 42	22.70
Luppewala Three	Bahawalpur	28° 49' 58" N - 71° 12' 41" E	Hakra Wares	Mughal 1997: 42	6.30
Luppewala Two	Bahawalpur	28° 48' 53" N - 71° 12' 55" E	Kot Diji	Mughal 1997: 44	5.50
Lurewala	Bahawalpur	29° 05' 34" N - 71° 34' 56" E	Cemetery H	Stein 1943a: 158-59 Mughal 1997: 51 Dalal 1980: 11	15.90
Lyari River Area	Karachi	24° 56' 00" N - 67° 03' 00" E	Kili Ghul Mohammad?	Anonymous 1964: 9	
Machiala Mota	Amreli	21° 41' 00" N - 71° 14' 00" E	Late Historic RED POLISHED WARE Lustrous Red Ware	Rao 1963a: 206 Possehl 1980: 108 Joshi et al. 1984: 528	2.70
Machuki Damb	Makran	25° 41' 00" N - 62° 34' 00" E	Islamic Kulli?	Stein 1931: 59 Possehl 1986a: 150	2.50
Madak Kalat	Makran	26° 11' 00" N - 64° 28' 00" E	ISLAMIC/BRITISH Kechi Beg	Stein 1931: 111	
Madan Kundala Gondal	Rajkot		Sorath Harappan	IAR 1983-84: 18	
Madanapur	Hardoi		Copper Hoard	V. N. Misra 1976 Makkhan Lal 1984a: 36-7	
Madeva	Amreli	21° 50' 00" N - 71° 24' 00" E	Late Sorath Harappan Sorath Harappan	Rao 1963a: 206 Possehl 1980: 108 Joshi et al. 1984: 528	
Madhi	Amreli	21° 45' 00" N - 70° 50' 00" E	Lustrous Red Ware Late Sorath Harappan	Rao 1963a: 206 Possehl 1980: 109 Joshi et al. 1984: 528	

Madhopar	Jullunder		Mature Harappan	IAR 1956-57: 79	
Madhvya-no Timbo	Banaskantha	23° 44' 00" N - 71° 05' 00" E	Amri-Nal Burial Pottery	Ajithprasad and Sonawane, in press	0.10
Madiala Kalan	Ludhiana		Post-urban Harappan	IAR 1963-64: 91 Suraj Bhan 1975: 122	
Madina	Rohtak	28° 58' 00" N - 76° 28' 00" E	Post-urban Harappan	Joshi et al. 1984: 526	
Madopur	Jullunder		Mature Harappan	Pande & Ramachandran 1971: 40	
Magrejewali	Bahawalpur	28° 48' 05" N - 71° 21' 18" E	Cemetery H	Mughal 1997: 51	0.30
Mahadevio	Amreli	21° 54' 00" N - 71° 17' 00" E	Late Sorath Harappan Sorath Harappan	IAR 1960-61: 7 Possehl 1980: 109 Joshi et al. 1984: 528	13.20
Mahadevno Timbo	Amreli Late		Late Sorath Harappan Sorath Harappan	A. F. Cunningham, unpublished	1.00
Mahakalino Timbo	Ahmedabad		Sorath Harappan	IAR 1976-77: 15	
Mahatpur	Hoshiarpur	31° 55' 00" N - 75° 39' 00" E	Post-urban Harappan	Joshi et al. 1984: 526	
Mahawala Ther	Bahawalpur	28° 39' 13" N - 71° 01' 58" E	Mature Harappan	Mughal 1997: 48	9.40
Mahipura	Saharanpur	29° 58' 00" N - 77° 34' 00" E	Post-urban Harappan	Joshi et al. 1984: 523	
Mahiwali	Bahawalpur	28° 47' 03" N - 71° 20' 37" E	Mature Harappan	Mughal 1997: 48	2.00
Mahmoodpur	Muzaffarnagar		Medieval OCP	Srivastava 1982: 75-8	3.60
Maholi One	Sangrur		Post-urban Harappan	IAR 1982-83: 65	
Mahorana	Sangrur	30° 29' 00" N - 75° 57' 00" E	Mature Harappan Sothi-Siswal	Y. D. Sharma 1982a Joshi et al. 1984: 520, 527 Y. D. Sharma 1987	
Mai Ghari	Karachi		Amri-Nal Kili Ghul Mohammad?	A. R. Khan 1968a: 5	
Mai Manoori Bhir	Multan	29° 50' 00" N - 71° 48' 00" E	Mature Harappan Kot Diji	A. N. Khan 1988b: 85	
Mainpuri	Mainpuri		Copper Hoard	Anderson 1883: 403 Makkhan Lal 1984a: 36-7	
Majhadpur	Hardoi		Copper Hoard	B. B. Lal 1951: 29 Makkhan Lal 1984a: 36-7	
Majo Mill	Quetta-Pishin	30° 34' 00" N - 67° 04' 00" E	Islamic/British Quetta Damb Sadaat Kechi Beg	Fairservis 1971c: 399	
Majra Roran	Karnal	29° 47' 27" N - 76° 42' 58" E	Post-urban Harappan	Singh 1981: 57 Joshi et al. 1984: 524	
Majri Jattan	Patiala	30° 38' 00" N - 76° 13' 00" E	Post-urban Harappan	Joshi et al. 1984: 527	
Makansar	Rajkot		Sorath Harappan	IAR 1957-58: 19	
Makvana	Bhavnagar	21° 57' 00" N - 71° 40' 00" E	Sorath Harappan	IAR 1960-61: 8 Rao 1963a: 206 Possehl 1980: 109 Joshi et al. 1984: 528	
Malakpur	Kurukshetra	30° 02' 00" N - 76° 38' 00" E	Post-urban Harappan	Joshi et al. 1984: 524	

Malasaratalavdi	Ahmedabad		Sorath Harappan	IAR 1974-75: 68	
Malasband	Jhalawan	26° 58' 00" N - 65° 30' 00" E	Islamic-British Kechi Beg	Stein 1931: 148	
Malaud	Ludhiana	30° 38' 00" N - 75° 57' 00" E	Post-urban Harappan Mature Harappan	Joshi et al. 1984: 522, 527	
Malazai	Quetta-Pishin	30° 23' 00" N - 66° 53' 00" E	Islamic Early Historic Pirak II Quetta	de Cardi 1983: 17-8	
Malgam	Rajkot	22° 01' 00" N - 71° 26' 00" E	Late Sorath Harappan Sorath Harappan	Possehl 1980: 109 Joshi et al. 1984: 528	10.30
Malghori Damb	Sarawan	29° 03' 00" N - 66° 25' 00" E	Kechi Beg Togau	Stein 1931: 185 Mughal 1972a: 148 de Cardi 1983: 24	
Malgodh	Rajkot	22° 00' 00" N - 70° 34' 00" E	Sorath Harappan	IAR 1957-58: 19 Possehl 1980: 110 Joshi et al. 1984: 530	
Malhalewala Ther	Bahawalpur	29° 10' 40" N - 72° 09' 48" E	Kot Diji	Mughal 1997: 44 Stein 1943a: 123 Dalal 1980: 9	19.00
Malhar Khera	Jind	29° 22' 28" N - 76° 34' 25" E	PGW Post-urban Harappan	Joshi et al. 1984: 525 Mohan 1988: 106	6.50
Malikpur	Kurukshetra		Post-urban Harappan (OCP)	Kumar 1978: 53	4.00
Malion-Ka Tiba	Jaipur		OCP	IAR 1973-74: 24	
Maliuwali One	Rahimyar Khan	28° 30' 55" N - 70° 44' 56" E	Mature Harappan	Mughal 1997: 48	1.30
Malki	Sarawan	29° 05' 00" N - 66° 24' 00" E	Partho-Sassanian Early Historic Iron Age Kechi Beg Togau Burj Basket-marked	de Cardi 1983: 24	
Mallawala Toba	Ganganagar		Mature Harappan	Joshi et al. 1984: 522	
Malluwali Two	Rahimyar Khan	28° 30' 52" N - 70° 44' 45" E	Mature Harappan	Mughal 1997: 48	1.30
Malsian	Jullunder	31° 07' 00" N - 75° 22' 00" E	Post-urban Harappan	Joshi et al. 1984: 526	
Malvan	Surat	21° 06' 00" N - 72° 43' 00" E	Late Sorath Harappan Sorath Harappan	IAR 1967-68: 10-2 Possehl 1980: 110 Joshi et al. 1984: 529	1.80
Malyali	Sikar		OCP and Microliths	IAR 1981-82: 62	
Mamlika	Gurgaon	27° 55' 00" N - 77° 08' 00" E	Post-urban Harappan	Suraj Bhan 1975: 112, 126 Joshi et al. 1984: 519, 526	
Mammai Damb	Kharan	27° 56' 00" N - 65° 50' 00" E	Kulli Amri-Nal	Stein 1931: 30	0.60
Mamro One	Sukkur	27° 29' 20" N - 69° 01' 20" E	Mature Harappan	Lambrick 1946: 51 Flam 1981a: 235 Mallah 1994: 152	
Mamro Two	Sukkur	27° 28' 30" N - 69° 00' 30" E	Mature Harappan	Lambrick 1946: 51 Flam 1981a: 235	13.90
Mana	Rohtak	28° 50' 00" N - 76° 36' 00" E	Post-urban Harappan	Joshi et al. 1984: 526	

Manal Majra	Karnal	29° 33' 00" N - 76° 54' 00" E	Post-urban Harappan	Suraj Bhan 1975: 125 Suraj Bhan and Shaffer 1978: 62 Joshi et al. 1984: 524	0.60
Manar	Broach	21° 42' 00" N - 72° 47' 00" E	Sorath Harappan	Possehl 1980: 110 Joshi et al. 1984: 530	
Manda	Jammu	32° 54' 00" N - 74° 48' 00" E	Kushan Red Ware Mature Harappan Sothi-Siswal	Joshi et al. 1984: 520	
Mandha	Jaipur		PGW OCP	IAR 1972-73: 29	
Mandkaula	Gurgaon	28° 08' 00" N - 77° 10' 00" E	Post-urban Harappan Sothi-Siswal	Joshi et al. 1984: 519, 526	
Mandla	Saharanpur	30° 04' 00" N - 77° 39' 00" E	OCP	IAR 1966-67: 43 Joshi et al. 1984: 523	
Mandoli	Delhi		Kushan PGW Mature Harappan	Possehl, unpublished	0.50
Mandowala	Saharanpur	30° 05' 00" N - 77° 45' 00" E	OCP	IAR 1964-65: 44 Joshi et al. 1984: 523	
Mandriyara Mohra	Kutch	23° 30' 00" N - 70° 16' 00" E	Medieval Mature Harappan	IAR 1986-87: 29	
Manela	Ropar	30° 50' 00" N - 76° 21' 00" E	Post-urban Harappan	Joshi et al. 1984: 527	
Mangali One	Hissar	29° 02' 00" N - 75° 44' 00" E	Sothi-Siswal	IAR 1987-88: 21	
Mangali Two	Hissar	29° 02' 00" N - 75° 44' 00" E	Sothi-Siswal	IAR 1987-88: 21	
Mangalpur	Jind	29° 31' 41" N - 76° 04' 07" E	Post-urban Harappan Sothi-Siswal	Singh 1981: 116 Joshi et al. 1984: 519, 525	0.90
Mangli Nichi	Ludhiana	30° 52' 00" N - 75° 57' 00" E	Medieval Kushan Post-urban Harappan (Bara)	IAR 1980-81: 48	40.00
Manhairu	Mahendragarh	28° 43' 00" N - 76° 14' 00" E	Mature Harappan	Suraj Bhan 1975: 126 Joshi et al. 1984: 519, 526	
Manikpur Sharif	Ropar		Post-urban Harappan	IAR 1962-63: 17 Suraj Bhan 1975: 122	
Manju Kota	Jaipur		OCP	IAR 1973-74: 24	
Manoharpur	Jind	29° 21' 00" N - 76° 24' 00" E	PGW Post-urban Harappan	Suraj Bhan 1975: 124 Joshi et al. 1984: 519, 525	
Manpura	Bulandshahr	28° 31' 00" N - 78° 01' 00" E	Post-urban Harappan	Shastri 1915: 4 IAR 1961-62: 103 Joshi et al. 1984: 523 Makkhan Lal 1984a: 36-7	
Mansadevi	Ropar		Mature Harappan	IAR 1975-76: 76	
Manupura	Ludhiana	30° 76' 00" N - 76° 15' 00" E	Post-urban Harappan	Suraj Bhan 1975: 122 Joshi et al. 1984: 527	
Marastan	Makran	26° 02' 50" N - 64° 11' 50" E	Kulli	Stein 1931: 107 Possehl 1986a: 148	0.20
Marechiwala	Bahawalpur	28° 48' 22" N - 71° 14' 02" E	Cemetery H	Mughal 1997: 51	1.80
Marhanwala One	Ropar		OCP	IAR 1971-72: 23	

Marhanwala Two	Ropar			OCP	IAR 1971-72: 23	
Markhan	Thar Parkar	24° 32' 00" N	-	Mature Harappan	Baloch 1973	
		68° 48' 00" E			Baloch 1975	
					A. R. Khan 1979a: map	
					Flam 1981a: 236	
Marki Mas	Jhalawan	27° 10' 00" N	-	Londo	Raikes 1968b: 150	0.40
		66° 25' 00" E		Kulli		
				Amri-Nal		
				Kechi Beg		
Masaudpur	Hissar	29° 12' 47" N	-	Post-urban Harappan	IAR 1980-81: 16	7.80
		75° 58' 12" E		Mature Harappan	Joshi et al. 1984: 520, 521,	
				Sothi-Siswal	526	
					Mohan 1988: 107	
Mashak	Dadu	26° 26' 00" N	-	Jhukar-Trihni	Majumdar 1934: 63-4	
		67° 35' 00" E		Mature Harappan	Flam 1981a: 237	
Mashinewala	Bahawalpur	28° 42' 33" N	-	Mature Harappan	Mughal 1997: 48	4.90
		70° 59' 15" E				
Mashula	Ganganagar	29° 12' 00" N	-	Mature Harappan	Stein 1943a: 73	5.90
		73° 33' 00" E			Dalal 1980: 26	
					Joshi et al. 1984: 522	
Mata Ghundai	Quetta-Pishin	30° 45' 00" N	-	Quetta	Stein 1929a: 84	
		67° 10' 00" E		Damb Sadaat		
				Kechi Beg		
Mata Kaudani	Zhob	31° 15' 00" N	-	Early Historic	Stein 1929a: 41-43	1.50
		69° 20' 00" E		Waziri		
Mata-no Thumdo	Banaskantha	23° 59' 00" N	-	Anarta-Rangpur IIC	Ajithprasad and Sonawane, in	1.10
		71° 26' 30" E		Anarta-Rangpur IIB	press	
Mataji-no	Surendranagar	23° 25' 35" N	-	Lustrous Red Ware	IAR 1982-83: 28	
Timbo		71° 51' 50" E			Hegde and Sonawane 1986: 31	
Matar Sham	Hissar	29° 10' 00" N	-	Post-urban Harappan	Suraj Bhan 1975: 124	
		75° 35' 00" E		Sothi-Siswal	Joshi et al. 1984: 519, 526	
Matewalno	Ahmedabad			Sorath Harappan	IAR 1974-75: 68	
Tekro						
Mathan	Samrala			Post-urban Harappan	Suraj Bhan 1975: 122	
Mathana	Saharanpur	30° 00' 00" N	-	Post-urban Harappan	Joshi et al. 1984: 523	
		77° 44' 00" E				
Mathura	Mathura			Copper Hoard	Makkhan Lal 1984a: 36-7	
Matki Jharauli	Saharanpur	30° 04' 00" N	-	OCP	IAR 1966-67: 43	
		77° 35' 00" E		Mature Harappan	Joshi et al. 1984: 521, 523	
Maudi Three	Karnal	29° 47' 00" N	-	Post-urban Harappan	Singh 1981: 336	1.50
		76° 46' 00" E			Joshi et al. 1984: 524	
Maudi Two	Karnal	29° 47' 40" N	-	Post-urban Harappan	Suraj Bhan 1975: 125	
		76° 46' 30" E			Singh 1981: 336	
Mayal Chah	Makran	27° 19' 00" N	-	Kulli?	Stein 1931: 42	
Damb		65° 05' 00" E			Possehl 1986a: 150	
Mayapur	Saharanpur	29° 56' 00" N	-	Post-urban Harappan	Joshi et al. 1984: 523	
		78° 08' 00" E				
Mazena Damb	Jhalawan	26° 58' 45" N	-	Kulli	Stein 1931: 148-49	12.00
		65° 30' 00" E			Possehl 1986a: 147	
Meerut	Meerut	29° 00' 00" N	-	Post-urban Harappan	Joshi et al. 1984: 523	
		77° 45' 00" E				
Meghapar	Rajkot			Lustrous Red Ware	Chitalwala 1979: 115	0.10
Meghper	Kutch			Mature Harappan	IAR 1980-81: 10	

Mehgam	Broach	21° 42' 00" N 72° 45' 00" E	-	Sorath Harappan	IAR 1957-58: 15-7 Rao 1963a: 189-90, 205 Possehl 1980: 110 Joshi et al. 1984: 529	
Mehi	Jhalawan	27° 13' 00" N 65° 42' 00" E	-	Kulli	Stein 1931: 153-63 Possehl 1986a: 147	9.90
Mehmudabad	Bahawalpur	29° 05' 55" N 71° 07' 06" E	-	Mature Harappan	Mughal 1997: 48	3.90
Mehra	Kurukshetra	30° 02' 20" N 77° 04' 36" E	-	Early Historic Post-urban Harappan	Kumar 1978: 71-2 Joshi et al. 1984: 524	5.00
Mehranwala	Ropar	30° 55' 00" N 76° 50' 00" E	-	Post-urban Harappan Mature Harappan	IAR 1954-55: 59 Suraj Bhan 1975: 122 Joshi et al. 1984: 524	
Mehrgarh	Kachi	29° 25' 00" N 67° 35' 00" E	-	BMAC Transitional Kot Diji Kechi Beg Togau Burj Basket-marked Kili Ghul Mohammad	Jarrige 1977, 1979, 1982 Jarrige, Jarrige, Meadow and Quivron 1995	
Mehrianwala Ther	Bahawalpur	28° 45' 30" N 71° 06' 27" E	-	Mature Harappan	Mughal 1997: 48	3.50
Mehrianwali Two	Bahawalpur	28° 45' 20" N 71° 06' 30" E	-	Mature Harappan	Mughal 1997: 48	2.30
Mehrindawala Ther	Bahawalpur	28° 42' 11" N 71° 04' 41" E	-	Mature Harappan	Mughal 1997: 48	7.00
Mehruband Ther	Bahawalpur	28° 48' 46" N 71° 22' 10" E	-	Mature Harappan	Mughal 1997: 48	6.80
Mehtawari	Diu	20° 44' 00" N 70° 55' 00" E	-	NBP(?) Lustrous Red Ware	IAR 1981-82: 14	
Mehwali	Bahawalpur	28° 39' 55" N 71° 02' 19" E	-	Mature Harappan	Mughal 1997: 48	7.80
Mehwali Two	Bahawalpur	28° 39' 30" N 71° 02' 04" E	-	Hakra Wares	Mughal 1997: 42	10.60
Melana Four	Bhavnagar	21° 55' 40" N 71° 46' 50" E	-	Sorath or Late Sorath Harappan	Possehl, unpublished	
Men Damb	Jhalawan	27° 07' 00" N 65° 35' 00" E	-	Kulli	Stein 1931: 150-151 Possehl 1986a: 147	1.80
Mepla-no Thumdo	Banaskantha	23° 46' 00" N 71° 09' 00" E	-	Anarta-Rangpur IIC Anarta-Rangpur IIB	Ajithprasad and Sonawane, in press	0.50
Merechi Kanda	Bahawalpur	28° 49' 25" N 71° 14' 20" E	-	Hakra Wares	Mughal 1997: 42	3.60
Merechi Kanda Three	Bahawalpur	28° 49' 40" N 71° 13' 29" E	-	Kot Diji	Mughal 1997: 44	3.70
Merechi Kanda Two	Bahawalpur	28° 49' 51" N 71° 14' 20" E	-	Hakra Wares	Mughal 1997: 42	10.70
Merujh	Sukkur	27° 15' 00" N 69° 00' 00" E	-	Mature Harappan	Lambrick 1946: 52 Flam 1981a: 238	
Metal Maha No Timbo	Ahmedabad	22° 47' 00" N 72° 14' 00" E	-	Sorath Harappan	Joshi et al. 1984: 530	
Midhana	Sonepat	29° 00' 00" N 76° 23' 00" E	-	Post-urban Harappan	Joshi et al. 1984: 525	

Site	District	Coordinates		Period	Reference	Area
Mirana	Bahawalpur	28° 57' 35" N 71° 18' 05" E	-	Mature Harappan	Mughal 1997: 48	16.90
Mirchpur	Hissar	29° 19' 30" N 76° 11' 30' E	-	Post-urban Harappan Mature Harappan Sothi-Siswal	IAR 1980-81: 16 Mohan 1988: 108 Joshi et al. 1984: 519, 521, 526	4.50
Miri Qalat	Makran	26° 02' 00" N 63° 00' 45" E	-	Medieval Shahi Tump Kulli-Harappan Amri-Nal	Stein 1931: 54-56 Field 1959: 79-80 Possehl 1986a: 149 Besenval and Sanlaville 1990: 114-15, 123-26	3.70
Mirn-jee-Serri	Sukkur			Mature Harappan	Mallah 1994: 190-91	0.40
Mirpur	Ambala			Post-urban Harappan	Kumar 1978: 44	
Mirpur, Rupnagar	Ropar	30° 13' 00" N 77° 19' 00" E	-	Post-urban Harappan	Joshi et al. 1984: 524	
Mirpur, Saharanpur	Saharanpur	29° 55' 00" N 77° 16' 00" E	-	Post-urban Harappan	Joshi et al. 1984: 523	
Mirzapur	Kurukshetra	29° 58' 00" N 76° 48' 00" E	-	Medieval Cemetery Kushan Post-urban Harappan	U.V. Singh 1976: 27-8, 1977 Shaffer 1981: 85 Joshi et al. 1984: 524	1.80
Mishk	Jhalawan	28° 27' 00" N 67° 05' 00" E	-	Kulli-Harappan Amri-Nal	de Cardi 1983: 33	
Misri	Mahendragarh	28° 41' 00" N 76° 16' 00" E	-	Post-urban Harappan	Suraj Bhan 1975: 126 Joshi et al. 1984: 526	
Mitathal	Bhiwani	28° 53' 10" N 76° 10' 20" E	-	Copper Hoard Post-urban Harappan Mature Harappan	Suraj Bhan 1975: 4, 125 Joshi et al. 1984: 519, 521, 526 Makkhan Lal 1984a: 34-5 Mohan 1988: 108	7.20
Miyoli	Kurukshetra	29° 48' 45" N 76° 33' 45" E	-	Post-urban Harappan	Joshi et al. 1984: 524 Kumar 1978: 60	6.00
Moana	Jind	29° 26' 12" N 76° 34' 47" E	-	Post-urban Harappan Sothi-Siswal	Joshi et al. 1984: 519, 525 Mohan 1988: 110	1.80
Mobi Damb	Sarawan	29° 57' 00" N 66° 45' 00" E	-	Islamic-British Quetta Damb Sadaat Kechi Beg	de Cardi 1983: 20	
Moda				Sorath Harappan	Chitalwala 1985: key to Figure 8	
Modpar				Sorath Harappan	Chitalwala 1985: key to Figure 8	
Moghul Ghundai	Zhob	31° 26' 00" N 69° 15' 00" E	-	Buddhist Kot Diji	Stein 1929a: 43-9 Fairservis 1959: 329	0.60
Moghul Kala	Loralai	30° 26' 30" N 69° 50' 00" E	-	Islamic-British Kot Diji	Stein 1929a: 53, pl.7	0.90
Mohammadpur	Sangrur	30° 32' 00" N 75° 55' 00" E	-	Post-urban Harappan	Suraj Bhan 1975: 122 Joshi et al. 1984: 527	
Mohanpur	Ambala	30° 02' 00" N 76° 30' 00" E	-	Post-urban Harappan	Suraj Bhan 1975: 123 Joshi et al. 1984: 524	
Mohenjo-daro	Larkana	27° 18' 00" N 68° 07' 00" E	-	Jhukar Mature Harappan	Marshall 1925-26: 74 Marshall 1931a Mackay 1937-38 Anonymous 1964: 38-39 Flam 1981a: 239-40	100.00

Mohiuddinpur	Saharanpur	30° 00' 00" N	-	OCP	IAR 1966-67: 43	
		77° 38' 00" E		Mature Harappan	Joshi et al. 1984: 521, 523	
Mohna	Kurukshetra			Post-urban Harappan	Suraj Bhan 1975: 125	
Moholi	Sangrur	30° 38' 00" N	-	Post-urban Harappan	Joshi et al. 1984: 520, 522, 527	
		75° 45' 00" E		Mature Harappan		
				Sothi-Siswal		
Mojgarh Ther	Bahawalpur	29° 01' 07" N	-	Kot Diji	Mughal 1997: 44	4.50
		72° 08' 26" E				
Moniwala	Rahimyar Khan	28° 38' 20" N	-	Hakra Wares	Mughal 1997: 42	22.90
		70° 43' 12" E				
Mor Karima	Ludhiana	30° 50' 00" N	-	Kushan	IAR 1980-81: 49	5.00
		75° 37' 00" E		Mature Harappan(?)		
Mora	Jamnagar	22° 28' 00" N	-	Late Sorath Harappan	Rao 1963a: 206	1.00
		70° 14' 00" E		Sorath Harappan	Possehl 1980: 110	
					Joshi et al. 1984: 528	
					K. K. Bhan 1989: 238	
Morkhi	Jind	29° 17' 12" N	-	Post-urban Harappan	Suraj Bhan 1975: 125	4.00
		76° 33' 16" E		Sothi-Siswal	Joshi et al. 1984: 519	
					Mohan 1988: 110	
Morpur	Jamnagar	22° 16' 00" N	-	Lustrous Red Ware	IAR 1978-79: 7	
		69° 49' 00" E			Rao 1963a: 206	
					Possehl 1980: 110	
					Joshi et al. 1984: 528	
					K. K. Bhan 1986: 20	
Morvo	Kutch	23° 50' 00" N	-	Mature Harappan	IAR 1967-68: 17	
		70° 42' 00" E			Joshi 1972: 114	
					Possehl 1980: 110	
					Joshi et al. 1984: 529	
Motachoprika	Ahmedabad	22° 21' 30" N	-	Sorath Harappan	Possehl, unpublished	2.10
		71° 48' 00" E				
Motadevalia				Sorath Harappan	Chitalwala 1985: key to Figure 8	
Motasar Tibba One	Ganganagar	29° 09' 00" N	-	Mature Harappan	Dalal 1980: 26	
		73° 28' 00" E			Joshi et al. 1984: 522	
Motasar Tibba Two	Ganganagar	29° 09' 00" N	-	Mature Harappan	Dalal 1980: 26	
		73° 27' 00" E			Joshi et al. 1984: 522	
Moti Gop	Jamnagar	22° 19' 00" N	-	Late Sorath Harappan	K. K. Bhan 1986: 17	
		69° 30' 00" E		Sorath Harappan		
Moti Kalavad	Jamnagar			Lustrous Red Ware	IAR 1961-62: 10-1	
Moti Parbadi	Rajkot			Lustrous Red Ware	Chitalwala 1979: 115	2.00
Moti Pipli	Banaskantha	23° 49' 25" N	-	Anarta-Harappan		2.70
		71° 31' 00" E		Amri-Nal Burial	K. K. Bhan 1994: 86-7	
				Pottery		
Motidharai	Bhavnagar	21° 57' 00" N	-	Historic	IAR 1955-56: 70	0.40
		71° 54' 00" E		Sorath Harappan	IAR 1957-58: 18-9	
Mowari	Larkana	27° 32' 30" N	-	Mature Harappan	Flam, unpublished	
		67° 19' 00" E		Amri-Nal		
Mubarak Ther West	Bahawalpur	28° 55' 00" N	-	Mature Harappan	Stein 1943a: 172	4.10
		71° 07' 00" E			Dalal 1980: 13	
Mubarakwala Ther	Bahawalpur	28° 55' 07" N	-	Cemetery H	Stein 1943a: 172	14.70
		71° 09' 30" E			Mughal 1997: 51	
					Dalal 1980: 13	
Mujahidpur	Hardoi			OCP & Copper Hoard	IAR 1978-79: 101	
Mul Madhavpur	Jamnagar			Lustrous Red Ware	IAR 1961-62: 10-1	

Site	District	Coordinates		Period/Ware	Reference	Size
Mulaheri One	Muzaffarnagar	29° 23' 15" N 77° 40' 10" E	-	OCP/Post-urban Harappan	Gaur and Lal 1992: 378	
Mulaheri Two	Muzaffarnagar	29° 23' 15" N 77° 40' 10" E	-	OCP/Post-urban Harappan	Gaur and Lal 1992: 378	
Mulana	Ambala	30° 16' 50" N 77° 02' 40" E	-	Post-urban Harappan (OCP)	Kumar 1978: 38 Joshi et al. 1984: 524	3.00
Mullada Two	Surendranagar	23° 18' 00" N 71° 44' 00" E	-	Lustrous Red Ware	K. K. Bhan 1994: 86-7	0.60
Mulpadar, Bhanvad	Jamnagar	21° 56' 00" N 69° 45' 00" E	-	Sorath Harappan	Possehl 1980: 110 Joshi et al. 1984: 529	
Mulpadar, Kalianpur	Jamnagar	21° 56' 00" N 69° 45' 00" E	-	Late Sorath Harappan Sorath Harappan	IAR 1957-58: 19 Possehl 1980: 114 Joshi et al. 1984: 528 K. K. Bhan 1989: 238	5.00
Mulparda	Jamnagar			Sorath Harappan	IAR 1979-80: 25	
Mulu	Kutch			Mature Harappan	IAR 1979-80: 17	
Mundetha	Gurgaon	27° 55' 00" N 77° 08' 00" E	-	Post-urban Harappan	Suraj Bhan 1975: 112, 126 Joshi et al. 1984: 519	
Mundh Two	Jind	29° 31' 00" N 76° 33' 00" E	-	Post-urban Harappan	Suraj Bhan 1975: 125 Joshi et al. 1984: 525	
Mundigak	Kandahar	31° 55' 00" N 65° 30' 00" E	-	Quetta Damb Sadaat Kechi Beg Togau	Casal 1961a Ball and Gardin 1982: 187-8	18.70
Mungatoda	Jamnagar			Sorath Harappan	IAR 1980-81: 13	
Mungli Damb	Larkana	27° 32' 30" N 67° 32' 00" E	-	Amri-Nal (w/ Kot Diji)	Flam, unpublished	
Munkola	Gurgaon	28° 30' 00" N 76° 54' 00" E	-	Post-urban Harappan	Suraj Bhan 1975: 112, 126 Joshi et al. 1984: 526	
Munkola One	Gurgaon			Post-urban Harappan	Suraj Bhan 1975: 126	
Munkola Two	Gurgaon			Post-urban Harappan	Suraj Bhan 1975: 126	
Murgha Mehtarzai	Zhob	30° 44' 00" N 67° 35' 30" E	-	Islamic-British Waziri Kot Diji Kechi Beg	Stein 1929a: 80	
Musa Khel	Mianwali	32° 39' 00" N 71° 44' 00" E	-	Late Kot Diji Kot Diji	Dani 1970-71: 32	3.10
Musafarwali	Bahawalpur	28° 46' 47" N 71° 08' 06" E	-	Hakra Wares	Mughal 1997: 42	27.60
Musafarwali Two	Bahawalpur	28° 46' 22" N 71° 09' 02" E	-	Hakra Wares	Mughal 1997: 42	2.10
Nada	Chandigarh	30° 47' 00" N 76° 48' 00" E	-	Post-urban Harappan	IAR 1975-76: 39 Joshi et al. 1984: 527	
Nadana	Jind	29° 15' 06" N 76° 27' 04" E	-	Post-urban Harappan	Singh 1981: 91 Joshi et al. 1984: 525	1.70
Nadapa				Sorath Harappan	Chitalwala 1985: key to Figure 8	
Nag/Zamuran	Makran	26° 23' 45" N 62° 51' 15" E	-	Shahi Tump Dasht	Besenval and Sanlaville 1990: 121	
Nagadia	Jamnagar	21° 55' 00" N 69° 33' 00" E	-	Lustrous Red Ware Microliths	IAR 1979-80: 25	
Nagaman	Patiala			PGW Post-urban Harappan	Kumar 1978: 79	4.00
Nagar	Jullunder	31° 02' 00" N	-	Harappan/PGW Overlap	Suraj Bhan 1975: 122	

		75° 50' 00" E		IAR 1976-77: 42	
				Joshi et al. 1984: 526	
Nagari Kheri	Jind		Post-urban Harappan	Suraj Bhan & Shaffer 1978: 62	5.70
Nageshri	Bhavnagar		Lustrous Red Ware	Chitalwala 1985: key to Figure 8	
Nageswar	Jamnagar	22° 18' 00" N -	Mature Harappan	IAR 1980-81: 14	1.40
		69° 02' 00" E		IAR 1983-84: 18-9	
				K. K. Bhan 1986: 21	
				Hegde, Bhan, Sonawane, Krishnan	
				and Shah 1990	
Nagoor	Sukkur		Mature Harappan	Mallah 1994: 192-95	50.00
Naguran One	Jind	29° 26' 10" N -	PGW	Singh 1981: 90	1.20
		76° 22' 25" E	Post-urban Harappan		
Naguran Two	Jind	29° 26' 10" N -	Post-urban Harappan	Singh 1981: 90	0.80
		76° 21' 25" E			
Nagwada Five	Surendranagar	23° 17' 50" N -	Lustrous Red Ware	Ajithprasad and Sonawane, in	0.10
		71° 43' 00" E		press	
Nagwada Four	Surendranagar	23° 17' 20" N -	Mature Harappan	IAR 1984-85: 19	0.50
		71° 41' 30" E	Anarta	K. K. Bhan 1994: 86-7	
Nagwada One	Surendranagar	23° 18' 15" N -	Anarta-Harappan	IAR 1984-85: 19	1.60
		71° 42' 45" E	Amri-Nal Burial		
			Pottery		
Nagwada Three	Surendranagar	23° 18' 50" N -	Lustrous Red Ware	IAR 1984-85: 19	0.70
		71° 42' 30" E		K. K. Bhan 1994: 86-7	
Nagwada Two	Surendranagar	23° 19' 00" N -	Lustrous Red Ware	IAR 1984-85: 19	1.50
		71° 43' 15" E		K. K. Bhan 1994: 86-7	
Nagwan	Patiala	30° 07' 00" N -	Mature Harappan	Joshi et al. 1984: 522	
		76° 23' 00" E			
Naharnwala	Bahawalpur	28° 50' 13" N -	Kot Diji	Mughal 1997: 42	6.10
		71° 30' 00" E	Hakra Wares		
Naharwali	Bahawalpur	28° 50' 28" N -	Hakra Wares	Mughal 1997: 42	7.30
		71° 23' 20" E			
Naharwali 'B'	Bahawalpur	28° 49' 55" N -	Hakra Wares	Mughal 1997: 42	2.00
		71° 23' 33" E			
Nahli	Meerut	29° 14' 00" N -	Post-urban Harappan	Joshi et al. 1984: 523	
		77° 33' 00" E			
Nahrenwala	Bahawalpur	28° 50' 13" N -	Kot Diji	Mughal 1997: 42, 44	6.10
		71° 30' 00" E	Hakra Wares		
Nahriwala	Bhatinda	30° 05' 00" N -	Post-urban Harappan	Joshi, 1986: 139	16.00
		75° 25' 00" E			
Nainan	Kurukshetra	29° 47' 00" N -	Post-urban Harappan	Joshi et al. 1984: 524	
		76° 32' 00" E			
Naing Gar	Dadu	26° 18' 00" N -	Amri-Nal	Lambrick 1944: 64	
Jabal		67° 31' 00" E		Flam 1981a: 267	
Naiwala Theh	Bhatinda	29° 50' 00" N -	Mature Harappan	Joshi et al. 1984: 520	16.00
		75° 30' 00" E	Sothi-Siswal	Joshi 1986: 139	
Nakamshakh	Bannu	32° 30' 00" N -	Kili Ghul Mohammad?	Khan, Knox and Thomas 1987: 85	
		70° 42' 00" E			
Nakarahiya	Sitapur		Copper Hoard	K. N. Dikshit 1968: 50	
				Makkhan Lal 1984a: 36-7	
Nakharauli	Ambala	30° 20' 36" N -	Post-urban Harappan	Kumar 1978: 48	4.00
		77° 06' 20" E			
Nal	Jhalawan	27° 44' 00" N -	Early Kulli	Marshall 1904-05	5.70
		66° 16' 00" E	Amri-Nal	Hargreaves 1929	

Site	District	Coordinates	Period/Culture	Reference	Size
				Stein 1931: 166-168	
				Possehl 1986a: 147	
Nal Village	Jhalawan	27° 42' 00" N - 66° 11' 30" E	Early Historic Kulli?	Stein 1931: 169	
Nala	Muzaffarnagar	29° 17' 20" N - 77° 16' 40" E	OCP/Post-urban Harappan	Gaur and Lal 1992: 378	
Nalhera	Meerut	29° 10' 00" N - 77° 21' 00" E	Post-urban Harappan	Joshi et al. 1984: 523	
Nalhera Bakal	Saharanpur	29° 59' 00" N - 77° 30' 00" E	Post-urban Harappan	Joshi et al. 1984: 523	
Namdai	Sarawan		Amri-Nal Kechi Beg Togau	Fairservis 1971c: 402	
Nammal Lake Cave	Campbellpur	32° 20' 00" N - 71° 45' 00" E	Kot Diji	M. Salim 1992: 44-5	
Nanauli	Saharanpur		Mature Harappan(?)	IAR 1964-65: 44	
Nandgarh One	Jind	29° 10' 54" N - 76° 28' 50" E	Post-urban Harappan Sothi-Siswal	Singh 1981: 90 Joshi et al. 1984: 519, 525 Mohan 1988: 112	1.90
Nandgarh Two	Jind	29° 11' 54" N - 76° 28' 50" E	Post-urban Harappan	Singh 1981: 90-1 Joshi et al. 1984: 519, 525 Mohan 1988: 112	1.30
Nandlalpur	Jaipur		Copper Hoard	Parmar 1977: 63-4 Makkhan Lal 1984a: 36-7	
Nandu Khera	Kurukshetra	29° 59' 00" N - 76° 39' 00" E	Post-urban Harappan	Joshi et al. 1984: 524	
Nandu Khera	Kurukshetra	29° 59' 44" N - 76° 39' 50" E	Early Historic PGW Post-urban Harappan	Joshi et al. 1984: 524	5.00
Nani Chandur	Mehsana	23° 35' 00" N - 71° 37' 30" E	Lustrous Red Ware Anarta Microliths	K. K. Bhan 1994: 86-7	1.00
Nanichoprika	Ahmedabad	22° 22' 00" N - 71° 46' 00" E	Sorath Harappan	Possehl, unpublished	2.20
Nar	Kheda	22° 28' 00" N - 72° 42' 00" E	Sorath Harappan	IAR 1972-73: 11 IAR 1974-75: 13 Momin 1979: 138-39 Momin 1984	8.00
Narani	Jind	29° 15' 00" N - 76° 25' 00" E	Post-urban Harappan	Joshi et al. 1984: 525	
Narapa	Kutch	23° 29' 00" N - 69° 09' 00" E	Mature Harappan	IAR 1967-68: 17 Possehl 1980: 110 Joshi et al. 1984: 529	
Nariankhera	Sirsa		Rang Mahal Post-urban Harappan	IAR 1983-84: 32	
Narkatari	Kurukshetra	29° 57' 50" N - 76° 48' 00" E	NBP PGW Post-urban Harappan	Kumar 1978: 72	
Narmana One	Jamnagar	22° 15' 00" N - 70° 09' 00" E	Late Sorath Harappan Sorath Harappan	Rao 1963a: 206 Possehl 1980: 110 Joshi et al. 1984: 528 K. K. Bhan 1989: 238	0.50
Naru Waro	Khairpur	27° 25' 00" N -	Mature Harappan	Anonymous 1964b: 43-4	34.80

Dharo		68° 41' 00" E			Flam 1981a: 241-42
Narukheri	Karnal	29° 38' 00" N - 76° 59' 00" E	PGW Post-urban Harappan		Joshi et al. 1984: 524
Naryana	Karnal	29° 46' 00" N - 76° 55' 00" E	Post-urban Harappan		Joshi et al. 1984: 524
Nasirpur, Saharanpur	Saharanpur	29° 45' 00" N - 77° 51' 00" E	Post-urban Harappan		Joshi et al. 1984: 523
Nasirpur, Shahjhanpur	Shahjahanpur		Copper Hoard		K. N. Dikshit 1968: 47 Makkhan Lal 1984a: 36-7
Nasitpur	Bhavnagar		Sorath Harappan		IAR 1980-81: 12
Nathwan	Hissar	29° 06' 53" N - 75° 36' 00" E	Mature Harappan		IAR 1980-81: 16 Joshi et al. 1984: 521 Mohan 1988: 112	0.70
Naugawan	Patiala	30° 07' 00" N - 76° 23' 00" E	Post-urban Harappan		Joshi et al. 1984: 527
Naujhalwala	Bahawalpur	29° 13' 27" N - 71° 49' 00" E	Mature Harappan		Mughal 1997: 48	0.60
Nauli	Jullunder	31° 23' 00" N - 75° 40' 00" E	Post-urban Harappan		Joshi et al. 1984: 526
Naura	Patiala	30° 26' 00" N - 76° 06' 00" E	PGW Post-urban Harappan		IAR 1976-77: 43 Joshi et al. 1984: 527
Nausharo	Kachi	29° 22' 00" N - 67° 35' 00" E	Pirak III Mature Harappan Early to Mature Harappan Kot Diji		Jarrige 1986: 63-130 Jarrige 1990a: 239	1.80
Navagam	Surat	21° 16' 00" N - 72° 56' 00" E	Sorath Harappan		Joshi et al. 1984: 530
Navapur			Sorath Harappan		Chitalwala 1985: key Figure 8
Navarsa	Kurukshetra	29° 55' 40" N - 77° 04' 40" E	Post-urban Harappan		Kumar 1978: 73 Joshi et al. 1984: 524	1.00
Navinal	Kutch	22° 50' 00" N - 69° 35' 00" E	Mature Harappan		Rao 1963a: 206 Possehl 1980: 111 Joshi et al. 1984: 528
Nawan Gaon	Saharanpur	29° 53' 00" N - 77° 26' 00" E	Post-urban Harappan Mature Harappan		Joshi et al. 1984: 521, 523
Nawanbans	Saharanpur	29° 54' 00" N - 77° 17' 00" E	Post-urban Harappan Mature Harappan Sothi-Siswal		IAR 1965-66: 54 Nath 1982 Joshi et al. 1984: 523
Nazarabad	Makran	26° 06' 00" N - 62° 26' 30" E	Shahi Tump Amri-Nal Kechi Beg		Stein 1931: 84-85 Field 1959: 81 Besenval and Sanlaville 1990: 111
Nazganijo Kund	Dadu	26° 52' 00" N - 67° 17' 00" E	Amri-Nal		Krishna Deva and McCown 1949: 28-9 Flam 1981a: 262	0.30
Neghar Damb	Kalat	28° 16' 00" N - 66° 18' 00" E	Londo Anjira Amri-Nal Kechi Beg Togau Burj Basket-marked		Stein 1931: 18-9 Mughal 1972: 149 de Cardi 1983: 28	0.30
Nehriwala Theh	Bhatinda	30° 05' 00" N - 75° 33' 00" E	Post-urban Harappan		Joshi et al. 1984: 527

Nelavada	Amreli		Late Sorath Harappan Sorath Harappan	A. F. Cunningham, unpublished	0.50
Nenuni Dhar	Kutch	23° 51' 00" N - 69° 44' 00" E	Mature Harappan	IAR 1967-68: 17 Possehl 1980: 111 Joshi et al. 1984: 528-9	
Ner Nesdo	Kutch		Mature Harappan Sorath Harappan	IAR 1980-81: 10 Chitalwala 1985: key Figure 8	
Neshdo	Amreli	21° 53' 00" N - 71° 23' 00" E	Late Sorath Harappan Sorath Harappan	Possehl 1980: 111 Joshi et al. 1984: 528	2.1
Netra Khirasara	Kutch		Red Polished Ware Mature Harappan	IAR 1969-70: 6 IAR 1976-77: 74	
Newan	Ludhiana	30° 44' 00" N - 76° 21' 00" E	Post-urban Harappan	Joshi et al. 1984: 527	
Niai Buthi	Las Bela	26° 15' 00" N - 66° 26' 00" E	Kulli-Harappan Amri-Nal Kechi Beg	Stein 1943a: 215-16 A. R. Khan 1979a: 73-4	1.30
Nidana	Karnal		Post-urban Harappan	Suraj Bhan 1975: 125	
Nidani	Jind	29° 15' 32" N - 76° 25' 04" E	Early Historic Post-urban Harappan Sothi-Siswal	Singh 1981: 91 Joshi et al. 1984: 519	2.10
Niguran Two	Jind	29° 26' 00" N - 76° 22' 00" E	Post-urban Harappan	Joshi et al. 1984: 525	
Nikawa One	Jamnagar	22° 11' 00" N - 70° 36' 00" E	Late Sorath Harappan Sorath Harappan	K. K. Bhan 1986: 18	
Nindowari	Jhalawan	26° 57' 00" N - 66° 04' 00" E	Kulli-Harappan	Casal 1966: 10-21 Casal 1968: 51-5 Possehl 1986a: 149 de Cardi 1983: 39-40	50.00
Niorai	Etah		Copper Hoard	Anderson 1883: 396 Makkhan Lal 1984a: 36-7	
Nirpalpur	Saharanpur	30° 01' 00" N - 77° 29' 00" E	OCP Mature Harappan	IAR 1964-65: 44 K. N. Dikshit 1982a: 115 Joshi et al. 1984: 523	
Nisang Two	Karnal	29° 42' 00" N - 76° 45' 00" E	Post-urban Harappan	Suraj Bhan 1975: 125 Joshi et al. 1984: 524	
Niwaniwala Ther East	Bahawalpur	28° 47' 22" N - 71° 10' 00" E	Mature Harappan	Mughal 1997: 48	9.60
Niwaniwala Ther West	Bahawalpur	28° 47' 25" N - 71° 09' 54" E	Hakra Wares	Mughal 1997: 42	2.30
Niwaniwala Three	Bahawalpur	28° 47' 33" N - 71° 10' 25" E	Hakra Wares	Mughal 1997: 42	0.30
Niwaniwala Two	Bahawalpur	28° 47' 23" N - 71° 10' 09" E	Mature Harappan	Mughal 1997: 48	0.10
Nodiz Damb	Makran		Islamic Shahi Tump Kulli	Field 1959 Possehl 1986a: 149	
Noh	Bharatpur	27° 13' 00" N - 77° 30' 00" E	Kushan NBP PGW Black & Red Ware OCP	IAR 1963-64: 28-9 IAR 1964-65: 34-5 IAR 1965-66: 38 IAR 1966-67: 30-1 IAR 1968-69: 26 IAR 1970-71: 31-2 IAR 1971-72: 41-2	6.70

Nohar	Ganganagar	29° 10' 00" N - 74° 45' 00" E	Mature Harappan Sothi-Siswal	Dalal 1980: 26 K. N. Dikshit 1980: 35 Joshi et al. 1984: 522	2.00
Nohto	Thar Parkar	24° 58' 00" N - 69° 32' 00" E	Jhangar Jhukar	Lambrick 1964: 89	
Nokjo Shahdinzai	Jhalawan	27° 10' 30" N - 65° 39' 00" E	Islamic-British Londo Kulli Amri-Nal	Stein 1931: 152-53 Possehl 1986a: 147	7.50
Noor Garh	Gurgaon	28° 21' 00" N - 76° 36' 00" E	Post-urban Harappan	Joshi et al. 1984: 526	
Noor Shah Ther	Bahawalpur	28° 46' 48" N - 71° 00' 35" E	Mature Harappan	Mughal 1997: 48	1.30
Noor Shah-jee-Bhit	Sukkur	27° 36' 00" N - 68° 54' 00" E	Mature Harappan	Mallah 1994: 196	
Nuka	Dadu	26° 18' 00" N - 67° 37' 00" E	Mature Harappan	Flam 1981a: 293-95 Nissen 1983: 7	1.70
Nundara	Jhalawan	26° 28' 00" N - 65° 25' 00" E	Nal Kechi Beg	Stein 1931: 138-144 Possehl 1986a: 148	3.30
Nuran Kheri	Sonepat	29° 13' 00" N - 76° 33' 00" E	Post-urban Harappan	Joshi et al. 1984: 525	
Nushki	Chagai	29° 33' 00" N - 66° 02' 00" E	Early Islamic Partho-Sassanian Early Historic Iron Age Quetta Amri-Nal Kechi Beg	Fairservis 1956a: 199 de Cardi 1983: 21	
Oddi Bhit	Sukkur		Mature Harappan	Mallah 1994: 153-55	1.00
Odherio Timbo	Mehsana	23° 36' 20" N - 71° 49' 00" E	Rangpur IIC Anarta	K. K. Bhan 1994: 86-7	1.00
Oinwala Ther	Bahawalpur	28° 50' 15" N - 71° 22' 45" E	Hakra Wares	Mughal 1997: 42	2.40
Old Balor	Makran	26° 03' 00" N - 64° 25' 00" E	Kulli Togau	Stein 1931: 110 Possehl 1986a: 148	0.40
Oliya Peer	Jamnagar	21° 16' 00" N - 70° 01' 00" E	Lustrous Red Ware Sorath Harappan	IAR 1980-81: 13 K. K. Bhan 1983: 248-49	0.40
Onchi Ther	Rahimyar Khan	28° 31' 11" N - 70° 36' 20" E	Mature Harappan	Mughal 1997: 48	2.80
Orangi	Karachi	24° 59' 00" N - 67° 08' 00" E	Amri-Nal	Majumdar 1934: 144 Ghurye 1936: 5-6 Flam 1981a: 353	
Ori-no Thumdo	Banaskantha	23° 50' 00" N - 71° 09' 00" E	Anarta-Lustrous Red Ware	Ajithprasad and Sonawane, in press	0.40
Oriyo Timbo	Bhavnagar	21° 53' 12" N - 71° 36' 16" E	Lustrous Red Ware Microliths	Possehl 1980: 111 Joshi et al. 1984: 528 IAR 1984-85: 13 Rissman & Chitalwala 1990	4.40
Oriyodada-no Timbo	Surendranagar	23° 23' 00" N - 71° 48' 00" E	Lustrous Red Ware	Hegde and Sonawane 1986: 31 K. K. Bhan 1994: 86-7	2.50
Orumana	Mehsana	23° 36' 00" N - 71° 53' 40" E	Lustrous Red Ware Anarta	K. K. Bhan 1994: 86-7	0.20
Othmanjo Buthi	Karachi	25° 29' 00" N - 67° 53' 00" E	Amri-Nal	Majumdar 1934: 139-41 Flam 1981a: 345	7.40

P-10	Quetta-Pishin	30° 40' 00" N 66° 59' 00" E	-	Damb Sadaat Kechi Beg	Fairservis 1971c: 401	
Pabumath	Kutch	23° 37' 00" N 70° 31' 00" E	-	Late Sorath Harappan Mature Harappan	IAR 1977-78: 21 Possehl 1980: 111 Joshi et al. 1984: 528-29	1.50
Padadhari	Rajkot			Lustrous Red Ware	IAR 1978-79: 5	
Padaliya	Chittorgarh			Copper Hoard	Agrawala 1979: 91 Makkhan Lal 1984a: 36-7	
Padar	Rajkot	21° 59' 00" N 70° 50' 00" E	-	Sorath Harappan	IAR 1957-58: 19 Possehl 1980: 111 Joshi et al. 1984: 530	
Padra	Kheda	22° 28' 00" N 72° 33' 00" E	-	Lustrous Red Ware Sorath Harappan	Momin 1976: 53 Momin 1979: 118-19 Momin 1984	6.00
Padri	Bhavnagar	21° 20' 21" N 72° 06' 32" E	-	Sorath Harappan	Shinde 1991, 1992a	7.50
Pahlwan	Jind	29° 39' 00" N 76° 12' 00" E	-	OCP Sothi-Siswal	Suraj Bhan & Shaffer 1978: 62 Joshi et al. 1984: 519, 525	2.30
Paijo Kotiro	Dadu	26° 50' 00" N 67° 28' 00" E	-	Mature Harappan Amri-Nal	Krishna Deva and McCown 1949: 14-6 Flam 1981a: 267	
Pajrana	Saharanpur	30° 10' 00" N 77° 40' 00" E	-	OCP	IAR 1964-65: 44 Joshi et al. 1984: 523	
Pak	Makran	26° 04' 00" N 64° 13' 00'"E	-	Shahi Tump Kulli Amri-Nal	Stein 1931: 107-108 Possehl 1986a: 148	0.70
Pal	Rajkot	22° 18' 00" N 70° 43' 00" E	-	Sorath Harappan Microliths	IAR 1964-65: 12 Possehl 1980: 111 Joshi et al. 1984: 530	2.00
Palawa	Alwar			OCP	IAR 1980-81: 55	
Pali	Hissar	29° 10' 10" N 76° 04' 06" E	-	PGW Mature Harappan Sothi-Siswal	Suraj Bhan 1975: 124 Joshi et al. 1984: 519, 521 Mohan 1988: 113	10.00
Pallanpur	Ropar	30° 52' 00" N 76° 41' 00" E	-	Post-urban Harappan	IAR 1976-77: 43 Joshi et al. 1984: 527	
Palwal	Kurukshetra	29° 57' 00" N 76° 52' 00" E	-	Post-urban Harappan	Kumar 1978: 73 Joshi et al. 1984: 524	1.60
Pancha Pipro	Jamnagar	22° 02' 00" N 70° 05' 00" E	-	Lustrous Red Ware Sorath Harappan	IAR 1980-81: 13 K. K. Bhan 1989: 238	2.40
Pandi Wahi	Dadu	26° 40' 00" N 67° 22' 00" E	-	Mature Harappan Amri-Nal	Majumdar 1934: 91-5 Flam 1981a: 270-71 Nissen 1983: 7	1.50
Panditonka Tila	Kurukshetra	29° 45' 00" N 76° 34' 00" E	-	Kushan PGW Post-urban Harappan	U. V. Singh 1976: 28 Joshi et al. 1984: 524	
Panjalsa	Ambala	30° 27' 30" N 77° 07' 20" E	-	Post-urban Harappan	Kumar 1978: 48	
Panju Damb	Jhalawan	27° 19' 00" N 66° 25' 00" E	-	Early Historic Iron Age Togau	Stein 1931: 175	13.80
Panodi	Makran	25° 50' 00" N 62° 28' 00" E	-	Kulli Amri-Nal Kechi Beg	Stein 1931: 59 Possehl 1986a: 150	
Pansina	Surendranagar	22° 31' 00" N	-	Late Sorath Harappan	Rao 1963a: 206	

		71° 55' 00" E	Sorath Harappan	Possehl 1980: 111	
				Joshi et al. 1984: 529	
Paoli	Jind	29° 04' 39" N -	Copper Hoard	IAR 1968-69: 64	8.50
		76° 26' 30" E	Mature Harappan	Suraj Bhan 1975: 125	
			Sothi-Siswal	Joshi et al. 1984: 519, 524	
				Mohan 1988: 116	
Papra	Gurgaon	27° 54' 00" N -	Post-urban Harappan	Suraj Bhan 1975: 112, 126	
		77° 08' 00" E		Joshi et al. 1984: 519, 526	
Papreki	Saharanpur	29° 57' 00" N -	Post-urban Harappan	Joshi et al. 1984: 523	
		77° 37' 00" E			
Parachh	Chandigarh	30° 48' 00" N -	Post-urban Harappan	Joshi et al. 1984: 527	
		76° 46' 00" E			
Parait	Ludhiana		Post-urban Harappan	IAR 1980-81: 49	
				IAR 1984-85: 62	
Parhara	Bahawalpur	28° 44' 57" N -	Hakra Wares	Mughal 1997: 42	1.50
		71° 11' 35" E			
Parharewala 'A'	Bahawalpur	28° 04' 56" N -	Mature Harappan	Stein 1943a: 166	15.30
		71° 11' 13" E		Mughal 1997: 48	
				Dalal 1980: 12	
Parharewala 'B'	Bahawalpur	28° 04' 00" N -	Hakra Wares	Mughal 1997: 4232	0.60
		71° 11' 00" E		Dalal 1980: 12	
Paria, Waro Mohra	Kutch	23° 06' 00" N - 70° 05' 00" E	Medieval Post-urban Harappan	IAR 1986-87: 29	
Pariaj	Kheda	22° 32' 00" N -	Sorath Harappan	Momin 1984	
		72° 37' 00" E		Momin 1979: 128	
Pariar	Unnao	26° 35' 00" N -	Sunga-Kushan	Fuhrer 1891	
		80° 20' 00" E	NBP	V. Smith 1907: 53	
			PGW	IAR 1953-54: 38	
			Black Slip/Blk & Red	IAR 1978-79: 60-1	
			OCP & Copper Hoard	B. B. Lal and Dikshit 1982	
				Makkhan Lal 1984a: 36-7	
Parihati	Midnapur		Copper Hoard	Nag and Chakrabarty 1980: 97-100	
				Makkhan Lal 1984a: 40-1	
Parvala			Sorath Harappan	Chitalwala 1985: key Figure 8	
Pasawal	Kurukshetra	29° 57' 00" N -	Post-urban Harappan	Joshi et al. 1984: 524	
		76° 15' 00" E			
Pasegam	Bhavnagar	21° 51' 14" N -	Recent	IAR 1960-61: 8	16.20
		71° 38' 48" E	Red Polished Ware	Rao 1963a: 206	
			Late Sorath Harappan	Possehl 1980: 111	
			Sorath Harappan	Joshi et al. 1984: 528	
Patan	Hissar	29° 05' 35" N -	Mature Harappan	Suraj Bhan 1975: 124	1.10
		75° 38' 40" E		Joshi et al. 1984: 519	
				Mohan 1988: 116	
Patana	Bhavnagar		Sorath Harappan	IAR 1980-81: 12	
Patdi	Rajkot		Sorath Harappan	IAR 1965-66: 12	
Patel Raniji Ka Magsa	Kutch	23° 06' 00" N - 70° 11' 00" E	Post-urban Harappan	IAR 1986-87: 29	
Patel-nu Khetar	Banaskantha	23° 51' 00" N - 71° 30' 00" E	Arnata-Lustrous Red Ware	Ajithprasad and Sonawane, in press	0.20
Pathani Damb One	Kachi	28° 31' 00" N - 67° 26' 00" E	Mature Harappan Kot Diji	de Cardi 1964: 28-9 Flam 1981a: 255	
				de Cardi 1983: 35	
Pathani Damb	Kachi	28° 31' 00" N -	Early Historic	de Cardi 1983: 36	

Three		67° 26' 00" E		Mature Harappan		
Pathani Damb	Kachi	28° 31' 00" N	-	Pirak I	de Cardi 1983: 36	
Two		67° 26' 00" E		Mature Harappan		
Pathori	Saharanpur	29° 50' 00" N	-	Post-urban Harappan	Joshi et al. 1984: 523	
		77° 37' 00" E				
Patti Kalyana	Karnal	29° 12' 22" N	-	Medieval	Singh 1981: 71-2	0.70
		77° 01' 43" E		PGW	Joshi et al. 1984: 524	
				Post-urban Harappan		
Pavateswar Mahadev	Ahmedabad	22° 10' 00" N	-	Late Sorath Harappan	IAR 1957-58: 66	
		71° 54' 00" E		Sorath Harappan	Possehl 1980: 112	
					Joshi et al. 1984: 529	
Payuna Bhit	Bahawalpur	28° 49' 10" N	-	Cemetery H	Mughal 1997: 51	5.50
		71° 22' 25" E				
Payunewala Bhit Three	Bahawalpur	28° 48' 53" N	-	Hakra Wares	Mughal 1997: 42	0.20
		71° 22' 10" E				
Payunewala Bhit Two	Bahawalpur	28° 58' 53" N	-	Hakra Wares	Mughal 1997: 42	1.20
		71° 22' 10" E				
Peedal One	Kurukshetra	30° 01' 00" N	-	Post-urban Harappan	Kumar 1978: 53	3.00
		76° 20' 00" E			Joshi et al. 1984: 524	
Peedal Two	Kurukshetra	30° 00' 00" N	-	Post-urban Harappan	Kumar 1978: 53	2.20
		76° 20' 00" E		(OCP)		
Peerni Durga	Jamnagar	22° 17' 00" N	-	Lustrous Red Ware	IAR 1980-81: 13	0.30
		70° 04' 00" E			K. K. Bhan 1983: 256-57	
					K. K. Bhan 1989: 238	
Peervala	Jamnagar	22° 05' 00" N	-	Sorath Harappan	IAR 1980-81: 13	1.00
		70° 01' 00" E			K. K. Bhan 1989: 239	
Pepadia Timbo	Banaskantha	23° 50' 00" N	-	Rangpur IIC	Ajithprasad and Sonawane, in	0.10
		71° 30' 00" E		Rangpur IIB	press	
Periano Ghundai	Zhob	31° 22' 00" N	-	Waziri-Mature	Noetling 1898a: 460-70	14.40
		69° 23' 00" E		Harappan	Stein 1929a: 31-41	
				Kot Diji		
				Kechi Beg	Fairservis 1959: 329	
				Togau		
Phagla	Ludhiana	30° 56' 00" N	-	Medieval	IAR 1980-81: 48	1.00
		75° 57' 00" E		Kushan		
				Post-urban Harappan		
Phala	Jamnagar	22° 18' 00" N	-	Late Sorath Harappan	IAR 1954-55: 59	1.00
		70° 32' 00" E		Sorath Harappan	Rao 1963a: 206	
					Possehl 1980: 112	
					Joshi et al. 1984: 528	
					K. K. Bhan 1989: 238	
Phang	Karachi	25° 42' 00" N	-	Kot Diji	Majumdar 1934: 13-34	0.40
		67° 38' 00" E			Lambrick 1944: 60-1	
					Flam 1981a: 334-35	
Phaphrana	Karnal	29° 21' 26" N	-	Post-urban Harappan	Singh 1981: 58-9	0.90
		76° 38' 34" E			Joshi et al. 1984: 524	
Phukhi Ther	Bahawalpur	29° 04' 00" N	-	Cemetery H	Mughal 1997: 51	7.30
		71° 28' 13" E				
Phul Timbo	Bhavnagar	21° 50' 51" N	-	Red Polished Ware	Possehl 1980: 112	4.20
		71° 43' 30" E		Lustrous Red Ware	Joshi et al. 1984: 528	
Phul Wadi	Bhavnagar	21° 51' 00" N	-	Red Polished Ware	Possehl 1980: 112	6.00
		71° 40' 00" E		Lustrous Red Ware	Joshi et al. 1984: 528	
Phulabad Qalat	Makran	26° 06' 00" N	-	Shahi Tump	Besenval and Sanlaville 1990:	
		62° 24' 15" E		Dasht	111	

Site	District	Coordinates		Period	Reference	Size
Phusi Damb	Jhalawan	27° 05' 00" N 66° 11' 00" E	-	Early Historic Iron Age Kulli-Harappan Amri-Nal Kechi Beg Togau	deCardi 1964 Raikes 1968b: 114 de Cardi 1983: 39 Possehl 1986a: 149	10.50
Pidarak Oasis	Makran	25° 50' 45" N 63° 14' 15" E	-	Dasht	Besenval and Sanlaville 1990: 108	
Piki	Saharanpur	30° 02' 00" N 77° 36' 00" E	-	OCP Mature Harappan	IAR 1966-67: 43 Joshi et al. 1984: 521, 523	
Pilakhni	Saharanpur	30° 01' 00" N 77° 29' 00" E	-	Post-urban Harappan Mature Harappan	IAR 1963-64: 92 K. N. Dikshit 1982a: 114 Joshi et al. 1984: 521	
Pinaundian	Patiala	30° 26' 00" N 76° 26' 00" E	-	Post-urban Harappan	Joshi et al. 1984: 527	
Pindara	Jind	29° 19' 20" N 76° 22' 28" E	-	Post-urban Harappan Sothi-Siswal	Mohan 1988: 117	5.00
Pinjaura	Saharanpur	29° 56' 00" N 77° 33' 00" E	-	OCP Mature Harappan	IAR 1966-67: 43 Joshi et al. 1984: 521, 523	
Pinjupura	Jind	29° 39' 00" N 76° 12' 00" E	-	Post-urban Harappan Sothi-Siswal	Singh 1981: 117 Joshi et al. 1984: 519, 525	1.40
Pipalia	Rajkot			Sorath Harappan	IAR 1980-81: 11	
Pipalsa	Muzaffarnagar			Early Historic NBP OCP	Srivastava 1982: 83-6	5.00
Pipaltha One	Jind	29° 45' 33" N 76° 06' 35" E	-	Sothi-Siswal	Singh 1981: 117 Joshi et al. 1984: 519 Mohan 1988: 117	0.50
Pipaltha Three	Jind	29° 45' 00" N 76° 06' 30" E	-	Early Historic Post-urban Harappan	Singh 1981: 118 Joshi et al. 1984: 525 Mohan 1988: 118	1.30
Pipartoda One	Jamnagar	22° 02' 00" N 70° 05' 00" E	-	Lustrous Red Ware	K. K. Bhan 1986: 20	
Pipartoda Two	Jamnagar	22° 02' 00" N 70° 05' 00" E	-	Lustrous Red Ware	K. K. Bhan 1986: 20	
Piplan	Dera Ismail Khan	32° 10' 00" N 71° 06' 00" E	-	Kot Diji	Dani 1970-71: 32, Fig. 1	
Pipli, Gujarat	Bhavnagar			Sorath Harappan	IAR 1980-81: 12	
Pipli, Haryana	Kurukshetra	29° 58' 00" N 76° 63' 00" E	-	Post-urban Harappan	Kumar 1978: 74 Joshi et al. 1984: 524	
Pipllage	Amreli			Lustrous Red Ware	IAR 1978-79: 5	
Pir Alizai	Quetta-Pishin	30° 38' 00" N 66° 42' 30" E	-	Quetta	Stein 1929a: 86-87	0.90
Pir Haidar Shahr	Jhalawan	28° 16' 00" N 66° 06' 00" E	-	Kechi Beg Togau	de Cardi 1983: 31	0.30
Pir Hassan Shah	Kharan	28° 33' 00" N 65° 28' 00" E	-	Islamic-British Early Islamic Early Historic Londo Kulli Amri-Nal	Stein 1931: 27-8	15.00
Pir Mango	Karachi	25° 02' 00" N 67° 08' 00" E	-	Amri-Nal	Anonymous 1964b: 8 Flam 1981a: 354	

Pir Shah Jurio	Karachi	24° 53' 00" N 66° 58' 00" E	-	Mature Harappan	A. R. Khan 1968a: 3	
Piriya-no Timbo	Mehsana	23° 33' 35" N 71° 52' 30" E 71° 51' 00" E	-	Lustrous Red Ware	Ajithprasad and Sonawane, in press	4.00
Pirno Dhoro	Amreli			Late Sorath Harappan Sorath Harappan	A. F. Cunningham, unpublished	1.90
Pirojpur	Mehsana	23° 25' 00" N 71° 50' 00" E	-	Lustrous Red Ware	IAR 1978-79: 71 Joshi et al. 1984: 529 K. K. Bhan 1994: 86-7	0.20
Pirwada Khetar	Kutch	23° 20' 00" N 70° 00' 00" E	-	Mature Harappan	IAR 1965-66: 17 Possehl 1980: 112 Joshi et al. 1984: 529	
Pitar	Jamnagar	22° 41' 00" N 70° 32' 00" E	-	Late Sorath Harappan Sorath Harappan	Rao 1963a: 206 Possehl 1980: 112 Joshi et al. 1984: 528	
Pitaria	Rajkot	21° 35' 00" N 70° 55' 00" E	-	Late Sorath Harappan Sorath Harappan	IAR 1957-58: 20 Rao 1963a: 206 Possehl 1980: 112 Joshi et al. 1984: 528	
Pithad	Rajkot	21° 57' 00" N 70° 44' 00" E	-	Sorath Harappan	IAR 1959-60: 68 Joshi et al. 1984: 530	
Pithad One	Jamnagar	22° 41' 00" N 70° 32' 00" E	-	Late Sorath Harappan Sorath Harappan	K. K. Bhan 1986: 18	
Pithadia, Jamnagar	Jamnagar	22° 24' 00" N 70° 29' 00" E	-	Late Sorath Harappan Sorath Harappan	Bhan 1989: 239	1.50
Pithadia, Rajkot	Rajkot	21° 46' 00" N 70° 40' 00" E	-	Lustrous Red Ware Late Sorath Harappan	IAR 1957-58: 18-9 Joshi et al. 1984: 530 Possehl 1980: 112	
Pithal Puri	Sikar			OCP	IAR 1981-82: 62	
Pithavajal				Sorath Harappan	Chitalwala 1985: key Figure 8	
Pokhran	Karachi	25° 49' 00" N 67° 44' 00" E	-	Amri-Nal	Majumdar 1934: 128-29 Flam 1981a: 321	0.80
Pokhran Landi	Karachi	25° 49' 10" N 67° 44' 00" E	-	Mature Harappan Amri-Nal	Majumdar 1934: 127-28 Flam 1981a: 319	
Pondi	Rewa			Copper Hoard	B. B. Lal 1951: 22-3 Makkhan Lal 1984a: 38-9	
Popatpura	Kheda	22° 35' 00" N 72° 32' 00" E	-	Lustrous Red Ware Sorath Harappan	Momin 1979: 119-20 Momin 1984	
Prahag B	Makran	25° 17' 15" N 63° 25' 15" E	-	Mature Harappan Dasht	Besenval and Sanlaville 1990: 92	
Prahag C	Makran	25° 17' 15" N 63° 25' 15" E	-	Mature Harappan Dasht	Besenval and Sanlaville 1990: 92	
Prahag D	Makran	25° 17' 30" N 63° 26' 15" E	-	Mature Harappan Dasht	Besenval and Sanlaville 1990: 92-3	
Prahag 'A'	Makran	25° 17' 00" N 63° 27' 45" E	-	Kulli-Harappan Amri-Nal	Besenval and Sanlaville 1990: 91-2	5.00
Puchur Damb	Jhalawan	27° 16' 00" N 66° 23' 00" E	-	Islamic-British Kulli Anjira Kechi Beg Togau	Raikes 1968b: 148-49	
Pujam	Karnal	29° 51' 00" N	-	Early Historic	Suraj Bhan 1975: 125	

		76° 55' 00" E	PGW Post-urban Harappan	Joshi et al. 1984: 521, 524	
Pujana	Saharanpur	29° 41' 00" N - 77° 21' 00" E	Post-urban Harappan	Joshi et al. 1984: 523	
Pundari	Kurukshetra	29° 45' 46" N - 76° 33' 25" E	Post-urban Harappan	Kumar 1978: 60 Joshi et al. 1984: 524	2.20
Pur Balian Two	Muzaffarnagar	29° 21' 22" N - 77° 40' 00" E	OCP/Post-urban Harappan	Gaur and Lal 1992: 378	
Purani Rewari	Jaipur		OCP	IAR 1972-73: 29	
Puranpur	Saharanpur	29° 58' 00" N - 78° 00' 00" E	Post-urban Harappan	Joshi et al. 1984: 523	
Puthar	Karnal	29° 12' 51" N - 76° 52' 13" E	Early Historic Post-urban Harappan	Singh 1981: 72 Joshi et al. 1984· 524	0.70
Pypaliya			Sorath Harappan	Chitalwala 1985: key Figure 8	
Q-06	Quetta-Pishin	29° 46' 00" N - 66° 58' 00" E	Quetta Damb Sadaat Kechi Beg Togau	Fairservis 1956a: 196	0.30
Q-17	Quetta-Pishin	30° 14' 00" N - 66° 54' 00" E	Damb Sadaat Kechi Beg Togau Burj Basket-marked	Fairservis 1956a: 197 de Cardi 1983: 19	0.60
Q-18	Quetta-Pishin	30° 11' 00" N - 66° 53' 00" E	Early Islamic Damb Sadaat Kechi Beg Togau	Fairservis 1956a: 197	0.30
Q-20	Quetta-Pishin	30° 15' 00" N - 66° 56' 00" E	Quetta Damb Sadaat	Fairservis 1971c: 400	
Q-23	Quetta-Pishin	30° 16' 00" N - 66° 59' 00" E	Kechi Beg Togau	Fairservis 1956a: 198	0.20
Q-25	Quetta-Pishin	30° 21' 00" N - 66° 56' 00" E	Early Historic Iron Age Damb Sadaat Kechi Beg Togau Burj Basket-marked	Fairservis 1956a: 198	1.50
Q-26	Quetta-Pishin	30° 19' 00" N - 66° 52' 00" E	Damb Sadaat Kechi Beg	Fairservis 1956a: 198	1.10
Q-28	Quetta-Pishin	30° 19' 00" N - 66° 52' 00" E	Damb Sadaat Kechi Beg	Fairservis 1956a: 198	0.30
Q-30	Quetta-Pishin	30° 16' 00" N - 66° 58' 00" E	Modern Islamic-British Early Islamic Early Historic Iron Age Togau	Fairservis 1956a: 198	0.20
Q-32	Quetta-Pishin	30° 18' 00" N - 66° 57' 00" E	Modern Islamic-British Early Islamic Early Historic Kechi Beg Togau	Fairservis 1956a: 198	16.70
Q-33	Quetta-Pishin	29° 47' 00" N -	Quetta	Fairservis 1956a: 196	0.30

		67° 04' 00" E		Damb Sadaat Kechi Beg Togau		
Q-35	Quetta-Pishin	30° 13' 00" N 66° 47' 00" E	-	Quetta Damb Sadaat Kechi Beg Togau	Fairservis 1956a: 199	0.40
Q-36	Quetta-Pishin	29° 58' 00" N 66° 57' 00" E	-	Iron Age Damb Sadaat Kechi Beg Togau	Fairservis 1956a: 196	0.20
Qadain	Alwar			OCP	IAR 1980-81: 55	
Qadarwali Theri	Bahawalpur	29° 12' 00" N 72° 29' 00" E	-	Kot Diji	Stein 1943a: 133 Dalal 1980: 11	5.40
Qadir Bux Theri	Bahawalpur	28° 46' 37" N 71° 24' 07" E	-	Hakra Wares	Mughal 1997: 42	0.70
Qasaiwala	Bahawalpur	28° 42' 10" N 71° 19' 13" E	-	Mature Harappan	Mughal 1997: 48	1.70
Quabulpur One	Karnal	29° 38' 48" N 76° 42' 35" E	-	Post-urban Harappan	Singh 1981: 59 Joshi et al. 1984: 524	4.00
Quabulpur Two	Karnal	29° 38' 00" N 76° 42' 00" E	-	Post-urban Harappan	Singh 1981: 59-60 Joshi et al. 1984: 524	3.50
Quetta Miri	Quetta-Pishin	30° 15' 00" N 66° 59' 00" E	-	Early Historic Iron Age Quetta Damb Sadaat Kechi Beg Togau	Fairservis 1956a: 197	23.00
Quraish Ther	Bahawalpur	29° 14' 37" N 72° 42' 37" E	-	Kot Diji	Mughal 1997: 44	5.90
R. D. 66	Bahawalpur	29° 13' 06" N 72° 52' 04" E	-	Hakra Wares	Mughal 1997: 42	0.05
R. D. 89	Ganganagar	29° 12' 30" N 73° 04' 00" E	-	Sothi-Siswal Hakra Wares	Mughal 1997: 421980: 34	
R. D. 92	Ganganagar	29° 12' 30" N 73° 03' 30" E	-	Mature Harappan Sothi-Siswal	Dalal 1980: 34	
Radhana	Jind	29° 15' 00" N 76° 20' 53" E	-	Post-urban Harappan Sothi-Siswal	Singh 1981: 92 Joshi et al. 1984: 519, 525	1.80
Rafiabbad	Budaun			OCP	IAR 1978-79: 22	
Rahatpur	Muzaffarnagar	29° 39' 00" N 79° 19' 00" E	-	Post-urban Harappan	K. N. Dikshit 1981: 72 Joshi et al. 1984: 523	
Rahlavadar	Bhavnagar			Modern Late Sorath Harappan	Possehl 1980: 218	
Rahmanwali	Bahawalpur	28° 38' 52" N 71° 13' 13" E	-	Hakra Wares	Mughal 1997: 42	1.00
Rahon	Jullunder	31° 02' 00" N 76° 05' 00" E	-	Post-urban Harappan	Joshi et al. 1984: 526	
Raichandwala	Jind	29° 23' 52" N 76° 25' 05" E	-	Post-urban Harappan	Singh 1981: 92-3 Joshi et al. 1984: 525	1.10
Raipur-Jagir	Sikar			OCP	IAR 1981-82: 62	
Rais Sher Mohammad	Jhalawan	28° 19' 00" N 66° 08' 00" E	-	Early Historic Iron Age Amri-Nal	de Cardi 1983: 29-30 Mughal 1972a: 149	0.02

Site	District	Coordinates	Period	Reference	Size
			Kechi Beg		
			Togau		
Raison Two	Karnal	29° 53' 00" N - 76° 48' 00" E	Late Medieval Early Historic PGW	B. Datt 1980: 132 Singh 1981: 337 Joshi et al. 1984: 524	
Raja Karna Ka Qila One	Kurukshetra	29° 58' 00" N - 76° 49' 00" E	Post-urban Harappan Medieval NBP PGW Post-urban Harappan	IAR 1971-72: 23-4 Suraj Bhan 1975: 123 U. V. Singh 1976: 24-7 Joshi et al. 1984: 524	
Raja Karna Ka Qila Two	Kurukshetra	29° 58' 10" N - 76° 49' 10" E	Medieval NBP PGW Post-urban Harappan	IAR 1971-72: 23-4 Suraj Bhan 1975: 123 U. V. Singh 1976: 24-7 Joshi et al. 1984: 524	
Raja Sirkap	Faridkot	30° 39' 00" N - 74° 46' 00" E	Mature Harappan Sothi-Siswal	IAR 1958-59: 73 Suraj Bhan 1975: 122 Joshi et al. 1984: 520, 522	
Rajathali	Rajkot	21° 55' 00" N - 71° 01' 00" E	Sorath Harappan	IAR 1957-58: 19 Possehl 1980: 113 Joshi et al. 1984: 530	
Rajbai	Rahimyar Khan	28° 30' 55" N - 70° 53' 27" E	Mature Harappan	Mughal 1997: 48	3.10
Rajda	Jamnagar	22° 11' 00" N - 70° 36' 00" E	Lustrous Red Ware	K. K. Bhan 1986: 18	
Rajdhana	Saharanpur	30° 00' 00" N - 77° 28' 00" E	OCP	IAR 1964-65: 44 Joshi et al. 1984: 523	
Rajgarh, Jindh	Jind	29° 08' 00" N - 76° 22' 00" E	Post-urban Harappan	Joshi et al. 1984: 525 Singh 1981: 118	1.20
Rajgarh, Patiala	Patiala	30° 25' 00" N - 76° 45' 00" E	Post-urban Harappan	Joshi et al. 1984: 527	
Rajipipala			Sorath Harappan	Chitalwala 1985: key Figure 8	
Rajo-daro One	Dadu	26° 58' 00" N - 67° 23' 00" E	Kot Diji	Krishna Deva and McCown 1949: 14-6, 25 Flam 1981a: 265-66	0.70
Rajo-Daro Two	Dadu	26° 58' 00" N - 67° 23' 00" E	Mature Harappan	Krishna Deva and McCown 1949: 14-6, 25 Flam 1981a: 265-66	0.05
Rajpipla Eight	Bhavnagar	21° 51' 00" N - 71° 34' 00" E	Red Polished Ware Late Sorath Harappan	Possehl 1980: 231 Joshi et al. 1984: 529	
Rajpipla Five	Bhavnagar	21° 51' 00" N - 71° 34' 00" E	Late Sorath Harappan	Joshi et al. 1984: 529	
Rajpipla Four	Bhavnagar	21° 51' 00" N - 71° 34' 00" E	Late Historic Late Sorath Harappan Sorath Harappan	Possehl 1980: 113 Joshi et al. 1984: 529	2.00
Rajpipla Nine	Bhavnagar	21° 51' 00" N - 71° 34' 00" E	Late Sorath Harappan	Joshi et al. 1984: 529	
Rajpipla One	Bhavnagar	21° 51' 00" N - 71° 33' 00" E	Late Sorath Harappan Sorath Harappan	Possehl 1980: 113 Joshi et al. 1984: 528	3.90
Rajpipla Seven	Bhavnagar	21° 52' 00" N - 71° 33' 00" E	Lustrous Red Ware	Possehl 1980: 114 Joshi et al. 1984: 529	1.30
Rajpipla Six	Bhavnagar	21° 52' 00" N - 71° 38' 00" E	Red Polished Ware Late Sorath Harappan Sorath Harappan	Possehl 1980: 113 Joshi et al. 1984: 529	2.00

Rajpipla Three	Bhavnagar	21° 51' 00" N 71° 33' 00" E	-	Late Sorath Harappan Sorath Harappan	Possehl 1980: 113 Joshi et al. 1984: 529	0.50
Rajpipla Two	Bhavnagar	21° 51' 00" N 71° 33' 00" E	-	Late Historic Lustrous Red Ware	Possehl 1980: 113 Joshi et al. 1984: 529	1.10
Rajpur Parsu	Bijnor	29° 10' 00" N 78° 10' 00" E	-	Post-urban Harappan	V. Smith 1905: 231 B. B. Lal 1954-55: 146 Makkhan Lal 1984a: 366-7 Joshi et al. 1984: 523	
Rajpura	Hissar	29° 11' 03" N 76° 05' 08" E	-	Mature Harappan	IAR 1980-81: 16, 119 Joshi et al. 1984: 521	9.80
Rajpura Two	Jind	29° 10' 50" N 76° 03' 30" E	-	Sothi-Siswal	Mohan 1988: 119	3.00
Rajwadio Timbo Two	Mehsana	23° 35' 00" N 71° 51' 00" E	-	Lustrous Red Ware	K. K. Bhan 1994: 86-7	0.20
Rakhighari	Hissar	29° 17' 30" N 76° 06' 50" E	-	Mature Harappan Sothi-Siswal	IAR 1963-64: 90 Suraj Bhan 1975: 95-101, 124 IAR 1980-81: 16 Joshi et al. 1984: 520	40.00
Ramba One	Karnal	29° 48' 00" N 77° 00' 00" E	-	Post-urban Harappan	Suraj Bhan 1975: 125 Joshi et al. 1984: 524	
Ramba Two	Karnal	29° 48' 00" N 77° 00' 00" E	-	Post-urban Harappan	Suraj Bhan 1975: 125 Joshi et al. 1984: 524	
Ramgarh Pandwan One	Jind	29° 40' 23" N 76° 17' 00" E	-	Early Historic Post-urban Harappan	Singh 1981: 118 Joshi et al. 1984: 525 Mohan 1988: 121	1.70
Ramgarh Pandwan Two	Jind	29° 39' 46" N 76° 18' 00" E	-	Post-urban Harappan	Singh 1981: 118 Joshi et al. 1984: 525 Mohan 1988: 121	1.20
Ramjalra	Jaipur			OCP	IAR 1972-73: 29	
Ramjipura	Nimar			Copper Hoard	IAR 1962-63: 99 Makkhan Lal 1984a: 38-9	
Ramkali	Jind	29° 12' 26" N 76° 25' 16" E	-	PGW Post-urban Harappan	Singh 1981: 92-3 Joshi et al. 1984: 525 Mohan 1988: 124	1.40
Ramnagar	Alwar			OCP	IAR 1980-81: 55	
Rampar				Sorath Harappan	Chitalwala 1985: key Figure 8	
Rampar Vekarano Timbo	Kutch			Mature Harappan	IAR 1967-68: 9 Possehl 1980: 114	
Rampara	Kutch	23° 30' 00" N 70° 45' 00" E	-	Mature Harappan	Joshi et al. 1984: 529	
Rampara One	Bhavnagar	21° 58' 00" N 71° 29' 00" E	-	Sorath or Late Sorath Harappan	Possehl 1980: 114 Joshi et al. 1984: 529	0.50
Rampara Two	Bhavnagar	21° 58' 00" N 71° 29' 00" E	-	Late Sorath Harappan Sorath Harappan	Possehl 1980: 114 Joshi et al. 1984: 529	1.10
Rampur, Gujarat	Jamnagar	22° 17' 00" N 70° 04' 00" E	-	Lustrous Red Ware	K. K. Bhan 1986: 20	
Rampur, Punjab	Ropar	30° 36' 00" N 76° 47' 00" E	-	Post-urban Harappan	Joshi et al. 1984: 527	
Ramvav	Kutch	23° 32' 00" N 70° 28' 00" E	-	Mature Harappan	IAR 1977-78: 20. Joshi et al. 1984: 529	
Ran Pethani Nadi	Karachi			Amri-Nal Microliths	A. R. Khan 1968a: 8	
Rana Ghundai	Loralai	30° 24' 00" N	-	Buddhist	Noetling 1899: 101	1.40

				Waziri	Stein 1929a: 51-3	
		68° 45' 00" E		Kot Diji	Ross 1946	
				Kechi Beg	Fairservis 1959: 289	
				Togau		
				Burj Basket-marked		
				Kili Ghul Mohammad?		
Rana-Ki Radi	Jaipur			OCP	IAR 1973-74: 24	
Randal Dadwa	Rajkot			Lustrous Red Ware	IAR 1983-84: 17	1.00
				Sorath Harappan		
Randalio,	Amreli	21° 48' 00" N	-	Late Sorath Harappan	IAR 1958-59: 19	
Amreli		71° 03' 00" E			IAR 1983-84: 17	
					Joshi et al. 1984: 528	
Randalio,	Jamnagar	21° 49' 00" N	-	Sorath Harappan	Rao 1963a: 206	
Jamnagar		71° 03' 00" E			Possehl 1980: 114	
Rangel	Saharanpur	29° 56' 00" N	-	Post-urban Harappan	Joshi et al. 1984: 521, 523	
		77° 40' 00" E		Mature Harappan		
Rangpur	Surendranagar	22° 23' 56" N	-	Lustrous Red Ware	Rao 1963a: 4-175, 206	
		71° 55' 19" E		Late Sorath Harappan	Possehl 1980: 114	
				Sorath Harappan	Joshi et al. 1984: 530	
Rani Ran	Jind	29° 42' 30" N	-	Post-urban Harappan	Suraj Bhan & Shaffer 1978: 62	2.00
		76° 21' 32" E		Mature Harappan	Singh 1981: 100	
				Sothi-Siswal	Joshi et al. 1984: 519, 521, 525	
					Mohan 1988: 70	
Ranigam	Bhavnagar	21° 58' 00" N	-	Sorath Harappan	IAR 1960-61: 7	
		71° 43' 00" E			Rao 1963a: 206	
					Possehl 1980: 114	
					Joshi et al. 1984: 529	
Raniono Timbo	Bhavnagar			Sorath Harappan	IAR 1984-85: 14	
Ranke	Ludhiana	30° 57' 00" N	-	Post-urban Harappan	IAR 1980-81: 49	
		75° 37' 00" E				
Ranol-no Timbo	Surendranagar	23° 23' 00" N	-	Rangpur IIB-C	IAR 1984-85: 19	4.00
		71° 38' 00" E		Anarta	K. K. Bhan 1994: 86-7	
Ranparda	Jamnagar	21° 55' 00" N	-	Late Sorath Harappan	IAR 1957-58: 19	
		69° 23' 00" E		Sorath Harappan	Rao 1963a: 206	
					K. K. Bhan 1986: 19	
Ranpur	Jamnagar			Sorath Harappan	IAR 1980-81: 13	
Raowal	Ludhiana	30° 54' 00" N	-	Post-urban Harappan	IAR 1980-81: 49	
		75° 32' 00" E				
Rappwala Ther	Bahawalpur	28° 38' 55" N	-	Mature Harappan	Mughal 1997: 48	7.60
		71° 10' 20" E				
Rasnal	Jamnagar	22° 41' 00" N	-	Late Sorath Harappan	IAR 1958-59: 69	
		70° 35' 00" E		Sorath Harappan	K. K. Bhan 1986: 18	
Rasulpur	Saharanpur	30° 00' 00" N	-	Post-urban Harappan	Joshi et al. 1984: 523	
		77° 34' 00" E				
Ratan Dehra	Kurukshetra	30° 00' 20" N	-	Post-urban Harappan	Kumar 1978: 74	1.50
		76° 52' 00" E			Joshi et al. 1984: 524	
Ratan Heri	Ropar	30° 21' 00" N	-	Post-urban Harappan	Joshi et al. 1984: 524	
		76° 56' 00" E				
Ratankheri	Ambala			Post-urban Harappan	Kumar 1978: 39	1.50
Ratna Kheri	Saharanpur	29° 57' 00" N	-	Post-urban Harappan	K. N. Dikshit 1982a: 115	
		77° 30' 00" E		Mature Harappan	Joshi et al. 1984: 523	
Ratta Khera	Kurukshetra	30° 07' 00" N	-	Post-urban Harappan	Suraj Bhan 1975: 122	
Khuram		76° 27' 00" E		Mature Harappan	Joshi et al. 1984: 519, 521,	
				Sothi-Siswal	524	

Ratta One	Rahimyar Khan	28° 25' 40" N 70° 37' 45" E	-	Mature Harappan	Mughal 1997: 48	4.20
Ratta Theh	Hissar	29° 43' 15" N 75° 42' 15" E	-	PGW Post-urban Harappan Mature Harappan Sothi-Siswal	Suraj Bhan 1975: 124 IAR 1980-81: 16 Joshi et al. 1984: 520, 521, 526 Mohan 1988: 124	24.00
Ratta Ther	Bahawalpur	29° 02' 55" N 71° 31' 19" E	-	Cemetery H	Stein 1943a: 159 Mughal 1997: 51 Dalal 1980: 11	12.30
Ratta Three	Rahimyar Khan	28° 24' 30" N 70° 35' 58" E	-	Mature Harappan	Mughal 1997: 48	4.90
Ratta Two	Rahimyar Khan	28° 24' 29" N 70° 35' 50" E	-	Mature Harappan	Mughal 1997: 48	8.70
Rattakhera	Kurukshetra	30° 05' 00" N 76° 16' 00" E	-	Post-urban Harappan	Suraj Bhan 1975: 122 Joshi et al. 1984: 524	
Rattakhera Kuhram	Kurukshetra			Post-urban Harappan (OCP)	Kumar 1978: 54	
Rawalwas Kalan	Hissar	29° 04' 00" N 75° 35' 00" E	-	Sothi-Siswal	IAR 1987-88: 21	
Rawewala	Bahawalpur	28° 57' 05" N 71° 28' 45" E	-	Cemetery H	Mughal 1997: 51	5.40
Rehman Dheri	Dera Ismail Khan	31° 57' 00" N 70° 46' 00" E	-	Late Kot Diji Kot Diji	Dani 1970-71: 28 Durrani 1986 Durrani 1988	19.00
Reko Cave	Jhalawan	28° 06' 00" N 66° 38' 00" E	-	Londo Amri-Nal?	de Cardi 1983: 31	
Rel	Kheda	22° 28' 00" N 72° 30' 00" E	-	Sorath Harappan	IAR 1972-73: 10 Momin 1979: 120 Momin 1984	6.00
Reri Malakpur	Saharanpur	29° 55' 00" N 77° 29' 00" E	-	OCP Mature Harappan	IAR 1966-67: 43 Joshi et al. 1984: 521, 523	
Rewari	Mahendragarh			Copper Hoard	K. N. Dikshit 1968: 49 Suraj Bhan 1975: 126 Makkhan Lal 1984: 34-5	
Rhaurani Khera	Kurukshetra			PGW Post-urban Harappan	Kumar 1978: 305	
Rindhana	Sonepat	29° 07' 00" N 76° 30' 00" E	-	Post-urban Harappan Sothi-Siswal	Joshi et al. 1984: 519, 525	
Ritauli	Jind	29° 24' 20" N 76° 30' 10" E	-	PGW Post-urban Harappan	Suraj Bhan 1975: 125 Joshi et al. 1984: 521, 525 Mohan 1988: 126	11.00
Rizvi Karuna	Quetta-Pishin	30° 15' 00" N 66° 55' 00" E	-	Kechi Beg Togau Burj Basket-marked	Mughal 1972a: 149	
Rodinjo One	Kalat			Kechi Beg	Mughal 1972a: 149	
Rodkan	Makran	26° 06' 00" N 64° 24' 00" E	-	Islamic-British Early Islamic Kulli Amri-Nal Kechi Beg	Stein 1931: 109-110 Possehl 1986a: 148	0.90
Rohatwala	Bahawalpur	29° 07' 08" N 71° 42' 31" E	-	Cemetery H	Mughal 1997: 51	1.70
Roheljo Kund	Dadu	26° 53' 00" N	-	Amri-Nal	Krishna Deva and McCown 1949:	1.00

		67° 18' 00" E		16-25	Flam 1981a: 263	
Rohira	Sangrur	30° 38' 00" N 75° 50' 00" E	-	Medieval Sunga-Kushan PGW Post-urban Harappan Mature Harappan Sothi-Siswal	Suraj Bhan 1975: 122 IAR 1982-83: 65-6 Joshi et al. 1984: 520, 522, 527	9.00
Rohta	Patiala	30° 22' 00" N 76° 12' 00" E	-	Post-urban Harappan	Joshi et al. 1984: 527	
Rohtak	Rohtak	28° 53' 00" N 76° 35' 00" E	-	Post-urban Harappan	Suraj Bhan 1975: 125 Joshi et al. 1984: 526	
Rojdi	Rajkot	21° 51' 47" N 70° 55' 08" E	-	Medieval Red Polished Ware Late Sorath Harappan Sorath Harappan	IAR 1957-58: 18-9 Rao 1963a: 206 Chitalwala 1979: 115 Possehl and Raval 1989	7.50
Rookhi	Sonepat	29° 03' 00" N 76° 41' 00" E	-	Sothi-Siswal	Joshi et al. 1984: 519	
Ropar	Ropar	30° 58' 00" N 76° 32' 00" E	-	PGW Mature Harappan Sothi-Siswal	Suraj Bhan 1975: 122 Y. D. Sharma 1982a: 151 Joshi et al. 1984: 520	8.00
Rukhi	Sonepat	29° 03' 00" N 76° 41' 00" E	-	Post-urban Harappan	Suraj Bhan 1975: 125 Joshi et al. 1984: 525	
Runjan Damb	Jhalawan	27° 24' 00" N 65° 45' 00" E	-	Kulli	Stein 1931: 164 Possehl 1986a: 147	1.80
Runwali	Bahawalpur	28° 41' 43" N 71° 14' 30" E	-	Mature Harappan	Mughal 1997: 48	0.90
Rupalon	Ludhiana	31° 47' 00" N 76° 07' 00" E	-	Early Medieval Mature Harappan	IAR 1981-82: 55	8.00
Rupamore	Jamnagar	21° 60' 00" N 69° 45' 00" E	-	Sorath or Late Sorath Har	IAR 1978-79: 7 K. K. Bhan 1986: 16	
Sabdalpur	Saharanpur	29° 56' 00" N 77° 21' 00" E	-	Post-urban Harappan	Joshi et al. 1984: 523	
Sabharo	Sukkur	27° 24' 00" N 69° 09' 00" E	-	Mature Harappan	Mallah 1994: 197-98	0.70
Sadabad	Mathura			Copper Hoard	Srivastava 1973: 41 Makkhan Lal 1984a: 36-7	
Sadha Majra	Jind	29° 29' 00" N 76° 08' 00" E	-	Post-urban Harappan Sothi-Siswal	Joshi et al. 1984: 519, 525	
Sadwala Kanda	Bahawalpur	28° 48' 35" N 71° 06' 36" E	-	Hakra Wares	Mughal 1997: 42	4.50
Safuwala Four	Bahawalpur	28° 38' 50" N 71° 00' 00" E	-	Mature Harappan	Mughal 1997: 48	0.10
Safuwala Ther	Bahawalpur	28° 38' 11" N 70° 58' 35" E	-	Hakra Wares	Mughal 1997: 42	1.30
Safuwala Three	Bahawalpur	28° 38' 48" N 71° 00' 11" E	-	Hakra Wares	Mughal 1997: 43	8.10
Safuwala Two	Bahawalpur	28° 38' 12" N 70° 58' 32" E	-	Hakra Wares	Mughal 1997: 43	0.30
Saga	Karnal	29° 46' 00" N 76° 53' 00" E	-	Early Historic PGW Post-urban Harappan	Singh 1981: 60 Joshi et al. 1984: 524	5.00
Saguna	Palamau			Copper Hoard	Coggin-Brown 1915a: 125-26 Makkhan Lal 1984a: 38-9	

Sahib Khan	Quetta-Pishin	30° 36' 00" N 67° 03' 00" E	-	Quetta Damb Sadaat Kechi Beg Togau	Fairservis 1956a: 201	0.40
Sahnewali	Bhatinda	29° 55' 00" N 75° 06' 00" E	-	Post-urban Harappan	Joshi et al. 1984: 527	
Sai Timbo	Mehsana	23° 33' 00" N 71° 54' 00" E	-	Lustrous Red Ware	Joshi et al. 1984: 529 K. K. Bhan 1994: 86-7	5.40
Sai-no Tikro	Kheda	22° 28' 00" N 72° 31' 00" E	-	Sorath Harappan	Joshi et al. 1984: 530	
Said Qala	Kandahar	31° 38' 00" N 65° 35' 00" E	-	Damb Sadaat	Shaffer 1978b Ball and Gardin 1982: 230	3.50
Saipai	Etah	26° 27' 00" N 78° 58' 00" E	-	OCP & Copper Hoard	IAR 1970-71: 38 IAR 1971-72: 46-7 Wahal 1971-72: 12-3 Makkhan Lal 1984a: 36-7	0.50
Saiyid Maurez Damb	Sarawan	29° 26' 00" N 66° 27' 00" E	-	Londo Quetta Amri-Nal Kechi Beg Togau Burj Basket-marked	Stein 1931: 186-187 deCardi 1983: 22-3	6.30
Saka Kalat	Jhalawan	27° 34' 00" N 65° 52' 00" E	-	Londo Kulli	Stein 1931: 165-166 Possehl 1986a: 147	3.70
Saket Colony	Meerut			OCP	IAR 1981-82: 103	
Salari	Larkana	27° 10' 00" N 67° 20' 00" E	-	Mature Harappan Amri-Nal	Flam, unpublished	
Salarpura	Saharanpur	29° 49' 00" N 77° 16' 00" E	-	Post-urban Harappan Mature Harappan	IAR 1965-66: 54 Joshi et al. 1984: 523	
Salepur	Saharanpur	29° 56' 00" N 77° 21' 00" E	-	Post-urban Harappan Mature Harappan	Joshi et al. 1984: 521, 523	
Salepur Bhokri	Saharanpur	30° 02' 00" N 77° 35' 00" E	-	PGW OCP	IAR 1966-67: 43 Joshi et al. 1984: 523	
Salimgarh	Hissar	29° 10' 30" N 75° 32' 45" E	-	Post-urban Harappan Sothi-Siswal	Suraj Bhan 1975: 124 Joshi et al. 1984: 520, 526 Mohan 1988: 127	3.20
Salimgarh Two	Hissar	29° 11' 20" N 75° 33' 11" E	-	Post-urban Harappan	Mohan 1988: 128	2.90
Salimpur Mahdud	Saharanpur	29° 56' 00" N 77° 04' 00" E	-	Post-urban Harappan	Joshi et al. 1984: 523	
Salu Khan	Sarawan	29° 18' 00" N 66° 29' 00" E	-	Anjira Amri-Nal Kechi Beg	Stein 1931: 186	1.80
Samadhiala, Bhavnagar	Bhavnagar	21° 52' 00" N 71° 38' 00" E	-	Late Sorath Harappan Sorath Harappan	Possehl 1980: 115 Joshi et al. 1984: 529	1.00
Samadhiala, Surendranagar	Surendranagar	22° 19' 00" N 71° 42' 00" E	-	Sorath Harappan	Possehl 1980: 115 Joshi et al. 1984: 530	
Samagogha	Kutch	22° 55' 00" N 69° 40' 00" E	-	Late Sorath Harappan Mature Harappan	Possehl 1980: 115 Joshi et al. 1984: 528	
Samarala	Ludhiana	31° 47' 00" N 76° 07' 00" E	-	Mature Harappan	IAR 1981-82: 55	8.00
Sambhalkha	Muzaffarnagar	29° 25' 00" N 77° 20' 00" E	-	Post-urban Harappan	K. N. Dikshit 1981: 72 Joshi et al. 1984: 523	
Sambhi One	Karnal	29° 49' 00" N	-	Post-urban Harappan	Suraj Bhan 1975: 125	

		76° 49' 00" E			Joshi et al. 1984: 524	
Samdo	Jind	29° 29' 31" N	-	PGW	Singh 1981: 93	0.20
		76° 23' 51" E		Post-urban Harappan	Joshi et al. 1984: 525	
Samel Heri	Ropar	30° 20' 00" N	-	Post-urban Harappan	Joshi et al. 1984: 524	
		76° 57' 00" E				
Sami	Makran	26° 02' 00" N	-	Islamic	Besenval and Sanlaville 1990:	
		63° 25' 00" E		Zangian	116	
				Shahi Tump		
				Kulli-Harappan		
				Dasht		
Sami Hill	Makran	26° 02' 00" N	-	Islamic	Besenval and Sanlaville 1990:	
		63° 25' 00" E		Zangian	117	
				Shahi Tump		
				Kulli-Harappan		
				Dasht		
Samlehri	Ambala			Post-urban Harappan (OCP	Kumar 1978: 39	
Sampan Kheri	Kurukshetra			Post-urban Harappan (OCP	Kumar 1978: 61	3.00
Sanalo	Jamnagar	22° 12' 00" N	-	Lustrous Red Ware	Rao 1963a: 207	
		70° 25' 00" E		Late Sorath Harappan		
Sanara Timbo	Jamnagar			Sorath Harappan	IAR 1978-79: 7	
Sanasi Buthi	Dadu	26° 19' 00" N	-	Mature Harappan	Lambrick 1944: 65	
		67° 35' 00" E			Flam 1981a: 290	
Sanasiwala	Rahimyar Khan	28° 27' 37" N	-	Mature Harappan	Mughal 1997: 48	2.50
		70° 52' 00" E				
Sand	Ambala	30° 10' 00" N	-	Post-urban Harappan	IAR 1963-64: 27	
		77° 15' 00" E		(OCP)	Suraj Bhan 1975: 124	
					Joshi et al. 1984: 524	
Sandhai	Ropar	30° 10' 00" N	-	Post-urban Harappan	Joshi et al. 1984: 524	
		77° 15' 00" E				
Sandhanawala Ther	Bahawalpur	29° 13' 56" N	-	Mature Harappan	Mughal 1997: 44, 48	10.00
		72° 50' 15" E		Kot Diji	Stein 1943a: 145-46	
					Dalal 1980: 11	
Sandhya	Kurukshetra			Post-urban Harappan	Kumar 1978: 302	
Sang	Zhob	31° 27' 00" N	-	Kechi Beg	Stein 1929a: 50	
		69° 22' 30" E		Togau		
				Burj Basket-marked		
Sangan	Jind	29° 48' 17" N	-	Post-urban Harappan	Singh 1981: 120	1.00
		76° 13' 59" E			Joshi et al. 1984: 525	
Sangatpura	Jind	29° 20' 00" N	-	Post-urban Harappan	Suraj Bhan 1975: 124	
		76° 14' 00" E			Joshi et al. 1984: 525	
Sanghewala	Bahawalpur	28° 44' 30" N	-	Mature Harappan	Mughal 1997: 48	5.40
		71° 58' 44" E				
Sanghi	Rohtak	29° 02' 00" N	-	Post-urban Harappan	Suraj Bhan 1975: 125	
		76° 37' 00" E			Joshi et al. 1984: 519, 526	
Sanghol	Ludhiana	30° 47' 00" N	-	Kushan	IAR 1968-69: 25	9.00
		76° 24' 00" E		PGW	Suraj Bhan 1975: 122	
				Post-urban Harappan	Joshi et al. 1984: 520	
Sangroli	Kurukshetra	29° 50' 00" N	-	Post-urban Harappan	Joshi et al. 1984: 524	
		76° 30' 00" E				
Sankatrawalo Thumdo	Banaskantha	23° 54' 00" N	-	Anarta-Rangpur IIC	Ajithprasad and Sonawane, in	0.30
		71° 20' 00" E		Anarta-Rangpur IIB	press	

Site	District	Coordinates		Period	Reference	Size
Santhali				Sorath Harappan	Chitalwala 1985: key Figure 8	
Santhli Five	Banaskantha	23° 54' 15" N	71° 29' 50" E	Rangpur IIC Microlithic	Ajithprasad and Sonawane, in press	0.30
Santhli Four	Banaskantha	23° 54' 00" N	71° 28' 50" E	Amri-Nal Burial Pottery Microlithic	Ajithprasad and Sonawane, in press	0.01
Santhli One	Banaskantha	23° 54' 10" N	71° 30' 00" E	Anarta (Pre-Harappan)	Ajithprasad and Sonawane, in press	0.60
Santhli Six	Banaskantha	23° 54' 00" N	71° 30' 20" E	Rangpur IIC Microlithic	Ajithprasad and Sonawane, in press	0.30
Santhli Three	Banaskantha	23° 53' 50" N	71° 29' 00" E	Anarta? Microlithic	Ajithprasad and Sonawane, in press	0.02
Santhli Two	Banaskantha	23° 54' 00" N	71° 29' 10" E	Amri-Nal Burial Pottery Microlithic	Ajithprasad and Sonawane, in press	0.60
Sanukewala	Bahawalpur	28° 51' 41" N	71° 10' 34" E	Mature Harappan	Mughal 1997: 48	14.80
Sanukewala Three	Bahawalpur	28° 51' 50" N	71° 10' 25" E	Mature Harappan	Mughal 1997: 48	0.70
Sanukewala Two	Bahawalpur	28° 51' 40" N	71° 10' 16" E	Mature Harappan Hakra Wares	Mughal 1997: 448	5.40
Sapar Kheri	Kurukshetra	29° 47' 00" N	76° 30' 00" E	Post-urban Harappan	Joshi et al. 1984: 524	
Sapara	Kutch			Mature Harappan	IAR 1979-80: 17	
Saparwadi	Jamnagar			Sorath Harappan	IAR 1980-81: 13	
Saprod Nangal	Jullunder	31° 15' 00" N	75° 43' 00" E	Post-urban Harappan	Joshi et al. 1984: 526	
Sarangpur	Ropar	30° 46' 00" N	76° 48' 00" E	OCP Mature Harappan Sothi-Siswal	IAR 1964-65: 33 Suraj Bhan 1975: 123 Joshi et al. 1984: 527	
Sardar Khel Damb	Sarawan			Quetta Amri-Nal Kechi Beg Togau	Anonymous 1964b: 17	1.50
Sardargarh Two	Ganganagar	29° 24' 00" N	73° 45' 00" E	Mature Harappan	Dalal 1980: 26 Joshi et al. 1984: 522	
Sari Damb	Makran	26° 58' 00" N	64° 02' 00" E	Shahi Tump Kulli Amri-Nal	Stein 1931: 44 Possehl 1986a: 150	
Sarkari Kumar	Saharanpur	30° 02' 00" N	77° 33' 00" E	OCP	IAR 1966-67: 43 Joshi et al. 1984: 523	
Sarkari Sheikh	Saharanpur	30° 00' 00" N	77° 36' 00" E	OCP Mature Harappan	IAR 1966-67: 43 Joshi et al. 1984: 521, 523	
Sarkhadolino Timbo	Mehsana			Lustrous Red Ware	K. K. Bhan 1994: 86-7	0.80
Sarola	Kurukshetra	29° 02' 00" N	76° 15' 00" E	PGW OCP	Kumar 1978: 54 Joshi et al. 1984: 524	3.00
Sarthauli	Shahjahanpur			Copper Hoard	B. B. Lal 1951: 28-9 Makkhan Lal 1984a: 36-7	
Saruppur Taga	Saharanpur	29° 56' 00" N	77° 18' 00" E	OCP	IAR 1965-66: 54 Joshi et al. 1984: 523	
Sarwania One	Jamnagar	22° 09' 00" N	70° 22' 00" E	Late Sorath Harappan Sorath Harappan	K. K. Bhan 1986: 18	
Sasa	Patiala			PGW	Kumar 1978: 79-80	2.20

			Post-urban Harappan		
Sasi	Patiala	30° 07' 00" N - 76° 20' 00" E	Post-urban Harappan	Suraj Bhan 1975: 122 / Joshi et al. 1984: 522	
Sasiyano Timbo	Mehsana	23° 35' 00" N - 71° 51' 10" E	Lustrous Red Ware	Hegde and Sonawane 1986: 30 / K. K. Bhan 1994: 86-7	2.20
Satoj-Sar	Patiala		Pre-Kushan / PGW / Mature Harappan	IAR 1979-80: 105	
Satrand Khas Two	Hissar		Mature Harappan	IAR 1980-81: 16	
Satrod Khurd One	Hissar	29° 08' 57" N - 75° 46' 48" E	Mature Harappan / Sothi-Siswal	Joshi et al. 1984: 520 / Mohan 1988: 129	4.00
Satrod Khurd Three	Hissar	29° 08' 45" N - 75° 46' 11" E	Sothi-Siswal	Suraj Bhan 1975: 124 / Joshi et al. 1984: 520 / Mohan 1988: 130	
Satrod Khurd Two	Hissar	29° 08' 45" N - 75° 46' 11" E	Mature Harappan	Suraj Bhan 1975: 124 / Joshi et al. 1984: 520	3.80
Satuki East	Bahawalpur	29° 14' 14" N - 72° 47' 54" E	Hakra Wares	Mughal 1997: 43	
Satuki West	Bahawalpur	29° 14' 13" N - 72° 47' 45" E	Hakra Wares	Mughal 1997: 43	
Saudevalio	Jamnagar	22° 00' 00" N - 69° 44' 00" E	Sorath Harappan	Joshi et al. 1984: 529	
Saunkhr Three	Karnal	29° 47' 00" N - 76° 53' 00" E	Sothi-Siswal	Joshi et al. 1984: 519	
Saunkhra One	Karnal	29° 48' 35" N - 76° 51' 55" E	Post-urban Harappan	Singh 1981: 61 / Joshi et al. 1984: 524	2.40
Saunkhra Three	Karnal	29° 48' 05" N - 76° 51' 20" E	Post-urban Harappan / Sothi-Siswal	Singh 1981: 61-2 / Joshi et al. 1984: 524	0.70
Saunkhra Two	Karnal	29° 47' 35" N - 76° 50' 55" E	Post-urban Harappan / Sothi-Siswal	Singh 1981: 61-2 / Joshi et al. 1984: 524	
Sauransanda	Bahawalpur	28° 45' 40" N - 71° 19' 20" E	Mature Harappan	Mughal 1997: 48	1.20
Savani	Jamnagar	20° 58' 00" N - 70° 28' 00" E	Sorath Harappan	IAR 1977-78: 19 / Joshi et al. 1984: 529	
Savarniya	Bikaner		Copper Hoard	K. N. Dikshit 1968: 49 / IAR 1968-69: 69 / Makkhan Lal 1984a: 36-7	
Savni			Sorath Harappan	Chitalwala 1985: key Figure 8	
Sayra			Sorath Harappan	Chitalwala 1985: key Figure 8	
Seed Farm	Bhavnagar	21° 57' 52" N - 71° 35' 15" E	Late Sorath Harappan / Sorath Harappan	Possehl 1980: 115 / Joshi et al. 1984: 529	1.90
Seel	Patiala	30° 20' 00" N - 76° 32' 00" E	Post-urban Harappan	Joshi et al. 1984: 527	
Seer Dheri	Bannu	32° 52' 10" N - 70° 36' 00" E	Late Kot Diji	Allchin, Allchin, Durrani and Khan 1985: 193	1.10
Segak	Makran	26° 01' 00" N - 64° 17' 00" E	Kulli / Amri-Nal	Stein 1931: 109, pl 8 / Possehl 1986a: 148	1.80
Sejpura	Ganganagar		Mature Harappan	Pande & Ramachandran 1971: 41	
Selari	Kutch	23° 42' 00" N - 70° 37' 00" E	Mature Harappan	IAR 1967-68: 17 / Possehl 1980: 115 / Joshi et al. 1984: 529	
Senalo	Jamnagar	22° 12' 00" N - 70° 25' 00" E	Lustrous Red Ware / Late Sorath Harappan	Possehl 1980: 115 / Joshi et al. 1984: 528	

Serfraguvar	Jhunjhunu		OCP	IAR 1980-81: 56	
Serikoran Damb	Makran	26° 57' 00" N - 64° 05' 00" E	Kulli Amri-Nal Kechi Beg	Stein 1931: 44	
Shadiwala Ther	Rahimyar Khan	28° 30' 28" N - 70° 55' 30" E	Mature Harappan	Mughal 1997: 48	1.30
Shah Ghar Ther	Rahimyar Khan	28° 26' 45" N - 70° 27' 40" E	Mature Harappan	Mughal 1997: 48	12.90
Shahabad	Hardoi		NBP PGW Copper Hoard	IAR 1966-67: 81 IAR 1965-66: Makkhan Lal 1984a: 36-7	
Shahi Tump	Makran	26° 00' 30" N - 63° 00' 15" E	Shahi Tump Kulli	Stein 1931: 88-103, pl 7 Besenval and Sanlaville 1990: 113	0.70
Shahiwala	Bahawalpur	29° 02' 35" N - 71° 21' 41" E	Cemetery H	Mughal 1997: 51	20.00
Shahjo Kotiro	Karachi	25° 35' 00" N - 67° 50' 00" E	Kulli-Harappan	Majumdar 1934: 137-39 Flam 1981a: 340	
Shahpur, Hissar	Hissar	29° 09' 59" N - 75° 36' 51" E	Sothi-Siswal	Suraj Bhan 1975: 124 Joshi et al. 1984: 520 Mohan 1988: 130	9.00
Shahr Kuloi	Sarawan	29° 29' 00" N - 66° 28' 00" E	Quetta	de Cardi 1983: 22	1.60
Shahr Sardar	Sarawan	29° 27' 00" N - 66° 29' 00" E	Quetta Amri-Nal Kechi Beg	de Cardi 1983: 22	0.90
Shahrak Pogunsh	Makran	26° 02' 00" N - 63° 20' 00" E	Shahi Tump Kulli? Dasht	Besenval and Sanlaville 1990: 115	
Shaikhanwala Ther	Bahawalpur	29° 01' 17" N - 71° 11' 21" E	Cemetery H	Mughal 1997: 51	1.50
Shakar Khan Damb	Jhalawan	27° 45' 30" N - 66° 17' 00" E	Kili Ghul Mohammad	Stein 1931: 168	
Shakarrpur	Saharanpur	29° 48' 00" N - 77° 57' 00" E	Post-urban Harappan	Joshi et al. 1984: 523	
Shakhupur Manchuri	Karnal		Post-urban Harappan	Suraj Bhan & Shaffer 1978: 62	1.10
Shakpur Machuri	Karnal	29° 35' 00" N - 76° 45' 00" E	Post-urban Harappan	Joshi et al. 1984: 525	
Shamgarh	Karnal	29° 47' 00" N - 76° 49' 00" E	Post-urban Harappan	Suraj Bhan 1975: 125 Joshi et al. 1984: 524	
Shami Damb	Makran	26° 44' 00" N - 63° 16' 00" E	Islamic Early Historic Londo Kulli	Stein 1931: 51 Possehl 1986a: 150	2.50
Shamli-Shamla	Muzaffarnagar		PGW OCP/Post-urban Harappan	Gaur and Lal 1992: 378	
Sheikhri Two	Bahawalpur	28° 41' 24" N - 71° 03' 05" E	Mature Harappan	Mughal 1997: 48	1.50
Sheikhwali	Bahawalpur	28° 30' 05" N - 70° 58' 18" E	Mature Harappan	Mughal 1997: 48	6.50
Sheorajpur	Kanpur		Copper Hoard	B. B. Lal 1951: 29 Makkhan Lal 1984a: 36-7	

Site	District	Coordinates		Period/Ware	Reference	Size
Sheri Khan Tarakai	Bannu	32° 49' 00" N 70° 27' 00" E	-	Kechi Beg	Khan, Knox and Thomas 1986 Khan, Knox and Thomas 1988 Khan, Knox and Thomas 1991a: 35-63	21.00
Sherpur	Saharanpur	29° 53' 00" N 77° 39' 00" E	-	OCP Mature Harappan	IAR 1966-67: 43 Joshi et al. 1984: 521, 523	
Sherpura	Ganganagar	29° 10' 00" N 75° 15' 00" E	-	Sothi-Siswal	IAR 1977-78: 47 K. N. Dikshit 1980: 34 Joshi et al. 1984: 520, 522	2.00
Sheruwala Ther	Bahawalpur	28° 43' 52" N 71° 13' 20" E	-	Mature Harappan	Mughal 1997: 48	22.20
Sheruwala Three	Bahawalpur	28° 44' 05" N 71° 13' 10" E	-	Hakra Wares	Mughal 1997: 43	6.00
Sheruwala Two	Bahawalpur	28° 43' 55" N 71° 14' 25" E	-	Hakra Wares	Mughal 1997: 43	15.10
Shidiwala 'A'	Bahawalpur	28° 46' 43" N 71° 13' 43" E	-	Hakra Wares	Mughal 1997: 43	0.80
Shidiwala 'B'	Bahawalpur			Mature Harappan	Mughal 1997: 48	5.70
Shiharu-no Thumdo	Banaskantha	23° 50' 20" N 71° 30' 00" E	-	Anarta-Rangpur IIC	Ajithprasad and Sonawane, in press	0.30
Shikarpur	Muzaffarnagar	29° 23' 00" N 77° 39' 00" E	-	OCP	IAR 1986-87: 80	
Shikarpur	Kutch	23° 07' 00" N 70° 35' 00" E	-	Mature Harappan	IAR 1986-87: 80	5.30
Shikarpur One	Muzaffarnagar	29° 25' 40" N 77° 29' 40" E	-	OCP/Post-urban Harappan	Gaur and Lal 1992: 379	
Shikarwala Ther	Bahawalpur	28° 45' 49" N 71° 24' 32" E	-	Mature Harappan	Stein 1943a: 167-68 Mughal 1997: 48 Dalal 1980: 12	4.00
Shimoyno Dhoro	Rajkot			Lustrous Red Ware	Chitalwala 1979: 115	0.70
Shisak	Rajkot			Lustrous Red Ware	Chitalwala 1979: 115	1.00
Shishpur, Karnal	Karnal	29° 14' 39" N 76° 49' 03" E		Post-urban Harappan Sothi-Siswal	Singh 1981: 73 Joshi et al. 1984: 519, 524	0.70
Shortughai		37° 18' 00" N 69° 30' 00" E	-	Post-urban Harappan Mature Harappan	Ball and Gardin 1982: 255 Francfort 1989b	2.50
Shrinagar	Jamnagar	21° 39' 00" N 69° 37' 00" E	-	Late Sorath Harappan Sorath Harappan	Rao 1963a: 207 Possehl 1980: 116 Joshi et al. 1984: 528	
Shukartal	Saharanpur	29° 55' 00" N 77° 17' 00" E	-	OCP	IAR 1965-66: 54 Joshi et al. 1984: 523	
SI-6	Karachi			Mature Harappan	Fairservis 1971c: 410	
Siah Damb, Jhau	Jhalawan	26° 21' 00" N 65° 40' 00" E	-	Kulli Amri-Nal	Stein 1931: 135, pl 10 Possehl 1986a: 147	17.60
Siah Damb, Surab	Jhalawan	28° 34' 00" N 66° 11' 00" E	-	Amri-Nal Kechi Beg Togau Burj Basket-marked	deCardi 1965: 103-10 deCardi 1983: 28	1.50
Siamlo Kalan One	Jind	29° 12' 45" N 76° 24' 10" E	-	Post-urban Harappan Sothi-Siswal	Singh 1981: 93-4 Joshi et al. 1984: 519	2.00
Siamlo Kalan Two	Jind	29° 12' 10" N 76° 23' 51" E	-	Post-urban Harappan Sothi-Siswal	Singh 1981: 94 Joshi et al. 1984: 519	2.10
Sianzai	Sarawan	29° 05' 00" N 66° 15' 00" E	-	Amri-Nal	Mughal 1972a: 149	

Sibri Two	Kachi	29° 20' 00" N 67° 35' 00" E	-	Kechi Beg Togau	Jarrige, Jarrige, Meadow and Quivron 1995: 76	
Siddhuwala Ther	Bahawalpur	28° 57' 28" N 71° 13' 28" E	-	Cemetery H	Stein 1943a: 171 Mughal 1997: 51 Dalal 1980: 13	3.70
Siddhuwali 'B'	Bahawalpur	28° 57' 43" N 71° 13' 40" E	-	Mature Harappan	Mughal 1997: 48	0.30
Siddhuwali 'C'	Bahawalpur	28° 58' 00" N 71° 14' 02" E	-	Kot Diji	Mughal 1997: 44	0.90
Siddhuwali 'D'	Bahawalpur	28° 58' 13" N 71° 14' 11" E	-	Mature Harappan	Mughal 1997: 48	1.80
Siddhuwali 'E'	Bahawalpur	28° 58' 23" N 71° 14' 01" E	-	Cemetery H	Mughal 1997: 51	4.90
Siddhuwali 'F'	Bahawalpur	28° 58' 18" N 71° 13' 25" E	-	Cemetery H	Mughal 1997: 51	5.90
Sidsar	Bhavnagar			Sorath Harappan Microliths	IAR 1980-81: 12	
Sihnewali	Bhatinda	29° 55' 00" N 75° 30' 00" E	-	Post-urban Harappan	Joshi 1986: 139	25.00
Sikrera	Muzaffarnagar	29° 18' 00" N 77° 58' 00" E	-	Post-urban Harappan	Joshi et al. 1984: 523	
Sikri, Muzaffarnagar	Muzaffarnagar	29° 32' 00" N 77° 55' 00" E	-	Post-urban Harappan	Joshi et al. 1984: 523	
Sikri, Saharanpur	Saharanpur	29° 53' 00" N 77° 38' 00" E	-	OCP	IAR 1964-65: 44 Joshi et al. 1984: 523	
Sila Kheri One	Jind	29° 23' 00" N 76° 37' 12" E	-	Historic Post-urban Harappan	Dhattarwal 1978: 34 Joshi et al. 1984: 525 Mohan 1988: 132	3.80
Sinad	Jind	29° 45' 50" N 76° 13' 00" E	-	Post-urban Harappan	Singh 1981: 120 Joshi et al. 1984: 525 Mohan 1988: 133	0.20
Sindhvi Khera	Jind	29° 17' 04" N 76° 24' 35" E	-	Post-urban Harappan	Singh 1981: 94 Joshi et al. 1984: 525	3.80
Singauli Taga	Meerut	28° 55' 00" N 77° 23' 00" E	-	Mature Harappan	K. N. Dikshit 1982a: 115	2.20
Singen Kalat	Jhalawan	28° 25' 00" N 67° 06' 00" E	-	Londo Anjira Amri-Nal Kechi Beg Togau Burj Basket-marked	de Cardi 1983: 33	
Singharwali	Bahawalpur	28° 47' 35" N 71° 20' 12" E	-	Cemetery H	Mughal 1997: 51	0.05
Singhra	Karnal	29° 42' 00" N 76° 50' 00" E	-	Post-urban Harappan Sothi-Siswal	Suraj Bhan & Shaffer 1978: 62 Joshi et al. 1984: 519, 525	0.70
Singhwa	Hissar	29° 02' 00" N 76° 17' 00" E	-	Post-urban Harappan Sothi-Siswal	Suraj Bhan 1975: 125 Joshi et al. 1984: 520, 526	
Singhwal	Jind	29° 35' 50" N 76° 13' 20" E	-	Early Medieval Post-urban Harappan	Singh 1981: 120-21 Joshi et al. 1984: 525 Mohan 1988: 133	0.40
Singi Kalat	Makran	26° 16' 30" N 64° 58' 30" E	-	Kulli	Stein 1931: 116, pl 8 Possehl 1986a: 148	6.00
Singot Damb	Jhalawan	27° 20' 00" N 66° 19' 00" E	-	Kulli Togau?	Raikes 1968b: 149 Possehl 1986a: 149	

Sinjawi Ghundai	Loralai			Partho-Sassanian Mature Harappan Kot Diji	Mughal 1972a: 149	
Sirsa Ther	Budaun			Medieval Kushan PGW OCP	IAR 1978-79: 22	
Sisai Bola One	Hissar	29° 10' 00" N 76° 01' 00" E	-	Post-urban Harappan	IAR 1980-81: 16 Joshi et al. 1984: 526	
Sisai Bola Two	Hissar	29° 10' 00" N 76° 01' 00" E	-	Post-urban Harappan	IAR 1980-81: 16 Joshi et al. 1984: 526	
Sisai Kali Ravan Four	Hissar	29° 09' 00" N 76° 00' 00" E	-	Post-urban Harappan	IAR 1980-81: 16 Joshi et al. 1984: 526	
Sisai Kali Ravan One	Hissar	29° 09' 00" N 76° 00' 00" E	-	Post-urban Harappan	IAR 1980-81: 16 Joshi et al. 1984: 526	
Sisai Kali Ravan Two	Hissar	29° 09' 00" N 76° 00' 00" E	-	Post-urban Harappan	IAR 1980-81: 16 Joshi et al. 1984: 526	
Sisai One	Hissar	29° 11' 47" N 76° 03' 20" E	-	Post-urban Harappan	Suraj Bhan 1975: 124 Mohan 1988: 134	6.00
Sisai Three	Hissar	29° 10' 00" N 76° 00' 00" E	-	Mature Harappan	Suraj Bhan 1975: 124 Joshi et al. 1984: 521	
Sisai Two	Hissar	29° 12' 02" N 76° 02' 50" E	-	Post-urban Harappan	Suraj Bhan 1975: 124 Mohan 1988: 134	10.00
Sisana	Rohtak	29° 56' 00" N 76° 51' 00" E	-	Sothi-Siswal	Joshi et al. 1984: 519	
Sisanah	Rohtak	28° 56' 00" N 76° 51' 00" E	-	Post-urban Harappan	Joshi et al. 1984: 526	
Siswal	Hissar	29° 13' 12" N 75° 30' 30" E	-	Post-urban Harappan Mature Harappan Sothi-Siswal	Suraj Bhan 1975: 103-09, 12 Joshi et al. 1984: 520, 521, 526 Mohan 1988: 136	6.00
Siswan	Ropar	30° 50' 00" N 76° 42' 00" E	-	Post-urban Harappan	Joshi et al. 1984: 527	
Site 63	Makran	25° 13' 45" N 63° 28' 30" E	-	Mature Harappan	Besenval and Sanlaville 1990: 93	
Site 64	Makran	25° 13' 45" N 63° 28' 30" E	-	Mature Harappan	Besenval and Sanlaville 1990: 93	
Site 70	Makran	25° 15' 55" N 63° 26' 00" E	-	Shahi Tump Mature Harappan Dasht	Besenval and Sanlaville 1990: 93	
Site Near Kuki Damb	Jhalawan	28° 44' 00" N 66° 21' 00" E	-	Amri-Nal Kechi Beg	Stein 1931: 17 de Cardi 1983: 26-7	6.70
Siwana Mal One	Jind	29° 15' 12" N 76° 35' 20" E	-	Post-urban Harappan	Mohan 1988: 136	4.90
Siwana Mal Two	Jind	29° 16' 07" N 76° 35' 04" E	-	Post-urban Harappan	Mohan 1988: 138	3.60
Soont-no Timbo	Banaskantha	23° 56' 00" N 71° 20' 00" E	-	Anarta-Rangpur IIC	Ajithprasad and Sonawane, in press	0.03
Sodhra	Sukkur			Mature Harappan	Mallah 1994: 160-61	3.80
Sohavi	Ludhiana	30° 45' 00" N 76° 24' 00" E	-	Post-urban Harappan	Joshi et al. 1984: 527	
Sohniwali	Bahawalpur	28° 45' 04" N 71° 00' 58" E	-	Hakra Wares	Mughal 1997: 43	22.00

Sohniwali Two	Bahawalpur	28° 44' 50" N 71° 01' 30" E	-	Hakra Wares	Mughal 1997: 43	4.20
Sohren Damb One	Makran	26° 30' 00" N 65° 28' 00" E	-	Kulli Amri-Nal	Stein 1931: 131, 137	1.10
Solath	Jind	29° 23' 00" N 76° 31' 00" E	-	Post-urban/PGW Overlap(?) Harappan Post-urban	Suraj Bhan & Shaffer 1978: 62 Joshi et al. 1984: 525	3.90
Somnath	Jamnagar	20° 47' 00" N 70° 30' 00" E	-	Lustrous Red Ware Prabhas (Rojdi B-C) Pre-Prabhas	IAR 1955-56: 7 Rao 1963a: 206 Possehl 1980: 12 Joshi et al. 1984: 5	9.00
Sonaria	Jamnagar	22° 00' 00" N 69° 46' 00" E	-	Late Sorath Harappan Sorath Harappan	K. K. Bhan 1988: 239	2.20
Sorah Site	Sukkur			Mature Harappan	Mallah 1994: 162-64	8.20
Sorak Damb	Jhalawan	27° 26' 00" N 66° 28' 00" E	-	Partho-Sassanian Complex B Londo Kulli-Harappan Amri-Nal Kechi Beg	Stein 1931: 176 Raikes 1968b: 112, 146 Possehl 1986a: 149	0.30
Sosan	Faridkot	30° 50' 00" N 75° 00' 00" E	-	Post-urban Harappan	Joshi et al. 1984: 527	
Sothi	Ganganagar	29° 11' 00" N 74° 50' 00" E	-	Mature Harappan Sothi-Siswal	K. N. Dikshit 1980 K. N. Dikshit 1984a Joshi et al. 1984: 520	4.00
Sotka Koh	Makran	25° 25' 15" N 63° 27' 15" E	-	Mature Harappan	Dales 1962a: 86-92 Besenval and Sanlaville 1990: 95	16.00
Spina Ghundai	Quetta-Pishin	30° 57' 00" N 66° 40' 00" E	-	Early Islamic Partho-Sassanian	Stein 1929a: 82 Fairservis 1956a: 200	0.40
Spur Number Three	Larkana	27° 18' 00" N 68° 07' 20" E		Mature Harappan Early Historic Iron Age Quetta Damb Sadaat Kechi Beg	Hussain 1989	
Sra Kala	Quetta-Pishin	30° 38' 00" N 66° 59' 00" E	-	Partho-Sassanian Quetta Damb Sadaat Kechi Beg	Stein 1929a: 82-83 Mughal 1972a: 149	2.60
Sraduk	Makran	27° 01' 00" N 64° 11' 00" E	-	Islamic-British Early Islamic Kulli Amri-Nal Kechi Beg	Stein 1931: 45 Possehl 1986a: 150	5.00
Stupa Tikri	Sukkur			Mature Harappan	Mallah 1994: 156-59	
Subri Khwaja	Saharanpur	29° 53' 00" N 77° 37' 00" E	-	Post-urban Harappan	Joshi et al. 1984: 523	
Sudhel	Ropar	30° 10' 00" N 77° 14' 00" E	-	Post-urban Harappan	Joshi et al. 1984: 524	
Suhavi	Ludhiana			Post-urban Harappan	Suraj Bhan 1975: 122	

Sujnipur	Mehsana	23° 46' 00" N - 72° 12' 00" E	Lustrous Red Ware	Rao 1963a: 189, 207 Possehl 1980: 116 Joshi et al. 1984: 529 K. K. Bhan 1994: 86-7	
Suketri	Ropar	30° 45' 00" N - 76° 50' 00" E	Post-urban Harappan	Joshi et al. 1984: 524	
Suketri	Ambala		Post-urban Harappan	Joshi et al. 1984: 524	1.50
Sulla	Bahawalpur		Mature Harappan Sothi-Siswal	F. A. Khan 1959a: 192	
Sullewala	Bahawalpur	28° 53' 44" N - 71° 27' 53" E	Mature Harappan	Mughal 1997: 48	4.40
Sultanpur, Gujarat	Rajkot	21° 45' 00" N - 70° 50' 00" E	Late Sorath Harappan	IAR 1958-59: 19 Rao 1963a: 207 Possehl 1980: 16 Joshi et al. 1984: 528	
Sultanpur, Haryana	Gurgaon	27° 56' 00" N - 77° 08' 00" E	Post-urban Harappan Mature Harappan	Suraj Bhan 1975: 112 Joshi et al. 1984: 519	
Sumer Damb	Jhalawan	27° 09' 30" N - 66° 26' 00" E	Amri-Nal Kechi Beg	Raikes 1968b: 150-51	0.20
Suneri Damb	Jhalawan	27° 27' 00" N - 65° 45' 00" E	Islamic-British Early Islamic Partho-Sassanian Early Historic Londo Kechi Beg	Stein 1931: 164-65	3.50
Sunet	Ludhiana	30° 50' 00" N - 75° 50' 00" E	Early Medieval Gupta Sunga-Kushan Black Slipped Ware PGW Post-urban Harappan	IAR 1983-84: 67-8	
Suniarheri	Patiala	30° 27' 00" N - 76° 26' 00" E	Post-urban Harappan	Joshi et al. 1984: 527	
Sur Jangal	Loralai	30° 16' 00" N - 68° 30' 00" E	Kechi Beg Togau	Stein 1929a: 73-77 Fairservis 1959: 293-300	1.60
Surab Valley 'A'	Jhalawan	28° 23' 00" N - 66° 10' 00" E	Togau Burj Basket-marked	de Cardi 1983: 28	
Surain Damb	Makran	26° 45' 00" N - 63° 53' 00" E	Shahi Tump Kulli Amri-Nal	Field 1959: 84, 88-9, 185 Possehl 1986a: 149	1.50
Surajpur	Ropar		Mature Harappan	IAR 1975-76: 76	
Surbra	Jind	29° 29' 35" N - 76° 04' 21" E	Post-urban Harappan Sothi-Siswal	Singh 1981: 121 Joshi et al. 1984: 525	1.40
Surkh Damb	Jhalawan	28° 18' 00" N - 66° 16' 00" E	Anjira Amri-Nal Kechi Beg	Stein 1931: 19 de Cardi 1983: 27	2.90
Surkotada	Kutch	23° 37' 00" N - 70° 50' 00" E	Mature Harappan Early to Mature Harappan	IAR 1964-65: 12 Possehl 1980: 116 Joshi et al. 1984: 528	1.40
Suryavadar One	Jamnagar	21° 56' 00" N - 69° 45' 00" E	Late Sorath Harappan Sorath Harappan	K. K. Bhan 1986a: 19	
Sutana	Karnal	29° 22' 10" N - 76° 52' 50" E	Post-urban Harappan	Singh 1981: 73 Joshi et al. 1984: 525	1.20

Sutkagen-dor	Makran	25° 30' 00" N	-	Kulli-Harappan	Stein 1931: 60-71	4.50
		62° 00' 00" E			Possehl 1986a: 150	
Suwaiki	Ganganagar	29° 20' 00" N	-	Mature Harappan	Stein 1943a: 47	
		73° 48' 00" E		Sothi-Siswal	Dalal 1980: 8, 35	
Taghazi Damb	Kharan	27° 49' 45" N	-	Londo	Stein 1931: 31-32	
		65° 50' 45" E		Kulli	Possehl 1986a: 150	
Tahirpur	Saharanpur	29° 55' 00" N	-	PGW	IAR 1964-65: 44	
		77° 32' 00" E		OCP	Joshi et al. 1984: 523	
Talavadino Timbo	Ahmedabad			Sorath Harappan	IAR 1966-67: 8	
Talewadi	Jamnagar	22° 02' 00" N	-	Lustrous Red Ware	IAR 1980-81: 13	2.00
		70° 05' 00" E			K. K. Bhan 1989: 242	
Taloor-ji Bhit	Khairpur	26° 43' 00" N	-	Mature Harappan	Kazi 1992	6.40
		68° 26' 00" E				
Talu	Hissar	28° 59' 00" N	-	Post-urban Harappan	Joshi et al. 1984: 526	
		76° 09' 00" E				
Talwandino Timbo	Ahmedabad	22° 45' 00" N	-	Sorath Harappan	Joshi et al. 1984: 530	
		72° 20' 00" E				
Talwara	Ludhiana	30° 55' 00" N	-	Post-urban Harappan	Joshi et al. 1984: 522, 527	
		75° 44' 00" E		Mature Harappan		
Talwara, Hissar	Hissar	29° 41' 30" N	-	PGW	Suraj Bhan 1975: 122	2.90
		75° 38' 42" E		Mature Harappan	Joshi et al. 1984: 520	
					Mohan 1988: 138	
Tamajuri	Midnapur			Copper Hoard	Anderson 1883: 485-86	
					Makkhan Lal 1984a: 40-1	
Tando Rahim Khan	Dadu	26° 30' 00" N	-	Early to Mature Harappan	Majumdar 1934: 86	0.70
		67° 33' 00" E		Amri-Nal	Flam 1981a: 272-73	
Tandwal	Ambala	30° 27' 00" N	-	PGW	Suraj Bhan 1975: 123	
		77° 04' 00" E		Post-urban Harappan	Joshi et al. 1984: 524	
Tang	Makran	25° 46' 30" N	-	Dasht	Besenval and Sanlaville 1990: 107	
		62° 17' 45" E				
Tankaria	Jamnagar	21° 56' 00" N	-	Late Sorath Harappan	IAR 1979-80: 25	6.00
		69° 25' 00" E		Sorath Harappan	Rao 1963a: 207	
					Possehl 1980: 116	
					Joshi et al. 1984: 528	
					K. K. Bhan 1989: 239	
Taraghada	Rajkot	21° 44' 00" N	-	Lustrous Red Ware	IAR 1958-59: 19	20.00
		70° 26' 00" E		Sorath Harappan	Possehl 1980: 117	
					Joshi et al. 1984: 530	
Tarakai Ghundai	Bannu	32° 49' 00" N	-	Kot Diji	Khan, Knox and Thomas 1989: 284	3.50
		70° 24' 00" E			Khan, Knox and Thomas 1991a: 31-4	
Tarakai Qila	Bannu	32° 55' 00" N	-	Late Kot Diji	Allchin, Allchin, Durrani and Khan 1985: 9, 133-34	8.00
		70° 23' 00" E			Khan, Knox and Thomas 1991a: 20	
Tarana Four	Jamnagar	22° 43' 00" N	-	Late Sorath Harappan	IAR 1979-80: 25	0.30
		70° 27' 00" E		Sorath Harappan	K. K. Bhan 1989: 239	
Tarana One	Jamnagar	22° 43' 00" N	-	Sorath or Late Sorath Har	IAR 1979-80: 25	
		70° 27' 00" E				
Tarana Three	Jamnagar	22° 43' 00" N	-	Sorath or Late Sorath Harappan	K. K. Bhan 1989: 239	60.00
		70° 27' 00" E				

Tarana Two	Jamnagar	22° 43' 00" N - 70° 27' 00" E		Late Sorath Harappan Sorath Harappan	IAR 1960-61: 8 Possehl 1980: 117 Joshi et al. 1984: 529 K. K. Bhan 1986: 18	
Tarasamra	Bhavnagar			Sorath Harappan	IAR 1980-81: 12	
Tarat Qalat Two	Makran	25° 48' 45" N - 62° 41' 15" E		Shahi Tump Dasht	Besenval and Sanlaville 1990: 102	
Tarkhanwala Dera	Ganganagar	29° 15' 00" N - 73° 12' 00" E		Mature Harappan Sothi-Siswal	Ghosh 1962: 3 Dalal 1980: 26, 34 Joshi et al. 1984: 522	
Tarshikhad	Ahmedabad			Sorath Harappan	IAR 1974-75: 68	
Tarsoolwala	Bahawalpur	29° 04' 08" N - 71° 51' 06" E		Mature Harappan	Mughal 1997: 48	13.50
Taskola	Jaipur			OCP	IAR 1973-74: 24	
Tatana	Bhavnagar	21° 58' 00" N - 71° 40' 00" E		Late Sorath Harappan Sorath Harappan	Possehl 1980: 117 Joshi et al. 1984: 529	5.30
Tatarpur Kalan	Saharanpur			Mature Harappan	IAR 1965-66: 54 K. N. Dikshit 1982a: 115	
Tauli	Saharanpur	29° 56' 00" N - 77° 27' 00" E		OCP	IAR 1965-66: 54 Joshi et al. 1984: 523	
Taung	Dadu	25° 46' 00" N - 67° 34' 00" E		Historic Jhangar Mature Harappan Amri-Nal	Lambrick 1941 Lambrick 1944: 61-2 Flam 1981a: 327-29	0.50
Tegak	Jhalawan	28° 19' 00" N - 66° 09' 00" E		Londo Kulli Togau	deCardi 1964 de Cardi 1983: 30 Possehl 1986a: 148	1.10
Teli Wala	Saharanpur	29° 57' 00" N - 77° 58' 00" E		Post-urban Harappan	Joshi et al. 1984: 523	
Telod	Broach	21° 42' 00" N - 72° 46' 00" E		Sorath Harappan	IAR 1957-58: 15 Rao 1963a: 190, 207 Possehl 1980: 117 Joshi et al. 1984: 529	
Tetariyo	Amreli	21° 49' 00" N - 71° 06' 00" E		Late Sorath Harappan Sorath Harappan	IAR 1958-59: 19 Rao 1963a: 207 Possehl 1980: 17 Joshi et al. 1984: 528	
Thakowala	Rahimyar Khan	28° 36' 50" N - 70° 57' 00" E		Mature Harappan	Mughal 1997: 48	5.10
Thale Damb	Makran	26° 00' 45" N - 63° 53' 00" E		Kulli Amri-Nal	Stein 1931: 104-105 Possehl 1986: 148 Besenval and Sanlaville 1990: 118	1.20
Thana Bhawan	Muzaffarnagar	29° 35' 00" N - 77° 25' 00" E		Post-urban Harappan	K. N. Dikshit 1981: 72 Joshi et al. 1984: 523	
Tharo Waro Daro	Sukkur			Mature Harappan	Mallah 1994: 199-202	50.00
Tharro Hill	Nawabshah	24° 50' 00" N - 67° 49' 00" E		Mature Harappan? Amri-Nal Kili Ghul Mohammad Microliths?	Majumdar 1934: 20-2 Lambrick 1942a: 109-10 Flam 1981a: 243	12.50
Tharulawala Ther	Bahawalpur	28° 41' 12" N - 71° 17' 47" E		Mature Harappan	Mughal 1997: 48	1.20

Tharwala	Bahawalpur	28° 37' 16" N	-	Mature Harappan	Mughal 1997: 48	1.50
		71° 00' 49" E				
Thathaula	Saharanpur	29° 46' 00" N	-	Post-urban Harappan	Joshi et al. 1984: 523	
		77° 59' 00" E				
Thebachada One	Rajkot	22° 22' 00" N	-	Late Sorath Harappan	IAR 1961-62: 10	5.00
		70° 51' 00" E			Possehl 1980: 117	
					Joshi et al. 1984: 528	
Thebachada Two	Rajkot	22° 22' 00" N	-	Lustrous Red Ware	Chitalwala 1979: 115	1.00
		70° 51' 00" E				
Theekariya	Jaipur			OCP	IAR 1973-74: 24	
Then Lahara	Ludhiana	30° 35' 00" N	-	Kushan	IAR 1980-81: 48	6.00
		75° 20' 00" E		Post-urban Harappan		
Ther	Sukkur	27° 34' 00" N	-	Mature Harappan	Lambrick 1946: 50-1	0.40
		69° 06' 00" E			Flam 1981a: 245	
					Mallah 1994: 165-66	
Theraj	Hissar	29° 44' 00" N	-	Sothi-Siswal	Suraj Bhan 1975: 122	
		75° 08' 00" E			Joshi et al. 1984: 520, 526	
Theriwala	Bahawalpur	29° 05' 48" N	-	Hakra Wares	Mughal 1997: 43	18.90
		72° 48' 24" E				
Therri Bahadur Shah	Jacobabad	28° 23' 00" N	-	Mature Harappan	Anonymous 1965: 6	3.80
		68° 22' 00" E			Flam 1981a: 250	
Thikariya-no Timbo	Mehsana	23° 31' 40" N	-	Lustrous Red Ware	Hegde and Sonawane 1986: 30	3.40
		71° 45' 20" E		Anarta	K. K. Bhan 1994: 86-7	
					Joshi et al. 1984: 529	
Thirana	Karnal	29° 25' 00" N	-	Post-urban Harappan	Suraj Bhan & Shaffer 1978: 62	5.70
		76° 50' 00" E			Joshi et al. 1984: 525	
Thok Valley One	Jhalawan	28° 44' 00" N	-	Togau	Stein 1931: 17	2.50
		66° 21' 00" E		Burj Basket-marked		
Thoom Thali	Bahawalpur	28° 46' 20" N	-	Hakra Wares	Mughal 1997: 43	14.10
		71° 21' 20" E				
Thoriwala	Bahawalpur	28° 36' 10" N	-	Mature Harappan	Mughal 1997: 43, 48	0.60
		71° 01' 50" E		Hakra Wares		
Thuwa	Jind	29° 31' 36" N	-	Early Historic	Singh 1981: 95	2.10
		76° 21' 00" E		Post-urban Harappan	Joshi et al. 1984: 525	
					Mohan 1988: 139	
Tigrana	Bhiwani	28° 53' 15" N	-	Post-urban Harappan	Suraj Bhan 1975: 125	5.00
		76° 08' 12" E		Mature Harappan	Joshi et al. 1984: 519, 526	
				Sothi-Siswal	IAR 1987-88: 21	
					Mohan 1988: 139	
Tigri	Sikar			OCP	IAR 1973-74: 24	
Tihani Qalat	Makran	25° 49' 45" N	-	Zangian	Besenval and Sanlaville 1990:	
		62° 44' 15" E		Dasht	103	
Tikrat Dehri	Rahimyar Khan	28° 03' 00" N	-	Mature Harappan	Stein 1943a: 101	
		70° 09' 00" E			Dalal 1980: 8	
Tikri Damb	Jhalawan	26° 23' 00" N	-	Kulli	Stein 1931: 133-134	
		65° 24' 00" E		Amri-Nal	Possehl 1986a: 147	
Tikrol	Saharanpur	29° 44' 00" N	-	Post-urban Harappan	K. N. Dikshit 1981: 72	
		77° 22' 00" E		Mature Harappan	Joshi et al. 1984: 521, 523	
Timaram	Rajkot	21° 53' 00" N	-	Sorath Harappan	IAR 1957-58: 19	
		70° 30' 00" E			Possehl 1980: 117	
					Joshi et al. 1984: 530	
Timbi One	Jamnagar			Sorath Harappan	IAR 1980-81: 13	
				Microliths		

Timbo One	Jamnagar		Sorath Harappan	IAR 1980-81: 13	
Timbo One	Mehsana	23° 43' 00" N - 71° 36' 00" E	Lustrous Red Ware	K. K. Bhan 1994: 86-7	0.70
Timbo Two	Jamnagar		Sorath Harappan	IAR 1980-81: 13	
Timbo Two	Mehsana	23° 43' 10" N - 71° 37' 00" E	Lustrous Red Ware	K. K. Bhan 1994: 86-7	0.60
Timran	Rajkot		Lustrous Red Ware	Chitalwala 1979: 115	4.50
Toda	Muzaffarnagar	29° 17' 00" N - 77° 32' 00" E	Kushan PGW OCP	Gaur and Lal 1992: 379	
Todi Khera	Jind	29° 25' 20" N - 76° 42' 12" E	Medieval Post-urban Harappan	Joshi et al. 1984: 525 Mohan 1988: 141	2.90
Todia Timbo	Kutch		Mature Harappan	IAR 1955-56: 70	
Todio	Kutch	23° 05' 00" N - 68° 55' 00" E	Mature Harappan	Rao 1963a: 188, 207 Possehl 1980: 118 Joshi et al. 1984: 529	
Togau	Sarawan	29° 04' 00" N - 66° 18' 00" E	Amri-Nal Kechi Beg Togau Burj Basket-marked	de Cardi 1951 Mughal 1972a: 149 de Cardi 1983: 23	
Toji Damb	Kharan	28° 53' 00" N - 65° 40' 00" E	Early Historic? Iron Age? Kulli Amri-Nal Kechi Beg	Stein 1931: 22-5 Possehl 1986a: 151	0.70
Tokaria Timbo	Mehsana	23° 28' 00" N - 71° 49' 30" E	Lustrous Red Ware Microliths	IAR 1982-83: 28 K. K. Bhan 1994: 86-7	3.60
Tor Ghundai	Sarawan	29° 45' 00" N - 66° 20' 00" E	Quetta Amri-Nal Kechi Beg	Fairservis 1956a: 199 de Cardi 1983: 20	7.50
Tor Warai	Sarawan	29° 46' 00" N - 66° 20' 00" E	Quetta Amri-Nal Kechi Beg	de Cardi 1983: 20	
Trekoe	Bahawalpur	28° 49' 17" N - 71° 19' 15" E	Cemetery H Mature Harappan	Stein 1943a: 162-63 Mughal 1997: 48, 51 Dalal 1980: 11	12.00
Trihni	Dadu	26° 23' 00" N - 67° 42' 00" E	Trihni	Majumdar 1934: 60-3 Mackay 1943: 35-7	
Trillar	Bahawalpur	29° 10' 42" N - 72° 12' 30" E	Hakra Wares	Mughal 1997: 43	2.90
Tump Qalat	Makran	26° 06' 00" N - 62° 22' 15" E	Islamic Dasht	Besenval and Sanlaville 1990: 110	
Tumpak	Makran	26° 07' 00" N - 61° 55' 00" E	Kulli	Stein 1931: 83	
Tup Takhtikhel	Bannu	32° 29' 00" N - 70° 42' 00" E	Kili Ghul Mohammad?	Khan, Knox and Thomas 1987: 85	
Tupi	Larkana	27° 44' 00" N - 67° 32' 00" E	Mature Harappan Amri-Nal (w/ Kot Diji)	Flam, unpublished	
Tuppewala Three	Bahawalpur		Cemetery H	Mughal 1997: 51	0.90
Turanwala	Bahawalpur	29° 03' 52" N - 71° 28' 15" E	Cemetery H	Mughal 1997: 51	3.00

Turawewala 'B'	Bahawalpur	28° 46' 40" N - 71° 30' 05" E	Hakra Wares	Mughal 1997: 43	3.50
Turawewala 'C'	Bahawalpur	28° 47' 05" N - 71° 30' 45" E	Hakra Wares	Mughal 1997: 43	1.00
Turawewali Theri	Bahawalpur	28° 46' 36" N - 71° 30' 12" E	Hakra Wares	Mughal 1997: 43	1.00
Turewala	Bahawalpur		Cemetery H	F. A. Khan 1959a: 192	
Ubhad	Surat		Sorath Harappan Microliths	IAR 1982-83: 31	
Uchcha Gaon	Patiala	30° 22' 00" N - 76° 21' 00" E	Post-urban Harappan	Joshi et al. 1984: 527	
Uchcha Khera	Patiala	30° 34' 00" N - 76° 38' 00" E	Post-urban Harappan	IAR 1976-77: 43 Joshi et al. 1984: 527	
Udepur			Sorath Harappan	Chitalwala 1985: key Figure 8	
Ujalbas	Ganganagar		Mature Harappan	Pande & Ramachandran 1971: 42	
Ujhana One	Jind	29° 41' 53" N - 76° 07' 03" E	Post-urban Harappan	Singh 1981: 122 Joshi et al. 1984: 525 Mohan 1988: 142	0.70
Ujhana Two	Jind	29° 43' 45" N - 76° 08' 30" E	Post-urban Harappan Sothi-Siswal	Singh 1981: 122 Joshi et al. 1984: 525 Mohan 1988: 142	1.10
Un	Muzaffarnagar	29° 35' 00" N - 77° 15' 00" E	Post-urban Harappan	K. N. Dikshit 1981: 72 Joshi et al. 1984: 523	
Una	Jamnagar		Sorath Harappan(?)	IAR 1956-57: 70	
Unknown	Jabalpur		Copper Hoard	Mohapatra 1964: 45-7 Makkhan Lal 1984a: 40-1	
Unknown	Unknown		Copper Hoard	Mohapatra 1964: 45-7 Makkhan Lal 1984a: 40-1	
Unknown	Mayurbhanj		Copper Hoard	Mohapatra 1964: 45-7 Makkhan Lal 1984a: 40-1	
Unknown	Chota Nagpur		Copper Hoard	Mohapatra 1964: 45-7 Makkhan Lal 1984a: 40-1	
Unknown	Hardoi		Copper Hoard	Mohapatra 1964: 45-7 Makkhan Lal 1984a: 40-1	
Unknown	Ranchi		Copper Hoard	Mohapatra 1964: 45-7 Makkhan Lal 1984a: 40-1	
Unknown	Hazaribagh		Copper Hoard	Mohapatra 1964: 45-7 Makkhan Lal 1984a: 40-1	
Unknown	Etah		Copper Hoard	Mohapatra 1964: 45-7 Makkhan Lal 1984a: 40-1	
Unknown	Mayurbhanj		Copper Hoard	Mohapatra 1964: 45-7 Makkhan Lal 1984a: 40-1	
Unknown	Ranchi		Copper Hoard	Mohapatra 1964: 45-7 Makkhan Lal 1984: 40-1	
Unnamed Damb	Dera Ismail Khan		Late Kot Diji Kot Diji Kechi Beg	Fairservis 1971c: 413	
Unnamed Site Five	Jhalawan		Amri-Nal Kechi Beg	Fairservis 1971c: 405	
Uplana	Kurukshetra		Post-urban Harappan	Suraj Bhan 1975: 125	
Uplana Four	Karnal	29° 35' 40" N - 76° 40' 25" E	Post-urban Harappan	Singh 1981: 63 Joshi et al. 1984: 525	

Uplana Three	Karnal	29° 35' 10" N - 76° 39' 25" E	Post-urban Harappan	Singh 1981: 63 Joshi et al. 1984: 525	1.00
Uplana Two	Karnal	29° 36' 10" N - 76° 39' 51" E	Post-urban Harappan	Singh 1981: 63 Joshi et al. 1984: 525	
Urdana	Jind	29° 28' 36" N - 76° 33' 16" E	Post-urban Harappan Sothi-Siswal	Singh 1981: 96 Joshi et al. 1984: 525	
Urlana Khurd One	Karnal	29° 21' 00" N - 76° 43' 00" E	Post-urban Harappan	Singh 1981: 74 Joshi et al. 1984: 525	0.50
Urlana Khurd Two	Karnal	29° 22' 12" N - 76° 40' 50" E	Post-urban Harappan Mature Harappan Sothi-Siswal	Singh 1981: 74 Joshi et al. 1984: 519, 521, 525 Mohan 1988: 143	2.50
Uruske Zhara	Zhob	31° 11' 30" N - 69° 17' 00" E	Waziri	Stein 1929a: 49	1.90
Vachali Ghodi	Rajkot		Lustrous Red Ware	IAR 1978-79: 5	
Vada	Kutch	23° 29' 00" N - 69° 07' 00" E	Mature Harappan	IAR 1967-68: 17 Possehl 1980: 118 Joshi et al. 1984: 529	
Vadalan	Amritsar	31° 49' 00" N - 76° 48' 00" E	Mature Harappan	Joshi et al. 1984: 521	
Vadalan Garanthian	Gurdaspur	31° 50' 00" N - 75° 17' 00" E	Post-urban Harappan	Joshi et al. 1984: 526	
Vadasada	Rajkot	21° 47' 00" N - 70° 45' 00" E	Sorath Harappan	IAR 1958-59: 19 Possehl 1980: 118 Joshi et al. 1984: 530	
Vadera	Amreli	21° 36' 00" N - 71° 06' 00" E	Late Sorath Harappan Sorath Harappan	IAR 1978-79: 6 Joshi et al. 1984: 530	1.80
Vadgam	Kheda	22° 19' 00" N - 72° 28' 00" E	Sorath Harappan	IAR 1964-65: 11 Joshi et al. 1984: 528	4.00
Vadgam	Surendranagar	23° 21' 00" N - 71° 48' 00" E	Lustrous Red Ware	IAR 1964-65: 11 Joshi et al. 1984: 528 K. K. Bhan 1994: 86-7	1.00
Vadia-no Timbo	Mehsana	23° 34' 00" N - 71° 53' 00" E	Lustrous Red Ware	IAR 1982-83: 28 Joshi et al. 1984: 529 K. K. Bhan 1994: 86-7	0.90
Vadli	Rajkot		Lustrous Red Ware Sorath Harappan	Chitalwala 1979: 115	1.20
Vagad	Ahmedabad	22° 19' 00" N - 71° 52' 00" E	Sorath Harappan	Sonawane and Mehta 1985	13.50
Vaghania Juna	Amreli		Lustrous Red Ware	IAR 1978-79: 5	
Vaghatalav	Kheda	22° 32' 00" N - 72° 27' 00" E	Lustrous Red Ware Sorath Harappan	Momin 1979: 123-24 Momin 1984	0.20
Vagrano Dhoro	Amreli		Late Sorath Harappan Sorath Harappan	A. F. Cunningham, unpublished	
Vaharvo	Bhavnagar	21° 50' 50" N - 71° 43' 55" E	Late Historic Red Polished Ware Late Sorath Harappan Sorath Harappan	IAR 1960-61: 8 Rao 1963a: 207 Possehl 1980: 118 Joshi et al. 1984: 529	12.00
Vaidwali Mohra	Kutch		Post-urban Harappan	IAR 1985-86: 17	
Vainiwal	Sahiwal	30° 06' 00" N - 72° 58' 00" E	Mature Harappan Kot Diji	Mughal 1972a: 6	7.40
Valabhi	Bhavnagar	21° 53' 00" N - 71° 53' 00" E	Sorath Harappan	IAR 1979-80: 24 Mehta 1982	4.0

Valotri	Kheda	22° 32' 00" N	-	Sorath Harappan	IAR 1972-73: 11	
		72° 35' 00" E			IAR 1974-75: 13	
					Momin 1984	
Valpura	Bhavnagar	21° 57' 00" N	-	Sorath Harappan	Joshi et al. 1984: 530	
		71° 42' 00" E				
Valwala Two	Bahawalpur	28° 37' 25" N	-	Hakra Wares	Mughal 1997: 43	11.20
		70° 58' 50" E				
Valwali	Bahawalpur	28° 37' 34" N	-	Hakra Wares	Mughal 1997: 43	2.90
		70° 58' 30" E				
Vaniavadar	Amreli	21° 39' 00" N	-	Red Polished Ware	Rao 1963a: 207	2.00
		71° 09' 00" E		Late Sorath Harappan	Possehl 1980: 118	
				Sorath Harappan	Joshi et al. 1984: 528	
Vankiner	Jamnagar	21° 50' 00" N	-	Late Sorath Harappan	IAR 1979-80: 25	2.00
		69° 25' 00" E		Sorath Harappan	Rao 1963a: 207	
					Possehl 1980: 118	
					Joshi et al. 1984: 528	
Vanta Vash	Surendranagar			Sorath Harappan	IAR 1979-80: 100	
Various Sites	Manbhum			Copper Hoard	Campbell 1916	
					Makkhan Lal 1984a: 38-9	
Varudimatano Timbo	Ahmedabad			Sorath Harappan	IAR 1976-77: 14	
Varwala	Jamnagar			Sorath Harappan	IAR 1979-80: 29	
Vasai	Jamnagar	22° 24' 00" N	-	Lustrous Red Ware	Rao 1963a: 183, 207	9.00
		70° 00' 00" E		Late Sorath Harappan	Possehl 1980: 119	
				Sorath Harappan	Joshi et al. 1984: 528	
					K. K. Bhan 1983: 156-57	
Vasavad				Sorath Harappan	Chitalwala 1985: key Figure 8	
Vegadi	Rajkot	21° 47' 00" N	-	Lustrous Red Ware	IAR 1958-59: 19	6.00
		70° 30' 00" E		Sorath Harappan	Chitalwala 1979: 115	
					Possehl 1980: 118	
Vejalpur	Broach			HARAPPAN STONE TOOLS	IAR 1958-59: 69	
Veranatha Timbo	Mehsana	23° 39' 00" N	-	Lustrous Red Ware	K. K. Bhan 1994: 86-7	0.20
		71° 54' 10" E				
Veraval	Jamnagar	22° 22' 00" N	-	Lustrous Red Ware	K. K. Bhan 1986: 21	
		69° 05' 00" E				
Veraval Moti	Jamnagar	22° 17' 00" N	-	Lustrous Red Ware	K. K. Bhan 1986: 20	
		70° 04' 00" E				
Virpur, Gondal	Rajkot			Sorath Harappan	Chitalwala 1985: key Figure 8	
Virpur, Jamnagar	Jamnagar	22° 07' 00" N	-	Lustrous Red Ware	Rao 1963a: 183, 207	1.00
		70° 56' 00" E		Late Sorath Harappan	Possehl 1980: 119	
				Sorath Harappan	K. K. Bhan 1983: 157-58	
					Joshi et al. 1984: 528	
Vokda-no Thumdo	Banaskantha	23° 50' 15" N	-	Anarta-Rangpur IIC	Ajithprasad and Sonawane, in	0.20
		71° 20' 00" E		Anarta-Rangpur IIB	press	
Waddanwala	Bahawalpur	28° 36' 30" N	-	Mature Harappan	Mughal 1997: 48	8.90
		71° 52' 14" E				
Waddenwali	Bahawalpur	28° 52' 10" N	-	Hakra Wares	Mughal 1997: 43	5.70
		71° 26' 22" E				
Wadh Thana	Jhalawan	27° 22' 00" N	-	Islamic-British	Stein 1931: 173, 175	
		66° 37' 00" E		Kulli	Raikes 1968b: 148	
					de Cardi 1983: 38	
Wahir Two	Jhalawan	27° 36' 00" N	-	Kulli	Stein 1931: 174-75	7.50

		66° 30' 00" E		Amri-Nal	Possehl 1986a: 150	
Wakkarwala	Bahawalpur	29° 07' 22" N 71° 57' 12" E	-	Kot Diji	Mughal 1997: 44	1.20
Warawar	Bahawalpur			Mature Harappan	Mughal 1997: 48	2.70
Wariyal Ther	Bahawalpur	29° 09' 50" N 71° 57' 30" E	-	Mature Harappan	Mughal 1997: 48	2.30
Wariyal 'A'	Bahawalpur	29° 10' 40" N 71° 54' 14" E	-	Kot Diji	Mughal 1997: 44	6.20
Wariyal 'B'	Bahawalpur	29° 10' 43" N 71° 54' 43" E	-	Cemetery H	Mughal 1997: 51	3.60
Wariyal 'C'	Bahawalpur	29° 10' 50" N 71° 54' 50" E	-	Hakra Wares	Mughal 1997: 43	0.40
Wariyal 'D'	Bahawalpur	29° 10' 57" N 71° 54' 55" E	-	Kot Diji	Mughal 1997: 44	2.20
Wariyal 'E'	Bahawalpur	29° 09' 39" N 71° 57' 13" E	-	Mature Harappan	Mughal 1997: 48	1.00
Wariyal 'F'	Bahawalpur	29° 09' 22" N 71° 56' 50" E	-	Mature Harappan	Mughal 1997: 48	0.50
Wariyal 'G'	Bahawalpur	29° 08' 17" N 71° 57' 04" E	-	Cemetery H	Mughal 1997: 51	2.20
Wariyal 'H'	Bahawalpur	29° 08' 25" N 71° 57' 10" E	-	Cemetery H Mature Harappan	Mughal 1997: 51	0.30
Warthan	Surat	21° 22' 00" N 72° 51' 00" E	-	Red Polished Ware Late Sorath Harappan	IAR 1961-62: 14, 16	1.00
Wasuwala Ther	Bahawalpur	28° 46' 10" N 71° 09' 22" E	-	Mature Harappan	Mughal 1997: 48	6.50
Wavriwala	Bahawalpur	28° 50' 58" N 71° 26' 18" E	-	Cemetery H	Mughal 1997: 51	9.60
Wutaki Damb	Makran	26° 37' 01" N 63° 24' 59" E	-	Medieval Kulli?	Stein 1931: 51	0.20
Yaqubpur				Post-urban Harappan	IAR 1981-82: 15	
Yarak	Bannu	32° 31' 00" N 70° 41' 00" E	-	Kili Ghul Mohammad?	Khan, Knox and Thomas 1989: 288	
Zahrazai	Sarawan	29° 24' 00" N 66° 29' 00" E	-	Quetta Amri-Nal Kechi Beg	de Cardi 1983: 22	
Zari Damb	Jhalawan	28° 18' 00" N 66° 08' 00" E	-	Amri-Nal Kechi Beg Togau	de Cardi 1983: 30-1	
Zayak North	Kharan	27° 55' 00" N 65° 54' 00" E	-	Complex B Londo Kulli Amri-Nal Kechi Beg Togau	Stein 1931: 32-33 Possehl 1986a: 151	1.50
Zayak Southeast	Jhalawan	27° 54' 40" N 65° 53' 40" E	-	Historic Kulli Amri-Nal Kechi Beg	Stein 1931: 32-34 Field 1959 Possehl 1986a: 151	
Zekhada	Banaskantha	23° 51' 00" N 71° 28' 00" E	-	Anarta Harappan	Mehta 1982 K. Bhan 1994: 86-7	4.50
Ziarat Bharam Shahi	Bahawalpur	29° 03' 00" N 72° 21' 00" E	-	Kot Diji	Stein 1943a: 127-28 Dalal 1980: 10	3.70

Zidi	Jhalawan	27° 43' 00" N -	Anjira	Stein 1931: 173	0.90
		66° 47' 00" E	Amri-Nal	de Cardi 1951: 59-64	
			Kechi Beg	de Cardi 1983: 37	
			Togau		
Zik	Makran	26° 12' 00" N -	Kulli	Stein 1931: 112	5.00
		64° 47' 00" E	Amri-Nal	Possehl 1986a: 148	
			Kechi Beg		

APPENDIX-B

Mineral Localities

MATERIAL	COUNTRY	STATE	DISTRICT / LOC	BIBLIOGRAPHY
Agate	India	Gujarat	Ahmedabad	N. L. Sharma and K. S. V. Ram 1964: 197
				Fentress 1976: 308
Agate	India	Gujarat	Bhadar River	S. R. Rao 1985: 585
Agate	India	Gujarat	Bhavnagar	N. L. Sharma and K. S. V. Ram 1964: 197
				Fentress 1976: 308
				B. C. Roy 1953: 133
Agate	India	Gujarat	Junagadh	N. L. Sharma and K. S. V. Ram 1964:197
				Fentress 1976: 308
				B. C. Roy 1953: 133
Agate	India	Gujarat	Kapadvanj, Kaira District	S. R. Rao 1985: 585
Agate	India	Gujarat	Kutch	GLP observation
Agate	India	Gujarat	Majam River, Kaira District	S. R. Rao 1985: 585
Agate	India	Gujarat	Rajkot, near Wankaner	B. C. Roy 1953: 134
Agate	India	Gujarat	Rajpipla on the Narmada River	Bose 1908: 182
				Fentress 1976: 308
Agate	India	Gujarat	Rangpur, Ahmedabad District	S. R. Rao 1985: 585
Agate	India	Jammu and Kashmir	Rudok	Pascoe 1931: 681
				Fentress 1976: 308
Agate	Pakistan	Baluchistan	Kalat, Wad Valley and Pab Hills	Minchin 1907a: 162
Alabaster	India	Rajasthan	Ajmer	Holland and Fermor 1910: 143
				Fentress 1976: 306
				Wadia 1966: 454
Alabaster	India	Rajasthan	Alwar	Hackett 1880: 230
				Fentress 1976: 306
				Wadia 1966: 454
Alabaster	India	Rajasthan	Jaipur	Hackett 1880: 230
				Fentress 1976: 306
Alabaster	India	Rajasthan	Jodhpur	Holland and Fermor 1910: 143
				Fentress 1976: 306
				Wadia 1966: 454

Alabaster	India	Rajasthan	Kishangar	Holland and Fermor 1910: 143
				Fentress 1976: 306
Alabaster	India	Rajasthan	Udaipur	Hackett 1880: 230
				Fentress 1976: 306
Alabaster	Pakistan	Baluchistan	Western Bugti	Blanford 1883: 133 و
				Fentress 1976: 306
Alabaster	Pakistan	Northwest Frontier Province	Near Khyber Pass	Coggin-Brown and Dey 1923: 87
				Fentress 1976: 306
Alabaster	Pakistan	Swat	Mardan	Coggin-Brown and Dey 1923:88
				Fentress 1976: 306
Amazonite	India	Andhra Pradesh	Nellore District	N. L. Sharma
				K. S. V. Ram 1964: 104
Amazonite	India	Bihar	Hazaribagh District	N. L. Sharma
				K. S. V. Ram 1964: 104
Amazonite	India	Jammu and Kashmir	Padar District	Pascoe 1931: 678
				Fentress 1976: 309
Amazonite	India	Tamil Nadu	Nilgiri Hills	Pascoe 1931: 678
				Fentress 1976: 309
Amethyst	India	Himachal Pradesh	Simla	Coggin-Brown and Dey 1923: 133
				Fentress 1976: 308
Amethyst	India	Jammu and Kashmir	Kashmir	N. L. Sharma and K. S. V. Ram 1964: 193
				Fentress 1976: 308
Amethyst	India	Maharashtra(?)	Rajmahal	Coggin-Brown and Dey 1923: 133
				Fentress 1976: 308
Amethyst	India	Rajasthan	Jaipur	N. L. Sharma and K. S. V. Ram 1964: 193
				Fentress 1976: 308
Amethyst	India & Pakistan	Punjab	Sutlej Valley	Coggin-Brown and Dey 1923: 133
				Fentress 1976: 308
Antimony	Afghanistan		Toba Plateau	Government of India 1908d: 34
Antimony	Pakistan	Northwest Frontier Province	Chitral	Wadia 1966: 470
Antimony	Pakistan	Northwest Frontier Province	Shigri glacier	Wadia 1966: 470
Arsenic	India	Haryana	Gurgaon District	Government of India 1985: Vol. 1, 432
Arsenic	India	Jammu & Kashmir	Lashteal, Baramula and Zaskar	Government of India 1985: Vol. 1, 432
Arsenic	India	Rajasthan	associated with the Batai and Bagor copper mines near Khetri	Government of India 1985: Vol. 1, 432
Arsenic	India	Uttar Pradesh	mountain districts	Government of India 1985: Vol. 1, 432
Arsenic	India	Gujarat	Panch Mahals District	Government of India 1985: Vol. 1, 432
Azurite	Pakistan	Baluchistan	Kharan (Sainkak)	Vredenburg 1901: 293
Basalt	India	Gujarat	Kutch	Wadia 1966: 292-93
Basalt	India	Gujarat	Saurashtra	Wadia 1966: 292-93
Basalt	India	Madhya Pradesh	Madhya Pradesh	Wadia 1966: 292-93
Basalt	India	Maharashtra	Maharashtra	Wadia 1966: 292-93
Basalt	Pakistan	Kirthar Range	Kirthar Range	Coggin-Brown and Dey 1923: 198

Bitumen	Pakistan	Baluchistan	Kachi, Sibi	Coggin-Brown and Dey 1923: 138 Fentress 1976: 309 Wadia 1966: 466
Bitumen	Pakistan	Punjab	Isakhel on the Indus	Pascoe 1931: 682 Fentress 1976: 309
Chert	India	Punjab	Kirama Hills	Heron and Crookshank 1955: 207 Fentress 1976: 309
Chert	Pakistan	Sindh	Rohri Hills	Fentress 1976: 309
Chromium	Pakistan	Baluchistan	Baluchistan	Wadia 1966: 471
Copper	Afghanistan	Kabul	Safed Koh	Pascoe 1931: 676
Copper	Afghanistan	Kabul	Tezin, east of Kabul	Government of India 1908d: 34
Copper	Afghanistan	Kandahar	Rich ores at Nesh, 60 miles north of Kandahar	Government of India 1908d: 34
Copper	Afghanistan	Northern Afghanistan	Shadkani Pass, Sagur River	Government of India 1908d: 34
Copper	Afghanistan	Northern Afghanistan	Shah Maksud Range	Government of India 1908d: 34
Copper	Afghanistan	Northern Afghanistan	Silawat Pass	Government of India 1908d: 34
Copper	India	Gujarat	Banaskantha, near Ambamata	Agrawal, Krishnamurthy, Kusumgar and Pant 1977: 230
Copper	India	Gujarat	Banaskantha, near Kumbharia	Agrawal, Krishnamurthy and Kusumgar 1985: 98
Copper	India	Gujarat	Banaskantha, near Mount Abu, former Danta State	B. C. Roy 1951: 136
Copper	India	Gujarat	Baroda, at Jhari near Chota Udaipur	B. C. Roy 1951: 136
Copper	India	Gujarat	Sabarkantha, Rohira in Sirohi	B. C. Roy 1951: 136
Copper	India	Jammu and Kashmir	Kashmir	Pascoe 1931: 676 Fentress 1976: 307
Copper	India	Punjab	Bikaner	B. C. Roy 1959: 301 Fentress 1976: 307
Copper	India	Punjab	Julunder	Allami 1965: 57 Fentress 1976: 307
Copper	India	Punjab	Kangra	Government of Punjab 1883b: 17 Fentress 1976: 307
Copper	India	Punjab	Patiala	Gee 1948: 57 Fentress 1976: 307
Copper	India	Rajasthan	Ajmer	Hackett 1880: 231 Fentress 1976: 307
Copper	India	Rajasthan	Alwar, extensive old workings	Hackett 1880: 231 Fentress 1976: 307 Lahiri 1990: 425
Copper	India	Rajasthan	Banswara	Lahiri 1990: 427
Copper	India	Rajasthan	Bharatpur	B. C. Roy 1959: 301 Fentress 1976: 307
Copper	India	Rajasthan	Bhilawar	Lahiri 1990: 426
Copper	India	Rajasthan	Bhilwara	Lahiri 1990: 426
Copper	India	Rajasthan	Bikaner	Lahiri 1990: 427
Copper	India	Rajasthan	Chittorgarh, extensive old workings	Lahiri 1990: 426-27
Copper	India	Rajasthan	Dungarpur	Lahiri 1990: 427

Copper	India	Rajasthan	Jaipur	Hackett 1880: 231 Fentress 1976: 307 Lahiri 1990: 427
Copper	India	Rajasthan	Jhunjhunu, many sites of old mining and smelting	Lahiri 1990: 424
Copper	India	Rajasthan	Jodhpur	B. C. Roy 1959: 301 Fentress 1976: 307
Copper	India	Rajasthan	Sikar	Lahiri 1990: 425
Copper	India	Rajasthan	Udaipur	Hackett 1880: 231 Fentress 1976: 307 Lahiri 1990: 427
Copper	Pakistan	Baluchistan	Kalat, Saruna and Khidran country (rich deposits)	Minchin 1907a: 162
Copper	Pakistan	Baluchistan	Kharan, Drana Koh	Vredenburg 1901: 293
Copper	Pakistan	Baluchistan	Kharan, Koh-i Malik Shah	Vredenburg 1901: 294
Copper	Pakistan	Baluchistan	Kharan, Miss-i Dick area	Hassan 1989
Copper	Pakistan	Baluchistan	Kharan, Pud-kash area	Hassan 1989
Copper	Pakistan	Baluchistan	Kharan, Ras Koh	Vredenburg 1901: 291
Copper	Pakistan	Baluchistan	Kharan, Robat	Vredenburg 1901: 292
Copper	Pakistan	Baluchistan	Kharan, Robat area	Hassan 1989
Copper	Pakistan	Baluchistan	Kharan, Sainkak	Vredenburg 1901: 293
Copper	Pakistan	Baluchistan	Khuzdar	Hassan 1989
Copper	Pakistan	Baluchistan	Las Bela, Porali River	Hassan 1989
Copper	Pakistan	Baluchistan	Sarawan	Fentress 1976: 307 Hassan 1989
Copper	Pakistan	Northwest Frontier Province	Chitral	Coggin-Brown and Dey 1923: 107 Fentress 1976: 307
Copper	Pakistan	Northwest Frontier Province	Waziristan	Coggin-Brown and Dey 1923: 107 Fentress 1976: 307
Copper	Pakistan	Punjab	Salt Range	Government of Punjab 1883a: 14 Fentress 1976: 307
Copper, malachite	Pakistan	Baluchistan	Kalat, Wad Valley and Pab Hills	Minchin 1907a: 162
Copper, malachite	Pakistan	Baluchistan	Kharan, Sainkak	Vredenburg 1901: 293
Gold	Afghanistan		North slope of Hindu Kush	Government of India 1908d: 34
Gold	Afghanistan	Kandahar	Kandahar City, three miles north	Government of India 1908d: 34
Gold	India	Ganges Valley	Ganges Valley	Godley 1926 (Heroditus, Book III, 98-102)
Gold	India	Gujarat	Baroda, near Chota Udaipur	Ziauddin and Narayanaswami 1974: 96, 148
Gold	India	Gujarat	Satapur (Alech Hills)	Ziauddin and Narayanaswami 1974: 96, 148
Gold	India	Jammu and Kashmir	Achinthang	Ziauddin and Narayanaswami 1974: 135, 149

Gold	India	Jammu and Kashmir	Balistan Fentress 1976: 307	Holland and Fermor 1910: 92
Gold	India	Jammu and Kashmir	Dras Valley Fentress 1976: 307	Holland and Fermor 1910: 92
Gold	India	Jammu and Kashmir	Kapalu	Ziauddin and Narayanaswami 1974: 149
Gold	India	Jammu and Kashmir	Kharbu	Ziauddin and Narayanaswami 1974: 149
Gold	India	Jammu and Kashmir	Ladakh	Holland and Fermor 1910: 92 Fentress 1976: 307
Gold	India	Jammu and Kashmir	Skio	Ziauddin and Narayanaswami 1974: 135, 149
Gold	India	Karnataka	Hutti	Ziauddin and Narayanaswami 1974: 58-60
Gold	India	Karnataka	Kolar	Ziauddin and Narayanaswami 1974: 49-58
Gold	India	Rajasthan	Ajmer, near Sunarkuri	Ziauddin and Narayanaswami 1974: 144, 154
Gold	India	Rajasthan	Jodhpur, near Raipur	Ziauddin and Narayanaswami 1974: 144, 154
Gold	India	Rajasthan	Jodhpur, near Sagaramgarh	Ziauddin and Narayanaswami 1974: 144, 154
Gold	India	Rajasthan	Sirohi, near Rohira	Ziauddin and Narayanaswami 1974: 144, 154
Gold	Pakistan	West Punjab	Indus	Ansari 1993
Gold (washing)	India	Punjab	Kangra	Government of Punjab 1883b: 8 Fentress 1976: 307
Gold (washing)	India	Rajasthan	Jaipur	B. C. Roy 1959: 123 Fentress 1976: 307
Gold (washing)	India	Rajasthan	Jodhpur	B. C. Roy 1959: 123 Fentress 1976: 307
Gold (washing)	India	Rajasthan	Sirohi	B. C. Roy 1959: 123 Fentress 1976: 307
Gold (washing)	Pakistan	Northwest Frontier Province	Peshawar, along the Indus and Kabul Rivers	Holland and Fermor 1910:148 Fentress 1976: 307
Gold (washing)	Pakistan	Punjab	Hazara	Government of Punjab 1883e: 17 Fentress 1976: 307
Gold (washing)	Pakistan	Punjab	Jhang	Government of Punjab 1883d: 10 Fentress 1976: 307
Gold (washing)	Pakistan	Punjab	Kohat	Government of Punjab 1883c: 8 Fentress 1976: 307
Gold (washing)	Paksitan	Punjab	Hoshiarpur	Government of Punjab 1883d: 10 Fentress 1976: 307
Gold, placer	Afghanistan		Streams of the Koh-i Baba, central Afghanistan	Government of India 1908d: 34
Gold, placer	Afghanistan	Kabul	Streams of the Kohistan, Laghman and Kunar	Government of India 1908d: 34
Gold?	India	Rajasthan	Jhunjhunu	Lahiri 1990: 424
Gypsum	Pakistan	Baluchistan	Kacchi	Blanford 1883: 88 Fentress 1976: 306
Gypsum	Pakistan	Baluchistan	Quetta (Mashalak Range)	Blanford 1883: 88 Fentress 1976: 306
Gypsum	Pakistan	Punjab	Jhelum	Government of Punjab 1883a: 13 Fentress 1976: 306

Gypsum	Pakistan	Punjab	Salt Range Fentress 1976: 306	Holland and Fermor 1910: 128
Gypsum	Pakistan	Sindh	Kirthar Range Fentress 1976: 306	Holland and Fermor 1910: 127
Haematite	Pakistan	Baluchistan	Kharan (Koh-i Malik Shah)	Vredenburg 1901: 294
Haematite	India	Punjab	Punjab	Fentress 1976: 309
Haematite	India	Rajasthan	Rajasthan	Fentress 1976: 309
Jadeite	Turkmenistan		Karakash Valley	Wadia 1966: 490
Jasper	India	Gujarat	Tankara, Saurashtra	S. R. Rao 1985: 586
Jasper	Pakistan	Baluchistan	Baluchistan, Kalat, Wad Valley and Pab Hills	Minchin 1907a: 162
Kaolin clay	India	Gujarat	Saurashtra	Wadia 1966: 449
Lapis lazuli	Afghanistan	Badakhshan	Badakhshan, Sar-i Sang	Salah et. al. 1977: 281.
Lapis lazuli	Pakistan	Baluchistan	Chagai Hills	Delmas and Casanova 1990
Lapis lazuli	Russia		Ural Mountains	Delmas and Casanova 1990
Lapis lazuli	Tadjakistan		Pamirs and Lake Baikal area	Ivanov 1976
Lead	Afghanistan		Frinjal, Gorband Valley	Government of India 1908d: 34
Lead	India	Jammu and Kashmir	Baramula, Buniyar area	Wadia 1966: 87
Lead	India	Jammu and Kashmir	Urhampur, near Nigote	Wadia 1966: 87
Lead	India	Punjab	Kangra	Government of Punjab 1883b: 13 Fentress 1976: 308
Lead	India	Punjab	Kangra, near Taboo	Wadia 1966: 88
Lead	India	Punjab	Kulu	Wadia 1966: 87-8
Lead	India	Rajasthan	Ajmer	B. C. Roy 1959: 49 Fentress 1976: 308
Lead	India	Rajasthan	Alwar	B. C. Roy 1959: 49 Fentress 1976: 308
Lead	India	Rajasthan	Jaipur	B. C. Roy 1959: 49 Fentress 1976: 308
Lead	India	Rajasthan	Udaipur, near Zawar	Wadia 1966: 88
Lead	India	Uttar Pradesh	Almora, near Kharahi	Wadia 1966: 88
Lead	India	Uttar Pradesh	Tehri Garhwal, near Pindki	Wadia 1966: 88
Lead	Pakistan	Baluchistan	Kalat	Hassan 1989
Lead	Pakistan	Baluchistan	Khuzdar (Surmai Village)	Hassan 1989
Lead	Pakistan	Punjab	Jhelum	Government of Punjab 1883a: 15 Fentress 1976: 308
Lead, galena	Pakistan	Baluchistan	Kharan (Sainkak)	Vredenburg 1901: 293
Limestone	Pakistan	Baluchistan	Quetta	Coggin-Brown and Dey 1923: 145 Fentress 1976: 307
Limestone	Pakistan	Punjab	Abbotabad	Coggin-Brown and Dey 1923: 113 Fentress 1976: 307
Limestone	Pakistan	Punjab	Hazara	Government of Punjab 1883e: 17 Fentress 1976: 307
Limestone	Pakistan	Punjab	Hoshiarpur	Government of Punjab 1883d: 10 Fentress 1976: 307
Limestone	Pakistan	Punjab	Jhelum	Government of Punjab 1883a: 15 Fentress 1976: 307
Limestone	Pakistan	Punjab	Kohat	Government of Punjab 1883c: 8 Fentress 1976: 307
Limestone	Pakistan	Sindh	Hyderabad	Aitken 1907: 77
Limestone	Pakistan	Sindh	Kotri	Aitken 1907: 77

Limestone	Pakistan	Sindh	Rohri Hills	Aitken 1907: 77
Ochre	India	Gujarat	Baroda	N. L. Sharma and K. S. V. Ram 1964: 167
Ochre	India	Gujarat	Broach	N. L. Sharma and K. S. V. Ram 1964: 167
Ochre	India	Gujarat	Jamnagar	N. L. Sharma and K. S. V. Ram 1964: 167
Ochre	India	Gujarat	Junagadh	N. L. Sharma and K. S. V. Ram 1964: 167
Ochre	India	Gujarat	Kutch	N. L. Sharma and K. S. V. Ram 1964: 167 Fentress 1976: 309
Ochre	India	Gujarat	Panchmahal	N. L. Sharma and K. S. V. Ram 1964: 167
Ochre	India	Gujarat	Surendranagar	N. L. Sharma and K. S. V. Ram 1964: 167
Ochre	India	Jammu and Kashmir	Uri Tehsil	N. L. Sharma and K. S. V. Ram 1964: 167
Ochre	India	Punjab	Kangra	N. L. Sharma and K. S. V. Ram 1964: 167
Ochre	India	Rajasthan	Alwar	N. L. Sharma and K. S. V. Ram 1964: 167
Ochre	India	Rajasthan	Bikaner	N. L. Sharma and K. S. V. Ram 1964: 167
Ochre	India	Rajasthan	Bundi	N. L. Sharma and K. S. V. Ram 1964: 167
Ochre	India	Rajasthan	Jaipur	N. L. Sharma and K. S. V. Ram 1964: 167
Ochre	India	Rajasthan	Jaisalmer	N. L. Sharma and K. S. V. Ram 1964: 167
Ochre	India	Rajasthan	Udaipur	N. L. Sharma and K. S. V. Ram 1964: 167
Ochre	India	Uttar Pradesh	Mirzapur	N. L. Sharma and K. S. V. Ram 1964: 167
Ochre	Oman	Hormuz	Oman, Hormuz	Pascoe 1931: 680 Fentress 1976: 309
Onyx	India	Gujarat	Vijarkhi, Jamnagar District	S. R. Rao 1985: 586
Pumice	Pakistan	Baluchistan	Kharan (Koh-i Sultan)	Vredenburg 1901: 280
Quartz			Kirana Hills	Government of Punjab 1883c: 16 Fentress 1976: 308
Quartz	India	Gujarat	Idar	Fentress 1976: 308
Quartz	India	Gujarat	Kathiawar	Pascoe 1931: 681 Fentress 1976: 308
Quartz	India	Jammu and Kashmir	Kashmir	Coggin-Brown and Dey 1923: 96 Fentress 1976: 308
Quartz	India	Rajashtan	Ajmer	N. L. Sharma and K. S. V. Ram 1964: 192 Fentress 1976: 308
Quartz	India	Rajashtan	Jaipur	N. L. Sharma and K. S. V. Ram 1964: 192 Fentress 1976: 308
Quartz	Pakistan	Punjab	Salt Range	Government of Punjab 1883c: 16 Fentress 1976: 308

Rubies	Afghanistan		Jagdalak, between Kabul and Jalalabad	Government of India 1908d: 34
Salt	India	Gujarat	Kutch	Wadia 1966: 155
Salt	Pakistan	Punjab	Hazara	Government of Punjab 1883e: 12 Fentress 1976: 306
Salt	Pakistan	Punjab	Jhelum	Government of Punjab 1883a: 13 Fentress 1976: 306
Salt	Pakistan	Punjab	Kohat, Salt Range	Wynne 1875: 153 Fentress 1976: 306
Salt	Pakistan	Sindh	Southeastern Sindh	Wadia 1966: 155
Sandstone	India	Rajasthan	Jaipur	
Sandstone	Pakistan	Punjab	Jhelum	Government of Punjab 1883a: 13 Fentress 1976: 306
Serpentine	India	Punjab	Punjab	Wadia 1966: 490
Silver	Afghanistan		Frinjal, Gorband Valley	Government of India 1908d: 34
Silver	Afghanistan	Herat	Mines near Herat	Government of India 1908d: 34
Silver	Afghanistan	Panjshir	Panjshir Valley	Government of India 1908d: 34
Silver	India	Himachal Pradesh	Bushahir, in Sutlej Valley at 11,000 feet elevation	Wadia 1966: 89
Silver	India	Himachal Pradesh	Kulu	Pascoe 1931: 675 Fentress 1976: 307
Silver	India	Himachal Pradesh	Simla	N. L. Sharma and K. S. V. Ram 1964: 207 Fentress 1976: 307
Silver	India	Jammu and Kashmir	Riasi District	N. L. Sharma and K. S. V. Ram 1964: 207 Fentress 1976: 307
Silver	India	Karnataka	Kolar Goldfield	Wadia 1966: 89
Silver	India	Punjab	Kangra District	N. L. Sharma and K. S. V. Ram 1964: 207 Fentress 1976: 307
Silver	India	Rajasthan	Udaipur	B. C. Roy 1959: 239 Fentress 1976: 307 N. L. Sharma and K. S. V. Ram 1964: 207
Silver	India	Rajasthan	Udaipur, Zawar	Wadia 1966: 89 N. L. Sharma and K. S. V. Ram 1964: 207
Silver	Pakistan	Baluchistan	Khuzdar (Surmai Village)	Hassan 1989
Slate	India	Himachal Pradesh	Kangra	Fentress 1976: 309
Slate	India	Jammu and Kashmir	Kashmir	Fentress 1976: 309
Slate	India	Rajasthan	Rajasthan	Coggin-Brown and Dey 1923: 138 Fentress 1976: 309
Slate	Pakistan	Northwest Frontier Province	Nowshera	Fentress 1976: 309
Sodalite	India	Rajasthan	Kishangar	Coggin-Brown and Dey 1923: 75 Fentress 1976: 309
Steatite	India	Jammu & Kashmir,	Raisi District	Government of India 1985: Vol. 10, 33
Steatite	India	Jammu & Kashmir,	Udhampur District	Government of India 1985: Vol. 10, 33
Steatite	India	Rajasthan	Bhilwara District	Government of India 1985: Vol. 10, 34

Steatite	India	Gujarat	Sabarkantha District, near Himatnagar (former Idar State)	Government of India 1985: Vol. 10, 33 N. L. Sharma and K. S. V. Ram 1964: 213 Fentress 1976: 306
Steatite	India	Rajasthan	Ajmer	B. C. Roy 1951: 130 B. C. Roy 1959: 186 Fentress 1976: 306
Steatite	India	Rajasthan	Alwar	B. C. Roy 1959: 186 Fentress 1976: 306 Wadia 1966: 159
Steatite	India	Rajasthan	Banswara	Wadia 1966: 159
Steatite	India	Rajasthan	Dungarpur	Wadia 1966: 159
Steatite	India	Rajasthan	Jaipur	Government of India 1985: Vol. 10, 34 Hackett 1880: 245 Fentress 1976: 306 Wadia 1966: 159 B. C. Roy 1951: 129
Steatite	India	Rajasthan	Jodhpur	B. C. Roy 1959: 186 Fentress 1976: 306
Steatite	India	Rajasthan	Udaipur	Government of India 1985: Vol. 10, 34 B. C. Roy 1959: 186 Fentress 1976: 306 Wadia 1966: 159
Steatite	India	Uttar Pradesh	Almora	Wadia 1966: 159
Steatite	India	Uttar Pradesh	Hamirpur, near Garahuri	Wadia 1966: 159
Steatite	India	Uttar Pradesh	Jhansi, near Bijri	Wadia 1966: 159
Steatite	India	Uttar Pradesh	Jhansi, near Dhaukua	Wadia 1966: 159
Steatite	Pakistan	Northwest Frontier Province	Peshawar (Nowshera)	Coggin-Brown and Dey 1923: 25 Fentress 1976: 306
Steatite	Pakistan	Punjab	Abbotabad	Coggin-Brown and Dey 1923: 25 Fentress 1976: 306
Tin	Afghanistan		Central	Salah et al. 1977: 165-90
Tin	India	Bihar	Hazaribagh	Ball 1898: 147 Fentress 1976: 308
Tin	India	Gujarat	Banaskantha	N. L. Sharma and K. S. V. Ram 1964: 215 Fentress 1976: 308
Tin	India	Gujarat	Panch Mahals, near Jambughoda	B. C. Roy 1951: 145
Tin	India	Rajasthan	Bhilwara	N. L. Sharma and K. S. V. Ram 1964: 215 Fentress 1976: 308
Turquoise	India	Rajasthan	Rajasthan, Ajmer Hills	Coggin-Brown and Dey 1923: 117 Fentress 1976: 309
Turquoise	Iran		Damghan	Bulgarelli 1981: 67
Turquoise	Iran		Kirman	Pogue 1915: 40
Turquoise	Iran		Nishapur	Bulgarelli 1981: 67
Turquoise	Iran		Sar-i Cheshme	Bulgarelli 1981: 67
Turquoise	Iran		Yazd	Pogue 1915: 40

Turquoise	Uzbekistan and Kazakhstan	Central Asia	Kyzyl Kum	Vinogradov, Lopatin and Mamedov 1965 Bulgarelli 1981: 66
Zinc	India	Rajasthan	Udaipur region	Wadia 1966: 486
Zinc	Pakistan	Baluchistan	Khuzdar (Surmai Village)	Hassan 1989

BIBLIOGRAPHY

Abbott, J.
1924   *Sind: A re-interpretation of the unhappy valley*. Bombay: Oxford University Press for the University of Bombay.

Abdul Ali, A. F. M.
1935   Earthquakes in India. *Indian Culture*, 1(3): 467-76.

Adams, Robert McC.
1965   *Land Behind Baghdad*. Chicago: University of Chicago Press.

Adams, Robert McC.
1972   Demography and the "Urban Revolution" in lowland Mesopotamia. In, Brian Spooner, ed., *Population Growth: Anthropological implications*. Cambridge: MIT Press: 60-3.

Adams, Robert McC.
1974a   Historic patterns of Mesopotamian irrigation agriculture. In, Theodore E. Downing and McGuire Gibson eds., *Irrigation's Impact on Society*. Tucson: University of Arizona, Anthropological Papers No. 25: 1-6.

Adams, Robert McC.
1974b   Anthropological perspectives on ancient trade. *Current Anthropology*, 15(3): 239-58.

Adams, Robert McC.
1981   *Heartland of Cities*. Chicago: University of Chicago Press.

Adams, Robert McC. and Hans J. Nissen
1972   *The Uruk Countryside*. Chicago: University of Chicago Press.

Agrawal, D. P.
1964   Harappa culture: new evidence for a shorter chronology. *Science*, 3609: 950-52.

Agrawal, D. P.
1969   The copper hoards problem: a technological angle. *Asian Perspectives*, 12: 113-19.

848

Agrawal, D. P.
1969-70 The metal technology of the Indian protohistoric cultures: its archaeological
         implications. *Puratattva*, 3: 15-22.

Agrawal, D. P.
1970   Metal technology of the Harappa Culture and its socio-economic implications. *Indian
         Journal of the History of Science*, 5(2): 238-52.

Agrawal, D. P.
1971   *The Copper Bronze Age in India*. Delhi: Munshiram Manoharlal.

Agrawal, D. P.
1972-73 Genesis of Harappa culture. *Puratattva*, 6: 37-41.

Agrawal, D. P.
1976   Problems of protohistoric copper artifacts and their ore correlation. In, Udai Vir Singh,
         ed., *Archaeological Congress and Seminar: 1972*. Kurukshetra: B.N. Chakravarty
         University of Kurukshetra: 85-9.

Agrawal, D. P.
1982a   *The Archaeology of India*. Copenhagen: Scandinavian Institute of Asian Studies
         Monograph Series No. 46.

Agrawal, D. P.
1982b   Palaeoclimate and geochronology of the arid regions of India: some suggestions. In,
         Proceedings of the Workshop on the Problems of the Deserts of India. Delhi: Geological
         Survey of India, Special Publication No. 49: 105-12.

Agrawal, D. P.
1982c   The technology of the Indus Civilization. In, R. K. Sharma, ed., *Indian Archaeology:
         New perspectives*. Delhi: Agam Kala Prakashan: 83-112.

Agrawal, D. P.
1982d   The Indian Bronze Age cultures and their metal technology. In, F. Wendorf and A. E.
         Close, eds., *Advances in World Archaeology*, 1: 213-64.

Agrawal, D. P.
1984   Metal technology of the Harappans. In, B. B. Lal and S. P. Gupta, eds., *Frontiers of
         the Indus Civilization*. Delhi: Books and Books: 163-67.

Agrawal, D. P.
1987   Environmental changes in India during the last 4 million years. *Journal of the
         Palaeontological Society of India*, 32: 1-4.

Agrawal, D. P. and R. K. Sood
1982   Ecological factors and the Harappan Civilization. In, Gregory L. Possehl, ed., *Harappan
         Civilization: A contemporary perspective*. Delhi: Oxford & IBH and the American
         Institute of Indian Studies: 223-31.

Agrawal, D. P. and Sheela Kusumgar
1974a   *Prehistoric Chronology and Radiocarbon Dating in India*. Delhi: Munshiram Manoharlal.

Agrawal, D. P. and Sheela Kusumgar
1974b   On the calibration of C-14 dates. *Puratattva*, 7: 70-3.

Agrawal, D. P., R. V. Krishnamurthy and Sheela Kusumgar
1978   On the affiliation of the Daimabad Bronzes: some fresh data. Paper presented at the International Archaeometry Symposium, Bonn, March 1978.

Agrawal, D. P., R. V. Krishnamurthy and Sheela Kusumgar
1978   New data on the copper hoards and the Daimabad bronzes. *Man and Environment*, 2: 41-6.

Agrawal, D. P., R. V. Krishnamurthy and Sheela Kusumgar
1981   Arsenical coppers in the Indian Bronze Age. In, M. S. Nagaraja Rao, ed., *Mandu: Recent research in Indian archaeology and art history, the Shri M. N. Deshpande festschrift*. Delhi: Agam Kala Prakashan: 9-16.

Agrawal, D. P., R. V. Krishnamurthy and Sheela Kusumgar
1985   Physical Research Laboratory radiocarbon date list *V. Radiocarbon*, 27(1): 95-110.

Agrawal, D. P., R. V. Krishnamurthy, Sheela Kusumgar and R. K. Pant
1977   Physical Research Laboratory radiocarbon date list II. *Radiocarbon*, 19(2): 229-36.

Agrawal, D. P., et al.
1978   The chronology of Indian prehistory from the Mesolithic Period to the Iron Age. *Journal of Human Evolution*, 7: 37-44.

Agrawala, R. C.
1979   More copper finds from Rajasthan. *Man and Environment*, 3: 91-2.

Agrawala, R. C.
1981   Recent explorations in Rajasthan. *Man and Environment*, 5: 59-63.

Agrawala, R. C. and Vijay Kumar
1982   Ganeshwar-Jodhpura culture: new traits in Indian archaeology. In, Gregory L. Possehl, ed., *Harappan Civilization: A contemporary perspective*. Delhi: Oxford & IBH and the American Institute of Indian Studies: 125-34.

Agrawala, R. C. and Vijay Kumar
1995   Excavation at Jodhpura (District Jaipur). In, R.C. Gaur *Excavations at Lal Qila: A habitational OCP site & a unique copper-hoard from Kiratpur*. Jaipur: Publication Scheme: 213-15.

Agrawala, V. S.
1947-48　Terracotta figurines of Ahichchhatra, District Bareilly, U. P. *Ancient India*, 4: 104-179.

Aitken, E. H.
1907　*Gazetteer of the Province of Sind*. Karachi: Government of Bombay.

Ajithprasad, P. and V. S. Sonawane
in press　The Harappa Culture in North Gujarat: a regional perspective. In, Gregory L. Possehl and Vasant Shinde, eds., *Harappans and Others in Gujarat*. Delhi: Oxford & IBH.

Al Khalifa, Shaikha Haya Ali and Michael Rices, editors
1986　*Bahrain Through the Ages, the Archaeology*. London: KPI Limited.

Alcock, Leslie
1952　Exploring Pakistan's past: the first year's work. *Pakistan Quarterly*, 2(1): 12-6.

Alcock, Leslie
1956　The pottery, site Q8, cut 3. In, Walter A. Fairservis, Jr., *Excavations in the Quetta Valley, West Pakistan*. Anthropological Papers of the American Museum of Natural History, 45(2): 362-71.

Alcock, Leslie
1986　A pottery sequence from Mohenjo Daro: R. E. M. Wheeler's 1950 "Citadel Mound" excavations. In, George F. Dales and J. Mark Kenoyer, *Excavations at Mohenjo Daro, Pakistan: The pottery*. Philadelphia: The University Museum: 493-551.

Alder, Garry
1975　Introduction. In, Charles Masson, *Narrative of Various Journeys in Balochistan, Afghanistan and the Punjab: Including a residence in those countries from 1826-1838*. 3 Vols. Graz: Akademische Druck-u Verlagsanstalt: v-xxi.

Alekseyev, V. P.
1964　Anthropological types of the early population of India. In, V. V. Struve and G. M. Bongard-Levin, eds., *Ancient India*. Moscow: Nauk Publishing: 19-30 (In Russian).

Algaze, Guillermo
1993　*The Uruk World System: The dynamics of expansion of Early Mesopotamian Civilization*. Chicago: University of Chicago Press.

Ali, S. M.
1942　Population and settlement in the Ghaggar Plain. *Indian Geographical Journal*, 17(3): 157-82.

Ali, Salim
1946　The wild ass of Kutch. *Journal of the Bombay Natural History Society*, 46(3): 472-77.

Ali, Salim and S. Dillon Ripley
1983   *Handbook of the Birds of India and Pakistan: Compact edition.* Delhi: Oxford University Press.

Allami, Abu'l-Fazl
1965   *A'in-i Akbari.* Translated by H. Blochman. Delhi: Aediesh Book Depot.

Allchin, Bridget
1966   *The Stone-Tipped Arrow.* New York: Barnes and Noble.

Allchin, Bridget
1972   Hunters or pastoral nomads? Late Stone Age settlements in western and central India. In, Peter J. Ucko and Ruth Tringham, eds., *Man, Settlement and Urbanism.* London: Gerald Duckworth & Co.: 115-19.

Allchin, Bridget
1977   Hunters, pastoralists and early agriculturalists in South Asia. In, J. V. S. Megaw, ed., *Hunters, Gatherers and First Farmers Beyond Europe.* Leicester: Leicester University Press: 127-43.

Allchin, Bridget
1979a   Stone blade industries of early settlements in Sind as indicators of geographical and socio-economic change. In, M. Taddei, ed., *South Asian Archaeology 1977.* Naples: Instituto Universitario Orientale, Seminario di Studi Asiatici,Series Minor 6: 173-221.

Allchin, Bridget
1979b   The agate and carnelian industry of western India and Pakistan. In, J. E. van Lohuizen-de Leeuw, ed., *South Asian Archaeology 1975.* Leiden: E. J. Brill: 91-105.

Allchin, Bridget
1981   The Palaeolithic of the Potwar Plateau, Punjab, Pakistan: a fresh approach. *Paleorient,* 7(1): 123-34.

Allchin, Bridget
1986   Earliest traces of man on the Potwar Plateau, Pakistan: a report of the British Archaeological Mission to Pakistan. *South Asian Studies,* 2: 69-83.

Allchin, B. and F.R.
1968   *The Birth of Indian Civilization.* Baltimore: Penguin Books.

Allchin, B. and F. R.
1982a   Lewan: An Early Harappan manufacturing site in the Bannu Basin. In, Gregory L. Possehl, ed., *Harappan Civilization: A recent perspective,* 2nd edition. Delhi: Oxford & IBH and the American Institute of Indian Studies: 521-53.

Allchin, B. and F.R.
1982b   *The Rise of Civilization in India and Pakistan. Cambridge:* Cambridge University Press.

852

Allchin, Bridget, Andrew Goudie and Karunarkara Hegde
1978   *The Prehistory and Palaeogeography of the Great Indian Desert*. New York: Academic Press.

Allchin, F. R.
1962   Upon the antiquity and methods of gold mining in ancient India. *Journal of the Economic and Social History of the Orient*, 5: 195-211.

Allchin, F. R.
1969a   Early cultivated plants in India and Pakistan. In, Peter J. Ucko and G. W. Dimbleby, eds., *The Domestication and Exploitation of Plants and Animals*. London: Gerald Duckworth & Co.: 325-29.

Allchin, F. R.
1969b   Early domestic animals in India and Pakistan. In, Peter J. Ucko and G. W. Dimbleby, eds., *The Domestication and Exploitation of Plants and Animals*. London: Gerald Duckworth & Co.: 317-22.

Allchin, F. R.
1981   Antiquity of gold mining in the Gadag region—Karnataka. In, M. S. Nagaraja Rao, ed., *Madhu: Recent researches in Indian archaeology and art history, the Shri M. N. Deshpande festschrift*. Delhi: Agam Kala Prakashan: 81-83.

Allchin, F. R.
1982   How old is the city of Taxila? *Antiquity*, 56: 8-14.

Allchin, F. R. and J. P. Joshi
1970   Malvan—further light on the southern extension of the Indus Civilization. *Journal of the Royal Asiatic Society of Great Britain and Ireland*: 20-8.

Allchin, F. R. and Jagat Pati Joshi
1995   *Excavations at Malvan*. Memoirs of the Archaeological Survey of India, 92.

Allchin, F. R. and R. Knox
1989   Preliminary report on the excavations at Lewan, 1977-78. In, H. Hartel, ed., *South Asian Archaeology 1979*. Berlin: Dietrich Reimer Verlag: 241-44.

Allchin, F. R., B. Allchin, F. A. Durrani and M. Farid Khan, eds.
1985   *Lewan and the Bannu Basin: Excavation and survey of sites and environments in North West Pakistan*. British Archaeological Reports, International Series, No. 310.

Alur, K. R.
1971   *Animal Remains from Bagor*. Unpublished report, Deccan College, Pune.

Alur, K. R.
1980   Faunal remains from the Vindhyas and the Ganga Valley. In, G. R. Sharma, V. D. Misra, D. Mandal, B. B. Misra and J. N. Pal, *The Beginnings of Agriculture*. Allahabad: Abinash Prakashan: 201-27.

Anderson, J.
1883   *Cataloque of Archaeological Collections in the Indian Museum*. 2 Vols. Calcutta: The Indian Museum.

Anderson, J. D.
1943   Researches into the prehistory of the Chinese. *Bulletin of the Museum of Far Eastern Antiquities*, 15(1): 1-304.

Andouze, F. and Catherine Jarrige
1991   Nomadic pastoralists and sedentary agriculturalists in the Kachi Plain, Baluchistan. *Studies in History*, 7(2): 231-54.

Andrews, Fred H.
1944   Sir Aurel Stein: the man. *Indian Arts and Letters*, 18(2): 4-6.

Angel, J. Lawrence
1971   Early Neolithic skeletons from Catal Huyuk: demography and pathology. *Anatolian Studies*, 21: 77-98.

Angel, J. Lawrence
1984   Health as a critical factor in changes from hunting to developed farming in the eastern Mediterranean. In, Mark Nathan Cohen and George J. Armelagos, eds., *Paleopathology at the Origins of Agriculture*. New York: Academic Press: 51-73.

Anonymous
1938a   Dacoits murder archaeologist, Mr. N. G. Majumdar. *The Madras Mail*, Saturday, 12 November: 14.

Anonymous
1938b   Organization of archaeological research in India. *Nature*, 141(3582): 1131.

Anonymous
1939a   Sir L. Woolley's report: a missing link in India, blank era of 2,000 years. *The Times*, Thursday, 13 July: 17-8.

Anonymous
1939b   Anthropological studies in India. *Nature*, 144(3652): 721-23.

Anonymous
1939c   Work of the Archaeological Survey of India. *Nature*: 144(3652): 758-59.

Anonymous
1939d   Indian archaeology and Indian problems. *Nature*, 144(3659): 1006.

Anonymous
1941   Annex 3, Committee on Indic and Iranian Studies. *Bulletin of the American Council of Learned Societies*, 33: 529-30.

854

Anonymous
1943   Ernest Mackay, 63, an archaeologist. *The Times*, 6 October: 22.

Anonymous
1953   *Medical Plants*. Gazetteer of Bombay State, Maharashtra State Gazetteers, Revised Edition A(1). Bombay: Government of Bombay.

Anonymous
1957   *Timbers*. Gazetteer of Bombay State, Maharashtra State Gazetteers, Revised Edition A(2). Bombay: Government of Bombay.

Anonymous
1961   *Miscellaneous Plants*. Gazetteer of Bombay State, Maharashtra State Gazetteers, General Series A(3) Botany, 2nd ed. Bombay: Government of Maharashtra.

Anonymous
1963   *Gold Mining Industry in India*. Geological Survey of India, Memoir No. 1.

Anonymous
1964a   Departmental excavations: Mohenjo-daro, Kot Diji, Naru Waro Dharo, Mainamati, Charsada, Banbhore, Lahore Fort. *Pakistan Archaeology*, 1: 37-56.

Anonymous
1964b   Departmental exploration. *Pakistan Archaeology*, 1: 8-20.

Anonymous
1968   Excavations: Amri. *Pakistan Archaeology*, 5: 47-50.

Anonymous
1989   *Les Cites Oubliees de Indus: Archaeologie du Pakistan*. Paris: Musee National des Arts Asiatiques, Guimet: 208 pp.

Anonymous
1992   *Handbook of Agriculture*. Delhi: Indian Council of Agricultural Research.

Ansari, Ishtiaq
1993   Kerigar: Gold pickers of Indus. *Journal of Pakistan Archaeologists' Forum*, 2(1-2): 155-66.

Ansari, Z. D. and M. K. Dhavalikar
1975   *Excavations at Kayatha*. Pune: Deccan College Postgraduate and Research Institute.

Anthony, David W.
1985   *The Social and Economic Implications of the Domestication of the Horse*. PhD Dissertation, Department of Anthropology, University of Pennsylvania

Anthony, David W.
1986   The "Kurgan Culture," Indo-European origins and the domestication of the horse: a reconsideration. *Current Anthropology*, 27(4): 291-313.

Anthony, David W.
1991   The archaeology of Indo-European Origins. *Journal of Indo-European Studies*, 19(3-4): 193-222.

Anthony, David W.
1996   Current thoughts on the domestication of the horse in Asia. *South Asian Studies* 13:315-16

Anthony, David and D. Brown
1989   Looking a gift horse in the mouth: identification of the earliest bitted equids and the microscopic analysis of bit wear. In. P. Crabtree, D. Campanya and K. Ryan, eds., *Early Animal Domestication in Cultural Context*. Philadelphia: MASCA Research Papers in Science and Archaeology, Supp to Vol. 6: 98-116.

Anthony, David and Dorcas Brown
1991   The origins of horseback riding. *Antiquity*, 65(246): 22-38.

Anthony, David and Nicoli Vinogradov
1995   The birth of the chariot. *Archaeology*, 48(2): 36-41.

Aravamuthan, T. G.
1942   *Some Survivals of the Harappa Culture*. Bombay: Karnatak Publishing House.

Ardeleanu-Jansen, Alexandra
1984   Stone sculptures from Mohenjo-daro. In, M. Jansen and G. Urban, eds., *Reports on Field Work Carried out at Mohenjo-daro, Pakistan 1982-83 by the IsMEO-Aachen University Mission: Interim Reports, Volume 1*. Aachen/Rome: RWTH/IsMEO: 139-57.

Ardeleanu-Jansen, Alexandra
1987   The theriomorphic stone sculpture from Mohenjo-daro reconsidered. In, Michael Jansen and Guntur Urban eds., *Reports on Field Work Carried Out at Mohenjo-daro, Pakistan, 1983-84: Interim Reports, Volume 2*. Aachen/Rome:RWTH/IsMEO: 59-68.

Ardeleanu-Jansen, Alexandra
1989   A short note on steatite sculpture from Mohenjo-Daro. In, Karen Frifelt and Per Sorensen, eds., *South Asian Archaeology 1985*. London: Curzon Press, Scandinavian Institute of Asian Studies, Occasional Papers No. 4: 196-210.

Ardeleanu-Jansen, Alexandra
1992   New evidence on the distribution of artifacts: an approach towards a qualitative-quantitative assessment of the terracotta figurines of Mohenjo-daro. In, Catherine Jarrige, ed., *South Asian Archaeology 1989*. Madison: Prehistory Press, Monographs in World Prehistory, 14: 5-14.

856

Ardeleanu-Jansen, Alexandra
1993a   Who fell in the well? Digging up a well in Mohenjo-daro. In, Adalbert J. Gail and Gerd J. R. Mevissen, eds., *South Asian Archaeology 1991*. Stuttgart: Franz Steiner Verlag: 1-15.

Ardeleanu-Jansen, Alexandra
1993b   *Die Terrakotten in Mohenjo-daro: Eine unterschung zur keramischen kleinplastik in Mohenjo-daro, Pakistan (ca. 2300-1900 v. Chr.)*. Aachen University Mission Occasional Papers, edited by Michael Jansen and G. Urban. Aachen: Reinisch Westfalische Technische Hochschule.

Ardeleanu-Jansen, Alexandra, Ute Franke and Michael Jansen
1983   An approach toward the replacement of artifacts into the architectural context of the Great Bath at Mohenjo-daro. In, G. Urban and M. Jansen, eds., *Forschungsprojekt DFG Mohenjodaro*. Aachen: Reinische-Westfalischen Technischen Hockschule: 43-69.

Arne, Ture J.
1925   Painted Stone Age pottery from the Province of Honan, China. *Palaeontologica Sinica*, Series D, Vol. 1, fascicle 2: 1-34.

Ashfaque, Syed M. and Salma Sultana
1989   In search of Sangala of Alexander's campaign. *Journal of the Pakistan Historical Society*, 37(2): 159-85.

Asthana, Shashi
1976   *History and Archaeology of India's Contacts with Other Countries, from Earliest Times to 300 B.C.* Delhi: B. R. Publishing Corporation.

Asthana, Shashi
1982   Harappan trade in metals and minerals: a regional approach. In, Gregory L. Possehl, ed., *Harappan Civilization: A contemporary perspective*. Delhi: Oxford & IBH and the American Institute of Indian Studies: 271-85.

Asthana, Shashi
1985   *Pre-Harappan Cultures of India and the Borderlands*. Delhi: Books and Books.

Asthana, Shashi
1987   Revised chronological framework for prehistoric cultures of northern Baluchistan. In, B. M. Pande and B. D. Chattopadhyaya, eds., *Archaeology and History: Essays in memory of Sh. A. Ghosh*. 2 Vols. Delhi: Agam Kala Prakashan: 69-74.

Atri, C. M.
1982   Gujarat: Harappan sites. Ahmedabad: Department of Archaeology, mss.

Aufrey, J. C. and E. Tchernov
1989   Origine du commensalisme de la souris domestique (*Mus musculus domesticus*) vis-

a-vis de l'homme. *Comptes Rendus de L'academie Des Sciences Paris*, 307 (Serie III): 517-22.

Aurenche, Olivier, editor
1984   *Nomades et Sedentaries: Perspectives ethnoarcheologique*. Paris: Editions Recherche sue des Civilisations.

Ayyar, V. Ramanath and K. P. Aithal
1964   Karpasa cotton: its origin and spread in ancient India. *Adyar Library Bulletin*, 28(1-2): 1-39.

Babu, B. S. R.
1995   Excavations at Bhorgarh. *Puratattva*, 25: 88-90.

Baillie, Alexander F.
1890   *Kurrachee: (Karachi), Past: present: and future*. Calcutta: Thacker, Spink & Company.

Baker, W. E.
1840   Report on the line levels between the Jumna and Sutlej Rivers. *Journal of the Asiatic Society of Bengal*, 9: 688-94.

Balfour, Edward
1885   *The Cyclopaedia of India: And of Eastern and Southern Asia, commercial, industrial and scientific*. 3 Vols, 3rd edition. London: Bernard Quaritch.

Ball, V.
1898   On the occurrence of gold in the District Singhbun. *Records of the Geological Survey of India*, 2(1): 11-4.

Ball, Warwick, with Jean-Claude Gardin
1982   *Archaeological Gazetteer of Afghanistan*. 2 Vols. Paris: C. N. R. S. Editions Recherche sur les Civilizations, Synthese.

Balland, Daniel
1991   Nomadism and politics: the case of Afghan nomads in the Indian Subcontinent. *Studies in History*, 7(2): 205-30.

Baloch, N. A.
1973   In search of the Indus culture sites in Sind. *Bulletin of the Institute of Sindology*, 3(2-3): 11-33.

Baloch, N. A.
1975   A few Harappan sites explored in Sind. In, Ahmad Nabi Khan ed., *Proceedings of International Symposium on Moenjodaro, 1973*. Karachi: National Book Foundation: 79-85.

Banerjee, S. and S. Chakrabarti
1973   Remains of the great one-horned rhinoceros from Rajasthan. *Science and Culture*.

858

Banerji, R. D.
1918-19   Jhukar. *Annual Progress Report of the Archaeological Survey of India, Western Circle, 1918-19*: 58

Banerji, R. D.
1920-21   Mohenjo-daro. *Progress Report of the Archaeological Survey of India, Western Circle, for the Year Ending 1 March 1920*: 79-80.

Banerji, R. D.
1922-23   Exploration, Western Circle, Sind, Mohenjo-daro. *Annual Report of the Archaeological Survey of India, 1922-23*: 102-04.

Banerji, R. D.
1925-26   Exploration, Eastern Circle, Bengal. *Annual Report of the Archaeological Survey of India, 1925-26*: 107-17.

Banerji, R. D.
1926   *Mohenjo-Daro: A long forgotten report*. First printed in 1984. Varanasi: Prithvi Prakashan.

Bar-Yosef, Ofer
1989   The PPNA in the Levant—an overview. *Paleorient*, 15(1): 57-63.

Bar-Yosef, Ofer and Anatoly
1992   *Pastoralism in the Levant: Archaeological materials in anthropological perspective*. Madison: Prehistory Press, Monographs in World Archaeology.

Bar-Yosef, Ofer and Anna Belfer-Cohen
1989   The origins of sedentism and farming communities in the Levant. *Journal of World Archaeology*, 3(4): 447-98.

Bar-Yosef, Ofer and Anna Belfer-Cohen
1991   From sedentary hunter-gatherers to territorial farmers in the Levant. In, Susan A. Gregg, ed., *Between Bands and States*. Urbana-Champaign: Center for Archaeological Investigations, Occasional Paper 9: 181-202.

Bar-Yosef, Ofer and Anna Belfer-Cohen
1992   From foraging to farming in the Mediterranean Levant. In, Anne Birgitte Gebauer and T. Douglas Price, eds., *Transition to Agriculture in Prehistory*. Madison: Prehistory Press, Monographs in World Archaeology, 4: 21-48.

Bar-Yosef, Ofer and David Alon
1988   Nahal Hemar Cave: The excavations. *Atiqot*, 18: 1-30.

Bar-Yosef, Ofer and Francois R. Valla, editors
1991a   *The Natufian Culture in the Levant*. Ann Arbor: International Monographs in Prehistory, Archaeological Series.

Bar-Yosef, Ofer and Francois R. Valla
1991b   The Natufian Culture—an introduction. In, Ofer Bar-Yosef and Francois R. Valla, eds., *The Natufian Culture in the Levant*. Ann Arbor: International Monographs in Prehistory, Archaeological Series 1: 1-10.

Bar-Yosef, Ofer and Mordechai E. Kislev
1989   Early farming communities in the Jordan Valley. In, David R. Harris and G. C. Hillman, eds., *Foraging and Farming: The evolution of plant exploitation*. London: Unwin Hyman. One World Archaeology, 13: 633-42.

Bar-Yosef, Ofer and Richard H. Meadow
1995   The origins of agriculture in the Near East. In, T. Douglas Price and Anne Birgitte Gebauer, eds., *Last Hunters, First Farmers: New perspectives on the prehistoric transition to agriculture*. Santa Fe: School of American Research: 39-95.

Barfield, Thomas J.
1993   *The Nomadic Alternative*. Englewood Cliffs: Prentice-Hall.

Barnicot, N.
1969   Human nutrition: evolutionary perspectives. In, Peter J. Ucko and G. W. Dimbleby, eds., *The Domestication and Exploitation of Plants and Animals*. London: Gerald Duckworth & Co.: 525-30.

Barros, Joao de
1563-1615 *Decadas de Asia*. 4 Vols. Lisbon and Madrid.

Barros, Joao de
1945-46 *Decadas: Seleccao, prefacio e notas de Antonio Baiao*. 4 Vols. Coleccao de Classecas sa da Costa. Lisboa: Livraria sa da Costa.

Barth, Fredrik
1956   Ecologic relationships of ethnic groups in Swat, North Pakistan. *American Anthropologist*, 58: 1079-89.

Barth, Fredrik
1961   *Nomads of South Persia*. Oslo: Oslo University Press.

Barth, Fredrik, editor
1969   *Ethnic Groups and Boundaries: The social organization of cultural differences*. Boston: Little, Brown and Co.

Barton, George A.
1928a   On the so-called Sumero-Indian seals. *American Schools of Oriental Research Annual for 1926-1927*, 8: 79-95.

Barton, George A.
1928b   The palaeographic affinities of the seals from Harappan and Mohenjo-daro. *All-India Oriental Conference*, Session 5, Lahore (Title only).

Barton, George A.
1929   Whence came the Sumerians? *Journal of the American Oriental Society*, 49: 263-68.

Barton, George A.
1930   A comparative list of the signs in the so-called Indo-Sumerian seals. *American Schools of Oriental Research Annual for 1928-1929*, 10: 75-94.

Basham, Arthur L.
1967   *The Wonder That Was India*. 3rd ed. New York: Taplinger Publishing Company.

Basu, Arabinda and Anadi Pal
1980   *Human Remains from Burzahom*. Calcutta: Anthropological Survey of India, Memoir No. 56.

Bates, Daniel G. and Susan H. Lees
1977   The role of exchange in productive specialization. *American Anthropologist*, 79: 824-41.

Bautze, J.
1985   The problem of the *khadga (Rhinoceros unicornis)* in light of archaeological finds and art. In, J. Schotsmans and M. Taddei, eds., *South Asian Archaeology 1983*. Naples: Instituto Universitario Orientale, Dipartmento di Studi Asiatici, Series Minor 23: 405-34.

Beck, Brenda
1976   The Ramayana in South India. Presentation to the Department of South Asia Regional Studies, University of Pennsylvania.

Beck, Lois
1986   *The Qashqa'i of Iran*. New Haven: Yale University Press.

Belcher, William R.
1991   Fish resources in an early urban context at Harappa. In, Richard H. Meadow, ed., *Harappa Excavations 1986-1990: A multidisciplinary approach to third millennium urbanization*. Madison: Prehistory Press, Monographs in World Archaeology, 3: 107-20.

Belcher, William R.
1993   Riverine and maritime fish resource utilization of the Indus Valley Tradition. *Journal of Pakistan Archaeologists' Forum*, 2(1-2): 241-79.

Belcher, William R.
1994a   Butchery practices and the ethnoarchaeology of South Asia fisherfolk. In, W. Van Neer, ed., *Fish Exploitation in the Past*. Tervuren: Annals du Musee Royal de l'Afrique Central, Sciences, Zoologiques, No. 274: 170-76.

Belcher, William R.
1994b   Riverine fisheries and habitat exploitation of the Indus Valley tradition: an example from Harappa, Pakistan. In, Asko Parpola and Petteri Koskikallio, eds., *South Asian Archaeology 1993*. 2 Vols. Helsinki: Annales Academiae Scientiarum Fennicae, Series B, Volume 271: 71-80.

Belcher, William R.
1994c   Multiple approaches towards reconstruction of fishing technology: net making and the Indus Valley Tradition. In J.M. Kenoyer, ed., *From Sumer to Meluhha: Contributions to the archaeology of South and West Asia in memory of George F. Dales, Jr.* Madison: Wisconsin Archaeological Reports 3L: 129–41.

Belfer-Cohen, Anna
1991   The Natufian in the Levant. *Annual Review of Anthropology*, 20: 167-86.

Bellasis, A. F.
1857   Further observations on the ancient and ruined city of Brahminabad in Sind. *Journal of the Bombay Branch of the Royal Asiatic Society*, 5: 467-74.

Bernal, Martin
1987   *Black Athena: The Afroasiatic roots of Classical civilization; the fabrication of ancient Greece 1785-1985.* Vol. I. London: Free Association Books.

Bernal, Martin
1991   *Black Athena: The Afroasiatic roots of Classical civilization; the archaeological and documentary evidence.* Vol. II. London: Free Association Books.

Berthoud, T., R. Besenval, J. P. Carbonnel, F. Cesbron, J. Liszak-Hours
1977   *Les Anciennes Mines D'Afghanistan (Rapport Preliminarie).* Paris: Commissariat a l'Energie Atomique, Laboratorie de Researche des Musees de France, Unite de Researche Archaeologique, No. 7.

Besenval, M. Roland
1990   Les populations nomades et l'exploitation des resources minerales dans les zones arides et semi-arides: donnees ethnologiques et problemes archeologiques. Le cas du plateau iranien aux 4e et 3e millenaires. In, H.P. Francfort, ed., *Nomades et Sedentaires en Asie Central.* Paris: Editions CNRS: 53-6.

Besenval, M. Roland
1992   Recent archaeological surveys in Pakistani Makran. In, Catherine Jarrige, ed., *South Asian Archaeology 1989.* Madison: Prehistory Press, Monographs in World Archaeology, 14: 25-35.

Besenval, M. Roland
1994   The 1992-1993 field seasons at Miri Qalat: new contributions to the chronology of Protohistoric settlement in Pakistani Makran. In, Asko Parpola and P. Koskikallio, eds., *South Asian Archaeology 1993.* 2 Vols. Helsinki: Annales Academiae Scientiarum Fennicae, Series B, Volume 271: 81-91.

Besenval, M. Roland and P. Marquis
1993   Excavations in Miri Qalat (Pakistani Makran)—results of the first field season (1990). In, Adalbert J. Gail and Gerd J. R. Mevissen, eds., *South Asian Archaeology 1991.* Stuttgart: Franz Steiner Verlag: 31-48.

862

Besenval, M. Roland and P. Sanlaville
1990   Cartography of ancient settlements in central southern Pakistani Makran: new date. *Mesopotamia*: 79-146.

Betts, Alison V. G.
1988   Excavations at Dhuweila, eastern Jordan. *Levant*, 20: 7-21.

Betts, Alison V. G., Klaas van der Borg, Ari de Jong, Catherine McClintock and Mark van Strydonck
1994   Early cotton in North Arabia. *Journal of Archaeological Science*, 21: 489-99.

Bhan, Kuldeep K.
1983   *The Archaeology of Jamnagar District, Gujarat*. PhD Dissertation, Department of Archaeology and Ancient History, Maharaja Sayajirao University of Baroda.

Bhan, Kuldeep K.
1986   Recent explorations in the Jamnagar District of Saurashtra. *Man and Environment*, 10: 1-21.

Bhan, Kuldeep K.
1989   Late Harappan settlements of western India, with special reference to Gujarat. In, Jonathan Mark Kenoyer, ed., *Old Problems and New Perspectives in the Archaeology of South Asia*. Madison: Wisconsin Archaeological Reports, 2: 219-42.

Bhan, Kuldeep K.
1994   Cultural development of the Prehistoric period in North Gujarat with reference to Western India. *South Asian Studies*, 10: 71-90.

Bhandarkar, D. R.
1911-12   Excavation. *Progress Report of the Archaeological Survey of India: Western Circle, for the year ending 31 March 1912*.

Bhola Nath
1959   Remains of the horse and Indian elephant from the prehistoric site of Harappa (West Pakistan). *Proceedings of the First All-India Congress of Zoologists*, Pt. 2, Scientific Papers: 1-14.

Bhola Nath
1962   Prehistoric animals of India and their bearing on early Indian cultures. *Proceedings of the Second All-India Congress of Zoologists*: 6-16.

Bhola Nath
1963   Animal remains from Rangpur. In, S. R. Rao, Excavations at Rangpur and other explorations in Gujarat. *Ancient India*, 18-19: 153-60.

Bhola Nath
1968   Animal remains from Rupar and Bara sites, Ambala District, East Punjab. *Indian Museum Bulletin*, 3(1-2): 69-115.

Bhola Nath and G. V. Sreenivasa Rao
1985   Animal remains from Lothal excavations. In, S. R. Rao, *Lothal: A Harappan port town, 1955-62*. Memoirs of the Archaeological Survey of India, No. 78, Vol. 2: 636-50.

Bhola Nath and M. K. Biswas
1969   Animal remains from Alamgirpur. *Indian Museum Bulletin*, 4(1): 43-52.

Biagi, Paolo and Mauro Cremaschi
1988   The early Palaeolithic sites of the Rohri Hills (Sind, Pakistan) and their environmental significance. *World Archaeology*, 19(3): 421-33.

Biagi, Paolo and Mauro Cremaschi
1990   Geoarchaeological investigations on the Rohri Hills (Sind, Pakistan). In, Maurizio Taddei, ed., *South Asian Archaeology 1987*. Roma: Instituto Italiano per il Medio ed Estremo Oriente, Serie Orientale Roma, 66(1):30-42.

Biagi, Paolo and Mauro Cremaschi
1991   The Harappan flint quarries of the Rohri Hills (Sind-Pakistan). *Antiquity*, 65(246): 97-102.

Bibby, T. Geoffrey
1969   *Looking for Dilmun*. New York: Alfred Knopf.

Billimoria, N. M.
1947   The Great Indian Desert with special reference to the former existence of the sea in the Indus Valley (with two maps). *Journal of the Sind Historical Society*, 8(2): 85-127.

Binford, Lewis R.
1962   Archaeology as anthropology. *American Antiquity*, 28(2): 217-25.

Binford, Lewis R.
1965   Archaeological systematics and the study of culture process. *American Antiquity*, 31(2): 203-10.

Binford, Lewis R.
1967   Smudge pits and hide smoking: the use of analogy in archaeological reasoning. *American Antiquity*, 32(1): 1-12.

Binford, Lewis R.
1968a   Archaeological perspectives. In, Sally R. Binford and Lewis R. Binford, eds., *New Perspectives in Archaeology*. Chicago: Aldine Publishing Co: 5-32.

Binford, Lewis R.
1968b   Post-Pleistocene adaptations. In, Sally R. Binford and Lewis R. Binford, eds., *New Perspectives in Archaeology*. Chicago: Aldine Publishing Co: 313-41.

Binford, Lewis R.

1968c   Methodological considerations of the archaeological use of ethnographic data. In, R. B. Lee and I. DeVore, eds., *Man the Hunter*. Chicago: Aldine Publishing Co.: 268-73.

Binford, Lewis R.

1968d   Some comments on historical versus processual archaeology. *Southwestern Journal of Anthropology*, 24: 267-75.

Bird, Junius B.

1956   Fabrics, basketry and matting as revealed by impressions on pottery. In, Walter A. Fairservis, Jr., *Excavations in the Quetta Valley, West Pakistan*. New York: Anthropological Papers of the American Museum of Natural History, 45(2): 372-77.

Biscione, Raffaele

1973   Dynamics of an early South Asian urbanization: the first period of Shahr-i Sokhta and its connections with Southern Turkmenia. In, Norman Hammond, ed., *South Asian Archaeology*. Park Ridge: Noyse Press: 105-18.

Bisht, Ravi Singh

1976a   *Banawali*. Chandigarh: Public Relations Department, Government of Haryana.

Bisht, Ravi Singh

1976b   Transformation of the Harappan culture in Panjab with special reference to the excavations at Sanghol and Chandigarh. In, U. V. Singh, ed., *Archaeological Congress and Seminar: 1972*. Kurukshetra: B. N. Chakravarty University Kurukshetra: 16-22.

Bisht, Ravi Singh

1977   *Banawali: A look back into the Pre-Indus and Indus Civilizations*. Chandigarh: Special Board of Archaeology, Government of Haryana.

Bisht, Ravi Singh

1978   Banawali: a new Harappan site in Haryana. *Man and Environment*, 2: 86-8.

Bisht, Ravi Singh

1982   Excavations at Banawali: 1974-77. In, Gregory L. Possehl, ed., *Harappan Civilization: A contemporary perspective*. Delhi: Oxford & IBH and the American Institute of Indian Studies: 113-24.

Bisht, Ravi Singh

1984   Structural remains and town-planning of Banawali. In, B.B. Lal and S. P. Gupta, eds., *Frontiers of the Indus Civilization*. Delhi: Books and Books: 89-97.

Bisht, Ravi Singh

1987   Further excavation at Banawali: 1983-84. In, B. M. Pande and B. D. Chattopadhyaya, eds., *Archaeology and History: Essays in memory of Sh. A. Ghosh*. 2 Vols. Delhi: Agam Kala Prakashan: 135-156.

Bisht, Ravi Singh

1989a   A new model of the Harappan town planning as revealed at Dholavira in Kutch: a surface study of its plan and architecture. In, Bhaskar Chatterjee, ed., *History and Archaeology: Prof. H. D. Sankalia felicitation volume*. Delhi: Ramanand Vidya Bhawan: 397-408.

Bisht, Ravi Singh

1989b   The Harappan colonization of Kutch: an ergonomic study with reference to Dholavira and Surkotada. In, Krishna Deva and Lallanji Gopal, eds., *History and Art*. Delhi: Ramanand Vidya Bhavan: 265-72.

Bisht, Ravi Singh

1991   Dholavira: a new horizon of the Indus Civilization. *Puratattva*, 20: 71-82.

Bisht, Ravi Singh and Shashi Asthana

1979   Banawali and some other recently excavated Harappan sites in India. In, M. Taddei, ed., *South Asian Archaeology 1977*. Naples: Instituto Universitario Orientale, Seminario di Studi Asiatici, Series Minor 6: 223-40.

Bissing, Frederich W., von

1927   Ein vor etwa 15 Jahren erworbenes "Harappa-Siegel." *Archiv fur Orientforschung*, 4: 21-2.

Blanford, W. T.

1880   The Geology of Western Sind. *Memoirs of the Geological Survey of India*, 17.

Blanford, W. T.

1883   Geological Notes on the Hills in the Neighborhood of Sind and Punjab Frontier Between Quetta and Dera Ghazi Khan. *Memoirs of the Geological Survey of India*, 20: 1-209.

Blanford, W. T.

1888-91   *The Fauna of British India, Including Ceylon and Burma: Mammalia*. London: Taylor and Francis.

Bloch, Jules

1924   Sanskrit et Dravidien. *Bulletin de la Societe de Linguistique de Paris*, 25: 1-21.

Boas, Franz

1940   *Race, Language and Culture*. New York: Macmillan Company.

Bokonyi, Sandor

1969   Archaeological problems and methods of recognizing animal domestication. In, P. J. Uco and G. W. Dimbelby, eds., *The Domestication and Exploitation of Plants and Animals*. London: Gerald Duckworth & Co.: 219-29.

Bokonyi, Sandor

1996   Horse remains from the prehistoric site of Surkotada, Kutch, late 3rd millennium BC. *South Asian Studies*, 13:297-307.

866

Bonte, Pierre
1990   French Marxist perspectives on nomadic pastoral societies. In, Carl Salzman and John G. Galaty, eds., *Nomads in a Changing World*. Naples: Instituto Universitario Orientale, Dipartmento di Studi Asiatica, Series Minor XXXII: 40-101.

Bor, N. L.
1960   *Grasses of Burma, Ceylon, India and Pakistan (Excluding Bambuseae)*. London: Pergamon Press.

Bose, P. N.
1908   Notes on the geology and mineral resources of Rajpipla State. *Records of the Geological Survey of India*, 37: 167-90.

Boserup, Esther
1965   *The Conditions of Agricultural Growth: The economics of agrarian change under population pressure*. Chicago: Aldine Publishing Company.

Boserup, Esther
1981   *Population and Technological Change: A study of long-term trends*. Chicago: University of Chicago Press.

Bower, B.
1993   The write stuff: Researchers debate the origins and effects of literacy. *Science News*, 143: 152-54.

Braidwood, Linda S. and Robert J. Braidwoods, editors
1982   *Prehistoric Village Archaeology in South-Eastern Turkey*. Oxford: British Archaeological Reports, S138.

Braidwood, Linda S., Robert J. Braidwood, Bruce Howe, Charles A. Reed and Patty Jo Watson, editors
1983   *Prehistoric Archaeology Along the Zagros Flanks*. Chicago: The Oriental Institute of the University of Chicago, Studies in Ancient Oriental Civilization, No. 105.

Braidwood, Robert J.
1952   *The Near East and the Foundations for Civilization*. Eugene: Condon Lectures, Oregon State System of Higher Education.

Braidwood, Robert J.
1975   *Prehistoric Men*. 8th ed. New York: Scott-Foresman and Company.

Braidwood, Robert J. and Bruce Howe
1960   *Prehistoric Investigations in Iraqi Kurdistan*. Chicago: The Oriental Institute of the University of Chicago, Studies in Ancient Oriental Civilization, No. 31.

Braidwood, Robert J., Bruce Howe and Charles A. Reed
1961   The Iranian prehistoric project. *Science*, 133: 2008-10.

Braidwood, Robert J., Halet Cambel, Charles L. Redman and Patty Jo Watson
1971   Beginnings of village-farming communities in southeastern Turkey. *Proceedings of the National Academy of Sciences,* 86(6): 1236-40.

Bray, Denys DeS.
1909-34   *The Brahui Language.* 3 Vols. Calcutta: Superintendent of Government Printing.

Bray, Denys DeS.
1913   *The Life-history of a Brahui.* London: Prize Publication Fund 4.

Briant, Pierre
1982   *Etat et pasteurs au Moyen-Orient ancien.* Cambridge/Paris: Cambridge University Press/Editions de la Maison des sciences de l'homme.

Brinkman, R. and C. M. Rafiq
1971   *Landforms and soil parent materials of West Pakistan.* Lahore: Soil Survey of Pakistan.

Bronson, Bennet
1977   The earliest farming: demography as cause and consequence. In, C. A. Reed, ed., *Origins of Agriculture.* The Hague: Mouton: 23-48.

Brown, Dorcas and David Anthony
1995   *Bit wear and horseback riding.* Paper presented at "Early Horsekeepers of the Eurasian Steppes, 4500-1500 BC." June 19-24. Petropavlovsk, Kazakhstan.

Brown, W. Norman
1938   The excavations at Chanhu-daro. *American Journal of Archaeology,* 42:127.

Brown, W. Norman
1939   The beginnings of civilization in India. *Journal of the American Oriental Society,* 59: 32-44.

Brown, W. Norman
1957   The sanctity of the cow in Hinduism. *The Madras University Journal,* 28: 29-49.

Brunswig, Robert H.
1973   Prospective tree-ring calibration of the Indus Civilization radiocarbon chronology. *Man,* 8: 543-54.

Brunswig, Robert H.
1975   Radiocarbon dating and the Indus Civilization: calibration and chronology. *East and West,* 25(1-2): 111-45.

Brunton, John
1939   *John Brunton's Book: Being the memoirs of John Brunton, engineer, from a manuscript in his own hand, written for his grandchildren and now first printed.* Cambridge: Cambridge University Press.

Bryson, Reid A.
1975   The lessons of climatic history. *Environment and Conservation*, 2: 163-79.

Bryson, Reid A. and A. M. Swain
1981   Holocene variations of monsoon rainfall in Rajasthan. *Quaternary Research*, 16: 135-45.

Buckley, Robert Burton
1893   *Irrigation Works in India and Egypt*. London: E. & S. N. Spoon.

Bulgarelli, G. M.
1981   Turquoise working in the Helmand Civilization—some observations. In, H. Hartel, ed., *South Asian Archaeology* 1979. Berlin: Dietrich Reimer Verlag: 65-9.

Bulliet, Richard W.
1975   *The Camel and the Wheel*. Cambridge: Harvard University Press.

Burnes, James
1829   *A Narrative of a Visit to the Court of Sinde*. Bombay: Summachar Press.

Burnes, Sir Alexander
1833-34   Substance of a geographical memoir on the Indus. *Journal of the Royal Geographical Society*, 3: 113-56; 4: 287-90

Burnes, Sir Alexander
1834   *A Voyage on the Indus*. London: John Murray.

Burnes, Sir Alexander
1835a   *Travels Into Bokhara: Containing the narrative of "A Voyage on the Indus"*. 3 Vols. London: John Murray.

Burnes, Sir Alexander
1835b   Memoir on the eastern branch of the River Indus. *Transactions of the Royal Asiatic Society*, 3: 550-88.

Burt, Lieutenant J. S.
1834   Description of the mode of extracting salt from the damp sand-beds of the River Jumna, as practiced by the inhabitants of Bundelkhand. *Journal of the Asiatic Society of Bengal*, 3: 33-7.

Burton, Richard F.
1851a   *Scinde, or the Unhappy Valley*. 2 Vols. London: Richard Bentley.

Burton, Richard F.
1851b   *Sind: And the races that inhabit the Valley of the Indus*. *London*: William H. Allen & Co.

Burton, Richard F.
1877   *Sind Revisited: With notices of the Anglo-Indian Army, Railroads...* 2 Vols. London: Richard Bentley.

869

Buth, Ghulam Mohammad
1986   *Central Asia and Western Himalaya: A forgotten link.* Jodhpur: Scientific Publishers.

Buth, Ghulam Mohammad, Maqsooda Khan and Farooq A. Lone
1986   Antiquity of rice and its introduction in Kashmir. In, Ghulam Mohammad Buth, ed.,
           Central Asia and Western Himalaya: A forgotten link. Jodhpur: Scientific Publishers:
           63-7.

Buth, Ghulam Mohammad, Ravi Singh Bisht and G. S. Gaur
1982   Investigation of palaeoethnobotanical remains from Semthan, Kashmir. *Man and
           Environment,* 6: 41-5.

Butler, B. E.
1950   A theory of prior streams as a causal factor of soil occurrence in the riverine plain of
           southeastern Australia. *Australian Journal of Agricultural Research,* 1: 231-52.

Butzer, Karl W.
1976   *Early Hydraulic Civilization in Egypt: A study in cultural ecology.* Chicago: University
           of Chicago Press, Prehistoric Archaeology and Ecology Series.

Byrd, Bryan F.
1989   The Natufian: settlement variability and economic adaptations in the Levant at the
           end of the Pleistocene. *Journal of World History,* 3: 159-97.

COHMAP
1988   Climatic changes of the last 18,000 years: observations and model simulations. *Science,*
           241: 1043-52.

Caldwell, Joseph R.
1964   Interaction spheres in prehistory. In, Joseph R. Caldwell and Robert L. Hall, eds.,
           Hopewellian Studies. Springfield: Illinois State Museum Scientific Papers, 12: 133-
           43.

Caldwell, Robert
1874   *A Comparative Grammar of the Dravidian or South-Indian Family of Languages.*
           London: Kegan Paul, Trench and Trubner.

Campbell, A.
1916   A note on the occurence of copper celts in Manbhum. *Journal of the Bihar and
           Orissa Research Society,* 2: 85-6.

Cane, Scott
1989   Australian Aboriginal seed grinding and its archaeological record: a case study from
           the Western Desert. In, David R. Harris and G. C. Hillman, eds., *Foraging and
           Farming: The evolution of plant exploitation.* London: Unwin Hyman: 99-119.

Cappieri, Mario
1959   La popolarizione prehistoria della civilta dell'Indio. *Revista di Scienze Prehistoriche,*
           14: 123-74.

870

Cappieri, Mario
1960   *L'India Prehistorica*. Firenze: Sansoni.

Cappieri, Mario
1965   Ist die Indus-Kultur und ihre Bevolkerung Wirklich Verschwunden? *Anthropos*, 60: 719-62.

Cappieri, Mario
1970   *The Population of the Indus Civilization*. Field research projects, Occasional Papers II. Miami.

Cappieri, Mario
1971   The population of the Indus Civilization. In, Walter A. Fairservis, Jr. *The Roots of Ancient India*. New York: Macmillan: 425-42.

de Cardi, Beatrice
1950   On the borders of Pakistan: recent exploration. *Journal of the Royal India, Pakistan and Ceylon Society, Arts and Letters*, 24(2):54.

de Cardi, Beatrice
1951   A new prehistoric ware from Baluchistan. *Iraq*, 13(2): 63-75.

de Cardi, Beatrice
1959   New wares and fresh problems from Baluchistan. *Antiquity*, 33: 15-24.

de Cardi, Beatrice
1964   British expeditions to Kalat, 1948 and 1957. *Pakistan Archaeology*, 1: 20-29.

de Cardi, Beatrice
1965   Excavation and reconnaissance in Kalat, West Pakistan: the prehistoric sequence in the Surab region. *Pakistan Archaeology*, 2: 86-182.

de Cardi, Beatrice
1983   *Archaeological Surveys in Baluchistan, 1948 and 1957*. London: Institute of Archaeology, Occasional Publication No. 8.

de Cardi, Beatrice
1984   Some third and fourth millennium sites in Sarawan and Jhalawan, Baluchistan, in relation to the Mehrgarh sequence. In, Bridget Allchin, ed., *South Asian Archaeology 1981*. Cambridge: Cambridge University Press: 61-8.

Cardona, George
1988   *Panini: His work and traditions*. Volume One, Background and Introduction. Varanasi: Motilal Banarsidass.

Carless, T. G.
1837   Memoir on the delta of the Indus. In, R. Hughes Thomas, ed., 1855, *Memoirs on Sind*. Bombay: Selections From the Records of the Bombay Government, Vol. 1, No. 17, New Series: 459-500.

Carless, T. G.
1838a   Memoir to accompany the survey of the delta of the Indus. *Journal of the Royal Geographical Society*, 8: 328-66.

Carless, T. G.
1838b   Memoir on the bay, harbour and trade of Kurachee. In, R. Hughes Thomas, ed., 1855, *Memoirs on Sind*. Bombay: Selections From the Records of the Bombay Government, Vol. 1, No. 17, New Series: 189-208.

Carless, T. G.
1838c   Memoir on the Province of Lus and a narrative of a journey to Beila. In, R. Hughes Thomas, ed., 1855, *Memoirs on Sind*. Selections from the Records of the Bombay Government, Vol. 1, No. 17, New Series: 299-319.

Carless, T. G.
1839   Account of a journey to Beylah. *Journal of the Asiatic Society of Bengal*, 8: 184-202.

Carneiro, Robert L. and Daisy F. Hulse
1966   On determining the probable rate of population growth during the Neolithic. *American Anthropologist*, 68(1): 177-81.

Carter, G. E. L.
1932   Old sites on the Lower Indus. *The Indian Antiquary*, 61: 86-90.

Carter, Howard and A. C. Mace
1923   *The Tomb of Tut-Ankhamen*. 3 Vols. London: Cassell and Company.

Casal, Jean-Marie
1961a   *Fouilles de Mundigak*. 2 Vols. Paris: Memoires de la Delegation Archaeologique Francais en Afghanistan, Tome 17.

Casal, Jean-Marie
1961b   Rapport provisoire sur les fouilles executees a Amri (Pakistan) en 1959-1960. *Arts Asiatiques*, 8: 11-26.

Casal, Jean-Marie
1964a   *Fouilles d'Amri*. 2 Vols. Paris: Publications de la Commission des Fouilles Archaeologiques, Fouilles du Pakistan.

Casal, Jean-Marie
1964b   Fresh digging at Amri. *Pakistan Archaeology*, 1: 57-65.

Casal, Jean-Marie
1966   Nindowari—a Chalcolithic site in south Baluchistan. *Pakistan Archaeology*, 3: 10-21.

Casal, Jean-Marie
1968   Nindo Damb. *Pakistan Archaeology*, 5: 51-5.

872

Casal, Jean-Marie
1969   *La Civilisation de l'Indus et ses Enigmes.* Paris: Fayard.

Casanova, Michele
1992   The sources of the lapis lazuli found in Iran. In, Catherine Jarrige, ed., *South Asian Archaeology 1989*. Madison: Prehistory Press, Monographs in World Archaeology, 14: 49-56.

Casanova, Michele
1994   Lapis lazuli beads in Susa and Central Asia: a preliminary study. In, Asko Parpola and Petteri Koskikallio, eds., *South Asian Archaeology 1993*. 2 Vols. Helsinki: Annales Academiae Scientiarum Fennicae, Series B, Volume 271: 137-45.

Casson, L.
1989   *The Periplus Maris Erythraei: Text with introduction, translation and commentary.* Princeton: Princeton University Press.

Cauvin, J.
1978   *Les Premiers Villages de Syrie-Palestine du IXeme au VIIeme Millenaire Avant J.C.* Lyon: Maison de l'Orient.

Cauvin, J.
1990   Les origines prehistorique de nomadisme pastoral dans les pays du Levant: le cas de l'oasis d'El Kowm (Syrie). In, Henri-Paul Francfort, ed., *Nomades et Sedentaires en Asie Centrale: Apports de l'archeologie et de l'ethnologie.* Paris:Editions CNRS: 69-80.

Chakrabarti, Dilip K.
1978   Lapis lazuli in early India. *Man and Environment*, 2: 51-8.

Chakrabarti, Dilip K.
1978a   Seals as evidence of Indus-West Asia interrelations. In, Debiprasad Chattopadhyay, ed., *History and Society: Essays in honor of Professor Niharranjan Ray.* Calcutta: K. P. Bagchi & Company: 93-116.

Chakrabarti, Dilip K.
1978b   The Nippur Indus seal and Indus chronology. *Man and Environment*, 2: 88-90.

Chakrabarti, Dilip K.
1978c   Reserved slip ware in the Harappan context. *Puratattva*, 8: 158-64.

Chakrabarti, Dilip K.
1979a   Size of Harappan settlements. In, D. P. Agrawal and Dilip Chakrabarti, eds., *Essays in Indian Protohistory.* Delhi: B. R. Publishing Corporation: 205-15.

Chakrabarti, Dilip K.
1979b   The problem of tin in early India - a preliminary survey. *Man and Environment*, 3: 61-74.

Chakrabarti, Dilip K.
1981   Indian archaeology: The first phase, 1784-1861. In, Glyn Daniel, ed., *Towards a History of Archaeology*. London: Thames and Hudson: 169-85.

Chakrabarti, Dilip K.
1982   'Long barrel-cylinder' beads and the issue of Pre-Sargonic contact between the Harappan Civilization and Mesopotamia. In, Gregory L. Possehl, ed., *Harappan Civilization: A contemporary perspective*. Delhi: Oxford & IBH and the American Institute of Indian Studies: 265-70.

Chakrabarti, Dilip K.
1987   The pre-industrial mines of India. *Puratattva*, 16: 65-71.

Chakrabarti, Dilip K.
1988   *A History of Indian Archaeology: From the beginning to 1947*. Delhi: Munshiram Manoharlal.

Chandra, A. N.
1980   *The Rig-Vedic Culture and the Indus Civilization*. Calcutta: Ratna Prakashan.

Chase, A. K.
1989   Domestication and domiculture in northern Australia: a social perspective. In, David R. Harris and G. C. Hillman, eds., *Foraging and Farming: The evolution of plant exploitation*. London: Unwin Hyman: 42-54.

Chatterjee, B. K. and G. D. Kumar
1962   Etude comparee et analyse racial des restes humains de Harappa, Pakistan Occidental. *L'Anthropologie*, 66 335-37.

Chatterjee, B. K. and G. D. Kumar
1964   *Comparative Study and Racial Analysis of Human Remains of Indus Valley Civilization*. Calcutta: W. Newman and Co.

Childe, V. Gordon
1926   *The Aryans: A study of Indo-European origins*. London: Kegan Paul, Trench and Trubner.

Childe, V. Gordon
1928   *The Most Ancient East: The Oriental prelude to European prehistory*. London: Kegan Paul, Trench, Trubner & Company.

Childe, V. Gordon
1934   *New Light on the Most Ancient East: The Oriental prelude to European prehistory*. 1st edition. London: Kegan Paul, Trench, Trubner & Company.

Childe, V. Gordon
1936   *Man Makes Himself*. 1st edition. London: Watts & Company.

Childe, V. Gordon
1937   The Indus Civilization. *Antiquity*, 11: 351.

Childe, V. Gordon
1939   India and the west before Darius. *Antiquity*, 13: 5-15.

Childe, V. Gordon
1941   *Man Makes Himself*. 2nd edition. London: Watts & Company.

Childe, V. Gordon
1950   The urban revolution. *Town Planning Review*, 21: 3-17.

Childe, V. Gordon
1953   *New Light on the Most Ancient East*. American printing of the 3rd edition. New York: Frederick A. Praeger.

Chitalwala, Y. M.
1979   Harappan and Post-Harappan settlement patterns in Rajkot District of Saurashtra. In, D. P. Agrawal and Dilip Chakrabarti, eds., *Essays in Indian Protohistory*. Delhi: B. R. Publishing Corporation: 113-21.

Chitalwala, Y. M.
1985   Late Harappan cultures. In, S. B. Deo and K. Paddayya, eds., *Recent Advances in Indian Archaeology: Proceedings of the seminar held in Poona in 1983*. Poona: Deccan College Post-graduate and Research Institute: 58-64.

Chitalwala, Y. M. and P. K. Thomas
1978   Faunal remains from Khanpur and their bearing on culture, ecomony and environment. *Bulletin of the Deccan College Research Institute*, 37(1-4): 11-14.

Chowdhury, K. A.
1983   The plant remains. In, R. C. Gaur, *Excavations at Atranjikhera: Early Civilization of the Upper Ganges Basin*. Delhi: Motilal Banarsidass and Center for Advanced Study, Department of History, Aligarh Muslum University: 457-60.

Chowdhury, K. A. and S. S. Ghosh
1951   Plant remains from Harappa 1946. *Ancient India*, 7: 3-19.

Claire, John
1827   *The Shepherd's Calendar*. Edited by Eric Robinson and Geoffery Summerfield. 1973 edition. Oxford: Oxford University Press.

Clason, A. T.
1974   Archaeozoological study in India: aspects of stock-breeding and hunting in Prehistoric and Early Historic times. In, J. E. van Lohuizen-de Leeuw and J. M. M. Ubaghs, eds., *South Asian Archaeology 1973*. Leiden: E. J. Brill: 90-100.

Clason, A. T.
1977   Wild and domestic animals in prehistoric India. *Eastern Anthropologist*, 30: 241-89.

Clason, A. T.
1979   *Wild and Domestic Animals in Prehistoric India*. Lucknow: Ethnographic & Folk Culture Society.

Clason, A. T.
1984   Animal-man relationship in southern Asia during the Holocene. In, Bridget Allchin, ed., *South Asian Archaeology 1981*. Cambridge: Cambridge University Press: 341-43.

Clayton, W. D.
1972   Gramineae. In, F. N. Hepper, ed., *Flora of West Tropical Africa*. 2nd ed., London: Crown Agents: Vol. 3, Pt. 2: 349-512.

Cleuziou, Serge
1980   Three seasons at Hili: toward a chronology and cultural history of the Oman Peninsula in the 3rd millennium B.C. *Proceedings of the Seminar on Arabian Studies*, 10: 19-23.

Cleuziou, Serge
1981   Oman peninsula in early second millennium B. C. In, H. Hartel, ed., *South Asian Archaeology 1979*. Berlin: Dietrich Reimer Verlag: 279-93.

Cleuziou, Serge
1982   Hili and the beginnings of oasis life in eastern Arabia. *Proceedings of the Seminar for Arabian Studies*, 12: 15-22.

Cleuziou, Serge
1984   Oman peninsula and its relations eastward during third millennium. In, B. B. Lal and S. P. Gupta, eds., *Frontiers of the Indus Civilization*. Delhi: Books and Books: 371-93.

Cleuziou, Serge
1986   Dilmun and Makkan during the third and early second millennia B. C. In, Shaikha Haya Ali Al Khalifa and Michael Rice, eds., *Bahrain Through the Ages, the Archaeology*. New York: KPI Limited: 143-58.

Cleuziou, Serge
1989a   The chronology of Protohistoric Oman as seen from Hili. In, Paolo M. Costa and Maurizio Tosi, eds., *Oman Studies: Papers on the archaeology and history of Oman*. Roma: IsMEO, Serie Orientale Roma, 63: 47-77.

Cleuziou, Serge
1989b   The Early Dilmun Period (third and second milennium B.C.). In, P. Lombard and M. Kervan eds., *Bahrain National Museum Archaeological Collection: A selection of Pre-Islamic antiquities from excavations 1954-1975*. Vol. 1. Bahrain:Ministry of Education: 11-36.

Cleuziou, Serge
1992   The Oman Peninsula and the Indus Civilization: a reassessment. *Man and Environment*, 17(2): 93-103.

Cleuziou, Serge and Lorenzo Costantini
1980   Premiers elements sur l'agriculture protohistorique de l'Arabie orientale. *Paleorient*, 6: 245-51.

Cleuziou, Serge and Lorenzo Costantini
1982   A l'origin des oasis. *La Recherche*, 137: 1180-82.

Cleuziou, Serge and Maurizio Tosi
1986   *The Joint Hadd Project: Summary Report on the First Season*. Rome: The Joint Hadd Project

Cleuziou, Serge and Maurizio Tosi
1988   *The Joint Hadd Project: Summary Report on the Second Season, November 1986-January 1987*. Naples: The Joint Hadd Project.

Cleuziou, Serge and Maurizio Tosi
1989   The southeastern frontier of the ancient Near East. In, Karen Frifelt and Per Sorensen, eds., *South Asian Archaeology 1985*. London: Curzon Press, Scandinavian Institute of Asian Studies, Occasional Papers No. 4:15-48.

Cleuziou, Serge, Julian Reade and Maurizio Tosi, editors
1989   *The Joint Hadd Project: Summary report on the third season: October 1987-February 1988*. Rome: The Joint Hadd Project.

Clutton-Brock, Juliet
1965   *The fauna. Excavations at Langhnaj: 1944-63*. Part 2. Poona: Deccan College Postgraduate and Research Institute.

Clutton-Brock, Juliet, Vishnu-Mittre and A. N. Gulati
1961   *Technical Reports on Archaeological Remains*. Poona: Deccan College Postgraduate and Research Institute.

Coatman, J.
1925-26 *India in 1925-26*. Calcutta: Government of India.

Coatman, J.
1927-28 *India in 1927-28*. Calcutta: Government of India.

Cockburn, J.
1883   On the recent existence of *Rhinoceros indicus* in the north-western provinces, and a description of a tracing of an archaic rock painting from Mirzapur representing the hunting of this animal. *Journal of the Royal Asiatic Society of Bengal*, 52(2): 56-64.

Coggin-Brown, J.
1915a   Note on a copper celt found in Palamau District. *Journal of the Bihar and Orissa Research Society*, 1: 125-26.

Coggin-Brown, J.
1915b   Notes on two copper axes. *Journal of the Bihar and Orissa Research Society*, 1: 127-28.

Coggin-Brown, J.
1916   Further relics of the copper age. *Journal of the Bihar and Orissa Research Society*, 2: 386-87.

Coggin-Brown, J. and A. K. Dey
1923   *India's Mineral Wealth*. Oxford: Oxford University Press.

Cohen, Joel E.
1995   *How Many People Can the Earth Support?* London: W. W. Norton & Company.

Cohen, Mark Nathan
1977a   *The Food Crisis in Prehistory: Overpopulation and the origins of agriculture*. New Haven: Yale University Press.

Cohen, Mark Nathan
1977b   Population pressure and the origins of agriculture: an archaeological example from the coast of Peru. In, C. A. Reed, ed., *Origins of Agriculture*, The Hague: Mouton: 135-77.

Cohen, Mark Nathan
1984   Introduction. In, Mark Nathan Cohen and George J. Armelagos, eds., *Paleopathology at the Origins of Agriculture*. New York: Academic Press: 1-11.

Cohen, Mark Nathan and George J. Armelagos
1984a   *Paleopathology at the Origins of Agriculture*. New York: Academic Press.

Cohen, Mark Nathan and George J. Armelagos
1984b   Palaeopathology at the origins of agriculture: editors' summation. In, Mark Nathan Cohen and George J. Armelagos, eds., *Paleopathology at the Origins of Agriculture*. New York: Academic Press: 585-601.

COHMAP
1988   Climatic changes of the last 18,000 years: observations and model simulations. *Science* 241: 1043-52.

Cohen, Yehudi A.
1974   Comments on "Anthropological perspectives on ancient trade" by Robert McC. Adams. *Current Anthropology*, 15(3): 250-1.

Compagnoni, Bruno and Maurizio Tosi
1975 The camel: its distribution & state of domestication in the Middle East during the 3rd mill. B.C...from Shahr-i-Sokhta. In, R. H. Meadow and M. A. Zeder, eds., *Approaches to Faunal Analysis in the Middle East*. Peabody Museum Bull. No. 2: 91-103

Conrad, Roswitha
1974 The domestic animals in the early cultures of India. *Puratattva*, 7: 76-7.

Contenson, H., de
1971 Tell Ramad, a village of Syria in the 7th and 6th millennia BC. *Archaeology*, 24(3): 278-85.

Coomaraswamy, Ananda
1929 A very ancient Indian seal. *Bulletin of the Museum of Fine Arts*, 27: 28-9.

Cooper, Jerold S.
1983 *The Curse of Agade*. Baltimore: Johns Hopkins University Press.

Corbet, G. B. and J. E. Hill
1992 *The Mammals of the Indomalayan Region: A systematic review*. Oxford: Oxford University Press, Natural History Museum Publications.

Cornwall, Peter B.
1946 On the location of Dilmun. *Bulletin of the American Schools of Oriental Research*, 103: 3-11.

Correll, D. S. and M. C. Johnston
1970 *Manual of the Vascular Plants of Texas*. Renner: Texas Research Foundation.

Costantini, Lorenzo
1979 Plant remains from Pirak. In, Jean-Francois Jarrige and Marielle Santoni, *Fouilles de Pirak*. 2 Vols. Paris: Publications de la Commission des Fouilles Archaeologique, Fouilles du Pakistan, No. 2: 326-33.

Costantini, Lorenzo
1981 Palaeoethnobotany at Pirak: a contribution to the second millennium B. C. agriculture of the Sibi-Kacchi Plain, Pakistan. In, H. Hartel, ed., *South Asian Archaeology 1979*. Berlin: Dietrich Reimer Verlag: 271-77.

Costantini, Lorenzo
1984 The beginnings of agriculture in the Kachi Plain: the evidence from Mehrgarh. In, Bridget Allchin, ed., *South Asian Archaeology 1981*. Cambridge: Cambridge University Press: 29-33.

Costantini, Lorenzo
1985 Considerazioni su alcuni reperti di palma da dattero e sul centro di origine e l'area di coltivazione della "Phoenix dactylifera" L. In, G. Gnoli and L Lanciotti eds., *Orientalia Iosephi Tucci Memoriae Dicata*. Rome: IsMEO: 209-17.

Costantini, Lorenzo and Loredana Costantini Biasini
1985   Agriculture in Baluchistan between the 7th and 3rd Millennium B.C. *Newsletter of Baluchistan Studies*, 2: 16-30.

Costantini, Lorenzo
1990a   Harappan agriculture in Pakistan: the evidence of Nausharo. In Taddei, Maurizio, editor, *South Asian Archaeology 1987*. Roma: Instituto Italiano per il Medio ed Estremo Oriente, Serie Orientale Roma, 66(1): 321-32.

Costantini, Lorenzo
1990b   Ecology and farming of the protohistoric communities in the central Yemeni highlands. In deMaigre, A., editor, *The Bronze Age Culture of Hawlan At-Tiyal and Al-Hada* (Republic of Yemen). 2 Vols Rome:Instituto Italiano per il Medio de Estremo Oriente, Centro Studi e Scavi Archeologici, pp. 187-204.

Courty, M. A.
1985   Le milieu physique et utilisation du sol. In, Henri-Paul Francfort, ed., *Prospections Archaeologiques au Nord-Ouest de l'Inde: Rapport preliminarie 1983-84*. Paris: Editions Recherche sur les Civilizations, Memoire No. 62, Travaux de la Mission Archaeologique Franciase en Inde, No. 1: 11-31.

Courty, M. A.
1989   Integration of sediment and soil information in the reconstruction of protohistoric and historic landscapes of the Ghaggar Plain, north-west India. In, Karen Frifelt and Per Sorensen, eds., *South Asian Archaeology 1985*. Scandinavian Institute of Asian Studies, Occasional Papers No. 4: 255-59.

Cousens, Henry
1929   *The Antiquities of Sind With an Historical Outline*. Archaeological Survey of India, New Imperial Series, 46.

Cowan, C. Wesley and Patty Jo Watson
1992   Some concluding remarks. In, C. Wesley Cowan and Patty Jo Watson, eds., *The Origins of Agriculture: An international perspective*. Washington DC: Smithsonian Institution Press: 207-12.

Craddock, P. T.
1991   Old ways in the Kolar gold field. *Gold Bulletin & Gold Patent Digest*, 24(1): 127-31.

Craddock, Paul T., Ian C. Freestone, L. K. Gujar, A. Middleton and L. Willies
1989   The production of lead, silver and zinc in early India. In, Andreas Hauptmann, Ernst Pernicka and Gunther A. Wagner, eds., *Old World Archaeometallurgy*. Bochum: Selbstverlag des Deutchen Bergbau-Museums: 51-69.

Cribb, Roger
1991   *Nomads in Archaeology*. Cambridge: Cambridge University Press.

880

Cumming, Sir John
1939   *Revealing India's Past: A co-operative record of archaeological conservation and exploration in India and beyond.* London: The India Society.

Cunningham, Anne
1979   Notes on explorations in Amreli District and other parts of Saurashtra. Manuscript.

Cunningham, Sir Alexander
1871   Ramnagar and Ahichchatra *Archaeological Survey of India, Four Reports for the Years 1862-63-64-65.* Vol. 1: 255-65.

Cunningham, Sir Alexander
1875   Harappa. *Annual Report of the Archaeological Survey of India,* 5: 105-08.

Curtin, Philip
1975   *Economic Change in Pre-Colonial Africa.* 2 Vols. Madison: University of Wisconsin Press.

Curzon, George N., Lord
1900   Ancient monuments in India. *Annual Progress Report of the Archaeological Survey, Northwestern Provinces and Oudh Circle for the Year Ending 31st March 1900.* Appendix H. Delhi : Archaeological Survery of India.

Curzon, George N., Lord
1923   Introduction: George Birdwood Memorial Lecture. *Journal of the Royal Society of Arts,* 71 (3690): 659.

Dalal, Katy Feroze
1980   A short history of archaeological exploration in Bikanir and Bahawalpur along the 'Lost' Sarasvati River. *Indica,* 17(1): 3-40.

Dalal, Katy Feroze
1981   RD 89: a new Hakra Ware site? *Man and Environment,* 5: 77-86.

Dalal, Katy Feroze
1987   Binjor 1—a Pre-Harappan site on the Indo-Pak border. In, B. M. Pande and B. D. Chattopadhyaya, eds., *Archaeology and History: Essays in memory of Sh. A. Ghosh.* 2 Vols. Delhi: Agam Kala Prakashan: 75-111.

Dales, George F.
1962a   Harappan outposts on the Makran coast. *Antiquity,* 36: 86-92.

Dales, George F.
1962b   A search for ancient seaports. *Expedition,* 4(2): 2-10.

Dales, George F.
1964   The University of Pennsylvania expedition to Makran. *Pakistan Archaeology,* 1: 36-7.

Dales, George F.
1965a   New investigations at Mohenjo-daro. *Archaeology*, 18: 145-50.

Dales, George F.
1965b   Re-opening the Mohenjo-daro excavations. *Illustrated London News*, May 29: 25-7.

Dales, George F.
1965c   Civilization and floods in the Indus Valley. *Expedition*, 7(2): 2-10.

Dales, George F.
1966a   The decline of the Harappans. *Scientific American*, 214(5): 93-100.

Dales, George F.
1966b   Relation of Indus Valley floods to decline of Harappan Civilization. *American Philosophical Society Yearbook*, 1965. Philadelphia: American Philosophical Society: 508-12.

Dales, George F.
1966c   A suggested chronology for Afghanistan, Baluchistan and the Indus Valley. In, Robert Ehrich, ed., *Chronologies in Old World Archaeology*. Chicago: University of Chicago Press: 257-84.

Dales, George F.
1968   The South Asia Section. *Expedition*, 11(1): 38-45.

Dales, George F.
1971   Early human contacts from the Persian Gulf through Baluchistan and southern Afghanistan. In, William G. McGinnies, Bram J. Goldman and Patricia Paylore, eds., *Food Fiber and the Arid Lands*. Tucson: University of Arizona Press: 145-70.

Dales, George F.
1973   Archaeological and radiocarbon chronologies for protohistoric South Asia. In, Norman Hammond, ed., *South Asian Archaeology*. Park Ridge: Noyes Press: 157-69.

Dales, George F.
1974a   Excavations at Balakot, Pakistan 1973. *Journal of Field Archaeology*, 1: 3-22.

Dales, George F.
1974b   Current research: South Asia. *American Antiquity*, 39: 505-06.

Dales, George F.
1976   New inscriptions from Moenjodaro, Pakistan. In, Barry L. Eichler, ed., *Kramer Anniversary Volume: Cuneiform studies in honor of Samuel Noah Kramer*. Kevelaer: Verlag Butzon and Bercker: 111-23.

Dales, George F.
1979a   The Balakot Project: summary of four years excavations in Pakistan. In, M. Taddei, ed., *South Asian Archaeology 1977*. Naples: Instituto Universitario Orientale, Seminario di Studi Asiatici, Series Minor 6: 241-74.

882

Dales, George F.
1979b   The Balakot Project: summary of four years of excavations in Pakistan. *Man and Environment*, 3: 45-53.

Dales, George F.
1981   Reflections on four years of excavations at Balakot. In, Ahmad Hasan Dani, ed., *Indus Civilization: New perspectives*. Islamabad: Quaid-i-Azam University: 25-32.

Dales, George F.
1982   Mohenjodaro miscellany: some unpublished, forgotten or misinterpreted features. In, Gregory L. Possehl, ed., *Harappan Civilization: A contemporary perspective*. Delhi: Oxford & IBH and the American Institute of Indian Studies: 97-106.

Dales, George F.
1985   Stone sculpture from the Protohistoric Helmand Civilization, Afghanistan. In, G. Gnoli and L. Lanciotti, *Orientalia Iosephi Tucci Memoriae Dicta*. Roma: Instituto Italiano per Il Medio ed Estremo Oriente, Serie Minor 56(1): 219-24.

Dales, George F.
1986   Addendum to Alcock's supplement. In, George F. Dales and J. Mark Kenoyer *Excavations at Mohenjo Daro, Pakistan: The pottery*. Philadelphia: The University Museum: 552-54.

Dales, George F. and Carl P. Lipo
1992   *Explorations on the Makran Coast, Pakistan: A search for paradise*. Berkeley: Contributions of the Archaeological Research Faculty, University of California, Berkeley, 50.

Dales, George F. and J. Mark Kenoyer
1977   Shell working at ancient Balakot, Pakistan. *Expedition*, 19(2): 13-9.

Dales, George F. and J. Mark Kenoyer
1986   *Excavations at Mohenjo Daro, Pakistan: The pottery*. Philadelphia: The University Museum, University of Pennsylvania.

Dales, George F. and J. Mark Kenoyer
1987   Preliminary Report on the University of California at Berkeley's Second Season at Harappa, Pakistan: January-April 1987. Manuscript, photocopy.

Dales, George F. and J. Mark Kenoyer
1988   Preliminary Report on the Third Season (January - March 1988) of Research at Harappa, Pakistan. Manuscript, photocopy.

Dales, George F. and J. Mark Kenoyer
1989   Preliminary Report on the Fourth Season (January 15 - March 31, 1989) of Research at Harappa, Pakistan. Manuscript, photocopy.

Dales, George F. and J. Mark Kenoyer
1990   Excavation at Harappa—1989. *Pakistan Archaeology*, 25: 241-80.

Dales, George F. and J. Mark Kenoyer
1992a   Harappa 1989: summary of the fourth season. In, Catherine Jarrige, ed., *South Asian Archaeology 1989*. Madison: Prehistory Press, Monographs in World Archaeology, 14: 57-68.

Dales, George F. and J. Mark Kenoyer
1992b   Excavation at Harappa. *Pakistan Archaeology*, 27: 31-88.

Dales, George F. and J. Mark Kenoyer
1993a   The Harappa Project 1986-1989: New investigation at an ancient Indus city. In, Gregory L. Possehl, ed., *Harappan Civilization: A recent perspective*. 2nd ed. Delhi: Oxford & IBH and the American Institute of Indian Studies: 469-520.

Dales, George F. and J. Mark Kenoyer
1993b   Excavation and overview. In, G. F. Dales and J. M. Kenoyer, The Harappa Project 1986-89: new investigations at an ancient Indus city. In, Gregory L. Possehl, ed., *Harappan Civilization: A recent perspective*. 2nd ed. Delhi: Oxford & IBH and the AIIS: 469-95.

Dames, M. Longworth
1886   Old seals found at Harappa. *The Indian Antiquary*, 15: 1.

Dames, Mansel Longworth
1918   *The Book of Duarte Barbosa*. 2 Vols. London: The Hakluyt Society.

Dana, Edward S.
1949   *A Texbook of Mineralogy*. 4th ed. revised by W. R. Ford. New York: John Wiley and Sons.

Dani, Ahmad Hasan
1950   Hariyupiya in the Rigveda. *Varendra Research Society Monographs*, 8: 17-24.

Dani, Ahmad Hasan
1970-71   Excavations in the Gomal Valley. *Ancient Pakistan*, 5: 1-177.

Dani, Ahmad Hasan
1983   Neolithic problem and the patterns of culture in Pakistan. *Journal of Central Asia*, 6(1): 41-50.

Daniel, J. C.
1983   *The Book of Indian Reptiles*. Bombay: Bombay Natural History Society.

Dar, Saifur Rahman
1983   Khadianwala: the first Kot Dijian site discovered on the right bank of the river Ravi. *Journal of Central Asia*, 6(2): 17-34.

Datt, Braham
1980   *Settlements of Painted Grey Ware in Haryana*. PhD Dissertation, Department of Ancient Indian History, Culture and Archaeology, Kurukshetra University.

884

Datta, J. M.
1962   Demographic notes on Harappa skeletons. In, P. Gupta, P. C. Dutta and A. Basu, *Human Skeletal Remains from Harappa*. Memoirs of the Anthropological Survey of India, No. 9: 7-12.

Dave, J.
1965   *Report of the Committee on the Economic and Social Conditions of the Gujarati Gopalak*. Ahmedabad: Gujarat State Gopalak Society. (in Gujarati).

Davies, O. and K. Gordon-Grey
1977   Tropical African cultigens from Shongwenl excavations, Natal. *Journal of Archaeological Sciences*, 4: 153-62.

Davis, Richard S.
1978   The Palaeolithic. In, F. R. Allchin and N. Hammond, eds., *The Archaeology of Afghanistan: From earliest times to the Timurid Period*. New York: Academic Press: 37-70.

Davis, S. J. M.
1982   Climatic change and the advent of domestication: the succession of ruminant artiodactyls in the Late Pleistocene-Holocene in the Israel region. *Paleorient*, 8(2): 5-15.

Dayton, John E.
1971   The problem of tin in the ancient world. *World Archaeology*, 3(1): 49-70, 98-104.

DeLisle, D. G.
1963   Taxonomy and distribution of the genus Canchrus. *Iowa State Journal of Science*, 37: 259-351.

Debaine-Francfort, C.
1988   Etude comparative de materiels lithiques protohistoriques chinois (Chine metropolitaine at Asie centrale). Paris: Actes de Colloque Franco-Soviteique, Paris 19-26 November 1985. *L'Aise Centrale et Ses Rapports Avec Les Civilizations Orientales Des Origines a l'Age du Fer*: 197-206.

Della Casa, Carlo and Daniel a Sagramoso, editors
1990   *Luigi Pio Tessitori: Atti del covegno internazionale di Udine (12-14 Novembre 1987)*. Brescia: Paideria Editrice. Biblioteca Indiana, 4.

Delmas, A. B. and M. Casanova
1990   The lapis lazuli sources in the ancient east. In, Maurizio Taddei, ed., *South Asian Archaeology 1987*. Roma: Instituto Italiano per il Medio ed Estremo Oriente, Serie Orientale Roma, 66(1): 493-505.

Dennell, R. W.
1984   The importance of the Potwar Plateau, Pakistan, to studies of early man. In, Bridget Allchin, ed., *South Asian Archaeology 1981*. Cambridge: Cambridge University Press: 10-19.

885

Dennell, R. W.
1990   Report on the 1989 field season of the British Archaeological Mission to Pakistan. *South Asian Studies*, 6: 249-53.

Dennell, R. W.
1991   Report of the 1990 field season of the British Archaeological Mission to Pakistan. *South Asian Studies*, 7: 161-65.

Dennell, R. W., L. Hurcombe, R. Jenkinson and H. Rendell
1990   Preliminary results of the Palaeolithic programe of the British Archaeological Mission to Pakistan, 1983-87. In, Maurizio Taddei, ed., *South Asian Archaeology 1987*. Roma: Instituto Italiano per il Medio ed Estremo Oriente, Serie Orientale Roma, 66(1): 17-30.

Dennell, R. W., L. M. Hurcombe, R. Coard, M. Beech, M. Anwar and S. ul Haq
1993   The 1990 field season for the British Archaeological Mission to Pakistan in the Baroth area of the Pabbi Hills, northern Pakistan. In, A. Gail and G. Mevissen eds., *South Asian Archaeology 1991*. Stuttgart: Franz Steiner Verlag: 49-64.

Deotare, B. C. and M. D. Kajale
1996   Quaternary pollon analysis and palaeoenvironmental studies of the salt basins at Panchpadra and Thob, western Rajasthan, India: preliminary observations. *Man and Environment*, 21(1): 24-31.

Deshmukh, P. R.
1954   The Indus civilization in the Rig Veda. *Proceedings of the Indian History Congress*, 18th session: 115-22.

Deshmukh, P. R.
1982   *Indus Civilization, Rigveda and Hindu Culture*. Nagpur: Saroj Prakashan.

Deshpande, M. N.
1977   The Harappan settlements in the Ganga-Yamuna Doab. Paper presented at the conference titled, *Indus Civilization: Problems and issues*. Organized by B. B. Lal and S. C. Malik. Simla: Indian Institute of Advanced Study.

Desse, Jean
1989   Etude archaeozoologique. In, Henri-Paul Francfort, *Fouilles de Shortughai: Recherches sur l'Asie Centrale Protohistorique*. Vol. 1. Paris: Diffusion de Boccard: 187-206.

Desse, Jean and Nathanlie Desse-Berset
1990   La faune: les mammiferes et les poissons. In, Yves Calvet and Jacqueline Gachet, eds., *Failaka: Fouilles Francaises 1986-88*. Paris: Diffusion Boccard, Travaux de la Maison de l'Orient, 18: 51-70.

Dhattarwal, D. S.
1978   *Archaeology of Safidon Tehsil, District Jind (Haryana)*. M. Phil. Dissertation,

886

Department of Ancient Indian History, Culture and Archaeology, Kurukshetra University.

Dhavalikar, M. K.
1982   Daimabad bronzes. In, Gregory L. Possehl, ed., *Harappan Civilization: A contemporary perspective*. Delhi: Oxford & IBH and the American Institute of Indian Studies: 361-66.

Dhavalikar, M. K.
1992   Kuntasi: an Harappan port in western India. In, Catherine Jarrige, ed., *South Asian Archaeology 1989*. Madison: Prehistory Press, Monographs in World Archaeology, 14: 73-82.

Dhavalikar, M. K.
1993   Harappans in Saurashtra: the merchantile model as seen from recent excavations at Kuntasi. In, Gregory L. Possehl, ed., *Harappan Civilization: A recent perspective*. 2nd ed. Delhi: Oxford & IBH and the American Institute of Indian Studies: 555-68.

Dhavalikar, M. K. and Gregory L. Possehl
1992   The Pre-Harappan period at Prabhas Patan and the Pre-Harappan Phase in Gujarat. *Man and Environment*, 17(1): 71-8.

Dhavalikar, M. K., V. Shinde and S. Atre
1990   *Excavations at Kaothe*. Poone: Deccan College Post-Graduate and Research Institute.

Digard, J.-P.
1990   Les relations nomades-sedentaires au Moyen-Orient. Elements d-une polemique. In, Henri-Paul Francfort, ed., *Nomades et Sedentaires en Asie Centrale: Apports de l'archeologie et de l'ethnologie*. Paris: Editions CNRS: 97-112.

Dikshit, K.N.
1967   Exploration along the right bank of river Sutlej in Punjab. *Journal of Indian History*, 45(2): 561-68.

Dikshit, K. N.
1968   The copper hoards in the light of recent discoveries. *Bulletin of Ancient Indian History and Archaeology*, 2: 43-50.

Dikshit, K. N.
1969   Nature of Harappan wares in Sutlej Valley. In, B. P. Sinha, ed., *Potteries in Ancient India*. Patna: Department of Ancient Indian History and Archaeology, Patna University: 56-66.

Dikshit, K. N.
1977   Saharanpur District. Appendix I, M. N. Deshpande, The Harappan settlements in the Ganga-Yamuna Doab. Paper presented at, Indus Civilization: Problems and issues. Organized by B. B. Lal and S. C. Malik. Simla: Indian Institute of Advanced Study.

Dikshit, K. N.
1979a   Old channels of Ghaggar in Rajasthan - revisited. *Man and Environment*, 3: 105-6.

Dikshit, K. N.
1979b   The ochre colored ware settlement in Ganga-Yamuna Doab. In, D. P. Agrawal and Dilip Chakrabarti, eds., *Essays in Indian Protohistory*. Delhi: B. R. Publishing Corporation: 285-99.

Dikshit, K. N.
1980   A critical review of the pre-Harappan cultures. *Man and Environment*, 4: 32-43.

Dikshit, K. N.
1981   The excavations at Hulas and further exploration of the upper Ganga-Yamuna Doab. *Man and Environment*, 5: 70-6.

Dikshit, K. N.
1982a   The distribution of Harappan wares in Gangetic Valley. In, R. K. Sharma, ed., *Indian Archaeology: New perspectives*. Delhi: Agam Kala Prakashan: 113-23.

Dikshit, K. N.
1982b   Hulas and the Late Harappan complex in western Uttar Pradesh. In, Gregory L. Possehl, ed., *Harappan Civilization: A contemporary perspective*. Delhi: Oxford & IBH and the American Institute of Indian Studies: 339-51.

Dikshit, K. N.
1984a   The Sothi Complex: old records and fresh observations. In, B. B. Lal and S. P. Gupta, eds., *Frontiers of the Indus Civilization*. Delhi: Books and Books: 531-37.

Dikshit, K. N.
1984b   The Pre-Harappan culture of Rajasthan. *Bharati*, 2: 55-70.

Dikshit, K. N.
1984c   Late Harappa in northern India. In, B. B. Lal and S. P. Gupta, eds., *Frontiers of the Indus Civilization*. Delhi: Books and Books: 253-69.

Dikshit, K. N.
1987   The Sothi culture. In, B. M. Pande and B. D. Chattopadhyaya, eds., *Archaeology and History: Essays in memory of Sh. A. Ghosh*. 2 Vols. Delhi: Agam Kala Prakashan: 113-115.

Dikshit, K. N. and A. K. Sinha
1982   The Ganeshwar culture—an appraisal. *Puratattva*, 11: 120-2.

Dikshit, K. N., Rao Bahadur
1924-25   Explorations, Western Circle, Sind, Mohenjo-daro. *Annual Report of the Archaeological Survey of India, 1924-25*: 63-73.

Dikshit, K. N., Rao Bahadur
1925-26a   Exploration, Western Circle, Upper Sind Frontier District. *Annual Report of the Archaeological Survey of India, 1925-26*: 98-100.

888

Dikshit, K. N., Rao Bahadur
1925-26b Exploration, Western Circle, Upper Sind Frontier District, Limojunjo. *Annual Report of the Archaeological Survey of India, 1925-26*: 98-9.

Dikshit, K. N., Rao Bahadur
1925-26c Exploration, Western Circle, Upper Sind Frontier District, Badah. *Annual Report of the Archaeological Survey of India, 1925-26*: 99.

Dikshit, K. N., Rao Bahadur
1925-26d Exploration, Western Circle, Upper Sind Frontier District, Lohumjo-daro. *Annual Report of the Archaeological Survey of India, 1925-26*: 99-100.

Dikshit, K. N., Rao Bahadur
1935 The work of the Archaeological Survey of India. *Annual Bibliography of Indian Archaeology*, Kern Institute, Leiden, 1935: 1-2.

Dikshit, M. G.
1949 *Etched Beads in India*. Poona: Deccan College Postgraduate and Research Institute, Monograph Series No. 4.

Dikshit, M. G.
1950 Excavations at Rangpur: 1947. *Bulletin of the Deccan College Research Institute*, 11(1): 3-55.

Dikshit, M. G.
1952 Beads from Ahichchhatra, U. P. *Ancient India*, 8: 33-63.

Dikshit, M. G.
1957 New evidence of Harappa culture from Saurashtra. *Vallabh Vidyanagar Research Bulletin*, 1(1): 23-5.

Din, Malik Muhammad
1904 *Bahawalpur State*. Lahore: The Civil and Military Gazette Press. Punjab State Gazetteers, Vol. 36A.

Douglas, James
1893a *Bombay and Western India: A series of stray papers*. 2 Vols. London: S. Low Marston.

Douglas, James
1893b Cannibal and ogre. *Bombay and Western India: A series of stray papers*. 2 Vols. London: S. Low Marston: Vol. 2, 351-62.

Draper, Patricia
1975 !Kung women: contrasts in sexual egalitarianism in the foraging and sedentary contexts. In, R. Reiter, ed., *Toward an Anthropology of Women*. New York: Monthly Review Press: 77-109.

Duerst, J. U.
1908   Animal remains from the excavation of Anau and the horse of Anau in its relation to
           the history and to the races of domesticated horses. In, R. Pumpelly, *Explorations in
           Turkestan, Expedition of 1904*. Washington DC: The Carnegie Institute: 341-442.

Dupree, Louis
1958   *Shamshir Ghar: Historic Cave Site in Kandahar Province, Afghanistan*. New York:
           Anthropological Papers of the American Museum of Natural History, 46(2): 141-311
           pp.

Dupree, Louis
1963   *Deh Morasi Ghundai: A Chalcolithic site in south-central Afghanistan*. New York:
           Anthropological Papers of the American Museum of Natural History, 50(2): 59-135.

Dupree, Louis
1964   Prehistoric surveys and excavations in Afghanistan, 1959-60 and 1961-63. *Science*,
           146(3644): 638-40.

Dupree, Louis
1972a   *Prehistoric Research in Afghanistan (1959-1966)*. Philadelphia: Transactions of the
           American Philosophical Society, 62(4): 3-84.

Dupree, Louis
1972b   Tentative conclusions and tentative chronological charts. In, Louis Dupree, *Prehistoric
           Research in Afghanistan (1959-1966)*. Philadelphia: Transactions of the American
           Philosophical Society, 62(4): 74-82.

Dupree, Louis
1989   Evolution of the wheat-barley, sheep-goat-cattle complex: a gentle approach by gender.
           In, Jonathan Mark Kenoyer, ed., *Old Problems and New Perspectives in the
           Archaeology of South Asia*. Madison: Wisconsin Archaeological Reports, 2:115-16.

Durante, S.
1977   The use of imported sea-shells at Shahr-i-Sokhta: trading between inland Iran and
           the Indian Ocean. In, P. Basaglia et. al., eds., *La Citta' Bruciata del Deserto Salato*.
           Venezia: Erizzo: 223-28.

During Caspers, Elisabeth C. L.
1972   *Etched Carnelian Beads*. Bulletin of the Institute of Archaeology, London University,
           No. 10.

Durrani, Farzand A.
1965   Climate of the lower Indus in ancient times. *Journal of the University of Peshawar*,
           10: 33-7.

Durrani, Farzand A.
1981   Rehman Dheri and the birth of civilization in Pakistan. *Bulletin of the Institute of
           Archaeology*, 18: 191-207.

890

Durrani, Farzand A.
1984 Some Early Harappan sites in Gomal and Bannu Valleys. In, B. B. Lal and S. P. Gupta, eds., *Frontiers of the Indus Civilization.* Delhi: Books and Books: 505-10.

Durrani, Farzand A.
1986 *Rehman Dheri and the Origins of the Indus Civilization.* 2 Vols. PhD Dissertation, Department of Anthropology, Temple University.

Durrani, Farzand A.
1988 Excavations in the Gomal Valley: Rehman Dheri excavation report, No. 1. *Ancient Pakistan,* 6: 1-204.

Durrani, Farzand A. and Rita P. Wright
1992 Excavation at Rehman Dheri: the pottery typology and technology. In, Gregory L. Possehl, ed., *South Asian Archaeology Studies.* Delhi: Oxford & IBH: 145-62.

Durrani, Farzand A., Ihsan Ali and G. Erdosy
1991 Further excavations at Rehman Dheri. *Ancient Pakistan,* 7: 61-151.

Dutta, Arup Kumar
1991 *Unicornis: The great Indian one-horned rhinoceros.* Delhi: Konark Publishers.

Dutta, Pratap C.
1972 The Bronze Age Harappans: a re-examination of the skulls in the context of the population concept. *American Journal of Physical Anthropology,* 36: 391-96.

Dutta, Pratap C.
1975 Race concept and palaeoanthropology: a research model for interpreting ancient human remains. *L'Anthropologie* 13:35–46.

Dutta, Pratap C.
1983 *The Bronze Age Harappans: A Bio-anthropological study of the skeletons discovered at Harappa.* Calcutta: Anthropological Survey of India.

Dutta, Pratap C., Anadi Pal, Pabitra Gupta and Bimal C. Dutta
1987 *Ancient Human Remains from Rupar.* Calcutta: Memoirs of the Anthropological Survey of India, No. 77.

Dyson-Hudson, R. and N. Dyson-Hudson
1980 Nomadic pastoralism. *Annual Review of Anthropology,* 9: 15-61.

Edens, Christopher
1993 Indus-Arabian interaction during the Bronze Age: a review of the evidence. In, Gregory L. Possehl, ed., *Harappan Civilization: A recent perspective.* 2nd ed. Delhi: Oxford & IBH and the American Institute of Indian Studies: 335-63.

Elfenbein, J. H.
1983 The Brahui problem again. *Indo-Iranian Journal,* 25: 103-25.

Elfenbein, J. H.
1987   A periplous of the 'Brahui problem.' *Studia Iranica*, 16: 215-33.

Ellerman, J. R. and T. C. S. Morrison-Scott
1966   *Checklist of Palaearctic and Indian Mammals, 1758-1946*. 2nd ed. London: British Museum (Natural History).

Elliot, Sir Henry M.
1867-77   *The History of India as Told by its Own Historians: The Muhammadan Period*. Edited by Prof. John Dowson. 8 Vols. London: Trubner and Company.

Elliot, Sir Henry M.
1871   *The History of India as Told by its Own Historians: The Muhammadan Period*. Edited by Prof. John Dowson. Vol. 2. London: Trubner and Company.

Ellis, Francis Whyte
1816   Note to the introduction. In, A.D. Campbell, ed., *A grammar of the Teloogoo Language*. Madras: College Press of Fort St. George.

Elphinstone, Montstuart
1819   *An Account of the Kingdom of Cabul and its Dependencies in Persia, Tartary and India: Comprising a view of the Afghan Nation and a history of Dooranee monarchy*. 2 Vols. London: Longman, Hurst and Ree, Orm and Brown & John Murray.

Ember, Carol
1978   Myths about hunter gatherers. *Ethnology*, 17: 439-48.

Enault, Jean-Francois
1979   *Fouilles de Pirak*. 2 Vols. Paris: Publications de la Commission des Fouilles Archaeologique, Fouilles du Pakistan, No. 2, Vol. 2.

Enault, Jean-Francois and Jean-Francois Jarrige
1973   Chalcolithic pottery from four sites in the Bolan area of Baluchistan, West Pakistan. In, Norman Hammond, ed., *South Asian Archaeology*. Park Ridge: Noyes Press: 181-96.

Engles, J. M. M., J. G. Hawkes and M. Worede
1991   *Plant Genetic Resources of Ethiopia*. Cambridge: Cambridge University Press.

Erskine, K. D.
1908   *The Western Rajputana States Residency and Bikaner Agency: Statistical Tables*. Allahabad: The Pioneer Press. Rajputana Gazetteers, Vol. 3B.

Erskine, K. D.
1909   *The Western Rajputana States Residency and Bikaner Agency*. Allahabad: The Pioneer Press. 2 Vols. Rajputanta Gazetteers, Vol. 3A.

892

Fabri, C. L.
1937   A Sumero-Babylonian inscription discovered at Mohenjo daro. *Indian Culture*, 3: 663-73.

Fairclough, H. Rushton, translator
1986   *Virgil: Eclogues georgics Aeneid.* 2 Vols. Cambridge: Harvard University Press, Loeb Classical Library.

Fairservis, Walter A., Jr.
1956a   *Excavations in the Quetta Valley, West Pakistan.* New York: Anthropological Papers of the American Museum of Natural History, 45(2): 169-402

Fairservis, Walter A., Jr.
1956b   The chronology of the Harappan Civilization and the Aryan invasions: recent archaeological research. *Man*, 56(173): 153-56.

Fairservis, Walter A., Jr.
1959   *Archaeological Surveys in the Zhob and Loralai Districts, West Pakistan.* New York: Anthropological Papers of the American Museum of Natural History, 47(2): 277-448.

Fairservis, Walter A., Jr.
1961a   *Archaeological Studies in the Seistan Basin of Southwestern Afghanistan and Eastern Iran.* New York: Anthropological Papers of the American Museum of Natural History, 48(1): 1-128.

Fairservis, Walter A., Jr.
1961b   The Harappan Civilization: new evidence and more theory. New York: American Museum of Natural History, *Novitates*, No. 2055.

Fairservis, Walter A., Jr.
1961c   Baluchistan find: ruins of a 4000-year-old culture still standing in West Pakistan. *Natural History*, 70(6): 22-29.

Fairservis, Walter A., Jr.
1961d   Possible light on the Indus Valley civilization: huge sites in Baluchistan recently discovered and awaiting the spade. *Illustrated London News*, August 26: 324-27.

Fairservis, Walter A., Jr.
1964   The American Museum of Natural History expeditions to West Pakistan. *Pakistan Archaeology*, 1: 29-34.

Fairservis, Walter A., Jr.
1967   The origin, character and decline of an early civilization. New York: American Museum of Natural History, *Novitates*, No. 2302.

Fairservis, Walter A., Jr.
1971a   *The Roots of Ancient India.* New York: Macmillan.

Fairservis, Walter A., Jr.
1971b   Population estimates for selected sites in the Indo-Iranian borderlands, based on statistics of modern settlements in West Pakistan. In, Walter A. Fairservis, Jr. *The Roots of Ancient India*. New York: Macmillan.

Fairservis, Walter A., Jr.
1971c   Sites of the Indo-Iranian borderlands and the Indus River Valley. In, Walter A. Fairservis, Jr. *The Roots of Ancient India*. New York: Macmillan: 398-414.

Fairservis, Walter A., Jr.
1971d   Sites of the Kandahar area. In, Walter A. Fairservis, Jr. *The Roots of Ancient India*. New York: Macmillan: 393-94.

Fairservis, Walter A., Jr.
1973   Preliminary report on excavations at Allahdino (first season 1973). *Pakistan Archaeology*, 9: 95-102.

Fairservis, Walter A., Jr.
1975   *The Roots of Ancient India*. 2nd ed. Chicago: University of Chicago Press.

Fairservis, Walter A., Jr.
1976   *Excavations at the Harappan Site of Allahdino: The seals and other inscribed material.* New York: Papers of the Allahdino Expedition No. 1: 117 pp.

Fairservis, Walter A., Jr.
1982   Allahdino: an excavation of a small Harappan site. In, Gregory L. Possehl, ed., *Harappan Civilization: A contemporary perspective*. Delhi: Oxford & IBH and the American Institute of Indian Studies: 107-12.

Fairservis, Walter A., Jr.
1983   The Script of the Indus Valley Civilization. *Scientific American*, 248(3): 58-66.

Fairservis, Walter A., Jr.
1986   Cattle and the Harappan Chiefdoms of the Indus Valley. *Expedition*, 28(2): 43-50.

Fairservis, Walter A., Jr.
1992   *The Harappan Civilization and its Writing: A model for the decipherment of the Indus script*. Delhi: Oxford & IBH.

Fairservis, Walter A., Jr. and Franklin C. Southworth
1989   Linguistic archaeology and the Indus Valley Culture. In, Jonathan Mark Kenoyer, ed., *Old Problems and New Perspectives in the Archaeology of South Asia*. Madison: Wisconsin Archaeological Reports, 2: 133-41.

Falk, Harry
1991   Silver, lead and zinc in early Indian literature. *South Asian Studies*, 7: 111-17.

894

Falkenstein, Adam
1963   Zu den Inschriftenfunden der Grabung in Uruk-Warka, 1960-61. Berlin: Deutsches
        Archaologisches Institut Abteilung Baghdad. *Baghdader Mitteilungen* 2: 1-82.

Falkenstein, Adam
1964   Sumerische religiose Texte 5: Enki und die Weltordnung. *Zeitschrift Fur Assyriologie*,
        56: 44-129.

Farwell, Byron
1989   *Armies of the Raj: From the Great Indian Mutiny to Independence, 1858-1947.* New
        York, W. W. Norton & Company.

Fein, Jay S. and Pamela L. Stephens, editors
1987   *Monsoons.* New York: John Wiley and Sons.

Fentress, Marcia
1976   *Resource Access, Exchange Systems and Regional Interaction in the Indus Valley: An
        investigation of archaeological variability at Harappa and Moenjodaro.* PhD
        Dissertation, Department of Oriental Studies, University of Pennsylvania.

Field, Henry
1959   *An Anthropological Reconnaissance in West Pakistan, 1955.* Cambridge: Papers of
        the Peabody Museum of Archaeology and Ethnology, Harvard University, 52.

Fife, J. G.
1857   Report on the upper portion of the Eastern Nara. *Selections from the Records of the
        Bombay Government*, NS 45.

Flam, Louis
1981a   *The Palaeogeography and Prehistoric Settlement Patterns in Sind, Pakistan (4000-
        2000 B. C.).* PhD Dissertation, University of Pennsylvania.

Flam, Louis
1981b   Towards an ecological analysis of prehistoric settlement pattern in Sind, Pakistan.
        Man and Environment, 5: 52-8.

Flam, Louis
1982a   Suggested archaeological evidence for complex social organizations in prehistoric
        Sind. In, Stephen Pastner and Louis Flam, eds., *Anthropology in Pakistan.* Ithaca:
        Cornell University South Asia Occasional Papers and Theses, No. 8: 219-30.

Flam, Louis
1982b   Towards an ecological analysis of prehistoric settlement patterns in Sind, Pakistan.
        Sindhological Studies, Summer: 1-13.

Flam, Louis
1982c   Introduction to part II: ecological perspectives on the past. In, Stephen Pastner and
        Louis Flam, eds., *Anthropology in Pakistan.* Ithaca: Cornell University, South Asia
        Occasional Papers and Theses, No. 8: 122-23.

Flam, Louis
1984   Palaeogeography and prehistoric settlement patterns of the lower Indus Valley, Sind, Pakistan. In, Kenneth A. R. Kennedy and Gregory L. Possehl, eds., *Studies in the Archaeology and Palaeoanthropology of South Asia*. Delhi: Oxford & IBH and the American Institute of Indian Studies: 77-87.

Flam, Louis
1986a   Recent explorations in Sind: palaeogeography, regional ecology and prehistoric settlement patterns. In, Jerome Jacobson, ed, *Studies in the Archaeology of India and Pakistan*. Delhi: Oxford & IBH and the American Institute of Indian Studies: 65-89.

Flam, Louis
1986b   The Indus River and Arab Period in Sindh. *Sindhological Studies*, Summer: 5-14.

Flam, Louis
1987   Recent explorations in Sind: palaeogeography, regional ecology and prehistoric settlement patterns. *Sindhological Studies*, Summer: 5-32.

Flam, Louis
1993a   Excavations at Ghazi Shah, Sindh, Pakistan. In, Gregory L. Possehl, ed., *Harappan Civilization: A recent perspective*. 2nd ed. Delhi: Oxford & IBH and the American Institute of Indian Studies: 457-67.

Flam, Louis
1993b   Fluvial geomorphology of the lower Indus Basin (Sindh, Pakistan) and the Indus Civilization. In, John F. Shroder, Jr., ed., *Himalaya to the Sea: Geology, geomorphology and the Quaternary*. London: Routledge: 265-87.

Flannery, Kent V.
1968   Archaeological systems theory and early Mesoamerica. *Anthropological Archaeology in America*. Washington D. C.: The Anthropological Society of Washington: 67-87.

Flannery, Kent V.
1969   Origins and ecological effects of early domestication in Iran and the Near East. In, Peter Ucko and G. W. Dimbleby, eds., *The Domestication and Exploitation of Plants and Animals*. London: Gerald Duckworth & Co.: 73-100.

Flannery, Kent V.
1986   *Guila Naquitz: Archaic foraging and early agriculture in Oaxaca, Mexico*. New York: Academic Press.

Flannery, Kent V.
1995   Prehistoric social evolution. In, Carol. R. Ember and Melvin Ember eds., *Research Frontiers in Anthropology*. Englewood Cliffs: Prentice-Hall: 1-26.

Fleet, J. F.
1912   Seals from Harappa. *Journal of the Royal Asiatic Society of Great Britain and Ireland*, 698-701.

896

Foote, Robert Bruce
1916   *The Foote Collection of Indian Prehistoric and Protohistoric Antiquities: Notes on their ages and distribution.* Madras: Government of Madras.

Ford, Richard I.
1972   Barter, gift or violence: an anlysis of Tewa intertribal exchange. In, E. N. Wilmsen, ed., *Social Exchange and Interaction.* Museum of Anthropology, University of Michigan, Anthropological Papers Number 46: 2-45.

Forde, C. Darryl
1963   *Habitat, Economy and Society.* New York: E. P. Dutton & Company.

Fox, Richard G.
1969   Professional primitives: hunters and gatherers of nuclear South Asia. *Man in India,* 49(2): 139-60.

Francfort, Henri-Paul
1985a   *Prospections Archaeologiques au Nord-Ouest de L'inde: Rapport Preliminare 1983-84.* Paris: Editions Recherche sur les Civilizations, Memoire No. 62, Travaux de la Mission Archaeologique Franciase en Inde, No. 1.

Francfort, Henri-Paul
1985b   Distribution des sites. In, Henri-Paul Francfort, ed., *Prospections Archaeologiques au Nord-Ouest de l'Inde: Rapport preliminarie 1983-84.* Paris: Editions Recherche sur les Civilizations, Memoire No. 62, Travaux de la Mission Archaeologique Franciase en Inde, No. 1.

Francfort, Henri-Paul
1986a   La civilization de l'Indis face au desert. *La Recherche,* 181:1271.

Francfort, Henri-Paul
1986b   Preliminary report (1983-1984): archaeological and evnironmental researches in the Ghaggar (Saraswati) Plains. *Man and Environment,* 10: 97-100.

Francfort, Henri-Paul
1987   Le development proto-historique du bassin de la Ghaggar (nord-ouest de l'Inde). *Information Bulletin.* Moscow: UNESCO, International Association for the Study of the Cultures of Central Asia, 12: 93-5.

Francfort, Henri-Paul
1988a   A propos de l'urbanization du site de Shortughai (Afghanistan). *Bulletin du Centre Genevois D'Anthropologie,* 1: 15-34.

Francfort, Henri-Paul
1988b   Le development protohistorique du bassin de la Ghaggar (nord-ouest de l'Inde). In, Jean-Claude Gardin, ed., *L'Asie Centrale et Ses Rapports Avec Les Civilisations Orientales, Des Origines a l'Age du Fer.* Paris: MMAFAC, Diffusion Boccard, 1: 109-19.

Francfort, Henri-Paul
1989a   The Indo-French archaeological project in Haryana and Rajasthan. In, Karen Frifelt and Per Sorensen, eds., *South Asian Archaeology 1985*. London: Curzon Press, Scandinavian Institute of Asian Studies, Occasional Papers No.4. London: Curzon Press: 260-64.

Francfort, Henri-Paul
1989b   *Fouilles de Shortughai: Recherches sur l'Asie Centrale Protohistorique*. 2 Vols. Paris: Diffusion de Boccard.

Francfort, Henri-Paul, editor
1990   *Nomades et Sedentaires en Asie Centrale: Apports de l'archeologie et de l'ethnologie*. Paris: Editions du Centre National de la Recherche Scientifique.

Francfort, Henri-Paul, editor
1992   Evidence for Harappan irrigation in Haryana and Rajasthan. *The Eastern Anthropologist*, 45(1-2): 87-103.

Frankfort, Henri
1933   *Tell Asmar, Khafaje and Khorsabad: Second preliminary report of the Iraq Expedition*. Chicago: The Oriental Institute of the University of Chicago, Studies in Ancient Oriental Civilization, No. 16.

Frankfort, Henri
1939   *Sculpture of the Third Millennium B.C. from Tell Asmar and Khafaje*. Chicago: The Oriental Institute of the University of Chicago, Studies in Ancient Oriental Civilization, No. 43.

Franklin, Alan, Jacqueline S. Olin and Theodore A. Wertime, editors
1978   *The Search for Ancient Tin*. Washington D. C.: The Smithsonian Institution and the National Bureau of Standards.

Fraser, I. S.
1958   *Report on a Reconnaissance Survey of the Landforms, Soils and Present Land Use of the Indus Plains, West Pakistan*. Wahington D.C.: Colombo Plan Cooperative Project.

Frenchman, Katy Nariman
1972   *Prehistoric Pottery Industries Along the 'Lost' Sarasvati River of the Great Indian Desert*. 2 Vols. PhD Dissertation, Department of Archaeology, Deccan College.

Frere, H. B. E.
1853   Descriptive notices of antiquities in Scinde. *Journal of the Bombay Branch of the Royal Asiatic Society*, 5(19): 349-62.

Friederichs, Heinz F.
1933   Die zoologische und kulturhistorische bedeutung der tierdarstellungen von Mohenjo-daro am Indus. *Der Alte Orient*, 32(3/4): 1-20.

898

Frifelt, Karen
1976   Evidence of a third millennium BC town in Oman. *Journal of Oman Studies*, 2: 57-74.

Frifelt, Karen
1979   The Umm an-Nar and Jemdet Nasr of Oman and their relations abroad. In, J. E. van Lohuizen-de Leeuw, ed., *South Asian Archaeology 1975*. Leiden: E. J. Brill: 43-57.

Frifelt, Karen
1985   Further evidence of the third millennium B. C. town at Bat in Oman. *Journal of Oman Studies*, 7: 89-104.

Frifelt, Karen
1986   Burial mounds near Ali excavated by the Danish Expedition. In, Shaikha Haya Ali Al Khalifa and Michael Rice, eds., *Bahrain Through the Ages, the Archaeology*. New York: KPI Limited: 125-34.

Frifelt, Karen
1989   Third millennium irrigation and oasis culture in Oman. In, Jonathan Mark Kenoyer, ed., *Old Problems and New Perspectives in the Archaeology of South Asia*. Madison: Wisconsin Archaeological Reports, 2: 105-13.

Fuhrer, A.
1891   *Monumental Antiquities and Inscriptions of the N. W. Provinces and Oudh*. Allahabad: Government Press.

Fuhrer, A.
1891-92 *Progress Report of the Epigraphical and Architectural Branches of the N. W. Provinces and Oudh*. Allahabad: Government Press: 1-4.

Gadd, C. J.
1932   Seals of ancient Indian style found at Ur. *Proceedings of the British Academy*, 18: 191-210.

Gadd, C. J.
1933   A seal of Mohenjo daro type. *British Museum Quarterly*, 7(1): 5-6.

Gadd, C. J. and Sidney Smith
1924   The new links between Indian and Babylonian Civilization. *Illustrated London News*, October 4: 614-16.

Gardener, P.
1980   Lexicostatistics and Dravidian differentiation in situ. *Indian Linguistics*, 41: 170-80.

Garnett, David, editor
1939   *The Letters of T. E. Lawrence*. New York: Doubleday, Doran: 869 pp.

Garrod, Dorothy A. E.
1932   A new Mesolithic industry: the Natufian of Palestine. *Journal of the Royal Anthropological Institute*, 62: 257-69.

Garrod, Dorothy A. E.
1957   The Natufian culture: the life and economy of a Mesolithic people in the Near East. *Proceedings of the British Academy*, 43: 211-27.

Garrod, Dorothy A. E. and D. A. M. Bate
1937   *The Stone Age of Mount Carmel.* Vol. I. Oxford: Oxford University Press.

Garwood, Major J. F.
1887   Notes on the ancient mounds in the Quetta District. *Journal of the Asiatic Society of Bengal*, 56(1): 161-63.

Gaur, R. C.
1983   *Excavations at Atranjikhera: Early Civilization of the Upper Ganga Basin.* Delhi: Motilal Banarsidass and Center of Advanced Study, Department of History, Aligarh Muslim University: 518 pp.

Gaur, R. C.
1988   Excavations at Daulatpur (District Bulandshahr) — a camp site of the OCP Period. In, Purushottam Singh and O. P. Tandon, eds., *Archaeological Studies*. Varanasi: Bharat Kala Bhavan: 53-6.

Gaur, R. C.
1989   Lal Qila excavation and the OCP problem. In, D. P. Agrawal and A. Ghosh, eds., *Radiocarbon and Indian Archaeology*. Bombay: Tata Institute of Fundamental Research: 154-63.

Gaur, R. C.
1995   Excavation at Daulatpur (District Bulandshahr): a camp site of the OCP Period. In, R. C. Gaur *Excavations at Lal Qila: A habitational OCP site & a unique Copper-Hoard from Kiratpur*. Jaipur: Publication Scheme: 215-19.

Gaur, R.C. and Lal, Makhan
1992   Archaeological exploration in Muzaffarnagar District, U.P. Paper presented in Section V of the Indian History Congress. Published as: Lal, Makkhan (1998) Mapping the archaeological sites and emerging patterns. *Puratattva*, 28.

Gaussen, H., P. Legris, F. Blasco, V. H. Mehr-Homji and J. P. Troy
1968   *Notice de le Feuille Kathiawar*. Pondichery: Institute Francais, Carte Internationale de Tapis Vegetal.

Gebauer, Anne Birgitte and T. Douglas Price, editors
1992   *Transitions to Agriculture in Prehistory*. Madison: Prehistory Press, Monographs in World Archaeology, No. 4.

900

Geddes, David S.
1981   Les moutons mesolithiques dans le Midi de la France: implications pour les origines de l'elevage en Mediterranee occidentale. *Bulletin de la Societe Prehistorique Francaise: Compte Rendu des Seances*, 78(8): 227.

Geddes, David S.
1983   Neolithic transhumance in the Mediterranean Pyrenees. *World Archaeology*, 15(1): 51-66.

Geddes, David S.
1984   Settlement and subsistence during the Mesolithic and Neolithic in the Aude River Valley (France). In, W. H. Waldren, R. Chapman, J. Lewthwaite and Rex-Claire Kennard, *Early Settlement in the Western Mediterranean Islands and Peripheral Areas.* Oxford: BAR International Series, 229: 180-87.

Geddes, David S.
1985   Mesolithic domesticated sheep in west Mediterranean Europe. *Journal of Archaeological Science*, 12: 25-48.

Gee, E. R.
1948   Mineral resources of northwest India. *Records of the Geological Survey of Pakistan*, 1: 1-29.

Geldner, Karl Friedrich
1951   *Der Rig-Veda.* Cambridge: Harvard University Press. Harvard Oriental Series, 33-35.

Ghirshman, Roman
1938   *Fouilles de Sialk: Pres Kashan, 1933, 1934, 1937.* Paris: 2 Vols. Musee du Louvre, Department of Antiquities Orientales, Serie Archaeologique Vol 5.

Ghose, Bimal, Amal Kar and Zahid Husain
1979   The lost courses of the Sarasvati River in the Great Indian Desert: new evidence from Landsat imagery. *The Geographical Journal*, 145(3): 446-51.

Ghose, Bimal, Amal Kar and Zahid Husain
1980   Comparative role of the Aravalli and the Himalayan river systems in the fluvial sedimentation of the Rajasthan Desert. *Man and Environment*, 4: 8-12.

Ghosh, A.
1937   American excavations at Chanhu-daro in Sind. *Science and Culture*, Calcutta, 2: 347–49.

Ghosh, A.
1946   Introduction: The pottery of Ahichchhatra, District Bareilly, U. P. *Ancient India*, 1: 37-40.

Ghosh, A.
1947-48   Taxila (Sirkap), 1944-45. *Ancient India*, 4: 41-84.

Ghosh, A.
1952   The Rajputana desert: its archaeological aspect. *Bulletin of the National Institute of Sciences in India*, 1: 37-42.

Ghosh, A.
1953a   Fifty years of the Archaeological Survey of India. *Ancient India*, 9: 29-52.

Ghosh, A.
1953b   Exploration in Bikanir. *East and West*, 4(1): 31-4.

Ghosh, A.
1956   Exploration in Bikanir, India. *Miscellanea Asiatica Occidentalis*, 18: 102-15. American Documentation Institution Microfilm No. 5070.

Ghosh, A.
1959   Explorations in Bikanir. In, Henry Field, *An Anthropological Reconnaissance in West Pakistan, 1955*. Cambridge: Papers of the Peabody Museum of Archaeology and Ethnology, Harvard University, 52: 212-16.

Ghosh, A.
1961   A hundred years of Indian archaeology. *Cultural Forum*, 4(2): 4-13.

Ghosh, A.
1962   The archaeological background. In, P. Gupta, P. C. Dutta and A. Basu, *Human Skeletal Remains from Harappa*. Memoirs of the Anthropological Survey of India, No. 9: 1-5.

Ghosh, A.
1965a   The Indus Civilization: its origins, authors, extent and chronology. In, V. N. Misra and M. S. Mate, eds., *Indian Prehistory: 1964*. Poona: Deccan College Post-graduate and Research Institute: 113-24.

Ghosh, A.
1965b   Reply to, Comments on: The Indus Civilization: its origins, authors, extent and chronology. In, V. N. Misra and M. S. Mate, eds., *Indian Prehistory: 1964*. Poona: Deccan College Post-graduate and Research Institute.

Ghosh, A., editor
1989a   *An Encyclopaedia of Indian Archaeology*. 2 Vols. Delhi: Munshiram Manoharlal.

Ghosh, A.
1989b   Sarasvati Valley. In, A. Ghosh, ed., *An Encyclopaedia of Indian Archaeology*. Vol. 2, Delhi: Munshiram Manoharlal Publishers, 2: 394-97.

Ghosh, A. and K. C. Panigrahi
1946   The pottery of Ahichchhatra, District Bareilly, U. P. *Ancient India*, 1: 37-59.

Ghosh, N. C.
1989   Chandigarh. In, A. Ghosh, ed., *An Encyclopaedia of Indian Archaeology*. 2 Vols. Delhi: Munshiram Manoharlal : 94.

Ghosh, S. S. and Krishna Lal
1963   Plant remains from Rangpur. In, S. R. Rao, Excavation at Rangpur and other explorations in Gujarat. *Ancient India*, 18-19: 161-75.

Ghurye, G. S.
1936   An account of an exploratory tour in certain parts of Sind in search of pre-historic culture. *Journal of the University of Bombay, Arts and Law*, 8(6): 1-18.

Ghurye, G. S.
1939   Two sites in Kathiawar. *Journal of the University of Bombay*, 8(1): 3-12.

Gibb, H. A. R.
1929   *Ibn Battuta: Travels in Asia and Africa, 1325-54*. London: Roultedge and Kegan Paul.

Gibb, H. A. R.
1957   *The Travels of Ibn Battuta, A.D. 1325-1354*. London: The Hakluyt Society.

Gimbutas, Maria
1973   Old Europe 7000-3500 BC, the earliest European cultures before the infiltration of the Indo-European peoples. *Journal of Indo-European Studies*, 1: 1-20.

Gimbutas, Maria
1977   The first wave of Eurasian steppe pastoralists into Copper Age Europe. *Journal of Indo-European Studies*, 5: 277-338.

Glover, Ian C. and Charles Higham
1996   New evidence for rice cultivation in South, Southeast Asia. In, David R. Harris ed., *The Origins and Spread of Agriculture and Pastoralism in Eurasia*. London: University College, London: 413-41.

Godley, A. D., translator
1926   *Herodotus*. Revised edition, 4 Vols. Cambridge: Harvard University Press, Loeb Classical Library.

Gollan, Klim
1985   Prehistoric dogs in Australia: an Indian origin? In, V. N. Misra and Peter Bellwood, eds., *Recent Advances in Indo-Pacific Prehistory*. Delhi: Oxford & IBH: 439-43.

Gonda, J.
1991   *The Functions and Significance of Gold in the Veda*. Leiden: E. J. Brill.

Good, Irene
1995   A review of Pre-Han textile evidence in Asia. *Antiquity*, 69(266): 959-68.

Goody, Jack
1986   *The Logic of Writing and the Organization of Society*. Cambridge: Cambridge University Press.

Goody, Jack
1987   *The Interface Between the Written and the Oral*. Cambridge: Cambridge University Press.

Gopal, L.
1961   Textiles in ancient India. *Journal of the Economic and Social History of the Orient*, 4: 53-72.

Gordon, D. H.
1958   *The Pre-Historic Background of Indian Culture*. Bombay: Bhulabhai Memorial Trust.

Gorman, Chester
1970a   Excavations at Spirit Cave, north Thailand. *Asian Perspectives*, 13: 79-107.

Gorman, Chester
1970b   The Hoabinhian and after: subsistence patterns in Southeast Asia during the late Pleistocene and early Recent periods. *World Archaeology*, 2(3): 300-20.

Gorman, Chester
1977   A priori models and Thai prehistory: a reconsideration of the beginnings of agriculture in southeastern Asia. In, C. A. Reed, ed., *Origins of Agriculture*, The Hague: Mouton: 321-55.

Gould, F. W.
1975   *The Grasses of Texas*. College Station : Texas A & M University Press.

Gould, Stephen J. and N. Eldridge
1977   Punctuated equilibria: the tempo and mode of evolution reconsidered. *Palaeobiology*, 3: 115-51.

Gourdin, W. H. and W. D. Kingery
1975   The beginnings of pyrotechnology: Neolithic and Egyptian lime plaster. *Journal of Field Archaeology*, 2: 133-50.

Government of Bombay
1879   *Kaira and Panch Mahals*. Bombay: Government Central Press. Gazetteer of the Bombay Presidency, Vol. 3.

Government of Bombay
1880   *Cutch, Palanpur and Mahi Kantha*. Bombay: Government Central Press. Gazetteer of the Bombay Presidency, Vol. 5.

904

Government of Bombay
1884   *Kathiawar*. Bombay: Government Central Press. Gazetteer of the Bombay Presidency,
            Vol. 8.

Government of Gujarat
1964a   *District Census Handbook 7: Kutch*. Census of India 1961, Gujarat, Vol. 5, No. 7.

Government of Gujarat
1964b   *District Census Handbook 4: Bhavnagar*. Census of India 1961, Gujarat, Vol. 5, No. 4.

Government of Gujarat
1964c   *District Census Handbook 2: Rajkot*. Census of India 1961, Gujarat, Vol. 5, No. 2.

Government of Gujarat
1964d   *District Census Handbook 10: Mehsana*. Census of India 1961, Gujarat, Vol. 5, No. 10.

Government of Gujarat
1964e   *District Census Handbook 16: Surat*. Census of India 1961, Gujarat, Vol. 5, No. 16.

Government of Gujarat
1964f   *Agate Industry of Cambay*. Census of India 1961, Selected Crafts of Gujarat, Vol. 5,
            Pt. 7-a(1).

Government of India
1884a   *Gazetteer of the Bannu District, 1883-84*. Lahore: Punjab Government.

Government of India
1884b   *Gazetteer of the Dera Ismail Khan District, 1883-84*. Lahore: Punjab Government.

Government of India
1884c   *Gazetteer of the Gujranwala District, 1883-84*. Lahore: Punjab Government.

Government of India
1884d   *Gazetteer of the Hazara District, 1883-84*. Lahore: Punjab Government.

Government of India
1884e   *Gazetteer of the Kohat District, 1883-84*. Lahore: Punjab Government.

Government of India
1884f   *Gazetteer of the Lahore District, 1883-84*. Lahore: Punjab Government.

Government of India
1884g   *Gazetteer of the Montgomery District, 1883-84*. Lahore: Punjab Government.

Government of India
1895   *Gazetteer of the Rawalpindi District, 1893-94*. Lahore: Punjab Government.

Government of India
1898   *Gazetteer of the Dera Ghazi Khan District, 1893-97*. Revised edition. Lahore: Punjab Government.

Government of India
1899   *Gazetteer of the Peshawar District, 1897-98*. Lahore: Punjab Government.

Government of India
1908a   *Imperial Gazetteer of India: Provincial Series, North-West Frontier Province*. Calcutta: Superintendent of Government Printing.

Government of India
1908b   *Imperial Gazetteer of India: Provincial Series, Punjab*. 2 Vols. Calcutta: Superintendent of Government Printing.

Government of India
1908c   *Imperial Gazetteer of India: Provincial Series, Baluchistan*. Calcutta: Superintendent of Government Printing.

Government of India
1908d   *Imperial Gazetteer of India: Afghanistan and Nepal*. Calcutta: Superintendent of Government Printing.

Government of India
1908e   *Imperial Gazetteer of India: Provincial Series, Rajputana*. Calcutta: Superintendent of Government Printing.

Government of India
1908f   *Imperial Gazetteer of India: Provincial Series, United Provinces*. 2 Vols. Calcutta: Superintendent of Government Printing.

Government of India
1908g   *Imperial Gazetteer of India: Provincial Series, Bombay Presidency*. 2 Vols. Calcutta: Superintendent of Government Printing.

Government of India
1915   *Gazetteer of the Mianwali District, 1915*. Lahore: Punjab Government.

Government of India
1921   *Gazetteer of the Gujrat District, 1921*. Lahore: Punjab Government.

Government of India
1926   *Gazetteer of the Lahore District, 1923-24*. Lahore: Punjab Government.

Government of India
1932   *Gazetteer of the Attock District, 1930*. Lahore: Punjab Government.

906

Government of India
1934   Department of Education, Health and Lands, Simla, 13th September 1934, No. F.
           41-1/33. *The Gazette of India*, 15 September 1934: 1103-05.

Government of India
1937   *List of Members of the Most Exalted Order of the Star of India and the Most Exalted
           Order of the Indian Empire*. Delhi: Manager of Publications.

Government of India
1964   *The Search for Minerals in India*. Delhi: Publications Division.

Government of India
1985   *The Wealth of India: A dictionary of Indian raw materials & industrial products*. 2nd
           ed. 12 Vols. Delhi: Council of Scientific & Industrial Research.

Government of India
1990   *Indian Agriculture Brief*. 23rd edition. Delhi: Directorate of Economics and Statistics,
           Department of Agriculture and Cooperation, Ministry of Agriculture.

Government of the Punjab
1883a   *Gazetteer of the Jhelum District*. Lahore: Punjab Government Press.

Government of the Punjab
1883b   *Gazetteer of the Kangra District*. Lahore: Punjab Government Press.

Government of the Punjab
1883c   *Gazetteer of the Kohat District*. Lahore: Punjab Government Press.

Government of the Punjab
1883d   *Gazetteer of Hoshiarpur District*. Lahore: Punjab Government Press.

Government of the Punjab
1883e   *Gazetteer of the Hazara District*. Lahore: Punjab Government Press.

Government of the Punjab
1907   *Gazetteer of Rawalpindi District*. Lahore: Punjab Government Press. Punjab District
           Gazetteers, Vol. 28A.

Government of the Punjab
1915   *Gazetteer of Mianwali District*. Lahore: Superintendent of Government Printing. Punjab
           District Gazetteers, Vol. 30A.

Graziosi, Paulo
1960   *Palaeolithic Art*. New York: McGraw Hill Company.

Graziosi, Paulo
1964   *Prehistoric Research in Northwestern Punjab: Anthropological Research in Chitral*.

Italian Expeditions to the Karakorum (K2) and Hindu Kush, Scientific Reports, V. Prehistory-Anthropology, Vol. 1. Leiden E. J. Brill.

Griffith, Ralph T. H., translator
1893   *Hymns of the Samaveda*. 1986 reprint. Delhi: Munshiram Manoharlal.

Griffith, Ralph T. H., translator
1895-96 *Hymns of the Atharvaveda*. 2 Vols. 1987 reprint. Delhi: Munshiram Manoharlal.

Griffith, Ralph T. H., translator
1896   *The Hymns of the Rigveda*. 2 Vols. 2nd edition. 1987 reprint. Delhi: Munshiram Manoharlal.

Griffith, Ralph T. H., translator
1899   *The Texts of the White Yajurveda*. 1987 reprint. Delhi: Munshiram Manoharlal.

Grigson, Caroline
1984   Some thoughts on unicorns and other cattle depicted at Mohenjo-daro and Harappa. In, Bridget Allchin, ed., *South Asian Archaeology 1981*. Cambridge: Cambridge University Press: 166-69.

Grigson, Caroline
1985   *Bos indicus and Bos namadicus and the problem of autochthonous domestication in India*. In, V. N. Misra and Peter Bellwood, eds., *Recent Advances in Indo-Pacific Prehistory*. Delhi: Oxford & IBH: 425-28.

Guha, B. S.
1935   Racial affinities of the peoples of India. *Census of India*, Vol. 1 (India), Part III-A (Ethnographical): 2-22.

Guha, B. S. and B. K. Chatterjee
1946   A Chalcolithic site in northern Baluchistan: report on skeletal remains. *Journal of Near Eastern studies*, 5(4): 315-16.

Gulati, A. N. and A. James Turner
1928   A note on the early history of cotton. *Indian Central Cotton Committee*, Bulletin No. 17, Technological Series No. 12.

Gulati, A. N. and A. James Turner
1929   A note on the early history of cotton. *Journal of the Textile Institute*. Transactions, 20: t1-t9.

Gupta, Hari Pal
1976   Holocene palynology from Meander Lake in the Ganga Valley, District Pratapgarh, U.P. *The Palaeobotanist*, 25: 109-119.

908

Gupta, P. L.
1971   Copper hoards in India. Paper presented at the 28th International Congress of Orientalista, Canberra.

Gupta, S. K.
1977a   Holocene silting in the Little Rann of Kutch. In, D. P. Agrawal and B. M. Pande, eds., *Ecology and Archaeology of Western India*. Delhi: Concept Publishing: 201-05.

Gupta, S. K.
1977b   Quaternary sea-level changes on the Saurashtra coast. In, D. P. Agrawal and B. M. Pande, eds., *Ecology and Archaeology of Western India*. Delhi: Concept Publishing: 181-94.

Gupta, S. P.
1963   The Indian copper hoards: the problems of homogeneity, stages of development, origin, authorship and dating. *Journal of the Bihar Research Society*, Patna, 49(1,4): 147-66.

Gupta, S. P.
1965   Further copper hoards: a reassessment in the light of new evidence. *Journal of the Bihar Research Society*, 51(1-4): 1-7.

Gupta, S. P.
1967   The mountainous Neolithic cultures of Central Asia and North India. *The Anthropologist*, 14: 125-36.

Gupta, S. P.
1972-73   A model for understanding the first urbanization in India. *Puratattva*, 6: 42-50.

Gupta, S. P.
1972a   *Disposal of the Dead and Physical Types in Ancient India*. Delhi: Oriental Publishers.

Gupta, S. P.
1972b   The dichotomy of Harappan and pre-Harappan cultures. In, Omi Manchanda, ed., *A Study of Harappan Pottery*. Delhi: Oriental Publishers: 394-405.

Gupta, S. P.
1976   The problem of missing link in the process of first urbanization in India. In, Udai Vir Singh, ed., *Archaeological Congress and Seminar: 1972*. Kurukshetra: B.N. Chakravarty University Kurukshetra: 157-65.

Gupta, S. P.
1978   Origin of the form of Harappa culture: a new proposition. *Puratattva*, 8: 141-6.

Gupta, S. P.
1979   *Archaeology of Soviet Central Asia and the Indian Borderlands.* 2 Vols. Delhi: B. R. Publishing Corporation.

Gupta, S. P., editor
1989   *An Archaeological Tour Along the Ghaggar-Hakra River.* Meerut: Kusumanjali Prakashan.

Gupta, S. P. and A. Kesarwani
1983   Herding as the backdrop to the growth of agriculture in West Asia and South Asia. *Puratattva*, 12: 101-11.

Gupta, S. P. and K. N. Dikshit
1984   The Central Asian and north-west South Asian Neolithic: a processual study. *Man and Environment*, 8: 103-8.

Haaland, Randi
1987   Socio-economic differentiation in the Neolithic Sudan. *British Archaeological Reports, International Series*, 350.

Haaland, Randi
1995a   Sedentism, cultivation and plant domestication in the Holocene Middle Nile region. *Journal of Field Archaeology*, 22: 157-74.

Haaland, Randi
1995b   Theory and evidence in archaeological interpretation of the transition from gathering to domestication: The puzzle of the late emergence of domesticated sorghum in the Nile Valley. Manuscript.

Haaland, Randi
in press   The process of cultivation and domestication of African sorghum and its dispersal to southern Arabia and India. *South Asian Studies*, 13.

Hackett, C. A.
1880   Salt in Rajputana. *Records of the Geological Survey of India*, 5(13).

Hackin, J.
1933   *Nouvelles Researches Archaeologiques a Bamian.* Memoires de la Delegation Archaeologique Francaise en Afghanistan Vol. 3, No. 2.

Haig, M. R.
1887   Ibun Batuta in Sindh. *Journal of the Royal Asiatic Society*, 19: 393-412.

Haig, M. R.
1894   *The Indus Delta Country.* London: Kegan Paul, Trench and Trubner.

Halbfass, Wilhelm
1988   *India and Europe: An essay in understanding.* Albany: State University of New York Press.

910

Halim, M. Abdul
1972a   Excavation at Sarai Khola, Part I. *Pakistan Archaeology*, 7: 23-89.

Halim, M. Abdul
1972b   Excavations at Sarai Khola, Part II. *Pakistan Archaeology*, 8: 1-112.

Halim, M. Abdul and Massimo Vidale
1984   Kilns, bangles and coated vessels. In, M. Jansen and G. Urban, eds., *Reports on Field Work Carried out at Mohenjo-daro, Pakistan 1982-83 by the IsMEO-Aachen University Mission: Interim Reports*, Volume 1. Aachen/Rome:RWTH/IsMEO: 63-97.

Hamilton, Douglas
1892   *Records of Sport in Southern India.* London: R. H. Porter.

Hargreaves, Harold
1925-26a Exploration, Frontier Circle, Baluchistan. *Annual Report of the Archaeological Survey of India, 1925-26*: 59-72.

Hargreaves, Harold
1925-26b Exploration, Nal. *Annual Report of the Archaeological Survey of India, 1925-26*: 63-72.

Hargreaves, Harold
1927-28 Introduction. *Annual Report of the Archaeological Survey of India, 1927-28*: 1-3.

Hargreaves, Harold
1929   *Excavations in Baluchistan 1925, Sampur Mound, Mastung and Sohr Damb, Nal.* Memoirs of the Archaeological Survey of India, No. 35: 89 pp.

Harlan, Jack R.
1967   A wild wheat harvest in Turkey. *Archaeology*, 20: 197-201.

Harlan, Jack R.
1971   Agricultural origins: centers and noncenters. *Science*, 174: 468-74.

Harlan, Jack R.
1976a   Plant and animal distribution in relation to domestication. In, Sir Joseph Hutchinson, Grahame Clark, E. M. Jope and R. Riley, eds., The early history of agriculture. *Philosophical Transactions of the Royal Society of London*, B,Biological Sciences, 275(936): 13-25.

Harlan, Jack R.
1976b   Plants and animals that nourish man. *Scientific American*, 235(3), September: 88-97.

Harlan, Jack R.
1977   The origins of cereal agriculture in the Old World. In, C. A. Reed, ed., *Origins of Agriculture*, The Hague: Mouton: 357-83.

Harlan, Jack R.
1989a   Wild-grass seed harvesting in the Sahara and Sub-Sahara of Africa. In, David R.

Harris and G. C. Hillman, eds., *Foraging and Farming: The evolution of plant exploitation*. London: Unwin Hyman. One World Archaeology, 13: 79-98.

Harlan, Jack R.
1989b   Tropical African cereals. In, David R. Harris and G. C. Hillman, eds., *Foraging and Farming: The evolution of plant exploitation*. London: Unwin Hyman. One World Archaeology, 13: 335-43.

Harlan, Jack R.
1992   Indigenous African agriculture. In, C. Wesley Cowan and Patty Jo Watson, eds., *The Origins of Agriculture: An international perspective*. Washington DC: Smithsonian Institution Press: 59-70.

Harlan, Jack R. and Ann Stemler
1976   The races of sorghum in Africa. Jack R. Harlan, Jan M. L. DeWet and Ann B. L. Stemler, eds., *Origins of African Plant Domestication*. The Hague: Mouton: 465-78.

Harlan, Jack R. and D. Zohary
1966   Distribution of wild wheats and barley. *Science*, 153: 1074-80.

Harlan, Jack R. and Jan M. J. deWet
1971   On the quality of evidence for origin and dispersal of cultivated plants. *Current Anthropology*, 14(1-2): 51-5.

Harlan, Jack R., Jan M. J. deWet, and Ann B. L. Stemler
1976   *Origins of African Plant Domestication*. The Hague: Mouton.

Harris, David R.
1972   The origins of agriculture in the tropics. *American Scientist*, 60: 180-93.

Harris, David R.
1977   Alternative pathways toward agriculture. In, C. A. Reed, ed., *Origins of Agriculture*. The Hague: Mouton: 179-243.

Harris, David R.
1989   An evolutionary continuum of people-plant interaction. In, David R. Harris and G. C. Hillman, eds., *Foraging and Farming: The evolution of plant exploitation*. London: Unwin Hyman: 11-26.

Harris, David R. and G. C. Hillman, editors
1989   *Foraging and Farming: The evolution of plant exploitaton*. London: Unwin Hyman. One World Archaeology, 13.

Hartkamp-Jonxis, E.
1979   Some explorations in the visual organization of scenes on Rajasthani cloth paintings in honor of Pabuji. In, J. E. van Lohuizen-de Leeuw, ed., *South Asian Archaeology 1975*. Leiden: E. J. Brill: 175-87.

912

Hasdorf, Christine and Virginia S. Popper, editors
1988   *Current Paleoethnobotany: Analytical Methods and Cultural Interpretations of Archaeological Plant Remains.* Chicago: University of Chicago Press.

Hassan, Mohammad Usman
1989   Prehistoric mines around Khuzdar Baluchistan. *Journal of Central Asia*, 12(1): 107-16.

Hawkes, Jacquetta
1982   *Adventurer in Archaeology: The biography of Sir Mortimer Wheeler.* New York: St. Martins Press.

Hawkins, R. E.
1986   *Encyclopedia of Indian Natural History.* Delhi: Oxford University Press for the Bombay Natural History Society.

Hayden, Brian
1981a   Research and development in the Stone Age. *Current Anthropology*, 22: 519-48.

Hayden, Brian
1981b   Subsistence and ecological adaptations of modern hunter/gatherers. In, Robert S. O. Harding and G. Teeleki, eds., *Omnivorous Primates.* New York: Columbia University Press: 344-422.

Hegde, K. T. M.
1978   Sources of ancient tin in India. In, A. D. Franklin, J. S. Olin and T. A. Wertime, eds. *The Search for Ancient Tin.* Washington D. C.: The Smithsonian Institution and the National Bureau of Standards: 39-42.

Hegde, K. T. M.
1989   Boom town: Harappa. *The Future Perfect 2001*, December: 19-22.

Hegde, K. T. M. and V. H. Sonawane
1986   Landscape and settlement pattern of Harappa culture villages in the Rupen estuary. *Man and Environment*, 10: 23-32.

Hegde, K. T. M., K. K. Bhan, V. H. Sonawane
1984-85   Excavations at Nageshwar—1984: a preliminary report. *Journal of the Maharaja Sayajirao University of Baroda (Humanities)*, 33-34(1): 3-12.

Hegde, K. T. M., K. K. Bhan, V. H. Sonawane, K. Krishnan and D. R. Shah
1990   *Excavation at Nageshwar, Gujarat: A Harappan shell working site on the Gulf of Kutch.* Baroda: Maharaja Sayajirao University Archaeology Series 18.

Hegde, K. T. M., R. V. Karanth and S. P. Sychanthavong
1982   On the composition and technology of Harappan microbeads. In, Gregory L. Possehl,

ed., *Harappan Civilization: A contemporary perspective*. Delhi: Oxford & IBH and the American Institute of Indian Studies: 239-44.

Hegde, K. T. M., V. H. Sonawane, K. K. Bhan, Ajit Prasad and K. Krishnan
1990   Excavation at Nagwada—1987-88: a preliminary report. In, N. C. Ghosh and S. Chakrabarti, eds., *Adaptation and Other Essays: Proceedings of the archaeology conference, 1988*. Santiniketan: Visva-Bharati Research Publications: 191-95.

Hegde, K. T. M., V. H. Sonawane, D. R. Shah, K. K. Bhan, Ajitprasad, K. Krishnan, and A. Pratapa Chandran
1988   Excavation at Nagwada—1986 and 1987: A preliminary report. *Man and Environment*, 12: 55-65.

Heine-Geldern, Robert, von
1956a   The coming of the Aryans and the end of the Harappa civilization. *Man*, 56: 136-40.

Heine-Geldern, Robert, von
1956b   The origin of ancient civilizations and Toynbee's theories. *Diogenes*, 3: 81-99.

Helbaek, Hans
1966a   Palaeobotany at Beidha. *Palestine Exploration Quarterly*, Jan-June: 64-5.

Helbaek, Hans
1966b   Appendix A: Pre-pottery Neolithic farming at Beidha, a preliminary report. *Palestine Exploration Quarterly*, Jan.-June: 61-6.

Helm, June
1962   The ecological approach in anthropology. *American Journal of Sociology*, 67.

Helmer, D.
1989   Le development de la domestication au Proche-Orient de 9500 a 7500 BP: Les nouvelles donnes d'El Kown et de Ras Shamra. *Paleorient*, 15(1): 111-21.

Hemmy, A. S.
1931   System of weights at Mohenjo-daro. In, Sir John Marshall, ed., *Mohenjo-daro and the Indus Civilization*, 3 Vols. London: Arthur Probsthain: 589-98.

Hemmy, A. S.
1937-38 System of weights at Mohenjo-daro. In, Ernest J. H. Mackay, *Further Excavations at Mohenjo-Daro*. Delhi: Government of India: 601-12.

Hemphill, Brian
1993   Discrete trait analysis. In, G. F. Dales and J. M. Kenoyer, The Harappa Project 1986-89: new investigations at an ancient Indus city. In, Gregory L. Possehl, ed., *Harappan Civilization: A recent perspective*. 2nd ed. Delhi: Oxford& IBH and the American Institute of Indian Studies: 500-01.

914

Hemphill, Brian E., John R. Lukacs and Kenneth A. R. Kennedy
1991   Biological adaptations and affinities of Bronze Age Harappans. In, Richard H. Meadow, ed., *Harappa Excavations 1986-1990: A multidisciplinary approach to third millennium urbanization*. Madison: Prehistory Press, Monographs in World Archaeology, 3: 137-82.

Henrickson, E. F.
1985   The early development of pastoralism in the Central Zagros highlands (Luristan). *Iranica Antiqua*, 20: 1-42.

Henry, Donald O.
1977   An examination of the artifactual variability in the Natufian of Palestine. *Eretz-Israel*, 13: 229-40.

Henry, Donald O.
1989   *From Foraging to Agriculture: The Levant at the end of the Ice Age*. Philadelphia: University of Pennsylvania Press.

Hermann, Georgina
1968   Lapis lazuli: the early phases of its trade. *Iraq*, 30: 21-54.

Hermann, Georgina and P. R. S. Moorey
1980-83   Lapis lazuli. *Reallexikon Der Assyriologie Und Vorderasiatischen Archaologie*, 6: 489-92.

Hermanns, M.
1951   Were animals first domesticated and bred in India? *Journal of the Bombay Branch of the Royal Asiatic Society*. New series, 27(1): 134-73.

Heron, A. M. and H. Crookshank
1955   Directory of economic minerals of Pakistan. *Records of the Geological Survey of Pakistan*, 7(2): 1-145.

de Hevesy, Guillaume
1932   Ecriture de l'Ile Paques. *Bulletin de la Societe Des Americanistes de Belgique*, Decembre: 120-27.

de Hevesy, Guillaume
1933a   Oceanie et Inde prearyenne: Mohenjodaro et l'Ille de Paques. *Bulletin de l'Association Francaise Des Amis de l'Orient*, 14-15: 29-50.

de Hevesy, Guillaume
1933b   Sur ecriture Oceanienne paraissant d'origine neolithique. *Bulletin de la Societe Prehistorique Francaise*, 30(7-8): 434-439.

de Hevesy, Guillaume
1934a   On a writing oceanique of Neolithic origin. *Journal of Indian History*, 13(1): 1-17.

de Hevesy, Guillaume
1934b   Los geroglificos de la Isla de Pascua y de India. *Zig-Zag*, Santiago de Chile, 5 April.

de Hevesy, Guillaume
1934c   Osterinselschrift und Indusschrift. *Orientalistische Literaturzeitung*, Monatsschrift fur die Wissenschaft vom Gansen Orient und Seinen Besiehungen zu den Angrenzenden Kulturkreisen, Leipzig, 37 (11): 666-74.

de Hevesy, Guillaume
1938a   The scripts of the Indus Valley and Easter island. *Man*, 183: 159-60.

de Hevesy, Guillaume
1938b   The Easter Island and Indus Valley scripts (and a critical study by Mr. Metraux). *Anthropos*, 33: 808-14.

Hiebert, Fredrik and Carl C. Lamberg-Karlovsky
1992   Central Asia and the Indo-Iranian borderlands. *Iran*, 30: 1-15.

Higgs, Eric S.
1972   *Papers in Economic Prehistory*. Cambridge: Cambridge University Press.

Higgs, Eric S.
1975   *Palaeoeconomy*. Cambridge: Cambridge University Press.

Higgs, Eric S. and M. R. Jarman
1972   The origins of animal and plant husbandry. In, E. S. Higgs, ed., *Papers in Economic Prehistory*. New York: Cambridge University Press: 3-13.

Hillman, G. C.
1989   Upper Palaeolithic plant foods from Wadi Kubbaniya in Upper Egypt: dietary diversity, infant weaning and seasonality in a riverine settlement. In, D. R. Harris and G. C. Hillman, eds., *Foraging and Farming*. London: Unwin Hyman. One World Archaeology, 13: 207-39.

Hillman, G. C. and M. S. Davies
1990   Measured domestication rates in wild wheats and barley under primitive cultivation and their archaeological implications. *Journal of World Prehistory*, 4: 157-222.

Hillman, G. C., S. M. Colledge and D. R. Harris
1989   Plant-food economy during the Epipalaeolithic period at Tell Abu Hureyra, Syria: dietary diversity, seasonality and modes of exploitation. In, D. R. Harris and G. C. Hillman, eds., *Foraging and Farming*. London: Unwin Hyman. One World Archaeology, 13: 240-68.

Hirsch, Hans
1963   Die Inschriften der Konige von Agade. *Archiv Fur Orientforschung*, 20: 1-82.

916

His Majesty, The King Emperor
1911   *List of Members of the Most Exalted Order of the Indian Empire, 1911.* London: His Majesty's Stationary Office.

His Majesty, The King Emperor
1913   *List of Members of the Most Exalted Order of the Indian Empire, 1913.* London: His Majesty's Stationary Office.

Hodder, Ian
1979   Economic and social stress and material culture patterning. *American Antiquity*, 44: 446-54.

Holdich, Sir Thomas Hungerford
1904   *India.* London: Macmillan and Co.

Holdich, T. A.
1894   *Notes on Antiquities, Ethnography and History of Las Bela and Makran.* Calcutta: Archaeological Survey of India.

Hole, Frank
1968   Evidence of social organization from western Iran, 8000-4000 B.C. In, Sally R. Binford and Lewis R. Binford, eds., *New Perspectives in Archaeology.* Chicago: Aldine Publishing Co: 245-66.

Hole, Frank
1974   Tepe Tula'i: an early campsite in Khuzistan, Iran. *Paleorient*, 2(2): 219-42.

Hole, Frank
1975   The sondage at Tapphe Tula'i. In Firouz Bagherzadeh, ed., *Proceedings of the 3rd Annual Symposium on Archaeological Research in Iran.* Tehran: Iranian Centre for Archaeological Research: 63-76.

Hole, Frank
1984   A reassessment of the Neolithic Revolution. *Paleorient*, 10(2): 49-60.

Hole, Frank
1989   A two part, two stage model of domestication. In, Juliet Clutton-Brock, ed., *The Walking Larder.* London: Unwin Hyman: 97-104.

Hole, Frank, Kent V. Flannery and James A. Neeley
1969   *Prehistory and Human Ecology of the Deh Luran Plain: An early village sequence from Khuzistan, Iran.* Ann Arbor: University of Michigan, Museum of Anthropology, Memoir, 1.

Holland, Sir Thomas H.
1914   The origin of desert salt deposits. *Proceedings of Liverpool Geology*, Section 2.

Holland, Sir Thomas H. and W. A. K. Christie
1909   The origin of the salt deposits in Rajputana. *Records of the Geological Survey of India*, 5(38): 154-86.

Holland, Sir Thomas H., and L. Leigh Fermor
1910   A uniquennial review of the mineral production of India during the years 1904 to 1908. *Records of the Geological Survey of India*, 39: 1-280.

Holmes, D. A.
1968   The recent history of the Indus. *The Geographical Journal*, 134(3): 367-82.

Hooja, Rima
1988   *The Ahar Culture and Beyond: Settlements and frontiers of 'Mesolithic' and early agricultural sites in south-eastern Rajasthan, c. 3rd-2nd Millennia B.C.* Oxford: British Archaeological Reports International Series 412.

Hopf, Maria
1983   Jericho plant remains. In, Kathleen M. Kenyon and T. A. Holland, *Excavations at Jericho*, V. London: British School of Archaeology in Jerusalem: 576-621.

Hopkins, J.
1967   Identification of the domestication of animals without morphological changes. Manuscript, University of Chicago.

Hora, Sunder Lal
1951a   Knowledge of the ancient Hindus concerning fish and fisheries of India, 3, Matsyavinoda or a chapter on angling in Manasollasa by King Somesvara (1127 AD). *Journal of the Asiatic Society, Letters*, 17: 145-69.

Hora, Sunder Lal
1951b   Maintenance of irrigation-tanks through fishery revenue in ancient India. *Journal of the Asiatic Society, Letters*, 17: 41-50

Hora, Sunder Lal
1952   Fish in the Ramajana. *Journal of the Asiatic Society, Letters*, 18: 63-9

Hora, Sunder Lal
1954-55 Angling in ancient India. *Ancient India*, 10-11: 152-56.

Hora, Sunder Lal
1956   Fish paintings of the third millennium B.C. from Nal (Baluchistan) and their zoogeographical significance. *Memoirs of the Indian Museum*, 14(2): 73-84.

Hughes, A. W.
1877   *The Country of Baluchistan: Its geography, topography, ethnography and history.* London: George Bell and Sons.

918

Hughes-Buller, Ralph
1903-04   Gabarbands in Baluchistan. *Annual Report of the Archaeological Survey of India, 1903-04*: 194-201.

Hughes-Buller, Ralph
1906   *Makran District*. Bombay: Government of India. Baluchistan District Gazetteer Series, Vol. 7 (bound with Kharan District, Vol. 7A).

Hughes-Buller, Ralph
1907a   *Quetta-Pishin District*. Ajmer: Government of India. Baluchistan District Gazetteer Series, Vol. 5.

Hughes-Buller, Ralph
1907b   *Chagai District*. Karachi: Government of India. Baluchistan District Gazetteer Series, Vol. 4 (bound with Bolan Pass and Nushki Railway District, Vol. 4): 252 pp.

Hunter, G. R.
1929   *The Script of Harappa and Mohenjo-Daro and its Connection with Other Scripts*. PhD Dissertation, Oxford University.

Hunter, G. R.
1932   Mohenjo daro — Indus epigraphy. *Journal of the Royal Asiatic Society of Great Britain and Ireland*: 466-503.

Hunter, G. R.
1934   *The Script of Harappa and Mohenjo-Daro and its Connection with Other Scripts*. London: Kegan Paul, Trench, Trubner & Co. Ltd.

Huntingford, G. W. B.
1980   *The Periplus of the Erythraean Sea*. London: The Hakuyt Society, Second Series No. 151.

Huntington, Ellsworth
1924   *Climate and Civilization*. 3rd ed. New Haven: Yale University Press.

Hussain, Majid
1989   Salvage excavation at Moenjodaro. *Journal of the Pakistan Historical Society*, 37(1): 89-98.

Hutchins, Francis G.
1985   *Animal Fables of India: Narayana's Hitopadeshe, or friendly counsel*. West Franklin: Amarta Press.

Hutchinson, Sir Joseph, editor
1974a   *Evolutionary Studies in World Crops: Diversity and change in the Indian Subcontinent*. Cambridge: Cambridge University Press.

Hutchinson, Sir Joseph
1974b   Crop plant evolution in the Indian subcontinent. In, Sir Joseph Hutchinson, ed., *Evolutionary Studies in World Crops: Diversity and Change in the Indian Subcontinent.* Cambridge: Cambridge University Press: 151-60.

Hutchinson, Sir Joseph
1976   India: local and introduced crops. In, Sir Joseph Hutchinson, Grahame Clark, E. M. Jope and R. Riley, eds., The early history of agriculture. *Philosophical Transactions of the Royal Society of London*, B, Biological Sciences, 275(936): 129-38.

Imbelloni, J.
1939   Recent discoveries in the Middle-Indus area and their relation to the Easter Island script. *Journal of the Polynesian Society*, 48: 60-66.

Inden, Ronald
1968   Early India: Literary Evidence for a Revised Chronology. Unpublished manuscript, University of Chicago.

Inden, Ronald
1990   *Imaging India.* Oxford: Basil Blackwell.

India Meterological Department
1962   Monthly and Annual Norms of Rainfall and of Rainy Days Based on Records from 1906 to 1950. *Memoirs of the India Meterological Department,* Vol. 31, Part 3 Delhi.

Indian Archaeology, A Review
1953-93   Report of the Archaeological Survey of India. Delhi: Archaeological Survey of India.

Ingalls, Daniel H. H.
1968   *Sanskrit Poetry: From Vidyakara's 'Treasury.'* Cambridge: The Belknap Press of Harvard University Press.

Inglis, James
1888   *Tent Life in Tiger Land.* Sydney: A. Hutchinson & Son.

Inverarity, J. D.
1861   Report on the rise, progress and results of the late overflow of the River Indus, which endangered the towns of Shikarpoor and Jacobabod. *Transactions of the Bombay Geographical Society*, 16: 48-65.

Irons, J. and N. Dyson-Hudsons
1972   *Perspectives on Nomadism.* Leiden: E. J. Brill: 122-32.

Ivanov, V. G.
1976   The geochemistry of formation of the rocks of the lazurite deposits of the southern Baikal region. *Geochemistry International*, 13(1): 26-31.

920

Jacob, John
1857   Report on the upper portion of the Eastern Nara, its sources of supply and the feasibility of restoring it as a permanent stream. *Selections from the Records of the Bombay Government*, NS 45: 1-105.

Jacobsen, Thorkild
1973   *Enmerkar Epics: Mesopotamia and Iran in the third millennium B.C.* Boston: Museum of Fine Arts.

Jacobsen, Thorkild and Robert McC. Adams
1958   Salt and silt in ancient Mesopotamian agriculture. *Science*, 128(3334): 1251-58.

Jairath, Virjendra Kumar
1986   *Archaeology of the Northern Part of Bhavnagar District, Gujarat State, up to the 15th Century A.D.* 2 Vols. PhD Dissertation, Department of Archaeology and Ancient Indian History, Maharaja Sayajirao University of Baroda.

Janaki, V. A.
1980   *The Commerce of Cambay from the Earliest Period to the Nineteenth Century*. Baroda: Maharaja Sayajirao University of Baroda, Geography Monograph, 10.

Janaway, R. C. and Robin A. E. Coningham
1995   A review of archaeological textile evidence from South Asia. *South Asian Studies*, 11: 157-74.

Jansen, Michael
1979   Architectural problems of the Harappa culture. In, M. Taddei, ed., *South Asian Archaeology 1977*. Naples: Instituto Universitario Orientale, Seminario di Studi Asiatici, Series Minor 6: 405-31.

Jansen, Michael
1981   Settlement patterns in the Harappa Culture. In, H. Hartel, ed., *South Asian Archaeology 1979*. Berlin: Dietrich Reimer Verlag: 251-69.

Jansen, Michael
1983   Preliminary results of three years' documentation at Mohenjo-daro. In, G. Urban and M. Jansen, eds., *Forschungsprojekt DFG Mohenjodaro*. Aachen: Veroffentlichung des Geogatischen Instituts der Reinisch-Westfalischen Technischen Hochschule, Nr. 34: 21-35.

Jansen, Michael
1984a   Architectural remains in Mohenjo-daro. In, B.B. Lal and S. P. Gupta, eds., *Frontiers of the Indus Civilization*. Delhi: Books and Books: 75-88.

Jansen, Michael
1984b   Preliminary results of two years' documentation in Mohenjo-daro. In, Bridget Allchin, ed., *South Asian Archaeology 1981*. Cambridge: Cambridge University Press: 135-53.

Jansen, Michael
1985   Mohenjo-daro HR-A, house I, a temple? Analysis of an architectural structure. In, J. Schotsmans and M. Taddei, eds., *South Asian Archaeology 1983*. Naples: Instituto Universitario Orientale, Dipartimento di Studi Asiatici, Series Minor 23: 157-206.

Jansen, Michael
1986   *Die Indus Zivilization: Wiederentdeckung Einer Fruhen Hochkultur*. Koln: DuMont Buchverlag.

Jansen, Michael
1987   Preliminary resulte on the 'forma urbis' research at Mohenjo-Daro. In, Michael Jansen and Guntur Urban eds., *Reports on Field Work Carried Out at Mohenjo-daro, Pakistan, 1983-84: Interim Reports*. Volume 2. Aachen/Rome: RWTH/IsMEO: 9-22.

Jansen, Michael
1989a   Early cities: a comparative study of urban development. *Lahore Museum Journal*, 2(1): 5-14.

Jansen, Michael
1989b   Some problems regarding the forma urbis Mohenjo-Daro. In, Karen Frifelt and Per Sorensen, eds., *South Asian Archaeology 1985*. London: Curzon Press, Scandinavian Institute of Asian Studies, Occasional Papers No. 4: 247-56.

Jansen, Michael
1993a   Mohenjo-daro: Type site of the earliest urbanization process in South Asia. In, H. Spodek and D. M. Srinivasan, eds., *Urban Form and Meaning in South Asia*. Washington DC: National Gallery of Art. Studies in the History of Art, 31. Center for Advanced Study in the Visual Arts Symposium Papers 15: 33-51.

Jansen, Michael
1993b   *Mohenjo-daro: Stadt der brunnen und kanale (City of wells and drains), Wasserlexus vor 4500 jharan (Water splendor 4500 years ago)*. Dual German-English text. Bergisch Gladbach: Frontinus-Gesellschaft e. V.

Jansen, Michael and Gunter Urban, editors
1983   *Reports on Field Work Carried Out at Mohenjo-Daro, Pakistan 1982-83 by the IsMEO-Aachen Univeristy Mission: Interim Reports*. Volume 1. Aachen/Rome: RWTH/IsMEO.

Jansen, Michael and Gunter Urban, editors
1984   Concerning the contradictory spellings of the name "Mohenjo-Daro." In, M. Jansen and G. Urban, eds., *Reports on Field Work Carried out at Mohenjo-daro, Pakistan 1982-83 by the IsMEO-Aachen University Mission: Interim Reports*. Volume 1. Aachen/Rome: RWTH/IsMEO: 5.

Jansen, Michael and Gunter Urban
1985   *Mohenjo Daro: Report of the Aachen University Mission 1979-1985*. Section One: Data Collection. Volume One: Catalogue and Concordance of the Field Registers, 1924-38. Part One: The HR-Area Field Register, 1925-27. Leiden: E. J. Brill.

922

Jansen, Michael and Gunter Urban, editors
1987   *Reports on Field Work Carried Out at Mohenjo-Daro, Pakistan 1983-84 by the IsMEO-Aachen Univeristy Mission: Interim Reports.* Volume 2. Aachen/Rome: RWTH/ IsMEO.

Jansen, Michael and Maurizio Tosi, editors
1988   *Reports on Field Work Carried Out at Mohenjo-daro, Pakistan 1983-86 by the IsMEO-Aachen University Mission: Interim Reports.* Aachen/Roma: RWTH and IsMEO.

Jansen, Michael, Marie Mulloy and Gunter Urban
1991   *Forgotten Cities on the Indus: Early Civilization in Pakistan from the 8th to the 2nd millennium B.C.* Mainz: Verlag Philipp von Zabern.

Jarman, Michael R. and P. F. Wilkinson
1972   Criteria of animal domestication. In, E. S. Higgs, ed., *Papers in Economic Prehistory*, New York: Cambridge University Press: 83-96.

Jarrige, Catherine
1984   Terracotta human figurines from Nindowari. In, Bridget Allchin, ed., *South Asian Archaeology 1981*. Cambridge: Cambridge University Press: 129-34.

Jarrige, Catherine
1991   The terracotta figurines from Mehrgarh. In, Michael Jansen, Maire Mulloy and Gunter Urban, eds., *Forgotten Cities on the Indus: Early civilization in Pakistan from the 8th to the 2nd millennium B.C.* Mainz: Verlag Philipp von Zabern: 87-94.

Jarrige, Catherine
1992   Une tete d'elephant en terre cuite de Nausharo (Pakistan). *Arts Asiatiques*, 47: 132-36.

Jarrige, Catherine
1994   The Mature Indus phase at Nausharo as seen from a block of Period III. In, Asko Parpola and Petteri Koskikallio, eds., *South Asian Archaeology 1993*. 2 Vols. Helsinki: Annales Academiae Scientiarum Fennicae, Series B, Volume 271: 281-94.

Jarrige, Catherine and Maurizio Tosi
1981   The natural resources of Mundigak: some observations on the location of the site in relation to its economic space. In, H. Hartel, ed., *South Asian Archaeology 1979*. Berlin: Dietrich Reimer Verlag: 115-42.

Jarrige, Catherine, Jean-Francois Jarrige, Richard H. Meadow and Gonzaque Quivron
1995   *Mehrgarh: Field reports 1974-1985, from Neolithic times to the Indus Civilization.* Karachi: Department of Culture and Tourism of Sindh, Pakistan, Department of Archaeology and Museums, French Ministry of Foreign Affairs.

Jarrige, Jean-Francois
1977   Nouvelles researches archaeologiques au Baluchistan: les fouilles de Mehrgarh. Paris: *Le Plateau Iranien et l'Asie Centrale des Origins a la Conquete Islamique*. Colloques Internationaux du C. N. R. S., No. 567: 79-94.

Jarrige, Jean-Francois
1979   Excavations at Mehrgarh—Pakistan. In, J. E. van Lohuizen-de Leeuw, ed., *South Asian Archaeology 1975*. Leiden: E. J. Brill: 76-87.

Jarrige, Jean-Francois
1981   Economy and society in the Early Chalcolithic/Bronze Age of Baluchistan: new perspectives from recent excavations at Mehrgarh. In, Herbert Hartel, ed., *South Asian Archaeology 1979*. Berlin: Dietrich Reimer verlag: 93-114.

Jarrige, Jean-Francois
1982   Excavations at Mehrgarh: their significance for understanding the background of the Harappan Civilization. In, Gregory L. Possehl, ed., *Harappan Civilization: A contemporary perspective*. Delhi: Oxford & IBH and the American Institute of Indian Studies: 79-84.

Jarrige, Jean-Francois
1983   Nindowari, a 3rd millennium site in southern Baluchistan. *Newsletter of Baluchistan Studies*, 1: 47-50.

Jarrige, Jean-Francois
1984a   Chronology of the earlier periods of the Greater Indus as seen from Mehrgarh, Pakistan. In, Bridget Allchin, ed., *South Asian Archaeology 1981*. Cambridge: Cambridge University Press: 21-9.

Jarrige, Jean-Francois
1984b   Towns and villages of hill and plain. In, B. B. Lal and S. P. Gupta, eds., *Frontiers of the Indus Civilization*. Delhi: Books and Books: 289-300.

Jarrige, Jean-Francois
1986   Excavations at Mehrgarh-Nausharo. *Pakistan Archaeology*, 10-22: 63-131.

Jarrige, Jean-Francois
1987a   Excavations at Mehrgarh-Nausharo: The Twelfth Season: 1985-86, A Preliminary Report. Paris: Musee Guimet, French Archaeological Mission to Pakistan.

Jarrige, Jean-Francois
1987b   Problemes de datation du site neolithique Mehrgarh, Baluchistan, Pakistan. In, O. Aurenche, J. Evin and F. Hours, eds., *Chronologies in the Near East*. British Archaeological Reports International Series, 379: 381-86.

Jarrige, Jean-Francois
1988a   Excavation at Nausharo. *Pakistan Archaeology*, 23: 149-203.

Jarrige, Jean-Francois
1988b   Les styles de Geoksyur et de Quetta et la question des rapports entre les regions au Nord et au Sud de l'Hindu Kush a la fin du 4e et au debut du 3e millenaires. In, J.-

924

C. Gardin, ed., *L'Asie Centrale et ses Rapports avec les Civilisations Orientales des Originls al L'Age du Fes*. Paris: MMAFAC, Diffusion Boccard: 95-102.

Jarrige, Jean-Francois
1989   Excavation at Nausharo 1987-88. *Pakistan Archaeology*, 24: 21-68.

Jarrige, Jean-Francois
1990a   Excavations at Nausharo: 1988-89. *Pakistan Archaeology*, 25: 193-240.

Jarrige, Jean-Francois
1990b   *Excavations at Mehrgarh-Naushero: The sixteenth season, 1989-90, A Preliminary Report*. Paris: Musee Guimet, French Archaeological Mission to Pakistan.

Jarrige, Jean-Francois
1990c   Sedentarite et semi-nomadisme dans la plaine de Kachi du 7e au 2e millennaire avant notre ere. In, Henri-Paul Francfort, ed., *Nomades et Sedentaires en Asie Centrale: Apports de l'archeologie et de l'ethnologie*. Paris: Editions CNRS: 157-68.

Jarrige, Jean-Francois
1991a   Mehrgarh: its place in the development of ancient cultures in Pakistan. In, Michael Jansen, Maire Mulloy and Gunter Urban, eds., *Forgotten Cities on the Indus: Early civilization in Pakistan from the 8th to the 2nd millennium B.C.* Mainz: Verlag Philipp von Zabern: 34-50.

Jarrige, Jean-Francois
1991b   *Excavations at Mehrgarh-Naushero: The seventeenth season, 1990-91. A Preliminary Report*. Paris: Musee Guimet, French Archaeological Mission to Pakistan.

Jarrige, Jean-Francois
1992   *Excavations at Mehrgarh-Naushero: The eighteenth season, 1991-92. A Preliminary Report*. Paris: Musee Guimet, French Archaeological Mission to Pakistan.

Jarrige, Jean-Francois
1993a   The question of the beginnings of the Mature Harappan Civilization as seen from Nausharo excavations. In, Adalbert J. Gail and Gerd J. R. Mevissen, eds., *South Asian Archaeology 1991*. Stuttgart: Franz Steiner Verlag: 149-64.

Jarrige, Jean-Francois
1993b   *Excavations at Mehrgarh-Naushero: The nineteenth season, 1992-93. A Preliminary Report*. Paris: Musee Guimet, French Archaeological Mission to Pakistan.

Jarrige, Jean-Francois
1994a   The final phase of Indus occupation at Nausharo and its connection with the following cultural complex of Mehrgarh VIII. In, Asko Parpola and Petteri Koskikallio, eds., *South Asian Archaeology 1993*. 2 Vols. Helsinki: Annales Academiae Scientiarum Fennicae, Series B, Volume 271: 295-313.

Jarrige, Jean-Francois
1994b   *Excavations at Mehrgarh-Naushero: The twentieth season, 1993-94*. A Preliminary Report. Paris: Musee Guimet, French Archaeological Mission to Pakistan.

Jarrige, Jean-Francois
1995a   Introduction. In, C. Jarrige, J.-F. Jarrige, R. H. Meadow and G. Quivron, *Mehrgarh: Field reports 1974-1985, from Neolithic times to the Indus Civilization*. Karachi: Department of Culture and Tourism of Sindh, Department of Archaeology and Museums, French Ministry of Foreign Affairs: 51-103.

Jarrige, Jean-Francois
1995b   *Excavations at Mehrgarh-Naushero: The twenty-first season, 1994-95. A Preliminary Report*. Paris: Musee Guimet, French Archaeological Mission to Pakistan.

Jarrige, Jean-Francois
1996   *Excavations at Mehrgarh-Naushero: The twenty-second season, 1995-96. A Preliminary Report*. Paris: Musee Guimet, French Archaeological Mission to Pakistan.

Jarrige, Jean-Francois and M. U. Hassan
1989   Funerary complexes in Baluchistan at the end of the third millennium in the light of recent discoveries at Mehrgarh and Quetta. In, K. Frifelt and P. Sorensen, eds., *South Asian Archaeology 1985*. Scandinavian Institute of Asian Studies, Occasional Papers No. 4: 150-66.

Jarrige, Jean-Francois and Marielle Santoni
1979   *Fouilles de Pirak*. 2 Vols. Paris: Publications de la Commission des Fouilles Archaeologique, Fouilles du Pakistan, No. 2, Vol. 1: 411 and 36 pp.

Jarrige, Jean-Francois and Monique Lechevallier
1979   Excavations at Mehrgarh, Baluchistan: their significance in the prehistorical context of the Indo-Pakistan borderlands. In, M. Taddei, ed., *South Asian Archaeology 1977*. Naples: Instituto Universitario Orientale, Seminario di Studi Asiatici, Series Minor 6: 463-535.

Jarrige, Jean-Francois and Monique Lechevallier
1980   Les fouilles de Mehrgarh, Pakistan: problems chronologiques. *Paleorient*, 6: 253-58.

Jarrige, Jean-Francois and Richard H. Meadow
1980   The antecedents of civilization in the Indus Valley. *Scientific American*, 243(2): 122-33.

Jarrige, Jean-Francois and Richard H. Meadow
1992   Melange Fairservis: a discourse on relations between Kachi and Sindh in prehistory. In, Gregory L. Possehl, ed., *South Asian Archaeology Studies*. Delhi: Oxford & IBH: 163-78.

926

Jauhar, Prem P.
1981   Cytogenetics and breeding of Pearl Millet and related species. *Progress and Topics in Cytogenetics*, edited by Avery A. Sandberg. New York: Alan R. Liss.

Joglekar, P. P.
1990   Shanka or conch: a confusion in archaeology. *Bulletin of the Deccan College Post-Graduate and Research Institute*, 50: 241-44.

Johnson, Gregory A.
1972   A test of the utility of central place theory in archaeology. In, Peter J. Ucko, Ruth Tringham and G. W. Dimbleby, eds., *Man, Settlement and Urbanism*. London: Gerald Duckworth & Co.: 769-85.

Johnston, Arch C. and Lisa R. Kanter
1990   Earthquakes in stable continental shelf. *Scientific American*, 262(3): 68-75.

Jones, Sir William
1788   The Third Anniversary Discourse: On the Hindus. *Asiatic Researches*, 1: 343-55

Jorgensen, David W., Michael D. Harvey, Stanley A. Schumm and Louis Flam
1993   Morphology and dynamics of the Indus River: Implications for the Mohenjo-daro site. In, John F. Shroder, Jr., ed., *Himalaya to the Sea: Geology, geomorphology and the Quaternary*. London: Routledge: 288-326.

Joshi, Jagat Pati
1966   Exploration in northern Kutch. *Journal of the Oriental Institute, Maharaja Sayajirao University of Baroda*, 16(1): 62-9.

Joshi, Jagat Pati
1972   Excavations at Sur Kotada and new light on Harappan migration. *Journal of the Oriental Institute, Maharaja Sayajirao University of Baroda*: 22: 98-144.

Joshi, Jagat Pati
1976   Excavations at Bhagwanpura. In, S. P. Gupta and K. S. Ramachnadran, eds., *Mahabharata: Myth and reality, differing views*. Delhi: Agam Prakashan: 238-39.

Joshi, Jagat Pati
1977   Overlap of Late Harappan Culture and Painted Grey Ware Culture in Haryana, Punjab and Jammu. Paper presented at: Indus Civilization: Problems and issues. Organized by B.B.Lal and S.C.Malik. Simla Indian Institute of Advanced Study.

Joshi, Jagat Pati
1978a   A note on the excavation at Bhagwanpura. *Puratattva*, 8: 178-80.

Joshi, Jagat Pati
1978b   Interlocking of late Harappa culture and Painted Grey Ware culture in the light of recent excavations. *Man and Environment*, 2: 98-101.

Joshi, Jagat Pati
1984   Harappa Culture: Emergence of a new picture. *Puratattva*, 13-14: 51-4.

Joshi, Jagat Pati
1986   Settlement patterns in the third, second and first millennia in India—with special reference to recent discoveries in Punjab. In, K. C. Varma et. al. eds., *Rtambhara: Studies in Indology*. Ghaziabad: Society for Indic Studies: 134-39.

Joshi, Jagat Pati
1990a   *Excavation at Surkotada 1971-72 and Exploration in Kutch*. Memoirs of the Archaeological Survey of India, 87.

Joshi, Jagat Pati
1990b   Exploration in Kutch. In, Jagat Pati Joshi, *Excavation at Surkotada 1971-72 and Exploration in Kutch*. Memoirs of the Archaeological Survey of India, 87: 393-435.

Joshi, Jagat Pati
1993   *Excavation at Bhagwanpura 1975-76 and Other Explorations and Excavations 1975-81 in Haryana, Jammu & Kashmir and Punjab*. Memoirs of the Archaeological Survey of India, 89.

Joshi, Jagat Pati and Asko Parpola
1987   *Corpus of Indus Seals and Inscriptions. Vol. 1, Collections in India*. Helsinki: Suomalainen Tiedeakatemia, Suomalaisen Tiedeakatemian Toimituksia Annales Academiae Scientiarum Fennicae, Sarja, Series B, NIDE, Tome 239.

Joshi, Jagat Pati and F. R. Allchin
1972   Malvan. In, S. B. Deo, ed., *Archaeological Congress and Seminar Papers*. Nagpur: Nagpur University: 36-42.

Joshi, Jagat Pati and Madhu Bala
1982   Manda: a Harappan site in Jammu and Kashmir. In, Gregory L. Possehl, ed., *Harappan Civilization: A contemporary perspective*. Delhi: Oxford & IBH and the American Institute of Indian Studies: 185-95.

Joshi, Jagat Pati and Madhu Bala
1993   Explorations and excavations in Haryana, Jammu & Kashmir and Punjab. In, Jagat Pati Joshi, *Excavation at Bhagwanpura 1975-76 and Other Explorations and Excavations 1975-81 in Haryana, Jammu & Kashmir and Punjab*. Memoirs of the Archaeological Survey of India, 89: 227-56.

Joshi, Jagat Pati, Madhu Bala and Jassu Ram
1984   The Indus Civilization: a reconsideration on the basis of distribution maps. In, B. B. Lal and S. P. Gupta, eds., *Frontiers of the Indus Civilization*. Delhi: Books and Books: 511-30.

Joshi, R. V.
1978   *Stone Age Cultures of Central India*. Poona: Deccan College Post-graduate and Research Institute.

928

Kajale, M. D.
1988   Plant economy. In, M. K. Dhavalikar, H. D. Sankalia and Z. D. Ansari, *Excavations at Inamgaon*. Vol. 1, Part ii. Pune: Deccan College Post-Graduate and Research Institute: 727-822.

Kajale, M. D.
1991   Current status of Indian palaeoethnobotany: introduced and indigenous food plants with a discussion of the historical and evolutionary development of Indian agriculture and agricultural systems in general. In, J. M. Renfrew, ed., *New Light on Early Farming*. Edinburgh: Edinburgh University Press: 155-89.

Kale, Vivek P.
1993   Report on the field-workshop on palaeoseismicity at Allah Bund, Kutch, Gujarat. Report submitted to Professor S. N. Rajaguru, Convenor.

Kamminga, J.
1981   Commment on Brian Hayden. *Current Anthropology*, 22: 535-36.

Karanth, R. V.
1988   Silica bead industry in Cambay, Gujarat State, India. *Journal of the Geological Society of India*, 31: 426-31.

Karanth, R. V.
1990   The diamond drill used in the Cambay bead industry. *Journal of Gemology*, 22(2): 91-6.

Karanth, R. V.
1992   The ancient gem industry in Cambay. *Man and Environment*, 17(1): 61-70.

Karttunen, Klaus
1981   The reliability of the *Indica* of Ctesias. *Studia Orientalia*, 50: 105-07.

Karttunen, Klaus
1989   India in Early Greek Literature. *Studia Orientalia*, 65: 1-293.

Kashyap, P. C.
1984   *Surviving Harappan Civilization*. Delhi: Abhinav Publications.

Kavoori, P. S.
1991   Transhumance in western Rajasthan: trends and transformations. *Studies in History*, 7(2): 255-78.

Kaw, R. N.
1979   The Neolithic of Kashmir. In, D. P. Agrawal and Dilip K. Chakrabarti, eds., *Essays in Indian Protohistory*. Delhi: B.R. Publishing Corporation: 219-28.

Kaw, R. N.
1989   Burzahom. In, A. Ghosh, ed., *An Encyclopaedia of Indian Archaeology*. 2 Vols. Delhi: Munshiram Manoharlal: 86-90.

Kaye, George Rusby and Edward Hamilton Johnson
1937   *Catalogue of Manuscripts in European Languages*. Vol. 2, Pt. 2, Minor Collections and Miscellaneous Manuscripts, Section 1. London: The India Office Library.

Kazi, Muhammad Mukhtiar
1989   Lakhueen-jo-daro. *Journal of Central Asia*, 12(1): 89-106.

Kazi, Muhammad Mukhtiar
1992   Taloor-ji-Bhitt, an Indus Site. *Journal of Central Asia*, 15(1): 90-130.

Keay, John
1977   *When Men and Mountains Meet: The Explorers of the Western Himalayas, 1820-75*. London: John Murray.

Keeley, Lawrence H.
1995   Protoagricultural practices among hunter-gatherers: a cross-cultural survey. In, T. Douglas Price and Anne Birgitte Bebauer, eds., *Last Hunters, First Farmers*. Santa Fe: School of American Research: 243-72.

Keith, Sir Arthur
1931   The ancient Mesopotamia of India: Town planning 5000 years ago at Mohenjo-daro. *Illustrated London News*, December 19: 1000-04.

Kennedy, Kenneth A. R.
1970-71 The palaeontology of human populations. *The Cornell Plantations*, 26(4): 51-64.

Kennedy, Kenneth A. R.
1976   *Human Variation in Time and Space*. Dubuque: William C. Brown Publishers.

Kennedy, Kenneth A. R.
1982a   Skulls, Aryans and flowing drains: the interface of archaeology and skeletal biology in the study of the Harappan Civilization. In, G. L. Possehl, ed., *Harappan Civilization: A contemporary perspective*. Delhi: Oxford & IBH and the American Institute of Indian Studies: 289-95.

Kennedy, Kenneth A. R.
1982b   Biological anthropology of human skeletal remains from Bagor: osteology. In, J.R. Lukacs, V.N. Misra and K.A.R. Kennedy, *The Human Skeletal Remains. Bagor and Tilwara: Late Mesolithic Cultures of Northwest India*, Vol. I. Pune: Deccan College Postgraduate and Research Institute: 27-51.

Kennedy, Kenneth A. R.
1984a   Trauma and disease in the ancient Harappans. In, B. B. Lal and S. P. Gupta, eds., *Frontiers of the Indus Civilization*. Delhi: Books and Books: 425-36.

Kennedy, Kenneth A. R.
1984b   Growth, nutrition and pathology in changing paleodemographic settings in South Asia.

930

In, Mark Nathan Cohen and George J. Armelagos, eds., *Paleopathology at the Origins of Agriculture*. New York: Academic Press: 169-92.

Kennedy, Kenneth A. R.
1990   Reconstruction of trauma, disease, and lifeways of prehistoric peoples of South Asia from the skeletal record. In, Maurizio Taddei, ed., *South Asian Archaeology 1987*. Roma: Instituto Italiano per il Medio ed Estremo Oriente, Serie Orientale Roma, 66(1): 61-77.

Kennedy, Kenneth A. R.
1993   Morphometric analysis. In, G. F. Dales and J. M. Kenoyer, The Harappa Project 1986-89: new investigations at an ancient Indus city. In, Gregory L. Possehl, ed., *Harappan Civilization: A recent perspective*. 2nd ed. Delhi: Oxford & IBH and the American Institute of Indian Studies: 496-97.

Kennedy, Kenneth A. R.
1996   Skeletal identification of massacre victims in archaeological contexts: a forensic anthropological approach. In, C. Margabandhu and K. S. Ramachandran, eds., *Spectrum of Indian Culture (Professor S. B. Deo felicitation volume)*. 2 Vols. Delhi: Agam Kala Prakashan: 77-83.

Kennedy, Kenneth A. R. and Peggy C. Caldwell
1984   South Asian prehistoric human skeletal remains and burial practices. In, John R. Lukacs, ed., *The People of South Asia: The biological anthropology of India, Pakistan and Nepal*. New York: Plenum Press:159-97.

Kennedy, Kenneth A. R., John Chimet, Todd Drisotell and David Meyers
1984   Principal-components analysis of prehistoric South Asian crania. *American Journal of Physical Anthropology*, 64(2): 105-18.

Kenoyer, Jonathan Mark
1983   *Shell Working Industries of the Indus Civilization: An archaeological and ethnographic perspective*. PhD Dissertation, Department of South and Southeast Asian Studies, University of California, Berkeley.

Kenoyer, Jonathan Mark
1984a   Chipped stone tools from Mohenjo-daro. In, B. B. Lal and S. P. Gupta, eds., *Frontiers of the Indus Civilization*. Delhi: Books and Books: 117-32.

Kenoyer, Jonathan Mark
1984b   Shell industries at Mohenjo daro, Pakistan. In, M. Jansen and G. Urban, eds., *Reports on Field Work Carried out at Mohenjo-daro, Pakistan 1982-83 by the IsMEO-Aachen University Mission: Interim Reports*, Volume 1. Aachen/Rome:RWTH/IsMEO: 99-115.

Kenoyer, Jonathan Mark
1984c   Shell working industries of the Indus civilization: a summary. *Paleorient*, 10(1): 49-63.

Kenoyer, Jonathan Mark
1985   Shell working at Mohenjo-daro, Pakistan. In, J. Schotsmans and M. Taddei, eds., *South Asian Archaeology 1983*. Naples: Instituto Universitario Orientale, Dipartimento di Studi Asiatici, Series Minor 23: 297-344.

Kenoyer, Jonathan Mark
1986   The Indus bead industry: contributions to bead technology. *Ornament*, Autumn: 18-23.

Kenoyer, Jonathan Mark
1989   Socio-economic structures of the Indus Civilization as reflected in specialized crafts and the question of ritual segregation. In, Jonathan Mark Kenoyer, ed., *Old Problems and New Perspectives in the Archaeology of South Asia*. Madison: Wisconsin Archaeological Reports, 2: 183-92.

Kenoyer, Jonathan Mark
1991a   Urban processes in the Indus tradition: a preliminary model from Harappa. In, Richard H. Meadow, ed., *Harappa Excavations 1986-1990: A multidisciplinary approach to third millennium urbanization*. Madison: Prehistory Press, Monographs in World Archaeology, 3: 29-60.

Kenoyer, Jonathan Mark
1991b   Shell-working in the Indus Civilization. In, Michael Jansen, Maire Mulloy and Gunter Urban, eds., *Forgotten Cities on the Indus: Early civilization in Pakistan from the 8th to the 2nd millennium B.C.* Mainz: Verlag Philippvon Zabern: 216-19.

Kenoyer, Jonathan Mark
1992a   Harappan craft specialization and the question of urban segregation and stratification. *The Eastern Anthropologist*, 45(1-2): 39-54.

Kenoyer, Jonathan Mark
1992b   Socio-ritual artifacts of Upper Palaeolithic hunter-gatherers in South Asia. In, Gregory L. Possehl, ed., *South Asian Archaeology Studies*. Delhi: Oxford & IBH: 233-52.

Kenoyer, Jonathan Mark and Richard H. Meadow
1992   Harappa Archaeological Project 1992: End of season report (January 12-April 3, 1992). Berkeley, Cambridge, Madison: The Harappa Archaeological Project (photocopy).

Kenoyer, Jonathan Mark, J. D. Clark, J. N. Pal and G. R. Sharma
1983   An Upper Palaeolithic shrine in India? *Antiquity*, 57: 88-94.

Kenoyer, Jonathan Mark, Massimo Vidale and Kuldeep K. Bhan
1991   Contemporary stone bead making in Khambhat India: patterns of craft specialization and organization of production as reflected in the archaeological record. *World Archaeology*, 23(1): 44-63.

Kenyon, Kathleen M.
1957   *Digging up Jericho*. London: Ernest Benn.

932

Khan, Abdur Rauf
1968a   *Ancient Settlements in the Karachi Region*. Karachi: Department of Geography, Karachi University.

Khan, Abdur Rauf
1968b   Ancient settlements in the Karachi region. *Dawn*, Sunday Magazine Section, July 21 and 28: 12

Khan, Abdur Rauf
1973   *New Archaeological Sites in Las Bela*. Karachi: Department of Geography, Karachi University.

Khan, Abdur Rauf
1979a   Studies in geomorphology and prehistory of Sind. *Grassroots*, 3(2): 1-112.

Khan, Abdur Rauf
1979b   New archaeological sites in Las Bela—a Neolithic settlement discovered. In, A. Rauf Khan, Studies in geomorphology and prehistory of Sind. *Grassroots*, 3(2): 62-79.

Khan, Abdur Rauf
1979c   Ancient settlements in the Karachi region. In, A. Rauf Khan, Studies in geomorphology and prehistory of Sind. *Grassroots*, 3(2): 1-24.

Khan, Abdur Rauf
1979d   Palaeolithic sites discovered in the lower Sind and their significance in the prehistory of the country. In, A. Rauf Khan, Studies in geomorphology and prehistory of Sind. *Grassroots*, 3(2): 80-2.

Khan, Abdur Rauf
1979e   The Rann of Kutch: its history and evolution. In, A. Rauf Khan, Studies in geomorphology and prehistory of Sind. *Grassroots*, 3(2): 89-112.

Khan, Abdur Rauf
1979f   "Kot Kori"—a site of the Indus Civilization on the edge of the Rann of Kutch. In, A. Rauf Khan, Studies in geomorphology and prehistory of Sind. *Grassroots*, 3(2): 83-8.

Khan, Abdur Rauf
1979g   "Kot Kori"—a site of Indus Civilization in lower Sind. *Sindhological Studies*, Summer: 68-73.

Khan, Abdur Rauf
1981   Kot Kori: a site of the Indus Civilization in lower Sind. In, Ahmad Hasan Dani, ed., *Indus Civilization: New perspectives*. Islamabad: Quaid-i-Azam University: 43-5.

Khan, Ahmad Nabi
1988a   *Proceedings of Third South Asian Archaeological Congress, Islamabad—1988*. Karachi: Department of Archaeology and Museums.

Khan, Ahmad Nabi
1988b   Archaeology in Pakistan 1987-88—a review. In, Ahmad Nabi Khan, ed., *Proceedings of Third South Asian Archaeological Congress, Islamabad—1988*. Karachi: Department of Archaeology and Museums: 74-104.

Khan, F. A.
1959a   Fresh light on the ancient cultures of Baluchistan and Bahawalpur. In, Henry Field, *An Anthropological Reconnaissance in West Pakistan, 1955*. Cambridge: Papers of the Peabody Museum of Archaeology and Ethnology, Harvard University, 52:181-211.

Khan, F. A.
1959b   *Preliminary report on the Kot Diji excavations, 1957-58*. Karachi: Government of Pakistan, Department of Archaeology.

Khan, F. A.
1964   *Kot Diji*. Karachi: Government of Pakistan, Department of Archaeology.

Khan, F. A.
1965   Excavations at Kot Diji. *Pakistan Archaeology*, 2: 11-85.

Khan, Farid
1986   Archaeological Sites in the Bannu Basin. In, F. R. Allchin, B. Allchin, F. A. Durrani and M. Farid Khan, eds., *Lewan and the Bannu Basin*. Oxford: British Archaeological Reports International Series, 310: 183-95.

Khan, Farid
1990   A Neolithic settlement in Bannu. *Ancient Ceylon*, 10: 175-82.

Khan, Farid
1991   The antiquity of crane-catching in the Bannu Basin. *South Asian Studies*, 7: 97-9.

Khan, Farid, J. R. Knox and K. D. Thomas
1986   Sheri Khan Tarakai: a new site in the North West Frontier Province of Pakistan. *Journal of Central Asia*, 9(1): 13-34.

Khan, Farid, J. R. Knox and K. D. Thomas
1987   The Bannu Archaeological Project: a study of prehistoric settlement in Bannu District, Pakistan. *South Asian Studies*, 3: 83-90.

Khan, Farid, J. R. Knox and K. D. Thomas
1988   Prehistoric and Protohistoric settlement in Bannu District. *Pakistan Archaeology*, 23: 99-148.

Khan, Farid, J. R. Knox and K. D. Thomas
1989   New perspectives on early settlement in Bannu District, Pakistan. In, Karen Frifelt and Per Sorensen, eds., *South Asian Archaeology 1985*. London: Curzon Press,

934

Scandinavian Institute of Asian Studies, Occasional Papers No. 4.London: Curzon Press: 281-91.

Khan, Farid, J. R. Knox and K. D. Thomas
1990a   The Bannu Archaeological Project: investigations at Sheri Khan Tarakai 1987-9. *South Asian Studies*, 6: 241-47.

Khan, Farid, J. R. Knox and K. D. Thomas
1990b   Sheri Khan Tarakai: a Neolithic village in Bannu District, NWFP. In, Maurizio Taddei, ed., *South Asian Archaeology 1987*. Roma: Instituto Italiano per il Medio ed Estremo Oriente, Serie Orientale Roma, 66(1): 111-127.

Khan, Farid, J. R. Knox and K. D. Thomas
1990c   Towards a model for protohistoric subsistence systems in Bannu District, NWFP. In, Maurizio Taddei, ed., *South Asian Archaeology 1987*. Roma: Instituto Italiano per il Medio ed Estremo Oriente, Serie Orientale Roma, 66(1): 129-41.

Khan, Farid, J. R. Knox and K. D. Thomas
1991a   *Explorations and Excavations in Bannu District, North-west Frontier Province, Pakistan, 1985-88*. London: British Museum, Department of Oriental Antiquities, Occasional Paper No. 50.

Khan, Farid, J. R. Knox and K. D. Thomas
1991b   Tradition, identity and individuality: exploring the cultural relationship of Sheri Khan Tarakai. *Pakistan Archaeology*, 26(1): 156-74.

Khan, Muhammad
1990a   Archaeological discoveries in District Kharan (Baluchistan). *Journal of the Pakistan Historical Society*, 38(1): 77-86.

Khan, Muhammad
1990b   Recent archaeological discoveries in Makran; Baluchistan. *Journal of the Pakistan Historical Society*, 38(4): 355-71.

Khan, Qasim Ali
1990   Lakheen-jo-daro: a Harappan site in Sukkur. *Journal of the Pakistan Historical Society*, 38(2): 163-70.

Khanna, Gurcharan Singh
1988   *Reasessing the Mesolithic of India: With Special Reference to the Site of Bagor, Rajasthan*. PhD Dissertation, Department of Anthropology, University of California, Berkeley.

Khanna, Gurcharan Singh
1992   Patterns of mobility in the Mesolithic of Rajasthan. In, Catherine Jarrige, ed., *South Asian Archaeology 1989*. Madison: Prehistory Press, Monographs in World Archaeology, 14: 153-60.

Khatana, Ram Parshad
1992   *Tribal Migration in Himalayan Frontiers: A study of Gujjar Bakarwal Transhumance Economy*. Delhi: Vintage Press.

Khatri, J. S. and M. Acharya
1995   Kunal: A new Indus-Saraswati site. *Puratattva*, 25: 84-6.

Khatri, J. S. and M. Acharya
in press Kunal. In, Gregory L. Possehl, ed., *South Asian Archaeology, An Encyclopaedia*. Delhi: Oxford & IBH.

Khazanov, Anatoli Michailovich
1994   *Nomads and the Outside World*. Translated by Julia Crookenden. Madison: University of Wisconsin Press.

Khlopin, I. N.
1963   *Eneolit Juznyh Oblastej Srednej Azii: Pamjatniki rannego Eneolita juznoj Turkemnii*. Moscow-Leningrad: Nauka.

Khlopin, I. N.
1969   *Pamjatniki Razvitogo Eneolita Jugo-Vostocnoj Turkmenii*. Leningrad: Nauka.

Khlopin, I. N.
1960   Dashlydzhi-Tepe i eneoliticheskiye zemledel'tsy yuzhnogo Turkmenistana. *Trudy YuT AKE*, 10: 134-224.

Khuhro, Hamida
1974   Introduction. Reprint of *A Narrative of a Visit to the Court of Sinde by* James Burnes originally published in 1829. Karachi: Oxford University Press: vii-xxviii.

Kincaid, C. A.
1925   *Folk Tales of Sind and Guzerat*. 1979 reprint. Ahmedabad: New Order Book Co.

King, L. W.
1909   An early mention of cotton: the cultivation of Gossypium arboreum, of tree-cotton, in Assyria in the seventh century BC. *Proceedings of the Society for Biblical Archaeology*, 31: 339-43.

Kingery, David W., Pamela B. Vandiver and Martha Prickett
1988   The beginnings of pyrotechnology, Part II: production and use of lime and gypsum plaster in the Pre-Pottery Neolithic Near East. *Journal of Field Archaeology*, 15: 219-44.

Kinnier, N. B.
1920   The past and present distribution of the lion in South East Asia. *Journal of the Bombay Natural History Society*, 27(1): 33-9.

936

Kirch, Patrick Vinton
1984   *The Evolution of Polynesian Chiefdoms.* Cambridge: Cambridge University Press: 314 pp.

Kirk, G. S.
1975   The Homeric poems as history. In, I. E. S. Edwards, et. al. eds., *Cambridge Ancient History*, 2(2), History of the Middle East and the Agean Region, c. 1380-1000 B.C. Cambridge: Cambridge University Press: 820-50.

Kirkbride, Diana
1966   Five seasons at the Pre-Pottery Neolithic village of Beidha in Jordan. *Palestine Exploration Quarterly*, Jan-June: 8-72.

Kislev, M. E., Ofer Bar-Yosef and A. Gopher
1986   Early Neolithic domesticated and wild cereals from Netiv Hagdud region in the Jordan Valley. *Israel Journal of Botany*, 35: 197-201.

Klein, Richard G. and Kathryn Cruz-Uribe
1984   *The Analysis of Animal Bones from Archaeological Sites.* Chicago: University of Chicago Press.

Klickowska, M.
1984   Plants of the Neolithic Kadero (Central Sudan): a palaeoethnobotanical study of the plant impressions on pottery. In, L. Krzyaniak and M. Kobuslewicz, eds., *Origins and Early Development of Food Producing Cultures in North-Eastern Africa.* Poznan: Polsak Academic Nauk: 321-26.

Knappe, Karl-Adolf
1964   *Durer: Das graphische werk.* Wein & Munchen: Verlag von Anton School.

Kohl, Philip L.
1974   *Seeds of Upheaval: The production of chlorite at Tepe Yahya and an analysis of commodity production and trade in Southwest Asia in the third millennium.* PhD Dissertation, Department of Anthropology, Harvard University.

Kohl, Philip L.
1975   Carved chlorite vessels: a trade in finished commodities in the mid-third millennium. *Expedition*, 18(1): 18-31.

Kohl, Philip L.
1976   Steatite carvings of the early third millennium B. C. *American Journal of Archaeology*, 80(1): 73-5.

Kohl, Philip L.
1984   *Central Asia: Palaeolithic beginnings to the Iron Age.* Paris: Centre National de la Recherche Scientifique, Editions Recherche sur les Civilizations, "Synthese," No. 14.

Kohler-Rollefson, Ilse
1992   A model for the development of nomadic pastoralism on the Transjordan Plateau. In, O, Bar-Yosef and A. Khazanov, eds., *Pastoralism in the Levant: Archaeological materials in anthropological perspectives*. Madison: Prehistory Press, Monographs in World Archaeology, 10: 11-18.

Koster, H. A. and C. Chang, editors
1994a   *Pastoralists at the Periphery*. Tucson: University of Arizona Press.

Koster, H. A. and C. Chang, editors
1994b   Introduction. In, H. A. Koster and C. Chang, ed.s, *Pastoralists at the Periphery*. Tucson: University of Arizona Press: 1-22.

Kramer, Samuel N.
1963   Dilmun: quest for paradise. *Antiquity*, 37: 111-15.

Kramer, Samuel N.
1964   The Indus Civilization and Dilmun, the Sumerian paradise land. *Expedition*, 6(3): 44-52.

Krishna Deva
1982   Contributions of Aurel Stein and N. G. Majumdar to research into the Harappan Civilization with special reference to their methodology. In, G. L. Possehl, ed., *Harappan Civilization: A contemporary perspective*. Delhi: Oxford & IBH and the American Institute of Indian Studies: 387-93.

Krishna Deva and Donald E. McCown
1949   Further exploration in Sind: 1938. *Ancient India*, 5: 12-30.

Krishna Deva and R. E. M. Wheeler
1946a   Appendix A, Northern Black Polished Ware, the pottery of Ahichchhatra *Ancient India*, 1: 55-8.

Krishna Deva and R. E. M. Wheeler
1946b   Appendix B, Note on the Painted Grey Wares at Ahichchhatra. *Ancient India*, 1: 58-9.

Krishna Rao, P. R.
1962   *Monthly and Annual Norms of Rainfall and Rainy Days: Based on Records from 1901-1950*. Memoirs of the India Meteorological Department, 31(3).

Krishna, C.
1966   Copper celt from Ramjipura, District East Nimar. *Bulletin of the Deccan College Research Institute*, 25:197.

Krishnan, A. and K. P. Thanvi
1982   Study on the variability of rainfall and evaluation of rainfall types in western Rajasthan. In, *Proceedings of the Workshop on the Problems of the Deserts of India*. Delhi: Geological Survey of India, Special Publication No. 49: 156-60.

938

Krishnaswamy, N.
1951   Origin and distribution of cultuvated plants of South Asia: millets. *Indian Journal of Genetics and Plant Breeding*, 11: 67-74.

Kroeber, A. L.
1939   *Cultural and Natural Areas of North America*. Berkeley: University of California Press.

Krzyzaniak, Lech
1978   New light on early food-production in the Central Sudan. *Journal of African History*, 19: 159-72.

Krzyzaniak, Lech
1991   Early farming in the middle Nile basin: recent dioscoveries at Kadero. *Antiquity*, 65(248): 515-32.

Kumar, Manmohan
1978   *Archaeology of Ambala and Kurukshetra Districts (Haryana)*. PhD Dissertation, Department of Ancient Indian History, Culture and Archaeology, Kurukshetra University.

Kumar, Tuk-Tuk
1988   *History of Rice in India: Mythology, culture and agriculture*. Delhi: Gian Publishing House.

Kuraishi, M. H.
1935-36 Excavations at Harappa. *Annual Report of the Archaeological Survey of India, 1935-36*: 35-6.

Kuzmina, Elene
1994   *Otkuda Prishli Indoarii?* Moskva: Rossiiskii Institut Kul'turologii.

Lahiri, Dipankar
1968   Minerology in ancient India. *Indian Journal of the History of Science*, 3: 1-8.

Lahiri, Nayanjot
1990   Harappa as a centre of trade and trade routes: a case study of the resource-use, resource-access and lines of communication in the Indus Civilization. *The Indian Economic and Social History Review*, 27(4): 405-444.

Lal, B. B.
1951   Further copper hoards from the Gangetic basin and a review of the problem. *Ancient India*, 7: 20-39

Lal, B. B.
1954-55 Excavations at Hastinapura and other explorations in the Upper Ganga and Sutlej Basins 1950-52. *Ancient India*, 10-11: 5-151.

Lal, B. B.
1963   A picture emerges—an assessment of the Carbon-14 datings of the protohistoric cultures of the Indo-Pakistan subcontinent. *Ancient India*, 18-19: 208-21.

Lal, B. B.
1979   Kalibangan and Indus Civilization. In, D. P. Agrawal and Dilip Chakrabarti, eds., *Essays in Indian Protohistory*. Delhi: B. R. Publishing Corporation: 65-97.

Lal, B. B.
1981   Some reflections on the structural remains at Kalibangan. In, Ahmad Hasan Dani, ed., *Indus Civilization: New perspectives*. Islamabad: Quaid-i-Azam University: 47-54.

Lal, B. B.
1984   Sir Mortimer Wheeler—the man: some reminiscences. In, B. B. Lal and S. P. Gupta, eds., *Frontiers of the Indus Civilization*. Delhi: Books and Books: vii-ix.

Lal, B. B.
1989   H. D. Sankalia. *Man and Environment*, 14(2): 125-27.

Lal, B. B.
1992   Antecedents of the signs used in the Indus script: a discussion. In, Gregory L. Possehl, ed., *South Asian Archaeology Studies*. Delhi: Oxford & IBH: 54-56.

Lal, B. B.
1997   *The Earliest Civilization of South Asia: Rise, maturity and decline.* New Delhi: Aryan Books International.

Lal, B. B. and B. K. Thapar
1967   Excavations at Kalibangan: new light on Indian civilization. *Cultural Forum*, 9(4): 78-88.

Lal, B. B. and K. N. Dikshit
1982   Pariar — an eastern outpost of the Painted Grey Ware. *Puratattva*, 11: 26-31.

Lal, B. B. (Dr.)
1971-72   Appendix F — The ochre-coloured pottery — a geochronological study. *Puratattva*, 5: 49-58.

Lal, Makkhan
1979   New copper hoards from Bithur, Khanpur District, Uttar Pradesh. *Archaeological Studies*, 4: 34-7.

Lal, Makkhan
1980   The date of the Painted Grey Ware Culture: a review. *Bulletin of the Deccan College Research Institute*, 39: 65-77.

940

Lal, Makkhan
1982   *Early Human Colonisation Patterns in the Ganga-Yamuna Doab*. PhD Dissertation, Department of Archaeology, Deccan College.

Lal, Makkhan
1984a   *Settlement History and Rise of Civilization in Ganga-Yamuna Doab: From 1500 BC to 300 AD*. Delhi: B. R. Publishing Corporation.

Lal, Makkhan
1984b   Summary of four seasons of explorations in Kanpur district, Uttar Pradesh. *Man and Environment*, 8: 61-80.

Lamb, H. H., R. P. W. Lewis and A. Woodruff
1966   *World climate from 8000 to 0 B.C*. Proceedings of the International Meterological Symposium. London: Royal Meterological Service.

Lamberg-Karlovsky, Carl C.
1969   Further notes on the shaft-hole pick-axe from Khurab, Makran. *Iran*, 7: 163-68.

Lamberg-Karlovsky, Carl C.
1972   Trade mechanisms in Indus-Mesopotamian interrelations. *Journal of the American Oriental Society*, 92(1): 222-29.

Lamberg-Karlovsky, Carl C. and Thomas W. Beale
1986   *Excavations at Tepe Yahya, Iran, 1967-75: The Early Periods*. Cambridge: Peabody Museum.

Lambert, W. G.
1960   *Babylonian Wisdom Literature*. Oxford: At the Clarendon Press.

Lambrick, H. T.
1941   The 'Miri' at Taung. *Journal of the Sind Historical Society*, 5(2): 92-111.

Lambrick, H. T.
1942a   Amateur excursions in archaeology: Lower Sind 1941. *Journal of the Sind Historical Society*, 6(2): 104-12.

Lambrick, H. T.
1942b   *Sind*. Delhi: Census of India, 1941, Vol. 12, Tables.

Lambrick, H. T.
1944   Amateur excursions in archaeology II: 1942, Kohistan. *Journal of the Sind Historical Society*, 7(3): 59-69.

Lambrick, H. T.
1946   Amateur excursions in archaeology, No. III: Eastern Sind, 1943-46. *Journal of the Sind Historical Society*, 8(1):45-65.

Lambrick, H. T.
1952   *Sir Charles Napier and Sind*. Oxford: Clarendon Press.

Lambrick, H. T.
1960   *John Jacob of Jacobabad*. London: Cassell.

Lambrick, H. T.
1964   *Sind: A general introduction*. History of Sind Series, Vol. 1. Hyderabad (Pakistan): Sindhi Adabi Board.

Lambrick, H. T.
1967   The Indus flood-plain and the 'Indus Civilization.' *The Geographical Journal*, 133: 483-94.

Lambrick, H. T.
1971   Stratigraphy at Mohenjo-daro. *Journal of the Oriental Institute, Maharaja Sayajirao University of Baroda*, 20(4): 363-69.

Lambrick, H. T.
1972   *The Terrorist*. London: Ernest Benn Limited.

Lambrick, H. T.
1973   *Sind: Before the Muslim conquest*. History of Sind Series, Vol. 2. Hyderabad (Pakistan): Sindhi Adabi Board.

Landsberger, Benno
1962   The fauna of ancient Mesopotamia. The series *Har-ra* = hubullu: tablets xiv-xviii. Roma: Pontificum Institutum Biblicum. *Materials for the Sumerian Lexicon*, Vol. 8, Pt. 2.

Langdon, Stephen H.
1929   The Dynasty of Akkad and Lagash. In, J. B. Bury, S. A. Cook and F. E. Adcock, eds., *Cambridge Ancient History*. Vol. 1, Egypt and Babylonia to 1580 BC. 2nd ed. Cambridge: Cambridge University Press: 402-551.

Langdon, Stephen H.
1931   The Indus script. In, Sir John Marshall, ed., *Mohenjo-daro and the Indus Civilization*, 3 Vols. London: Arthur Probsthain: 423-55.

Langdon, Stephen H.
1932   Another Indus valley seal. *Journal of the Royal Asiatic Society of Great Britain and Ireland*: 47-48.

Langdon, Stephen H.
1934a   Introduction. In, G. R. Hunter, *The Script of Harappa and Mohenjo-Daro and its Connection with Other Scripts*. London: Kegan Paul, Trench, Trubner & Co. Ltd: ix-xii.

942

Langdon, Stephen H.
1934b   Mr. L. C. Watelin, excavations at Kish. *The Times*, Obituary, 5 July.

Lassen, Christian
1874   *Indische Alterthumskunde*. 4 Vols., 2nd ed. Leipzig: Verlag von L. A. Kittler.

Lavachery, Henri
1935   La mission Franco-Belge dans l'Ile de Paques (Jillet 1934-Avril 1935). *Bulletin des Musees Royale d'Art et Histoire*: Mai-Juin: 50-63.

Lawrence, Barbara
1982   Principal food animals at Cayonu. In, Linda S. Braidwood and Robert J. Braidwood, eds., *Prehistoric Village Archaeology in South-Eastern Turkey*. Oxford: British Archaeological Reports, S138: 175-99.

Leach, Edmund R.
1964   *Political Systems of Highland Burma: A Study of Kachin Social Structure*. London School of Economics Monographs on Social Anthropology, No. 44.

Lechevallier, Monique
1978   *Abu Ghosh et Beisamoun, Deux Gisements du VIIe Millenaire Avant L'ere Chertienne en Israel*. Paris, Association Paleorient. Memoires et Traveaux de Centre de Researches Prehistoriques Francais de Jerusalem 2.

Lechevallier, Monique
1984   Flint industry of Mehrgarh. In, Bridget Allchin, ed., *South Asian Archaeology 1981*. Cambridge: Cambridge University Press: 41-51.

Lechevallier, Monique and Gonzague Quivron
1981   The Neolithic in Baluchistan: new evidences from Mehrgarh. In, H. Hartel, ed., *South Asian Archaeology 1979*. Berlin: Dietrich Reimer Verlag: 71-92.

Lechevallier, Monique and Gonzague Quivron
1985   Results of recent excavations at the Neolithic site of Mehrgarh. In, J. Schotsmans and M. Taddei, eds., *South Asian Archaeology 1983*. Naples: Instituto Universitario Orientale, Dipartimento di Studi Asiatici, Series Minor 23: 69-90.

Lechevallier, Monique, Richard Meadow and G. Quivron
1982   Depots d'animaux dans le sepultures neolithiques de Mehrgarh, Pakistan. *Paleorient*, 8(1): 99-106.

Lee, Richard B.
1968   What hunters do for a living or how to make out on scarce resources. In, Richard B. Lee and Irvin DeVore, *Man the Hunter*. Chicago: Aldine: 30-43.

Lee, Richard B.
1969   !Kung Bushman subsistence: an input-output analysis. In, Andrew Vaida, ed.,

Ecological Studies in Cultural Anthropology. Garden City: Natural History Press: 47-9.

Lee, Richard B.
1972a   Population growth and the beginnings of sedentary life among the !Kung bushmen. In, Brian Spooner, ed., *Population Growth: Anthropological implications*. Cambridge: MIT Press: 329-42.

Lee, Richard B.
1972b   Work effort, group structure and land-use in contemporary hunter-gatherers. In, Peter J. Ucko, Ruth Tringham and G. W. Dimbleby, eds., *Man, Settlement and Urbanism*. London: Gerald Duckworth & Co.: 177-85.

Lee, Richard B. and Irvin DeVore, editors
1968   *Man the Hunter*. Chicago: Aldine.

Lee, Richard B. and Irvin DeVore, editors
1976   *Kalahari Hunter Gatherers*. Cambridge: Harvard University Press.

Lees, Susan and Daniel G. Bates
1974   The origins of specialized nomadic populations: a systemic model. *American Antiquity*, 39: 187-93.

Legrain, Leon
1947   *Ur Excavation Texts III: Business Documents of the Third Dynasty of Ur. London*, Philadelphia: The British Museum and The University Museum.

Lele, V. S.
1982   Development of the Little Rann of Kutch, western India. In, *Proceedings of the Workshop on the Problems of the Deserts of India*. Delhi: Geological Survey of India, Special Publication No. 49: 214-16.

Leroi-Gourhan, A.
1974   Etudes palynologiques des derniers 11,000 ans en Syrie semi-desertiques. *Paleorient*, 2: 443-51.

Leshnik, Lawrence S.
1968   Prehistoric explorations in North Gujarat and parts of Rajasthan. *East and West*, 18 (3-4): 295-310.

Leshnik, Lawrence S.
1972   Pastoral nomadism in the archaeology of India and Pakistan. *World Archaeology*, 4(2): 150-66.

Leshnik, Lawrence S. and Gunther D. Sontheimers
1975   *Pastoralists and Nomads in South Asia*. Wiesbaden: Otto Harrassowitz. Schriftenreihe de Sudasien Institute der Universitat Heidelberg.

944

Levi-Strauss, C.
1969   *The Elementary Structure of Kinship.* London: Eyre and Spottiswoode.

Lewis, Henry T.
1972   The role of fire in the domestication of plants and animals in Southwest Asia: an hypothesis. *Man,* 7(2): 195-222.

Leyden, John and William Erskine, translators
1921   *Memoirs of Zehir-Ed-Din Muhammad Babur: Emperor of Hindustan.* 2 Vols. London: Humphrey Milford, Oxford University Press.

Lieberman, D. E., T. W. Deacon and R. H. Meadow
1990   Computer image enhancement and analysis of cementum increments as applied to teeth of Gazelle gazella. *Journal of Archaeological Science,* 17: 519-33.

van Lohuizen-de Leeuw, J. E.
1974   Moenjo Daro—a cause of common concern. In, J. E. van Lohuizen-de Leeuw and J. J. M. Ubaghs, eds., *South Asian Archaeology 1973.* Leiden: E. J. Brill: 1-11.

Lovell, Nancy C.
1993a   Palaeodietary reconstruction. In, G. F. Dales and J. M. Kenoyer, The Harappa Project 1986-89: new investigations at an ancient Indus city. In, G. L. Possehl, ed., *Harappan Civilization: A recent perspective.* 2nd ed. Delhi:Oxford & IBH and the American Institute of Indian Studies: 497-98.

Lovell, Nancy C.
1993b   Palaeopathology. In, George F. Dales and J. Mark Kenoyer, The Harappa Project 1986-89: new investigations at an ancient Indus city. In, Gregory L. Possehl, ed., *Harappan Civilization: A recent perspective.* 2nd ed. Delhi: Oxford& IBH and the American Institute of Indian Studies.

Lower Indus Project
1965a   *Lower Indus Report: Physical Resources.* Vol. 1, Climate. Karachi: Ferozsons.

Lower Indus Project
1965b   *Lower Indus Report: Physical Resources.* Vol. 2, Geomorphology, Soils and Watertable. Karachi: Ferozsons.

Lower Indus Project
1965c   *Lower Indus Report: Physical Resources.* Vol. 3, River Indus. Karachi: Ferozsons.

Lower Indus Project
1965d   *Lower Indus Report: Physical Resources.* Vol. 4, Torrents. Karachi: Ferozsons.

Lower Indus Project
1965e   *Lower Indus Report: Physical Resources.* Vol. 5, Surface Water Storage. Karachi: Ferozsons.

Lower Indus Project
1966   *Lower Indus Project, Main Report.* 2 Vols. London: Red Lion House.

Lowie, Robert H.
1912   The principle of convergence in ethnology. *Journal of American Folk-Lore*, 25(45): 24-42.

Luckenbill, D. D.
1924   *The Annals of Sennacherib.* Chicago: Oriental Institute of the University of Chicago

Lukacs, John R.
1982   Biological anthropology of human skeletal remains from Bagor: dentition. In, John R. Lukcs, V. N. Misra and Kenneth A. R. Kennedy, *The Human Skeletal Remains.* Bagor and Tilwara: Late Mesolithic Cultures of Northwest India, Vol. I.Pune: Deccan College Postgraduate and Research Institute: 61-85.

Lukacs, John R.
1983   Human dental remains from early Neolithic levels at Mehrgarh, Baluchistan. *Current Anthropology*, 24(3): 390-93.

Lukacs, John R.
1985   Dental pathology and tooth size at Mehrgarh: an anthropological assessment. In, J. Schotsmans and M. Taddei, eds., *South Asian Archaeology 1983.* Naples: Instituto Universitario Orientale, Dipartimento di Studi Asiatici, Series Minor 23: 121-50.

Lukacs, John R.
1989   Biological affinities from dental morphology: the evidence from Neolithic Mehrgarh. In, Jonathan Mark Kenoyer, ed., *Old Problems and New Perspectives in the Archaeology of South Asia.* Madison: Wisconsin Archaeological Reports, 2:75-88.

Lukacs, John R.
1993   Dental anthropology. In, George F. Dales and J. Mark Kenoyer, The Harappa Project 1986-89: new investigations at an ancient Indus city. In, Gregory L. Possehl, ed., *Harappan Civilization: A recent perspective.* 2nd ed. Delhi: Oxford& IBH and the American Institute of Indian Studies: 498-500.

Lukacs, John R. and R. F. Pastor
1988   Activity-induced patterns of dental abrasion in prehistoric Pakistan: evidence from Mehrgarh. *American Journal of Physical Anthropology*, 76(3): 377-98.

Lukacs, John R., V. N. Misra and Kenneth A. R. Kennedy
1982   *The Human Skeletal Remains. Bagor and Tilwara: Late Mesolithic cultures of Northwestern India.* Vol. 1. Pune: Deccan College Postgraduate and Research Institute: 61-85.

Lyell, Sir Charles
1853   *Principles of Geology.* 9th ed. Boston: Little, Brown and Company.

Macdonell, A. A. and A. B. Keith.
1912   *Vedic Index of Names and Subjects.* 2 Vols. London.

Mackay, Dorothy
1945   Ancient river beds and dead cities. *Antiquity,* 19: 135-44.

Mackay, Ernest J. H.
1925-26 Exploration, Western Circle, Mohenjo-daro (Area DK). *Annual Report of the Archaeological Survey of India, 1925-26:* 87-93.

Mackay, Ernest J. H.
1925a   *Report on the Excavations of the 'A' Cemetery at Kish, Mesopotamia.* Part 1. Chicago: Field Museum of Natural History, Anthropology Memoirs, 1(1).

Mackay, Ernest J. H.
1925b   Sumerian connections with ancient India. *Journal of the Royal Asiatic Society of Great Britain and Ireland:* 697-701.

Mackay, Ernest J. H.
1926-27 "L" Area. *Annual Report of the Archaeological Survey of India, 1926-27:* 89-97.

Mackay, Ernest J. H.
1927-28 Excavations at Mohenjo-daro. *Annual Report of the Archaeological Survey of India, 1927-28:* 67-76.

Mackay, Ernest J. H.
1928-29 Excavations at Mohenjo-daro. *Annual Report of the Archaeological Survey of India, 1928-29:* 67-75.

Mackay, Ernest J. H.
1929-30 Excavations at Mohenjo-daro. *Annual Report of the Archaeological Survey of India, 1929-30:* 98-109.

Mackay, Ernest J. H.
1929a   *A Sumerian Palace and the 'A' Cemetery at Kish, Mesopotamia.* Part II. Chicago: Field Museum of Natural History, Anthropology Memoirs, Vol. 1, No. 2.

Mackay, Ernest J. H.
1929b   Bahrain. In, E. J. H. Mackay, G. Harding and F. Petrie, eds., *Bahrain and Hemamieh.* London: British School of Archaeology in Egypt, 47: 1-29.

Mackay, Ernest J. H.
1930-34 Excavations at Mohenjo-daro. *Annual Reports of the Archaeological Survey of India for the Years 1930-31, 1931-32, 1932-33 & 1933-34,* Part One: 51-71.

Mackay, Ernest J. H.
1931a   Personal ornaments. In, Sir John Marshall, ed., *Mohenjo-daro and the Indus Civilization,* 3 Vols. London: Arthur Probsthain: 509-48.

Mackay, Ernest J. H.
1931b   Further links between ancient Sind, Sumer and elsewhere. *Antiquity*, 5(20): 459-73.

Mackay, Ernest J. H.
1931c   *Report on the Excavations at Jemdet Nasr*. Chicago: Field Museum of Natural History, Anthropology Memoirs, Vol. 1, No. 3.

Mackay, Ernest J. H.
1931d   Seals, seal impressions and copper tablets, with tabulation. In, Sir John Marshall, ed., *Mohenjo-daro and the Indus Civilization*, 3 Vols. London: Arthur Probsthain: 370-405.

Mackay, Ernest J. H.
1931e   Ivory, shell, faience and other objects of technical interest. In, Sir John Marshall, ed., *Mohenjo-daro and the Indus Civilization*, 3 Vols. London: Arthur Probsthain: 562-88.

Mackay, Ernest J. H.
1931f   Figurines and model animals. In Marshall, Sir John, editor, *Mohenjo-daro and the Indus Civilization*. 3 Vols. London: Arthur Probsthain: 338-55.

Mackay, Ernest J. H.
1931g   Statuary. In Marshall, Sir John, editor, *Mohenjo-daro and the Indus Civilization*. 3 Vols. London: Arthur Probsthain: 356-64.

Mackay, Ernest J. H.
1931h   Faience and stone vessels. In Marshall, Sir John, editor, *Mohenjo-daro and the Indus Civilization*. 3 Vols. London: Arthur Probsthain: 365-69.

Mackay, Ernest J. H.
1931i   Seals, seal impressions and copper tablets, with tabulation. In Marshall, Sir John, editor, *Mohenjo-daro and the Indus Civilization*. 3 Vols. London: Arthur Probsthain: 370-405.

Mackay, Ernest J. H.
1931j   Household objects, tools and implements. In Marshall, Sir John, editor, *Mohenjo-daro and the Indus Civilization*. 3 Vols. London: Arthur Probsthain: 456-80.

Mackay, Ernest J. H.
1931k   Copper and bronze utensils and other objects: technique and description of metal vessels, tools, implements and other objects. In Marshall, Sir John, editor, *Mohenjo-daro and the Indus Civilization*. 3 Vols. London: Arthur Probsthain: 488-508.

Mackay, Ernest J. H.
1931l   Personal ornaments. In Marshall, Sir John, editor, *Mohenjo-daro and the Indus Civilization*. 3 Vols. London: Arthur Probsthain: 509-48.

948

Mackay, Ernest J. H.
1931m   Games and toys. In Marshall, Sir John, editor, *Mohenjo-daro and the Indus Civilization*. 3 Vols. London: Arthur Probsthain: 549-61.

Mackay, Ernest J. H.
1931n   Ivory, shell, faience and other objects of technical interest. In Marshall, Sir John, editor, *Mohenjo-daro and the Indus Civilization*. 3 Vols. London: Arthur Probsthain: 562-88.

Mackay, Ernest J. H.
1933a   A Sumerian representation of an Indian stand. *Journal of the Royal Asiatic Society of Great Britain and Ireland*: 335-38.

Mackay, Ernest J. H.
1933b   An important link between ancient India and Elam. *Antiquity*, 6: 356-57.

Mackay, Ernest J. H.
1934   The Indus Civilization: some connections with Sumer, Elam and the west. *Journal of the Royal Central Asian Society*, 21(3): 420-43.

Mackay, Ernest J. H.
1935   *The Indus Civilization*. London: Luzac & Co.

Mackay, Ernest J. H.
1935-36 Excavations at Chanhu-daro. *Annual Report of the Archaeological Survey of India, 1935-36*: 38-44

Mackay, Ernest J. H.
1936a   Excavations at Chanhu-daro by the American School of Indic and Iranian Studies and the Museum of Fine Arts, Boston: Season 1935-36. *Bulletin of the Museum of Fine Arts*, 34(205): 83-92.

Mackay, Ernest J. H.
1936b   Great new discoveries of ancient Indian culture on a virgin prehistoric site in Sind. *Illustrated London News*, November 21: 860-64; 908-11.

Mackay, Ernest J. H.
1937a   Bead making in ancient Sind. *Journal of the American Oriental Society*, 57: 1-15.

Mackay, Ernest J. H.
1937b   Early culture at Chanhu-daro. *Discovery*, September: 286-89.

Mackay, Ernest J. H.
1937c   Excavations at Chanhu-daro by the American School of Indic and Iranian Studies and the Museum of Fine Arts, Boston, Season 1935-36. Washington DC: Smithsonian Institution. *Smithsonian Report for 1937*: 469-78.

Mackay, Ernest J. H.
1937-38 *Further Excavations at Mohenjo-daro*. 2 Vols. Delhi: Government of India.

Mackay, Ernest J. H.
1943 *Chanhu-daro Excavations 1935-36*. New Haven: American Oriental Society, American Oriental Series, Vol. 20.

Mackay, Ernest J. H.
1948 *Early Indus Civilizations*. 2nd ed. Revised by Dorothy Mackay. London: Luzac & Co.

Mackay, Ernest J. H., G. L. Harding and F. Petrie
1929 *Bahrain and Hemamieh*. London: Publications of the British School of Archaeology in Egypt, No. 47.

MacMurdo, J.
1834a An account of the country of Sindh. *Journal of the Royal Asiatic Society*, 1: 223-57.

MacMurdo, J.
1834b Dissertation on the River Indus. *Journal of the Royal Asiatic Society*, 1: 21-44.

MacMurdo, J.
1839 Observations on the Sindoo or River Indus. *Transactions of the Bombay Geographical Society*, 2: 124-35.

Madhu Bala
1975 A survey of protohistoric investigation in Jammu and Kashmir and review of present position. *The Anthropologist*, 22(1-2): 1-16.

Madhu Bala
1981 Recently explored sites in Punjab. *Man and Environment*, 5: 67-9.

Madhu Bala
1992 *Archaeology of Punjab*. Delhi: Agam Kala Prakashan.

Maggi, Roberto, Paolo Biaggi, Robert Travers and Renato Nishet
1985 Excavations at the RH5 and RH6 sites, Qurm, Winter 1985-1986. *East and West*, 35: 407-17.

Magrath, R. N.
1839 Some observations upon Sind and the River Indus as far up as Bukkur. *Transactions of the Bombay Geographical Society*, 2: 25-31.

Mahadevan, Iravatham
1977 *The Indus Script: Texts, concordance and tables*. Memoirs of the Archaeological Survey of India, 77.

Majidzadeh, Y.
1982 Lapis lazuli and the Great Khorasan road. *Paleorient*, 8(1): 59-70.

950

Majumdar, Abhijit
1994   Disposal of the dead during the Chalcolithic Period of Gujarat (A Study of Harappan burial customs). MA Dissertation, Department of Archaeology and Ancient History, Maharaja Sayajirao University of Baroda.

Majumdar, N. G.
1927-28 Excavations at Jhukar. *Annual Report of the Archaeological Survey of India, 1927-28*: 76-83.

Majumdar, N. G.
1929-30 Explorations in Sind. *Annual Report of the Archaeological Survey of India, 1929-30*: 110-21.

Majumdar, N. G.
1930-34 Explorations in Sind. *Annual Reports of the Archaeological Survey of India for the Years 1930-31, 1931-32, 1932-33 & 1933-34*, Part One: 90-106.

Majumdar, N. G.
1934   *Explorations in Sind*. Memoirs of the Archaeological Survey of India, No. 48.

Majumdar, N. G.
1939   Prehistoric and Protohistoric civilization. In, Sir John Cumming, ed., *Revealing India's Past*. London: The India Society: 91-117.

Mallah, Qasid Hussain
1994   *The Survey/Exploration of Historic Monuments, Archaeological Sites and Ancient Settlement Pattern in Sukkur District*. Khairpur: MPhil Thesis, Department of Archaeology, Shah Abdul Latif University.

Mallory, J. P.
1989   *In Search of the Indo-Europeans: Language, archaeology and myth*. New York: Thames and Hudson.

Mallowan, M. E. L., Sir
1977a   *Mallowan's Memoirs*. New York: Dodd, Mead & Company.

Mallowan, M. E. L., Sir
1977b   Recollections of C. Leonard Woolley. *Expedition*, 20(1): 3-4.

Manchanda, Omi
1972   *A Study of Harappan Pottery*. Delhi: Oriental Publishers.

Mann, H. S. and R. P. Singh
1977   Crop production in the Indian arid zone. *Desertification and its Control*. New Delhi: Indian Council of Agricultural Research: 215-24.

Margabandhu, C. and R. P. Sharma
1981   Explorations along the Sahibi River in District Gurgaon. *Puratattva*, 10: 14-9.

Marshall, Sir John
1904-05 A new type of pottery from Baluchistan. *Annual Report of the Archaeological Survey of India, 1904-05*: 105-06.

Marshall, Sir John
1907   *Conservation of Ancient Monuments*. Calcutta: Manager of Publications.

Marshall, Sir John
1918-19 Editorial comment on L. P. Tessitori. *Annual Report of the Archaeological Survey of India, 1918-19*: 22.

Marshall, Sir John
1920-21 Harappa. *Annual Report of the Archaeological Survey of India, 1920-21*: 15-7.

Marshall, Sir John
1922   The monuments of ancient India. In, E. J. Rapson, ed., *The Cambridge History of India*. Cambridge: Cambridge University Press: 612-49.

Marshall, Sir John
1923-24 Exploration and Research, Harappa and Mohenjo-daro. *Annual Report of the Archaeological Survey of India, 1923-24*: 47-51.

Marshall, Sir John
1923a   *Conservation Manual for the Care of Ancient Monuments*. Delhi: Archaeological Survey of India.

Marshall, Sir John
1923b   The George Birdwood Memorial Lecture: Influence of race on early Indian art. *Journal of the Royal Society of Arts*, 71 (3690): 659-66.

Marshall, Sir John
1924   First light on a long forgotten civilization. *Illustrated London News*, September 20: 528-32, 548.

Marshall, Sir John
1924-25 The prehistoric civilization of the Indus. *Annual Report of the Archaeological Survey of India, 1924-25*: 60-3.

Marshall, Sir John
1925-26 Exploration, Western Circle, Mohenjo-daro. *Annual Report of the Archaeological Survey of India, 1925-26*: 72-98.

Marshall, Sir John
1926a   Unveiling the prehistoric civilization of the Indus. *Illustrated London News*, 27 February: 346-49.

Marshall, Sir John
1926b   Unveiling the prehistoric civilization of the Indus. *Illustrated London News*, 6 March: 398-400.

952

Marshall, Sir John
1926c   Prehistoric India. *The Times, Weekly*, 4 March: 186.

Marshall, Sir John
1926-27a The Indus Culture. *Annual Report of the Archaeological Survey of India, 1926-27*: 51-60.

Marshall, Sir John
1926-27b Personnel. *Annual Report of the Archaeological Survey of India, 1926-27*: 246-47.

Marshall, Sir John
1928a   A new chapter in Indian archaeology. *Illustrated London News*, 7 January: 12-5.

Marshall, Sir John
1928b   A new chapter in Indian archaeology. *Illustrated London News*, 14 January: 42-5.

Marshall, Sir John
1928c   India 5000 years ago. Mohenjodaro. The excavated cities. *The Times*, 4 January: 13.

Marshall, Sir John, editor
1931a   *Mohenjo-Daro and the Indus Civilization*. 3 Vols. London: Arthur Probsthain.

Marshall, Sir John
1931b   The country, climate and rivers. In, Sir John Marshall, ed., *Mohenjo-daro and the Indus Civilization*, 3 Vols. London: Arthur Probsthain: 1-7.

Marshall, Sir John
1931c   The site and its excavation. In, Sir John Marshall, ed., *Mohenjo-daro and the Indus Civilization*, 3 Vols. London: Arthur Probsthain: 8-14.

Marshall, Sir John
1931d   Extent of the Indus Civilization. In, Sir John Marshall, ed., *Mohenjo-daro and the Indus Civilization*, 3 Vols. London: Arthur Probsthain: 91-101.

Marshall, Sir John
1931e   The buildings. In, Sir John Marshall, ed., *Mohenjo-daro and the Indus Civilization*, 3 Vols. London: Arthur Probsthain: 15-26.

Marshall, Sir John
1931f   Other antiquities and art. In, Sir John Marshall, ed., *Mohenjo-daro and the Indus Civilization*, 3 Vols. London: Arthur Probsthain: 27-47.

Marshall, Sir John
1931g   Religion. In, Sir John Marshall, ed., *Mohenjo-daro and the Indus Civilization*, 3 Vols. London: Arthur Probsthain: 48-78.

Marshall, Sir John
1931h   The age and authors of the Indus Civilization. In, Sir John Marshall, ed., *Mohenjo-daro and the Indus Civilization*, 3 Vols. London: Arthur Probsthain: 102-12.

Marshall, Sir John
1939   The story of the Archaeological Department in India. In, Sir John Cumming, ed., *Revealing India's Past*. London: The India Society: 1-33.

Marshall, Sir John
1951   *Taxila*. 3 Vols. Cambridge: Cambridge University Press.

Masson, Charles
1834   Memoir on the ancient coins found at Beghram, in the kohistan of Kabul. *Journal of the Asiatic Society of Bengal*, 3: 152-75

Masson, Charles
1836a   Second memoir on the ancient coins found at Beghram, in the kohistan of Kabul. *Journal of the Asiatic Society of Bengal*. 5: 1-28.

Masson, Charles
1836b   Third memoir on the ancient coins discovered at the site called Beghram, in the kohistan of Kabul. *Journal of the Asiatic Society of Bengal*, 5: 537-46.

Masson, Charles
1842   *Narrative of Various Journeys in Baluchistan, Afghanistan and the Punjab: Including a residence in those countries from 1826 to 1838*. 3 Vols. London: Richard Bently.

Masson, Charles
1843   *Narrative of Various Journeys in Baluchistan, Afghanistan the Punjab and Kalat, Including an Account of the Insurrection in that Place in 1840 and a Memoir of Eastern Balochistan*. 4 Vols. London: Richard Bently.

Masson, V. M.
1960   Kara Teroe Mean Artyk. *Trudy Iu TAKE*, 10: 319-463.

Masson, V. M. and V. I. Sarianidi
1972   *Central Asia: Turkmenia before the Achaemenids*. New York: Praeger.

Maurer, Walter H.
1986   *Pinnacles of India's Past: Selections from the Rgveda*. Philadelphia: University of Pennsylvania Studies in South Asia, 2.

Mauss, Marcel
1966   *The Gift: Forms and functions of exchange in archaic societies*. Translated by Ian Cunnison. London: Cohen and West.

Maxwell-Hyslop, K. R.
1955   Note on a shaft-hole axe-pick from Khurab, Makran. *Iraq*, 17.

McAlpin, David W.
1980   Is Brahui really Dravidian? *Proceedings of the Berkeley Linguistic Society*, 6: 66-72.

954

McAlpin, David W.
1981   *Proto-Elamo-Dravidian: The evidence and its implications*. Philadelphia: Transactions of the American Philosophical Society, 71(3).

McConaghey, A.
1907   Chagai District: Statistical and Explanatory Notes. *Baluchistan District Gazetteer Series*, Vol. 4, Volume B (bound with Bolan Pass and Nushki Railway District, Vol. 4). Karachi: The Merchantile Steam Press.

McCorriston, Joy and Frank Hole
1991   The ecology of seasonal stress and the origins of agriculture in the Near East. *American Anthropologist*, 93(1): 46-69.

McCown, Donald E.
1942   *The Comparative Stratigraphy of Early Iran*. Chicago: The Oriental Institute of the University of Chicago, Studies in Ancient Oriental Civilization No. 23.

McCown, Donald E.
1946a   A Chalcolithic site in northern Baluchistan: prefatory remarks. *Journal of Near Eastern Studies*, 5(4): 284-91.

McCown, Donald E.
1946b   An examination of the pottery from Niain Buthi, Las Bela. Delhi: Archaeological Survey of India, ms.

McCown, Donald E.
1947   Appendix B, Distribution of Harappa pottery. In, R. E. M. Wheeler, Harappa 1946: the defenses and Cemetery R-37. *Ancient India*, 3: 129-30.

McCown, Donald E. and R. C. Haines
1967   *Nippur I: Temple of Enlil, scribal quarter and soundings*. Chicago: The Oriental Institute of the University of Chicago, Studies in Ancient Oriental Civilization, No. 97.

McCown, Donald E., R. C. Haines and R. D. Biggs.
1978   *Nippur II: The north temple and sounding* E. Chicago: The Oriental Institute of the University of Chicago, Studies in Ancient Oriental Civilization, No. 97.

McCown, Theodore D. and Sir Arthur Keith
1939   *The Stone Age of Mount Carmel*. Vol. II. Oxford: Oxford University Press.

McCrindle, John Watson
1882   *Ancient India as Described by Ktesias the Knidian*. London: Trubner & Co.

McEvilley, Thomas
1981   An archaeology of yoga. *Res*, 1: 44-77.

McKean, Margaret Bernard
  1983   *The Palynology of Balakot, a Preharappan and Harappan Age Site in Las Bela, Pakistan*. PhD Dissertation, Department of Anthropology, Souther Methodost University.

Meadow, Richard H.
  1973   A chronology for the Indo-Iranian borderlands and southern Baluchistan, 4000-2000 B.C. In, D. P. Agrawal and A. Ghosh, eds., *Radiocarbon and Indian Archaeology*. Bombay: Tata Institute of Fundamental Research: 190-204.

Meadow, Richard H.
  1979a   Prehistoric subsistence at Balakot: initial consideration of the faunal remains. In, M. Taddei, ed., *South Asian Archaeology 1977*. Naples: Instituto Universitario Orientale, Seminario di Studi Asiatici, Series Minor 6: 275-315.

Meadow, Richard H.
  1979b   A preliminary report on the faunal remains from Pirak. In, Jean-Francois Jarrige and M. Santoni, *Fouilles de Pirak*. Publications de la Commission des Fouilles Archaeologiques. Fouilles du Pakistan, No. 2, Vol. 1.

Meadow, Richard H.
  1981   Early animal domestication in South Asia: a first report of the faunal remains from Mehrgarh, Pakistan. In, H. Hartel, ed., *South Asian Archaeology 1979*. Berlin: Dietrich Reimer Verlag: 143-79.

Meadow, Richard H.
  1982   From hunting to herding in prehistoric Baluchistan. In, Stephen Pastner and Louis Flam, eds., *Anthropology in Pakistan*. Ithaca: Cornell University SAOPT, No. 8: 145-53.

Meadow, Richard H.
  1984a   Animal domestication in the Middle East: a view from the eastern margin. In, Juliet Clutton-Brock and Caroline Grigson, eds., *Animals and Archaeology: 3. Early Herders and Their Flocks*. Oxford: British Archaeological Reports, S202: 309-37.

Meadow, Richard H.
  1984b   Notes on the faunal remains from Mehrgarh with a focus on cattle (Bos). In, Bridget Allchin, ed., *South Asian Archaeology 1981*. Cambridge: Cambridge University Press: 34-40.

Meadow, Richard H.
  1984c   A camel skeleton from Mohenjo-daro. In, B. B. Lal and S. P. Gupta, eds., *Frontiers of the Indus Civilization*. Delhi: Books and Books: 137-39.

Meadow, Richard H.
  1986   Faunal exploitation in the greater Indus Valley: a review of recent work to 1980. In,

956

J. Jacobson, ed., *Studies in the Archaeology of India and Pakistan*. Delhi: Oxford & IBH and the American Instiitute of Indian Studies: 43-64.

Meadow, Richard H.
1987   Faunal exploitation patterns in eastern Iran and Baluchistan: a review of recent investigations. In, Edenda Curaverunt, G. Gnoli and L. Lanciotti, eds., *Orientalia Josephi Tucci Memoriae Dicata*. Roma: Istituto Italiano per il Medo ed Estremo Oriente, Serie Orientale Roma, 56(2), Vol. 2: 881-916.

Meadow, Richard H.
1988   The faunal remains from Jalilpur, 1971. *Pakistan Archaeology*, 23: 204-220.

Meadow, Richard H.
1989a   Continuity and change in the agriculture of the Greater Indus Valley: the palaeoethnobotanical and zooarchaeological evidence. In, Jonathan Mark Kenoyer, ed., *Old Problems and New Perspectives in the Archaeology of South Asia*. Madison: Wisconsin Archaeological Reports, 2: 61-74.

Meadow, Richard H.
1989b   Prehistoric wild sheep and sheep domestication on the eastern margin of the Middle East. In, P. Crabtree, D. Campana and K. Ryan, eds., *Early Animal Domestication and its Cultural Context*. Philadelphia: MASCA Research Papers in Science and Archaeology, Special Supp. to Vol. 6: 24-36.

Meadow, Richard H., editor
1991a   *Harappa Excavations 1986-1990: A multidisciplinary approach to third millennium urbanism*. Madison: Prehistory Press, Monographs in World Archaeology, 3.

Meadow, Richard H.
1991b   Domestication and exploitation of plants and animals in the Greater Indus Valley. In, M. Jansen, Maire Mulloy and Gunter Urban, eds., *Forgotten Cities on the Indus: Early civilization in Pakistan from the 8th to the 2nd millennium B.C.* Mainz: Verlag Philipp von Zabern: 51-8.

Meadow, Richard H.
1992   Inconclusive remarks on pastoralism, nomadism and other animal-related matters. In, O. Bar-Yosef and A. Khazanov, eds., *Pastoralism in the Levant: Archaeological materials in anthropological perspectives*. Madison: Prehistory Press, Monographs in World Archaeology, 10: 261-69.

Meadow, Richard H.
1993a   Animal domestication in the Middle East: a revised view from the eastern margin. In, Gregory L. Possehl, ed., *Harappan Civilization: A recent perspective*. 2nd ed. Delhi: Oxford & IBH and the American Institute of Indian Studies: 295-320.

Meadow, Richard H.
1993b   Faunal studies. In, G. F. Dales and J. M. Kenoyer, The Harappa Project 1986-89: new

investigations at an ancient Indus city. In, Gregory L. Possehl, ed., *Harappan Civilization: A recent perspective*. 2nd ed. Delhi: Oxford & IBH and the American Institute of Indian Studies: 513-15.

Meadow, Richard H.
1996   The origins and spread of agriculture and pastoralism in northwestern South Asia. In, David R. Harris, ed., *The Origins and Spread of Agriculture and Pastoralism in Eurasia*. London: Institute of Archaeology, University College, London: 390–412.

Meadow, Richard H. and Ajita Patel
1997   A comment on "Horse remains from Surkotada, Kutch, late 3rd millennium BC" by Sandor Bokonyi. *South Asian Studies*, 13:308–15.

Meadow, Richard H. and Hans-Peter Uerpmann, editors
1986   *Equids in the Ancient World*. Wiesbaden: Dr. Lugwig Reichert Verlag.

Meadow, Richard H., J. Mark Kenoyer and Rita Wright.
1996   *Harappa Archaeological Research Project: Harappa excavations* 1996. Cambridge: Peabody Museum, ms.

Meher-Homji, V. M.
1970   Some phytogeographic aspects of Rajasthan, India. *Vegetatio*, 21: 299-30.

Mehra, K. L.
1963   Considerations on the African origin of *Eleusine coracana*(L.). *Current Science*, 32: 300-01.

Mehra, K. L.
1991   Prehistoric Ethiopia and India: contacts through sorghum and miillet genetic resources. In, J. M. M. Engles, J. G. Hawkes and M. Woorede, eds., *Plant Genetic Resources of Ethiopia*. Cambridge: Cambridge University Press: 160-68.

Mehra, K. L. and R. K. Arora
1985   Some considerations on the domestication of plants in India. In, V. N. Misra and Peter Bellwood, eds., *Recent Advances in Indo-Pacific Prehistory*. Delhi: Oxford & IBH: 275-79.

Mehta, R. N.
1965   Mitali: a microlithic site. *Journal of the Oriental Institute, Maharaja Sayajirao University of Baroda*, 15(2): 173-74.

Mehta, R. N.
1967   Stone Age sites in Valia and Mangrol Taluka and Surat Districts. *Journal of the Oriental Institute, Maharaja Sayajirao University of Baroda*, 27(2): 142-48.

Mehta, R. N.
1982   Some rural Harappan settlements in Gujarat. In, Gregory L. Possehl, ed., *Harappan*

958

Civilization: A contemporary perspective. Delhi: Oxford & IBH and the American Institute of Indian Studies: 167-74.

Mehta, R. N.
1984   Valabhi—a station of Harappan cattle breeders. In, B. B. Lal and S. P. Gupta, eds., *Frontiers of the Indus Civilization.* Delhi: Books and Books: 227-30.

Mehta, R. N. and S. N. Chowdhary, K. T. M. Hegde and D. R. Shah
1975   *Excavation at Dhatva.* Baroda: Maharaja Sayajirao University, Archaeology Series, No. 12: 70 pp.

Mehta, R. N., S. N. Chowdhary, K. T. M. Hegde and D. R. Shah
1971   *Excavation at Jokha.* Baroda: Maharaja Sayajirao University, Archaeology Series, No. 11: 81 pp.

Mehta, R. N., K. N. Momin and D. R. Shah
1980   *Excavation at Kanewal.* Baroda: Maharaja Sayajirao University, Archaeology Series, No. 17.

Meissner, Bruno
1910   Akklimatisationsversuche mesopotamischer Fursten. *Mitteilungen ver Vorderasiatisch Gesellschaft,* 15.

Meissner, Bruno
1981   *Akkadesches Handwortenbuch.* 3 Vols. Weisbaden: Otto Harrassovitz.

Mellaart, James
1965   *Earliest Civilizations of the Near East.* London: Thames and Hudson.

Mellaart, James
1975   *The Neolithic of the Near East.* New York: Charles Scribners Sons.

Memnon, M. M.
1963   Manchar Lake: a study of its fishing industry. *Pakistan Geographical Review,* 18(2): 13-24.

Metraux, Alfred
1938a   The proto-Indian script and the Easter Island tablets (a critical study). *Anthropos,* 33: 218-39.

Metraux, Alfred
1938b   Two Easter Island tablets in the Bernice Pauahi Bishop Museum, Honolulu. *Man,* 1: 1-4.

Meyers, J. Thomas
1971   The origins of agriculture: an evaluation of three hypotheses. In, Stuart Struever, ed., *Prehistoric Agriculture.* Garden City: The Natural History Press, American Museum Source Books in Anthropology: 101-21.

Micozzi, M. S.
1991   *Postmortem Changes in Human and Animal Remains: A systematic approach.* Springfield: Charles C. Thomas.

Miller, Joseph
1976   *The Bagaravat/Devnarayan Epic Recitation Texts.* MA Thesis, Department of South Asia Regional Studies, University of Pennsylvania.

Miller, Naomi F.
1984   The use of dung as fuel: an ethnographic example and an archaeological application. *Paleorient,* 10(2): 71-9.

Miller, Naomi F.
1991   The Near East. In, Willem van Zeist, Krystyna Wasylikowa and Karl-Ernst Behre eds., *Progress in Old World Palaeoethnobotany.* Rotterdam: A. A. Balkema: 133-60.

Miller, Naomi F.
1992   The origins of plant cultivation in the Near East. In, C. Wesley Cowan and Patty Jo Watson, eds., *The Origins of Agriculture: An international perspective.* Washington DC: Smithsonian Institution Press: 39-58.

Miller, Naomi F. and Tristine Lee Smart
1984   Intentional Burning of dung as fuel: a mechanism for the incorporation of charred seeds into the archaeological record. *Journal of Ethnobotany,* 4(1): 15-28.

Minchin, C. F.
1907a   *Jhalawan District.* Bombay: Government of India. Baluchistan District Gazetteer Series, Vol. 6B (bound with Sarawan District, Vol. 6 and Kachhi District, Vol. 6B).

Minchin, C. F.
1907b   *Kachhi District.* Bombay: Government of India. Baluchistan District Gazetteer Series, Vol. 6 (bound with Sarawan District, Vol. 6 and Jhalawan District, Vol. 6B).

Minchin, C. F.
1907c   *Kharan District.* Bombay: Government of India. Baluchistan District Gazetteer Series, Vol. 7A (bound with Makran District, Vol. 7).

Minchin, C. F.
1907d   *Las Bela.* Allahabad: Government of India. Baluchistan District Gazetteer Series, Vol. 8.

Minchin, C. F.
1907e   *Loralai District.* Bombay: Government of India. Baluchistan District Gazetteer Series, Vol. 2.

Minchin, C. F.
1907f   *Loralai District: Statistical tables and explanatory notes.* Bombay: Government of India. Baluchistan District Gazetteer Series, Vol. 2B.

960

Minchin, C. F.
1907g   *Sarawan District*. Bombay: Government of India. Baluchistan District Gazetteer Series, Vol. 6 (bound with Kachhi District, Vol. 6A and Jhalawan District, Vol. 6B).

Minchin, C. F.
1907h   *Zhob District*. Bombay: Government of India. Baluchistan District Gazetteer Series, Vol. 1.

Minchin, C. F.
1907i   *Zhob District: Statistical tables and explanatory notes*. Bombay: Government of India. Baluchistan District Gazetteer Series, Vol. 1B.

Minchin, C. F.
1907j   *Marri, Bugti Country*. Allahabad: Government of India. Baluchistan District Gazetteer Series, Vol. 3.

Mirsky, Jeannette
1977   *Sir Aurel Stein: Archaeological explorer*. Chicago: University of Chicago Press.

Misra, P. K.
1975   The Gaudula lohars. In. L. S. Leshink and G. D. Sontheimer, eds., *Pastoralists and Nomads in South Asia*. Wiesbaden: Otto Harrassowitz. Schriftenreihe des Sudasien Instituts der Universitat Heidelberg: 235-46.

Misra, P. K. and K. C. Malhotra, editors
1982   *Nomads in India: Proceedings of the National Seminar*. Calcutta: Anthropological Survey of India.

Misra, Satya Swarup
1992   *The Aryan Problem, a Linguistic Approach*. Delhi: Munshiram Manoharlal.

Misra, V. N.
1967   *Pre- and Proto-History of the Berach Basin South Rajasthan*. Poona: Deccan College Postgraduate and Research Institute.

Misra, V. N.
1970a   Cultural significance of three copper arrow-heads from Rajasthan India. *Journal of Near Eastern studies*, 29(4): 221-31.

Misra, V. N.
1970b   Evidence for a new Chalcolithic culture in south Rajasthan. *The Indian Antiquary*, 3rd Series 4(1-4): 85-95.

Misra, V. N.
1971a   Two late Mesolithic settlements in Rajasthan—a brief review of investigations. *Poona University Journal (Humanities)*, 35: 59-77.

Misra, V. N.
1971b   Two microlithic sites in Rajasthan—a preliminary investigation. *The Eastern Anthropologist*, 24(3): 237-88.

Misra, V. N.
1972   Burials from prehistoric Bagor, Rajasthan. In, S. B. Deo, ed., *Archaeological Congress and Seminar Papers*. Nagpur: Nagpur University: 58-65.

Misra, V. N.
1973a   Bagor: a late Mesolithic settlement in north-west India. *World Archaeology*, 5(1): 92-100.

Misra, V. N.
1973b   A new prehistoric ceramic from Rajasthan. *East and West*, 23(3-4): 295-305.

Misra, V. N.
1973c   Problems of palaeoecology, palaeoclimate and chronology of Mesolithic cultures of north-west India. In, D. P. Agrawal and A. Ghosh, eds., *Radiocarbon and Indian Archaeology*. Bombay: Tata Institute of Fundamental Research: 58-72.

Misra, V. N.
1974   Archaeological and ethnographic evidence for the hafting and use of microliths and related tools. *Puratattva*, 7: 3-12.

Misra, V. N.
1976   A new copper hoard from Madnapur, District Hardoi, Uttar Pradesh. Paper presented at the VIII annual Conference of the Indian Archaeological Society, Jaipur.

Misra, V. N.
1982   Bagor: the archaeological setting. In, John R. Lukacs, V. N. Misra and Kenneth A. R. Kennedy, *The Human Skeletal Remains. Bagor and Tilwara: Late Mesolithic cultures of Northwest India*, Vol. I. Pune: Deccan College Postgraduate and Research Institute: 9-20.

Misra, V. N.
1984   Climate, a factor in the rise and fall of the Indus Civilization—evidence from Rajasthan and beyond. In, B. B. Lal and S. P. Gupta, eds., *Frontiers of the Indus Civilization*. Delhi: Books and Books: 461-89.

Mitchiner, John E.
1978   *Studies in the Indus Valley Inscriptions*. Delhi: Oxford & IBH: 66 pp.

Mockler, E., Major
1877   On ruins in Makran. *Journal of the Royal Asiatic Society of Great Britain and Ireland*, 9: 121-34.

Mohan, Vijneshu
1988   *The Harappan Civilization: A study in variation and regionalism in Haryana, India.*
        MS Thesis, Faculty of Oriental Studies, Cambridge University.

Mohapatra, G. C.
1964   Prehistory. In, N. K. Sahu, ed., *Utkal University History of Orissa.* Vol. 1,
        Bhubaneswar: Utkal University: 1-54.

Momin, K. N.
1971   2 Chalcolithic settlements in Bhalbara. *Journal of the Maharaja Sayajirao University
        of Baroda,* 22-23: 51-6.

Momin, K. N.
1976   Chalcolithic settlements in Bhalbara Taluka, Cambay, Gujarat. In, Udai Vir Singh,
        ed., *Archaeological Congress and Seminar: 1972.* Kurukshetra: B.N. Chakravarty
        University Kurukshetra: 51-54.

Momin, K. N.
1979   *Archaeology of Kheda District (Gujarat) up to 1500 A.D..* PhD Dissertation,
        Department of Archaeology and Ancient Indian History and Culture, Maharaja
        Sayajirao University of Baroda.

Momin, K. N.
1980   Loliyana: an important archaeological site. *Journal of the Maharaja Sayajirao
        University of Baroda,* 29(1):: 59-64.

Momin, K. N.
1982   Excavations at Kanewal. In, R. K. Sharma, ed., *Indian Archaeology: New perspectives.*
        Delhi: Agam Kala Prakashan: 142-47.

Momin, K. N.
1984   Village Harappans in Kheda District of Gujarat. In, B. B. Lal and S. P. Gupta, eds.,
        Frontiers of the Indus Civilization. Delhi: Books and Books: 231-34.

Moneer, Q. M.
1930-34 Mr. Moneer's work during 1933-34. *Annual Reports of the Archaeological Survey of
        India for the Years 1930-31, 1931-32, 1932-33 & 1933-34,* Part One: 72.

Moneer, Q. M.
1936-37 Conservation, Bombay Presidency and Sind. *Annual Report of the Archaeological
        Survey of India, 1936-37:* 16-22.

Moore, A. M. T.
1989   The transition from foraging to farming in Southwest Asia: present problems and
        future directions. In, David R. Harris and G. C. Hillman, eds., *Foraging and Farming:*

The evolution of plant exploitation. London: Unwin Hyman. One World Archaeology, 13: 620-32.

Mortensen, Peder
1972   Seasonal camps and early villages in the Zagros. In, Peter J. Ucko, Ruth Tringham and G. W. Dimbelby eds., *Man Settlement and Urbanism*. London: Gerald Duckworth & Co.: 293-97.

Mughal, M. Rafique
1968a   Excavations: Harappa, 1966 (Cemetery R-37). *Pakistan Archaeology*, 5: 63-8.

Mughal, M. Rafique
1968b   *The Pre-Harappan religious motifs*. M. A. Paper, Department of South Asia Regional Studies, University of Pennsylvania.

Mughal, M. Rafique
1970   *The Early Harappan Period in the Greater Indus Valley and Baluchistan*. PhD Dissertation, Department of Anthropology, University of Pennsylvania.

Mughal, M. Rafique
1972a   A summary of excavations and explorations in Pakistan. *Pakistan Archaeology*, 8: 113-58.

Mughal, M. Rafique
1972b   Excavation at Jalilpur. *Pakistan Archaeology*, 8: 117-24.

Mughal, M. Rafique
1972c   Excavation at Zarif Karuna. *Pakistan Archaeology*, 8: 125-26.

Mughal, M. Rafique
1972d   Excavations at Sarai Khola. *Pakistan Archaeology*, 8: 113-17.

Mughal, M. Rafique
1972e   Exploration in central Punjab: Sahiwal District. *Pakistan Archaeology*, 8: 127-31.

Mughal, M. Rafique
1972f   Exploration in northern Punjab: Campbellpur and Rawalpindi Districts. *Pakistan Archaeology*, 8: 131-32.

Mughal, M. Rafique
1972g   Explorations in northern Baluchistan. *Pakistan Archaeology*, 8: 137-50.

Mughal, M. Rafique
1972h   Explorations in southern Sind. *Pakistan Archaeology*, 8: 133-37.

Mughal, M. Rafique
1972i   Introduction to the pottery of Periods I and II of Sarai Khola. In, M. Abdul Halim, Excavations at Sarai Khola, Part II. *Pakistan Archaeology*, 8: 34-39.

964

Mughal, M. Rafique
1972j   The Sarai Khola pottery types of the early Periods I and II. In, M. Abdul Halim,
         Excavations at Sarai Khola, Part II. *Pakistan Archaeology*, 8: 40-76.

Mughal, M. Rafique
1973   *Present state of research on the Indus Valley Civilization.* Karachi: Department of
         Archaeology.

Mughal, M. Rafique
1974a   Explorations in northern Baluchistan, 1972: new evidence and fresh interpretation.
         In, Firoz Bagherzadeh, ed., *Proceedings of the Annual Symposium on Archaeological
         Research in Iran.* Tehran: Iranian Centre for Archaeological Research: 276-86.

Mughal, M. Rafique
1974b   New evidence of Early Harappan Culture from Jalilpur, Pakistan. *Archaeology*, 27(2):
         106-13.

Mughal, M. Rafique
1975   Present state of research on the Indus Valley Civilization. In, Ahmad Nabi Khan ed.,
         Proceedings of International Symposium on Moenjodaro, 1973. Karachi: National
         Book Foundation: 37-57.

Mughal, M. Rafique
1977   Cultural links between Pakistan and Iran during the prehistoric period (5000-1000
         BC). *Iran and Pakistan: A Common Culture.* Islamabad.

Mughal, M. Rafique
1980a   New archaeological evidence from Bahawalpur. *Man and Environment*, 4: 93-8.

Mughal, M. Rafique
1980b   The Early Harappan cultural phase: a reply. *Puratattva*, 9: 84-8.

Mughal, M. Rafique
1980c   The origins of the Indus Civilization. *Sindhological Studies*, 1(1), Summer: 5-14.

Mughal, M. Rafique
1981   New archaeological evidence from Bahawalpur. In, Ahmad Hasan Dani, ed., *Indus
         Civilization: New perspectives.* Islamabad: Quaid-i-Azam University: 33-41.

Mughal, M. Rafique
1982   Recent archaeological research in the Cholistan desert. In, Gregory L. Possehl, ed.,
         Harappan Civilization: A contemporary perspective. Delhi: Oxford & IBH and the
         American Institute of Indian Studies: 85-95.

Mughal, M. Rafique
1983   Current research trends on the rise of the Indus Civilization. In, G. Urban and M.
         Jansen, eds., *Forschungsprojekt DFG Mohenjodaro.* Aachen: Veroffentlichung des

Geogatischen Instituts der Reinisch-Westfalischen Technischen Hochschule, Nr. 34: 13-20.

Mughal, M. Rafique
1984   The Post-Harappan Phase in Bahawalpur distt., Pakistan. In, B. B. Lal and S. P. Gupta, eds., *Frontiers of the Indus Civilization*. Delhi: Books and Books: 499-503.

Mughal, M. Rafique
1985   The significance of some Pre- and Protohistoric discoveries in the Karakorum area. *Journal of Central Asia*, 8(2): 213-35.

Mughal, M. Rafique
1988   Genesis of the Indus Valley Civilization. *Lahore Museum Journal*, 1: 45-54.

Mughal, M. Rafique
1989   The development of Protohistoric research in Pakistan: 1970-85. *Journal of Central Asia*, 12(1): 47-77.

Mughal, M. Rafique
1990a   Further evidence of the Early Harappan Culture in the Greater Indus Valley: 1971-90. *South Asian Studies*, 6: 175-200.

Mughal, M. Rafique
1990b   The Harappan settlement systems and patterns in the Greater Indus Valley. *Pakistan Archaeology*, 25: 1-72.

Mughal, M. Rafique
1990c   The protohistoric settlement patterns in the Cholistan Desert. In, Maurizio Taddei, ed., *South Asian Archaeology 1987*. Roma: Instituto Italiano per il Medio ed Estremo Oriente, Serie Orientale Roma, 66(1): 143-56.

Mughal, M. Rafique
1990d   The Harappan "twin capitals" and reality. *Journal of Central Asia*, 13(1): 155-62.

Mughal, M. Rafique
1991a   Cultural patterns of ancient Pakistan and neighboring regions circa 7000-1500 BC. *Pakistan Archaeology*, 26(1): 218-37.

Mughal, M. Rafique
1991b   The rise of the Indus Civilization. In, Michael Jansen, Maire Mulloy and Gunter Urban, eds., *Forgotten Cities on the Indus: Early civilization in Pakistan from the 8th to the 2nd millennium B.C.* Mainz: Verlag Philipp von Zabern: 104-10.

Mughal, M. Rafique
1992a   Jhukar and the Late Harappan cultural mosaic of the Greater Indus Valley. In, Catherine Jarrige, ed., *South Asian Archaeology 1989*. Madison: Prehistory Press, Monographs in World Archaeology, 14: 213-22.

Mughal, M. Rafique
1992b   The consequences of river changes for the Harappan settlements in Cholistan. *The Eastern Anthropologist*, 45(1-2): 105-16.

Mughal, M. Rafique
1992c   The geographical extent of the Indus Civilization during the Early, Mature and Late Harappan times. In, Gregory L. Possehl, ed., *South Asian Archaeology Studies*. Delhi: Oxford & IBH: 123-43.

Mughal, M. Rafique
1994   The Harappan nomads of Cholistan. In, Bridget Allchin, ed., *Living Traditions: Studies in the ethnoarchaeology of South Asia*. Delhi: Oxford & IBH: 53-68.

Mughal, M. Rafique
1995   A preliminary review of archaeological surveys in Punjab and Sindh: 1993-95. Draft statement circulated at the 13th South Asian Archaeology Conference, Cambridge, England, July 2-7, 1995.

Mughal, M. Rafique
1997   *Ancient Cholistan: Archaeology and architecture*. Lahore: Ferozsons.

Muhly, James D.
1973   *Copper and Tin*. Hamden Connecticut: Archon Books.

Mukharjee, G. N.
1935   Prehistoric copper celts. *Indian Historical Quarterly*, 11: 517-28.

Mukherjee, Rathin and Kalidas Saha
1988   Record of guar (*Bos gaurus*, H. Smith) from the prehistoric site at Kalibangan, Rajasthan, India. *Science and Culture*, 54(9).

Mukherji, S. N.
1968   *Sir William Jones*. Cambridge: Cambridge University Press.

Munn, L.
1934   Economics, dealing especially with the ancient gold mining activity in the area. *Journal of the Hyderabad Geological Survey*, 2: 77-104.

Munn, L.
1936   Observations and notes on the methods of ancient gold mining in southern India. *Transactions of the Mining and Geological Institute of India*, 30: 103-16.

Murray, James A.
1884   *The Vertebrate Zoology of Sind: A systematic account*. New York: Richardson and Company.

Murton, Brian J.
1987   Monsoons in agricultural proverbs in Tamilnadu. In, Jay S. Fein and Pamela L. Stephens, eds., *Monsoons*. New York: John Wiley and Sons: 77-102.

Murty, Y. G. K, G. R. Kulkarni and S. K. Gupta
1969   Interim report on the rate of silting in the Rann of Kutch and Quaternary movements of Saurashtra coast line. Geological Survey of India, Unpublished manuscript.

Nag, Arun K. and Dilip K. Chakrabarti
1980   "Copper hoards" from west Bengal. *Puratattva*, 9: 97-100.

Nanavati, J. M., R. N. Mehta and S. N. Chowdhary
1971   *Somnath—1956*. Department of Archaeology, Gujarat State and Department of Archaeology and Ancient History, Maharaja Sayajirao University, Monograph No. 1.

Nanda, Rajni
1992   *The History of Gold in India*. Delhi: Munshiram Manoharlal.

Napier, Priscilla
1990   *I Have Sind: Charles Napier in India, 1841-1844*. London: Michael Russell.

Naseem, Mohammad
1982   *The Neolithic Cultures of North Western Indo-Pakistan Sub-Continent*. Delhi: Ramanand Vidya Bhavan.

Nash, Manning
1966   *Primitive and Peasant Economic Systems*. Scranton: Chandler Publishing Co.

Nath, Shankar
1982   Pre-Harappan pottery from Distt. Saharanpur, U.P. *Puratattva*, 11: 122-23.

Nazim, M., Dr.
1934-35 Exploration in the Northern Circle: Harappa. *Annual Report of the Archaeological Survey of India, 1934-35*: 31-3.

Nearchus
1875   The lost river of the Indian Desert. *Calcutta Review*, 60: 323-51.

Netting, Robert McC.
1971   *The Ecological Approach in Cultural Study*. Reading: Addison-Wesley, McCaleb Modile in Anthropology.

Nisbet, Renato
1985   Evidence for sorghum at site RH5, Qurm, Muscat. *East and West*, 35(4): 415-17.

Nissen, Hans J.
1983   Report on the preliminary archaeological reconnaissance of the area of north western Sind (between Lake Manchar and Sukkur). Berlin: Free University of Berlin (photocopied).

968

Nissen, Hans J.
1994   An archaeological surface survey in northwestern Sindh, Pakistan. In, J. M. Kenoyer, ed., *From Sumer to Meluhha: Contributions to the archaeology of South and West Asia in memory of George F. Dales, Jr.* Madison: Wisconsin Archaeological Reports 3: 51-8.

Noetling, Fritz W.
1898a   Uber eine prahistorische neiderlassung im oberen Zhob-thal in Baluchistan. *Zeitschrift Fur Ethnologie: Berliner Gesellschaft fur Anthropologie Ethnologie und Urgeschichte,* 30: 460-71.

Noetling, Fritz W.
1898b   Reise nach Baluchistan. *Zeitschrift Fur Ethnologie: Berliner Gesellschaft fur Anthropologie Ethnologie und Urgeschichte,* 30: 250-51.

Noetling, Fritz W.
1899   Uber eine prahistorische neiderlassungen in Baluchistan. *Zeitschrift Fur Ethnologie: Berliner Gesellschaft fur Anthropologie Ethnologie und Urgeschichte,* 31: 100-10.

O'Flaherty, Wendy D.
1970   In defense of Sir John Marshall. *Journal of Tamil Studies,* 2(1): 277-85.

O'Flaherty, Wendy Doniger
1981   *The Rig Veda: An anthology.* Baltimore: Penguin Books.

Oldham, C. E. A. W.
1944   Sir Aurel Stein, 1862-1943. *Proceedings of the British Academy,* 29:19.

Oldham, C. F.
1874   Notes on the Lost River of the Indian desert. *Calcutta Review,* 59: 1-27.

Oldham, C. F.
1893   The Sarasvati and the Lost River of the Indian desert. *Journal of the Royal Asiatic Society of Great Britain and Ireland,* 25: 49-76.

Oldham, R. D.
1887   On probable changes in the geography of the Punjab and its rivers; a historico-geographical study. *Journal of the Asiatic Society of Bengal,* 55: 322-43.

Oldham, R. D.
1926   The Cutch (Kachh) earthquake of 16th June 1819 with a revision of the great earthquake of 12 June 1897. *Memoir of the Geological Survey of India,* 46(2): 71-147.

Olmstead, A. T.
1948   *History of the Persian Empire.* Chicago: University of Chicago Press.

Olszewski, D. I.
1988   The North Syrian Epipaleolithic and its relationship to the Natufian complex. *Levant*, 20: 127-37.

Oppenheim, A. Leo
1964   *Mesopotamia: Portrait of a Dead Civilization*. Chicago: University of Chicago Press.

Pakistan Census of Agriculture 1960
1963   Data by Districts: By Detailed Size Classification. Karachi: Agricultural Census Organization, Ministry of Agriculture and Works, West Pakistan Report I, Vol. 2.

Pal, Yash, Baldev Sahni, R. K. Sood and D. P. Agrawal
1980   Remote sensing of the 'lost' Sarasvati River. *Proceedings of the Indian Academy of Sciences* (Earth and Planetary Sciences), 89(3): 317-31.

Pande, B. M.
1970   The Neolithic in Kashmir: new discoveries. *The Anthropologist*, 17(1-2): 25-41.

Pande, B. M.
1972   A Neolithic "tectiform" from Burzahom, District Srinagar, Kashmir. *Journal of the Indian Anthropological Society*, 7(2): 175-77.

Pande, B. M.
1973   Neolithic hunting scene on a stone slab from Burzahom, Kashmir. *Asian Perspectives*, 14: 134-38.

Pande, B. M.
1977   Archaeological remains along the ancient Sarasvati. In, D. P. Agrawal and B. M. Pande, eds., *Ecology and Archaeology of Western India*. Delhi: Concept Publishing: 55-60.

Pande, B. M.
1982   History of research on the Harappan culture. In, Gregory L. Possehl, ed., *Harappan Civilization: A contemporary perspective*. Delhi: Oxford & IBH and the American Institute of Indian studies: 395-403.

Pande, B. M. and K. S. Ramachandran
1971   *Bibliography of the Harappan Culture*. Coconut Grove: Field Research Projects.

Pandya, P. P.
1954   Explorations in Halar and Sorath Districts, Saurashtra. *Journal of the Maharaja Sayajirao University of Baroda*, 3(2): 1-12.

Pandya, Suman
1981   *Sarasvati Floods: Causes, consequences, solutions*. Ahmedabad: Suman Pandya (in Gujarati).

970

Pandya, Suman
1982   *The End of Lothal*. Ahmedabad: Suman Pandya (in Gujarati).

Pandya, Suman
1987   Protohistoric floods at Lothal: a critical study. In, B. M. Pande and B. D. Chattopadhyaya, eds., *Archaeology and History: Essays in memory of Sh. A. Ghosh*. 2 Vols. Delhi: Agam Kala Prakashan: 177-186.

Pandya, Suman
1991   *More About Lothal*. Ahmedabad: Jasu H. Pandya for Pandya Brothers.

Panigrahi, K. C.
1946   The pottery types: the pottery of Ahichchhatra. *Ancient India*, 1: 40-55.

Pant, R. K.
1979   Microwear studies on Burzahom Neolithic tools. *Man and Environment*, 3: 11-7.

Parikh, R. T.
1978   *Archaeology of Banaskantha District (North Gujarat) up to 1500 A.D*. PhD Dissertation, Department of Archaeology and Ancient Indian History, Maharaja Sayajirao University of Baroda.

Parmar, B. M. S.
1977   A copper hoard from Nandlalpura, District Jaipur, Rajasthan. *Man and Environment*, 1: 63-4.

Parpola, Asko
1984a   Interpreting the Indus script, I. In, B. B. Lal and S. P. Gupta, eds., *Frontiers of the Indus Civilization*. Delhi: Books and Books: 179-91.

Parpola, Asko
1984b   New correspondences between Harappan and Near Eastern glyptic art. In, Bridget Allchin, ed., *South Asian Archaeology 1981*. Cambridge: Cambridge University Press: 176-95.

Parpola, Asko
1985   The Sky-Garment: a study of the Harappan religion and its relation to the Mesopotamian and later India religion. *Studia Orientalia*, 57: 8-216.

Parpola, Asko
1986   The Indus Script: a challenging puzzle. *World Archaeology*, 17(3): 399-419.

Parpola, Asko
1994   *Deciphering the Indus Script*. Cambridge: Cambridge University Press.

Parpola, Asko
1995   The problem of Aryans and the Soma: textual-linguistic and archaeological evidence.

In, George Erdosy, ed., *The Indo-Aryans of Ancient South Asia: Language, material culture and ethnicity*. Berlin: Walter de Gruyter: 353-81.

Parry, M. and A. B. Lord
1954   *Serbocroatin Heroic Songs I*. Cambridge: Harvard University Press.

Pascoe, Sir Edwin
1931   Minerals and metals. In, Sir John Marshall, ed., *Mohenjo-daro and the Indus Civilization*, 3 Vols. London: Arthur Probsthain: 674-85.

Patel, Ajita
1987   Map of sites in the Rupen River estuary. Manuscript.

Patel, P. P.
1993   Seismicity and geomorphology of Kachchh with reference to envrionmental implications. Deccan College, Pune. Background Papers for the Field Workshop on Palaeoseismicity in the Epicentral Zone of 1819 Kutch Earthquake, March 10-13, 1993.

Payne, Sebastian
1968   The origins of domestic sheep and goats: a reconsideration in light of fossil evidence. *Proceedings of the Prehistoric Society*, 34: 368-84

Peake, R. H.
1928   The copper mountain of Magan. *Antiquity*, 2: 452-54.

Pedde, Friedhelm
1993a   *Keramik Aus Nor-Baluchistan: Sie Sammlungen Noetling und Henckmann im Museen fur Indische Kunst, Staatliche Museen zu Berlin, Preussischer Kulturbesitz*. Berlin, Verlag von Dietrich Reimer. Deutsches Archaologisches Institut Abteilung Tehran, Materialien zur Iranischen Archaologie, Band 1.

Pedde, Friedhelm
1993b   Pottery from northern Baluchistan—the Noetling Collection in the Museum of Indian Art, Berlin. In, Adalbert J. Gail and Gerd J. R. Mevissen, eds., *South Asian Archaeology 1991*. Stuttgart: Franz Steiner Verlag: 215-30.

Pehrson, Robert N.
1966   *The Social Organization of the Marri Baluch*. Compiled by Fredrik Barth. New York: Wenner-Gren Foundation for Anthropological Research. Viking Fund Publications in Anthropology.

Pels, Simon
1964   The present and ancestral Murray River system. *Australian Geographical Studies*, 2: 111-19.

Pendall, Elise and Ronald Amundson
1990a   Soil/landform relationships surrounding the Harappa archaeological site, Pakistan. *Geoarchaeology*, 5(4): 301-22.

972

Pendall, Elise and Ronald Amundson
1990b   The stable isotope chemistry of pedogenic carbonate in an alluvial soil from the Punjab, Pakistan. *Soil Science*, 149(4): 199-211

Pendall, Elise and Ronald Amundson
1993   Soil survey. In, George F. Dales and J. Mark Kenoyer, The Harappa Project 1986-89: new investigations at an ancient Indus city. In, Gregory L. Possehl, ed., *Harappan Civilization: A recent perspective*. 2nd ed. Delhi: Oxford & IBH and the American Institute of Indian Studies: 515-17.

Perkins, Dexter
1964   Prehistoric fauna from Shanidar, Iraq. *Science*, 144: 1565-66.

Perkins, Dexter
1972   The fauna from the Aq Kupruk Caves: a brief note. In, Louis Dupree, *Prehistoric Research in Afghanistan (1959-1966)*. Philadelphia: Transactions of the American Philosophical Society, 62(4): 73.

Perrot, Jean
1968   *La Prehistoire Palestinienne*. Paris: Letouzey et Ane. Supplement au Dictionnaire de la Bible, VIII.

Phillips, L. L.
1976   Cotton. In, N. W. Simmonds, ed., *Evolution of Crop Plants*. London: Longman: 196-200.

Phogat, Silak Ram
1970   Archaeological remains at Kalayat. *Kurukshetra University Research Journal* (Arts and Humanities), 4 (1-2): 137-40.

Piddocke, Stuart
1965   The potlatch system of the southern Kwakiutl: a new perspective. *Southwestern Journal of Anthropology*, 21: 244-64.

Piggott, Stuart
1944   Prehistoric copper hoards in the Ganges Basin. *Antiquity*, 18(72): 173-82.

Piggott, Stuart
1947   A new prehistoric ceramic from Baluchistan. *Ancient India*, 3: 131-42.

Piggott, Stuart
1950   *Prehistoric India to 1000 B.C.* Baltimore: Penguin Books.

Pilleri, Giorgio
1980   *The Secrets of the Blind Dolphins*. Karachi: Sind Wildlife Management Board.

Piperno, Marcello and Maurizio Tosi
1973   Lithic technology behind the ancient lapis lazuli trade. *Expedition*, 16: 15-23.

Pithawala, Maneck B.
1952   *The Problem of Baluchistan: Development and conservation of water resources, soils and natural vegetation.* Karachi: Ministry of Economic Affairs.

Pithawala, Maneck B.
1959   *A Physical and Economic Geography of Sind (The Lower Indus Basin).* Karachi: Sindhi Adabi Board.

Pithawala, Maneck B. and Khan M. Shamshad
1953   *The Climate of Karachi and How to Live in It.* Karachi: Maneck B. Pithawala and Khan M. Shamshad.

Pogue, J. E.
1915   Turquoise. *Memoirs of the National Academy of Science,* 12(2): 1-154.

Poliakov, Leon
1977   *The Aryan Myth: A history of racist and nationalist ideas in Europe.* New York: New American Library.

Possehl, Gregory L.
1967   The Mohenjo daro floods: a reply. *American Anthropologist,* 69(1): 32-40.

Possehl, Gregory L.
1974   *Variation and Change in the Indus Civilization: A study of prehistoric Gujarat with special reference to the Post-urban Harappan.* PhD Dissertation, Department of Anthropology, University of Chicago.

Possehl, Gregory L.
1975   The chronology of gabarbands and palas in western South Asia. *Expedition,* 17(2): 33-37.

Possehl, Gregory L.
1976   Lothal: a gateway settlement of the Harappan Civilization. In, Kenneth A. R. Kennedy and Gregory L. Possehl, eds., *Ecological Backgrounds of South Asian Prehistory.* Ithaca: Cornell University South Asia Program, Occasional Papers and Theses, No. 4: 118-31.

Possehl, Gregory L.
1977   The end of a state and the continuity of a tradition. In, Richard Fox, ed., *Realm and Region in Traditional India.* Durham: Carolina Academic Press: 234-54.

Possehl, Gregory L., editor
1979a   *Ancient Cities of the Indus.* Durham: Carolina Academic Press.

Possehl, Gregory L.
1979b   An extensive bibliography of the Indus Civilization, including references cited in the text. In, Gregory L. Possehl, ed., *Ancient Cities of the Indus.* Durham: Carolina Academic Press: 363-422.

974

Possehl, Gregory L.
1979c   Pastoral nomadism in the Indus Civilization: an hypothesis. In, M. Taddei, ed., *South Asian Archaeology 1977*. Naples: Instituto Universitario Orientale, Seminario di Studi Asiatici, Series Minor 6: 537-51.

Possehl, Gregory L.
1980   *Indus Civilization in Saurashtra*. Delhi: B. R. Publishing Corporation.

Possehl, Gregory L., editor
1982a   *Harappan Civilization: A contemporary perspective*. Delhi: Oxford & IBH and the American Institute of Indian Studies.

Possehl, Gregory L.
1982b   The Harappan Civilization: a contemporary perspective. In, Gregory L. Possehl, ed., *Harappan Civilization: A contemporary perspective*. Delhi: Oxford & IBH and the American Institute of Indian Studies: 15-28.

Possehl, Gregory L.
1982c   Discovering ancient India's earliest cities: the first phase of research. In, Gregory L. Possehl, ed., *Harappan Civilization: A contemporary perspective*. Delhi: Oxford & IBH and the American Institute of Indian Studies: 405-13.

Possehl, Gregory L.
1982d   Cambay bead making: an ancient craft in modern India. *Expedition*, 23(4): 39-46.

Possehl, Gregory L.
1984   A note on Harappan settlement patterns in the Punjab. In, Kenneth A. R. Kennedy and Gregory L. Possehl, eds., *Studies in the Archaeology and Palaeoanthropology of South Asia*. Delhi: Oxford & IBH and the American Institute of Indian Studies: 83-87.

Possehl, Gregory L.
1986a   *Kulli: An exploration of ancient civilization in South Asia*. Durham: Carolina Academic Press.

Possehl, Gregory L.
1986b   African millets in South Asian prehistory. In, Jerome Jacobson, ed., *Studies in the Archaeology of India and Pakistan*. Delhi: Oxford & IBH and the American Institute of Indian Studies: 237-56.

Possehl, Gregory L.
1988   Radiocarbon dates from South Asia. *Man and Environment*, 12: 169-96.

Possehl, Gregory L.
1989   *Radiocarbon Dates for South Asian Archaeology*. Philadelphia: The University Museum, An Occasional Publication of the Asian Section.

Possehl, Gregory L.
1990a   An archaeological adventurer in Afghanistan: Charles Masson. *South Asian Studies*, 6: 111-24.

Possehl, Gregory L.
1990b   Revolution in the urban revolution: the emergence of Indus urbanization. *Annual Review of Anthropology*, 19: 261-82.

Possehl, Gregory L.
1990c   Some further thoughts on unicorns. In, C. P. Sinha, ed., *Archaeology and Art: Krishna Deva felicitation volume*. 2 Vols. Delhi: Ramanand Vidya Bhavan: 44-8.

Possehl, Gregory L.
1991   A short history of archaeological discovery at Harappa. In, Richard H. Meadow, ed., *Harappa Excavations 1986-1990: A Multidisciplinary Approach to Third Millennium Urbanization*. Madison: Prehistory Press, Monographs in World Archaeology, 3: 5-11.

Possehl, Gregory L.
1992a   The Harappan cultural mosaic: ecology revisited. In, Catherine Jarrige, ed., *South Asian Archaeology 1989*. Madison: Prehistory Press, Monographs in World Archaeology, 14: 237-44.

Possehl, Gregory L.
1992b   The Harappan Civilization in Gujarat: The Sorath and Sindhi Harappans. *The Eastern Anthropologist*, 45(1-2): 117-54.

Possehl, Gregory L.
1993a   Sir Leonard Woolley evaluates Indian archaeology. *Harappan Studies*, 1: 1-56.

Possehl, Gregory L.
1993b   The date of Indus urbanization: a proposed chronology for the Pre-urban and Urban Harappan Phases. In, Adalbert J. Gail and Gerd J. R. Mevissen, eds., *South Asian Archaeology 1991*. Stuttgart: Franz Steiner Verlag: 231-49.

Possehl, Gregory L., editor
1993c   *Harappan Civilization: A recent perspective*. 2nd revised edition. Delhi: Oxford & IBH and the American Institute of Indian Studies.

Possehl, Gregory L.
1994   Govindbhai-no vadi: A modern farmer's garden in Gujarat and its ethnoarchaeological significance. In, Bridget Allchin, ed., *Living Traditions: Studies in the ethnoarchaeology of South Asia*. Delhi: Oxford & IBH: 193-204.

Possehl, Gregory L.
1996a   *Indus Age: The writing system*. Delhi: Oxford & IBH and Philadelphia: University of Pennsylvania Press.

Possehl, Gregory L.
1996b   The date of the Nal cemetery. In, C. Margabandhu and K. S. Ramachandran, eds., *Spectrum of Indian Culture (Professor S. B. Deo felicitation volume)*. 2 Vols. Delhi: Agam Kala Prakashan: 67-76.

Possehl, Gregory L.
1996c   Meluhha. In, Julian E. Reade, ed., *The Indian Ocean in Antiquity*. London: Kegan Paul International in Association with the British Museum: 133-208.

Possehl, Gregory L.
in press a Prehistoric plant exchanges between Africa and the Indian Subcontinent. In, David Harris, ed., *Prehistoric Plant Exchanges*. London: The Lineaean Society.

Possehl, Gregory L.
in press b Seafaring Merchants of Meluhha. In, Bridget Allchin, ed., *South Asian Archaeology 1995*. Delhi: Oxford and IBH.

Possehl, Gregory L.
in press c The date of the Surkotada cemetery: A reassessment in light of recent archaeological work in Gujarat. In, Jagat Pati Joshi, ed., *The B. B. Lal felicitation volume*. Delhi.

Possehl, Gregory L. and Dinker P. Mehta
1994   Excavations at Rojdi 1992-93. In, Asko Parpola and Petteri Koskikallio, eds., *South Asian Archaeology 1993*. 2 Vols. Helsinki: Annales Academiae Scientiarum Fennicae, Series B, Volume 271: 603-14.

Possehl, Gregory L. and Kenneth A. R. Kennedy
1979   Hunter-gatherer/agriculturalist exchange in prehistory: an Indian example. *Current Anthropology*, 20(3): 592-93.

Possehl, Gregory L. and M. H. Raval
1989   *Harappan Civilization and Rojdi*. Delhi: Oxford & IBH and the American Institute of Indian Studies.

Possehl, Gregory L. and Paul C. Rissman
1992   The chronology of prehistoric India: from earliest times to the Iron Age. In, Robert Ehrich, ed., *Chronologies in Old World Archaeology*, 3rd ed. 2 Vols. Chicago: University of Chicago Press: 465-90 & 447-74.

Possehl, Gregory L., Y. M. Chitalwala, Paul C. Rissman, Gail E. Wagner, Pamela Crabtree and Julia Longenecker
1985   Preliminary report on the second season of excavations at Rojdi: 1983-84. *Man and Environment*, 9: 80-100.

Possehl, Gregory L., Y. M. Chitalwala, Paul C. Rissman and Gail E. Wagner
1984   Excavations at Rojdi: 1982-83. *Puratattva*, 13-14: 155-63.

Postans, T. and R. C. Knight
1844   Reports and the Manchur Lake and Aral and Narra Rivers. *Journal of the Royal Asiatic Society*, 8: 381-89.

Potts, Daniel T.
1983   *Dilmun: New studies in the archaeology and early history of Bahrain.* Berlin: Dietrich Reimer Verlag.

Potts, Daniel T.
1990   *The Arabian Gulf in Antiquity.* 2 Vols. Oxford: Clarendon Press.

Potts, Daniel T.
1993   The late Prehistoric, Protohistoric and Early Historic Periods in eastern Arabia (ca. 5000-1200 B. C.). *Journal of World Prehistory*, 7(2): 163-212.

Pough, Frederick H.
1976   *A Field Guide to Rocks and Minerals.* 4th ed. Boston: Houghton Mifflin.

Poulain-Josien, Therese
1964   Etude de la faune. In, Jean-Marie Casal, *Fouilles d'Amri*, 2 Vols. Paris: Publications de la Commission des Fouilles Archaeologiques, Fouilles du Pakistan: 164-69.

Pran Nath
1932   The scripts on the Indus valley seals, II. *The Indian Historical Quarterly*, 8, supplement: 1-32.

Pran Nath
1986   *The Scripts on the Indus Valley Seals: With an appendix containing extracts from the Sumerian and Indian literature throwing light upon the words occurring in the inscriptions of the Indus Valley, Elam and Crete.* Varanasi: Indological Book House, reprint.

Prashad, Baini
1934   Animal remains. In, N. G. Majumdar, *Explorations in Sind.* Memoirs of the Archaeological Survey of India, No. 48: 155-57.

Prashad, Baini
1936   *Animal Remains from Harappa.* Memoirs of the Archaeological Survey of India, 51.

Prater, S. H.
1971   *The Book of Indian Mammals.* 3rd edition. Bombay: Oxford University Press and the Bombay Natural History Society.

Price, T. Douglas and Anne Birgitte Gebauer
1995   *Last Hunters, First Farmers: New perspectives on the transition to agriculture.* Santa Fe: School of American Research.

978

Prickett, Martha
1986   *Man, Land and Water: Settlement distribution and the development of irrigation agriculture in the upper Rud-i Gusk drainage, Southeastern Iran*. PhD Dissertation, Department of Anthropology, Harvard University.

Prufer, Olaf H.
1952   *Nalagarh 1951: Interim report on the excavations carried out at Dher Majra*. Calcutta: Jamia Millia Islamia Historical Research Foundation.

Prufer, Olaf H.
1956   The prehistory of the Sisra valley, Punjab, India. *Quartar*, 7-8: 91-123, 120-21 (German summary).

Pugh, Judy F.
1983   Into the almanac: time, meaning and action in North Indian society. *Contributions to Indian Sociology*, NS 17(1): 27-49.

Punekar, S. M.
1984   *Mohenjodaro Seals: Read and identified*. Delhi: Caxton Publications.

Puri, B. M.
1981   D. R. Bhandarkar and Indian historigraphy. *Indian History Congress: Proceedings of the forty-second session*, 35-41.

Puri, Kidar Nath
1936-37 Excavations at Mohenjo-daro. *Annual Report of the Archaeological Survey of India, 1936-37*: 41.

Purnia, D. S.
1976   *Archaeology of Gurgaon and Mahendragadh Districts (Haryana)*. PhD Dissertation, Department of Ancient Indian History, Culture and Archaeology, Kurukshetra University.

Pyne, Stephen J.
1991   *Burning Bush: A fire history of Australia*. New York: Henry Holt & Company.

Qasim, Ali Qasim
1990   Lakhueen-jo-daro. *The Archaeology*, 2(1): 5–7.

Quivron, Gonzague
1980   Les marques incisees sur les poteries de Mehrgarh au Baluchistan, du milieu de IVe millenaire a la premier moitie du IIIe millenaire. *Paleorient*, 6: 269-80.

Quivron, Gonzague
1991   The Neolithic settlement at Mehrgarh: architecture from the beginning of the 7th to the first half of the 6th millennium BC. In, Michael Jansen, M. Mulloy and G. Urban,

eds., *Forgotten Cities on the Indus: Early civilization in Pakistan from the 8th to the 2nd millennium B.C.* Mainz: Verlag Philipp von Zabern: 59-65.

Radhawa, M. S., V. Nath, S. Vaidya, H. M. Patel, M. D. Patel and B. B. Kadam
1968   *Farmers of India.* Vol. 4. New Delhi: Indian Council of Agricultural Research.

Raghunath, S. N.
1977   Palaeoclimate at Lothal—a reconstruction. In, D. P. Agrawal and B. M. Pande, eds., *Ecology and Archaeology of Western India.* Delhi: Concept Publishing: 105-06.

Raghunath, S. N.
1984   Lothal 'dockyard' was a fishing engine. *Quarterly Journal of the Mythic Society,* 75(3): 294-300.

Raikes, Robert L.
1964   The end of the ancient cities of the Indus. *American Anthropologist,* 66(2): 284-99.

Raikes, Robert L.
1965a   The Mohenjo-daro floods. *Antiquity,* 39: 196-203.

Raikes, Robert L.
1965b   The ancient gabarbands of Baluchistan. *East and West,* 15(1-2): 3-12.

Raikes, Robert L.
1967   The Mohenjo-daro floods—further notes. *Antiquity,* 41: 64-6.

Raikes, Robert L.
1968a   Kalibangan: death from natural causes. *Antiquity,* 42: 286-91.

Raikes, Robert L.
1968b   Archaeological explorations in southern Jhalawan and Las Bela. *Origini,* 2: 103-71.

Raikes, Robert L.
1979   The Mohenjo-daro floods: the debate continues. In, M. Taddei, ed., *South Asian Archaeology 1977.* Naples: Instituto Universitario Orientale, Seminario di Studi Asiatici, Series Minor 6: 561-66.

Raikes, Robert L.
1984   Mohenjo-daro environment. In, B. B. Lal and S. P. Gupta, eds., *Frontiers of the Indus Civilization.* Delhi: Books and Books: 455-60.

Raikes, Robert L. and George F. Dales
1977   The Mohenjo-daro floods reconsidered. *Journal of the Palaeontological Society of India,* 20: 251-60.

Raikes, Robert L. and George F. Dales
1986   Reposte to Wasson's sedimentological basis of the Mohenjo-daro flood hypothesis. *Man and Environment,* 10: 33-44.

980

Raikes, Robert L. and Robert H. Dyson, Jr.
1961   The prehistoric climate of Baluchistan and the Indus Valley. *American Anthropologist*, 63: 265-81.

Ralph, Elizabeth and Henry Michael and Mark A. Han
1973   Radiocarbon and reality. *MASCA Newsletter*, 9(1):1-20.

Ram, Silak
1972   *Archaeology of Rohtak and Hissar Districts (Haryana)*. PhD Dissertation, Department of Ancient Indian History, Culture and Archaeology, Kurukshetra University.

Ramachandran, K. S.
1975   *Radiocarbon Dates of Archaeological Sites in India*. Hyderabad: The Government of Andhra Pradesh. Archaeological Series, 42.

Ramakrishna, V. S.
1988   Climatic changes in relation to desertification in Indian arid zone. In, A. K. Tiwari, ed., *Desertification: Monitoring and Control*. Jodhpur: Scientific Publishers: 99-115.

Ramaswamy, C.
1968   Monsoon over the Indus Valley during the Harappan period. *Nature*, 217(5129): 628-29.

Ramaswamy, S. M., P. C. Bakliwal and R. P. Verma
1991   Remote sensing and river migration in western India. *Remote Sensing*, 12(12): 2597-2609.

Ramesh Rao, K. and Krishna Rao
1985   Plant remains from Lothal. In, S. R. Rao, *Lothal: A Harappan port town, 1955-62*. Memoirs of the Archaeological Survey of India, No. 78, Vol. 2: 667-84.

Rao, B. K.
1961   Recent survey of gold. *Memoir of the Indian Bureau of Mines, Economic Minerals*, 10(2): 44-5.

Rao, S. R.
1963a   Excavations at Rangpur and other explorations in Gujarat. *Ancient India*, 18-19: 5-207.

Rao, S. R.
1963b   A "Persian Gulf" seal from Lothal. *Antiquity*, 37: 96-9.

Rao, S. R.
1973   *Lothal and the Indus Civilization*. Bombay: Asia Publishing House.

Rao, S. R.
1979   *Lothal: A Harappan Port Town, 1955-62*. Memoirs of the Archaeological Survey of India, No. 78, Vol. 1.

Rao, S. R.
1985   *Lothal: A Harappan Port Town, 1955-62*. Memoirs of the Archaeological Survey of India, No. 78, Vol. 2.

Rao, V. V.
1972-73 Ornithology in protohistoric archaeology of India. *Puratattva*, 6: 56-9.

Rao, V. V.
1990   Pot burials. In, Jagat Pati Joshi, *Excavation at Surkotada 1971-72 and Exploration in Kutch*. Memoirs of the Archaeological Survey of India, 87: 364-71

Ratan, R. and A. Chandra
1982   Palynological investigations of the Arabian Sea: Pollen/spores from the recent sediments of the Gulf of Kachchh, India. *The Palaeobotanist*, 31(2): 165-75.

Rathbun, Ted A.
1984   Skeletal pathology from Paleolithic through the Metal Ages in Iran and Iraq. In, Mark Nathan Cohen and George J. Armelagos, eds., *Paleopathology at the Origins of Agriculture*. New York: Academic Press: 137-66.

Ratnagar, Shereen
1981   *Encounters: The westerly trade of the Harappa Civilization*. Delhi: Oxford University Press.

Ratnagar, Shereen
1987   Pastoralists in the prehistory of Baluchistan. *Studies in History*, 3(2): 137-54.

Ratnagar, Shereen
1991   Pastoralism as an issue in historical reseach. *Studies in History*, 7(2): 181-94.

Raverty, Henry G.
1892a   *The Mihran of Sind and its tributaries: a geographical and historical study*. Journal of the Asiatic Society of Bengal: 61(1) & extra number: 155-206 & 297-508.

Raverty, Henry G.
1892b   *The Mihran of Sind, and its Tributaries*. 1979 reprint. Lahore: Sang-e-Meel Publications.

Reade, Julian E.
1979   *Early Etched Beads and the Indus-Mesopotamia Trade*. London: British Museum, Department of Western Asiatic Antiquities, No. 1.

Reddy, Seetha Narahari
1994   *Plant Usage and Subsistence Modeling: An ethnoarchaeological approach to the Late Harappan of Northwest India*. Phd Dissertation, Department of Anthropology, University of Wisconsin.

982

Redfield, Robert
1953   *The Primitive World and its Transformations*. Ithaca: Cornell University Press.

Redman, Charles L.
1978   *The Rise of Civilization: From early farmers to urban society in the ancient Near East*. San Francisco: W. H. Freeman and Company.

Reed, A.
1920   *Guide to the Antiquities of the Bronze Age*. London: British Museum.

Reed, Charles A.
1977a   *Origins of Agriculture*. The Hague: Mouton.

Reed, Charles A.
1977b   Origins of agriculture: discussion and some conclusions. In, Charles A. Reed, ed., *Origins of Agriculture*. The Hague: Mouton: 879-953.

Reed, Charles A.
1977c   A model for the origin of agriculture in the Near East. In, Charles A. Reed, ed., *Origins of Agriculture*. The Hague: Mouton: 543-67.

Rendell, Helen M.
1981   A preliminary investigation of the sedimentary history of the Bannu Basin in the Late Holocene. In, H. Hartel, ed., *South Asian Archaeology 1979*. Berlin: Dietrich Reimer Verlag: 219-25.

Rendell, Helen M.
1984   The Pleistocene sequence in the Soan Valley, northern Pakistan. In, Bridget Allchin, ed., *South Asian Archaeology 1981*. Cambridge: Cambridge University Press: 3-9.

Renfrew, Colin
1987   *Archaeology & Language: The puzzle of Indo-European origins*. Cambridge: Cambridge University Press.

Renfrew, Colin
1989   The origins of Indo-European languages. *Scientific American*, 261: 106-14.

Renfrew, Jane M.
1991   *New Light on Early Farming: Recent developments in palaeoethnobotany*. Edinburgh: Edinburgh University Press.

Rindos, David
1984   *The Origins of Agriculture: An evolutionary perspective*. New York: Academic Press.

Ripinsky, M. M.
1975   The camel in ancient Arabia. *Antiquity*, 49(196): 295-98.

Ripinsky, M. M.
1982   Pleistocene camel distribution in the Old World. *Antiquity*, 56(216): 48-50.

Ripinsky, M. M.
1983   Camel ancestry and domestication in Egypt and the Sahara. *Archaeology*, 36(3): 21-7.

Risley, Herbert H.
1915   *The People of India*. 2nd edition with an Introduction by William Crooke. Calcutta: Thacker and Spink.

Rissman, Paul C.
1985   *Migratory Pastoralism in Western India in the Second Millennium BC: The evidence from Oriyo Timbo*. PhD Dissertation, Department of Anthropology, University of Pennsylvania.

Rissman, Paul C.
1986   Seasonal aspects of man/cattle interaction in Bronze Age western India. *Journal of Ethnobiology*, 6(2): 257-77.

Rissman, Paul C.
1989   The status of research on animal domestication in India and its cultural context. In, P. Crabtree, D. Campana and K. Ryan, eds., *Early Animal Domestication and its Cultural Context*. Philadelphia: MASCA Research Papers in Science and Archaeology, Special Supplement to Vol. 6: 14-23.

Rissman, Paul C. and Y. M. Chitalwala
1990   *Harappan Civilization and Oriyo Timbo*. Delhi: Oxford & IBH and the American Institute of Indian Studies.

Roberts, T. J.
1977   *The Mammals of Pakistan*. London: Ernest Benn Limited.

Roberts, T. J.
1991-92 *The Birds of Pakistan*. 2 Vols. Karachi: Oxford University Press.

Robinson, M. and R. N. L. B. Hubbard
1977   The transport of pollen in the bracts of hulled cereals. *Journal of Archaeological Science*, 4: 197-99.

Robson, E. Iliff, translator
1929   *Arrian: History of Alexander and Indica*. 2 Vols. Cambridge: Harvard University Press, Loeb Classical Library.

Rocher, Rosane
1978   *India and Indology: Selected articles by W. Norman Brown*. Delhi: Motilal Banarsidass.

Rodgers, W. A.
1991   Environmental change and the evolution of pastoralism in South Asia: a discussion. *Studies in History*, 7(2): 195-204.

984

Rogers, Alexander, translator and Henry Beveridge
1909-14   *The Tuzuk-i-Jhangiri or Memoirs of Jahangir.* 2 Vols. 1968 reprint Odhi: Munshiram Manohar lal.

Rollefson, Gary O.
1983   Ritual and ceremony of Neolithic Ain Ghazal (Jordan). *Paleorient,* 9: 29-38.

Rollefson, Gary O.
1986   Neolithic Ain Ghazal (Jordan): ritual and ceremony II. *Paleorient,* 12: 45-52.

Ross, Alan S. C.
1936   Preliminary notice of some late eighteenth century numerals from Easter Island. *Man,* 120: 94-5.

Ross, Alan S. C.
1938   *The 'Numeral-Signs' of the Mohenjodaro Script.* Memoirs of the Archaeological Survey of India, 57.

Ross, Alan S. C.
1939   The direction of the Mohenjo-daro script. In, S. M. Katre and P. K. Gode, eds., *A Volume of Indian and Iranian Studies Presented to Sir E. Denison Ross.* The New Indian Antiquary, extra series 2: 554-58.

Ross, E. J.
1946   A Chalcolithic site in northern Baluchistan: Rana Ghundai. *Journal of Near Eastern Studies,* 5(4): 291-315.

Ross, Frank E.
1933   New light on Charles Masson. *The Indian Antiquary,* 63: 221-22.

Ross, Sir E. Denison
1932   India and Easter Island: similarity of early scripts. *The Times,* Letter to the Editor, 21 September: 6.

Rottlander, R. C. A.
1984   The Harappan linear measurement unit. In, M. Jansen and G. Urban, eds., *Reports on Field Work Carried out at Mohenjo-daro, Pakistan 1982-83 by the IsMEO-Aachen University Mission: Interim Reports.* Volume 1. Aachen/Rome: RWTH/IsMEO: 201-05.

Rowley-Conway, Peter
1991   Sorghum from Qasr Ibrim, Egyptian Nubia, c. 800 BC- AD 1811: A preliminary study. In, Jane Renfrew, ed., *New Light on Early Farming: Recent developments in palaeoethnobotany.* Edinburgh: Edinburgh University Press: 191-212.

Roy, B. B.
1928   Harappa and the Vedic Hariyupa. *Journal of the Bihar and Orissa Research Society,* 14(1): 129-30.

Roy, B. C.
1951   *Mineral Resources of Bombay*. Bombay: Government Central Press.

Roy, B. C.
1953   *The Economic Geology and Mineral Resources of Saurashtra*. Rajkot: Government of Saurashtra, Department of Industry and Supply.

Roy, B. C.
1959   Geological Map of Rajasthan. Economic Geology and Mineral Resources of Rajasthan. *Memoirs of the Geological Survey of India*, 86.

Roy, Baskar and S. S. Merh
1977   Geomorphology of the Rann of Kutch and climatic changes. In, D. P. Agrawal and B. M. Pande, eds., *Ecology and Archaeology of Western India*. Delhi: Concept Publishing: 195-200.

Roy, S. C.
1915   A note on the remains of the ancient Asuras in the Ranchi District. *Journal of the Bihar and Orissa Research Society*, 1: 229-59.

Roy, S. C.
1916   Relics of the copper age found in Chhota Nagpur. *Journal of the Bihar and Orissa Research Society*, 2: 481-84.

Roy, Sourindranath
1953   Indian archaeology from Jones to Marshall (1784-1902). *Ancient India*, 9: 4-28.

Roy, T. N.
1961   *The Story of Indian Archaeology: 1784-1947*. Delhi: Government of India.

Rydh, Hanna
1959   *Rang Mahal*. Lund: CWK Gleerup Publishers.

Sah, S. C. D. and R. K. Kar
1969   Palynology of the Laki sediments in Kutch 3. Pollen from the bore-holes around Jhulrai, Baranda and Panandhro. *The Palaeobotanist*, 18(2): 127-42.

Sahi, M. D. N.
1990   Excavations at Jakhera—1985-87: an interim report. In, N. C. Ghosh and Subrata Chakrabarti, eds., *Adaptation and Other Essays: Proceedings of the archaeology conference, 1988*. Santiniketan: Visva-Bharati Research Publications: 217-22.

Sahlins, Marshall D.
1958   *Social Stratification in Polynesia*. Seattle: University of Washington Press.

Sahlins, Marshall D.
1965   On the sociology of primitive exchange. In, M. Banton, ed., *The Relevance of Models for Social Anthropology*. London: Tavistock, ASA Monograph No. 1: 139-227.

986

Sahlins, Marshall D.
1972   *Stone Age Economics*. Chicago: Aldine.

Sahni, Rai Bahadur Daya Ram
1916-17 Harappa, District Montgomery. *Annual Progress Report of the Superintendent, Hindu and Buddhist Monuments, Northern Circle, for the Year Ending 31st March 1917*. Lahore: Government Printing, Punjab: 7.

Sahni, Rai Bahadur Daya Ram
1920-21a Excavations at Harappa. *Annual Progress Report of the Superintendent, Hindu and Buddhist Monuments, Northern Circle, for the Year Ending 31st March 1921*. Lahore: Civil and Military Gazette Press: 8-26.

Sahni, Rai Bahadur Daya Ram
1920-21b Exploration, Hindu and Buddhist Monuments, Punjab, Harappa. *Annual Report of the Archaeological Survey of India, 1920-21*: 15-7.

Sahni, Rai Bahadur Daya Ram
1923-24 Exploration and Research, Northern Circle, Punjab, Harappa. *Annual Report of the Archaeological Survey of India, 1923-24*: 52-4.

Sahni, Rai Bahadur Daya Ram
1924-25 Explorations, Northern Circle, Punjab, Harappa. *Annual Report of the Archaeological Survey of India, 1924-25*: 73-80.

Sahni, Rai Bahadur Daya Ram
1925-26 Exploration, Western Circle, Mohenjo-daro (Area VS). *Annual Report of the Archaeological Survey of India, 1925-26*: 93-98.

Sahni, Rai Bahadur Daya Ram
1926-27 Mohenjo-daro. *Annual Report of the Archaeological Survey of India, 1926-27*: 60-88.

Sahni, Rai Bahadur Daya Ram
1931a HR area (continued) Section B. In, Sir John Marshall, ed., *Mohenjo-daro and the Indus Civilization*, 3 Vols. London: Arthur Probsthain: 187-213.

Sahni, Rai Bahadur Daya Ram
1931b VS area. In, Sir John Marshall, ed., *Mohenjo-daro and the Indus Civilization*, 3 Vols. London: Arthur Probsthain: 214-32.

Sahu, B. P.
1988   *From Hunters to Breeders: Faunal background to Early India*. Delhi: Anamika Prakashan.

Said, Edward W.
1979   *Orientalism*. New York: Vantage Books.

Said, Edward W.
1993   *Culture and Imperialism*. New York: Vantage Books.

Saidel, Benjamin
1993   Round house or square? Architectural form and socio-economic organization in the PPNB. *Journal of Mediterranean Archaeology*, 6(1): 65-108.

Saizieu, B. Bartheleme de
1990   Le cimetiere Neolithique de Mehrgarh (Balochistan Pakistanis) apport de l'analyse factorielle. *Paleorient*, 16(1): 23-43.

Salah, A. S., V.M. Chmyriov, A. Shareq, K.F. Stazhilo-Alekseev, V.I. Drobov, N.A. Azimi, P.J. Gannon, B.K. Lubemov, A.Kh. Kafarskiy, E.P. Malyarov
1977   *Mineral Resources of Afghanistan.* Kabul: Ministry of Mines and Industries. United Nations Development Programme AFG/74/012.

Sali, S. A.
1970   The Harappan culture as revealed through surface explorations in the Tapti basin. *Journal of the Oriental Institute, Maharaja Sayajirao University of Baroda*, 20: 93-101.

Sali, S.A.
1986   *Daimabad, 1976-79.* Memoirs of the Archaeological Survey of India, No. 83.

Salim, M.
1991   Dhok Gangaal: a Painted Grey Ware site in Islamabad. *Ancient Pakistan*, 27: 27-33.

Salim, M.
1991   Painted Grey Ware sites around Islamabad. *Pakistan Archaeology*, 26(1): 144-55.

Salim, M.
1992   Archaeological exploration in Punjab, NWFP, Pakistan. *Journal of Central Asia*, 15(1): 34-77.

Salzman, Carl and John G. Galaty, editors
1990   *Nomads in a Changing World.* Napoli: Instituto Universitario Orientale, Dipartmento di Studi Asiatici, Series Minor, 32.

Salzman, Philip Carl and John G. Galaty
1990   Nomads in a changing world: issues and problems. In, Carl Salzman and John G. Galaty, eds., *Nomads in a Changing World.* Napoli: Instituto Universitario Orientale, Dipartmento di Studi Asiatica, Series Minor 32: 3-48.

Samzun, Anaick
1988   La ceramique chalcolithique de Mehrgarh III et ses relations avec celle de l'Asie centrale (Namazga I-II). In, Jean-Claude Gardin, ed., *L'Asie Centrale et Ses Rapports Avec Les Civilisations Orientales, Des Origines a l'Age du FerParis*: MMAFAC, Diffusion Boccard, 1: 125-34.

Samzun, Anaick
1991   The early Chalcolithic: Mehrgarh Period III. In, Michael Jansen, Maire Mulloy and

988

Gunter Urban, eds., *Forgotten Cities on the Indus: Early civilization in Pakistan from the 8th to the 2nd millennium B.C.* Mainz: Verlag Philipp von Zabern: 66-72.

Samzun, Anaick and P. Sellier
1983   Decouverts d'une necroploe chalcolithique a Mehrgarh, Pakistan. *Paleorient*, 9(2): 69-79.

Samzun, Anaick and P. Sellier
1985   First anthropological and cultural evidences for the funerary practices of the Chalcolithic population of Mehrgarh, Pakistan. In, J. Schotsmans and M. Taddei, eds., *South Asian Archaeology 1983*. Naples: Instituto Universitario Orientale, Dipartimento di Studi Asiatici, Series Minor 23: 91-120.

Sanderson, G. P.
1864   *The Wild Beasts of India*. 1983 Reprint. Delhi: Mittal Publications.

Sankalia, H. D.
1965   Archaeology. *Excavations at Langhnaj: 1944-63*. Part 1. Poona: Deccan College Post-graduate and Research Institute.

Sankalia, H. D.
1969   Kot Diji and Hissar III. *Antiquity*, 43: 142-44.

Sankalia, H. D.
1974   *The Prehistory and Protohistory of India and Pakistan*. 2nd ed. Poona: Deccan College Post-graduate and Research Institute.

Sankalia, H. D.
1978   *Born for Archaeology: An autobiography*. Delhi: B. R. Publishers.

Sankalia, H. D.
1981   Ancient name of Kutch. *Journal of the Oriental Institute, Maharaja Sayajirao University of Baroda*, 31(2): 183-84.

Sankalia, H. D., S. B. Deo and Zainuddin Dawood Ansari
1969   *Excavations at Ahar (Tambavati)*. Poona: Deccan College Post-graduate and Research Institute.

Sankarananda, Swami
1962   *Hindu States of Sumeria*. Calcutta: Firma Mukhapadhyay.

Santhanam, V. and J. B. Hutchinson
1974   Cotton. In, Sir Joseph Hutchinson, ed., *Evolutionary Studies in World Crops: Diversity and Change in the Indian Subcontinent*. Cambridge: Cambridge University Press: 89-100.

Santoni, Marielle
1980   Dur Khan, in site de l'Age du Fer dans la plaine de Kachi, Baluchistan Pakistan. *Paleorient* 6:287–302.

Santoni, Marielle
1984   Sibri and the south cemetery of Mehrgarh: 3rd millennium connections between the northern Kachi Plain (Pakistan) and Central Asia. In, B. Allchin, ed., *South Asian Archaeology 1981*. Cambridge: Cambridge University Press: 52-60.

Santoni, Marielle
1988   Aspects materiels des cultures de Sibri et Mehrgarh VIII (plaine de Kachi, Baluchistan, Pakistan).. a la fin du 3e et au debut du 2e millenaires. In, J.-C. Gardin, ed., *L'Asie Centrale et ses Rapports avec les Civilisations Orientales des Origines a l'Age du Fer*. Paris: MMAFAC, Diffusion Boccard, 1: 135-42.

Santoni, Marielle
1989   Potters and pottery during the third millennium B.C. (Periods VI and VII). In, Karen Frifelt and Per Sorensen, eds., *South Asian Archaeology 1985*. London: Curzon Press, Scandinavian Institute of Asian Studies, Occasional PapersNo. 4: 176-85.

Saraswat, K. S.
1993   Plant Economy of Late Harappans at Hulas. *Puratattva*, 23: 1-12.

Sarianidi, Viktor I.
1960   Eneolithic site of Geoksyur. *Trudi Iu TAKE*, 10: 225-318.

Sarianidi, Viktor I.
1971   The lapis lazuli route in the ancient Near East. *Archaeology*, 24: 12-5.

Sarkar, H.
1953   Fish-hooks from the Indus Valley. *Journal of the Asiatic Society, Science*, 19: 133-39.

Sastri, K. N.
1957   *New Light on the Indus Civilization*. Vol. 1. Delhi: Atma Ram & Sons.

Sastri, K. N.
1965   *New Light on the Indus Civilization*. Vol. 2. Delhi: Atma Ram & Sons.

Sathe, V. G. and S. Atre
1989   The problem of the camel in the Indus Civilization. *Bulletin of the Deccan College Post-Graduate and Research Institute*, Vol. 47-48: 301-06.

Sauer, Carl O.
1952   *Agricultural Origins and Dispersals*. New York: American Geographical Society.

Savithri, R. and Vishnu-Mittre
1977   Further contribution on Protohistoric ragi - *Eleusine coracana* Gaertn. *The Palaeobotanist*, 26(1): 10-15.

990

Sayce, A. H.
1924   Remarkable discoveries in India. *Illustrated London News*, September 27: 566.

Schaller, George B.
1967   *The Deer and the Tiger*. Chicago: University of Chicago Press.

Schaller, George B.
1977   *Mountain Monarchs*. Chicago: University of Chicago Press.

Scheil, V. E.
1925   Un nouveau sceau Hindon pseudo-Sumerian. *Revue d'Assyriologie et d'Archeologie Orientale*, 22(2): 55-6.

Schiemann, Elisabeth
1948   *Weizen, Roggen, Gerste: Systematik, geschichte und verwendung*. Jena: Fischer Verlag.

Schiffer, Michael B.
1986   Radiocarbon dating and the "old wood" problem: the case of the Hohokam chronology. *Journal of Archaeological Science*, 13: 13-30.

Schmidt, Erich F.
1937   *Excavations at Tepe Hissar, Damghan*. Philadelphia: The University Museum.

Schmidt, Robert G. and R. Williams Matthews
1992   Mineral commodity sources for ancient peoples of the Lower Indus River Valley. Open file report 92-519, computer disk. Washington DC: Department of the Interior, U. S. Geological Survey.

Schoff, Wilfred H., translator
1912   *The Periplus of the Erythraean Sea*. New York: Longmans, Green and Company.

Scholz, Fred
1974   Der modern Wandel in der nomadischen Belutschen-und Brahui-Stammen der Gebirgsprovinz Belutschistan (Pakistan). *Sociologus*, 24: 117-37.

Scholz, Fred
1983   Baluchistan: a brief introduction to the geography of Pakistan's mountainous province. *Newsletter of Baluchistan Studies*, 1: 13-8.

Schoninger, M. J.
1981   The agricultural "revolution": its effects of human diet in prehsitoric Iran and Israel. *Paleorient*, 7: 73-91.

Schuiling, R. D.
1983   The position of Indian tin occurrences in the tin-belts of Gondwana. *Journal of the Geological Society of India*, 24: 101-05.

Schumm, Stanley A.
1965   Quaternary paleohydrology. In, H. E. Wright and D. G. Frey, eds., *Quaternary in the United States*. Princeton: Princeton University Press: 783-94.

Schumm, Stanley A.
1968   River adjustments to altered hydrologic regimen—Murrumbidgee River and palaeochannels, Australia. *United States Geological Survey Professional Paper*. Washington D.C.: U.S. Geological Survey.

Schumm, Stanley A.
1969   River metamorphosis. *Journal of the Hydraulics Division, Proceedings of the American Society of Civil Engineers*, 95(1): 255-73.

Sellier, Pascal
1985   Position et disposition des ossements; observations pourune approche dynamique des sepultures neolithiques et chalcolithique de Mehrgarh, Pakistan. *Methodes d'Etude des Sepultures*, Vol. 1. Paris: Centre National du Researche Scientifique, RCP 742: 39-42.

Sellier, Pascal
1987   Les seplutures de Mehrgarh: de l'analyse osteologique a la reconstruction de rituel funeraire. *Annales Fyssen*, 3: 17-35.

Sellier, Pascal
1988   La necropole neolithique de Mehrgarh. *Les Cites Oubliees de l'Indus, Archaeologie du Pakistan*. Paris: Musee Guimet: 58-64, 81-2.

Sellier, Pascal
1989   Hypotheses and estimators for the demographic interpretation of the Chalcolithic population from Mehrgarh, Pakistan. *East and West,* 39: 11-42.

Sellier, Pascal
1990   Anthropologie de terrain et gestes funeraires: le cimetiere neolithique de Mehrgarh (Pakistan). Les Nouvilles de l'Archeologie, special issue, C. Masset and P. Sellier eds., *La Paleoanthropologie Funeraire*, 40: 19-21.

Sellier, Pascal
1991   Mehrgarh: the funerary rites and the archaeology of death. In, Michael Jansen, Maire Mulloy and Gunter Urban, eds., *Forgotten Cities on the Indus: Early civilization in Pakistan from the 8th to the 2nd millennium B.C.* Mainz: Verlag Philipp von Zabern: 75-86.

Sellier, Pascal
1992   The contribution of palaeoanthropology to the interpretation of a functional funerary structure: the graves from Neolithic Mehrgarh Period IB. In, Catherine Jarrige, ed., *South Asian Archaeology 1989*. Madison: Prehistory Press, Monographs in World Archaeology, 14: 253-66.

992

Sen, Amal Kumar, Gheeslal and C. T. Abraham
1982   Land use in Bikaner District. In, *Proceedings of the Workshop on the Problems of the Deserts of India*. Delhi: Geological Survey of India, Special Publication No. 49: 303-12.

Sethna, K. D.
1981   *Karpasa in prehistoric India: A chronological and cultural clue*. New Delhi: Biblia Impex Private.

Sethna, K. D.
1992   *The Problem of Aryan Origins: From an Indian point of view*. 2nd enlarged edition. New Delhi: Aditya Prakashan.

Sewell, R. B. Seymour and B. S. Guha
1931a   Zoological remains. In, Sir John Marshall, ed., *Mohenjo-daro and the Indus Civilization*, 3 Vols. London: Arthur Probsthain: 649-73.

Sewell, R. B. Seymour and B. S. Guha
1931b   Human remains. In, Sir John Marshall, ed., *Mohenjo-daro and the Indus Civilization*, 3 Vols. London: Arthur Probsthain: 599-648.

Shaffer, Jim G.
1974   *Allahdino and the Mature Harappan: A preliminary report on the cultural stratigraphy*. Cleveland: Department of Anthropology, Case Western Reserve University.

Shaffer, Jim G.
1977   Harappan external trade: a critical assessment. Paper presented at the conference titled, *Indus Civilization: Problems and issues*. Organized by B. B. Lal and S. C. Malik. Simla: Indian Institute of Advanced Study.

Shaffer, Jim G.
1978a   The later prehistoric periods. In, F. R. Allchin and N. Hammond, eds., *The Archaeology of Afghanistan: From earliest times to the Timurid period*. New York: Academic Press: 71-186.

Shaffer, Jim G.
1978b   *Prehistoric Baluchistan: With excavation report on Said Qala Tepe*. Delhi: B. R. Publishing Corporation.

Shaffer, Jim G.
1981   The Protohistoric period in the eastern Punjab: a preliminary assessment. In, Ahmad Hasan Dani, ed., *Indus Civilization: New perspectives*. Islamabad: Quaid-i-Azam University: 65-102.

Shaffer, Jim G.
1986a   Cultural development in the eastern Punjab. In, J. Jacobson, ed., *Studies in the*

Archaeology of India and Pakistan. Delhi: Oxford & IBH and the American Institute of Indian Studies: 195-235.

Shaffer, Jim G.
1986b   The archaeology of Baluchistan: a review. *Newsletter of Baluchistan Studies*, 3: 63-111.

Shaffer, Jim G.
1987   One hump or two: the impact of the camel on Harappan society. In, Edenda Curaverunt, G. Gnoli and L. Lanciotti, eds., *Orientalia Josephi Tucci Memoriae Dicata*. Roma: Istituto Italiano per il Medo ed Estremo Oriente, Serie OrientaleRoma, 56(2), Vol. 3: 1315-28.

Shaffer, Jim G.
1992   The Indus Valley, Baluchistan and Helmand traditions: Neolithic through Bronze Age. In, Robert W. Ehrich, ed., *Chronologies in Old World Archaeology*. 3rd ed. 2 Vols. Chicago: University of Chicago Press: 441-64 & 425-46.

Shaffer, Jim G. and Diane A. Lichtenstein
1989   Ethnicity and change in the Indus Valley Cultural Tradition. In, Jonathan Mark Kenoyer, ed., *Old Problems and New Perspectives in South Asian Archaeology*. Madison: Wisconsin Archaeological Reports, 2: 117-26.

Shah, D. R.
1971a   A note on unmodified animal remains from Bagor. *The Eastern Anthropologist*, 24: 319-20.

Shah, D. R.
1971b   Bones. In, R. N. Mehta and S. N. Chowdhary, *Excavation at Jokha*. Baroda: Maharaja Sayajirao University Archaeology Series, No. 11: 70-4.

Shah, D. R.
1975   Animal remains from Dhatva. In, R. N. Mehta and S. N. Chowdhary, *Excavation at Dhatva*. Baroda: Maharaja Sayajirao University Archaeology Series, No. 12: 57-60.

Shah, D. R.
1980   Animal remains from Kanewal. In, R. N. Mehta, K. N. Momin and D. R. Shah, *Excavations at Kanewal*. Baroda: Maharaja Sayajirao University Archaeology Series, No. 17: 74-6.

Shah, G. L.
1974   *Flora of Gujarat State.* 2 Vols. Vallabh Vidyanagar: Sardar Patel University.

Shah, Sayid Ghulam Mustafa and Asko Parpola
1991   *Corpus of Indus Seals and Inscriptions.* Vol. 2, Collections in Pakistan. Helsinki: Suomalainen Tiedeakatemia, Suomalaisen Tiedeakatemian Toimituksia Annales Academiae Scientiarum Fennicae, Sarja, Series B, NIDE, Tome 240.

994

Shaikh, Nilofer
1989   *The Trade of the Mohenjo-Darins*. PhD Dissertation, Department of Archaeology,
        Shah Abdul Latif University of Sindh, Khairpur.

Shamashastry, R., translator
1960   *Kautilya's Arthashastra*. Mysore: Mysore Printing and Publishing House.

Sharif, Muhammad
1989   Archaeological exploration around Multan, 1988. *Pakistan Archaeology*, 24: 195-221.

Sharma, A. K.
1967   Neolithic human burials from Burzahom, Kashmir. *Journal of the Oriental Institute,
        Maharaja Sayajirao University of Baroda*, 16(3): 239-42.

Sharma, A. K.
1968   Animal burials from Burzahom—a Neolithic settlement in Kashmir. *Journal of the
        Oriental Institute, Maharaja Sayajirao University of Baroda*, 18(1-2): 40-4.

Sharma, A. K.
1982a   The Harappan cemetery at Kalibangan: a study. In, Gregory L. Possehl, ed., *Harappan
        Civilization: A contemporary perspective*. Delhi: Oxford & IBH and the American
        Institute of Indian Studies: 297-91.

Sharma, A. K.
1982b   Excavations at Gufkral - 1981. *Puratattva*, 11: 19-25.

Sharma, A. K.
1982c   Gufkral 1981: an aceramic Neolithic site in the Kashmir Valley. *Asian Perspectives*,
        25(2): 24-41.

Sharma, A. K.
1983   Animal bones from Gufkral — evidence of human and non-human activities.
        Puratattva, 12: 31-6.

Sharma, A. K.
1986   Neolithic Gufkral. In, Ghulam Mohammad Buth, ed., *Central Asia and Western
        Himalaya: A forgotten link*. Jodhpur: Scientific Publishers: 13-7.

Sharma, A. K.
1990   Animal bone remains. In, Jagat Pati Joshi, *Excavation at Surkotada 1971-72 and
        Exploration in Kutch*. Memoirs of the Archaeological Survey of India, 87: 372-83.

Sharma, A. K.
1991   Neolithic Gufkral. In, C. Margabandhu, K. S. Ramachandran, A. P. Sagar and D. K.
        Sinha, eds., *Indian Archaeological Heritage: Shri K. V. Soundara Rajan festschrift*.
        Delhi: Agam Kala Prakashan: 101-10.

Sharma, A. K.
1992   Early iron users of Gufkral. In, B. U. Nayak and N. C. Ghosh, eds., *New Trends in Indian Art and Archaeology: S. R. Rao's 70th birthday felicitation volume*. 2 Vols. Delhi: Aditya Prakashan, 1: 63-8.

Sharma, A. K.
1993   Animal skeletal remains. In, Jagat Pati Joshi, *Excavation at Bhagwanpura 1975-76 and Other Explorations and Excavations 1975-81 in Haryana, Jammu & Kashmir and Punjab*. Memoirs of the Archaeological Survey of India, 89: 143-48.

Sharma, G. B. and M. Kumar
1983   Excavation at Rohira. *Puratattva*, 12: 125-7.

Sharma, G. R.
1971-72 Appendix B — Excavations at Baharia, District Shahjahanpur. *Puratattva*, 5: 42-3.

Sharma, G. R., V. D. Mishra, D. Mandal, B. B. Mishra and J. N. Pal
1980   *Beginnings of Agriculture*. Allahabad: Abinash Prakashan.

Sharma, N. L. and K. S. V. Ram
1964   *An Introduction to India's Economic Minerals*. Dhanbad: Asia Press.

Sharma, R. P.
1972   Proto-historic exploration along the bank of the Yamuna in Distt. Meerut. In, S. B. Deo, ed., *Archaeological Congress and Seminar Papers*. Nagpur: Nagpur University: 117-18.

Sharma, R. P.
1982   Khatoli — a protohistoric site in Haryana. *Puratattva*, 11: 123-25.

Sharma, R. S.
1990   A tribute to Luigi Pio Tessitori. In, Carlo Della Casa and Daniela Sagramoso, eds., *Luigi Pio Tessitori*. Brescia: Paideria Editrice. Biblioteca Indiana, 4: 13-24.

Sharma, Shubh Kiran
1995   Scientific Studies of Kunal Site, Distt. Hissar, Haryana. *Puratattva*, 25: 86-8.

Sharma, Y. D.
1953   Exploration of historical sites. *Ancient India*, 9: 116-69.

Sharma, Y. D.
1956   Past patterns in living as unfolded by excavations at Rupar. *Lalit Kala*, 1-2: 121-29.

Sharma, Y. D.
1971-72 Appendix A — Salvage of archaeological evidence from Bahadrabad. *Puratattva*, 5: 39-42.

996

Sharma, Y. D.
1973   Value of common painted ceramic designs from different sites as a guide to chronology with special reference to pottery from Bara (Punjab). In, D. P. Agrawal and A. Ghosh, eds., *Radiocarbon and Indian Archaeology*. Bombay: Tata Institute of Fundamental Research: 222-30.

Sharma, Y. D.
1976   Transformation of the Harappa Culture in the Panjab. In, Udai Vir Singh, ed. *Archaeological Congress and Seminar: 1972*. Kurukshetra: B. N. Chakravarty University, Kurukshetra: 5-15.

Sharma, Y. D.
1982a   Harappan complex on the Sutlej (India). In, Gregory L. Possehl, ed., *Harappan Civilization: A contemporary perspective*. Delhi: Oxford & IBH and the American Institute of Indian Studies: 141-65.

Sharma, Y. D.
1982b   The Pre-Harappans in Punjab. *Puratattva*, 11: 34-8.

Sharma, Y. D.
1983   Domeli: fresh light on Neolithic culture of Punjab. In, K. V. Raman, et. al., eds., *Srinidhih: Perspectives in Indian archaeology, art and culture, Shri K. R. Srinivasan festschrift*: 1-10.

Sharma, Y. D.
1987   Fresh light on the Bara culture from Mahorana. In, B. M. Pande and B. D. Chattopadhyaya, eds., *Archaeology and History: Essays in memory of Sh. A. Ghosh*. 2 Vols. Delhi: Agam Kala Prakashan: 157-176.

Sharma, Y. D.
1989   Ropar. In, A. Ghosh, ed., *An Encyclopaedia of Indian Archaeology*. 2 Vols. Delhi: Munshiram Manoharlal Publishers, Vol. 2: 377-81.

Sharpe, A.
1965   Topographica Indica. *Orientalia Gandensia*, 2: 189-256.

Shastri, H.
1915   Recent additions to our knowledge of the Copper Age antiquities of the Indian empire. *Journal of the Asiatic Society of Bengal*, N. S. 11: 1-7.

Sherratt, Andrew
1980   Water, soil and seasonality in early cereal cultivation. *World Archaeology*, 11(3): 313-30.

Shinde, Vasant
1991   A horn-headed human figure on a Harappan jar from Padri, Gujarat. *Man and Environment*, 16(2): 87-89.

Shinde, Vasant
1992a   Excavations at Padri—1990-91: a preliminary report. *Man and Environment*, 17(1):
         79-86.

Shinde, Vasant
1992b   Settlement archaeology of Kaothe: a Chalcolithic site in the Tapti Basin. *Puratattva*,
         22: 47-52.

Shinde, Vasant and E. Thomas
1993   A unique Harappan copper fish-hook from Padri, Gujarat. *Man and Environment*,
         18(2): 145-47.

Shinde, Vasant and S. B. Kar
1992   Padri ware: a new painted ceramic found in Harappan levels at Padri in Gujarat. *Man
         and Environment*, 17(2): 105-110.

Shroder, John F., Jr., editor
1993   *Himalaya to the Sea: Geology, geomorphology and the Quaternary*. London:
         Routledge.

Siddiqi, S. I.
1944   River changes in the Ghaggar plain. *Indian Geographical Journal*, 19: 139-46.

Siddiqi, S. I.
1945   Physiography of the River Sutlej. *Indian Geographical Journal*, 20(2): 69-75.

Siddique, M.
1992   Exploration of ancient settlements around Multan. *Journal of Central Asia*, 15(2):
         34-44.

Silveright, R.
1907   Cutch and the Ran. *The Geographical Journal*, 29: 518-39.

Singh, Amar
1981   *Archaeology of Karnal and Jind Districts (Haryana)*. PhD Dissertation, Department
         of Ancient Indian History, Culture and Archaeology, Kurukshetra University.

Singh, Gurdip
1971   The Indus Valley Culture seen in the context of Post-glacial climatic and ecological
         studies in northwest India. *Archaeology and Physical Anthropology in Oceania*, 6(2):
         177-89.

Singh, Gurdip
1977   Climatic changes in the Indian Desert. *Desertification and its Control*. New Delhi:
         Indian Council of Agricultural Research: 25-30.

Singh, Gurdip
1985   The challenge of discovering human impact on Quaternary vegetation through man-
         made fires. *Man and Environment*, 9:1-2.

998

Singh, Gurdip, R. J. Wasson and D. P. Agrawal
1990   Vegetational and seasonal climatic changes since the last full glacial? in the Thar Desert, northwestern India. *Review of Palaeobotany and Palynology*, 64: 351-58.

Singh, Gurdip, R. D. Joshi and A. B. Singh
1972   Stratigraphic and radiocarbon evidence for the age and development of three salt lake deposits in Rajasthan, India. *Quaternary Research*, 2(4): 496-505.

Singh, Gurdip, R. D. Joshi, S. K. Chopra and A. B. Singh
1974   Late Quaternary history of vegetation and climate of the Rajasthan Desert, India. *Philosophical Transactions of the Royal Society of London*, B, Biological Sciences, 267(889): 467-501.

Singh, Gurdip, S. K. Chopra and A. B. Singh
1973   Pollen-rain from vegetation of North-west India. *New Phytology*, 72: 191-206.

Singh, Khushwant
1987   The Indian monsoon in literature. In, Jay S. Fein and Pamela L. Stephens, eds., *Monsoons*. New York: John Wiley and Sons: 35-49.

Singh, Purushottam
1974   *Neolithic Cultures of Western Asia*. New York: Seminar Press.

Singh, Purushottam
1991   *The Neolithic Origins*. Delhi: Agam Kala Prakashan.

Singh, Ranjit Pratap
1990   *Agriculture in Protohistoric India*. Delhi: Pratibha Prakashan.

Singh, Ranjit Pratap
1990   Millet cultivation in ancient India. In, C. P. Sinha, ed., *Archaeology and Art: Krishna Deva felicitation volume*. 2 Vols. Delhi: Ramanand Vidya Bhavan: 12-8.

Singh, Sarva Daman
1963   The elephant and the Aryans. *Journal of the Royal Asiatic Society of Great Britain and Ireland*: 1-6.

Singh, Sheo Bahadur
1976   Protohistoric sites in South Panchala. *Kurukshetra University Research Journal (Arts and Humanities)*, 10: 7-15.

Singh, Udai Vir
1976   Recent archaeological discoveries in the vicinity of Thanesar. *Kurukshetra University Research Journal (Arts and Humanities)*, 10: 24-30.

Singh, Udai Vir
1977   Late Harappan culture as revealed by the excavations at Mirzapur and Daulatpur, District Kurukshetra (Haryana). Paper presented at, *Indus Civilization: Problems and*

issues. Organized by B. B. Lal and S. C. Malik. Simla: Indian Institute of Advanced Study: 1-7.

Singh, Udai Vir and Suraj Bhan
1982   A note on the excavation at Balu, distt. Jind (Haryana). In, R. K. Sharma, ed., *Indian Archaeology: New perspectives*. Delhi: Agam Kala Prakashan: 124-26.

Sinha, R. K.
1975   Ancient tin working in Bihar. *Quarterly Journal of the Mining and Metallurgical Society of India*, 31: 75-7.

Sinha, Subrata
1977   Origin of salinity in Rajasthan salt lakes. In, D. P. Agrawal and B. M. Pande, eds., *Ecology and Archaeology of Western India*. Delhi: Concept Publishing: 147-56.

Smith, Andrew
1984-87 Development of Khoikhoi society in Southern Africa: implications for pastoral archaeology. *Origini*, 13: 409-24.

Smith, Bruce D.
1989   Origins of agriculture in eastern North America. *Science*, 246: 1566-71.

Smith, Philip E. L.
1972a   *The Consequences of Food Production*. Addison-Wesley Module in Anthropology, No. 31.

Smith, Philip E. L.
1972b   Changes in population pressure in archaeological explanation. *World Archaeology*, 4(1): 5-18.

Smith, Philip E. L.
1976   Reflections on four seasons of excavations at Tappeh Ganj Dareh. In, Firoz Bagherzadeh, ed., *Proceedings of the IVth Annual Symposium on Archaeological Research in Iran*. Tehran: Iran Bastam: 11-22.

Smith, Sidney
1927   *Early History of Assyria to 1000 BC. New York*: E. P. Dutton & Co.

Smith, Sidney
1933   Obituary of Archibald H. Sayce. *Man*, 68-69: 69-70.

Smith, Vincent A.
1905   The Copper Age and prehistoric bronze implements of India. *The Indian Antiquary*, 34: 229-44.

1000

Smith, Vincent A.
1907   The copper age and prehistoric implements of India—supplement. *The Indian Antiquary*, 36: 53-5.

Snead, Rodman E.
1963   *A Study of the Physical Geography of the Las Bela Coastal Plain*. New Orleans: Institute of Coastal Studies, University of Louisiana.

Snead, Rodman E.
1966   *Physical Geography Reconnaissance: Las Bela Coastal Plain West Pakistan*. Baton Rouge: Lousiana State University.

Snead, Rodman E.
1967   Recent morphological changes along the coast of West Pakistan. *Annual of the Association of American Geographers*, 57: 550-65.

Snead, Rodman E.
1969   *Physical Geography Reconnaissance: West Pakistan Coastal Zone*. Albuquerque: University of New Mexico, Publications in Geography, No. 1.

Snead, Rodman E.
1993   Uplifted marine terraces along the Makran Coast of Pakistan and Iran. In, John F. Shroder, Jr., ed., *Himalaya to the Sea: Geology, geomorphology and the Quaternary*. London: Routledge: 327-62.

Snelgrove, A. K.
1967   *Geohydrology of the Indus River, West Pakistan*. Hyderabad: Sind University Press.

Solecki, Ralph S.
1955   Shanidar Cave, a Palaeolithic site in northern Iraq. *Annual Report of the Board of Regents of the Smithsonian Institution*, 1954. Publication No. 4190: 389-425.

Solecki, Ralph S.
1963   Prehistory in the Shanidar Valley, Northern Iraq. *Science*, 139: 179-93.

Solecki, Ralph S.
1978   Contemporary Kurdish winter-time inhabitants of Shanidar cave, Iraq. *World Archaeology*, 10(3): 318-30.

Solecki, Rose L.
1964   Zawi Chemi Shanidar, a post-Pleistocene village site in northern Iraq. *Report of the 6th International Congress on the Quaternary*, 4: 405-12.

Solecki, Rose L.
1981   *An Early Village Site at Zawi Chemi Shanidar*. Malibu: Undena Publications. Bibliotheca Mesopotamica, 13.

Sollberger, Edmond
1965   *Royal Inscriptions, Part 2.* Ur Excavation Texts VIII, London/Philadelphia: British Museum/The University Museum.

Sonawane, V. H. and P. Ajithprasad
1994   Harappa culture and Gujarat. *Man and Environment*, 19(1-2): 129-39.

Sonawane, V. H. and R. N. Mehta
1985   Vagad — a rural Harappan settlement in Gujarat. *Man and Environment*, 9: 38-44.

Sorley, H. T.
1959   *The Former Province of Sind (Including Khairpur State).* The Gazetteer of West Pakistan. Karachi: Government of West Pakistan.

Southworth, Franklin C.
1976   Cereals in South Asian prehistory: a look at the linguistic evidence. In, K. A. R. Kennedy and G. L. Possehl, eds., *Ecological Backgrounds of South Asian Prehistory*. Ithaca: Cornell University South Asia Occasional Papers and Theses, No. 4: 52-74.

Southworth, Franklin C.
1979   Lexical evidence for early contacts between Indo-Aryan and Dravidian. In, M. Deshpande and P. Hook, eds., *Aryan and Non-Aryan in India*. Ann Arbor: University of Michigan, Center for South and Southeast Asian Studies.

Southworth, Franklin C.
1988   Ancient economic plants of South Asia: linguistic archaeology and early agriculture. In, M. A. Jazayery and W. Winter, eds., *Languages and Cultures: Studies in honor of Edgar C. Polome*. New York: Mouton de Gruyer, Trends in Linguistics, Studies and Monographs, 36: 649-68.

Southworth, Franklin C.
1990   The reconstruction of prehistoric South Asian language contact. In, E. H. Benedict, ed., *The Uses of Linguistics*. New York, The New York Academy of Sciences, Annals of the New York Academy of Sciences, 583.

Southworth, Franklin C.
1992   Linguistics and archaeology: prehistoric implications of some South Asian plant names. In, Gregory L. Possehl, ed., *South Asian Archaeology Studies*. Delhi: Oxford & IBH: 81-6.

Spate, O. H. K. and A. T. A. Learmonth
1967   *India and Pakistan: A general and regional geography*. 3rd ed. London: Methuen & Co.

Spooner, Brian
1971   Towards a generative model of nomadism. *Anthropological Quarterly*, 22: 198-210.

Spooner, Brian
1972a   The status of nomadism as a cultural phenomenon in the Middle East. In, J. Irons

1002

and N. Dyson-Hudson, eds., *Perspectives on Nomadism*. Leiden: E. J. Brill: 122-32.

Spooner, Brian, editor
1972b   *Population Growth: Anthropological implications*. Cambridge: MIT Press.

Spooner, Brian
1973   The cultural ecology of pastoral nomads. *Addison-Wesley Module in Anthropology*, 45.

Spooner, Brian
1975   Nomadism in Baluchistan. In. L. S. Leshink and G. D. Sontheimer, eds., *Pastoralists and Nomads in South Asia*. Wiesbaden: Otto Harrassowitz. Schriftenreihe des Sudasien Instituts der Universitat Heidelberg: 68-91.

Spooner, D. Brainerd
1922-23   Conservation, introduction. *Annual Report of the Archaeological Survey of India, 1922-23*: 1-3.

Srinivasan, Doris
1975-76   The so-called proto-Siva seal from Mohenjo-daro: an iconographical assessment. *Archives of Asian Art*, 29: 47-58.

Srinivasan, Doris
1984   Unhinging Siva from the Indus Civilization. *Journal of the Royal Asiatic Society of Great Britain and Ireland*: 77-89.

Srivastava, A. K.
1973   Treasure trove finds from Mathura District. *Bulletin of Archaeology and Museums of Uttar Pradesh*, 11-12: 37-41.

Srivastava, H. L.
1936-37   Harappa Museum. *Annual Report of the Archaeological Survey of India, 1936-37*: 138.

Srivastava, H. L.
1939-41   Excavations at Harappa. *Annual Report of the Archaeological Survey of India, 1936-37*: 39-41.

Srivastava, Om Prakash
1982   *A Study of Antiquarian Remains in the Sadar Tahsil of District Muzaffarnagar*. MsP Dissertation, Department of History, Aligarh Muslum University.

Stack-Kane, Victoria
1989   Animal remains from Rojdi. In, Gregory L. Possehl and M. H. Raval, *Harappan Civilization and Rojdi*. Delhi: Oxford & IBH: 182-84.

Stacul, Giorgio
1966   Notes on the discovery of a necropolis near Kherai in the Gorband Valley (Swat - West Pakistan). *East and West*, 16(3-4): 261-274.

Stacul, Giorgio
1967   Excavations in a rock shelter near Ghaligai (Swat, Pakistan). *East and West*, 17(3-4): 185-219.

Stacul, Giorgio
1969   Excavation near Ghaligai (1968) and the chronological sequence of Protohistorical cultures in the Swat Valley (West Pakistan). *East and West*, 19(1-2): 44-91.

Stacul, Giorgio
1970a   An archaeological survey near Kalam (Swat Kohistan). *East and West*, 20: 87-91.

Stacul, Giorgio
1970b   The grey pottery in the Swat Valley and the Indo-Iranian connections (ca. 1500-300 B.C.) *East and West*, 20: 92-102.

Stacul, Giorgio
1971   Cremation graves in northwest Pakistan and their Eurasian connections: remarks and hypotheses. *East and West*, 21(1-2): 9-19.

Stacul, Giorgio
1974   New archaeological evidence on north-west Indo-Pakistan (3rd-1st millennia B.C.). *East and West*, 24(3-4): 239-243.

Stacul, Giorgio
1975   The fractional burial custom in the Swat Valley and some connected problems. *East and West*, 25: 323-32.

Stacul, Giorgio
1976   Excavation at Loebanr III (Swat, Pakistan). *East and West*, 26: 13-30.

Stacul, Giorgio
1977   Dwelling- and storage-pits at Loebanr III (Swat, Pakistan): 1976 excavation report. *East and West*, 27: 227-53.

Stacul, Giorgio
1978   Excavation at Bir-kot-ghundai (Swat, Pakistan). *East and West*, 28: 137-150.

Stacul, Giorgio
1979a   Early Iron Age in the Northwest of Sub-continent. In, D. P. Agrawal and D. K. Chakrabarti, eds., *Essays in Indian Protohistory*. Delhi: B. R. Publishing: 341-345.

Stacul, Giorgio
1979b   The sequence and proto-historical periods at Aligrama (Swat, Pakistan). In, J. E. van Lohuizen-de Leeuw, ed., *South Asian Archaeology 1975*. Leiden: E. J. Brill: 88-90.

Stacul, Giorgio
1980a   Bir-kot-ghundai (Swat, Pakistan): 1978 excavation report. *East and West*, 30(1-2): 55-65.

1004

Stacul, Giorgio
1980b   Loebanr III (Swat, Pakistan): 1979 excavation report. *East and West*, 30(1-2): 67-76.

Stacul, Giorgio
1981   On periods and cultures in the Swat Valley and beyond. *Puratattva*, 10:89-91.

Stacul, Giorgio
1984a   Cultural change in the Swat Valley and beyond, c. 3000-1400 B.C. In, Bridget Allchin, ed., *South Asian Archaeology 1981*. Cambridge: Cambridge University Press: 205-12.

Stacul, Giorgio
1984b   Harappan Post-urban evidence in the Swat Valley. In, B. B. Lal and S. P. Gupta, eds., *Frontiers of the Indus Civilization*. Delhi: Books and Books: 271-75.

Stacul, Giorgio
1985   A Harappan Post-urban outpost in the Swat Valley. In, J. Schotsmans and M. Taddei, eds., *South Asian Archaeology 1983*. Naples: Instituto Universitario Orientale, Dipartimento di Studi Asiatici, Series Minor 23: 357-68.

Stacul, Giorgio
1987   *Prehistoric and Protohistoric Swat, Pakistan (c. 3000-1400 B.C.)*. Rome: Instituto Italiano per il Medio ed Estremo Oriente.

Stacul, Giorgio
1989   Continuity and change in the Swat Valley (18th-15th centuries B.C.). In, Jonathan Mark Kenoyer, ed., *Old Problems and New Perspectives in the Archaeology of South Asia*. Madison: Wisconsin Archaeological Reports, 2: 249-51.

Stacul, Giorgio
1992a   Further evidence on "The Inner Asian Complex" from Swat. In, Gregory L. Possehl, ed., *South Asian Archaeology Studies*. Delhi: Oxford & IBH: 111-22.

Stacul, Giorgio
1992b   Swat, Pirak and connected problems (mid-2nd millennium BC). In, Catherine Jarrige, ed., *South Asian Archaeology 1989*. Madison: Prehistory Press, Monographs in World Archaeology, 14: 267-70.

Stacul, Giorgio
1993   Kalako-deray, Swat: an archaeological complex from the early/mid-2nd millennium B.C. In, Adalbert J. Gail and Gerd J. R. Mevissen, eds., *South Asian Archaeology 1991*. Stuttgart: Franz Steiner Verlag: 265-72.

Starr, Richard F. S.
1941   *Indus Valley Painted Pottery: A Comparative Study of the Designs on the Painted Wares of the Harappa Culture*. Princeton: Princeton University Press.

Stech, Tamara and Vincent Pigott
1986   The metals trade in Southwest Asia in the third millennium B. C., *Iraq*, 48: 39-64.

Stein, Sir Aurel
1905   *Report on Archaeological Survey Work in the North-West Frontier Province and Baluchistan for the Period from January 2nd, 1904 to March 31st, 1905*. Peshawar: North-West Frontier Province Government Press, for the Archaeological Survey of India.

Stein, Sir Aurel
1925-26 Officers on Special Duty: Sir Aurel Stein's work. *Annual Report of the Archaeological Survey of India, 1925-26*: 159-63.

Stein, Sir Aurel
1926-27 Officers on Special Duty: Sir Aurel Stein's work. *Annual Report of the Archaeological Survey of India, 1926-27*: 221-25.

Stein, Sir Aurel
1927   Alexander's campaign in the Indian north-west frontier. *The Geographical Journal*, 70: 5-6.

Stein, Sir Aurel
1927-28 Officers on Special Duty: Sir Aurel Stein's work. *Annual Report of the Archaeological Survey of India, 1927-28*: 163-78.

Stein, Sir Aurel
1928a   Note on archaeological explorations in Waziristan and Northern Baluchistan. *The Indian Antiquary*, 58: 54-6.

Stein, Sir Aurel
1928b   An archaeological tour along the Waziristan border. *The Geographical Journal*, April: 378-80.

Stein, Sir Aurel
1928c   Alexander's campaign on the North-West Frontier. *The Indian Antiquary*, 58: 15-7.

Stein, Sir Aurel
1929a   *An Archaeological Tour in Waziristan and Northern Baluchistan*. Memoirs of the Archaeological Survey of India, No. 37.

Stein, Sir Aurel
1929b   *On Alexander's Track to the Indus: Personal narrative of explorations on the North-west Frontier of India carried out under the orders of H. M. Indian Government*. London: Macmillan and Company.

Stein, Sir Aurel
1930   *An Archaeological Tour in Upper Swat and Adjacent Hill Tracts*. Memoirs of the Archaeological Survey of India, No. 42.

1006

Stein, Sir Aurel
1931   *An Archaeological Tour in Gedrosia*. Memoirs of the Archaeological Survey of India, No. 43.

Stein, Sir Aurel
1932   The site of Alexander's passage of the Hydaspes and the battle with Poros. *The Geographical Journal*, 80: 32-46.

Stein, Sir Aurel
1934   The Indo-Iranian borderlands: their prehistory in the light of geography and of recent explorations. *Man*, 160: 140-41.

Stein, Sir Aurel
1937   *Archaeological Reconnaissances in North-Western India and South-Eastern Iran*. London: Macmillan and Company.

Stein, Sir Aurel
1940   *Old Routes of Western Iran*. London: Macmillan and Company, Limited.

Stein, Sir Aurel
1942   A survey of ancient sites along the 'lost' Sarasvati River. *The Geographical Journal*, 99: 173-82.

Stein, Sir Aurel
1943a   *An archaeological tour along the Ghaggar-Hakra River, 1940-42*. American Documentation Institute Microfilm No. ADI-4861.

Stein, Sir Aurel
1943b   On Alexander's route into Gedrosia: An archaeological tour in Las Bela. *The Geographical Journal*, 102(5-6): 193-227.

Steward, Julian H.
1929a   Irrigation without agriculture. *Papers of the Michigan Academy of Sciences, Arts and Letters*, 12: 149-56.

Steward, Julian H.
1929b   Diffusion and independent invention: a critique of logic. *American Anthropologist*, 31: 491-95.

Steward, Julian H.
1955   *Theory of Culture Change*. Urbana: University of Illinois Press.

Subbarao, Bendapudi
1952   Archaeological explorations in the Mahi Valley. *Journal of the Maharaja Sayajirao University*, 1: 33-72.

Subbarao, Bendapudi
1958   *The Personality of India*. 2nd ed. Baroda: Maharaja Sayajirao University Archaeology Series 3.

Subharayappa, B.V.
1995   Rigvedic people and their identity. In: A.K. Srinivasan and S. Nagaraja, eds., *Sri Nagabhinandanam (Dr. M.S. Nagaraja Rao Felicitation Volume)*. bangalore: Dr. M.S. Nagaraja Rao Felicitation Committee: 83–98.

Sullivan, Hugh Patrick
1964   A re-examination of the religion of the Indus Civilization. *History of Religions*, 4: 115-25.

Sundersen, D.
1976   *Livestock Breeding in India*. Delhi: Vikas Publishing House.

Suraj Bhan
1967   New light on the Ochre Colored Ware problem. *Research Bulletin, Arts*, Punjab University, 52(3): 1-9.

Suraj Bhan
1969   Excavations at Mitathal (Hissar) 1968. *Journal of Haryana Studies*, 4(1): 1-15.

Suraj Bhan
1971-72 Appendix D — Siswal: a pre-Harappan site in Drishadvati Valley. *Puratattva*, 5: 44-6.

Suraj Bhan
1972   *Prehistoric Archaeology of the Saraswati and Drusaduati Valleys*. PhD Dissertation, Department of Archaeology, Maharaja Sayajirao University of Baroda.

Suraj Bhan
1973   The sequence and spread of prehistoric cultures in the upper Sarasvati Basin. In, D. P. Agrawal and A. Ghosh, eds., *Radiocarbon and Indian Archaeology*. Bombay: Tata Institute of Fundamental Research: 252-63.

Suraj Bhan
1975   *Excavation at Mitathal (1968) and Other Explorations in the Sutlej-Yamuna Divide*. Kurukshetra: Kurukshetra University.

Suraj Bhan
1989   Dher Majra. In, A. Ghosh, ed., *An Encyclopaedia of Indian Archaeology*. Delhi: Munshiram Manoharlal, 1: 127-28.

Suraj Bhan and Jim G. Shaffer
1978   New Discoveries in Northern Haryana. *Man and Environment*, 2: 59-68.

Suryavanshi, Bhagwansingh
1962   *The Abhiras, Their History and Culture*. Baroda: Maharaja Sayajiro University of Baroda.

1008

Swain, A. M.; J. E. Kutzbach and S. Hastenrath
1983   Estimates of Holocene precipitation for Rajasthan, India, based on pollen and lake-level data. *Quaternary Research*, 19: 1-17.

Talon, P.
1986   Le cotton et la Soie en Mesopotamie? *Akkadica*, 47: 75-8.

Tchernov, E.
1984   Commensal animals and human settlement in the Middle East. In, Juliet Clutton-Brock and Caroline Grigson eds., *Animals and Archaeology: 3. Early Herders and Their Flocks*. Oxford: British Archaeological Reports, International Series, 202: 91-105.

Tchernov, E. and Ofer Bar-Yosef
1982   Animal exploitation in the Pre-Pottery Neolithic B period at Wadi Tbeik, southern Sinai. *Paleorient*, 8(2): 17-37.

Telegrin, Dimitri
1995   About the absolute age of the settlement and cemetery of Dereivka on the middle Dneper. Paper presented at "Early Horsekeepers of the Eurasian Steppes, 4500-1500 BC." June 19-24. Petropavlovsk, Kazakhstan.

Terra, Hellmut, de and G. Evelyn Hutchinson
1936   Data on post-glacial climatic change in North-west India. *Current Science*, 5(1): 5-9.

Terra, Hellmut, de and T. T. Paterson
1939   *Studies on the Ice Age of India*. Washington D. C.: Carnegie Institute Publication, No. 493.

Tessitori, Luigi P.
1914   Bardic and historical survey of Rajputana. Scheme for the bardic and historical survey of Rajputana. *Journal of the Asiatic Society of Bengal*, 10 (NS): 373-410.

Tessitori, Luigi P.
1915   Notes on the grammar of the Old Western Rajasthani with special reference to Apabhramca and to Gujarati and Marwari. *Indian Antiquary*, 44: 3-11, 30-36, 52-58, 74-81, 96-105, 119-26, 159-63.

Tessitori, Luigi P.
1916   Notes on the grammar of the Old Western Rajasthani with special reference to Apabhramca and to Gujarati and Marwari. *Indian Antiquary*, 45: 6-7, 93-9.

Tessitori, Luigi P.
1917-18 Exploration, Bikaner. *Annual Report of the Archaeological Survey of India, 1917-18*: 21-3.

Tessitori, Luigi P.
1917a   Bardic and Historical Survey of Rajputana: Vacanika Rathora Ratana Singhaji ri Mahesadasota ri Khiriya Jaga ri Kahi. Part I, Dingala text with notes and glossary. *Bibliotheca Indica*, 1411 (NS): 1-139.

Tessitori, Luigi P.
1917b   A Descriptive Catalogue of Bardic and Historical Manuscripts. Section 1, Prose Chronicles, Part I, Jodhpur State, fasc. I. *Bibliotheca Indica*, 1409 (NS): 1-69.

Tessitori, Luigi P.
1918   A Descriptive Catalogue of Bardic and Historical Manuscripts. Section 1, Prose Chronicles, Part II, Bikaner State, fasc. I. *Bibliotheca Indica*, 1412 (NS): 2-94.

Tessitori, Luigi P.
1918-19 Exploration, Bikaner. *Annual Report of the Archaeological Survey of India*, 1918-19: 22-3.

Tessitori, Luigi P.
1919   Bardic and Historical Survey of Rajputana: Veli Krisana Rukamani ri Rathora raja Prithi Raja ri Kahi. *Bibliotheca Indica*, 1423 (NS): 1-143.

Tessitori, Luigi P.
1920   A progress report on the work done during the year 1917 in connection with the bardic and historical survey of Rajputana. *Journal of the Asiatic Society of Bengal*, 15 (NS): 5-79.

Tessitori, Luigi P.
1921   A progress report on the work done during the year 1918 in connection with the bardic and historical survey of Rajputana. *Journal of the Asiatic Society of Bengal*, 16 (NS): 251-79.

Tessitori, Luigi P.
n.d.   Exploration in Rajasthan. Delhi: Archaeological Survey of India, mss.

Thapar, B. K.
1973a   New traits of the Indus Civilization at Kalibangan: an appraisal. In, Norman Hammond, ed., *South Asian Archaeology*. Park Ridge: Noyes Press: 85-104.

Thapar, B. K.
1973b   Synthesis of the multiple data as obtained from Kalibangan. In, D. P. Agrawal and A. Ghosh, eds., *Radiocarbon and Indian Archaeology*. Bombay: Tata Institute of Fundamental Research: 264-71.

Thapar, B. K.
1974   Problems of the Neolithic cultures in India: a retrospect. *Puratattva*, 7:61-65.

Thapar, B. K.
1975   Kalibangan: A Harappan metropolis beyond the Indus Valley. *Expedition*, 17(2): 19-32.

Thapar, B. K.
1978   Early farming communities in India. *Journal of Human Evolution*, 7: 11-22.

Thapar, B. K.
1982   The Harappan Civilization: some reflections on its environments and resources and their exploitation. In, Gregory L. Possehl, ed., *Harappan Civilization: A contemporary perspective*. Delhi: Oxford & IBH and the American Institute of Indian Studies: 3-13.

Thapar, B. K.
1984   Fresh light on the Neolithic cultures of India. *Puratattva*, 13-14: 37-43.

Thapar, B. K.
1987   Fresh light on the Neolithic cultures of India. In, B. M. Pande and B. D. Chattopadyaya, eds., *Archaeology and History: Essays in memory of Sh. A. Ghosh*. 2 Vols. Delhi: Agam Kala Prakashan: 247-254.

Thapar, B. K.
1989   Kalibangan, -1 and -2. In, A. Ghosh, ed., *An Encyclopaedia of Indian Archaeology*. 2 Vols. Delhi: Munshiram Manoharlal, Vol. 2: 194-96.

Thaplyal, K. K. and S. P. Shukla
1976   Copper celts with circular depressions—some observations. In, Udai Vir Singh, ed., *Archaeological Congress and Seminar: 1972*. Kurukshetra: B. N. Chakravarty University Kurukshetra: 98-101.

Thaw, U Aung
1971   The Neolithic culture of the Padah-Lin Caves. *Asian Perspectives*, 14: 123-33.

Thiebault, Stephanie
1989   A note on the ancient vegetation of Baluchistan based on charcoal analysis of the latest periods from Mehrgarh, Pakistan. In, Karen Frifelt and Per Sorensen, eds., *South Asian Archaeology 1985*. London: Curzon Press, Scandinavian Institute of Asian Studies, Occasional Papers No. 4: 186-88.

Thiebault, Stephanie
1992   Complementary results in anthracological analysis from sites in Baluchistan. In, Catherine Jarrige, ed., *South Asian Archaeology 1989*. Madison: Prehistory Press, Monographs in World Archaeology, 14: 271-76.

Thomas, Kenneth D.
1983a   Agricultural subsistence systems of the third millennium BC in north-west Pakistan: a speculative outline. In, M. Jones, ed., *Integrating the Subsistence Economy*. Oxford: British Archaeological Reports International Series, 181:279-314.

Thomas, Kenneth D.
1983b   Tarakai Qila: site, economy and environment. In, B. Proudfoot, ed., *Site, Environment and Economy*. Oxford: British Archaeological Reports International Series, 173: 127-44.

Thomas, Kenneth D.
1986a   Environment and subsistence in the Bannu Basin. In, F. R. Allchin, B. Allchin, F. A. Durrani and M. Farid Khan, eds., *Lewan and the Bannu Basin*. Oxford: British Archaeological Reports International Series, No. 310: 13-33.

Thomas, Kenneth D.
1986b   Palaeobiological investigations. In, F. R. Allchin, B. Allchin, F. A. Durrani and M. Farid Khan eds., *Lewan and the Bannu Basin*. British Archaeological Reports, International Series, No. 310: 121-137.

Thomas, Kenneth D. and F. R. Allchin
1986   Radiocarbon dating some early sites in N. W. Pakistan. *South Asian Studies*, 2: 37-44.

Thomas, P. K.
1975   The role of animals in the food economy of the Mesolithic culture of Western and Central India. In, A. T. Clason, ed., *Archaeozoological Studies*. Amsterdam: North-Holland: 322-28.

Thomas, P. K.
1977   *Archaeozoological Aspects of the Prehistoric Cultures of Western India*. PhD Dissertation, Department of Archaeology, Deccan College.

Thomas, P. K.
1984   The faunal background of the Chalcolithic culture of western India. In, J. Clutton-Brock and C. Greigson, eds., *Animals and Archaeology: 3. Early Herders and Their Flocks*. B.A.R. International Series, 202: 355-62.

Tikkanen, Bertil
1988   On Burushaski and other ancient substrata in northwestern South Asia. *Studia Orientalia*, 64: 303-25.

Tilak, Bal Gangadhar
1904   *The Arctic Home in the Vedas*. Poona: Tilak Brothers.

Tobler, A. J.
1950   *Excavations at Tepe Gawra*. Vol. 2. Philadelphia: The University Museum.

Tod, James
1829-32   *Annals and Antiquities of Rajasthan: Or the Central and Western Rajput States of India*. 2 Vols. London: Routledge & Kegan Paul.

Tod, James
1894   *Annals and Antiquities of Rajasthan: Or the Central and Western Rajput States of India*. Revision of the original published in 1829-32. 2 Vols. Calcutta: S. K. Lahiri and Company.

1012

Todd, Joan M.
1985   Baltic amber in the ancient Near East: a preliminary investigation. *Journal of Baltic Studies*, 16: 292-301.

Tosi, Maurizio
1969   Excavations at Shahr-i Sokhta. Preliminary report on the second campaign, September-December, 1968. *East and West*, 19(3-4): 283-386.

Tosi, Maurizio
1970   On the route for lapis lazuli, parts 1 and 2. *The Illustrated London News*, January 24: 24-5; February 7: 24-5.

Tosi, Maurizio
1974a   The lapis lazuli trade across the Iranian Plateau in the 3rd millennium B. C. Napoli: Instituto Universitario Orientale. *Gururajamanjarika: Studi in onore di Giuseppe Tucci*: 3-22.

Tosi, Maurizio
1974b   The problem of turquoise in Protohistoric trade on the Iranian Plateau. *Studi di Paletnologia, Paleoantropologia, Paleontologia E Geologia Del Quaternario*, 2: 147-62

Tosi, Maurizio
1980   Karneol. *Reallexikon Der Assyriologie und Vorderasiaticschen Archalogie*, 5: 448-52.

Tosi, Maurizio
1986a   Early maritime cultures of the Arab Gulf and the Indian Ocean. In, Shaikha Haya Ali Al Khalifa and Michael Rice, eds., *Bahrain Through the Ages, the Archaeology*. New York: KPI Limited: 94-107.

Tosi, Maurizio
1986b   Prehistoric archaeology in Oman: the first 30 years. In, P. M. Costa and M. Tosi eds., *Oman Studies*. Orientalia Romana 7. Rome: IsMEO. 135-61.

Tosi, Maurizio
1986c   The emerging picture of prehistoric Arabia. *Annual Review of Anthropology*, 15: 461-90.

Tosi, Maurizio
1991   The Indus Civilization beyond the Indian Subcontinent. In, Michael Jansen, Maire Mulloy and Gunter Urban, eds., *Forgotten Cities on the Indus: Early civilization in Pakistan from the 8th to the 2nd millennium B.C.* Mainz: Verlag Philipp von Zabern: 111-28.

Tremenheere, C. W.
1867   On the lower portion of the River Indus. *Journal of the Royal Geographical Society*, 37: 68-91.

Turner, A. James and A. N. Gulati
1929a   A note on the early history of cotton. Bombay: *Indian Central Cotton Committee Bulletin*, 17, Technological Series No. 12.

Turner, A. James and A. N. Gulati
1929b   The early history of cotton. *Agricultural Journal of India*, 24(1): 14-20.

Turner, C. G.
1979   Dental anthropological indications of agriculture among the Jomon people of central Japan. *American Journal of Physical Anthropology*, 51(4): 619-36.

Unger-Hamilton, R.
1989   Epipalaeolithic Palestine and the beginnings of plant cultivation: The evidence from harvesting experiments and microwear studies. *Current Anthropology*, 30: 88-103.

Urban, Gunter and Michael Jansen, editors
1983   *Forschungprojekt DFG Mohenjo-Daro: Dokumentation in der archaologie, techniken, methoden, analysen.* Aachen: Veroffentlichung des Geogatischen Instituts der Reinisch-Westfalischen Technischen Hochschule, Nr.34.

Urban, Thomas
1987   State of research on the architecture in 'Moneer' area, Mohenjo-daro. In, Michael Jansen and Gunter Urban eds., *Reports on Field Work Carried Out at Mohenjo-daro, Pakistan, 1983-84:* Interim Reports, Volume 2. Aachen/Rome: RWTH/IsMEO:23-32.

Vansina, Jan
1961   *Oral Tradition: A study in historical methodology.* Chicago: Aldine.

Varma, Supriya
1991   Villages abandoned: the case for mobile pastoralism in post-Harappan Gujarat. *Studies in History*, 7(2): 279-300.

Vasu, Srisa Chandra
1990   *The Astashyayi of Panini.* 2 Volume Reprint. Delhi: Low Priced Publications.

Vats, M. S.
1923-24 Exploration and Research, Sind, Mohenjo-daro. *Annual Report of the Archaeological Survey of India, 1923-24*: 51-2.

Vats, M. S.
1926-27 Harappa. *Annual Report of the Archaeological Survey of India, 1926-27*: 97-108.

Vats, M. S.
1927-28 Excavations at Harappa. *Annual Report of the Archaeological Survey of India, 1927-28*: 83-90.

Vats, M. S.
1928-29 Excavations at Harappa. *Annual Report of the Archaeological Survey of India, 1928-29*: 76-85.

1014

Vats, M. S.
1929-30a Excavations at Harappa. *Annual Report of the Archaeological Survey of India, 1929-30*: 121-31.

Vats, M. S.
1929-30b Kotla Nihang. *Annual Report of the Archaeological Survey of India, 1929-30*: 131-32.

Vats, M. S.
1930-34a Excavations at Harappa. *Annual Reports of the Archaeological Survey of India for the Years 1930-31, 1931-32, 1932-33 & 1933-34*, Part One: 72-90.

Vats, M. S.
1930-34b Excavations at Harappa: excavations during 1930-31. *Annual Reports of the Archaeological Survey of India for the Years 1930-31, 1931-32, 1932-33 & 1933-34*, Part One: 73-85.

Vats, M. S.
1930-34c Excavations at Harappa: excavations during 1931-32. *Annual Reports of the Archaeological Survey of India for the Years 1930-31, 1931-32, 1932-33 & 1933-34*, Part One: 85-8.

Vats, M. S.
1930-34d Excavations at Harappa: excavations during 1932-33, further work in the 'workmen's quarters.' *Annual Reports of the Archaeological Survey of India for the Years 1930-31, 1931-32, 1932-33 & 1933-34*, Part One: 88-9.

Vats, M. S.
1930-34e Excavations at Harappa: excavations during 1933-34, brick platform in the southern slope of Mound F. *Annual Reports of the Archaeological Survey of India for the Years 1930-31, 1931-32, 1932-33 & 1933-34*, Part One: 89-90.

Vats, M. S.
1930-34f The Chalcolithic site at Chak Purbane Sayal. *Annual Reports of the Archaeological Survey of India for the Years 1930-31, 1931-32, 1932-33 & 1933-34*, Part One: 106-07.

Vats, M. S.
1934-35 Trial excavations at Rangpur, Limbdi State, Kathiawar. *Annual Report of the Archaeological Survey of India, 1934-35*: 34-8.

Vats, M. S.
1935-36a Excavation in Khairpur State, Diji-ji-Tikri. *Annual Report of the Archaeological Survey of India, 1935-36*: 36-7.

Vats, M. S.
1935-36b Excavation in Khairpur State, Kotasur. *Annual Report of the Archaeological Survey of India, 1935-36*: 37-8.

Vats, M. S.
1935-36c Conservation, Bombay Presidency and Sind. *Annual Report of the Archaeological Survey of India, 1935-36*: 18-21.

Vats, M. S.
1937   Excavations at Harappa. *Annual Bibliography of Indian Archaeology*, 12: 1-9.

Vats, M. S.
1940   *Excavations at Harappa*. 2 Vols. Delhi: Government of India.

Vavilov, Nicoli I.
1949-50 The Origin, Variation, Immunity and Breeding of Cultivated Plants. Translated by K. Starr Chester. *Chronica Botanica*, 16(1-6): 1-366.

Vavilov, Nicoli I.
1957   *World Resources of Cereals, Leguminous Seed Crops and Flax, and Their Utilization in Plant Breeding*. Moscow.

Vinogradov, A. V.
1979   Studies of Stone Age sites in northern Afghanistan. *Ancient Bactria*, 2: 7-62. (in Russian).

Vinogradov, A. V., S. V. Lopatin, E. D. Mamedov
1965   Kyzylkum desert sites. *Sovetskaya Ethnografija*, 2: 114-34.

Vishnu-Mittre
1969   Remains of rice and millet. In, H. D. Sankalia, S. B. Deo and Z. D. Ansari, *Excavations at Ahar (Timbavati)*. Poona: Deccan College Post-graduate and Research Insititute: 229-36.

Vishnu-Mittre
1971   Neolithic plant economy at Chirand, Bihar. *The Palaeobotanist*, 21(1): 18-22.

Vishnu-Mittre
1974   The beginnings of agriculture: palaeobotanical evidence in India. In, Sir Joseph Hutchinson, ed., *Evolutionary Studies in World Crops: Diversity and change in the Indian Subcontinent*. Cambridge: Cambridge University Press: 3-30.

Vishnu-Mittre
1978   Origin and history of agriculture in the Indian Subcontinent. *Journal of Human Evolution*, 7: 31-6.

Vishnu-Mittre
1982   The Harappan Civilization and the need for a new approach. In, Gregory L. Possehl, ed., *Harappan Civilization: A contemporary perspective*. Delhi: Oxford & IBH and the American Institute of Indian Studies: 31-9.

Vishnu-Mittre and Chhaya Sharma
1973   Pollen analysis of the salt flat at Malvan, Gujarat. The *Palaeobotanist*, 22(2): 118-23.

1016

Vishnu-Mittre and Chhaya Sharma
1978   Pollen analysis of Nal Lake, Gujarat. *The Palaeobotanist*, 26: 96-104.

Vishnu-Mittre and R. Savithri
1973   Supposed remains of rice (*Oryza* sp.) in the terracotta cakes and pai at Kalibangan, Rajasthan. *The Palaeobotanist*, 22(2): 124-26.

Vishnu-Mittre and R. Savithri
1974   Ancient plant economy at Noh, Rajasthan. Puratattva 7:77-80.

Vishnu-Mittre and R. Savithri
1976   *Setaria* spp. in the ancient plant economy of India. *The Palaeobotanist*, 25: 559-64.

Vishnu-Mittre and R. Savithri
1982   Food economy of the Harappans. In, Gregory L. Possehl, ed., *Harappan Civilization: A contemporary perspective*. Delhi: Oxford & IBH and the American Institute of Indian Studies: 205-221.

Voigt, Mary M.
1985   Village on the Euphrates: excavations at Neolithic Gritille in Turkey. *Expedition*, 27(1): 10-24.

Voigt, Mary M. and Richard S. Ellis
1981   Excavations at Gritille, Turkey 1981. *Paleorient*, 7(2): 87-100.

Vredenburg, E. W.
1901   A Geological Sketch of the Baluchistan Desert and Part of Eastern Persia. *Memoirs of the Geological Survey of India*, 31(2): 179-302.

Waddell, L. A.
1925a   *The Indo-Sumerian Seals Deciphered: Discovering Sumerians of Indus Valley as Phoenicians, Barats, Goths & Famous Vedic Aryans, 3100-2300 B.C.* London: Luzac & Co.

Waddell, L. A.
1925b   Sumerians in India. *The Indian Historical Quarterly*, 1: 21-25.

Waddell, L. A.
1926   Indo-Sumerian seals. *Journal of the Royal Asiatic Society of Great Britain and Ireland*: 115-16.

Wadia, D. N.
1966   *Geology of India*. 3rd ed. New York: Macmillan.

Wadley, Susan
1983   The rains of estrangement: understanding the Hindu yearly cycle. *Contributions to Indian Sociology*, 17(1): 51-85.

Wahal, L. M.
1971-72 Session on OCP, comment on Saipai. *Puratattva*, 5: 12-3.

Wakankar, V. S.
1967 Kayatha Excavation Number. *Journal of Vikram University*: 1-52.

Walker, Benjamin
1968 *Hindu World: An encyclopedic survey of Hinduism.* 2 Vols. London: George Allen & Unwin.

Wasson, R. J.
1984 The sedimentological basis of the Mohenjo-daro flood hypothesis. *Man and Environment*, 8: 88-90.

Wasson, R. J.
1987 The sedimentological basis of the Mohenjo-daro flood hypothesis — a further comment. *Man and Environment*, 11: 122-3.

Wasson, R. J., G. I. Smith and D. P. Agrawal
1984 Late Quaternary sediments, minerals and inferred geochemical history of Didwana Lake, Thar Desert, India. *Palaeogrography, Palaeoclimatology, Palaeoecology*, 46: 345-72.

Watson, William
1970 *Cultural Frontiers in Ancient East Asia.* Edinburgh: Edinburgh University Press.

Watt, G.
1908 *The Commercial Products of India.* 1969 reprint. New Delhi: Today Tomorrows.

Weber, Steven A.
1989 *Plants and Harappan Subsistence: An example of stability and change from Rojdi.* PhD Dissertation, Department of Anthropology, University of Pennsylvania.

Weber, Steven A.
1990 Millets in South Asia: Rojdi as a case study. In, Maurizio Taddei, ed., *South Asian Archaeology 1987*. Roma: Instituto Italiano per il Medio ed Estremo Oriente, Serie Orientale Roma, 66(1): 333-48.

Weber, Steven A.
1991 *Plants and Harappan Subsistence: An example of stability and change from Rojdi.* Delhi: Oxford & IBH and the American Institute of Indian Studies.

Weber, Steven A. and Vishnu-Mittre
1989 Palaeobotanical research at Rojdi. In, Gregory L. Possehl and M. H. Raval, *Harappan Civilization and Rojdi*. Delhi: Oxford & IBH and the American Institute of Indian Studies: 177-81.

Weiner, Annette B.
1992 *Inalienable Possessions: The paradox of keeping-while-giving.* Berkeley: University of California Press.

1018

Weisgerber, Gerd
1980   ...und kupfer in Oman. *Der Anschnitt*, 32: 62-110.

Weisgerber, Gerd
1981   Mehr als kupfer in Oman—ergebnisse der expedition 1981. *Der Anschnitt*, 33: 174-263.

Weisgerber, Gerd
1983   Copper production during the third millennium BC in Oman and the question of Makkan. *Journal of Oman Studies*, 6(1): 269-76.

Weisgerber, Gerd
1984   Makan and Meluhha—third millennium BC copper production in Oman and the evidence of contact with the Indus Valley. In, B. Allchin, ed., *South Asian Archaeology 1981*. Cambridge: Cambridge University Press: 196-201.

Wertime, Theodore A.
1973   Pyrotechnology: man's first industrial uses of fire. *American Scientist*, 61(6): 670-82.

West, W. D.
1936   Preliminary geological report on the Baluchistan (Quetta) earthquake of May 31st, 1935. *Records of the Geological Survey of India*, 69(2): 58-130.

Westphal-Hellbusch, Sigrid and Heinz Westphal
1968   *Zur Geschichte un Kultur der Jat.* Berlin: Duncker & Humblot.

Westphal-Hellenbusch, Sigrid
1975   Changes in the meaning of ethnic names as exemplified by the Jat, Rabari, Bhavard and Charan in Northwestern India. In. L. S. Leshink and G. D. Sontheimer, eds., *Pastoralists and Nomads in South Asia*. Wiesbaden: Otto Harrassowitz: 117-38.

Wheeler, R. E. M.
1946a   Archaeological planning for India: some of the factors. *Ancient India*, 2: 125-33.

Wheeler, R. E. M.
1946b   India's earliest civilization: recent excavations in the Indus basin. *Illustrated London News*, August 19: 158–59.

Wheeler, R. E. M.
1947-48   Brahmagiri and Chandravalli 1947: megalithic and other cultures in the Chitaldrug District, Mysore State. *Ancient India*, 4: 180-310.

Wheeler, R. E. M.
1947a   Harappa 1946: the defenses and cemetery R-37. *Ancient India*, 3: 58-130.

Wheeler, R. E. M.
1947b   Harappan chronology and the Rigveda. In, R. E. M. Wheeler, Harappa, 1946: the defenses and Cemetery R-37. *Ancient India*, 3: 78-85.

Wheeler, R. E. M.
1947c   Sociological aspects of the Harappa Civilization. In, R. E. M. Wheeler, Harappa, 1946: the defenses and Cemetery R-37. *Ancient India*, 3: 74-8.

Wheeler, R. E. M.
1947d   Archaeology in Afghanistan. *Antiquity*, 21: 57-65.

Wheeler, R. E. M.
1949   Archaeological fieldwork in India: planning ahead. *Ancient India*, 5: 4-11.

Wheeler, R. E. M.
1950a   Newly found at Mohenjo-daro: a huge 4000-year-old granary. *Illustrated London News*, May 20: 782-83.

Wheeler, R. E. M.
1950b   New light on the Indus Civilization: the Mohenjo-daro granary. *Illustrated London News*, May 27: 813-16.

Wheeler, R. E. M.
1950c   Man in 4000 year old Mohenjo-daro. *Illustrated London News*, June 3: 854-55.

Wheeler, R. E. M.
1950d   *Mohen-Jo-Daro*. Karachi: Government of Pakistan.

Wheeler, R. E. M.
1950e   *Five Thousand Years of Pakistan: An archaeological outline*. London: Royal India & Pakistan Society.

Wheeler, R. E. M., A. Ghosh and Krishna Deva
1946   Arikamedu: an Indo-Roman trading-station on the east coast of India. *Ancient India*, 2: 17-124.

Wheeler, Sir Mortimer
1953   *The Indus Civilization*. 1st edition. Supplementary Volume to the Cambridge Ancient History of India. Cambridge: At the University Press.

Wheeler, Sir Mortimer
1954   *Archaeology from the Earth*. Oxford: Oxford University Press.

Wheeler, Sir Mortimer
1955   *Still Digging*. New York: E. P. Dutton.

Wheeler, Sir Mortimer
1958   Sir John Marshall. *The Times*, 21 August: 10.

Wheeler, Sir Mortimer
1960   *The Indus Civilization*. 2nd edition. Supplementary Volume to the Cambridge Ancient History of India. Cambridge: Cambridge University Press.

1020

Wheeler, Sir Mortimer
1962   *Charsada: A metropolis of the North-west Frontier*. Oxford: For the Government of Pakistan and the British Academy by Oxford University Press.

Wheeler, Sir Mortimer
1966   *Civilizations of the Indus Valley and Beyond*. New York: McGraw-Hill.

Wheeler, Sir Mortimer
1968   *The Indus Civilization*. 3rd edition. Supplementary Volume to the Cambridge Ancient History of India. Cambridge: At the University Press.

Wheeler, Sir Mortimer
1971   Marshall, Sir John Hubert. In, E. T. Williams and Helen M. Palmer, eds., *The Dictionary of National Biography: 1951-60*. Oxford: Oxford University Press: 698-99.

Wheeler, Sir Mortimer
1976   *My Archaeological Mission to India and Pakistan*. London: Thames and Hudson.

Whitehouse, Ruth
1968   The early Neolithic sequence of southern Italy. *Antiquity*, 42: 188-93.

Whitehouse, Ruth
1971   The last hunter-gatherers in southern Italy. *World Archaeology*, 2(3): 241-54.

Whitten, D. G. A and J. R. V. Brooks
1972   *The Penguin Dictionary of Geology*. New York: Penguin Books.

Whitteridge, Gordon
1986   *Charles Masson of Afghanistan: Explorer, archaeologist, numismatist and intelligence agent*. Warminster: Aris & Philips.

Whyte, Robert Orr
1964   *The Fodder and Grassland Resources of India*. New Delhi: Indian Council of Agricultural Research.

Wigboldus, Jouke S.
1996   Early presence of African millets near the Indian Ocean. In, Julian Reade, ed., *The Indian Ocean in Antiquity*. London: Kegan Paul International in Cooperation with the British Museum: 75-86.

Wilhelmy, Herbert
1968a   Verschollene stadte im Indusdelta. *Geographische Zeitschrift*, 56(4): 256-94.

Wilhelmy, Herbert
1969   Urstromtal am ostrand der Indusebene und der Sarasvati-problem. In, Karlheinz Kaiser, ed., Glazialmorphologie, Glacial Morphologie. *Zeitschrift Fur Geomorphologie*, Supplementband 8: 76-93.

Willcox, George H.
1992   Some differences between crops of Near Eastern origin and those from the tropics. In, Catherine Jarrige, ed., *South Asian Archaeology 1989*. Madison: Prehistory Press, Monographs in World Archaeology, 14: 291-99.

Wilson, Horace Hayman
1841   *Ariana Antiqua: A descriptive account of the antiquities and coins of Afghanistan.* London: The East India Company.

Wilson, Horace Hayman
1850-88 *Rig-Veda Sanhita: A collection of ancient Hindu hymns of the Rig-Veda, the oldest anthority on the religious and social institutions of the Hindus.* 6 Vols. London: W. H. Allen.

Winstone, H. V. F.
1990   *Woolley of Ur: The life of Sir Leonard Woolley.* London: Secker & Warburg.

Wood, Lt. John
1838   Report on the River Indus accompanied by a chart in five sheets. In, R. Hughes Thomas, ed., 1855, *Memoirs on Sind*. Bombay: Selections From the Records of the Bombay Government, Vol. 1, No. 18, New Series: 541-88.

Wood, Lt. John
1841   *A Personal Narrative of a Journey to the Source of the Oxus River.* London: John Murray.

Wood, W. Arden
1924   Rivers and man in the Indus-Ganges Plains. *Scottish Geographical Magazine*, 40: 1-15.

Woodburn, J.
1968   An introduction to Hadza ecology. In, Richard B. Lee and Irvin DeVore, eds., *Man the Hunter*. Chicago: Aldine: 49-55.

Woolley, Sir C. Leonard
1939a   *A Report on the Work of the Archaeological Survey of India.* Delhi: Government of India.

Woolley, Sir C. Leonard
1939b   Archaeological research in India. *Nature*, 144(3652): 758.

Woolley, Sir C. Leonard
1940   The George Birdwood Memorial Lecture: Some aspects and problems of Indian archaeology. *Journal of the Royal Society of Arts*, 88(4546): 183-97.

Wright, Gary A.
1971   Origins of food production in Southwestern Asia: a survey of ideas. *Current Anthropology*, 12(4-5): 447-77.

1022

Wright, Henry T.
1977   Recent research on the origin of the state. *Annual Review of Anthropology*, 6: 379-97.

Wright, Rita P.
1984   *Technology, Style and Craft Specialization: Spheres of interaction on the Indo-Iranian borderlands, third millennium B.C.* PhD Dissertation, Department of Anthropology, Harvard University.

Wright, Rita P.
1985   Technology and style in ancient ceramics. In, W. D. Kingery, ed., *Ceramics and Civilization: Ancient technology to modern science*. American Ceramic Society, Vol. 1: 5-25.

Wright, Rita P.
1987   The frontiers of prehistoric Baluchistan and the development of the Indus Civilization. In, K. M. Trinkaus, ed., *Polities and Partitions: Human boundaries and the growth of complex societies*. Tucson: Arizona State Series, No. 36:1-23.

Wright, Rita P.
1989   New perspectives on third millennium painted grey wares. In, Karen Frifelt and Per Sorensen, eds., *South Asian Archaeology 1985*. London: Curzon Press, Scandinavian Institute of Asian Studies, Occasional Papers No. 4: 137-49.

Wyart, J. P. Bariand and J. Filippi
1981   Lapis lazuli from Sar-i Sang, Badakhshan, Afghanistan. *Gems and Gemology*, 17(4): 184-90.

Wynne, A. B.
1872   Geology of Kutch. *Memoirs of the Geological Survey of India*, 9(1).

Wynne, A.B.
1875   The Trans-Indus Salt Region in the Kohat District. *Memoirs of the Geological Survey of India*, 11: 1-189.

Xu Chaolong
1990   The Kot Dijians and the Harappans: their simultaneity—another possible interpretation. In, Maurizio Taddei, ed., *South Asian Archaeology 1987*. Roma: Instituto Italiano per il Medio ed Estremo Oriente, Serie Orientale Roma, 66(1): 157-201.

Xu Chaolong
1994   Cultural changes in Sindh prior to the Mature Harappan Period? A clue drawn from the comparative study of the pottery. In, J. Mark Kenoyer, ed., *From Sumer to Meluhha: Contributions to the archaeology of South and West Asia in memory of George F. Dales*, Jr. Madison: Wisconsin Archaeological Reports 3: 59-70.

Yen, Douglas E.
1989   The domestication of environment. In, David R. Harris and G. C. Hillman, eds., *Foraging and Farming: The evolution of plant exploitation*. London: Unwin Hyman: 55-78.

Yesner, David
1980a   Maritime hunter-gatherers. *Current Anthropology*, 21: 727-50.

Yesner, David
1980   Nutrition and cultural anthropology. In, N. W. Jerome, R. F. Kandel and G. H. Pelto, eds., *Nutritional Anthropology*. Pleasantville, New York: Redgrave: 85-116.

Young, G. M.
1946   A new hoard from Taxila (Bhir Mound). *Ancient India*, 1: 27-36.

Yudkin, J.
1969   Archaeology and the nutritionist. In, Peter J. Ucko and G. W. Dimbleby, eds., *The Domestication and Exploitation of Plants and Animals*. London: Gerald Duckworth & Co.: 547-54.

Yule, Colonel Sir Henry and A. C. Burnell
1903   *Hobson-Jobson: A glossary of colloquial Anglo-Indian words and phrases, and of kindred terms, etymological, historical, geographical and discursive*. New edition edited by William Crooke. 1990 reprint. Calcutta: Rupa and Company.

Yule, Colonel Sir Henry, translator
1926   *The Book of Marco Polo The Venitian: Concerning the kingdoms and marvels of the east*. 3 Vols., 3rd edition. London: John Murray.

Yule, Paul
1985   *Metalwork of the Bronze Age in India*. Munchen: C. H. Beck'sche Verlagsbuchhandlung. Prahistorische Bronzefunde, Abteilung 20, Band 8.

Yusuf, Mazhar
1987   Gulf of Sindhi or the Rann of Cutch. *Sindhological Studies*, Summer: 76-83.

Zarins, Juris A.
1989   Eastern Saudi Arabia and external relations: selected ceramic and textual evidence— 3500-1900. In, Karen Frifelt and Per Sorensen, eds., *South Asian Archaeology 1985*. London: Curzon Press, Scandinavian Institute of Asian Studies, Occasional Papers No. 4: 74-103.

Zarins, Juris A.
1992   Archaeological and chronological problems within the greater Southwest Asian arid zone, 8500-1850 B.C. In, Robert W. Ehrich, ed., *Chronologies in Old World Archaeology*. 3rd ed. 2 Vols. Chicago: University of Chicago Press: 42-62 & 61-76.

van Zeist, Willem, and J. A. H. Bakker-Heeres
1982   Archaeobotanical studies in the Levant. I, Neolithic sites in the Damascus basin: Aswad, Ghoraifa, Ramad. *Palaeohistoria*, 24: 165-256.

van Zeist, Willem, and J. A. H. Bakker-Heeres
1986   Archaeobotanical studies in the Levant. III, Late Palaeolithic Mureybit. *Palaeohistoria*, 26: 171-99.

1024

van Zeist, Willem, and J. A. H. Bakker-Heeres
1979   Some economic and ecological aspects of the plant husbandry of Tell Aswad. *Paleorient*, 5: 161-69.

van Zeist, Willem, and Sytze Bottema
1966   Palaeobotanical investigations at Ramad. *Annales Archeologiques Syriennes*, 16: 179-80.

van Zeist, Willem, and Sytze Bottema
1991   *Late Quaternary Vegetation of the Near East*. Weisbaden: Dr. Ludweg Reichert Verlag. Beihefts zum Tubinger Atlas des Vorderen Orienta, Reihe A (Naturwissenschaften) Nr. 18: 1-156.

van Zeist, Willem, Krystyna Wasylikowa and Karl-Ernst Behre.
1991   *Progress in Old World Palaeoethnobotany*. Rotterdam: A. A. Balkema.

van Zeist, Willem, and H. Woldring
1980   Holocene vegetation and climate of northwestern Syria. *Palaeohistoria*, 22: 111-25.

Zeuner, Frederick E.
1950   *Stone Age and Pleistocene Chronology of Gujarat*. Poona: Deccan College Post-graduate and Research Institute, Monograph Series 6.

Zeuner, Frederick E.
1951   *Prehistory in India*. Poona: Deccan College Post-graduate and Research Institute.

Zeuner, Frederick E.
1952   Microlithic culture of Langhnaj, Gujarat. *Man*, 52(182): 129-31.

Zeuner, Frederick E.
1953   *Environment of Early Man with Special Reference to Tropical Regions*. Baroda: Maharaja Sayajirao University of Baroda.

Zeuner, Frederick E.
1955   The identity of the camel on the Khurab pick. *Iraq*, 17(2): 162-63.

Zeuner, Frederick E.
1959   On the origin of the cinder mounds of the Bellary District, India. *Journal of the Institute of Archaeology*, 2: 37-44.

Zeuner, Frederick E.
1963   *A History of Domesticated Animals*. New York: Harper and Row.

Zeuner, Frederick E. and Bridget Allchin
1956   The microlithic sites of Tinnevelly District, Madras State. *Ancient India*, 12: 4-20.

Ziauddin, M. and S. Narayanaswami
1974   Gold Resources of India. *Bulletins of the Geological Survey of India*, Series A, Economic Geology, No. 38, Pts. I & II.

Zohary, Daniel
1970   Centers of diversity and centers of origin. In, D. H. Frankel and E. Bennett, eds., *Genetic Resources in Plants—their exploitation and conservation.* London: International Biological Programmes: 33-42.

Zohary, Daniel
1989   Domestication of the Southwest Asian Neolithic crop assemblage of cereals, pulses and flax: the evidence from living plants. In, David R. Harris and G. C. Hillman, eds., *Foraging and Farming: The evolution of plant exploitation.* London: Unwin Hyman. One World Archaeology, 13: 358-73.

Zohary, Daniel and M. Hopf
1973   Domestication of pulses in the Old World. *Science*, 182: 87-94.

Zohary, Daniel and M. Hopf
1988   *Domestication of Plants in the Old World: The origin and spread of cultivated plants in West Asia, Europe and the Nile Valley.* Oxford: Clarendon Press.

Zohary, Michael
1973   *Geobotanical Foundations of the Middle East.* 2 Vols. Stuttgart/Amsterdam: Gustav Fischer Verlag/Swets & Zeitlinger: 739 pp.

DETAILED TABLE OF CONTENTS

1030

1034

1040

GENERAL INDEX

1054

Lal, B.B. 132
Lal Chhato 282
Lambis truncata sebae 228, 229
Lambis truncata truncata 229
Lambrick, Hugh Trevor 136, 294
Langdon, Stephen 93
Langur 209
lapis lazuli 235
Larkana 159, 303
Larkhana district 61
Las Bela 161, 270, 321
  microliths in 441
  subsistence regime 321
Late Glacial hunter-gatherers 428
Late Harappan 92, 701
Late Kot Diji 711
Late Kot Diji Phase 648
Late Kot Dijian Phase 24
Late Period 68
Latin 39, 41
Lawrence, T.E. 80
Laws of Thermodynamics 13
lead 6
Lens culinaris 239
Lens esculenta 547
Lens sp. 238
lentil 547
leopard 200, 266, 317
leopard-cat 200, 266
Levant 428
Lewan 141
lifeways and peoples
  their diversity 157
limestone 237, 307
linear culture historical sequences 25
Linum sp. 238
lion 197, 331
Little Rann of Kutch 328, 335
lizards 223
Loebanr III 548
lohar 165
Lohumjo-daro 84
Lolium sp. 424
Londo Ware 305
Long Lane Group 34
Loralai 160, 339
  agricultural regime 344
Loralai District 103, 159
Loralai District in Baluchistan 55
Lord Curzon of Kedleston 56
Lord Wavell 129
Lothal 139, 189, 192, 204, 213, 336
  boat model 289
Lower Indus Basin 299
Lower Indus Project 298
Lower Town of the Mature Harappan 690
Lowland Gujarat 331
Ludhiana 358

Lunkaransar lake 259
Lustrous Red Ware Phase 24
Lynx 200

M

maat 10
Macaca mulatta 209
Macedonian 102
Macedonian army 108
Mackay, Ernest J.H. 77, 78, 80, 95, 100, 101, 133, 134
Madhya Pradesh 177
Madras 132
Magan
  ships 290
Mahagara Neolithic Pirak I 246
Mahagara rice 246
Maharaja Sayajiro University of Baroda 92
Maharashtra 194, 565
Mahayana Buddhist monastic site 47
Mahayogi 133
Mahommedan town 49
Major Clark 52
Majumdar, N.G. 69, 83, 116
  murder of 86
Majumdar's sequence 140
Makhialah Hills 352
Makran 53, 104, 310, 323
  agriculture in 324
  flora 325
  microliths in 441
Makran Coastal Range 323
Makran Subsistence Regime 325
Makrani 161
maldhari 158
maldhari people 167
Mallavali Theri 365
Malvan 264
mammals, domesticated 175
Manasarover Lake 279
Manda 711
mandalas 5
Mangro 225
Manis crassicaudata 317
Manu 11
  Laws of 10
marble 237
Mari
  kingdom of 155
Markhor 181, 182, 183, 317
Marri-Bugti 160, 339, 343
Marri-Bugti country 159
Marri-Bugti Hills 270, 282
Marshall Era 57
Marshall, Sir John 1, 11, 38, 58, 59, 67, 68, 72, 78, 87, 93, 100, 134, 143, 258
  and the Indus Civilization 109
  appointment of 56
  campaign at Mohenjo-daro 42